Children's
Picturebook
Price Guide

2006—2007 Edition

Children's Picturebook Price Guide

Finding, Assessing, and Collecting Contemporary Illustrated Books

2006—2007 Edition

Linda and Stan Zielinski

ISBN-10:   0-9779394-0-5
ISBN-13:   978-0-9779394-0-4
LCCN: 2006903277

Published by
  Flying Moose Books L.L.C.
  P.O. Box 2251
  Park City, Utah   84098

www.flyingmoosebooks.com

First Edition
9 8 7 6 5 4 3 2 1 0

Printed in the United States of America

For Ruby, Jessica, and Quintin

Table Of Contents

Table Of Contents

Introduction

Illustrated children's picturebooks are enjoyable to behold. Flipping through a book, one is impressed by the craft of illustration, the nuances of color and shading, and their effect on the tone of the story. By flipping through several books, one learns to appreciate the subtleties of story boarding—the sequencing of picture to story—and the impact on the story's pace and viewpoint. By flipping through many books, one comes to recognize the artistic and creative effort that goes into every single book. Yes, we do love collecting children's picturebooks.

Our passion for collecting children's illustrated picturebooks is like many other collecting hobbies — the thrill of the hunt; the greater thrill of the find; investigation; confirmation; uncovering and recording forgotten tidbits of information; conversing with like-minded collectors; participating in lively discussions over differences that amount to irreconcilable differences of the heart, not of the mind.

To our chagrin, there has been a lack of information relative to collecting illustrated children's picturebooks, especially as compared to collecting books in general. We hope to partially fill the gap with this Price Guide. This Price Guide is focused on children's illustrated picturebooks, covering the period from 1930 to present, with an emphasis on illustrators whose works are still being published today.

OBJECTIVE

The objective of this Price Guide is to expand the children's picturebook collecting hobby by providing visibility to the estimated market value of first edition picturebooks. Our hope is that the general population will come to understand that first edition children's picturebooks have significant market value, and in turn, will lead to new collectors being attracted to the hobby. Because of this, the primary audience for this Price Guide is the book collector, rather than the bookseller. A secondary objective is to provide booksellers and collectors with structured information concerning the picturebook collecting hobby.

If this Price Guide is successful, collectible booksellers will stock and sell more children's picturebooks, bringing more first editions into the market place. Not only will this improve the availability of collectible children's picturebooks, but it will also improve the liquidity within the hobby.

THE BOOK LIST

The roots of this Price Guide originated from our own children's book collection. We began collecting children's picturebooks over fifteen years ago, and, as most collectors are apt to do, created a list as books were acquired. At the start, the list was limited to the books we owned. We began developing a wish list of books to obtain. At first, we used the "Other Books By" the illustrator, which is a list found in nearly every book we acquired. In the mid-1990's, the emergence of the internet made it more convenient to add to our book collection. Similarly, we began performing electronic searches on illustrators we collected, and over time, compiled fairly complete listings of their books. So, here we are today, with over 4,000 first edition children's books in our collection and nearly 23,000 books in our database. The Price Guide includes books from over 700 children's book illustrators, including books from:

- Each Caldecott Medal and Honor award winning illustrator
- Each Kate Greenaway Medal winning illustrator

INCLUSIONS AND EXCLUSIONS: ILLUSTRATORS AND THEIR BOOKS

As stated earlier, this Price Guide is focused on children's illustrated picturebooks, covering the period from 1930 to present, with an emphasis on illustrators whose works are still published today. Subsequently, the Price Guide is sorted alphabetically by the illustrator's last name, rather than by the author's last name. This is contrary to normal convention—our experience shows that collectors concentrate on the illustrator of picturebooks, rather than the authors—therefore "alphabetical by illustrator" is practical for this Price Guide.

An illustrated children's 'picturebook' is one in which the text and the illustrations are synergistic in telling the story – the two are intertwined such that one enhances the other, and vice-versa. The illustrations are not an augment to the story, but are intrinsic to the story. Books included in our definition of 'picturebooks' should meet the following criteria:

- A full-page illustration on every page or every other page
- Illustrations are credited to an illustrator (i.e. not an anonymous artist)
- Published in hardcover format, with a dust jacket

Many notable picturebook illustrators have contributed to children's chapter books, which have only an occasional illustration to accompany a reading story. We have included these type chapter books in the Price Guide. Also, some picturebooks are issued without dust jackets, yet include art by a notable illustrator—we have included these type books in the Price Guide.

By and large, we have excluded hard cover chapter books in which only the dust jacket cover art was completed by a notable children's picturebook illustrator. Soft cover picturebooks (i.e. paperbacks) have been nearly totally excluded from this Price Guide. To our knowledge, the only soft cover books included are the Mercer Mayer *Little Critter* books and also the original 1939 edition of *Rudolph the Red-Nosed Reindeer*, by Robert May, illustrated by Denver Gillen.

BOOK PRICING

We have over fifteen years of experience in the children's picturebook market, which includes very active participation in acquisition and collecting. Coupled with this experience, there are five primary sources for book prices in this Price Guide:

1. Antiquarian and used book stores
2. Antiquarian book fairs
3. Internet book markets
4. Catalogs distributed by children's booksellers
5. eBay auctions

Among these five sources, prices for the same book in similar condition can vary widely. For additional information, see Chapter 5, "Price Guide Illumination."

Being the first edition of the Price Guide and covering nearly 23,000 books, there are going to be pricing mistakes due to a number of reasons, including, but not limited to: typographical errors; bibliographical errors and oversights; and incorrect and incomplete market information[1]. As this publication matures, the pricing accuracy will increase. The intention is to provide a Price Guide which reflects current market retail conditions.

This Price Guide is not an offer to buy or sell any book, nor should the authors be held liable for any losses suffered from transactions made due to information in this book. Many factors affect the perceived value of any collectible, inclusive of illustrated children's picturebooks. The book buyer must weigh all factors before deciding to purchase a collectible first edition children's picturebook. In Chapter Two, "Collectibility And Value," we discuss in detail some key factors that impact a book's value.

ESTIMATION AND EXTRAPOLATION

Many of the books listed in this Price Guide do not come up for sale or auction on a routine or recent basis. Because of this, the book prices have had to be estimated, by extrapolation, from other information such as prices of books of similar authorship, similar vintage, similar condition, similar demand, and similar supply. An extrapolation of a book's price is only an adequate substitute for the market value of the book—the true indicator is a bookseller finding a book buyer who is willing to pay a certain amount for a book. Even then, the sale of a particular book is no guarantee that the same or similar book can be sold for the same or similar amount. Circumstances will always enter into the collectible book buying equation.

SPECULATIVE COLLECTING

The intention of this Price Guide, and future editions, is to estimate the current market values of first edition children's picturebooks. Values will change from year-to-year as the supply and demand balance changes for each individual book. Similar to most collectible hobbies,

---

1   Please email us at bookprices@1stedition.net for comments or information which would help increase the accuracy of book market prices in this Price Guide.

children's picturebook collectors would like a tool to measure the relative value of their collection over time. It is the nature of most collectors, regardless of the hobby, that they would like to be rewarded for their savvy decision making, and estimated market value is a key method of validation. So, children's book collectors do have a speculative interest, however it is not the primary driver for adding to their collection (See Chapter 3, "Approaches To Collecting").

We do want the picturebook collecting hobby to expand with people who love the books and appreciate the illustrations and creative talents involved. We do not want the hobby to expand with people whose primary interest is making money from their book collecting investment. This type of expansion is not sustainable, because once 'book values' cease to appreciate, the speculators will leave the hobby.

In general, we believe that first edition children's picturebooks are undervalued in the current market. In this Price Guide, we often provide opinions about particular books which have potential market appreciation or which we think are undervalued. We recognize that these opinions are tilted toward the speculative interest of a collector, however that should only be of minor importance when one is considering adding such book or books to one's collection. The monetary appreciation of any collectible picturebook is certainly not guaranteed; the aesthetic appreciation certainly is.

IDENTIFYING CONTEMPORARY FIRST EDITION PICTUREBOOKS

In general, on most contemporary first editions, the copyright page will have the words "First Edition," "First Printing" or "First Impression," in conjunction with a numbering or lettering (less common) systems. *It is important to understand that a book with "First Edition" or "First Printing" on the copyright page does not mean the book is a first edition in the collectible sense.* Rather, the correct "number line" sequence is of vital importance. In many cases the number line alone is present, without "First Edition" verbiage on the copyright page, to indicate a true first edition.

Thankfully, understanding the "number line" sequence for properly identifying a contemporary first edition picturebook is not too complicated. Chapter 4, "Identifying First Editions," provides information which should assist the new collector.

Chapter 1
Today's Golden Era Of Picturebooks

A Growing Hobby—Picturebook Collecting

Collecting contemporary illustrated children's picturebooks is a rapidly growing hobby. Thousands of collectible first edition picturebooks are listed for sale through the leading internet book association catalogs. Hard-to-find books are quickly absorbed by a collecting public. The competition is fierce for books in high demand, as evidenced almost daily on the prominent internet auction sites, and by the prices above the cover price realized by first editions of recent award winning books.

The growth in the picturebook collecting hobby is due to a number of reasons: the high approachability of the picturebook; the large number of quality illustrators actively creating today, and, most of all, the growing appreciation for the sheer beauty of the illustrations. The art of the illustrations has by-and-large been underappreciated by the 'knowing public', however that is changing as more of the illustrators are being 'found' by reputable art galleries. Lithographs and serigraphs by well-known picturebook illustrators are becoming more common.

The internet is intrinsic to the growth of the hobby by increasing the availability of collectible first edition picturebooks; increasing the visibility of picturebook prices; and increasing the participation in online book auctions. Because of this, the internet increases the liquidity of first edition collectible picturebooks. The internet has created an efficient market place for collectible books.

Yet, even with this popular interest and high growth, there has been a lack of information available relative to collecting children's picturebooks, and especially so when compared to book collecting in general. Most booksellers only have a rudimentary understanding of the collectible children's picturebook market. Also, many of the booksellers that do specialize in children's books often concentrate on the antiquarian collectible or are only interested in books by selected well–known illustrators.

Why Collect Picturebooks?

Collecting picturebooks is a bit different than collecting books in general. Picturebooks, by design, are more approachable. There is an easy appreciation for their attractiveness the instant the unacquainted flips through the pages of illustrations. This same 'instant expertise' cannot be said for antiquarian book collecting in general; often, experience must be garnered, hard earned, regarding the collectibility of a book. Appreciation of an antiquarian book is knowledge gathered through experience.

The illustrations in a picturebook are intrinsic to the story, and often are more descriptive of the story's intent than the text itself. The positive reinforcement and feedback for owning a first edition picturebook does not have to be entirely personal, and can to a large degree be from sharing the book with others. Anyone, including the inexperienced, can appreciate the artwork. And of course, first edition picturebooks can be shared through the highly preferred method of entertaining or educating children, which, after all, is their primary purpose. Collecting children's picturebooks should be a participative hobby.

The Golden Era of Children's Picturebooks

We are in a golden era of children's picturebook illustration. There has never been a period where the number of high quality children's book illustrators has been so plentiful. This is not meant to demean or denigrate the great illustrators of the past, since there have been many who are as good, perhaps even better, than the best of today. But without question, active today, the quantity of quality children's book illustrators is without parallel. To understand why this is so, one must understand a little about the development and evolution of the contemporary children's picturebook[2].

Development And Evolution Of The Picturebook Market

In the late 19th and early 20th century, illustrated children's picturebooks were not economically feasible or accessible to a majority of the population, so the books were produced and marketed to a minority of relatively affluent families. Children's literacy was more the exception than the rule, since children were critical providers of labor to both the agrarian and industrial economies. Therefore education, by and large, was considered of secondary importance. Books specifically produced for the entertainment of children were rare, as the industry of children's literature was quite immature. The methods, quality, and economics of multi-color printing technologies were not cost effective for mass market picturebooks. Some cheap periodicals appealing to the juvenile reader started to appear in the early 20th century, often with uncredited illustrations. Only a few illustrators made their living by illustrating children's books during this period.

The small number of artists who were making their living illustrating children's books were extremely talented, as one can appreciate by looking through any of the books augmented

---

2   From research and experience, we have knitted together this development and evolution of today's picturebook market to answer the question, "Why are there more children's book illustrators earning a living practicing their craft today than at anytime in the past?" The brief answer to this question offered in the chapter should be viewed as a hypothesis, until an experienced historian produces a definitive text.

with pictures by Arthur Rackham, Cicely Barker, Willie Pogany, Edmund Dulac, William H. Robinson, Howard Pyle, or Charles Robinson, to name just a few. Generally, these finely illustrated books had eight to twelve pages of illustrated pictures or plates accompanying a classic children's storybook. So, from the artist's perspective, the attention to those relatively few pages were quite high, and the examples are often exquisite.

Because of the high quality of illustration, this early 20th century period is often labeled the "Golden Age of Children's Book Illustration"[3]. But, these were definitely not 'picturebooks' as we understand the category today since the books had very few illustrations. Rather a combination of elements came together to start the children's picturebook industry:

- Compulsory Education
- Children's Literature
- Printing Technology
- Child Labor Laws

COMPULSORY EDUCATION

In 1852, Massachusetts was the first state to mandate a public education requirement for children. Over the next sixty years, compulsory education spread across the states, until finally in 1918, Mississippi became the last state to pass similar legislation[4]. Obviously, this spurred the start of a major transition within the United States: from a country with a majority of illiterate children to a country with a majority of literate children.

Still, mandated schooling was not rigorously enforced, and truancy was endemic across the country. Juvenile literacy was still the exception. Children were considered to be part of the working class, and, for all but the rich, an underlying foundation to the agrarian and industrialized economies. Children did not fully leave the work force until 1936, when the Fair Labor Act resulted in children entering schools in large numbers.

CHILDREN'S LITERATURE

The notion of books specifically for children was rare during the mid-19th century. Books for entertainment or enjoyment were especially rare. The books that were made for children, by and large, were religious or educational in nature. The idea that children should be, could be, entertained by what they read was a relatively novel idea.

Lewis Carroll's *Alice's Adventures in Wonderland* (Macmillan) in 1866 was one of the first highly successful entertainment books for children, and led to other commercially successful books in the latter part of the 19th century. Helen Bannerman's *Little Black Sambo* (Grant Richards) was published in 1899, and went through numerous printings and versions during the first decade of the 20th century. L. Frank Baum's *Wizard of Oz* (George M. Hill Co.) was published in 1900, and Baum created a number of other successful Oz-oriented books in the period from 1900-1910. Beatrix Potter's *The Tale of Peter Rabbit* (Frederick Warne) was published in 1902 to immediate success. Peter Rabbit was Potter's first of many "The Tales Of...," including *The Tale of Squirrel Nutkin*, *The Tale of Benjamin Bunny*, *The Tale of Tom Kitten*,

---

3   Dalby, Richard. The Golden Age of Children's Book Illustration. Gallery Books, 1991.

4   Richardson, John G, "Variation in Date of Enactment of Compulsory School Attendance Laws," Sociology of Education vol. 53 (July 1980)

and *The Tale of Jemima Puddle-Duck*, to name but a few which were published in the years leading up to 1910.

In 1913, Cupples & Leon published a series of dust jacketed 'All About' books which emulated the form and size of the Frederick Warne Beatrix Potter books. There were fifteen titles in the Cupples & Leon series, including *All About Peter Rabbit*, *All About The Three Bears*, *All About Mother Goose*, and *All About Little Red Hen*. The latter, along with several others, was illustrated by Johnny Gruelle.

In 1918, Gruelle wrote and illustrated *Raggedy Ann*, published by P.F. Volland, and in 1920 followed up with *Raggedy Andy Stories*. The two books were the cornerstone of a Volland series of children's books, each issued in an individual box, with dust jacket. The front of the box had a paste on cover that matched the illustration on the dust jacket cover. Other Gruelle books in the series included *Beloved Belinda*, *Eddie Elephant*, and *Friendly Fairies*. Other illustrators in the series included Janet Laura Scott, John Rae, and Katherine Sturges Dodge.

These successes, and others that followed in their footsteps, helped establish the children's market as a viable commercial vehicle, leading up to 1920.

PRINTING TECHNOLOGY—OFFSET LITHOGRAPHY

Perhaps the largest impact on the development of the picturebook was the advancement in printing technology, which made tremendous progress in the late 19th century and early part of the 20th century. In particular, the technology for offset lithography made high quality color printing economical to use for mass produced books.

It is important to understand a little of the process of lithography, since it will lead the reader to a higher appreciation for picturebooks by illustrators of the 1920's and 1930's, the era in which the technology was fast developing. In addition, the advancements in lithography play a very important role in the picturebook industry today.

Prior to the advent of lithography, gravure was the principle method of producing a high quality image to paper. Gravure is the process of engraving the image onto a metal or wood plate, applying ink to the engraving, then transferring the image to paper by impression. The engraving process was tedious, labor intensive, and not very conducive to correction. A lot of skill and technique was required to create the engraving, and the illustrator by necessity was highly connected to the engraving process.

Compared to gravure, lithography is much simpler to execute. Originally, lithography was simply drawing onto a stone using a waxy substance. The stone was then wet, and when an oily ink mixture was applied, it would adhere to the wax and repel from the wet stone areas. Pressing paper to the stone would then transfer the image to paper. In this way, etching an image into metal or wood was no longer required. This greatly economized the process of lithography over gravure, in terms of time, labor, and materials. The economics for producing illustrations in books was greatly improved[5].

In order to do multiple colors using lithography, multiple stones would be used, one for each color. On each stone an image needs to be created, each image particular to a particular color. For example, one image would be made just for blue ink, another for just the red ink, and so forth. Then, ink of a particular color is applied to each stone image, and the paper is pressed

---

5   Weber, Wilhelm. A History of Lithography, Thames & Hudson, 1966.

in steps. In this way, each step applies a color. When one speaks of a four-color press, then the steps might be red, blue, green and black.

Originally, with lithography, the illustrator would draw directly onto flat stones. Over time, methods were created which allowed the illustrations to be drawn onto special paper, which could be transferred onto the stones. During the course of the 19th century, these lithographic stones were gradually replaced with metal plates, in which the image was made via a photographic process. These plates were less expensive and easier to work with, and evolved into the use of curved plates. Curved plates allowed for rotary presses, which greatly increased the economies of books printed by lithographic techniques[6]. By the turn of the 20th century, rotary lithographic presses were becoming more and more common.

Better performing inks and color evolved in conjunction with the developments in the lithographic press. The ink's "magic" was in adhering to the paper and not to the impressioning device. The science of lithographic ink greatly improved the quality and economics of illustrations in print.

BEGINNING OF THE MODERN PICTUREBOOK

So, leading up 1920, the following socio-economic threads were coming together:

- More and more children were becoming literate, as the country had a sixty year history with compulsory education; the last state mandate was passed in 1918.
- Children's literature had become accepted, blossoming in the late 19th century and early part of the 20th century, and it was not unusual for publishers to target juvenile readers.
- Advancement in lithography technologies caused step–change reductions in the cost of printing. As rotary presses proliferated around the country, industry pressure was increased to find economically viable publishing content.
- Advancement in lithography technologies made it easier for artists to create high quality mass produced images, as a complex technique (etching) was removed from the publishing process.

The combination of social, technical, and economic elements came together in the mid– and late–1920's and the children's picturebook industry was born[7].

Wanda Gag's *Millions of Cats* (Coward-McCann) published in 1928, could arguably be called the first notable picturebook. Wanda Gag was a successful graphic artist, and this, her first picturebook, won a Newbery Medal runner-up award[8]. Started in 1922, the Newbery is presented annually by the American Library Association (ALA) "for the most distinguished American children's book published the previous year." *Millions of Cats* was the first picturebook to receive an award. It is the first milestone picturebook, and is still in print today, nearly eighty years after its initial publication!

---

6   Weber, Wilhelm. A History of Lithography, Thames & Hudson, 1966.

7   For a detailed look at the history of the picturebook, every serious collector should own a copy of *American Picturebooks from Noah's Ark to the Beast Within* (1976, Macmillan), by Barbara Bader. The book is an incredibly detailed view of picturebooks and illustrators which played an important part in the evolution of the art form.

8   Today, a Newbery runner-up is referred to as a Newbery Honor award.

Wanda Gag followed with *The Funny Thing* (Coward-McCann) in 1929, *Snippy and Snappy* (Coward-McCann) in 1931, and then *The ABC Bunny* (Coward-McCann) in 1933, which garnered her a second Newbery runner-up award. Gag's books helped to prove that children's picturebooks could be commercially successful.

Other early milestone picturebooks followed *Millions of Cats*. In 1930, Marjorie Flack authored and illustrated *Angus and the Ducks* (Doubleday, Doran), followed in 1931 by *Angus And The Cats* (Doubleday, Doran), then in 1932 *Angus Lost* (Doubleday, Doran). Flack authored another milestone book in 1933, *The Story About Ping* (Viking), illustrated by Kurt Wiese. All of these books are still being published today.

Platt & Munk played a part in the early development of the picturebook market with publication of the "Never Grow Old Series" of children's hardcover picturebooks, issued with dust jackets. Beginning in 1930, the nine book series included retellings of several Mother Goose stories, and also included a 'new' edition of Helen Bannerman's *Little Black Sambo*, this time illustrated by Eulalie Banks. To the general population, this is probably the most familiar of all the versions of *Little Black Sambo*, and stayed in print until the early 1970's.

However, the most popular book from the "Never Grow Old Series" was the 1930 publication of *The Little Engine That Could*, illustrated by Lois Lenski. This version stayed in print until 1954, when it was illustrated anew by George and Dorothy Hauman. The Hauman version is still in print today. Significantly, *The Little Engine That Could* spawned an entire line of books and related paraphernalia—a recent query on the Penguin Books website produced over twenty versions or line extensions of the book. In 2001, *The Little Engine That Could* stood 30th on Publisher Weekly's list of the top bestselling children's hardcover books[9]. Additionally, and significantly, the book brought the refrain "I think I can! I think I can!" into the public's consciousness.

In 1933, Jean de Brunhoff's *Babar* was introduced to American readership in *The Story Of Babar* (Smith and Haas). Originally published in French, Merle Haas translated the work into English, and was then published by "Harrison Smith and Robert Haas." Smith and Haas published *The Travels of Babar* in 1934, then *Babar The King* in 1935[10]. In 1935, Random House became the publisher of Babar books, and has continued publishing books in the Babar franchise up to the present day. So, by the mid-1930's, the children's picturebook market was firmly established.

In 1936, Munro Leaf's *Ferdinand* (Viking) was published, illustrated by Robert Lawson. Immediately successful, *Ferdinand* went into multiple printings within months of publication. *Ferdinand* was the first picturebook to crossover into pop culture. Walt Disney produced an animated feature film, and in conjunction published a Walt Disney Studio's version of the story, along with corresponding merchandising materials. *Ferdinand* was a national phenomenon, and Life Magazine featured a story on the book, film, and creators in their February 21, 1938 issue. The story's anti-war sentiment struck a nerve in a pre-war America.

---

9   Publisher Weekly's 2001 list of bestselling hardcover children's book sales through the year 2000.

10 The original Smith and Haas published Babar books are rare in first printings. The three books were published with dust jackets, and were larger in format then the corresponding publication by Random House. The Random House editions also had dust jackets, and are also difficult to find in first printings.

CHILD LABOR LAW & CALDECOTT AWARDS

The Elson Basic Reader (Scott, Foresman & Co.), introducing the public to "Dick and Jane," was published in 1930, and this early reader series exploded in popularity in the late 1930's and early 1940's, especially after Congress passed the Fair Labor Act, which dramatically impacted, favorably, the percentage of children to attend school.

CHILD LABOR

In 1938, Congress passed the Fair Labor Standards Act effectively making it illegal for children under 14 years of age to work full time. Education had been mandated on a state-by-state basis beginning in 1852, through 1918, but the public did not wholeheartedly embrace the enforcement of truancy, in part because of the beneficial economic impact of working children.

The Fair Labor Standards Act of 1938[11] was enforced at a federal level, and caused a large number of children of school age to leave the work place and enter the school place. In turn, the increase in the number of formally educated children greatly increased the quantity and variety of beginning reader books. Beginning reader books nearly always included clarifying or instructive pictures. As more children became literate, the demand for entertainment books increased, and the result was a step change increase in the capitalistic forces to create picture-books for the market. The proverbial snowball was launched down the hill, and the Fair Labor Act became a significant milestone in the development of the picturebook industry.

DR. SEUSS

In 1937, Theodor Seuss Geisel's first book for children was published, *And To Think That I Saw It On Mulberry Street* (Random House). Prior to the publication of Mulberry Street, Seuss was a successful graphic artist and humorist. Look Magazine published a feature article on Seuss in the June 7, 1938 issue, titled "On Unheard of Animals," an article about some of his crazy animal creations.

Mulberry Street was immediately successful, and Seuss followed up with *The 500 Hats Of Bartholomew Cubbins* in 1938, followed by *The King's Stilts* in 1939, and *Horton Hatches An Egg* in 1940, all published by Random House. Each of these books was commercially successful, and Seuss and his children's books became nationally popular. Life Magazine featured an article on Seuss in the Dec. 15, 1941 issue, and Newsweek published an article on Dr. Seuss creations in the Feb. 9, 1942 issue. WWII served as a break in Seuss's book career, then from 1947 to 1956 Seuss had twelve children's picturebooks published, each of which are still in print today. More on Seuss later.

CALDECOTT AWARDS

In 1938, the American Library Association (ALA) began presenting annually the Caldecott Medal to the most distinguished children's book illustration published in the year. The Caldecott Medal was established as a sister award to the ALA's Newbery Medal, which was awarded to a children's books for literary merit and presented annually beginning in 1922. Therefore,

---

11   The Act set a minimum age limit of 16 for work during school hours for companies engaged in interstate commerce, and 14 for work outside school hours in non-manufacturing companies.

in 1938, a highly creditable organization began presenting an award annually to a picturebook and illustrator, lending great credence to the blossoming art form.

Interestingly, in the decade leading up to the first Caldecott Awards, three of Wanda Gag's picturebooks won Newbery awards for their literary merit, probably hastening the inception of an annual award for children's illustration! The Caldecott Awards continue to be presented today, and have grown in stature and prestige over the past 70 years (see Chapter 2 for detailed information on the Caldecott awards).

The first Caldecott Medal was awarded in 1938 to Dorothy Lathrop for her illustrations in *Animals Of The Bible* (Frederick Stokes), written by Helen Dean Fish. Thomas Handforth won the second Caldecott Medal in 1939, for *Mei Li* (Doubleday), which he also wrote. Nearly all of the Caldecott Medal winning books are still in print today.

Ludwig Bemelman's *Madeline* (Simon & Schuster) was published in 1939 to some fanfare. The original publication of the book was preceded by a feature in the September 4, 1939 issue of *Life Magazine. Madeline* was also selected as a Caldecott Medal runner-up, which today is called a Caldecott Honor book.

So, by the end of the 1930's, the children's picturebook, barely a decade old in its established form, was firmly entrenched as a successful commercial vehicle.

LITTLE GOLDEN BOOKS

In 1942, Simon & Schuster began publishing the Little Golden Books, a series of inexpensive, well illustrated, high quality children's books. The first twelve books were all published simultaneously, in hard cover format with dust jackets. At a price of 25 cents, the series was met with instant commercial success.

The books went into multiple printings nearly immediately, devoured by a population hungry for a children's book of this sort. Inexpensive, yet of high quality and high durability, the Little Golden Books fulfilled an unmet need of the country's growing juvenile reading population. From a parent's perspective, LGB's were a worthy economic alternative to the comic book.

The eighth book in the series, *Poky Little Puppy*, is the top selling children's book of all time according to a 2001 list of bestselling children's hardback books compiled by Publisher's Weekly (see Appendix 4 for the Publisher's Weekly list of 100 bestselling children's hardcover books). But *Poky Little Puppy* is not the only hugely successful LGB—four of the top eight books on the Publisher's Weekly list are Little Golden Books! Many of the books have become icons within the picturebook marketplace—*Poky Little Puppy, Tootle, Scuffy The Tugboat, The Little Red Hen* among others. Several of the illustrators for the Little Golden Books later became staples within the picturebook industry. Corinne Malvern, Tibor Gergely, Gustaf Tenggren, Feodor Rojankovsky, Richard Scarry, Eloise Wilkin, and Garth Williams are just a few of the illustrator's who contributed to this astonishingly successful book publishing phenomenon.

Many book collectors do not realize that the first thirty-five LGB's were issued with dust jackets —from 1942 to 1947—at a standard 25-cent price. These dust jacketed versions also have a blue cloth spine. It is amazingly difficult to find a first edition, first printing with a nice condition dust jacket. Actually, it is very difficult to find a dust jacketed version of any of the 1940's printings, first edition or later printing.

There is an active collecting community of first edition Little Golden Books. *Collecting Little Golden Books* (Krause Publications), by Steve Santi, is the authoritative price guide, so we have not included the complete listing in our price guide. Online auctions for first printings are especially competitive, so don't expect to purchase the early first editions cheaply. High quality and high demand, coupled with very limited supply, begets high prices.

During the mid-forties to early-fifties, the American Library Association's Caldecott Awards continued adding to the credibility of illustrated picturebooks as an acceptable art form. During that time, many prominent artists were either

FIRST TWELVE LITTLE GOLDEN BOOKS	
TITLE	**ILLUSTRATOR**
1. The Three Little Kittens	Masha
2. Bedtime Stories	Gustaf Tenggren
3. The Alphabet From A To Z	Vivienne Blake
4. Mother Goose	Miss Elliott
5. Prayers For Children	Rachel Taft Dixon
6. The Little Red Hen	Rudolf Freund
7. Nursery Songs	Corinne Malvern
8. The Poky Little Puppy	Gustaf Tenggren
9. The Golden Book Of Fairy Tales	Winfield Hoskins
10. Baby's Book	Bob Smith
11. The Animals Of Farmer Jones	Rudolf Freund
12. This Little Piggy	Roberta Pavlin

at the top of their craft or at the beginning of a lustrous career, and had won either a Caldecott Medal or Honor award. These included such notables as Marcia Brown, Barbara Cooney, Roger Duvoisin, Margaret Bloy Graham, Berta and Elmer Hader, Robert Lawson, Robert McCloskey, Dr. Seuss, Maurice Sendak, Ingri & Edgar Parin d'Aulaire, Leo Politi, Tasha Tudor, and Leonard Weisgard. By 1955, such picturebook classics as *Thidwick*, *Ferdinand*, *Madeline*, *Make Way For Ducklings*, *The Little House*, *Curious George*, and *Eloise*, had all been published.

CAT IN THE HAT AND THE BEGINNER BOOKS

Up until the mid-1950s, there was a degree of separation between illustrated educational books and illustrated picturebooks. That all changed, dramatically and with much national fanfare, with the 1957 publication of Dr. Seuss's *The Cat In The Hat* (Random House). Here was an early reader, full of 220 madly rhyming words, which made its way into our elementary school classrooms.

The Cat In The Hat is a tremendously important book. Not just an important picturebook or an important children's book, but an important book without any qualifiers! The publication of the book in 1957 forever changed the way in which children would learn to read and be educated. Reading COULD be fun!

Prior to the publication of his first children's book in 1937, *And To Think That I Saw It On Mulberry Street* (Random House, 1937)), Theodor Seuss Geisel was a prominent and successful humorist illustrator for such magazines as *Judge* and *Life*. By the time of *The Cat In The Hat's* publication, Dr. Seuss was a very successful children's book illustrator, having published twelve children's books, three of which had won Caldecott Honor awards. Actually, prior to the publication of *The Cat In The Hat*, one could easily say that Dr. Seuss had already had two successful illustration careers, one as a humorist and one as a picturebook creator.

Mr. Geisel created *The Cat In The Hat* in reaction to a *Life Magazine* article by John Hersey, published in the May 24, 1954 issue, titled "Why Do Students Bog Down On First R? A LOCAL COMMITTEE SHEDS LIGHT ON A NATIONAL PROBLEM: READING." In the article, Hersey was critical of the then current state of school primers,

> "In the classroom boys and girls are confronted with books that have insipid illustrations depicting the slicked-up lives of other children. [Existing primers] feature abnormally courteous, unnaturally clean boys and girls." "In bookstores, anyone can buy brighter, livelier books featuring strange and wonderful animals and children who behave naturally, i.e., sometimes misbehave. Given incentive from school boards, publishers could do as well with primers."

Hersey's arguments were enumerated in some ten pages of Life Magazine, which was the leading periodical of its time. After detailing many issues contributing to the dilemma with student's reading, toward the end of the article, Hersey redundantly asked:

> "Why should [school primers] not have pictures that widen rather than narrow the associative richness the children give to the words they illustrate—drawings like those of the wonderfully imaginative geniuses among children's illustrators, Tenniel, Howard Pyle, "Dr. Seuss," Walt Disney?"

Geisel responded to this "challenge" by rigidly limiting himself to a small set of words from an elementary school vocabulary list, then crafted a story based upon two randomly selected words—cat and hat. The results of this personal challenge are nothing short of amazing!

Successful before the publication of the *The Cat In The Hat*, after it's publication, Dr. Seuss became an 'overnight' national phenomenon. After the publication of *The Cat In The Hat*, numerous feature articles were published in *Life*, *Look* and other prominent periodicals. The book's characters, along with other Seuss creations, were extended into toys and other products, occurring long before co-merchandising and line extensions became commonplace for children's character marketing.

The Cat In The Hat was published by Random House. However because of it's success, an independent publishing company was formed, called Beginner Books. Geisel was the president and editor. Beginner Books was chartered as a series of books oriented toward various stages of early reading development. The second book in the series was nearly as popular, *The Cat In The Hat Comes Back*, published in 1958.

Springing from this series of beginning readers were such standards as *A Fly Went By* (1958), *Sam and the Firefly* (1958), *Green Eggs and Ham* (1960), *Go, Dog. Go!* (1961), *Hop On Pop* (1963), and *Fox in Socks* (1965), each a monument in the picturebook industry, and also significant in the historical development of early readers. All are still in print and remain very popular over forty years after their initial publication[12].

Creators in the Beginner Book series were such luminaries as Jan & Stan Berenstain, P. D. Eastman, Roy McKie, and Helen Palmer (Mr. Geisel's wife). The Beginner Books dominated

---

12   From 1957 to 1960, Random House was the distributor of Beginner Books. In 1960, Random House purchased Beginner Books, and it became a division of Random House.

the children's picturebook market of the 1960's, and still plays a significant role today within the phases of students' reading development.

Early Readers

In 1957, on the heels of Beginner Books' *The Cat In The Hat*, came *Little Bear*, the first of the "I Can Read" series of books, published by Harper & Brothers. Written by Else Holmelund Minarik and illustrated by a then relatively unknown Maurice Sendak, the two collaborated on three other "I Can Read" books over the next three years.

From 1958 to 1960, Syd Hoff wrote and illustrated four "I Can Read" books: *Danny And The Dinosaur*, *Sammy The Seal*, *Julius*, and *Oliver*. Each of these books is still in print today, and has served several generations of developing student readers. By 1960, sixteen "I Can Read" books had been published by Harper & Brothers. The early success of the "I Can Read" books and the Beginner Books, both from a commercial and learn-to-read perspective, initiated the blurring between educational and entertainment books.

This phenomenon favorably impacted the consumer market for children's books. The economic forces that percolate early reader books to market became more formalized, forming a business infrastructure for the picturebook industry. As a result, more and more illustrators could begin to economically support themselves by illustrating children's picturebooks.

By the 1970's, printing technology had evolved so much that the illustrator became less and less involved with the printing process. The advent of photography to create negatives for lithographic printing meant that the illustrator could focus on their medium of expression, rather than on the techniques necessary to get the image onto a press. Today's illustrators do not have to be involved in the color separation process, although some choose to do so.

The Involved Parent

Still, up until the 1970's, the educational selection of books was in large part the business of the ALA librarians and the country's educators, since these organizations largely controlled the books our children were formally exposed to in schools. This changed beginning in the late 1970's and early 1980's, as credible journalists and educators went public with scathing exposes and rebuttals of the shortcomings and failures of our public education system, forever changing the laissez-faire attitude of parental involvement in their child's elementary education. Parents began becoming more connected to the educational development of their children, which fueled a greater involvement in what their children were reading.

This social unrest toward public education was in part why the U.S. Secretary of Education created the National Commission on Excellence in Education in 1981, and directed it to present a report on the quality of education in America for him and the American people. The Commission's report, published in April of 1983, was titled "Our Nation At Risk."[13]

> "Our Nation is at risk. Our once unchallenged preeminence in commerce, industry, science, and technological innovation is being overtaken by competitors throughout the world. This report is concerned with only one of the many causes and dimensions of the problem, but it is the one

---

13   National Commission On Excellence In Education; David P. Gardner, Chairman. A Nation at Risk: The Imperative for Educational Reform. 1983.

that under girds American prosperity, security, and civility. We report to the American people that while we can take justifiable pride in what our schools and colleges have historically accomplished and contributed to the United States and the well-being of its people, the educational foundations of our society are presently being eroded by a rising tide of mediocrity that threatens our very future as a Nation and a people. What was unimaginable a generation ago has begun to occur—others are matching and surpassing our educational attainments."

In response to "Our Nation At Risk," a measure of books, newspaper and journal articles were published in the mid- and late- eighties, both citing, supporting, and countering the findings of the commission (and continue to be published today[14]). It is our opinion that a by-product of this mass of social dialogue was a shift within the group of informed and concerned parents, away from total dependency on the public school system, and toward joint responsibility for the education of our children. This shift is still in process and has created a social group we refer to as the involved parent.

Today's involved parent, in this modern era of illustrated children's picturebooks, is motivated to not only read to their children to improve their reading and language skills, but is highly participative in the selection of the particular books. This pervasive participation is increasing variety and diversity of the demand. It's also improving quality, since the competition for the readers' eyes and minds is fierce among publishers, and they realize quality begets sales. So there is improved quality of the word, obviously, and also improved quality of the illustration, since writers understand that good composition, storyboarding, and pictures help tell and sell the stories.

The 'primary reader books', such as the Dick and Jane series, has almost entirely vanished from our elementary school curriculum. Instead, it has been replaced by commercially produced early reader books, typified by the Beginner Book series. The beginning reader books now used in the elementary school system must both educate and entertain. No longer is the selection of the early reader books wholly the responsibility of the educational administration across the country.

In 2006, the American Library Association started awarding the Theodor Seuss Geisel Award to the most distinguished beginning reader book.

> "The Theodor Seuss Geisel Award, [...] will be given annually beginning in 2006 to the author(s) and illustrator(s) of the most distinguished contribution to the body of American children's literature known as beginning reader books published in the United States during the preceding year. The award is to recognize the author(s) and illustrator(s) of a beginning reader book who demonstrate great creativity and imagination in his/her/their literary and artistic achievements to engage children in reading."[15]

An interesting aspect is that the award is presented to both the author and illustrator, in "artistic achievements to engage children to reading." Quite a noble purpose. In addition to the recog-

---

14   See Selected Bibliography.
15   American Library Association

nition the Theodor Seuss Geisel Award provides to deserving creators, it is also a validation of the contribution of the illustrations to the effect of the picturebook upon the reader.

TODAY'S GOLDEN ERA OF THE PICTUREBOOK

So put it all together and what does it mean? The manner and methods of education has changed. The home environment has changed, increasing the number of children and adults exposed to quality children's picturebooks. The population has grown dramatically. The book publishing industry has changed, is very 'results' oriented, and the means of book distribution and marketing has become significantly more productive. All of these factors, and others, translates into a children's book industry that is orders-of-magnitude larger in size than that of the past.

Because of these market economies, there are a large number of illustrators who are earning a living by illustrating children's books, more than ever before. Understandably, quantity does not necessarily beget quality. However, printing technologies have advanced to the point where the artist can be completely detached from the methods of printing, and therefore can completely focus on their craft. Illustrators have the creative freedom to create in whatever medium they are most comfortable. The printing technology no longer constrains the artist, and does not dictate the type and method of illustration! Because of this, the artwork today in picturebooks is of the highest caliber, especially in terms of composition and originality. Numerous colleges and universities have curriculum related to the form. This makes for a very rich picturebook collecting environment.

The pictures are intrinsic to the story; the story is intrinsic to the pictures. Wordless children's picturebooks are better crafted then anytime in the past, due in large part to academic material and training surrounding the child's need and perspective. The variety of the types of art—abstract, cartoon, collage, impressionistic, realistic—is without precedence. No single type dominates the landscape, so virtually every aficionado's particular favorite is represented by many artists. This makes for a very rich collecting environment.

A number of new illustrators are entering the market every year, finding themselves, and finding an audience. Each year, several of these new illustrators develop into market mainstays, creators who will produce at least a book a year, for years to come. This makes for a very rich collecting environment.

All across the country, numerous collectible picturebooks lie dormant on underexposed bookseller's shelves, or sit boxed in someone's attic. The artwork is underappreciated by the general population, and in turn, the books are underappreciated by the collecting public. Most adults have fond memories of childhood picturebooks, which translates into latent demand. The books were stops on our way to adulthood, just as they are in the journey of today's children, and tomorrow's. For the fortunate reader whose life includes a child or children learning to read, then you have the opportunity to create some picturebook memories, some future stops along the way. This makes for a very rich collecting environment.

What's A Book About Picturebooks Without Any Pictures?

You are probably asking yourself that question. We love children's picturebook illustrations, however as time was getting closer to press there arose a multitude of permission issues, so we opted for what you hold in your hand. In the introduction to Chapter 1, "A Growing Hobby—Picturebook Collecting," we mentioned the growing popularity of the original artwork for children's picturebooks. Over the years, we have acquired several pieces, including the cover piece for this book, by David Christiana. It's from *The Magical, Mystical, Marvelous Coat*, by Catherine Ann Cullen, illustrated by David Christiana, published by Little, Brown in 2001. David was kind enough to give permission to use the artwork for this Price Guide.

If you are interested in acquiring some original children's picturebook illustrations, or limited edition prints, then some potential sources:

Storyopolis in Los Angeles has a very large selection of original artwork from a number of picturebook illustrators. "Storyopolis represents the world's finest children book illustrators, editorial artists, and cartoonists." They also have limited edition prints. One can view what is available on their website, at http://www.storyopolis.com/artistlist.asp.

Every Picture Tells A Story advertises that they are "the foremost gallery of the Art of Illustration -- children's book art, fantasy and editorial works. Choose from over 70 of the greatest illustrators of all time and your favorite characters from literature. From Seuss to Steadman -- you can share and collect unique and cherished artworks -- both classic and contemporary." You can visit their website at http://www.every-picture.com/.

In December 2005, *Chemers Gallery* in Los Angeles held their 14th Annual Children's Book Illustration Show. The show featured original artwork from Scott Gustafson, Julie Downing, Paige Miglio, Jane Dyer, Matt Faulkner, and Winslow Pels, with the proceeds going to a local charity. Each year, Chemers holds a similar show with different children's book illustrators. See their website at http://www.chemersgallery.com, special events.

Chapter 2
Factors Affecting Collectibility

TODAY'S PICTUREBOOK COLLECTING HOBBY

From a collecting perspective, first edition children's illustrated picturebooks are largely under-appreciated by the general population. This is in part due to the familiarity of the books—"I used to read that when I was a child!"—which propagates the notion that the books are common collectibles. The books *are* common, the first editions are not. Still, the market prices of first edition picturebooks remain relatively modest. This is unfortunate, but as a result, the hobby is reasonably inexpensive to practice. The price of 'buyer's remorse' is not too costly—the consolation is owning a nicely illustrated picturebook! Another positive aspect to this 'general under appreciation', is that inexpensive collectible picturebooks can still be found on bookseller's shelves all across the country.

The antiquarian book collecting industry is a tad elitist and not accessible to everyone. It is certainly not a 'drive-up-to-the-window-and-order' type of hobby. This is not meant to be a criticism, just highlighting the reality—the antiquarian book industry has a high barrier to entry, in terms of acquiring knowledge through experience.

There are several publications and online reference systems where one can uncover the authoritative value of an antiquarian illustrated children's book, but it takes a bit more work for the novice to know whether the book is of good collectible value[16]. The antiquarian book collecting market tends to be very supply oriented, meaning that small printings, with only a small number of known available copies, command the most value and the most attention. Rarity tends to drive value. Rarity, coupled with publishing significance, drives very high value.

---

16   There are several exceptions to this, including the Oz books, Alice books, and Pooh books, which have active interest and very wide popularity, but this is the exception rather than the rule for most finely illustrated books of the early 20th century.

On the other hand, the children's picturebook market is, and will continue to be, very demand oriented. The value and collectibility of a book will be determined most by the number of people who have been exposed to the book, and the deep interest of a small portion of those who will want to own a first edition copy. The hobby of collecting children's picturebooks is highly accessible, and does not require years of personal research to come to an understanding of a book's beauty, collectibility, and value. Many people have grown up and been educated by these books and their illustrators. Rarity, in and of itself, will not drive value. Popularity and demand will.

The value of any collectible is essentially an economic balance between the supply and demand within the hobby. The supply of the collectible is dependent upon the original production quantity, less the number that are damaged or discarded over time. The demand for the collectible is impacted by different criteria, factors particular to the item in question. Since the supply side of any collectible is fixed after its production, then the heaviest impact on the appreciation of a collectible over time are the factors which impact demand.

Every collecting hobby has some key factors that determine an item's collectibility and value. For example, with comic books, a hobby with a highly established valuation method, value is determined by the comic's title, the characters involved, the writer & artist, the story, whether it introduces new characters, the publisher, the age or era, the supply, and the condition of the book. All of these items affect the collecting population's demand for the particular issue, which in turn, determines the comic book's price within the market. Similar factors could be enumerated for coins, stamps, baseball cards, Disneyana material, and Pez dispensers. So, as with any collecting hobby, illustrated children's picturebooks have several key factors that determine their collectibility and value.

PREREQUISITES TO COLLECTIBILITY

Before detailing the key factors to collectible children's picturebooks, one should pause to consider that there are prerequisites for a book to have *any* collectibility or value. In the case of illustrated children's picturebooks, the prerequisites to collectibility and value are no different then of book collecting in general: a book's identification as a true first edition and the condition of the book.

As you become more and more involved in book collecting, it will become vital that you are able to assess and identify contemporary first editions from most major publishing houses. To get you started in this endeavor, refer to Chapter 4, "Identifying First Editions," for information on identifying first editions from some popular children's book publishers. Similarly, as your interest in the hobby grows, it is important that you understand how to assess or grade a book's condition. Subsequently, Chapter 6, "Book Grading," provides information about generally accepted book condition guidelines.

One could argue that the two prerequisites, first edition identification and a book's condition, should be included as the *most important* key factors affecting a book's collectibility and value. If this argument sets you at ease, then fine, for it matters not how one categorizes the influences on a book's collectibility and value, just so we agree upon some common understanding of the influences.

SIX KEY FACTORS

It may come as a surprise to some, but the key factors to a picturebook's collectibility and value are not manifestly created. Similar to other collecting hobbies, the factors evolve over time. With regard to collecting first edition picturebooks, to our knowledge, the factors that affect value have not yet been documented within the hobby. So, the factors that we put forth are a starting point for dialogue within the picturebook collecting hobby, which will create some controversy and discourse. Over time, this collaborative tension will lead to evaluation and evolution of the factors generally accepted to affect a book's value and collectibility. Eventually these factors will become solidified within the picturebook collecting hobby

With that said, it is with some degree of uncertainty that we offer these six key factors in determining the collectibility and value of a first edition children's picturebook. After all, it is difficult to determine exactly why anybody collects anything, so to itemize six key factors to collecting children's picturebooks would seem a frivolous endeavor. Also, one would be quite naïve to think that these six are the only factors which contribute to a picturebook's value. Still, our insanity prevails—the six key factors are, in no particular order, and with the spirit of stirring up some controversy:

1. Aesthetic Quality of the Illustrations and the Story
2. Eminence of the Illustrator
3. Book's Illustration Awards
4. Pop Culture
5. Copies Sold / High Printings
6. Franchise Books

The six factors are intimately connected, so it is difficult to individually describe one without intermingling the description with the other factors. One factor will invariably impact other factors. Not one to retreat from a challenge, we will try nonetheless.

FACTOR 1: AESTHETIC QUALITY OF THE ILLUSTRATIONS AND STORY

It almost goes without saying, but we want to clearly state that the quality and appeal of the illustrations and story should be the key factor in determining a picturebook's collectibility. Therefore, since the role of the beholder is such a singularly personal affair, avoid collecting books in which the artwork or story is not appealing to you. Hopefully, this will not be an epiphany to the readers of this Price Guide.

The quality of the illustrations and story is the single most important factor in your picturebook collection appreciating over time. Perhaps this appreciation will not come in monetary or material ways, but in satisfaction of the heart, which as any true bibliophile will attest, is why we collect books in the first place. Still, one would hope that the general collecting pubic will at some point 'catch on' to the quality of your discerning eye, and as a result enhance the collectibility and value of your collection[17]. Similar to all collecting hobbies, higher demand leads to higher collectibility and value.

---

17   The opportunity always exists to discover previously unrecognized talent amid the thousands of picturebooks published each year.

22

Many, many books have become perennial staples within the picturebook industry due to the high appeal of the story and illustrations. Some contemporary books that quickly come to mind: *Guess How Much I Love You?* (Candlewick, 1995), written by Sam McBratney and illustrated by Anita Jeram; *The Rainbow Fish* (North-South, 1992), written and illustrated by Marcus Pfister ; *The Very Hungry Caterpillar* (Philomel, 1969), written and illustrated by Eric Carle; and *If You Give A Mouse A Cookie* (Harpercollins, 1985), written by Laura Numeroff and illustrated by Felicia Bond. Each of these books became popular before the illustrators or authors were widely known—they might be renowned today as a direct result of the success of the book! In all cases, the books have sold many, many more copies than the original print run, and subsequently went into multiple print runs.[18] It was the aesthetic quality of the story and the illustrations which contributed to the huge success of each of these books. Because of this appeal, the demand and collectibility was increased for first edition copies within the hobby.

BREAKTHROUGH ILLUSTRATIONS

There are numerous types of illustration styles for children's picturebooks, and some are certain to be more appealing to you than others. The same can be said for everybody. Because of this, during specific periods over the past seventy years, particular illustration styles have been more popular than others. It is difficult to pinpoint *why* the public embraces one illustration style over another—it is not as difficult to identify *when* one style became more popular than another. Usually, this change in trend can be traced to a single book—to the artistic interpretation of a visionary illustrator.

Throughout the history of the picturebook industry, some notable books advanced the art of children's picturebook illustrations, and in turn influenced the composition of other books that followed. First editions of these books with "breakthrough illustrations" have enhanced collectibility within the hobby.

Note that the table is not meant to be a list of important picturebooks from the collecting hobby's historical perspective, but instead are significant *in advanc-*

Picturebooks With Breakthrough Illustrations

Year	Title	Illustrator
1928	Millions of Cats	Wanda Gàg
1931	The Magic Rug	Ingri & Edgar Parin d'Aulaire
1933	The Story About Ping	Kurt Wiese
1937	And To Think I Saw It On Mulberry Street	Theodor Seuss Geisel
1939	Madeline	Ludwig Bemelmans
1946	Little Lost Lamb	Leonard Weisgard
1949	Song of the Swallows	Leo Politi
1954	A Very Special House	Maurice Sendak
1959	Little Blue And Little Yellow	Leo Leonni
1963	Where The Wild Things Are	Maurice Sendak
1967	The Emperor And The Kite	Ed Young
1970	The Kingdom Under The Sea	Jan Pienkowski
1972	Snow-White And The Seven Dwarfs	Nancy Ekholm Burkert
1975	Why Mosquitoes Buzz In People's Ears	Leo & Diane Dillon
1979	Garden of Abdul Gasazi	Chris Van Allsburg
1982	Where The Buffaloes Begin	Stephen Gammell
1984	Little Red Riding Hood	Trina Schart Hyman
1985	Hansel And Gretel	Paul Zelinsky
1988	Mirandy And Brother Wind	Jerry Pinkney
1988	Free Fall	David Wiesner
1993	The Stinky Cheese Man	Lane Smith
2002	My Friend Rabbit	Eric Rohmann

18 As a matter of fact, each of these books has been so successful that it made the 2001 list by Publisher's Weekly of the Bestselling Children's Books, refer to Factor 5, this chapter. In addition, several of the books became "Franchise Books," refer to Factor 6, this chapter.

ing the art of picturebook illustration. At the time of their publishing, they influenced other creators to what was a new style of children's picturebook illustration. When viewed today, the artwork in each of these books has a comforting familiarity; when viewed in their year of publication, *the artwork was a breakthrough.*

FACTOR 2: EMINENCE OF THE ILLUSTRATOR

One of the key factors in determining the collectibility and value of an illustrated children's picturebook is the 'eminence' of the illustrator. Without any intention of pretentiousness, when we speak of "eminence" of an illustrator, we mean their standing as a collectible illustrator of children's picturebooks, and not their prominence in society in general. This eminence is a combination of several interrelated factors, primarily being the following:

- Longevity in the business
- Productivity, or number of different books that have been published
- General popularity
- Awards for Illustration

EMINENCE: LONGEVITY IN THE BUSINESS

One of the most important factors to an artist's eminence as a collectible children's illustrator is their longevity as an illustrator, which speaks to the length of time they have been a published picturebook illustrator. The longer an illustrator has been creating illustrated books, the larger their eminence, and in turn, the more collectible their books become. For example, an illustrator who has had books published for forty years has more eminence than one who has had books published for only ten years, all other things being equal.

This does not necessarily mean that one illustrator's books are more collectible than another's simply because of their longevity in the business, since the other factors affecting an illustrator's eminence must be taken into consideration, such as general popularity, productivity, and illustration awards.

Another impact of longevity is the earlier an individual book is published in an illustrators' career, the higher the collectibility and value of a book, all other things being equal. This is especially true of the first book by a long-standing illustrator. In sports card collecting, this first instance is referred to as the player's 'rookie card' and is nearly always the most valuable card for a particular player. Similarly, in comic book collecting, the first issue of a series is usually the most valuable. In our opinion, the current state of the collectible children's picturebook market does not place enough emphasis on the first book by a celebrated illustrator.

This effect of higher value on 'earliest publishing date' does not hold true when other factors come into play. Examples of this are when a book published later wins an industry award or introduces a franchise character. Both of these are collectibility enhancing factors that will increase demand for the first edition of the particular book as compared to books published earlier in an artist's career.

EMINENCE: PRODUCTIVITY

Productivity refers to the number of different books the artist has illustrated. In general, the greater the number of books the artist has had published, the higher the eminence of the illustrator, and the more collectibility their books will have.

Longevity and productivity would seem to go hand in hand, but that's not always the case. There are many instances of relatively new children's book illustrators with a high number of books published, more than one per year, just as there are plenty of illustrators who have been in the business for 30+ years who have not published as many as one book per year. Steven Kellogg and Mercer Mayer come quickly to mind as two illustrators who are very productive, often having published more than one book per year. Both longevity and productivity increases the collectibility of an illustrator's particular books, and obviously are a result of the success of their books in the publishing industry.

EMINENCE: GENERAL POPULARITY

The general popularity of an illustrator is essentially based upon how many copies of the illustrator's books have been sold over time. Obviously, quality artwork, along with both productivity and longevity in the industry, contribute to the number of books an artist has illustrated, which in turn directly affects how many copies of their books have been purchased by readers.

It makes common sense that the more popular an illustrator is, the more collectible their books become. This is especially important since the children's picturebook hobby tends to be more demand driven than supply driven. It is imperative that the collector understand this key point—*scarcity of supply does not drive collectibility and value nearly as much as popularity of the demand for a particular book*!

As an example of this, Dr. Seuss books have sold the most copies of children's picturebooks, over 400 million worldwide, according to Random House, and first print runs were relatively high owing to the expected popularity of the books. Yet even with this high supply, first edition Dr. Seuss books command very high prices, routinely fetching several hundreds of dollars, and for the highly popular titles, several thousands of dollars. It is the high demand for the book that fuels the high prices, not necessarily the absolute scarcity of supply.

Another aspect is that a single hugely successful book will favorably enhance the collectibility of an illustrator's other books. An example of this is David Christiana's illustrations for Disney's *Fairy Dust and the Quest for the Egg* (2005), written by Newbery award winning author Gail Carson Levine. Christiana is one of our favorite children's book illustrators, yet his books have been generally underappreciated by the book collecting hobby. It is doubtful that Fairy Dust will have the opportunity to appreciate much in value due to the high number of first print copies, however Christiana's other works will benefit from the popularity of this book and its upcoming sequels[19].

EMINENCE: AWARDS FOR ILLUSTRATION

The number and caliber of awards that an illustrator or their books have received is another key factor of their eminence within the industry. Whereas the aesthetic quality of picturebook illustrations is a singularly personal affair (i.e. only *you* know what *you* like), awards are a validation of the quality of the illustrations by others within the children's book industry. Does this mean that a book or its illustrator needs to have received an award to make it collectible? Absolutely not. But, awards do increase the eminence of the artist. In earning these awards,

19   According to Disney website, https://licensing.disney.com/Login/minisite.do?siteId=disney_fairies, "The Walt Disney Company will provide unparalleled and synergistic support for Disney Fairies across its business units. […] The entertainment experience will continue with a series of chapter books planned for spring 2006 …"

the eminence of the illustrator is increased, subsequently the collectibility and value of their other books is increased.

As an example of this, David Small's eminence in the industry is burgeoning by winning the 2001 Caldecott Medal for *So You Want To Be President?*, which is in addition to his winning the 1996 Caldecott Honor for the book *The Gardener.* In turn, the collectibility and value of all of his other books are positively enhanced: a) larger number of people will be interested in seeing Mr. Small's books; b) in turn, a number of people will actually be exposed to them; c) a large portion of these people will like what they see; d) many of these people will want to add these books to their collection. Since the demand for first edition copies of David Small's books will increase over time, while the supply of them remains fixed, the collectibility and value will be enhanced.

Maurice Sendak and Marcia Brown are other examples of illustrators with higher eminence due in part to the number of children's book illustration awards that they and their books have earned over the years[20]. Later in the book, we describe some of the major children's book illustration awards, and the impact on the collectibility and value of the particular book that won the award.

AN END TO EMINENCE

Longevity, productivity, popularity, and awards, when mixed, juggled, stirred, and tossed together, tumbles out and equates to an illustrator's eminence. So, the critical question arises, "How important is the eminence of an illustrator in the value and collectibility of a book?" We think the answer is, "Very."

The eminence of an illustrator is a combination of many things, all of which are additive over time. Probably the most popular illustrator is Theodor Geisel, a.k.a. Dr. Seuss, and no wonder. He wrote and illustrated over 40 children's books over a 50 year span (longevity and productivity); he won several Caldecott awards—and a Pulitzer prize (awards); his books have been made into movies and TV programs; his books have sold hundreds of millions of copies worldwide; and his books crossed over into mainstream public education, forever changing the way children learn to read (popularity). Other illustrators of high eminence, again, in a collecting sense, are Maurice Sendak, Tasha Tudor, Wanda Gag, Barbara Cooney, Tomie dePaola, Trina Schart Hyman, Chris Van Allsburg, and Rosemary Wells to name just a few.

In a later chapter we propose a categorization method to help classify the collectibility and eminence of a number of popular illustrators. Of course, this continues a trend, and is offered in the spirit of generating some controversy and dialogue within the hobby.

FACTOR 3: AWARDS

The illustrated children's picturebooks that win awards, by definition, are of the highest caliber. In nearly all cases, the winning book will be increasingly sought after by readers, and therefore will sell more copies and stay in print longer than otherwise. Because of this increased demand and exposure for the particular book, the collectibility and value of first edition copies are enhanced by the receipt of an industry award for illustration.

---

20   Maurice Sendak has won eight Caldecott awards—one Caldecott Medal and seven Caldecott Honor awards. Marcia Brown has won nine Caldecott awards—three Caldecott Medal and six Caldecott Honor awards!

There are a number of awards given annually to illustrated children's picturebooks, the most significant awards being the following:

- Caldecott Medal and Honor
- Horn Book / Boston Globe
- Kate Greenaway Medal
- Golden Kite
- Coretta Scott King Award
- Irma Simonton Black Award

CALDECOTT MEDAL AND HONOR AWARDS

The Caldecott Medal has been awarded annually since 1938 to the artist of the "most distinguished American picturebook for children." The Medal is named in honor of the nineteenth-century English illustrator Randolph J. Caldecott, and is awarded by the Association for Library Service to Children, a division of the American Library Association (ALA). The Award is restricted to artists who are citizens or residents of the United States. As stated in the ALA terms for the Caldecott Medal,

> "The Medal shall be awarded annually to the artist of the most distinguished American picturebook for children published in the United States during the preceding year. There are no limitations as to the character of the picturebook except that the illustrations be original work. Honor Books may be named. These shall be books that are also truly distinguished."

The Caldecott Honor books were not always called such; in the early years, these distinguished books were referred to as "runners-up." Regarding the changing of this terminology, from the ALA:

> "From the beginning of the awarding of the Newbery and Caldecott Medals, committees could, and usually did, cite other books as worthy of attention. Such books were referred to as Newbery or Caldecott "runners-up." In 1971 the term "runners-up" was changed to "honor books." The new terminology was made retroactive so that all former runners-up are now referred to as Newbery or Caldecott Honor Books."

The Caldecott Awards are the most prestigious in the industry. There is only one Caldecott Medal book awarded each year, and one or more Caldecott Honor books. Ponder the odds. Thousands of illustrated children's picturebooks are published each year, and only one is singled out to win the Caldecott Medal! Because of this, first editions of each of the Caldecott Medal books are highly collectible, and sought after by many book collectors and booksellers. First edition copies of the early Caldecott Medal books are extremely difficult to find.

There are a number of reasons for the high esteem of the Caldecott awards. A primary reason is the high credibility of the American Library Association within the children's book industry, and in particular, that of selection process. We have never heard of reliable arguments asserting the Caldecott selection process has been influenced by biased factors or entities. Another reason for the high esteem of the Caldecott awards is the longevity of the process, and of course the continued success of many of the awarded books.

As an example of this, simply take a look at the number of Caldecott winning books which are still in publication decades after they were first published (see Chapter 3, "Approaches To Collecting," for a complete list of the Caldecott Medal books, and Appendix 1, "Caldecott Honor Award Books," for a complete list of the Caldecott Honor books). Some might argue that winning the award is the reason the book is still in publication, but we strenuously disagree. Our argument is, over time, a book, the story, and its illustrations must be appealing to a wide audience, in many cases over the span of several generations, before it can be printed with the magnitude of many Caldecott award winning books. In our opinion, the Caldecott awards have consistently selected books which have high audience appeal over time.

In many cases, the Caldecott award winning illustrator was selected years before their popularity had risen. As an example, Chris Van Allsburg's 1980 Caldecott Honor award for *The Garden of Abdul Gasazi* comes quickly to mind. This was Van Allsburg's first book, before *Jumanji* or *The Polar Express*, and the Caldecott selection group had the boldness to select this first book by this relatively unknown illustrator. In retrospect, one can appreciate the incredible foresight of this selection.

Another prime example is *Madeline*, written and illustrated by Ludwig Bemelmans, which was awarded a Caldecott Honor in 1940. *Madeline* is still in print today, has crossed over to TV, and had a major motion picture made over 50 years after it's initial publication. No one would argue that the Caldecott award given to the book somehow created *Madeline's* enormous success over the past sixty–five years—the quality of the book is the primary reason for its tremendous success over time. Again, this is an example of incredible foresight by the Caldecott selection committee. In reviewing the Caldecott award lists, one comes upon case after case of similar long-term success stories.

Some collectors and booksellers feel the Caldecott selections have been politicized over the years. In our opinion, whether politicized or not, it is superfluous to the credibility and proven record of the Caldecott selection process over the nearly seventy years it has been awarded. The examples listed above are just a few of the many instances of bold and foresightful selections.

BOSTON GLOBE—HORN BOOK AWARD

The Boston Globe newspaper and The Horn Book, Inc., have co-sponsored the Boston Globe–Horn Book Awards since 1967. The Boston Globe-Horn Book presents awards "for excellence in literature for children and young adults," and they are considered to be among the most prestigious in the industry. Eligible books must be published in the United States, though they may be written or illustrated by citizens of any country.

Each year a committee of distinguished professionals in the field of children's literature evaluates submissions from U.S. publishers. The committee selects winners in three categories; Picturebook, Fiction, and Nonfiction. Honor books may also be awarded in each category, and, on occasion, special citations will be given a book for its high quality and overall creative excellence.

KATE GREENAWAY MEDAL

The Kate Greenaway Medal has been awarded annually since 1956 by The Library Association of London for "outstanding illustration in a children's book." The Library Association awards only one Greenaway Medal each year, so it is quite prestigious. To be eligible, books must be published in the United Kingdom during the preceding year.

The Greenaway Medal is awarded to the artist who has "produced the most distinguished work in the illustration of children's books." It is awarded based on the nominations submitted to members of the Library Association's Youth Libraries Group, from general Library Association members. The nominated books are assessed upon a number of elements, including the design, the format and production, as well as artistic merit. For a complete listing of the Kate Greenaway Award winning books, see the chapter on "Some Approaches to Collecting."

GOLDEN KITE AWARD

The Golden Kite Award is presented annually by the Society of Children's Book Writers and Illustrators to "excellence in the field of children's books"[21]. It is notable in that it is the only award presented to children's book creators by their fellow authors and artists.

In addition to categories for fiction and non-fiction, Golden Kite Statuettes are awarded for picturebook text and picturebook illustration. Also, an Honor Book plaque is awarded in each category. The awards are given to the creative works that "genuinely appeal to the interests and concerns of children."[22]

CORETTA SCOTT KING AWARD

The Coretta Scott King Book Award is presented annually by the Coretta Scott King Committee of the American Library Association's Ethnic Multicultural Information Exchange Round Table. Originating in 1970, the award was initially given to authors only; beginning in 1974, an award for illustration was initiated.

> "The award is given to an African American author and an African American illustrator for an outstandingly inspirational and educational contribution. The books promote understanding and appreciation of the culture of all peoples and their contribution to the realization of the American dream. The Award is further designed to commemorate the life and works of Dr. Martin Luther King, Jr. and to honor Mrs. Coretta Scott King for her courage and determination to continue the work for peace and world brotherhood.

The purpose of the award is to encourage the artistic expression of the African American experience via literature and the graphic arts, including biographical, historical and social history treatments by African American authors and illustrators."

IRMA SIMONTON BLACK AWARD

Since 1972, the Bank Street College of Education in New York has annually presented the Irma Simonton Black Award for excellence. Irma Simonton Black was a writer and editor of over 29

---

21   Society of Children's Book Writers and Illustrators
22   Society of Children's Book Writers and Illustrators

children's books. In 1937, she was a founding member of the Bank Street Writers Laboratory. Upon her death in 1972, the Bank Street College of Education established the Irma Simonton Black Award for Excellence in Children's Literature. The Award was presented in Irma's name only until 1992, when James Black's name was added in recognition of his ardent support of the Award. From the Bank Street website:

> "The Award goes to an outstanding book for young children—a book in which text and illustrations are inseparable, each enhancing and enlarging on the other to produce a singular whole.The Award is unusual in that children are the final judges of the winning book. The process is as follows:

> From the many children's books published each year, an adult group of writers, librarians and educators choose approximately twenty to twenty five books that they consider the best candidates for the Award. These books are then sent (in four sets) to the four 8-9s and 9-10s classrooms at the Bank Street School for Children. Over the course of five weeks the children read and discuss all of the books before selecting four finalists. These four--called the Irma Simonton Black and James H. Black Honor Books--are placed in classrooms or libraries in several different schools, in New York and elsewhere. The children in these classrooms read, examine, discuss, and re-read the books over a four week period, before they select the winning book. Twelve schools in five states participated in the selection of the 2004 award, with over 2500 children voting on the books."

FACTOR 4: POP CULTURE

The value and collectibility of individual books are greatly affected if they cross over into popular culture. In many cases, this single factor can inflate the value of a book more than any other single factor, since the hobby is primarily driven by the demand for a particular book or illustrator's books. It makes common sense that high public popularity will increase the demand for the first edition of the particular book, while the supply remains fixed from the original print run.

In many cases, the popularity of the book transcends the popularity of the illustrator. For example, more people in the general population know of the *Magic School Bus* series, than know that Bruce Degan illustrates them. Another example of this is the highly popular *Harry Potter* series, with covers illustrated by Mary Grandpre. She brought Harry to life with her spirited cover illustrations in the American printings of the series, although most people do not know of her illustrated children's picturebooks. As more people become aware of this in the future, there is a good likelihood of Grandpre's picturebooks increasing in collectibility, of course enabled by the high aesthetic appeal of her creative work.

POP CULTURE: MOVIES AND TELEVISION

The most common means of moving into pop culture is by a book being made into a successful movie or long running cartoon. *The Grinch That Stole Christmas*, *Curious George*, *The Cat In*

The Hat, Jumanji, Polar Express, and *Zathura* come to mind as prominent examples of books being made into major motion pictures. There are many other examples.

William Joyce's **Rolie Polie Olie** and Maurice Sendak's **Little Bear** are two examples of books that crossed over into children's animated TV programs. In these cases, not only do the particular books have greatly enhanced collectibility, but the illustrator's other books are positively affected because of the increased popularity and demand side exposure.

Pop Culture: Learn To Read Standards

Another means of increased pop culture exposure is via high emphasis in the area of education or child development skills. *The Cat in the Hat* quickly comes to mind, as does the entire series of Beginner Books, including both the Seuss and non-Seuss books, such classics as **Go, Dog. Go, Have You Seen My Mother?, A Fly Went By,** and **Put Me In The Zoo**, Mercer Mayer's **Little Critter** series of books also fit within this category, as does Richard Scarry's entire sequence of easy readers, and the "I Can Read" series by Harper & Row.

Pop Culture: Be A Book First

The collectibility and value of an illustrated children's picturebook is much more positively enhanced if the book was published first, prior to cross-over into an alternative media. In other words, the book's collectibility is increased if the supply side has been constrained relative to the enhanced demand due to the cross-over into pop culture. Such is the case for *Jumanji*, or "the *Grinch*." But, the first printings of the Disney books that accompany their animated feature films are printed in such high numbers that there is not a large opportunity for the demand base to greatly exceed the supply base. In this example, the supply base plays a larger influence on the collectibility of the book.

Another example of this are Berkeley Breathed's books, which are immensely entertaining, extremely well illustrated, and gems of children's literature. However these books do not have a huge collectibility upside due to the immense popularity of Mr. Breathed's work, which is a result of the Bloom County cartoon strip that ran successfully in newspapers for years and years. Because of this high popularity, the first printings of his books are printed in very large numbers, which is great for Mr. Breathed and his publisher, but maybe not so great in terms of enhancing his books' collectibility[23].

Factor 5: Copies Sold / High Printings

In general, the more copies sold over time, or the greater number of printings, the more collectible will be the true first printing of a picturebook. The caveat is the first print run cannot be a large percentage of the books that were printed. It makes common sense, but bears repeating: the demand increases over time while the original supply of true first printings actually decreases over time, through attrition (i.e. damaged or discarded), or by being absorbed into book collectors' libraries. In either case, the availability or supply of the first edition book is reduced to the collecting marketplace.

---

23   Having said this, we feel the book "A Wish For Wings That Work" is one of our top ten contemporary books that a collector should have in their picturebook library. In addition to being Breathed's first original book after retiring from the Bloom County strip, it is a wonderful Christmas story and a modern classic. We can only hope that he continues to produce at least one book a year hereafter.

Picturebooks get into high print runs for a number of reasons, many of which have been previously mentioned. The key factor to a book's long-term popularity is the high appeal of the illustration and story, and especially if that appeal is generational in nature—refer to Key Factor #1 in this chapter, "Aesthetic Quality Of The Illustrations And The Story." Another leading cause is the book crossing over into popular culture, cementing demand for years to come.

Chapter 3, "Approaches To Collecting," contains a section on bestselling children's books, compiled by Publisher's Weekly. The number one bestselling children's book is a Little Golden Book, *The Poky Little Puppy*, which has sold over 14 million copies. Since only a small percentage of those were first edition printings, the number of copies sold, which is directly related to the number of people who have read the book (and therefore are potential collectors), is a major contributing factor to the high collectibility and market value of the book.

Another example is Shel Silverstein's *The Giving Tree*, published initially in 1964, and has sold over 5.6 million copies. Although Silverstein had several books published prior to *The Giving Tree*, it was his first of several phenomenally successful books. Because of this, the initial printing of *The Giving Tree* is relatively small compared to the total number of copies sold, therefore the first edition copies have a high market value. Silverstein's *Where The Sidewalk Ends* has sold even more copies, some 6.2 million copies, however the first edition copy does not have near the market value of *The Giving Tree*. Since *Where The Sidewalk Ends* was published in 1974, after a decade of successful sales of the *The Giving Tree*, the publisher had a good idea of success in the market, and therefore there were substantially higher first printing copies produced.

The number of printings is probably more important then the number of copies sold, although obviously the two are interrelated. As an example of this, the Disney books that accompany their marquee animated movies are sold in very high numbers, but don't get into especially high number of print runs. The number of first editions of these Disney books is quite high relative to the number of total books sold. There is not a high chance for high appreciation in the future[24].

On the other hand, a book such as *The Polar Express*, by Chris Van Allsburg, has had over 70 printings in its twenty-some year publication history, which is quite remarkable for a relatively new book. The collectibility and value of *The Polar Express* is enhanced by the combination of the high number of copies sold, meaning a large number of children and adults who have read or been exposed to the book, and the relatively low number of first editions that were initially printed. There are many, many examples of this, and most of the books in the Chapter 8, "Most Valuable Books," reflect this trait.

FACTOR 6: FRANCHISE BOOKS

There are a number of books which have become franchise books for their creator(s). In these cases, the book is the introduction of a character or characters, which the creator uses in many subsequent books. In all cases, the collectibility of the first book in the series is enhanced. Numerous examples of franchise books come to mind, such as *Madeline, Babar,* or *Eloise*.

---

24   The collectibility of the Disney books based upon their animated feature film is slightly enhanced since they are a 'cross-over' collectible, appealing to both the Disneyana collector and the picturebook collector.

The first edition book introducing the franchise character or characters usually has high market value relative to a particular illustrator's other books. In many cases the initial franchise book was under printed relative to the demand for the book, since the popularity of the character was unknown at the time of the first printing. Related to this, the first book in the franchise was printed in substantially lower quantities than other books in the franchise, since success was paved for the later books.

In many cases the other first edition books in the successful, multi-year, multi-book franchise will also have higher collectibility, all other things being equal. The *Petunia* books, written and illus-

FRANCHISE BOOKS—SELECTED EXAMPLES		
YEAR	**ILLUSTRATOR**	**TITLE**
1932	Lois Lenski	The Little Family
1933	Jean de Brunhoff	The Story of Babar
1939	Ludwig Bemelmans	Madeline
1941	H. A. Rey	Curious George
1950	Roger Duvoisin	Petunia
1955	Hilary Knight	Eloise
1955	Crockett Johnson	Harold And The Purple Crayon
1957	Theodor Geisel	The Cat In The Hat
1957	Maurice Sendak	Little Bear
1962	Stan & Jan Berenstain	The Big Honey Hunt
1975	Mercer Mayer	Just For You (Little Critter)
1976	Marc Brown	Arthur's Nose
1999	William Joyce	Rolie Polie Olie
1997	Hollie Hobby	Toot & Puddle
2000	Ian Falconer	Olivia

trated by Roger Duvoisin, who illustrated over 118 books, tend to have a higher market value than Duvoisin's numerous other books. The same can be said for Hilary Knight's Eloise books, as compared to the other books that he illustrated. There are many, many examples of franchise books, and the table provides but a few examples from various eras within the picturebook industry. The astute collector should be aware of new books which have long-term franchise potential.

Chapter 3
Approaches to Collecting

There are a number of different approaches to collecting first edition children's picturebooks. Most collectors will develop a primary focus, theme, or approach, and leverage it to build their book collection over time. Often, they will incorporate, or mix, several themes to tailor the collection to their particular desires. We will call this mix of themes a collecting strategy. It is a year-over-year plan of building a book collection, and is in constant evolution to meet the expanding interests of the collector.

COLLECTING STRATEGIES

Even for the rare individual with the unlimited budget, there should be some strategy to building their collection. A focused collecting strategy is much more important for collectors who have limited resources of time and money. As a start to formulating a collecting strategy, always concentrate on illustrators whose artwork you particularly enjoy (see Chapter 2, Factor 1, "Aesthetic Quality of the Illustrations and Story"), coupled with stories you find entertaining, interesting, or meaningful.

Since a strategy is a combination of different collecting approaches, in this section we wanted to offer several of the more prominent approaches to collecting illustrated children's picturebooks. In addition, this section provides some valuable information to assist in your collecting pursuits, and is compiled in such a way to allow you to make informed collecting decisions.

Again, a disclaimer applies: these are just examples of common approaches and are not offered as the only definitive means—the fun of the hobby is to find and develop your own particular angles, and combine them to form a unique strategy toward collecting children's picturebooks. By being aware that these collecting approaches are fairly common, and variations are often included in most collectors' strategies, you will gain important insight into the scarcity and value of certain books in the marketplace.

COLLECTING APPROACH: CALDECOTT AWARD BOOKS

A tried and true method to collecting illustrated children's picturebooks is to collect Caldecott Medal and Caldecott Honor award books. For years, even prior to the internet, booksellers were well aware of the collectibility of Caldecott award winning books. Subsequently, many booksellers carry Caldecott award winning books in their inventory, even those booksellers who normally don't specialize in children's books. As a result, of course in large part due to the credibility of the award, collecting Caldecott award books has a rich history and a fairly wide collecting audience.

The American Library Association has awarded 69 books with the Caldecott Medal and 216 books with the Caldecott Honor, since the inception of the awards in 1938. First edition copies of these 285 books are pursued by thousands upon thousands of collectors and booksellers, so, as you might expect from this high demand, the price for these books can be quite high. It is not unusual for a very recent first edition Caldecott Medal winning book to bring 50% to 100% above the publisher's retail price, even a book printed in the last 2—3 years! Older Caldecott award books fetch easily into the hundreds of dollars, and a select few are valued at over $1,000! The following is a complete list of the Caldecott Medal books awarded by the American Library Association, from the award's inception in 1938, through the 2006 award:

CALDECOTT MEDAL WINNERS 1938-2006						
YEAR	TITLE	ILLUSTRATOR	VG-	VG	VG+	FINE
1938	Animals Of The Bible	Dorothy P. Lathrop	$960	$1,200	$1,600	
1939	Mei Li	Thomas Handforth	$960	$1,200	$1,600	
1940	Abraham Lincoln	Ingri & Edgar d'Aulaire	$960	$1,200	$1,600	
1941	They Were Strong And Good	Robert Lawson	$560	$740	$920	
1942	Make Way For Ducklings	Robert McCloskey	$4,400	$6,000	$7,400	
1943	The Little House	Virginia Lee Burton	$3,000	$4,000	$5,000	
1944	Many Moons	Louis Slobodkin	$460	$620	$780	
1945	Prayer For A Child	Elizabeth Orton Jones	$220	$280	$360	
1946	The Rooster Crows	Maud & Miska Petersham	$440	$600	$740	
1947	The Little Island	Leonard Weisgard	$300	$400	$500	
1948	White Snow, Bright Snow	Roger Duvoisin	$280	$380	$480	
1949	The Big Snow	Berta & Elmer Hader	$440	$580	$720	
1950	Song Of The Swallows	Leo Politi	$280	$360	$460	
1951	The Egg Tree	Katherine Milhous	$320	$440	$540	
1952	Finders Keepers	Nicholas Mordvinoff	$260	$360	$440	
1953	The Biggest Bear	Lynd Ward	$600	$800	$1,000	
1954	Madeline's Rescue	Ludwig Bemelmans	$580	$780	$980	
1955	Cinderella, Or The Little Glass Slipper	Marcia Brown	$580	$760	$960	
1956	Frog Went A-Courtin	Feodor Rojankovsky	$480	$640	$800	
1957	Time Of Wonder	Robert McCloskey	$540	$720	$900	
1958	A Tree Is Nice	Marc Simont	$240	$320	$400	
1959	Chanticleer And The Fox	Barbara Cooney	$360	$480	$600	
1960	Nine Days To Christmas	Marie Hall Ets	$220	$300	$380	
1961	Baboushka And The Three Kings	Nicolas Sidjakov	$160	$200	$260	
1962	Once A Mouse	Marcia Brown	$320	$420	$520	

CALDECOTT MEDAL WINNERS 1938-2006						
YEAR	TITLE	ILLUSTRATOR	VG-	VG	VG+	FINE
1963	The Snowy Day	Ezra Jack Keats	$220	$280	$360	
1964	Where The Wild Things Are	Maurice Sendak	$6,200	$8,200	$10,200	
1965	May I Bring A Friend?	Beni Montresor	$200	$280	$340	
1966	Always Room For One More	Nonny Hogrogian	$200	$280	$340	
1967	Sam, Bangs, And Moonshine	Evaline Ness	$300	$400	$500	
1968	Drummer Hoff	Ed Emberley	$220	$300	$380	
1969	The Fool Of The World And The Flying Ship	Uri Shulevitz	$200	$260	$320	
1970	Sylvester And The Magic Pebble	William Steig	$280	$360	$460	
1971	A Story, A Story	Gail E. Haley		$180	$260	$340
1972	One Fine Day	Nonny Hogrogian		$180	$260	$340
1973	The Funny Little Woman	Blair Lent		$220	$320	$420
1974	Duffy And The Devil	Margot Zemach		$160	$240	$320
1975	Arrow To The Sun	Gerald McDermott		$220	$320	$420
1976	Why Mosquitoes Buzz In People's Ears	Leo & Diane Dillon		$200	$280	$380
1977	Ashanti To Zulu: African Traditions	Leo & Diane Dillon		$140	$220	$300
1978	Noah's Ark	Peter Spier		$180	$280	$360
1979	The Girl Who Loved Wild Horses	Paul Goble		$180	$260	$340
1980	Ox-Cart Man	Barbara Cooney		$180	$260	$340
1981	Fables	Arnold Lobel		$100	$160	$200
1982	Jumanji	Chris Van Allsburg		$500	$760	$1,000
1983	Shadow	Marcia Brown		$120	$180	$240
1984	The Glorious Flight	Alice & Martin Provensen		$120	$180	$240
1985	Saint George And The Dragon	Trina Schart Hyman		$160	$220	$300
1986	Polar Express	Chris Van Allsburg		$700	$1,000	$1,400
1987	Hey, Al	Richard Egielski		$80	$120	$160
1988	Song And Dance Man	Stephen Gammell		$120	$180	$240
1989	Owl Moon	John Schoenherr		$160	$220	$300
1990	Lon Po Po	Ed Young		$90	$120	$180
1991	Black And White	David Macaulay		$60	$80	$120
1992	Tuesday	David Wiesner		$100	$140	$200
1993	Mirette On The High Wire	Emily Arnold McCully		$70	$100	$140
1994	Grandfather's Journey	Allen Say		$70	$100	$140
1995	Smoky Night	David Diaz		$60	$90	$120
1996	Officer Buckle And Gloria	Peggy Rathmann		$60	$80	$120
1997	Golem	David Wisniewski		$40	$60	$80
1998	Rapunzel	Paul O. Zelinsky		$50	$70	$100
1999	Snowflake Bentley	Mary Azarian		$80	$120	$160
2000	Joseph Had A Little Overcoat	Simms Taback		$40	$60	$80
2001	So You Want To Be President?	David Small		$40	$60	$90
2002	The Three Pigs	David Wiesner		$35	$50	$70
2003	My Friend Rabbit	Eric Rohmann		$40	$60	$90
2004	The Man Who Walked Between The Towers	Mordicai Gerstein		$35	$50	$70
2005	Kitten's First Full Moon	Kevin Henkes		$25	$40	$50
2006	The Hello, Goodbye Window	Christopher Raschka		$25	$40	$50

Of the books published in the past twenty years, *Song And Dance Man*, *Owl Moon*, *Snowflake Bentley*, and *My Friend Rabbit* are slightly harder to find in first edition format than their peer group. Each of these books was under printed in their first print run, and subsequently went into multiple printings after the book and illustrator were awarded with the Caldecott Medal.

See Appendix 1 for a complete listing of the Caldecott Honor books from 1938 through the 2006 award process.

COLLECTING APPROACH: CALDECOTT AWARD ILLUSTRATORS

As stated earlier, the American Library Association has awarded 69 books with the Caldecott Medal, and 216 books with the Caldecott Honor. The 285 award books were created by 159 different illustrators (see Appendix 2 for a complete listing of the Caldecott award winning illustrators). Collecting the works of these Caldecott award winning illustrators is a very common and reliable method of collecting illustrated children's picturebooks. In this case, the population of available books is increased an order-of-magnitude, from the 285 award winning books, into the thousands of books created by these illustrators through the course of their careers. Most collectors focus on Caldecott illustrator's whose artwork is especially appealing or meaningful to them, rather than collecting all books by any of the winning illustrators.

Only seven illustrators have won more than one Caldecott Medal award: Marcia Brown, Barbara Cooney, Leo & Diane Dillon, Nonny Hogrogian, Robert McCloskey, David Wiesner, and Chris Van Allsburg. Of these, only Marcia Brown has won three, while the rest have each won two Caldecott Medals. Any of the books illustrated by any of these multiple Caldecott Medalists should be considered highly collectible.

THREE OR MORE CALDECOTT AWARDS				THREE OR MORE CALDECOTT AWARDS			
Illustrator	Total	Medal	Honor	Illustrator	Total	Medal	Honor
Marcia Brown	9	3	6	Berta & Elmer Hader	3	1	2
Maurice Sendak	8	1	7	David Macaulay	3	1	2
Marie Hall Ets	6	1	5	Ed Young	3	1	2
Robert McCloskey	5	2	3	Leo Politi	3	1	2
Jerry Pinkney	5		5	Leonard Weisgard	3	1	2
David Wiesner	4	2	2	Marc Simont	3	1	2
Blair Lent	4	1	3	Margot Zemach	3	1	2
Evaline Ness	4	1	3	Robert Lawson	3	1	2
Paul O. Zelinsky	4	1	3	Roger Duvoisin	3	1	2
Trina Schart Hyman	4	1	3	Stephen Gammell	3	1	2
Clare Turlay Newberry	4		4	Uri Shulevitz	3	1	2
Leo Lionni	4		4	Molly Bang	3		3
Chris Van Allsburg	3	2	1	Peter Parnall	3		3
Nonny Hogrogian	3	2	1	Taro Yashima	3		3
Arnold Lobel	3	1	2	Theodor Seuss Geisel	3		3

The table lists the thirty illustrators who have won three or more Caldecott awards (including both Medal and Honor awards). All of the books illustrated by any of these multiple Caldecott winners should be considered highly collectible. Many of these illustrators are active today, so first edition copies of their non-Caldecott award books can be found in the market at very reasonable prices[25]. The active illustrators are: Molly Bang, Stephen Gammell, David Macaulay, Jerry Pinkney, Maurice Sendak, Uri Shulevitz, Chris Van Allsburg, David Wiesner, Ed Young, and Paul Zelinsky.

Collecting Approach: Children's Illustrators

Another common approach to collecting illustrated children's picturebooks is to focus on particular illustrators either because you: a) enjoy their illustrations; b) think their books will appreciate in market value c) think their books are relatively undervalued and underappreciated by the collecting public. Similar to collecting Caldecott Award winning illustrators, this approach is often generational in nature, either coinciding with books from the collector's childhood or that of their children's.

Chapter 2 introduced the concept of an illustrator's 'eminence', defined as an indicator of their standing as a collectible illustrator of children's picturebooks, and not their prominence in society in general. We further explained some factors which positively impact an illustrator's eminence.

With the intention of stirring up some needed controversy within the bibliophile industry, we have developed an approach of segmenting illustrators into five distinct categories. These categories are not meant in any way to reflect upon the quality or aesthetic appeal of the illustrations, or about the merits of the books containing their artwork. Instead, the intention is to try to apportion the illustrators into segments of collectibility and value[26]. The categories we suggest are: Luminary Collectible; Prestige Collectible; Highly Collectible; Choice Collectible; and Rising Collectible.

> **Luminary**—Reserved for illustrators whose books have reached the highest level of collectibility. These creators have been published for decades, and their books have been endeared by the public and sold millions of copies. The illustrator and their books have received prestigious awards a number of times and several have crossed over into pop culture. Their books are recognized as fine collectibles by general booksellers. These illustrators have had a meaningful impact on society in a manner outside of general book selling or publication. Only Theodor Seuss Geisel, Maurice Sendak, Chris Van Allsburg, and Wanda Gag currently meet these criteria.
>
> **Prestige**—Reserved for illustrators whose books have been published for decades, and their books have been endeared by the public and sold millions of copies. The illustrator and their books have received prestigious awards a number of times, and several books might have crossed over into pop culture. Their books are recognized as fine collectibles by children's booksellers and many general booksellers.

---

25   Barbara Cooney won two Caldecott Medals, for *Chanticleer and the Fox* (1959) and *Ox-Cart Man* (1980). Since these were her only Caldecott awards, she did not make the list of illustrators with three or more awards.

26   We enjoy and admire the artwork of any illustrator with the talent to be published, and hope that none of them are offended by this categorization, since no such offense is intended.

HIGHLY COLLECTIBLE—Reserved for illustrators whose books have been published for several years, perhaps decades, and their books endeared by the public and been very successfully sold. The illustrator, and their books, might have received prestigious awards, and several books might have crossed over into pop culture. Their books are recognized as highly collectible by children's booksellers.

CHOICE COLLECTIBLE—Reserved for illustrators whose books have been published for several years, and their books endeared by the public and been very successfully sold. Their books might have received a prestigious award. Their books are recognized as collectible by many children's booksellers.

RISING COLLECTIBLE—Illustrators who have several books published, and have measured success in the marketplace, but have not yet garnered major awards or received critical acclaim. Often their books are modestly priced relative to their body of work. Their books are recognized as collectible by many astute children's booksellers.

The collectible children's book market currently classifies illustrators along these lines, or something similar, however to date, a nomenclature has not yet been developed. We propose the above, yet are very open to alternatives. An accepted norm would assist newcomers to the hobby in evaluating potential books they might want to add to their collection. We have assessed over 700 illustrators along the above categories to assist us with our book collecting hobby.

PRODUCTIVE ILLUSTRATORS

Illustrators who have had a number of different books published are very collectible—productivity increases the collectibility of an illustrator's particular books, and obviously are a result of the success of their books in the publishing industry. In all cases, the illustrator's craft is appreciated by the book buying public (else why have so many books been published?). In turn, the illustrator's first edition books have solid collectible interest.

The table, "Illustrator's Books in Price Guide," is a list of the top fifty most prolific illustrator's in the Price Guide, in terms of number of books published. Incredibly, there are over 6,000 books in the Price Guide with artwork from these fifty illustrators! Obviously, each illustrator on the list is an accomplished artist, whose books appeal to a very wide audience over a number of generations.

Some of our favorite illustrators are in the top 50 most productive illustrators, including several who have not garnered a Caldecott Award to date, yet whose books are very collectible. The following is a list of eight illustrators who are generally underappreciated by the book collecting market, yet whose books are very collectible: Mercer Mayer; Tomie dePaola; Cyndy Szekeres; David McPhail; Steven Kellogg; Lynn Munsinger; Kay Chorao; and Michael Hague.

At this point in time, we are not making claim that the numbers in the table represent the number of books that these illustrators have completed during their career. They have completed at least this many books. At this time, the Price Guide database is not complete enough for us to make that claim, and probably never will. We are certain our research, extensive as it is, has not uncovered every single book by every single illustrator in this first edition of the Price Guide.

ILLUSTRATOR'S BOOKS IN PRICE GUIDE		
Rank	Illustrator	Books
1.	Kurt Wiese	280
2.	Mercer Mayer	250
3.	Paul Galdone	249
4.	Tomie dePaola	234
5.	Stan & Jan Berenstain	215
6.	Marc Brown	172
7.	Emily Arnold McCully	161
8.	Robert M. Quackenbush	148
9.	Leonard Everett Fisher	145
10.	Victor G. Ambrus	137
11.	Lillian Hoban	135
12.	Anne F. Rockwell	133
13.	Tony Ross	129
14.	James Stevenson	125
15.	Cyndy Szekeres	124
16.	Leonard Weisgard	123
17.	Quentin Blake	120
18.	Barry Moser	119
19.	Roger Duvoisin	118
20.	Richard Scarry	118
21.	Ted Lewin	116
22.	Michael Foreman	115
23.	Trina Schart Hyman	114
24.	Ronald Himler	112
25.	Aliki (Aliki Brandenburg)	109

ILLUSTRATOR'S BOOKS IN PRICE GUIDE		
Rank	Illustrator	Books
26.	Edward Gorey	109
27.	David McPhail	108
28.	Steven Kellogg	105
29.	Doug Cushman	104
30.	Lois Lenski	103
31.	Marc Simont	102
32.	Diane De Groat	101
33.	Lynd Ward	101
34.	Jim Arnosky	100
35.	Shirley Hughes	100
36.	Edward Ardizzone	99
37.	Glen Rounds	98
38.	G. Brian Karas	97
39.	Lynn Munsinger	95
40.	Marylin Hafner	94
41.	Erik Blegvad	91
42.	James Marshall	90
43.	Rosemary Wells	87
44.	Arnold Lobel	86
45.	Chris Demarest	85
46.	Demi	85
47.	Kay Chorao	83
48.	Maurice Sendak	82
49.	Lucy Cousins	81
50.	Michael Hague	80

COLLECTING APPROACH: OTHER ILLUSTRATION AWARDS

In Chapter 2, "Factors Affecting Collectibility," we mentioned several of the notable children's book awards that increase an illustrator's eminence within the industry. Since winning book illustration awards increase an illustrator's eminence, it would follow that collecting books which have won awards would be a reliable collecting strategy.

Once a book wins an illustration award, it has validation, to a certain degree, of appealing artwork and good craftsmanship. Therefore, the book will generally stay in print for a length of time, and likely extend into multiple printings. Because of this, the first edition copies of award winning books are very collectible, and have solid market place demand.

KATE GREENAWAY AWARD

In Chapter 2, we provided background information regarding the Kate Greenaway Medal for children's book illustration. It is generally accepted to be the most prestigious award for children's illustration given in the United Kingdom—it is the British equivalent to the Caldecott Medal. However, oddly enough, the Kate Greenaway Medal winning books have not received the same level of collector interest as the Caldecott Medal. In that regard, they are affordable as compared to the first edition Caldecott Medal book from the same award year.

Most of the winning books have been published by an American publisher, generally in response to the book winning the award—very few Kate Greenaway Award winning books were published in the U.S. during its original publication year in the U.K.. Many of the Kate Greenaway Award winning illustrators are very successful in the U.S., including Edward Ardizzone, Brian Wildsmith, Raymond Briggs, Helen Oxenbury, Quentin Blake, Victor Ambrus, Michael Foreman, and P.J. Lynch. The following table is a listing of the Kate Greenaway winning books, through the 2004 award year.

KATE GREENAWAY AWARD WINNING BOOKS						
YEAR	TITLE	ILLUSTRATOR	VG-	VG	VG+	FINE
1956	Tim All Alone	Edward Ardizzone	$280	$380	$480	
1957	Mrs. Easter And The Storks	V.H. Drummond	$100	$140	$180	
1959	Kashtanka And A Bundle Of Ballads	William Stobbs	$50	$60	$80	
1960	Old Winkle And The Seagulls	Gerald Rose	$100	$140	$180	
1961	Mrs. Cockle's Cat	Antony Maitland	$100	$120	$160	
1962	ABC	Brian Wildsmith	$70	$90	$120	
1963	Borka	John Burningham	$140	$200	$240	
1964	Shakespeare's Theatre	C. Walter Hodges	$60	$80	$100	
1965	The Three Poor Tailors	Victor G. Ambrus	$70	$100	$120	
1966	The Mother Goose Treasury	Raymond Briggs	$200	$260	$320	
1967	Charley, Charlotte, And The Golden Canary	Charles Keeping	$80	$120	$140	
1968	A Dictionary Of Chivalry	Pauline Baynes	$80	$120	$140	
1969	The Quangle Wangle's Hat	Helen Oxenbury		$70	$100	$140
1970	Mr. Gumpy's Outing	John Burningham		$100	$160	$200
1971	The Kingdom Under The Sea	Jan Pienkowski		$70	$100	$140
1972	The Woodcutter's Duck	Krystyna Turska		$40	$60	$90
1973	Father Christmas	Raymond Briggs		$100	$160	$220
1974	The Wind Blew.	Pat Hutchins		$60	$90	$120
1975	Horses In Battle And Mishka	Victor G. Ambrus		$50	$70	$90
1976	The Post Office Cat	Gail E. Haley		$60	$80	$120
1977	Dogger	Shirley Hughes		$60	$80	$120
1978	Each Peach Pear Plum	Janet Ahlberg		$90	$140	$180
1979	The Haunted House	Jan Pienkowski		$50	$80	$100
1980	Mister Magnolia	Quentin Blake		$60	$80	$120
1981	The Highwayman	Charles Keeping		$50	$70	$100
1982	Long Neck And Thunder Foot	Michael Foreman		$70	$100	$140
1983	Gorilla	Anthony Browne		$70	$100	$140
1984	Hiawatha's Childhood	Errol Le Cain		$50	$80	$100
1985	Sir Gawain And The Loathly Lady	Juan Wijngaard		$30	$40	$60
1986	Snow White In New York	Fiona French		$40	$60	$80
1987	Crafty Chameleon	Adrienne Kennaway		$60	$80	$120
1988	Can't You Sleep Little Bear?	Barbara Firth		$80	$120	$160
1989	War Boy	Michael Foreman		$50	$80	$100
1990	The Whales' Song	Gary Blythe		$25	$40	$50
1991	The Jolly Christmas Postman	Janet Ahlberg		$50	$80	$100
1992	Zoo	Anthony Browne		$40	$60	$90

KATE GREENAWAY AWARD WINNING BOOKS						
YEAR	TITLE	ILLUSTRATOR	VG-	VG	VG+	FINE
1993	Black Ships Before Troy	Alan Lee		$40	$60	$80
1994	Way Home	Gregory Rogers		$25	$40	$50
1995	The Christmas Miracle Of Jonathan Toomey	P.J. Lynch		$35	$50	$70
1996	The Baby Who Wouldn't Go To Bed	Helen Cooper		$50	$70	$90
1997	When Jessie Came Across The Sea	P.J. Lynch		$30	$40	$60
1998	Pumpkin Soup	Helen Cooper		$40	$60	$80
1999	Alice's Adventures In Wonderland	Helen Oxenbury		$35	$50	$70
2000	I Will Not Ever Never Eat A Tomato	Lauren Child		$30	$50	$60
2001	Pirate Diary	Chris Riddell		$35	$50	$70
2002	Jethro Byrde	Bob Graham		$25	$35	$50
2003	Ella's Big Chance	Shirley Hughes		$25	$40	$50

OTHER CHILDREN'S ILLUSTRATION AWARDS

In addition to the Caldecott awards and the Kate Greenaway Award, there are four other significant awards which have collector interest. In Chapter 2, "Factors Affecting Collectibility," we provided background information on the Boston Globe—Horn Book. Golden Kite Awards; the Irma Simonton Black Award, and the Coretta Scott King Awards for illustration. To see full lists of the award winning books, please see the following internet links:

Boston Globe—Horn Book	www.hbook.com/awards/bghb/past.asp
Golden Kite Award	www.scbwi.org/awards/gk_list.htm
Irma Simonton Black Award	http://streetcat.bankstreet.edu/html/winners.html
Coretta Scott King Award	www.ala.org/ala/emiert/corettascottkingbookawards

COLLECTING APPROACH: BEST SELLING BOOKS

True first editions of the best selling books are collectible for a number of reasons. First, since so many people have read the book, the demand for the book is quite high. Second, to have such a high number of sales usually means that the book has had many print runs, therefore the first print books are in short supply relative to the total number of books sold.

Publisher's Weekly completed a survey in 2001 which identified the "All-Time Bestselling Hardcover Children's Books." Publisher's Weekly provides the following background:

> "The figures in these lists cover sales from the original date of publication through the end of 2000. We asked publishers to supply us with figures for hardcover books that have sold more than 750,000 copies and paperback books with sales over one million copies. The lists are based on actual sales as reported by publishers; they reflect domestic sales only, and do not include book club and international sales. Books in the public domain generally are not listed, since aggregate sales figures are not available. Some publishers were unable to supply accurate cumulative numbers, often because the originating publisher was acquired by another. Therefore, some titles had to be left off, and others are ranked according to whatever sales figures were available."

Most of the books on this list are collectible in first edition format, although there are some aberrations. For example, the Disney movie books—#28 *The Lion King*; #80 *The 101 Dalmatians*; #82 *Beauty and the Beast*; #87 *The Little Mermaid*; and #95 *Aladdin*—all make the list due to the widespread popularity of the animated feature films, but there is little chance that the first editions will ever be highly valuable since so many copies of the first editions were printed Also, the Barney books—#51 *Barney's Favorite Mother Goose Rhymes* Vol. 1; #57 *Barney's Farm Animals*; #59 *Baby Bop's Toys*; #71 *Barney's Magical Picnic*; #81 *Barney's Color Surprise*—have little chance of substantial value appreciation, since the first editions were produced in such high quantities.

Not all of the books on the list meet the 'criteria' of this price guide, since there are numerous chapter books on the list (notably the Nancy Drew books), but whose first editions are, of course, still collectible in the general book collecting or the general children's book collecting hobbies. Some interesting tidbits:

- *The Poky Little Puppy*, the top selling book of all time, is a Little Golden Book, and is extremely difficult to find in first edition with the original dust jacket.

- Four of the top eight bestselling books are Little Golden Books (#1 *The Poky Little Puppy*; #3 *Tootle*; #7 *Saggy Baggy Elephant*; and #8 *Scuffy The Tugboat*). All of the early Little Golden Books with dust jackets are considered to be highly collectible, whether in first edition form or not, and likely to appreciate in value. Fine condition dust jackets are becoming more difficult to find.

- Ten of the top 40 bestselling books are by Theodor Geisel, aka Dr. Seuss! His top selling book is the classic *Green Eggs and Ham*, which is the fourth bestselling children's book with sales of over 8 million copies!

- There are three Caldecott Medal winning books in the top 100 bestselling books—#44 *Polar Express*; #63 *Where The Wild Things Are*; and #96 *Make Way For Ducklings*.

- Shel Silverstein has four books on the list of top 100 bestselling books, with #12 *Where The Sidewalk Ends* (1974), #14 *The Giving Tree* (1964), #22 *A Light In The Attic* (1981), and #52 *Falling Up* (1996). *The Giving Tree* is especially difficult to find in collectible, first edition format.

As for collecting potential, books on the list which we think are underappreciated in the current market:

- The first edition copies of the four Little Golden Books (see above), all but *Saggy Baggy Elephant* (1947) were issued with dust jackets.

- #15 *The Littlest Angel* (1946), illustrated by Catherine Evans and authored by Charles Tazewell, currently is not too difficult to find in collectible, first edition format.

- #20 *The Very Hungry Caterpillar* (1969) by Eric Carle, is very difficult to find in first edition format. Carle's other book in the top 100, #89 *The Very Quiet Cricket* (1990) is becoming harder to find.

- There are four non-Seuss Beginner Books on the list which are very under-appreciated by the book collecting market. #24 *Are You My Mother* (1960) and #34 *Go, Dog. Go!*, both by P.D. Eastman, #60 *Put Me In The Zoo*, by Robert Lopshire, and #91 *A Fly Went By* (1958), illustrated by Fritz Siebel are relatively hard to find in first condition format, yet generally not significantly expensive.

- #41 *Where's Waldo?* (1987) by Martin Handford, was into multiple printings nearly immediately after initial publication, making first editions difficult, but not impossible to find. Note that two other Waldo books are in the top 100 bestselling, #43 *The Great Waldo Search* (1989), and #45 *Find Waldo Now* (1989). All three books were issued without dust jackets.

- #69 *If You Give A Mouse A Cookie* (1985), illustrated by Felicia Bond, written by Laura Numeroff, is a modern classic. This is the first of six books that the two have collaborated on, so should be considered a franchise book.

- #74 *Guess How Much I Love You* (1995), illustrated by Anita Jeram, and written by Sam McBratney is another modern classic, and already is into a high number of printings. First edition, first printings are still relatively affordable at this time.

COLLECTING APPROACH: FAIRY TALES & OTHER GENRE

Another approach to collecting illustrated children's picturebooks is to focus on fairy tales or other specific genre books. These genre books might be alphabet, Brother's Grimm, Mother Goose, Aesop Fables, or any of a number of books centered on a particular theme. Whichever the case may be, there are a large number of particular fairy tale or genre books available to the book collector.

One reason for the large quantity of published genre books is quite simple: fairy tale, alphabet, and Mother Goose books are always in high demand by the general reading population. This demand exists from generation to generation, as new young readers are constantly being formally educated, and books of these types are part of the educational process. Because of this continued demand, consistent over many years, accomplished illustrators look to the challenge of creating a milestone version of the classic tale.

Another reason for the large quantity of genre books in print is more subtle, and has to do with the evolution of the career of successful book illustrators. When they begin their career, the new illustrator is often illustrating another author's work—in most cases the new illustrators are not the authors of their first pieces of work. After several of their books are published, and they have reached a certain level of success, the illustrator frequently has a choice to author their own book, thereby enjoying the benefit of receiving all of the publishing royalties designated for the book's creator.

In many cases, the illustrator, as a first time author, will choose to use a story that is in the public domain, rather than attempt to write a completely original story. Since Cinderella, Sleeping Beauty, Snow White, Mother Goose rhymes, and a multitude of other famous stories are in the public domain, the illustrator is free to select, modify, and put their own spin on the classic tale. As a result, there are many, many illustrated versions of each of the classic fairy tales available in the book marketplace. The same can be said for the many alphabet books in print. The cynic might wonder: "Do we really need another version of Cinderella?," or "How many surprise endings are there to ABC?" We do not know the answer to these questions, however, because of the great multitude of ABC, Grimm, Mother Goose, Aesop, and fairy tale books published over the years, they make for a very rich collecting approach.

Chapter 4
Identifying First Editions

FIRST EDITION DEFINITION

Book collectors and booksellers are meticulous in their meaning of "First Edition." In the book collecting industry, "First Edition" is always meant to be the first printing of the first edition of the book. This is the same meaning as the "First State" of the first edition. Most of the bookselling associations have a code of ethics that their members follow, and lend great credibility to members of these associations. Notable among these are the Antiquarian Booksellers Association of America (ABAA).

In the collectible bookselling market, it must be clearly stated in the book's description if the book is a later printing or later state of the first edition. The only exception is when the bookseller does not know that an earlier printing or 'state' of the book exists. If the bookseller is unsure if an earlier printing exists, then the book's description should indicate this insecurity.

It is very important for the novice book collector or bookseller to understand that the meaning and use of the term "First Edition" is different in the publishing industry than in the book collecting industry. Many publishers use the term 'First Edition' on the copyright page to indicate a book that has been reprinted without changes from its first printing. It is not uncommon for printers to employ the words "First Edition" on the copyright page on books even up to the eighth and ninth printing.

This use of the words "First Edition" on later printings of books has caused numerous headaches in recent years for book collectors, as more novice and amateur booksellers offer books for sale on the internet. A large number of novice or casual sellers do not distinguish the difference between the collecting definition of "First Edition," and the printing industry's use of the term. This is especially prevalent on eBay auctions, and the prudent potential book buyer should make an inquiry to the seller to obtain exact copyright page information.

For the reader to become proficient at identifying first editions, the following are acceptable authoritative guides:

- *Pocket Guide to the Identification of First Editions*; edited by William M. McBride.
- *First Editions: A Guide to Identification*; edited by: E. N. Zempel and Linda A. Verkler.
- *First Editions: A Field Guide for Collectors of English & American Literature*; A. K. Ward.

Each of these guides will provide solid reference to identifying first edition markings for different publishing houses. These books do not provide first edition 'identification points' for specific collectible children's books.

IDENTIFYING CONTEMPORARY FIRST EDITION PICTUREBOOKS

In general, on most contemporary first editions, the copyright page will have the words "First Edition," "First Printing," or "First Impression," in conjunction with a numbering or lettering

NUMBERING SYSTEM: 1—10	NUMBERING SYSTEM: 0—9	LETTERING SYSTERM
In the case of the 1-to-10 numbering system, look for a sequence such as: 1 2 3 4 5 6 7 8 9 10 **or** 1 3 5 7 9 10 8 6 4 2 The true First Edition will include the '1' in the sequence. If the sequence is missing the '1' and the '2', therefore the numbers look like: 3 4 5 6 7 8 9 10 **or** 3 5 7 9 10 8 6 4 In this case, the book is the third printing, even if the copyright page includes the words "First Edition." No reputable bookseller would represent a book such as this as a first edition. Informed auction sellers also should not represent a book such as this as a first edition.	In the case of the 0-to-9 numbering system, look for a sequence such as: 0 1 2 3 4 5 6 7 8 9 The true first edition will include the 'o' in the sequence. If the sequence is missing the 'o' and the '1', therefore the numbers look like: 2 3 4 5 6 7 8 9 In this case, the book is the third printing, even if the copyright page includes the words "First Edition." No reputable bookseller would represent a book such as this as a first edition. Informed auction sellers also should not represent a book such as this as a first edition.	In the case of the lettering system, look for a sequence such as: A B C D E The true first edition will include the 'A' in the sequence. If the sequence is missing the 'A' and the 'B', therefore the letters look like: C D E In this case, the book is the third printing, even if the copyright page includes the words "First Edition." No reputable bookseller would represent a book such as this as a first edition. Informed auction sellers also should not represent a book such as this as a first edition.

(less common) systems. *It is important to understand that a book with "First Edition" or "First Printing" on the copyright page does not mean the book is a first edition in the collectible sense.* Rather, the correct "number line" sequence is of vital importance.

First Edition Identification For Specific Publishers

In order to assist the reader in identifying first edition books, we have included the following table of identifying marks for a few prominent printing companies. This list is not intended to be complete, and is provided only to give the novice collector a flavor of how to identify true first editions. The previously mentioned reference books will provide much more detailed information on many more publishing houses. Please note that for some publishers, the first edition of the book will only include the correct number line sequence, and will not have the words "First Edition" or "First Printing" on the copyright page.

PUBLISHER	FIRST PRINTING IDENTIFIER
Clarion Books	10 9 8 7 6 5 4 3 2 1
Dial Books for Young Readers	First Edition 1 3 5 7 9 10 8 6 4 2
Doubleday	'Month, Year' 10 9 8 7 6 5 4 3 2 1
Dutton Children's Books	First Edition 10 9 8 7 6 5 4 3 2 1
Farrar, Straus, & Giroux	First Edition, 'Year'
Greenwillow Books (William Morrow)	First Edition 10 9 8 7 6 5 4 3 2 1
Harcourt Brace	First edition A B C D E
Harcourt Brace (Gulliver Books)	First edition A C E F D B
Harpercollins	1 2 3 4 5 6 7 8 9 10 First Edition
Harry N. Abrams	First Edition
Houghton Mifflin	10 9 8 7 6 5 4 3 2 1
Hyperion Books for Children	First Edition 1 3 5 7 9 10 8 6 4 2
Knopf	10 9 8 7 6 5 4 3 2 1
Knopf (If printed outside US.)	First American Edition 10 9 8 7 6 5 4 3 2 1
Little, Brown	First Edition 10 9 8 7 6 5 4 3 2 1
Lothrop, Lee & Shepard	First Edition 1 2 3 4 5 6 7 8 9 10
Michael di Capua Books	First Edition, 'Year'
Morrow	1 2 3 4 5 6 7 8 9 10

PUBLISHER	FIRST PRINTING IDENTIFIER
Morrow Junior Books	10 9 8 7 6 5 4 3 2 1
Orchard Books	10 9 8 7 6 5 4 3 2 1
Philomel	10 9 8 7 6 5 4 3 2 1 First Impression
Putnam's	1 3 5 7 9 10 8 6 4 2 First Impression
Random House (modern)	1 2 3 4 5 6 7 8 9 0
Simon & Schuster Books for Young Readers	10 9 8 7 6 5 4 3 2 1
Simon & Schuster	First Edition 10 9 8 7 6 5 4 3 2 1
Viking	10 9 8 7 6 5 4 3 2 1

IDENTIFYING CALDECOTT MEDAL BOOKS

Within the hobby, to our knowledge, a method for identifying first printings of Caldecott Medal winning books has not yet been published. We present the following list for identifying a majority of the Caldecott Medal books[27].

Animals Of The Bible (1937) Dust jacket spine: Lathrop misspelled "Lathop." Copyright page: Line states "COPYRIGHT, 1937, DOROTHY P. LATHROP" and no other publication dates.

Mei Li (1938) Copyright page: Line states "CL," followed by line "Copyright, 1938 by Thomas Handforth. All Rights Reserved. First edition."

Abraham Lincoln (1939)
Copyright page: Line states "FIRST EDITION," followed by line "COPYRIGHT, 1939, BY DOUBLEDAY, DORAN & COMPANY, INCORPORATED."

They Were Strong And Good (1940) Copyright page: Line states "FIRST PUBLISHED SEPTEMBER 1940" and no other publication dates.

Make Way For Ducklings (1941) Copyright page: Line states "First published August 1941" and no other publication dates.

Many Moons (1943) Copyright page: Line states "COPYRIGHT, 1943 BY," followed by line "JAMES THURBER," followed by threes lines beginning with "All rights reserved…," followed by line "I." No other publication dates.

Prayer For A Child (1944) Title page: Line with "New York · The Macmillan Company · 1944." Front DJ flap, bottom right price "$1.50."

The Rooster Crows (1945) Last line on copyright page: "Published 1945." Title page line: "New York   Macmillan Company   1945."

The Little Island (1946) Copyright page: Line states "FIRST EDITION."

White Snow, Bright Snow (1947) Front flap: "WHITE SNOW BRIGHT SNOW" followed by synopsis; bottom line "Ages 4 - 8 $2.00." No additional printing on copyright page.

---

27   We intend to have the first identification points for the omitted Caldecott Medal books in a future edition, once we have the particular points verified by reputable sources.

IDENTIFYING CALDECOTT MEDAL BOOKS (cont)

Song Of The Swallows (1949) Copyright page: "Copyright 1949 by Charles Scribner's Sons · Printed in the United States of America." On later printings, beneath this line, "Copyright, 1948, by Leo Politi" has been added. It is the absence of the 1948 copyright which signifies a first edition.

The Egg Tree (1950) Copyright page: Line with "THE PERMISSION OF CHARLES SCRIBNER'S SONS," followed by line with "A" (last line on the copyright page).

The Biggest Bear (1952) Front flap price "$2.75." Title page states "1952."

Madeline's Rescue (1953)
Copyright page: Line with "Published by The Viking Press in April 1953"

Cinderella (1954)
Copyright page: Line with "Printed in the United States of America · A"

Frog Went A-Courtin (1955)
Copyright page: Line with "FIRST EDITION." DJ price "$2.50."

Chanticleer And The Fox (1958) No additional printings on copyright page. Front flap states "CHANTICLEER AND THE FOX," followed by synopsis, then "(004 - 008)" at bottom right. Back flap has short bio of Barbara Cooney.

Nine Days To Christmas (1959)
Copyright page: "First Published in 1959 by The Viking Press, Inc."

Baboushka And The Three Kings (1960)
Front Flap: Top right "$2.50." Copyright page: No additional printings.

Once A Mouse (1961) Copyright page: Line with "Copyright © 1961 Marcia Brown," followed by line "All Rights Reserved'" followed by line "A-9.61 [RJ]."

Where The Wild Things Are (1963) Front flap: Top right "$3.50," followed by "Where The Wild Things Are" followed by synopsis. Rear flap: Three paragraph biography for Maurice Sendak. Dust jacket flaps do not mention Wild Things winning Caldecott Medal.

Always Room For One More (1965) Copyright page: Line with "Printed in the United States of America / 960610-1115 / First Edition."

Sam, Bangs, And Moonshine (1966) Copyright page: Line with "LIBRARY OF CONGRESS CATALOG CARD NUMBER: AC 66-10113," followed by line with "FIRST EDITION."

Drummer Hoff (1967) Absence of later printings on copyright page and dust jacket. Front flap: Three paragraph synopsis of book. Rear flap: "About the Emberleys" followed by two paragraph biography.

The Funny Little Woman (1972) Copyright page: Last line with "SBN: 0-525-30265-4 LCC: 75-179046   Printed n the U.S.A.   First Edition."

IDENTIFYING CALDECOTT MEDAL BOOKS (cont)

Duffy And The Devil (1973) Copyright page: Line with "Typography by Atha Tehon," followed by line with "First edition, 1973."

Arrow To The Sun (1974) Last page: Number line "1 2 3 4 5 6 7   79 78 77 76 75 74."

Why Mosquitoes Buzz In People's Ears (1975) Copyright page: Line with "Pictures copyright © 1975 by Leo and Diane Dillon," followed by line with "All Rights Reserved | First Printing."

Ashanti To Zulu: African Traditions (1976) Copyright page: Line with "Pictures copyright © 1976 by Leo and Diane Dillon," followed by line with "All Rights Reserved · First Printing."

Noah's Ark (1977) Copyright page: Line with "All Rights Reserved   Printed in the United States of America   First Edition."

The Girl Who Loved Wild Horses (1978) Copyright page: Line ends with "Manufactured in the United States of America   1 2 3 80 79 78."

Ox-Cart Man (1979) Copyright page: Line with "First Edition," followed by six lines, then line "1 2 3 4 5 83 82 81 80 79."

Fables (1980) Copyright page: Line with "Printed in the U.S.A. All rights reserved," followed by line with "First Edition."

Jumanji (1981) Copyright page: Number line "H 10 9 8 7 6 5 4 3 2 1."

Shadow (1982) Copyright page: Line with "permission of Charles Scribner's Sons.," followed by number line "1 3 5 7 9 11 13 15 17 19 ND / C 20 18 16 14 12 10 8 6 4 2."

The Glorious Flight (1983) Copyright page (in back): Line with "First edition," followed by three lines, then line with "1 2 3 4 5 87 86 85 84 83."

Saint George And The Dragon (1984) Copyright page: "FIRST EDITION"

Polar Express (1985) Copyright page: Number line "H 10 9 8 7 6 5 4 3 2 1."

Hey, Al (1986) Copyright page: Line with "Typography by Cynthia Krupat," followed by line with "First edition, 1986."

Song And Dance Man (1987)
Copyright page (in back): Number line "1 3 5 7 9 10 8 6 4 2."

Lon Po Po (1989)
Copyright page (in back): Line with "ISBN 0-399-21619-7.   First Impression."

Black And White (1990) Copyright page (in back): Line with "Printed in the United States of America," followed by number line "H O R 10 9 8 7 6 5 4 3 2 1."

Tuesday (1991) Copyright page: Number line "H O R 10 9 8 7 6 5 4 3 2 1."

Mirette On The High Wire (1992) Copyright page: Number line " 1 3 5 7 9 10 8 6 4 2," followed by line "First Impression."

IDENTIFYING CALDECOTT MEDAL BOOKS (cont)

Grandfather's Journey (1993)
Copyright page: Number line "H O R 10 9 8 7 6 5 4 3 2 1."

Smoky Night (1994)
Copyright page: Line with "First edition," followed by line with "A B C D E."

Officer Buckle And Gloria (1995) Copyright page: Number line "1 3 5 7 9 10 8 6 4 2" followed by line with "First Impression."

Golem (1996) Copyright page: Number line "B V G 10 9 8 7 6 5 4 3 2 1 ".

Rapunzel (1997) Copyright page: Line with "First Edition" followed by line with number line "1 3 5 7 9 10 8 6 4 2."

Snowflake Bentley (1998) Copyright page: Line with "Manufactured in the United States of America," followed by line with "H O R 10 9 8 7 6 5 4 3 2 1."

Joseph Had A Little Overcoat (1999)
Copyright page: Number line "1 3 5 7 9 10 8 6 4 2."

So You Want To Be President? (2000) Copyright page (in back): Line with "1 3 5 7 9 10 8 6 4 2" followed by line with "First Impression."

The Three Pigs (2001) Copyright page: Number line "L B M 10 9 8 7 6 5 4 3 2 1."

My Friend Rabbit (2002)
Copyright page: Line with "First edition" followed by line with "10 9 8 7 6 5 4 3 2 1."

The Man Who Walked Between The Towers (2003) Copyright page: Line with "ISBN 0-7613-1791-0 (trade edition)," followed by number line with "1 3 5 7 9 10 8 6 4 2." Followed by line with "ISBN 0-7613-2868-8 (library binding)," followed by number line with "1 3 5 7 9 10 8 6 4 2." Also, on page 13, cable is "five-eighths of an inch thick." on 1st printing books; 2nd and later printings have correction, with cable "seven-eighths of an inch thick."

Kitten's First Full Moon (2004)
Copyright page: Number line "First Edition 10 9 8 7 6 5 4 3 2 1."

The Hello, Goodbye Window (2005) Copyright page: Line with "LIBRARY OF CONGRESS CONTROL NUMBER : 2004113496   DESIGNED BY CHRISTINE KETTNER FIRST EDITION, 2005."

IDENTIFYING SOME KEY FIRST EDITION BOOKS

It would be a daunting task to list the first edition identification points for all the key books listed in the Price Guide. Therefore, we include in the following table the first edition identification points for only a few key books.

Millions Of Cats (1928) Copyright page: Line with "Printed in U.S.A." followed by line with "By the Jersey City Publishing Co.." Subsequent printings omitted Jersey City Publishing lines.

IDENTIFYING SOME KEY FIRST EDITION BOOKS (cont)

The Little Engine That Could (1930) DJ: No copyright or trademark on cover; blank (white) dust jacket flaps. Book has red boards, and front paste-on which matches front DJ illustration; 'Stories That Never Grow Old' has nine titles, starting with The Rooster, The Mouse, and the Little Red Hen and ending with The Little Engine That Could.

Ferdinand (1936)
Copyright page: "First Published September 1936" with no additional printings.

Madeline (1939)
Title page: Line with "Simon & Schuster" followed by line with "1939."

The myth has propagated on the internet that the first printing book includes an error that was corrected in subsequent printings, with 12 girls 'breaking bread' instead of 11 (with Madeline in the hospital, there is supposed to be only 11 girls dining). This "12 girl error" was used in many, many subsequent printings, and is therefore not a method to identifying a true first printing.

Rudolph The Red-Nosed Reindeer (1939) Soft covered format. Tri-motor plane on page 9. Later editions have a plane with four motors.

Eloise (1955) Copyright page: Line states "NEW YORK 20, N.Y.," followed by line "FIRST PRINTING," followed by line "LIBRARY OF CONGRESS CATALOG CARD NUMBER: 55-11039." Page 50 on the true first state book makes reference to 'Lily Dache'; in later state copies this reference is changed to "Coco Chanel."

Harold And The Purple Crayon (1955) Title page: "Harper & Brothers." Dust jacket with $1.50 price.

The Giving Tree (1964) Front flap: Top right "2.50," then "The Giving Tree" followed by synopsis; bottom left "0964." Copyright page: Four lines of text only. "THE GIVING TREE," followed by "Copyright © 1964 Shel Silverstein," followed by "Printed in the United States of America. All rights reserved.," then last line reads "Library of Congress catalog card number: 64-11840." Back flap: "Some reviews of LAFCADIO," followed by three reviews. Back DJ photo only on left half of DJ (not full back photo) of full torso (later editions have only head shot) with "Shel Silverstein" beneath photo.

IDENTIFYING DR. SEUSS FIRST EDITIONS

Identifying Dr. Seuss first editions books is enormously difficult. It is so difficult that we often think, facetiously, it is due to a Random House conspiracy that has persevered for over sixty years—the complexity is too high to be random coincidence.

Any person seriously in the market for Dr. Seuss books should own a copy of *First Editions of Dr. Seuss Books* (2002), by Helen Younger, Marc Younger, and Dan Hirsch. Within the hobby, this book is considered the definitive guide to correctly identifying Dr. Seuss first editions, providing detailed information on each book, along with full color examples of books and dust jackets. Given the cost of making a mistake with Dr. Seuss first editions, the Younger/Hirsch book is an invaluable resource.

We had been collecting Dr. Seuss books for many years prior to the publication of the Younger/Hirsch book, and in the process had compiled our own list of points to help us identify many of the older first editions. In all cases, we either own, or have had in our possession, the first edition book with the identifying points listed. The information differs in several cases from that presented in Younger/Hirsch, since it is a result of our own research. So, we will provide the following modest partial list of 'what we know'[28].

We have included only the children's books that Dr. Seuss both wrote and illustrated, and have excluded those he wrote only, as either Dr. Seuss or as his pseudonym Theo LeSieg[29], and which others illustrated. This list should not be considered complete, but it should help to group identification of some of the Seuss first editions. Again, the Younger/Hirsch book should be obtained for a much more complete listing (contains books Geisel wrote under the Theo LeSieg pseudonym) and for detailed information.

GROUP A: STATED 'FIRST PRINTING"

This group of books is the easiest to identify since they state "First Printing" on the copyright page.

The Seven Lady Godivas (1939) Copyright page states 'First Printing."

Horton Hatches The Egg (1940) Copyright page states 'First Printing."

Cat In The Hat Comes Back (1958) Copyright page states 'First Printing." Also, for the dust jacket, the graphic matches the front book boards, with the snowball just to the left of the Cat's tail. In later printings, the snowball was omitted from both the cover of the book and dust jacket.

GROUP B: BOOK EXTERIOR UNIQUE TO FIRST PRINTING / DJ CAN BE PRICE CLIPPED

For this group of books, one can identify the first edition book or dust jacket easily, without even opening the book. The book boards and dust jacket graphics are unique to first printings and were changed on subsequent printings.

Bartholomew And The Oobleck (1949) Blue boards and blue dust jacket are unique to first printings.

If I Ran The Circus (1956) Pink boards and pink dust jacket are unique to first printings.

Horton Hears A Who (1954) On both back DJ and back board, the graphic is the same, and must have full Horton ear, with five branches on tree in upper right. On later editions, a portion of Horton's ear was "cut off" to make room for reviewer's comments.

---

28 As the picturebook collecting hobby evolves, the identification of Seuss first editions will also evolve. New information will be uncovered/discovered with time. Also, one can expect the precision will increase with regard to proper identification of valuable first editions.

29 Geisel wrote one book under the pseudonym "Rosetta Stone," *Because A Little Bug Went Ka-Choo!*, published by Beginner Books in 1975, and illustrated by Michael Firth.

GROUP C: DJ UNIQUE TO FIRST PRINTING / DJ CAN BE PRICE CLIPPED

For this group of books, the graphics on the dust jacket is unique to the first printing. These unique graphics might be on the front, back, or flaps. Because of this, it is not necessary to have a price on the dust jacket. The dust jacket price is of no consequence.

Thidwick The Big-Hearted Moose (1948) White 'starburst' on dust jacket front cover. First printing book has red boards, however this alone does not identify a first printing book. We have several early state copies with red boards, and also there is no 'starburst' graphic on the dust jacket.

Yertle The Turtle (1958) The back dust jacket has 13 photos of previous Seuss books.

One Fish, Two Fish, Red Fish, Blue Fish (1960) The top of the back dust jacket states "EXPERTS IN THE READING FIELD ACCLAIM," followed by three reviews on *One Fish, Two Fish, Red Fish, Blue Fish*. These reviews take up the majority of the printed area on the dust jacket back, so there is no listing of Beginner Books as can be found on subsequent printings.

Green Eggs And Ham (1960) Dust jacket front cover must have 'Beginner Book' sticker, rather than being printed. The back dust jacket has two lists. The first list of fifteen "Books For Beginners" starts with *The Cat In The Hat* and ends with *The King's Wish*. The second list of three "For BEGINNING Beginners" books contains *Green Eggs And Ham*, then *Put Me In The Zoo*, followed by, *Are You My Mother?*[30]

The Sneetches And Other Stories (1961) The back dust jacket flap lists "Twenty books by Dr. Seuss." Subsequent printings list "Twenty-three books by Dr. Seuss" on the back dust jacket flap.

Sleep Book (1962) Two list boxes on back dust jacket of previously published books by Dr. Seuss. The first list of sixteen books starts with *Yertle* and ends with *Mulberry Street*. The second list of four books starts with *Cat In The Hat* and ends with *Green Eggs And Ham*. Subsequent printings included *The Sleep Book* in the listings.

Hop On Pop (1963) The top of the dust jacket back states "About HOP ON POP, educators say:" followed by five reviews. These reviews take up the majority of the printed area on the dust jacket back, so there is no listing of Beginner Books as can be found on subsequent printings.

Dr. Seuss's ABC (1963) Three list boxes on back dust jacket of previously published books, including Dr. Seuss books and other Beginner Books. The third list ends with *Little Black Goes To The Circus*. Subsequent printings include Beginner Books published later than 1963.

Fox In Socks (1965) Three list boxes on back dust jacket of previously published books, including Dr. Seuss books and other Beginner Books. Third list ends with *Little Black*

---

30 For years we erroneously thought we owned a first edition copy of *Green Eggs and Ham*, a copy with the correct back dust jacket cover. Then, in 2000, a copy with the sticker came up for auction on eBay, going for what was then a remarkable $3000. Since then, we have seen several copies of the 'sticker' version for sale at the San Francisco Antiquarian Book Fair. They are very rare.

Goes To The Circus. In the second state book, the third list ends with "Fox In Sox," which is curiously misspelled (should be Socks).

I Had Trouble In Getting To Solla Sollew (1965) Two lists on back dust jacket of previously published books by Dr. Seuss. The first list is of the eighteen large format Dr. Seuss books, and is in chronological order, starting with *Mulberry Street* and ending with *Solla Sollew*. The second list of seven Dr. Seuss "Beginning Reader" books, starts with *ABC* and ends with *Fox In Socks* (spelled correctly).

Foot Book (1968) The top of the dust jacket back states "BRIGHT and EARLY BOOKS," then beneath it "…revolutionize the approach to reading for young readers.," followed by four reviews. These reviews take up the majority of the printed area on the dust jacket back, so there is no listing of Beginner Books or Bright and Early Books as can be found on subsequent printings.

GROUP D: DJ PRICE UNIQUE TO FIRST PRINTING

For this group of books, the book itself cannot be identified as a first printing without the dust jacket and price. In this group, the book and dust jacket graphic remained unchanged for later printings, whereas the price on the dust jacket changed.

If I Ran The Zoo (1950) DJ price of "200/200" must be present on front flap top right. Later printings have same book and dust jacket, however with "250/250" price.

Scrambled Eggs Super (1953) DJ price of "$2.50" must be present on front flap top right. Later printings have same book and dust jacket, however with "$2.95" price.

On Beyond Zebra (1955) DJ price of "250/250" must be present on the front flap top right. Later printings have same book and dust jacket, however with "295/295" price.

Cat In The Hat (1957) DJ price of "200/200" must be present on front flap top right. Later printings have similar book with same dust jacket, however with "195/195" price. Also, the first printing has a single book binding signature (later printings had three signatures)[31]. Be sure to differentiate the replica dust jacket from the 1985 *Cat In The Hat* reproduction book. The only difference in the dust jackets are the words, "Printed in U.S.A." printed on the back flap bottom of the replica dust jacket.

GROUP E: DJ PRICE WITH LOCATION UNIQUE TO FIRST PRINTING

In this group, the dust jacket price must be present and in the right location. In these books, later printings were priced at the same amount, however the location of price on the dust jacket was changed.

McElligot's Pool (1947) Dust jacket price of "$2.50" must be present on back flap, bottom left. Also note that the fish has an open mouth on the front board[32].

---

31 This point is not documented in Younger/Hirsch. We have inspected over fifteen different copies of the first state book, and all have had a single book binding signature. We have inspected over forty different copies of early state books (version with the slanted "For Beginning Readers" logo on both the front board and dust jacket), and all have had three book binding signatures.

32 First edition points for *McElligot's Pool* are a bit complex so please refer to Younger/Hirsch for details on variants.

How The Grinch Stole Christmas (1957) Dust jacket price of "250/250" must be present on front flap bottom right. Advertisement on back book must match DJ back, which lists *Cat In The Hat* for $2.00.

The following table is a synopsis of the first edition identification points for Dr. Seuss books, sorted by the "Group," and also provides the book's value estimate from the Price Guide.[33]

	IDENTIFYING FIRST EDITION DR. SEUSS BOOKS				
YEAR	**TITLE**	**GROUP**	**VG-**	**VG**	**VG+**
1939	The Seven Lady Godivas	A	$ 320	$ 440	$ 540
1940	Horton Hatches The Egg	A	$ 4,400	$ 6,000	$ 7,400
1958	Cat In The Hat Comes Back	A	$ 180	$ 240	$ 300
1949	Bartholomew And The Oobleck	B	$ 1,400	$ 1,800	$ 2,200
1954	Horton Hears A Who	B	$ 1,200	$ 1,600	$ 2,000
1956	If I Ran The Circus	B	$ 840	$ 1,200	$ 1,400
1948	Thidwick: The Big-Hearted Moose	C	$ 1,800	$ 2,400	$ 3,000
1958	Yertle The Turtle And Other Stories	C	$ 140	$ 180	$ 220
1960	One Fish, Two Fish, Red Fish, Blue Fish	C	$ 380	$ 520	$ 640
1960	Green Eggs And Ham	C	$ 2,800	$ 3,800	$ 4,800
1961	The Sneetches And Other Stories	C	$ 160	$ 200	$ 260
1962	Dr. Seuss's Sleep Book	C	$ 120	$ 160	$ 200
1963	Hop On Pop	C	$ 320	$ 420	$ 520
1963	Dr. Seuss's ABC	C	$ 320	$ 420	$ 520
1965	Fox In Socks	C	$ 160	$ 200	$ 260
1965	I Had Trouble In Getting To Solla Sollew	C	$ 160	$ 210	$ 260
1967	The Cat In The Hat Song Book	C	$ 70	$ 90	$ 120
1968	Foot Book	C	$ 960	$ 1,200	$ 1,600
1950	If I Ran The Zoo	D	$ 960	$ 1,200	$ 1,600
1953	Scrambled Eggs Super	D	$ 960	$ 1,200	$ 1,600
1955	On Beyond Zebra	D	$ 840	$ 1,200	$ 1,400
1957	The Cat In The Hat	D	$ 2,400	$ 3,200	$ 4,000
1947	McElligot's Pool	E	$ 1,800	$ 2,400	$ 3,000
1957	How The Grinch Stole Christmas	E	$ 1,200	$ 1,600	$ 2,000
1937	And To Think That I Saw It On Mulberry Street	YH	$ 5,000	$ 6,800	$ 8,400
1938	The 500 Hats Of Bartholomew Cubbins	YH	$ 3,800	$ 5,000	$ 6,200
1939	The King's Stilts	YH	$ 3,200	$ 4,200	$ 5,200
1959	Happy Birthday To You	YH	$ 160	$ 200	$ 260

33   Note: YH Group—see Younger, Helen, Younger Marc, and Hirsch, Dan. *First Editions of Dr. Seuss Books: A Guide to Identification*. Custom Communications, 2002.

Chapter 5
Price Guide Illumination

This Price Guide is focused on illustrated children's picturebooks, concentrating on the period from 1930 to present, with an emphasis on illustrators whose works are still published today. Subsequently, the Price Guide is sorted alphabetically by illustrator's last name.

An illustrated children's 'picturebook' is one in which the text and the illustrations are synergistic in telling the story—the two are intertwined such that one enhances the other, and vice-versa. The illustrations are not an augment to the story, but are intrinsic to the story. Books included in our definition of 'picturebooks' should meet the following criteria:

- A full-page illustration on every page or every other page.
- Illustrations are credited to an illustrator (i.e. not an anonymous artist).
- Published in hardcover format, with a dust jacket.

Many notable picturebook illustrators have contributed to children's chapter books, which have only an occasional illustration to accompany a reading story. Since it is important to capture the full bibliography of many of these notable children's picturebook illustrators, at least in their contribution to children's books, we have included these chapter books in the Price Guide. Also, some picturebooks are issued without dust jackets, yet include art by a notable illustrator—an example which comes quick to mind is Mercer Mayer and his *Little Critter* books. Here again, in the spirit of comprehensiveness, we have included these books in the Price Guide.

By and large, we have excluded hard cover chapter books in which ONLY the dust jacket cover art was completed by a notable children's picturebook illustrator. However, we have included those books, when the illustrator's cover art only might contribute to the market value of the artist's other books. The two notable inclusions are Mary Grandpre's cover artwork for the U.S. editions of the *Harry Potter* series of books[34], and also Eric Rohmann's covers for the U.S. editions of Philip Pullman's *Dark Materials* trilogy.

Soft cover picturebooks (i.e. paperbacks) have been nearly totally excluded from this Price Guide[35]. To our knowledge, the only soft cover books included are the Mercer Mayer *Little Critter* books published in soft cover format, and also the 1939 first edition of *Rudolph the Red-Nosed Reindeer*, by Robert May, illustrated by Denver Gillen.

BOOK PRICING

Since this is the first edition of the Price Guide, and covering nearly 23,000 books, there are pricing mistakes due to a number of reasons, including, but not limited to: typographical errors; bibliographical errors and oversights; and incorrect and incomplete market information[36]. As this publication matures, the pricing accuracy will increase. The intention is to provide a Price Guide which reflects current market retail conditions.

This Price Guide is not an offer to buy or sell any book, nor should the authors be held liable for any losses suffered from transactions made due to information in this book. Many factors affect the perceived value of any collectible, inclusive of illustrated children's picturebooks. In Chapter 2, "Factors Affecting Collectibility," we discuss in detail the factors that impact a book's value, so there is no need to reiterate it here. The book buyer must personally weigh all factors before deciding to purchase a collectible first edition children's picturebook.

We have over fifteen years of experience in the children's picturebook market, which includes very active participation in acquisition and collecting. Coupled with this experience, there are five primary sources for book prices in this Price Guide:

1. Antiquarian and used book stores
2. Antiquarian book fairs
3. Internet book markets
4. Catalogs distributed by children's booksellers
5. eBay auctions

Among these five sources, prices for the same book in similar condition can vary widely. This is primarily because the demand-side of the market (i.e. the potential buyers) for each source is dramatically different.

To expand upon this, consider the differences in number and type of potential buyers at an antiquarian book fair, as compared to the potential buyers for the internet book markets. The buyers at a antiquarian book fair are relatively few in number (as compared to the internet population), however they are by and large, experienced, sophisticated book collectors with a well focused interest. They have paid admission, and taken the time to attend and browse. When this type of collector finds a book they desire at a book fair, they are more likely to pay toward the top end of the market. Once the transaction is completed, the buyer can take ownership of the book immediately.

---

34   The high collectibility and value of the 1st edition *Harry Potter* books should favorable impact the collectibility and demand of Mary Grandpre's other picturebooks.

35   Please email us at errata@1stedition.net for soft cover books which have been inadvertently included in this Price Guide.

36   Please email us at bookprices@1stedition.net for comments or information which would help increase the accuracy of book market prices in this Price Guide.

The conditions for buying collectible first editions on the internet is considerably different. The object for sale cannot be physically inspected, therefore the prospective buyer must rely on the experience and credibility of the seller for an accurate description. Also, once the transaction has been agreed upon, the buyer must wait days, perhaps weeks, for delivery of the book. The slightly higher risks will impact, however marginally, the price that the buyer is willing to pay for a book sold via the internet.

Also, time and circumstance have little bearing on an internet listing—books can be bought anytime, from anywhere. Because of this, along with the multitude of books available for purchase on the internet, the prospective buyer will be more selective. If one were looking for a first edition copy of *Once A Mouse*, one would likely purchase an acceptable copy immediately at a book fair, whereas one might value shop for weeks on the internet.

ESTIMATION AND EXTRAPOLATION

Since many of the books listed in this Price Guide do not come up for sale or auction on a routine or recent basis, the book prices have had to be estimated, by extrapolation, from other information, such as prices of books of similar authorship, similar vintage, similar condition, similar demand, and similar supply. An extrapolation of a book's price is only an adequate estimate for the market value of the book—the true indicator is a bookseller finding a book buyer who is willing to pay a certain amount for a book. Even then, the sale of a particular book is no guarantee that the same or similar book can be sold for the same or similar amount. Circumstances will always enter into the equation.

The eBay auctions should be discussed further. We have been successful collectible book buyers on eBay for eight years, and have purchased over a thousand first edition books during that time. On average, our eBay book purchases have been well below the retail price we would have had to pay for a similar book bought at another market place. In most cases, the price would be below 'wholesale', if one considers that wholesale is 50% of retail. Why is this so?

In many cases, there were an insufficient number of potential buyers for the auction to reach the book's market value. It takes a lot of work to find first edition picturebooks for sale on eBay. In most cases, other potential buyers did not perform the work to find the book for auction on eBay, therefore the competition for the book was small. In some cases, the book seller did not know the market value of the book they were selling, set no reserve, or too low of a reserve, and the book sold for a song. Therein lies one of the key objectives of this Price Guide—to provide better visibility to the value of collectible children's picturebooks.

VERY GOOD+ AND FINE

Through our many years of book collecting experience, we have found that it is very difficult to find dust jacketed children's picturebooks published before 1970 in better than "Very Good+" condition. Because of this, we have estimated the market value of books published pre-1970 in "Very Good+" condition. For books published from 1970 to present, we have estimated the market value of dust jacketed children's picturebooks in "Fine" condition.

What is the difference in a "VG+" and "Fine" condition book? In both cases, the book itself should be in nearly new condition, with no flaws. The "VG+" book might have a previous owner's signature, whereas the "Fine" book will have no marks. By and large, the biggest difference is in the condition of the dust jacket. The "VG+" book might have some soiling, some creases or wrinkles, or some very small closed tears (no more than a couple). The dust jacket of a book graded as "Fine" condition will not have any closed tears or significant wrinkles or creases.

So what is the market value of a picturebook published pre-1970, in "Fine" condition? It's difficult to say. As an example, in the Price Guide, we have estimated the "VG+" value of *Where The Wild Things Are* at around $10,000; in "Fine" condition, the book would probably sell for somewhere between $15,000 to $20,000! In the Price Guide, we have estimated the "VG+" value of *Bartholomew And The Oobleck* at around $2200; in "Fine" condition, the book would probably sell for somewhere between $3,000 to $4,000.

SELECTED AUTHORS

Some illustrators have high eminence in the market place. Similarly, several children's book authors have more eminence than others—the author's books have higher collectibility. Two key examples are picturebooks written by Margaret Wise Brown, or by Jane Yolen. The Price Guide reflects slightly higher value for books authored by either of these two for a particular illustrator. There are numerous other examples.

Theodor Seuss Geisel, a.k.a. Dr. Seuss, wrote twelve books under the pseudonym Theo LeSieg, in which he was not the illustrator, all published by Beginner Books. Each of these is very collectible.

DR. SEUSS AUTHORED BOOKS (AS THEO LESEIG)						
TITLES	ILLUSTRATOR	YEAR	VG-	VG	VG+	FINE
Ten Apples Up On Top!	Roy McKié	1961	$ 220	$ 280	$ 360	
I Wish That I Had Duck Feet	B. Tobey	1965	$ 300	$ 400	$ 500	
Come Over To My House	Richard Erdoes	1966	$ 200	$ 260	$ 320	
Eye Book	Roy McKié	1968	$ 420	$ 560	$ 700	
My Book About Me	Roy McKié	1969	$ 120	$ 160	$ 200	
In A People House	Roy McKié	1972		$ 220	$ 320	$ 420
The Many Mice Of Mr. Brice	Roy McKié	1973		$ 160	$ 240	$ 320
Wacky Wednesday	George Booth	1974		$ 100	$ 160	$ 220
Would You Rather Be A Bullfrog?	Roy McKié	1975		$ 160	$ 220	$ 300
Hooper Humperdink ... ? Not Him!	Charles E. Martin	1976		$ 100	$ 160	$ 220
Please Try To Remember The First Of Octember!	Art Cumings	1977		$ 120	$ 180	$ 240
Tooth Book	Roy McKié	1981		$ 100	$ 160	$ 220

Books written by Newbery Medal winning authors also tend to command a premium in the market. The American Library Association has been awarding the Newbery Award since 1922 (from the ALA website):

> "The Newbery Medal was named for eighteenth-century British book-seller John Newbery. It is awarded annually by the Association for Library Service to Children, a division of the American Library Association, to the author of the most distinguished contribution to American literature for children."

Since the Newbery award winning books are chapter books and by-and-large are not illustrated children's books, they have not been included as part of the picturebook Price Guide. However, there are some exceptions, and many Newbery award winning books are augmented with illustrations by a picturebook illustrator. As we have stated earlier, for the sake of completeness, we have included these type of chapter books in the Price Guide. There are 81 Newbery award winning books which include pictures and/or cover art by illustrators listed in the Price Guide, which includes 28 Newbery Medal books! See Appendix 4 for a complete list.

Pop Culture Afterthought

For books published prior to 1990, there are not too many instances of a movie, television, or person of celebrity authoring or illustrating a children's picturebook. Fred Gwynne (Car 54 and The Munsters) comes to mind for his many author/illustrator books, as does Kay Thompson (Broadway stage) for her authorship of the Eloise books. Past these two, one has to reach deep in their experience base to recall other examples.

From 1990 through 1998, the actor Dom Deluise authored five wonderful children's picturebooks, augmented by the equally wonderful illustrations of Christopher Santoro. In the past couple of years, the authorship by actor or celebrity has picked up some momentum.

The list of pop culture celebrities who have authored children's picturebooks includes Billy Crystal, Madonna, Jerry Seinfeld, John Lithgow, Jay Leno, and Jamie Lee Curtis to name but a few. The cynic might question their qualifications, "Why would I want to buy a children's picturebook written by Madonna?" Obviously, in the opinion of their publishers, there is a belief that their celebrity will lead to strong sales. A strange thing occurred on the way to market—by and large, the picturebooks written by such celebrities are very good! Why is this? For one, the illustrators employed are of very high caliber—one assumes the illustrator selection process is rigorous. Secondly, the editors are of a similar high caliber. Lastly, each author has a nice story to tell.

Normally, the first printings of these books are fairly high in number, therefore should not experience substantial future market appreciation. However, there is a benefit to the illustrators of books authored by celebrities, since so many more people are exposed to their artwork than might be otherwise. For example, the other books by Loren Long, the illustrator for Madonna's *Mr. Peabody's Apples*, have benefited, in the collectibility sense, from this increased exposure[37].

Autographed First Editions

For the most part, autographed first editions command a premium in the collectible picturebook market. In general, this premium ranges from 20% to 30% above the grade price.

The Books Of Wonder bookstore in New York has a collector's club where signed first editions are available at cover price from newly published children's book titles, including both chapter books and picturebooks. If you are interested in collecting autographed children's books at a reasonable price, then this is a superb place to start. Books Of Wonder is the best known

---

37 Mr. Long *might* have benefited professionally, since we have no way of knowing whether his work on Madonna's book helped him in getting the work for the re-make of *The Little Engine That Could*. By the way, in our opinion this is the best illustrated version of the classic.

bookstore in New York[38], with substantial customer traffic, therefore it has a lot of author and illustrator book signings. Also, should you decide to sell these signed books at some future date, the Books Of Wonder collector club receipts provide solid validation that the signatures are authentic. Storyopolis in Los Angeles has available a wide array of author and illustrator signed children's books as well.

SIGNED LIMITED EDITIONS

By and large, we have omitted books that were originally issued in signed, limited edition format. These books are limited to a certain number, signed by both the author and illustrator, and come encased with a special slipcase. Often they will also come with a limited edition print, similarly signed and numbered.

Whereas most signed limited editions are issued simultaneously with the publication of the normal first printing book, Barry Moser and Edward Gorey have numerous books issued only in limited slipcase fashion. Following the spirit of complete bibliographies, we have included those in the Price Guide.

There are some very collectible signed limited editions. Wanda Gag's *Millions of Cats* was issued in signed, limited, slipcase format along with the first printing of the book in 1928, which included a small etching. During the 1930's, Platt & Munk issued *The Little Engine That Could* in a boxed, limited format with blue cloth binding. One of the most difficult limited edition books to find is *Rudolph The Red-Nosed Reindeer*, issued by Montgomery Ward in a boxed, hardcover edition given to employees, friends and family of the creators, Robert May and Denver Gillen.

As for modern collectibles, to commemorate the movie, Houghton Mifflin produced a slipcased edition of *Polar Express*, limited to 175 copies, signed by Chris Van Allsburg, Tom Hanks, and director Robert Zemeckis.

> "A limited edition of 175 numbered and meticulously hand-bound copies of the beloved holiday classic *The Polar Express* are available. This special leather-bound, boxed and numbered edition of *The Polar Express* [...] This is the first edition to utilize modern digital printing technology, undertaken by securing the original art. The results are spectacular. For the first time, the colors and details of Chris's paintings are reproduced with the accuracy and vibrancy he had originally intended. The result is a quality of reproduction with the highest degree of fidelity, overseen on press by the artist himself."

So, if the above is used as an indicator, signed, limited edition books are advancing in technique in terms of production quality and also in intent. The reader's comments are welcome in terms of adding books issued in signed, limited format to future editions of the Price Guide.

---

38 In the movie, You've Got Mail, the bookstore in the film was based upon Books of Wonder. It has been reported that Meg Ryan worked the counter for a day as part of her preparation.

Chapter 6
Book Grading

The value of a first edition book is extremely dependent upon its condition. The difference in value between a particular first edition book in "Fine" versus "Very Good" condition can be as much as 50%. Because of this, an accurate description of a book's condition is vitally important to collectors and booksellers.

Many bookselling and book collecting associations include a statement in their charter or creed related to providing accurate descriptions of books. Because of this, buying a book from an association, such as an ABAA member, carries a greater degree of confidence.

Due to the importance of condition, a fairly uniform approach toward book grading has been adopted by the book collecting industry. AB Bookman's Weekly, a now defunct book collecting periodical, created and endorsed a set of book grading terms which over the years have come to be accepted as an industry standard. Most books on book collecting provide good information on how to properly assess the condition of a book – the roots can generally be traced back to AB Bookman's Weekly. The same can be said for the reference material available on many of the book collecting or book association's internet sites, although many do not give due credit to AB Bookman's Weekly. The following are grading terms based upon the AB Bookman's Weekly:

As New   is to be used only when the book is in the same immaculate condition in which it was published. There can be no defects, no missing pages, no library stamps, etc., and the dustjacket (if it was issued with one) must be perfect, without any tears.

Fine   approaches the condition of "As New," but without being crisp. For the use of the term "Fine" there must also be no defects, etc., and if it has a small defect, or looks worn, this should be noted.

Very Good can describe a used book that does show some small signs of wear—but no tears—on either binding or paper. Any defects must be noted.

Good describes the average used and worn book that has all pages or leaves present. Any defects must be noted.

Fair is a worn book that has complete text pages (including those with maps or plates) but may lack endpapers, half-title, etc. (which must be noted). Binding, jacket (if any), etc. may also be worn. All defects must be noted.

Poor describes a book that is sufficiently worn; that its only merit is as a 'Reading Copy' because it does have the complete text, which must be legible. Any missing maps or plates should still be noted. This copy may be soiled, scuffed, stained or spotted and may have loose joints, hinges, pages, etc.

Ex-library must always be designated as such no matter what the condition of the book.

Book Club must always be noted as such no matter what the condition of the book.

Dustjacket In all cases, the lack of a dustjacket should be noted if the book was issued with one.

Virtually all professional bookselling associations and reputable booksellers use the above book grading terminology, most with some minor variation or another. Some practices are becoming more common:

- It has become a fairly prevalent to denote "As New" as "Mint"—the terms have become nearly synonymous.
- Many booksellers have adopted a "Near Fine" term to denote books with a single minor defect that keeps it from being "Fine."
- Many booksellers have adopted a plus or minus sign ('+' or '-') to the terms to provide increased granularity to the grading scale. For instance "VG+" or "VG-." To our knowledge, a standard has not yet been wholly agreed upon within the industry regarding the clear meaning of these gradient descriptions, therefore one should come to know the individual bookseller to understand completely the application to the particular book.

EX-LIBRARY

Books that have been circulated in public libraries, "Ex-library" or "Ex-lib" books, as they are generally referred to within the hobby, have very little collectible value. These books will have a library card pocket inside the book, and a card catalog identifier glued to the outside of the dust jacket at the spine. Sometimes the pocket has been removed or the page containing the pocket has been sliced from the book, but in either case the collectibility of the book is not positively affected by the removal.

We will not put forth an estimate as to their value, since they only have value when a buyer (demand-side) can be found—there are very few collectors who pursue "Ex-Lib" books. Because of this, the demand for such books is extremely low, and given such a thin marketplace, it's fruitless to make an extrapolation for the book's marketplace value. Ex-library books are not considered collectible within the hobby.

DUST JACKETS

Books without dust jackets, when one was originally issued with the first printing, have a greatly reduced market value, however they do have some collectible interest. Our experience indicates that the value for a first edition book, without its dust jacket, is about 10%-to-20% of the value of the same book, in similar condition, with the dust jacket intact. Even worn or damaged dust jackets add significant value to first edition picturebooks.

The dust jacket's presence has more importance within the children's picturebook hobby than for book collecting in general. This is because the artwork selected for the dust jacket cover is one of the most important marketing decisions made by the book's creators and publisher. In many cases, the initial retail purchase decision of a picturebook is made entirely due to attractive or interesting cover artwork. The old adage, "You can't judge a book by its cover!," does not necessarily apply to children's picturebooks. The same cannot be said for books in general.

The lives of picturebook collectors' are complicated by the fact that so many dust jackets of picturebooks are discarded almost immediately upon purchase, since they often interfere with the child opening and reading the book, or are torn asunder through the enthusiastic enjoyment of the book by the child. This general trend only increases the value of first edition picturebooks with intact dust jackets, since the existing supply-side quantity is diminished.

In many instances, the dust jackets serve to fully identify the book as a genuine first edition. This is especially true on Seuss books and other Random House offerings, but is also true of other picturebooks. The dust jacket often has the price on the top right or bottom right of the front flap, and this information could be vital to identification as a true first edition. Sometimes the front or back flap might contain a listing of previously published titles by the author or illustrator that are essential to proper identification as a true first edition printing.

Beginner Books

It is difficult to find a sequential listing of the Beginner Books, so we offer the following table. Note that many of the books were published simultaneously.

The First Fifty Beginner Books

Series	Year	Title	VG+	Illustrator	Author
B-01	1957	The Cat In The Hat	$4,000	Dr. Seuss	Dr. Seuss
B-02	1958	Cat In The Hat Comes Back	$300	Dr. Seuss	Dr. Seuss
B-03	1958	A Fly Went By	$260	Fritz Siebel	Mike McClintock
B-04	1958	The Big Jump & Other Stories	$180	Katherine Evans	Benjamin Elkin
B-05	1958	A Big Ball Of String	$180	Marion Holland	Marion Holland
B-06	1958	Sam And The Firefly	$260	P.D. Eastman	P. D. Eastman
B-07	1959	You Will Go To The Moon	$60	Lee J. Ames	Mae & Ira Freeman
B-08	1959	Cowboy Andy	$180	E. Raymond Kinstler	Edna W. Chandler
B-09	1959	The Whales Go By	$180	Paul Galdone	Fred Phleger
B-10	1959	Stop That Ball!	$180	Fritz Siebel	Mike McClintock
B-11	1959	Bennett Cerf's Book Of Laughs	$180	Carl Rose	Bennett Cerf
B-12	1959	Ann Can Fly	$180	Robert Lopshire	Fred Phleger
B-13	1960	One Fish, Two Fish, Red Fish, Blue Fish	$640	Dr. Seuss	Dr. Seuss
B-14	1960	The King's Wish & Other Stories	$120	Leonard Shortall	Benjamin Elkin
B-15	1960	Bennett Cerf's Book Of Riddles	$180	Roy McKié	Bennett Cerf
B-16	1960	Green Eggs And Ham	$4,800	Dr. Seuss	Dr. Seuss
B-17	1960	Put Me In The Zoo	$320	Robert Lopshire	Robert Lopshire
B-18	1960	Are You My Mother?	$260	P.D. Eastman	P. D. Eastman
B-19	1961	Ten Apples Up On Top!	$360	Roy McKié	Theo LeSieg (Seuss)
B-20	1961	Go, Dog. Go!	$360	P.D. Eastman	P. D. Eastman
B-21	1961	Little Black, A Pony	$120	James Schucker	Robert Farley
B-22	1961	Look Out For Pirates	$120	H. B. (Herman) Vestal	Iris Vinton
B-23	1961	Fish Out Of Water	$240	P.D. Eastman	Helen Palmer
B-24	1961	Bennett Cerf's More Riddles	$140	Roy McKié	Bennett Cerf
B-25	1962	Robert The Rose Horse	$120	P.D. Eastman	Joan Heilbroner
B-26	1962	I Was Kissed By A Seal At The Zoo	$120	Lynn (photos) Fayman	Helen Palmer
B-27	1962	Snow	$140	Roy McKié	P. D. Eastman
B-28	1962	The Big Honey Hunt	$240	Stan & Jan Berenstain	Same
B-29	1963	Hop On Pop	$520	Dr. Seuss	Dr. Seuss
B-30	1963	Dr. Seuss's ABC	$520	Dr. Seuss	Dr. Seuss
B-31	1963	Do You Know What I'm Going To Do Next Saturday?	$80	Lynn Fayman (photos)	Helen Palmer
B-32	1963	Summer	$140	Roy McKié	Alice Low
B-33	1963	Little Black Goes To The Circus	$120	James Schucker	Walter Farley
B-34	1964	Bennett Cerf's Book Of Animal Riddles	$120	Roy McKié	Bennett Cerf
B-35	1964	Why I Built The Boogle House	$100	Lynn Fayman (photos)	Helen Palmer
B-36	1964	The Bike Lesson	$160	Stan & Jan Berenstain	Same
B-37	1964	How To Make Flibbers	$160	Robert Lopshire	Robert Lopshire
B-38	1965	Fox In Socks	$260	Dr. Seuss	Dr. Seuss
B-39	1965	The King, The Mice And The Cheese	$120	Eric Gurney	Nancy Gurney
B-40	1965	I Wish That I Had Duck Feet	$500	B. Tobey	Theo LeSieg (Seuss)
B-41	1966	The Bears' Picnic	$160	Stan & Jan Berenstain	Same
B-42	1966	Don And Donna Go To Bat	$160	B. Tobey	Al Perkins
B-43	1966	You Will Live Under The Sea	$80	Ward Brackett	Fred Phleger
B-44	1966	Come Over To My House	$320	Richard Erdoes	Theo LeSieg (Seuss)
B-45	1967	Babar Loses His Crown	$140	Laurent de Brunhoff	Laurent de Brunhoff
B-46	1967	The Bear Scouts	$140	Stan & Jan Berenstain	Same
B-47	1967	The Digging-Est Dog	$100	Eric Gurney	Al Perkins
B-48	1967	Travels Of Doctor Dolittle	$100	Philip Wende	Al Perkins (adapted)
B-49	1968	Doctor Dolittle And The Pirates	$100	Philip Wende	Al Perkins (adapted)
B-50	1968	Off To The Races	$100	Leo Summers	Fred Phleger

Chapter 7
Where To Find
First Edition Picturebooks

Finding children's picturebooks is easy, while finding collectible first editions is relatively more difficult. In part, the entertainment in book collecting as a worthwhile pastime is by confronting and overcoming this difficulty. There is a thrill in finding the desired through the tedium of the hunt. There are four key areas to find collectible first edition children's picturebooks:

1. Book Stores
2. Internet—Book Services
3. Children's Booksellers
4. eBay

BOOK STORES

The best place to find collectible first edition books is by visiting book stores and personally searching their shelves for books of your particular interest. We have visited hundreds of book stores over the years, and are always delighted to come upon a first edition picturebook to add to our collection. There is no substitute to holding the children's picturebook in hand, browsing the story, and looking at the illustrations—there have been innumerable times that we stumbled upon wonderful illustrations by an artist we previously had not known, by using this 'technique'. Feel free to share this technique with friends—it is not proprietary, and to date, to our knowledge, no person or organization has patented the procedure, therefore royalties are not a barrier.

We want this Price Guide to be a vehicle for booksellers to sell more children's picture-books. To meet this objective, we need new collectors to enter the hobby. The 'New Books' type bookstores should embrace the information in this Price Guide, especially the transparency of picturebook values provided to the collecting public. The collecting of contemporary first edition books is a hands-on hobby, and the brick-and-mortar chains would have a distinct advantage over the online chains, since the latter are not set-up for their order-pickers to identify first edition copies as they work through their daily fulfillment of orders. The brick-and-mortar stores are an ideal place for the informed collector (one who can identify true first edition printings) to browse the in-store inventory and select collectible first edition, first print books. This is a distinct competitive advantage for the "New Books" brick-and-mortar store, however small.

The "Used Book" type bookstores will be a bit more hesitant to offer this Price Guide to their customers. In general, the store owner's personal collection of books about book collecting can be found behind the counter, out of reach of the perusing customers. The majority of the Used Bookstore income is the accumulated margin from sales volume on book turnover—buying, and then selling slightly used books at a fair profit. The "Used Book" store is the market maker, in a scenario which is repeated with multiplicity across nearly every city in America.

A small portion of the typical "Used Book" store revenue comes from buying collectible first editions at well below market prices, locating a collector for the book, then selling the book at a fair market price, which results in a sizeable profit. The bookseller has gathered knowledge of the collectible book market through years of research and a lifetime of experience, therefore the profit is only a fair return on the long–term investment of their time.

As a result, this is not necessarily a usurious profit. However, it is a profit that will shrink as the public becomes better educated about the market value for their collectible picturebooks. The "Used Book" store is already feeling competitive pressure from the internet, which is quickly becoming the primary market maker for collectible first edition books. So, some "Used Book" store owners will be hesitant to embrace an educated collecting public—it will potentially limit their opportunity to buy collectible first edition picturebooks at used book prices.

We hope a majority of "Used Book" booksellers will recognize the long-term benefit of expanding the hobby, and by becoming a local fair market exchange for collectible children's picturebooks. We will promote this spirit of education, and hope booksellers will follow suit.

INTERNET—BOOK SERVICES

The internet is a rich source of collectible books. Many booksellers now list through one of the many services that are now available. The advantage of using these types of services is that in all but the rarest of cases you will be buying from someone who truly knows books, and knows how to properly identify and grade books. The disadvantage is that you will normally pay full market price or somewhere close to it. Of course, this is not a disadvantage at all if you really want the book and cannot find it elsewhere.

All of the online bookselling associations and cooperatives have search engines with fairly advanced capabilities. Since there are 20 to 30 million books offered on the internet at any one time, you are very likely to find virtually any book, author, or illustrator that you might be interested in—perhaps not in a first edition, collectible format, but at least a reading copy should be available.

Some of the good internet used book services are:

Addall	www.addall.com
Advanced Book Exchange	www.abebooks.com
Alibris	www.alibris.com
Amazon	www.amazon.com
Antiquarian Booksellers Association Of America	www.abaa.org
Barnes and Nobles (select Out-of-Print tab)	www.barnesandnoble.com
Bibliofind	www.bibliofind.com

The inclusion of the organization in the list above does not constitute endorsement, implied or otherwise, of any material in this price guide.

CHILDREN'S BOOKSELLERS

There are a multitude of established booksellers who specialize in children's books, however they may or may not operate walk-in stores. These booksellers either distribute mailing lists, and/or market their books via their website, Bibliofind, Advanced Book Exchange, or one of the other internet book services. In most cases, one can navigate through the bookselling association website to find booksellers specializing in children's books. Also, you can use a search engine for "children's books" with the word "collectible" to find children's book specialists.

INTERNET—EBAY

eBay is the leading online auction service for goods of all types, and has grown over the past several years into a rich source of collectible books, including children's picturebooks. eBay has become a vital marketplace for used and out-of-print books. The sheer number of offerings at any one time is enormous, in large part due to the exposure a book-for-sale will have when posted by a member of the eBay community, which is open to anyone to join. Because of this high public exposure, there are a large number of regular booksellers on eBay. Many reputable booksellers have become regular sellers and buyers on eBay.

But most members who offer books on eBay are not professional booksellers, therefore it is often unclear as to whether the book being offered is a true first printing of a first edition. The prudent prospective bidder should email the eBay bookseller to gather specific first print information; normally the seller will respond in a prompt, courteous manner – it's to their benefit. As time goes by, more and more sellers are becoming educated as to first edition identification methods. Still, new sellers are constantly entering the eBay fray, so it's up to the buyer to find as much information as possible about a book prior to bidding.

PICTURES

Another nice feature of eBay auctions is the use of pictures by the bookseller. Many of the other internet book selling services do not yet offer images of the item being sold. In some cases an image service is offered, however it is too costly or difficult for the bookseller to implement. In either case, the prospective book buyer has only the written description to determine the actual condition or state of the book, without benefit of a picture. In most cases this is sufficient, since the booksellers have a lot of professional experience, although a visual example would still be helpful.

70

TRANSPARENCY OF AUCTION RESULTS

eBay also provides a good transparency of pricing. Once an auction closes, the auction results remain available for public viewing for ninety days. In addition, all of the bids on a particular auction are open for public scrutiny. By archiving this information, the modestly motivated collector can begin documentation of prevailing prices on books of their interest. This is an important value-added feature of eBay auctions.

ADVANCED SEARCH CAPABILITIES

Because of the high number of children's books offered for sale at any one time, most of which are not of the collectible fabric, it is imperative for the prospective bidder to leverage the item search capabilities on eBay. eBay's search capabilities are quite advanced, and provide a lot of flexibility to develop and save some refined searches. The search 'diction' is fairly simple, and allows the user to save highly customized searches that you can perform 2 or 3 times a week. The auctions on eBay usually have a 5 to 10 day time limit, therefore if you execute a particular search about once every three days, you are very likely not to miss the auction of a book in which you might be interested. This might seem time consuming to some, but the eBay searches are much more time efficient as compared to the other means of discovering, then buying a collectible picturebook.

FEEDBACK

eBay uses a very formalized system of user 'feedback' to assist buyers and sellers in establishing a reputable reputation. Feedback can only be given by the buyer and seller involved in a completed eBay auction, and must be in one of three categories (positive, negative, neutral), accompanied by a comment. Each eBay user's feedback is available for viewing by the entire eBay population, so a high number of positive comments serve to 'validate', to a degree, the selling integrity of the seller. Selling items will command better prices and more bidders if the seller has a high number of positive feedbacks, coupled with an absence of negative feedbacks.

This 'feedback' system has served eBay quite well, and although not perfect, it is quite reliable. The eBay services do a fairly responsible job of policing their members, but the determined can always find means of circumventing the system. The prudent bidder should take care when items are offered for sale by members new to the eBay community and who have little or no feedback.

SELLING FIRST EDITION PICTUREBOOKS ON EBAY

In a future edition, we will provide various methods and other information related to selling your first edition collectible picturebooks. Prior to that time, should you decide to sell your first edition picturebook on eBay, we offer several important tips.

- It is of the utmost importance that you provide detailed information regarding the first edition identification points for your book in the eBay description. This is probably the single most important item relative to getting a price close to market price for the book being sold.

- Use pictures, and also provide a detailed description of the condition of both the book and dust jacket.

- Indicate "First Edition" or " 1st Edition" in the item's description.

Chapter 8
Most Valuable Books

There are 44 picturebooks in the Price Guide which have an estimated market value of $1,000 or more. The list is a virtual "Who's Who?" of American picturebooks, topped by *Where The Wild Things Are*. Most of the books are staples within the picturebook industry—the list includes such classics as *Make Way For Ducklings*, *The Story Of Ferdinand*, *Millions Of Cats*, *Madeline*, *Curious George*, *Harold And The Purple Crayon*, *Eloise*, and *Babar*. Fifteen of the books are by Theodor Geisel, a.k.a. Dr. Seuss! Virginia Lee Burton has two books in the top ten, *Mike Mulligan And His Steam Shovel* and *The Little House*. Nine of the books are Caldecott Medal books, while seven of the books are Caldecott Honor books. *The Polar Express* (1985), by Chris Van Allsburg, is the most recently published book with an estimated market value over $1,000.

Probably the most difficult book to find in collectible first edition condition would be Robert McCloskey's, *Make Way For Ducklings*. In all our years of collecting, we have seen only a couple come to market. *Harold And The Purple Crayon* is nearly as difficult to find, as our the three Smith and Haas published *Babar* books. The early Seuss books are also difficult to find in collectible, first edition state. The Seuss books published after 1954, starting with *On Beyond Zebra*, can be found in collectible condition with a modest amount of effort. The exception to this, to a certain extent, is the first state ("200/200") of Seuss's milestone book, *The Cat In The Hat*, and to a large extent, is the first state (stickered) of *Green Eggs and Ham*—the first state of *Green Eggs* does not surface too often. As for the other books in the list, we have found that most of them come to market several times per year.

For this list and the lists that follow, note the key factors that impact the collectibility of the books. First, each is a high quality story with imaginative or inventive illustrations, therefore the reading public has recurrently purchased the books for decades. Because of this, the books have stayed in print since their original publication and gone into many, many printings. Many of the books have earned a children's picturebook award, while many of the illustrators have won numerous awards. All of the illustrators have high esteem within the book publishing market place. Many of the book's characters became franchise characters, where one or more sequels were published, and line extensions have been made into other consumer product areas (i.e. toys, games, dolls, costumes, decorations, etc...). Lastly, many of the books or characters have crossed over into pop culture, either via a TV or feature film adaptation.

\multicolumn{8}{c}{MOST VALUABLE PICTUREBOOKS}
YEAR	TITLE	ILLUSTRATOR	VG-	VG	VG+	FINE
1963	Where The Wild Things Are	Maurice Sendak	$6,200	$8,200	$10,200	
1937	And To Think That I Saw It On Mulberry Street	Theodor Geisel	$5,000	$6,800	$8,400	
1940	Horton Hatches The Egg	Theodor Geisel	$4,400	$6,000	$7,400	
1941	Make Way For Ducklings	Robert McCloskey	$4,400	$6,000	$7,400	
1938	The 500 Hats Of Bartholomew Cubbins	Theodor Geisel	$3,800	$5,000	$6,200	
1939	The King's Stilts	Theodor Geisel	$3,200	$4,200	$5,200	
1936	The Story Of Ferdinand	Robert Lawson	$3,000	$4,000	$5,000	
1942	The Little House	Virginia Lee Burton	$3,000	$4,000	$5,000	
1960	Green Eggs And Ham	Theodor Geisel	$2,800	$3,800	$4,800	
1939	Mike Mulligan And His Steam Shovel	Virginia Lee Burton	$2,600	$3,400	$4,200	
1928	Millions Of Cats	Wanda Gág	$2,400	$3,200	$4,000	
1939	Madeline	Ludwig Bemelmans	$2,400	$3,200	$4,000	
1957	The Cat In The Hat	Theodor Geisel	$2,400	$3,200	$4,000	
1933	The Story Of Babar	Jean de Brunhoff	$2,200	$3,000	$3,800	
1941	Curious George	H.A. Rey	$2,200	$3,000	$3,800	
1938	Pumpkin Moonshine	Tasha Tudor	$2,000	$2,800	$3,400	
1947	McElligot's Pool	Theodor Geisel	$1,800	$2,400	$3,000	
1948	Thidwick: The Big-Hearted Moose	Theodor Geisel	$1,800	$2,400	$3,000	
1955	Harold And The Purple Crayon	Crockett Johnson	$1,800	$2,400	$3,000	
1955	Eloise	Hilary Knight	$1,800	$2,400	$3,000	
1934	The Travels Of Babar	Jean de Brunhoff	$1,600	$2,000	$2,600	
1935	Babar The King	Jean de Brunhoff	$1,600	$2,000	$2,600	
1947	Curious George Takes A Job	H.A. Rey	$1,400	$2,000	$2,400	
1949	Bartholomew And The Oobleck	Theodor Geisel	$1,400	$1,800	$2,200	
1954	Horton Hears A Who	Theodor Geisel	$1,200	$1,600	$2,000	
1957	How The Grinch Stole Christmas	Theodor Geisel	$1,200	$1,600	$2,000	
1937	Animals Of The Bible	Dorothy P. Lathrop	$960	$1,200	$1,600	
1938	Mei Li	Thomas Handforth	$960	$1,200	$1,600	
1939	Abraham Lincoln	Ingri & Edgar Parin d'Aulaire	$960	$1,200	$1,600	
1939	Alexander The Gander	Tasha Tudor	$960	$1,200	$1,600	
1950	If I Ran The Zoo	Theodor Geisel	$960	$1,200	$1,600	
1953	Scrambled Eggs Super	Theodor Geisel	$960	$1,200	$1,600	
1968	Foot Book	Theodor Geisel	$960	$1,200	$1,600	
1933	The ABC Bunny	Wanda Gág	$840	$1,200	$1,400	
1948	Blueberries For Sal	Robert McCloskey	$840	$1,200	$1,400	
1955	On Beyond Zebra	Theodor Geisel	$840	$1,200	$1,400	
1956	If I Ran The Circus	Theodor Geisel	$840	$1,200	$1,400	
1985	Polar Express	Chris Van Allsburg		$700	$1,000	$1,400
1939	Little Toot	Hardie Gramatky	$720	$960	$1,200	
1942	Cecily G. And The 9 Monkeys	H.A. Rey	$720	$960	$1,200	
1953	Journey Cake, Ho!	Robert McCloskey	$720	$960	$1,200	
1953	A Very Special House	Maurice Sendak	$720	$960	$1,200	
1952	The Biggest Bear	Lynd Ward	$600	$800	$1,000	
1981	Jumanji	Chris Van Allsburg		$500	$ 760	$1,000

Most Valuable Books – 1930's

As one might expect, since the picturebook industry was in its formative years, the collectible books from the 1930's are some of the most valuable. The first three Seuss children's books are at the top of the list. Seventeen of the books are on the 'over $1,000' list above.

The Little Engine That Could is one of the most valuable books from the 1930's, and is a significantly important book in the context of the history of collectible, illustrated picturebooks. Published in 1930, illustrated by Lois Lenski, *The Little Engine That Could* is one of the top selling children's books of all time, and is still in print today, robustly, over seventy-five years after it was first published!

The author for the story was originally credited to Watty Piper, but that was simply a house name used by Platt & Munk during the early twentieth century, and, somewhat amazingly, the real author for the story is still contended today[39].

	Most Valuable Picturebooks – 1930's				
Year	**Title**	**Illustrator**	**VG-**	**VG**	**VG+**
1937	And To Think That I Saw It On Mulberry Street	Theodor Geisel	$5,000	$6,800	$8,400
1938	The 500 Hats Of Bartholomew Cubbins	Theodor Geisel	$3,800	$5,000	$6,200
1939	The King's Stilts	Theodor Geisel	$3,200	$4,200	$5,200
1936	The Story Of Ferdinand	Robert Lawson	$3,000	$4,000	$5,000
1939	Mike Mulligan And His Steam Shovel	Virginia Lee Burton	$2,600	$3,400	$4,200
1939	Madeline	Ludwig Bemelmans	$2,400	$3,200	$4,000
1933	The Story Of Babar	Jean de Brunhoff	$2,200	$3,000	$3,800
1938	Pumpkin Moonshine	Tasha Tudor	$2,000	$2,800	$3,400
1934	The Travels Of Babar	Jean de Brunhoff	$1,600	$2,000	$2,600
1935	Babar The King	Jean de Brunhoff	$1,600	$2,000	$2,600
1937	Animals Of The Bible	Dorothy P. Lathrop	$960	$1,200	$1,600
1938	Mei Li	Thomas Handforth	$960	$1,200	$1,600
1939	Abraham Lincoln	Ingri & Edgar Parin d'Aulaire	$960	$1,200	$1,600
1939	Alexander The Gander	Tasha Tudor	$960	$1,200	$1,600
1933	The ABC Bunny	Wanda Gág	$840	$1,200	$1,400
1939	Little Toot	Hardie Gramatky	$720	$960	$1,200
1932	The Little Family	Lois Lenski	$580	$780	$980
1930	The Little Engine That Could	Lois Lenski	$560	$740	$920
1931	Snippy And Snappy	Wanda Gág	$560	$740	$920
1938	Snow White And The Seven Dwarfs	Wanda Gág	$500	$680	$840

---

39   For detailed information regarding the authorship controversy for *The Little Engine That Could*, see Roy Plotnick's website http://tigger.uic.edu/~plotnick/littleng.htm.

MOST VALUABLE BOOKS – 1940's

Tasha Tudor created seven of the twenty most valuable picturebooks from the 1940's, while Dr. Seuss created four books on the list. H.A. Rey has three *Curious George* books on the list, all of which are fairly difficult to find in first edition collectible format. Although Rey's book, *Cecily G. And The 9 Monkeys* is the second American book featuring Curious George, the book's British and French version precede the 1941 American printing of *Curious George*. The British version, published in 1939, was titled *Raffy And The 9 Monkeys*; the French version, also published in 1939, was titled *Rafi et les 9 Singes*. For the purist, either of these two books are actually the first appearance, in book form, of the Curious George character.

McCloskey's two books on the list, *Make Way For Ducklings* and *Blueberries For Sal* are both difficult to find in first edition collectible format. Based upon our experience, *Make Way For Ducklings* is one of the most difficult picturebooks to find in a first edition.

The Caldecott awards make a significant impact on the list, since there are five Medal books and four Honor books on the list. The Medal books are: *Make Way For Ducklings*, *The Little House*, *Many Moons*, *The Rooster Crows*, and *The Big Snow*.

MOST VALUABLE PICTUREBOOKS – 1940's					
YEAR	TITLE	ILLUSTRATOR	VG-	VG	VG+
1940	Horton Hatches The Egg	Theodor Geisel	$4,400	$6,000	$7,400
1941	Make Way For Ducklings	Robert McCloskey	$4,400	$6,000	$7,400
1942	The Little House	Virginia Lee Burton	$3,000	$4,000	$5,000
1941	Curious George	H.A. Rey	$2,200	$3,000	$3,800
1947	McElligot's Pool	Theodor Geisel	$1,800	$2,400	$3,000
1948	Thidwick: The Big-Hearted Moose	Theodor Geisel	$1,800	$2,400	$3,000
1947	Curious George Takes A Job	H.A. Rey	$1,400	$2,000	$2,400
1949	Bartholomew And The Oobleck	Theodor Geisel	$1,400	$1,800	$2,200
1948	Blueberries For Sal	Robert McCloskey	$840	$1,200	$1,400
1942	Cecily G. And The 9 Monkeys	H.A. Rey	$720	$960	$1,200
1940	The County Fair	Tasha Tudor	$480	$640	$800
1940	Thistly B	Tasha Tudor	$480	$640	$800
1941	A Tale For Easter	Tasha Tudor	$480	$640	$800
1941	Snow Before Christmas	Tasha Tudor	$480	$640	$800
1942	Poo-Poo And The Dragons	Robert Lawson	$460	$620	$780
1942	Dorcas Porkus	Tasha Tudor	$460	$620	$780
1943	Many Moons	Louis Slobodkin	$460	$620	$780
1944	Mother Goose	Tasha Tudor	$460	$600	$760
1945	The Rooster Crows	Maud & Miska Petersham	$440	$600	$740
1948	The Big Snow	Berta & Elmer Hader	$440	$580	$720

Most Valuable Books – 1950's

Seven Dr. Seuss books make the list of most valuable picturebooks from the 1950's, headed by *The Cat In The Hat*. *Harold And The Purple Crayon* is the second most valuable book on the list, however it is probably the most difficult book on the 1950's list to obtain in collectible first edition condition. Robert McCloskey's classic book, *Journey Cake, Ho!*, is also very difficult to find in first edition, as is Lynd Ward's Caldecott Medal winning book, *The Biggest Bear*.

The first *Eloise* book is the third most valuable book from the 1950's. Being the first book in the *Eloise* franchise, it is much more difficult to find then the other books in the series. The subsequent books in the series, *Eloise In Paris* (1956), *Eloise At Christmastime* (1959), *Eloise In Moscow* (1959), and *Eloise in London* (1961) are not extremely difficult to find in first edition, collectible condition since they were initially printed in higher quantity than the original *Eloise*.

Four Caldecott Medal books and three Caldecott Honor books are on the list.

MOST VALUABLE PICTUREBOOKS – 1950's					
Year	**Title**	**Illustrator**	**VG-**	**VG**	**VG+**
1957	The Cat In The Hat	Theodor Geisel	$2,400	$3,200	$4,000
1955	Harold And The Purple Crayon	Crockett Johnson	$1,800	$2,400	$3,000
1955	Eloise	Hilary Knight	$1,800	$2,400	$3,000
1954	Horton Hears A Who	Theodor Geisel	$1,200	$1,600	$2,000
1957	How The Grinch Stole Christmas	Theodor Geisel	$1,200	$1,600	$2,000
1950	If I Ran The Zoo	Theodor Geisel	$960	$1,200	$1,600
1953	Scrambled Eggs Super	Theodor Geisel	$960	$1,200	$1,600
1955	On Beyond Zebra	Theodor Geisel	$840	$1,200	$1,400
1956	If I Ran The Circus	Theodor Geisel	$840	$1,200	$1,400
1953	Journey Cake, Ho!	Robert McCloskey	$720	$960	$1,200
1953	A Very Special House	Maurice Sendak	$720	$960	$1,200
1952	The Biggest Bear	Lynd Ward	$600	$800	$1,000
1952	Curious George Rides A Bike	H.A. Rey	$580	$780	$980
1953	Madeline's Rescue	Ludwig Bemelmans	$580	$780	$980
1954	Cinderella, Or The Little Glass Slipper	Marcia Brown	$580	$760	$960
1957	Harold's Trip To The Sky	Crockett Johnson	$540	$720	$900
1957	Time Of Wonder	Robert McCloskey	$540	$720	$900
1957	Curious George Gets A Medal	H.A. Rey	$540	$720	$900
1958	Curious George Flies A Kite	H.A. Rey	$520	$700	$880
1958	Increase Rabbit	Tasha Tudor	$520	$700	$880

MOST VALUABLE BOOKS – 1960's

Where The Wild Things Are, the most valuable picturebook in the Price Guide, heads the list of most valuable books from the 1960's. The list includes four books written and illustrated by Dr. Seuss, and remarkably, includes two other books that he wrote (as Theo LeSieg) but did not illustrate—*The Eye Book*, illustrated by Roy McKie, and *I Wish That I Had Duck Feet*, illustrated by B. Tobey.

The Giving Tree, the timeless story by Shel Silverstein, has been in print since its initial publication in 1964, and is still briskly sold in new book stores. It is the fifth most valuable book from the 1960's, and is difficult to find in first edition condition ($2.50/DJ).

The *Nutshell Library* is a boxed sleeve set of four tiny books by Maurice Sendak, comprising *Alligators All Around*, *Chicken Soup with Rice*, *One was Johnny*, and *Pierre*. The true first edition set can only by identified by the $2.95 price sticker on the *Nutshell Library* box.

Five Caldecott Medal books are on the list.

MOST VALUABLE PICTUREBOOKS – 1960's					
YEAR	**TITLE**	**ILLUSTRATOR**	**VG-**	**VG**	**VG+**
1963	Where The Wild Things Are	Maurice Sendak	$6,200	$8,200	$10,200
1960	Green Eggs And Ham	Theodor Geisel	$2,800	$3,800	$4,800
1968	Foot Book	Theodor Geisel	$960	$1,200	$1,600
1960	A Picture For Harold's Room	Crockett Johnson	$500	$680	$840
1964	The Giving Tree	Shel Silverstein	$460	$620	$780
1968	Eye Book	Roy McKié	$420	$560	$700
1960	One Fish, Two Fish, Red Fish, Blue Fish	Theodor Geisel	$380	$520	$640
1962	Nutshell Library	Maurice Sendak	$320	$440	$540
1963	Curious George Learns The Alphabet	H.A. Rey	$320	$420	$520
1963	Hop On Pop	Theodor Geisel	$320	$420	$520
1963	Dr. Seuss's ABC	Theodor Geisel	$320	$420	$520
1965	I Wish That I Had Duck Feet	B. Tobey	$300	$400	$500
1966	Sam, Bangs, And Moonshine	Evaline Ness	$300	$400	$500
1969	Sylvester And The Magic Pebble	William Steig	$280	$360	$460
1964	Dorrie And The Blue Witch	Patricia Coombs	$240	$320	$400
1960	Inch By Inch	Leo Lionni	$220	$300	$380
1960	Becky's Birthday	Tasha Tudor	$220	$300	$380
1967	Drummer Hoff	Ed Emberley	$220	$300	$380
1961	Madeline In London	Ludwig Bemelmans	$220	$280	$360
1961	Once A Mouse	Marcia Brown	$220	$280	$360

MOST VALUABLE BOOKS – 1970's

Chris Van Allsburg's first book, *The Garden Of Abdul Gasazi*, won a Caldecott Honor award, and leads the list of most valuable picturebooks published in the 1970's. It is difficult to find in first edition, collectible condition, as is Gerald McDermott's Caldecott Medal winning book, *Arrow To The Sun.*

The Caldecott award books dominate the list, with fourteen Caldecott Medal or Honor books. Remarkably, all ten Caldecott Medal winning books made this top twenty list from the decade! Leo and Diane Dillon won back-to-back Caldecott Medals with *Why Mosquitoes Buzz In People's Ears* and *Ashanti to Zulu*. Both of these books should have some market place upside, in terms of value appreciation.

Dr. Seuss illustrated only a single book on the list, *Mr. Brown Can Moo! Can You?*, however he authored four other books on the list as Theo LeSieg (*In A People House, The Many Mice Of Mr. Brice, Would You Rather Be A Bullfrog?, Please Try To Remember The First Of Octember!*), which were illustrated by others!

	MOST VALUABLE PICTUREBOOKS – 1970's				
YEAR	**TITLE**	**ILLUSTRATOR**	**VG**	**VG+**	**FINE**
1979	The Garden Of Abdul Gasazi	Chris Van Allsburg	$480	$700	$940
1972	The Funny Little Woman	Blair Lent	$220	$320	$420
1972	In A People House	Roy McKié	$220	$320	$420
1974	Arrow To The Sun	Gerald McDermott	$220	$320	$420
1975	Why Mosquitoes Buzz In People's Ears	Leo & Diane Dillon	$200	$280	$380
1977	Noah's Ark	Peter Spier	$180	$280	$360
1970	A Story, A Story	Gail E. Haley	$180	$260	$340
1971	One Fine Day	Nonny Hogrogian	$180	$260	$340
1978	The Girl Who Loved Wild Horses	Paul Goble	$180	$260	$340
1979	Ox-Cart Man	Barbara Cooney	$180	$260	$340
1973	The Many Mice Of Mr. Brice	Roy McKié	$160	$240	$320
1973	Duffy And The Devil	Margot Zemach	$160	$240	$320
1970	In The Night Kitchen	Maurice Sendak	$160	$220	$300
1975	Strega Nona	Tomie dePaola	$160	$220	$300
1975	Would You Rather Be A Bullfrog?	Roy McKié	$160	$220	$300
1976	Ashanti To Zulu: African Traditions	Leo & Diane Dillon	$140	$220	$300
1972	Anansi The Spider	Gerald McDermott	$140	$220	$280
1975	Just For You	Mercer Mayer	$140	$200	$260
1977	Please Try To Remember The First Of Octember!	Art Cumings	$120	$180	$240
1970	Mr. Brown Can Moo! Can You?	Theodor Geisel	$120	$180	$240

Most Valuable Books – 1980's

The two Chris Van Allsburg Caldecott Medal winning books are at the top of the most valuable books from the 1980's. Of the two, *Jumanji* is more difficult to find in fine first edition condition, however there is more demand for the *Polar Express*. Currently, these are the only two books published since 1970 with an estimated market value of over $1,000. Van Allsburg has two other books on the list, *The Wreck Of The Zephyr* and *The Mysteries Of Harris Burdick*.

For the second decade in a row, the ten Caldecott Medal winning books make the top twenty valuable books of the decade! In addition, three Caldecott Honor books make the list. Of the Caldecott Medal winning books, *Owl Moon* and *Song And Dance Man* are probably the two most difficult to acquire.

A Visit To William Blake's Inn, by Alice and Martin Provensen, is a dual award book, winning a Caldecott Honor award, and, more importantly from a collectibility perspective, won the 1982 Newbery Medal! Because of this, the book probably has some positive market expectations.

MOST VALUABLE PICTUREBOOKS – 1980's					
YEAR	TITLE	ILLUSTRATOR	VG	VG+	FINE
1985	Polar Express	Chris Van Allsburg	$700	$1,000	$1,400
1981	Jumanji	Chris Van Allsburg	$500	$760	$1,000
1981	A Visit To William Blake's Inn	Alice & Martin Provensen	$160	$240	$320
1982	The World Of The Dark Crystal	Brian Froud	$160	$220	$300
1984	Saint George And The Dragon	Trina Schart Hyman	$160	$220	$300
1987	Owl Moon	John Schoenherr	$160	$220	$300
1987	Song And Dance Man	Stephen Gammell	$120	$180	$240
1982	Shadow	Marcia Brown	$120	$180	$240
1983	The Glorious Flight	Alice & Martin Provensen	$120	$180	$240
1981	Where The Buffaloes Begin	Stephen Gammell	$100	$160	$220
1981	Tooth Book	Roy McKié	$100	$160	$220
1980	Fables	Arnold Lobel	$100	$160	$200
1982	Ben's Dream	Chris Van Allsburg	$100	$160	$200
1983	Little Red Riding Hood	Trina Schart Hyman	$100	$140	$200
1983	The Wreck Of The Zephyr	Chris Van Allsburg	$100	$140	$200
1984	The Mysteries Of Harris Burdick	Chris Van Allsburg	$90	$140	$180
1989	Lon Po Po	Ed Young	$90	$120	$180
1987	Where's Waldo?	Martin Handford	$80	$120	$160
1987	Hey Al!	Richard Egielski	$80	$120	$160
1981	On Market Street	Anita Lobel	$80	$120	$160

MOST VALUABLE BOOKS – 1990's

This list is dominated by the seven Caldecott Medal award books, headed by David Wiesner's *Tuesday*. *Tuesday* is becoming moderately difficult to find, and Wiesner's regard within the market place has been enhanced by winning a second Caldecott Medal with *The Three Pigs*, and a second Caldecott Honor for *Sector 7*. In our opinion, David Wiesner's wordless books are the best that have been crafted. As an aside, Wiesner also illustrated *E.T., The Storybook*, published in 1982, which is 97th on the Publisher's Weekly list of bestselling children's books.

The collectibility of William Steig's *Shrek!* has obviously been enhanced by the enormous popularity of the two animated feature films (it should be noted that the book was issued without a dust jacket), and is the second most valuable picturebook published in the 1990's.

Snowflake Bentley, *Seven Blind Mice*, and *Rainbow Fish* are probably the three most difficult books on the list to find in a first edition state, so should have some potential future appreciation.

	MOST VALUABLE PICTUREBOOKS – 1990's				
YEAR	TITLE	ILLUSTRATOR	VG	VG+	FINE
1991	Tuesday	David Wiesner	$100	$140	$200
1990	Shrek!	William Steig	$80	$120	$160
1998	Snowflake Bentley	Mary Azarian	$80	$120	$160
1992	Mirette On The High Wire	Emily Arnold McCully	$70	$100	$140
1993	Grandfather's Journey	Allen Say	$70	$100	$140
1992	Seven Blind Mice	Ed Young	$60	$90	$120
1994	Smoky Night	David Diaz	$60	$90	$120
1990	Black And White	David Macaulay	$60	$80	$120
1995	Officer Buckle And Gloria	Peggy Rathmann	$60	$80	$120
1991	The Jolly Christmas Postman	Janet Ahlberg	$50	$80	$100
1992	The Sleepy Book	Patrice Aggs	$50	$80	$100
1990	Puss In Boots	Fred Marcellino	$50	$70	$100
1997	Rapunzel	Paul O. Zelinsky	$50	$70	$100
1996	The Baby Who Wouldn't Go To Bed	Helen Cooper	$50	$70	$90
1992	Zoo	Anthony Browne	$40	$60	$90
1992	Working Cotton	Carole M. Byard	$40	$60	$90
1992	The Rainbow Fish	Marcus Pfister	$40	$60	$90
1992	The Dark Thirty	Brian Pinkney	$40	$60	$90
1992	Grandma According To Me	Ted Rand	$40	$60	$90
1992	The Giraffe That Walked To Paris	Roger Roth	$40	$60	$90

80

MOST VALUABLE ILLUSTRATORS

The table lists the top 100 illustrators with the highest average estimated market value for their collectible children's books. As one might expect, Dr. Seuss is at the top of the list.

	HIGHEST AVERAGE BOOK VALUE		
	ILLUSTRATOR	VALUE	BOOKS
1.	Theodor Geisel	$1,183	53
2.	Virginia Lee Burton	$1,083	12
3.	Robert McCloskey	$1,005	14
4.	Wanda Gág	$917	12
5.	H.A. Rey	$564	27
6.	Jean de Brunhoff	$522	25
7.	Johnny Gruelle	$511	37
8.	Thomas Handforth	$492	5
9.	Helen Sewell	$436	47
10.	Nancy Ekholm Burkert	$431	10
11.	Crockett Johnson	$425	24
12.	Maurice Sendak	$393	82
13.	Robert Lawson	$363	41
14.	Willy Pogány	$348	21
15.	Tasha Tudor	$340	64
16.	Ingri & Edgar Parin d'Aulaire	$296	24
17.	Harrison Cady	$282	53
18.	Dorothy P. Lathrop	$277	30
19.	Jean Charlot	$265	22
20.	Marjorie Flack	$263	26
21.	Janet Laura Scott	$259	16
22.	Chris Van Allsburg	$253	18
23.	Lois Lenski	$245	103
24.	Ludwig Bemelmans	$244	46
25.	Hardie Gramatky	$235	15
26.	Marguerite De Angeli	$234	38
27.	Marcia Brown	$214	31
28.	Clare Turlay Newberry	$213	21
29.	Shel Silverstein	$198	13
30.	Jules Feiffer	$198	10
31.	Esther Holden Averill	$195	11
32.	Roy McKié	$184	22
33.	James Henry Daugherty	$181	54
34.	Elizabeth Orton Jones	$177	23
35.	Edward Ardizzone	$176	99
36.	Gustaf Tenggren	$176	39
37.	Taro Yashima	$176	10
38.	Maud & Miska Petersham	$173	59
39.	Edna Groff Deihl	$170	16
40.	Berta & Elmer Hader	$166	71
41.	Boris Artzybasheff	$166	14
42.	Kate Seredy	$166	32
43.	Holling Clancy Holling	$161	16
44.	Edward Gorey	$154	109
45.	Rachel Field	$147	24
46.	Hilary Knight	$142	54
47.	Leo Politi	$140	32
48.	Fern Bisel Peat	$140	32
49.	Kurt Wiese	$139	280
50.	Katherine Milhous	$133	21
51.	Eulalie (Eulalie Banks)	$132	52
52.	William Pène Du Bois	$132	69
53.	P.D. Eastman	$132	18
54.	Emma L. Brock	$131	67
55.	Peggy Bacon	$128	25
56.	Feodor Rojankovsky	$128	60
57.	Nicholas Mordvinoff	$127	15
58.	Lynd Ward	$127	101
59.	Marie Hall Ets	$126	21
60.	Dorothy M. Kunhardt	$124	10
61.	Wesley Dennis	$123	36
62.	Munro Leaf	$120	32
63.	Mary GrandPré	$119	20
64.	Corinne Malvern	$118	21
65.	Fritz Siebel	$117	11
66.	Ralph Steadman	$115	23
67.	Helen Stone	$115	21
68.	Patricia Coombs	$115	29
69.	Louis Slobodkin	$113	72
70.	Raymond Briggs	$113	37
71.	Remy Charlip	$113	20
72.	Esphyr Slobodkina	$112	24
73.	Ruth Carroll	$109	39
74.	Masha	$109	15
75.	Brett Helquist	$109	20
76.	Conrad Buff	$108	15
77.	Everett Shinn	$107	14
78.	Marjorie Torrey	$106	14
79.	Garth Williams	$105	69
80.	Bettina	$105	16
81.	Barbara Cooney	$102	67
82.	Roger Duvoisin	$102	118
83.	Leo Lionni	$102	33
84.	Hildegard Woodward	$101	10
85.	Bernard Martin	$101	21
86.	Mariana	$101	19
87.	Morgan Dennis	$99	36
88.	Pelagie Doane	$99	39
89.	Bernarda Bryson	$96	11
90.	Evaline Ness	$95	50
91.	V.H. Drummond	$95	14
92.	Laurent de Brunhoff	$93	67
93.	Margaret Bloy Graham	$93	28
94.	Tomi Ungerer	$89	50
95.	Blair Lent	$89	22
96.	Leonard Weisgard	$88	123
97.	Beni Montresor	$86	18
98.	Eric Carle	$85	74
99.	Clement Hurd	$85	80
100.	Ezra Jack Keats	$85	71

APPENDIX 1

Caldecott Honor Award Winning Books

	CALDECOTT HONOR BOOKS 1938-2006			
YEAR	TITLE	ILLUSTRATOR	VG+	FINE
1938	Four & Twenty Blackbirds	Robert Lawson	$380	
1938	Seven Simeons	Boris Artzybasheff	$260	
1939	Andy And The Lion	James Henry Daugherty	$360	
1939	Barkis	Clare Turlay Newberry	$360	
1939	The Forest Pool	Laura Adams Armer	$300	
1939	Wee Gillis	Robert Lawson	$360	
1940	Cock-A-Doodle Doo	Berta & Elmer Hader	$340	
1940	Madeline	Ludwig Bemelmans	$4,000	
1940	The Ageless Story	Lauren Ford	$240	
1941	April's Kittens	Clare Turlay Newberry	$320	
1942	An American ABC	Maud & Miska Petersham	$360	
1942	In My Mother's House	Velino Herrera	$240	
1942	Nothing At All	Wanda Gág	$380	
1942	Paddle-To-The-Sea	Holling Clancy Holling	$360	
1943	Dash & Dart	Conrad Buff	$240	
1943	Marshmallow	Clare Turlay Newberry	$320	
1944	A Child's Good Night Book	Jean Charlot	$340	
1944	Good-Luck Horse	Plato Chan	$240	
1944	Pierre Pidgeon	Arnold Edwin Bare	$180	
1944	Small Rain	Elizabeth Orton Jones	$280	
1944	The Mighty Hunter	Berta & Elmer Hader	$340	
1945	In The Forest	Marie Hall Ets	$220	
1945	Mother Goose	Tasha Tudor	$760	
1945	The Christmas Anna Angel	Kate Seredy	$300	
1945	The Magic Monkey	Plato Chan	$220	
1945	Yonie Wondernose	Marguerite De Angeli	$340	
1946	Bhimsa, The Dancing Bear	Roger Duvoisin	$220	
1946	Little Lost Lamb	Leonard Weisgard	$220	
1946	My Mother Is Most Beautiful Woman In World	Ruth Gannett	$220	
1946	Sing Mother Goose	Marjorie Torrey	$220	
1946	You Can Write Chinese	Kurt Wiese	$220	
1947	In Our Town	Garth Williams	$260	
1947	Pedro, The Angel Of Olvera Street	Leo Politi	$320	
1947	Rain Drop Splash	Leonard Weisgard	$220	
1947	Sing In Praise	Marjorie Torrey	$220	
1947	Timothy Turtle	Tony Palazzo	$220	
1948	Bambino The Clown	Georges Schreiber	$220	
1948	McElligot's Pool	Theodor Geisel	$3,000	
1948	Roger And The Fox	Hildegard Woodward	$220	
1948	Song Of Robin Hood	Virginia Lee Burton	$320	
1948	Stone Soup	Marcia Brown	$400	
1949	All Around The Town	Helen Stone	$300	
1949	Blueberries For Sal	Robert McCloskey	$1,400	
1949	Juanita	Leo Politi	$260	
1950	America's Ethan Allen	Lynd Ward	$220	
1950	Bartholomew And The Oobleck	Theodor Geisel	$2,200	

\multicolumn{5}{c}{**CALDECOTT HONOR BOOKS 1938-2006**}
YEAR	**TITLE**	**ILLUSTRATOR**	**VG+**	**FINE**
1950	Dick Whittington And His Cat	Marcia Brown	$340	
1950	Henry-Fisherman	Marcia Brown	$340	
1950	The Happy Day	Marc Simont	$220	
1950	The Wild Birthday Cake	Hildegard Woodward	$220	
1951	If I Ran The Zoo	Theodor Geisel	$1,600	
1951	Russet And The Two Reds	Nicholas Mordvinoff	$240	
1951	Skipper John's Cook	Marcia Brown	$320	
1951	T-Bone, The Baby-Sitter	Clare Turlay Newberry	$300	
1951	The Most Wonderful Doll In The World	Helen Stone	$280	
1952	All Falling Down	Margaret Bloy Graham	$300	
1952	Feather Mountain	Elizabeth Olds	$200	
1952	Mr. T. W. Anthony Woo	Marie Hall Ets	$200	
1952	Puss In Boots	Marcia Brown	$320	
1953	Ape In A Cape	Fritz Eichenberg	$200	
1953	Bear Party	William Pène Du Bois	$300	
1953	Five Little Monkeys	Juliet Kepes	$200	
1953	One Morning In Maine	Robert McCloskey	$560	
1953	The Steadfast Tin Soldier	Marcia Brown	$320	
1953	The Storm Book	Margaret Bloy Graham	$260	
1954	A Very Special House	Maurice Sendak	$1,200	
1954	Journey Cake, Ho!	Robert McCloskey	$1,200	
1954	When Will The World Be Mine?	Jean Charlot	$300	
1955	Green Eyes	Abe Birnbaum	$160	
1955	The Thanksgiving Story	Helen Sewell	$220	
1955	Wheel On The Chimney	Tibor Gergely	$280	
1956	Book Of Nursery And Mother Goose Rhymes	Marguerite De Angeli	$280	
1956	Crow Boy	Taro Yashima	$280	
1956	Play With Me	Marie Hall Ets	$180	
1957	1 Is One	Tasha Tudor	$400	
1957	Anatole	Paul Galdone	$280	
1957	Gillespie And The Guards	James Henry Daugherty	$280	
1957	Lion	William Pène Du Bois	$280	
1957	Mister Penny's Race Horse	Marie Hall Ets	$180	
1958	Anatole And The Cat	Paul Galdone	$240	
1958	Fly High, Fly Low	Don Freeman	$180	
1959	The House That Jack Built	Antonio Frasconi	$180	
1959	Umbrella	Taro Yashima	$260	
1959	What Do You Do, Dear?	Maurice Sendak	$400	
1960	Houses From The Sea	Adrienne Adams	$180	
1960	The Moon Jumpers	Maurice Sendak	$380	
1961	Inch By Inch	Leo Lionni	$380	
1962	Little Bear's Visit	Maurice Sendak	$260	
1962	The Fox Went Out On A Chilly Night	Peter Spier	$260	
1963	Mr. Rabbit And The Lovely Present	Maurice Sendak	$240	
1963	The Day We Saw The Sun Come Up	Adrienne Adams	$160	

CALDECOTT HONOR BOOKS 1938-2006				
YEAR	**TITLE**	**ILLUSTRATOR**	**VG+**	**FINE**
1963	The Sun Is A Golden Earring	Bernarda Bryson	$140	
1964	All In The Morning Early	Evaline Ness	$240	
1964	Mother Goose And Nursery Rhymes	Philip Reed	$120	
1964	Swimmy	Leo Lionni	$300	
1965	A Pocketful Of Cricket	Evaline Ness	$240	
1965	Rain Makes Applesauce	Marvin Bileck	$160	
1965	The Wave	Blair Lent	$180	
1966	Hide And Seek Fog	Roger Duvoisin	$160	
1966	Just Me	Marie Hall Ets	$160	
1966	Tom Tit Tot	Evaline Ness	$220	
1967	One Wide River To Cross	Ed Emberley	$160	
1968	Frederick	Leo Lionni	$260	
1968	Seashore Story	Taro Yashima	$220	
1968	The Emperor And The Kite	Ed Young	$140	
1969	Why The Sun And The Moon Live In The Sky	Blair Lent	$160	
1970	Alexander And The Wind-Up Mouse	Leo Lionni	$220	
1970	Goggles!	Ezra Jack Keats	$140	
1970	Pop Corn & Ma Goodness	Robert Andrew Parker	$140	
1970	The Judge, An Untrue Tale	Margot Zemach	$140	
1970	Thy Friend, Obadiah	Brinton Turkle	$140	
1971	Frog And Toad Are Friends	Arnold Lobel	$140	$180
1971	In The Night Kitchen	Maurice Sendak	$220	$300
1971	The Angry Moon	Blair Lent	$120	$160
1972	Hildilid's Night	Arnold Lobel	$100	$140
1972	If All The Seas Were One Sea	Janina Domanska	$100	$140
1972	Moja Means One	Tom Feelings	$100	$140
1973	Anansi The Spider	Gerald McDermott	$220	$280
1973	Hosie's Alphabet	Leonard Baskin	$140	$200
1973	Snow White And The Seven Dwarfs	Nancy Ekholm Burkert	$140	$200
1974	Cathedral: The Story Of Its Construction	David Macaulay	$90	$120
1974	Three Jovial Huntsmen	Susan Jeffers	$180	$240
1974	When Clay Sings	Tom Bahti	$80	$100
1975	Jambo Means Hello	Tom Feelings	$90	$120
1976	Strega Nona	Tomie dePaola	$220	$300
1976	The Desert Is Theirs	Peter Parnall	$100	$140
1977	Fish For Supper	M. B. Goffstein	$100	$140
1977	Hawk, I'm Your Brother	Peter Parnall	$100	$140
1977	It Could Always Be Worse	Margot Zemach	$80	$120
1977	The Amazing Bone	William Steig	$120	$180
1977	The Contest	Nonny Hogrogian	$100	$140
1977	The Golem	Beverly Brodsky	$80	$120
1978	Castle	David Macaulay	$60	$80
1979	Freight Train	Donald Crews	$120	$160
1979	The Treasure	Uri Shulevitz	$80	$100
1979	The Way To Start A Day	Peter Parnall	$90	$120
1980	Ben's Trumpet	Rachel Isadora	$80	$100

CALDECOTT HONOR BOOKS 1938-2006				
YEAR	**TITLE**	**ILLUSTRATOR**	**VG+**	**FINE**
1980	The Garden Of Abdul Gasazi	Chris Van Allsburg	$700	$940
1980	The Grey Lady And The Strawberry Snatcher	Molly Bang	$80	$100
1981	Mice Twice	Joseph Low	$70	$100
1981	The Bremen Town Musicians	Ilse Plume	$70	$100
1981	Truck	Donald Crews	$70	$100
1982	A Visit To William Blake's Inn	Alice & Martin Provensen	$240	$320
1982	On Market Street	Anita Lobel	$120	$160
1982	Outside Over There	Maurice Sendak	$60	$90
1982	Where The Buffaloes Begin	Stephen Gammell	$160	$220
1983	A Chair For My Mother	Vera B. Williams	$70	$90
1983	Ten, Nine, Eight	Molly Bang	$70	$90
1983	When I Was Young In The Mountains	Diane Goode	$80	$120
1984	Little Red Riding Hood	Trina Schart Hyman	$140	$200
1985	Hansel And Gretel	Paul O. Zelinsky	$90	$120
1985	Have You Seen My Duckling?	Nancy Tafuri	$60	$90
1985	The Story Of A Jumping Mouse	John Steptoe	$60	$90
1986	King Bidgood's In The Bathtub	Don Wood	$60	$80
1986	The Relatives Came	Stephen Gammell	$90	$120
1987	Alphabatics	Suse MacDonald	$60	$80
1987	Rumpelstiltskin	Paul O. Zelinsky	$80	$120
1987	The Village Of Round And Square Houses	Ann Grifalconi	$60	$80
1988	Mufaro's Beautiful Daughters	John Steptoe	$80	$120
1989	Free Fall	David Wiesner	$60	$90
1989	Goldilocks And The Three Bears	James Marshall	$80	$100
1989	Mirandy And Brother Wind	Jerry Pinkney	$80	$100
1989	The Boy Of The Three-Year Nap	Allen Say	$80	$100
1990	Bill Peet: An Autobiography	Bill Peet	$60	$80
1990	Color Zoo	Lois Ehlert	$50	$70
1990	Hershel And The Hanukkah Goblins	Trina Schart Hyman	$80	$100
1990	The Talking Eggs	Jerry Pinkney	$80	$100
1991	More More More Said The Baby	Vera B. Williams	$50	$70
1991	Puss In Boots	Fred Marcellino	$70	$100
1992	Tar Beach	Faith Ringgold	$50	$60
1993	Seven Blind Mice	Ed Young	$90	$120
1993	The Stinky Cheese Man	Lane Smith	$40	$60
1993	Working Cotton	Carole M. Byard	$60	$90
1994	In The Small, Small Pond	Denise Fleming	$40	$60
1994	Owen	Kevin Henkes	$60	$80
1994	Peppe The Lamplighter	Ted Lewin	$40	$60
1994	Yo! Yes?	Christopher Raschka	$60	$80
1995	John Henry	Jerry Pinkney	$60	$80
1995	Swamp Angel	Paul O. Zelinsky	$60	$80
1995	Time Flies	Eric Rohmann	$60	$80
1996	Alphabet City	Stephen T. Johnson	$50	$70
1996	The Faithful Friend	Brian Pinkney	$50	$70
1996	Tops & Bottoms	Janet Stevens	$50	$70

\	CALDECOTT HONOR BOOKS 1938-2006	\	\	\
YEAR	**TITLE**	**ILLUSTRATOR**	**VG+**	**FINE**
1996	Zin! Zin! Zin!: A Violin	Marjorie Priceman	$50	$70
1997	Hush!: A Thai Lullaby	Holly Meade	$50	$60
1997	Starry Messenger: Galileo Galilei	Peter Sis	$50	$60
1997	The Graphic Alphabet	David Pelletier	$40	$50
1997	The Paperboy	Dav Pilkey	$50	$60
1998	Harlem	Christopher Myers	$35	$50
1998	The Gardener	David Small	$40	$60
1998	There Was An Old Lady Who Swallowed A Fly	Simms Taback	$40	$60
1999	Duke Ellington	Brian Pinkney	$40	$50
1999	No, David!	David Shannon	$60	$80
1999	Snow	Uri Shulevitz	$40	$50
1999	Tibet Through The Red Box	Peter Sis	$40	$50
2000	A Child's Calendar	Trina Schart Hyman	$50	$70
2000	Sector 7	David Wiesner	$50	$70
2000	The Ugly Duckling	Jerry Pinkney	$50	$70
2000	When Sophie Gets Angry-Really, Really Angry	Molly Bang	$40	$60
2001	Casey At The Bat	Christopher Bing	$50	$70
2001	Click, Clack, Moo	Betsy Lewin	$50	$60
2001	Olivia	Ian Falconer	$60	$90
2001	The Stray Dog	Marc Simont	$30	$40
2002	Martin's Big Words	Bryan Collier	$40	$50
2002	The Dinosaurs Of Waterhouse Hawkins	Brian Selznick	$35	$50
2003	Hondo & Fabian	Peter McCarty	$50	$60
2003	Noah's Ark	Jerry Pinkney	$35	$50
2003	The Spider And The Fly	Tony DiTerlizzi	$50	$60
2004	Don't Let The Pigeon Drive The Bus	Mo Willems	$40	$60
2005	Coming On Home Soon	Earl B. Lewis	$40	$50
2005	The Knuffle Bunny	Mo Willems	$25	$35
2005	The Red Book	Barbara Lehman	$25	$35
2006	Hot Air	Marjorie Priceman	$20	$30
2006	Rosa	Bryan Collier	$20	$30
2006	Song Of The Water Boatman	Beckie Prange	$20	$30
2006	Zen Shorts	Jon J. Muth	$20	$30

Appendix 2

Caldecott Award
Winning Illustrators

The following is an alphabetized list of each of the Caldecott Medal and Honor award winning illustrators, including the number of awards they have won, through the 2005 award year:

CALDECOTT AWARD ILLUSTRATORS			
ILLUSTRATOR	**TOTAL**	**MEDAL**	**HONOR**
Adrienne Adams	2		2
Laura Adams Armer	1		1
Boris Artzybasheff	1		1
Mary Azarian	1	1	
Tom Bahti	1		1
Molly Bang	3		3
Arnold Edwin Bare	1		1
Leonard Baskin	1		1
Ludwig Bemelmans	2	1	1
Marvin Bileck	1		1
Christopher Bing	1		1
Abe Birnbaum	1		1
Beverly Brodsky	1		1
Marcia Brown	9	3	6
Bernarda Bryson	1		1
Conrad Buff	1		1
Nancy Ekholm Burkert	1		1
Virginia Lee Burton	2	1	1
Carole M. Byard	1		1
Plato Chan	2		2
Jean Charlot	2		2
Margaret Chodos-Irvine	1		1
Bryan Collier	1		1
Barbara Cooney	2	2	
Donald Crews	2		2
James Henry Daugherty	2		2
Ingri & Edgar Parin d'Aulaire	1	1	
Marguerite De Angeli	2		2
Tomie dePaola	1		1
David Diaz	1	1	
Leo & Diane Dillon	2	2	
Tony DiTerlizzi	1		1
Janina Domanska	1		1
William Pène Du Bois	2		2
Roger Duvoisin	2	1	1
Richard Egielski	1	1	
Lois Ehlert	1		1
Fritz Eichenberg	1		1
Ed Emberley	2	1	1
Marie Hall Ets	6	1	5

CALDECOTT AWARD ILLUSTRATORS			
ILLUSTRATOR	**TOTAL**	**MEDAL**	**HONOR**
Ian Falconer	1		1
Tom Feelings	2		2
Denise Fleming	1		1
Lauren Ford	1		1
Antonio Frasconi	1		1
Don Freeman	1		1
Wanda Gág	1		1
Paul Galdone	2		2
Stephen Gammell	3	1	2
Ruth Gannett	1		1
Theodor Geisel	3		3
Tibor Gergely	1		1
Mordicai Gerstein	1	1	
Paul Goble	1	1	
M. B. Goffstein	1		1
Diane Goode	1		1
Margaret Bloy Graham	2		2
Ann Grifalconi	1		1
Berta & Elmer Hader	3	1	2
Gail E. Haley	1	1	
Thomas Handforth	1	1	
Kevin Henkes	2	1	1
Velino Herrera	1		1
Nonny Hogrogian	3	2	1
Holling Clancy Holling	1		1
Trina Schart Hyman	4	1	3
Rachel Isadora	1		1
Susan Jeffers	1		1
Steve Jenkins	1		1
Stephen T. Johnson	1		1
Elizabeth Orton Jones	2	1	1
Ezra Jack Keats	2	1	1
Juliet Kepes	1		1
Dorothy P. Lathrop	1	1	
Robert Lawson	3	1	2
Barbara Lehman	1		1
Blair Lent	4	1	3
Betsy Lewin	1		1
Ted Lewin	1		1
Earl B. Lewis	1		1

CALDECOTT AWARD ILLUSTRATORS			
ILLUSTRATOR	**TOTAL**	**MEDAL**	**HONOR**
Leo Lionni	4		4
Anita Lobel	1		1
Arnold Lobel	3	1	2
Joseph Low	1		1
David Macaulay	3	1	2
Suse MacDonald	1		1
Fred Marcellino	1		1
James Marshall	1		1
Peter McCarty	1		1
Robert McCloskey	5	2	3
Emily Arnold McCully	1	1	
Gerald McDermott	2	1	1
Holly Meade	1		1
Katherine Milhous	1	1	
Beni Montresor	1	1	
Nicholas Mordvinoff	2	1	1
Christopher Myers	1		1
Evaline Ness	4	1	3
Clare Turlay Newberry	4		4
Elizabeth Olds	1		1
Tony Palazzo	1		1
Robert Andrew Parker	1		1
Peter Parnall	3		3
Bill Peet	1		1
David Pelletier	1		1
Maud & Miska Petersham	2	1	1
Dav Pilkey	1		1
Brian Pinkney	1		1
Jerry Pinkney	5		5
Ilse Plume	1		1
Leo Politi	3	1	2
Marjorie Priceman	1		1
Alice & Martin Provensen	2	1	1
Christopher Raschka	1		1
Peggy Rathmann	1	1	
Philip Reed	1		1
Faith Ringgold	1		1
Eric Rohmann	2	1	1
Feodor Rojankovsky	1	1	
Allen Say	2	1	1

CALDECOTT AWARD ILLUSTRATORS			
ILLUSTRATOR	**TOTAL**	**MEDAL**	**HONOR**
John Schoenherr	1	1	
Georges Schreiber	1		1
Brian Selznick	1		1
Maurice Sendak	8	1	7
Kate Seredy	1		1
Helen Sewell	1		1
David Shannon	1		1
Uri Shulevitz	2	1	1
Nicolas Sidjakov	1	1	
Marc Simont	3	1	2
Peter Sis	2		2
Louis Slobodkin	1	1	
David Small	2	1	1
Lane Smith	1		1
Peter Spier	2	1	1
William Steig	2	1	1
John Steptoe	2		2
Janet Stevens	1		1
Helen Stone	2		2
Simms Taback	2	1	1
Nancy Tafuri	1		1
Marjorie Torrey	2		2
Tasha Tudor	2		2
Brinton Turkle	1		1
Chris Van Allsburg	3	2	1
Lynd Ward	2	1	1
Leonard Weisgard	3	1	2
Kurt Wiese	1		1
David Wiesner	4	2	2
Mo Willems	2		2
Garth Williams	1		1
Vera B. Williams	2		2
David Wisniewski	1	1	
Don Wood	1		1
Hildegard Woodward	2		2
Taro Yashima	3		3
Ed Young	3	1	2
Paul O. Zelinsky	4	1	3
Margot Zemach	3	1	2

Appendix 3

Publisher's Weekly
All-Time Bestselling
Children's Books

Sales Rank	Copies Sold	Title	Year	Author	Illustrator
1.	14,898,341	The Poky Little Puppy	1942	Janette Sebring Lowrey	Gustaf Tenggren
2.	9,380,274	The Tale Of Peter Rabbit	1902	Beatrix Potter	Beatrix Potter
3.	8,560,277	Tootle	1945	Gertrude Crampton	Tibor Gergely
4.	8,143,088	Green Eggs And Ham	1960	Dr. Seuss	Dr. Seuss
5.	7,913,765	Harry Potter And The Goblet Of Fire	2000	J.K. Rowling	Mary GrandPré
6.	7,562,710	Pat The Bunny	1940	Dorothy Kunhardt	Dorothy Kunhardt
7.	7,476,395	Saggy Baggy Elephant	1947	Kathryn & Byron Jackson	Gustaf Tenggren
8.	7,366,073	Scuffy The Tugboat	1946	Gertrude Crampton	Tibor Gergely
9.	7,220,982	The Cat In The Hat	1957	Dr. Seuss	Dr. Seuss
10.	6,335,585	Harry Potter And The Chamber Of Secrets	1999	J.K. Rowling	Mary GrandPré
11.	6,314,391	Harry Potter And The Prisoner Of Azkaban	1999	J.K. Rowling	Mary GrandPré
12.	6,228,042	Where The Sidewalk Ends	1974	Shel Silverstein	Shel Silverstein
13.	6,164,454	One Fish, Two Fish, Red Fish, Blue Fish	1960	Dr. Seuss	Dr. Seuss
14.	5,603,187	The Giving Tree	1964	Shel Silverstein	Shel Silverstein
15.	5,471,709	The Littlest Angel	1946	Charles Tazewell	Katherine Evans
16.	5,420,890	Hop On Pop	1963	Dr. Seuss	Dr. Seuss
17.	5,353,426	Oh, The Places You'll Go!	1990	Dr. Seuss	Dr. Seuss
18.	5,187,656	Dr. Seuss's ABC	1960	Dr. Seuss	Dr. Seuss
19.	5,087,304	Harry Potter And The Sorcerer's Stone	1998	J.K. Rowling	Mary GrandPré
20.	4,849,704	The Very Hungry Caterpillar	1969	Eric Carle	Eric Carle
21.	4,281,314	The Children's Bible	1965		
22.	4,269,048	A Light In The Attic	1981	Shel Silverstein	Shel Silverstein
23.	4,163,244	The Tale Of Benjamin Bunny	1904	Beatrix Potter	Beatrix Potter
24.	4,135,762	Are You My Mother?	1960	P.D. Eastman	P.D. Eastman
25.	4,082,500	The Rainbow Fish	1992	Marcus Pfister	Marcus Pfister
26.	4,043,578	The Cat In The Hat Comes Back	1958	Dr. Seuss	Dr. Seuss
27.	3,981,291	Richard Scarry's Best Word Book	1963	Richard Scarry	Richard Scarry
28.	3,900,150	Disney's The Lion King	1994	Justine Korman (adapted)	Don Williams
29.	3,839,474	The Tale Of Jemina Puddle-Duck	1908	Beatrix Potter	Beatrix Potter
30.	3,757,178	The Little Engine That Could	1930	Watty Piper	Lois Lenski
31.	3,680,135	Fox In Socks	1965	Dr. Seuss	Dr. Seuss
32.	3,613,958	Goodnight Moon (Board Book)	1991	Margaret Wise Brown	Clement Hurd
33.	3,600,000	The Real Mother Goose	1916	Blanche F. Wright	
34.	3,482,666	Go, Dog. Go!	1961	P.D. Eastman	P.D. Eastman
35.	3,446,646	How The Grinch Stole Christmas	1964	Dr. Seuss	Dr. Seuss
36.	3,172,366	The Tale Of Squirrel Nutkin	1903	Beatrix Potter	Beatrix Potter
37.	3,079,464	The Tale Of Tom Kitten	1907	Beatrix Potter	Beatrix Potter
38.	3,054,401	Macmillan Dictionary For Children	1975	Judith Levy (edited)	
39.	2,952,331	Winnie-The-Pooh	1926	A.A. Milne	Ernest Shepard
40.	2,923,826	My Book About Me	1969	Dr. Seuss	Roy McKie

Sales Rank	Copies Sold	Title	Year	Author	Illustrator
41.	2,911,195	Where's Waldo?	1987	Martin Handford	Martin Handford
42.	2,861,949	Just Imagine	1992		
43.	2,819,598	The Great Waldo Search	1989	Martin Handford	Martin Handford
44.	3,544,116	The Polar Express	1985	Chris Van Allsburg	Chris Van Allsburg
45.	2,730,622	Find Waldo Now	1989	Martin Handford	Martin Handford
46.	2,609,201	Cat's Cradle	1993	Anne Akers Johnson	Sarah Boore
47.	2,524,642	The Cat In The Hat Beginner Book Dictionary	1964	P.D. Eastman	P.D. Eastman
48.	2,441,836	Goodnight Moon	1947	Margaret Wise Brown	Clement Hurd
49.	2,400,904	Walt Disney's Storyland	1962	Walt Disney	
50.	2,347,750	The Secret Of Shadow Ranch (Nancy Drew #5)	1931	Carolyn Keene	
51.	2,343,018	Barney's Favorite Mother Goose Rhymes Vol.1	1993		
52.	2,319,722	Falling Up	1996	Shel Silverstein	Shel Silverstein
53.	2,273,429	The Secret Of The Old Clock (Nancy Drew #1)	1930	Carolyn Keene	
54.	2,241,218	Richard Scarry's Best Mother Goose Ever	1964	Richard Scarry	Richard Scarry
55.	2,209,774	The Tower Treasure (Hardy Boys #1)	1927	Franklin Dixon	
56.	2,199,550	Guess How Much I Love You (Board Book)	1996	Sam McBratney	Anita Jeram
57.	2,174,283	Barney's Farm Animals	1993		
58.	2,139,084	I Can Read With My Eyes Shut	1978	Dr. Seuss	Dr. Seuss
59.	2,136,818	Baby Bop's Toys	1993		
60.	2,065,102	Put Me In The Zoo	1960	Robert Lopshire	Robert Lopshire
61.	2,040,125	The Touch Me Book	1961	Pat and Eve Witte	
62.	2,034,130	I Am A Bunny	1963	Ole Risom	Richard Scarry
63.	1,972,147	Where The Wild Things Are	1964	Maurice Sendak	Maurice Sendak
64.	1,934,275	Never Talk To Strangers	1967	Irma Joyce	
65.	1,896,663	Oh, The Thinks You Can Think!	1975	Dr. Seuss	Dr. Seuss
66.	1,863,024	Richard Scarry's Best Storybook Ever	1968	Richard Scarry	Richard Scarry
67.	1,856,687	When We Were Very Young	1924	A.A. Milne	Ernest Shepard
68.	1,821,457	The Hidden Staircase (Nancy Drew #2)	1930	Carolyn Keene	
69.	1,786,320	If You Give A Mouse A Cookie	1985	Laura Numeroff	Felicia Bond
70.	1,753,185	The Little Prince	1943	Antoine de Saint-Exupéry	A. de Saint-Exupéry
71.	1,743,700	Barney's Magical Picnic	1993	Stephen White	
72.	1,712,433	The House On The Cliff (Hardy Boys #2)	1927	Franklin Dixon	
73.	1,691,855	Scarry's Cars And Trucks And Things That Go	1968	Richard Scarry	Richard Scarry
74.	1,630,908	Guess How Much I Love You	1995	Sam McBratney	Anita Jeram
75.	1,609,000	Animalia	1987	Graeme Base	Graeme Base
76.	1,548,785	The Bungalow Mystery (Nancy Drew #3)	1930	Carolyn Keene	
77.	1,543,297	Eloise	1955	Kay Thompson	Hilary Knight
78.	1,537,560	Charlotte's Web	1952	E.B. White	Garth Williams
79.	1,535,595	Moo Baa La La La (Board Book)	1982	Sandra Boynton	Sandra Boynton
80.	1,520,900	Disney's 101 Dalmatians	1991	Ronald Kidd (adapted)	Bill Langley

Sales Rank	Copies Sold	Title	Year	Author	Illustrator
81.	1,509,244	Barney's Color Surprise	1993		
82.	1,479,350	Disney's Beauty And The Beast	1991	Ronald Kidd (adapted)	Ron Dias
83.	1,476,792	Scholastic Children's Dictionary	1996		
84.	1,471,000	Eloise Wilkin's Mother Goose	1961	Eloise Wilkin	Eloise Wilkin
85.	1,467,944	Oh Say Can You Say?	1979	Dr. Seuss	Dr. Seuss
86.	1,467,645	The Secret Of The Old Mill (Hardy Boys #3)	1930	Franklin Dixon	
87.	1,467,300	Disney's The Little Mermaid	1991	Ronald Kidd (adapted)	Sue Di Cicco
88.	1,421,064	Love Is A Special Way Of Feeling	1960	Joan Walsh Anglund	Joan Walsh Anglund
89.	1,403,629	The Very Quiet Cricket	1990	Eric Carle	Eric Carle
90.	1,390,000	The Magic Locket	1988	Elizabeth Koda-Callan	
91.	1,375,505	A Fly Went	1958	Mike McClintock	Fritz Siebel
92.	1,371,225	The Going To Bed Book	1982	Sandra Boynton	Sandra Boynton
93.	1,360,839	There's A Wocket In My Pocket!	1974	Dr. Seuss	Dr. Seuss
94.	1,354,626	Big Bird's Color Game	1980		
95.	1,354,500	Aladdin	1992	Ronald Kidd (adapted)	Darrell Baker
96.	1,352,712	Make Way For Ducklings	1941	Robert McCloskey	Robert McCloskey
97.	1,342,863	ET: The Extra-Terrestrial Storybook	1983	William Kotzwinkle	David Wiesner
98.	1,339,547	Mr. Brown Can Moo, Can You? (Board Book)	1996	Dr. Seuss	Dr. Seuss
99.	1,338,315	Dr. Seuss's ABC (Board Book)	1996	Dr. Seuss	Dr. Seuss
100.	1,331,991	The Mystery Of Lilac Inn (Nancy Drew #4)	1930	Carolyn Keene	

Appendix 4

Newbery Award Books
With Illustrations

The Newbery awards have been given by the American Library Association since 1922:

> The Newbery Medal was named for eighteenth-century British bookseller John Newbery. It is awarded annually by the Association for Library Service to Children, a division of the American Library Association, to the author of the most distinguished contribution to American literature for children.

Within the book collecting marketplace, the Newbery Medal winning books are generally more collectible than the Caldecott Medal winning books. Since the Newbery award winning books are chapter books, they have not been included as part of the picturebook Price Guide. However, many of the Newbery award winning books are augmented with illustrations by picturebook illustrators included in the Price Guide. As we have stated earlier, for the sake of completeness, we have included these type of chapter books in the Price Guide.

There are 81 Newbery award winning books which include pictures and/or cover art by illustrators listed in the Price Guide. This includes 28 Newbery Medal books! Twenty-four of these books were both written and illustrated by one of the picturebook illustrators, including Robert Lawson and Wanda Gag.

NEWBERY MEDAL AND HONOR BOOKS—PICTUREBOOK ILLUSTRATORS						
YEAR	**TITLE**		**WINNING AUTHOR(S)**	**ILLUSTRATOR**	**VG+**	**FINE**
1922	The Golden Fleece	NH	Padraic Colum	Willy Pogány	$460	
1928	Gay-Neck	NM	Dhan Gopal Mukerji	Boris Artzybasheff	$540	
1929	Millions Of Cats	NH	Wanda Gág	Wanda Gág	$4,000	
1930	Hitty, Her First Hundred Years	NM	Rachel Field	Dorothy P. Lathrop	$940	
1931	The Cat Who Went To Heaven	NM	Elizabeth Coatsworth	Lynd Ward	$780	
1932	Waterless Mountain	NM	Laura Adams Armer	Laura Adams Armer	$1,200	
1932	The Fairy Circus	NH	Dorothy P. Lathrop	Dorothy P. Lathrop	$520	
1933	Young Fu Of The Upper Yangtze	NM	Elizabeth Foreman Lewis	Kurt Wiese	$760	
1934	The ABC Bunny	NH	Wanda Gág	Wanda Gág	$1,400	
1936	Caddie Woodlawn	NM	Carol Ryrie Brink	Kate Seredy	$1,000	
1936	Honk, The Moose	NH	Kate Seredy	Kurt Wiese	$480	
1936	The Good Master	NH	Phil Stong	Kate Seredy	$260	
1937	Phoebe Fairchild	NH	Lois Lenski	Lois Lenski	$380	
1937	The Golden Basket	NH	Ludwig Bemelmans	Ludwig Bemelmans	$480	
1938	The White Stag	NM	Kate Seredy	Kate Seredy	$560	
1938	Pecos Bill	NH	James Bowman	Laura Bannon	$140	
1939	Mr Popper's Penguins	NH	Richard & Florence Atwater	Robert Lawson	$400	
1940	Daniel Boone	NM	James Daugherty	James Daugherty	$640	
1940	The Singing Tree	NH	Kate Seredy	Kate Seredy	$240	
1941	The Long Winter	NH	Laura Ingalls Wilder	Helen Sewell	$1,200	
1942	The Matchlock Gun	NM	Walter D. Edmonds	Paul Lantz	$540	
1942	Indian Captive	NH	Lois Lenski	Lois Lenski	$320	
1942	Little Town On The Prairie	NH	Laura Ingalls Wilder	Helen Sewell	$1,200	
1943	Adam Of The Road	NM	Elizabeth Gray Vining	Robert Lawson	$400	
1943	The Middle Moffat	NH	Eleanor Estes	Louis Slobodkin	$380	

	NEWBERY MEDAL AND HONOR BOOKS—PICTUREBOOK ILLUSTRATORS					
YEAR	TITLE		WINNING AUTHOR(S)	ILLUSTRATOR	VG+	FINE
1944	Johnny Tremain	NM	Esther Forbes	Lynd Ward	$520	
1944	Rufus M.	NH	Eleanor Estes	Louis Slobodkin	$240	
1945	Rabbit Hill	NM	Robert Lawson	Robert Lawson	$360	
1945	The Hundred Dresses	NH	Alice Dalgliesh	Louis Slobodkin	$220	
1945	The Silver Pencil	NH	Eleanor Estes	Katherine Milhous	$200	
1946	Strawberry Girl	NM	Lois Lenski	Lois Lenski	$1,200	
1946	Justin Morgan Had A Horse	NH	Marguerite Henry	Wesley Dennis	$220	
1947	Miss Hickory	NM	Carolyn Sherwin Bailey	Ruth Gannett	$500	
1947	Big Tree	NH	Mary Buff	Conrad Buff	$160	
1948	The Twenty-One Balloons	NM	William Pène Du Bois	William Pène Du Bois	$280	
1948	Misty Of Chincoteague	NH	Marguerite Henry	Wesley Dennis	$220	
1948	Pancakes-Paris	NH	Claire Huchet Bishop	Georges Schreiber	$140	
1949	King Of The Wind	NM	Marguerite Henry	Wesley Dennis	$480	
1949	My Father's Dragon	NH	Ruth Stiles Gannett	Ruth Chrisman Gannett	$220	
1949	Seabird	NH	Holling C. Holling	Holling C. Holling	$260	
1950	The Door In The Wall	NM	Marguerite De Angeli	Marguerite De Angeli	$460	
1952	Ginger Pye	NM	Eleanor Estes	Louis Slobodkin	$440	
1952	Minn Of The Mississippi	NH	Holling C. Holling	Holling C. Holling	$240	
1952	The Apple And The Arrow	NH	Mary Buff	Conrad Buff	$140	
1953	Secret Of The Andes	NM	Ann Nolan Clark	Jean Charlot	$440	
1953	Charlotte's Web	NH	Alice Dalgliesh	Garth Williams	$980	
1953	The Bears On Hemlock Mountain	NH	E. B. White	Helen Sewell	$200	
1954	... And Now Miguel	NM	Joseph Krumgold	Jean Charlot	$440	
1954	Hurry Home, Candy	NH	Mary Buff	Conrad Buff	$540	
1954	Magic Maize	NH	Meindert De Jong	Maurice Sendak	$140	
1954	Shadrach	NH	Meindert De Jong	Maurice Sendak	$360	
1955	The Wheel On The School	NM	Meindert De Jong	Maurice Sendak	$800	
1955	The Courage Of Sarah Noble	NH	Alice Dalgliesh	Leonard Weisgard	$200	
1957	Black Fox Of Lorne	NH	Marguerite De Angeli	Marguerite De Angeli	$220	
1957	The House Of Sixty Fathers	NH	Meindert De Jong	Maurice Sendak	$520	
1958	The Great Wheel	NH	Robert Lawson	Robert Lawson	$280	
1959	Along Came A Dog	NH	Meindert De Jong	Maurice Sendak	$400	
1961	The Cricket In Times Square	NH	George Selden	Garth Williams	$260	
1966	The Animal Family	NH	Randall Jarrell	Maurice Sendak	$340	
1968	The Fearsome Inn	NH	Isaac Bashevis Singer	Nonny Hogrogian	$140	
1969	To Be A Slave	NH	Isaac Bashevis Singer	Tom Feelings	$100	
1969	When Shlemiel Went To Warsaw	NH	Julius Lester	Margot Zemach	$140	
1971	Kneeknock Rise	NH	Natalie Babbitt	Natalie Babbitt	$70	$90
1972	Annie And The Old One	NH	Miska Miles	Peter Parnall	$50	$60
1973	Julie Of The Wolves	NM	Jean Craighead George	John Schoenherr	$180	$240
1973	Frog And Toad Together	NH	Arnold Lobel	Arnold Lobel	$120	$180
1975	Figgs & Phantoms	NH	Ellen Raskin	Ellen Raskin	$60	$80
1977	Roll Of Thunder, Hear My Cry	NM	Mildred Taylor	Jerry Pinkney	$180	$260
1977	Abel's Island	NH	William Steig	William Steig	$80	$120
1979	The Westing Game	NM	Ellen Raskin	Ellen Raskin	$180	$240

NEWBERY MEDAL AND HONOR BOOKS—PICTUREBOOK ILLUSTRATORS							
YEAR	**TITLE**		**WINNING AUTHOR(S)**	**ILLUSTRATOR**	**VG+**	**FINE**	
1982	A Visit To William Blake's Inn	NM	Nancy Willard	A. & M. Provensen	$240	$320	
1983	Doctor DeSoto	NH	William Steig	William Steig	$70	$90	
1984	Dear Mr. Henshaw	NM	Beverly Cleary	Paul O. Zelinsky	$140	$200	
1985	Like Jake And Me	NH	Mavis Jukes	Lloyd Bloom	$50	$70	
1987	The Whipping Boy	NM	Sid Fleischman	Peter Sis	$160	$200	
1989	Joyful Noise	NM	Paul Fleischman	Eric Beddows	$120	$160	
1989	In The Beginning	NH	Virginia Hamilton	Barry Moser	$50	$70	
1993	The Dark Thirty	NH	Patricia McKissack	Brian Pinkney	$60	$90	
2000	26 Fairmount Avenue	NH	Tomie dePaola	Tomie dePaola	$50	$70	
2001	The Wanderer	NH	Sharon Creech	David Diaz	$60	$90	
2004	Olive's Ocean	NH	Kevin Henkes	Kevin Henkes	$35	$50	

All of the books above are considered very collectible.

Allen, Marjorie. 100 Years Of Children's Books In America. New York: Facts On File, 1996.

Bader, Barbara, American Picturebooks from Noah's Ark to The Beast Within. Macmillan, 1976.

Cullinan, Bernice and Galda, Lee, Literature and the Child, third edition; Harcourt Brace, 1994.

Cummins, Julie. Children's Book Illustration and Design, Volume II. PBC International, 1998.

Dalby, Richard, The Golden Age of Children's Book Illustration, Gallery Books, 1991.

Flesch, Rudolph. Why Johnny Can't Read--And What You Can Do About It. Harper & Brothers, 1955.

Greer, Colin. The Great School Legend: A Revisionist Interpretation of American Public Education. Basic Books, 1972.

Gross, Michael. The Conspiracy of Ignorance: The Failure of American Public Schools. Harper, 2000.

Hanrahan, Joyce, Works of Maurice Sendak, 1947 – 1994, Peter E. Randall Publisher, 1995.

Hearn, Patric, Clark Trinkett, and Clark, Nichols. Myth, Magic, and Mystery, One Hundred Years of American Children's Book Illustration. Robert Rinehart Publishers, 1996.

Hirsch, E.D. Jr. The Schools We Need: Why We Don't Have Them. Doubleday, 1996.

Hirsch, E.D. Jr. What Your First Grader Needs to Know. Doubleday, 1991.

Hirsch, E.D. Jr. What Your Second Grader Needs to Know. Doubleday, 1991.

Hunt, Peter, Children's Literature, An Illustrated History, Oxford University Press, 1995.

Klemin, Diana. The Illustrated Book, Its Art and Craft. Bramhall House, 1970.

Marting, Douglas, The Telling Line, Essays on fifteen comtemporary book illustrators, Delacorte Press, 1990.

MacDonald, Ruth, Dr. Seuss; Twayne Publishers, 1988.

McBride, Bill. A Pocket Guide to the Identification of First Editions, fifth revised edition. William M. McBride, 1995.

McEwan, Elaine. Angry Parents, Failing Schools. Shaw, 2000.

National Commission On Excellence In Education; David P. Gardner, Chairman. A Nation at Risk: The Imperative for Educational Reform. 1983

Pitz, Henry. Illustrating Children's Books, History, Technique, Production. Watson-Guptill Publications, 1963.

Ravitch, Diane. The Troubled Crusade. Basic Books, 1983.

Ravatch, Diane. Left Back:A Century of Battles over School Reform. Simon & Schuster, 2000.

Roginski, Jim, Newbery and Caldecott Medalists and Honor Book Winners, Libraries Unlimited, 1982.

Santi, Steve; Collecting Little Golden Books, 4th edition, Krause Publications, 2000.

Shulevitz, Uri, Writing With Pictures, How To Write And Illustrate Children's Books, Watson-Guptill Publications,1985.

Smith, Irene. A History of the Newbery and Caldecott Medals. The Viking Press, 1957.

Younger, Helen, Younger Marc, and Hirsch, Dan. First Editions of Dr. Seuss Books: A Guide to Identification. Custom Communications, 2002.

Zempel, Edward and Verkler, Linda. First Editions, A Guide To Identification, 2nd edition.

The Spoon River Press, 1989.

Price Guide

SCOPE—The Price Guide is focused on illustrated children's picturebooks, covering the period from 1930 to present, with an emphasis on illustrators whose works are still published today. Subsequently, the Price Guide is sorted alphabetically by illustrator's last name.

PICTUREBOOK DEFINED—An illustrated children's 'picturebook' is one in which the text and the illustrations are synergistic in telling the story—the two are intertwined such that one enhances the other, and vice-versa. The illustrations are not an augment to the story, but are intrinsic to the story. Books included in our definition of 'picturebooks' should meet the following criteria:

- A full-page illustration on every page or every other page.
- Illustrations are credited to an illustrator (i.e. not an anonymous artist).
- Published in hardcover format, with a dust jacket.

CHAPTER BOOKS—Many notable picturebook illustrators have contributed to children's chapter books, which have only an occasional illustration to accompany a reading story. Since it is important to capture the full bibliography of many of these notable children's picturebook illustrators, we have included these chapter books in the Price Guide. Also, some picturebooks are issued without dust jackets, yet include art by a notable illustrator—here again, in the spirit of comprehensiveness, we have included these books in the Price Guide.

DUST JACKET ART ONLY—By and large, we have excluded hard cover chapter books in which only the dust jacket cover art was completed by a notable children's picturebook illustrator. However, we have included those books, with the illustrator's cover art only, which might contribute to the market value of the artist's other books.

PRICING ERRORS—This being the first edition of the Price Guide, and covering nearly 23,000 books, there are pricing mistakes due to a number of reasons, including, but not limited to: typographical errors; bibliographic errors and oversights; and incorrect and incomplete market information. As this publication matures, the pricing accuracy will increase. The intention is to provide a Price Guide which reflects current market retail conditions.

CAVEAT EMPTOR—This Price Guide is not an offer to buy or sell any book, nor should the authors be held liable for any losses suffered from transactions made due to information in this book. Many factors affect the perceived value of any collectible, inclusive of illustrated children's picturebooks. In Chapter Two, "Collectibility And Value" we discuss in detail some factors that impact a book's value. The book buyer must personally weigh all factors before deciding to purchase a collectible first edition children's picturebook.

"VERY GOOD+" AND "FINE"—In this Price Guide, the estimated market value of books published before 1970 is in "Very Good+" condition. For books published from 1970 to present, the estimated market value of dust jacketed children's picturebooks is in "Fine" condition.

PRICE GUIDE KEY TO AWARDS ABBREVIATIONS			
CH	Caldecott Honor	NH	Newbery Honor
CM	Caldecott Medal	NM	Newbery Medal
CSKM	Coretta Scott King Medal	NYT	NY Times Best Illustrated
GM	Kate Greenaway Medal		

Abolafia   Yossi

Year	Title	VG-	VG	VG+	Fine	Author	Award	Pub
1982	Buffy And Albert		$20	$30	$40	Charlotte Pomerantz		Green
1983	Harry's Visit		$14	$20	$30	Barbara Ann Porte		Green
1983	It's Valentine's Day		$14	$20	$30	Jack Prelutsky		Green
1984	Harry's Dog		$14	$20	$30	Barbara Ann Porte		Green
1984	What I Did Last Summer		$14	$20	$30	Jack Prelutsky		Green
1985	Harry's Mom		$14	$20	$25	Barbara Ann Porte		Green
1985	My Parents Think I'm Sleeping		$14	$20	$25	Jack Prelutsky		Green
1985	My Three Uncles		$14	$20	$25	Yossi Abolafia		Green
1987	Donovan Scares The Monsters		$12	$18	$25	Susan Love Whitlock		Green
1987	Yanosh's Island		$12	$18	$25	Yossi Abolafia		Green
1988	A Fish For Mrs. Gardenia		$12	$18	$25	Yossi Abolafia		Green
1988	Leo And Emily's Zoo		$12	$18	$25	Franz Brandenberg		Green
1989	Harry In Trouble		$12	$18	$25	Barbara Ann Porte		Green
1989	The Birthday Thing		$12	$18	$25	Kevin Kiser		Green
1991	Fox Tale		$12	$16	$20	Yossi Abolafia		Green
1991	Harry Gets An Uncle		$12	$16	$20	Barbara Ann Porte		Green
1992	Taxicab Tales		$12	$16	$20	Barbara Ann Porte		Green
1993	Stop, Thief!		$10	$16	$20	Robert Kalan		Green
1994	Busybody Brandy		$10	$16	$20	Jessie Haas		Green
1994	Harry's Birthday		$10	$16	$20	Barbara Ann Porte		Green
1994	Ten Old Pails		$10	$16	$20	Nicholas Heller		Green
1996	Clean House		$10	$14	$18	Jessie Haas		Green
1996	Moving Day		$10	$14	$18	Robert Kalan		Green
1997	Harry's Pony		$10	$14	$18	Barbara Ann Porte		Green

Abrams   Lester

Year	Title	VG-	VG	VG+	Fine	Author	Award	Pub
1972	The Four Donkeys		$30	$50	$60	Lloyd Alexander		HR&W

Ackley   Peggy Jo

Year	Title	VG-	VG	VG+	Fine	Author	Award	Pub
1983	If Christmas Were A Poem		$14	$20	$25	Ronnie Sellers		Caed
1984	When Springtime Comes		$14	$20	$25	Ronnie Sellers		Caed
1995	Bitty Bear Gets Dressed		$8	$10	$14	Kristi Jacobek		Pleasnt
1995	Bitty Bear's Autumn Fun		$8	$10	$14	Peggy Jo Ackley		Pleasnt
1995	Bitty Bear's Bedtime		$8	$10	$14	Kristi Jacobek		Pleasnt
1995	Bitty Bear's Birthday		$8	$10	$14	Kristi Jacobek		Pleasnt
1995	Bitty Bear's Spring Fun		$8	$10	$14	Peggy Jo Ackley		Pleasnt
1995	Bitty Bear's Summer Fun		$8	$10	$14	Peggy Jo Ackley		Pleasnt
1995	Bitty Bear's Tasty Treats		$8	$10	$14	Kristi Jacobek		Pleasnt
1995	Bitty Bear's Winter Fun		$8	$10	$14	Peggy Jo Ackley		Pleasnt
1997	Bitty Bear's Frosty Fun		$8	$10	$14	Kristi Jacobek		Pleasnt
1998	Bitty Bear Picks Apples		$8	$10	$14	Kristi Jacobek		Pleasnt
1999	Bitty Bear Takes A Trip		$8	$10	$14	Kristi Jacobek		Pleasnt
1999	Bitty Bear's Big Top Fun		$8	$10	$14	Kristi Jacobek		Pleasnt

Adams   Adrienne

Year	Title	VG-	VG	VG+	Fine	Author	Award	Pub
1931	The World On A Farm	$100	$140	$180		Gertrude Chandler Warner		Friend
1942	Bag Of Smoke	$80	$100	$140		Lonzo Anderson		Viking
1943	The Boy Jones	$80	$100	$140		Patricia Gordon		Viking
1950	The 13th Is Magic	$160	$200	$260		Joan Howard		LL&S
1952	The Summer Is Magic	$140	$200	$240		Joan Howard		LL&S
1953	Captain Ramsay's Daughter	$50	$70	$90		Elizabeth Fraser Torjesen		LL&S
1954	Impunity Jane	$50	$70	$90		Rumer Godden		Viking
1954	Jenny	$50	$70	$90		Mary Kennedy		LL&S
1954	Pulling Strings	$50	$70	$90		Madeleine Myers		Holt
1956	The Blue Mountain	$50	$70	$90		Beth Hurley Lewis		Knopf
1956	The Fairy Doll	$50	$70	$90		Rumer Godden		Viking
1957	Mouse House	$50	$70	$90		Rumer Godden		Viking
1957	The Easter Bunny	$50	$70	$90		Priscilla/Otto Friedrich		LL&S
1957	The Light In The Tower	$50	$70	$90		Joan Howard		LL&S
1958	The Story Of Holly And Ivy	$50	$60	$80		Rumer Godden		Viking
1959	Houses From The Sea	$100	$140	$180		Alice E. Goudey	CH	Scribnr
1959	The Littlest Witch	$50	$60	$80		Jeanne Massey		Knopf

Adams   Adrienne

Year	Title	VG-	VG	VG+	Fine	Author	Award	Pub
1960	Candy Floss	$40	$50	$70		Rumer Godden		Viking
1960	Going Barefoot	$40	$50	$70		Aileen Fisher		Crowell
1960	The Shoemaker And The Elves	$40	$50	$70		Jacob & Wilhelm Grimm		Scribnr
1961	Thumbelina	$50	$70	$90		Hans Christian Andersen		Scribnr
1961	Where Does Everyone Go?	$40	$50	$70		Aileen Fisher		Crowell
1962	Mary's Marvelous Mouse	$40	$50	$70		Mary Frances Shura		Knopf
1962	The Day We Saw The Sun Come Up	$100	$120	$160		Alice E. Goudey	CH	Scribnr
1962	What Makes A Shadow?	$40	$50	$70		Clyde Robert Bulla		Crowell
1964	Butterfly Time	$35	$50	$60		Alice Goudey		Scribnr
1964	Snow White And Rose Red	$35	$50	$60		Jacob & Wilhelm Grimm		Scribnr
1964	The Mouse Palace	$35	$50	$60		Frances Carpenter		McHill
1964	The Nearsighted Knight	$35	$50	$60		Mary Frances Shura		Knopf
1965	Cabbage Moon	$70	$100	$120		Jan Wahl		HR&W
1965	The Ugly Duckling	$35	$50	$60		Hans Christian Andersen		Scribnr
1966	Ponies Of Mykillengi	$35	$50	$60		John Lonzo Anderson		Scribnr
1966	The Twelve Dancing Princesses	$35	$50	$60		Andrew Lang		HR&W
1967	The White Rat's Tale	$35	$40	$60		Barbara Schiller		HR&W
1968	Bag Of Smoke	$25	$30	$40		Lonzo Anderson		Knopf
1968	Jorinda And Joringel	$35	$40	$60		Jacob & Wilhelm Grimm		Scribnr
1968	Two Hundred Rabbits	$35	$40	$60		Lonzo Anderson		Viking
1969	The Laird Of Cockpen	$35	$40	$60		Sorche Nic Leodhas		HR&W
1970	Painting The Moon		$25	$40	$50	Carl Withers		Dutton
1970	Summer's Coming In		$25	$40	$50	Natalia Belting		HR&W
1971	A Woggle Of Witches		$50	$80	$100	Adrienne Adams		Scribnr
1971	Mr Biddle And The Birds		$25	$40	$50	John Lonzo Anderson		Scribnr
1972	Poetry Of Earth		$25	$40	$50	Adrienne Adams		Scribnr
1973	Izzard		$25	$40	$50	John Lonzo Anderson		Scribnr
1973	Twice Upon A Time		$25	$40	$50	Irwin Shapiro		Xerox
1974	The Halloween Party		$25	$40	$50	John Lonzo Anderson		Scribnr
1975	Hansel And Gretel		$25	$35	$50	Jacob & Wilhelm Grimm		Scribnr
1976	The Easter Egg Artists		$25	$35	$50	Adrienne Adams		Scribnr
1977	The River Bank		$25	$35	$50	Kenneth Grahame		Scribnr
1978	Arion And The Dolphins		$25	$35	$50	John Lonzo Anderson		Scribnr
1978	The Christmas Party		$25	$35	$50	Adrienne Adams		Scribnr
1979	The Wounded Duck		$20	$30	$40	Peter Barnhart		Scribnr
1980	The Boy Jones		$16	$25	$30	Joan Howard		Gregg
1980	The Great Valentine's Day Balloon Race		$20	$30	$40	Adrienne Adams		Scribnr
1981	A Halloween Happening		$20	$30	$40	Adrienne Adams		Scribnr
1983	The Easter Bunny That Overslept		$18	$25	$35	Priscilla Friedrich		LL&S
1985	A Woggle Of Witches		$14	$20	$25	Adrienne Adams		Scribnr

Adams   Jean Ekman

Year	Title	VG-	VG	VG+	Fine	Author	Award	Pub
2000	Clarence Goes Out West And Meets A Purple Horse		$6	$10	$12	Jean Ekman Adams		RMoon
2001	Clarence And The Great Surprise		$6	$10	$12	Jean Ekman Adams		RMoon
2003	Clarence and the Purple Horse		$8	$10	$14	Jean Ekman Adams		RMoon

Agee   Jon

Year	Title	VG-	VG	VG+	Fine	Author	Award	Pub
1982	If Snow Falls		$25	$35	$50	Jon Agee		Pan
1983	Ellsworth		$25	$35	$50	Jon Agee		Pan
1984	Moon Valley		$20	$30	$40	Jon Agee		Pan
1985	Ludlow Laughs		$20	$30	$40	Jon Agee		FSG
1988	The Incredible Painting Of Felix Clousseau		$18	$25	$35	Jon Agee		FSG
1989	Dishes All Done		$18	$25	$35	Lucia Monfried		Dutton
1989	Sitting In My Box		$18	$25	$35	Dee Lillegard		Dutton
1989	The Toy Box		$18	$25	$35	Mary H. Heyward		Dutton
1991	Go Hang A Salami! I'm A Lasagna Hog! & Other Palindromes		$16	$25	$30	Jon Agee		FSG
1992	The Return Of Freddy Legrand		$16	$25	$30	Jon Agee		FSG
1993	Flapstick		$16	$25	$30	Jon Agee		Dutton
1994	So Many Dynamos! & Other Palindromes		$14	$20	$30	Jon Agee		FSG
1995	Mr. Lee		$14	$20	$25	Jennifer Jacobson		OCP
1996	Dmitri The Astronaut		$12	$18	$25	Jon Agee		HCollins
1997	Mean Margaret		$12	$18	$25	Tor Seidler		HCollins
1997	The Halloween House		$12	$18	$25	Erica Silverman		FSG
1998	Who Ordered The Jumbo Shrimp?		$12	$16	$20	Jon Agee		HCollins

Agee   Jon

Year	Title	VG-	VG	VG+	Fine	Author	Award	Pub
1999	Sit On A Potato Pan, Otis!		$12	$16	$20	Jon Agee		FSG
2000	Elvis Lives		$10	$14	$18	Jon Agee		FSG
2001	Milo's Hat Trick		$10	$14	$18	Jon Agee		Hyper
2002	Jon Agee's Palindromania		$8	$12	$16	Jon Agee		FSG
2002	Potch & Polly		$8	$12	$16	William Steig		FSG
2003	Z Goes Home		$8	$12	$16	Jon Agee		Hyper

Aggs   Patrice

Year	Title	VG-	VG	VG+	Fine	Author	Award	Pub
1992	Soft And Noisy		$10	$15	$20	Judy Hindley		Hyper
1992	The Sleepy Book		$15	$22	$30	Judy Hindley		Orchard
1993	Florizella And The Wolves		$10	$15	$20	Philippa Gregory		Candle
1993	Why Count Sheep?		$10	$15	$20	Karen Wallace		Hyper
1993	Why The Sea Is Salt		$10	$15	$20	Vivian French		Candle
1994	Mr. Pam Pam And The Hullabazoo		$9	$14	$18	Trish Cooke		Candle
1995	Bye-Bye, Babies!		$9	$14	$18	Angela Shelf Medearis		Candle
1995	Eat Up, Babies!		$12	$16	$20	Patrice Aggs		Candle
1995	Eat, Babies, Eat!		$9	$14	$18	Angela Shelf Medearis		Candle
1995	Un, Deux, Trois		$9	$14	$18	Opal Dunn		Barrn
1998	A Treasury Of Ballet Stories		$9	$14	$18	Caroline Plaisted		Kfisher
1999	The Visitor		$9	$14	$18	Patrice Aggs		Orchard
2001	Kingfisher Treasury Of Princess Stories		$8	$12	$16	Fiona Waters		Kfisher

Ahlberg   Janet

Year	Title	VG-	VG	VG+	Fine	Author	Award	Pub
1972	My Growing Up Book		$120	$160	$220	Bernard Max Garfinkel		P&Munk
1977	Burglar Bill		$40	$60	$90	Allan Ahlberg		Green
1977	Jeremiah In The Dark Woods		$40	$60	$90	Allan Ahlberg		Kestrel
1977	The Old Joke Book		$40	$60	$90	Allan Ahlberg		Viking
1978	Cops And Robbers		$40	$60	$90	Allan Ahlberg		Green
1978	Jeremiah In The Dark Woods		$40	$60	$90	Allan Ahlberg		Viking
1978	Mathematics In The Toy Store		$40	$60	$90	Vincent F. O'Connor		Rain
1978	The Vanishment Of Thomas Tull		$40	$60	$90	Allan Ahlberg		Scribnr
1979	Each Peach Pear Plum		$90	$140	$180	Allan Ahlberg	GM	Viking
1980	Funnybones		$40	$60	$80	Allan Ahlberg		Green
1980	The Little Worm Book		$40	$60	$80	Allan Ahlberg		Viking
1981	Peek-A-Boo!		$40	$60	$80	Allan Ahlberg		Viking
1982	Mr. Biff The Boxer		$40	$60	$80	Allan Ahlberg		Golden
1982	Mrs. Wobble The Waitress		$40	$60	$80	Allan Ahlberg		Golden
1982	The Baby's Catalogue		$40	$60	$80	Allan Ahlberg		LBrown
1985	Playmates		$35	$50	$70	Allan Ahlberg		VK
1985	Yum Yum		$35	$50	$70	Allan Ahlberg		VK
1986	The Cinderella Show		$30	$50	$60	Allan Ahlberg		VK
1986	The Jolly Postman		$30	$50	$60	Allan Ahlberg		LBrown
1988	--Starting school		$30	$50	$60	Allan Ahlberg		VK
1988	The Clothes Horse & Other Stories		$30	$50	$60	Allan Ahlberg		VK
1989	Bye Bye Baby		$30	$40	$60	Allan Ahlberg		LBrown
1991	The Jolly Christmas Postman		$50	$80	$100	Allan Ahlberg	GM	Heine
1992	The Bear Nobody Wanted		$25	$35	$50	Allan Ahlberg		Viking
1993	It Was A Dark And Stormy Night		$25	$35	$50	Allan Ahlberg		Viking
1998	Baby Sleeps		$10	$16	$20	Allan Ahlberg		LBrown
1998	Blue Buggy		$10	$16	$20	Allan Ahlberg		LBrown
1998	Doll And Teddy		$10	$16	$20	Allan Ahlberg		LBrown
1998	See The Rabbit		$10	$16	$20	Allan Ahlberg		LBrown

Alain

Year	Title	VG-	VG	VG+	Fine	Author	Award	Pub
1956	It's Spring!	$40	$60	$70		Janice		LL&S
1956	The Elephant And The Flea	$40	$60	$70		Alain		Whittle
1957	The Magic Stones	$40	$60	$70		Alain		Whittle
1959	Minette	$40	$60	$70		Janice		Whittle
1964	One, Two, Three, Going To Sea	$35	$50	$60		Alain		YScott

Alborough — Jez

Year	Title	VG-	VG	VG+	Fine	Author	Award	Pub
1984	Bare Bear		$30	$40	$60	Jez Alborough		Knopf
1985	Running Bear		$20	$30	$40	Jez Alborough		Knopf
1986	Can You Hear Me, Grandad?		$14	$20	$30	Pat Thomson		DelaP
1987	The Grass Is Always Greener		$14	$20	$30	Jez Alborough		Dial
1989	Cupboard Bear		$14	$20	$25	Jez Alborough		Ideals
1989	Martin's Mice		$14	$20	$25	Dick King-Smith		Crown
1990	Beaky		$12	$18	$25	Jez Alborough		HM
1992	Where's My Teddy		$12	$18	$25	Jez Alborough		Candle
1993	Clothesline		$12	$16	$20	Jez Alborough		Candle
1993	Cuddly Dudley		$12	$16	$20	Jez Alborough		Candle
1994	Hide And Seek		$12	$16	$20	Jez Alborough		Candle
1994	It's The Bear!		$12	$16	$20	Jez Alborough		Candle
1995	There's Something At The Mail Slot		$10	$16	$20	Jez Alborough		Candle
1996	Can You Jump Like A Kangaroo?		$10	$16	$20	Jez Alborough		Candle
1996	Can You Peck Like A Hen?		$10	$16	$20	Jez Alborough		Candle
1997	Watch Out! Big Bro's Coming		$10	$14	$18	Jez Alborough		Candle
1998	My Friend Bear		$10	$14	$18	Jez Alborough		Candle
1999	Whose Socks Are Those?		$10	$14	$18	Jez Alborough		Candle
2000	Duck In The Truck		$8	$12	$16	Jez Alborough		HCollins
2000	Hug		$8	$12	$16	Jez Alborough		Candle
2002	Eddie and the Bear in Big and Small		$12	$16	$20	Jez Alborough		Walker
2002	Fix-It Duck		$8	$10	$14	Jez Alborough		HCollins
2003	Captain Duck		$8	$10	$14	Jez Alborough		HCollins
2003	Some Dogs Do		$8	$10	$14	Jez Alborough		Candle

Alcorn — John

Year	Title	VG-	VG	VG+	Fine	Author	Award	Pub
1966	The Fireside Book of Children's Songs	$35	$50	$60		John Alcorn		S&S
1966	Wonderful Time	$35	$50	$60		Phyllis McGinley		Lippin
1967	Pocahontas In London	$35	$40	$60		Jan Wahl		DelaP
1969	Never Make Fun Of A Turtle, My Son	$35	$40	$60		Martin Gardner		S&S

Aldridge — Alan

Year	Title	VG-	VG	VG+	Fine	Author	Award	Pub
1970	Ann in the Moon		$30	$50	$60	Frances Francis		Bedrik
1973	The Butterfly Ball And The Grasshopper's Feast		$30	$50	$60	William Plomer		JCape
1977	The Adventures & Brave Deeds Of The Ship's Cat		$25	$35	$50	Richard Adams		Knopf
1979	The Peacock Party		$20	$30	$40	George E. Ryder		Viking
1980	The Lion's Cavalcade		$20	$30	$40	Ted Walker		JCape
1982	Phantasia Of Dockland, Rockland, And Dodos		$20	$30	$40	Harry Willock		Ball

Alexander — Martha

Year	Title	VG-	VG	VG+	Fine	Author	Award	Pub
1966	Big Sister And Little Sister	$50	$60	$80		Charlotte Zolotow		H&Row
1967	Grandfathers Are To Love	$35	$40	$60		Lois Wyse		PMagP
1967	Grandmothers Are To Love	$35	$40	$60		Lois Wyse		PMagP
1969	Blackboard Bear	$40	$60	$80		Martha Alexander		Dial
1969	Four Bears in a Box	$35	$40	$60		Martha Alexander		Dial
1970	Bobo's Dream		$25	$40	$50	Martha Alexander		Dial
1970	We Never Get to Do Anything		$25	$40	$50	Martha Alexander		Dial
1971	Charles		$25	$40	$50	Liesel Skorpen		H&Row
1971	Nobody Asked Me If I Wanted A Baby Sister		$25	$40	$50	Martha Alexander		Dial
1971	When The New Baby Comes I'm Moving Out		$25	$40	$50	Martha Alexander		Dial
1972	And My Mean Old Mother Will Be Sorry, Blackboard Bear		$25	$40	$50	Martha Alexander		Dial
1974	Too Hot for Ice Cream		$25	$40	$50	Jean Van Leeuwen		Penguin
1976	I Sure Am Glad To See You, Blackboard Bear		$25	$35	$50	Martha Alexander		Dial
1977	The Everyday Train		$25	$35	$50	Amy Ehrlich		Dial
1995	You're A Genius, Blackboard Bear		$10	$16	$20	Martha Alexander		Candle

Aliki — (Aliki Brandenburg)

Year	Title	VG-	VG	VG+	Fine	Author	Award	Pub
1961	The Story Of William Tell	$70	$90	$120		Aliki		Bedrik
1961	What's For Lunch, Charley?	$50	$60	$80		Margaret Hodges		Dial
1962	Alaska: A Book To Begin On	$50	$60	$80		Aliki		Pan
1962	My Five Senses	$50	$60	$80		Aliki		Crowell

Aliki   (Aliki Brandenburg)

Year	Title	VG-	VG	VG+	Fine	Author	Award	Pub
1962	My Hands	$50	$60	$80		Aliki		Crowell
1962	New Ways In Math	$50	$60	$80		Helen Clare		P-Hall
1962	The Lazy Little Lulu	$50	$60	$80		James Holding		Morrow
1962	The Wish Workers	$50	$60	$80		Aliki		Dial
1962	This Is The House Where Jack Lives	$50	$60	$80		Joan Heilbroner		Harper
1962	What Can I Buy?	$50	$60	$80		Mickey Marks		Dial
1963	Mr. Moonlight And Omar	$50	$60	$80		James Holding		Morrow
1963	The Story Of Johnny Appleseed	$50	$60	$80		Aliki		P-Hall
1963	This Is My Family	$50	$60	$80		Howard F. Fehr		HR&W
1964	Bees And Beelines	$50	$60	$80		Judy Hawes		Crowell
1964	Everything Has A Shape	$50	$60	$80		Bernice Kohn Hunt		P-Hall
1964	Everything Has A Size	$50	$60	$80		Aliki		Crowell
1964	George And The Cherry Tree	$50	$60	$80		Aliki		Dial
1964	More New Ways In Math	$50	$60	$80		Arthur Jonas		P-Hall
1964	The Story Of William Penn	$50	$60	$80		Aliki		P-Hall
1965	A Weed Is A Flower	$40	$60	$70		Aliki		P-Hall
1965	Is It Blue As A Butterfly?	$40	$60	$70		Rebecca Kalusky		P-Hall
1965	Mother's Day	$40	$60	$70		Mary Kay Phelan		Crowell
1965	One Day It Rained Cats And Dogs	$40	$60	$70		Bernice Kohn Hunt		CM
1966	Is That A Happy Hippopotamus?	$40	$60	$70		Sean Morrison		Crowell
1966	Keep Your Mouth Closed, Dear	$40	$60	$70		Aliki		Dial
1967	Five Dolls And The Monkey	$60	$80	$100		Pauline Clarke		P-Hall
1967	Five Dolls In The Snow	$60	$80	$100		Pauline Clarke		P-Hall
1967	New Year's Day	$40	$50	$70		Aliki		Crowell
1967	Three Gold Pieces	$40	$50	$70		Aliki		Pan
1968	At Home	$40	$50	$70		Esther Rudomin Hautzig		Macmil
1968	Birds At Night	$40	$50	$70		Roma Gans		Crowell
1968	Diogenes	$40	$50	$70		Aliki		P-Hall
1968	Five Dolls And The Duke	$60	$80	$100		Pauline Clarke		P-Hall
1968	Five Dolls And Their Friends	$60	$80	$100		Pauline Clarke		P-Hall
1968	Hush Little Baby	$40	$50	$70		Aliki		P-Hall
1968	Mrs. Neverbody's Recipes	$40	$50	$70		Wilma Yeo		Lippin
1968	Oh Lord, I Wish I Was A Buzzard	$40	$50	$70		Polly Greenberg		Macmil
1969	My Visit To The Dinosaurs	$40	$50	$70		Aliki		Crowell
1969	The Eggs	$40	$50	$70		Aliki		Pan
1970	I Once Knew A Man		$25	$40	$50	Franz Brandenberg		Macmil
1970	Weighing & Balancing		$25	$40	$50	Jane Jonas Srivastava		Crowell
1972	Fossils Tell Of Long Ago		$25	$40	$50	Aliki		Crowell
1972	June 7!		$25	$40	$50	Aliki		Macmil
1973	Fresh Cider And Pie		$25	$40	$50	Franz Brandenberg		Macmil
1973	The Long Lost Coelacanth		$25	$40	$50	Aliki		Crowell
1974	Ears And Tails And Common Sense		$25	$40	$50	Philip Sherlock		Crowell
1974	Go Tell Aunt Rhody		$25	$35	$50	Aliki		Macmil
1974	Green Grass And White Milk		$25	$40	$50	Aliki		Crowell
1975	A Secret For Grandmother's Birthday		$25	$35	$50	Franz Brandenberg		Green
1975	Averages		$25	$35	$50	Jane Jonas Srivastava		Crowell
1975	No School Today!		$35	$50	$70	Franz Brandenberg		Macmil
1976	A Robber! A Robber!		$25	$35	$50	Franz Brandenberg		Green
1976	At Mary Bloom's		$25	$35	$50	Aliki		Green
1976	Corn Is Maize		$25	$35	$50	Aliki		Crowell
1976	I Wish I Was Sick, Too!		$25	$35	$50	Franz Brandenberg		Green
1977	Nice New Neighbors		$25	$35	$50	Franz Brandenberg		Green
1977	The Many Lives Of Benjamin Franklin		$25	$35	$50	Aliki		P-Hall
1977	What Can You Make Of It?		$25	$35	$50	Franz Brandenberg		Green
1977	Wild And Woolly Mammoths		$25	$35	$50	Aliki		Crowell
1978	A Picnic, Hurrah!		$25	$35	$50	Franz Brandenberg		Green
1978	Six New Students		$25	$35	$50	Franz Brandenberg		Green
1978	The Twelve Months: A Greek Folktale		$25	$35	$50	Aliki		Green
1979	Everyone Ready?		$20	$30	$40	Franz Brandenberg		Green
1979	Mummies Made In Egypt		$20	$30	$40	Aliki		Crowell
1979	The Two Of Them		$20	$30	$40	Aliki		Green
1980	It's Not My Fault		$18	$25	$35	Franz Brandenberg		Green
1981	Digging Up Dinosaurs		$16	$25	$30	Aliki		Crowell
1981	Leo And Emily		$16	$25	$30	Franz Brandenberg		Green
1982	Leo And Emily's Big Ideas		$16	$25	$30	Franz Brandenberg		Green
1982	We Are Best Friends		$16	$25	$30	Aliki		Green
1983	A Medieval Feast		$16	$25	$30	Aliki		Crowell

Aliki   (Aliki Brandenburg)

Year	Title	VG-	VG	VG+	Fine	Author	Award	Pub
1983	Aunt Nina And Her Nephews And Nieces		$16	$25	$30	Franz Brandenberg		Green
1983	Use Your Head, Dear		$16	$25	$30	Aliki		Green
1984	Aunt Nina's Visit		$16	$25	$30	Franz Brandenberg		Green
1984	Feelings		$16	$25	$30	Aliki		Green
1984	Leo And Emily And The Dragon		$16	$25	$30	Franz Brandenberg		Green
1985	Dinosaurs Are Different		$14	$20	$30	Aliki		Crowell
1985	The Hit Of The Party		$14	$20	$30	Franz Brandenberg		Green
1986	Cock-A-Doodle-Doo		$14	$20	$30	Franz Brandenberg		Green
1986	Go Tell Aunt Rhody		$14	$20	$30	Aliki		Macmil
1986	How A Book Is Made		$14	$20	$30	Aliki		Crowell
1986	Jack And Jake		$14	$20	$30	Aliki		Green
1987	Evolution		$14	$20	$30	Joanna Cole		Crowell
1987	Overnight At Mary Bloom's		$14	$20	$30	Aliki		Green
1987	Welcome, Little Baby		$14	$20	$30	Aliki		Green
1987	What's Wrong With A Van?		$14	$20	$30	Franz Brandenberg		Green
1988	Dinosaur Bones		$18	$25	$35	Aliki		Crowell
1989	Aunt Nina, Good Night		$14	$20	$25	Franz Brandenberg		Green
1989	The King's Day		$14	$20	$25	Aliki		Crowell
1990	Manners		$12	$18	$25	Aliki		Green
1990	My Feet		$12	$18	$25	Aliki		Crowell
1991	Christmas Tree Memories		$12	$18	$25	Aliki		HCollins
1991	The Listening Walk		$12	$18	$25	Paul Showers		HCollins
1992	I'm Growing!		$12	$18	$25	Aliki		HCollins
1992	Milk From Cow To Carton		$12	$18	$25	Aliki		HCollins
1993	Communication		$12	$16	$20	Aliki		Green
1993	My Visit To The Aquarium		$12	$16	$20	Aliki		HCollins
1994	The Gods And Goddesses Of Olympus		$18	$25	$35	Aliki		HCollins
1995	Best Friends Together Again		$10	$16	$20	Aliki		Green
1995	Tabby		$10	$16	$20	Aliki		HCollins
1996	Hello! Good-Bye!		$10	$16	$20	Aliki		Green
1996	Those Summers		$10	$16	$20	Aliki		HCollins
1996	Wild And Woolly Mammoths		$10	$16	$20	Aliki		HCollins
1997	My Visit To The Zoo		$10	$14	$18	Aliki		HCollins
1998	Painted Words		$10	$14	$18	Aliki		Green
1999	William Shakespeare & The Globe		$10	$14	$18	Aliki		HCollins
2000	All By Myself!		$8	$12	$16	Aliki		HCollins
2001	One Little Spoonful		$8	$12	$16	Aliki		HFest
2003	Ah, Music		$8	$10	$14	Aliki		HCollins

Allen   Thomas B.

Year	Title	VG-	VG	VG+	Fine	Author	Award	Pub
1987	In Coal Country		$20	$30	$40	Judith Hendershot		Knopf
1990	Time To Go		$12	$16	$20	Beverly & David Fiday		GB
1994	Sewing Quilts		$10	$16	$20	Ann W. Turner		Macmil
1996	Once In The Country		$10	$14	$18	Tony Johnston		Putnam
1996	When Artie Was Little		$10	$14	$18	Harriet Schwartz		Knopf

Alley   R.W.

Year	Title	VG-	VG	VG+	Fine	Author	Award	Pub
1988	The Clever Carpenter		$10	$14	$18	R.W. Alley		Random
1990	Mrs. Toggle's Zipper		$8	$12	$16	Robin Pulver		4Winds
1991	Mrs. Toggle's And The Dinosaur		$8	$12	$16	Robin Pulver		S&S
1994	Family Reunion		$8	$12	$16	Marilyn Singer		Macmil
1994	Mrs. Toggle's Beautiful Blue Shoe		$8	$12	$16	Robin Pulver		4Winds
1995	There's A Dragon About		$8	$10	$14	Richard Schotter		Orchard
1996	Old Winter		$8	$10	$14	Judith Benét Richardson		Orchard
1997	The New Dog		$8	$10	$14	Barbara Shook Hazen		Dial
2000	Mrs. Toggle's Class Picture Day		$6	$10	$12	Robin Pulver		Scholas
2002	Little Flower		$6	$10	$12	Gloria Rand		Holt

Ambrus   Victor G.

Year	Title	VG-	VG	VG+	Fine	Author	Award	Pub
1963	The Cossacks	$50	$70	$90		Barbara Bartos-Höppner		Walck
1964	High and Haunted Island	$35	$50	$60		Nan Chauncy		WNorton
1964	Save The Khan	$35	$50	$60		Barbara Bartos-Höppner		Walck

Ambrus   Victor G.

Year	Title	VG-	VG	VG+	Fine	Author	Award	Pub
1965	A Cavalcade Of Kings	$35	$50	$60		Eleanor Farjeon		Walck
1965	A Cavalcade Of Queens	$35	$50	$60		Eleanor Farjeon		Walck
1965	A Turkish Village	$35	$50	$60		Mary Gough		Oxford
1966	Henri's Hands For Pablo Picasso	$35	$50	$60		Helen Kay		AS
1966	Nobody's Garden	$35	$50	$60		Cordelia Jones		Scribnr
1966	Storm Over The Blue Hills	$35	$50	$60		Alan C. Jenkins		Norton
1966	The Greyhound	$35	$50	$60		Helen Griffiths		DoubleD
1966	The Merchant Navy	$35	$50	$60		James Lennox Kerr		Oxford
1966	The Three Poor Tailors	$70	$100	$120		Victor G. Ambrus	GM	HBrace
1966	The Young Pretenders	$35	$50	$60		Barbara Leonie Picard		Crit
1967	A Sapphire For September	$35	$40	$60		Hesba Brinsmead-Hungerford		Oxford
1967	Brave Soldier Janosh	$35	$40	$60		Victor G. Ambrus		HBrace
1967	No Beat Of Drum	$35	$40	$60		Hester Burton		World
1967	Prisoners In The Snow	$35	$40	$60		Arthur Catherall		LL&S
1967	The Challenge Of The Green Knight	$35	$40	$60		Ian Serraillier		Walck
1967	The Journey Of The Eldest Son	$35	$40	$60		J. G. Fyson		CM
1967	The Pieces Of Home	$35	$40	$60		Miska Miles		LBrown
1967	The Three Brothers Of Ur	$35	$40	$60		J. G. Fyson		CM
1967	The Wild Horse Of Santander	$35	$40	$60		Helen Griffiths		DoubleD
1967	Thunder In The Sky	$35	$40	$60		K. M. Peyton		World
1967	Vendetta	$35	$40	$60		Shirley Deane		Viking
1968	Camerons Ahoy!	$35	$40	$60		Jane Duncan		Macmil
1968	Flambards	$35	$40	$60		K. M. Peyton		World
1968	Robin In The Greenwood	$35	$40	$60		Ian Serraillier		Walck
1968	Shannon	$35	$40	$60		Barbara J. Berry		Follett
1968	Stallion Of The Sands	$35	$40	$60		Helen Griffiths		Hutch
1968	Stranger In The Hills	$35	$40	$60		Madeleine A. Polland		DoubleD
1968	The Glass Man And The Golden Bird	$35	$40	$60		Ruth Manning-Sanders		Roy
1968	The Great Bow	$35	$40	$60		Reginald Maddock		RandMc
1968	The Little Cockerel	$35	$40	$60		Victor G. Ambrus		HBrace
1968	When Jays Fly To Bárbmo	$35	$40	$60		Margaret Balderson		Oxford
1968	Young Mark	$35	$40	$60		E. M. Almedingen		FSG
1969	Big Ben	$35	$40	$60		David Harry Walker		HM
1969	Flambards In Summer	$35	$40	$60		K. M. Peyton		Oxford
1969	Folk Tales From The North	$35	$40	$60		Winifred Finlay		FWatts
1969	In Spite Of All Terror	$35	$40	$60		Hester Burton		World
1969	Jonnikin And The Flying Basket	$35	$40	$60		Ruth Manning-Sanders		Dutton
1969	Kidnapped By Accident	$35	$40	$60		Arthur Catherall		LL&S
1969	Knights Of God	$35	$40	$60		Patricia Lynch		HR&W
1969	The Edge Of The Cloud	$35	$40	$60		K. M. Peyton		World
1969	The Horse	$35	$40	$60		Siegfried Stander		World
1969	The Mystery Of Stonehenge	$35	$40	$60		Franklyn M. Branley		Crowell
1970	Beyond The Weir Bridge		$25	$40	$50	Hester Burton		Crowell
1970	Flambards In Summer		$25	$40	$50	K. M. Peyton		World
1970	Folk Tales From Moor And Mountain		$25	$40	$50	Winifred Finlay		Roy
1970	Haki, The Shetland Pony		$25	$40	$50	Kathleen Fidler		RandMc
1970	Red Sea Rescue		$25	$40	$50	Arthur Catherall		LL&S
1970	Robin And His Merry Men		$25	$40	$50	Ian Serraillier		Walck
1970	Slave Of The Huns		$25	$40	$50	Géza Gárdonyi		Bobbs
1970	The Diverting History Of John Gilpin		$25	$40	$50	William Cowper		AS
1970	The Seven Skinny Goats		$25	$40	$50	Victor G. Ambrus		HBrace
1970	The Story Of Britain		$25	$40	$50	R. J. Unstead		TNelson
1971	Stirabout Stories		$25	$40	$50	Barbara Sleigh		Bobbs
1972	A Christmas Fantasy		$25	$40	$50	Carolyn Haywood		Morrow
1972	Heather, Oak, And Olive		$25	$40	$50	Rosemary Sutcliff		Dutton
1972	Stranger In The Storm		$25	$40	$50	Charles Paul May		AS
1972	Tales Of Ancient Persia		$25	$40	$50	Barbara Leonie Picard		Oxford
1972	Tank Commander		$25	$40	$50	Ronald Welch		Oxford
1972	The Henchmans At Home		$25	$40	$50	Hester Burton		Crowell
1972	The Rebel		$25	$40	$50	Hester Burton		Crowell
1972	The Sultan's Bath		$25	$40	$50	Victor G. Ambrus		HBJ
1973	A Cavalcade Of Magicians		$25	$40	$50	Roger Lancelyn Green		Walck
1973	Hunted In Their Own Land		$25	$40	$50	Nan Chauncy		Seabury
1973	Kodi's Mare		$25	$40	$50	Bonnie Highsmith		AS
1973	Riders Of The Storm		$25	$40	$50	Hester Burton		Crowell
1973	Russian Blue		$25	$40	$50	Helen Griffiths		Holiday
1973	The Traitor Within		$25	$40	$50	Alexander Cordell		TNelson

Ambrus   Victor G.

Year	Title	VG-	VG	VG+	Fine	Author	Award	Pub
1974	Cap O' Rushes & Other Folk Tales		$25	$40	$50	Winifred Finlay		K&W
1974	Kate Rider		$25	$40	$50	Hester Burton		Oxford
1974	The Kingdom And The Cave		$25	$40	$50	Joan Aiken		DoubleD
1975	A Country Wedding		$25	$35	$50	Victor G. Ambrus		AW
1975	Horses In Battle		$25	$35	$50	Victor G. Ambrus		Oxford
1975	Horses In Battle And Mishka		$50	$70	$90	Victor G. Ambrus	GM	Oxford
1975	Just A Dog		$25	$35	$50	Helen Griffiths		Holiday
1975	Kate Ryder		$25	$35	$50	Hester Burton		Crowell
1975	The Colt At Taparoo		$25	$35	$50	Elyne Mitchell		Hutch
1975	The Mysterious Appearance Of Agnes		$25	$35	$50	Helen Griffiths		Holiday
1975	Witch Fear		$25	$35	$50	Helen Griffiths		Hutch
1976	A Valentine Fantasy		$25	$35	$50	Carolyn Haywood		Morrow
1976	Favourite Tales From Shakespeare		$25	$35	$50	Bernard Miles (adapted)		Hamlyn
1976	The Farthest-Away Mountain		$25	$35	$50	Lynne Reid Banks		DoubleD
1976	The World Of Dinosaurs		$25	$35	$50	Richard Moody		Hamlyn
1977	Chasing The Goblins Away		$25	$35	$50	Tobi Tobias		FWarne
1977	Running Wild		$25	$35	$50	Helen Griffiths		Holiday
1977	The Book Of Magical Horses		$25	$35	$50	Margaret Mayo		Hastings
1978	Mishka		$40	$60	$90	Victor G. Ambrus	GM	FWarne
1978	The Very Special Baby		$25	$35	$50	Robert E. Swindells		P-Hall
1979	Robin Hood, His Life And Legend		$20	$30	$40	Bernard Miles		RandMc
1979	The Last Summer		$20	$30	$40	Helen Griffiths		Holiday
1979	The Maplin Bird		$20	$30	$40	K. M. Peyton		Gregg
1980	Blackface Stallion		$18	$25	$35	Helen Griffiths		Holiday
1980	The King's Monster		$18	$25	$35	Carolyn Haywood		Morrow
1980	The Valiant Little Tailor		$18	$25	$35	Victor G. Ambrus		Oxford
1980	When Jays Fly To Bárbmo		$18	$25	$35	Margaret Balderson		Gregg
1981	Dracula's Bedtime Storybook		$16	$25	$30	Victor G. Ambrus		Oxford
1981	Encyclopedia Of Legendary Creatures		$16	$25	$30	Tom McGowen		RandMc
1982	Flambards		$16	$25	$30	K. M. Peyton		Philo
1982	Grandma, Felix, And Mustapha Biscuit		$16	$25	$30	Victor G. Ambrus		Morrow
1982	Just So Stories		$16	$25	$30	Rudyard Kipling		RandMc
1982	Tales Of King Arthur		$16	$25	$30	James Riordan		RandMc
1983	Santa Claus Forever!		$16	$25	$30	Carolyn Haywood		Morrow
1984	Favorite Stories Of The Ballet		$16	$25	$30	James Riordan		RandMc
1984	Favorite Tales From Shakespeare		$16	$25	$30	Bernard Miles (adapted)		CP
1985	Tales From The Arabian Nights		$14	$20	$30	James Riordan		RandMc
1986	How The Reindeer Saved Santa		$14	$20	$30	Carolyn Haywood		Morrow
1987	How The First Letter Was Written		$14	$20	$30	Rudyard Kipling		Bedrik
1989	El Cid		$14	$20	$25	Geraldine McCaughrean		Oxford
1990	Dracula's Late-Night TV Show		$12	$18	$25	Victor G. Ambrus		Oxford
1990	Son Of Dracula		$12	$18	$25	Victor G. Ambrus		Oxford
1991	Count, Dracula		$12	$18	$25	Victor G. Ambrus		Oxford
1991	The Rabbi's Wisdom		$12	$18	$25	Erica Gordon		Bedrik
1991	What's The Time, Dracula?		$12	$18	$25	Victor G. Ambrus		Oxford
1992	Dracula's Bedtime Storybook		$12	$18	$25	Victor G. Ambrus		Oxford
1992	Never Laugh At Bears		$12	$18	$25	Victor G. Ambrus		Bedrik
1993	A Treasury Of Stories From Around The World		$12	$16	$20	Linda M. Jennings		Kfisher
1993	The Odyssey		$12	$16	$20	Geraldine McCaughrean		Oxford
1994	Favorite Fairy Tales Told In France		$12	$16	$20	Virginia Haviland (adapted)		Beech
1994	Horse Stories		$12	$16	$20	Christine Pullein-Thompson		Kfisher
1994	The Shoemaker's Boy		$12	$16	$20	Joan Aiken		S&S
1995	Don Quixote		$10	$16	$20	Michael Harrison (adapted)		Oxford
1995	The Canterbury Tales		$10	$16	$20	G. McCaughrean (adapted)		Oxford
1996	Black Beauty		$10	$16	$20	Anna Sewell		DK
1996	Moby Dick		$10	$16	$20	G. McCaughrean (adapted)		Oxford
1996	Pinocchio		$10	$16	$20	James Riordan (adapted)		Oxford
1996	Thundering Hooves		$10	$16	$20	Christine Pullein-Thompson		Kfisher
1997	Roman Aromas		$10	$14	$18	Mary J. Dobson		Oxford
1997	The Random House Book Of Horse Stories		$10	$14	$18	Felicity Trotman		Random
1998	Eric The Red		$10	$14	$18	Neil Grant		Oxford
1998	King Arthur		$10	$14	$18	James Riordan		Oxford
2000	The Iliad		$8	$12	$16	Nick McCarty (adapted)		Kfisher
2000	The Three Musketeers		$8	$12	$16	Michael Leitch (adapted)		DK
2001	The Story Of Mother Teresa		$8	$12	$16	Stewart Ross		Thames
2002	Great Expectations		$8	$10	$14	James Riordan (adapted)		Oxford
2003	The Farthest-Away Mountain		$8	$10	$14	Lynne Reid Banks		DelaP

Ames   Lee J.

Year	Title	VG-	VG	VG+	Fine	Author	Award	Pub
1954	Circus Parade	$20	$30	$35		Phyllis R. Fenner		Knopf
1957	Exploring The Animal Kingdom	$20	$25	$35		Millicent Selsam		GardenC
1959	You Will Go To The Moon	$35	$40	$60		Mae & Ira Freeman		BB
1962	All About The Planet Earth	$18	$25	$30		Patricia Lauber		Random
1963	City Street Games	$18	$25	$30		Jocelyn Ames		HR&W
1967	Life In The Universe	$16	$20	$30		Alvin/ Virginia Silverstein		VNost
1967	Tool Chest	$16	$20	$30		Anthony Rowley		Singer
1968	The Brain Of Man	$16	$20	$30		John McNeel		Putnam
1968	The Origin Of Life	$16	$20	$30		Alvin/ Virginia Silverstein		VNost
1969	By Land, By Sea, By Air	$16	$20	$30		Jerome Edward Leavitt		Putnam
1969	Carl Linnaeus	$16	$20	$30		Alvin/ Virginia Silverstein		JohnDay
1969	Great Ideas Of Science	$16	$20	$30		Isaac Asimov		HM
1970	Harold Urey, The Man Who Explored From Earth To Moon		$14	$20	$25	Alvin/ Virginia Silverstein		JohnDay
1971	Hide-And-Seek ABC		$14	$20	$25	Adelaide Holl		P&Munk
1971	My Sister The Horse		$14	$20	$25	Barbara Klimowicz		Abing
1971	Telephone Systems		$14	$20	$25	Herbert Spencer Zim		Morrow
1972	The Muscular System		$14	$20	$25	Alvin/ Virginia Silverstein		P-Hall
1972	The Skin: Coverings And Linings Of Living Things		$14	$20	$25	Alvin/ Virginia Silverstein		P-Hall
1972	Tractors		$14	$20	$25	Herbert Spencer Zim		Morrow
1973	Commercial Fishing		$14	$20	$25	Herbert Spencer Zim		Morrow
1973	The Great Green Apple War		$14	$20	$25	Barbara. Klimowicz		Abing
1974	Pipes And Plumbing Systems		$12	$18	$25	Herbert Spencer Zim		Morrow
1982	The Battle Of The Dinosaurs		$10	$16	$20	David C. Knight		P-Hall
1985	Dinosaurs That Swam And Flew		$10	$14	$18	David C. Knight		P-Hall
1986	Amazing Mouths And Menus		$10	$14	$18	Mary Blocksma		P-Hall

Anderson   Wayne

Year	Title	VG-	VG	VG+	Fine	Author	Award	Pub
1976	Ratsmagic		$50	$70	$90	Christopher Logue		Pan
1979	The Flight of Dragons		$40	$60	$80	Peter Dickinson		H&Row
1979	The Magic Circus		$40	$60	$80	Christopher Logue		Viking
1984	A Mouse's Tale		$35	$50	$70	Naomi Lewis		H&Row
1990	Thumbelina		$18	$25	$35	James Riordan (adapted)		Putnam
1992	Dragon		$16	$25	$30	David Passes		GreenT
1995	Journey To The Haunted Planet		$14	$20	$25	A. J. Wood		Templar
1996	Invasion Of The Giant Bugs		$14	$20	$25	A. J. Wood		HFest
1996	Wayne Anderson's Horrorble Book		$14	$20	$25	Wayne Anderson		DK
1997	Jug Of Milk		$12	$18	$25	Ben Butterworth		Sund
1997	Pocketful Of Gold		$12	$18	$25	Ben Butterworth		Sund
1997	Story Without End		$12	$18	$25	Ben Butterworth		Sund
1997	Too Small		$12	$18	$25	Ben Butterworth		Sund
1998	The Flight Of Dragons		$12	$16	$20	Peter Dickinson		Over
2001	The Tin Forest		$10	$14	$18	Helen Ward		Dutton
2003	The Dragon Machine		$8	$12	$16	Helen Ward		Dutton
2003	Year Of The Goat		$8	$12	$16	Nigel Suckling		Fairfax
2003	Year Of The Horse		$8	$12	$16	Nigel Suckling		Fairfax

Andreasen   Dan

Year	Title	VG-	VG	VG+	Fine	Author	Award	Pub
1991	Felicity Learns A Lesson		$12	$18	$25	Valerie Tripp		Pleasnt
1991	Felicity's Surprise		$12	$18	$25	Valerie Tripp		Pleasnt
1991	Love, David		$12	$18	$25	Dianne Case		LodeS
1991	Meet Felicity		$12	$18	$25	Valerie Tripp		Pleasnt
1991	The Boonsville Bombers		$12	$18	$25	Alison Herzig		Viking
1992	Changes For Felicity		$12	$18	$25	Valerie Tripp		Pleasnt
1992	Felicity Saves The Day		$12	$18	$25	Valerie Tripp		Pleasnt
1992	Happy Birthday, Felicity		$12	$18	$25	Valerie Tripp		Pleasnt
1992	The Bite Of The Gold Bug		$12	$18	$25	Barthe DeClements		Viking
1993	Joshua T. Bates Takes Charge		$12	$16	$20	Susan Richards Shreve		Knopf
1993	The President Is Dead		$12	$16	$20	Virginia T. Gross		Viking
1994	Brigid, Bewitched		$12	$16	$20	Kathleen Leverich		Random
1994	By The Dawn's Early Light		$12	$16	$20	Steven Kroll		Scholas
1995	Brigid Beware!		$10	$16	$20	Kathleen Leverich		Random
1995	Brigid The Bad		$10	$16	$20	Kathleen Leverich		Random
1995	Grandma's Smile		$10	$16	$20	Elaine Moore		LL&S
1996	Black Sky River		$10	$16	$20	Tres Seymour		Orchard

Andreasen   Dan

Year	Title	VG-	VG	VG+	Fine	Author	Award	Pub
1996	Little House In Brookfield		$10	$16	$20	Maria D. Wilkes		HCollins
1996	Pony Express!		$10	$16	$20	Steven Kroll		Scholas
1997	Eagle Song		$10	$14	$18	Joseph Bruchac		Dial
1997	Little Town At The Crossroads		$10	$14	$18	Maria D. Wilkes		HCollins
1997	New Dawn On Rocky Ridge		$10	$14	$18	Roger Lea MacBride		HCollins
1997	Touch The Sky Summer		$10	$14	$18	Jean Van Leeuwen		Dial
1998	Changes For Samantha		$10	$14	$18	Valerie Tripp		Pleasnt
1998	Halley Came To Jackson		$10	$14	$18	Mary-Chapin Carpenter		HCollins
1998	Happy Birthday, Samantha!		$10	$14	$18	Valerie Tripp		Pleasnt
1998	Little Clearing In The Woods		$10	$14	$18	Maria D. Wilkes		HCollins
1998	Meet Samantha		$10	$14	$18	Susan S. Adler		Pleasnt
1998	On The Banks Of The Bayou		$10	$14	$18	Roger Lea MacBride		HCollins
1998	Pioneer Girl		$10	$14	$18	William Anderson		HCollins
1998	Samantha Learns A Lesson		$10	$14	$18	Susan S. Adler		Pleasnt
1998	Samantha Saves The Day		$10	$14	$18	Valerie Tripp		Pleasnt
1998	Samantha's Surprise		$10	$14	$18	Rose Schur		Pleasnt
1998	We Played Marbles		$10	$14	$18	Tres Seymour		Orchard
1999	Bachelor Girl		$10	$14	$18	Roger Lea MacBride		HCollins
1999	Felicity's New Sister		$10	$14	$18	Valerie Tripp		Pleasnt
1999	Little House By Boston Bay		$10	$14	$18	Melissa Wiley		HCollins
1999	Samantha's Winter Party		$10	$14	$18	Valerie Tripp		Pleasnt
1999	Streets Of Gold		$10	$14	$18	Rosemary Wells		Dial
2000	Felicity's Dancing Shoes		$8	$12	$16	Valerie Tripp		Pleasnt
2000	Naomi Judd's Guardian Angels		$8	$12	$16	Naomi Judd		HCollins
2000	On Top Of Concord Hill		$8	$12	$16	Maria D. Wilkes		Harper
2000	Rose Red And The Bear Prince		$8	$12	$16	Jacob & Wilhelm Grimm		HCollins
2000	Samantha Saves The Wedding		$8	$12	$16	Valerie Tripp		Pleasnt
2000	The Stars That Shine		$8	$12	$16	Julie Clay		S&S
2001	Across The Rolling River		$8	$12	$16	Celia Wilkins		HCollins
2001	Felicity Takes A Dare		$8	$12	$16	Valerie Tripp		Pleasnt
2001	Felicity's Story Collection		$8	$12	$16	Valerie Tripp		Pleasnt
2001	On Tide Mill Lane		$8	$12	$16	Melissa Wiley		HCollins
2001	Samantha And The Missing Pearls		$8	$12	$16	Valerie Tripp		Pleasnt
2001	Samantha's Story Collection		$8	$12	$16	Susan S. Adler		Pleasnt
2001	Tattered Sails		$8	$12	$16	Verla Kay		Putnam
2002	A Quiet Place		$8	$10	$14	Douglas Wood		S&S
2002	Felicity Discovers A Secret		$8	$10	$14	Valerie Tripp		Pleasnt
2002	Love Song For A Baby		$8	$10	$14	Marion Dane Bauer		S&S
2002	Night Flight		$8	$10	$14	Sydelle Kramer		G&D
2002	Sailor Boy Jig		$8	$10	$14	Margaret Wise Brown		McEld
2002	Samantha's Blue Bicycle		$8	$10	$14	Valerie Tripp		Pleasnt
2002	Samantha's Friendship Fun		$8	$10	$14	Tamara England		AG
2002	The House In The Mail		$8	$10	$14	Rosemary Wells		Viking
2002	The Road From Roxbury		$8	$10	$14	Melissa Wiley		HCollins
2003	Joan Of Arc		$8	$10	$14	Shana Corey		Random
2003	Little City By The Lake		$8	$10	$14	Celia Wilkins		HCollins
2003	River Boy		$8	$10	$14	William Anderson		HCollins
2003	Samantha's Special Talent		$8	$10	$14	Sarah Masters Buckey		Pleasnt
2003	The Balloon Man		$8	$10	$14	Bruce Balan		S&S
2003	With A Little Help From Daddy		$8	$10	$14	Dan Andreasen		McEld
2004	A Special Day For Mommy		$8	$10	$14	Dan Andreasen		McEld
2004	Across The Puddingstone Dam		$8	$10	$14	Melissa Wiley		HCollins
2004	Keeping Up With Roo		$8	$10	$14	Sharlee Mullins Glenn		Putnam
2004	Little Spotted Cat		$8	$10	$14	Alyssa Satin Capucilli		Dial
2004	Sam And The Bag		$8	$10	$14	Alison Jeffries		Harcort
2004	The Attic Christmas		$8	$10	$14	B. G. Hennessy		Putnam

Anglund   Joan Walsh

Year	Title	VG-	VG	VG+	Fine	Author	Award	Pub
1948	To Church We Go	$100	$140	$180		Robbie Trent		W&F
1958	A Friend Is Someone Who Likes You	$80	$120	$140		Joan Walsh Anglund		HBrace
1959	Look Out The Window	$60	$80	$100		Joan Walsh Anglund		HBrace
1959	The Brave Cowboy	$80	$120	$140		Joan Walsh Anglund		HBrace
1959	The Golden Treasury Of Poetry	$40	$60	$70		Louis Untermeyer (adapted)		Golden
1960	In A Pumpkin Shell, A Mother Goose ABC	$50	$70	$90		Joan Walsh Anglund		HBrace
1960	Love Is A Special Way Of Feeling	$50	$70	$90		Joan Walsh Anglund		HBrace

Anglund   Joan Walsh

Year	Title	VG-	VG	VG+	Fine	Author	Award	Pub
1961	Christmas Is A Time Of Giving	$50	$70	$90		Joan Walsh Anglund		HBrace
1961	Cowboy And His Friends	$80	$100	$140		Joan Walsh Anglund		HBrace
1962	Nibble Nibble Mousekin	$50	$70	$90		Joan Walsh Anglund		HBrace
1963	Cowboy's Secret Life	$80	$100	$140		Joan Walsh Anglund		HBrace
1963	Spring Is A New Beginning	$50	$70	$90		Joan Walsh Anglund		HBrace
1964	A Pocketful Of Proverbs	$50	$70	$90		Joan Walsh Anglund		HBrace
1964	Childhood Is A Time Of Innocence	$50	$70	$90		Joan Walsh Anglund		HBrace
1965	A Book Of Good Tidings From The Bible	$50	$60	$80		Joan Walsh Anglund		HBrace
1966	A Year Is Round	$50	$60	$80		Joan Walsh Anglund		HBrace
1966	What Color Is Love?	$50	$60	$80		Joan Walsh Anglund		HBrace
1967	A Cup Of Sun; A Book Of Poems	$50	$60	$80		Joan Walsh Anglund		HBrace
1968	A Is For Always; An ABC Book	$50	$60	$80		Joan Walsh Anglund		HBrace
1969	Morning Is A Little Child	$50	$60	$80		Joan Walsh Anglund		HBrace
1970	A Slice Of Snow; A Book Of Poems		$30	$50	$60	Joan Walsh Anglund		HBJ
1971	Do You Love Someone?		$30	$50	$60	Joan Walsh Anglund		HBJ
1971	The Golden Book Of Poems For The Very Young		$30	$50	$60	Joan Walsh Anglund		Golden
1972	The Cowboy's Christmas		$40	$60	$80	Joan Walsh Anglund		Athenm
1973	A Child's Book Of Old Nursery Rhymes		$30	$40	$60	Joan Walsh Anglund		Athenm
1974	Goodbye, Yesterday; A Book Of Poems		$30	$40	$60	Joan Walsh Anglund		Athenm
1975	A Birthday Book		$25	$40	$50	Joan Walsh Anglund		DetProd
1977	The Christmas Cookie Book		$25	$40	$50	Joan Walsh Anglund		DetProd
1978	The Joan Walsh Anglund Storybook		$25	$40	$50	Joan Walsh Anglund		Random
1979	Emily And Adam Book Of Opposites		$25	$35	$50	Joan Walsh Anglund		Random
1979	The Adam Book		$25	$35	$50	Joan Walsh Anglund		Random
1980	Almost A Rainbow: A Book Of Poems		$25	$35	$50	Joan Walsh Anglund		Random
1982	Rainbow Love		$20	$30	$40	Joan Walsh Anglund		DetProd
1983	A Christmas Book		$20	$30	$40	Joan Walsh Anglund		Random
1983	The Circle Of The Spirit		$20	$30	$40	Joan Walsh Anglund		Random
1984	Memories Of The Heart		$20	$30	$40	Joan Walsh Anglund		Random
1985	Baby Brother		$20	$30	$40	Joan Walsh Anglund		Random
1985	Teddy Bear Tales		$20	$30	$40	Joan Walsh Anglund		Random
1986	Christmas Is Here		$18	$25	$35	Joan Walsh Anglund		Random
1987	A Book Of Poetry		$18	$25	$35	Joan Walsh Anglund		Random
1987	The Song Of Love		$18	$25	$35	Joan Walsh Anglund		Scribnr
1988	Christmas Is Love		$18	$25	$35	Joan Walsh Anglund		HBJ
1988	How Many Days Has Baby To Play?		$18	$25	$35	Joan Walsh Anglund		HBJ
1989	A Little Book Of Poems & Prayers		$18	$25	$35	Joan Walsh Anglund		S&S
1990	Crocus In The Snow: A Book Of Poems		$14	$20	$25	Joan Walsh Anglund		Random
1991	A Mother Goose Book		$14	$20	$25	Joan Walsh Anglund		HBJ
1992	A Child's Year		$12	$18	$25	Joan Walsh Anglund		Golden
1992	Love Is A Baby		$12	$18	$25	Joan Walsh Anglund		HBJ
1992	The Way Of Love		$12	$18	$25	Joan Walsh Anglund		Random
1993	A Bedtime Book		$12	$18	$25	Joan Walsh Anglund		S&S
1993	A Friend Is Someone Who Likes You		$12	$18	$25	Joan Walsh Anglund		HBJ
1993	Peace Is A Circle Of Love		$12	$18	$25	Joan Walsh Anglund		HBrace
1993	The Friend We Have Not Met		$12	$18	$25	Joan Walsh Anglund		Random
1994	Wings Of Hope: A Book Of Poems		$12	$18	$25	Joan Walsh Anglund		Random
1995	Angels: A Book Of Poems		$12	$16	$20	Joan Walsh Anglund		Random
1995	Joan Walsh Anglund's Mother Goose Pop-Up Book		$12	$16	$20	Joan Walsh Anglund		LSimon
1995	Mother Goose Pop-Up Book		$12	$16	$20	Joan Walsh Anglund		LSimon
1996	Merry Christmas, Baby		$10	$16	$20	Joan Walsh Anglund		Western
1996	Poems Of Childhood		$10	$16	$20	Joan Walsh Anglund		HBrace
1996	Sweet Dreams		$10	$16	$20	Joan Walsh Anglund		LSimon
1997	Love Always Remembers		$10	$16	$20	Joan Walsh Anglund		Random
1997	Love Is Forever		$10	$16	$20	Joan Walsh Anglund		HBJ
1998	A Patchwork Of Love		$10	$16	$20	Joan Walsh Anglund		AM
1998	The Jewels Of The Spirit		$10	$16	$20	Joan Walsh Anglund		AM
1999	A Christmas Alphabet		$10	$14	$18	Joan Walsh Anglund		AM
1999	In All Thy Ways		$10	$14	$18	Joan Walsh Anglund		HShaw
1999	My Busy Day		$10	$14	$18	Joan Walsh Anglund		LSimon
1999	My Busy Year		$10	$14	$18	Joan Walsh Anglund		LSimon
1999	Prayer Is A Gentle Way		$10	$14	$18	Joan Walsh Anglund		HShaw
2000	Be My Friend		$8	$12	$16	Joan Walsh Anglund		LSimon
2000	Between Friends		$8	$12	$16	Joan Walsh Anglund		AM
2000	Happy Birthday		$8	$12	$16	Joan Walsh Anglund		AM
2001	A Christmas Sampler		$8	$12	$16	Joan Walsh Anglund		Harcort
2002	Babies Are A Bit Of Heaven		$8	$12	$16	Joan Walsh Anglund		S&S

Anglund   Joan Walsh

Year	Title	VG-	VG	VG+	Fine	Author	Award	Pub
2002	The Christmas Candy Book		$8	$12	$16	Joan Walsh Anglund		AM
2003	Litte Angels Alphabet Of Love		$8	$10	$14	Joan Walsh Anglund		S&S
2003	The Adventures Of The Brave Cowboy		$8	$10	$14	Joan Walsh Anglund		MLF
2004	Love Is The Best Teacher		$8	$10	$14	Joan Walsh Anglund		AM

Anno   Mitsumasa

Year	Title	VG-	VG	VG+	Fine	Author	Award	Pub
1971	Upside-Downers		$50	$80	$100	E.M. Weatherby		Weather
1972	Dr. Anno's Magical Midnight Circus		$35	$50	$70	Mitsumasa Anno		Weather
1975	Anno's Alphabet		$60	$80	$120	Mitsumasa Anno	NYT	Crowell
1976	In Shadowland		$50	$70	$90	Mitsumasa Anno		Orchard
1977	Anno's Counting Book		$40	$60	$90	Mitsumasa Anno		HCollins
1978	Anno's Journey		$40	$60	$80	Mitsumasa Anno		Collins
1979	Anno's Animals		$30	$50	$60	Mitsumasa Anno		Collins
1979	The King's Flower		$30	$50	$60	Mitsumasa Anno		Collins
1980	Anno's Italy		$30	$50	$60	Mitsumasa Anno		Collins
1980	Anno's Medieval World		$30	$50	$60	Ursula Synge (translated)		Philo
1981	Anno's Magical ABC: An Anamorphic Alphabet		$30	$40	$60	Mitsumasa Anno		Philo
1982	Anno's Britain		$30	$40	$60	Mitsumasa Anno		Philo
1982	Anno's Counting House		$30	$40	$60	Mitsumasa Anno		Philo
1983	Anno's Mysterious Multiplying Jar		$30	$40	$60	Masaichiro Anno		Philo
1983	Anno's U.S.A		$30	$40	$60	Mitsumasa Anno		Philo
1984	Anno's Flea Market		$25	$40	$50	Mitsumasa Anno		Philo
1985	Anno's Hat Tricks		$25	$40	$50	Akihiro Nozaki		Philo
1986	Socrates And The Three Little Pigs		$18	$25	$35	Tuyosi Mori		Philo
1987	Anno's Math Games		$18	$25	$35	Mitsumasa Anno		Philo
1987	Anno's Sundial		$18	$25	$35	Mitsumasa Anno		Philo
1988	Anno's Peekaboo		$18	$25	$35	Mitsumasa Anno		Philo
1988	In Shadowland		$18	$25	$35	Mitsumasa Anno		Orchard
1989	Anno's Aesop: A Book Of Fables		$18	$25	$35	Aesop		Orchard
1989	Anno's Faces		$18	$25	$35	Mitsumasa Anno		Philo
1989	Topsy-Turvies		$18	$25	$35	Mitsumasa Anno		Weather
1990	Anno's Masks		$16	$25	$30	Mitsumasa Anno		Philo
1991	Anno's Math Games III		$16	$25	$30	Mitsumasa Anno		Philo
1992	The Animals: Selected Poems		$16	$25	$30	Michio Mado		McEld
1993	Anno's Twice Told Tales		$14	$20	$30	Jacob & Wilhelm Grimm		Philo
1995	Anno's Magic Seeds		$12	$18	$25	Mitsumasa Anno		Philo
1998	The Magic Pocket		$12	$16	$20	Michio Mado		McEld
2004	Anno's Spain		$8	$10	$14	Mitsumasa Anno		Philo

Ardizzone   Edward

Year	Title	VG-	VG	VG+	Fine	Author	Award	Pub
1929	In A Glass Darkly	$380	$500	$620		Sheridan Le Fanu		PDavies
1936	Little Tim And The Brave Sea Captain	$960	$1,200	$1,600		Edward Ardizzone		Oxford
1939	My Uncle Silas	$320	$440	$540		H. E Bates		JCape
1939	The Local	$520	$680	$860		Maurice Gorham		Cassel
1946	Peacock Pie	$200	$260	$320		Walter De La Mare		Faber
1947	Nicholas and the Fast Moving Diesel	$280	$380	$480		Edward Ardizzone		E&S
1948	Paul The Hero of the Fire	$280	$380	$480		Edward Ardizzone		Penguin
1948	The Otterbury Incident	$120	$160	$220		C. Day Lewis		World
1949	Tim To The Rescue	$280	$360	$460		Edward Ardizzone		Oxford
1951	Tim And Charlotte	$180	$240	$300		Edward Ardizzone		Oxford
1952	The Blackbird In The Lilac	$120	$160	$200		James Reeves		Oxford
1953	Tim In Danger	$260	$360	$440		Edward Ardizzone		Oxford
1954	That Yew Tree's Shade	$120	$160	$200		Cyril Hare		Faber
1955	The Little Bookroom	$100	$140	$180		Eleanor Farjeon		Oxford
1956	Tim All Alone	$280	$380	$480		Edward Ardizzone	GM	Oxford
1957	Ding Dong Bell	$80	$120	$140		Percy Marshall Young		Dobson
1957	Prefabulous Animiles	$80	$120	$140		James Reeves		Heine
1957	Sugar For The Horse	$80	$120	$140		H. E Bates		MJoseph
1957	The Boy Down Kitchener Street	$80	$120	$140		Leslie Allen Paul		Faber
1958	Jim At The Corner	$80	$120	$140		Eleanor Farjeon		Walck
1958	Pinky Pye	$80	$120	$140		Eleanor Estes		HBrace
1958	The Minnow Leads To Treasure	$80	$120	$140		Philippa Pearce		Gregg
1958	Tim & Lucy Go To Sea	$120	$160	$220		Edward Ardizzone		Walck
1959	Elfrida And The Pig	$80	$120	$140		John Symonds		Harrap

Ardizzone　　　Edward

Year	Title	VG-	VG	VG+	Fine	Author	Award	Pub
1959	Nicholas And The Fast-Moving Diesel	$180	$240	$300		Edward Ardizzone		Walck
1959	The Godstone and the Blackmore	$120	$160	$200		T. H. White		Putnam
1960	Italian Peepshow	$80	$100	$140		Eleanor Farjeon		Walck
1960	Johnny The Clockmaker	$120	$160	$200		Edward Ardizzone		Walck
1960	Merry England	$80	$100	$140		Cyril Ray		Vista
1960	The Witch Family	$80	$100	$140		Eleanor Estes		HBJ
1960	Titus In Trouble	$80	$100	$140		James Reeves		Walck
1961	Down In The Cellar	$80	$100	$140		Nicholas Stuart Gray		Dobson
1962	Mrs. Malone	$80	$100	$140		Eleanor Farjeon		Walck
1962	Peter Pan	$80	$100	$140		J. M. Barrie		Scribnr
1962	Tim's Friend Towser	$120	$160	$200		Edward Ardizzone		Walck
1963	A Ring of Bells	$80	$100	$140		John Betjemin		HM
1963	Kaleidoscope	$80	$100	$140		Eleanor Farjeon		Walck
1964	Ann At Highwood Hall	$70	$100	$120		Robert Graves		Cassel
1964	Diana And Her Rhinoceros	$70	$100	$120		Edward Ardizzone		Walck
1964	Hello, Elephant	$70	$100	$120		Jan Wahl		HR&W
1964	Nurse Matilda	$100	$140	$180		Christianna Brand		Brock
1964	Peter The Wanderer	$70	$100	$120		Edward Ardizzone		Walck
1964	The Land of Right Up and Down	$140	$180	$240		Eva-Lis Wuorio		World
1964	The Thirty-Nine Steps	$70	$100	$120		John Buchan		Dent
1965	The Old Nurse's Stocking-Basket	$70	$100	$120		Eleanor Farjeon		Walck
1965	Tim And Ginger	$70	$100	$120		Edward Ardizzone		Walck
1966	A Book For Eleanor Farjeon	$70	$100	$120		Eleanor Farjeon		Walck
1966	Ann At Highwood Hall	$70	$100	$120		Robert Graves		DoubleD
1966	Long Ago When I Was Young	$70	$100	$120		Edith Nesbit		FWatts
1966	Sarah And Simon And No Red Paint	$70	$100	$120		Edward Ardizzone		DelaP
1966	The Eleanor Farjeon Book	$70	$100	$120		Eleanor Farjeon		HHamil
1966	The Land Of Green Ginger	$70	$100	$120		Noel Langley		Penguin
1966	The Muffletumps	$70	$100	$120		Jan Wahl		HR&W
1966	The Secret Shoemakers	$70	$100	$120		James Reeves		AS
1966	Timothy's Song	$70	$100	$120		William J. Lederer		Lutten
1967	Kali And The Golden Mirror	$70	$90	$120		Eva-Lis Wuorio		World
1967	Miranda The Great	$70	$90	$120		Eleanor Estes		HBrace
1967	The Dragon	$70	$90	$120		Archibald Marshall		Dutton
1967	The Little Girl And The Tiny Doll	$70	$90	$120		Aingelda Ardizzone		DelaP
1967	The Magic Summer	$70	$90	$120		Noel Streatfeild		Random
1968	A Likely Place	$70	$90	$120		Paula Fox		Macmil
1968	Nurse Matilda Goes To Town	$70	$90	$120		Christianna Brand		Dutton
1968	Rhyming Will	$70	$90	$120		James Reeves		McHill
1968	Robinson Crusoe	$70	$90	$120		Daniel Defoe		FWatts
1968	The Truants, & Other Poems	$70	$90	$120		J. H Walsh		RandMc
1968	Tim To The Lighthouse	$70	$90	$120		Edward Ardizzone		Walck
1969	A Riot Of Quiet	$70	$90	$120		Virginia Sicotte		HR&W
1969	Special Branch Willie	$70	$90	$120		Dorothy Clewes		HHamil
1970	Dick Whittington		$60	$80	$120	Kathleen Lines		Walck
1970	Fire-Brigade Willie		$60	$80	$120	Dorothy Clewes		HHamil
1970	The Angel And The Donkey		$60	$80	$120	James Reeves		McHill
1970	The Wrong Side Of The Bed		$60	$80	$120	Edward Ardizzone		DoubleD
1971	How The Moon Began		$50	$80	$100	James Reeves		AS
1971	Lucy Brown And Mr. Grimes		$80	$120	$160	Edward Ardizzone		Walck
1971	The Tunnel Of Hugsy Goode		$50	$80	$100	Eleanor Estes		HBJ
1972	Rain, Rain, Don't Go Away		$50	$80	$100	Shirley Morgan		Dutton
1972	The Old Ballad Of The Babes In The Wood		$50	$80	$100	Edward Ardizzone		Walck
1972	The Second-Best Children In The World		$50	$80	$100	Mary Lavin		HM
1973	Complete Poems		$50	$80	$100	James Reeves		Heine
1973	The Little Fire Engine		$70	$100	$140	Graham Greene		DoubleD
1973	Tim's Last Voyage		$70	$100	$140	Edward Ardizzone		Walck
1974	The Little Horse Bus		$50	$70	$100	Graham Greene		DoubleD
1974	The Little Steamroller		$50	$70	$100	Graham Greene		DoubleD
1974	The Little Train		$50	$70	$100	Graham Greene		DoubleD
1975	More Prefabulous Animiles		$50	$70	$90	James Reeves		Heine
1975	The Night Ride		$50	$70	$90	Aingelda Ardizzone		Windmil
1976	Ardizzone's Kilvert		$50	$70	$90	Robert Francis Kilvert		JCape
1977	Exploits Of Don Quixote		$40	$60	$90	James Reeves		Black
1977	Stories From The Bible		$40	$60	$90	Walter De La Mare		Faber
1978	Arcadian Ballads		$40	$60	$90	James Reeves		Heine
1978	Ship's Cook Ginger		$40	$60	$90	Edward Ardizzone		Macmil

Ardizzone   Edward

Year	Title	VG-	VG	VG+	Fine	Author	Award	Pub
1978	The James Reeves Story Book		$40	$60	$90	James Reeves		Heine
1979	Ardizzone's Hans Andersen		$40	$60	$80	Hans Christian Andersen		Athenm
1979	The Nine Lives Of Island Mackenzie		$40	$60	$80	Ursula Moray Williams		C&Weed
1980	A Child's Christmas In Wales		$40	$60	$80	Dylan Thomas		Godine
1980	Ardizzone's English Fairy Tales		$40	$60	$80	Joseph Jacobs		Deutsch
1984	The Little Bookworm		$50	$80	$100	Eleanor Farjeon		Godine
2000	Minnow On The Say		$14	$20	$25	Philippa Pearce		Green
2003	The Alley		$10	$16	$20	Eleanor Estes		Harcort

Armer   Laura Adams

Year	Title	VG-	VG	VG+	Fine	Author	Award	Pub
1931	Waterless Mountain	$720	$960	$1,200		Laura Adams Armer	NM	Longman
1933	Dark Circle Of Branches	$100	$140	$180		Laura Adams Armer		Longman
1935	Southwest	$100	$140	$180		Laura Adams Armer		Longman
1937	The Trader's Children	$100	$140	$180		Laura Adams Armer		Longman
1938	The Forest Pool	$180	$240	$300		Laura Adams Armer	CH	Longman

Arnold   Tedd

Year	Title	VG-	VG	VG+	Fine	Author	Award	Pub
1985	Colors		$25	$35	$50	Tedd Arnold		LSimon
1985	Opposites		$25	$35	$50	Tedd Arnold		LSimon
1985	Sounds		$25	$35	$50	Tedd Arnold		LSimon
1986	Looking For Zebra		$16	$25	$30	Ron Atlas		LSimon
1986	My First Drawing Book		$16	$25	$30	Tedd Arnold		Workman
1987	A Room For Benny		$16	$25	$30	Ron Atlas		LSimon
1987	No Jumping On The Bed!		$16	$25	$30	Tedd Arnold		Dial
1988	My First Baking Book		$16	$25	$30	Rena Coyle		Workman
1988	Ollie Forgot		$16	$25	$30	Tedd Arnold		Dial
1989	My First Camera Book		$16	$25	$30	Anne Kostick		Workman
1990	Cross Stitch Patterns For Mother Goose's		$12	$18	$25	Tedd Arnold		Dutton
1990	Mother Goose's Words Of Wit And Wisdom		$12	$18	$25	Tedd Arnold		Dial
1991	My First Computer Book		$12	$18	$25	D. Schiller		Workman
1992	My First Garden Book		$12	$18	$25	Carole Ottesen		Workman
1992	The Signmaker's Assistant		$12	$18	$25	Tedd Arnold		Dial
1993	Green Wilma		$12	$16	$20	Tedd Arnold		Dial
1993	Inside A Barn In The Country		$12	$16	$20	Alyssa Satin Capucilli		Scholas
1994	My Working Mom		$12	$16	$20	Peter Glassman		Morrow
1994	The Roly- Poly Spider		$12	$16	$20	Jill Sardegna		Scholas
1995	Five Ugly Monsters		$10	$16	$20	Tedd Arnold		Scholas
1995	No More Water In The Tub!		$10	$16	$20	Tedd Arnold		Dial
1996	Bialosky's Bedtime		$10	$14	$18	Tedd Arnold		Workman
1996	Bialosky's Big Mess		$10	$14	$18	Tedd Arnold		Workman
1996	Bialosky's Bumblebees		$10	$14	$18	Tedd Arnold		Workman
1996	Bialosky's House		$10	$14	$18	Tedd Arnold		Workman
1996	Tracks		$10	$14	$18	David Galef		Morrow
1997	Huggly Gets Dressed		$10	$14	$18	Tedd Arnold		Cart
1997	My Dog Never Says Please		$10	$14	$18	Tedd Arnold		Dial
1997	Parts		$10	$14	$18	Tedd Arnold		Dial
1998	Huggly And The Toy Monster		$8	$12	$16	Tedd Arnold		Cart
1998	Huggly Takes A Bath		$8	$12	$16	Tedd Arnold		Cart
1998	In The Haunted House On The Hill		$8	$12	$16	Alyssa Satin Capucilli		Scholas
1999	Axle Annie		$8	$12	$16	Robin Pulver		Dial
2000	Huggly's Pizza		$8	$10	$14	Tedd Arnold		Cart
2000	Inside A Zoo In The City		$8	$10	$14	Alyssa Satin Capucilli		Cart
2001	Huggly's Big Mess		$8	$10	$14	Tedd Arnold		Cart
2001	Huggly's Christmas		$8	$10	$14	Tedd Arnold		Cart
2001	More Parts		$8	$10	$14	Tedd Arnold		Dial
2002	Giant Children		$8	$10	$14	Brod Bagert		Dial
2002	Huggly's Snow Day		$8	$10	$14	Tedd Arnold		Cart
2002	Huggly's Thanksgiving Parade		$8	$10	$14	Tedd Arnold		Scholas
2002	Huggly's Trip To The Beach		$8	$10	$14	Tedd Arnold		Cart
2003	Huggly Goes Camping		$8	$10	$14	Tedd Arnold		Cart
2003	Huggly's Valentines		$8	$10	$14	Tedd Arnold		Cart
2003	Lasso Lou And Cowboy Mccoy		$8	$10	$14	Barbara Larmon Failing		Dial
2004	Catalina Magdalena		$6	$10	$12	Tedd Arnold		Cart
2004	Even More Parts		$6	$10	$12	Tedd Arnold		Dial

Arnosky   Jim

Year	Title	VG-	VG	VG+	Fine	Author	Award	Pub
1976	Chicken Forgets		$40	$60	$80	Miska Miles		LBrown
1976	Fitting In		$30	$40	$60	Melvin & Gilda Berger		CM&G
1976	Swim, Little Duck		$40	$60	$80	Miska Miles		LBrown
1977	I Was Born In A Tree And Raised By Bees		$25	$35	$50	Jim Arnosky		Putnam
1977	Look! How Your Eyes See		$25	$35	$50	Marcel J. Sislowitz		Coward
1977	Small Rabbit		$25	$35	$50	Miska Miles		LBrown
1978	Nathaniel		$25	$35	$50	Jim Arnosky		AW
1978	Outdoors On Foot		$25	$35	$50	Jim Arnosky		CM&G
1978	Porcupine Baby		$25	$35	$50	Berniece Freschet		Putnam
1978	Possum Baby		$25	$35	$50	Berniece Freschet		Putnam
1979	A Kettle Of Hawks		$20	$30	$40	Jim Arnosky		CM&G
1979	Crinkleroot's Book Of Animal Tracks		$20	$30	$40	Jim Arnosky		Putnam
1979	Delta Baby & 2 Sea Songs		$20	$30	$40	Richard Kennedy		AW
1979	Joel And The Great Merlini		$20	$30	$40	Eloise Jarvis McGraw		Pan
1979	Moose Baby		$20	$30	$40	Berniece Freschet		Putnam
1979	Mud Time And More		$20	$30	$40	Jim Arnosky		AW
1979	The Covered Bridge House & Other Poems		$20	$30	$40	Kaye Starbird		4Winds
1980	Bear Underground		$16	$25	$30	Betty V, Boegehold		DoubleD
1980	The Year Of The Apple		$16	$25	$30	Michael New		AW
1980	What's That You Said?		$16	$25	$30	Ann E. Weiss		HBJ
1981	Black Bear Baby		$16	$25	$30	Berniece Freschet		Putnam
1981	Chipper's Choices		$16	$25	$30	Betty V, Boegehold		CM&G
1981	Raindrop Stories		$16	$25	$30	P. Bassett & M.F. Bartlett		4Winds
1981	Rocky The Cat		$16	$25	$30	A. R. Swinnerton		AW
1981	Shadow Bear		$16	$25	$30	Joan Hiatt. Harlow		DoubleD
1981	Up A Tall Tree		$16	$25	$30	Anne F. Rockwell		DoubleD
1982	Drawing From Nature		$14	$20	$30	Jim Arnosky		LL&S
1982	Freshwater Fish & Fishing		$14	$20	$30	Jim Arnosky		4Winds
1982	Mouse Numbers & Letters		$14	$20	$30	Jim Arnosky		HBJ
1983	A Passion In The Desert		$14	$20	$30	Honoré de Balzac		Creat
1983	Mouse Writing		$14	$20	$30	Jim Arnosky		HBJ
1983	Secrets Of A Wildlife Watcher		$14	$20	$30	Jim Arnosky		LL&S
1983	Wood Duck Baby		$14	$20	$30	Berniece Freschet		Putnam
1984	Drawing Life In Motion		$14	$20	$30	Jim Arnosky		LL&S
1984	Raccoon Baby		$14	$20	$30	Berniece Freschet		Putnam
1985	Watching Foxes		$16	$25	$30	Jim Arnosky		LL&S
1986	Deer At The Brook		$14	$20	$30	Jim Arnosky		LL&S
1986	Flies In The Water, Fish In The Air		$14	$20	$30	Jim Arnosky		LL&S
1987	Raccoons And Ripe Corn		$14	$20	$30	Jim Arnosky		LL&S
1987	Sketching Outdoors In Spring		$14	$20	$30	Jim Arnosky		LL&S
1988	Gray Boy		$14	$20	$30	Jim Arnosky		LL&S
1988	Sketching Outdoors In Autumn		$14	$20	$30	Jim Arnosky		LL&S
1988	Sketching Outdoors In Summer		$14	$20	$30	Jim Arnosky		LL&S
1988	Sketching Outdoors In Winter		$14	$20	$30	Jim Arnosky		LL&S
1989	Come Out, Muskrats		$14	$20	$25	Jim Arnosky		LL&S
1989	Crinkleroot's Book Of Animal Tracking		$14	$20	$25	Jim Arnosky		BradP
1989	In The Forest		$14	$20	$25	Jim Arnosky		LL&S
1990	Crinkleroot's Guide To Walking In Wild Places		$10	$14	$18	Jim Arnosky		BradP
1991	Fish In A Flash!		$10	$14	$18	Jim Arnosky		BradP
1991	The Empty Lot		$10	$14	$18	Dale Fife		Sierra
1992	Crinkleroot's Guide To Knowing The Birds		$10	$14	$18	Jim Arnosky		BradP
1992	Crinkleroot's Guide To Knowing The Trees		$10	$14	$18	Jim Arnosky		BradP
1992	Long Spikes		$10	$14	$18	Jim Arnosky		Clarion
1992	Otters Under Water		$10	$14	$18	Jim Arnosky		Putnam
1993	Crinkleroot's 25 Birds Every Child Should Know		$10	$14	$18	Jim Arnosky		BradP
1993	Crinkleroot's 25 Fish Every Child Should Know		$10	$14	$18	Jim Arnosky		BradP
1993	Every Autumn Comes The Bear		$10	$14	$18	Jim Arnosky		Putnam
1993	Sketching Outdoors In All Seasons		$10	$14	$18	Jim Arnosky		Country
1994	All About Alligators		$10	$14	$18	Jim Arnosky		Scholas
1994	All Night Near The Water		$10	$14	$18	Jim Arnosky		Putnam
1994	Crinkleroot's 25 Mammals Every Child Should Know		$10	$14	$18	Jim Arnosky		BradP
1994	Crinkleroot's 25 More Animals Every Child Should Know		$10	$14	$18	Jim Arnosky		BradP
1995	All About Owls		$8	$12	$16	Jim Arnosky		Scholas
1995	I See Animals Hiding		$8	$10	$14	Jim Arnosky		Scholas
1995	Little Champ		$8	$10	$14	Jim Arnosky		Putnam
1996	All About Deer		$8	$10	$14	Jim Arnosky		Scholas
1996	Crinkleroot's Guide To Knowing Butterflies & Moths		$8	$10	$14	Jim Arnosky		S&S

Arnosky   Jim

Year	Title	VG-	VG	VG+	Fine	Author	Award	Pub
1996	Nearer Nature		$8	$10	$14	Jim Arnosky		LL&S
1997	All About Rattlesnakes		$8	$10	$14	Jim Arnosky		Scholas
1997	Bring 'Em Back Alive!		$8	$10	$14	Jim Arnosky		LBrown
1997	Crinkleroot's Guide To Knowing Animal Habitats		$8	$10	$14	Jim Arnosky		S&S
1997	Rabbits And Raindrops		$8	$10	$14	Jim Arnosky		Putnam
1997	Watching Water Birds		$8	$10	$14	Jim Arnosky		NGS
1998	All About Turkeys		$8	$10	$14	Jim Arnosky		Scholas
1998	Crinkleroot's Visit To Crinkle Cove		$8	$10	$14	Jim Arnosky		S&S
1998	Little Lions		$8	$10	$14	Jim Arnosky		Putnam
1998	Watching Desert Wildlife		$8	$10	$14	Jim Arnosky		NGS
1999	Arnosky's Ark		$8	$10	$14	Jim Arnosky		NGS
1999	Big Jim And The White Legged Moose		$8	$10	$14	Jim Arnosky		LL&S
1999	Crinkleroot's Nature Almanac		$8	$10	$14	Jim Arnosky		S&S
1999	Mouse Letters		$8	$10	$14	Jim Arnosky		Clarion
1999	Mouse Numbers		$8	$10	$14	Jim Arnosky		Clarion
2000	A Manatee Morning		$6	$10	$12	Jim Arnosky		S&S
2000	All About Turtles		$6	$10	$12	Jim Arnosky		Scholas
2000	Beaver Pond, Moose Pond		$6	$10	$12	Jim Arnosky		NGS
2000	Rattlesnake Dance		$6	$10	$12	Jim Arnosky		Putnam
2000	Wild And Swampy		$6	$10	$12	Jim Arnosky		HCollins
2001	Mouse Colors		$6	$10	$12	Jim Arnosky		Clarion
2001	Mouse Shapes		$6	$10	$12	Jim Arnosky		Clarion
2001	Raccoon On His Own		$6	$10	$12	Jim Arnosky		Putnam
2001	Wolves		$6	$10	$12	Jim Arnosky		NGS
2002	All About Frogs		$6	$10	$12	Jim Arnosky		Scholas
2002	Field Trips		$6	$10	$12	Jim Arnosky		HCollins
2002	Turtle In The Sea		$6	$10	$12	Jim Arnosky		Putnam
2002	Wild Ponies		$6	$10	$12	Jim Arnosky		NGS
2003	All About Sharks		$6	$10	$12	Jim Arnosky		Scholas
2003	Armadillo's Orange		$6	$10	$12	Jim Arnosky		Putnam
2004	All About Lizards		$6	$10	$12	Jim Arnosky		Scholas
2004	Beachcombing		$6	$10	$12	Jim Arnosky		Dutton
2004	Following The Coast		$6	$10	$12	Jim Arnosky		HCollins

Artzybasheff   Boris

Year	Title	VG-	VG	VG+	Fine	Author	Award	Pub
1927	Gay-Neck	$320	$440	$540		Dhan Gopal Mukerji	NM	Dutton
1927	The Wonder Smith And His Son	$140	$180	$220		Ella Young		Longman
1928	Ghond, The Hunter	$80	$100	$140		Dhan Gopal Mukerji		Dutton
1929	Three And The Moon	$80	$100	$140		Jacques Dorey		Knopf
1931	Poor Shaydullah	$70	$100	$120		Boris Artzybasheff		Macmil
1932	White Horses	$70	$100	$120		Hugh Chisholm		Ashlar
1933	Aesop's Fables	$70	$100	$120		Aesop		Viking
1934	Son Of The Sword	$70	$100	$120		Youel B. Mirza		Viking
1935	The Circus Of Dr. Lao	$70	$100	$120		Charles G. Finney		Viking
1936	Black Thunder	$70	$100	$120		Arna W. Bontemps		Macmil
1937	Seven Simeons	$160	$200	$260		Boris Artzybasheff	CH	Viking
1940	Nansen	$70	$90	$120		Anna Gertrude Hall		Viking
1941	Let George Do It!	$70	$90	$120		Boris Artzybasheff		AIG
1942	The Tree Of Life	$70	$90	$120		Ruth Smith		Viking

Aruego   José

Year	Title	VG-	VG	VG+	Fine	Author	Award	Pub
1969	The King And His Friends	$25	$30	$40		José Aruego		Scribnr
1969	Whose Mouse Are You?	$25	$30	$40		Robert Kraus		Macmil
1970	Juan And The Asuangs		$16	$25	$30	José Aruego		Scribnr
1970	Parakeets And Peach Pies		$16	$25	$30	Aruego Kay		PMagP
1970	Symbiosis: A Book Of Unusual Friendships		$16	$25	$30	José Aruego		Scribnr
1970	Toucans Two, & Other Poems		$16	$25	$30	Jack Prelutsky		Macmil
1971	Leo The Late Bloomer		$16	$25	$30	Robert Kraus		Windmil
1971	Look What I Can Do		$16	$25	$30	José Aruego		Scribnr
1971	Pilyo The Piranha		$16	$25	$30	José Aruego		Macmil
1971	The Day They Parachuted Cats On Borneo		$16	$25	$30	Charlotte Pomerantz		YScott
1971	What Is Pink?		$16	$25	$30	Christina Georgina Rossetti		Macmil
1971	Zoo Doings, & Other Poems		$16	$25	$30	Jack Prelutsky		HHamil
1972	Good Night		$16	$25	$30	Elizabeth Coatsworth		Macmil

Aruego   José

Year	Title	VG-	VG	VG+	Fine	Author	Award	Pub
1979	Never Say Ugh To A Bug		$14	$20	$25	Norma Farber		Green

Aruego   José (w/Ariane Dewey)

Year	Title	VG-	VG	VG+	Fine	Author	Award	Pub
1972	A Crocodile's Tale		$16	$25	$30	José Aruego		Scribnr
1972	Milton The Early Riser		$16	$25	$30	Robert Kraus		Windmil
1972	The Chick And The Duckling		$16	$25	$30	Mirra Ginsburg		Macmil
1973	Herman The Helper		$16	$25	$30	Robert Kraus		Windmil
1974	Marie Louise & Christophe		$16	$25	$30	Natalie Carlson		Scribnr
1974	Mushroom In The Rain		$16	$25	$30	Mirra Ginsburg		Macmil
1974	Owliver		$16	$25	$30	Robert Kraus		Windmil
1975	How The Sun Was Brought Back To The Sky		$14	$20	$30	Mirra Ginsburg		Macmil
1975	Marie Louise's Heyday		$14	$20	$30	Natalie Carlson		Scribnr
1975	Sea Frog, City Frog		$14	$20	$30	Dorothy Van Woerkom		Macmil
1975	Three Friends		$14	$20	$30	Robert Kraus		Windmil
1976	Boris Bad Enough		$14	$20	$25	Robert Kraus		S&S
1976	Two Greedy Bears		$14	$20	$25	Mirra Ginsburg		Macmil
1977	If Dragon Flies Made Honey		$14	$20	$25	David Kherdian		Green
1977	Noel The Coward		$14	$20	$25	Robert Kraus		Windmil
1977	Runaway Marie Louise		$14	$20	$25	Natalie Carlson		Scribnr
1977	The Strongest One Of All		$14	$20	$25	Mirra Ginsburg		Green
1978	Mitchell Is Moving		$14	$20	$25	Marjorie Weinman Sharmat		Macmil
1978	Rum Pum Pum		$14	$20	$25	Maggie Duff		Macmil
1979	Musical Max		$14	$20	$25	Robert Kraus		Windmil
1979	We Hide, You Seek		$14	$20	$25	José Aruego		Green
1980	Animal Families		$12	$18	$25	Robert Kraus		Windmil
1980	Another Mouse To Feed		$12	$18	$25	Robert Kraus		Windmil
1980	Gregory, The Terrible Eater		$12	$18	$25	Mitchell Sharmat		4Winds
1980	Mert The Blurt		$12	$18	$25	Robert Kraus		Windmil
1980	Mouse Work		$12	$18	$25	Robert Kraus		Windmil
1981	Lizard's Song		$12	$18	$25	George Shannon		Green
1981	Marie Louise & Christophe At The Carnival		$12	$18	$25	Natalie Carlson		Scribnr
1981	Where Does The Sun Go At Night?		$12	$18	$25	Mirra Ginsburg		Green
1982	Dance Away		$12	$18	$25	George Shannon		Green
1983	The Surprise		$12	$16	$20	George Shannon		Green
1984	One Duck, Another Duck		$12	$16	$20	Charlotte Pomerantz		Green
1986	Where Are You Going, Little Mouse		$10	$16	$20	Robert Kraus		Green
1986	Where Are You Going, Little Mouse?		$10	$16	$20	Robert Kraus		Green
1987	Alligator Arrived With Apples		$10	$16	$20	Crescent Dragonwagon		Macmil
1987	Come Out And Play, Little Mouse		$10	$16	$20	Robert Kraus		Green
1988	Rockabye Crocodile		$10	$14	$18	José Aruego		Green
1989	Five Little Ducks		$10	$14	$18	Raffi		Crown
1989	Pork And Beans		$10	$14	$18	Jovial Bob Stine		Scholas
1992	Merry-Go-Round		$8	$12	$16	Mirra Ginsburg		Green
1993	Alligators & Others All Year Long!		$8	$12	$16	Crescent Dragonwagon		Macmil
1993	Birthday Rhymes, Special Times		$8	$12	$16	Bobbye S. Goldstein		DelaP
1995	April Showers		$8	$10	$14	George Shannon		Green
1996	They Thought They Saw Him		$8	$10	$14	Craig Strete		Green
1997	Star Of The Circus		$8	$10	$14	Michael R. Sampson		Holt
1998	Antarctic Antics		$8	$10	$14	Judy Sierra		HBrace
1998	Little Louie The Baby Bloomer		$8	$10	$14	Robert Kraus		HCollins
1999	Lizard's Home		$8	$10	$14	George Shannon		Green
1999	Safe, Warm, And Snug		$8	$10	$14	Stephen R. Swinburne		HBrace
2000	Mouse In Love		$6	$10	$12	Robert Kraus		Orchard
2000	The Big, Big Wall		$6	$10	$12	Reginald Howard		Harcort
2001	How Chipmunk Got His Stripes		$6	$10	$12	Joséph & James Bruchac		Dial
2001	Splash!		$6	$10	$12	Ariane Dewey		Harcort
2002	Rosa Raposa		$6	$10	$12	F. Isabel Campoy		Harcort
2002	The Littlest Wolf		$6	$10	$12	Larry Dane Brimner		HCollins
2002	Weird Friends		$6	$10	$12	José Aruego		Harcort
2003	Lizard's Guest		$6	$10	$12	George Shannon		Green
2003	Turtle's Race With Beaver		$6	$10	$12	Joséph & James Bruchac		Dial
2004	Duck, Duck, Goose		$6	$10	$12	Karen Beaumont		HCollins
2004	Raccoon's Last Race		$6	$10	$12	Joséph & James Bruchac		Dial

Asch   Frank

Year	Title	VG-	VG	VG+	Fine	Author	Award	Pub
1968	George's Store	$60	$80	$100		Frank Asch		McHill
1969	Linda	$60	$80	$100		Frank Asch		McHill
1970	Elvira Everything		$70	$100	$140	Frank Asch		H&Row
1971	Blue Balloon		$40	$60	$90	Frank Asch		McHill
1972	Rebecka		$30	$50	$60	Frank Asch		H&Row
1973	In the Eye of the Teddy		$30	$50	$60	Frank Asch		H&Row
1974	Gia And The One Hundred Dollars Worth Of Bubblegum		$30	$40	$60	Frank Asch		McHill
1977	Monkey Face		$25	$35	$50	Frank Asch		PMagP
1977	The Inside Kid		$25	$35	$50	Lise Gladstone		McHill
1978	City Sandwich		$25	$35	$50	Frank Asch		Green
1978	Moon Bear		$25	$35	$50	Frank Asch		Scribnr
1978	Sand Cake		$25	$35	$50	Frank Asch		PMagP
1978	Turtle Tale		$25	$35	$50	Frank Asch		Dial
1979	Country Pie		$20	$30	$40	Frank Asch		Green
1979	Little Devil's 1, 2, 3		$20	$30	$40	Frank Asch		Scribnr
1979	Little Devil's ABC		$20	$30	$40	Frank Asch		Scribnr
1979	Popcorn		$20	$30	$40	Frank Asch		PMagP
1980	Starbaby		$18	$25	$35	Frank Asch		Scribnr
1980	The Last Puppy		$18	$25	$35	Frank Asch		P-Hall
1981	Bread And Honey		$16	$25	$30	Frank Asch		PMagP
1981	Goodnight Horsey		$16	$25	$30	Frank Asch		P-Hall
1981	Just Like Daddy		$16	$25	$30	Frank Asch		P-Hall
1982	Happy Birthday, Moon		$16	$25	$30	Frank Asch		P-Hall
1982	Milk And Cookies		$16	$25	$30	Frank Asch		PMagP
1983	Mooncake		$16	$25	$30	Frank Asch		P-Hall
1984	Moongame		$16	$25	$30	Frank Asch		P-Hall
1984	Pearl's Promise		$16	$25	$30	Frank Asch		DelaP
1984	Skyfire		$16	$25	$30	Frank Asch		P-Hall
1985	Bear Shadow		$12	$18	$25	Frank Asch		P-Hall
1985	Bear's Bargain		$12	$18	$25	Frank Asch		P-Hall
1986	Goodbye House		$12	$18	$25	Frank Asch		P-Hall
1986	I Can Blink		$12	$18	$25	Frank Asch		Crown
1986	I Can Roar		$12	$18	$25	Frank Asch		Crown
1987	Pearl's Pirates		$12	$18	$25	Frank Asch		DelaP
1988	Oats And Wild Apples		$12	$18	$25	Frank Asch		Holiday
1989	Baby In The Box		$12	$16	$20	Frank Asch		Holiday
1989	Journey To Terezor		$12	$16	$20	Frank Asch		Holiday
1992	Dear Brother		$25	$35	$50	Vladimir Vagin		Scholas
1992	Little Fish, Big Fish		$10	$16	$20	Frank Asch		Scholas
1992	Short Train, Long Train		$10	$16	$20	Frank Asch		Scholas
1993	Moonbear's Canoe		$10	$16	$20	Frank Asch		LSimon
1993	Moonbear's Friend		$10	$16	$20	Frank Asch		LSimon
1993	Moondance		$10	$16	$20	Frank Asch		Scholas
1994	Hands Around Lincoln School		$10	$16	$20	Frank Asch		Scholas
1994	The Earth And I		$10	$16	$20	Frank Asch		GB
1995	Water		$10	$14	$18	Frank Asch		HBrace
1997	Moonbear's Pet		$10	$14	$18	Frank Asch		S&S
1998	Barnyard Lullaby		$8	$12	$16	Frank Asch		S&S
1998	Good Night, Baby Bear		$8	$12	$16	Frank Asch		HBrace
1998	Goodnight, Baby Bear		$8	$12	$16	Frank Asch		HBrace
1999	Baby Bird's First Nest		$8	$12	$16	Frank Asch		GB
1999	Moonbear's Dream		$8	$12	$16	Frank Asch		S&S
2000	The Sun Is My Favorite Star		$8	$10	$14	Frank Asch		HBrace
2001	Baby Duck's New Friend		$8	$10	$14	Devin Asch		HBrace
2002	Like A Windy Day		$8	$10	$14	Devin Asch		Harcort
2003	The Sun, The Moon, And The Stars		$8	$10	$14	Nancy Elizabeth Wallace		HM

Ashforth   Camilla

Year	Title	VG-	VG	VG+	Fine	Author	Award	Pub
1992	Horatio's Bed		$10	$16	$20	Camilla Ashforth		Candle
1992	Monkey Tricks		$10	$16	$20	Camilla Ashforth		Candle
1993	Calamity		$10	$16	$20	Camilla Ashforth		Candle
1995	Humphrey Thud		$10	$14	$18	Camilla Ashforth		Candle
1996	Baby's Book Of Favorite Things		$10	$14	$18	Camilla Ashforth		Candle
1999	Who Do You Love?		$8	$12	$16	Martin Waddell		Candle
2002	Willow At Christmas		$8	$10	$14	Camilla Ashforth		Candle

Ashforth   Camilla

Year	Title	VG-	VG	VG+	Fine	Author	Award	Pub
2002	Willow By The Sea		$8	$10	$14	Camilla Ashforth		Candle
2002	Willow On The River		$8	$10	$14	Camilla Ashforth		Candle

Atkinson   Allen

Year	Title	VG-	VG	VG+	Fine	Author	Award	Pub
1975	The Windows Of Forever		$18	$25	$35	John Morressy		Walker
1982	Fairy Tales		$14	$20	$25	Jacob & Wilhelm Grimm		Wander
1982	The Tale Of Peter Rabbit & Other Stories		$14	$20	$25	Beatrix Potter		Knopf
1983	Cecily Parsley's Nursery Rhymes		$14	$20	$25	Beatrix Potter		Bantam
1983	The Tailor Of Gloucester		$14	$20	$25	Beatrix Potter		Bantam
1983	The Tale Of Mr. Jeremy Fisher		$14	$20	$25	Beatrix Potter		Bantam
1983	The Tale Of Tom Kitten		$14	$20	$25	Beatrix Potter		Bantam
1983	The Velveteen Rabbit		$14	$20	$25	Margery W. Bianco		Knopf
1984	Mother Goose's Nursery Rhymes		$12	$18	$25	Allen Atkinson		Ariel
1985	Humpty Dumpty & Other Favorites		$12	$16	$20	Allen Atkinson		Bantam
1985	Little Boy Blue & Other Favorites		$12	$16	$20	Allen Atkinson		Bantam
1985	Mary Had A Little Lamb		$12	$16	$20	Allen Atkinson		Bantam
1985	The Cat And The Fiddle & Other Favorites		$12	$16	$20	Allen Atkinson		Bantam
1985	The Wizard Of Oz		$12	$16	$20	L. Frank Baum		LSimon
1986	Babes In Toyland		$10	$14	$18	James Howe		HBJ
1986	Jack And Jill & Other Favorites		$10	$14	$18	Allen Atkinson		Bantam
1986	Little Bo-Peep & Other Favorites		$10	$14	$18	Allen Atkinson		Bantam
1986	Mystery Of The Windy Meadow		$10	$14	$18	Ski Michaels		Troll
1986	Old King Cole & Other Favorites		$10	$14	$18	Allen Atkinson		Bantam
1986	Simple Simon & Other Favorites		$10	$14	$18	Allen Atkinson		Bantam
1987	Jack In The Green		$10	$14	$18	Allen Atkinson		Crown
1988	Peter And The Wolf		$10	$14	$18	David Eastman		Troll

Austin   Margot

Year	Title	VG-	VG	VG+	Fine	Author	Award	Pub
1939	Moxie And Hanty And Bunty	$80	$100	$140		Margot Austin		Scribnr
1940	David's Silver Dollar	$70	$90	$120		Elizabeth Briggs Squires		P&Munk
1940	Mother Goose Rhymes	$70	$90	$120		Watty Piper (pseud.)		P&Munk
1940	Once Upon A Springtime	$70	$90	$120		Margot Austin		Scribnr
1940	Tumble Bear	$70	$90	$120		Margot Austin		Scribnr
1941	Barney's Adventure	$50	$70	$90		Margot Austin		Dutton
1941	Peter Churchmouse	$50	$70	$90		Margot Austin		Dutton
1941	Willamette Way	$50	$70	$90		Margot Austin		Scribnr
1942	Effelli	$50	$70	$90		Margot Austin		Dutton
1942	Gabriel Churchkitten	$50	$70	$90		Margot Austin		Dutton
1943	Manuel's Kite String	$50	$70	$90		Margot Austin		Scribnr
1943	Trumpet	$50	$70	$90		Margot Austin		Dutton
1944	Lutie	$50	$70	$90		Margot Austin		Dutton
1944	Mother Goose Rhymes	$50	$70	$90		Watty Piper (pseud.)		P&Munk
1948	Gabriel Churchkitten And The Moths	$50	$60	$80		Margot Austin		Dutton
1949	Poppet	$50	$60	$80		Margot Austin		Dutton
1950	The Three Silly Kittens	$40	$50	$70		Margot Austin		Dutton
1951	Growl Bear	$40	$50	$70		Margot Austin		Dutton
1952	First Prize For Danny	$40	$50	$70		Margot Austin		Dutton
1954	William's Shadow	$35	$50	$60		Margot Austin		Dutton
1955	Brave John Henry	$35	$50	$60		Margot Austin		Dutton
1956	Churchmouse Stories	$35	$50	$60		Margot Austin		Dutton
1957	Archie Angel	$35	$50	$60		Margot Austin		Dutton
1960	Cousin's Treasure	$25	$35	$50		Margot Austin		Dutton
1963	The Very Young Mother Goose	$25	$35	$50		Margot Austin		P&Munk

Averill   Esther Holden

Year	Title	VG-	VG	VG+	Fine	Author	Award	Pub
1944	The Adventures Of Jack Ninepins	$160	$220	$280		Esther Holden Averill		H&B
1944	The Cat Club	$160	$220	$280		Esther Holden Averill		H&B
1947	The School For Cats	$160	$200	$260		Esther Holden Averill		H&B
1949	Jenny's Moonlight Adventure	$160	$200	$260		Esther Holden Averill		H&B
1951	When Jenny Lost Her Scarf	$120	$160	$200		Esther Holden Averill		H&B
1952	Jenny's Adopted Brothers	$120	$160	$200		Esther Holden Averill		H&B
1957	Jenny Goes To Sea	$100	$140	$180		Esther Holden Averill		H&B

Averill — Esther Holden

Year	Title	VG-	VG	VG+	Fine	Author	Award	Pub
1960	The Fire Cat	$120	$160	$220		Esther Holden Averill		H&B
1969	The Hotel Cat	$70	$90	$120		Esther Holden Averill		H&Row
1972	Captains Of The City Streets		$30	$50	$60	Esther Holden Averill		H&Row
1973	Jenny And The Cat Club		$50	$80	$100	Esther Holden Averill		H&Row

Azarian — Mary

Year	Title	VG-	VG	VG+	Fine	Author	Award	Pub
1973	The Wild Flavor		$60	$90	$120	Marilyn Kluger		CM&G
1981	A Farmer's Alphabet		$50	$70	$100	Mary Azarian		4Winds
1982	The Tale Of John Barleycorn		$50	$70	$90	Mary Azarian		Godine
1984	The Man Who Lived Alone		$40	$60	$90	Donald Hall		Godine
1985	The Wildman		$40	$60	$80	Martin Steingesser		Coyote
1987	Gridley Firing		$40	$60	$80	James Hayford		NEP
1989	Sea Gifts		$35	$50	$70	George Shannon		Godine
1996	A Symphony For The Sheep		$25	$35	$50	C. M. Millen		HM
1998	Barn Cat		$20	$30	$40	Carol Saul		LBrown
1998	Faraway Summer		$16	$25	$30	Johanna Hurwitz		Morrow
1998	Snowflake Bentley		$80	$120	$160	Jacqueline Martin	CM	HM
2000	A Gardener's Alphabet		$14	$20	$25	Mary Azarian		HM
2000	The Four Seasons Of Mary Azarian		$14	$20	$25	Lilias MacBean Hart		Godine
2001	The Race Of The Birkebeiners		$12	$18	$25	Lise Lunge-Larsen		HM
2001	When The Moon Is Full		$12	$18	$25	Penny Pollock		LBrown
2002	From Dawn Till Dusk		$12	$16	$20	Natalie Kinsey-Warnock		HM
2002	Louisa May & Mr. Thoreau's Flute		$12	$16	$20	Julie Dunlap		Dial
2003	Kneeling Orion		$10	$16	$20	Kate Barnes		Godine
2004	A Christmas Like Helen's		$8	$12	$16	Natalie Kinsey-Warnock		HM
2004	Miss Bridie Chose A Shovel		$8	$12	$16	Leslie Connor		HM

Babbitt — Natalie

Year	Title	VG-	VG	VG+	Fine	Author	Award	Pub
1966	The Forty-Ninth Magician	$40	$60	$70		Samuel F. Babbitt		Pan
1967	Dick Foote And The Shark	$40	$50	$70		Natalie Babbitt		FSG
1968	Phoebe's Revolt	$40	$50	$70		Natalie Babbitt		FSG
1969	The Search for Delicious	$40	$50	$70		Natalie Babbitt		FSG
1970	Knee Knock Rise		$50	$70	$90	Natalie Babbitt	NH	FSG
1970	The Something		$30	$50	$60	Natalie Babbitt		FSG
1971	Goody Hall		$25	$40	$50	Natalie Babbitt		FSG
1972	Small Poems		$25	$40	$50	Valerie Worth		FSG
1975	Tuck Everlasting		$25	$35	$50	Natalie Babbitt		FSG
1976	More Small Poems		$25	$35	$50	Valerie Worth		FSG
1977	The Eyes Of The Amaryllis		$25	$35	$50	Natalie Babbitt		FSG
1978	Still More Small Poems		$25	$35	$50	Valerie Worth		FSG
1980	Curlicues		$20	$30	$40	Valerie Worth		FSG
1982	Herbert Rowbarge		$16	$25	$30	Natalie Babbitt		FSG
1986	Small Poems Again		$14	$20	$30	Valerie Worth		FSG
1987	All The Small Poems		$14	$20	$30	Valerie Worth		FSG
1987	The Devil's Other Storybook		$14	$20	$30	Natalie Babbitt		FSG
1989	Nellie		$14	$20	$25	Natalie Babbitt		FSG
1994	Bub, Or, The Very Best Thing		$10	$16	$20	Natalie Babbitt		HCollins
1999	Second Sight		$8	$12	$16	Avi		Philo
2001	Elsie Times Eight		$8	$10	$14	Natalie Babbitt		Hyper
2002	Peacock & Other Poems		$8	$10	$14	Valerie Worth		FSG

Bacon — Peggy

Year	Title	VG-	VG	VG+	Fine	Author	Award	Pub
1919	The True Philosopher & Other Cat Tales	$180	$240	$300		Peggy Bacon		4Seas
1927	The Lion-Hearted Kitten & Other Stories	$160	$220	$280		Peggy Bacon		Macmil
1928	Mercy And The Mouse & Other Stories	$160	$220	$280		Peggy Bacon		Macmil
1929	The Ballad Of Tangle Street	$160	$220	$280		Peggy Bacon		Macmil
1931	The Terrible Nuisance & Other Tales	$100	$140	$180		Peggy Bacon		HBrace
1933	Thirty Fables In Slang	$100	$140	$180		George Ade		Arrow
1934	Off With Their Heads!	$100	$140	$180		Peggy Bacon		McBride
1935	Cat-Calls	$70	$100	$120		Peggy Bacon		McBride
1938	Buttons	$60	$80	$100		Thomas P. Robinson		Viking
1939	The Mystery At East Hatchett	$60	$80	$100		Peggy Bacon		Viking

Bacon   Peggy

Year	Title	VG-	VG	VG+	Fine	Author	Award	Pub
1942	Cindy	$50	$70	$90		Dorothy Keeley Aldis		Putnam
1942	Josephine	$50	$70	$90		Kathleen Coyle		H&B
1942	My Yankee Mother	$50	$70	$90		Herbert E. French		Vnguard
1944	A Treasury Of Cat Stories	$50	$70	$90		Era Zistel		Ginn
1945	Peter Makebelieve	$50	$70	$90		Adrian Van Sinderen		YaleUP
1947	The Cat That Jumped Out Of The Story	$50	$60	$80		Ben Hecht		Winston
1952	The Leftover Elf	$50	$60	$80		Mary Stolz		H&B
1957	The Good American Witch	$80	$120	$140		Peggy Bacon		FWatts
1962	The Cat And Mrs. Cary	$40	$50	$70		Doris Gates		Viking
1962	The Oddity	$50	$70	$90		Peggy Bacon		Pan
1965	The Auction Pony	$35	$50	$60		Linell Nash Smith		LBrown
1966	Rama, The Gypsy Cat	$35	$50	$60		Betsy Cromer Byars		Viking
1967	Return To Hackberry Street	$35	$40	$60		Christine Noble Govan		World
1967	The Ghost Of Opalina	$35	$40	$60		Peggy Bacon		LBrown
1968	The Magic Touch	$70	$90	$120		Peggy Bacon		LBrown

Bahti   Tom

Year	Title	VG-	VG	VG+	Fine	Author	Award	Pub
1969	Before You Came This Way	$30	$40	$50		Byrd Baylor		Dutton
1973	When Clay Sings		$50	$80	$100	Byrd Baylor	CH	Scribnr

Baker   Alan

Year	Title	VG-	VG	VG+	Fine	Author	Award	Pub
1977	Benjamin And The Box		$25	$40	$50	Alan Baker		Lippin
1978	Benjamin Bounces Back		$25	$40	$50	Alan Baker		Lippin
1978	The Battle Of Bubble And Squeak		$25	$40	$50	Philippa Pearce		Deutsch
1980	Benjamin's Dreadful Dream		$25	$35	$50	Alan Baker		Lippin
1980	Creatures Great And Small		$25	$35	$50	Michael H. Gabb		Lerner
1981	Mythical Beasts		$25	$35	$50	Deirdre Headon		Hutch
1982	Benjamin's Book		$25	$35	$50	Alan Baker		LL&S
1982	The Butterfly That Stamped		$25	$35	$50	Rudyard Kipling		Bedrik
1984	Dinosaurs		$20	$30	$40	Kate Petty		FWatts
1984	Snakes		$20	$30	$40	Kate Petty		FWatts
1985	Spiders		$20	$30	$40	Kate Petty		FWatts
1986	Benjamin's Portrait		$20	$30	$40	Alan Baker		LL&S
1988	The Odyssey		$18	$25	$35	Robin Lister		DoubleD
1988	The Story Of King Arthur		$18	$25	$35	Robin Lister		Kfisher
1990	Benjamin's Balloon		$14	$20	$30	Alan Baker		LL&S
1990	Goodnight, William		$14	$20	$30	Alan Baker		Deutsch
1990	Gorilla Rescue		$14	$20	$30	Jill Bailey		Steck-V
1990	Mission Rhino		$14	$20	$30	Jill Bailey		Steck-V
1990	Project Panda		$14	$20	$30	Jill Bailey		Steck-V
1990	Save The Tiger		$14	$20	$30	Jill Bailey		Steck-V
1991	Stop, Look And Listen, Mr. Toad!		$14	$20	$30	Kate Petty		Barrn
1991	Two Tiny Mice		$14	$20	$30	Alan Baker		Dial
1992	Both Sides Now		$14	$20	$25	Joni Mitchell		Scholas
1992	Itsy-Bitsy Beasties		$14	$20	$25	Michael Rosen		CRB
1992	Mr. Toad To The Rescue		$14	$20	$25	Kate Petty		Barrn
1992	Mr. Toad's Narrow Escapes		$14	$20	$25	Kate Petty		Barrn
1992	Where's Mouse		$14	$20	$25	Alan Baker		Kfisher
1993	A Bug In A Jug & Other Funny Rhymes		$14	$20	$25	Gloria Patrick		Heath
1993	Mike And Lottie		$14	$20	$25	Verna Wilkins		ChildP
1994	Black And White Rabbit's ABC		$12	$18	$25	Alan Baker		Kfisher
1994	Brown Rabbit's Shape Book		$12	$18	$25	Alan Baker		Kfisher
1994	Gray Rabbit's 1, 2, 3		$12	$18	$25	Alan Baker		Kfisher
1994	White Rabbit's Color Book		$12	$18	$25	Alan Baker		Kfisher
1995	Brown Rabbit's Day		$12	$16	$20	Alan Baker		Kfisher
1995	Gray Rabbit's Odd One Out		$12	$16	$20	Alan Baker		Kfisher
1996	I Thought I Heard--		$12	$16	$20	Alan Baker		CBeach
1996	Little Rabbit's First Word Book		$12	$16	$20	Alan Baker		Kfisher
1996	Mouse's Christmas		$12	$16	$20	Alan Baker		CBeach
1997	Little Rabbits' Play And Learn Book		$10	$16	$20	Alan Baker		Kfisher
1997	Mouse's Halloween		$10	$16	$20	Alan Baker		Millbk
1997	The Story Of King Arthur		$10	$16	$20	Robin Lister		Kfisher
1998	Little Rabbit's Bedtime		$10	$16	$20	Alan Baker		Kfisher
1998	Little Rabbit's First Number Book		$10	$16	$20	Kate Petty		Kfisher

Baker   Alan

Year	Title	VG-	VG	VG+	Fine	Author	Award	Pub
1998	Little Rabbit's Snacktime		$10	$16	$20	Alan Baker		Kfisher
1999	Little Rabbit's First Time Book		$10	$16	$20	Alan Baker		Kfisher
1999	The Arctic		$10	$16	$20	Alan Baker		Bedrik
1999	The Desert		$10	$16	$20	Alan Baker		Bedrik
1999	The Ocean		$10	$16	$20	Alan Baker		Bedrik
1999	The Rain Forest		$10	$16	$20	Alan Baker		Bedrik
2001	Little Rabbits On The Farm		$8	$12	$16	Alan Baker		Kfisher
2001	Red Dog		$8	$12	$16	Louis De Bernières		Pan
2002	Seasons		$8	$12	$16	David Stewart		FWatts

Baker   Leslie

Year	Title	VG-	VG	VG+	Fine	Author	Award	Pub
1987	The Third Story Cat		$30	$50	$60	Leslie Baker		LBrown
1988	Winter Harvest		$16	$25	$30	Jane Chelsea Aragon		LBrown
1990	Morning Beach		$14	$20	$30	Leslie Baker		LBrown
1991	All Those Secrets Of The World		$14	$20	$30	Jane Yolen		LBrown
1992	The Antique Store Cat		$14	$20	$25	Leslie Baker		LBrown
1993	Honkers		$14	$20	$25	Jane Yolen		LBrown
1996	When Snow Lay Soft on the Mountain		$12	$16	$20	Patricia Hermes		LBrown
1998	Rabbit and the Moon		$10	$16	$20	Douglas Wood		S&S
1999	Paris Cat		$10	$16	$20	Leslie Baker		LBrown
2000	Cats of Myth		$10	$14	$18	Gerald & Loretta Hausman		S&S

Balet   Jan B.

Year	Title	VG-	VG	VG+	Fine	Author	Award	Pub
1945	The Golden Ladle	$70	$100	$120		Zack/Herz Hanle		Ziff-D
1948	Amos And The Moon	$50	$60	$80		Jan B. Balet		Oxford
1949	Ned And Ed And The Lion	$40	$50	$70		Jan B. Balet		Oxford
1951	What Makes An Orchestra	$35	$40	$60		Jan B. Balet		Oxford
1952	Rosalinda	$35	$40	$60		Helen Wing		RandMc
1953	The Lazy Lion	$35	$40	$60		Helen Wing		RandMc
1954	Rumpelstiltskin	$35	$40	$60		Patricia Jones		RandMc
1955	Columbine, The White Cat	$30	$40	$50		Patricia Jones		ContC
1956	Fair, Brown and Trembling	$30	$40	$50		Patricia Jones		ContC
1957	Bean Blossom Hill	$30	$40	$50		Martha Bennett King		ContC
1958	The Birthday Angel	$30	$40	$50		Martha Bennett King		Charles
1959	Amos And The Moon	$30	$40	$50		Jan B. Balet		Walck
1959	Papa Pompino	$30	$40	$50		Martha Bennett King		ContC
1959	The Five Rollatinis	$30	$40	$50		Jan B. Balet		Lippin
1960	The Snow Queen	$25	$35	$50		Martha Bennett King		ContC
1962	The Princess On The Pea	$25	$35	$50		Hans Christian Andersen		PMagP
1963	The Mice, the Monks and the Christmas Tree	$25	$35	$50		George Seldon		Macmil
1964	Adding: A Poem	$25	$35	$50		Christina Roseti		HR&W
1967	Joanjo	$25	$30	$40		Jan B. Balet		DelaP
1967	Just One Me	$25	$30	$40		Aileen Brothers		Folio
1967	The Gift	$25	$30	$40		Jan B. Balet		DelaP
1968	The King And The Broom Maker	$25	$30	$40		Jan B. Balet		DelaP
1969	The Fence	$25	$30	$40		Jan B. Balet		DelaP
1971	Ladismouse		$20	$30	$40	Jan B. Balet		Walck

Bang   Molly

Year	Title	VG-	VG	VG+	Fine	Author	Award	Pub
1973	Men From The Village Deep In The Mountains		$50	$70	$100	Molly Bang		Macmil
1973	The Goblins Giggle, & Other Stories		$50	$70	$100	Molly Bang		Scribnr
1975	The Old Woman And The Red Pumpkin		$40	$60	$80	Betsy Bang		Macmil
1976	Wiley And The Hairy Man		$40	$60	$80	Molly Bang		Macmil
1977	The Buried Moon & Other Stories		$35	$50	$70	Molly Bang		Scribnr
1978	The Old Woman And The Rice Thief		$35	$50	$70	Betsy Bang		Green
1978	Tuntuni, The Tailor Bird		$35	$50	$70	Betsy Bang		Green
1979	The Grey Lady And The Strawberry Snatcher		$50	$80	$100	Molly Bang	CH	4Winds
1980	The Demons Of Rajpur		$30	$40	$60	Betsy Bang		Green
1981	Tye May And The Magic Brush		$30	$40	$60	Molly Bang		Green
1982	Ten, Nine, Eight		$50	$70	$90	Molly Bang	CH	Green
1983	Dawn		$25	$40	$50	Molly Bang		Morrow
1984	David's Landing		$25	$40	$50	Judith Benét Richardson		WHHC

Bang   Molly

Year	Title	VG-	VG	VG+	Fine	Author	Award	Pub
1985	The Paper Crane		$25	$35	$50	Molly Bang		Green
1988	Delphine		$18	$25	$35	Molly Bang		Morrow
1991	Picture This		$14	$20	$30	Molly Bang		LBrown
1991	Yellow Ball		$14	$20	$30	Molly Bang		Morrow
1992	Red Dragonfly On My Shoulder		$14	$20	$25	Sylvia Cassedy		HCollins
1993	From Sea To Shining Sea		$14	$20	$25	Amy L Cohn		Scholas
1994	One Fall Day		$12	$18	$25	Molly Bang		Green
1996	Chattanooga Sludge		$12	$16	$20	Molly Bang		HBrace
1996	Goose		$12	$16	$20	Molly Bang		BSP
1997	Common Ground		$10	$16	$20	Molly Bang		BSP
1999	When Sophie Gets Angry-Really, Really Angry		$30	$40	$60	Molly Bang	CH	BSP
2000	Nobody Particular		$10	$14	$18	Molly Bang		Holt
2001	Harley		$8	$12	$16	Star Livingstone		SeaStar
2001	Tiger's Fall		$8	$12	$16	Molly Bang		Holt
2002	Little Rat Sets Sail		$8	$12	$16	Monika Bang-Campbell		Harcort
2004	Hello Sunshine, Good Night Moonligh		$8	$10	$14	John Wallace		Abrams
2004	Jungle Drums		$8	$10	$14	Graeme Base		Abrams
2004	Little Rat Rides		$8	$10	$14	Monika Bang-Campbell		Harcort
2004	My Light		$8	$10	$14	Molly Bang		BSP
2004	Truckdogs		$8	$10	$14	Graeme Base		Abrams
2005	In My Heart		$6	$10	$12	Molly Bang		LBrown

Bannon   Laura

Year	Title	VG-	VG	VG+	Fine	Author	Award	Pub
1937	Pecos Bill	$80	$120	$140		James Bowman	NH	JuniorL
1939	Manuela's Birthday In Old Mexico	$40	$50	$70		Laura Bannon		AWhit
1944	Gregorio And The White Llama	$40	$50	$70		Laura Bannon		AWhit
1946	Patty Paints A Picture	$35	$50	$60		Laura Bannon		AWhit
1946	Red Mittens	$35	$50	$60		Laura Bannon		HM
1946	Tortilla Girl	$35	$50	$60		May F. McElravy		AWhit
1947	Baby Roo	$35	$50	$60		Laura Bannon		HM
1947	Rogue Reynard	$35	$50	$60		Alice Mary Norton		HM
1948	Watchdog	$35	$50	$60		Laura Bannon		AWhit
1949	Billy And The Bear	$35	$50	$60		Laura Bannon		HM
1950	Big Brother	$35	$40	$60		Laura Bannon		AWhit
1951	Horse On A Houseboat	$35	$40	$60		Laura Bannon		AWhit
1952	Mind Your Child's Art	$35	$40	$60		Laura Bannon		P&C
1952	The Best House In The World	$35	$40	$60		Laura Bannon		HM
1953	The Wonderful Fashion Doll	$35	$40	$60		Laura Bannon		HM
1953	When The Moon Is New	$35	$40	$60		Laura Bannon		AWhit
1954	Hat For A Hero	$35	$40	$60		Laura Bannon		AWhit
1955	Burro Boy And His Big Trouble	$30	$40	$50		Laura Bannon		Abing
1955	The Little Sister Doll	$30	$40	$50		Laura Bannon		AWhit
1956	The Scary Thing	$30	$40	$50		Laura Bannon		HM
1957	The Tide Won't Wait	$30	$40	$50		Laura Bannon		AWhit
1958	Jo-Jo, The Talking Crow	$30	$40	$50		Laura Bannon		HM
1959	Katy Comes Next	$30	$40	$50		Laura Bannon		AWhit
1959	Whistle For A Pilot	$30	$40	$50		Laura Bannon		HM
1960	Hop-High, The Goat	$25	$35	$50		Laura Bannon		Bobbs
1960	The Famous Baby-Sitter	$25	$35	$50		Laura Bannon		AWhit
1960	The Other Side Of The World	$25	$35	$50		Laura Bannon		HM
1961	The Gift Of Hawaii	$25	$35	$50		Laura Bannon		AWhit
1962	Hawaiian Coffee Picker	$25	$35	$50		Laura Bannon		HM
1962	Who Walks The Attic?	$25	$35	$50		Laura Bannon		AWhit
1963	Little People Of The Night	$25	$35	$50		Laura Bannon		HM
1963	The Contented Horse Trader	$25	$35	$50		Laura Bannon		AWhit
1963	Toby's Friends	$25	$35	$50		Laura Bannon		AWhit
1964	Make Room For Rags	$25	$35	$50		Laura Bannon		HM
1964	Twirlup On The Moon	$25	$35	$50		Laura Bannon		AWhit
1972	Rogue Reynard		$35	$50	$70	Andre Norton		Dell

Bare   Arnold Edwin

Year	Title	VG-	VG	VG+	Fine	Author	Award	Pub
1943	Pierre Pidgeon	$100	$140	$180		Lee Kingman	CH	HM
1945	Ilenka	$35	$50	$60		Lee Kingman		HM
1946	Mooky And Tooky	$35	$50	$60		Janet Field Heath		Howell

Bare   Arnold Edwin

Year	Title	VG-	VG	VG+	Fine	Author	Award	Pub
1947	The Golden Goose	$35	$50	$60		Jacob & Wilhelm Grimm		HM
1948	Peter Paints The U. S. A	$35	$50	$60		Jean Poindexter Colby		HM
1952	Maui's Summer	$25	$35	$50		Arnold Edwin Bare		HM

Barklem   Jill

Year	Title	VG-	VG	VG+	Fine	Author	Award	Pub
1980	Autumn Story		$12	$18	$25	Jill Barklem		Philo
1980	Spring Story		$12	$18	$25	Jill Barklem		Philo
1980	Summer Story		$12	$18	$25	Jill Barklem		Philo
1980	The Brambly Hedge Books		$12	$18	$25	Jill Barklem		Philo
1980	Winter Story		$12	$18	$25	Jill Barklem		Philo
1981	The Big Book Of Brambly Hedge		$12	$18	$25	Jill Barklem		Philo
1983	The Secret Staircase		$12	$16	$20	Jill Barklem		Philo
1986	The High Hills		$10	$16	$20	Jill Barklem		Philo
1990	The Four Seasons Of Brambly Hedge		$10	$14	$18	Jill Barklem		Philo
1991	Sea Story		$10	$14	$18	Jill Barklem		Philo
1993	The World Of Brambly Hedge		$10	$14	$18	Jill Barklem		Philo
1995	Poppy's Babies		$8	$12	$16	Jill Barklem		Philo

Barnes   Catherine

Year	Title	VG-	VG	VG+	Fine	Author	Award	Pub
1946	Cinderella	$35	$40	$60		Nila Mack		Harrisn
1946	Famous Fairy Tales	$60	$80	$100		Various Authors		PiedP
1946	Understood Betsy	$35	$40	$60		Dorothy Canfield Fisher		Holt
1947	Pom Pom: The Fuzzy Dog	$35	$40	$60		Virginia Cunningham		Whitman
1948	Let's Pretend	$35	$40	$60		Nila Mack		Whitman
1951	Linda Clayton	$30	$40	$50		Marjory Hall		Sloane
1952	Saralee's Silver Spoon	$30	$40	$50		Marjory Hall		Sloane
1953	Greetings From Glenna	$30	$40	$50		Marjory Hall		F&W
1958	The Runaway Flea Circus	$25	$35	$50		Patricia Lauber		Random

Barnum   Jay Hyde

Year	Title	VG-	VG	VG+	Fine	Author	Award	Pub
1940	Champion's Choice	$40	$50	$70		John Roberts Tunis		HBrace
1940	The Kid From Tomkinsville	$40	$50	$70		John Tunnis		HBrace
1946	The Boats On The River	$35	$50	$60		Marjorie Flack		Viking
1949	Too Many Cherries	$35	$50	$60		Carl Carmer		Viking
1950	Shortstop Shadow	$30	$40	$50		Howard Brier		Random
1950	The Little Red Horse	$30	$40	$50		Ruth Sawyer		Viking
1952	Cinder Cyclone	$30	$40	$50		Howard Brier		Random
1952	Little Giant of the North	$30	$40	$50		Alida Malkus		Winston
1952	The New Fire Engine	$30	$40	$50		Jay Hyde Barnum		Morrow
1952	The Vanilla Village	$30	$40	$50		Priscilla Carden		Ariel
1953	The Little Old Truck	$30	$40	$50		Jay Hyde Barnum		Morrow
1953	The Popcorn Dragon	$30	$40	$50		Jane Thayer		Morrow
1955	Buddy And The Old Pro	$25	$35	$50		John Roberts Tunis		Morrow
1955	Two-Bow Bill	$25	$35	$50		Gladys Brown		Morrow
1957	Charley and the New Car	$25	$35	$50		Jane Thayer		Morrow
1958	Motorcycle Dog	$25	$35	$50		Jay Hyde Barnum		Morrow

Barrett   Angela

Year	Title	VG-	VG	VG+	Fine	Author	Award	Pub
1985	The Dragon Wore Pink		$12	$16	$20	Christopher Hope		Athenm
1988	Can It Be True		$10	$16	$20	Susan Hill		Viking
1997	The Emperor's New Clothes		$8	$12	$16	Hans Christian Andersen		Candle

Barrett   Ron

Year	Title	VG-	VG	VG+	Fine	Author	Award	Pub
1969	Old MacDonald Had An Apartment	$30	$40	$50		Judi Barrett		Athenm
1970	Animals Should Definitely Not Wear Clothing		$16	$25	$30	Judi Barrett		Athenm
1978	Cloudy With A Chance Of Meatballs		$14	$20	$25	Judith Barrett	NYT	Athenm
1983	The Pop-Up White House		$35	$50	$70	John Boswell		Bantam
1984	Hi-Yo Fido!		$16	$25	$30	Ron Barrett		Crown
1989	Animals Should Definitely Not Act Like People		$10	$16	$20	Judi Barrett		Athenm
1997	Pickles to Pittsburgh		$10	$16	$20	Judi Barrett		Athenm

Barron   Rex

Year	Title	VG-	VG	VG+	Fine	Author	Award	Pub
1994	Eggbert, The Slightly Cracked Egg		$10	$14	$18	Tom Ross		Putnam
1996	Irma The Flying Bowling Ball		$8	$12	$16	Tom Ross		Putnam
1996	The Day The Daisies Danced		$8	$12	$16	Dee Lillegard		Putnam
1997	The Wild Bunch		$8	$12	$16	Dee Lillegard		Putnam
1999	The Big Bug Ball		$8	$12	$16	Dee Lillegard		Putnam
2000	Fed Up!		$8	$10	$14	Rex Barron		Putnam
2004	Showdown At The Food Pyramid		$6	$10	$12	Rex Barron		Putnam

Barry   Robert E.

Year	Title	VG-	VG	VG+	Fine	Author	Award	Pub
1957	This Is The Story Of Faint George	$30	$40	$50		Robert E. Barry		HM
1958	Just Pepper	$30	$40	$50		Robert E. Barry		HM
1959	Boo	$30	$40	$50		Robert E. Barry		HM
1961	Next Please	$25	$35	$50		Robert E. Barry		HM
1963	Mr Willowby's Christmas Tree	$40	$60	$80		Robert E. Barry		McHill
1965	The Musical Palm Tree	$25	$30	$40		Robert E. Barry		McHill
1967	Animals Around The World	$25	$30	$40		Robert E. Barry		McHill
1968	The Riddle Of Castle Hill	$25	$30	$40		Robert E. Barry		McHill
1971	Ramon And The Pirate Gull		$20	$30	$40	Robert E. Barry		McHill
1975	Snowman's Secret		$18	$25	$35	Edward Frascino		Macmil

Barton   Byron

Year	Title	VG-	VG	VG+	Fine	Author	Award	Pub
1969	A Girl Called Al	$60	$80	$100		Constance C. Greene		Viking
1971	Elephant		$30	$50	$60	Byron Barton		Seabury
1972	Where's Al?		$30	$50	$60	Byron Barton		Seabury
1973	Applebet Story		$30	$50	$60	Byron Barton		Viking
1973	Buzz, Buzz, Buzz		$30	$50	$60	Byron Barton		Macmil
1973	The Checker Players		$30	$50	$60	Alan Venable		Lippin
1974	Harry Is A Scaredy-Cat		$30	$40	$60	Byron Barton		Macmil
1974	Jack And Fred		$30	$40	$60	Byron Barton		Macmil
1975	Angles Are Easy As Pie		$30	$40	$60	Robert Froman		Crowell
1975	Hester		$30	$40	$60	Byron Barton		Green
1975	I Know You, Al		$30	$40	$60	Constance C. Greene		Viking
1976	Bullfrog Grows Up		$30	$40	$60	Rosamond Dauer		Green
1976	How Little And How Much		$30	$40	$60	Franklyn M. Branley		Crowell
1977	Bullfrog Builds A House		$25	$40	$50	Rosamond Dauer		Green
1977	Roman Numerals		$25	$40	$50	David A. Adler		Crowell
1977	The Snopp On The Sidewalk		$25	$40	$50	Jack Prelutsky		Green
1978	Arthur's New Power		$25	$40	$50	Russell Hoban		Crowell
1978	Drakestail		$25	$40	$50	Jan Wahl		Green
1979	Wheels		$25	$40	$50	Byron Barton		Crowell
1980	Bullfrog And Gertrude Go Camping		$20	$30	$40	Rosamond Dauer		Green
1980	Gila Monsters Meet You At The Airport		$20	$30	$40	Marjorie Weinman Sharmat		Macmil
1980	Good Morning, Chick		$20	$30	$40	Mirra Ginsburg		Green
1980	The Tamarindo Puppy & Other Poems		$20	$30	$40	Charlotte Pomerantz		Green
1981	Building A House		$20	$30	$40	Byron Barton		Green
1981	Jump, Frog, Jump!		$20	$30	$40	Robert Kalan		Green
1982	Airport		$20	$30	$40	Byron Barton		Crowell
1982	My Dog And The Key Mystery		$20	$30	$40	David A. Adler		FWatts
1984	Truck Song		$18	$25	$35	Diane Siebert		Crowell
1984	Where's The Bear?		$18	$25	$35	Charlotte Pomerantz		Green
1986	Airplanes		$16	$25	$30	Byron Barton		Crowell
1986	Boats		$16	$25	$30	Byron Barton		Crowell
1986	Trains		$16	$25	$30	Byron Barton		Crowell
1986	Trucks		$16	$25	$30	Byron Barton		Crowell
1987	Machines At Work		$16	$25	$30	Byron Barton		Crowell
1988	I Want To Be An Astronaut		$16	$25	$30	Byron Barton		Crowell
1989	Dinosaurs, Dinosaurs		$16	$25	$30	Byron Barton		Crowell
1990	Bones, Bones, And Dinosaur Bones		$14	$20	$30	Byron Barton		Crowell
1990	Bones, Bones, Dinosaur Bones		$14	$20	$30	Byron Barton		H&Row
1991	The Three Bears		$14	$20	$30	Byron Barton (adapted)		HCollins
1993	The Little Red Hen		$14	$20	$25	Byron Barton		HCollins
1995	Big Machines		$12	$16	$20	Byron Barton		HFest
1995	Dinosaurs		$12	$16	$20	Byron Barton		HFest
1995	The Wee Little Woman		$12	$16	$20	Byron Barton		HCollins

Barton — Byron

Year	Title	VG-	VG	VG+	Fine	Author	Award	Pub
1995	Tools		$12	$16	$20	Byron Barton		HFest
1995	Zoo Animals		$12	$16	$20	Byron Barton		HFest
1998	Little Factory		$10	$16	$20	Sarah Weeks		LauraG
2001	My Car		$8	$12	$16	Byron Barton		Green

Base — Graeme

Year	Title	VG-	VG	VG+	Fine	Author	Award	Pub
1982	Adventures With My Worst Best Friend		$25	$40	$50	Max Dann		Oxford
1983	My Grandma Lived In Gooligulch		$16	$25	$30	Graeme Base		TNelson
1986	Animalia		$14	$20	$25	Graeme Base		Abrams
1989	Jabberwocky		$12	$18	$25	Lewis Carroll		Abrams
1989	The Eleventh Hour: A Curious Mystery		$12	$18	$25	Graeme Base		Abrams
1992	The Sign Of The Seahorse		$12	$16	$20	Graeme Base		Abrams
1999	The Worst Band In The Universe		$8	$12	$16	Graeme Base		Abrams
2001	The Water Hole		$8	$10	$14	Graeme Base		Abrams

Baskin — Leonard

Year	Title	VG-	VG	VG+	Fine	Author	Award	Pub
1962	Creatures Of Darkness	$50	$70	$90		Esther Baskin		LBrown
1972	Hosie's Alphabet		$100	$140	$200	Hosie Baskin	CH	Viking
1973	Mandrakes		$35	$50	$70	Thom Gunn		Rainbow
1975	Season Songs		$35	$50	$70	Ted Hughes		Viking
1976	Moon Whales & Other Moon Poems		$30	$50	$60	Ted Hughes		Viking
1978	Adam And The Sacred Nine		$30	$50	$60	Ted Hughes		Rainbow
1979	Hosie's Aviary		$30	$50	$60	Tobias Baskin		Viking
1981	Hosie's Zoo		$30	$40	$60	Tobias Baskin		Viking
1981	Under The North Star		$30	$40	$60	Ted Hughes		Viking
1983	The Owl Papers		$25	$40	$50	Jonathan Evan Maslow		Dutton
1984	Imps, Demons, Hobgoblins, Witches, Fairies & Elves		$25	$40	$50	Leonard Baskin		Pan
1985	A Book Of Dragons		$25	$35	$50	Hosie Baskin		Knopf
1986	Flowers And Insects		$25	$35	$50	Ted Hughes		Knopf
1992	Alberic The Wise		$16	$25	$30	Norton Juster		S&S
1993	Did You Say Ghosts?		$16	$25	$30	Richard Michelson		Macmil
1996	Animals That Ought To Be		$12	$16	$20	Richard Michelson		S&S
1999	A Book Of Flies Real Or Otherwise		$10	$16	$20	Richard Michelson		MCaven
2000	Ten Times Better		$10	$14	$18	Richard Michelson		MCaven

Bayley (Morse) — Dorothy

Year	Title	VG-	VG	VG+	Fine	Author	Award	Pub
1935	If This Be I, As I Suppose It Be	$50	$70	$90		Margaret W.C. Deland		DApple
1936	Stories To Shorten The Road	$35	$50	$60		Effie Power		Dutton
1937	Flaxen Braids	$35	$50	$60		Annette Turngren		TNelson
1937	From Umar's Pack	$35	$50	$60		Effie Power		Dutton
1938	Giotto Tended The Sheep	$35	$50	$60		S. Wheeler & O. Deucher		Dutton
1939	All Over Town	$35	$50	$60		Carol Ryrie Brink		Macmil
1939	Julia Ann	$35	$50	$60		Rachel M. Varble		DD
1939	Millet Tilled The Soil	$35	$50	$60		S. Wheeler & O. Deucher		Dutton
1939	The Phantom Of The Forest	$35	$50	$60		Ann Hark		Lippin
1940	Out Of The Net	$30	$40	$50		Mary D. Edmonds		Oxford
1940	The Weather House People	$30	$40	$50		Marie McSwigan		Lippin
1940	Wings At My Window	$30	$40	$50		Ada Clapham Govan		Macmil
1941	Let Us Be Merry	$30	$40	$50		Agnes Louise Dean		Knopf
1941	Stars To Steer By	$30	$40	$50		Louis Untermeyer		HBrace
1941	The Middle Button	$30	$40	$50		Kathryn Worth		DoubleD
1941	Twelve Daughters Of Democracy	$30	$40	$50		Eleanor Maria Sickels		Viking
1941	Vanished Island	$30	$40	$50		Cornelia Meigs		Macmil
1942	The Hickory Limb	$30	$40	$50		Margaret Ann Hubbard		Macmil
1942	Training Sylvia	$30	$40	$50		Eliza Orne White		HM
1947	Lightning Strikes Twice	$30	$40	$50		Marguerite S. Dickson		TNelson
1947	Racing The Red Sail	$30	$40	$50		Alice Geer Kelsey		Longman
1948	Down In Dixie	$25	$35	$50		Wilhelmina Harper		Dutton
1948	Sail Away	$25	$35	$50		Robb White		DoubleD
1948	Somebody Else's Shoes	$25	$35	$50		Florence Lowe		Rinehrt
1949	The Hidden Burro	$25	$35	$50		Delia Goetz		Morrow
1949	Tree Of Freedom	$25	$35	$50		Rebecca Caudill		Viking

Bayley (Morse)   Dorothy

Year	Title	VG-	VG	VG+	Fine	Author	Award	Pub
1950	Cherries Are Ripe	$25	$35	$50		Helen Reynolds		TNelson
1950	Sylvan City	$25	$35	$50		Grace Trotter		Viking
1951	Wish On The Moon	$25	$35	$50		Dean Marshall		Dutton
1952	Boy Of The Pyramids	$25	$35	$50		Ruth Fosdick Jones		Random
1952	Everybody's Island	$25	$35	$50		Amy Morris Lillie		Dutton
1953	Candle In The Sky	$25	$35	$50		Elizabeth Bleecker Meigs		Dutton
1953	Promenade All	$25	$35	$50		Helen Markley Miller		DoubleD
1953	Sink The Basket	$25	$35	$50		Sally Elizabeth Knapp		Crowell
1954	It Happened To Hannah	$25	$35	$50		Ruth Rounds		Dutton
1954	Sing Morning Star	$25	$35	$50		Elizabeth Bleecker Meigs		Dutton
1954	Will And Charlie Mayo	$25	$35	$50		Marie Hammontree		Bobbs
1955	Samuel Morse	$25	$30	$40		Dorothea J. Snow		Bobbs
1956	Lucky Days	$25	$30	$40		Laura Pardee		Dutton
1957	Dust In The Gold Sack	$25	$30	$40		Helen Markley Miller		DoubleD
1957	The Holiday Shop	$25	$30	$40		Mickey Klar Marks		Holt
1957	The Honest Dollar	$25	$30	$40		Dorothy Simpson		Lippin
1957	The Little Red Schoolhouse	$25	$30	$40		Carolyn Sherwin Bailey		Viking
1957	The Singing Boones	$25	$30	$40		Marian T. Place		Viking
1958	A Lesson For Janie	$25	$30	$40		Dorothy Simpson		Lippin
1958	Escape To Freedom	$25	$30	$40		Ruth Fosdick Jones		Random
1958	Mystery Of The Wooden Indian	$25	$30	$40		Elizabeth Hoffman Honness		Lippin
1959	Tosco, The Stubborn One	$25	$30	$40		Robert Parker MacLeod		Crowell
1960	Grasshopper Year	$25	$30	$40		Neola Tracy Lane		Lippin
1960	Liza Of The Hundredfold	$25	$30	$40		Elizabeth H. Lansing		Crowell
1961	Best Friends At School	$25	$30	$40		Mary Bard		Lippin
1961	Miney And The Blessing	$25	$30	$40		Miriam Evangeline Mason		Macmil
1961	New Horizons	$25	$30	$40		Dorothy Simpson		Lippin
1961	On Call	$25	$30	$40		Catherine Herzel		HR&W
1961	Young Viking Of Brooklyn	$25	$30	$40		Harriett H. Carr		Viking
1962	The Path Above The Pines	$25	$30	$40		Belle Dorman Rugh		HM
1963	A Summer's Duckling	$20	$30	$35		Daniel Lang		H&Row
1963	Pony Girl	$20	$30	$35		Jan Young		McKay
1964	Cyrus Holt And The Civil War	$20	$30	$35		Anna Gertrude Hall		Viking
1966	Our Country's Freedom	$20	$25	$35		Frances Cavanah		RandMc
1967	The Lost Waters	$20	$25	$35		Belle Dorman Rugh		HM
1968	Katy Kelly Of Cripple Creek	$20	$25	$35		Ruth H. Wissmann		DoddM

Bayley   Nicola

Year	Title	VG-	VG	VG+	Fine	Author	Award	Pub
1976	The Tyger Voyage		$30	$50	$60	Richard Adams		Knopf
1977	Nicola Bayley's Book Of Nursery Rhymes		$20	$30	$40	Nicola Bayley		Knopf
1977	One Old Oxford Ox		$20	$30	$40	Nicola Bayley		Athenm
1981	The Patchwork Cat		$16	$25	$30	William Mayne		Knopf
1983	The Mouldy		$14	$20	$30	William Mayne		Knopf
1984	Crab Cat		$14	$20	$30	Nicola Bayley		Knopf
1984	Elephant Cat		$14	$20	$30	Nicola Bayley		Knopf
1984	Parrot Cat		$14	$20	$30	Nicola Bayley		Knopf
1984	Polar Bear Cat		$14	$20	$30	Nicola Bayley		Knopf
1984	Spider Cat		$14	$20	$30	Nicola Bayley		Knopf
1986	As I Was Going Up And Down		$14	$20	$25	Nicola Bayley		Macmil
1988	Boy		$12	$18	$25	Paul Manning		Macmil
1988	Clown		$12	$18	$25	Paul Manning		Macmil
1988	Cook		$12	$18	$25	Paul Manning		Macmil
1988	Fisherman		$12	$18	$25	Paul Manning		Macmil
1990	The Mousehole Cat		$12	$16	$20	Antonia Barber		Macmil
1992	Copycats		$12	$16	$20	Nicola Bayley		Candle
1993	Fun With Mrs. Thumb		$10	$16	$20	Jan Mark		Candle
1998	The Necessary Cat		$10	$14	$18	Nicola Bayley		Candle
2000	All For The Newborn Baby		$8	$12	$16	Phyllis Root		Candle
2001	Katje, The Windmill Cat		$8	$10	$14	Gretchen Woelfle		Candle

Baynes   Pauline

Year	Title	VG-	VG	VG+	Fine	Author	Award	Pub
1950	The Lion, The Witch, And The Wardrobe	$5,600	$7,400	$9,200		C.S. Lewis		Macmil
1950	The Lion, The Witch, And The Wardrobe	$8,000	$10,800	$13,400		C.S. Lewis		GBles
1951	Prince Caspian	$3,800	$5,000	$6,200		C.S. Lewis		GBles

Bemelmans   Ludwig

Year	Title	VG-	VG	VG+	Fine	Author	Award	Pub
1985	Madeline's Christmas		$50	$70	$100	Ludwig Bemelmans		VK
1985	Tell Them It Was Wonderful		$12	$18	$25	Ludwig Bemelmans		Viking
1993	Mad About Madeline		$25	$35	$50	Ludwig Bemelmans		Viking
1999	Madeline In America		$16	$25	$30	John Bemelmans Marciano		Levine

Benson   Patrick

Year	Title	VG-	VG	VG+	Fine	Author	Award	Pub
1984	The Blue Book Of Hob Stories		$12	$18	$25	William Mayne		Philo
1984	The Green Book Of Hob Stories		$12	$18	$25	William Mayne		Philo
1984	The Red Book Of Hob Stories		$12	$18	$25	William Mayne		Philo
1984	The Twelve Days Of Christmas		$12	$18	$25	Folk Song		Philo
1984	The Yellow Book Of Hob Stories		$12	$18	$25	William Mayne		Philo
1985	The Baron Rides Out		$40	$60	$80	Adrian Mitchell		Philo
1986	The Baron On The Island Of Cheese		$40	$60	$80	Adrian Mitchell		Walker
1987	The Baron All At Sea		$40	$60	$80	Adrian Mitchell		Walker
1987	The Tough Princess		$40	$60	$80	Martin Waddell		Philo
1988	Herbert Five Stories		$18	$25	$35	Ivor Cutler		LL&S
1989	Robin Hood		$18	$25	$35	Sarah Hayes		Holt
1989	The Story Of Three Whales		$18	$25	$35	Giles Whittell		GarethS
1991	Little Penguin		$14	$20	$30	Patrick Benson		Philo
1991	The Minpins		$14	$20	$30	Roald Dahl		Viking
1992	Owl Babies		$14	$20	$25	Martin Waddell		Candle
1993	A Christmas Carol		$14	$20	$25	Charles Dickens		Candle
1993	Fly Fishing: Memories Of Angling Days		$14	$20	$25	J.R. Hartley		HCollins
1993	Prince Oliver Doesn't Want To Take A Bath		$14	$20	$25	Odile Hellmann-Hurpoil		CW
1994	The Willows In Winter		$12	$18	$25	William Horwood		StMart
1995	The Little Boat		$12	$16	$20	Kathy Henderson		Candle
1995	The Wind In The Willows		$12	$16	$20	Kenneth Grahame		StMart
1996	Let The Lynx Come In		$12	$16	$20	Jonathan London		Candle
1996	Toad Triumphant		$12	$16	$20	William Horwood		StMart
1997	The Book Of Hob Stories		$10	$16	$20	William Mayne		Candle
1999	The Sea-Thing Child		$10	$16	$20	Russell Hoban		Candle
2001	Squeak's Good Idea		$8	$12	$16	Max Eilenberg		Candle
2001	The Willows At Christmas		$8	$12	$16	William Horwood		StMart
2002	Mole And The Baby Bird		$8	$12	$16	Marjorie Newman		Bloom
2004	Christopher Mouse		$8	$10	$14	William Wise		Bloom

Berenstain   Michael

Year	Title	VG-	VG	VG+	Fine	Author	Award	Pub
1977	The Castle Book		$30	$50	$60	Michael Berenstain		DMcKay
1978	The Ship Book		$30	$50	$60	Michael Berenstain		DMcKay
1979	The Armor Book		$30	$50	$60	Michael Berenstain		DMcKay
1979	The Lighthouse Book		$30	$50	$60	Michael Berenstain		DMcKay
1980	The Troll Book		$25	$35	$50	Michael Berenstain		Random
1981	The Sorcerer's Scrapbook		$25	$35	$50	Michael Berenstain		Random
1982	The Creature Catalog		$25	$35	$50	Michael Berenstain		Random
1983	King Kong		$25	$35	$50	Judith Conaway		Random
1986	Peat Moss And Ivy And The Birthday Present		$20	$30	$40	Michael Berenstain		Random
1986	Peat Moss And Ivy's Backyard Adventure		$20	$30	$40	Michael Berenstain		Random
1987	Peat Moss And Ivy Meet Santa Claws		$20	$30	$40	Michael Berenstain		Random
1987	The Day Of The Dinosaur		$20	$30	$40	Stan & Jan Berenstain		Random
1988	After The Dinosaurs		$18	$25	$35	Stan & Jan Berenstain		Random
1989	The Biggest Dinosaurs		$18	$25	$35	Michael Berenstain		Golden
1989	The Horned Dinosaur		$18	$25	$35	Michael Berenstain		Western
1989	The Panda Club's Tree House		$18	$25	$35	Michael Berenstain		Western
1989	The Spike-Tailed Dinosaur		$18	$25	$35	Michael Berenstain		Golden
1990	Ready For School		$14	$20	$30	Michael Berenstain		Western
1990	The Panda's New Pet		$14	$20	$30	Michael Berenstain		Western
1991	C-A-T Spells Cat		$14	$20	$30	Michael Berenstain		Golden
1991	Faster, Slower, Higher, Lower		$14	$20	$30	Michael Berenstain		Western
1991	Flying Dinosaurs		$14	$20	$30	Michael Berenstain		Western
1991	Long, Long, Ago		$14	$20	$30	Michael Berenstain		Western
1992	Michael Berenstain's Butterfly Book		$14	$20	$25	Michael Berenstain		Western
1992	Michael Berenstain's Hop, Waddle, Swim!		$14	$20	$25	Michael Berenstain		Western
1992	Michael Berenstain's When I Grow Up		$14	$20	$25	Michael Berenstain		Western
1995	The B. Bear Scouts And The Humongous Pumpkin		$12	$16	$20	Stan & Jan Berenstain		Scholas

Berenstain   Michael

Year	Title	VG-	VG	VG+	Fine	Author	Award	Pub
1995	The B. Bear Scouts In Giant Bat Cave		$12	$16	$20	Stan & Jan Berenstain		Scholas
1996	Ghost Versus Ghost		$12	$16	$20	Stan & Jan Berenstain		Scholas
1996	The B. Bear Scouts And The Coughing Catfish		$12	$16	$20	Stan & Jan Berenstain		Scholas
1996	The B. Bear Scouts And The Sci-Fi Pizza		$12	$16	$20	Stan & Jan Berenstain		Scholas
1997	The B. Bear Scouts And The Run-Amuck Robot		$10	$16	$20	Stan & Jan Berenstain		Scholas
1997	The B. Bear Scouts And The Sinister Smoke Ring		$10	$16	$20	Stan & Jan Berenstain		Scholas
1998	The B. Bear Scouts And The Missing Merit Badges		$10	$16	$20	Stan & Jan Berenstain		Scholas
1998	The B. Bear Scouts And The Ripoff Queen		$10	$16	$20	Stan & Jan Berenstain		Scholas
1998	The B. Bear Scouts And The Search For Naughty Ned		$10	$16	$20	Stan & Jan Berenstain		Scholas
1998	The B. Bear Scouts Scream Their Heads Off		$10	$16	$20	Stan & Jan Berenstain		Scholas
1999	The B. Bear Scouts And The Stinky Milk Mystery		$10	$16	$20	Stan & Jan Berenstain		Scholas
1999	The B. Bear Scouts And The White-Water Mystery		$10	$16	$20	Stan & Jan Berenstain		Scholas
2003	The Berenstain Bears Save Christmas		$8	$10	$14	Stan & Jan Berenstain		HCollins

Berenstain   Stan & Jan

Year	Title	VG-	VG	VG+	Fine	Author	Award	Pub
1951	Berenstain's Baby Book	$80	$100	$140		Stan & Jan Berenstain		Macmil
1952	Sister	$50	$70	$90		Stan & Jan Berenstain		Schuman
1952	Tax-Wise	$50	$70	$90		Stan & Jan Berenstain		Schuman
1956	Baby Makes Four	$50	$70	$90		Stan & Jan Berenstain		Macmil
1958	It's All In The Family	$50	$60	$80		Stan & Jan Berenstain		Dutton
1960	And Beat Him When He Sneezes	$50	$60	$80		Stan & Jan Berenstain		McHill
1961	Call Me Mrs	$50	$60	$80		Stan & Jan Berenstain		Macmil
1961	It's Still In The Family	$50	$60	$80		Stan & Jan Berenstain		Dutton
1962	The Big Honey Hunt	$140	$200	$240		Stan & Jan Berenstain		BB
1964	The Bike Lesson	$90	$120	$160		Stan & Jan Berenstain		BB
1965	Flipsville	$40	$60	$70		Stan & Jan Berenstain		DelaP
1966	The Bears' Picnic	$90	$120	$160		Stan & Jan Berenstain		BB
1967	Mr. Dirty Vs. Mrs. Clean	$80	$120	$140		Stan & Jan Berenstain		Dell
1967	The Bear Scouts	$80	$120	$140		Stan & Jan Berenstain		BB
1968	Inside, Outside, Upside Down	$80	$120	$140		Stan & Jan Berenstain		BB
1968	The Bears' Vacation	$80	$120	$140		Stan & Jan Berenstain		BB
1969	Bears On Wheels	$80	$120	$140		Stan & Jan Berenstain		BB
1970	Old Hat, New Hat		$60	$80	$120	Stan & Jan Berenstain		BB
1970	The Bears' Christmas		$70	$100	$140	Stan & Jan Berenstain		BB
1971	Bears In The Night		$50	$80	$100	Stan & Jan Berenstain		BB
1971	The Berenstains' B Book		$50	$80	$100	Stan & Jan Berenstain		BB
1972	C Is For Clown		$50	$80	$100	Stan & Jan Berenstain		BB
1973	The Bears' Almanac		$50	$80	$100	Stan & Jan Berenstain		BB
1973	The Berenstain Bears' Nursery Tales		$50	$80	$100	Stan & Jan Berenstain		BB
1974	He Bear, She Bear		$50	$70	$100	Stan & Jan Berenstain		BB
1974	The Berenstain Bears' New Baby		$50	$70	$100	Stan & Jan Berenstain		BB
1975	The Bear Detectives		$50	$70	$90	Stan & Jan Berenstain		BB
1975	The Bears' Nature Guide		$50	$70	$90	Stan & Jan Berenstain		BB
1976	The Berenstain Bears' Counting Book		$50	$70	$90	Stan & Jan Berenstain		BB
1977	The Berenstain Bears' Science Fair		$40	$60	$90	Stan & Jan Berenstain		BB
1978	Berenstain Bears Go To School		$40	$60	$90	Stan & Jan Berenstain		BB
1978	Papa's Pizza		$25	$35	$50	Stan & Jan Berenstain		BB
1978	The B. Bears And The Spooky Old Tree		$40	$60	$90	Stan & Jan Berenstain		BB
1980	The B. Bears And The Missing Dinosaur Bone		$25	$35	$50	Stan & Jan Berenstain		BB
1980	The Berenstain Bears' Christmas Tree		$25	$35	$50	Stan & Jan Berenstain		BB
1981	The B. Bears And The Sitter		$25	$35	$50	Stan & Jan Berenstain		BB
1981	The Berenstain Bears Go To The Doctor		$25	$35	$50	Stan & Jan Berenstain		BB
1981	The Berenstain Bears' Moving Day		$25	$35	$50	Stan & Jan Berenstain		BB
1981	The Berenstain Bears Visit The Dentist		$25	$35	$50	Stan & Jan Berenstain		BB
1982	The Berenstain Bears Get In A Fight		$20	$30	$40	Stan & Jan Berenstain		BB
1982	The Berenstain Bears Go To Camp		$20	$30	$40	Stan & Jan Berenstain		BB
1982	The Berenstain Bears In The Dark		$20	$30	$40	Stan & Jan Berenstain		BB
1982	The Berenstain Bears' Storybook Tree House		$20	$30	$40	Stan & Jan Berenstain		BB
1983	The B. Bears And The Messy Room		$20	$30	$40	Stan & Jan Berenstain		BB
1983	The B. Bears And The Truth		$20	$30	$40	Stan & Jan Berenstain		BB
1983	The Berenstain Bears' Trouble With Money		$20	$30	$40	Stan & Jan Berenstain		BB
1984	The B. Bears And The Dinosaurs		$20	$30	$40	Stan & Jan Berenstain		BB
1984	The B. Bears And The Neighborly Skunk		$20	$30	$40	Stan & Jan Berenstain		BB
1984	The Berenstain Bears And Mama's New Job		$20	$30	$40	Stan & Jan Berenstain		BB
1984	The Berenstain Bears And Too Much TV		$20	$30	$40	Stan & Jan Berenstain		BB

Berenstain, Stan & Jan

Year	Title	VG-	VG	VG+	Fine	Author	Award	Pub
1984	The Berenstain Bears Meet Santa Bear		$20	$30	$40	Stan & Jan Berenstain		BB
1985	Stan & Jan Berenstain's "It's All In The Family"		$20	$30	$40	Stan & Jan Berenstain		BB
1985	The Berenstain Bears And Too Much Junk Food		$20	$30	$40	Stan & Jan Berenstain		BB
1985	The Berenstain Bears Forget Their Manners		$20	$30	$40	Stan & Jan Berenstain		BB
1985	The Berenstain Bears Learn About Strangers		$20	$30	$40	Stan & Jan Berenstain		BB
1985	The Berenstain Bears On The Moon		$20	$30	$40	Stan & Jan Berenstain		BB
1986	The B. Bears And The Bad Habit		$18	$25	$35	Stan & Jan Berenstain		BB
1986	The B. Bears And The Trouble With Friends		$18	$25	$35	Stan & Jan Berenstain		BB
1986	The B. Bears And The Week At Grandma's		$18	$25	$35	Stan & Jan Berenstain		BB
1986	The Berenstain Bears And Too Much Birthday		$18	$25	$35	Stan & Jan Berenstain		BB
1986	The Berenstain Bears Get Stage Fright		$18	$25	$35	Stan & Jan Berenstain		BB
1986	The Berenstain Bears Go Out For The Team		$18	$25	$35	Stan & Jan Berenstain		BB
1986	The Berenstain Bears' Knight To Remember		$18	$25	$35	Stan & Jan Berenstain		BB
1986	The Berenstain Bears' Trouble At School		$18	$25	$35	Stan & Jan Berenstain		BB
1986	The Berenstain Bears, No Girl's Allowed		$18	$25	$35	Stan & Jan Berenstain		BB
1987	The B. Bears And The Big Road Race		$18	$25	$35	Stan & Jan Berenstain		BB
1987	The B. Bears And The Mansion Mystery		$18	$25	$35	Stan & Jan Berenstain		BB
1987	The B. Bears And The Missing Honey		$18	$25	$35	Stan & Jan Berenstain		BB
1987	The Berenstain Bears Blaze A Trail		$18	$25	$35	Stan & Jan Berenstain		BB
1987	The Berenstain Bears On The Job		$18	$25	$35	Stan & Jan Berenstain		BB
1987	The Berenstain Kids		$18	$25	$35	Stan & Jan Berenstain		BB
1988	The B. Bears And The Bad Dream		$18	$25	$35	Stan & Jan Berenstain		BB
1988	The B. Bears And The Double Dare		$18	$25	$35	Stan & Jan Berenstain		BB
1988	The B. Bears And The Ghost Of The Forest		$18	$25	$35	Stan & Jan Berenstain		BB
1988	The Berenstain Bears Get The Gimmies		$18	$25	$35	Stan & Jan Berenstain		BB
1988	The Berenstain Bears Ready, Get Set, Go!		$18	$25	$35	Stan & Jan Berenstain		BB
1989	The B. Bears And The In-Crowd		$18	$25	$35	Stan & Jan Berenstain		BB
1989	The Berenstain Bears And Too Much Vacation		$18	$25	$35	Stan & Jan Berenstain		BB
1989	The Berenstain Bears Trick Or Treat		$18	$25	$35	Stan & Jan Berenstain		BB
1990	The B. Bears And The Prize Pumpkin		$16	$25	$30	Stan & Jan Berenstain		BB
1990	The B. Bears And The Slumber Party		$16	$25	$30	Stan & Jan Berenstain		BB
1990	The Berenstain Bears' Trouble With Pets		$16	$25	$30	Stan & Jan Berenstain		BB
1991	The Berenstain Bears Are A Family		$16	$25	$30	Stan & Jan Berenstain		BB
1991	The Berenstain Bears At The Super-Duper Market		$16	$25	$30	Stan & Jan Berenstain		BB
1991	The Berenstain Bears Don't Pollute (Anymore)		$16	$25	$30	Stan & Jan Berenstain		BB
1991	The Berenstain Bears' Four Seasons		$16	$25	$30	Stan & Jan Berenstain		BB
1991	The Berenstain Bears Say Good Night		$16	$25	$30	Stan & Jan Berenstain		BB
1992	The B. Bears And The Broken Piggy Bank		$16	$25	$30	Stan & Jan Berenstain		Western
1992	The B. Bears And The Trouble With Grownups		$16	$25	$30	Stan & Jan Berenstain		BB
1992	The Berenstain Bears And Too Much Pressure		$16	$25	$30	Stan & Jan Berenstain		BB
1992	The Berenstain Bears' Big Rummage Sale		$16	$25	$30	Stan & Jan Berenstain		Western
1992	The Berenstain Bears Hug And Make Up		$16	$25	$30	Stan & Jan Berenstain		Western
1992	The Berenstain Bears Visit Fun Park		$16	$25	$30	Stan & Jan Berenstain		Western
1992	The Berenstain Bears's Perfect Fishing Spot		$16	$25	$30	Stan & Jan Berenstain		Western
1993	The B. Bears And The Baby Chipmunk		$14	$20	$30	Stan & Jan Berenstain		Western
1993	The B. Bears And The Bully		$14	$20	$30	Stan & Jan Berenstain		BB
1993	The B. Bears And The Drug Free Zone		$14	$20	$30	Stan & Jan Berenstain		BB
1993	The B. Bears And The Female Fullback		$14	$20	$30	Stan & Jan Berenstain		BB
1993	The B. Bears And The Good Deed		$14	$20	$30	Stan & Jan Berenstain		Western
1993	The B. Bears And The Hiccup Cure		$14	$20	$30	Stan & Jan Berenstain		Western
1993	The B. Bears And The Jump Rope Contest		$14	$20	$30	Stan & Jan Berenstain		Western
1993	The B. Bears And The Nerdy Nephew		$14	$20	$30	Stan & Jan Berenstain		BB
1993	The B. Bears And The New Girl In Town		$14	$20	$30	Stan & Jan Berenstain		BB
1993	The B. Bears And The Red-Handed Thief		$14	$20	$30	Stan & Jan Berenstain		BB
1993	The B. Bears And The Spooky Old House		$14	$20	$30	Stan & Jan Berenstain		Western
1993	The B. Bears And The Wheelchair Commando		$14	$20	$30	Stan & Jan Berenstain		BB
1993	The B. Bears And The Wishing Star		$14	$20	$30	Stan & Jan Berenstain		Western
1993	The Berenstain Bears Accept No Substitutes		$14	$20	$30	Stan & Jan Berenstain		BB
1993	The Berenstain Bears All Year 'Round		$14	$20	$30	Stan & Jan Berenstain		Western
1993	The Berenstain Bears' Bedtime Battle		$14	$20	$30	Stan & Jan Berenstain		Golden
1993	The Berenstain Bears' Family Get-Together		$14	$20	$30	Stan & Jan Berenstain		Western
1993	The Berenstain Bears Get A Checkup		$14	$20	$30	Stan & Jan Berenstain		Western
1993	The Berenstain Bears Gotta Dance!		$14	$20	$30	Stan & Jan Berenstain		BB
1993	The Berenstain Bears Learn About Colors		$14	$20	$30	Stan & Jan Berenstain		BB
1993	The Berenstain Bears' Pet Show		$14	$20	$30	Stan & Jan Berenstain		Western
1993	The Berenstain Bears Visit Farmer Ben		$14	$20	$30	Stan & Jan Berenstain		Western
1993	The Berenstain Bears With Nothing To Do		$14	$20	$30	Stan & Jan Berenstain		Western

BERENSTAIN   Stan & Jan

Year	Title	VG-	VG	VG+	Fine	Author	Award	Pub
1994	The B. Bears And The Big Picture		$14	$20	$25	Stan & Jan Berenstain		Western
1994	The B. Bears And The Dress Code		$14	$20	$25	Stan & Jan Berenstain		BB
1994	The B. Bears And The Galloping Ghost		$14	$20	$25	Stan & Jan Berenstain		BB
1994	The B. Bears And The Giddy Grandma		$14	$20	$25	Stan & Jan Berenstain		BB
1994	The B. Bears And The Green-Eyed Monster		$14	$20	$25	Stan & Jan Berenstain		BB
1994	The B. Bears And The School Scandal Sheet		$14	$20	$25	Stan & Jan Berenstain		BB
1994	The B. Bears And The Summer Job		$14	$20	$25	Stan & Jan Berenstain		Western
1994	The Berenstain Bears At Big Bear Fair		$14	$20	$25	Stan & Jan Berenstain		Western
1994	The Berenstain Bears At Camp Crush		$14	$20	$25	Stan & Jan Berenstain		BB
1994	The Berenstain Bears' Birthday Boy		$14	$20	$25	Stan & Jan Berenstain		Western
1994	The Berenstain Bears Lost In A Cave		$14	$20	$25	Stan & Jan Berenstain		Western
1994	The Berenstain Bears' New Neighbors		$14	$20	$25	Stan & Jan Berenstain		BB
1994	The Berenstain Bears Visit Uncle Tex		$14	$20	$25	Stan & Jan Berenstain		Western
1995	The B. Bears And The Showdown At Chainsaw Gap		$12	$18	$25	Stan & Jan Berenstain		BB
1995	The Berenstain Bears And Too Much Teasing		$12	$18	$25	Stan & Jan Berenstain		BB
1995	The Berenstain Bears Count Their Blessings		$12	$18	$25	Stan & Jan Berenstain		BB
1995	The Berenstain Bears In The Freaky Funhouse		$12	$18	$25	Stan & Jan Berenstain		BB
1995	The Berenstain Bears' Media Madness		$12	$18	$25	Stan & Jan Berenstain		BB
1996	The Berenstain Bears At The Teen Rock Cafe		$12	$18	$25	Stan & Jan Berenstain		BB
1996	The Berenstain Bears Cook-It		$12	$18	$25	Stan & Jan Berenstain		BB
1996	The Berenstain Bears Draw-It		$12	$18	$25	Stan & Jan Berenstain		BB
1996	The Berenstain Bears Fly-It		$12	$18	$25	Stan & Jan Berenstain		BB
1996	The Berenstain Bears Grow-It		$12	$18	$25	Stan & Jan Berenstain		BB
1996	The Berenstain Bears In Big Bear City		$12	$18	$25	Stan & Jan Berenstain		BB
1996	The Berenstain Bears In Maniac Mansion		$12	$18	$25	Stan & Jan Berenstain		BB
1996	The Berenstain Bears' Sampler		$12	$18	$25	Stan & Jan Berenstain		BB
1996	The Berenstain Bears Yike! Yike! Where's My Trike?		$12	$18	$25	Stan & Jan Berenstain		BB
1997	Berenstains' A Book		$12	$16	$20	Stan & Jan Berenstain		BB
1997	Berenstains' C Book		$12	$16	$20	Stan & Jan Berenstain		BB
1997	The B. Bears And The Bermuda Triangle		$12	$16	$20	Stan & Jan Berenstain		BB
1997	The B. Bears And The Blame Game		$12	$16	$20	Stan & Jan Berenstain		BB
1997	The B. Bears And The Ghost Of The Auto Graveyard		$12	$16	$20	Stan & Jan Berenstain		BB
1997	The B. Bears And The Haunted Hayride		$12	$16	$20	Stan & Jan Berenstain		BB
1997	The B. Bears And The Homework Hassle		$12	$16	$20	Stan & Jan Berenstain		BB
1997	The Berenstain Bears And Queenie's Crazy Crush		$12	$16	$20	Stan & Jan Berenstain		BB
1997	The Berenstain Bears' Big Book Of Science And Nature		$12	$16	$20	Stan & Jan Berenstain		BB
1997	The Berenstain Bears' Home Sweet Tree		$12	$16	$20	Stan & Jan Berenstain		BB
1997	The Berenstain Bears' Thanksgiving		$12	$16	$20	Stan & Jan Berenstain		Scholas
1997	The Berenstain Bears The Whole Year Through		$12	$16	$20	Stan & Jan Berenstain		Scholas
1998	The B. Bears And The Big Date		$12	$16	$20	Stan & Jan Berenstain		BB
1998	The B. Bears And The Love Match		$12	$16	$20	Stan & Jan Berenstain		BB
1998	The B. Bears And The Perfect Crime (Almost)		$12	$16	$20	Stan & Jan Berenstain		BB
1998	The Berenstain Bears Big Bear, Small Bear		$12	$16	$20	Stan & Jan Berenstain		BB
1998	The Berenstain Bears By The Sea		$12	$16	$20	Stan & Jan Berenstain		BB
1998	The Berenstain Bears' Comic Valentine		$12	$16	$20	Stan & Jan Berenstain		Scholas
1998	The Berenstain Bears' Easter Surprise		$12	$16	$20	Stan & Jan Berenstain		Scholas
1998	The Berenstain Bears Get The Don't Haftas		$12	$16	$20	Stan & Jan Berenstain		BB
1998	The Berenstain Bears Get The Screamies		$12	$16	$20	Stan & Jan Berenstain		BB
1998	The Berenstain Bears Get Their Kicks		$12	$16	$20	Stan & Jan Berenstain		BB
1998	The Berenstain Bears Go Platinum		$12	$16	$20	Stan & Jan Berenstain		BB
1998	The Berenstain Bears Lend A Helping Hand		$12	$16	$20	Stan & Jan Berenstain		BB
1998	The Berenstain Bears Play Ball		$12	$16	$20	Stan & Jan Berenstain		Scholas
1998	The Berenstain Bears Ride The Thunderbolt		$12	$16	$20	Stan & Jan Berenstain		BB
1999	My New Bed		$10	$16	$20	Stan & Jan Berenstain		BB
1999	My Potty And I		$10	$16	$20	Stan & Jan Berenstain		BB
1999	My Trusty Car Seat		$10	$16	$20	Stan & Jan Berenstain		BB
1999	The B. Bears And The Big Question		$10	$16	$20	Stan & Jan Berenstain		BB
1999	The B. Bears And The G-Rex Bones		$10	$16	$20	Stan & Jan Berenstain		BB
1999	The Berenstain Bears Catch The Bus		$10	$16	$20	Stan & Jan Berenstain		BB
1999	The Berenstain Bears Get The Noisies		$10	$16	$20	Stan & Jan Berenstain		BB
1999	The Berenstain Bears Get The Scaredies		$10	$16	$20	Stan & Jan Berenstain		BB
1999	The Berenstain Bears Go Hollywood		$10	$16	$20	Stan & Jan Berenstain		BB
1999	The Berenstain Bears Go Up And Down		$10	$16	$20	Stan & Jan Berenstain		BB
1999	The Berenstain Bears In The House Of Mirrors		$10	$16	$20	Stan & Jan Berenstain		BB
1999	The Berenstain Bears In The Wax Museum		$10	$16	$20	Stan & Jan Berenstain		BB
1999	The Berenstain Bears Lost In Cyberspace		$10	$16	$20	Stan & Jan Berenstain		BB
1999	The Berenstain Bears' Mad, Mad, Mad Toy Craze		$10	$16	$20	Stan & Jan Berenstain		BB

Berenstain   Stan & Jan

Year	Title	VG-	VG	VG+	Fine	Author	Award	Pub
1999	The Berenstain Bears Think Of Those In Need		$10	$16	$20	Stan & Jan Berenstain		BB
1999	The Birds, The Bees, And The Berenstain Bears		$10	$16	$20	Stan & Jan Berenstain		BB
2000	Me First! Me First!		$10	$14	$18	Stan & Jan Berenstain		BB
2000	My Every Day Book		$10	$14	$18	Stan & Jan Berenstain		BB
2000	The B. Bears And The Big Blooper		$10	$14	$18	Stan & Jan Berenstain		BB
2000	The B. Bears And The Escape Of The Bogg Brothers		$10	$14	$18	Stan & Jan Berenstain		BB
2000	The B. Bears And The Great Ant Attack		$10	$14	$18	Stan & Jan Berenstain		BB
2000	The Berenstain Bears And Baby Makes Five		$10	$14	$18	Stan & Jan Berenstain		BB
2000	The Berenstain Bears Get The Twitchies		$10	$14	$18	Stan & Jan Berenstain		BB
2000	The Berenstain Bears Go In And Out		$10	$14	$18	Stan & Jan Berenstain		BB
2000	The Berenstain Bears' That Stump Must Go!		$10	$14	$18	Stan & Jan Berenstain		BB
2001	Feeding Time		$10	$14	$18	Stan & Jan Berenstain		BB
2001	My Blankie And I		$10	$14	$18	Stan & Jan Berenstain		BB
2001	The B. Bears And The Excuse Note		$10	$14	$18	Stan & Jan Berenstain		BB
2001	The B. Bears And The Haunted Lighthouse		$10	$14	$18	Stan & Jan Berenstain		BB
2001	The B. Bears And The Missing Watermelon Money		$10	$14	$18	Stan & Jan Berenstain		BB
2001	The B. Bears And The Tic-Tac-Toe Mystery		$10	$14	$18	Stan & Jan Berenstain		BB
2001	The Berenstain Bears Dollars And Sense		$10	$14	$18	Stan & Jan Berenstain		BB
2001	The Berenstain Bears-- Phenom In The Family		$10	$14	$18	Stan & Jan Berenstain		BB
2001	The Goofy, Goony Guy		$10	$14	$18	Stan & Jan Berenstain		BB
2001	The Runamuck Dog Show		$10	$14	$18	Stan & Jan Berenstain		BB
2001	The Wrong Crowd		$10	$14	$18	Stan & Jan Berenstain		BB
2002	Down A Sunny Dirt Road		$8	$12	16	Stan & Jan Berenstain		BB
2002	Ride Like The Wind		$8	$12	16	Stan & Jan Berenstain		BB
2002	The B. Bears And The Real Easter Eggs		$8	$12	16	Stan & Jan Berenstain		BB
2002	The Berenstain Bears' Report Card Trouble		$8	$12	16	Stan & Jan Berenstain		BB
2003	The B. Bears And The Papa's Day Surprise		$8	$12	16	Stan & Jan Berenstain		BB
2003	The Berenstain Bears' Funny Valentine		$8	$12	16	Stan & Jan Berenstain		BB
2003	Too Small For The Team		$8	$12	16	Stan & Jan Berenstain		BB
2004	The B. Bears And The Mama's Day Surprise		$8	$10	14	Stan & Jan Berenstain		BB
2004	We Like Kites		$8	$10	14	Stan & Jan Berenstain		BB

Berenzy   Alix

Year	Title	VG-	VG	VG+	Fine	Author	Award	Pub
1985	America's Very Own Ghosts		$25	$35	$50	Daniel Cohen		DoddM
1987	Touch The Moon		$16	$25	$30	Marion Dane Bauer		Clarion
1988	The Last Slice Of Rainbow & Other Stories		$16	$25	$30	Joan Aiken		H&Row
1989	A Frog Prince		$16	$25	$30	Alix Berenzy		Holt
1992	Cannonball River Tales		$14	$20	$25	David Rounds		Sierra
1995	Rapunzel		$12	$16	$20	Alix Berenzy		Holt
1996	Into The Sea		$12	$16	$20	Brenda Z. Guiberson		Holt
1998	A Glory Of Unicorns		$10	$16	$20	Bruce Coville		Scholas
1998	Home At Last		$10	$16	$20	April Pulley Sayre		Holt
2001	My Kingdom For A Horse		$8	$12	16	Betty Ann Schwartz		Holt

Berger   Barbara

Year	Title	VG-	VG	VG+	Fine	Author	Award	Pub
1981	Brothers Of The Wind		$18	$25	$35	Jane Yolen		Philo
1982	Animalia		$16	$25	$30	Barbara Berger		Carts
1984	Grandfather Twilight		$16	$25	$30	Barbara Berger		Philo
1997	Burpee Seed Starter		$10	$16	$20	Maureen Heffernan		Macmil
2000	Angels On A Pin		$8	$12	16	Barbara Berger		Philo

Bergsma   Jody

Year	Title	VG-	VG	VG+	Fine	Author	Award	Pub
1985	Touching		$12	$16	$20	Sandy Kleven		Watcorn
1997	Dreambirds		$8	$12	16	David Ogden		Illum
1997	The Right Touch		$8	$12	16	Sandy Kleven		Illum
1998	Sky Castle		$8	$12	16	Sandra Hanken		Illum
1999	Dragon		$8	$12	16	Jody Bergsma		Illum
2000	The Little Wizard		$8	$10	14	Jody Bergsma		Illum
2002	Faerie		$8	$10	14	Jody Bergsma		Gallery

Bernal   Richard

Year	Title	VG-	VG	VG+	Fine	Author	Award	Pub
1989	Night, Zoo		$10	$16	$20	Richard Bernal		Calico
1990	Night, Mother Goose		$10	$14	$18	Richard Bernal		ContB
1991	Aesop's Fables		$10	$14	$18	Fiona Black		Ariel
1992	Peter And The Wolf		$10	$14	$18	Samantha Easton		AM
1993	Jack And The Beanstalk		$10	$14	$18	Jennifer Greenway		AM
1993	London Bridge Is Falling Down		$10	$14	$18	Richard Bernal		PubIntl
1993	The Ants Go Marching One By One		$10	$14	$18	Richard Bernal		PubIntl
1994	The Little Red Barn		$10	$14	$18	Mallory Loehr		Random
1997	Smasher		$8	$12	$16	Dick King-Smith		Random
1998	A Very Scary Cave		$8	$12	$16	Kari Smalley Gibson		G&H
1998	Classic Animal Tales		$8	$12	$16	Richard Bernal		PubIntl
1998	Mooki's Secret		$8	$12	$16	Kari Smalley Gibson		G&H
2000	Fifteen Flamingos		$8	$10	$14	Elspeth Campbell Murphy		Bethny
2004	Jag's New Friend		$6	$10	$12	LeAnn Rimes		Dutton

Berson   Harold

Year	Title	VG-	VG	VG+	Fine	Author	Award	Pub
1958	In Happy Hollow	$70	$100	$120		Rutherford Montgomery		DoubleD
1958	Loretta Mason Potts	$50	$60	$80		Mary Chase		Lippin
1958	The Silver Button	$50	$60	$80		Helen Diehl Olds		Knopf
1959	Larry And The Freedom Man	$50	$60	$80		Margaret Hagler		LL&S
1959	Seventh Son Of A Seventh Son	$50	$60	$80		William Littlefield		LL&S
1959	The Nutcracker	$50	$60	$80		Daniel Walden		Lippin
1960	A Pint Of Judgment	$40	$50	$70		Elizabeth Morrow		Knopf
1960	Belling The Cat	$40	$50	$70		Leland B. Jacobs		Golden
1961	Mince Pie And Mistletoe	$40	$50	$70		Phyllis McGinley		Lippin
1961	Mr. Kipling's Elephant	$40	$50	$70		Margaret Otto		Knopf
1962	The Nightingale	$40	$50	$70		Hans Christian Andersen		Lippin
1964	Swanhilda-Of-The-Swans	$35	$50	$60		Dana Faralla		Lippin
1965	Raminagrobis And The Mice	$40	$60	$70		Harold Berson		Seabury
1965	The Dancing Camel	$40	$60	$70		Betsy Cromer Byars		Viking
1965	The Elephant On Ice	$40	$60	$70		James Playsted Wood		Seabury
1965	The Perfect Pitch	$40	$60	$70		Beman Lord		Walck
1965	The Wonderful Flying-Go-Round	$40	$60	$70		Dana Faralla		World
1966	Pop! Goes The Turnip	$40	$60	$70		Harold Berson		G&D
1966	The Bad Child's Book Of Beasts	$40	$60	$70		Hilaire Belloc		G&D
1967	A Treasury Of Mother Goose	$40	$50	$70		Oscar Weigle		G&D
1967	The Day The Spaceship Landed	$40	$50	$70		Beman Lord		Walck
1967	The Pelican Chorus	$40	$50	$70		Edward Lear		PMagP
1967	Watermelons, Walnuts, And The Wisdom Of Allah	$40	$50	$70		Barbara K. Walker		PMagP
1967	When Will I Whistle?	$40	$50	$70		Mary McBurney Green		FWatts
1968	Hubba-Hubba	$40	$50	$70		Ruth Philpott Collins		Crown
1968	The Celebrated Jumping Frog Of Calaveras County	$40	$50	$70		Mark Twain		FWatts
1968	The Wild Beast	$40	$50	$70		N. S. Leskov		F&W
1969	A Bear Named George	$40	$50	$70		Miriam Young		Crown
1969	King Midas And The Golden Touch	$80	$120	$140		Al Perkins		BB
1969	Pigs And Pirates	$40	$50	$70		Barbara K. Walker		Dwhite
1969	Shot-Put Challenge	$40	$50	$70		Beman Lord		Walck
1969	The King And The Whirlybird	$40	$50	$70		Mabel Watts		PMagP
1969	Why The Jackal Won't Speak To The Hedgehog	$40	$50	$70		Harold Berson		Seabury
1970	Festival In The Park		$25	$40	$50	Helen Copeland		Crown
1970	Folktales Of The Irish Countryside		$25	$40	$50	Kevin Danaher		Dwhite
1970	Shrimp's Soccer Goal		$25	$40	$50	Beman Lord		Walck
1970	The Dragon That Lived Under Manhattan		$25	$40	$50	E. W. Hildick		Crown
1970	The Spaceship Returns		$25	$40	$50	Beman Lord		Walck
1970	What A Beautiful Noise		$25	$40	$50	Harry Behn		World
1971	Ittki Pittki		$25	$40	$50	Miriam Chaikin		PMagP
1971	Sunday In Centreville		$25	$40	$50	G. Allen Foster		Dwhite
1972	Balarin's Goat		$25	$40	$50	Harold Berson		Crown
1972	How The Devil Gets His Due		$25	$40	$50	Harold Berson		Crown
1972	K Mouse And Bo Bixby		$25	$40	$50	Nan Hayden Agle		Seabury
1972	The Bluejay Boarders		$25	$40	$50	Harold Keith		Crowell
1972	The Thief Who Hugged A Moonbeam		$25	$40	$50	Harold Berson		Seabury
1973	Carlos Goes To School		$25	$40	$50	Eloise A. Anderson		FWarne
1973	Henry Possum		$25	$40	$50	Harold Berson		Crown
1973	More Poetry For Holidays		$25	$40	$50	Nancy Larrick		Garrard

Berson   Harold

Year	Title	VG-	VG	VG+	Fine	Author	Award	Pub
1973	Pirates In The Park		$25	$40	$50	Thom Roberts		Crown
1973	The Good Guys And The Bad Guys		$25	$40	$50	Osmond Molarsky		Walck
1974	Hang In At The Plate		$25	$40	$50	Fred Bachman		Walck
1974	House Cat		$25	$40	$50	Ann Finlayson		FWarne
1974	New Patches For Old		$25	$40	$50	Barbara K. Walker		PMagP
1974	The Boy, The Baker, The Miller, And More		$25	$40	$50	Harold Berson		Crown
1975	A Moose Is Not A Mouse		$25	$35	$50	Harold Berson		Crown
1975	The Mule Who Refused To Budge		$25	$35	$50	Lionel Wilson		Crown
1976	Abu Ali		$25	$35	$50	Dorothy Van Woerkom		Macmil
1976	I'm Bored, Ma!		$25	$35	$50	Harold Berson		Crown
1976	The Rats Who Lived In The Delicatessen		$25	$35	$50	Harold Berson		Crown
1977	Kassim's Shoes		$25	$35	$50	Harold Berson		Crown
1978	My Trip To Alpha I		$25	$35	$50	Alfred Slote		H&Row
1978	The Friends Of Abu Ali		$25	$35	$50	Dorothy Van Woerkom		Macmil
1978	Yetta, The Trickster		$25	$35	$50	Andrea Griffing Zimmerman		Seabury
1979	Joseph And The Snake		$20	$30	$40	Harold Berson		Macmil
1980	Charles And Claudine		$20	$30	$40	Harold Berson		Macmil
1980	The Greedy Shopkeeper		$20	$30	$40	Irene Mirkovi c		HBJ
1980	Truffles For Lunch		$20	$30	$40	Harold Berson		Macmil
1982	Barrels To The Moon		$20	$30	$40	Harold Berson		CM&G
1983	The Turkey Girl		$18	$25	$35	Betty Baker		Macmil

Bettina

Year	Title	VG-	VG	VG+	Fine	Author	Award	Pub
1943	Poo-Tsee, The Water-Tortoise	$80	$100	$140		Bettina Ehrlich		C&Weed
1945	Cocolo	$70	$100	$120		Bettina Ehrlich		C&Weed
1949	Cocolo Comes To America	$70	$90	$120		Bettina Ehrlich		H&B
1950	Cocolo's Home	$70	$90	$120		Bettina Ehrlich		H&B
1951	Castle In The Sand	$70	$90	$120		Bettina Ehrlich		H&B
1952	A Horse For The Island	$70	$90	$120		Bettina Ehrlich		H&B
1954	Piccolo	$70	$90	$120		Bettina Ehrlich		H&B
1954	The Swans Of Ballycastle	$70	$90	$120		Walter Anthony Hackett		Ariel
1956	The Magic Christmas Tree	$60	$80	$100		Lee Kingman		Ariel
1957	Pantaloni	$90	$120	$160		Bettina Ehrlich		H&B
1959	Trovato	$60	$80	$100		Bettina Ehrlich		Ariel
1960	Paolo And Panetto	$50	$70	$90		Bettina Ehrlich		FWatts
1963	Dolls	$50	$70	$90		Bettina Ehrlich		Ariel
1964	Of Uncles And Aunts	$50	$70	$90		Bettina Ehrlich		Norton
1966	The Goat Boy	$50	$60	$80		Bettina Ehrlich		Norton
1967	Sardines And The Angel	$50	$60	$80		Bettina Ehrlich		Oxford

Biers   Clarence

Year	Title	VG-	VG	VG+	Fine	Author	Award	Pub
1925	A Riddle Book For Silent Reading	$60	$80	$100		Lily Lee Dootson		RandMc
1925	Sunny Crest Farmyard	$100	$120	$160		Fannie R. Buchanan		RandMc
1935	The Five Little Bears	$50	$70	$90		Sterling North		RandMc
1935	Who Am I?	$50	$70	$90		Lily Lee Dootson		RandMc
1936	The Five Little Raccoons	$50	$60	$80		Gladys Buchanan		RandMc
1938	Snow-White And Rose-Red	$50	$60	$80		Jacob & Wilhelm Grimm		RandMc
1941	Choo-Choo, The Little Switch Engine	$50	$60	$80		Wallace Carter Wadsworth		RandMc
1942	Number 9	$50	$60	$80		Wallace Carter Wadsworth		RandMc
1942	The Lazy Automobile	$50	$60	$80		Wallace Carter Wadsworth		RandMc
1943	Cocky, The Little Helicopter	$50	$60	$80		Marjorie Barrows		RandMc
1944	Jojo	$50	$60	$80		Marjorie Barrows		RandMc
1944	The Happy Giraffe	$50	$60	$80		Frances Cavanah		W&F
1948	Dipsy Donkey	$40	$60	$70		Clarence Biers		Whitman
1949	Scamper	$40	$60	$70		Marjorie Barrows		RandMc
1950	Tut!	$40	$50	$70		Marjorie Barrows		GardenC

Bileck   Marvin

Year	Title	VG-	VG	VG+	Fine	Author	Award	Pub
1955	Nipper Shiffer's Donkey	$60	$80	$100		Fingal Ruth Rosenquist		H&B
1955	Sugarplum	$50	$70	$90		Johanna Johnston		Knopf
1964	Rain Makes Applesauce	$90	$120	$160		Julian Scheer	CH	Holiday
1966	Penny	$40	$60	$70		Beatrice S. De Regniers		Viking

Bileck — Marvin

Year	Title	VG-	VG	VG+	Fine	Author	Award	Pub
1970	Timi, The Tale Of A Griffin		$30	$50	$60	Barbara Constance Freeman		G&D

Billout — Guy

Year	Title	VG-	VG	VG+	Fine	Author	Award	Pub
1979	By Camel Or By Car		$25	$40	$50	Guy Billout		P-Hall
1980	Stone & Steel		$18	$25	$35	Guy Billout		P-Hall
1981	Thunderbolt & Rainbow		$18	$25	$35	Guy Billout		P-Hall
1982	Squid & Spider		$16	$25	$30	Guy Billout		P-Hall
1993	The Journey		$12	$16	$20	Guy Billout		Creat
2002	Something's Not Quite Right		$8	$10	$14	Guy Billout		Godine

Bing — Christopher

Year	Title	VG-	VG	VG+	Fine	Author	Award	Pub
2000	Casey At The Bat		$35	$50	$70	Ernest Lawrence Thayer	CH	Hand
2001	The Midnight Ride Of Paul Revere		$12	$18	$25	Henry Wadsworth Longfellow		Hand
2003	The Story Of Little Black Sambo		$10	$16	$20	Helen Bannerman		Hand

Birnbaum — Abe

Year	Title	VG-	VG	VG+	Fine	Author	Award	Pub
1954	Green Eyes	$90	$120	$160		Abe Birnbaum	CH	Caed
1966	Did A Bear Just Walk There!	$35	$40	$60		Ann Rand		HBrace

Blackwood — Gladys Rourke

Year	Title	VG-	VG	VG+	Fine	Author	Award	Pub
1940	Dilly Dally Sally	$50	$70	$90		Marguerite Henry		SaalF
1940	Jano And Jeni	$50	$70	$90		Maria Vrooman		AWhit
1940	Secrets At The Mardi Gras	$50	$70	$90		Joan Constantino		AWhit
1942	Geraldine Belinda	$80	$100	$140		Marguerite Henry		P&Munk
1943	Their First Igloo On Baffin Island	$50	$70	$90		Marguerite Henry		AWhit
1944	Anno And Tauno	$50	$70	$90		Marguerite Henry		AWhit
1945	The Coco Dancer	$50	$70	$90		Flora Rue		AWhit
1952	Whistle For Cindy	$50	$60	$80		Gladys Rourke Blackwood		AWhit
1955	The Eskimo Store	$40	$60	$70		Ann Lange		AWhit

Blake — Quentin

Year	Title	VG-	VG	VG+	Fine	Author	Award	Pub
1961	The Wonderful Button	$100	$120	$160		Evan Hunter		SaalF
1963	Tales Of A Wicked Uncle	$50	$60	$80		Rupert Croft-Cooke		Bedford
1964	Uncle Stories	$140	$180	$240		J.P. Martin		CM
1966	Aristide	$40	$60	$70		Robert Tibber		Dial
1967	Agaton Sax And The Diamond Thieves	$40	$50	$70		Evelyn Ramsden		DelaP
1967	In A Glass Lightly	$60	$80	$100		Quentin Blake		Metheun
1967	Living With Technology	$40	$50	$70		H.P. Rickman		H&S
1967	Puzzles For Pleasure And Leisure	$40	$50	$70		Thomas L. Hirsch.		AS
1967	Uncle Cleans Up	$80	$120	$140		J. P. Martin.		CM
1968	Albert The Dragon And The Centaur	$60	$80	$100		Quentin Blake		AS
1969	Agaton Sax And The Scotland Yard Mystery	$60	$80	$100		Quentin Blake		DelaP
1969	Alphabet Soup	$40	$50	$70		John Yeoman		Faber
1969	Gillygaloos And Gollywhoppers	$60	$80	$100		Quentin Blake		AS
1969	Patrick	$40	$50	$70		Quentin Blake		Walck
1969	The Bear's Winter House	$40	$50	$70		John Yeoman		World
1969	The First Elephant Comes To Ireland	$40	$50	$70		Quentin Blake		Follett
1970	Agaton Sax And The Incredible Max Brothers		$30	$50	$60	Quentin Blake		DelaP
1970	Agaton Sax And The Max Brothers		$30	$50	$60	Quentin Blake		Deutsch
1970	Angelo		$30	$50	$60	Quentin Blake		JCape
1970	Kibby's Big Feat		$30	$50	$60	Thomas I. Corddry		Follett
1970	The Bear's Water Picnic		$30	$50	$60	Quentin Blake		Macmil
1971	Puzzles And Quizzles		$30	$50	$60	Quentin Blake		AS
1971	Sixes And Sevens		$30	$50	$60	John Yeoman		Macmil
1971	The Ages Of Man: From Sav-Age To Sew-Age		$30	$50	$60	Quentin Blake		AHP
1971	The Birds		$30	$50	$60	Dudley Fitts		LUP
1972	Mouse Trouble		$30	$50	$60	Quentin Blake		Macmil
1973	Snuff		$30	$50	$60	Quentin Blake		Lippin
1974	Agaton Sax And The League Of Silent Exploders		$30	$40	$60	Quentin Blake		Deutsch
1974	Arabel's Raven		$30	$40	$60	Quentin Blake		DoubleD

Blake   Quentin

Year	Title	VG-	VG	VG+	Fine	Author	Award	Pub
1974	Beatrice And Vanessa		$30	$40	$60	John Yeoman		HHamil
1974	Great Day For Up!		$90	$140	$180	Theodor Geisel		BB
1974	How Tom Beat Captain Najork		$40	$60	$80	Quentin Blake		Athenm
1974	Mind Your Own Business		$30	$40	$60	Quentin Blake		Phillip
1974	The Bread Bin		$30	$40	$60	Bernard Cribbins		BBC
1975	Agaton Sax And The Haunted House		$30	$40	$60	Nils-Olof Franzen		Deutsch
1975	Kidnapped At Christmas: A Play		$30	$40	$60	Willis Hall		Fogel
1975	The Witch's Cat		$30	$40	$60	Quentin Blake		AW
1976	A Near Thing For Captain Najork		$40	$60	$80	Russell Hoban	NYT	Athenm
1976	Horseshoe Harry And The Whale		$30	$40	$60	Adele de Leeuw		PMagP
1976	Lady Monster Has A Plan		$30	$40	$60	Ellen Blance		Bowmar
1976	Mortimer's Tie		$30	$40	$60	Joan Aiken		BBC
1976	The Bed Book		$30	$40	$60	Sylvia Plath		Faber
1976	The Improbable Book Of Records		$30	$40	$60	John Yeoman		Athenm
1977	Nonstop Nonsense		$25	$40	$50	Margaret Mahy		JMDent
1977	Of Quarks, Quasars, & Other Quirks		$25	$40	$50	Sara Brewton		Crowell
1977	Wouldn't You Like To Know		$25	$40	$50	Michael Rosen		Deutsch
1978	Agaton Sax And Lispington's Grandfather Clock		$25	$40	$50	Nils-Olof Franzen		Deutsch
1978	The Enormous Crocodile		$50	$80	$100	Roald Dahl		Knopf
1978	The Great Piratical Rumbustification		$25	$40	$50	Margaret Mahy		JMDent
1978	The Young Performing Horse		$25	$40	$50	John Yeoman		PMagP
1978	Willie The Squowse		$25	$40	$50	Ted Allan		Hastings
1979	The Wild Washerwomen: A New Folk Tale		$25	$40	$50	John Yeoman		Green
1980	Ace Dragon Ltd		$20	$30	$40	Russell Hoban		JCape
1980	Black Mischief		$20	$30	$40	Evelyn Waugh		Folio
1980	Custard And Company: Poems		$20	$30	$40	Ogden Nash		LBrown
1980	Mister Magnolia		$60	$80	$120	Quentin Blake	GM	JCape
1980	What Difference Does It Make, Danny?		$20	$30	$40	Helen Young		Deutsch
1981	Agaton Sax And The Big Rig		$20	$30	$40	Nils-Olof Franzen		Deutsch
1981	Arabel And Mortimer		$20	$30	$40	Joan Aiken		DoubleD
1981	George's Marvellous Medicine		$40	$60	$80	Roald Dahl		JCape
1981	The Twits		$40	$60	$80	Roald Dahl		Knopf
1981	You Can't Catch Me!		$20	$30	$40	Michael Rosen		Deutsch
1982	George's Marvelous Medicine		$40	$60	$80	Roald Dahl		Knopf
1982	Roald Dahl's Revolting Rhymes		$40	$60	$80	Quentin Blake		Knopf
1982	The BFG		$40	$60	$80	Roald Dahl		FSG
1983	Cyril Bonhamy And The Great Drain Robbery		$18	$25	$35	Jonathan Gathorne-Hardy		JCape
1983	Mortimer's Cross		$18	$25	$35	Joan Aiken		H&Row
1983	Quentin Blake's Nursery Rhyme Book		$18	$25	$35	Quentin Blake		H&Row
1983	Quick, Let's Get Out Of Here		$18	$25	$35	Michael Rosen		Deutsch
1983	The Witches		$35	$50	$70	Roald Dahl		FSG
1984	Dirty Beasts		$35	$50	$70	Roald Dahl		JCape
1985	Cyril Bonhamy And Operation Ping		$18	$25	$35	Jonathan Gathorne-Hardy		JCape
1985	How The Camel Got His Hump		$18	$25	$35	Rudyard Kipling		Bedrik
1985	Mortimer Says Nothing		$18	$25	$35	Joan Aiken		H&Row
1985	The Giraffe And The Pelly And Me		$35	$50	$70	Roald Dahl		FSG
1985	The Story Of The Dancing Frog		$18	$25	$35	Quentin Blake		Knopf
1986	Can You Get Warts From Touching Toads?		$16	$25	$30	Peter Rowan		Messner
1986	Smelly Jelly Smelly Fish		$16	$25	$30	Michael Rosen		P-Hall
1986	The Rain Door		$16	$25	$30	Russell Hoban		Crowell
1986	Under The Bed		$16	$25	$30	Michael Rosen		P-Hall
1987	Down At The Doctor's: The Sick Book		$16	$25	$30	Michael Rosen		P-Hall
1987	Hard-Boiled Legs		$16	$25	$30	Michael Rosen		P-Hall
1987	Mrs. Armitage On Wheels		$16	$25	$30	Quentin Blake		Knopf
1987	Spollyollydiddlytiddlyitis		$16	$25	$30	Michael Rosen		Walker
1987	The Marzipan Pig		$16	$25	$30	Russell Hoban		FSG
1988	Matilda		$60	$90	$120	Roald Dahl		JCape
1988	Our Village Poems		$16	$25	$30	John Yeoman		Athenm
1989	Monsters		$16	$25	$30	Russell Hoban		Scholas
1989	Quentin Blake's ABC		$16	$25	$30	Quentin Blake		Knopf
1989	Rhyme Stew		$30	$40	$60	Roald Dahl		JCape
1990	Esio Trot		$25	$40	$50	Roald Dahl		Viking
1990	Old Mother Hubbard's Dog Dresses Up		$14	$20	$30	John Yeoman		HM
1990	Old Mother Hubbard's Dog Needs A Doctor		$14	$20	$30	John Yeoman		HM
1990	Old Mother Hubbard's Dog Takes Up Sport		$14	$20	$30	John Yeoman		HM
1991	All Join In		$14	$20	$30	Quentin Blake		LBrown
1991	Mr. Horrox And The Gratch		$14	$20	$30	James Reeves		Weather

Blake   Quentin

Year	Title	VG-	VG	VG+	Fine	Author	Award	Pub
1992	Cockatoos		$14	$20	$25	Quentin Blake		LBrown
1992	Dick King-Smith's Alphabeasts		$14	$20	$25	Quentin Blake		Macmil
1992	Here Comes Mcbroom: Three More Tall Tales		$14	$20	$25	Sid Fleischman		Green
1992	Mcbroom's Wonderful One-Acre Farm		$14	$20	$25	Sid Fleischman		Green
1992	The Vicar Of Nibbleswicke		$25	$35	$50	Roald Dahl		Viking
1993	The Singing Tortoise & Other Animal Folktales		$14	$20	$25	John Yeoman		Tambour
1994	My Year		$20	$30	$40	Roald Dahl		Viking
1994	Simpkin		$12	$18	$25	Quentin Blake		Viking
1995	A Christmas Carol		$12	$16	$20	Charles Dickens		McEld
1995	James and the Giant Peach		$20	$30	$40	Roald Dahl		Viking
1995	The Do-It-Yourself House That Jack Built		$12	$16	$20	John Yeoman		Athenm
1995	The Magic Finger		$12	$16	$20	Roald Dahl		Viking
1996	Clown		$12	$16	$20	Quentin Blake		Holt
1998	Mrs. Armitage And The Big Wave		$10	$16	$20	Quentin Blake		HBrace
1998	The Twelve Days Of Christmas		$10	$16	$20	John Julius Norwich		StMart
1998	Zagazoo		$10	$16	$20	Quentin Blake		Orchard
2000	Ten Frogs		$10	$14	$18	Quentin Blake		diCapua
2000	Trouble On Thunder Mountain		$10	$14	$18	Russell Hoban		Orchard
2000	Wizzil		$10	$14	$18	William Steig		FSG
2002	Loveykins		$8	$12	$16	Quentin Blake		Peach
2002	Magic Pencil		$8	$12	$16	Quentin Blake		LangArt
2003	Mrs Armitage		$8	$10	$14	Quentin Blake		Peach
2003	Tell Me A Picture		$8	$10	$14	Quentin Blake		Millbk
2004	Father Christmas's Last Present		$8	$10	$14	Marie-Aude Murail		Peach

Blathwayt   Benedict

Year	Title	VG-	VG	VG+	Fine	Author	Award	Pub
1987	Tangle And The Firesticks		$16	$25	$30	Benedict Blathwayt		Knopf
1988	Bear's Adventure		$16	$25	$30	Benedict Blathwayt		Knopf
1989	Tangle And The Silver Bird		$16	$25	$30	Benedict Blathwayt		Knopf
1993	Stories From Firefly Island		$14	$20	$25	Benedict Blathwayt		Green

Blegvad   Erik

Year	Title	VG-	VG	VG+	Fine	Author	Award	Pub
1956	Greenwillow	$70	$100	$120		B. J. Chute		Dutton
1956	Myrtle Albertina's Secret	$70	$100	$120		Lillian Pohlmann		CM
1956	The Amazing Vacation	$70	$100	$120		Dan Wickenden		HBrace
1957	Bed-Knob And Broomstick	$50	$70	$90		Mary Norton		HBrace
1957	Oddity Land	$50	$70	$90		Edward Anthony		DoubleD
1957	The Late Spring	$50	$70	$90		Jean Fritz		CM
1958	Flivver, The Heroic Horse	$50	$60	$80		Lee Kingman		DoubleD
1958	Journey To Christmas	$50	$60	$80		B. J. Chute		Dutton
1958	Myrtle Albertina's Song	$50	$60	$80		Lillian Pohlmann		CM
1958	The Swineherd	$50	$60	$80		Hans Christian Andersen		HBrace
1959	Having A Friend	$50	$60	$80		Betty Miles		Knopf
1959	The Adventures Of Rinaldo	$50	$60	$80		Isabella Holt		LBrown
1959	The Emperor's New Clothes	$50	$60	$80		Hans Christian Andersen		HBrace
1959	The Gammage Cup	$50	$60	$80		Carol Kendall		HBJ
1960	Jack Mack	$50	$60	$80		Robert Paul Smith		CM
1960	Plenty Of Fish	$50	$60	$80		Millicent Selsam		H&B
1960	The Little Old Train	$50	$60	$80		Margaret Otto		Knopf
1961	Mud Pies & Other Recipes	$50	$60	$80		Marjorie Winslow		Macmil
1961	The Last Of The Wizards	$50	$60	$80		Rona Jaffe		S&S
1961	Where's Willie?	$50	$60	$80		Seymour Reit		Golden
1962	Dusty & The Fiddlers	$50	$60	$80		Miska Miles		LBrown
1962	Elephi	$50	$60	$80		Jean Stafford		FSG
1962	See What I Found	$50	$60	$80		Myra Cohn Livingston		HBrace
1962	The Diamond in the Window	$140	$200	$240		Jane Langton		H&Row
1963	A Year Is A Window	$50	$60	$80		Richard Webber Jackson		DoubleD
1963	I'm Not Me	$50	$60	$80		Myra Cohn Livingston		HBrace
1964	Elisabeth, The Treasure Hunter	$50	$60	$80		Felice Holman		Macmil
1964	Happy Birthday!	$50	$60	$80		Myra Cohn Livingston		HBrace
1964	Pony In The Schoolhouse	$50	$60	$80		Miska Miles		LBrown
1964	The Five Pennies	$50	$60	$80		Barbara Brenner		Knopf
1966	Elisabeth And The Marsh Mystery	$40	$60	$70		Felice Holman		Macmil
1966	I'm Waiting	$40	$60	$70		Myra Cohn Livingston		HBrace

Blegvad   Erik

Year	Title	VG-	VG	VG+	Fine	Author	Award	Pub
1966	The Good-Byes Of Magnus Marmalade	$40	$60	$70		Doris Orgel		Putnam
1967	Beginning-To-Read Poetry	$40	$50	$70		Sally Clithero		Follett
1967	The Swing In The Summerhouse	$40	$50	$70		Jane Langton		H&Row
1968	One Is For The Sun	$40	$50	$70		Lenore Blegvad		HBrace
1969	Emily's Autumn	$40	$50	$70		Janice May Udry		AWhit
1969	Phoebe And The Prince	$40	$50	$70		Doris Orgel		Putnam
1969	The Cat & The Coffee Drinkers	$40	$50	$70		Max Steele		H&Row
1969	The Cat From Nowhere	$40	$50	$70		Monica Stirling		HBrace
1969	The Diamond In The Window	$40	$50	$70		Jane Langton		HHamil
1969	The Great Hamster Hunt	$40	$50	$70		Lenore Blegvad		HBrace
1970	Bonnie Bess, The Weathervane Horse		$30	$50	$60	Alvin R. Tresselt		PMagP
1970	Miss Bianca In The Orient		$30	$50	$60	Margery Sharp		LBrown
1970	The Conscience Pudding		$30	$50	$60	Edith Nesbit		CM
1971	Miss Bianca In The Antarctic		$30	$50	$60	Margery Sharp		LBrown
1971	The Astonishing Stereoscope		$30	$50	$60	Jane Langton		H&Row
1971	The Finches' Fabulous Furnace		$30	$50	$60	Roger W. Drury		LBrown
1971	The Tenth Good Thing About Barney		$30	$50	$60	Judith Viorst		Athenm
1972	Miss Bianca And The Bridesmaid		$30	$50	$60	Margery Sharp		LBrown
1972	Moon-Watch Summer		$30	$50	$60	Lenore Blegvad		HBJ
1972	The Gift Of The Magi		$30	$50	$60	O. Henry		HawB
1973	The Complete Book Of Dragons		$30	$50	$60	Edith Nesbit		Macmil
1973	The Narrow Passage		$30	$50	$60	Oliver Butterworth		LBrown
1973	The Winds' Child		$30	$50	$60	Mark Taylor		Athenm
1974	Mittens For Kittens & Other Rhymes About Cats		$30	$40	$60	Lenore Blegvad		Athenm
1974	Polly's Tiger		$30	$40	$60	Joan Phipson		Dutton
1974	The Five In The Forest		$30	$40	$60	Jan Wahl		Follett
1974	The Mushroom Center Disaster		$30	$40	$60	N. M. Bodecker		Athenm
1975	The Dollhouse Caper		$30	$40	$60	Jean S. O'Connell		Crowell
1975	The Winter Bear		$30	$40	$60	Ruth Craft		Athenm
1976	Hark! Hark! The Dogs Do Bark		$30	$40	$60	Lenore Blegvad		Athenm
1976	May I Visit?		$30	$40	$60	Charlotte Zolotow		H&Row
1977	Blueberries Lavender		$25	$40	$50	Nancy Dingman Watson		AW
1977	Burnie's Hill		$25	$40	$50	Erik Blegvad		Athenm
1977	Pleasant Fieldmouse's Valentine Trick		$25	$40	$50	Jan Wahl		Windmil
1977	The Pleasant Fieldmouse Storybook		$25	$40	$50	Jan Wahl		P-Hall
1978	24 Poems From A Child's Garden Of Verses		$25	$40	$50	Robert Louis Stevenson		Random
1978	Someone New		$25	$40	$50	Charlotte Zolotow		H&Row
1978	This Little Pig-A-Wig		$25	$40	$50	Lenore Blegvad		Athenm
1979	Yesterday's Snowman		$25	$40	$50	Gail Mack		Pan
1980	The Three Little Pigs		$25	$35	$50	Erik Blegvad		Athenm
1980	Yellow Fairy Book		$25	$35	$50	Andrew Lang		Kestrel
1981	Rare Treasures From Grimm		$25	$35	$50	Jacob & Wilhelm Grimm		DoubleD
1982	The Parrot In The Garret		$25	$35	$50	Lenore Blegvad		Athenm
1983	Cat Walk		$25	$35	$50	Mary Stolz		H&Row
1984	Peter And The Troll Baby		$20	$30	$40	Jan Wahl		Golden
1985	Anna Banana And Me		$20	$30	$40	Lenore Blegvad		Athenm
1986	This Is Me		$20	$30	$40	Lenore Blegvad		Random
1987	I Like To Be Little		$20	$30	$40	Charlotte Zolotow		Crowell
1988	Rainy Day Kate		$18	$25	$35	Lenore Blegvad		McEld
1989	Little Little Sister		$18	$25	$35	Jane Louise Curry		McEld
1991	Water Pennies & Other Poems		$16	$25	$30	N. M. Bodecker		McEld
1994	Twelve Tales		$14	$20	$30	Hans Christian Andersen		McEld
1995	A Sound Of Leaves		$14	$20	$25	Lenore Blegvad		McEld
1995	With One White Wing		$14	$20	$25	Elizabeth Spires		McEld
1998	Hurry, Hurry, Mary Dear!		$12	$16	$20	N. M. Bodecker		McEld
1999	Riddle Road		$12	$16	$20	Elizabeth Spires		McEld
2000	Around My Room		$10	$14	$18	William Jay Smith		FSG
2002	Seasons		$8	$12	$16	Charlotte Zolotow		HCollins
2003	Seagoing Clocks		$8	$12	$16	Louise Borden		McEld

Bloom   Lloyd

Year	Title	VG-	VG	VG+	Fine	Author	Award	Pub
1984	Like Jake And Me		$35	$50	$70	Mavis Jukes	NH	Knopf
1988	Yonder		$10	$16	$20	Tony Johnston		Dial
1999	When Uncle Took The Fiddle		$8	$12	$16	Libba Moore Gray		Orchard

Blythe   Gary

Year	Title	VG-	VG	VG+	Fine	Author	Award	Pub
1991	The Whales' Song		$25	$40	$50	Dyan Sheldon	GM	Dial
1993	The Garden		$14	$20	$25	Dyan Sheldon		Hutch
1994	Under The Moon		$12	$18	$25	Dyan Sheldon		Dial
1996	This Is The Star		$12	$16	$20	Joyce Dunbar		HBrace
2000	Beauty And The Beast		$10	$14	$18	Geraldine McCaughrean		CRB
2004	Bram Stoker's Dracula		$8	$10	$14	Jan Needle (adapted)		Candle

Boddy   Joe

Year	Title	VG-	VG	VG+	Fine	Author	Award	Pub
1982	We Seized Our Rifles		$12	$18	$25	Eugene Lee Silliman (edited)		MountP
1983	A.J. Goes To Germany		$12	$16	$20	Lowell Dickmeyer		Dillon
1983	Lyndsey Sees The Midnight Sun		$12	$16	$20	Lowell Dickmeyer		Dillon
1983	Paul Meets The Masters		$12	$16	$20	Lowell Dickmeyer		Gem
1984	Abram, Abram, Where Are We Going?		$12	$16	$20	Fredrick & Patricia McKissack		Chariot
1984	Hana Discovers Japan		$12	$16	$20	Lowell Dickmeyer		Dillon
1984	Look What You've Done Now, Moses		$12	$16	$20	Fredrick & Patricia McKissack		Chariot
1984	Special Strengths		$12	$16	$20	Gail Radley		Bellwd
1984	The Adams See Australia		$12	$16	$20	Lowell Dickmeyer		Dillon
1984	The Eagles Fly To Scotland		$12	$16	$20	Lowell Dickmeyer		Dillon
1984	Trimotor And Trail		$12	$16	$20	Earl Cooley		MountP
1985	I'm So-So, So What?		$12	$16	$20	Charlotte Graeber		TNelson
1985	My Mr. T Doll		$12	$16	$20	Charlotte Graeber		TNelson
1985	Phony Baloney: The Counterfeit Kid		$12	$16	$20	Charlotte Graeber		TNelson
1985	Tackle Block Stop		$12	$16	$20	Charlotte Graeber		TNelson
1985	The Best Bike Ever		$12	$16	$20	Charlotte Graeber		TNelson
1985	The Hand-Me-Down Cap		$12	$16	$20	Charlotte Graeber		TNelson
1985	The Hard Luck Mutt		$12	$16	$20	Charlotte Graeber		TNelson
1985	The Muscle Tussle		$12	$16	$20	Charlotte Graeber		TNelson
1985	The Not-So-Great Place		$12	$16	$20	Charlotte Graeber		TNelson
1985	The Sidewalk Mockers		$12	$16	$20	Charlotte Graeber		TNelson
1985	The Silver Squawk Box		$12	$16	$20	Charlotte Graeber		TNelson
1985	The Somebody Kid		$12	$16	$20	Charlotte Graeber		TNelson
1986	Dinky, The Pint-Sized Dragon		$10	$16	$20	Sheila Coleman		TNelson
1986	In The Beginning There Was No Sky		$10	$16	$20	Walter, Jr. Wangerin		TNelson
1986	Little Miss Ruthie Mae		$10	$16	$20	Sheila Coleman		TNelson
1986	Mchappy, The Unhappy Clown		$10	$16	$20	Sheila Coleman		TNelson
1986	The Seven Days Of Creation		$10	$16	$20	Dann J. Ettner		Concord
1987	Blue Ben		$10	$16	$20	Carol Greene		Millik
1987	Catherine Marshall's Storybook		$10	$16	$20	David Hazard (edited)		Chosen
1987	Lost And Found		$10	$16	$20	Martha Whitmore Hickman		Abing
1987	Seven Special Days		$10	$16	$20	Henrietta D. Gambill		StandP
1987	Tall Corn: A Tall Tale		$10	$16	$20	Dorothy Van Woerkom		Millik
1988	The Glassmakers Of Gurven		$10	$16	$20	Marlys Boddy		Abing
1989	First Steamboat Down The Mississippi		$10	$16	$20	George S. Fichter		Pelican
1989	Mixed-Up Sam		$10	$16	$20	Elaine Moore		Millik
1989	The First Zoo		$10	$16	$20	Henrietta D. Gambill		StandP
1989	The Mystery Of The Missing Scarf		$10	$16	$20	Mary Blount Christian		Millik
1989	The North Pole Mystery		$10	$16	$20	Mary Blount Christian		Millik
1989	The Pet Day Mystery		$10	$16	$20	Mary Blount Christian		Millik
1989	The Ufo Mystery		$10	$16	$20	Mary Blount Christian		Millik
1990	David And Goliath		$10	$14	$18	Henrietta D. Gambill		StandP
1990	Forbidden Gates: A Story Of Stephen		$10	$14	$18	Denise Williamson		W&H
1990	Rebecca Of Sunnybrook Farm		$10	$14	$18	Eric & Kate Wiggin (adapted)		W&H
1990	River Of Danger: A Story Of Samuel Kirkland		$10	$14	$18	Denise Williamson		W&H
1990	Robinson Rabbit, What Do You Hear?		$10	$14	$18	Rebecca Laird		Augsb
1990	The Bremen Town Musicians		$10	$14	$18	Eugene Evans		Unicorn
1991	A Christmas Carol		$10	$14	$18	Charles Dickens		Unicorn
1991	ABC Book Of Feelings		$10	$14	$18	Marlys Boddy		Concord
1991	Dinosaurs In God's World Long Ago		$10	$14	$18	Henrietta D. Gambill		StandP
1991	The King's Reward: A Story Of Vincent De Paul		$10	$14	$18	Denise Williamson		W&H
1992	Hallelujah The Clown		$10	$14	$18	Kathy Long		Augsb
1992	Silent Night: A Mouse Tale		$10	$14	$18	Betsy Hernandez		Sparrow
1992	The Sword In The Stone		$10	$14	$18	Grace Maccarone		Scholas
1993	K'tonton's Sukkot Adventure		$10	$14	$18	Sadie Rose Weilerstein		JPS
1994	Piggyback Ninja		$10	$14	$18	Neal Shusterman		Lowell
1995	K'tonton's Yom Kippur Kitten		$8	$12	$16	Sadie Rose Weilerstein		JPS

Boddy   Joe

Year	Title	VG-	VG	VG+	Fine	Author	Award	Pub
1996	The Fox		$8	$12	$16	Janice Boland		RCOwen

Bodecker   N. M.

Year	Title	VG-	VG	VG+	Fine	Author	Award	Pub
1956	The Bulls and the Bees	$50	$70	$90		Roger Eddy		Crowell
1958	The Time Garden	$160	$200	$260		Edward Eager		HBrace
1962	Seven Day Magic	$140	$200	$240		Edward Eager		HBrace
1963	The Snake In The Carpool	$50	$60	$80		Miriam Schlein		AS
1965	Is There A Mouse In The House?	$40	$60	$70		Josephine Gibson		Macmil
1971	Miss Jaster's Garden		$30	$50	$60	N. M. Bodecker		Golden
1972	Good Night, Little A.B.C.		$30	$50	$60	Robert Kraus		Spring
1972	Good Night, Little One		$30	$50	$60	Robert Kraus		Spring
1972	Good Night, Richard Rabbit		$30	$50	$60	Robert Kraus		Spring
1973	It's Raining Said John Twaining		$30	$50	$60	N. M. Bodecker		McEld
1973	It's Raining, Said John Twaining		$30	$50	$60	N. M. Bodecker		Athenm
1973	Mattie Fritts And The Flying Mushroom		$30	$50	$60	Michael Jennings		Windmil
1973	Sylvester, The Mouse With The Musical Ear		$30	$50	$60	Adelaide Holl		Golden
1974	Let's Marry Said The Cherry		$30	$40	$60	N. M. Bodecker		Athenm
1975	The Night-Lite Storybook		$30	$40	$60	Robert Kraus		Windmil
1976	A Little At A Time		$30	$40	$60	David A. Adler		Random
1976	Hurry, Hurry, Mary Dear!		$30	$40	$60	N. M. Bodecker		Athenm
1980	A Person From Britain Head Shape Of A Mitten		$25	$35	$50	N. M. Bodecker		Athenm
1981	The Lost String Quartet		$25	$35	$50	N. M. Bodecker		Athenm
1982	Pigeon Cubes & Other Verse		$25	$35	$50	N. M. Bodecker		Athenm
1983	Snowman Sniffles & Other Verse		$25	$35	$50	N. M. Bodecker		Athenm

Bolling   Vickey

Year	Title	VG-	VG	VG+	Fine	Author	Award	Pub
1996	Jack And Jill's Spill		$8	$12	$16	Lisa Ann Marsoli		Chron
1996	Rocky Bobocky		$8	$12	$16	Emily Ellison		LP
1997	Proud		$8	$12	$16	Fred Penner		LP
1998	Look, Look! I Wrote A Book!		$8	$12	$16	Linda Ball		GoodY

Bond   Felicia

Year	Title	VG-	VG	VG+	Fine	Author	Award	Pub
1981	Poinsettia & Her Family		$35	$50	$70	Felicia Bond		Crowell
1981	The Sky Is Full Of Stars		$35	$50	$70	Franklyn M. Branley		Crowell
1982	How Little Porcupine Played Christmas		$25	$35	$50	Joseph Slate		Crowell
1982	The Firelings		$25	$35	$50	Carol Kendall		Athenm
1983	Christmas In The Chicken Coop		$25	$35	$50	Felicia Bond		Crowell
1983	Four Valentines In A Rainstorm		$25	$35	$50	Felicia Bond		Crowell
1983	Mary Betty Lizzie Mcnutt's Birthday		$25	$35	$50	Felicia Bond		Crowell
1983	The Halloween Performance		$25	$35	$50	Felicia Bond		Crowell
1984	Mama's Secret		$20	$30	$40	Maria Polushkin		4Winds
1984	Poinsettia And The Firefighters		$20	$30	$40	Felicia Bond		Crowell
1985	If You Give A Mouse A Cookie		$40	$60	$80	Laura Joffe Numeroff		H&Row
1986	Getting Oxygen		$20	$30	$40	Stephen P. Kramer		Crowell
1987	How To Think Like A Scientist		$20	$30	$40	Stephen P. Kramer		Crowell
1987	Wake Up, Vladimir		$20	$30	$40	Felicia Bond		Crowell
1989	Big Red Barn		$18	$25	$35	Margaret Wise Brown		H&Row
1990	The Right Number Of Elephants		$16	$25	$30	Jeff Sheppard		H&Row
1991	If You Give A Moose A Muffin		$30	$50	$60	Laura Joffe Numeroff		HCollins
1993	The Big Green Pocketbook		$16	$25	$30	Candice Ransom		HCollins
1994	Christmas In The Manger		$14	$20	$30	Nola Buck		HFest
1995	Mouse Cookies		$14	$20	$25	Laura Joffe Numeroff		HCollins
1996	Tumble Bumble		$12	$18	$25	Felicia Bond		Front
1998	If You Give A Pig A Pancake		$12	$16	$20	Laura Joffe Numeroff		LauraG
2000	If You Take A Mouse To The Movies		$10	$14	$18	Laura Joffe Numeroff		HCollins
2002	If You Take A Mouse To School		$8	$12	$16	Laura Joffe Numeroff		HCollins

Bonsall   Crosby

Year	Title	VG-	VG	VG+	Fine	Author	Award	Pub
1962	Who's A Pest?	$70	$90	$120		Crosby Bonsall		Harper
1963	The Case Of The Hungry Stranger	$50	$60	$80		Crosby Bonsall		H&Row
1963	What Spot?	$50	$60	$80		Crosby Bonsall		H&Row

Bonsall   Crosby

Year	Title	VG-	VG	VG+	Fine	Author	Award	Pub
1965	The Case Of The Cat's Meow	$40	$60	$70		Crosby Bonsall		H&Row
1966	The Case Of The Dumb Bells	$40	$60	$70		Crosby Bonsall		H&Row
1971	The Case Of The Scaredy Cats		$30	$50	$60	Crosby Bonsall		H&Row
1973	Mine's The Best		$30	$50	$60	Crosby Bonsall		H&Row

Booth   George

Year	Title	VG-	VG	VG+	Fine	Author	Award	Pub
1974	Wacky Wednesday		$100	$160	$220	Theo LeSieg (pseud/Seuss)		BB

Bourgeois   Florence

Year	Title	VG-	VG	VG+	Fine	Author	Award	Pub
1935	Beachcomber Bobbie	$40	$60	$70		Florence Bourgeois		DoubleD
1936	Molly And Michael	$40	$60	$70		Florence Bourgeois		DoubleD
1937	Peter, Peter, Pumpkin Grower	$40	$60	$70		Florence Bourgeois		DoubleD

Bowers   Tim

Year	Title	VG-	VG	VG+	Fine	Author	Award	Pub
1986	The Toy Circus		$25	$35	$50	Jan Wahl		HBJ
1988	Pajamas		$16	$25	$30	Livingston Taylor		HBJ
1989	The Adventures Of Underwater Dog		$16	$25	$30	Jan Wahl		G&D
1990	The Rabbit Club		$14	$20	$30	Jan Wahl		HBJ
1992	A Day With No Math		$14	$20	$25	Marilyn Kaye		HBJ
1994	A Friend For Fraidy Cat		$12	$18	$25	Clare Mishica		StandP
1994	Two Prayers For Patches		$12	$18	$25	Kim Henry		StandP
1999	Sometimes I Wonder If Poodles Like Noodles		$10	$16	$20	Laura Joffe Numeroff		S&S
2000	Sam And Jack		$10	$14	$18	Alex Moran		Harcort
2000	The News Hounds In The Great Balloon Race		$10	$14	$18	Amy Axelrod		S&S
2001	Little Whistle		$8	$12	$16	Cynthia Rylant		HBrace
2001	Little Whistle's Dinner Party		$8	$12	$16	Cynthia Rylant		HBrace
2001	The News Hounds Catch A Wave		$8	$12	$16	Amy Axelrod		S&S
2002	A New Home		$8	$12	$16	Tim Bowers		Harcort
2002	Little Whistle's Medicine		$8	$12	$16	Cynthia Rylant		HBrace
2003	Little Whistle's Christmas		$8	$10	$14	Cynthia Rylant		Harcort
2003	One Wide Sky		$8	$10	$14	Debbie Wiles		Harcort
2003	Sherman Crunchley		$8	$10	$14	Laura Joffe Numeroff		Dutton

Boynton   Sandra

Year	Title	VG-	VG	VG+	Fine	Author	Award	Pub
1979	Gopher Baroque		$50	$80	$100	Sandra Boynton		Dutton
1979	Hester In The Wild		$50	$80	$100	Sandra Boynton		H&Row
1979	Hippos Go Berserk		$50	$80	$100	Sandra Boynton		LBrown
1980	If At First ..		$30	$40	$60	Sandra Boynton		LBrown
1984	A To Z		$25	$40	$50	Sandra Boynton		S&S
1985	Chloë And Maude		$25	$35	$50	Sandra Boynton		LBrown
1985	Good Night, Good Night		$25	$35	$50	Sandra Boynton		Random
1985	Hey! What's That?		$25	$35	$50	Sandra Boynton		Random
1988	The Story Of Grump And Pout!		$20	$30	$40	James McEwan		Crown
1993	Barnyard Dance!		$18	$25	$35	Sandra Boynton		Workman
1993	Birthday Monsters!		$18	$25	$35	Sandra Boynton		Workman
1993	Oh My Oh My Oh Dinosaurs!		$18	$25	$35	Sandra Boynton		Workman
1993	One, Two, Three!		$18	$25	$35	Sandra Boynton		Workman
1996	Grunt		$14	$20	$30	Sandra Boynton		Workman
1999	The Heart Of Cool		$12	$18	$25	James McEwan		S&S
2000	Hey! Wake Up!		$10	$16	$20	Sandra Boynton		Workman
2000	Pajama Time!		$10	$16	$20	Sandra Boynton		Workman
2001	Yay, You!		$10	$16	$20	Sandra Boynton		S&S
2002	Consider Love		$10	$14	$18	Sandra Boynton		S&S
2002	Philadelphia Chickens		$10	$14	$18	Sandra Boynton		Workman
2003	Snuggle Puppy		$8	$12	$16	Sandra Boynton		Workman
2004	Rhinoceros Tap		$8	$10	$14	Michael Ford		Workman

Brackett   Ward

Year	Title	VG-	VG	VG+	Fine	Author	Award	Pub
1966	You Will Live Under The Sea	$50	$60	$80		Fred Phleger		BB

146

Breathed   Berkeley

Year	Title	VG-	VG	VG+	Fine	Author	Award	Pub
1987	Billy and the Boingers Bootleg		$40	$60	$90	Berkeley Breathed		LBrown
1991	A Wish For Wings That Work		$25	$40	$50	Berkeley Breathed		LBrown
1992	The Last Basselope		$20	$30	$40	Berkeley Breathed		LBrown
1993	Goodnight Opus		$18	$25	$35	Berkeley Breathed		LBrown
1994	Red Ranger Came Calling		$18	$25	$35	Berkeley Breathed		LBrown
2000	Edwurd Fudwupper Fibbed Big		$10	$16	$20	Berkeley Breathed		LBrown
2003	Flawed Dogs		$8	$12	$16	Berkeley Breathed		LBrown

Brett   Jan

Year	Title	VG-	VG	VG+	Fine	Author	Award	Pub
1978	Woodland Crossings		$70	$100	$140	Stephen Krensky		Athenm
1979	Inside A Sand Castle & Other Secrets		$60	$90	$120	Mary Louise Cuneo		HM
1979	The Secret Clocks		$40	$60	$90	Seymour Simon		Viking
1980	St. Patrick's Day In The Morning		$35	$50	$70	Eve Bunting		Clarion
1981	Fritz And The Beautiful Horses		$35	$50	$70	Jan Brett		HM
1981	In The Castle Of Cats		$35	$50	$70	Betty V, Boegehold		Dutton
1981	Some Birds Have Funny Names		$35	$50	$70	Diana Harding Cross		Crown
1981	Young Melvin And Bulger		$35	$50	$70	Mark Taylor		DoubleD
1983	Some Plants Have Funny Names		$30	$50	$60	Diana Harding Cross		Crown
1983	The Valentine Bears		$30	$50	$60	Eve Bunting		Clarion
1984	The Great Rescue		$30	$50	$60	Mark Taylor		Parker
1984	You Are Special To Jesus		$30	$50	$60	Annetta Dellinger		Concord
1985	Annie And The Wild Animals		$30	$40	$60	Jan Brett		HM
1985	Old Devil Is Waiting: Three Folktales		$30	$40	$60	Dorothy Van Woerkom		HBJ
1986	Noelle Of The Nutcracker		$30	$40	$60	Pamela Jane		HM
1986	Scary, Scary Halloween		$30	$40	$60	Eve Bunting		Clarion
1986	The Mother's Day Mice		$30	$40	$60	Eve Bunting		Clarion
1986	The Twelve Days Of Christmas		$30	$40	$60	Jan Brett		DoddM
1987	Goldilocks And The Three Bears		$25	$40	$50	Jan Brett (adapted)		DoddM
1987	The Enchanted Book: A Tale From Krakow		$25	$40	$50	Bozena Smith (translated)		HBJ
1988	Happy Birthday, Dear Duck		$25	$40	$50	Eve Bunting		Clarion
1988	The First Dog		$25	$40	$50	Jan Brett		HBJ
1989	Beauty And The Beast		$25	$40	$50	Jan Brett		Clarion
1989	The Mitten		$25	$40	$50	Jan Brett		Putnam
1990	The Wild Christmas Reindeer		$20	$30	$40	Jan Brett		Putnam
1991	Berlioz The Bear		$18	$25	$35	Jan Brett		Putnam
1991	The Owl And The Pussycat		$18	$25	$35	Edward Lear		Putnam
1992	Trouble With Trolls		$18	$25	$35	Jan Brett		Putnam
1993	Christmas Trolls		$18	$25	$35	Jan Brett		Putnam
1994	Town Mouse, Country Mouse		$16	$25	$30	Jan Brett		Putnam
1995	Armadillo Rodeo		$16	$25	$30	Jan Brett		Putnam
1996	Comet's Nine Lives		$14	$20	$30	Jan Brett		Putnam
1997	The Hat		$14	$20	$25	Jan Brett		Putnam
1998	The Night Before Christmas		$12	$18	$25	Clement C. Moore		Putnam
1999	Gingerbread Baby		$12	$18	$25	Jan Brett		Putnam
2000	Hedge's Surprise		$10	$16	$20	Jan Brett		Putnam
2002	Daisy Comes Home		$10	$14	$18	Jan Brett		Putnam
2002	The Night Before Christmas		$10	$14	$18	Clement C. Moore		HCollins
2002	Who's That Knocking On Christmas Eve?		$10	$14	$18	Jan Brett		Putnam
2003	On Noah's Ark		$8	$12	$16	Jan Brett		Putnam
2004	The Umbrella		$8	$10	$14	Jan Brett		Putnam

Brewster   Patience

Year	Title	VG-	VG	VG+	Fine	Author	Award	Pub
1980	Dame Wiggins Of Lee And Her 7 Wonderful Cats		$35	$50	$70	Patience Brewster		Crowell
1981	Ellsworth And The Cats From Mars		$25	$35	$50	Patience Brewster		Clarion
1982	Good As New		$25	$35	$50	Barbara Douglass		LL&S
1982	Nobody		$25	$35	$50	Patience Brewster		Clarion
1983	How Do You Do, Mr. Birdsteps?		$25	$35	$50	Morse Hamilton		Avon
1983	I Met A Polar Bear		$25	$35	$50	Selma & Pauline Boyd		LL&S
1983	Who's Afraid Of The Dark?		$25	$35	$50	Morse Hamilton		Avon
1984	Sun, Rain		$20	$30	$40	Niki Yektai		4Winds
1984	Victoria's ABC Adventure		$20	$30	$40	Cathy Warren		LL&S
1985	Don't Touch My Room		$20	$30	$40	Patricia Larkin		LBrown
1987	Oh, Brother!		$20	$30	$40	Patricia Lakin		LBrown
1987	There's More-- Much More		$20	$30	$40	Sue Alexander		GB

Brewster   Patience

Year	Title	VG-	VG	VG+	Fine	Author	Award	Pub
1987	Valentine Poems		$20	$30	$40	Myra C. Livingston (selected)		Holiday
1988	Bear And Mrs. Duck		$18	$25	$35	Elizabeth Winthrop		Holiday
1989	Just Like Me		$18	$25	$35	Patricia Lakin		LBrown
1991	Bear's Christmas Surprise		$16	$25	$30	Elizabeth Winthrop		Holiday
1991	Princess Abigail And The Wonderful Hat		$16	$25	$30	Steven Kroll		Holiday
1991	Rabbit Inn		$16	$25	$30	Patience Brewster		LBrown
1991	Yoo Hoo, Moon!		$16	$25	$30	Mary Blocksma		Bantam
1993	Queen Of The May		$16	$25	$30	Steven Kroll		Holiday
1994	Two Bushy Badgers		$14	$20	$30	Patience Brewster		LBrown
1996	Bear And Roly-Poly		$12	$18	$25	Elizabeth Winthrop		Holiday
1997	Too Many Puppies		$12	$18	$25	Patience Brewster		Scholas
1999	A Hive For The Honeybee		$12	$16	$20	Soinbhe Lally		Levine
1999	The Bouncy Baby Bunny		$12	$16	$20	Joan Chase Bowden		Golden
2000	Pee Wee's Tale		$10	$14	$18	Johanna Hurwitz		SeaStar
2001	Lexi's Tale		$10	$14	$18	Johanna Hurwitz		SeaStar
2001	The Merbaby		$10	$14	$18	Teresa Bateman		Holiday
2002	Pee Wee & Plush		$8	$12	$16	Johanna Hurwitz		SeaStar

Briggs   Raymond

Year	Title	VG-	VG	VG+	Fine	Author	Award	Pub
1959	Peter's Busy Day	$60	$80	$100		Stephen Tring		HHamil
1962	Ring-A-Ring O'roses	$100	$120	$160		Raymond Briggs		CM
1963	Sledges To The Rescue	$100	$120	$160		Raymond Briggs		HHamil
1963	The White Land	$100	$120	$160		Raymond Briggs		CM
1964	Fee Fi Fo Fum	$90	$120	$160		Raymond Briggs		McCann
1965	Whistling Rufus	$90	$120	$160		William Mayne		Dutton
1966	The Hamish Hamilton Book Of Magical Beasts	$90	$120	$160		Ruth Manning-Sanders		HHamil
1966	The Mother Goose Treasury	$200	$260	$320		Raymond Briggs	GM	CM
1968	Jimmy Murphy And The White Duesenberg	$80	$120	$140		Bruce Carter		CM
1968	Lindbergh, The Lone Flier	$80	$120	$140		Nicholas Fisk		CM
1968	Nuvolari And The Alfa Romeo	$80	$120	$140		Bruce Carter		CM
1968	Richthofen, The Red Baron	$80	$120	$140		Nicholas Fisk		CM
1968	The Christmas Book	$80	$120	$140		James Reeves		Dutton
1968	The Hamish Hamilton Book Of Giants	$80	$120	$140		William Mayne		HHamil
1969	Shackleton's Epic Voyage	$80	$120	$140		Michael Brown		CM
1969	The Elephant And The Bad Baby	$80	$120	$140		Elfrida Vipont		Coward
1969	William Mayne's Book Of Giants	$80	$120	$140		William Mayne		Dutton
1970	A Book Of Magical Beasts		$60	$80	$120	Ruth Manning-Sanders		TNelson
1970	Jim And The Beanstalk		$60	$80	$120	Raymond Briggs		CM
1971	The Tale Of Three Landlubbers		$50	$80	$100	Ian Serraillier		CM
1972	The Fairy Tale Treasury		$50	$80	$100	Virginia Haviland (adapted)		CM
1973	Father Christmas		$100	$160	$220	Raymond Briggs	GM	CM&G
1975	Father Christmas Goes On Holiday		$50	$70	$90	Raymond Briggs		HHamil
1978	The Snowman		$90	$140	$180	Raymond Briggs		Random
1979	Fungus The Bogeyman		$40	$60	$80	Raymond Briggs		Random
1982	When The Wind Blows		$40	$60	$80	Raymond Briggs		Schock
1984	The Tin-Pot Foreign General		$35	$50	$70	Raymond Briggs		HHamil
1985	The Party		$35	$50	$70	Raymond Briggs		LBrown
1985	Walking In The Air		$35	$50	$70	Raymond Briggs		LBrown
1986	All In A Day		$30	$50	$60	Mitsumasa Anno		Philo
1987	Unlucky Wally		$30	$50	$60	Raymond Briggs		HHamil
1990	The Snowman Storybook		$25	$40	$50	Raymond Briggs		Random
1994	The Bear		$20	$30	$40	Raymond Briggs		Random
1995	The Man		$20	$30	$40	Raymond Briggs		Random
1999	Ethel & Ernest		$16	$25	$30	Raymond Briggs		Knopf
2002	A Bit More Bert		$12	$16	$20	Allan Ahlberg		FSG
2002	Ug		$12	$16	$20	Raymond Briggs		Knopf

Bright   Robert

Year	Title	VG-	VG	VG+	Fine	Author	Award	Pub
1943	The Travels Of Ching	$40	$50	$70		Robert Bright		WRScott
1944	Georgie	$40	$50	$70		Robert Bright		DD
1953	Hurrah For Freddie!	$35	$40	$60		Robert Bright		DoubleD
1954	Miss Pattie	$35	$40	$60		Robert Bright		DoubleD
1955	I Like Red	$30	$40	$50		Robert Bright		DoubleD
1956	Georgie To The Rescue	$30	$40	$50		Robert Bright		DoubleD

Bright — Robert

Year	Title	VG-	VG	VG+	Fine	Author	Award	Pub
1958	Georgie's Halloween	$30	$40	$50		Robert Bright		DoubleD
1959	My Red Umbrella	$30	$40	$50		Robert Bright		Morrow
1963	Georgie And The Robbers	$25	$35	$50		Robert Bright		DoubleD
1975	Georgie's Christmas Carol		$14	$20	$30	Robert Bright		DoubleD
1979	Georgie And The Buried Treasure		$14	$20	$25	Robert Bright		DoubleD
1983	Georgie And The Baby Birds		$12	$16	$20	Robert Bright		DoubleD
1983	Georgie And The Ball Of Yarn		$12	$16	$20	Robert Bright		DoubleD
1983	Georgie And The Little Dog		$12	$16	$20	Robert Bright		DoubleD
1983	Georgie And The Runaway Balloon		$12	$16	$20	Robert Bright		DoubleD

Brighton — Catherine

Year	Title	VG-	VG	VG+	Fine	Author	Award	Pub
1983	Two Little Nurses		$30	$50	$60	Siân Victory		Faber
1984	My Hands, My World		$20	$30	$40	Catherine Brighton		Macmil
1985	The Picture		$20	$30	$40	Catherine Brighton		Faber
1986	The Voice		$20	$30	$40	Walter De La Mare		DelaP
1987	Five Secrets In A Box		$20	$30	$40	Catherine Brighton		Dutton
1988	Hope's Gift		$18	$25	$35	Catherine Brighton		DoubleD
1989	Nijinsky		$18	$25	$35	Catherine Brighton		DoubleD
1990	Mozart		$16	$25	$30	Catherine Brighton		DoubleD
1991	Dearest Grandmama		$16	$25	$30	Catherine Brighton		DoubleD
1994	The Brontes		$14	$20	$30	Catherine Brighton		Chron
1997	My Napoleon		$12	$18	$25	Catherine Brighton		Millbk
1999	The Fossil Girl		$12	$16	$20	Catherine Brighton		Millbk
2001	Galileo's Treasure Box		$10	$14	$18	Catherine Brighton		Walker

Brinckloe — Julie

Year	Title	VG-	VG	VG+	Fine	Author	Award	Pub
1972	Agouhanna		$18	$25	$35	Claude Aubry		DoubleD
1973	The Young Prince And The Magic Cone		$16	$25	$30	Herbert Gold		DoubleD
1974	Nobody Wanted To Scare Her		$16	$25	$30	Alice Cromie		DoubleD
1974	The Bollo Caper		$16	$25	$30	Art Buchwald		DoubleD
1975	The Eleven Steps		$16	$25	$30	Lucy Freeman		DoubleD
1976	Gordon's House		$16	$25	$30	Julie Brinckloe		DoubleD
1984	Jamie's Turn		$12	$18	$25	Jamie DeWitt		Rain
1984	Lotta On Troublemaker Street		$12	$18	$25	Astrid Lindgren		Macmil
1985	A Stitch In Time For The Brothers Rhyme		$12	$18	$25	Julie Brinckloe		Rain
1985	Fireflies!		$12	$18	$25	Julie Brinckloe		Macmil
1986	The Hunky-Dory Dairy		$12	$16	$20	Anne Lindbergh		HBJ
1988	Playing Marbles		$12	$16	$20	Julie Brinckloe		Morrow
1990	Sideways Stories From Wayside School		$10	$16	$20	Louis Sachar		Knopf

Brock — Emma L.

Year	Title	VG-	VG	VG+	Fine	Author	Award	Pub
1923	Merrimeg	$140	$180	$240		William Bowen		Macmil
1924	Granny's Wonderful Chair	$140	$180	$240		Francis Browne		Macmil
1927	Highdays And Holidays	$140	$180	$220		Florence Adams		Dutton
1929	The Runaway Sardine	$120	$160	$220		Emma L. Brock		Knopf
1930	Baker's Dozen	$120	$160	$220		Mary Gould Davis		HBrace
1930	Nutcracker And The Mouse King	$120	$160	$220		E. T. A. Hoffmann		AWhit
1930	To Market! To Market!	$120	$160	$220		Emma L. Brock		Knopf
1931	Greedy Goat	$100	$140	$180		Emma L. Brock		Knopf
1931	The Greedy Goat	$100	$140	$180		Emma L. Brock		Knopf
1931	Wise Little Donkey	$100	$140	$180		Sophie Segur		AWhit
1932	Hansi The Stork	$100	$140	$180		Oscar Ludmann		AWhit
1932	Little House In Green Valley	$100	$140	$180		Clara Whitehall Hunt		HM
1932	One Little Indian Boy	$100	$140	$180		Emma L. Brock		Knopf
1932	Poogie And Sibella	$100	$140	$180		Nita Van Housen		AWhit
1933	Johnny-Cake	$100	$140	$180		Johnnie Jacobs		Putnam
1933	The Hen That Kept House	$100	$140	$180		Emma L. Brock		Knopf
1934	Little Fat Gretchen	$100	$140	$180		Emma L. Brock		Knopf
1934	Through Golden Windows	$100	$140	$180		Ada Randall		EMHale
1935	Golden Chick And The Magic Frying Pan	$100	$140	$180		Jeanne Chardon		AWhit
1935	Sandy's Kingdom	$100	$140	$180		Mary Gould Davis		HBrace
1936	Away With The Circus	$80	$120	$140		Winifred Esther Wise		AWhit

Brock   Emma L.

Year	Title	VG-	VG	VG+	Fine	Author	Award	Pub
1936	Beppo	$80	$120	$140		Emma L. Brock		AWhit
1936	The Traveling Gallery	$80	$120	$140		Besse Schiff		AWhit
1936	Three Golden Oranges	$80	$120	$140		Ralph Boggs		Longman
1937	Drusilla	$80	$120	$140		Emma L. Brock		Macmil
1937	Handbook Of Farming For Boys And Girls	$80	$120	$140		R.A. Power		EMHale
1937	Practical Farming	$80	$120	$140		R.A. Power		EMHale
1937	Sean And Sheela	$80	$120	$140		Marian King		AWhit
1937	The Pig With A Front Porch	$80	$120	$140		Emma L. Brock		Knopf
1938	Dolls	$80	$100	$140		Julie Robinson		AWhit
1938	High In The Mountains	$80	$100	$140		Emma L. Brock		AWhit
1938	Nobody's Mouse	$80	$100	$140		Emma L. Brock		Knopf
1938	Till Potatoes Grow On Trees	$80	$100	$140		Emma L. Brock		Knopf
1939	A Present For Auntie	$80	$100	$140		Emma L. Brock		Knopf
1939	Heedless Susan Who Sometimes Forgot To Remember	$80	$100	$140		Emma L. Brock		Knopf
1939	Masha, The Little Goose Girl	$80	$100	$140		Marguerita Rudolph		Macmil
1939	Picture Tales From Scandinavia	$80	$100	$140		Ruth Bryan Owen		FStokes
1940	At Midsummer Time	$70	$90	$120		Emma L. Brock		Knopf
1940	The Shining Tree	$70	$90	$120		Emma L. Brock		Knopf
1940	Too Fast For John	$70	$90	$120		Emma L. Brock		Knopf
1941	Then Came Adventure	$70	$90	$120		Emma L. Brock		Knopf
1942	Here Comes Kristie	$70	$90	$120		Emma L. Brock		Knopf
1943	The Topsy-Turvy Family	$70	$90	$120		Emma L. Brock		Knopf
1944	Mr. Wren's House	$60	$80	$100		Emma L. Brock		Knopf
1944	Uncle Bennie Goes Visiting	$60	$80	$100		Emma L. Brock		Knopf
1945	The Umbrella Man	$60	$80	$100		Emma L. Brock		Knopf
1946	The Birds' Christmas Tree	$60	$80	$100		Emma L. Brock		Knopf
1947	A Pet For Barbi	$60	$80	$100		Emma L. Brock		Knopf
1948	Little Duchess, Anne Of Brittany	$60	$80	$100		Emma L. Brock		Knopf
1949	Kristie And The Colt	$60	$80	$100		Emma L. Brock		Knopf
1949	Surprise Balloon	$60	$80	$100		Emma L. Brock		Knopf
1950	Three Ring Circus	$60	$80	$100		Emma L. Brock		Knopf
1951	Too Many Turtles	$50	$70	$90		Emma L. Brock		Knopf
1952	Kristie's Buttercup	$50	$70	$90		Emma L. Brock		Knopf
1953	Kristie Goes To The Fair	$50	$70	$90		Emma L. Brock		Knopf
1954	Ballet For Mary	$50	$70	$90		Emma L. Brock		Knopf
1955	Plug-Horse Derby	$50	$70	$90		Emma L. Brock		Knopf
1956	Come On-Along, Fish!	$50	$70	$90		Emma L. Brock		Knopf
1958	Skipping Island	$50	$60	$80		Emma L. Brock		Knopf
1959	Patty On Horseback	$50	$60	$80		Emma L. Brock		Knopf
1960	Pancakes And The Merry-Go-Round	$50	$60	$80		Emma L. Brock		Knopf
1961	The Plaid Cow	$50	$60	$80		Emma L. Brock		Knopf
1962	Mary's Secret	$50	$60	$80		Emma L. Brock		Knopf
1963	Mary's Camera	$50	$60	$80		Emma L. Brock		Knopf
1964	Good Old Kristie	$50	$60	$80		Emma L. Brock		HR&W
1964	Mary Makes A Cake	$50	$60	$80		Emma L. Brock		Knopf
1967	Mary On Roller Skates	$40	$50	$70		Emma L. Brock		Knopf

Brodsky   Beverly

Year	Title	VG-	VG	VG+	Fine	Author	Award	Pub
1974	The Crystal Apple		$40	$60	$80	Beverly Brodsky		Viking
1975	Forest Of The Night		$30	$40	$60	John Rowe Townsend		Lippin
1975	Sedna : An Eskimo Myth		$30	$40	$60	Beverly Brodsky		Viking
1976	The Golem		$60	$80	$120	Beverly Brodsky	CH	Lippin
1977	Jonah : An Old Testament Story		$25	$40	$50	Beverly Brodsky		Lippin
1979	Secret Places		$25	$40	$50	Beverly Brodsky		Lippin
1982	Gooseberries To Oranges		$25	$35	$50	Barbara Cohen		LL&S
1984	Here Come The Purim Players!		$20	$30	$40	Barbara Cohen		LL&S
1995	Dreamtime		$14	$20	$25	Beverly Brodsky		BSP
1995	The Dreamtime		$14	$20	$25	Beverly Brodsky		BSP
2002	Buffalo		$8	$12	$16	Beverly Brodsky		Winslow

Brown   Marc

Year	Title	VG-	VG	VG+	Fine	Author	Award	Pub
1971	What Makes The Sun Shine?		$30	$50	$60	Isaac Asimov		LBrown
1972	The Iron Lion		$30	$50	$60	Peter Dickinson		LBrown
1973	I Found Them In The Yellow Pages		$30	$50	$60	Norma Farber		LBrown

Brown   Marc

Year	Title	VG-	VG	VG+	Fine	Author	Award	Pub
1974	The Little Green Thumb Window Garden With Seeds		$30	$40	$60	Douglas Morse		Stodd
1975	Four Corners Of The Sky		$30	$40	$60	Theodore Clymer		LBrown
1976	Arthur's Nose		$90	$120	$180	Marc Brown		Joy
1976	One, Two, Three		$30	$40	$60	Marc Brown		LBrown
1977	Full House		$25	$40	$50	Marc Brown		AW
1977	How The Rabbit Stole The Moon		$25	$40	$50	Louise Moeri		HM
1978	Lenny And Lola		$25	$40	$50	Marc Brown		Dutton
1978	Little Owl		$25	$40	$50	Janwillem Van de Wetering		HM
1978	Moose And Goose		$25	$40	$50	Marc Brown		Dutton
1979	Arthur's Eyes		$50	$80	$100	Marc Brown		LBrown
1979	Rabbit's New Rug		$25	$40	$50	Judy Delton		PMagP
1979	The Cloud Over Clarence		$25	$40	$50	Marc Brown		Dutton
1979	There Goes Feathertop		$25	$40	$50	Norma Farber		Dutton
1979	Why The Tides Ebb And Flow		$25	$40	$50	Joan Chase Bowden		HM
1980	Arthur's Valentine		$50	$70	$100	Marc Brown		LBrown
1980	Finger Rhymes		$25	$35	$50	Marc Brown		Dutton
1980	Pickle Things		$25	$35	$50	Marc Brown		PMagP
1980	Witches Four		$25	$35	$50	Marc Brown		PMagP
1981	The Banza		$25	$35	$50	Diane Wolkstein		Dial
1981	The True Francine		$25	$35	$50	Marc Brown		LBrown
1981	Your First Garden Book		$25	$35	$50	Marc Brown		LBrown
1982	Arthur Goes To Camp		$30	$50	$60	Marc Brown		LBrown
1982	Arthur's Halloween		$30	$50	$60	Marc Brown		LBrown
1982	Count To Ten		$25	$35	$50	Marc Brown		Western
1982	Dinosaurs, Beware!		$25	$35	$50	Stephen Krensky		LBrown
1982	What's So Funny, Ketu?		$25	$35	$50	Verna Aardema		Dial
1982	Wings On Things		$25	$35	$50	Marc Brown		BB
1983	Arthur's April Fool		$30	$50	$60	Marc Brown		LBrown
1983	Arthur's Thanksgiving		$30	$50	$60	Marc Brown		LBrown
1983	Perfect Pigs		$25	$35	$50	Stephen Krensky		LBrown
1983	Spooky Riddles		$25	$35	$50	Marc Brown		BB
1983	Swamp Monsters		$25	$35	$50	Mary Blount Christian		Dial
1983	The Silly Tail Book		$25	$35	$50	Marc Brown		PMagP
1983	What Do You Call A Dumb Bunny?		$25	$35	$50	Marc Brown		LBrown
1984	Arthur's Christmas		$30	$50	$60	Marc Brown		LBrown
1984	Little Witch's Big Night		$20	$30	$40	Deborah Hautzig		Random
1984	Oh, Kojo! How Could You!		$20	$30	$40	Verna Aardema		Dial
1984	The Bionic Bunny Show		$20	$30	$40	Laurene K. Brown		LBrown
1984	There's No Place Like Home		$20	$30	$40	Marc Brown		PMagP
1985	Arthur's Tooth		$25	$35	$50	Marc Brown		AMP
1985	Go West, Swamp Monsters!		$18	$25	$35	Mary Blount Christian		Dial
1985	Hand Rhymes		$18	$25	$35	Marc Brown		Dutton
1985	Happy Birthday, Little Witch		$18	$25	$35	Deborah Hautzig		Random
1986	A World Full Of Monsters		$16	$25	$30	John Troy McQueen		Crowell
1986	Arthur's Teacher Trouble		$25	$35	$50	Marc Brown		LBrown
1986	Dinosaurs Divorce		$16	$25	$30	Laurene K. Brown		AMP
1986	Read-Aloud Rhymes For The Very Young		$16	$25	$30	Jack Prelutsky		Knopf
1986	Visiting The Art Museum		$16	$25	$30	Laurene K. Brown		Dutton
1987	Arthur's Baby		$25	$35	$50	Marc Brown		Joy
1987	D.W. Flips		$16	$25	$30	Marc Brown		LBrown
1987	Play Rhymes		$16	$25	$30	Marc Brown		Dutton
1988	Dinosaurs Travel		$16	$25	$30	Laurene K. Brown		Joy
1988	Little Witch's Book Of Magic Spells		$16	$25	$30	Deborah Hautzig		Random
1988	Party Rhymes		$16	$25	$30	Marc Brown		Dutton
1989	Arthur's Birthday		$20	$30	$40	Marc Brown		Joy
1989	Baby Time		$16	$25	$30	Laurene K. Brown		Knopf
1989	The Family Read-Aloud Christmas Treasury		$16	$25	$30	Alice Low		Joy
1989	Yellow Fish, Blue Fish		$16	$25	$30	Laurene K. Brown		Heath
1990	Arthur's Pet Business		$16	$25	$30	Marc Brown		Joy
1990	Dinosaurs Alive And Well		$12	$18	$25	Laurene K. Brown		LBrown
1990	Toddler Time		$12	$18	$25	Laurene K. Brown		Joy
1991	Arthur Meets The President		$16	$25	$30	Marc Brown		Joy
1991	The Family Read-Aloud Holiday Treasury		$12	$18	$25	Alice Low		LBrown
1992	Arthur Babysits		$16	$25	$30	Marc Brown		Joy
1992	Dinosaurs To The Rescue!		$12	$18	$25	Laurene K. Brown		Joy
1993	Arthur's Family Vacation		$14	$20	$30	Marc Brown		LBrown
1993	Arthur's New Puppy		$14	$20	$30	Marc T. Brown		LBrown

Brown   Marc

Year	Title	VG-	VG	VG+	Fine	Author	Award	Pub
1993	D.W. Rides Again!		$12	$16	$20	Marc Brown		LBrown
1993	D.W. Thinks Big		$12	$16	$20	Marc Brown		Joy
1994	Arthur's Chicken Pox		$14	$20	$25	Marc Brown		LBrown
1994	Arthur's First Sleepover		$14	$20	$25	Marc Brown		LBrown
1994	Scared Silly!		$12	$16	$20	Marc Brown		LBrown
1995	Arthur Goes To School		$10	$16	$20	Marc Brown		Random
1995	Arthur's Reading Race		$10	$16	$20	Marc Brown		Random
1995	Arthur's Tv Trouble		$10	$16	$20	Marc Brown		LBrown
1995	D.W., The Picky Eater		$10	$16	$20	Marc Brown		LBrown
1995	Glasses For D.W		$10	$16	$20	Marc Brown		Random
1995	Monster's Lunchbox		$10	$16	$20	Marc Brown		LBrown
1995	Rex And Lilly Family Time		$10	$16	$20	Laurene K. Brown		LBrown
1995	Rex And Lilly Playtime		$10	$16	$20	Laurene K. Brown		LBrown
1996	Arthur And The True Francine		$10	$16	$20	Marc Brown		LBrown
1996	Arthur Writes A Story		$10	$16	$20	Marc Brown		LBrown
1996	Arthur's Neighborhood		$10	$16	$20	Marc Brown		Random
1996	When Dinosaurs Die		$10	$16	$20	Laurene K. Brown		LBrown
1997	Arthur Tricks The Tooth Fairy		$10	$14	$18	Marc Brown		Random
1997	Arthur's Computer Disaster		$10	$14	$18	Marc Brown		LBrown
1997	Arthur's Really Helpful Word Book		$10	$14	$18	Marc Brown		Random
1997	D.W.'S Color Book		$10	$14	$18	Marc Brown		Random
1997	Kiss Hello, Kiss Good-Bye		$10	$14	$18	Marc Brown		Random
1997	Rex And Lilly School Time		$10	$14	$18	Laurene K. Brown		LBrown
1997	Say The Magic Word		$10	$14	$18	Marc Brown		Random
1997	What's The Big Secret?		$10	$14	$18	Laurene K. Brown		LBrown
1997	Where's Arthur's Gerbil		$10	$14	$18	Marc Brown		Random
1998	Arthur Accused!		$10	$14	$18	Marc Brown		LBrown
1998	Arthur And The Crunch Cereal Contest		$10	$14	$18	Marc Brown		LBrown
1998	Arthur And The Lost Diary		$10	$14	$18	Stephen Krensky		LBrown
1998	Arthur And The Popularity Test		$10	$14	$18	Stephen Krennsky (adapted)		LBrown
1998	Arthur And The Scare-Your-Pants-Off Club		$10	$14	$18	Marc Brown		LBrown
1998	Arthur Counts!		$10	$14	$18	Marc Brown		Random
1998	Arthur Decks The Hall		$10	$14	$18	Marc Brown		Random
1998	Arthur Lost And Found		$10	$14	$18	Marc Brown		LBrown
1998	Arthur Makes The Team		$10	$14	$18	Marc Brown		LBrown
1998	Arthur On The Farm		$10	$14	$18	Marc Brown		Random
1998	Arthur Rocks With Binky		$10	$14	$18	Stephen Krennsky (adapted)		LBrown
1998	Arthur's Boo-Boo Book		$10	$14	$18	Marc Brown		Random
1998	Arthur's Mystery Envelope		$10	$14	$18	Marc Brown		LBrown
1998	Arthur's Really Helpful Bedtime Stories		$10	$14	$18	Marc Brown		Random
1998	Buster's Dino Dilemma		$10	$14	$18	Marc Brown		LBrown
1998	D.W.'S Lost Blankie		$10	$14	$18	Marc Brown		LBrown
1998	How To Be A Friend		$10	$14	$18	Laurene K. Brown		LBrown
1998	Locked In The Library!		$10	$14	$18	Marc Brown		LBrown
1998	The Mystery Of The Stolen Bike		$10	$14	$18	Marc Brown		LBrown
1998	Who's In Love With Arthur?		$10	$14	$18	Stephen Krennsky (adapted)		LBrown
1999	Arthur And The Cootie-Catcher		$10	$14	$18	Stephen Krensky		LBrown
1999	Arthur And The Poetry Contest		$10	$14	$18	Stephen Krensky		LBrown
1999	Arthur In A Pickle		$10	$14	$18	Marc Brown		Random
1999	Arthur, Clean Your Room!		$10	$14	$18	Marc Brown		Random
1999	Arthur's New Baby Book		$10	$14	$18	Marc Brown		Random
1999	Arthur's Underwear		$10	$14	$18	Marc Brown		LBrown
1999	Arthur's Valentine Countdown		$10	$14	$18	Marc Brown		Random
1999	Buster Makes The Grade		$10	$14	$18	Stephen Krensky		LBrown
1999	D.W., Go To Your Room!		$10	$14	$18	Marc Brown		LBrown
1999	Francine, Believe It Or Not		$10	$14	$18	Stephen Krennsky (adapted)		LBrown
1999	King Arthur		$10	$14	$18	Stephen Krennsky (adapted)		LBrown
1999	Muffy's Secret Admirer		$10	$14	$18	Stephen Krensky		LBrown
2000	Arthur And The Big Blow-Up		$8	$12	$16	Stephen Krensky		LBrown
2000	Arthur And The Perfect Brother		$8	$12	$16	Stephen Krensky		LBrown
2000	Arthur's Family Treasury		$8	$12	$16	Marc Brown		LBrown
2000	Arthur's Fire Drill		$8	$12	$16	Marc Brown		Random
2000	Arthur's Lost Puppy		$8	$12	$16	Marc Brown		Random
2000	Arthur's Perfect Christmas		$8	$12	$16	Marc Brown		LBrown
2000	Arthur's Teacher Moves In		$8	$12	$16	Marc Brown		LBrown
2000	Arthur's Truck Adventure		$8	$12	$16	Marc Brown		Random
2000	Binky Rules		$8	$12	$16	Stephen Krennsky (adapted)		LBrown

152

Brown   Marc

Year	Title	VG-	VG	VG+	Fine	Author	Award	Pub
2000	Buster Baxter, Cat Save		$8	$12	$16	Stephen Krennsky (adapted)		LBrown
2000	Buster's New Friend		$8	$12	$16	Stephen Krensky		LBrown
2000	Francine The Superstar		$8	$12	$16	Stephen Krensky		LBrown
2000	Marc Brown Arthur Chapter Books 1-3		$8	$12	$16	Stephen Krensky		LBrown
2001	Arthur And The Best Coach Ever		$8	$12	$16	Stephen Krensky		LBrown
2001	Arthur And The Goalie Ghost		$8	$12	$16	Stephen Krensky		LBrown
2001	Arthur And The Pen-Pal Playoff		$8	$12	$16	Stephen Krensky		iBrown
2001	Arthur And The Race To Read		$8	$12	$16	Stephen Krensky		LBrown
2001	Arthur And The Recess Rookie		$8	$12	$16	Stephen Krensky		LBrown
2001	Arthur And The Seventh Inning Stretcher		$8	$12	$16	Stephen Krensky		LBrown
2001	Arthur Style Guide		$8	$12	$16	Marc Brown		MBrown
2001	Arthur's First Kiss		$8	$12	$16	Marc Brown		Random
2001	Arthur's Hiccups		$8	$12	$16	Marc Brown		Random
2001	D.W.'S Library Card		$8	$12	$16	Marc Brown		LBrown
2001	Marc Brown		$8	$12	$16	Mae Woods		Abdo
2002	Arthur And The Comet Crisis		$8	$10	$14	Stephen Krensky		LBrown
2002	Arthur And The Double Dare		$8	$10	$14	Stephen Krensky		LBrown
2002	Arthur And The No-Brainer		$8	$10	$14	Marc Brown		LBrown
2002	Arthur, It's Only Rock 'N' Roll		$8	$10	$14	Marc Brown		LBrown
2002	Arthur's Animal Adventure		$8	$10	$14	Marc Brown		Random
2002	Arthur's Back-To-School Surprise		$8	$10	$14	Marc Brown		Random
2002	Marc Brown Arthur Chapter Books 4-6		$8	$10	$14	Stephen Krensky		LBrown
2003	Arthur And The 1,001 Dads		$8	$10	$14	Marc Brown		LBrown
2003	Arthur And The Bad-Luck Brain		$8	$10	$14	Stephen Krensky		LBrown
2003	Arthur And The School Pet		$8	$10	$14	Marc Brown		Random
2003	Arthur Plays The Blues		$8	$10	$14	Stephen Krennsky (adapted)		LBrown
2003	Arthur's Science Fair Trouble		$8	$10	$14	Marc Brown		Random
2003	Arthur's Spookiest Halloween		$8	$10	$14	Marc Brown		Random
2003	D.W.'S Guide To Preschool		$8	$10	$14	Marc Brown		LBrown
2004	Arthur And The Nerves Of Steal		$8	$10	$14	Stephen Krennsky (adapted)		LBrown
2004	Arthur And The New Kid		$8	$10	$14	Marc Brown		Random
2004	Arthur And The World Record		$8	$10	$14	Stephen Krennsky (adapted)		LBrown
2004	Arthur Loses His Marbles		$8	$10	$14	Stephen Krensky		LBrown
2004	Arthur's Heart Mix-Up		$8	$10	$14	Marc Brown		LBrown
2004	Wild About Books		$8	$10	$14	Judy Sierra		Knopf

Brown   Marcia

Year	Title	VG-	VG	VG+	Fine	Author	Award	Pub
1946	The Little Carousel	$160	$220	$280		Marcia Brown		Scribnr
1947	Stone Soup	$240	$320	$400		Marcia Brown	CH	Scribnr
1949	Dick Whittington And His Cat	$200	$280	$340		Marcia Brown	CH	Scribnr
1949	Henry-Fisherman	$200	$280	$340		Marcia Brown	CH	Scribnr
1950	Skipper John's Cook	$200	$260	$320		Marcia Brown	CH	Scribnr
1951	Puss In Boots	$200	$260	$320		Marcia Brown	CH	Scribnr
1952	The Steadfast Tin Soldier	$200	$260	$320		Marcia Brown	CH	Scribnr
1954	Anansi The Spider Man	$120	$160	$200		Philip Sherlock		Crowell
1954	Cinderella, Or The Little Glass Slipper	$580	$760	$960		Charles Perrault	CM	Scribnr
1956	The Flying Carpet	$100	$140	$180		Marcia Brown		Scribnr
1957	The Three Billy Goats Gruff	$100	$140	$180		Peter Christen Asbjønsen		HBrace
1958	Felice	$100	$140	$180		Marcia Brown		Scribnr
1959	Peter Piper's Alphabet	$100	$140	$180		Marcia Brown		Scribnr
1960	Tamarindo!	$100	$140	$180		Marcia Brown		Scribnr
1961	Once A Mouse	$320	$420	$520		Marcia Brown	CM	Scribnr
1963	The Wild Swans	$100	$120	$160		Hans Christian Andersen		Scribnr
1966	Backbone Of The King	$90	$120	$160		Marcia Brown		Scribnr
1967	The Neighbors	$80	$120	$140		Marcia Brown		Scribnr
1969	How, Hippo!	$80	$120	$140		Marcia Brown		Scribnr
1970	Giselle		$70	$100	$140	Violette Verdy		Dell
1972	The Bun		$70	$100	$140	Marcia Brown		HBJ
1972	The Snow Queen		$70	$100	$140	Marcia Brown		Scribnr
1974	All Butterflies		$60	$90	$120	Marcia Brown		Scribnr
1977	The Blue Jackal		$60	$80	$120	Marcia Brown		Scribnr
1979	Listen To A Shape		$50	$80	$100	Marcia Brown		FWatts
1979	Touch Will Tell		$50	$80	$100	Marcia Brown		FWatts
1979	Walk With Your Eyes		$50	$80	$100	Marcia Brown		FWatts
1982	Shadow		$120	$180	$240	Blaise Cendrars	CM	Scribnr

Brown   Marcia

Year	Title	VG-	VG	VG+	Fine	Author	Award	Pub
1984	Backbone Of The King		$35	$50	$70	Marcia Brown		UHaw
1986	Lotus Seeds		$30	$50	$60	Marcia Brown		Scribnr
1988	Sing A Song Of Popcorn		$30	$50	$60	Beatrice S. De Regniers		Scholas

Brown   Ruth

Year	Title	VG-	VG	VG+	Fine	Author	Award	Pub
1981	A Dark Dark Tale		$35	$50	$70	Ruth Brown		Dial
1982	Crazy Charlie		$25	$35	$50	Ruth Brown		RRourke
1983	If At First You Do Not See		$25	$35	$50	Ruth Brown		HR&W
1983	The Grizzly Revenge		$25	$35	$50	Ruth Brown		AP
1985	The Big Sneeze		$20	$30	$40	Ruth Brown		LL&S
1986	Our Cat Flossie		$20	$30	$40	Ruth Brown		Dutton
1986	The Christmas Day Kitten		$20	$30	$40	James Herriot		StMart
1987	Bonny's Big Day		$20	$30	$40	James Herriot		StMart
1987	Our Puppy's Vacation		$20	$30	$40	Ruth Brown		Dutton
1988	Blossom Comes Home		$18	$25	$35	James Herriot		StMart
1988	Ladybug, Ladybug		$18	$25	$35	Ruth Brown		Dutton
1989	The Market Square Dog		$18	$25	$35	James Herriot		StMart
1990	I Don't Like It!		$16	$25	$30	Ruth Brown		Dutton
1990	Oscar, Cat-About-Town		$16	$25	$30	James Herriot		StMart
1991	Alphabet Times Four		$16	$25	$30	Ruth Brown		Dutton
1991	Smudge, The Little Lost Lamb		$16	$25	$30	James Herriot		StMart
1991	The World That Jack Built		$16	$25	$30	Ruth Brown		Dutton
1992	James Herriot's Treasury		$16	$25	$30	James Herriot		StMart
1992	The Picnic		$16	$25	$30	Ruth Brown		Dutton
1993	In Search Of The Hidden Giant		$16	$25	$30	Jeanne Willis		Dutton
1994	Copycat		$14	$20	$30	Ruth Brown		Dutton
1994	Mr Bear & The Bear		$14	$20	$30	Frances Thomas		AP
1994	The Bear & Mr. Bear		$14	$20	$30	Frances Thomas		Dutton
1995	The Ghost Of Greyfriar's Bobby		$14	$20	$25	Ruth Brown		Dutton
1996	Ben's Christmas Carol		$12	$18	$25	Toby Forward		Dutton
1997	Baba Yaga & The Wise Doll		$12	$18	$25	Hiawyn Oram		Dutton
1997	Cry Baby		$12	$18	$25	Ruth Brown		Dutton
1997	Toad		$12	$18	$25	Ruth Brown		Dutton
1998	The Shy Little Angel		$12	$16	$20	Ruth Brown		Dutton
1999	Mad Summer Night's Dream		$12	$16	$20	Ruth Brown		Dutton
2000	Holly		$10	$14	$18	Ruth Brown		Holt
2000	Snail Trail		$10	$14	$18	Ruth Brown		Crown
2001	Ten Seeds		$10	$14	$18	Ruth Brown		Knopf

Browne   Anthony

Year	Title	VG-	VG	VG+	Fine	Author	Award	Pub
1977	A Walk In The Park		$40	$60	$80	Anthony Browne		HHamil
1977	Through The Magic Mirror		$40	$60	$80	Anthony Browne		Green
1980	Bear Hunt		$35	$50	$70	Anthony Browne		Athenm
1981	Hansel And Gretel		$35	$50	$70	Jacob & Wilhelm Grimm		MacRae
1983	Gorilla		$70	$100	$140	Anthony Browne	GM	Knopf
1984	Willy The Wimp		$30	$50	$60	Anthony Browne		Knopf
1985	Knock, Knock! Who's There?		$30	$40	$60	Sally Grindley		Knopf
1985	The Visitors Who Came To Stay		$30	$40	$60	Annalena McAfee		VK
1985	Willy The Champ		$30	$40	$60	Anthony Browne		Knopf
1986	Piggybook		$30	$40	$60	Anthony Browne		Knopf
1987	Kirsty Knows Best		$25	$40	$50	Annalena McAfee		Knopf
1988	Alice's Adventures In Wonderland		$25	$40	$50	Lewis Carroll		Knopf
1988	I Like Books		$25	$40	$50	Anthony Browne		Knopf
1988	Look What I've Got!		$25	$40	$50	Anthony Browne		Knopf
1989	Bear Goes To Town		$25	$40	$50	Anthony Browne		DoubleD
1989	The Little Bear Book		$25	$40	$50	Anthony Browne		DoubleD
1989	The Tunnel		$25	$40	$50	Anthony Browne		Knopf
1989	Things I Like		$25	$40	$50	Anthony Browne		Knopf
1990	Changes		$25	$35	$50	Anthony Browne		Knopf
1990	Trail Of Stones		$25	$35	$50	Gwen Strauss		Knopf
1991	Willy And Hugh		$25	$35	$50	Anthony Browne		Knopf
1992	The Night Shimmy		$20	$30	$40	Gwen Strauss		Knopf
1992	Zoo		$40	$60	$90	Anthony Browne	GM	Knopf
1994	Anthony Browne's King Kong		$20	$30	$40	Edgar Wallace		Turner

Browne — Anthony

Year	Title	VG-	VG	VG+	Fine	Author	Award	Pub
1994	The Big Baby		$20	$30	$40	Anthony Browne		Knopf
1994	The Daydreamer		$20	$30	$40	Ian McEwan		HCollins
1995	The Topiary Garden		$18	$25	$35	Janni Howker		Orchard
1995	Willy The Wizard		$18	$25	$35	Anthony Browne		Knopf
1998	Voices In The Park		$14	$20	$30	Anthony Browne		DK
1998	Willy The Dreamer		$14	$20	$30	Anthony Browne		Candle
2000	My Dad		$12	$18	$25	Anthony Browne		FSG
2000	Willy's Pictures		$12	$18	$25	Anthony Browne		Candle
2002	Animal Fair		$10	$16	$20	Anthony Browne		Candle
2003	The Shape Game		$10	$14	$18	Anthony Browne		FSG
2004	Into The Forest		$8	$12	$16	Anthony Browne		Candle
2005	My Mom		$6	$10	$12	Anthony Browne		FSG

Brunhoff — Jean de

Year	Title	VG-	VG	VG+	Fine	Author	Award	Pub
1933	The Story Of Babar	$2,200	$3,000	$3,800		Merle Haas (translated)		SmithH
1934	The Travels Of Babar	$1,600	$2,000	$2,600		Merle Haas (translated)		SmithH
1935	Babar The King	$1,600	$2,000	$2,600		Merle Haas (translated)		SmithH
1936	A B C Of Babar	$220	$300	$380		Jean de Brunhoff		Random
1936	Babar The King	$220	$300	$380		Jean de Brunhoff		Random
1936	The Story Of Babar	$340	$460	$580		Merle Haas (translated)		Random
1936	The Travels Of Babar	$220	$300	$380		Jean de Brunhoff		Random
1937	Zephir's Holidays	$220	$300	$380		Merle Haas (translated)		Random
1938	Babar And His Children	$220	$280	$360		Merle Haas (translated)		Random
1940	Babar And Father Christmas	$220	$280	$360		Merle Haas (translated)		Random
1940	Zephir's Holidays	$220	$280	$360		Jean de Brunhoff		Random
1942	Babar And Zephir	$200	$280	$340		Merle Haas (translated)		Random
1981	Babar's Anniversary Album		$70	$100	$140	Jean de Brunhoff		Random
1984	The Story Of Babar, The Little Elephant		$30	$50	$60	Jean de Brunhoff		Random
1985	The Travels Of Babar		$30	$40	$60	Jean de Brunhoff		Random
1986	Babar The King		$30	$40	$60	Merle Haas (translated)		Random
1989	Babar And His Children		$25	$40	$50	Jean de Brunhoff		Random
1995	A B C De Babar		$18	$25	$35	Jean de Brunhoff		Random
2000	Bonjour, Babar!		$12	$18	$25	Jean de Brunhoff		Random
2001	Babar And Father Christmas		$12	$16	$20	Merle Haas (translated)		Random
2002	Babar And His Children		$10	$16	$20	Merle Haas (translated)		Random
2002	Babar And Zephir		$10	$16	$20	Merle Haas (translated)		Random
2002	Babar The King		$10	$16	$20	Merle Haas (translated)		Random
2002	The Story Of Babar, The Little Elephant		$10	$16	$20	Merle Haas (translated)		Random
2002	The Travels Of Babar		$10	$16	$20	Merle Haas (translated)		Random

Brunhoff — Laurent de

Year	Title	VG-	VG	VG+	Fine	Author	Award	Pub
1948	Babar's Cousin, That Rascal Arthur	$280	$380	$480		Laurent de Brunhoff		Random
1949	Babar's Picnic	$200	$260	$320		Laurent de Brunhoff		Random
1952	Babar's Visit To Bird Island	$180	$240	$300		Laurent de Brunhoff		Random
1954	Babar's Fair	$160	$220	$280		Laurent de Brunhoff		Random
1957	Babar And The Professor	$160	$220	$280		Laurent de Brunhoff		Random
1961	Serafina The Giraffe	$70	$90	$120		Laurent de Brunhoff		World
1962	Babar's Castle	$100	$120	$160		Laurent de Brunhoff		Random
1962	Serafina's Lucky Find	$70	$90	$120		Laurent de Brunhoff		World
1963	Anatole And His Donkey	$70	$90	$120		Laurent de Brunhoff		Macmil
1963	Babar's French Lessons	$100	$120	$160		Laurent de Brunhoff		Random
1963	Babar's Spanish Lessons	$100	$120	$160		Laurent de Brunhoff		Random
1963	Captain Serafina	$70	$90	$120		Laurent de Brunhoff		World
1965	Babar Comes To America	$90	$120	$160		Laurent de Brunhoff		Random
1965	Bonhomme	$60	$80	$100		Laurent de Brunhoff		Pan
1967	Babar Loses His Crown	$80	$120	$140		Laurent de Brunhoff		BB
1967	The Cats Of The Eiffel Tower	$60	$80	$100		Auro Roselli		DelaP
1968	Babar's Games	$80	$120	$140		Laurent de Brunhoff		Random
1969	Babar At The Seashore	$80	$120	$140		Laurent de Brunhoff		Random
1969	Babar Goes On A Picnic	$80	$120	$140		Laurent de Brunhoff		Random
1969	Babar Goes Skiing	$80	$120	$140		Laurent de Brunhoff		Random
1969	Babar The Gardener	$80	$120	$140		Laurent de Brunhoff		Random
1970	Babar's Birthday Surprise		$70	$100	$140	Laurent de Brunhoff		Random
1971	Babar And The Doctor		$40	$60	$90	Laurent de Brunhoff		Random

Brunhoff   Laurent de

Year	Title	VG-	VG	VG+	Fine	Author	Award	Pub
1971	Babar The Artist		$40	$60	$90	Laurent de Brunhoff		Random
1971	Babar The Athlete		$40	$60	$90	Laurent de Brunhoff		Random
1971	Babar The Camper		$40	$60	$90	Laurent de Brunhoff		Random
1971	Gregory And Lady Turtle		$40	$60	$90	Laurent de Brunhoff		Pan
1972	Babar Visits Another Planet		$40	$60	$90	Laurent de Brunhoff		Random
1973	Meet Babar And His Family		$40	$60	$90	Laurent de Brunhoff		Random
1974	Bonhomme And The Huge Beast		$40	$60	$80	Laurent de Brunhoff		Pan
1975	Babar And The Wully-Wully		$40	$60	$80	Laurent de Brunhoff		Random
1976	Babar Saves The Day		$40	$60	$80	Laurent de Brunhoff		Random
1978	Babar's Mystery		$35	$50	$70	Laurent de Brunhoff		Random
1978	The One Pig With Horns		$35	$50	$70	Laurent de Brunhoff		Pan
1979	Babar Learns To Cook		$35	$50	$70	Laurent de Brunhoff		Random
1980	About Air		$25	$35	$50	Laurent de Brunhoff		Random
1980	About Earth		$25	$35	$50	Laurent de Brunhoff		Random
1980	About Fire		$25	$35	$50	Laurent de Brunhoff		Random
1980	About Water		$25	$35	$50	Laurent de Brunhoff		Random
1980	Babar The Magician		$35	$50	$70	Laurent de Brunhoff		Random
1981	Babar And The Ghost		$35	$50	$70	Laurent de Brunhoff		Random
1981	Babar's Anniversary Album		$35	$50	$70	Laurent de Brunhoff		Random
1983	Babar's ABC		$30	$50	$60	Laurent de Brunhoff		Random
1984	Babar's Book Of Color		$30	$50	$60	Laurent de Brunhoff		Random
1986	Babar's Counting Book		$30	$40	$60	Laurent de Brunhoff		Random
1987	Babar's Little Girl		$25	$40	$50	Laurent de Brunhoff		Random
1988	Babar's Little Circus Star		$25	$40	$50	Laurent de Brunhoff		Random
1989	Babar's Busy Year		$25	$40	$50	Laurent de Brunhoff		Random
1990	Isabelle's New Friend		$25	$35	$50	Laurent de Brunhoff		Random
1991	Babar's Family Album		$25	$35	$50	Laurent de Brunhoff		Random
1991	Babar's Picnic		$25	$35	$50	Laurent de Brunhoff		Random
1992	Babar's Bath Book		$20	$30	$40	Laurent de Brunhoff		Random
1992	Babar's Battle		$20	$30	$40	Laurent de Brunhoff		Random
1992	Babar's Car		$20	$30	$40	Laurent de Brunhoff		Random
1993	Babar's Peekaboo Fair		$20	$30	$40	Laurent de Brunhoff		Random
1993	The Rescue Of Babar		$20	$30	$40	Laurent de Brunhoff		Random
1994	Babar's French And English Word Book		$20	$30	$40	Laurent de Brunhoff		Random
2000	Babar And The Succotash Bird		$12	$18	$25	Laurent de Brunhoff		Abrams
2002	Babar's Battle		$10	$16	$20	Laurent de Brunhoff		Abrams
2002	Babar's Little Girl Makes A Friend		$10	$16	$20	Laurent de Brunhoff		Abrams
2002	Babar's Yoga For Elephants		$10	$16	$20	Laurent de Brunhoff		Abrams
2003	Babar And The Christmas House		$10	$14	$18	Laurent de Brunhoff		Abrams
2003	Babar Goes To School		$10	$14	$18	Laurent de Brunhoff		Abrams
2003	Babar's Museum Of Art		$10	$14	$18	Laurent de Brunhoff		Abrams
2004	Babar And The Gift For Mother		$8	$12	$16	Laurent de Brunhoff		Abrams
2004	Babar And The Runaway Egg		$8	$12	$16	Laurent de Brunhoff		Abrams
2004	Babar's Rescue		$8	$12	$16	Laurent de Brunhoff		Abrams

Bryan   Ashley

Year	Title	VG-	VG	VG+	Fine	Author	Award	Pub
1967	Moon, For What Do You Wait?	$60	$80	$100		Rabindranath Tagore		Athenm
1971	The Ox Of The Wonderful Horns		$30	$50	$60	Ashley Bryan		Athenm
1974	Walk Together Children		$30	$40	$60	Ashley Bryan		Athenm
1976	The Adventures Of Aku		$30	$40	$60	Ashley Bryan		Athenm
1977	The Dancing Granny		$25	$40	$50	Ashley Bryan		Athenm
1978	I Greet The Dawn		$25	$40	$50	Paul Laurence Dunbar		Athenm
1979	Jethro And The Jumbie		$25	$40	$50	Susan Cooper		Athenm
1979	Jim Flying High		$25	$40	$50	Mari Evans		DoubleD
1980	Beat The Story-Drum, Pum-Pum		$25	$35	$50	Ashley Bryan		Athenm
1985	The Cat's Purr		$20	$30	$40	Ashley Bryan		Athenm
1986	Lion And The Ostrich Chicks		$20	$30	$40	Ashley Bryan		Athenm
1989	Turtle Knows Your Name		$18	$25	$35	Ashley Bryan		Athenm
1992	Sing To The Sun		$16	$25	$30	Ashley Bryan		HCollins
1993	Christmas Gif'		$16	$25	$30	Charlemae Hill Rollins		Morrow
1993	The Story Of Lightning & Thunder		$16	$25	$30	Ashley Bryan		Athenm
1995	It's Kwanzaa Time!		$14	$20	$25	Linda Goss		Putnam
1995	The Story Of The Three Kingdoms		$14	$20	$25	Walter Dean Myers		HCollins
1995	What A Wonderful World		$14	$20	$25	George Weiss		Athenm
1996	The Sun Is So Quiet		$12	$18	$25	Nikki Giovanni		Holt

Bryan   Ashley

Year	Title	VG-	VG	VG+	Fine	Author	Award	Pub
1997	Ashley Bryan's ABC Of African-American Poetry		$12	$18	$25	Ashley Bryan		Athenm
1997	The House With No Door		$12	$18	$25	Brian Swann		HBrace
1998	Ashley Bryan's African Tales		$12	$16	$20	Ashley Bryan		Athenm
1998	Carol Of The Brown King		$12	$16	$20	Langston Hughes		Athenm
1998	Why Leopard Has Spots		$12	$16	$20	Won-Ldy Paye		Fulcrum
1999	Aneesa Lee And The Weaver's Gift		$12	$16	$20	Nikki Grimes		LL&S
1999	Jump Back, Honey		$12	$16	$20	Paul Laurence Dunbar		Hyper
1999	The Night Has Ears		$12	$16	$20	Ashley Bryan		Athenm
2000	Salting The Ocean		$10	$14	$18	Naomi Shihab Nye		Green
2003	Beautiful Blackbird		$8	$12	$16	Ashley Bryan		Athenm
2004	A Nest Full Of Stars		$8	$10	$14	James Berry		Green
2005	Spirituals		$6	$10	$12	Ashley Bryan		Athenm

Bryson   Bernarda

Year	Title	VG-	VG	VG+	Fine	Author	Award	Pub
1960	The Twenty Miracles Of Saint Nicolas	$80	$120	$140		Bernarda Bryson		LBrown
1962	The Sun Is A Golden Earring	$80	$100	$140		Natalia Belting	CH	HR&W
1963	The Return Of The Twelves	$50	$70	$90		Pauline Clarke		CM
1964	Calendar Moon	$50	$70	$90		Natalia Belting		HR&W
1964	The Zoo Of Zeus	$80	$100	$140		Bernarda Bryson		GP
1966	Gilgamesh; Man's First Story	$50	$60	$80		Bernarda Bryson		HR&W
1968	The Storyteller's Pack	$50	$60	$80		Frank R. Stockton		Scribnr
1970	The Grindstone Of God		$30	$50	$60	Carl Withers		HR&W
1972	Ben Shahn		$100	$140	$200	Ben Shahn		Abrams
1984	The Dreyfus Affair		$20	$30	$40	Ben Shahn		CrossR
1995	The Vanishing American Frontier		$14	$20	$25	Bernarda Bryson		WienAm

Buchanan   Heather

Year	Title	VG-	VG	VG+	Fine	Author	Award	Pub
1988	George And Matilda Mouse And The Doll's House		$18	$25	$35	Heather Buchanan		S&S
1991	George And Matilda Mouse And The Moon Rocket		$16	$25	$30	Heather Buchanan		S&S
1994	The Christmas Journey Of George & Matilda Mouse		$14	$20	$30	Heather Buchanan		LongMed

Buehner   Mark

Year	Title	VG-	VG	VG+	Fine	Author	Award	Pub
1990	The Adventures Of Taxi Dog		$25	$35	$50	Debra & Sal Barracca		Dial
1991	Maxi, The Hero		$16	$25	$30	Debra & Sal Barracca		Dial
1992	The Escape Of Marvin The Ape		$16	$25	$30	Caralyn Buehner		Dial
1993	A Job For Wittilda		$16	$25	$30	Caralyn Buehner		Dial
1994	Harvey Potter's Balloon Farm		$14	$20	$30	Jerdine Nolen		LL&S
1995	It's A Spoon, Not A Shovel		$14	$20	$25	Caralyn Buehner		Dial
1996	Fanny's Dream		$12	$18	$25	Caralyn Buehner		Dial
1997	My Life With The Wave		$12	$18	$25	Catherine Cowan (adapted)		LL&S
1998	I Did It, I'm Sorry		$12	$16	$20	Caralyn Buehner		Dial
1999	I Am The Cat		$12	$16	$20	Alice Schertle		LL&S
1999	My Monster Mama Loves Me So		$12	$16	$20	Laura Leuck		LL&S
2001	This First Thanksgiving Day		$10	$14	$18	Laura Krauss Melmed		HCollins
2002	Christmas Day In The Morning		$8	$12	$16	Pearl S. Buck		HCollins
2002	Snowmen At Night		$8	$12	$16	Caralyn Buehner		PFogel
2004	Niccolini's Song		$8	$10	$14	Mark Buehner		Dutton
2004	Superdog		$8	$10	$14	Caralyn Buehner		HCollins

Buff   Conrad

Year	Title	VG-	VG	VG+	Fine	Author	Award	Pub
1937	Dancing Cloud	$100	$140	$180		Mary Buff		Viking
1939	Kobi	$70	$90	$120		Mary Buff		Viking
1942	Dash & Dart	$140	$180	$240		Mary Buff	CH	Viking
1946	Big Tree	$90	$120	$160		Mary Buff	NH	Viking
1949	Peter's Pinto	$60	$80	$100		Mary Buff		Viking
1951	The Apple And The Arrow	$80	$100	$140		Mary Buff	NH	HM
1953	Magic Maize	$80	$100	$140		Mary Buff	NH	HM
1954	Hurry, Skurry, And Flurry	$50	$70	$90		Mary Buff		Viking
1957	Dancing Cloud, The Navajo Boy	$50	$70	$90		Mary Buff		Viking
1958	Elf Owl	$50	$60	$80		Mary Buff		Viking
1960	Trix And Vix	$50	$60	$80		Mary Buff		HM

Buff   Conrad

Year	Title	VG-	VG	VG+	Fine	Author	Award	Pub
1962	Forest Folk	$50	$60	$80		Mary Buff		Viking
1965	Peter's Pinto	$40	$60	$70		Mary Buff		WRichie
1966	Kemi, An Indian Boy Before The White Man Came	$40	$60	$70		Mary Buff		WRichie
1968	The Colorado, River Of Mystery	$40	$50	$70		Mary Buff		WRichie

Bullock   Kathleen

Year	Title	VG-	VG	VG+	Fine	Author	Award	Pub
1986	Hey Diddle Rock		$12	$16	$20	Patti Moran McCoy		Kids
1986	Hickory Dickory Rock		$12	$16	$20	Patti Moran McCoy		Kids
1986	Humpty Dumpty Rock		$12	$16	$20	Patti Moran McCoy		Kids
1986	Rock-A-Doodle-Doo		$12	$16	$20	Patti Moran McCoy		Kids
1988	The Bible Read-To-Me 1, 2, 3		$12	$16	$20	Joy MacKenzie		Chariot
1988	The Bible Read-To-Me ABC Book		$12	$16	$20	Joy MacKenzie		Chariot
1989	A Surprise For Mitzi Mouse		$12	$16	$20	Kathleen Bullock		S&S
1989	It Chanced To Rain		$12	$16	$20	Kathleen Bullock		S&S
1990	A Friend For Mitzi Mouse		$10	$16	$20	Kathleen Bullock		S&S
1991	The Rabbits Are Coming		$10	$16	$20	Kathleen Bullock		S&S
1991	The Twelve Days Of Christmas		$10	$16	$20	Kathleen Bullock		Budget
1993	She'll Be Comin' Round The Mountain		$10	$16	$20	Kathleen Bullock		S&S

Burgess   Anne

Year	Title	VG-	VG	VG+	Fine	Author	Award	Pub
1975	The Nunga Punga & The Booch		$16	$25	$30	Jean Wilson Kennedy		Scribnr
1977	The Summer Maker		$16	$25	$30	M. Bernstein & J. Kobrin		Scribnr
1980	Sloppy Kisses		$14	$20	$25	Elizabeth Winthrop		Macmil
1980	The Devil Take You, Barnabas Beane!		$14	$20	$25	Mary Blount Christian		Crowell
1981	Dusk To Dawn		$14	$20	$25	Helen Hill		Crowell
1990	Ready...Set...Read!		$10	$16	$20	Joanna Cole		DoubleD

Burkert   Nancy Ekholm

Year	Title	VG-	VG	VG+	Fine	Author	Award	Pub
1961	James And The Giant Peach	$2,000	$2,800	$3,400		Roald Dahl		Knopf
1963	Jean-Claude's Island	$70	$90	$120		Natalie Carlson		H&Row
1963	The Big Goose And The Little White Duck	$70	$90	$120		Meindert DeJong		H&Row
1965	A Child's Calendar	$60	$80	$100		John Updike		Knopf
1965	The Nightingale	$60	$80	$100		Hans Christian Andersen		H&Row
1968	The Scroobious Pip	$60	$80	$100		Ogden Nash		H&Row
1970	The Fir Tree		$50	$70	$90	Hans Christian Andersen		H&Row
1972	Snow White And The Seven Dwarfs		$100	$140	$200	Jacob & Wilhelm Grimm	CH	FSG
1980	Acts Of Light, Emily Dickinson: Poems		$35	$50	$70	Emily Dickinson		NYGS
1989	Valentine And Orson		$25	$40	$50	Nancy Ekholm Burkert		FSG

Burningham   John

Year	Title	VG-	VG	VG+	Fine	Author	Award	Pub
1963	Borka	$140	$200	$240		John Burningham	GM	Random
1964	ABC	$90	$120	$160		John Burningham		JCape
1964	Chitty Chitty Bang Bang	$140	$180	$240		Ian Fleming		Random
1965	Trubloff	$90	$120	$160		John Burningham		Random
1966	Cannonball Simp	$90	$120	$160		John Burningham		Bobbs
1967	Harquin: The Fox Who Went Down To The Valley	$80	$120	$140		John Burningham		Bobbs
1968	The Extraordinary Tug-Of-War, Retold	$80	$120	$140		Letta Schatz		Follett
1969	Seasons	$80	$120	$140		John Burningham		JCape
1970	Mr. Gumpy's Outing		$100	$160	$200	John Burningham	GM	HR&W
1972	Around The World In Eighty Days		$40	$60	$90	John Burningham		JCape
1975	The Baby		$40	$60	$80	John Burningham		Crowell
1975	The Rabbit		$40	$60	$80	John Burningham		Crowell
1975	The School		$40	$60	$80	John Burningham		Crowell
1975	The Snow		$40	$60	$80	John Burningham		Crowell
1976	Mr. Gumpy's Motor Car		$40	$60	$80	John Burningham		Crowell
1976	The Blanket		$40	$60	$80	John Burningham		Crowell
1976	The Cupboard		$40	$60	$80	John Burningham		Crowell
1976	The Dog		$40	$60	$80	John Burningham		Crowell
1976	The Friend		$40	$60	$80	John Burningham		Crowell
1977	Come Away From The Water, Shirley		$40	$60	$80	John Burningham		Crowell
1978	Time To Get Out Of The Bath, Shirley		$35	$50	$70	John Burningham		Crowell

Burningham   John

Year	Title	VG-	VG	VG+	Fine	Author	Award	Pub
1978	Would You Rather		$35	$50	$70	John Burningham		Crowell
1980	The Shopping Basket		$35	$50	$70	John Burningham		Crowell
1982	Avocado Baby		$30	$50	$60	John Burningham		Crowell
1983	Count Up		$30	$50	$60	John Burningham		Walker
1983	Five Down		$30	$50	$60	John Burningham		Walker
1983	Just Cats		$30	$50	$60	John Burningham		Viking
1983	Pigs Plus		$30	$50	$60	John Burningham		Walker
1983	Read One		$30	$50	$60	John Burningham		Walker
1983	Ride Off		$30	$50	$60	John Burningham		Walker
1983	The Wind In The Willows		$30	$50	$60	Kenneth Grahame		Viking
1984	Skip Trip		$30	$50	$60	John Burningham		Viking
1984	Sniff Shout		$30	$50	$60	John Burningham		Viking
1984	Wobble Pop		$30	$50	$60	John Burningham		Viking
1985	Cluck Baa		$30	$40	$60	John Burningham		Viking
1985	Granpa		$30	$40	$60	John Burningham		Crown
1985	Jangle Twang		$30	$40	$60	John Burningham		Viking
1985	John Burningham's 1 2 3		$30	$40	$60	John Burningham		Crown
1985	Slam Bang		$30	$40	$60	John Burningham		Viking
1986	John Burningham's ABC		$30	$40	$60	John Burningham		Crown
1986	John Burningham's Colors		$30	$40	$60	John Burningham		Crown
1986	John Burningham's Opposites		$30	$40	$60	John Burningham		Crown
1986	Where's Julius?		$30	$40	$60	John Burningham		Crown
1987	John Patrick Norman Mchennessy		$25	$40	$50	John Burningham		Crown
1989	Hey! Get Off The Train		$25	$40	$50	John Burningham		Crown
1989	Humbert, Mister Firkin & The Lord Mayor Of London		$25	$40	$50	John Burningham		Crown
1991	Aldo		$25	$35	$50	John Burningham		Crown
1992	England		$20	$30	$40	John Burningham		JCape
1993	Harvey Slumfenburger's Christmas Present		$20	$30	$40	John Burningham		Candle
1994	Courtney		$20	$30	$40	John Burningham		Crown
1996	Cloudland		$16	$25	$30	John Burningham		Crown
1999	Whaddayamean		$14	$20	$25	John Burningham		Crown
2000	Hushabye		$12	$18	$25	John Burningham		Knopf
2001	For Every Child		$12	$16	$20	Caroline Castle		PFogel
2001	Mr. Gumpy's Outing		$12	$16	$20	John Burningham		HR&W
2003	Colors		$10	$14	$18	John Burningham		Candle
2003	Letters		$10	$14	$18	John Burningham		Candle
2003	Numbers		$10	$14	$18	John Burningham		Candle
2003	Opposites		$10	$14	$18	John Burningham		Candle
2003	The Magic Bed		$10	$14	$18	John Burningham		Knopf

Burton   Virginia Lee

Year	Title	VG-	VG	VG+	Fine	Author	Award	Pub
1937	Choo Choo	$340	$460	$580		Virginia Lee Burton		HM
1937	Sad-Faced Boy	$340	$460	$580		Arna W. Bontemps		HM
1938	Belinda And The Singing Clock	$220	$300	$380		Ethel Calvert Phillips		HM
1939	Mike Mulligan And His Steam Shovel	$2,600	$3,400	$4,200		Virginia Lee Burton		HM
1941	Calico, The Wonder Horse	$220	$280	$360		Virginia Lee Burton		HM
1942	Don Coyote	$200	$280	$340		Leigh Peck		HM
1942	The Fast Sooner Hound	$200	$280	$340		Arna W. Bontemps		HM
1942	The Little House	$3,000	$4,000	$5,000		Virginia Lee Burton	CM	HM
1943	Katy And The Big Snow	$200	$280	$340		Virginia Lee Burton		HM
1947	Song Of Robin Hood	$200	$260	$320		Grace Castagnetta	CH	HM
1949	The Emperor's New Clothes	$200	$260	$320		Hans Christian Andersen		HM
1952	Maybelle, The Cable Car	$140	$200	$240		Virginia Lee Burton		HM

Bush   Timothy

Year	Title	VG-	VG	VG+	Fine	Author	Award	Pub
1993	James In The House Of Aunt Prudence		$20	$30	$40	Timothy Bush		Random
1994	Three At Sea		$14	$20	$30	Timothy Bush		Crown
1995	Grunt! The Primitive Cave Boy		$14	$20	$25	Timothy Bush		Crown
1998	Benjamin Mcfadden And The Robot Babysitter		$12	$16	$20	Timothy Bush		Crown
1999	Bach's Big Adventure		$12	$16	$20	Sallie Kethcam		Orchard
2000	Ferocious Girls, Steamroller Boys		$10	$14	$18	Timothy Bush		Orchard
2000	Wanna Buy An Alien?		$10	$14	$18	Eve Bunting		Clarion
2001	Math Man		$10	$14	$18	Teri Daniels		Orchard
2002	Christmas Cricket		$8	$12	$16	Eve Bunting		Clarion

Bush — Timothy

Year	Title	VG-	VG	VG+	Fine	Author	Award	Pub
2003	My Dad's Job		$8	$12	$16	Peter Glassman		S&S
2003	The Skeleton In The Smithsonian		$8	$12	$16	Ron Roy		Random
2004	A Spy In The White House		$8	$10	$14	Ron Roy		Random

Butterworth — Nick

Year	Title	VG-	VG	VG+	Fine	Author	Award	Pub
1982	B.B. Blacksheep And Company		$30	$50	$60	Nick Butterworth		G&D
1985	The Nativity Play		$20	$30	$40	Mick Inkpen		LBrown
1986	The House On The Rock		$20	$30	$40	Mick Inkpen		Mult
1986	The Lost Sheep		$20	$30	$40	Mick Inkpen		Mult
1986	The Precious Pearl		$20	$30	$40	Mick Inkpen		Mult
1986	The Two Sons		$20	$30	$40	Mick Inkpen		Mult
1987	Nice Or Nasty: Book Of Opposites		$20	$30	$40	Mick Inkpen		LBrown
1989	Just Like Jasper!		$18	$25	$35	Mick Inkpen		LBrown
1990	Nick Butterworth's Book Of Nursery Rhymes		$16	$25	$30	Nick Butterworth		Viking
1990	One Snowy Night		$16	$25	$30	Nick Butterworth		LBrown
1990	The School Trip		$16	$25	$30	Mick Inkpen		DelaP
1991	Amanda's Butterfly		$16	$25	$30	Nick Butterworth		HCollins
1992	Busy People		$16	$25	$30	Nick Butterworth		Candle
1992	My Grandpa Is Amazing		$16	$25	$30	Nick Butterworth		Candle
1992	One Blowy Night		$16	$25	$30	Nick Butterworth		LBrown
1992	Who Made Me?		$16	$25	$30	Malcolm & Meryl Doney		Zonder
1993	Jasper's Beanstalk		$16	$25	$30	Mick Inkpen		BradP
1993	Making Faces		$16	$25	$30	Nick Butterworth		Candle
1993	The Rescue Party		$16	$25	$30	Nick Butterworth		LBrown
1994	My Mom Is Excellent / Nick Butterworth		$14	$20	$30	Nick Butterworth		Candle
1994	The Secret Path		$14	$20	$30	Nick Butterworth		LBrown
1994	When It's Time For Bed		$14	$20	$30	Nick Butterworth		LBrown
1994	When There's Work To Do		$14	$20	$30	Nick Butterworth		LBrown
1994	When We Go Shopping		$14	$20	$30	Nick Butterworth		LBrown
1994	When We Play Together		$14	$20	$30	Nick Butterworth		LBrown
1995	All Together Now!		$14	$20	$25	Nick Butterworth		LBrown
1998	Jingle Bells		$12	$16	$20	Nick Butterworth		Orchard
1998	Wonderful Earth!		$12	$16	$20	N. Butterworth & M. Inkpen		TNelson
2000	Q Pootle 5		$10	$14	$18	Nick Butterworth		Athenm
2002	Albert The Bear		$8	$12	$16	Nick Butterworth		HCollins

Byard — Carole M.

Year	Title	VG-	VG	VG+	Fine	Author	Award	Pub
1971	Willy		$30	$50	$60	Helen Hayes King		DoubleD
1972	Nomi And The Magic Fish		$30	$50	$60	Phumla		DoubleD
1972	Under Christopher's Hat		$30	$50	$60	Dorothy M Callahan		Scribnr
1974	The Sycamore Tree & Other African Tales		$30	$40	$60	Po Lee		DoubleD
1975	Arthur Mitchell		$30	$40	$60	Tobi Tobias		Crowell
1977	Africa Dream		$25	$40	$50	Eloise Greenfield		JohnDay
1978	I Can Do It By Myself		$25	$40	$50	Lessie Jones Little		Crowell
1979	Cornrows		$25	$40	$50	Camille Yarbrough		CM&G
1979	Three African Tales		$25	$40	$50	Adjai Robinson		Putnam
1980	Grandmama's Joy		$25	$35	$50	Eloise Greenfield		Collins
1989	Have A Happy--		$18	$25	$35	Mildred Pitts Walter		LL&S
1989	The Black Snowman		$18	$25	$35	Phil Mendez		Scholas
1992	Working Cotton		$40	$60	$90	Sherley Anne Williams	CH	HBJ
2002	Angel City		$8	$12	$16	Tony Johnston		Philo

Byrd — Robert

Year	Title	VG-	VG	VG+	Fine	Author	Award	Pub
1970	Wiley And The Hairy Man		$50	$70	$90	Jack Stokes		MacSm
1971	The Possible Impossibles Of Ikkyu The Wise		$30	$50	$60	I. G. Edmonds		MacSm
1973	Heat		$30	$50	$60	Vicki Cobb		FWatts
1973	Poor Mister Splinterfitz!		$30	$50	$60	Robert Kraus		Spring
1974	Pinchpenny Mouse		$30	$40	$60	Robert Kraus		Windmil
1974	Rebecca Hatpin		$30	$40	$60	Robert Kraus		Windmil
1976	The Gondolier Of Venice		$30	$40	$60	Robert Kraus		Windmil
1978	The Detective Of London		$25	$40	$50	Robert Kraus		Windmil
1983	Charles Rat's Picnic		$25	$35	$50	Susan Saunders		Dutton

Byrd   Robert

Year	Title	VG-	VG	VG+	Fine	Author	Award	Pub
1985	Marcella Was Bored		$20	$30	$40	Robert Byrd		Dutton
1988	The Children's Aesop		$18	$25	$35	Stephanie Calmenson		DoubleD
1991	The Emperor's New Clothes		$16	$25	$30	Mike Levinson (retold)		Dutton
1992	All About How Things Are Made		$16	$25	$30	Kathleen Kain		World
1994	The Bear And The Bird King		$14	$20	$30	Jacob & Wilhelm Grimm		Dutton
1995	The Market		$14	$20	$25	Marilyn Jager Adams		OCP
1996	The Little Swineherd & Other Tales		$12	$18	$25	Paula Fox		Dutton
1999	Finn Maccoul And His Fearless Wife		$12	$16	$20	Robert Byrd		Dutton
2000	Saint Francis And The Christmas Donkey		$10	$14	$18	Robert Byrd		Dutton
2003	Leonardo, Beautiful Dreamer		$8	$12	$16	Robert Byrd		Dutton

Cady   Harrison

Year	Title	VG-	VG	VG+	Fine	Author	Award	Pub
1906	Racketty-Packetty House	$260	$360	$440		Frances Hodgson Burnett		Century
1906	The Troubles Of Queen Silver-Bell	$260	$360	$440		Frances Hodgson Burnett		Century
1907	Garden-Land	$260	$360	$440		Robert W. Chambers		DApple
1909	The Children's Book	$260	$360	$440		Frances Hodgson Burnett		Moffat
1910	Old Mother West Wind	$260	$340	$420		Thornton W. Burgess		LBrown
1910	The Water Goats	$260	$340	$420		Ellis Parker Butler		DP
1913	The Adventures Of Reddy Fox	$260	$340	$420		Thornton W. Burgess		LBrown
1914	The Adventures Of Peter Cottontail	$240	$320	$400		Thornton W. Burgess		LBrown
1915	The Adventures Of Chatterer The Red Squirrel	$240	$320	$400		Thornton W. Burgess		LBrown
1915	The Adventures Of Danny Meadow Mouse	$240	$320	$400		Thornton W. Burgess		LBrown
1915	The Adventures Of Grandfather Frog	$240	$320	$400		Thornton W. Burgess		LBrown
1915	The Adventures Of Sammy Jay	$240	$320	$400		Thornton W. Burgess		LBrown
1915	Tommy and the Wishing Stone	$240	$320	$400		Thornton W. Burgess		Century
1916	The Adventures Of Buster Bear	$240	$320	$400		Thornton W. Burgess		LBrown
1916	The Adventures Of Old Man Coyote	$240	$320	$400		Thornton W. Burgess		LBrown
1916	The Adventures Of Old Mr. Toad	$240	$320	$400		Thornton W. Burgess		LBrown
1916	The Adventures Of Prickly Porky	$240	$320	$400		Thornton W. Burgess		LBrown
1917	The Adventures Of Paddy Beaver	$240	$320	$400		Thornton W. Burgess		LBrown
1917	The Adventures Of Poor Mrs. Quack	$240	$320	$400		Thornton W. Burgess		LBrown
1918	Bugs And Wings & Other Things	$240	$320	$400		Annie Wood. Franchot		Dutton
1918	Happy Jack	$240	$320	$400		Thornton W. Burgess		LBrown
1918	The Adventures Of Bobby Coon	$240	$320	$400		Thornton W. Burgess		LBrown
1918	The Adventures Of Jimmy Skunk	$240	$320	$400		Thornton W. Burgess		LBrown
1919	The Adventures Of Ol' Mistah Buzzard	$220	$300	$380		Thornton W. Burgess		LBrown
1920	...Bowser The Hound	$180	$240	$300		Thornton W. Burgess		LBrown
1920	Old Granny Fox	$180	$240	$300		Thornton W. Burgess		LBrown
1921	Lightfoot The Deer	$180	$240	$300		Thornton W. Burgess		LBrown
1921	Tommy's Change Of Heart	$180	$240	$300		Thornton W. Burgess		LBrown
1921	Tommy's Wishes Come True	$180	$240	$300		Thornton W. Burgess		LBrown
1922	...Whitefoot, The Wood Mouse	$180	$240	$300		Thornton W. Burgess		LBrown
1922	Blacky The Crow	$180	$240	$300		Thornton W. Burgess		LBrown
1923	Buster Bear's Twins	$180	$240	$300		Thornton W. Burgess		LBrown
1924	Ant Ventures	$180	$240	$300		Blanche Elizabeth Wade		RandMc
1926	Jerry Muskrat At Home	$180	$240	$300		Thornton W. Burgess		LBrown
1928	Happy Jack Squirrel Helps Unc' Billy	$160	$220	$280		Thornton W. Burgess		Stoll&E
1928	The Neatness Of Bobby Coon	$160	$220	$280		Thornton W. Burgess		Stoll&E
1930	The Raggedies In Fairyland	$160	$220	$280		George Sherman Ripley		RandMc
1939	Mother West Wind's Children	$70	$90	$120		Thornton W. Burgess		LBrown
1941	Little Pete's Adventure	$70	$90	$120		Thornton W. Burgess		McLough
1942	Animal Stories	$70	$90	$120		Thornton W. Burgess		P&Munk
1942	Little Chuck's Adventure	$70	$90	$120		Thornton W. Burgess		McLough
1942	Little Red's Adventure	$70	$90	$120		Thornton W. Burgess		McLough
1944	50 Favorite Burgess Stories	$60	$80	$100		Thornton W. Burgess		G&D
1944	On The Green Meadows	$60	$80	$100		Thornton W. Burgess		LBrown
1944	The Adventures Of Johnny Chuck	$60	$80	$100		Thornton W. Burgess		LBrown
1945	At The Smiling Pool	$60	$80	$100		Thornton W. Burgess		LBrown
1946	The Crooked Little Path	$60	$80	$100		Thornton W. Burgess		LBrown
1947	The Dear Old Briar-Patch	$60	$80	$100		Thornton W. Burgess		LBrown
1950	At Paddy The Beaver's Pond	$30	$40	$50		Thornton W. Burgess		LBrown
1961	The Animal World Of Thornton Burgess	$25	$30	$40		Thornton W. Burgess		P&Munk
1968	Mother West Wind's Neighbors	$40	$50	$70		Thornton W. Burgess		LBrown
1990	Animal Tales		$10	$16	$20	Thornton W. Burgess		P&Munk
1992	The Spring Cleaning		$10	$16	$20	Frances Hodgson Burnett		Derry

Cannon   Janell

Year	Title	VG-	VG	VG+	Fine	Author	Award	Pub
1993	Stellaluna		$30	$40	$60	Janell Cannon		HBJ
1995	Trupp: A Fuzzhead Tale		$14	$20	$25	Janell Cannon		HBrace
1996	Purr--		$12	$18	$25	Janell Cannon		HBrace
1997	Verdi		$12	$18	$25	Janell Cannon		HBrace
2000	Crickwing		$10	$14	$18	Janell Cannon		Harcort
2002	Little Yau		$8	$12	$16	Janell Cannon		Harcort
2004	Pinduli		$8	$10	$14	Janell Cannon		Harcort

Caple   Kathy

Year	Title	VG-	VG	VG+	Fine	Author	Award	Pub
1980	Inspector Aardvark And The Perfect Cake		$35	$50	$70	Kathy Caple		Windmil
1985	The Biggest Nose		$20	$30	$40	Kathy Caple		HM
1986	The Purse		$20	$30	$40	Kathy Caple		HM
1987	Harry's Smile		$20	$30	$40	Kathy Caple		HM
1990	The Coolest Place In Town		$16	$25	$30	Kathy Caple		HM
1992	Fox And Bear		$16	$25	$30	Kathy Caple		HM
1994	The Wimp		$14	$20	$30	Kathy Caple		HM
1999	Starring Hillary		$12	$16	$20	Kathy Caple		CRB
2000	Hillary To The Rescue		$10	$14	$18	Kathy Caple		CRB
2000	The Friendship Tree		$10	$14	$18	Kathy Caple		Holiday
2000	Well Done, Worm		$10	$14	$18	Kathy Caple		Candle
2001	Wow, It's Worm!		$10	$14	$18	Kathy Caple		Candle
2004	Worm Gets A Job		$8	$10	$14	Kathy Caple		Candle

Carle   Eric

Year	Title	VG-	VG	VG+	Fine	Author	Award	Pub
1963	The Sun Is A Star	$100	$120	$160		Sune Engelbrektson		HR&W
1965	Aesop's Fables, For Modern Readers	$90	$120	$160		Aesop		PPauper
1966	On Friendship	$60	$80	$100		Louise Bachelder (edited)		PPauper
1967	Brown Bear, Brown Bear, What Do You See?	$120	$160	$220		Bill Martin Jr.		HR&W
1967	Flower Thoughts	$40	$50	$70		Louise Bachelder (edited)		PPauper
1967	The Say-With-Me ABC Book	$80	$120	$140		Eric Carle		HR&W
1968	1, 2, 3 To The Zoo	$80	$120	$140		Eric Carle		World
1968	In Search Of Meaning	$80	$120	$140		Carl Herman Voss		World
1968	The Whale With A Jail	$80	$120	$140		Nora Roberts Wanier		F&W
1969	The Very Hungry Caterpillar	$180	$240	$300		Eric Carle		Philo
1970	A Ghost Story		$70	$100	$140	Bill Martin Jr.		HR&W
1970	Pancakes, Pancakes!		$70	$100	$140	Eric Carle		Knopf
1970	Tales Of The Nimipoo		$70	$100	$140	Eleanor B. Heady		World
1970	The Boastful Fisherman		$70	$100	$140	William Knowlton		Knopf
1970	The Tiny Seed		$70	$100	$140	Eric Carle		Picture
1971	Do You Want To Be My Friend?		$70	$100	$140	Eric Carle		Crowell
1971	Feathered Ones And Furry		$70	$100	$140	Aileen Fisher		Crowell
1971	The Scarecrow Clock		$70	$100	$140	George Mendoza		HR&W
1972	The Secret Birthday Message		$70	$100	$140	Eric Carle		Crowell
1972	Walter The Baker		$70	$100	$140	Eric Carle (retold)		Knopf
1973	Do Bears Have Mothers Too?		$60	$90	$120	Aileen Fisher		Crowell
1973	Have You Seen My Cat?		$60	$90	$120	Eric Carle		FWatts
1973	I See A Song		$60	$90	$120	Eric Carle		Crowell
1974	All About Arthur (An Absolutely Absurd Ape)		$60	$90	$120	Eric Carle		FWatts
1974	Why Noah Chose The Dove		$60	$90	$120	Elizabeth Shub (translated)		FSG
1975	The Hole In The Dike		$60	$80	$120	Norma Green (retold)		Crowell
1975	The Mixed-Up Chameleon		$60	$80	$120	Eric Carle		Crowell
1976	Eric Carle's Storybook		$60	$80	$120	Eric Carle (retold)		FWatts
1977	The Grouchy Ladybug		$60	$80	$120	Eric Carle		Crowell
1978	Seven Stories By Hans Christian Andersen		$50	$80	$100	Eric Carle (retold)		FWatts
1978	Watch Out! A Giant!		$50	$80	$100	Eric Carle		Collins
1979	The Very Hungry Caterpillar		$35	$50	$70	Eric Carle		Philo
1980	Twelve Tales From Aesop		$40	$60	$80	Eric Carle (retold)		Philo
1981	The Honeybee And The Robber		$40	$60	$80	Eric Carle		Philo
1982	Catch The Ball!		$40	$60	$80	Eric Carle		Philo
1982	Let's Paint A Rainbow		$40	$60	$80	Eric Carle		Philo
1982	Otter Nonsense		$40	$60	$80	Norton Juster		Philo
1982	What's For Lunch?		$40	$60	$80	Eric Carle		Philo
1984	The Very Busy Spider		$35	$50	$70	Eric Carle		Philo
1985	Chip Has Many Brothers		$35	$50	$70	Hans Baumann		Philo

Carle   Eric

Year	Title	VG-	VG	VG+	Fine	Author	Award	Pub
1985	The Foolish Tortoise		$35	$50	$70	Richard Buckley		Picture
1985	The Greedy Python		$35	$50	$70	Richard Buckley		Picture
1985	The Mountain That Loved A Bird		$35	$50	$70	Alice McLerran		Picture
1986	All Around Us		$30	$50	$60	Eric Carle		Picture
1986	My Very First Book Of Growth		$30	$50	$60	Eric Carle		Crowell
1986	My Very First Book Of Homes		$30	$50	$60	Eric Carle		Crowell
1986	My Very First Book Of Motion		$30	$50	$60	Eric Carle		Crowell
1986	My Very First Book Of Touch		$30	$50	$60	Eric Carle		Crowell
1986	Papa, Please Get The Moon For Me		$30	$50	$60	Eric Carle		Picture
1987	A House For Hermit Crab		$30	$50	$60	Eric Carle		Picture
1987	Rooster's Off To See The World		$30	$50	$60	Eric Carle		Picture
1988	Eric Carle's Trasury Of Classic Stories		$30	$50	$60	Eric Carle		Orchard
1988	The Lamb And The Butterfly		$30	$50	$60	Arnold Sundgaard		Orchard
1989	Eric Carle's Animals, Animals		$30	$40	$60	Eric Carle		Philo
1990	Pancakes, Pancakes!		$25	$40	$50	Eric Carle		Picture
1990	The Very Quiet Cricket		$25	$40	$50	Eric Carle		Philo
1991	Eric Carle's Dragons & Other Creatures		$25	$40	$50	Laura Whipple (compiled)		Philo
1991	Polar Bear, Polar Bear, What Do You Hear?		$25	$40	$50	Bill Martin Jr.		Holt
1992	Draw Me A Star		$25	$35	$50	Eric Carle		Philo
1993	Today Is Monday		$25	$35	$50	Eric Carle		Philo
1993	Walter The Bear		$25	$35	$50	Eric Carle		Picture
1994	My Apron: A Story From My Childhood		$20	$30	$40	Eric Carle		Philo
1995	The Very Lonely Firefly		$20	$30	$40	Eric Carle		Philo
1997	Flora And Tiger		$18	$25	$35	Eric Carle		Philo
1997	From Head To Toe		$18	$25	$35	Eric Carle		HCollins
1998	Hello, Red Fox		$16	$25	$30	Eric Carle		S&S
1998	Stories For All Seasons		$16	$25	$30	Eric Carle		S&S
1998	The Very Clumsy Click Beetle		$16	$25	$30	Eric Carle		Philo
2000	Does A Kangaroo Have A Mother, Too?		$14	$20	$25	Eric Carle		HCollins
2000	Dream Snow		$14	$20	$25	Eric Carle		Philo
2002	Slowly, Slowly, Slowly, Said The Sloth		$12	$16	$20	Eric Carle		Philo
2003	Panda Bear, Panda Bear, What Do You See?		$10	$16	$20	Bill Martin		Holt
2003	Where Are You Going? To See My Friend		$10	$16	$20	Kazuo Iwamura		Orchard
2004	Mister Seahorse		$8	$12	$16	Eric Carle		Philo

Carlson   Nancy L.

Year	Title	VG-	VG	VG+	Fine	Author	Award	Pub
1982	Harriet & Walt		$25	$35	$50	Nancy L. Carlson		CRB
1982	Harriet And The Garden		$16	$25	$30	Nancy L. Carlson		CRB
1982	Harriet And The Roller Coaster		$16	$25	$30	Nancy L. Carlson		CRB
1982	Harriet's Halloween Candy		$16	$25	$30	Nancy L. Carlson		CRB
1982	Harriet's Recital		$16	$25	$30	Nancy L. Carlson		CRB
1983	Loudmouth George And The Big Race		$16	$25	$30	Nancy L. Carlson		CRB
1983	Loudmouth George And The Cornet		$16	$25	$30	Nancy L. Carlson		CRB
1983	Loudmouth George And The Fishing Trip		$16	$25	$30	Nancy L. Carlson		CRB
1983	Loudmouth George And The New Neighbors		$16	$25	$30	Nancy L. Carlson		CRB
1983	Loudmouth George And The Sixth-Grade Bully		$16	$25	$30	Nancy L. Carlson		CRB
1984	Bunnies And Their Hobbies		$16	$25	$30	Nancy L. Carlson		CRB
1985	Louanne In Making The Team		$16	$25	$30	Nancy L. Carlson		CRB
1985	Louanne In The Mysterious Valentine		$16	$25	$30	Nancy L. Carlson		CRB
1985	Louanne In The Perfect Family		$16	$25	$30	Nancy L. Carlson		CRB
1985	Louanne Pig In Witch Lady		$16	$25	$30	Nancy L. Carlson		CRB
1986	Louanne Pig In The Talent Show		$14	$20	$30	Nancy L. Carlson		CRB
1987	Arnie And The Stolen Markers		$14	$20	$30	Nancy L. Carlson		VK
1987	Baby And The Bear		$14	$20	$30	Susan Pearson		VK
1987	Bunnies And Their Sports		$14	$20	$30	Nancy L. Carlson		VK
1987	When Baby Went To Bed		$14	$20	$30	Susan Pearson		VK
1988	Arnie Goes To Camp		$14	$20	$30	Nancy L. Carlson		VK
1988	I Like Me!		$14	$20	$30	Nancy L. Carlson		VK
1989	Poor Carl		$14	$20	$25	Nancy L. Carlson		VK
1990	Arnie And The New Kid		$12	$18	$25	Nancy L. Carlson		Viking
1990	Watch Out For These Weirdos!		$12	$18	$25	Rufus Kline		Viking
1991	A Visit To Grandma's		$12	$18	$25	Nancy L. Carlson		Viking
1991	Take Time To Relax		$12	$18	$25	Nancy L. Carlson		Viking
1992	Lenore's Big Break		$12	$18	$25	Susan Pearson		Viking
1992	What If It Never Stops Raining?		$12	$18	$25	Nancy L. Carlson		Viking

Carlson   Nancy L.

Year	Title	VG-	VG	VG+	Fine	Author	Award	Pub
1993	Life Is Fun		$12	$16	$20	Nancy L. Carlson		Viking
1994	How To Lose All Your Friends		$12	$16	$20	Nancy L. Carlson		Viking
1994	The Masked Maverick		$12	$16	$20	Jacqueline K. Ogburn		LL&S
1995	Arnie And The Skateboard Gang		$10	$16	$20	Nancy L. Carlson		Viking
1995	What To Do When A Bug Climbs In Your Mouth		$10	$16	$20	Rick Walton		LL&S
1996	Sit Still		$10	$16	$20	Nancy L. Carlson		Viking
1997	ABC, I Like Me!		$10	$16	$20	Nancy L. Carlson		Viking
1997	Snowden		$10	$16	$20	Nancy L. Carlson		Viking
1998	It's Going To Be Perfect		$10	$14	$18	Nancy L. Carlson		Viking
1999	Look Out Kindergarten, Here I Come!		$10	$14	$18	Nancy L. Carlson		Viking
2000	Hooray For Grandparent's Day		$8	$12	$16	Nancy L. Carlson		Viking
2001	Harriet And George's Christmas Treat		$8	$12	$16	Nancy L. Carlson		CRB
2001	How About A Hug?		$8	$12	$16	Nancy L. Carlson		Viking
2001	My Best Friend Moved Away		$8	$12	$16	Nancy L. Carlson		Viking
2002	Smile A Lot!		$8	$10	$14	Nancy L. Carlson		CRB
2002	There's A Big, Beautiful World Out There!		$8	$10	$14	Nancy L. Carlson		Viking
2003	It's Not My Fault!		$8	$10	$14	Nancy L. Carlson		CRB
2004	Halloween		$8	$10	$14	Joyce K. Kessel		CRB
2004	Henry's Show And Tell		$8	$10	$14	Nancy L. Carlson		Viking
2004	My Family Is Forever		$8	$10	$14	Nancy L. Carlson		Viking
2004	Think Big!		$8	$10	$14	Nancy L. Carlson		CRB

Carrick   Donald

Year	Title	VG-	VG	VG+	Fine	Author	Award	Pub
1966	The Old Barn	$40	$60	$70		Carol Carrick		Bobbs
1967	The Brook	$30	$40	$50		Carol Carrick		Macmil
1969	Swamp Spring	$25	$35	$50		Carol Carrick		Macmil
1969	Tor, Wyoming Bighorn	$25	$35	$50		Ernestine Byrd		Scribnr
1970	A Clearing In The Forest		$25	$35	$50	Carol Carrick		Dial
1971	The Buffalo King; The Story Of Scotty Philip		$25	$35	$50	Nancy Veglahn		Scribnr
1971	The Tree		$25	$35	$50	Donald Carrick		Macmil
1971	Turtle Pond		$25	$35	$50	Berniece Freschet		Scribnr
1973	Beach Bird		$25	$35	$50	Carol Carrick		Dial
1973	Bear Mouse		$25	$35	$50	Berniece Freschet		Scribnr
1973	Drip, Drop		$25	$35	$50	Donald Carrick		Macmil
1973	Peter And Mr. Brandon		$25	$35	$50	Eleanor Schick		Macmil
1973	Sleep Out		$25	$35	$50	Carol Carrick		Seabury
1974	Christmas Tree Farm		$20	$30	$40	David Budbill		Macmil
1974	Lost In The Storm		$20	$30	$40	Carol Carrick		Seabury
1975	Grizzly Bear		$20	$30	$40	Berniece Freschet		Scribnr
1975	Old Mother Witch		$20	$30	$40	Carol Carrick		Seabury
1975	The Blue Lobster: A Life Cycle		$20	$30	$40	Carol Carrick		Dial
1976	The Accident		$20	$30	$40	Carol Carrick		Clarion
1976	The Deer In The Pasture		$20	$30	$40	Donald Carrick		Green
1976	Wind, Sand, And Sky		$20	$30	$40	Rebecca Caudill		Dutton
1977	A Wet And Sandy Day		$20	$30	$40	Joanne Ryder		H&Row
1977	Sand Tiger Shark		$20	$30	$40	Carol Carrick		Seabury
1977	The Foundling		$20	$30	$40	Carol Carrick		Seabury
1977	The Highest Balloon On The Common		$20	$30	$40	Carol Carrick		Green
1977	Walls Are To Be Walked		$20	$30	$40	Nathan Zimelman		Dutton
1978	Octopus		$20	$30	$40	Carol Carrick		Seabury
1978	Paul's Christmas Birthday		$20	$30	$40	Carol Carrick		Green
1978	Tawny		$20	$30	$40	Chas Carner		Macmil
1978	The Washout		$20	$30	$40	Carol Carrick		Seabury
1979	A Rabbit For Easter		$18	$25	$35	Carol Carrick		Green
1979	Latki And The Lightning Lizard		$18	$25	$35	Betty Baker		Macmil
1979	Some Friend!		$18	$25	$35	Carol Carrick		Clarion
1979	The Blue Horse, & Other Night Poems		$18	$25	$35	Siv Cedering Fox		Seabury
1980	The Climb		$18	$25	$35	Carol Carrick		Clarion
1980	The Crocodiles Still Wait		$18	$25	$35	Carol Carrick		Clarion
1981	Ben And The Porcupine		$18	$25	$35	Carol Carrick		Clarion
1981	The Empty Squirrel		$18	$25	$35	Carol Carrick		Green
1982	Harald And The Giant Knight		$16	$25	$30	Donald Carrick		Clarion
1982	The Longest Float In The Parade		$16	$25	$30	Carol Carrick		Green
1982	Truck And Loader		$16	$25	$30	Helen Haddad		Green
1982	Two Coyotes		$16	$25	$30	Carol Carrick		Clarion

Carrick   Donald

Year	Title	VG-	VG	VG+	Fine	Author	Award	Pub
1983	Alex Remembers		$16	$25	$30	Helen Griffith		Green
1983	More Alex And The Cat		$16	$25	$30	Helen Griffith		Green
1983	Patrick's Dinosaurs		$16	$25	$30	Carol Carrick		Clarion
1983	What A Wimp!		$16	$25	$30	Carol Carrick		Clarion
1984	Dark And Full Of Secrets		$16	$25	$30	Carol Carrick		Clarion
1984	Secrets Of A Small Brother		$16	$25	$30	Richard J. Margolis		Macmil
1985	Here I Am, An Only Child		$16	$25	$30	Marlene Fanta Shyer		Scribnr
1985	Milk		$16	$25	$30	Donald Carrick		Green
1985	Morgan And The Artist		$16	$25	$30	Donald Carrick		Clarion
1985	Stay Away From Simon!		$16	$25	$30	Carol Carrick		Clarion
1986	Doctor Change		$14	$20	$30	Joanna Cole		Morrow
1986	What Happened To Patrick's Dinosaurs?		$14	$20	$30	Carol Carrick		Clarion
1986	Yellow Blue Jay		$14	$20	$30	Johanna Hurwitz		Morrow
1987	Ghost's Hour, Spook's Hour		$14	$20	$30	Eve Bunting		Clarion
1987	Moss Gown		$14	$20	$30	William H. Hooks		Clarion
1987	Rosalie		$14	$20	$30	Joan Hewett		LL&S
1988	Going The Moose Way Home		$14	$20	$30	Jim Latimer		Scribnr
1988	Harald And The Great Stag		$14	$20	$30	Donald Carrick		Clarion
1988	Left Behind		$14	$20	$30	Carol Carrick		Clarion
1988	The Elephant In The Dark		$14	$20	$30	Carol Carrick		Clarion
1989	Aladdin And The Wonderful Lamp		$14	$20	$25	Carol Carrick		Scholas
1989	Big Jeremy		$14	$20	$25	Steven Kroll		Holiday
1989	Big Old Bones: A Dinosaur Tale		$14	$20	$25	Carol Carrick		Clarion
1989	The Wednesday Surprise		$14	$20	$25	Eve Bunting		Clarion
1990	In The Moonlight, Waiting		$12	$18	$25	Carol Carrick		Clarion
1990	When Moose Was Young		$12	$18	$25	Jim Latimer		Scribnr

Carrier   Lark

Year	Title	VG-	VG	VG+	Fine	Author	Award	Pub
1985	There Was A Hill		$30	$40	$60	Lark Carrier		Picture
1986	A Christmas Promise		$20	$30	$40	Lark Carrier		Picture
1987	Scout & Cody		$20	$30	$40	Lark Carrier		Picture
1988	Do Not Touch		$18	$25	$35	Lark Carrier		Picture
1989	The Snowy Path		$18	$25	$35	Lark Carrier		Picture
1990	A Perfect Spring		$16	$25	$30	Lark Carrier		Picture
1996	A Tree's Tale		$12	$18	$25	Lark Carrier		Dial
1999	On Halloween		$12	$16	$20	Lark Carrier		HFest
2001	Five Little Goblins		$10	$14	$18	Lark Carrier		HFest
2003	Five Little Chicks		$8	$12	$16	Lark Carrier		HFest
2004	Santa's Night		$8	$10	$14	Lark Carrier		HFest

Carroll   Ruth

Year	Title	VG-	VG	VG+	Fine	Author	Award	Pub
1932	Chimp And Chump	$140	$180	$220		Ruth Carroll		ReyHitc
1932	What Whiskers Did	$140	$180	$220		Ruth Carroll		Macmil
1934	Bounce And The Bunnies	$80	$120	$140		Ruth Carroll		ReyHitc
1935	Luck Of The Roll And Go	$80	$120	$140		Ruth & Latrobe Carroll		Macmil
1936	Chessie	$200	$260	$320		Ruth Carroll		Messner
1937	Another Singing Time	$80	$120	$140		Satis N. Coleman		ReyHitc
1937	Chessie And Her Kittens	$120	$160	$200		Ruth Carroll		Messner
1939	Flight Of The Silver Bird	$80	$100	$140		Ruth & Latrobe Carroll		Messner
1943	Scuffles	$70	$90	$120		Ruth & Latrobe Carroll		Walck
1945	School In The Sky	$60	$80	$100		Ruth & Latrobe Carroll		Macmil
1945	Watch The Puppy Grow	$60	$80	$100		William Hall		Crowell
1946	The Flying House	$60	$80	$100		Ruth & Latrobe Carroll		Macmil
1946	Watch The Kitten Grow	$60	$80	$100		William Hall		Crowell
1948	The Animals Came First	$60	$80	$100		Jean Louise Welch		Oxford
1949	Pet Tale	$60	$80	$100		Ruth & Latrobe Carroll		Oxford
1950	Where's The Bunny?	$60	$80	$100		Ruth Carroll		Oxford
1951	Peanut	$50	$70	$90		Ruth & Latrobe Carroll		Walck
1952	Salt And Pepper	$50	$70	$90		Ruth & Latrobe Carroll		Walck
1953	Beanie	$50	$70	$90		Ruth & Latrobe Carroll		Oxford
1954	Tough Enough	$120	$160	$200		Ruth & Latrobe Carroll		Oxford
1955	Digby, The Only Dog	$50	$70	$90		Ruth & Latrobe Carroll		Oxford
1956	Tough Enough's Trip	$70	$100	$120		Ruth & Latrobe Carroll		Oxford
1958	Tough Enough And Sassy	$70	$100	$120		Ruth & Latrobe Carroll		Walck

Carroll   Ruth

Year	Title	VG-	VG	VG+	Fine	Author	Award	Pub
1958	Tough Enough's Pony	$70	$100	$120		Ruth & Latrobe Carroll		Walck
1960	Tough Enough's Indians	$70	$90	$120		Ruth & Latrobe Carroll		Walck
1961	Old Mrs. Billups And The Black Cats	$50	$60	$80		Ruth Carroll		Walck
1962	Where's The Kitty?	$50	$60	$80		Ruth Carroll		Walck
1963	Runaway Pony, Runaway Dog	$50	$60	$80		Ruth & Latrobe Carroll		Walck
1964	From The Appalachians	$50	$60	$80		Ruth Carroll		Walck
1965	Danny And The Poi Pup	$40	$60	$70		Ruth & Latrobe Carroll		Walck
1966	The Picnic Bear	$40	$60	$70		Ruth & Latrobe Carroll		Walck
1968	Bumble Pup	$40	$50	$70		Ruth & Latrobe Carroll		Walck
1968	The Chimp And The Clown	$40	$50	$70		Ruth Carroll		Walck
1970	The Christmas Kitten		$30	$50	$60	Ruth & Latrobe Carroll		Walck
1972	The Managing Hen And The Floppy Hound		$30	$50	$60	Ruth & Latrobe Carroll		Walck
1973	Rolling Downhill		$30	$50	$60	Ruth Carroll		Walck
1973	The Witch Kitten		$30	$50	$60	Ruth Carroll		Walck
1974	The Dolphin And The Mermaid		$30	$40	$60	Ruth Carroll		Walck
1975	Hullabaloo, The Elephant Dog		$30	$40	$60	Ruth & Latrobe Carroll		Walck

Carter   Abby

Year	Title	VG-	VG	VG+	Fine	Author	Award	Pub
1988	Tess And Tim		$14	$20	$30	Marc Gave		PMagP
1990	Snakes Are Nothing To Sneeze At		$10	$16	$20	Gabrielle Charbonnet		Holt
1990	Travels With Tess And Tim		$10	$16	$20	Marc Gave		PMagP
1991	Twin Surprises		$10	$16	$20	Susan Beth Pfeffer		Holt
1992	Baseball Ballerina		$10	$16	$20	Kathryn Cristaldi		Random
1992	Great-Uncle Dracula		$10	$16	$20	Jayne Harvey		Random
1992	New Kid On Spurwink Ave		$10	$16	$20	Michael Crowley		LBrown
1992	Twin Troubles		$10	$16	$20	Susan Beth Pfeffer		Holt
1993	Great-Uncle Dracula And The Dirty Rat		$10	$16	$20	Jayne Harvey		Random
1993	I Thought I'd Take My Rat To School		$10	$16	$20	Dorothy M. Kennedy		LBrown
1993	Never Babysit The Hippopotamuses!		$10	$16	$20	Doug Johnson		Holt
1993	Shack And Back		$10	$16	$20	Michael Crowley		LBrown
1994	The Pink Party		$10	$14	$18	Maryann Macdonald		Hyper
1994	Tutu Much Ballet		$10	$14	$18	Gabrielle Charbonnet		Holt
1995	Edwin And Emily		$10	$14	$18	Suzanne Williams		Hyper
1995	Never Ride Your Elephant To School		$10	$14	$18	Doug Johnson		Holt
1995	Summer Legs		$10	$14	$18	Anita Hakkinen		Holt
1996	Annie Bananie Moves To Barry Avenue		$8	$12	$16	Leah Komaiko		DelaP
1996	Emily At School		$8	$12	$16	Suzanne Williams		Hyper
1997	Camp Sink Or Swim		$8	$12	$16	Gibbs Davis		Random
1997	The Invisible Day		$8	$12	$16	Marthe Jocelyn		Dutton
1998	Annie Bananie And The Pain Sisters		$8	$12	$16	Leah Komaiko		DelaP
1998	Annie Bananie And The People's Court		$8	$12	$16	Leah Komaiko		DelaP
1998	Check Under The Bed		$8	$12	$16	Judy Truesdell Mecca		Pleasnt
1998	Hairum-Scarum		$8	$12	$16	Christina Hamlett		Pleasnt
1998	No Copycats Allowed!		$8	$12	$16	Bonnie B. Graves		Hyper
1998	The Invisible Harry		$8	$12	$16	Marthe Jocelyn		Dutton
2000	Baseball Ballerina Strikes Out		$8	$10	$14	Kathryn Cristaldi		Random
2002	The Invisible Enemy		$8	$10	$14	Marthe Jocelyn		Tundra
2003	My Hippie Grandmother		$8	$10	$14	Reeve Lindbergh		Candle
2004	Slithery Jake		$6	$10	$12	Rose-Marie Provencher		HCollins

Cartwright   Reg

Year	Title	VG-	VG	VG+	Fine	Author	Award	Pub
1984	Norah's Ark: A Story		$30	$50	$60	Ann Cartwright		LSimon
1987	Peter And The Wolf		$20	$30	$40	Selina Hastings (retold)		Holt
1987	The Proud And Fearless Lion		$20	$30	$40	Ann Cartwright		Barrn
1988	My Cat		$18	$25	$35	Judy Taylor		Macmil
1988	My Dog		$18	$25	$35	Judy Taylor		Macmil
1988	The Canterbury Tales		$18	$25	$35	Selina Hastings (retold)		Holt
1988	The Man Who Wanted To Live Forever		$18	$25	$35	Selina Hastings		Holt
1989	In Search Of The Last Dodo		$18	$25	$35	Ann & Reg Cartwright		Joy
1989	The Last Dodo		$18	$25	$35	Ann Cartwright		Hutch
1990	Polly And The Privet Bird		$16	$25	$30	Ann Cartwright		Hutch
1990	The Winter Hedgehog		$16	$25	$30	Ann Cartwright		Macmil
1991	Birds, Beasts, And Fishes		$16	$25	$30	Ann Carter (selected)		Macmil
1993	The Firebird		$16	$25	$30	Selina Hastings (retold)		Candle

Cartwright Reg

Year	Title	VG-	VG	VG+	Fine	Author	Award	Pub
1995	James And The Rain		$14	$20	$25	Karla Kuskin		S&S
1996	The Boat Of Many Rooms		$12	$18	$25	J. Patrick Lewis		Athenm
1997	Mouse Creeps		$12	$18	$25	Peter Harris		Dial
1999	Three Golden Oranges		$12	$16	$20	Alma Flor Ada		Athenm
2000	What Does The Rabbit Say?		$10	$14	$18	Jacque Hall		DoubleD
2001	Going Home		$10	$14	$18	Ann Cartwright		DK
2001	The Lot At The End Of My Block		$10	$14	$18	Kevin Lewis		Hyper
2002	At The Edge Of The Woods		$8	$12	$16	Cynthia Cotten		Holt

Catrow David

Year	Title	VG-	VG	VG+	Fine	Author	Award	Pub
1983	The Story Of The Little Bighorn		$16	$25	$30	R. Conrad Stein		CP
1983	The Story Of Wounded Knee		$16	$25	$30	R. Conrad Stein		CP
1984	The Story Of The Johnstown Flood		$16	$25	$30	R. Conrad Stein		CP
1984	The Story Of The Oregon Trail		$16	$25	$30	R. Conrad Stein		CP
1985	The Story Of Apollo 11		$16	$25	$30	R. Conrad Stein		CP
1985	The Story Of The Trail Of Tears		$16	$25	$30	R. Conrad Stein		CP
1986	The Story Of The Battle Of Bull Run		$14	$20	$30	Zachery Kent		CP
1990	The Attic Mice		$16	$25	$30	Ethel Pochocki		Holt
1991	That's Good! That's Bad!		$16	$25	$30	Margery Cuyler		Holt
1992	Good Dogs		$16	$25	$30	Charles Ghigna		Hyper
1992	The Cataract Of Lodore		$16	$25	$30	Robert Southey		Holt
1993	Backstage With Clawdio		$16	$25	$30	Harriet Schwartz		Knopf
1994	The Million Dollar Bear		$14	$20	$30	William Kotzwinkle		Knopf
1995	Ridiculous Rhymes From A To Z		$14	$20	$25	John Walker		Holt
1995	She's Wearing A Dead Bird On Her Head!		$14	$20	$25	Kathryn Lasky		Hyper
1996	Over The River And Through The Wood		$12	$18	$25	Lydia Maria Child		Holt
1996	The Long, Long Letter		$12	$18	$25	Elizabeth Spurr		Hyper
1997	Who Said That?: Famous Americans Speak		$12	$18	$25	Robert Burleigh		Holt
1997	Why Lapin's Ears Are Long		$12	$18	$25	Sharon Arms Doucet		Orchard
1998	Rotten Teeth		$12	$16	$20	Laura Simms		HM
1998	Westward Ho, Carlotta!		$12	$16	$20	Candace Fleming		Athenm
2000	Cinderella Skeleton		$10	$14	$18	Robert D. San Souci		Harcort
2000	How Murray Saved Christmas		$10	$14	$18	Mike Reiss		PriceSS
2001	Stand Tall Molly Lou Melon		$10	$14	$18	Patty Lovell		Putnam
2002	Plantizilla		$8	$12	$16	Jerdine Nolen		Harcort
2002	Santa Claustrophobia		$8	$12	$16	Mike Reiss		PriceSS
2002	That's Good! That's Bad! In The Grand Canyon		$8	$12	$16	Margery Cuyler		Holt
2002	We The Kids		$8	$12	$16	David Catrow		Dial
2003	I'm Still Here In The Bathtub		$8	$12	$16	Alan Katz		McEld
2003	Little Pierre		$8	$12	$16	Robert D. San Souci (adapted)		Harcort
2003	The Boy Who Looked Like Lincoln		$8	$12	$16	Mike Reiss		PriceSS
2004	I Like Myself!		$8	$10	$14	Karen Beaumont		Harcort
2004	I Wanna Iguana		$8	$10	$14	Karen Kaufman Orloff		Putnam
2004	Lu And The Swamp Ghost		$8	$10	$14	James Carville		Athenm
2004	Where Did They Hide My Presents?		$8	$10	$14	Alan Katz		McEld

Cauley Lorinda Bryan

Year	Title	VG-	VG	VG+	Fine	Author	Award	Pub
1977	Bill Pickett		$16	$25	$30	Sibyl Hancock		HBJ
1977	Curley Cat Baby-Sits		$16	$25	$30	Pauline Watson		HBJ
1977	Pease Porridge Hot		$16	$25	$30	Lorinda B. Cauley		Putnam
1977	Rabbits' Search For A Little House		$20	$30	$40	Mary DeBall Kwitz		Crown
1978	The Bake-Off		$14	$20	$30	Lorinda B. Cauley		Putnam
1978	The House Of Five Bears		$14	$20	$30	Cynthia Jameson		Putnam
1978	The War Party		$14	$20	$30	William O. Steele		HBJ
1979	Ants Don't Get Sunday Off		$14	$20	$30	Penny Pollock		Putnam
1979	Small Bear Solves A Mystery		$14	$20	$30	Adelaide Holl		Garrard
1979	The Animal Kids		$14	$20	$30	Lorinda B. Cauley		Putnam
1979	The Ugly Duckling		$14	$20	$30	Lorinda B. Cauley		HBJ
1980	If You Say So, Claude		$14	$20	$25	Joan Lowery Nixon		FWarne
1980	Joseph Jacobs' The Story Of The 3 Little Pigs		$14	$20	$25	Joseph Jacobs		Putnam
1980	Old Hippo's Easter Egg		$14	$20	$25	Jan Wahl		HBJ
1980	The Slug Who Thought He Was A Snail		$14	$20	$25	Penny Pollock		Putnam
1980	Where's Henrietta's Hen?		$14	$20	$25	Berniece Freschet		Putnam
1981	Goldilocks And The Three Bears		$14	$20	$25	Lorinda B. Cauley		Putnam

Cauley   Lorinda Bryan

Year	Title	VG-	VG	VG+	Fine	Author	Award	Pub
1981	The Goose And The Golden Coins		$14	$20	$25	Lorinda B. Cauley (adapted)		HBJ
1981	The New House		$14	$20	$25	Lorinda B. Cauley		HBJ
1982	The Cock, The Mouse, And The Little Red Hen		$14	$20	$25	Lorinda B. Cauley		Putnam
1982	The Spit Bug Who Couldn't Spit		$14	$20	$25	Penny Pollock		Putnam
1982	The Three Little Kittens		$14	$20	$25	Lorinda B. Cauley		Putnam
1983	Jack And The Beanstalk		$14	$20	$25	Lorinda B. Cauley		Putnam
1983	The Elephant's Child		$14	$20	$25	Rudyard Kipling		HBJ
1984	Clancy's Coat		$12	$18	$25	Eve Bunting		FWarne
1984	The Goodnight Circle		$12	$18	$25	Carolyn Lesser		HBJ
1984	The Town Mouse And The Country Mouse		$12	$18	$25	Lorinda B. Cauley		Putnam
1985	The Beginning Of The Armadillos		$12	$18	$25	Rudyard Kipling		HBJ
1986	Puss In Boots		$12	$16	$20	Lorinda B. Cauley (adapted)		HBJ
1986	The Owl And The Pussycat		$12	$16	$20	Edward Lear		Putnam
1988	The Pancake Boy		$12	$16	$20	Lorinda B. Cauley		Putnam
1988	The Trouble With Tyrannosaurus Rex		$12	$16	$20	Lorinda B. Cauley		HBJ
1989	Old Macdonald Had A Farm		$12	$16	$20	Lorinda B. Cauley		Putnam
1991	Three Blind Mice		$10	$16	$20	John W. Ivimey		Putnam
1992	Clap Your Hands		$10	$16	$20	Lorinda B. Cauley		Putnam
1994	Treasure Hunt		$10	$14	$18	Lorinda B. Cauley		Putnam
2001	What Do You Know!		$8	$10	$14	Lorinda B. Cauley		Putnam

Cazet   Denys

Year	Title	VG-	VG	VG+	Fine	Author	Award	Pub
1980	The Duck With Squeaky Feet		$25	$35	$50	Denys Cazet		BradP
1981	Mud Baths For Everyone		$18	$25	$35	Denys Cazet		BradP
1983	Lucky Me		$16	$25	$30	Denys Cazet		BradP
1983	You Make The Angels Cry		$16	$25	$30	Denys Cazet		BradP
1984	Big Shoe, Little Shoe		$16	$25	$30	Denys Cazet		BradP
1984	Christmas Moon		$16	$25	$30	Denys Cazet		BradP
1985	Saturday		$16	$25	$30	Denys Cazet		BradP
1986	December 24th		$14	$20	$30	Denys Cazet		BradP
1987	A Fish In His Pocket		$14	$20	$30	Denys Cazet		Orchard
1988	Great-Uncle Felix		$14	$20	$30	Denys Cazet		Orchard
1988	Sunday		$14	$20	$30	Denys Cazet		BradP
1989	Good Morning, Maxine!		$14	$20	$25	Denys Cazet		BradP
1989	Mother Night		$14	$20	$25	Denys Cazet		Orchard
1990	Daydreams		$12	$18	$25	Denys Cazet		Orchard
1990	Never Spit On Your Shoes		$12	$18	$25	Denys Cazet		Orchard
1992	Are There Any Questions?		$12	$18	$25	Denys Cazet		Orchard
1992	I'm Not Sleepy		$12	$18	$25	Denys Cazet		Orchard
1992	The Great Squirrel Uprising		$12	$18	$25	Dan Elish		Orchard
1993	Annie, Bea, And Chi Chi Dolores		$12	$16	$20	Donna Maurer		Orchard
1993	Born In The Gravy		$12	$16	$20	Denys Cazet		Orchard
1994	Nothing At All!		$12	$16	$20	Denys Cazet		Orchard
1994	Where Can Daniel Be?		$12	$16	$20	Leah Komaiko		Orchard
1995	Dancing		$10	$16	$20	Denys Cazet		Orchard
1997	Night Lights		$10	$16	$20	Denys Cazet		Orchard
1998	Minnie And Moo Go Dancing		$10	$14	$18	Denys Cazet		DK
1998	Minnie And Moo Go To The Moon		$10	$14	$18	Denys Cazet		DK
1999	Minnie And Moo Go To Paris		$10	$14	$18	Denys Cazet		DK
1999	Minnie And Moo Save The Earth		$10	$14	$18	Denys Cazet		DK
2000	Minnie And Moo And The Thanksgiving Tree		$8	$12	$16	Denys Cazet		DK
2000	Never Poke A Squid		$8	$12	$16	Denys Cazet		Orchard
2001	Minnie And Moo Meet Frankenswine		$8	$12	$16	Denys Cazet		HCollins
2002	Minnie And Moo		$8	$10	$14	Denys Cazet		HCollins
2002	Minnie And Moo And The Potato From Planet X		$8	$10	$14	Denys Cazet		HCollins
2003	Minnie & Moo And The 7 Wonders Of The World		$8	$10	$14	Denys Cazet		Athenm
2004	Elvis The Rooster And The Magic Words		$8	$10	$14	Denys Cazet		HCollins

Chalk   Gary

Year	Title	VG-	VG	VG+	Fine	Author	Award	Pub
1987	Redwall		$280	$420	$560	Brian Jacques		Philo
1988	Mossflower		$140	$220	$280	Brian Jacques		Philo
1990	Mattimeo		$90	$120	$180	Brian Jacques		Philo
1992	Mariel Of Redwall		$60	$90	$120	Brian Jacques		Philo
1993	Salamandastron		$16	$25	$30	Brian Jacques		Philo

Chalk　　　　Gary

Year	Title	VG-	VG	VG+	Fine	Author	Award	Pub
1993	Yankee Doodle		$30	$40	$60	Gary Chalk		DK
1994	Martin The Warrior		$14	$20	$30	Brian Jacques		Philo
1994	Mr. Frog Went A-Courting		$14	$20	$30	Gary Chalk		DK
1994	The Boy Who Cried "Wolf!"		$14	$20	$30	Ellen Schecter (retold)		Bantam

Chalmers　　　　Mary

Year	Title	VG-	VG	VG+	Fine	Author	Award	Pub
1955	Come For A Walk With Me	$90	$120	$160		Mary Chalmers		H&B
1955	Here Comes The Trolley Car	$60	$80	$100		Mary Chalmers		H&B
1956	A Christmas Story	$60	$80	$100		Mary Chalmers		H&B
1956	A Hat For Amy Jean	$60	$80	$100		Mary Chalmers		H&B
1957	Every Day Is A World	$60	$80	$100		Raymond Bechtle		H&B
1957	George Appleton	$60	$80	$100		Mary Chalmers		H&B
1957	Kevin	$60	$80	$100		Mary Chalmers		H&B
1958	Boats Finds A House	$60	$80	$100		Mary Chalmers		H&B
1958	Throw A Kiss, Harry	$60	$80	$100		Mary Chalmers		H&B
1959	I Would Like To Be A Pony	$60	$80	$100		Dorothy Walter Baruch		H&B
1959	The Cat Who Liked To Pretend	$60	$80	$100		Mary Chalmers		H&B
1960	The Secret Language	$50	$60	$80		Ursula Nordstrom		H&B
1961	Mr. Cat's Wonderful Surprise	$50	$60	$80		Mary Chalmers		H&B
1961	The Three Funny Friends	$50	$60	$80		Charlotte Zolotow		H&B
1962	The Happy Birthday Present	$50	$60	$80		Joan Heilbroner		Harper
1964	Take A Nap, Harry	$50	$60	$80		Mary Chalmers		H&Row
1965	The House Of Thirty Cats	$40	$60	$70		Mary Calhoun		H&Row
1965	Three To Get Ready	$40	$60	$70		Betty V. Boegehold		H&Row
1966	The Crystal Tree	$40	$60	$70		Jennie D. Lindquist		H&Row
1967	Be Good, Harry	$40	$50	$70		Mary Chalmers		H&Row
1969	Goodnight, Andrew, Goodnight, Craig	$40	$50	$70		Marjorie Weinman Sharmat		H&Row
1970	I Write It		$30	$50	$60	Ruth Krauss		H&Row
1971	When Will It Snow?		$30	$50	$60	Syd Hoff		H&Row
1972	The Snuggle Bunny		$30	$50	$60	Nancy Jewell		H&Row
1973	Crickety Cricket!		$30	$50	$60	James S. Tippett		H&Row
1973	Letitia Rabbit's String Song		$30	$50	$60	Russell Hoban		CM&G
1974	When Daisies Pied, And Violets Blue		$30	$40	$60	William Shakespeare		CM&G
1975	The Day After Christmas		$30	$40	$60	Alice Bach		H&Row
1976	Oh No, Cat!		$30	$40	$60	Janice May Udry		CM&G
1977	Merry Christmas, Harry		$25	$40	$50	Mary Chalmers		H&Row
1978	Mule In The Mail		$25	$40	$50	Stephen Manes		CM&G
1980	Home At Last!		$25	$35	$50	Patricia Lauber		CM&G
1981	Come To The Doctor, Harry		$25	$35	$50	Mary Chalmers		H&Row
1986	Six Dogs, 23 Cats, 45 Mice, And 116 Spiders		$20	$30	$40	Mary Chalmers		H&Row
1988	Easter Parade		$18	$25	$35	Mary Chalmers		H&Row
1994	Marigold And Grandma On The Town		$14	$20	$30	Stephanie Calmenson		HCollins

Chambliss　　　　Maxie

Year	Title	VG-	VG	VG+	Fine	Author	Award	Pub
1981	Baby Talk		$18	$25	$35	D. Leb Tannenbaum		Avon
1982	Bathrooms		$14	$20	$25	Steven Kroll		Avon
1983	It's Me, Hippo!		$14	$20	$25	Mike Thaler		H&Row
1984	Ten Furry Monsters		$12	$18	$25	Stephanie Calmenson		PMagP
1984	When Mother Got The Flu		$12	$18	$25	Beverly Keller		CM
1985	Maude And Walter		$12	$18	$25	Zibby Oneal		Lippin
1986	Hippo Lemonade		$12	$16	$20	Mike Thaler		H&Row
1986	Who's Afraid Of Ernestine?		$12	$16	$20	Marjorie Weinman Sharmat		CM
1987	Donald Says Thumbs Down		$12	$16	$20	Nancy Evans Cooney		Putnam
1987	Eggs On Your Nose		$12	$16	$20	Ann McGovern		Macmil
1987	Fido		$12	$16	$20	Stephanie Calmenson		Scholas
1987	The Giggle Book		$12	$16	$20	Stephanie Calmenson		PMagP
1988	Dad's Car Wash		$12	$16	$20	Harry A. Sutherland		Athenm
1988	Where's Rufus?		$12	$16	$20	Stephanie Calmenson		PMagP
1989	I Can't Get My Turtle To Move		$12	$16	$20	Elizabeth Lee O'Donnell		Morrow
1989	Monsters!		$12	$16	$20	Diane Namm		Grolier
1989	Taking Care Of Tucker		$12	$16	$20	Pat Lowery Collins		Putnam
1990	Dog And Cat		$10	$16	$20	Paul Fehlner		CP
1990	Go Away Monsters, Lickety Split!		$10	$16	$20	Nancy Evans Cooney		Putnam
1990	Hannah The Hamster Hunter		$10	$16	$20	Marcia Leonard		Silver

Chambliss   Maxie

Year	Title	VG-	VG	VG+	Fine	Author	Award	Pub
1990	Mole's New Cap		$10	$16	$20	Mike Thaler		EEC
1990	The Mother's Day Sandwich		$10	$16	$20	Jillian Wynot		Orchard
1991	Come And Play, Hippo		$10	$16	$20	Mike Thaler		HCollins
1991	Fat Fanny, Beanpole Bertha, And The Boys		$10	$16	$20	Barbara Ann Porte		Orchard
1992	You Cheat!		$10	$16	$20	Jamie Gilson		BradP
1993	Eggs Over Easy		$10	$16	$20	Katharine Kenah		Dutton
1993	When Grandma Almost Fell Off The Mountain		$10	$16	$20	Barbara Ann Porte		Orchard
1994	Favorite Fairy Tales Told In England		$10	$14	$18	Virginia Haviland		Beech
1994	One Up, One Down		$10	$14	$18	Carol Snyder		Athenm
1994	Tomorrow Is Daddy's Birthday		$10	$14	$18	Ginger Wadsworth		CH
1994	We're Going On A Trip		$10	$14	$18	Christine Loomis		Morrow
1994	What Do You Do With A Potty		$10	$14	$18	Marianne Borgardt		Western
1994	When Aunt Lucy Rode A Mule		$10	$14	$18	Barbara Ann Porte		Orchard
1995	How I Was Adopted		$10	$14	$18	Joanna Cole		Morrow
1995	Monsters In My Mailbox		$10	$14	$18	Ellen Jackson		Troll
1996	Here Comes The Snow		$8	$12	$16	Angela Shelf Medearis		Scholas
1996	My Teacher Is The Tooth Fairy		$8	$12	$16	Mary Smith		Troll
1997	I'm A Big Brother		$8	$12	$16	Joanna Cole		Morrow
1997	I'm A Big Sister		$8	$12	$16	Joanna Cole		Morrow
1997	I'm Going To The Dentist		$8	$12	$16	Maxie Chambliss		LadyB
1997	I'm Going To The Doctor		$8	$12	$16	Kathryn Siegler		LadyB
1999	Meet My Monster		$8	$12	$16	Paul Z. Mann		RDigest
2000	My Big Boy Potty		$8	$10	$14	Joanna Cole		HCollins
2000	My Big Girl Potty		$8	$10	$14	Joanna Cole		HCollins
2001	When Mommy And Daddy Go To Work		$8	$10	$14	Joanna Cole		HCollins
2001	When You Were Inside Mommy		$8	$10	$14	Joanna Cole		HCollins
2002	Hobbeldy Clop		$8	$10	$14	Pat Brisson		Boyds
2004	Sharing Is Fun		$6	$10	$12	Joanna Cole		HCollins

Chan   Plato

Year	Title	VG-	VG	VG+	Fine	Author	Award	Pub
1943	Good-Luck Horse	$140	$180	$240		Chih-Yi Chan	CH	Whittle
1944	The Magic Monkey	$140	$180	$220		Christina Chan	CH	Whittle

Charlip   Remy

Year	Title	VG-	VG	VG+	Fine	Author	Award	Pub
1956	Curious Little Kitten	$70	$100	$120		Bernadine Cook		YScott
1956	Dress Up And Let's Have A Party	$100	$140	$180		Remy Charlip		WRScott
1957	Where Is Everybody?	$70	$100	$120		Remy Charlip		PMagP
1958	David's Little Indian	$100	$140	$180		Margaret Wise Brown		WRScott
1958	What Is The World	$70	$100	$120		Betty Miles		Knopf
1959	Moon Or A Button?	$100	$140	$180		Ruth Krauss		H&B
1960	Day Of Summer	$70	$90	$120		Betty Miles		Knopf
1961	Day Of Winter	$70	$90	$120		Betty Miles		Knopf
1961	Four Fur Feet	$100	$120	$160		Margaret Wise Brown		WRScott
1962	The Tree Angel	$70	$90	$120		Judith Martin		Knopf
1963	Jumping Beans	$70	$90	$120		Judith Martin		Knopf
1963	My Very Own Special Particular Private Personal Cat	$70	$90	$120		Stoddard Sandol		HM
1964	Fortunately	$60	$80	$100		Remy Charlip		PMagP
1965	The Dead Bird	$90	$120	$160		Margaret Wise Brown		H&Row
1967	What A Fine Day For...	$80	$120	$140		Ruth Krauss		PMagP
1973	Harlequin And The Gift Of Many Colors		$40	$60	$90	Burton Supree		PMagP
1975	Thirteen		$60	$80	$120	Jerry Joyner	NYT	PMagP
1999	I Love You		$14	$20	$25	Remy Charlip		Scholas
1999	Sleepytime Rhyme		$14	$20	$25	Remy Charlip		Green
2002	Baby Hearts And Baby Flowers		$10	$16	$20	Remy Charlip		Green

Charlot   Jean

Year	Title	VG-	VG	VG+	Fine	Author	Award	Pub
1930	The Book Of Christopher Columbus	$200	$280	$340		Paul Claudel		Oxford
1931	Tawnymore	$200	$280	$340		Monica Shannon		DD
1940	Tito's Hats	$180	$240	$300		Melchor G. Ferrer		GardenC
1941	The Story Of Chan Yuc	$180	$240	$300		Dorothy Rhoads		DD
1942	The Boy Who Could Do Anything	$180	$240	$300		Anita Brenner		WRScott
1943	A Child's Good Night Book	$200	$280	$340		Margaret Wise Brown	CH	WRScott

Charlot   Jean

Year	Title	VG-	VG	VG+	Fine	Author	Award	Pub
1949	Kittens, Cubs And Babies	$160	$200	$260		Miriam Schlein		WRScott
1949	Two Little Trains	$220	$300	$380		Margaret Wise Brown		H&B
1951	The Tibetan Venus	$120	$160	$200		John Bingham Morton		Sheed
1952	A Child's Good Morning	$180	$240	$300		Margaret Wise Brown		WRScott
1952	Secret Of The Andes	$260	$360	$440		Ann Nolan Clark	NM	Viking
1953	... And Now Miguel	$260	$360	$440		Joseph Krumgold	NM	Crowell
1953	Hero by Mistake	$180	$240	$300		Anita Brenner	NYT	WRScott
1953	When Will The World Be Mine?	$180	$240	$300		Miriam Schlein	CH	WRScott
1955	Julio	$100	$140	$180		Loretta Marie Tyman		AS
1955	Our Lady Of Guadalupe	$100	$140	$180		Helen Rand Parish		Viking
1955	Seven Stories About A Cat Named Sneakers	$100	$140	$180		Margaret Wise Brown		WRScott
1955	Sneakers	$100	$140	$180		Margaret Wise Brown		AW
1955	The Poppy Seeds	$100	$140	$180		Clyde Robert Bulla		Crowell
1956	The Corn Grows Ripe	$100	$140	$180		Dorothy Rhoads		Viking
1957	Dumb Juan & The Bandits	$100	$140	$180		Anita Brenner		YScott
1984	The Missing Boy And The Escapee		$40	$60	$90	Jean Charlot Charles		Adelphi

Cherry   Lynne

Year	Title	VG-	VG	VG+	Fine	Author	Award	Pub
1976	Coconut, The Tree Of Life		$20	$30	$40	Carolyn Meyer		Morrow
1977	What's The Time, Starling?		$16	$25	$30	Solveig Paulson Russell		McKay
1979	Emir's Education In The Proper Use Of Magical Powers		$14	$20	$30	Jane Roberts		DelaP
1979	Hidden Messages		$14	$20	$30	Dorothy Van Woerkom		Crown
1981	If I Were In Charge Of The World		$14	$20	$25	Judith Viorst		Athenm
1982	The Snail's Spell		$14	$20	$25	Joanne Ryder		FWarne
1982	What Has Ten Legs And Eats Cornflakes?		$14	$20	$25	Ron Roy		Clarion
1984	Rabbit Travels		$12	$18	$25	John McCormack		Dutton
1985	Harriet And William And The Terrible Creature		$12	$18	$25	Valerie Scho Carey		Dutton
1985	When I'm Sleepy		$12	$18	$25	Jane R. Howard		Dutton
1986	Big And Small, Short And Tall		$12	$16	$20	Ron Roy		Clarion
1987	Chipmunk Song		$12	$16	$20	Joanne Ryder		LodeS
1987	Grizzly Bear		$12	$16	$20	Lynne Cherry		Dutton
1987	Orangutan		$12	$16	$20	Lynne Cherry		Dutton
1987	Seal		$12	$16	$20	Lynne Cherry		Dutton
1987	Snow Leopard		$12	$16	$20	Lynne Cherry		Dutton
1988	Who's Sick Today?		$12	$16	$20	Lynne Cherry		Dutton
1989	Where Butterflies Grow		$12	$16	$20	Joanne Ryder		LodeS
1990	Archie, Follow Me		$10	$16	$20	Lynne Cherry		Dutton
1990	The Great Kapok Tree		$10	$16	$20	Lynne Cherry		HBJ
1992	A River Ran Wild: An Environmental History		$10	$16	$20	Lynne Cherry		HBJ
1994	The Armadillo From Amarillo		$10	$14	$18	Lynne Cherry		HBrace
1995	The Dragon And The Unicorn		$10	$14	$18	Lynne Cherry		HBrace
1997	Flute's Journey: The Life Of A Wood Thrush		$8	$12	$16	Lynne Cherry		HBrace
1998	The Shaman's Apprentice		$8	$12	$16	L. Cherry & M. Plotkin		HBrace
2003	How Groundhog's Garden Grew		$8	$10	$14	Lynne Cherry		BSP
2003	The Sea, The Storm And The Mangrove Tree		$8	$10	$14	Lynne Cherry		FSG

Chess   Victoria

Year	Title	VG-	VG	VG+	Fine	Author	Award	Pub
1965	I, Billy Shakespeare	$40	$60	$70		William Blatty		DoubleD
1967	Fletcher And Zenobia	$80	$120	$140		Edward Gorey		Mered
1968	Millicent The Monster	$40	$50	$70		Mary H. Lystad		HQuist
1969	The Witch Mobile	$40	$50	$70		Miriam Young		LL&S
1970	Once Upon A Time Is Enough		$30	$50	$60	Will Stanton		Lippin
1970	The Animals' Peace Day		$30	$50	$60	Jan Wahl		Crown
1971	Fletcher And Zenobia Save The Circus		$70	$100	$140	Edward Gorey		DoddM
1973	King Basil's Birthday		$30	$50	$60	Miriam Young		FWatts
1973	The Adventures Of Stanley Kane		$30	$50	$60	Stan J Goldberg		HBJ
1975	The King Who Could Not Sleep		$30	$40	$60	Benjamin Elkin		PMagP
1976	Bugs		$30	$40	$60	Mary Ann Hoberman		Viking
1976	Peacocks Are Very Special		$30	$40	$60	Sue Alexander		DoubleD
1977	A Ship In A Storm On The Way To Tarshish		$25	$40	$50	Norma Farber		Green
1978	Fables You Shouldn't Pay Any Attention To		$25	$40	$50	Florence Parry Heide		Lippin
1978	The Queen Of Eene		$25	$40	$50	Jack Prelutsky		Green
1979	Alfred's Alphabet Walk		$50	$80	$100	Victoria Chess		Green
1979	Tyrannosaurus Wrecks		$25	$40	$50	Noelle Sterne		Crowell

Chess   Victoria

Year	Title	VG-	VG	VG+	Fine	Author	Award	Pub
1979	Which Is The Witch?		$25	$40	$50	W. K. Jasner		Pan
1980	Cat And Dog And The Mixed-Up Week		$25	$35	$50	E. Miller & J. Cohen		FWatts
1980	Cat And Dog Give A Party		$25	$35	$50	E. Miller & J. Cohen		FWatts
1980	Cat And Dog Have A Contest		$25	$35	$50	E. Miller & J. Cohen		FWatts
1980	Cat And Dog Raise The Roof		$25	$35	$50	E. Miller & J. Cohen		FWatts
1980	Cat And Dog Take A Trip		$25	$35	$50	E. Miller & J. Cohen		FWatts
1980	Rolling Harvey Down The Hill		$25	$35	$50	Jack Prelutsky		Green
1980	Taking Care Of Melvin		$25	$35	$50	Marjorie Weinman Sharmat		Holiday
1981	Cat And Dog And The ABC's		$25	$35	$50	E. Miller & J. Cohen		FWatts
1981	Cat And Dog Have A Parade		$25	$35	$50	E. Miller & J. Cohen		FWatts
1981	Lost In The Store		$25	$35	$50	Larry Bograd		Macmil
1981	The Great Frog Swap		$25	$35	$50	Ron Roy		Pan
1982	Poor Esmé		$50	$70	$90	Victoria Chess		Holiday
1982	The Sheriff Of Rottenshot		$25	$35	$50	Jack Prelutsky		Green
1983	Slugs		$25	$35	$50	David Greenberg		LBrown
1984	Bim Dooley Makes His Move		$20	$30	$40	Alice Schertle		LL&S
1985	Tales For The Perfect Child		$20	$30	$40	Florence Parry Heide		LL&S
1985	The Twisted Witch & Other Spooky Riddles		$20	$30	$40	David A. Adler		Holiday
1986	A Little Touch Of Monster		$20	$30	$40	Emily Lampert		AMP
1987	Jim, Who Ran Away From His Nurse		$20	$30	$40	Hilaire Belloc		LBrown
1987	Once Around The Block		$40	$60	$80	Kevin Henkes		Green
1988	Princess Gorilla And A New Kind Of Water		$18	$25	$35	Verna Aardema		Dial
1989	Tommy At The Grocery Store		$18	$25	$35	Bill Grossman		H&Row
1990	A Hippopotamusn't & Other Animal Verses		$16	$25	$30	J. Patrick Lewis		Dial
1990	The Complete Story Of The Three Blind Mice		$16	$25	$30	John W. Ivimey		Joy
1991	Ghosts!		$16	$25	$30	Alvin Schwartz		HCollins
1992	Grim And Ghastly Goings-On		$16	$25	$30	Florence Parry Heide		LL&S
1992	Slither Mccreep And His Brother, Joe		$16	$25	$30	Tony Johnston		HBJ
1992	Spider Kane And The Mystery Under The May-Apple		$16	$25	$30	Mary Pope Osborne		Knopf
1993	Spider Kane & The Mystery At Jumbo Nightcrawler's		$16	$25	$30	Mary Pope Osborne		Knopf
1993	Ten Sly Piranhas		$16	$25	$30	William Wise		Dial
1994	The Bigness Contest		$14	$20	$30	Florence Parry Heide		Joy
1994	The Fat-Cats At Sea		$14	$20	$30	J. Patrick Lewis		Knopf
1995	Ridicholas Nicholas		$14	$20	$25	J. Patrick Lewis		Dial
1996	Good Night, Dinosaurs		$12	$18	$25	Judy Sierra		Clarion
1997	This For That		$12	$18	$25	Verna Aardema		Dial
1998	King Long Shanks		$12	$16	$20	Jane Yolen (adapted)		HBrace
1998	The Little Buggers		$12	$16	$20	J. Patrick Lewis		Dial
1999	Teeny Tiny Tingly Tales		$12	$16	$20	Nancy Van Laan		Athenm
2000	The Beautiful Butterfly		$10	$14	$18	Judy Sierra		Clarion
2003	The Scaredy Cats		$8	$12	$16	Barbara Bottner		S&S
2004	Baby Babka		$8	$10	$14	Jane Breskin Zalben		Clarion

Child   Lauren

Year	Title	VG-	VG	VG+	Fine	Author	Award	Pub
1999	Clarice Bean, That's Me		$14	$20	$25	Lauren Child		Candle
1999	I Want A Pet		$12	$16	$20	Lauren Child		Tricyc
2000	I Will Not Ever Never Eat A Tomato		$30	$50	$60	Lauren Child	GM	Orchard
2001	Beware Of The Storybook Wolves		$10	$14	$18	Lauren Child		Levine
2001	Clarice Bean, Guess Who's Babysitting?		$10	$14	$18	Lauren Child		Candle
2001	I Am Not Sleepy And I Will Not Go To Bed		$10	$14	$18	Lauren Child		Candle
2002	My Dream Bed		$8	$12	$16	Lauren Child		Levine
2002	That Pesky Rat		$8	$12	$16	Lauren Child		Candle
2002	What Planet Are You From Clarice Bean?		$8	$12	$16	Lauren Child		Candle
2003	Utterly Me, Clarice Bean		$8	$12	$16	Lauren Child		Candle
2003	Who's Afraid Of The Big Bad Book?		$8	$12	$16	Lauren Child		Hyper
2004	I Am Too Absolutely Small For School		$8	$10	$14	Lauren Child		Candle

Chorao   Kay

Year	Title	VG-	VG	VG+	Fine	Author	Award	Pub
1972	The Repair Of Uncle Toe		$40	$60	$90	Kay Chorao		FSG
1973	My Mama Says There Aren't Any Zombies		$30	$50	$60	Judith Viorst		Athenm
1974	Albert's Toothache		$20	$30	$40	Barbara Williams		Dutton
1974	Ida Makes A Movie		$30	$40	$60	Kay Chorao		Seabury
1974	Ralph And The Queen's Bathtub		$30	$40	$60	Kay Chorao		FSG
1974	The Witch's Egg		$30	$40	$60	Madeleine Edmondson		Seabury

Chorao — Kay

Year	Title	VG-	VG	VG+	Fine	Author	Award	Pub
1975	Henrietta, The Wild Woman Of Borneo		$20	$30	$40	Winifred Rosen		4Winds
1975	Kevin's Grandma		$20	$30	$40	Barbara Williams		Dutton
1975	Maudie's Umbrella		$30	$40	$60	Kay Chorao		Dutton
1976	Clyde Monster		$20	$30	$40	Robert L. Crowe		Dutton
1976	Molly's Moe		$30	$40	$60	Kay Chorao		Seabury
1976	Monster Poems		$20	$30	$40	Daisy Wallace (edited)		Holiday
1976	Someday, Said Mitchell		$20	$30	$40	Barbara Williams		Dutton
1976	The Hunt For Rabbit's Galosh		$20	$30	$40	Ann Schweninger		DoubleD
1977	Dracula's Cat / Frankenstein's Dog		$25	$40	$50	Jan Wahl		P-Hall
1977	I'm Terrific		$25	$40	$50	Marjorie Weinman Sharmat		Holiday
1977	Lester's Overnight		$25	$40	$50	Kay Chorao		Dutton
1977	That's Enough For One Day, J. P.!		$20	$30	$40	Susan Pearson		Dial
1977	The Baby's Lap Book		$25	$40	$50	Kay Chorao		Dutton
1978	Chester Chipmunk's Thanksgiving		$20	$30	$40	Barbara Williams		Dutton
1978	Henrietta And The Day Of The Iguana		$20	$30	$40	Winifred Rosen		4Winds
1978	Thornton, The Worrier		$25	$40	$50	Marjorie Weinman Sharmat		Holiday
1979	Molly's Lies		$25	$40	$50	Kay Chorao		Seabury
1979	The Nutcracker		$18	$25	$35	Janet Schulman (adapted)		Dutton
1979	Visiting Pamela		$18	$25	$35	Norma Klein		Dial
1980	Grumley The Grouch		$25	$35	$50	Marjorie Weinman Sharmat		Holiday
1980	Sometimes Mama And Papa Fight		$25	$35	$50	Marjorie Weinman Sharmat		H&Row
1980	Tyler Toad And The Thunder		$18	$25	$35	Robert L. Crowe		Dutton
1981	A Valentine For Cousin Archie		$18	$25	$35	Barbara Williams		Dutton
1981	Giant Journey		$18	$25	$35	Steven Kroll		Holiday
1981	Henrietta And The Gong From Hong Kong		$18	$25	$35	Winifred Rosen		4Winds
1981	Oink And Pearl		$25	$35	$50	Kay Chorao		H&Row
1982	Kate's Box		$25	$35	$50	Kay Chorao		Dutton
1982	Kate's Car		$25	$35	$50	Kay Chorao		Dutton
1982	Kate's Quilt		$25	$35	$50	Kay Chorao		Dutton
1982	Kate's Snowman		$25	$35	$50	Kay Chorao		Dutton
1982	The Boy With The Helium Head		$30	$50	$60	Phyllis Reynolds Naylor		Athenm
1982	The Thinking Place		$16	$25	$30	Barbara M. Joosse		Knopf
1983	But Not Billy		$25	$35	$50	Charlotte Zolotow		H&Row
1983	Lemon Moon		$25	$35	$50	Kay Chorao		Holiday
1983	Spiders In The Fruit Cellar		$16	$25	$30	Barbara M. Joosse		Knopf
1984	Rickety Witch		$16	$25	$30	Maggie S. Davis		Holiday
1984	The Baby's Bedtime Book		$20	$30	$40	Kay Chorao		Dutton
1984	Valentine For A Dragon		$16	$25	$30	Shirley Murphy		Athenm
1985	The Baby's Story Book		$20	$30	$40	Kay Chorao		Dutton
1986	The Baby's Good Morning Book		$20	$30	$40	Kay Chorao		Dutton
1986	Ups And Downs With Oink And Pearl		$20	$30	$40	Kay Chorao		H&Row
1987	George Told Kate		$20	$30	$40	Kay Chorao		Dutton
1987	The Child's Story Book		$20	$30	$40	Kay Chorao		Dutton
1988	Cathedral Mouse		$18	$25	$35	Kay Chorao		Dutton
1988	The Good-Bye Book		$18	$25	$35	Judith Viorst		Athenm
1989	Songs From Dreamland: Original Lullabies		$14	$20	$25	Lois Duncan		Knopf
1989	The Cherry Pie Baby		$18	$25	$35	Kay Chorao		Dutton
1990	Dracula's Cat / Frankenstein's Dog		$16	$25	$30	Jan Wahl		S&S
1990	The Baby's Lap Book		$16	$25	$30	Kay Chorao		Dutton
1990	The Child's Fairy Tale Book		$16	$25	$30	Kay Chorao		Dutton
1991	Baby's Christmas Treasury		$16	$25	$30	Varied Authors		Random
1991	Ida And Betty And The Secret Eggs		$16	$25	$30	Kay Chorao		Clarion
1992	Country Dawn To Dusk		$12	$18	$25	Riki Levinson		Dutton
1993	Rock, Rock, My Baby		$16	$25	$30	Kay Chorao		Random
1994	Annie And Cousin Precious		$14	$20	$30	Kay Chorao		Dutton
1994	Mother Goose Magic		$14	$20	$30	Kay Chorao		Dutton
1994	Peekaboo! Was It You?		$14	$20	$30	Kay Chorao		Random
1995	Carousel Round And Round		$14	$20	$25	Kay Chorao		Clarion
1995	Number One Number Fun		$14	$20	$25	Kay Chorao		Holiday
1995	The Book Of Giving		$14	$20	$25	Kay Chorao		Dutton
1996	The Christmas Story		$12	$18	$25	Kay Chorao		Holiday
1997	Jumpety-Bumpety Hop		$12	$18	$25	Kay Chorao		Dutton
1998	Little Farm By The Sea		$12	$16	$20	Kay Chorao		Holt
1998	The Cats Kids		$12	$16	$20	Kay Chorao		Holiday
1999	Knock At The Door		$12	$16	$20	Kay Chorao		Dutton
2000	Here Comes Kate		$10	$14	$18	Kay Chorao		Dutton
2000	Pig And Crow		$10	$14	$18	Kay Chorao		Holt

Chorao   Kay

Year	Title	VG-	VG	VG+	Fine	Author	Award	Pub
2000	The Little Country Town		$8	$12	$16	Jandelyn Southwell		Holt
2001	Baby's Christmas Treasury.		$10	$14	$18	Kay Chorao		Random
2001	Shadow Night		$10	$14	$18	Kay Chorao		Dutton
2002	Grayboy		$8	$12	$16	Kay Chorao		Holt
2002	Up And Down With Kate		$8	$12	$16	Kay Chorao		Dutton
2003	Rosie To The Rescue		$8	$10	$14	Bethany Roberts		Holt
2004	D Is For Drums		$8	$10	$14	Kay Chorao		Abrams
2004	The Baby's Book Of Baby Animals		$8	$10	$14	Kay Chorao		Dutton
2004	Whose House?		$8	$10	$14	Barbara Seuling		Harcort
2005	Grandma's Hurrying Child		$6	$10	$12	Jane Yolen		Harcort

Christiana   David

Year	Title	VG-	VG	VG+	Fine	Author	Award	Pub
1984	Fat Man In A Fur Coat		$30	$50	$60	Alvin Schwartz		FSG
1988	Gold & Silver, Silver & Gold		$18	$25	$35	Alvin Schwartz		FSG
1990	A Drawer In A Drawer		$16	$25	$30	David Christiana		FSG
1992	White Nineteens		$16	$25	$30	David Christiana		FSG
1993	The Alley Cat		$16	$25	$30	Brian Heinz		DoubleD
1994	A Tooth Fairy's Tale		$14	$20	$30	David Christiana		FSG
1995	Elfsong		$14	$20	$25	Ann W. Turner		HBrace
1995	Good Griselle		$14	$20	$25	Jane Yolen		HBJ
1995	The Mouse Bride		$14	$20	$25	Joy Cowley		Scholas
1996	The First Snow		$12	$18	$25	David Christiana		Scholas
1997	I Am The Mummy		$12	$18	$25	Eve Bunting		HBrace
1998	Silver Morning		$12	$16	$20	Susan Pearson		HBrace
1999	Poppy's Puppet		$12	$16	$20	Patricia Gauch		Holt
1999	The Tale I Told Sasha		$12	$16	$20	Nancy Willard		LBrown
2001	Magical, Mystical, Marvelous Coat		$10	$14	$18	Catherine Ann Cullen		LBrown
2001	The Christmas Promise		$10	$14	$18	Susan Bartoletti		BSP
2005	Fairy Dust and the Quest for the Egg		$8	$10	$14	Gail Carson Levine		Disney

Christopher   Denise

Year	Title	VG-	VG	VG+	Fine	Author	Award	Pub
1994	The Fool Of The World And The Flying Ship		$14	$20	$30	Christopher Denise		Philo
1996	The Great Redwall Feast		$10	$16	$20	Brian Jacques		Philo
1997	The Sea Man		$10	$16	$20	Jane Yolen		Philo
1998	Little Raccoon Catches A Cold		$10	$14	$18	Susan Canizares		Scholas
2000	Digger Pig And The Turnip		$8	$12	$16	Caron Lee Cohen		GLR
2000	Rabbit And Turtle Go To School		$8	$12	$16	Lucy Floyd		Harcort
2001	A Redwall Winter's Tale		$8	$12	$16	Brian Jacques		Philo
2002	Oliver Finds His Way		$8	$10	$14	Phyllis Root		Candle
2004	The Wishing Of Biddy Malone		$8	$10	$14	Joy Cowley		Philo

Chwast   Jacqueline

Year	Title	VG-	VG	VG+	Fine	Author	Award	Pub
1958	Whispers, & Other Poems	$70	$100	$120		Myra Cohn Livingston		HBrace
1959	Wide Awake	$50	$60	$80		Myra Cohn Livingston		HBrace
1961	The Cuckoo That Couldn't Count	$50	$60	$80		Jean Lee Latham		Macmil
1965	I Like You	$40	$60	$70		Sandol Stoddard		HM
1967	Elliott	$40	$50	$70		Peggy Clifford		HM
1967	When The Baby-Sitter Didn't Come	$40	$50	$70		Jacqueline Chwast		HBrace
1968	How Mr Berry Found A Home & Happiness Forever	$40	$50	$70		Jacqueline Chwast		S&S
1968	The First And Last Annual Pet Parade	$40	$50	$70		Mary Neville		Pan
1970	Aunt Bella's Umbrella		$30	$50	$60	William Cole		DoubleD
1970	Hooray For Us		$30	$50	$60	Sandol Stoddard		HM
1971	A Present From A Bird		$30	$50	$60	Jay Williams		PMagP
1972	Iggy		$30	$50	$60	Marcia Newfield		HM
1972	Play With The Wind		$30	$50	$60	Howard Everett Smith		McHill
1972	The Diary Of A Paper Boy		$30	$50	$60	Jean-Jacques Larrea		Putnam
1973	Tinker Tales		$30	$50	$60	Mary Dawson		PMagP
1975	Fire		$30	$40	$60	Gail Kay Haines		Morrow
1976	Don't Throw Another One, Dover!		$30	$40	$60	Beverly Keller		CM&G
1976	I Like Old Clothes		$30	$40	$60	Mary Ann Hoberman		Knopf
1976	Picnics And Parades		$30	$40	$60	Leonore Klein		Knopf
1977	Small Deer's Magic Tricks		$25	$40	$50	Betty V, Boegehold		CM&G

Chwast   Jacqueline

Year	Title	VG-	VG	VG+	Fine	Author	Award	Pub
1978	Pimm's Place		$25	$40	$50	Beverly Keller		CM&G
1978	X, A Fabulous Child's Story		$25	$40	$50	Lois Gould		DaughT
1992	A First Passover		$16	$25	$30	Leslie Swartz		MCP
1993	The Perilous Pit		$16	$25	$30	Orel Odinov Protopopescu	NYT	GreenT
1995	Starlight And Candles		$14	$20	$25	Fran Manushkin		S&S
1996	What Are Roses For?		$12	$18	$25	Sandol Stoddard		HM
1997	How Rabbit Lost His Tail		$12	$18	$25	Ann Tompert		HM
1999	The Hungry Black Bag		$12	$16	$20	Ann Tompert		HM

Chwast   Seymour

Year	Title	VG-	VG	VG+	Fine	Author	Award	Pub
1969	Sara's Granny And The Groodle	$25	$35	$50		Joan Gill		DoubleD
1969	Still Another Alphabet Book	$20	$30	$35		Martin Moskof		McHill
1970	Finding A Poem		$18	$25	$35	Eve Merriam		Athenm
1971	Still Another Number Book		$18	$25	$35	Martin Moskof		McHill
1971	The Pancake King		$18	$25	$35	Phyllis La Farge		DelaP
1972	Limerickricks		$18	$25	$35	Seymour Chwast		Random
1972	Mother Goooooose		$18	$25	$35	Seymour Chwast		Random
1972	Still Another Children's Book		$18	$25	$35	Martin Moskof		McHill
1973	The House That Jack Built		$16	$25	$30	Seymour Chwast		Random
1977	Sleepy Ida & Other Nonsense Poems		$16	$25	$30	Steven Kroll		Pan
1983	Bushy Bride		$14	$20	$25	Seymour Chwast		Creat
1983	Tall City, Wide Country		$14	$20	$25	Seymour Chwast		Viking
1986	Keeping Daddy Awake On The Way Home		$12	$16	$20	Harriet Ziefert		H&Row
1986	My Sister Says Nothing Ever Happens		$12	$16	$20	Harriet Ziefert		H&Row
1988	Just Enough Is Plenty		$12	$16	$20	Barbara Diamond Goldin		VK
1990	Harry's Bath		$10	$16	$20	Harriet Ziefert		Bantam
1991	The Alphabet Parade		$10	$16	$20	Seymour Chwast		HBJ
1992	Mathew Michael's Beastly Day		$10	$16	$20	Deborah Johnston		HBJ
1993	The Twelve Circus Rings		$10	$16	$20	Seymour Chwast		HBJ
1996	Mr. Merlin And The Turtle		$8	$12	$16	Seymour Chwast		Green
1997	Out Of The Bag		$8	$12	$16	Judith Martin		Hyper
1999	Traffic Jam		$8	$12	$16	Seymour Chwast		HM
2000	Moonride		$8	$10	$14	Harriet Ziefert		HM
2000	Ode To Humpty Dumpty		$8	$10	$14	Harriet Ziefert		HM
2000	The Wizard Who Wanted To Be Santa		$8	$10	$14	Gloria Nagy		Sheer
2002	Harry, I Need You!		$8	$10	$14	Seymour Chwast		HM
2003	My Daddy And Me		$8	$10	$14	Jerry Spinelli		Knopf

Clark   Emma Chichester

Year	Title	VG-	VG	VG+	Fine	Author	Award	Pub
1987	Listen To This		$14	$20	$30	Laura Cecil		Green
1988	The Story Of Horrible Hilda And Henry		$12	$16	$20	Emma Chichester Clark		LBrown
1989	Cissy Lavender		$12	$16	$20	Primrose Lockwood		LBrown
1989	Stuff And Nonsense		$12	$16	$20	Laura Cecil		Green
1990	Boo!		$10	$16	$20	Laura Cecil		Green
1990	Catch That Hat!		$10	$16	$20	Emma Chichester Clark		LBrown
1990	I Never Saw A Purple Cow		$10	$16	$20	Emma Chichester Clark		Walker
1990	Ragged Robin		$10	$16	$20	James Reeves		LBrown
1990	The Bouncing Dinosaur		$10	$16	$20	Emma Chichester Clark		FSG
1991	Beware Of The Aunts!		$10	$16	$20	Pat Thomson		McEld
1991	The Queen's Goat		$10	$16	$20	Margaret Mahy		Dial
1992	A Thousand Yards Of Sea		$10	$16	$20	Laura Cecil		Metheun
1992	Lunch With Aunt Augusta		$10	$16	$20	Emma Chichester Clark		Dial
1992	Tertius And Pliny		$10	$16	$20	Ben Frankel		HBJ
1993	Across T H E Blue Mountains		$10	$16	$20	Emma Chichester Clark		HBJ
1993	Greek Myths		$10	$16	$20	Geraldine McCaughrean		McEld
1993	The Minstrel And The Dragon Pup		$10	$16	$20	Rosemary Sutcliff		Candle
1994	Good Night, Stella		$10	$14	$18	Kate McMullan		Candle
1994	Time And The Clock Mice		$10	$14	$18	Peter Dickinson		DelaP
1994	Too Tired		$10	$14	$18	Ann Turnbull		HBrace
1995	Preposterous Pets		$10	$14	$18	Laura Cecil		Green
1995	Something Rich And Strange		$10	$14	$18	Gina Pollinger (adapted)		Kfisher
1995	The Frog Princess		$10	$14	$18	Laura Cecil		Green
1996	Thumbelina		$8	$12	$16	Jane Falloon (adapted)		McEld
1997	Little Miss Muffet's Count-Along Surprise		$8	$12	$16	Emma Chichester Clark		Bantam

Clark   Emma Chichester

Year	Title	VG-	VG	VG+	Fine	Author	Award	Pub
1997	Noah And The Space Ark		$8	$12	$16	Laura Cecil		CRB
1998	Greek Gods And Goddesses		$8	$12	$16	Geraldine McCaughrean		McEld
1999	Don't Worry, Alfie		$8	$12	$16	Mathew Price		Orchard
1999	I Love You, Blue Kangaroo!		$8	$12	$16	Emma Chichester Clark		DoubleD
1999	More!		$8	$12	$16	Emma Chichester Clark		DoubleD
1999	The Orchard Book Of Roman Myths		$8	$12	$16	Geraldine McCaughrean		Orchard
1999	Where's Alfie?		$8	$12	$16	Mathew Price		Orchard
2000	A Treasury Of Shakespeare's Verse		$8	$10	$14	Gina Pollinger (adapted)		Kfisher
2000	Patch And The Rabbits		$8	$10	$14	Mathew Price		Orchard
2000	Patch Finds A Friend		$8	$10	$14	Mathew Price		Orchard
2000	The Kingfisher Book Of Toy Stories		$8	$10	$14	Laura Cecil		Kfisher
2001	Roman Myths		$8	$10	$14	Geraldine McCaughrean		McEld
2001	Where Are You, Blue Kangaroo?		$8	$10	$14	Emma Chichester Clark		Random
2002	It Was You, Blue Kangaroo!		$8	$10	$14	Emma Chichester Clark		Random
2002	No More Kissing!		$8	$10	$14	Emma Chichester Clark		DoubleD
2003	Follow The Leader!		$8	$10	$14	Emma Chichester Clark		McEld
2003	Mimi's Book Of Counting		$8	$10	$14	Emma Chichester Clark		Charles
2003	Mimi's Book Of Opposites		$8	$10	$14	Emma Chichester Clark		Charles
2003	What Shall We Do, Blue Kangaroo?		$8	$10	$14	Emma Chichester Clark		Random

Clarke   Gus

Year	Title	VG-	VG	VG+	Fine	Author	Award	Pub
1990	Eddie And Teddy		$12	$18	$25	Gus Clarke		AP
1991	Along Came Eric		$10	$16	$20	Gus Clarke		LL&S
1992	Big Brave Brother Ben		$10	$16	$20	Kara May		LL&S
1992	How Many Days To My Birthday?		$10	$16	$20	Gus Clarke		AP
1993	E I E I O		$10	$16	$20	Gus Clarke		LL&S
1994	Ten Green Monsters		$10	$14	$18	Gus Clarke		Golden
1995	Helping Hector		$10	$14	$18	Gus Clarke		Western
1995	Too Many Teddies		$10	$14	$18	Gus Clarke		AP
1996	Naughty Monkey		$8	$12	$16	Gus Clarke		Western
1998	Lucy's Bedtime Book		$8	$12	$16	Gus Clarke		AP

Claverie   Jean

Year	Title	VG-	VG	VG+	Fine	Author	Award	Pub
1978	The Pied Piper Of Hamelin		$35	$50	$70	Kurt Baumann		Metheun
1980	The Happy Prince		$25	$35	$50	Oscar Wilde		Oxford
1981	The Princess On The Nut		$25	$35	$50	Michelle Nikly		Faber
1982	Puss In Boots		$25	$35	$50	Kurt Baumann (retold)		Faber
1985	My Daddy		$20	$30	$40	Mathew Price		Knopf
1985	Peekaboo!		$20	$30	$40	Mathew Price		Knopf
1985	Smile Please!!		$20	$30	$40	Mathew Price		Knopf
1986	Billy The Brave		$20	$30	$40	Anne-Marie Chapouton		NSBooks
1986	Happy Birthday!		$20	$30	$40	Mathew Price		Knopf
1986	My Mommy		$20	$30	$40	Mathew Price		Knopf
1986	Shopping		$20	$30	$40	Jean Claverie		Crown
1986	The Old House		$20	$30	$40	Hans Christian Andersen		NSBooks
1986	The Party		$20	$30	$40	Jean Claverie		Crown
1986	The Picnic		$20	$30	$40	Jean Claverie		Crown
1986	The Prince And The Lute		$20	$30	$40	Kurt Baumann		NSBooks
1986	Working		$20	$30	$40	Jean Claverie		Crown
1987	The Bear And Henry		$20	$30	$40	Arlene Blanchard		Barrn
1989	The Three Little Pigs		$18	$25	$35	Jean Claverie		NSBooks
1990	Little Lou		$16	$25	$30	Jean Claverie		Creat
1993	Little John's Fears: A Story		$16	$25	$30	Rene Escudie		CW
1993	The Bird Fisherman: A Story		$16	$25	$30	Nicole Schneegans		CW
1995	Julian		$14	$20	$25	Anne-Marie Chapouton		Kfisher
1996	Jean Claverie's Fairy Tale Theater		$12	$18	$25	Dawn Bentley (adapted)		Barrn

Clay   Jesse

Year	Title	VG-	VG	VG+	Fine	Author	Award	Pub
1992	Walt Disney's Alice's Tea Party		$10	$16	$20	Lyn Calder (adapted)		Disney
1995	Walt Disney's The Small One		$10	$14	$18	Alex Walsh (adapted)		Disney
1995	Walt Disney's Three Orphan Kittens		$10	$14	$18	Margaret Wise Brown		Disney

Clement   Rod

Year	Title	VG-	VG	VG+	Fine	Author	Award	Pub
1986	Snail Mail		$14	$20	$30	Hazel Edwards		Collins
1988	When Hippo Was Hairy		$12	$16	$20	Nick Greaves		Barrn
1991	Counting On Frank		$10	$16	$20	Rod Clement		GSteve
1993	When Lion Could Fly		$10	$16	$20	Nick Greaves		Barrn
1997	Edwina The Emu		$8	$12	$16	Sheena Knowles		Harper
1997	Grandpa's Teeth		$8	$12	$16	Rod Clement		HCollins
1997	Just Another Ordinary Day		$8	$12	$16	Rod Clement		HCollins
1999	Frank's Great Museum Adventure		$8	$12	$16	Rod Clement		HCollins

Clifford   Judy

Year	Title	VG-	VG	VG+	Fine	Author	Award	Pub
1979	The School Mouse And The Hamster		$14	$20	$30	Joan Harris		FWarne
1980	The Empty Window		$14	$20	$25	Eve Bunting		FWarne
1995	Midnight Magic		$10	$14	$18	Amy Gordon		BWB

Coalson   Glo

Year	Title	VG-	VG	VG+	Fine	Author	Award	Pub
1971	Three Stone Woman		$30	$50	$60	Glo Coalson		Athenm
1972	On Mother's Lap		$25	$35	$50	Ann Herbert Scott		McHill
1973	At The Mouth Of The Luckiest River		$25	$35	$50	Arnold A. Griese		Crowell
1973	Dexter.		$25	$35	$50	Clyde Robert Bulla		Crowell
1975	An Eskimo Birthday		$20	$30	$40	Tom D. Robinson		DoddM
1975	Morris And His Brave Lion		$20	$30	$40	Helen Spelman Rogers		McHill
1975	That's The Way It Is, Amigo		$20	$30	$40	Hila Colman		Crowell
1976	In A Bottle With A Cork On Top		$20	$30	$40	Gloria Skurzynski		DoddM
1977	The Chosen Baby		$20	$30	$40	Valentina Pavlovna Wasson		Lippin
1979	Bright Fawn And Me		$18	$25	$35	Jay Leech		Crowell
1980	By Myself		$18	$25	$35	Lee Bennett Hopkins		Crowell
1981	Today We Are Brother And Sister		$18	$25	$35	Arnold Adoff		LL&S
1994	Hi!		$12	$16	$20	Ann Herbert Scott		Philo
1996	Brave As A Mountain Lion		$10	$16	$20	Ann Herbert Scott		Clarion
1997	Daphne Eloise Slater		$10	$16	$20	Gina Willner-Pardo		Clarion
1997	Emily Just In Time		$10	$16	$20	Jan Slepian		Philo
2000	Blackberry Booties		$8	$12	$16	Tricia Gardella		Orchard
2001	The Moon's Lullaby		$8	$12	$16	Josephine Nobisso		Orchard

Cogancherry   Helen

Year	Title	VG-	VG	VG+	Fine	Author	Award	Pub
1979	Where Is Maria?		$18	$25	$35	Louise Gunther		Garrard
1980	Sometimes My Mom Drinks Too Much		$14	$20	$25	Kevin Kenny		Rain
1980	Who's Afraid Of The Dark?		$14	$20	$25	Muriel Stanek		AWhit
1980	Words In Our Hands		$14	$20	$25	Ada Bassett Litchfield		AWhit
1981	My Sister Is Different		$14	$20	$25	Betty Ren Wright		Rain
1981	Pride And Prejudice		$14	$20	$25	Diana Stewart (adapted)		Rain
1982	Wuthering Heights		$14	$20	$25	Betty Ren Wright (adapted)		Rain
1983	Don't Hurt Me, Mama		$14	$20	$25	Muriel Stanek		AWhit
1983	Wide Angle		$14	$20	$25	Linda Barrett Osborne		HBJ
1985	Millie Cooper, 3B		$12	$18	$25	Charlotte Herman		Dutton
1985	Who Is A Stranger, And What Should I Do?		$12	$18	$25	Linda Walvoord Girard		AWhit
1986	Don't Call Me Fatso		$12	$16	$20	Barbara Philips		Chariot
1987	Children Do, Grownups Don't		$12	$16	$20	Norma Simon		AWhit
1987	Dinnieabbiesister-R-R		$12	$16	$20	Riki Levinson		BradP
1988	Rebecca's Nap		$12	$16	$20	Fred Burstein		BradP
1990	All I Am		$10	$16	$20	Eileen Roe		BradP
1990	The Real Tooth Fairy		$10	$16	$20	Marilyn Kaye		HBJ
1991	Fourth Of July Bear		$10	$16	$20	Kathryn Lasky		Morrow
1992	Warm As Wool		$10	$16	$20	Scott R. Sanders		BradP
1992	Whispering In The Park		$10	$16	$20	Fred Burstein		BradP
1993	Here Comes The Mystery Man		$10	$16	$20	Scott R. Sanders		BradP
1994	Sarah, Also Known As Hannah		$10	$14	$18	Lillian Hammer Ross		AWhit
1995	Millie Cooper And Friends		$10	$14	$18	Charlotte Herman		Viking
1995	The Floating House		$10	$14	$18	Scott R. Sanders		Macmil

Cole   Babette

Year	Title	VG-	VG	VG+	Fine	Author	Award	Pub
1976	Daisy		$40	$60	$80	Jenny Butterworth		K&W
1976	The Unicorn Drum		$40	$60	$80	Annabel Farjeon		K&W
1978	Mice And Mendelson		$25	$40	$50	Joan Aiken		JCape
1979	Count Bakwerdz On The Carpet		$25	$40	$50	Norman Hunter		Bodley
1979	Nungu And The Hippopotamus		$35	$50	$70	Babette Cole		McHill
1980	Grasshopper And The Unwise Owl		$25	$35	$50	Jim Slater		HR&W
1980	Nungu And The Elephant		$35	$50	$70	Babette Cole		McHill
1980	Sneeze And Be Slain		$25	$35	$50	Norman Hunter		Bodley
1982	Don't Go Out Tonight		$30	$50	$60	Babette Cole		DoubleD
1983	The Wind In The Willows		$25	$35	$50	Kenneth Grahame		HR&W
1984	The Trouble With Mom		$20	$30	$40	Babette Cole		CM
1985	The Hairy Book		$20	$30	$40	Babette Cole		Random
1986	The Slimy Book		$20	$30	$40	Babette Cole		Random
1986	The Trouble With Dad		$20	$30	$40	Babette Cole		Putnam
1987	Princess Smartypants		$20	$30	$40	Babette Cole		Putnam
1987	The Trouble With Gran		$20	$30	$40	Babette Cole		Putnam
1988	Prince Cinders		$18	$25	$35	Babette Cole		Putnam
1988	The Smelly Book		$18	$25	$35	Babette Cole		S&S
1988	The Trouble With Grandad		$18	$25	$35	Babette Cole		Putnam
1989	King Change-A-Lot		$18	$25	$35	Babette Cole		Putnam
1989	Three Cheers For Errol!		$18	$25	$35	Babette Cole		Putnam
1990	Cupid		$16	$25	$30	Babette Cole		Putnam
1990	The Silly Book		$16	$25	$30	Babette Cole		DoubleD
1991	Babette Cole's Beastly Birthday Book		$16	$25	$30	Ron Van der Meer		DoubleD
1991	Hurray For Ethelyn		$16	$25	$30	Babette Cole		LBrown
1992	Tarzanna!		$16	$25	$30	Babette Cole		Putnam
1992	The Trouble With Uncle		$16	$25	$30	Babette Cole		LBrown
1993	Mommy Laid An Egg!		$16	$25	$30	Babette Cole		Chron
1993	Supermoo!		$16	$25	$30	Babette Cole		Putnam
1993	Winni Allfours		$16	$25	$30	Babette Cole		BWB
1995	Babette Cole's Ponies		$14	$20	$25	Babette Cole		Warner
1996	Drop Dead		$12	$18	$25	Babette Cole		Knopf
1996	The Bad Good Manners Book		$12	$18	$25	Babette Cole		Dial
1997	Babette Cole's Brother		$12	$18	$25	Babette Cole		WHBooks
1997	Babette Cole's Dad		$12	$18	$25	Babette Cole		WHBooks
1997	Babette Cole's Mum		$12	$18	$25	Babette Cole		WHBooks
1997	Dr. Dog		$12	$18	$25	Babette Cole		Knopf
1997	Two Of Everything		$12	$18	$25	Babette Cole		JCape
1998	The Un-Wedding		$12	$16	$20	Babette Cole		Knopf
1999	Bad Habits!		$12	$16	$20	Babette Cole		Dial
2000	Hair In Funny Places		$10	$14	$18	Babette Cole		Hyper
2001	The Silly Slimy Smelly Hairy Book		$10	$14	$18	Babette Cole		JCape
2002	Lady Lupin's Book Of Etiquette		$8	$12	$16	Babette Cole		Peach
2002	Truelove		$8	$12	$16	Babette Cole		Dial

Cole   Brock

Year	Title	VG-	VG	VG+	Fine	Author	Award	Pub
1979	The King At The Door		$14	$20	$30	Brock Cole		DoubleD
1980	No More Baths		$14	$20	$25	Brock Cole		DoubleD
1980	The Indian In The Cupboard		$120	$160	$220	Lynne Reid Banks		DoubleD
1981	Nothing But A Pig		$14	$20	$25	Brock Cole		DoubleD
1984	Gaffer Samson's Luck		$12	$18	$25	Jill Paton Walsh		FSG
1984	The Winter Wren		$12	$18	$25	Brock Cole		FSG
1986	The Giant's Toe		$12	$16	$20	Brock Cole		FSG
1987	The Goats		$12	$16	$20	Brock Cole		FSG
1989	Celine		$12	$16	$20	Brock Cole		FSG
1991	Alpha And The Dirty Baby		$10	$16	$20	Brock Cole		FSG
2000	Buttons		$8	$10	$14	Brock Cole		FSG
2001	Larky Mavis		$8	$10	$14	Brock Cole		FSG
2003	George Washington's Teeth		$8	$10	$14	Deborah Chandra		FSG

Collier   Bryan

Year	Title	VG-	VG	VG+	Fine	Author	Award	Pub
1999	These Hands		$14	$20	$25	Hope Lynne Price		Hyper
2000	Freedom River		$10	$14	$18	Doreen Rappaport		Hyper
2000	Uptown		$10	$14	$18	Bryan Collier		Holt

Collier   Bryan

Year	Title	VG-	VG	VG+	Fine	Author	Award	Pub
2001	Kiss It Up To God		$10	$14	$18	Nadine Mozon		Fly
2001	Martin's Big Words		$25	$40	$50	Doreen Rappaport	CH	Hyper
2002	I'm Your Child, God		$8	$12	$16	Marian Wright Edelman		Hyper
2002	Visiting Langston		$8	$12	$16	Willie Perdomo		Holt
2004	John's Secret Dreams		$8	$10	$14	Doreen Rappaport		Hyper
2004	What's The Hurry, Fox?		$8	$10	$14	Joyce Carol Thomas		HCollins
2005	Rosa		$14	$20	$30	Nikki Giovanni	CH	Holt

Collington   Peter

Year	Title	VG-	VG	VG+	Fine	Author	Award	Pub
1986	Little Pickle		$40	$60	$80	Peter Collington		Dutton
1987	The Angel And The Soldier Boy		$25	$40	$50	Peter Collington		Knopf
1988	My Darling Kitten		$25	$40	$50	Peter Collington		Knopf
1990	On Christmas Eve		$25	$35	$50	Peter Collington		Knopf
1992	The Midnight Circus		$20	$30	$40	Peter Collington		Knopf
1994	The Coming Of The Surfman		$20	$30	$40	Peter Collington		Knopf
1995	The Tooth Fairy		$18	$25	$35	Peter Collington		Knopf
1997	A Small Miracle		$16	$25	$30	Peter Collington		Knopf
2000	Clever Cat		$12	$18	$25	Peter Collington		Knopf

Collins   Ross

Year	Title	VG-	VG	VG+	Fine	Author	Award	Pub
1998	What If?		$8	$12	$16	Frances Thomas		Hyper
2002	Alfie Eats Soup		$8	$10	$14	Ross Collins		Levine
2002	Busy Night		$8	$10	$14	Ross Collins		Bloom

Colón   Raúl

Year	Title	VG-	VG	VG+	Fine	Author	Award	Pub
1995	Always My Dad		$18	$25	$35	Sharon Dennis Wyeth		Knopf
1995	My Mama Had A Dancing Heart		$14	$20	$25	Libba Moore Gray		Orchard
1997	Celebration!		$12	$18	$25	Jane Resh Thomas		Hyper
1997	Grandmother's Garden		$12	$18	$25	John Archambault		Silver
1997	Tomás And The Library Lady		$12	$18	$25	Pat Mora		Knopf
1998	A Weave Of Words		$12	$16	$20	Robert D. San Souci		Orchard
1998	Buoy, Home At Sea		$12	$16	$20	Bruce Balan		DelaP
1999	A Band Of Angels		$12	$16	$20	Deborah Hopkinson		Athenm
1999	Hercules		$12	$16	$20	Robert Burleigh		Whistle
2000	Secrets From The Dollhouse		$10	$14	$18	Ann W. Turner		HCollins
2000	The Snowman's Path		$10	$14	$18	Helena Clare Pittman		Dial
2001	A Shepherd's Gift		$10	$14	$18	Mary Calhoun		HCollins
2002	Pandora		$8	$12	$16	Robert Burleigh		Whistle
2002	Rise The Moon		$8	$12	$16	Eileen Spinelli		Dial
2003	Mightier Than The Sword		$8	$12	$16	Jane Yolen		Harcort
2004	Orson Blasts Off!		$8	$10	$14	Raúl Colón		Athenm

Conover   Chris

Year	Title	VG-	VG	VG+	Fine	Author	Award	Pub
1974	The Wish At The Top		$40	$60	$80	Clyde Robert Bulla		Crowell
1976	Six Little Ducks		$40	$60	$80	Chris Conover		Crowell
1976	Somebody Else's Child		$30	$40	$60	Roberta Silman		FWarne
1977	The School Mouse		$25	$40	$50	Dorothy Harris		FWarne
1978	Plenty Of Patches		$25	$40	$50	Marilyn Ratner		Crowell
1978	Where Did My Mother Go?		$25	$40	$50	Edna Mitchell Preston		4Winds
1979	The Bear And The Kingbird		$25	$40	$50	Lore Segal (translated)		FSG
1980	The Little Humpbacked Horse		$25	$35	$50	Margaret Hodges (retold)		FSG
1981	The Beast In The Bed		$25	$35	$50	Barbara Dillon		Morrow
1982	What's Happened To Harry?		$25	$35	$50	Barbara Dillon		Morrow
1984	The Wizard's Daughter		$30	$50	$60	Chris Conover		LBrown
1986	Froggie Went A-Courting		$30	$40	$60	Chris Conover		FSG
1987	The Adventures Of Simple Simon		$25	$40	$50	Chris Conover		FSG
1989	Mother Goose And The Sly Fox		$25	$40	$50	Chris Conover		FSG
1990	Moon Song		$16	$25	$30	Mildred Plew Merryman		Morrow
1992	Sam Panda And Thunder Dragon		$16	$25	$30	Chris Conover		FSG
2000	The Lion's Share		$10	$14	$18	Chris Conover		FSG
2004	Over The Hills And Far Away		$8	$10	$14	Chris Conover		FSG

Coombs   Patricia

Year	Title	VG-	VG	VG+	Fine	Author	Award	Pub
1964	Dorrie And The Blue Witch	$240	$320	$400		Patricia Coombs		LL&S
1966	Dorrie And The Weather-Box	$200	$260	$320		Patricia Coombs		LL&S
1967	Dorrie And The Witch Doctor	$160	$220	$280		Patricia Coombs		LL&S
1968	Dorrie And The Wizard's Spell	$140	$180	$240		Patricia Coombs		LL&S
1969	Lobo	$40	$50	$70		Gladys Y. Cretan		LL&S
1969	P. J., My Friend	$40	$50	$70		Noel B. Gerson.		DoubleD
1969	Pepi's Bell	$40	$50	$70		Shelagh Williamson		Singer
1970	Dorrie And The Haunted House		$80	$120	$160	Patricia Coombs		LL&S
1970	Lisa And The Grompet		$30	$50	$60	Patricia Coombs		LL&S
1971	Dorrie And The Birthday Eggs		$70	$100	$140	Patricia Coombs		LL&S
1971	Lobo And Brewster		$30	$50	$60	Gladys Y. Cretan		LL&S
1972	Dorrie And The Goblin		$70	$100	$140	Patricia Coombs		LL&S
1972	Mouse Cafe		$30	$50	$60	Patricia Coombs		LL&S
1973	Dorrie And The Fortune Teller		$60	$90	$120	Patricia Coombs		LL&S
1974	Dorrie And The Amazing Magic Elixir		$60	$90	$120	Patricia Coombs		LL&S
1975	Dorrie And The Witch's Imp		$60	$80	$120	Patricia Coombs		LL&S
1975	Molly Mullett		$30	$40	$60	Patricia Coombs		LL&S
1976	Dorrie And The Halloween Plot		$60	$80	$120	Patricia Coombs		LL&S
1977	Dorrie And The Dreamyard Monsters		$60	$80	$120	Patricia Coombs		LL&S
1977	The Magic Pot		$25	$40	$50	Patricia Coombs		LL&S
1978	Tilabel		$25	$40	$50	Patricia Coombs		LL&S
1979	Dorrie And The Screebit Ghost		$50	$80	$100	Patricia Coombs		LL&S
1980	Dorrie And The Witchville Fair		$50	$70	$100	Patricia Coombs		LL&S
1983	Dorrie And The Witches' Camp		$40	$60	$90	Patricia Coombs		LL&S
1984	The Magician And Mctree		$20	$30	$40	Patricia Coombs		LLee
1986	Dorrie And The Museum Case		$40	$60	$80	Patricia Coombs		LLee
1987	Bill And The Google-Eyed Goblins		$40	$60	$80	Alice Schertle		LL&S
1989	Dorrie And The Pin Witch		$35	$50	$70	Patricia Coombs		LLee
1992	Dorrie And The Haunted Schoolhouse		$30	$40	$60	Patricia Coombs		Clarion

Cooney   Barbara

Year	Title	VG-	VG	VG+	Fine	Author	Award	Pub
1940	Ake and His World	$140	$200	$240		Bertil Malmberg		F&R
1941	King Of Wreck Island	$140	$180	$240		Barbara Cooney		F&R
1942	The Kellyhorns	$140	$180	$240		Barbara Cooney		F&R
1943	Captain Pottle's House	$140	$180	$240		Barbara Cooney		F&R
1949	Christmas In The Barn	$120	$160	$220		Margaret Wise Brown		Crowell
1950	The Man Who Didn't Wash His Dishes	$80	$120	$140		Phyllis Krasilovsky		DoubleD
1952	Pepper	$80	$100	$140		Barbara Reynolds		Scribnr
1954	The Little Fir Tree (Reissued 1979)	$120	$160	$200		Margaret Wise Brown		Crowell
1955	Snow Birthday	$70	$100	$120		Helen Kay		Ariel
1956	Bambi	$70	$100	$120		Felix Salten		S&S
1956	Friends With God	$70	$100	$120		Catherine Marshall		McHill
1958	Chanticleer And The Fox	$360	$480	$600		Barbara Cooney (adapted)	CM	Crowell
1961	The Little Juggler	$70	$90	$120		Barbara Cooney		Hastings
1963	Favorite Fairy Tales Told In Spain	$70	$90	$120		Virginia Haviland (adapted)		LBrown
1965	Courtship, Merry Marriage & Feast Of Cock Robin	$60	$80	$100		Barbara Cooney		Scribnr
1965	Katie's Magic Glasses	$60	$80	$100		Jane. Goodsell		HM
1965	Shaun And The Boat, An Irish Story	$60	$80	$100		Anne Stearns Molloy		Hastings
1966	All In A Suitcase	$60	$80	$100		Samuel French Morse		LBrown
1966	Snow-White And Rose-Red	$60	$80	$100		Jacob & Wilhelm Grimm		DelaP
1966	The Courtship	$60	$80	$100		Barbara Cooney		Sadler
1967	A Little Prayer	$60	$80	$100		Barbara Cooney		Hastings
1967	Christmas	$60	$80	$100		Barbara Cooney		Crowell
1967	The Crows Of Pearblossom	$60	$80	$100		Aldous Huxley		Random
1969	A Garland Of Games & Other Diversions	$60	$80	$100		Suzanne R. Morse.		HR&W
1969	Christmas Folk	$60	$80	$100		Natalia Belting		HR&W
1969	The Owl And The Pussy-Cat	$60	$80	$100		Edward Lear		LBrown
1970	Dionysos And The Pirates		$50	$70	$90	Penelope Proddow (translated)		DoubleD
1970	The Lazy Young Duke Of Dundee		$50	$70	$90	William Wise		RandMc
1970	Wynken, Blynken, And Nod		$50	$70	$90	Eugene Field		Hastings
1971	Hermes, Lord Of Robbers		$40	$60	$90	Penelope Proddow (translated)		DoubleD
1972	Demeter And Persephone		$40	$60	$90	Penelope Proddow (translated)		DoubleD
1973	Down To The Beach		$40	$60	$90	May Garelick		4Winds
1973	Seven Little Rabbits		$40	$60	$90	John Becker		Walker
1973	The House Mouse		$40	$60	$90	Dorothy Harris		FWarne

Cooney   Barbara

Year	Title	VG-	VG	VG+	Fine	Author	Award	Pub
1973	Would You Rather Be A Tiger?		$40	$60	$90	Robyn Supraner		HM
1974	Squawk To The Moon, Little Goose		$40	$60	$80	Edna Mitchell Preston		Viking
1975	Burton And Dudley		$40	$60	$80	Marjorie Weinman Sharmat		Holiday
1975	Lexington And Concord, 1775		$40	$60	$80	Jean Colby		Hastings
1975	Sad Story Of The Little Bluebird & The Hungry Cat		$40	$60	$80	Edna Mitchell Preston		4Winds
1975	When The Sky Is Like Lace		$40	$60	$80	Elinor Lander Horwitz		Lippin
1977	Midsummer Magic		$40	$60	$80	Ellin Greene (compiled)		LL&S
1977	Plant Magic		$40	$60	$80	Aileen Fisher		Bowmar
1977	The Donkey Prince		$40	$60	$80	M. Jean Craig		DoubleD
1979	I Am Cherry Alive, The Little Girl Sang		$35	$50	$70	Delmore Schwartz		H&Row
1979	Ox-Cart Man		$180	$260	$340	Donald Hall	CM	Viking
1980	Emma		$35	$50	$70	Wendy Kesselman		DoubleD
1980	How The Hibernators Came To Bethlehem		$35	$50	$70	Norma Farber		Walker
1981	Tortillitas Para Mamma		$35	$50	$70	Margot C. Griego		Holt
1982	Little Brother And Little Sister		$30	$50	$60	Barbara Cooney		DoubleD
1982	Miss Rumphius		$30	$50	$60	Barbara Cooney		Viking
1984	Spirit Child: A Story Of The Nativity		$30	$50	$60	John Bierhorst		Morrow
1985	Peter And The Wolf		$30	$40	$60	Sergei Prokofiev		VK
1985	The Story Of Holly & Ivy		$30	$40	$60	Rumer Godden		VK
1986	Louhi, Witch Of North Farm		$30	$40	$60	Toni de Gerez		Viking
1988	Island Boy		$25	$40	$50	Barbara Cooney		Viking
1988	The Year Of The Perfect Christmas Tree		$25	$40	$50	Gloria Houston		Dial
1990	Hattie And The Wild Waves		$25	$35	$50	Barbara Cooney		Viking
1991	Roxaboxen		$25	$35	$50	Alice McLerran		LL&S
1992	Emily		$20	$30	$40	Michael Bedard		DoubleD
1992	Letting Swift River Go		$30	$40	$60	Jane Yolen		LBrown
1993	Animal Folk Songs		$20	$30	$40	Ruth Crawford Seeger		Linnet
1993	Kildee House		$20	$30	$40	Rutherford Montgomery		Walker
1994	Only Opal: The Diary Of A Young Girl		$20	$30	$40	Opal Whiteley		Philo
1994	The Remarkable Christmas Of The Cobbler's Sons		$20	$30	$40	Ruth Sawyer		Viking
1995	The Story Of Christmas		$18	$25	$35	Barbara Cooney		HCollins
1996	Eleanor		$16	$25	$30	Barbara Cooney		Viking
1998	Basket Moon		$14	$20	$30	Mary Lyn Ray		LBrown

Cooper   Floyd

Year	Title	VG-	VG	VG+	Fine	Author	Award	Pub
1988	Grandpa's Face		$25	$40	$50	Eloise Greenfield		Philo
1988	The Story Of Jackie Robinson		$18	$25	$35	Margaret Davidson		Dell
1989	Chita's Christmas Tree		$18	$25	$35	Elizabeth F. Howard		BradP
1990	Laura Charlotte		$16	$25	$30	Kathryn Osebold Galbraith		Philo
1990	Martin Luther King Jr		$16	$25	$30	Jacqueline Woodson		Silver
1991	When Africa Was Home		$16	$25	$30	Karen Lynn Williams		Orchard
1992	Imani's Gift At Kwanzaa		$16	$25	$30	Denise Burden-Patmon		MCP
1992	Petey		$16	$25	$30	Deborah Eaton		SBurdet
1992	The Girl Who Loved Caterpillars		$16	$25	$30	Jean Merrill		Philo
1993	Be Good To Eddie Lee		$16	$25	$30	Virginia M. Fleming		Philo
1993	Brown Honey In Broomwheat Tea		$16	$25	$30	Joyce Carol Thomas		HCollins
1993	Coyote Walks On Two Legs		$16	$25	$30	Gerald Hausman		Philo
1993	Pass It On		$16	$25	$30	Wade Hudson		Scholas
1994	Coming Home		$14	$20	$30	Floyd Cooper		Philo
1994	Happy Birthday, Dr. King!		$14	$20	$30	Kathryn D. Jones		MCP
1994	Meet Danitra Brown		$14	$20	$30	Nikki Grimes		LL&S
1995	Daddy, Daddy, Be There		$14	$20	$25	Candy Dawson Boyd		Philo
1995	Gingerbread Days		$14	$20	$25	Joyce Carol Thomas		HCollins
1995	How Sweet The Sound		$14	$20	$25	Wade Hudson		Scholas
1995	Jaguarundi		$14	$20	$25	Virginia Hamilton		BSP
1995	King Sejong's Secret		$14	$20	$25	Carol J. Farley		LL&S
1995	One April Morning		$14	$20	$25	Nancy Lamb		LL&S
1995	Papa Tells Chita A Story		$14	$20	$25	Elizabeth F. Howard		S&S
1995	Pulling The Lion's Tail		$14	$20	$25	Jane Kurtz		S&S
1996	Mandela		$12	$18	$25	Floyd Cooper		Philo
1996	Satchmo's Blues		$12	$18	$25	Alan Schroeder		DoubleD
1996	Si Won's Victory		$12	$18	$25	Bill Martin		CelebP
1997	Ma Dear's Aprons		$12	$18	$25	Patricia McKissack		Athenm
1997	Miz Berlin Walks		$12	$18	$25	Jane Yolen		Philo
1997	The Blacker The Berry		$12	$18	$25	Joyce Carol Thomas		HCollins

Cooper   Floyd

Year	Title	VG-	VG	VG+	Fine	Author	Award	Pub
1998	African Beginnings		$12	$16	$20	James Haskins		LL&S
1998	Cumbayah		$12	$16	$20	Floyd Cooper		Morrow
1998	Faraway Drums		$12	$16	$20	Virginia L. Kroll		LBrown
1998	I Have Heard Of A Land		$20	$30	$40	Joyce Carol Thomas	CSKH	HCollins
1998	Sea Girl And The Dragon King		$12	$16	$20	Ziporah Hildebrandt		Athenm
1998	Shake Rag		$12	$16	$20	Amy Littlesugar		Philo
1999	Bound For America		$12	$16	$20	James Haskins		LL&S
1999	Caddie, The Golf Dog		$12	$16	$20	Michael R. Sampson		TNelson
1999	Granddaddy's Street Songs		$12	$16	$20	Monalisa DeGross		Jump
1999	Tree Of Hope		$12	$16	$20	Amy Littlesugar		Philo
2000	A Child Is Born		$10	$14	$18	Margaret Wise Brown		Jump
2000	Sweet, Sweet Memory		$10	$14	$18	Jacqueline Woodson		Jump
2001	Freedom School, Yes!		$10	$14	$18	Amy Littlesugar		Philo
2002	Danitra Brown Leaves Town		$8	$12	$16	Nikki Grimes		HCollins
2003	Mississippi Morning		$8	$12	$16	Ruth Vander Zee		EerdB
2004	Jump!		$8	$10	$14	Floyd Cooper		Philo

Cooper   Helen

Year	Title	VG-	VG	VG+	Fine	Author	Award	Pub
1989	Solomon's Secret		$35	$50	$70	Saviour Pirotta		Dial
1990	Ella And The Rabbit		$35	$50	$70	Helen Cooper		Croc
1991	The Owl And The Pussycat		$30	$50	$60	Edward Lear		Dial
1993	The Bear Under The Stairs		$30	$40	$60	Helen Cooper		Dial
1993	The House Cat		$30	$40	$60	Helen Cooper		Scholas
1995	The Tale Of Bear		$25	$35	$50	Helen Cooper		Lothrop
1995	The Tale Of Duck		$25	$35	$50	Helen Cooper		Lothrop
1995	The Tale Of Frog		$25	$35	$50	Helen Cooper		Lothrop
1995	The Tale Of Pig		$25	$35	$50	Helen Cooper		Lothrop
1996	Little Monster Did It!		$25	$35	$50	Helen Cooper		Dial
1996	The Baby Who Wouldn't Go To Bed		$50	$70	$90	Helen Cooper	GM	DoubleD
1997	The Boy Who Wouldn't Go To Bed		$20	$30	$40	Helen Cooper		Dial
1998	Christmas Stories For The Very Young		$20	$30	$40	Sally Grindley		Kfisher
1998	Pumpkin Soup		$40	$60	$80	Helen Cooper	GM	FSG
2000	Chestnut Grey		$16	$25	$30	Helen Cooper		FLinc
2000	Toy Tales		$16	$25	$30	Helen Cooper		FSG
2001	Tatty Ratty		$14	$20	$30	Helen Cooper		FSG
2002	Tatty-Ratty		$12	$18	$25	Helen Cooper		FSG
2005	A Pipkin Of Pepper		$8	$10	$14	Helen Cooper		FSG

Cornell   Laura

Year	Title	VG-	VG	VG+	Fine	Author	Award	Pub
1983	Feed Me Or Else!		$16	$25	$30	Mary Anne Wollison		DoddM
1987	Annie Bananie		$12	$16	$20	Leah Komaiko		H&Row
1987	Zena And The Witch Circus		$12	$16	$20	Alice Low		Dial
1988	Earl's Too Cool For Me		$12	$16	$20	Leah Komaiko		H&Row
1992	Leonora O'grady		$10	$16	$20	Leah Komaiko		HCollins
1993	When I Was Little		$10	$16	$20	Jamie Lee Curtis		HCollins
1994	Letter Writer Book		$10	$14	$18	Nancy Cobb		RDigest
1994	Monster Of The Month Club		$10	$14	$18	Dian Curtis Regan		Holt
1994	Traveling Backward		$10	$14	$18	Toby Forward		Tambour
1995	Monsters In The Attic		$10	$14	$18	Dian Curtis Regan		Holt
1996	Contrary Bear		$8	$12	$16	Phyllis Root		LauraG
1996	Here's How		$8	$12	$16	Laura Cornell		Pleasnt
1996	Pie Magic		$8	$12	$16	Toby Forward		Tambour
1996	Tell Me Again About The Night I Was Born		$8	$12	$16	Jamie Lee Curtis		HCollins
1997	Little Baby Bobby		$8	$12	$16	Nancy Van Laan		Knopf
1997	The Ghost On Saturday Night		$8	$12	$16	Sid Fleischman		Green
1998	Before You Were Born		$8	$12	$16	Jennifer Rauch		Workman
1998	Today I Feel Silly & Moods That Make My Day		$8	$12	$16	Jamie Lee Curtis		HCollins
2000	Where Do Ballons Go?		$8	$10	$14	Jamie Lee Curtis		HCollins

Couch   Greg

Year	Title	VG-	VG	VG+	Fine	Author	Award	Pub
1992	The Man-In-The-Moon		$16	$25	$30	Jeff Brumbeau		ST&C
1996	The Windigo's Return		$10	$16	$20	Douglas Wood		S&S

Couch   Greg

Year	Title	VG-	VG	VG+	Fine	Author	Award	Pub
1997	First Palm Trees		$10	$16	$20	James Berry		S&S
1999	Moon Ball		$10	$14	$18	Jane Yolen		S&S
1999	The Cello Of Mr. O		$10	$14	$18	Jane Cutler		Dutton
1999	Wild Child		$10	$14	$18	Lynn Plourde		S&S
2001	I Know The Moon		$8	$12	$16	Stephen Axel Anderson		Philo
2001	Sun Dance, Water Dance		$8	$12	$16	Jonathan London		Dutton
2001	Winter Waits		$8	$12	$16	Lynn Plourde		S&S
2002	Spring's Sprung		$8	$10	$14	Lynn Plourde		S&S
2003	Halloween		$8	$10	$14	Harry Behn		NSBooks
2003	Summer's Vacation		$8	$10	$14	Lynn Plourde		S&S

Cousins   Lucy

Year	Title	VG-	VG	VG+	Fine	Author	Award	Pub
1989	Portly's Hat		$18	$25	$35	Lucy Cousins		Dutton
1990	Maisy Goes Swimming		$12	$18	$25	Lucy Cousins		LBrown
1990	Maisy Goes To Bed		$12	$18	$25	Lucy Cousins		LBrown
1990	The Little Dog Laughed		$12	$18	$25	Lucy Cousins		Dutton
1991	Country Animals		$12	$18	$25	Lucy Cousins		Tambour
1991	Farm Animals		$12	$18	$25	Lucy Cousins		Tambour
1991	Garden Animals		$12	$18	$25	Lucy Cousins		Tambour
1991	Pet Animals		$12	$18	$25	Lucy Cousins		Tambour
1991	What Can Rabbit Hear?		$12	$18	$25	Lucy Cousins		Walker
1991	What Can Rabbit See?		$12	$18	$25	Lucy Cousins		Walker
1992	Maisy Goes To School		$12	$18	$25	Lucy Cousins		Candle
1992	Maisy Goes To The Playground		$12	$18	$25	Lucy Cousins		Candle
1993	Noah's Ark		$12	$16	$20	Lucy Cousins		Candle
1995	Maisy's ABC		$10	$16	$20	Lucy Cousins		Candle
1995	Maisy's Pop-Up Playhouse		$10	$16	$20	Bruce Reifel		Candle
1995	Za-Za's Baby Brother		$10	$16	$20	Lucy Cousins		Candle
1996	Humpty Dumpty & Other Nursery Rhymes		$10	$16	$20	Lucy Cousins		Dutton
1996	Jack And Jill		$10	$16	$20	Lucy Cousins		Dutton
1996	Katy Cat And Beaky Boo		$10	$16	$20	Lucy Cousins		Candle
1997	Count With Maisy		$10	$16	$20	Lucy Cousins		Candle
1997	Katy Cat And Beaky Boo's Play Set		$10	$16	$20	Lisa Boggiss		Candle
1997	Little Miss Muffet		$10	$16	$20	Lucy Cousins		Dutton
1997	Maisy's Colors		$10	$16	$20	Lucy Cousins		Candle
1997	Wee Willie Winkie & Other Nursery Rhymes		$10	$16	$20	Lucy Cousins		Dutton
1997	What Can Pinky Hear?		$10	$16	$20	Lucy Cousins		Candle
1997	What Can Pinky See?		$10	$16	$20	Lucy Cousins		Candle
1998	Happy Birthday, Maisy		$10	$14	$18	Lisa Boggiss		Candle
1998	Maisy At The Farm		$10	$14	$18	Lisa Boggiss		Candle
1999	Dress Maisy		$10	$14	$18	Lucy Cousins		Candle
1999	Maisy Dresses Up		$10	$14	$18	Lucy Cousins		Candle
1999	Maisy Makes Gingerbread		$10	$14	$18	Lucy Cousins		Candle
1999	Maisy's Bedtime		$10	$14	$18	Lucy Cousins		Candle
1999	Maisy's Day		$10	$14	$18	Lucy Cousins		Candle
1999	Maisy's Mix-And-Match Mousewear		$10	$14	$18	Lucy Cousins		Candle
1999	Maisy's Pool		$10	$14	$18	Lucy Cousins		Candle
1999	Where Is Maisy?		$10	$14	$18	Lucy Cousins		Candle
1999	Where Is Maisy's Panda?		$10	$14	$18	Lucy Cousins		Candle
2000	Maisy Drives The Bus		$8	$12	$16	Lucy Cousins		Candle
2000	Maisy Takes A Bath		$8	$12	$16	Lucy Cousins		Candle
2000	Merry Christmas Maisy		$8	$12	$16	Lucy Cousins		Candle
2001	Doctor Maisy		$8	$12	$16	Lucy Cousins		Candle
2001	Maisy At The Beach		$8	$12	$16	Lucy Cousins		Candle
2001	Maisy At The Fair		$8	$12	$16	Lucy Cousins		Candle
2001	Maisy Drives		$8	$12	$16	Lucy Cousins		Candle
2001	Maisy Goes Shopping		$8	$12	$16	Lucy Cousins		Candle
2001	Maisy Plays		$8	$12	$16	Lucy Cousins		Candle
2001	Maisy's Big Flap Book		$8	$12	$16	Lucy Cousins		Candle
2001	Maisy's Favorite Animals		$8	$12	$16	Lucy Cousins		Candle
2001	Maisy's Favorite Clothes		$8	$12	$16	Lucy Cousins		Candle
2001	Maisy's Favorite Things		$8	$12	$16	Lucy Cousins		Candle
2001	Maisy's Favorite Toys		$8	$12	$16	Lucy Cousins		Candle
2001	Maisy's Garden Sticker Book		$8	$12	$16	Lucy Cousins		Candle
2001	Maisy's Morning On The Farm		$8	$12	$16	Lucy Cousins		Candle

Cousins   Lucy

Year	Title	VG-	VG	VG+	Fine	Author	Award	Pub
2002	Jazzy In The Jungle		$8	$10	$14	Lucy Cousins		Candle
2002	Maisy Cleans Up		$8	$10	$14	Lucy Cousins		Candle
2002	Maisy Likes Dancing		$8	$10	$14	Lucy Cousins		Candle
2002	Maisy Likes Music		$8	$10	$14	Lucy Cousins		Candle
2002	Maisy Makes Lemonade		$8	$10	$14	Lucy Cousins		Candle
2002	Maisy's Fire Engine		$8	$10	$14	Lucy Cousins		Candle
2002	Maisy's Noisy Day		$8	$10	$14	Lucy Cousins		Candle
2002	Maisy's Seasons		$8	$10	$14	Lucy Cousins		Candle
2002	Maisy's Train		$8	$10	$14	Lucy Cousins		Candle
2002	What's That Squeak, Maisy?		$8	$10	$14	Lucy Cousins		Candle
2003	Go, Maisy, Go!		$8	$10	$14	Lucy Cousins		Candle
2003	Maisy Loves You		$8	$10	$14	Lucy Cousins		Candle
2003	Maisy's Best Friends		$8	$10	$14	Lucy Cousins		Candle
2003	Maisy's Easter Egg Hunt		$8	$10	$14	Lucy Cousins		Candle
2003	Maisy's Rainbow Dream		$8	$10	$14	Lucy Cousins		Candle
2003	Maisy's Snowy Christmas Eve		$8	$10	$14	Lucy Cousins		Candle
2003	What Are You Doing, Maisy?		$8	$10	$14	Lucy Cousins		Candle
2003	Where Are You Going, Maisy?		$8	$10	$14	Lucy Cousins		Candle
2004	How Will You Get There, Maisy?		$8	$10	$14	Lucy Cousins		Candle
2004	Is This Maisy's House?		$8	$10	$14	Lucy Cousins		Candle
2004	Maisy Goes Camping		$8	$10	$14	Lucy Cousins		Candle
2004	Maisy's Christmas Sticker Book		$8	$10	$14	Lucy Cousins		Candle
2004	Maisy's Halloween		$8	$10	$14	Lucy Cousins		Candle
2004	Maisy's Pirate Treasure Hunt		$8	$10	$14	Lucy Cousins		Candle
2004	Maisy's Twinkly, Crinkly Counting Book		$8	$10	$14	Lucy Cousins		Candle
2004	Smile, Maisy!		$8	$10	$14	Lucy Cousins		Candle
2005	Ha Ha, Maisy!		$6	$10	$12	Lucy Cousins		Candle
2005	With Love From Maisy		$6	$10	$12	Lucy Cousins		Candle

Cowles   Fleur

Year	Title	VG-	VG	VG+	Fine	Author	Award	Pub
1968	Tiger Flower	$40	$50	$70		Robert Vavra		Collins
1974	Lion And Blue		$30	$40	$60	Robert Vavra		Reynal
1977	Romany Free		$25	$40	$50	Robert Vavra		Morrow
1980	The Love Of Tiger Flower		$25	$35	$50	Robert Vavra		Morrow
1986	To Be A Unicorn		$20	$30	$40	Robert Vavra		Reynal

Craft   K.Y. (Kinuko)

Year	Title	VG-	VG	VG+	Fine	Author	Award	Pub
1973	Gingerbread Children		$40	$60	$90	Ilo Orleans		Follett
1975	Bear, Wolf, And Mouse		$30	$40	$60	Jan Wahl		Follett
1975	Come Play With Me		$30	$40	$60	Margaret Hillert		Follett
1977	Classics		$25	$40	$50	Beverly Reingold		P&Munk
1977	Mother Goose ABC		$25	$40	$50	Kinuko Craft		P&Munk
1978	The Cookie House		$25	$40	$50	Margaret Hillert		Follett
1978	What Is It?		$25	$40	$50	Margaret Hillert		Follett
1979	The Black Swan		$25	$40	$50	Paula Hogan		Rain
1979	The Elephant		$25	$40	$50	Paula Hogan		Rain
1979	The Oak Tree		$25	$40	$50	Paula Hogan		Rain
1979	The Wolf And The Seven Kids		$25	$40	$50	Jacob & Wilhelm Grimm		Troll
1980	Tales Of The Ugly Ogres		$25	$35	$50	Corinne Denan		Troll
1980	Treasure Island		$25	$35	$50	June Edwards		Rain
1980	Washington Irving's Rip Van Winkle		$25	$35	$50	Carol Beach York (adapted)		Troll
1984	Bailey's Window		$20	$30	$40	Anne Lindbergh		HBJ
1986	Journey To Japan		$20	$30	$40	Joan Knight		VK
1989	The Twelve Dancing Princesses		$18	$25	$35	Marianna Mayer		Morrow
1994	Baba Yaga And Vasilisa The Brave		$14	$20	$30	Marianna Mayer		Morrow
1996	Cupid And Psyche		$12	$18	$25	M. Charlotte Craft		Morrow
1997	Pegasus		$12	$18	$25	Marianna Mayer		Morrow
1999	King Midas And The Golden Touch		$12	$16	$20	Charlotte Craft		Morrow
2000	Cinderella		$10	$14	$18	Charles Perrault		SeaStar
2001	The Adventures Of Tom Thumb		$10	$14	$18	Marianna Mayer		SeaStar
2002	Sleeping Beauty		$8	$12	$16	Mahlon F. Craft (adapted)		SeaStar
2003	The Christmas Moon		$8	$12	$16	Mahlon F. Craft		SeaStar

Craig   Helen

Year	Title	VG-	VG	VG+	Fine	Author	Award	Pub
1970	Wishing Gold		$50	$70	$90	Robert Nye		Macmil
1972	Animal Castle		$40	$60	$90	Tanith Lee		FSG
1972	Princess Hynchatti & Some Other Surprises		$40	$60	$90	Tanith Lee		Macmil
1983	Angelina Ballerina		$40	$60	$90	Katharine Holabird		Potter
1984	Angelina And The Princess		$40	$60	$90	Katharine Holabird		Potter
1985	Angelina At The Fair		$40	$60	$80	Katharine Holabird		Potter
1985	Angelina's Christmas		$40	$60	$80	Katharine Holabird		Potter
1985	Jam: A True Story		$30	$40	$60	Margaret Mahy		AMP
1985	Susie & Alfred In The Knight, Princess, & Dragon		$30	$40	$60	Helen Craig		Knopf
1986	Angelina On Stage		$40	$60	$80	Helen Craig		Potter
1986	Susie And Alfred In A Welcome For Annie		$30	$40	$60	Helen Craig		Knopf
1986	This Is The Bear		$30	$40	$60	Sarah Hayes		Lippin
1987	Angelina And Alice		$40	$60	$80	Katharine Holabird		Potter
1987	The One And Only Robin Hood		$25	$40	$50	Nigel Gray		Joy
1987	The Yellow House		$25	$40	$50	Blake Morrison		HBJ
1988	Alexander And The Dragon		$25	$40	$50	Katharine Holabird		Potter
1988	Porcellus, The Flying Pig		$25	$40	$50	Judy Corbalis		Dial
1988	This Is The Bear And The Picnic Lunch		$25	$40	$50	Sarah Hayes		Joy
1989	Angelina's Birthday Surprise		$35	$50	$70	Katharine Holabird		Potter
1990	Alexander And The Magic Boat		$25	$35	$50	Katharine Holabird		Potter
1990	Mary, Mary		$25	$35	$50	Sarah Hayes		McEld
1990	The Pumpkin Man And The Crafty Creeper		$20	$30	$40	Margaret Mahy		LL&S
1991	Angelina's Baby Sister		$25	$40	$50	Katharine Holabird		Potter
1992	Angelina Ballerina		$14	$20	$25	Katharine Holabird		Potter
1992	Angelina Dances		$18	$25	$35	Katharine Holabird		Random
1992	Christmas With Angelina		$18	$25	$35	Katharine Holabird		Random
1992	Crumbling Castle		$18	$25	$35	Sarah Hayes		Candle
1992	The Town Mouse And The Country Mouse		$18	$25	$35	Helen Craig		Candle
1992	This Is The Bear And The Scary Night		$18	$25	$35	Sarah Hayes		Joy
1993	Angelina Ice Skates		$18	$25	$35	Katharine Holabird		Potter
1993	I See The Moon, And The Moon Sees Me		$18	$25	$35	Helen Craig		HCollins
1994	Susie And Alfred In A Busy Day In Town		$16	$25	$30	Helen Craig		Candle
1995	Charlie And Tyler At The Seashore		$16	$25	$30	Helen Craig		Candle
1995	This Is The Bear And The Bad Little Girl		$16	$25	$30	Sarah Hayes		Candle
1996	One Windy Wednesday		$14	$20	$30	Phyllis Root		Candle
1998	The Bunny Who Found Easter		$12	$18	$25	Charlotte Zolotow		HM
1998	Turnover Tuesday		$12	$18	$25	Phyllis Root		Candle
1999	Gander's Pond		$12	$18	$25	Joyce Dunbar		Candle
1999	Panda's New Toy		$12	$18	$25	Joyce Dunbar		Candle
1999	The Bowl Of Fruit		$12	$18	$25	Joyce Dunbar		Candle
1999	The Random House Book Of Nursery Stories		$12	$18	$25	Helen Craig		Random
1999	The Secret Friend		$12	$18	$25	Joyce Dunbar		Candle
2000	Foggy Friday		$10	$16	$20	Phyllis Root		Candle
2000	Meow Monday		$10	$16	$20	Phyllis Root		Candle
2001	Angelina's Birthday		$10	$16	$20	Katharine Holabird		Pleasnt
2001	Soggy Saturday		$10	$16	$20	Phyllis Root		Candle
2002	Angelina And Henry		$10	$14	$18	Katharine Holabird		Pleasnt
2002	Angelina And The Rag Doll		$10	$14	$18	Katharine Holabird		Pleasnt
2002	Rosy's Visitors		$10	$14	$18	Judy Hindley		Candle

Crews   Donald

Year	Title	VG-	VG	VG+	Fine	Author	Award	Pub
1967	We Read: A To Z	$60	$80	$100		Donald Crews		H&Row
1970	ABC Science Experiments		$30	$50	$60	Harry Milgrom		Crowell
1971	Fractions Are Parts Of Things		$30	$50	$60	J Richard Dennis		Crowell
1972	ABC Of Ecology		$30	$50	$60	Harry Milgrom		Macmil
1973	Eclipse; Darkness In Daytime		$30	$50	$60	Franklyn M. Branley		Crowell
1978	Freight Train		$80	$120	$160	Donald Crews	CH	Green
1978	Rain		$25	$40	$50	Robert Kalan		Green
1979	Blue Sea		$25	$40	$50	Robert Kalan		Green
1979	The Talking Stone		$25	$40	$50	Dorothy De Wit		Green
1980	Truck		$50	$70	$100	Donald Crews	CH	Green
1981	Light		$25	$35	$50	Donald Crews		Green
1982	Carousel		$25	$35	$50	Donald Crews		Green
1982	Harbor		$25	$35	$50	Donald Crews		Green
1983	Parade		$25	$35	$50	Donald Crews		Green

Crews   Donald

Year	Title	VG-	VG	VG+	Fine	Author	Award	Pub
1984	School Bus		$20	$30	$40	Donald Crews		Green
1985	Bicycle Race		$20	$30	$40	Donald Crews		Green
1986	Flying		$20	$30	$40	Donald Crews		Green
1986	Ten Black Dots		$20	$30	$40	Donald Crews		Green
1988	How Many Snails?		$18	$25	$35	Paul Giganti		Green
1991	Bigmama's		$16	$25	$30	Donald Crews		Green
1992	Each Orange Had 8 Slices		$16	$25	$30	Paul Giganti		Green
1992	Shortcut		$16	$25	$30	Donald Crews		Green
1993	When This Box Is Full		$16	$25	$30	Patricia Lillie		Green
1995	Sail Away		$14	$20	$25	Donald Crews		Green
1995	Tomorrow's Alphabet		$14	$20	$25	George Shannon		Green
1996	More Than One		$12	$18	$25	Miriam Schlein		Green
1998	Night At The Fair		$12	$16	$20	Donald Crews		Green
1999	Cloudy Day/Sunny Day		$12	$16	$20	Donald Crews		GLR
2000	This Is The Sunflower		$10	$14	$18	Lola M. Schaefer		Green
2001	Inside Freight Train		$10	$14	$18	Donald Crews		HFest

Cruz   Ray

Year	Title	VG-	VG	VG+	Fine	Author	Award	Pub
1972	Alexander & The Terrible, Horrible, Very Bad Day		$18	$25	$35	Judith Viorst		Athenm
1973	Winter Hut		$18	$25	$35	Cynthia Johnson		CM&G
1978	Alexander, Who Used To Be Rich Last Sunday		$16	$25	$30	Judith Viorst		Athenm

Cuffari   Richard

Year	Title	VG-	VG	VG+	Fine	Author	Award	Pub
1967	The Wind In The Willows	$40	$50	$70		Kenneth Grahame		G&D
1969	Plants And Animals In The Air	$25	$35	$50		E. John De Waard		DoubleD
1969	Winter-Telling Stories	$25	$35	$50		Alice Lee Marriott		Crowell
1970	Cargo Ships		$25	$35	$50	Herbert Spencer Zim		Morrow
1970	Gregor Mendel		$25	$35	$50	Carla Greene		Dial
1970	James Madison		$25	$35	$50	Patricia Miles Martin		Putnam
1970	Old Ben		$25	$35	$50	Jesse Stuart		McHill
1970	The Winner		$25	$35	$50	Gene Smith		Cowles
1970	Who Will Wash The River?		$25	$35	$50	Wallace Orlowsky		CM
1971	Before The Dinosaurs		$25	$35	$50	Carla Greene		Bobbs
1971	Hot And Cold And In Between		$25	$35	$50	Robert Froman		G&D
1971	Jackie Robinson		$25	$35	$50	Kenneth Rudeen		Crowell
1971	Songs And Stories Of Afro-Americans		$25	$35	$50	Paul Glass		G&D
1971	Who Will Clean The Air?		$25	$35	$50	Wallace Orlowsky		CM&G
1972	Apollo Moon Rocks		$25	$35	$50	Marcus Langseth		CM&G
1972	Corvus The Crow		$25	$35	$50	Franklin Russell		4Winds
1972	Datra The Muskrat		$25	$35	$50	Franklin Russell		4Winds
1972	I Can Predict The Future		$25	$35	$50	Joseph Claro		LL&S
1972	Lotor The Raccoon		$25	$35	$50	Franklin Russell		4Winds
1972	Magnify And Find Out Why		$25	$35	$50	Julius Schwartz		McHill
1972	Mr. Charley's Chopsticks		$25	$35	$50	Doris Portwood Evans		CM&G
1972	The Carpenter Bee		$25	$35	$50	Ross E. Hutchins		AW
1972	The Magic Moth		$25	$35	$50	Virginia Lee		Seabury
1972	Water For Dinosaurs And You		$25	$35	$50	Roma Gans		Crowell
1973	Dancers On The Beach		$25	$35	$50	Edward R. Ricciuti		Crowell
1973	Little Yellow Fur		$25	$35	$50	Wilma Pitchford Hays		CM&G
1973	My Dad Lives In A Downtown Hotel		$25	$35	$50	Peggy Mann		DoubleD
1973	Ride The Crooked Wind		$25	$35	$50	Dale Fife		CM&G
1973	Small-Boy Chuku		$25	$35	$50	Alice Wellman		HM
1973	The Endless Pavement		$25	$35	$50	Jacqueline Jackson		Seabury
1974	All-Of-A-Sudden Susan		$20	$30	$40	Elizabeth Coatsworth		Macmil
1974	Grand Papa And Ellen Aroon		$20	$30	$40	F. N. Monjo		HR&W
1974	Standing In The Magic		$20	$30	$40	Gunilla Brodde Norris		Dutton
1974	The Hunters		$20	$30	$40	Daniel Jacobson		FWatts
1975	Mary's Monster		$20	$30	$40	Ruth Van Ness Blair		CM&G
1975	Mightiest Of Mortals, Heracles		$20	$30	$40	Doris Gates		Viking
1975	Slumps, Grunts, And Snickerdoodles		$20	$30	$40	Lila Perl		Seabury
1975	The Blazing Hills		$20	$30	$40	Sibyl Hancock		Putnam
1975	The Fishermen		$20	$30	$40	Daniel Jacobson		FWatts
1975	Time After Time		$20	$30	$40	Melvin Berger		CM&G
1976	How Did Numbers Begin?		$20	$30	$40	Mindel & Harry Sitomer		Crowell

Cuffari   Richard

Year	Title	VG-	VG	VG+	Fine	Author	Award	Pub
1976	My Plant		$20	$30	$40	Herbert H. Wong		AW
1976	No Boys Allowed		$20	$30	$40	Susan Terris		DoubleD
1976	The Ups And Downs Of Marvin		$20	$30	$40	Barbara Shook Hazen		Athenm
1976	Two That Were Tough		$20	$30	$40	Robert Burch		Viking
1976	Zenas And The Shaving Mill		$20	$30	$40	F. N. Monjo		CM&G
1977	Dollhouse Magic		$20	$30	$40	K. Roche		Dial
1977	Ecology		$20	$30	$40	John Hoke		FWatts
1977	The Gatherers		$20	$30	$40	Daniel Jacobson		FWatts
1977	The Rain Forest		$20	$30	$40	Wilda S. Ross		CM&G
1977	The Shad Are Running		$20	$30	$40	Judith St. George		Putnam
1978	Caves And Life		$20	$30	$40	Herbert Spencer Zim		Morrow
1978	Monsters From Outer Space?		$20	$30	$40	William Wise		Putnam
1978	The Dangers Of Noise		$20	$30	$40	Lucy Kavaler		Crowell
1978	The Wonderful Box		$20	$30	$40	Mildred Ames		Dutton
1978	Zero Is Not Nothing		$20	$30	$40	Mindel & Harry Sitomer		Crowell
1979	Balder And The Mistletoe		$18	$25	$35	Edna Barth		Seabury
1979	Family Secrets		$18	$25	$35	Susan Richards Shreve		Knopf

Cumings   Art

Year	Title	VG-	VG	VG+	Fine	Author	Award	Pub
1972	Percy The Parrot Passes The Puck		$30	$50	$60	Wayne Carley		Garrard
1972	Unlucky Day At Camp How-Ja-Do		$25	$35	$50	Wayne Carley		Garrard
1974	Percy The Parrot Yelled Quiet!		$20	$30	$40	Wayne Carley		Garrard
1977	Please Try To Remember The First Of Octember!		$120	$180	$240	Theo LeSieg (pseud/Seuss)		BB
1978	A Good Fish Dinner		$20	$30	$40	Barbara K. Walker		PMagP
1978	Charlie's Pets		$20	$30	$40	Kathryn F. Ernst		Crown
1979	Septimus Bean And His Amazing Machine		$18	$25	$35	Janet Quin-Harkin		PMagP
1980	Magic Growing Powder		$18	$25	$35	Janet Quin-Harkin		PMagP
1980	The Cat's Pajamas		$18	$25	$35	Ida Chittum		PMagP
1981	There's A Monster Eating My House		$18	$25	$35	Art Cumings		PMagP
1982	Ohm On The Range		$16	$25	$30	Charles Keller		P-Hall
1982	One-Minute Bedtime Stories		$16	$25	$30	Shari Lewis		DoubleD
1985	Astronuts		$16	$25	$30	Charles Keller		P-Hall
1985	Ecosystems And Food Chains		$16	$25	$30	Francene Sabin		Troll
1985	Mountains		$16	$25	$30	Keith Brandt		Troll

Cushman   Doug

Year	Title	VG-	VG	VG+	Fine	Author	Award	Pub
1979	Haunted Houses On Halloween		$25	$40	$50	Lillie Patterson		Garrard
1979	Little Brown Bear		$25	$40	$50	Elizabeth Norine Upham		P&Munk
1979	Monster For A Day		$25	$40	$50	F. Kaff		GingH
1980	Giants		$25	$35	$50	Doug Cushman		P&Munk
1980	Hickory Dickory Dock		$18	$25	$35	Leonard Kessler		Garrard
1980	The Silly Mother Hubbard		$18	$25	$35	Leonard Kessler		Garrard
1981	Trolls		$25	$35	$50	Doug Cushman		P&Munk
1982	Not Counting Monsters		$16	$25	$30	H. L. Ross		P&Munk
1982	Once Upon A Pig		$25	$35	$50	Doug Cushman		P&Munk
1983	Nasty Kyle The Crocodile		$16	$25	$30	Doug Cushman		G&D
1983	The Pudgy Fingers Counting Book		$16	$25	$30	Doug Cushman		G&D
1985	Chatty Chipmunk's Nutty Day		$16	$25	$30	Suzanne Gruber		Troll
1985	Tillie And Mert		$16	$25	$30	Ida Luttrell		H&Row
1986	Benny's Bad Day		$14	$20	$30	Michael Pellowski		Troll
1986	Mickey Takes A Bow		$14	$20	$30	Doug Cushman		LBrown
1987	Aunt Eater Loves A Mystery		$14	$20	$30	Doug Cushman		H&Row
1987	The Missing Mystery		$14	$20	$30	Doug Cushman		Check
1987	The Secret Of The Nile		$14	$20	$30	Jack Long		Check
1987	The Sunken Treasure		$14	$20	$30	Jack Long		Check
1987	The Vanishing Professor		$14	$20	$30	Jack Long		Check
1988	Bedtime Story		$14	$20	$30	Rose Greydanus		Troll
1988	Porcupine's Pajama Party		$14	$20	$30	Terry Webb Harshman		H&Row
1988	The Jolly Monsters		$14	$20	$30	Sharon Gordon		Troll
1988	The Monsters' Counting Book		$14	$20	$30	C. S. White		P&Munk
1988	Uncle Foster's Hat Tree		$14	$20	$30	Doug Cushman		Dutton
1989	A Shot For Baby Bear		$14	$20	$25	Dorothy Corey		AWhit
1989	Frida's Office Day		$14	$20	$25	Thomas Lewis		H&Row
1989	Itsy-Bitsy Giant		$14	$20	$25	Melanie Martin		Troll

Cushman   Doug

Year	Title	VG-	VG	VG+	Fine	Author	Award	Pub
1989	Mixed-Up Magic		$14	$20	$25	Michael Pellowski		Troll
1990	Aunt Morbelia And The Screaming Skulls		$12	$18	$25	Joan Davenport Carris		LBrown
1990	Camp Big Paw		$12	$18	$25	Doug Cushman		H&Row
1990	Possum Stew		$12	$18	$25	Doug Cushman		Dutton
1990	The Elves And The Shoemaker		$12	$18	$25	Marcia Leonard		Silver
1990	The Fourth Little Pig		$12	$18	$25	Teresa Noel Celsi		Rain
1990	The Three Little Pigs		$12	$18	$25	Marcia Leonard		Silver
1991	1 + 1 Take Away Two!		$12	$18	$25	Michael Berenstain		Western
1991	An Alligator Named Alligator		$12	$18	$25	Lois G. Grambling		Barrn
1992	Aunt Eater's Mystery Vacation		$12	$18	$25	Doug Cushman		HCollins
1992	Feed Me!		$12	$18	$25	William H. Hooks		Bantam
1992	How Do You Make A Bubble?		$12	$18	$25	William H. Hooks		Bantam
1992	The Early Bird		$12	$18	$25	Gary Richmond		Word
1993	Bicycle Bear		$12	$16	$20	Michaela Muntean		PMagP
1993	Crazy Gibberish		$12	$16	$20	Naomi Baltuck		Linnet
1993	The ABC Mystery		$12	$16	$20	Doug Cushman		HCollins
1994	A Good Sport		$12	$16	$20	Patricia Lakin		RainSV
1994	A True Partnership		$12	$16	$20	Patricia Lakin		RainSV
1994	Mouse & Mole And The Christmas Walk		$12	$16	$20	Doug Cushman		SAB
1994	Mouse & Mole And The Year-Round Garden		$12	$16	$20	Doug Cushman		SAB
1994	The Witch Who Couldn't Fly		$12	$16	$20	Mary Packard		Troll
1995	A Summer Job		$10	$16	$20	Patricia Lakin		RainSV
1995	Aunt Eater's Mystery Christmas		$10	$16	$20	Doug Cushman		HCollins
1995	Aware And Alert		$10	$16	$20	Patricia Lakin		RainSV
1995	Bicycle Bear Rides Again		$10	$16	$20	Michaela Muntean		PMagP
1995	Get Ready To Read!		$10	$16	$20	Patricia Lakin		RainSV
1995	Halloween Mice!		$10	$16	$20	Bethany Roberts		Clarion
1995	Information, Please		$10	$16	$20	Patricia Lakin		RainSV
1995	Mouse & Mole And The All-Weather Train Ride		$10	$16	$20	Doug Cushman		SAB
1995	Nat The Crab		$10	$16	$20	Alice Cary		OCP
1995	Red Letter Day		$10	$16	$20	Patricia Lakin		RainSV
1995	Signs Of Protest		$10	$16	$20	Patricia Lakin		RainSV
1995	Teddy Bear For Sale		$10	$16	$20	Gail Herman		Scholas
1995	The Mystery Illness		$10	$16	$20	Patricia Lakin		RainSV
1995	Trash And Treasure		$10	$16	$20	Patricia Lakin		RainSV
1995	Up A Tree		$10	$16	$20	Patricia Lakin		RainSV
1995	Where There's Smoke		$10	$16	$20	Patricia Lakin		RainSV
1996	Frogs		$10	$16	$20	Robin Dexter		Troll
1996	The Mystery Of King Karfu		$10	$16	$20	David Cushman		HCollins
1997	Halloween Pigs		$10	$16	$20	Rita Balducci		WStop
1997	The Turkey Saves The Day		$10	$16	$20	Shelagh Canning		Troll
1997	The Whiz Kids Plugged In		$10	$16	$20	Susan Goldman Rubin		Scholas
1997	The Wiz Kids Take Off!		$10	$16	$20	Susan Goldman Rubin		Scholas
1997	Valentine Mice!		$10	$16	$20	Bethany Roberts		Clarion
1998	Aunt Eater's Mystery Halloween		$10	$14	$18	Doug Cushman		HCollins
1999	The Mystery Of The Monkey's Maze		$10	$14	$18	Doug Cushman		HCollins
2000	Christmas Mice!		$8	$12	$16	Bethany Roberts		Clarion
2000	Inspector Hopper		$8	$12	$16	Doug Cushman		HCollins
2000	What Dads Can't Do		$8	$12	$16	Douglas Wood		S&S
2001	Crocodile And Hen		$8	$12	$16	Joan M. Lexau		HCollins
2001	Let's Try It Out In The Air		$8	$12	$16	S. Simon & N. Fauteax		S&S
2001	Let's Try It Out In The Water		$8	$12	$16	S. Simon & N. Fauteax		S&S
2001	Little Raccoon		$8	$12	$16	Lilian Moore		Holt
2001	Thanksgiving Mice!		$8	$12	$16	Bethany Roberts		Clarion
2001	What Moms Can't Do		$8	$12	$16	Douglas Wood		S&S
2002	Animal Train		$8	$10	$14	Jane Yolen		LSimon
2002	Birthday Mice!		$8	$10	$14	Bethany Roberts		Clarion
2002	But Mom, Everybody Else Does		$8	$10	$14	Kay Winters		Dutton
2002	Let's Try It Out On The Playground		$8	$10	$14	S. Simon & N. Fauteax		S&S
2002	Let's Try It Out With Cold Hands And Warm Feet		$8	$10	$14	S. Simon & N. Fauteax		S&S
2002	What Teachers Can't Do		$8	$10	$14	Douglas Wood		S&S
2003	Albert's Impossible Toothache		$8	$10	$14	Barbara Williams		Candle
2003	Dracula And Frankenstein Are Friends		$8	$10	$14	Katherine Brown Tegen		HCollins
2003	Easter Mice!		$8	$10	$14	Bethany Roberts		Clarion
2003	Inspector Hopper's Mystery Year		$8	$10	$14	Doug Cushman		HCollins
2003	Let's Try It Out In The Kitchen		$8	$10	$14	S. Simon & N. Fauteax		S&S
2003	Let's Try It Out With Towers And Bridges		$8	$10	$14	S. Simon & N. Fauteax		S&S

Cushman   Doug

Year	Title	VG-	VG	VG+	Fine	Author	Award	Pub
2003	What Did They See?		$8	$10	$14	John Schindel		Holt
2003	What Santa Can't Do		$8	$10	$14	Douglas Wood		S&S
2004	1, 2, 3, Counting Rhymes		$8	$10	$14	Matt Mitter		GarethS
2004	ABC		$8	$10	$14	Matt Mitter		GarethS
2004	Fourth Of July Mice!		$8	$10	$14	Bethany Roberts		Clarion
2004	Mystery At The Club Sandwich		$8	$10	$14	Doug Cushman		Clarion
2004	Never Ever Shout In A Zoo		$8	$10	$14	Karma Wilson		LBrown
2004	Space Cat		$8	$10	$14	Doug Cushman		HCollins
2004	What Time Is It, Mr. Crocodile?		$8	$10	$14	Judy Sierra		GB

Dabcovich   Lydia

Year	Title	VG-	VG	VG+	Fine	Author	Award	Pub
1972	A Trick Of Light		$30	$50	$60	Barbara Corcoran		Athenm
1972	Trail Boss In Pigtails		$25	$35	$50	Marjorie Stover		Athenm
1976	Nobody Comes To Dinner		$20	$30	$40	Frank Emerson Andrews		LBrown
1978	There Once Was A Woman Who Married A Man		$20	$30	$40	Norma Farber		AW
1980	Follow The River		$18	$25	$35	Lydia Dabcovich		Dutton
1982	Sleepy Bear		$16	$25	$30	Lydia Dabcovich		Dutton
1982	The Boy Who Would Be A Hero		$16	$25	$30	Marjorie Lewis		CM&G
1983	The Animal Hedge		$16	$25	$30	Paul Fleischman		Dutton
1984	Hurry Home, Grandma!		$16	$25	$30	Arielle North Olson		Dutton
1985	Mrs. Huggins And Her Hen Hannah		$16	$25	$30	Lydia Dabcovich		Dutton
1986	Up North In Winter		$14	$20	$30	Deborah Hartley		Dutton
1988	Busy Beavers		$14	$20	$30	Lydia Dabcovich		Dutton
1989	William And Grandpa		$14	$20	$25	Alice Schertle		LL&S
1990	Ducks Fly		$12	$18	$25	Lydia Dabcovich		Dutton
1991	The Night Ones		$12	$18	$25	Patricia Grossman		HBJ
1992	The Keys To My Kingdom		$12	$18	$25	Lydia Dabcovich		LL&S
1993	Feathers		$12	$16	$20	Ruth Gordon		Macmil
1995	Maisie		$10	$16	$20	Alice Schertle		LL&S
1996	The Polar Bear Son		$10	$16	$20	Lydia Dabcovich		Clarion
1998	Annushka's Voyage		$10	$14	$18	Edith Tarbescu		Clarion
2003	The Ghost On The Hearth		$8	$10	$14	Susan Milord		VFC

Daily   Don

Year	Title	VG-	VG	VG+	Fine	Author	Award	Pub
1993	The Wind In The Willows		$16	$25	$30	G.C. Barrett (adapted)		Courage
1994	The Jungle Book		$12	$16	$20	G.C. Barrett (adapted)		Courage
1995	Brer Rabbit		$10	$16	$20	David Borgenicht		Courage
1996	The Nutcracker		$10	$16	$20	Daniel Walden (adapted)		Courage
1997	Velveteen Rabbit		$10	$16	$20	Margery Williams		Courage
1998	The Twelve Days Of Christmas Cats		$10	$14	$18	Don Daily		Courage
1999	Aesop's Fables		$10	$14	$18	Don Daily (adapted)		Courage
2000	Callie Ann And Mistah Bear		$8	$12	$16	Robert D. San Souci		Dial
2000	The Twelve Days Of Christmas		$8	$12	$16	Don Daily (adapted)		Courage
2001	Grimm's Fairy Tales		$8	$12	$16	Danielle McCole (adapted)		Courage
2001	The Wind In The Willows		$8	$12	$16	Kenneth Grahame		Courage

Dale   Penny

Year	Title	VG-	VG	VG+	Fine	Author	Award	Pub
1986	The Stopwatch		$20	$30	$40	David Lloyd		H&Row
1987	Bet You Can't		$14	$20	$30	Penny Dale		Lippin
1989	Once There Were Giants		$14	$20	$25	Martin Waddell		DelaP
1991	The Elephant Tree		$12	$18	$25	Penny Dale		Putnam
1992	All About Alice		$12	$18	$25	Penny Dale		Candle
1992	Wake Up, Mr. B.!		$12	$18	$25	Penny Dale		Candle
1994	Ten Out Of Bed		$12	$16	$20	Penny Dale		Candle
1995	Daisy Rabbit's Tree House		$10	$16	$20	Penny Dale		Candle
1995	The Candlewick Book Of Bedtime Stories		$10	$16	$20	Penny Dale		Candle
1995	The Mushroom Hunt		$10	$16	$20	Simon Frazier		Candle
1995	When The Teddy Bears Came		$10	$16	$20	Martin Waddell		Candle
1997	Big Brother, Little Brother		$10	$16	$20	Penny Dale		Candle
1998	Ten Play Hide-And-Seek		$10	$14	$18	Penny Dale		Candle
1999	My Shadow		$10	$14	$18	Robert Louis Stevenson		Candle
1999	Rosie's Babies		$10	$14	$18	Martin Waddell		Candle

Dale   Penny

Year	Title	VG-	VG	VG+	Fine	Author	Award	Pub
2000	Night Night, Cuddly Bear		$8	$12	$16	Martin Waddell		Candle
2001	Ten In The Bed		$8	$12	$16	Penny Dale		Candle
2002	The Jamie And Angus Stories		$8	$10	$14	Anne Fine		Candle
2003	Princess, Princess		$8	$10	$14	Penny Dale		Candle

Dalton   Anne

Year	Title	VG-	VG	VG+	Fine	Author	Award	Pub
1977	The Shadow Of The Hawk		$20	$30	$40	James Reeves (retold)		Seabury
1982	The Blue Rose		$14	$20	$25	Maurice Baring		K&W
1985	Prince Starr		$12	$18	$25	Anne Dalton		K&W
1986	The King Of Kennelwick Castle		$12	$16	$20	Colin West		Lippin
1988	The King's Toothache		$12	$16	$20	Colin West		Lippin
1992	This Is The Way		$10	$16	$20	Anne Dalton		Scholas

Daly   Niki

Year	Title	VG-	VG	VG+	Fine	Author	Award	Pub
1978	The Little Girl Who Lived Down The Road		$20	$30	$40	Niki Daly		Collins
1979	Vim, The Rag Mouse		$14	$20	$30	Niki Daly		Athenm
1982	Joseph's Other Red Sock		$14	$20	$25	Niki Daly		Athenm
1985	Ben's Gingerbread Man		$12	$18	$25	Niki Daly		Viking
1985	Monsters Are Like That		$12	$18	$25	Niki Daly		VK
1985	Teddy's Ear		$12	$18	$25	Niki Daly		Viking
1986	Just Like Archie		$12	$16	$20	Niki Daly		VK
1986	Look At Me!		$12	$16	$20	Niki Daly		VK
1986	Not So Fast, Songololo		$12	$16	$20	Niki Daly		Athenm
1986	Thank You Henrietta		$12	$16	$20	Niki Daly		VK
1989	I Want To See The Moon		$12	$16	$20	Louis Baum		Over
1989	The Day Of The Rainbow		$12	$16	$20	Ruth Craft		VK
1990	Ashraf Of Africa		$10	$16	$20	Ingrid Mennen		Songo
1991	Charlie's House		$10	$16	$20	Reviva Schermbrucker		Viking
1991	Mama, Papa, And Baby Joe		$10	$16	$20	Niki Daly		Viking
1992	Papa Lucky's Shadow		$10	$16	$20	Niki Daly		McEld
1992	Somewhere In Africa		$10	$16	$20	Ingrid Mennen		Dutton
1993	All The Magic In The World		$10	$16	$20	Wendy Hartmann		Dutton
1993	Mary Malloy And The Baby Who Wouldn't Sleep		$10	$16	$20	Niki Daly		Golden
1994	One Round Moon And A Star For Me		$10	$14	$18	Ingrid Mennen		Orchard
1995	My Dad		$10	$14	$18	Niki Daly		McEld
1995	Red Light, Green Light		$10	$14	$18	Cari Best		Orchard
1995	The Herding Of The Snail		$10	$14	$18	Gus Ferguson		Firfield
1995	Why The Sun & Moon Live In The Sky		$10	$14	$18	Niki Daly		LL&S
1996	The Dancer		$8	$12	$16	Nola Turkington		H&R
1997	The Dinosaurs Are Back & It's All Your Fault, Edward!		$8	$12	$16	Wendy Hartmann		McEld
1998	Bravo, Zan Angelo!		$8	$12	$16	Niki Daly		FSG
1999	Jamela's Dress		$8	$12	$16	Niki Daly		FSG
1999	The Berry Basket		$8	$12	$16	Dinah M. Mbanze		Kwela
1999	The Boy On The Beach		$8	$12	$16	Niki Daly		McEld
1999	The Magic Pot		$8	$12	$16	Dinah M. Mbanze		Kwela
2000	Fly, Eagle, Fly!		$8	$10	$14	Christopher Gregorowski		McEld
2001	Daddy Island		$8	$10	$14	Philip Wells		BF
2001	What's Cooking, Jamela?		$8	$10	$14	Niki Daly		FSG
2002	Old Bob's Brown Bear		$8	$10	$14	Niki Daly		FSG
2003	Once Upon A Time		$8	$10	$14	Niki Daly		FSG
2003	The Squeaky, Creaky Bed		$8	$10	$14	Pat Thomson		Random
2004	The Greatest Skating Race		$6	$10	$12	Louise Borden		McEld
2004	Where's Jamela?		$6	$10	$12	Niki Daly		FSG

Daugherty   James Henry

Year	Title	VG-	VG	VG+	Fine	Author	Award	Pub
1926	Daniel Boone: Wilderness Scout	$220	$280	$360		Stewart Edward White		DP
1927	... The Story Of Bread	$220	$280	$360		Elizabeth Watson		H&B
1927	Kris And Kristina	$220	$280	$360		Marie Bruce		DoubleD
1927	The Story Of Milk And How It Came About	$220	$280	$360		Elizabeth Watson		H&B
1928	Abe Lincoln Grows Up	$90	$120	$160		Carl Sandburg		HBrace
1928	Irene Of Tundra Towers	$90	$120	$160		Elizabeth Burrows		DD
1928	The Blacksmith And The Blackbirds	$200	$280	$340		Edith Rickert		DD

Daugherty — James Henry

Year	Title	VG-	VG	VG+	Fine	Author	Award	Pub
1928	The Conquest Of Montezuma's Empire	$90	$120	$160		Andrew Lang		Longman
1928	The Story Of Textiles	$200	$280	$340		Elizabeth Watson		H&B
1928	Tuftoo The Clown	$90	$120	$160		Howard Roger Garis		DApple
1928	Wulnoth The Wanderer	$90	$120	$160		Herbert Escott Inman		Longman
1929	Uncle Toms Cabin	$90	$120	$160		Harriet Beecher Stowe		McCann
1930	Early Moon	$90	$120	$160		Carl Sandburg		HBrace
1930	John Brown's Body	$90	$120	$160		Stephen Vincent Benét		DD
1930	Judy Of The Whale Gates	$200	$280	$340		Elizabeth Burrows		DoubleD
1930	The Adventures Of Johnny Appleseed	$140	$180	$220		Henry Chapin		CM
1930	The Bold Dragoon & Other Ghostly Tales	$90	$120	$160		Washington Irving		Knopf
1931	Sir Nigel	$70	$100	$120		Arthur Conan Doyle		DoubleD
1932	The Railroad To Freedom	$70	$100	$120		Hildegarde Hoyt Swift		HBrace
1936	All Things New	$70	$100	$120		Sonia M. Daugherty		TNelson
1936	Their Weight In Wildcats	$70	$100	$120		James H. Daugherty		HBrace
1937	Girls Of Glen Hazard	$70	$90	$120		Maristan Chapman		DApple
1937	Green Gravel	$70	$90	$120		Dora Aydelotte		DApple
1938	Andy And The Lion	$220	$280	$360		James H. Daugherty	CH	Viking
1939	Daniel Boone	$380	$520	$640		James H. Daugherty	NM	Viking
1940	Call Of The Mountain	$70	$90	$120		Cornelia Meigs		LBrown
1940	Morgan's Fourth Son	$70	$90	$120		Margaret Isabel Ross		H&B
1940	Vanka's Donkey	$140	$200	$240		Sonia M. Daugherty		FStokes
1940	Wings Of Glory	$70	$90	$120		Sonia M. Daugherty		Oxford
1941	Barnaby Rudge	$70	$90	$120		Charles Dickens		THP
1941	Poor Richard	$140	$180	$240		James H. Daugherty		Viking
1944	An Outline Of Government In Connecticut	$140	$180	$220		James H. Daugherty		L&B
1944	Yankee Thunder	$60	$80	$100		Irwin Shapiro		Messner
1945	John Henry And The Double Jointed Steam-Drill	$140	$180	$220		Irwin Shapiro		Messner
1947	Lincoln's Gettysburg Address	$120	$160	$220		James H. Daugherty		AWhit
1948	Joe Magarac And His U.S.A. Citizen Papers	$120	$160	$220		Irwin Shapiro		Messner
1948	The Wild, Wild West	$120	$160	$220		James H. Daugherty		EMHale
1950	Better Known As Johnny Appleseed	$60	$80	$100		Mabel Leigh Hunt		Lippin
1950	The Landing Of The Pilgrims	$60	$80	$100		James H. Daugherty		Random
1951	A Long Way To Frisco	$50	$70	$90		Alfred Powers		LBrown
1951	Ten Brave Men	$50	$70	$90		Sonia M. Daugherty		Lippin
1952	Trappers And Traders Of The Far West	$50	$70	$90		James H. Daugherty		Random
1953	Marcus And Narcissa Whitman	$50	$70	$90		James H. Daugherty		Viking
1953	Ten Brave Women	$50	$70	$90		Sonia M. Daugherty		Lippin
1954	The Loudest Noise In The World	$120	$160	$200		Benjamin Elkin		Viking
1955	The Rainbow Book Of American History	$50	$70	$90		Earl Schenck Miers		World
1956	Gillespie And The Guards	$160	$220	$280		Benjamin Elkin	CH	Viking
1956	Out Of The Wilderness	$50	$70	$90		Virginia L. Eifert		DoddM
1956	The Magna Charta	$50	$70	$90		James H. Daugherty		Random
1957	The Last Of The Mohicans	$50	$70	$90		James Fenimore Cooper		World
1961	A Promise To Our Country	$100	$120	$160		James Calvert		Whittle
1962	The Three Musketeers	$50	$60	$80		Alexandre Dumas		Macmil
1967	Henry David Thoreau	$80	$120	$140		Henry David Thoreau		Viking
1971	The Sound Of Trumpets		$70	$100	$140	Ralph Waldo Emerson		Viking

d'Aulaire — Ingri & Edgar Parin

Year	Title	VG-	VG	VG+	Fine	Author	Award	Pub
1931	The Magic Rug	$240	$320	$400		Ingri & Edgar Parin d'Aulaire		DD
1933	Ola And Blakken	$220	$280	$360		Ingri & Edgar Parin d'Aulaire		DD
1933	The Conquest Of The Atlantic	$160	$200	$260		Ingri & Edgar Parin d'Aulaire		Viking
1934	The Lord's Prayer	$160	$200	$260		Ingri & Edgar Parin d'Aulaire		Viking
1935	Children Of The Northlights	$160	$200	$260		Ingri & Edgar Parin d'Aulaire		Viking
1936	George Washington	$340	$460	$580		Ingri & Edgar Parin d'Aulaire		DoubleD
1939	Abraham Lincoln	$960	$1,200	$1,600		Ingri & Edgar Parin d'Aulaire	CM	DoubleD
1939	Ola	$140	$200	$240		Ingri & Edgar Parin d'Aulaire		DoubleD
1940	Animals Everywhere	$140	$200	$240		Ingri & Edgar Parin d'Aulaire		DoubleD
1941	Leif The Lucky	$140	$180	$240		Ingri & Edgar Parin d'Aulaire		DoubleD
1943	Don't Count Your Chicks	$140	$180	$240		Ingri & Edgar Parin d'Aulaire		DoubleD
1944	Wings For Per	$140	$180	$220		Ingri & Edgar Parin d'Aulaire		DoubleD
1945	Too Big	$140	$180	$220		Ingri & Edgar Parin d'Aulaire		DoubleD
1946	Pocahontas	$140	$180	$220		Ingri & Edgar Parin d'Aulaire		DoubleD
1948	Nils	$120	$160	$220		Ingri & Edgar Parin d'Aulaire		DoubleD
1949	Foxie	$120	$160	$220		Ingri & Edgar Parin d'Aulaire		DoubleD

d'Aulaire — Ingri & Edgar Parin

Year	Title	VG-	VG	VG+	Fine	Author	Award	Pub
1950	Benjamin Franklin	$120	$160	$200		Ingri & Edgar Parin d'Aulaire		DoubleD
1952	Buffulo Bill	$120	$160	$200		Ingri & Edgar Parin d'Aulaire		DoubleD
1955	Columbus	$100	$140	$180		Ingri & Edgar Parin d'Aulaire		DoubleD
1955	Two Cars	$100	$140	$180		Ingri & Edgar Parin d'Aulaire		DoubleD
1958	The Magic Meadow	$100	$140	$180		Ingri & Edgar Parin d'Aulaire		DoubleD
1962	d'Aulaires' Book Of Greek Myths	$100	$120	$160		Ingri & Edgar Parin d'Aulaire		DoubleD
1967	d'Aulaires' Norse Gods And Giants	$80	$120	$140		Ingri & Edgar Parin d'Aulaire		DoubleD
1972	d'Aulaire's Trolls		$70	$100	$140	Ingri & Edgar Parin d'Aulaire		DoubleD

Davenier — Christine

Year	Title	VG-	VG	VG+	Fine	Author	Award	Pub
1998	Leon And Albertine		$10	$14	$18	Christine Davenier		Orchard
1999	The Low-Down Laundry Line Blues		$8	$12	$16	C. M. Millen		HM
1999	Very Best (Almost) Friends		$8	$12	$16	Paul B. Janeczko		Candle
2000	In Every Tiny Grain Of Sand		$8	$10	$14	Reeve Lindbergh		Candle
2000	Iris And Walter		$8	$10	$14	Elissa Haden Guest		HBrace
2000	Mabel Dancing		$8	$10	$14	Amy Hest		Candle
2001	The Other Dog		$8	$10	$14	Madeleine L'Engle		SeaStar
2002	Iris And Walter And Baby Rose		$8	$10	$14	Elissa Haden Guest		Harcort
2002	Iris And Walter, The Sleepover		$8	$10	$14	Elissa Haden Guest		Harcort
2002	That Makes Me Mad!		$8	$10	$14	Steven Kroll		SeaStar
2002	The First Thing My Mama Told Me		$8	$10	$14	Susan Marie Swanson		Harcort
2003	Full Moon Barnyard Dance		$8	$10	$14	Carole Lexa Schaefer		Candle
2003	Iris And Walter And Cousin Howie		$8	$10	$14	Elissa Haden Guest		Harcort
2004	Iris And Walter And The Substitute Teacher		$6	$10	$12	Elissa Haden Guest		Harcort

Davis — Jack E.

Year	Title	VG-	VG	VG+	Fine	Author	Award	Pub
1995	Menopaws		$14	$20	$25	Martha Sacks		10Speed
1998	Male Menopaws		$10	$14	$18	Martha Sacks		10Speed
1998	Music Over Manhattan		$10	$14	$18	Mark Karlins		DoubleD
1999	Mary Louise Loses Her Manners		$10	$14	$18	Diane Cuneo		DoubleD
2000	Bedhead		$8	$12	$16	Margie Palatini		S&S
2001	Marsupial Sue		$8	$12	$16	John Lithgow		S&S
2001	Metro Cat		$8	$12	$16	Marsha Diane Arnold		Golden
2001	Monster Goose		$8	$12	$16	Judy Sierra		Harcort
2002	My Last Chance Brother		$8	$10	$14	Amy Axelrod		Dutton
2003	Just A Minute		$8	$10	$14	Bonny Becker		S&S
2003	The Picture Of Morty & Ray		$8	$10	$14	Daniel Pinkwater		HCollins
2003	They'll Believe Me When I'm Gone		$8	$10	$14	Amy Axelrod		Dutton
2004	Hello Muddah, Hello Faddah		$8	$10	$14	Allan Sherman		Dutton
2004	Most Loved Monster		$8	$10	$14	Lynn Downey		Dial

Davis — Lambert

Year	Title	VG-	VG	VG+	Fine	Author	Award	Pub
1988	The Jolly Mon		$18	$25	$35	Jimmy Buffett		HBJ
1989	The Bells Of Christmas		$14	$20	$25	Virginia Hamilton		HBJ
1989	The Terrible Hodag		$14	$20	$25	Caroline Arnold		HBJ
1990	The Dark Way		$12	$18	$25	Virginia Hamilton		HBJ
1991	Trouble Dolls		$12	$18	$25	Jimmy Buffett		HBJ
1992	Rikki-Tikki-Tavi		$12	$18	$25	Rudyard Kipling		HBJ
1994	Baby Whales Drink Milk		$12	$16	$20	Barbara Juster Esbensen		HCollins
2000	The Snow Bear		$8	$12	$16	Liliana Stafford		Scholas
2003	Whales Passing		$8	$10	$14	Eve Bunting		BSP
2004	Swimming With Dolphins		$8	$10	$14	Lambert Davis		BSP

Davis — Susan

Year	Title	VG-	VG	VG+	Fine	Author	Award	Pub
1986	When Daddy Comes Home		$14	$20	$30	Linda Wagner Tyler		VK
1987	Waiting For Mom		$12	$16	$20	Linda Wagner Tyler		VK
1988	The Dinosaur Who Lived In My Backyard		$12	$16	$20	B. G. Hennessy		VK
1988	The Sick-In-Bed Birthday		$12	$16	$20	Linda Wagner Tyler		VK
1989	My Brother Oscar Thinks He Knows It All		$12	$16	$20	Linda Wagner Tyler		VK
1989	The Birthday Moon		$12	$16	$20	Lois Duncan		VK
1990	The After-Christmas Tree		$10	$16	$20	Linda Wagner Tyler		Viking

Davis   Susan

Year	Title	VG-	VG	VG+	Fine	Author	Award	Pub
1994	Who Is Sleeping?		$10	$14	$18	Andrew Gutelle		Time

Day   Alexandra

Year	Title	VG-	VG	VG+	Fine	Author	Award	Pub
1983	The Teddy Bears' Picnic		$25	$35	$50	Jimmy Kennedy		GreenT
1985	Good Dog, Carl		$40	$60	$80	Alexandra Day		GreenT
1987	When You Wish Upon A Star		$20	$30	$40	Ned Washington		GreenT
1988	Frank And Ernest		$18	$25	$35	Alexandra Day		Scholas
1989	Carl Goes Shopping		$25	$40	$50	Alexandra Day		FSG
1989	Paddy's Pay-Day		$18	$25	$35	Alexandra Day		VK
1990	Carl's Christmas		$25	$35	$50	Alexandra Day		FSG
1990	Frank And Ernest Play Ball		$16	$25	$30	Alexandra Day		Scholas
1990	River Parade		$16	$25	$30	Alexandra Day		Viking
1991	Carl's Afternoon In The Park		$16	$25	$30	Alexandra Day		FSG
1991	The Blue Faience Hippopotamus		$16	$25	$30	Joan Grant		GreenT
1992	Carl Pops Up		$16	$25	$30	Alexandra Day		S&S
1992	Carl's Masquerade		$16	$25	$30	Alexandra Day		FSG
1993	Carl Goes To Daycare		$16	$25	$30	Alexandra Day		FSG
1994	Carl Makes A Scrapbook		$14	$20	$30	Alexandra Day		FSG
1994	Frank And Ernest On The Road		$14	$20	$30	Alexandra Day		Scholas
1995	Carl's Birthday		$14	$20	$25	Alexandra Day		FSG
1996	A Bouquet		$12	$18	$25	Alexandra Day		BLB
1997	Mirror		$12	$18	$25	Christina Darling		FSG
1997	The Christmas We Moved To The Barn		$12	$18	$25	Cooper Edens		HCollins
1998	Follow Carl!		$12	$16	$20	Alexandra Day		FSG
1999	Boswell Wide-Awake		$12	$16	$20	Alexandra Day		FSG
2000	Carl's Christmas		$10	$14	$18	Alexandra Day		FSG
2001	Special Deliveries		$10	$14	$18	Cooper Edens		HCollins
2002	Puppy Trouble		$8	$12	$16	Alexandra Day		FSG
2004	The Flight Of The Dove		$8	$10	$14	Alexandra Day		FSG

De Angeli   Marguerite

Year	Title	VG-	VG	VG+	Fine	Author	Award	Pub
1927	The Little Duke, Richard The Fearless	$220	$280	$360		Charlotte Mary Yonge		Macmil
1929	The Lances Of Lynwood	$140	$180	$240		Charlotte Mary Yonge		Macmil
1931	A Candle In The Mist	$140	$180	$220		Florence Crannell Means		HM
1935	Ted And Nina Go To The Grocery Store	$200	$260	$320		Marguerite De Angeli		DD
1936	Henner's Lydia	$200	$260	$320		Marguerite De Angeli		DD
1936	Ted And Nina Have A Happy Rainy Day	$200	$260	$320		Marguerite De Angeli		DD
1937	Alice-All-By-Herself	$180	$240	$300		Elizabeth Coatsworth		Macmil
1937	Joan Wanted A Kitty	$180	$240	$300		Jane Brown Gemmill		Winston
1937	Petite Suzanne	$180	$240	$300		Marguerite De Angeli		DD
1938	Copper-Toed Boots	$180	$240	$300		Marguerite De Angeli		DD
1938	Strong Hearts and Bold	$180	$240	$300		Gertrude Crownfield		Lippin
1939	Skippack School	$180	$240	$300		Marguerite De Angeli		DD
1940	A Summer Day With Ted And Nina	$140	$200	$240		Marguerite De Angeli		DD
1940	Thee, Hannah!	$140	$200	$240		Marguerite De Angeli		DD
1941	Elin's Amerika	$140	$180	$240		Marguerite De Angeli		DD
1941	Prayers And Graces For Little Children	$140	$180	$240		Quail Hawkins		G&D
1942	They Loved To Laugh	$140	$180	$240		Kathryn Worth		DD
1942	Up The Hill	$140	$180	$240		Marguerite De Angeli		DD
1943	In And Out	$140	$180	$240		Thomas P. Robinson		Viking
1944	Turkey For Christmas	$140	$180	$220		Marguerite De Angeli		Westmin
1944	Yonie Wondernose	$200	$280	$340		Marguerite De Angeli	CH	DoubleD
1946	Bright April	$140	$180	$220		Marguerite De Angeli		DoubleD
1947	Jared's Island	$120	$160	$220		Marguerite De Angeli		DoubleD
1949	The Door In The Wall	$280	$360	$460		Marguerite De Angeli	NM	DD
1951	Just Like David	$120	$160	$200		Marguerite De Angeli		DoubleD
1952	A Little Book Of Prayers And Graces	$120	$160	$200		Quail Hawkins		DoubleD
1954	Side Saddle For Dandy	$120	$160	$200		Nancy Faulkner		DoubleD
1955	Book Of Nursery And Mother Goose Rhymes	$160	$220	$280		Marguerite De Angeli	CH	DoubleD
1956	Black Fox Of Lorne	$120	$160	$220		Marguerite De Angeli	NH	DoubleD
1964	Libraries And Reading	$90	$120	$160		Donald H. Hunt		Drexel
1964	The Goose Girl	$90	$120	$160		Jacob & Wilhelm Grimm		DoubleD
1965	The Ted And Nina Story Book	$90	$120	$160		Marguerite De Angeli		DoubleD
1966	The Empty Barn	$90	$120	$160		Arthur C. De Angeli		Westmin

De Angeli   Marguerite

Year	Title	VG-	VG	VG+	Fine	Author	Award	Pub
1969	Famous Modern Storytellers For Young People	$80	$120	$140		Norah Smaridge		DoddM
1974	Fiddlestrings		$60	$90	$120	Marguerite De Angeli		DoubleD
1975	The Lion In The Box		$60	$80	$120	Marguerite De Angeli		DoubleD
1977	Whistle For The Crossing		$60	$80	$120	Marguerite De Angeli		DoubleD
1981	Friendship & Other Poems		$50	$70	$100	Marguerite De Angeli		DoubleD

De Beer   Hans

Year	Title	VG-	VG	VG+	Fine	Author	Award	Pub
1987	Little Polar Bear		$20	$30	$40	Hans de Beer		NSBooks
1988	Ahoy There, Little Polar Bear		$25	$40	$50	Hans de Beer		NSBooks
1989	Ollie The Elephant		$18	$25	$35	Burny Bos		NSBooks
1990	Little Polar Bear Finds A Friend		$16	$25	$30	Hans de Beer		NSBooks
1990	Prince Valentino		$16	$25	$30	Bos Burny		NSBooks
1991	The Big Squirrel And The Little Rhinoceros		$16	$25	$30	Mischa Damjan		NSBooks
1992	Little Polar Bear And The Brave Little Hare		$16	$25	$30	Hans de Beer		NSBooks
1994	Bernard Bear's Amazing Adventure		$14	$20	$30	Hans de Beer		NSBooks
1994	Meet The Molesons		$14	$20	$30	Burny Bos		NSBooks
1995	Leave It To The Molesons!		$14	$20	$25	Burny Bos		NSBooks
1995	Little Bobo		$14	$20	$25	Serena Romanelli		NSBooks
1995	More From The Molesons		$14	$20	$25	Burny Bos		NSBooks
1995	On The Road With Poppa Whopper		$14	$20	$25	R. Schroder M. Busser		NSBooks
1996	King Bobble		$12	$18	$25	R. Schroder M. Busser		NSBooks
1996	Little Polar Bear, Take Me Home!		$12	$18	$25	Hans de Beer		NSBooks
1997	Little Bobo Saves The Day		$12	$18	$25	Serena Romanelli		NSBooks
1999	Little Polar Bear And The Husky Pup		$12	$16	$20	Hans de Beer		NSBooks
2000	Alexander The Great		$10	$14	$18	Burny Bos		NSBooks
2000	Fun With The Molesons		$10	$14	$18	Burny Bos		NSBooks
2001	Good Times With The Molesons		$10	$14	$18	Burny Bos		NSBooks
2002	Lars And Robby		$8	$12	$16	Gail Donovan		Night
2002	Lars Saves The Day		$8	$12	$16	Gail Donovan		Night
2002	Lars's Storybook Adventure		$8	$12	$16	Scott Peterson		Night
2002	Little Polar Bear And The Big Balloon		$8	$12	$16	Hans de Beer		NSBooks

De Groat   Diane

Year	Title	VG-	VG	VG+	Fine	Author	Award	Pub
1973	Luke Was There		$40	$60	$90	Eleanor L. Clymer		HR&W
1975	A Book For Jodan		$30	$40	$60	Marcia Newfield		Athenm
1975	Little Rabbit's Loose Tooth		$30	$40	$60	Lucy Bate		Crown
1975	My Friend Fish		$30	$40	$60	Mamie Hegwood		HR&W
1975	Nobody's Family		$30	$40	$60	Anne Snyder		HR&W
1975	Truth And Consequences		$30	$40	$60	Miriam Young		4Winds
1976	Antrim's Orange		$30	$40	$60	Sylvia Sunderlin		Scribnr
1976	Bubba And Babba		$30	$40	$60	Maria Polushkin		Crown
1976	Chasing Trouble		$30	$40	$60	Harriett Mandelay Luger		Viking
1976	Mr. Tamarin's Trees		$30	$40	$60	Kathryn F. Ernst		Crown
1976	One More Flight		$30	$40	$60	Eve Bunting		FWarne
1977	Alligator's Toothache		$40	$60	$80	Diane De Groat		Crown
1977	Owl's New Cards		$25	$40	$50	Kathryn F. Ernst		Crown
1978	Badger On His Own		$25	$40	$50	Ann Tompert		Crown
1978	How Your Mother And Father Met		$25	$40	$50	Tobi Tobias		McHill
1979	Anastasia Krupnik		$25	$40	$50	Lois Lowry		HM
1979	Animal Fact/Animal Fable		$25	$40	$50	Seymour Simon		Crown
1980	Part-Time Boy		$25	$35	$50	Elizabeth T. Billington		FWarne
1980	The Twins Strike Back		$25	$35	$50	Valerie Flournoy		Dial
1981	Don't Be Mad, Ivy		$25	$35	$50	Christine McDonnell		Dial
1981	Who Needs A Bear?		$25	$35	$50	Barbara Dillon		Morrow
1982	Anastasia At Your Service		$25	$35	$50	Lois Lowry		HM
1982	The Bad Dreams Of A Good Girl		$25	$35	$50	Susan Richards Shreve		Knopf
1982	The Toad Intruder		$25	$35	$50	Lynn Marie Luderer		HM
1982	Toad Food & Measle Soup		$25	$35	$50	Christine McDonnell		Dial
1982	Tough-Luck Karen		$25	$35	$50	Johanna Hurwitz		Morrow
1983	The Ewoks Join The Fight		$25	$35	$50	Bonnie Bogart		Random
1984	Albert The Running Bear's Exercise Book		$20	$30	$40	Barbara Isenberg		Clarion
1984	Dede Takes Charge!		$20	$30	$40	Johanna Hurwitz		Morrow
1984	I Don't Live Here!		$20	$30	$40	Pam Conrad		Dutton
1984	Lucky Charms & Birthday Wishes		$20	$30	$40	Christine McDonnell		Viking

De Groat   Diane

Year	Title	VG-	VG	VG+	Fine	Author	Award	Pub
1984	The Flunking Of Joshua T. Bates		$20	$30	$40	Susan Richards Shreve		Knopf
1985	And Don't Bring Jeremy		$20	$30	$40	Marilyn Levinson		HR&W
1985	The Story Of Superted		$20	$30	$40	Mike Young		Random
1986	Amanda & April		$20	$30	$40	Bonnie Pryor		Morrow
1986	Hurricane Elaine		$20	$30	$40	Johanna Hurwitz		Morrow
1986	Little Rabbit's Baby Brother		$20	$30	$40	Fran Manushkin		Crown
1986	The Great Ideas Of Lila Fenwick		$20	$30	$40	Kate McMullan		Dial
1986	When Mom And Dad Divorce		$20	$30	$40	Steven L. Nickman		Messner
1987	Albert The Running Bear Gets The Jitters		$20	$30	$40	Barbara Isenberg		Clarion
1987	Bears In Paris		$20	$30	$40	Niki Yektai		BradP
1987	Just For The Summer		$20	$30	$40	Christine McDonnell		VK
1987	The Christmas Revolution		$20	$30	$40	Barbara Cohen		LL&S
1987	The Gray Whales Are Missing		$20	$30	$40	Robin A. Thrush		HBJ
1988	All About Sam		$18	$25	$35	Lois Lowry		HM
1988	Great Advice From Lila Fenwick		$18	$25	$35	Kate McMullan		Dial
1988	The Orphan Game		$18	$25	$35	Barbara Cohen		LL&S
1988	Willow		$18	$25	$35	Cathy West		Random
1989	Stories From The Big Chair		$18	$25	$35	Ruth Wallace-Brodeur		McEld
1989	Where Is Everybody?		$18	$25	$35	Eve Merriam		S&S
1990	Aldo Peanut Butter		$16	$25	$30	Johanna Hurwitz		Morrow
1990	Be Brave, Baby Rabbit		$16	$25	$30	Fran Manushkin		Crown
1990	Hi Bears, Bye Bears		$16	$25	$30	Niki Yektai		Orchard
1990	Jace The Ace		$16	$25	$30	Joanne Rocklin		Macmil
1990	Merry Christmas, Amanda & April		$16	$25	$30	Bonnie Pryor		Morrow
1990	The Long Way Home		$16	$25	$30	Barbara Cohen		LL&S
1991	A Turkey For Thanksgiving		$16	$25	$30	Eve Bunting		Clarion
1991	Itchy Richard		$16	$25	$30	Jamie Gilson		Clarion
1991	The Great Eggspectations Of Lila Fenwick		$16	$25	$30	Kate McMullan		FSG
1992	An Elephant Never Forgets Its Snorkel		$16	$25	$30	Lisa Gollin Evans		Crown
1992	Annie Pitts, Artichoke		$20	$30	$40	Diane De Groat		S&S
1992	Attaboy, Sam!		$16	$25	$30	Lois Lowry		HM
1992	Our Teacher's Having A Baby		$16	$25	$30	Eve Bunting		Clarion
1992	Peter's Song		$16	$25	$30	Carol Saul		S&S
1992	The Great Summer Camp Catastrophe		$16	$25	$30	Jean Van Leeuwen		Dial
1992	Wait For Me		$16	$25	$30	Susan Richards Shreve		Tambour
1993	Amy Dunn Quits School		$16	$25	$30	Susan Richards Shreve		Tambour
1993	Dr. Ruth Talks To Kids		$16	$25	$30	Ruth K. Westheimer		Macmil
1993	Never Trust A Sister Over Twelve		$16	$25	$30	Stephen Roos		DelaP
1993	The Wrong-Way Rabbit		$16	$25	$30	Teddy Slater		Scholas
1994	Annie Pitts, Swamp Monster		$20	$30	$40	Diane De Groat		S&S
1994	Fruit Flies, Fish & Fortune Cookies		$14	$20	$30	A. C. LeMieux		Tambour
1994	It Goes Eeeeeeeeeeee!		$14	$20	$30	Jamie Gilson		Clarion
1994	Kinderkittens		$14	$20	$30	Stephanie Calmenson		Scholas
1994	Some Days, Other Days		$14	$20	$30	P. J. Petersen		Scribnr
1994	Sunshine Home		$14	$20	$30	Eve Bunting		Clarion
1995	Roses Are Pink, Your Feet Really Stink		$14	$20	$25	Diane De Groat		Morrow
1995	The Great Brain Is Back		$14	$20	$25	John Dennis Fitzgerald		Dial
1995	The Little Women Book		$14	$20	$25	Lucille Recht Penner		Random
1996	See You Around, Sam!		$12	$18	$25	Lois Lowry		HM
1997	A Pinky Is A Baby Mouse		$12	$18	$25	Pam Muñoz Ryan		Hyper
1997	Armadillos Sleep In Dugouts		$12	$18	$25	Pam Muñoz Ryan		Hyper
1998	Bug In A Rug		$12	$16	$20	Jamie Gilson		Clarion
1998	How I Saved Hanukkah		$12	$16	$20	Amy Goldman Koss		Dial
1998	Pots And Pans		$12	$16	$20	Patricia Hubbell		HFest
1998	Trick Or Treat, Smell My Feet		$14	$20	$30	Diane De Groat		Morrow
1999	Anna All Year Round		$12	$16	$20	Mary Downing Hahn		Clarion
1999	Happy Birthday To You, You Belong In A Zoo		$12	$16	$20	Diane De Groat		Morrow
1999	Our Thanksgiving		$12	$16	$20	Kimberly Weinberger		Scholas
1999	Zooman Sam		$12	$16	$20	Lois Lowry		HM
2000	Annie Pitts, Burger Kid		$10	$14	$18	Diane De Groat		SeaStar
2000	Gus & Gertie And The Missing Pearl		$10	$14	$18	Joan Lowery Nixon		SeaStar
2000	Jingle Bells, Homework Smells		$10	$14	$18	Diane De Groat		HCollins
2000	One Small Dog		$10	$14	$18	Johanna Hurwitz		HCollins
2001	Anna On The Farm		$10	$14	$18	Mary Downing Hahn		Clarion
2001	Gus & Gertie And The Lucky Charms		$10	$14	$18	Joan Lowery Nixon		SeaStar
2001	We Gather Together-- Now Please Get Lost!		$10	$14	$18	Diane De Groat		SeaStar
2002	Good Night, Sleep Tight		$8	$12	$16	Diane De Groat		SeaStar

De Groat   Diane

Year	Title	VG-	VG	VG+	Fine	Author	Award	Pub
2002	Lola The Elf		$8	$12	$16	Diane De Groat		Night
2003	Liar, Liar, Pants On Fire		$8	$12	$16	Diane De Groat		SeaStar
2003	Love, Lola		$8	$12	$16	Diane De Groat		Night

De Larrea   Victoria

Year	Title	VG-	VG	VG+	Fine	Author	Award	Pub
1967	Fighting The Unseen	$30	$40	$50		Suzanne Loebl		AS
1967	The Green Goose	$25	$30	$40		Theodora J. F. Koob		Lippin
1968	Leprechaun Tales	$20	$30	$35		Kathleen Green		Lippin
1968	Lucy	$20	$30	$35		Catherine Storr		P-Hall
1968	Orange October	$20	$30	$35		Gene Inyart Namovicz		FWatts
1968	The Blackmail Machine	$20	$30	$35		Felice Holman		Macmil
1968	The Good Day Mice	$20	$30	$35		Carol Beach York		FWatts
1968	The Pheasant On Route Seven	$20	$30	$35		Kaye Starbird		Lippin
1969	Good Charlotte	$20	$30	$35		Carol Beach York		FWatts
1969	Juba This And Juba That	$20	$30	$35		Virginia A. Tashjian		LBrown
1969	Lisa And Lottie	$20	$30	$35		Erich Kästner		Knopf
1969	Lucy Runs Away	$20	$30	$35		Catherine Storr		P-Hall
1969	No Room For Nicky	$20	$30	$35		Alicia Kaufmann		HawB
1970	Little Is Nice		$18	$25	$35	Alicia Kaufmann		HawB
1970	Me Is How I Feel: Poems		$18	$25	$35	Stacy Jo Crossen		McCall
1970	Rockabye To Monster Land		$18	$25	$35	Frances McKee		Putnam
1970	The Ten O'Clock Club		$18	$25	$35	Carol Beach York		FWatts
1971	Herbert's Treasure		$18	$25	$35	Alice Low		Putnam
1971	The Shades		$18	$25	$35	Betty Brock		H&Row
1972	Miss Know It All Returns		$18	$25	$35	Carol Beach York		FWatts
1973	The Friendly Woods		$16	$25	$30	Charles House		4Winds
1974	Baby Needs Shoes		$16	$25	$30	Dale Bick Carlson		Athenm
1980	Magical Beasts And Unbelievable Monsters		$14	$20	$25	Geraldine Woods		EMC
1980	The Helping Day		$14	$20	$25	Ann Bixby Herold		CM&G
1981	Abracatabby		$14	$20	$25	Catherine Hiller		CM&G
1981	Halloween Treats		$14	$20	$25	Carolyn Haywood		Morrow
1981	The Truth About Magical Beasts		$14	$20	$25	Geraldine Woods		Rourke
1983	Piñatas And Paper Flowers		$14	$20	$25	Lila Perl		Clarion
1984	Candles, Cakes, And Donkey Tails		$12	$18	$25	Lila Perl		Clarion
1984	Waiting For Mama		$12	$18	$25	Beatrice S. De Regniers		Clarion

De Mejo   Oscar

Year	Title	VG-	VG	VG+	Fine	Author	Award	Pub
1982	The Tiny Visitor		$25	$35	$50	Oscar De Mejo		Pan
1983	My America		$16	$25	$30	Oscar De Mejo		Abrams
1983	There's A Hand In The Sky		$16	$25	$30	Oscar De Mejo		Pan
1985	The Forty-Niner		$16	$25	$30	Oscar De Mejo		H&Row
1986	Lady With A Torch		$14	$20	$30	Eleanor Coerr		H&Row
1987	Journey To Boc Boc		$14	$20	$30	Oscar De Mejo		H&Row
1989	Does God Have A Big Toe?		$14	$20	$25	Marc Gellman		H&Row
1991	An Alphabet Of Rotten Kids!		$12	$18	$25	David Elliott		Philo
1992	La Bella Magellona And The Little Cavalier		$12	$18	$25	Oscar De Mejo		Philo
1992	Oscar De Mejo's ABC		$12	$18	$25	Oscar De Mejo		HCollins
1992	The Professor Of Etiquette		$12	$18	$25	Oscar De Mejo		Philo

De Veyrac   Robert

Year	Title	VG-	VG	VG+	Fine	Author	Award	Pub
1943	SHHhhhh......Bang	$70	$90	$120		Margaret Wise Brown		H&B
1944	The Big Fur Secret	$50	$60	$80		Margaret Wise Brown		H&B
1945	The House Of A Hundred Windows	$40	$60	$70		Margaret Wise Brown		H&B

Degen   Bruce

Year	Title	VG-	VG	VG+	Fine	Author	Award	Pub
1977	A Big Day For Scepters		$40	$60	$80	Stephen Krensky		Athenm
1977	Aunt Possum And The Pumpkin Man		$25	$40	$50	Bruce Degen		H&Row
1977	Forecast		$25	$40	$50	Malcolm Hall		CM&G
1978	Caricatures		$25	$40	$50	Malcolm Hall		CM&G
1979	Brimhall Turns To Magic		$25	$40	$50	Judy Delton		LL&S
1979	Ig Lives In A Cave		$25	$40	$50	Carol Chapman		Dutton

Degen   Bruce

Year	Title	VG-	VG	VG+	Fine	Author	Award	Pub
1979	Mr. Jameson & Mr. Phillips		$25	$40	$50	Marjorie Weinman Sharmat		H&Row
1979	Up And Down The River: Boat Poems		$25	$40	$50	Claudia Lewis		H&Row
1980	Commander Toad In Space		$25	$35	$50	Jane Yolen		CM&G
1980	My Mother Didn't Kiss Me Good-Night		$25	$35	$50	Charlotte Herman		Dutton
1980	The Little Witch And The Riddle		$25	$35	$50	Bruce Degen		H&Row
1981	Little Chick's Big Day		$25	$35	$50	Mary DeBall Kwitz		H&Row
1982	Commander Toad & The Planet Of The Grapes		$25	$35	$50	Jane Yolen		CM&G
1982	Dandelion Hill		$25	$35	$50	Clyde Robert Bulla		Dutton
1982	Deadlines		$25	$35	$50	Malcolm Hall		CM&G
1982	Upchuck Summer		$25	$35	$50	Joel L. Schwartz		DelaP
1983	Commander Toad And The Big Black Hole		$25	$35	$50	Jane Yolen		CM&G
1983	Jamberry		$25	$35	$50	Bruce Degen		H&Row
1983	Little Chick's Breakfast		$25	$35	$50	Mary DeBall Kwitz		H&Row
1984	Daddy's Coming Home		$20	$30	$40	Lyn Littlefield Hoopes		H&Row
1985	Commander Toad & The Dis-Asteroid		$20	$30	$40	Jane Yolen		CM&G
1985	Grandpa Bear		$20	$30	$40	Bonnie Pryor		Morrow
1985	Lonely Lula Cat		$20	$30	$40	Joseph Slate		H&Row
1986	Commander Toad And The Intergalactic Spy		$20	$30	$40	Jane Yolen		CM&G
1986	Grandpa Bear's Christmas		$20	$30	$40	Bonnie Pryor		Morrow
1986	Jesse Bear, What Will You Wear?		$30	$40	$60	Nancy Carlstrom		Macmil
1986	Magic School Bus At The Waterworks		$30	$50	$60	Joanna Cole		Scholas
1986	The Good-Luck Pencil		$20	$30	$40	Diane Stanley		4Winds
1986	The Josefina Story Quilt		$20	$30	$40	Eleanor Coerr		H&Row
1986	When It Comes To Bugs: Poems		$20	$30	$40	Aileen Fisher		H&Row
1987	Magic School Bus: Inside The Earth		$30	$50	$60	Joanna Cole		Scholas
1987	The Forgetful Bears Meet Mr. Memory		$20	$30	$40	Larry Weinberg		Scholas
1988	Better Not Get Wet, Jesse Bear		$18	$25	$35	Nancy Carlstrom		Macmil
1988	If You Were A Writer		$18	$25	$35	Joan Lowery Nixon		4Winds
1988	In The Middle Of The Puddle		$18	$25	$35	Mike Thaler		H&Row
1988	The Forgetful Bears Help Santa		$18	$25	$35	Larry Weinberg		Scholas
1989	Lion And Lamb		$18	$25	$35	W. Hooks & B. Brenner		Bantam
1989	Magic School Bus: Inside The Human Body		$30	$40	$60	Joanna Cole		Scholas
1990	Dinosaur Dances		$16	$25	$30	Jane Yolen		Putnam
1990	It's About Time, Jesse Bear		$25	$35	$50	Nancy Carlstrom		Macmil
1990	Lion And Lamb Step Out		$16	$25	$30	W. Hooks & B. Brenner		Bantam
1990	Magic School Bus: Lost In The Solar System		$25	$40	$50	Joanna Cole		Scholas
1991	Goblin Walk		$16	$25	$30	Tony Johnston		Putnam
1991	Teddy Bear Towers		$16	$25	$30	Bruce Degen		HCollins
1991	Ups And Downs With Lion And Lamb		$16	$25	$30	W. Hooks & B. Brenner		Bantam
1992	How Do You Say It Today, Jesse Bear?		$20	$30	$40	Nancy Carlstrom		Macmil
1992	Little Chick's Friend, Duckling		$16	$25	$30	Mary DeBall Kwitz		HCollins
1992	Magic School Bus On The Ocean Floor		$25	$35	$50	Joanna Cole		Scholas
1992	Riding Magic School Bus		$16	$25	$30	Joanna Cole		Scholas
1993	Mouse's Birthday		$16	$25	$30	Jane Yolen		Putnam
1994	A Beautiful Feast For A Big King Cat		$14	$20	$30	John Archambault		HCollins
1994	Happy Birthday, Jesse Bear!		$20	$30	$40	Nancy Carlstrom		Macmil
1994	Jesse Bear's Tra-La Tub		$20	$30	$40	Nancy Carlstrom		Aladd
1994	Jesse Bear's Tum-Tum Tickle		$20	$30	$40	Nancy Carlstrom		Aladd
1994	Jesse Bear's Wiggle-Jiggle Jump-Up		$20	$30	$40	Nancy Carlstrom		Aladd
1994	Jesse Bear's Yum-Yum Crumble		$20	$30	$40	Nancy Carlstrom		Aladd
1994	Magic School Bus: In The Time Of The Dinosaurs		$20	$30	$40	Joanna Cole		Scholas
1994	Will You Give Me A Dream?		$14	$20	$30	Joan Lowery Nixon		4Winds
1995	Magic School Bus Inside A Hurricane		$20	$30	$40	Joanna Cole		Scholas
1996	Let's Count It Out, Jesse Bear		$12	$18	$25	Nancy Carlstrom		S&S
1996	Magic School Bus. Inside A Beehive		$16	$25	$30	Joanna Cole		Scholas
1996	Sailaway Home		$12	$18	$25	Bruce Degen		Scholas
1997	Guess Who's Coming, Jesse Bear		$12	$18	$25	Nancy Carlstrom		S&S
1997	Hooray For Me, Hooray For You, Hooray For Blue		$12	$18	$25	Nancy Carlstrom		LSimon
1997	I Love You, Mama, Any Time Of Year		$12	$18	$25	Nancy Carlstrom		LSimon
1997	I Love You, Papa, In All Kinds Of Weather		$12	$18	$25	Nancy Carlstrom		LSimon
1997	Magic School Bus And The Electric Field Trip		$14	$20	$30	Joanna Cole		Scholas
1997	Magic School Bus Shows And Tells		$12	$18	$25	Joanna Cole		Scholas
1998	Commander Toad And The Voyage Home		$12	$16	$20	Jane Yolen		Putnam
1999	Magic School Bus Explores The Senses		$14	$20	$25	Joanna Cole		Scholas
1999	What A Scare, Jesse Bear		$12	$16	$20	Nancy Carlstrom		S&S
2000	Daddy Is A Doodlebug		$10	$14	$18	Bruce Degen		HCollins
2000	Shirley's Wonderful Baby		$10	$14	$18	Valiska Gregory		HCollins

Degen — Bruce

Year	Title	VG-	VG	VG+	Fine	Author	Award	Pub
2000	Where Is Christmas, Jesse Bear?		$12	$18	$25	Nancy Carlstrom		S&S
2001	Ms. Frizzle's Adventures		$10	$14	$18	Joanna Cole		Scholas
2001	Ms. Frizzle's Adventures: Ancient Egypt		$10	$14	$18	Joanna Cole		Scholas
2002	Climb The Family Tree, Jesse Bear!		$8	$12	$16	Nancy Carlstrom		S&S

Deihl — Edna Groff

Year	Title	VG-	VG	VG+	Fine	Author	Award	Pub
1922	The Little Kitten That Would Not Wash Its Face	$180	$240	$300		Edna Groff Deihl		Gabriel
1923	Aunt Este's Stories Of The Flower & Berry Babies	$120	$160	$200		Edna Groff Deihl		AWhit
1923	Aunt Este's Stories Of The Vegetable & Fruit Children	$120	$160	$200		Edna Groff Deihl		AWhit
1924	My Twin Kitties	$120	$160	$200		Edna Groff Deihl		Gabriel
1924	My Twin Puppies	$120	$160	$200		Edna Groff Deihl		Gabriel
1924	The Teddy Bear That Prowled At Night	$120	$160	$200		Mary La Fetra Russell		Gabriel
1925	The Three Books & Other Big Day Stories	$120	$160	$200		Edna Groff Deihl		AWhit
1927	Mother Brown Earth's Children	$100	$140	$180		Edna Groff Deihl		AWhit
1929	The Little Want-To-Be's ..	$100	$140	$180		Edna Groff Deihl		Gabriel
1930	Holiday-Time Stories	$90	$120	$160		Edna Groff Deihl		AWhit
1934	The Barnyard Village	$80	$120	$140		Edna Groff Deihl		AWhit
1941	The Little Dog That Would Not Wag His Tail	$80	$100	$140		Edna Groff Deihl		Gabriel
1942	The Little Chick That Would Not Go To Bed	$80	$100	$140		A. E. Kennedy		Gabriel
1942	The Little Rabbit That Would Not Eat	$80	$100	$140		A. E. Kennedy		Gabriel
1944	The Little Pig That Would Not Get Up	$70	$100	$120		A. E. Kennedy		Gabriel
1944	The Teddy Bear That Would Not Sleep	$70	$100	$120		Mary La Fetra Russell		Gabriel

Delamare — David

Year	Title	VG-	VG	VG+	Fine	Author	Award	Pub
1988	The Hawk's Tale		$25	$40	$50	John Balaban		HBJ
1990	The Steadfast Tin Soldier		$16	$25	$30	Katie Campbell (retold)		Unicorn
1991	The Christmas Secret		$16	$25	$30	David Delamare		GreenT
1991	The Nutcracker		$16	$25	$30	E. T. A. Hoffmann		Unicorn
1993	Cinderella		$16	$25	$30	David Delamare		S&S
1994	Mermaids And Magic Shows		$14	$20	$30	David Delamare		PTiger
1996	The Man In The Moon And The Hot Air Balloon		$12	$18	$25	David Delamare		Marlowe
1997	Midnight Farm		$12	$18	$25	Carly Simon		S&S

Delaney — Ned

Year	Title	VG-	VG	VG+	Fine	Author	Award	Pub
1976	One Dragon To Another		$20	$30	$40	Ned Delaney		HM
1976	Two Strikes, Four Eyes		$16	$25	$30	Ned Delaney		HM
1977	A Worm For Dinner		$16	$25	$30	Ned Delaney		HM
1978	Rufus The Doofus		$14	$20	$30	Ned Delaney		HM
1979	Bert And Barney		$14	$20	$30	Ned Delaney		HM
1980	Detective Bob And The Great Ape Escape		$14	$20	$25	David Lee Harrison		PMagP
1981	Eeeeeek!		$14	$20	$25	Patty Wolcott		AW
1982	The Secret Life Of Mr. Weird		$14	$20	$25	Jeffrey Allen		LBrown
1983	Aren't You Forgetting Something, Fiona!		$14	$20	$25	Joanna Cole		PMagP
1983	Otto		$14	$20	$25	Steven Kroll		PMagP
1983	Terrible Things Could Happen		$14	$20	$25	Ned Delaney		LL&S
1983	The Marigold Monster		$14	$20	$25	M.C. Delaney		Dutton
1985	Will You Cross Me?		$12	$18	$25	Marilyn Kaye		H&Row
1987	Bad Dog!		$12	$16	$20	Ned Delaney		Morrow
1988	Cosmic Chickens		$12	$16	$20	Ned Delaney		H&Row
1989	Old Enough For Magic		$12	$16	$20	Anola Pickett		H&Row
1991	The Cactus Flower Bakery		$10	$16	$20	Harry Allard		HCollins

Delessert — Etienne

Year	Title	VG-	VG	VG+	Fine	Author	Award	Pub
1966	The Tree	$60	$80	$100		E. Delessert & E. Schmid		HQuist
1967	The Endless Party	$40	$50	$70		Etienne Delessert		HQuist
1968	Story Number 1 For Children Under Three	$40	$50	$70		Eugène Ionesco		HQuist
1968	The Secret Seller	$40	$50	$70		Betty Jean Lifton		Norton
1970	Story Number 2 For Children Under Three		$30	$50	$60	Eugene Ionesco		HQuist
1971	How The Mouse Was Hit On The Head By A Stone		$30	$50	$60	Etienne Delessert		GoodB
1972	Just So Stories		$30	$50	$60	Rudyard Kipling		DoubleD
1972	The Pony Man		$30	$50	$60	Gordon Lightfoot		Harper

Delessert   Etienne

Year	Title	VG-	VG	VG+	Fine	Author	Award	Pub
1973	Being Green		$30	$50	$60	Joe Raposo		Western
1983	Prince Ring		$25	$35	$50	Heinz Edelmann		Creat
1984	A Christmas Memory		$20	$30	$40	Truman Capote		Creat
1984	Beauty And The Beast		$20	$30	$40	Delessert Aulnoy		Creat
1986	Hour Of Lead		$20	$30	$40	Anne Lindbergh		Redpth
1986	Mrs. Flowers		$20	$30	$40	Maya Angelou		Redpth
1986	The Pheasant Hunter		$20	$30	$40	William Saroyan		Redpth
1987	Ogden Nash's Zoo		$20	$30	$40	Ogden Nash		ST&C
1988	A Long Long Song		$18	$25	$35	Etienne Delessert		FSG
1988	Flowers For Algernon		$18	$25	$35	Daniel Keyes		Creat
1989	Food		$18	$25	$35	Ogden Nash		ST&C
1990	Ashes, Ashes		$16	$25	$30	Etienne Delessert		ST&C
1992	I Hate To Read!		$16	$25	$30	Rita Marshall		Creat
1993	Yok-Yok Best Friends		$16	$25	$30	Etienne Delessert		Creat
1993	Yok-Yok Magic Tricks		$16	$25	$30	Etienne Delessert		Creat
1994	Dance!		$14	$20	$30	Etienne Delessert		Creat
1994	Edwin Arlington Robinson		$14	$20	$30	Michael E Goodman		Creat
1994	Yok-Yok At Home		$14	$20	$30	Etienne Delessert		Creat
1994	Yok-Yok For The Birds		$14	$20	$30	Etienne Delessert		Creat
1994	Yok-Yok Let's Play		$14	$20	$30	Etienne Delessert		Creat
1994	Yok-Yok Moonlight		$14	$20	$30	Etienne Delessert		Creat
1994	Yok-Yok Nonsense		$14	$20	$30	Etienne Delessert		Creat
1994	Yok-Yok Nuts!		$14	$20	$30	Etienne Delessert		Creat
1994	Yok-Yok Snowflakes		$14	$20	$30	Etienne Delessert		Creat
1994	Yok-Yok Surprises		$14	$20	$30	Etienne Delessert		Creat
1994	Yok-Yok Weird?		$14	$20	$30	Etienne Delessert		Creat
1994	Yok-Yok What A Circus!		$14	$20	$30	Etienne Delessert		Creat
1999	The Cat Collection		$12	$16	$20	Etienne Delessert		Creat
2001	The Seven Dwarfs		$10	$14	$18	Etienne Delessert		Creat
2004	Who Killed Cock Robin?		$8	$10	$14	Etienne Delessert		Creat

Demarest   Chris

Year	Title	VG-	VG	VG+	Fine	Author	Award	Pub
1982	Benedict Finds A Home		$25	$35	$50	Chris Demarest		LL&S
1983	Clemens' Kingdom		$16	$25	$30	Chris Demarest		LL&S
1983	Hedgehog Adventures		$16	$25	$30	Betty Jo Stanovich		LL&S
1983	Pooks		$16	$25	$30	Elizabeth Isele		Lippin
1984	Hedgehog Surprises		$16	$25	$30	Betty Jo Stanovich		LL&S
1984	World Famous Muriel		$16	$25	$30	Sue Alexander		LBrown
1985	World Famous Muriel And The Scary Dragon		$16	$25	$30	Sue Alexander		LBrown
1986	Orville's Odyssey		$14	$20	$30	Chris Demarest		P-Hall
1987	Morton And Sidney		$14	$20	$30	Chris Demarest		Macmil
1988	No Peas For Nellie		$14	$20	$30	Chris Demarest		Macmil
1988	The Lunatic Adventure Of Kitman And Willy		$14	$20	$30	Chris Demarest		S&S
1989	Not Now! Said The Cow		$14	$20	$25	Joanne Oppenheim		Bantam
1989	Smedge		$14	$20	$25	Andrew Sharmat		Macmil
1989	The Butterfly Jar		$14	$20	$25	Jeffrey Moss		Bantam
1991	Kitman And Willy At Sea		$12	$18	$25	Chris Demarest		S&S
1991	The Cows Are Going To Paris		$12	$18	$25	David Kirby		CH
1991	The Donkey's Tale		$12	$18	$25	Joanne Oppenheim		Bantam
1991	The Other Side Of The Door		$12	$18	$25	Jeffrey Moss		Bantam
1991	The Scary Book		$12	$18	$25	Joanna Cole		Morrow
1992	Bob And Jack		$12	$18	$25	Jeffrey Moss		Bantam
1992	How Do You Wrap A Horse?		$12	$18	$25	Diana Klemin		CH
1992	My Little Red Car		$12	$18	$25	Chris Demarest		Boyds
1992	Two Badd Babies		$12	$18	$25	Jeffie Ross Gordon		CH
1992	What's On The Menu?		$12	$18	$25	Bobbye S. Goldstein		Viking
1992	Whooo's There?		$12	$18	$25	Lily Jones		RDigest
1993	Lindbergh		$12	$16	$20	Chris Demarest		Crown
1993	Smart Dog		$12	$16	$20	Ralph Leemis		CH
1993	Today I'm Going Fishing With My Dad		$12	$16	$20	N. L. Sharp		Boyds
1993	Uh-Oh! Said The Crow		$12	$16	$20	Joanne Oppenheim		Bantam
1994	Billy And The Magic String		$12	$16	$20	Susan Karnovsky		Troll
1994	Hieronymus White		$12	$16	$20	Jeffrey Moss		Ball
1994	Hooray For Grandma Jo!		$12	$16	$20	Thomas McKean		Crown
1994	Teacher's Pet		$12	$16	$20	Rita Walsh		Troll

Demarest   Chris

Year	Title	VG-	VG	VG+	Fine	Author	Award	Pub
1994	Time To Rhyme		$12	$16	$20	Marvin Terban		Wordsng
1994	When Cows Come Home		$12	$16	$20	David Lee Harrison		Boyds
1995	My Blue Boat		$10	$16	$20	Chris Demarest		HBrace
1995	Plane		$10	$16	$20	Chris Demarest		RWagon
1995	Ship		$10	$16	$20	Chris Demarest		HBrace
1995	What Would Mama Do?		$10	$16	$20	Judith Ross Enderle		Boyds
1996	Bus		$10	$16	$20	Chris Demarest		HBrace
1996	Casey In The Bath		$10	$16	$20	Cynthia C. DeFelice		FSG
1996	Derek's Dog Days		$10	$16	$20	Nancy Lee Charlton		HBrace
1996	Fall		$10	$16	$20	Chris Demarest		Harcort
1996	If Dogs Had Wings		$10	$16	$20	Larry Dane Brimner		Boyds
1996	Train		$10	$16	$20	Chris Demarest		HBrace
1996	Winter		$10	$16	$20	Chris Demarest		HBrace
1997	Spring		$10	$16	$20	Chris Demarest		HBrace
1997	Summer		$10	$16	$20	Chris Demarest		Harcort
1997	The Animals' Song		$10	$16	$20	David Lee Harrison		Boyds
1997	The Dad Of The Dad Of The Dad Of Your Dad		$10	$16	$20	Jeffrey Moss		Ball
1998	A Dozen Dozens		$10	$14	$18	Harriet Ziefert		Viking
1998	Farmer Nat		$10	$14	$18	Chris Demarest		HBrace
1998	Honk!		$10	$14	$18	Chris Demarest		Boyds
1998	Mike Swan, Sink Or Swim		$10	$14	$18	Deborah Heiligman		FCC
1998	The Case Of The Missing Monkeys		$10	$14	$18	Alice Pernick		Scholas
1998	Who Walks On This Halloween Night?		$10	$14	$18	Harriet Ziefert		S&S
1999	I Need A Valentine!		$10	$14	$18	Harriet Ziefert		LSimon
1999	The Cowboy ABC		$10	$14	$18	Chris Demarest		DK
1999	Who Loves Me Best?		$10	$14	$18	Kirsten Hall		RDigest
1999	Zookeeper Sue		$10	$14	$18	Chris Demarest		HBrace
2000	April Fool!		$8	$12	$16	Harriet Ziefert		Viking
2000	Beep Beep, Vroom Vroom!		$8	$12	$16	Stuart J. Murphy		HCollins
2000	Firefighters A To Z		$8	$12	$16	Chris Demarest		McEld
2000	I Can Jump Higher		$8	$12	$16	Paul Z. Mann		RDigest
2001	Bikes For Rent!		$8	$12	$16	Isaac Olaleye		Orchard
2001	Ding-Dong, Trick Or Treat!		$8	$12	$16	Harriet Ziefert		G&D
2001	My Best Friend		$8	$12	$16	Kirsten Hall		RDigest
2001	Someday We'll Have Very Good Manners		$8	$12	$16	Harriet Ziefert		Putnam
2002	Here Come Our Firefighters!		$8	$10	$14	Chris Demarest		LSimon
2002	I Invited A Dragon To Dinner		$8	$10	$14	Chris Demarest		Philo
2002	Smokejumpers One To Ten		$8	$10	$14	Chris Demarest		McEld
2002	Snowy Winter Day		$8	$10	$14	Estelle Feldman		Scholas
2002	The Bowwow Bake Sale		$8	$10	$14	Judith Bauer Stamper		G&D
2002	The Princess And The Pea		$8	$10	$14	Sarah Aronson (adapted)		LSimon
2003	Breakfast At Danny's Diner		$8	$10	$14	Judith Bauer Stamper		G&D
2003	Go, Fractions!		$8	$10	$14	Judith Bauer Stamper		G&D
2003	Hotshots!		$8	$10	$14	Chris Demarest		McEld
2003	She'll By Coming 'Round The Mountain		$8	$10	$14	Chris Demarest		Scholas
2003	Supertwins Meet The Dangerous Dino-Robots		$8	$10	$14	Brian James		Scholas
2003	The Supertwins And Tooth Trouble		$8	$10	$14	Brian James		Scholas
2003	The Supertwins Meet The Bad Dogs From Space		$8	$10	$14	Brian James		Scholas
2004	Leaping Beauty		$8	$10	$14	Gregory Maguire		HCollins
2004	Mayday! Mayday!		$8	$10	$14	Chris Demarest		McEld
2004	Supertwins And The Sneaky		$8	$10	$14	Brian James		Scholas
2004	T. Rex At Swan Lake		$8	$10	$14	L. Carrier & L. Hart		Dutton

Dematons   Charlotte

Year	Title	VG-	VG	VG+	Fine	Author	Award	Pub
1996	Looking For Cinderella		$10	$16	$20	Leigh Sauerwein (adapted)		Front
2001	Let's Go		$8	$10	$14	Charlotte Dematons		Front
2002	Robbie And Ronnie		$8	$10	$14	Christine Kliphuis		NSBooks
2002	Worry Bear		$8	$10	$14	Charlotte Dematons		Front
2003	The Yellow Balloon		$8	$10	$14	Charlotte Dematons		Front

Demi

Year	Title	VG-	VG	VG+	Fine	Author	Award	Pub
1976	The Old China Trade		$30	$40	$60	Francis R. Carpenter		CM&G
1978	All About Your Name, Anne		$20	$30	$40	Tom Glazer		DoubleD
1978	All About Your Name, David		$20	$30	$40	Tom Glazer		DoubleD

Demi

Year	Title	VG-	VG	VG+	Fine	Author	Award	Pub
1978	All About Your Name, Elizabeth		$20	$30	$40	Tom Glazer		DoubleD
1978	All About Your Name, James		$20	$30	$40	Tom Glazer		DoubleD
1978	All About Your Name, John		$20	$30	$40	Tom Glazer		DoubleD
1978	All About Your Name, Joseph		$20	$30	$40	Tom Glazer		DoubleD
1978	All About Your Name, Katherine		$20	$30	$40	Tom Glazer		DoubleD
1978	All About Your Name, Mary		$20	$30	$40	Tom Glazer		DoubleD
1978	All About Your Name, Susan		$20	$30	$40	Tom Glazer		DoubleD
1978	All About Your Name, William		$20	$30	$40	Tom Glazer		DoubleD
1979	Bong Nam And The Pheasants		$18	$25	$35	Yushin Yoo		P-Hall
1979	The Shape Of Water		$18	$25	$35	Augusta R. Goldin		DoubleD
1979	Under The Shade Of The Mulberry Tree		$18	$25	$35	Demi		P-Hall
1979	Where Is It?		$18	$25	$35	Demi		DoubleD
1980	Dragon Night & Other Lullabies		$18	$25	$35	Jane Yolen		Metheun
1980	Liang And The Magic Paintbrush		$18	$25	$35	Demi		HR&W
1980	The Leaky Umbrella		$18	$25	$35	Demi		P-Hall
1981	Follow The Line		$18	$25	$35	Demi		HR&W
1981	Three Little Elephants		$18	$25	$35	Demi		Random
1981	Tony's Tunnel		$18	$25	$35	Ann Sperry McGrath		HR&W
1981	Where Is Willie Worm?		$18	$25	$35	Demi		Random
1982	The Adventures Of Marco Polo		$16	$25	$30	Demi		HR&W
1982	The Peek-A-Boo ABC		$16	$25	$30	Demi		Random
1983	Make Noise, Make Merry		$16	$25	$30	Miriam Chaikin		Clarion
1984	Fat Gopal		$16	$25	$30	Jacquelin Singh		HBJ
1985	Demi's Find-The-Animal A.B.C		$16	$25	$30	Demi		G&D
1985	The Nightingale		$16	$25	$30	Anna Bier (adapted)		HBJ
1986	Demi's Count The Animals 1-2-3		$14	$20	$30	Demi		G&D
1986	Dragon Kites And Dragonflies		$14	$20	$30	Demi		HBJ
1986	Fuzzy Wuzzy Puppy		$14	$20	$30	Demi		G&D
1986	So Soft Kitty		$14	$20	$30	Demi		G&D
1987	A Chinese Zoo		$14	$20	$30	Demi		HBJ
1987	Chen Ping And His Magic Axe		$14	$20	$30	Demi		DoddM
1987	Demi's Opposites		$14	$20	$30	Demi		G&D
1987	Fleecy Lamb		$14	$20	$30	Demi		G&D
1987	Fluffy Bunny		$14	$20	$30	Demi		G&D
1987	The Hallowed Horse		$14	$20	$30	Demi		DoddM
1988	Cuddly Chick		$14	$20	$30	Demi		G&D
1988	Demi's Reflective Fables		$14	$20	$30	Demi		G&D
1988	Downy Duckling		$14	$20	$30	Demi		G&D
1988	Hans Christian Andersen's Thumbelina		$14	$20	$30	Demi (adapted)		DoddM
1989	Demi's Basket Of Books		$14	$20	$25	Demi		G&D
1989	Find Demi's Dinosaurs		$14	$20	$25	Demi		G&D
1990	Demi's Christmas Surprise		$12	$18	$25	Demi		G&D
1990	Find Demi's Baby Animals		$12	$18	$25	Demi		G&D
1990	The Empty Pot		$12	$18	$25	Demi		Holt
1990	The Magic Boat		$12	$18	$25	Demi		Holt
1991	Chingis Khan		$12	$18	$25	Demi		Holt
1991	Find Demi's Sea Creatures		$12	$18	$25	Demi		Putnam
1991	The Artist And The Architect		$12	$18	$25	Demi		Holt
1992	In The Eyes Of The Cat		$12	$18	$25	Demi		Holt
1992	Little Bitty Bunny		$12	$18	$25	Demi		G&D
1992	Little Chick Chick		$12	$18	$25	Demi		G&D
1993	Bamboo Hats And A Rice Cake		$12	$16	$20	Ann Tompert		Crown
1993	Demi's Dragons And Fantastic Creatures		$12	$16	$20	Demi		Holt
1993	Demi's Secret Garden		$12	$16	$20	Demi		Holt
1993	Little Baby Lamb		$12	$16	$20	Demi		G&D
1993	Little Lucky Ducky		$12	$16	$20	Demi		G&D
1994	Demi's Dozen Dinosaurs		$12	$16	$20	Demi		Holt
1994	Santa's Furry Friends		$12	$16	$20	Demi		Holt
1994	The Firebird		$12	$16	$20	Demi		Holt
1994	The Magic Tapestry		$12	$16	$20	Demi		Holt
1995	Eucalyptus Wings		$10	$16	$20	J. Alison James		Athenm
1995	The Magic Gold Fish		$10	$16	$20	Aleksandr Pushkin		Holt
1995	The Stonecutter		$10	$16	$20	Demi		Crown
1996	Buddha		$10	$16	$20	Demi		Holt
1996	Dragon's Tale & Other Fables Of The Chinese Zodiac		$10	$16	$20	Demi		Holt
1997	Buddha Stories		$10	$16	$20	Demi		Holt
1997	Grass Sandals		$10	$16	$20	Dawnine Spivak		Athenm

Demi

Year	Title	VG-	VG	VG+	Fine	Author	Award	Pub
1997	One Grain Of Rice		$10	$16	$20	Demi		Scholas
1998	Happy New Year!		$10	$14	$18	Demi		Crown
1998	The Dalai Lama		$10	$14	$18	Demi		Holt
1998	The Greatest Treasure		$10	$14	$18	Demi		Scholas
1999	Kites		$10	$14	$18	Demi		Crown
1999	The Donkey And The Rock		$10	$14	$18	Demi		Holt
2000	Liang And The Magic Paintbrush		$8	$12	$16	Demi		HR&W
2000	The Emperor's New Clothes		$8	$12	$16	Demi		McEld
2001	Gandhi		$8	$12	$16	Demi		McEld
2002	King Midas		$8	$10	$14	Demi		McEld
2003	Happy, Happy Chinese New Year!		$8	$10	$14	Demi		Crown
2003	Muhammad		$8	$10	$14	Demi		McEld
2003	The Legend Of Saint Nicholas		$8	$10	$14	Demi		McEld
2004	The Greatest Power		$8	$10	$14	Demi		McEld
2004	The Hungry Coat		$8	$10	$14	Demi		McEld

Dennis   Morgan

Year	Title	VG-	VG	VG+	Fine	Author	Award	Pub
1918	The Caravan Man	$100	$140	$180		Ernest Goodwin		HM
1920	The Real Diary Of The Worst Farmer	$70	$100	$120		Henry A. Shute		HM
1921	Tom Of The Raiders	$70	$90	$120		Austin Bishop		HBrace
1922	A Modern Trio In An Old Town	$70	$90	$120		Katharine Haviland Taylor		HBrace
1922	The Hop Pickers	$70	$90	$120		Flavia A. Camp Canfield		HBrace
1923	Saddle Bags	$70	$90	$120		Clifton Lisle		HBrace
1924	Tony From America	$70	$90	$120		Katharine Haviland Taylor		HBrace
1928	The Boy's Book Of Dogs	$70	$90	$120		Ralph Henry Barbour		DoddM
1930	Portrait Of A Dog	$60	$80	$100		Mazo De la Roche		LBrown
1933	Luck Of The Trail	$60	$80	$100		Esther Birdsall Darling		DD
1934	Gypsy Lad	$60	$80	$100		Sterner St. Paul Meek		Morrow
1934	Jock And Jill	$80	$120	$140		Maida Huneker		G&D
1937	...Sniff	$50	$60	$80		James S. Tippett		Heath
1937	A Friend In The Dark	$70	$90	$120		Ruth Adams Knight		G&D
1937	Shadow And The Stocking	$70	$90	$120		James S. Tippett		H&B
1938	Long Tails And Short	$50	$60	$80		Gladys (Bagg) Taber		MacSm
1938	The Rubaiyat Of Omar Ki-Yi	$70	$90	$120		Burges Johnson		Putnam
1941	Pete	$70	$90	$120		Thomas P. Robinson		Viking
1943	The Pup Himself	$70	$90	$120		Morgan Dennis		Viking
1943	Valiant Comrades	$50	$60	$80		Ruth Adams Knight		DD
1944	Crazy Dog	$60	$80	$100		Leon Ware		Whittle
1945	Burlap	$60	$80	$100		Morgan Dennis		Viking
1946	The Morgan Dennis Dog Book	$60	$80	$100		Morgan Dennis		Viking
1947	Every Dog Has His Say	$60	$80	$100		Edward Anthony		WGuptil
1950	The Dog Next Door	$40	$50	$70		Keith Robertson		Viking
1951	Skit And Skat	$50	$70	$90		Morgan Dennis		Viking
1951	The Cat That Went To College	$50	$70	$90		Frances Frost		Whittle
1952	Little Fox	$50	$70	$90		Frances Frost		Whittle
1952	Lost Dog Jerry	$40	$50	$70		Thomas P. Robinson		Viking
1952	Rags, The Firehouse Dog	$50	$70	$90		Elizabeth Morton		WP
1953	Everybody's Dog Book	$50	$70	$90		Beth Brown		WP
1954	Himself And Burlap On TV	$50	$70	$90		Morgan Dennis		Viking
1954	Pure Breds	$50	$70	$90		Morgan Dennis		WP
1955	Yipe	$50	$70	$90		David Malcolmson		LBrown
1958	The Sea Dog	$50	$60	$80		Morgan Dennis		Viking
1961	Kitten On The Keys	$50	$60	$80		Morgan Dennis		Viking

Dennis   Wesley

Year	Title	VG-	VG	VG+	Fine	Author	Award	Pub
1941	Flip	$140	$180	$240		Wesley Dennis		Viking
1942	Flip And The Cows	$70	$90	$120		Wesley Dennis		Viking
1944	Riders Of The Gabilans	$60	$80	$100		Graham Dean		Viking
1945	Justin Morgan Had A Horse	$140	$180	$220		Marguerite Henry	NH	W&F
1945	The Red Pony	$200	$280	$340		John Steinbeck		Viking
1946	Black Beauty	$90	$120	$160		Anna Sewell		World
1946	Golden Sovereign	$60	$80	$100		Dorothy Lyons		HBrace
1946	Holiday	$60	$80	$100		Wesley Dennis		Viking
1946	Now Listen, Warden	$60	$80	$100		Raymond Holland		Barnes

Dennis   Wesley

Year	Title	VG-	VG	VG+	Fine	Author	Award	Pub
1947	Benjamin West And His Cat Grimalkin	$60	$80	$100		Marguerite Henry		Bobbs
1947	Misty Of Chincoteague	$120	$160	$220		Marguerite Henry	NH	RandMc
1948	King Of The Wind	$280	$380	$480		Marguerite Henry	NM	RandMc
1949	Sea Star	$80	$120	$140		Marguerite Henry		RandMc
1950	Born To Trot	$80	$120	$140		Marguerite Henry		RandMc
1950	Palomino & Other Horses	$80	$120	$140		Wesley Dennis		World
1951	Flip And The Morning	$80	$100	$140		Wesley Dennis		Viking
1952	Fools Over Horses	$80	$100	$140		Helen Orr Watson		HM
1952	Portfolio Of Horses	$80	$100	$140		Wesley Dennis		RandMc
1953	Brighty Of The Grand Canyon	$80	$100	$140		Marguerite Henry		RandMc
1954	Justin Morgan Had A Horse	$50	$70	$90		Marguerite Henry		RandMc
1956	Cinnabar- The One O'Clock Fox	$50	$70	$90		Wesley Dennis		RandMc
1957	A Crow I Know	$50	$70	$90		Wesley Dennis		Viking
1957	Black Gold	$50	$70	$90		Marguerite Henry		RandMc
1961	Cammie's Choice	$50	$60	$80		Jane McIlvaine McClary		Bobbs
1962	Cammie's Challenge	$50	$60	$80		Jane McIlvaine McClary		Bobbs
1963	Stormy, Misty's Foal	$50	$60	$80		Marguerite Henry		RandMc
1964	A Horse Called Mystery	$50	$60	$80		Marjorie Reynolds		H&Row
1964	Portfolio Of Horse Paintings	$50	$60	$80		Marguerite Henry		RandMc
1964	White Stallion Of Lipizza	$50	$60	$80		Marguerite Henry		RandMc
1965	The Book Of Ponies	$40	$60	$70		Suzanne Wilding		StMart
1965	The Ice Bird	$40	$60	$70		Pauline B. Innis		RBLuce
1966	The Small War Of Sergeant Donkey	$40	$60	$70		Maureen Daly		DoddM
1966	Tumble	$40	$60	$70		Wesley Dennis		Hastings
1970	Album Of Dogs		$30	$50	$60	Marguerite Henry		RandMc
1976	A Pictorial Life Story Of Misty		$30	$40	$60	Marguerite Henry		RandMc
1977	One Man's Horse		$25	$40	$50	Marguerite Henry		RandMc

dePaola   Tomie

Year	Title	VG-	VG	VG+	Fine	Author	Award	Pub
1965	Sound	$60	$80	$100		Tomie dePaola		CM
1965	The Tiger And The Rabbit, & Other Tales	$60	$80	$100		Tomie dePaola		Lippin
1965	Wheels	$60	$80	$100		Tomie dePaola		CM
1967	Finders Keepers, Losers Weepers	$40	$50	$70		Joan M. Lexau		Lippin
1967	Tricky Peik, & Other Picture Tales	$40	$50	$70		Jeanne B. Hardendorff		Lippin
1968	Fight The Night	$60	$80	$100		Tomie dePaola		Lippin
1968	Joe And The Snow	$40	$50	$70		Tomie dePaola		HawB
1968	Poetry For Chuckles And Grins	$30	$40	$50		Leland B. Jacobs		Garrard
1968	Sound Science	$30	$40	$50		Melvin L. Alexenberg		P-Hall
1968	The Cabinet Of The President Of The United States	$30	$40	$50		James A. Eichner.		FWatts
1969	Hercules, The Gentle Giant	$60	$80	$100		Tomie dePaola		HawB
1969	Light And Sight	$25	$35	$50		Melvin L. Alexenberg.		P-Hall
1969	Parker Pig, Esquire	$60	$80	$100		Tomie dePaola		HawB
1969	Take This Hammer	$40	$50	$70		Sam and Beryl Epstein		HawB
1969	The Morning Glory	$40	$50	$70		Robert Bly		Kayak
1969	The Rocking-Chair Ghost	$40	$50	$70		Mary C. Jane.		Lippin
1970	How To Be A Puppeteer		$30	$50	$60	Tomie dePaola		McCall
1970	Rutherford T. Finds 21 B		$30	$50	$60	Tomie dePaola		Putnam
1970	The Folklore Of Love And Courtship		$30	$50	$60	Tomie dePaola		AHP
1970	The Folklore Of Weddings And Marriage		$30	$50	$60	Tomie dePaola		AHP
1970	The Journey Of The Kiss		$50	$70	$90	Tomie dePaola		HawB
1970	The Monsters' Ball		$50	$70	$90	Tomie dePaola		HawB
1970	Who Needs Holes?		$30	$50	$60	Sam and Beryl Epstein		HawB
1971	Hot As An Ice Cube		$30	$50	$60	Tomie dePaola		Crowell
1971	John Fisher's Magic Book		$30	$50	$60	Tomie dePaola		P-Hall
1971	Monsters Of The Middle Ages		$40	$60	$90	Tomie dePaola		Putnam
1971	Pick It Up		$30	$50	$60	Sam and Beryl Epstein		Holiday
1972	Mario's Mystery Machine		$30	$50	$60	Tomie dePaola		Putnam
1972	The Franklin Watts Concise Guide To Baby-Sitting		$25	$35	$50	Tomie dePaola		FWatts
1972	The Wind And The Sun		$40	$60	$90	Tomie dePaola		Ginn
1972	What Is Fear?		$25	$35	$50	Jean Rosenbaum		P-Hall
1973	Andy (That's My Name)		$30	$50	$60	Tomie dePaola		P-Hall
1973	Danny And His Thumb		$30	$50	$60	Kathryn F. Ernst		P-Hall
1973	Hold Everything		$30	$50	$60	Sam and Beryl Epstein		Holiday
1973	Let's Find Out About Communications		$30	$50	$60	Tomie dePaola		FWatts
1973	Look In The Mirror		$30	$50	$60	Sam and Beryl Epstein		Holiday

dePaola   Tomie

Year	Title	VG-	VG	VG+	Fine	Author	Award	Pub
1973	Nana Upstairs & Nana Downstairs		$30	$50	$60	Tomie dePaola		Putnam
1973	The Unicorn And The Moon		$40	$60	$90	Tomie dePaola		Ginn
1974	Charlie Needs A Cloak		$30	$40	$60	Tomie dePaola		P-Hall
1974	David's Windows		$30	$40	$60	Tomie dePaola		Putnam
1974	Star-Spangled Banana & Other Revolutionary Riddles		$30	$40	$60	Charles Keller		P-Hall
1974	Watch Out For The Chicken Feet In Your Soup		$30	$40	$60	Tomie dePaola		P-Hall
1975	Let's Find Out About Houses		$20	$30	$40	Martha & Charles Shapp		FWatts
1975	Michael Bird-Boy		$30	$40	$60	Tomie dePaola		P-Hall
1975	Old Man Whickutt's Donkey		$30	$40	$60	Tomie dePaola		PMagP
1975	Strega Nona	$160	$220	$300		Tomie dePaola	CH	P-Hall
1975	The Cloud Book		$20	$30	$40	Tomie dePaola		Holiday
1975	This Is The Ambulance Leaving The Zoo		$30	$40	$60	Norma Farber		Dutton
1976	Good Morning To You, Valentine: Poems		$30	$40	$60	Lee Bennett Hopkins		HBJ
1976	I Love You, Mouse		$30	$40	$60	John Graham		HBJ
1976	If He's My Brother		$30	$40	$60	Barbara Williams		Harvey
1976	The Mixed-Up Mystery Smell		$20	$30	$40	Eleanor Coerr		Putnam
1976	The Tyrannosaurus Game		$20	$30	$40	Steven Kroll		Holiday
1976	The Whatchamacallit Book		$20	$30	$40	Bernice Kohn Hunt		Putnam
1976	Things To Make And Do For Valentine's Day		$20	$30	$40	Tomie dePaola		FWatts
1976	When Everyone Was Fast Asleep		$30	$40	$60	Tomie dePaola		Holiday
1977	Beat The Drum, Independence Day Has Come		$20	$30	$40	Lee Bennett Hopkins		HBJ
1977	Can't You Make Them Behave, King George?		$25	$40	$50	Jean Fritz		CM&G
1977	Four Stories For Four Seasons		$20	$30	$40	Tomie dePaola		P-Hall
1977	Helga's Dowry: A Troll Love Story		$25	$40	$50	Tomie dePaola		HBJ
1977	Odd Jobs: Story		$20	$30	$40	Tony Johnston		Putnam
1977	Once Upon A Dinkelsbuhl		$20	$30	$40	Patricia Lee Gauch		Putnam
1977	Santa's Crash-Bang Christmas		$20	$30	$40	Steven Kroll		Holiday
1977	Simple Pictures Are Best		$20	$30	$40	Nancy Willard		HBJ
1977	The Ghost With The Halloween Hiccups		$25	$40	$50	Stephen Mooser		FWatts
1977	The Giants' Farm		$25	$40	$50	Jane Yolen		Seabury
1977	The Images Of Jesus		$20	$30	$40	Daniel O'Connor		WP
1977	The Quicksand Book		$20	$30	$40	Tomie dePaola		Holiday
1977	The Surprise Party		$20	$30	$40	Annabelle Prager		Pan
1978	Bill And Pete		$20	$30	$40	Tomie dePaola		Putnam
1978	Criss-Cross Applesauce		$20	$30	$40	B. A. King		BIP
1978	Fat Magic		$20	$30	$40	Steven Kroll		Holiday
1978	Four Scary Stories		$20	$30	$40	Tony Johnston		Putnam
1978	Jamie's Tiger		$20	$30	$40	Jan Wahl		HBJ
1978	Marc The Magnificent		$25	$40	$50	Sue Alexander		Pan
1978	Oh, Such Foolishness!: Poems		$20	$30	$40	William Cole		Lippin
1978	Pancakes For Breakfast		$20	$30	$40	Tomie dePaola		HBJ
1978	The Christmas Pageant		$20	$30	$40	Tomie dePaola		WP
1978	The Clown Of God		$20	$30	$40	Tomie dePaola		HBJ
1978	The Popcorn Book		$20	$30	$40	Tomie dePaola		Holiday
1979	Big Anthony And The Magic Ring		$25	$40	$50	Tomie dePaola		HBJ
1979	Easter Buds Are Springing: Poems For Easter		$25	$40	$50	Lee Bennett Hopkins		HBJ
1979	Flicks		$25	$40	$50	Tomie dePaola		HBJ
1979	Ghost Poems		$25	$40	$50	Daisy Wallace		Holiday
1979	My Daddy's Mustache		$25	$40	$50	Naomi Panush Salus		DoubleD
1979	Oliver Button Is A Sissy		$25	$40	$50	Tomie dePaola		HBJ
1979	Songs Of The Fog Maiden		$25	$40	$50	Tomie dePaola		Holiday
1979	The Cat On The Dovrefell: A Christmas Tale		$25	$40	$50	George Webbe Dasent		Putnam
1979	The Giants Go Camping		$25	$40	$50	Jane Yolen		Seabury
1979	The Kids' Cat Book		$25	$40	$50	Tomie dePaola		Holiday
1979	The Triumphs Of Fuzzy Fogtop		$25	$40	$50	Anne K. Rose		Dial
1980	Moon, Stars, Frogs, And Friends		$25	$35	$50	Patricia MacLachlan		Pan
1980	The Family Christmas Tree Book		$25	$35	$50	Tomie dePaola		Holiday
1980	The Knight And The Dragon		$25	$35	$50	Tomie dePaola		Putnam
1980	The Lady Of Guadalupe		$25	$35	$50	Tomie dePaola		Holiday
1980	The Legend Of Old Befana		$25	$35	$50	Tomie dePaola		HBJ
1980	The Little Friar Who Flew		$25	$35	$50	Patricia Lee Gauch		Putnam
1980	The Night Before Christmas		$25	$35	$50	Clement C. Moore		Holiday
1980	The Prince Of The Dolomites: An Old Italian Tale		$25	$35	$50	Tomie dePaola		HBJ
1980	The Walking Coat		$25	$35	$50	Pauline Watson		Walker
1980	The Wuggie Norple Story		$25	$35	$50	Daniel Pinkwater		4Winds
1981	Comic Adventures Of Old Mother Hubbard & Her Dog		$25	$35	$50	Tomie dePaola		HBJ
1981	Edward, Benjamin, And Butter		$25	$35	$50	Malcolm Hall		CM&G

dePaola   Tomie

Year	Title	VG-	VG	VG+	Fine	Author	Award	Pub
1981	Fin M'coul: The Giant Of Knockmany Hill		$25	$35	$50	Tomie dePaola		Holiday
1981	Funnyman's First Case		$25	$35	$50	Stephen Mooser		FWatts
1981	Now One Foot, Now The Other		$25	$35	$50	Tomie dePaola		Putnam
1981	Robin Goodfellow And The Giant Dwarf		$25	$35	$50	Michael Jennings		McHill
1981	The Friendly Beasts		$25	$35	$50	Tomie dePaola		Putnam
1981	The Hunter And The Animals		$25	$35	$50	Tomie dePaola		Holiday
1981	The Spooky Halloween Party		$25	$35	$50	Annabelle Prager		Pan
1982	Francis, The Poor Man Of Assisi		$25	$35	$50	Tomie dePaola		Holiday
1982	Giorgio's Village		$25	$35	$50	Tomie dePaola		Putnam
1982	Nicholas Bentley Stoningpot Iii		$25	$35	$50	Ann McGovern		Holiday
1982	Odd Jobs And Friends		$25	$35	$50	Tony Johnston		Putnam
1982	Strega Nona's Magic Lessons		$25	$35	$50	Tomie dePaola		HBJ
1982	The Good Giants And The Bad Pukwudgies		$25	$35	$50	Jean Fritz		Putnam
1983	Marianna May And Nursey		$25	$35	$50	Tomie dePaola		Holiday
1983	Noah And The Ark		$25	$35	$50	Tomie dePaola		WP
1983	Sing, Pierrot, Sing		$25	$35	$50	Tomie dePaola		HBJ
1983	Tattie's River Journey		$25	$35	$50	Shirley Murphy		Dial
1983	The Carsick Zebra & Other Animal Riddles		$25	$35	$50	David A. Adler		Holiday
1983	The Legend Of The Bluebonnet		$25	$35	$50	Tomie dePaola		Putnam
1983	The Story Of The Three Wise Kings		$25	$35	$50	Tomie dePaola		Putnam
1983	The Vanishing Pumpkin		$25	$35	$50	Tony Johnston		Putnam
1984	David And Goliath		$20	$30	$40	Tomie dePaola		WP
1984	Funnyman And The Penny Dodo		$20	$30	$40	Stephen Mooser		FWatts
1984	Mary Had A Little Lamb		$20	$30	$40	Sarah Josepha Hale		Holiday
1984	Miracle On 34th Street		$20	$30	$40	Valentine Davies		HBJ
1984	The First Christmas		$20	$30	$40	Tomie dePaola		Putnam
1984	The Mysterious Giant Of Barletta		$20	$30	$40	Tomie dePaola		HBJ
1985	The Quilt Story		$20	$30	$40	Tony Johnston		Putnam
1985	Tomie Depaola's Mother Goose		$20	$30	$40	Tomie dePaola		Putnam
1986	For Every Child A Star: A Christmas Story		$20	$30	$40	Thomas Yeomans		Holiday
1986	Katie & Kit At The Beach		$20	$30	$40	Tomie dePaola		S&S
1986	Katie, Kit & Cousin Tom		$20	$30	$40	Tomie dePaola		LSimon
1986	Katie's Good Idea		$20	$30	$40	Tomie dePaola		LSimon
1986	Merry Christmas, Strega Nona		$20	$30	$40	Tomie dePaola		HBrace
1986	Pajamas For Kit		$20	$30	$40	Tomie dePaola		LSimon
1986	Queen Esther		$20	$30	$40	Tomie dePaola		H&Row
1986	Teeny Tiny		$20	$30	$40	Jill Bennett		Putnam
1986	Tomie Depaola's Favorite Nursery Tales		$20	$30	$40	Tomie dePaola		Putnam
1986	Who's A Friend Of The Water-Spurting Whale?		$20	$30	$40	Sanna Anderson Baker		Chariot
1987	An Early American Christmas		$20	$30	$40	Tomie dePaola		Holiday
1987	Bill And Pete Go Down The Nile		$20	$30	$40	Tomie dePaola		Putnam
1987	Maggie And The Monster		$20	$30	$40	Elizabeth Winthrop		Holiday
1987	Shh! We're Writing The Constitution		$20	$30	$40	Jean Fritz		Putnam
1987	The Miracles Of Jesus		$20	$30	$40	Bible		Holiday
1987	The Mountains Of Quilt		$20	$30	$40	Nancy Willard		HBJ
1987	The Parables Of Jesus		$20	$30	$40	Bible		Holiday
1987	Tomie Depaola's Book Of Christmas Carols		$20	$30	$40	Tomie dePaola		Putnam
1987	What The Mailman Brought		$20	$30	$40	Carolyn Craven		Putnam
1988	Baby's First Christmas		$18	$25	$35	Tomie dePaola		Putnam
1988	Cookie's Week		$18	$25	$35	Cindy Ward		Putnam
1988	Hey Diddle Diddle & Other Mother Goose Rhymes		$18	$25	$35	Tomie dePaola		Putnam
1988	Pages Of Music		$18	$25	$35	Tony Johnston		Putnam
1988	Petook: An Easter Story		$18	$25	$35	Catherine Hiller		Holiday
1988	The Legend Of The Indian Paintbrush		$18	$25	$35	Tomie dePaola		Putnam
1988	Tomie Depaola's Book Of Poems		$18	$25	$35	Tomie dePaola		Putnam
1988	Tomie Depaola's Kitten Kids And The Big Camp-Out		$18	$25	$35	Tomie dePaola		Western
1988	Tomie Depaola's Kitten Kids And The Treasure Hunt		$18	$25	$35	Tomie dePaola		Western
1989	Haircuts For The Woolseys		$18	$25	$35	Tomie dePaola		Putnam
1989	My First Chanukah		$18	$25	$35	Tomie dePaola		Putnam
1989	The Art Lesson		$18	$25	$35	Tomie dePaola		Putnam
1989	Tony's Bread: An Italian Folktale		$18	$25	$35	Tomie dePaola		Putnam
1989	Too Many Hopkins		$18	$25	$35	Tomie dePaola		Putnam
1990	Little Grunt And The Big Egg:		$16	$25	$30	Tomie dePaola		Holiday
1990	My First Easter		$16	$25	$30	Tomie dePaola		Putnam
1990	My First Passover		$16	$25	$30	Tomie dePaola		Putnam
1990	The Badger And The Magic Fan		$16	$25	$30	Tony Johnston		Putnam
1990	Tomie Depaola's Book Of Bible Stories		$16	$25	$30	Tomie dePaola		Putnam

dePaola   Tomie

Year	Title	VG-	VG	VG+	Fine	Author	Award	Pub
1991	Bonjour, Mr. Satie		$16	$25	$30	Tomie dePaola		Putnam
1991	Hark! A Christmas Sampler		$16	$25	$30	Jane Yolen		Putnam
1991	My First Halloween		$16	$25	$30	Tomie dePaola		Putnam
1992	Jamie O'rourke And The Big Potato		$16	$25	$30	Tomie dePaola		Putnam
1992	Jingle, The Christmas Clown		$16	$25	$30	Tomie dePaola		Putnam
1992	My First Thanksgiving		$16	$25	$30	Tomie dePaola		Putnam
1992	Patrick: Patron Saint Of Ireland		$16	$25	$30	Tomie dePaola		Holiday
1992	The Great Adventure Of Christopher Columbus		$16	$25	$30	Jean Fritz		Putnam
1993	Strega Nona Meets Her Match		$16	$25	$30	Tomie dePaola		Putnam
1994	Christopher: The Holy Giant		$14	$20	$30	Tomie dePaola		Holiday
1994	Kit And Kat		$14	$20	$30	Tomie dePaola		G&D
1994	Mice Squeak, We Speak		$14	$20	$30	Tomie dePaola		Putnam
1994	The Legend Of The Poinsettia		$14	$20	$30	Tomie dePaola		Putnam
1994	The Tale Of Rabbit And Coyote		$14	$20	$30	Tony Johnston		Putnam
1995	Alice Nizzy Nazzy, The Witch Of Santa Fe		$14	$20	$25	Tony Johnston		Putnam
1995	Country Angel Christmas		$14	$20	$25	Tomie dePaola		Putnam
1995	Mary: The Mother Of Jesus		$14	$20	$25	Tomie dePaola		Holiday
1995	Tomie Depaola's Book Of The Old Testament		$14	$20	$25	Tomie dePaola		G&D
1996	Get Dressed, Santa!		$12	$18	$25	Tomie dePaola		G&D
1996	Strega Nona: Her Story		$12	$18	$25	Tomie dePaola		Putnam
1996	The Baby Sister		$12	$18	$25	Tomie dePaola		Putnam
1996	The Bubble Factory		$12	$18	$25	Tomie dePaola		G&D
1997	Antonio, The Bread Boy		$12	$18	$25	Tomie dePaola		Putnam
1997	Benny's Big Bubbles		$12	$18	$25	Jane O'Connor		G&D
1997	Days Of The Blackbird		$12	$18	$25	Tomie dePaola		Putnam
1997	The Eagle And The Rainbow		$12	$18	$25	Antonio Hernandez Madrigal		Fulcrum
1998	Big Anthony: His Story		$12	$16	$20	Tomie dePaola		Putnam
1998	Bill And Pete To The Rescue		$12	$16	$20	Tomie dePaola		Putnam
1998	H.C. Andersen's The Emperor's New Clothes		$12	$16	$20	Hans Christian Andersen		HBrace
1999	26 Fairmount Avenue		$35	$50	$70	Tomie dePaola	NH	Putnam
1999	Erandi's Braids		$12	$16	$20	Antonio Madrigal		Putnam
1999	The Night Of Las Posadas		$12	$16	$20	Tomie dePaola		Putnam
2000	Here We All Are		$10	$14	$18	Tomie dePaola		Putnam
2000	Jamie O'rourke And The Pooka		$10	$14	$18	Tomie dePaola		Putnam
2000	Strega Nona Takes A Vacation		$10	$14	$18	Tomie dePaola		Putnam
2000	Tomie Depaola's Rhyme Time		$10	$14	$18	Tomie dePaola		G&D
2001	Meet The Barkers		$10	$14	$18	Tomie dePaola		Putnam
2001	On My Way		$10	$14	$18	Tomie dePaola		Putnam
2001	The Holy Twins		$10	$14	$18	Kathleen Norris		Putnam
2002	A New Barker In The House		$8	$12	$16	Tomie dePaola		Putnam
2002	Adelita		$8	$12	$16	Tomie dePaola		Putnam
2002	Four Friends At Christmas		$8	$12	$16	Tomie dePaola		S&S
2002	Hide-And-Seek All Week		$8	$12	$16	Tomie dePaola		G&D
2002	Is That A Fact?		$8	$12	$16	Tony Stead		Sten
2002	Tomie's Little Christmas Pageant		$8	$12	$16	Tomie dePaola		Putnam
2002	T-Rex Is Missing!		$8	$12	$16	Tomie dePaola		G&D
2002	What A Year		$8	$12	$16	Tomie dePaola		Putnam
2003	Frida Kahlo		$8	$12	$16	Margaret Frith		G&D
2003	Marcos		$8	$12	$16	Tomie dePaola		Putnam
2003	Marcos Counts		$8	$12	$16	Tomie dePaola		Putnam
2003	Te Amo Sol Te Amo Luna		$8	$12	$16	Karen Pandell		Putnam
2003	Things Will Never Be The Same		$8	$12	$16	Tomie dePaola		Putnam
2003	Trouble In The Barkers' Class		$8	$12	$16	Tomie dePaola		Putnam
2004	Four Friends In Autumn		$8	$10	$14	Tomie dePaola		S&S
2004	Go Away, Girls!		$8	$10	$14	Ann Hackney		G&D
2004	Guess Who's Coming To Santa's For Dinner?		$8	$10	$14	Tomie dePaola		Putnam
2004	Mary Had A Little Lamb		$8	$10	$14	Sarah Josepha Hale		Putnam
2004	Pascual And The Kitchen Angels		$8	$10	$14	Tomie dePaola		Putnam
2004	T-Ball Trouble		$8	$10	$14	Gail Herman		G&D
2004	The Big Sleepover		$8	$10	$14	Gail Herman		G&D
2004	Tomie's Baa Baa Black Sheep & Other Rhymes		$8	$10	$14	Tomie dePaola		Putnam
2004	Tomie's Little Book Of Poems		$8	$10	$14	Tomie dePaola		Putnam
2004	Tomie's Three Bears & Other Tales		$8	$10	$14	Tomie dePaola		Putnam
2004	Triple Checkup		$8	$10	$14	Michelle Poploff		G&D

Devlin   Harry

Year	Title	VG-	VG	VG+	Fine	Author	Award	Pub
1962	The Wonderful Tree House	$50	$60	$80		Harold S. Longman		PMagP
1963	Old Black Witch!	$35	$40	$60		Wende Devlin		EB
1965	The Knobby Boys To The Rescue	$30	$40	$50		Wende Devlin		PMagP
1967	To Grandfather's House We Go	$30	$40	$50		Harry Devlin		4Winds
1968	Aunt Agatha, There's A Lion Under The Couch!	$30	$40	$50		Wende Devlin		VNost
1969	How Fletcher Was Hatched	$25	$35	$50		Wende Devlin		PMagP
1969	What Kind Of A House Is That?	$25	$35	$50		Harry Devlin		PMagP
1970	A Kiss For A Warthog		$25	$35	$50	Wende Devlin		Town
1970	Old Witch And The Polka-Dot Ribbon		$25	$35	$50	Wende Devlin		PMagP
1971	Cranberry Thanksgiving		$25	$35	$50	Wende Devlin		PMagP
1972	Old Witch Rescues Halloween!		$25	$35	$50	Wende Devlin		PMagP
1975	Harrydevlin's Tales Of Thunder And Lightning		$20	$30	$40	Harry Devlin		PMagP
1976	Cranberry Christmas		$20	$30	$40	Wende Devlin		PMagP
1978	Cranberry Mystery		$20	$30	$40	Wende Devlin		PMagP
1980	Hang On, Hester!		$18	$25	$35	Wende Devlin		LL&S
1982	Cranberry Halloween		$16	$25	$30	Wende Devlin		4Winds
1986	Cranberry Valentine		$14	$20	$30	Wende Devlin		4Winds
1988	Cranberry Birthday		$14	$20	$30	Wende Devlin		4Winds
1990	Cranberry Easter		$12	$18	$25	Wende Devlin		4Winds
1992	Cranberry Summer		$12	$18	$25	Wende Devlin		4Winds
1993	Cranberry Autumn		$12	$16	$20	Wende Devlin		4Winds
1994	A New Baby In Cranberryport		$12	$16	$20	Wende Devlin		Aladd
1994	Cranberry Moving Day		$12	$16	$20	Wende Devlin		Aladd
1994	Cranberry Trip To The Dentist		$12	$16	$20	Wende Devlin		Aladd
1994	Maggie Has A Nightmare		$12	$16	$20	Wende Devlin		Aladd
1995	The Trouble With Henriette		$10	$16	$20	Wende Devlin		S&S

Diaz   David

Year	Title	VG-	VG	VG+	Fine	Author	Award	Pub
1992	Neighborhood Odes		$30	$40	$60	Gary Soto		HBJ
1994	Smoky Night		$60	$90	$120	Eve Bunting	CM	HBrace
1996	Going Home		$25	$35	$50	Eve Bunting		HCollins
1996	Just One Flick Of A Finger		$25	$35	$50	Marybeth Lorbiecki		Dial
1996	Passing Strange		$25	$35	$50	Joseph A. Citro		ChapP
1996	Table For Two: An African Folktale		$25	$35	$50	Pauline Cartwright (retold)		CelebP
1996	The Inner City Mother Goose		$25	$35	$50	Eve Merriam		S&S
1996	Wilma Unlimited		$25	$35	$50	Kathleen Krull		HBrace
1997	December		$20	$30	$40	Eve Bunting		HBrace
1998	Be Not Far From Me		$20	$30	$40	Eric Kimmel (adapted)		S&S
1998	The Disappearing Alphabet		$20	$30	$40	Richard Wilbur		HBrace
1998	The Little Scarecrow Boy		$20	$30	$40	Margaret Wise Brown		HCollins
1999	Shadow Story		$18	$25	$35	Nancy Willard		HBrace
2000	Jump Rope Magic		$16	$25	$30	Afi Scruggs		BSP
2000	Roadrunner's Dance		$16	$25	$30	Rudolfo A. Anaya		Hyper
2000	The Gospel Cinderella		$16	$25	$30	Joyce Carol Thomas		HCollins
2000	The Wanderer		$40	$60	$90	Sharon Creech	NH	HCollins
2002	Angel Face		$12	$18	$25	Sarah Weeks		Athenm
2002	The Pot That Juan Built		$12	$18	$25	Nancy Andrews-Goebel		LeeLow
2003	Feliz Navidad!		$12	$16	$20	José Feliciano		Scholas
2004	A Baby In A Basket		$10	$14	$18	Sharon Creech		Cotler

Dillon   Leo & Diane

Year	Title	VG-	VG	VG+	Fine	Author	Award	Pub
1967	Claymore And Kilt	$40	$50	$70		Sorche Nic Leodhas		HR&W
1967	Dangerous Visions	$190	$210	$320		Harlan Ellison		DoubleD
1968	Dark Venture	$40	$50	$70		Audrey Beyer		Knopf
1968	Shamrock And Spear	$40	$50	$70		F. M. Pilkington		HR&W
1968	The Rider And His Horse	$40	$50	$70		Erik Haugaard		HM
1969	Why Heimdall Blew His Horn	$40	$50	$70		Frederick Laing		SBurdet
1970	The Ring In The Prairie		$70	$100	$140	John Bierhorst (edited)		Dial
1971	Gassire's Lute		$40	$60	$90	Alta Jablow (translated)		Dutton
1971	The Untold Tale		$30	$50	$60	Erik Haugaard		HM
1973	Behind The Back Of The Mountain		$40	$60	$90	Verna Aardema (retold)		Dial
1974	Burning Star		$30	$40	$60	Eth Clifford		HM
1974	Songs And Stories From Uganda		$30	$40	$60	W. Moses Serwadda		Crowell
1974	The Third Gift		$40	$60	$80	Jan Carew		LBrown

Dillon   Leo & Diane

Year	Title	VG-	VG	VG+	Fine	Author	Award	Pub
1974	Whirlwind Is A Ghost Dancing		$60	$90	$120	Natalia Belting		Dutton
1975	Song Of The Boat		$40	$60	$80	Lorenz Graham.		Crowell
1975	The Hundred Penny Box		$30	$40	$60	Sharon Bell Mathis		Viking
1975	Why Mosquitoes Buzz In People's Ears		$200	$280	$380	Verna Aardema (retold)	CM	Dial
1976	Ashanti To Zulu: African Traditions		$140	$220	$300	Margaret Musgrove	CM	Dial
1976	Selected Poems, 1923-1975		$30	$40	$60	Robert Penn Warren		Frank
1977	Who's In Rabbit's House?: A Masai Tale		$40	$60	$80	Verna Aardema (retold)		Dial
1978	Honey, I Love, & Other Love Poems		$25	$40	$50	Eloise Greenfield		Crowell
1979	Tales From Scandinavia		$25	$40	$50	Frederick Laing		SBurdet
1980	Children Of The Sun		$25	$35	$50	Jan Carew		LBrown
1980	Two Pairs Of Shoes		$25	$35	$50	P.L. Travers (retold)		Viking
1985	Brother To The Wind		$40	$60	$80	Mildred Pitts Walter		LL&S
1985	The People Could Fly		$40	$60	$80	Virginia Hamilton		Knopf
1987	The Porcelain Cat		$40	$60	$80	Michael Patrick Hearn		LBrown
1989	Moses' Ark: Stories From The Bible		$35	$50	$70	J.C. Exum & A. Bach		DelaP
1989	The Color Wizard		$35	$50	$70	Barbara Brenner		Bantam
1990	Aida		$35	$50	$70	Leontyne Price		HBJ
1990	The Tale Of The Mandarin Ducks		$35	$50	$70	Katherine Paterson	NYT	LodeS
1991	Miriam's Well		$30	$50	$60	J.C. Exum & A. Bach		DelaP
1991	Pish, Posh, Said Hieronymus Bosch		$30	$50	$60	Nancy Willard		HBJ
1991	The Race Of The Golden Apples		$30	$50	$60	Claire Martin		Dial
1992	Northern Lullaby		$25	$35	$50	Nancy Carlstrom		Philo
1993	Many Thousand Gone		$25	$35	$50	Virginia Hamilton		Knopf
1993	Switch On The Night		$25	$35	$50	Ray Bradbury		Knopf
1993	The Sorcerer's Apprentice		$25	$35	$50	Nancy Willard		BSP
1994	What Am I?		$20	$30	$40	N.N. Charles		BSP
1995	Her Stories		$20	$30	$40	Virginia Hamilton		BSP
1995	Wind Child		$20	$30	$40	Shirley Murphy		HCollins
1997	The Girl Who Dreamed Only Geese		$18	$25	$35	Howard Norman		HBrace
1998	To Every Thing There Is A Season		$16	$25	$30	Bible		BSP
2000	20,000 Leagues Under The Sea		$14	$20	$25	Jules Verne		HCollins
2000	The Girl Who Spun Gold		$14	$20	$25	Virginia Hamilton		BSP
2001	Enchantress From The Stars		$12	$18	$25	Sylvia Louise Engdahl		Walker
2001	Mansa Musa		$12	$18	$25	Khephra Burns		Harcort
2001	Two Little Trains		$12	$18	$25	Margaret Wise Brown		HCollins
2002	Rap A Tap Tap		$12	$16	$20	Leo & Diane Dillon		BSP
2003	One Winter's Night		$10	$16	$20	John Herman		Philo
2004	The Porcelain Cat		$8	$12	$16	Michael Patrick Hearn		Milk
2004	Where Have You Been?		$8	$12	$16	Margaret Wise Brown		HCollins

DiTerlizzi   Tony

Year	Title	VG-	VG	VG+	Fine	Author	Award	Pub
1998	Dinosaur Summer		$20	$30	$40	Tony DiTerlizzi		Arcad
2000	Jimmy Zangwow's Moon Pie Adventure		$12	$18	$25	Tony DiTerlizzi		S&S
2000	Ribeting Tales		$12	$18	$25	Nancy Springer		Philo
2001	Alien And Possum		$12	$16	$20	Greg Bear		S&S
2001	Ted		$12	$16	$20	Tony DiTerlizzi		S&S
2002	Alien & Possum Hanging Out		$8	$10	$14	Tony DiTerlizzi		S&S
2002	The Spider And The Fly		$30	$50	$60	Mary Howitt	CH	S&S
2003	Lucinda's Secret		$16	$25	$30	Holly Black		S&S
2003	The Field Guide		$35	$50	$70	Holly Black		S&S
2003	The Ironwood Tree		$10	$16	$20	Holly Black		S&S
2003	The Seeing Stone		$18	$25	$35	Holly Black		S&S
2004	The Wrath of Mulgarath		$10	$14	$18	Holly Black		S&S

Doane   Pelagie

Year	Title	VG-	VG	VG+	Fine	Author	Award	Pub
1932	The Haunted Attic	$50	$70	$90		Margaret Sutton		G&D
1936	The Tail Of The Sorry Sorrel Horse	$70	$100	$120		Elizabeth Hoffman Honness		TNelson
1937	Pinocchio: Put-Together Book	$70	$90	$120		Carlo Lorenzini		Gabriel
1937	Sammy Squirrel Goes To Town	$70	$90	$120		Elizabeth Hoffman Honness		TNelson
1938	Baby's Day In Rhymes And Pictures	$70	$90	$120		Margaret Sutton		G&D
1939	Lollypop	$70	$90	$120		Margaret Sutton		G&D
1940	Did You Ever?	$70	$90	$120		Elizabeth Hoffman Honness		Oxford
1940	Mother Goose	$70	$90	$120		Pelagie Doane		Random
1941	Favourite Nursery Songs	$70	$90	$120		Inez Bertail		Random

Doane   Pelagie

Year	Title	VG-	VG	VG+	Fine	Author	Award	Pub
1941	The Flight Of Fancy	$70	$90	$120		Elizabeth Hoffman Honness		Oxford
1941	Three Prayers For Children ..	$70	$90	$120		Pelagie Doane		G&D
1942	A Brand New Baby	$70	$90	$120		Margaret A. Stanger		Beacon
1942	A Child's Garden Of Verses	$70	$90	$120		Robert Louis Stevenson		GardenC
1942	Polly Peters	$70	$90	$120		Jane Quigg		Oxford
1942	Soldier Sammy	$70	$90	$120		Marion Gill MacNeil		Oxford
1943	Tell Me About God	$70	$90	$120		Mary Alice Jones		RandMc
1943	The Secret Of The Barred Window	$70	$90	$120		Margaret Sutton		G&D
1945	Animals Here And There	$60	$80	$100		Pelagie Doane		GardenC
1946	A Small Child's Bible	$60	$80	$100		Pelagie Doane		Oxford
1946	Angel Child	$60	$80	$100		Val Teal		RandMc
1946	Just Like Me	$60	$80	$100		Ruth MacKay		Abing
1946	The Rainbow Riddle	$60	$80	$100		Margaret Sutton		G&D
1947	Brother, Baby And I	$60	$80	$100		Pelagie Doane		G&D
1947	Little Steps	$60	$80	$100		Elsa Ruth Nast		G&D
1947	Peter's Birthday Party	$60	$80	$100		Edward Ernest		Oxford
1948	A Small Child's Book Of Verse	$60	$80	$100		Pelagie Doane		Oxford
1948	My First Dictionary	$60	$80	$100		Laura Oftedahl		G&D
1951	Prayers And Graces	$50	$70	$90		Dorothy Sheldon		G&D
1952	A Book Of Nature	$50	$70	$90		Pelagie Doane		Oxford
1953	The Boy Jesus	$50	$70	$90		Pelagie Doane		Oxford
1954	Bible Children	$50	$70	$90		Pelagie Doane		Lippin
1956	Littlest Ones	$50	$70	$90		Pelagie Doane		Oxford
1956	The First Day	$50	$70	$90		Pelagie Doane		Lippin
1957	One Rainy Night	$50	$70	$90		Pelagie Doane		Oxford
1958	The Big Trip	$50	$60	$80		Pelagie Doane		Walck
1958	The Story Of Moses	$50	$60	$80		Pelagie Doane		Lippin
1960	God Made The World	$50	$60	$80		Pelagie Doane		Lippin
1962	Understanding Kim	$50	$60	$80		Pelagie Doane		Lippin
1964	Fairy Elves	$50	$60	$80		Robin Palmer		Walck

Domanska   Janina

Year	Title	VG-	VG	VG+	Fine	Author	Award	Pub
1961	Ten And A Kid	$70	$90	$120		Sadie Rose Weilerstein		DoubleD
1961	The Song Of The Lop-Eared Mule	$50	$60	$80		Natalie Carlson		H&B
1962	Gas Station Gus	$50	$60	$80		Dorothy M. Kunhardt		H&B
1962	Mischievous Meg	$50	$60	$80		Astrid Lindgren		Viking
1962	The Golden Seed	$50	$60	$80		Maria Konopnicka		Scribnr
1963	I Like Weather	$50	$60	$80		Aileen Fisher		Crowell
1964	Nikkos And The Pink Pelican	$50	$60	$80		Ruth Tooze		Viking
1964	The Coconut Thieves	$50	$60	$80		Catharine Fournier		Scribnr
1965	Light	$40	$60	$70		Bernice Kohn Hunt		CM
1965	Why So Much Noise?	$40	$60	$70		Janina Domanska		H&Row
1966	The Black Heart Of Indri	$40	$60	$70		Dorothy Hoge		Scribnr
1967	Palmiero And The Ogre	$40	$50	$70		Janina Domanska		Macmil
1967	The Dragon Liked Smoked Fish	$40	$50	$70		Jerzy Laskowski		Seabury
1968	Look, There Is A Turtle Flying	$40	$50	$70		Janina Domanska		Macmil
1969	The Turnip	$40	$50	$70		Janina Domanska		Macmil
1970	Marilka		$30	$50	$60	Janina Domanska		Macmil
1971	If All The Seas Were One Sea		$70	$100	$140	Janina Domanska	CH	Macmil
1971	Under The Green Willow		$30	$50	$60	Elizabeth Coatsworth		Macmil
1972	I Saw A Ship A-Sailing		$30	$50	$60	Janina Domanska		Macmil
1973	Little Red Hen		$30	$50	$60	Janina Domanska (adapted)		Macmil
1973	Whizz!		$30	$50	$60	Edward Lear		Macmil
1974	What Do You See?		$30	$40	$60	Janina Domanska		Macmil
1975	Din Dan Don, It's Christmas		$30	$40	$60	Janina Domanska		Green
1976	Spring Is		$30	$40	$60	Janina Domanska		Green
1977	The Best Of The Bargain		$25	$40	$50	Janina Domanska		Green
1978	The Fifth Day		$25	$40	$50	Mary Q. Steele		Green
1978	The Tortoise And The Tree		$25	$40	$50	Janina Domanska		Green
1979	King Krakus And The Dragon		$25	$40	$50	Janina Domanska		Green
1980	The Bremen Town Musicians		$25	$35	$50	Grimm Bremer Stadtmusikanten		Green
1981	A Scythe, A Rooster, And A Cat		$25	$35	$50	Janina Domanska		Green
1982	Marek, The Little Fool		$25	$35	$50	Janina Domanska		Green
1983	What Happens Next?		$25	$35	$50	Janina Domanska		Green
1985	Busy Monday Morning		$20	$30	$40	Janina Domanska		Green

Domanska   Janina

Year	Title	VG-	VG	VG+	Fine	Author	Award	Pub
1986	The First Noel		$20	$30	$40	Janina Domanska		Green
1991	A Was An Angler		$16	$25	$30	Janina Domanska		Green

Dorcas   (Dorcas Couri)

Year	Title	VG-	VG	VG+	Fine	Author	Award	Pub
1946	The Elves And The Shoemaker	$35	$40	$60		Mary Patric (adapted)		PiedP
1948	The Night Before Christmas	$35	$40	$60		Clement C. Moore		G&D
1948	The Snowman Who Wanted To Stay	$35	$40	$60		Sarah Derman		Whitman

Downing   Julie

Year	Title	VG-	VG	VG+	Fine	Author	Award	Pub
1983	Clues In The Desert		$25	$35	$50	Emmett Davis		Rain
1983	Hannah's Alaska		$25	$35	$50	Joanne Reiser		Rain
1984	Pride And Prejudice		$16	$25	$30	Jane Austen		G&D
1985	Guess Who Took The Battered-Up Bike		$16	$25	$30	Raymond & Dorothy Moore		TNelson
1985	Oh, No! Miss Dent Is Coming To Dinner		$16	$25	$30	Raymond & Dorothy Moore		TNelson
1985	Quit? Not Me!		$16	$25	$30	Raymond & Dorothy Moore		TNelson
1985	Supercharged Infield		$16	$25	$30	Matt Christopher		LBrown
1986	Sonia Begonia		$14	$20	$30	Joanne Rocklin		Macmil
1987	Daniel's Gift		$14	$20	$30	Mary-Claire Helldorfer		BradP
1987	Margaret's Moves		$14	$20	$30	Berniece Rabe		Dutton
1987	Prince Boghole		$14	$20	$30	Erik Haugaard		Macmil
1989	Mr. Griggs' Work		$14	$20	$25	Cynthia Rylant		Orchard
1989	White Snow, Blue Feather		$14	$20	$25	Julie Downing		BradP
1990	Pulling My Leg: Story		$12	$18	$25	Joanne Carson		Orchard
1991	Mozart Tonight		$12	$18	$25	Julie Downing		BradP
1992	A Ride On The Red Mare's Back		$12	$18	$25	Ursula K. Le Guin		Orchard
1992	The Great Adventure Of Wo Ti		$12	$18	$25	Nathan Zimelman		Macmil
1992	Turtle Time		$12	$18	$25	Joanne Ryder		Knopf
1993	Cabbage Rose		$12	$16	$20	Mary-Claire Helldorfer		BradP
1993	Soon, Annala		$12	$16	$20	Riki Levinson		Orchard
1994	The Night Before Christmas		$12	$16	$20	Clement C. Moore		BradP
1995	Robin Hood In The Greenwood		$10	$16	$20	Jane Louise Curry		McEld
1995	The Magpies' Nest		$10	$16	$20	Joanna Foster		Clarion
1996	A First Bible Storybook		$10	$16	$20	Mary Hoffman		DK
1997	Watervoices		$10	$16	$20	Toby Speed		Putnam
1998	The Chicken Salad Club		$10	$14	$18	Marsha Diane Arnold		Dial
1998	Tom Mouse		$10	$14	$18	Ursula K. Le Guin		DK
1999	Come Aboard Noah's Ark		$10	$14	$18	Deborah Chancellor		DK
1999	Lullaby & Good Night		$10	$14	$18	Julie Downing		S&S
1999	Raggedy Ann And The Christmas Thief		$10	$14	$18	Nancy Willard		S&S
1999	The Christmas Story		$10	$14	$18	Deborah Chancellor		DK
2001	A First Book Of Fairy Tales		$8	$12	$16	Mary Hoffman		DK
2001	Caregivers' Comfort		$8	$12	$16	Julie Downing		CCC
2002	A First Book Of Jewish Bible Stories		$8	$10	$14	Mary Hoffman		DK
2002	Baby Animal Stories		$8	$10	$14	Julie Downing		PubIntl
2003	The Firekeeper's Son		$8	$10	$14	Linda Sue Park		Clarion
2003	Where Is My Mommy?		$8	$10	$14	Julie Downing		HCollins

Drew   Simon

Year	Title	VG-	VG	VG+	Fine	Author	Award	Pub
1986	A Book Of Bestial Nonsense		$20	$30	$40	Simon Drew		ACC
1987	Nonsense In Flight		$14	$20	$30	Simon Drew		ACC
1989	The Puffin's Advice		$14	$20	$25	Simon Drew		ACC
1990	Cat With Piano Tuna		$12	$18	$25	Simon Drew		ACC
1990	Still Warthogs Run Deep		$12	$18	$25	Simon Drew		ACC
1992	Camp David		$12	$18	$25	Simon Drew		ACC
1995	Simon Drew's Beastly Birthday Book.		$10	$16	$20	Simon Drew		ACC
1999	The Very Worst Of Simon Drew		$10	$14	$18	Simon Drew		ACC
2000	Spot The Book Title		$8	$12	$16	Simon Drew		ACC

Drummond   V.H.

Year	Title	VG-	VG	VG+	Fine	Author	Award	Pub
1939	Phewtus	$70	$90	$120		V.H. Drummond		Oxford
1944	Mrs. Easter's Parasol	$60	$80	$100		V.H. Drummond		Faber

Drummond   V.H.

Year	Title	VG-	VG	VG+	Fine	Author	Award	Pub
1945	Miss Anna Truly	$60	$80	$100		V.H. Drummond		Faber
1948	The Flying Postman	$60	$80	$100		V.H. Drummond		Penguin
1949	Miss Anna Truly	$60	$80	$100		V.H. Drummond		HM
1953	The Shaggy Dog Story	$50	$70	$90		Eric Partridge		Faber
1954	Mr. Finch's Pet Shop	$50	$70	$90		V.H. Drummond		Oxford
1957	Mrs. Easter And The Storks	$100	$140	$180		V.H. Drummond	GM	Faber
1957	The Twelfth	$50	$70	$90		J.K. Stanford		Country
1960	Little Laura On The River	$50	$60	$80		V.H. Drummond		Faber
1960	Little Laura's Cat	$50	$60	$80		V.H. Drummond		Faber
1960	Mrs. Easter And The Storks	$70	$90	$120		V.H. Drummond	GM	Barnes
1966	Phewtus The Squirrel	$40	$60	$70		V.H. Drummond		Const
1979	I'll Never Be Asked Again		$25	$40	$50	V.H. Drummond		Debrett

Du Bois   William Pène

Year	Title	VG-	VG	VG+	Fine	Author	Award	Pub
1936	Elisabeth	$220	$300	$380		William Pène Du Bois		TNelson
1936	Giant Otto	$340	$460	$580		William Pène Du Bois		Viking
1936	Otto At Sea	$220	$300	$380		William Pène Du Bois		Viking
1938	The Three Policemen	$160	$200	$260		William Pène Du Bois		Viking
1939	S.O.S. Geneva	$100	$120	$160		Richard Plant		Viking
1940	The Great Geppy	$140	$200	$240		William Pène Du Bois		Viking
1941	The Flying Locomotive	$140	$180	$240		William Pène Du Bois		Viking
1946	Harriett	$140	$180	$220		Charles Frederick McKinley		Viking
1947	The Island In The Square	$80	$120	$140		William Pène Du Bois		FSG
1947	The Twenty-One Balloons	$160	$220	$280		William Pène Du Bois	NM	Viking
1950	Peter Graves	$80	$120	$140		William Pène Du Bois		Viking
1951	Moon Ahead	$80	$100	$140		Leslie Greener		Viking
1951	The Mousewife	$120	$160	$200		Rumer Godden		Viking
1952	Bear Party	$180	$240	$300		William Pène Du Bois	CH	Viking
1952	Squirrel Hotel	$120	$160	$200		William Pène Du Bois		Viking
1952	Twenty And Ten	$120	$160	$200		Claire Huchet Bishop		Viking
1954	My Brother Bird	$80	$100	$140		Evelyn Perkins Ames		DoddM
1954	The Giant	$80	$100	$140		William Pène Du Bois		Viking
1955	The Rabbit's Umbrella	$70	$100	$120		George Plimpton		Viking
1956	A Season To Beware	$50	$70	$90		William Pène Du Bois		Putnam
1956	Lion	$160	$220	$280		William Pène Du Bois	CH	Viking
1957	Jexium Island	$70	$100	$120		Madeleine Grattan		Viking
1958	Kick The Dead Lion	$70	$100	$120		William Pène Du Bois		Viking
1958	Otto At Sea	$70	$100	$120		William Pène Du Bois		Viking
1958	The Falcon's Shadow	$70	$100	$120		William Pène Du Bois		Putnam
1959	Fierce John	$70	$100	$120		Edward Fenton		DoubleD
1959	Otto In Texas	$70	$100	$120		William Pène Du Bois		Viking
1960	The 3 Policemen	$70	$90	$120		William Pène Du Bois		Viking
1961	Billy The Barber	$100	$120	$160		Dorothy M. Kunhardt		H&B
1961	Otto In Africa	$70	$90	$120		William Pène Du Bois		Viking
1961	The Owl And The Pussy-Cat	$70	$90	$120		Edward Lear		DoubleD
1962	The Light Princess	$70	$90	$120		George MacDonald		Crowell
1962	The Three Little Pigs	$70	$90	$120		William Pène Du Bois		Viking
1963	Dr. Ox's Experiment	$70	$90	$120		Jules Verne		Macmil
1964	Elisabeth, The Cow Ghost	$60	$80	$100		William Pène Du Bois		Viking
1964	The Poison Belt	$60	$80	$100		Arthur Conan Doyle		Macmil
1965	A Certain Small Shepherd	$60	$80	$100		Rebecca Caudill		HR&W
1965	The Alligator Case	$60	$80	$100		William Pène Du Bois		H&Row
1966	Lazy Tommy Pumpkinhead	$60	$80	$100		William Pène Du Bois		H&Row
1966	The Magic Finger	$60	$80	$100		Roald Dahl		H&Row
1967	The Horse In The Camel Suit	$60	$80	$100		William Pène Du Bois		H&Row
1968	Pretty Pretty Peggy Moffitt	$60	$80	$100		William Pène Du Bois		H&Row
1968	The Tiger In The Teapot	$60	$80	$100		Betty Yurdin		HR&W
1969	Porko Von Popbutton	$60	$80	$100		William Pène Du Bois		H&Row
1970	Call Me Bandicoot		$50	$70	$90	William Pène Du Bois		H&Row
1970	Digging For China		$50	$70	$90	Richard Wilbur		DoubleD
1970	Otto And The Magic Potatoes		$50	$70	$90	William Pène Du Bois		Viking
1971	The Topsy-Turvy Emperor Of China		$40	$60	$90	Isaac Bashevis Singer		H&Row
1972	Bear Circus		$40	$60	$90	William Pène Du Bois		Viking
1972	Hare And The Tortoise & Tortoise And The Hare		$40	$60	$90	William Pène Du Bois		DoubleD
1972	Seal Pool		$40	$60	$90	Peter Matthiessen		DoubleD

Du Bois William Pène

Year	Title	VG-	VG	VG+	Fine	Author	Award	Pub
1972	William's Doll		$40	$60	$90	Charlotte Zolotow		H&Row
1973	Mother Goose For Christmas		$40	$60	$90	William Pène Du Bois		Viking
1974	My Grandson Lew		$40	$60	$80	Charlotte Zolotow		H&Row
1974	Where's Gomer?		$40	$60	$80	Norma Farber		Dutton
1975	The Unfriendly Book		$40	$60	$80	Charlotte Zolotow		H&Row
1976	It's Not Fair		$40	$60	$80	Charlotte Zolotow		H&Row
1976	Moving Day		$40	$60	$80	Tobi Tobias		Knopf
1976	The Runaway Flying Horse		$40	$60	$80	Paul-Jacques Bonzon		PMagP
1978	The Forbidden Forest		$35	$50	$70	William Pène Du Bois		H&Row
1978	We Came A-Marching ... 1, 2, 3		$35	$50	$70	Mildred Hobzek		PMagP
1979	The Sick Day		$35	$50	$70	Patricia MacLachlan		Pan
1982	Anna Witch		$30	$50	$60	Madeleine Edmondson		DoubleD
1982	The Planet Of Lost Things		$30	$50	$60	Mark Strand		Potter
1985	Gentleman Bear		$30	$40	$60	William Pène Du Bois		FSG
1985	The Night Book		$30	$40	$60	Mark Strand		Potter
1987	Little Red Riding Hood		$25	$40	$50	William Pène Du Bois		Random
1989	Bear In Mind		$25	$40	$50	Bobbye Goldstein (selected)		VK
1990	Just My Size		$25	$35	$50	May Garelick		H&Row

Duke Kate

Year	Title	VG-	VG	VG+	Fine	Author	Award	Pub
1983	The Guinea Pig ABC		$25	$35	$50	Kate Duke		Dutton
1984	Guinea Pigs Far And Near		$16	$25	$30	Kate Duke		Dutton
1985	Seven Froggies Went To School		$16	$25	$30	Kate Duke		Dutton
1988	What Would A Guinea Pig Do?		$14	$20	$30	Kate Duke		Dutton
1989	It's Too Noisy!		$14	$20	$25	Joanna Cole		Crowell
1989	Tingalayo		$14	$20	$25	Raffi		Crown
1990	Don't Tell The Whole World		$12	$18	$25	Joanna Cole		Crowell
1990	Roseberry's Great Escape		$12	$18	$25	Kate Duke		Dutton
1991	Good News		$12	$18	$25	Barbara Brenner		Bantam
1991	Let's Go Dinosaur Tracking!		$12	$18	$25	Miriam Schlein		HCollins
1992	Aunt Isabel Tells A Good One		$12	$18	$25	Kate Duke		Dutton
1992	Show-And-Tell Frog		$12	$18	$25	Joanne Oppenheim		Bantam
1993	If You Walk Down This Road		$12	$16	$20	Kate Duke		Dutton
1994	One Saturday Morning		$12	$16	$20	Barbara Baker		Dutton
1996	Aunt Isabel Makes Trouble		$10	$16	$20	Kate Duke		Dutton
1996	Mr. Garbage		$10	$16	$20	William H. Hooks		Bantam
1997	Archaeologists Dig For Clues		$10	$16	$20	Kate Duke		HCollins
1998	One Guinea Pig Is Not Enough		$10	$14	$18	Kate Duke		Dutton
1998	The Show-And-Tell Frog		$10	$14	$18	Joanne Oppenheim		GarethS
1999	Bedtime		$10	$14	$18	Kate Duke		Dutton
1999	Mr. Big Brother		$10	$14	$18	William H. Hooks		Bantam
1999	One Saturday Afternoon		$10	$14	$18	Barbara Baker		Dutton
1999	What Bounces?		$10	$14	$18	Kate Duke		Dutton
2000	Twenty Is Too Many		$8	$12	$16	Kate Duke		Dutton
2003	I Won't Get Lost		$8	$10	$14	Martha Lambert		HCollins

DuQuette Keith

Year	Title	VG-	VG	VG+	Fine	Author	Award	Pub
2003	They Call Me Woolly		$8	$10	$14	Keith DuQuette		Putnam
2004	Cock-A-Doodle Moooo!		$6	$10	$12	Keith DuQuette		Putnam

Duranceau Suzanne

Year	Title	VG-	VG	VG+	Fine	Author	Award	Pub
1984	Millicent And The Wind		$20	$30	$40	Robert N. Munsch		Annik
1992	Hickory, Dickory, Dock		$12	$18	$25	Robin Muller		Scholas
1995	Follow The Moon		$10	$16	$20	Sarah Weeks		HCollins
1995	Pockets		$10	$16	$20	Deborah Heiligman		Hyper
1999	Naomi Judd's Love Can Build A Bridge		$10	$14	$18	Naomi Judd		HCollins
1999	Piece Of Jungle		$10	$14	$18	Sarah Weeks		LauraG
2003	Without You		$8	$10	$14	Sarah Weeks		LauraG

Duvoisin Roger

Year	Title	VG-	VG	VG+	Fine	Author	Award	Pub
1932	A Little Boy Was Drawing	$160	$220	$280		Roger Duvoisin		Scribnr

Duvoisin   Roger

Year	Title	VG-	VG	VG+	Fine	Author	Award	Pub
1933	Donkey-Donkey	$360	$480	$600		Roger Duvoisin		Whitman
1935	All Aboard!	$160	$200	$260		Roger Duvoisin		G&D
1936	Mother Goose	$160	$200	$260		William Rose Benét		THP
1936	The Pied Piper Of Hamelin	$160	$200	$260		Robert Browning		G&D
1937	Riema	$100	$140	$180		Kathleen Morrow Elliot		Knopf
1938	And There Was America	$100	$120	$160		Roger Duvoisin		Knopf
1938	The Feast Of Lamps	$100	$120	$160		Charlet Root		Whitman
1939	Jo-Yo's Idea	$100	$120	$160		Kathleen Morrow Elliot		Knopf
1939	Rhamon, A Boy Of Kashmir	$100	$120	$160		Heluiz Chandler Washburne		Whitman
1940	Donkey-Donkey	$70	$90	$120		Roger Duvoisin		G&D
1940	The Dog Cantbark	$70	$90	$120		Marjorie Fischer		Random
1941	The Christmas Cake In Search Of Its Owner	$70	$90	$120		Roger Duvoisin		Oxford
1941	The Three Sneezes & Other Swiss Tales	$50	$60	$80		Roger Duvoisin		Knopf
1943	They Put Out To Sea	$35	$40	$60		Roger Duvoisin		Knopf
1944	A Child's Garden Of Verses	$60	$80	$100		Robert Louis Stevenson		Marchb
1944	Jumpy, The Kangaroo	$60	$80	$100		Janet Howard		LL&S
1945	Bhimsa, The Dancing Bear	$140	$180	$220		Christine Weston	CH	Scribnr
1945	I Won't Said The King	$60	$80	$100		Mildred Jordan		Knopf
1945	The Christmas Whale	$60	$80	$100		Roger Duvoisin		Knopf
1945	The Happy Time	$60	$80	$100		Robert Louis Fontaine		S&S
1945	Virgin With Butterflies	$35	$40	$60		Tom Powers		Bobbs
1946	At Daddy's Office	$60	$80	$100		Robert Jay Misch		Knopf
1946	Daddies, What They Do All Day	$60	$80	$100		Helen W. Puner		LL&S
1946	The Life And Adventures Of Robinson Crusoe	$35	$40	$60		Daniel Defoe		World
1947	Chanticleer	$60	$80	$100		Roger Duvoisin		G&D
1947	Moustachio	$60	$80	$100		Douglas Rigby		H&B
1947	White Snow, Bright Snow	$280	$380	$480		Alvin R. Tresselt	CM	LL&S
1948	Christmas Pony	$60	$80	$100		William Hall		Knopf
1948	Johnny Maple-Leaf	$60	$80	$100		Alvin R. Tresselt		LL&S
1948	The Four Corners Of The World	$35	$40	$60		Roger Duvoisin		Knopf
1948	The Steam Shovel That Wouldn't Eat Dirt	$60	$80	$100		Walter Retan		Aladd
1949	Sun Up	$60	$80	$100		Alvin R. Tresselt		LL&S
1950	Dozens Of Cousins	$60	$80	$100		Mabel Watts		Whittle
1950	Follow The Wind	$60	$80	$100		Alvin R. Tresselt		LL&S
1950	Hi, Mister Robin!	$60	$80	$100		Alvin R. Tresselt		LL&S
1950	Petunia	$120	$160	$200		Roger Duvoisin		Knopf
1950	The Christmas Forest	$60	$80	$100		Louise Fatio		Aladd
1950	Vavache	$60	$80	$100		Frederic Attwood		Aladd
1951	Anna, The Horse	$50	$70	$90		Louise Fatio		Whittle
1951	Petunia And The Song	$100	$140	$180		Roger Duvoisin		Knopf
1951	The Camel Who Took A Walk	$50	$70	$90		Jack Tworkov		Aladd
1952	A For The Ark	$50	$70	$90		Roger Duvoisin		LL&S
1952	Amahl And The Night Visitors	$50	$70	$90		Gian Carlo Menotti		McHill
1952	Petunia's Christmas	$100	$140	$180		Roger Duvoisin		Knopf
1952	The Talking Cat	$50	$70	$90		Natalie Carlson		H&B
1953	Petunia Takes A Trip	$100	$120	$160		Roger Duvoisin		Knopf
1954	Easter Treat	$50	$70	$90		Roger Duvoisin		Knopf
1954	The Happy Lion	$140	$180	$220		Louise Fatio		McHill
1954	The Night Before Christmas	$50	$70	$90		Clement C. Moore		GardenC
1955	Little Red Nose	$50	$70	$90		Miriam Schlein		AS
1955	One Step, Two...	$50	$70	$90		Charlotte Zolotow		LL&S
1955	One Thousand Christmas Beards	$50	$70	$90		Roger Duvoisin		Knopf
1955	The Happy Lion In Africa	$100	$140	$180		Louise Fatio		Whittle
1955	Two Lonely Ducks	$50	$70	$90		Roger Duvoisin		Knopf
1955	Wake Up, Farm!	$50	$70	$90		Alvin R. Tresselt		LL&S
1956	Bennie, The Bear Who Grew Too Fast	$50	$70	$90		Beatrice and Frazier Fraser		LL&S
1956	The House Of Four Seasons	$50	$70	$90		Roger Duvoisin		LL&S
1957	A Doll For Marie	$100	$140	$180		Louise Fatio		Whittle
1957	The Happy Lion Roars	$90	$120	$160		Louise Fatio		Whittle
1958	Fairy Tales From Switzerland	$50	$60	$80		Roger Duvoisin		Muller
1958	Petunia	$50	$60	$80		Roger Duvoisin		Knopf
1958	Petunia, Beware!	$50	$60	$80		Roger Duvoisin		Knopf
1958	Winkie's World	$50	$60	$80		William Hall		DoubleD
1959	Favorite Fairy Tales Told In France	$50	$60	$80		Virginia Haviland		LBrown
1959	Houn' Dog	$50	$60	$80		Mary Calhoun		Morrow
1959	The Three-Cornered Hat	$50	$60	$80		P. Antonio de Alarcón		LEC
1960	Angelique	$50	$60	$80		Janice		Whittle

Duvoisin   Roger

Year	Title	VG-	VG	VG+	Fine	Author	Award	Pub
1960	Day And Night	$50	$60	$80		Roger Duvoisin		Knopf
1960	Please Pass The Grass!	$50	$60	$80		Leone Adelson		McKay
1961	The Happy Hunter	$50	$60	$80		Roger Duvoisin		LL&S
1961	The Happy Lion's Quest	$50	$60	$80		Louise Fatio		Whittle
1961	Veronica	$50	$60	$80		Roger Duvoisin		Knopf
1962	Our Veronica Goes To Petunia's Farm	$50	$60	$80		Roger Duvoisin		Knopf
1962	The Miller, His Son, And Their Donkey	$50	$60	$80		Roger Duvoisin		Whittle
1962	Under The Trees & Through The Grass	$50	$60	$80		Alvin R. Tresselt		LL&S
1963	Lonely Veronica	$50	$60	$80		Roger Duvoisin		Random
1963	Spring Snow	$50	$60	$80		Roger Duvoisin		Knopf
1964	The Happy Lion And The Bear	$50	$60	$80		Louise Fatio		Whittle
1964	Veronica's Smile	$50	$60	$80		Roger Duvoisin		Knopf
1965	Days Of Sunshine, Days Of Rain	$40	$60	$70		Dean Frye		McHill
1965	Hide And Seek Fog	$90	$120	$160		Alvin R. Tresselt	CH	LL&S
1965	Petunia, I Love You	$40	$60	$70		Roger Duvoisin		Knopf
1965	The Rain Puddle	$40	$60	$70		Adelaide Holl		LL&S
1966	Around The Corner	$40	$60	$70		Jean B. Showalter		DoubleD
1966	Nubber Bear	$40	$60	$70		William Lipkind		HBrace
1967	Poems From France	$40	$50	$70		William Jay Smith		Crowell
1967	The Happy Lion's Vacation	$40	$50	$70		Louise Fatio		McHill
1967	The Missing Milkman	$40	$50	$70		Roger Duvoisin		Knopf
1967	The World In The Candy Egg	$40	$50	$70		Alvin R. Tresselt		LL&S
1968	The Old Bullfrog	$40	$50	$70		Berniece Freschet		Scribnr
1968	The Remarkable Egg	$40	$50	$70		Adelaide Holl		LL&S
1969	Earth And Sky	$40	$50	$70		Mona Dayton		H&Row
1969	It's Time Now!	$40	$50	$70		Alvin R. Tresselt		LL&S
1969	What Is Right For Tulip	$40	$50	$70		Roger Duvoisin		Knopf
1970	The Beaver Pond		$30	$50	$60	Alvin R. Tresselt		LL&S
1971	The Happy Lion's Treasure		$30	$50	$60	Louise Fatio		McHill
1971	Veronica And The Birthday Present		$30	$50	$60	Roger Duvoisin		Knopf
1972	The Web In The Grass		$30	$50	$60	Berniece Freschet		Scribnr
1973	Hector Penguin		$30	$50	$60	Louise Fatio		McHill
1973	Jasmine		$30	$50	$60	Roger Duvoisin		Knopf
1973	The Crocodile In The Tree		$30	$50	$60	Roger Duvoisin		Knopf
1974	See What I Am		$30	$40	$60	Roger Duvoisin		LL&S
1974	The Happy Lion's Rabbits		$30	$40	$60	Louise Fatio		McHill
1975	Marc And Pixie		$30	$40	$60	Louise Fatio		McHill
1975	Petunia's Treasure		$30	$40	$60	Roger Duvoisin		Knopf
1976	Periwinkle		$30	$40	$60	Roger Duvoisin		Knopf
1976	What Ever Happened To The Baxter Place		$30	$40	$60	Pat Ross		Pan
1976	Which Is The Best Place?		$30	$40	$60	Mirra Ginsburg		Macmil
1977	Crocus		$25	$40	$50	Roger Duvoisin		Knopf
1977	Hector And Christina		$25	$40	$50	Louise Fatio		McHill
1978	Mr And Mrs Button's Wonderful Watchdogs		$25	$40	$50	Janice Duvoisin		LL&S
1978	What Did You Leave Behind?		$25	$40	$50	Alvin R. Tresselt		LL&S
1979	Snowy And Woody		$25	$40	$50	Roger Duvoisin		Knopf
1980	The Happy Lioness		$25	$35	$50	Louise Fatio		McHill
1980	The Importance Of Crocus		$25	$35	$50	Roger Duvoisin		Knopf
1987	Petunia The Silly Goose Stories		$20	$30	$40	Roger Duvoisin		Knopf
1990	Autumn Harvest		$16	$25	$30	Alvin R. Tresselt		Mulbery

Dyer   Jane

Year	Title	VG-	VG	VG+	Fine	Author	Award	Pub
1985	Where Is Cuddles?		$20	$30	$40	Polly Thompson		Hasbro
1986	Penrod's Pants		$14	$20	$30	Mary Blount Christian		Macmil
1987	Penrod Again		$14	$20	$30	Mary Blount Christian		Macmil
1987	Piggins		$14	$20	$30	Jane Yolen		HBJ
1987	The Three Bears Rhyme Book		$14	$20	$30	Jane Yolen		HBJ
1988	Picnic With Piggins		$14	$20	$30	Jane Yolen		HBJ
1988	Piggins And The Royal Wedding		$14	$20	$30	Jane Yolen		HBJ
1989	My Father		$14	$20	$25	Judy Collins		LBrown
1990	Baby Bear's Bedtime Book		$12	$18	$25	Jane Yolen		HBJ
1990	Cozy In The Woods		$12	$18	$25	K.K. Ross		Random
1991	The Patchwork Lady		$12	$18	$25	Mary K. Whittington		HBJ
1992	Talking Like The Rain		$12	$18	$25	X. J. Kennedy		LBrown
1992	The Snow Speaks		$12	$18	$25	Nancy Carlstrom		LBrown

Dyer   Jane

Year	Title	VG-	VG	VG+	Fine	Author	Award	Pub
1993	If Anything Ever Goes Wrong At The Zoo		$12	$16	$20	Mary Jean Hendrick		HBJ
1993	Time For Bed		$12	$16	$20	Mem Fox		HBJ
1994	The Girl In The Golden Bower		$12	$16	$20	Jane Yolen		LBrown
1994	The Random House Book Of Bedtime Stories		$12	$16	$20	Jane Dyer		Random
1995	The Three Bears Holiday Rhyme Book		$10	$16	$20	Jane Yolen		HBrace
1996	Animal Crackers		$10	$16	$20	Jane Dyer		LBrown
1997	Child Of Faerie, Child Of Earth		$10	$16	$20	Jane Yolen		LBrown
1997	Cracked Corn And Snow Ice Cream		$10	$16	$20	Nancy Willard		HBrace
1998	Sophie's Masterpiece		$10	$14	$18	Eileen Spinelli		S&S
1998	When Mama Comes Home From Work		$10	$14	$18	Eileen Spinelli		S&S
1998	When Mama Comes Home Tonight		$10	$14	$18	Eileen Spinelli		S&S
1999	Blue Moon Soup		$10	$14	$18	Gary Goss		LBrown
1999	Here Is My Heart: Love Poems		$10	$14	$18	William Jay Smith (compiled)		LBrown
2000	I Love You Like Crazy Cakes		$8	$12	$16	Rose A. Lewis		LBrown
2000	Oh My Baby, Little One		$8	$12	$16	Kathi Appelt		Harcort
2000	Peekaboo Farm		$8	$12	$16	Jane Dyer		Random
2000	Whose Garden Is It?		$8	$12	$16	Mary Ann Hoberman		Harcort
2001	Good Morning Sweetie Pie		$8	$12	$16	Cynthia Rylant		S&S
2001	The Sick Day		$8	$12	$16	Patricia MacLachlan		Random
2002	Little Brown Bear Won't Go To School		$8	$10	$14	Jane Dyer		LBrown
2002	Little Brown Bear Won't Take A Nap!		$8	$10	$14	Jane Dyer		LBrown
2003	Babies On The Go		$8	$10	$14	Linda Ashman		Harcort
2003	Cinderella's Dress		$8	$10	$14	Nancy Willard		BSP
2004	Goodnight, Goodnight, Sleepyhead		$8	$10	$14	Ruth Krauss		HCollins
2004	Little Brown Bear And The Bundle Of Joy		$8	$10	$14	Jane Dyer		LBrown

Eastman   P.D.

Year	Title	VG-	VG	VG+	Fine	Author	Award	Pub
1958	Sam And The Firefly	$160	$200	$260		P. D. Eastman		BB
1960	Are You My Mother?	$160	$200	$260		P. D. Eastman		BB
1961	Fish Out Of Water	$140	$200	$240		Helen Palmer		BB
1961	Go, Dog, Go!	$220	$280	$360		P. D. Eastman		BB
1962	Robert The Rose Horse	$70	$90	$120		Joan Heilbroner		BB
1964	Cat In The Hat Dictionary	$200	$280	$340		Theodor Geisel		BB
1965	Cat In The Hat Beginner Book Dictionary In French	$90	$120	$160		Theodor Geisel		BB
1966	Cat In The Hat Beginner Book Dictionary In Spanish	$90	$120	$160		Theodor Geisel		BB
1967	Everything Happens To Aaron In The Autumn	$25	$30	$40		P. D. Eastman		Random
1967	Everything Happens To Aaron In The Spring	$25	$30	$40		P. D. Eastman		Random
1967	Everything Happens To Aaron In The Summer	$25	$30	$40		P. D. Eastman		Random
1967	Everything Happens To Aaron In The Winter	$25	$30	$40		P. D. Eastman		Random
1968	The Best Nest	$40	$50	$70		P. D. Eastman		BB
1969	Flap Your Wings	$40	$50	$70		P. D. Eastman		Random
1973	Big Dog ... Little Dog		$30	$50	$60	P. D. Eastman		Random
1973	I'll Teach My Dog 100 Words		$30	$50	$60	Michael K. Frith		BB
1974	The Alphabet Book		$30	$40	$60	P. D. Eastman		Random
1979	What Time Is It?		$25	$40	$50	P. D. Eastman		Random

Edelson   Wendy

Year	Title	VG-	VG	VG+	Fine	Author	Award	Pub
1976	Whose Garden?		$30	$40	$60	Marilyn Kratz		Harvey
1980	Hambone		$18	$25	$35	Caroline Fairless		Tundra
1987	Fiddler		$14	$20	$30	Stephen Cosgrove		Mult
1988	Billy Goats Gruff		$14	$20	$30	Stephen Cosgrove (retold)		Ideals
1988	Easter Bunnies		$14	$20	$30	Stephen Cosgrove		Ideals
1988	Goldilocks And The Three Bears		$14	$20	$30	Stephen Cosgrove (retold)		Ideals
1988	Humpity Dumpity		$14	$20	$30	Stephen Cosgrove (retold)		Ideals
1988	Shadow Chaser		$14	$20	$30	Stephen Cosgrove		Mult
1988	Three Blind Mice		$14	$20	$30	Stephen Cosgrove (retold)		Ideals
1989	Ira Wordworthy		$14	$20	$25	Stephen Cosgrove		Mult
1989	T.J. Flopp		$14	$20	$25	Stephen Cosgrove		Mult
1990	Hannah & Hickory		$12	$18	$25	Stephen Cosgrove		Mult
1990	Heidi's Rose		$12	$18	$25	Stephen Cosgrove		GAC
1990	Persimmony		$12	$18	$25	Stephen Cosgrove		Mult
1991	Derby Downs		$12	$18	$25	Stephen Cosgrove		CW
1991	Gossamer		$12	$18	$25	Stephen Cosgrove		CW
1992	The Velveteen Rabbit		$12	$18	$25	Margery Williams		Troll

Edelson   Wendy

Year	Title	VG-	VG	VG+	Fine	Author	Award	Pub
1995	The Baker's Dozen		$10	$16	$20	Aaron Shepard		Athenm
1996	Help Yourself, Little Red Hen!		$10	$16	$20	Alvin Granowsky (retold)		Steck-V
1996	Jeremy Fisher		$10	$16	$20	Wendy Edelson		PubIntl
1996	Little Mother Goose House		$10	$16	$20	Wendy Edelson		PubIntl
1996	Mrs. Tiggy-Winkle		$10	$16	$20	Wendy Edelson		PubIntl
1996	Peter Rabbit		$10	$16	$20	Beatrix Potter		PubIntl
1996	Two Bad Mice		$10	$16	$20	Wendy Edelson		PubIntl
1997	Jack And The Beanstalk		$10	$16	$20	Wendy Edelson		PubIntl
1997	Red Riding Hood		$10	$16	$20	Wendy Edelson		PubIntl
1998	Alex Fitzgerald, TV Star		$10	$14	$18	Kathleen Krull		Troll
1998	Alex Fitzgerald's Cure For Nightmares		$10	$14	$18	Kathleen Krull		Troll
2001	One Baby Jesus		$8	$12	$16	Patricia A. Pingry		Ccane
2004	The Christmas Story		$8	$10	$14	Patricia A. Pingry		Ccane

Edens   Cooper

Year	Title	VG-	VG	VG+	Fine	Author	Award	Pub
1979	If You're Afraid Of The Dark		$18	$25	$35	Cooper Edens		GreenT
1979	The Starcleaner Reunion		$14	$20	$30	Cooper Edens		GreenT
1980	Caretakers Of Wonder		$14	$20	$25	Cooper Edens		GreenT
1981	With Secret Friends		$14	$20	$25	Cooper Edens		GreenT
1986	19 Hats, 10 Teacups, An Empty Birdcage		$12	$16	$20	Cooper Edens		GreenT
1987	Now Is The Moon's Eyebrow		$12	$16	$20	Cooper Edens		GreenT
1988	Hugh's Hues		$12	$16	$20	Cooper Edens		GreenT
1989	Beauty And The Beast		$12	$16	$20	Cooper Edens		GreenT
1990	Hansel & Gretel		$10	$16	$20	Cooper Edens		GreenT
1990	Jack & The Beanstalk		$10	$16	$20	Cooper Edens		GreenT
1991	Little Red Riding Hood		$10	$16	$20	Cooper Edens		GreenT
1994	The Little World		$10	$14	$18	Cooper Edens		BLB
1998	If You're Still Afraid Of The Dark		$8	$12	$16	Cooper Edens		S&S

Egan   Tim

Year	Title	VG-	VG	VG+	Fine	Author	Award	Pub
1994	Friday Night At Hodges' Café		$12	$16	$20	Tim Egan		HM
1995	Chestnut Cove		$10	$14	$18	Tim Egan		HM
1996	Metropolitan Cow		$8	$12	$16	Tim Egan		HM
1997	Burnt Toast On Davenport Street		$8	$12	$16	Tim Egan		HM
1998	Distant Feathers		$8	$12	$16	Tim Egan		HM
1999	The Blunder Of The Rogues		$8	$12	$16	Tim Egan		HM
2001	A Mile From Ellington Station		$8	$10	$14	Tim Egan		HM
2002	The Experiments Of Doctor Vermin		$8	$10	$14	Tim Egan		HM
2003	Serious Farm		$8	$10	$14	Tim Egan		HM
2004	The Trial Of Cardigan Jones		$6	$10	$12	Tim Egan		HM

Egielski   Richard

Year	Title	VG-	VG	VG+	Fine	Author	Award	Pub
1976	The Letter, The Witch, And The Ring		$30	$40	$60	John Bellairs		Dial
1976	The Porcelain Pagoda		$30	$40	$60	F. N. Monjo		Viking
1977	Sid & Sol		$25	$40	$50	Arthur Yorinks		FSG
1979	I Should Worry, I Should Care		$25	$40	$50	Miriam Chaikin		H&Row
1980	Finders Weepers		$25	$35	$50	Miriam Chaikin		H&Row
1980	Louis The Fish		$25	$35	$50	Arthur Yorinks		FSG
1981	Mr. Wheatfield's Loft		$25	$35	$50	Isabel Langis Cusack		HR&W
1982	Getting Even		$25	$35	$50	Miriam Chaikin		H&Row
1982	Mary's Mirror		$25	$35	$50	Jim Aylesworth		HR&W
1983	It Happened In Pinsk		$25	$35	$50	Arthur Yorinks		FSG
1984	Lower! Higher! You're A Liar!		$20	$30	$40	Miriam Chaikin		H&Row
1985	Amy's Eyes		$20	$30	$40	Richard Kennedy		H&Row
1985	The Little Father		$20	$30	$40	Gelett Burgess		FSG
1986	Hey, Al		$80	$120	$160	Arthur Yorinks	CM	FSG
1988	Bravo Minski		$18	$25	$35	Arthur Yorinks		FSG
1988	Friends Forever		$18	$25	$35	Miriam Chaikin		H&Row
1989	Oh, Brother		$18	$25	$35	Arthur Yorinks		FSG
1989	The Tub People		$18	$25	$35	Richard Egielski		H&Row
1990	A Telling Of The Tales: Five Stories		$16	$25	$30	William J. Brooke		H&Row
1990	Ugh		$16	$25	$30	Arthur Yorinks		FSG

Egielski   Richard

Year	Title	VG-	VG	VG+	Fine	Author	Award	Pub
1991	Christmas In July		$16	$25	$30	Arthur Yorinks		HCollins
1992	The Lost Sailor		$16	$25	$30	Pam Conrad		HCollins
1993	The Tub Grandfather		$16	$25	$30	Pam Conrad		LauraG
1995	Buz		$14	$20	$25	Richard Egielski		LauraG
1995	Call Me Ahnighito		$14	$20	$25	Pam Conrad		HCollins
1996	Fire! Fire! Said Mrs. Mcguire		$12	$18	$25	Bill Martin Jr.		HBrace
1997	Perfect Pancakes, If You Please		$12	$18	$25	William Wise		Dial
1997	The Gingerbread Boy		$12	$18	$25	Richard Egielski		HCollins
1998	Jazper		$12	$16	$20	Richard Egielski		LauraG
1999	One Present From Flekman's		$12	$16	$20	Alan Arkin		HCollins
1999	The Tub People's Christmas		$12	$16	$20	Pam Conrad		LauraG
2000	Three Magic Balls		$10	$14	$18	Richard Egielski		HCollins
2001	Locust Pocus		$10	$14	$18	Douglas McKelvey		Philo
2001	The Web Files		$10	$14	$18	Margie Palatini		Hyper
2002	Slim And Jim		$8	$12	$16	Richard Egielski		HCollins
2003	The Fierce Yellow Pumpkin		$8	$12	$16	Margaret Wise Brown		HCollins
2003	The Small World Of Binky Braverman		$8	$12	$16	Rosemary Wells		Viking
2004	Saint Francis And The Wolf		$8	$10	$14	Richard Egielski		LauraG

Ehlert   Lois

Year	Title	VG-	VG	VG+	Fine	Author	Award	Pub
1965	Limericks	$40	$60	$70		Edward Lear		World
1966	What Is That Sound!	$30	$40	$50		Mary Le Duc O'Neill		Athenm
1972	Mathematical Games For One Or Two		$25	$35	$50	Mannis Charosh		Crowell
1973	The Great Flower Pie		$25	$35	$50	Andrea Di Noto		BradP
1976	What Do You Think I Saw?		$20	$30	$40	Nina Sazer		Pan
1977	The Visit		$20	$30	$40	Diane Wolkstein		Knopf
1979	Beginning To Learn About Shapes		$18	$25	$35	Richard L. Allington		Rain
1979	Number Families		$18	$25	$35	Jane Jonas Srivastava		Crowell
1987	Growing Vegetable Soup		$14	$20	$30	Lois Ehlert		HBJ
1988	Planting A Rainbow		$14	$20	$30	Lois Ehlert		HBJ
1989	Chicka Chicka Boom Boom		$14	$20	$25	Bill Martin		S&S
1989	Color Zoo		$35	$50	$70	Lois Ehlert	CH	H&Row
1989	Eating The Alphabet		$14	$20	$25	Lois Ehlert		HBJ
1989	Thump, Thump, Rat-A-Tat-Tat		$14	$20	$25	Gene Baer		H&Row
1990	Color Farm		$12	$18	$25	Lois Ehlert		Lippin
1990	Feathers For Lunch		$12	$18	$25	Lois Ehlert		HBJ
1990	Fish Eyes: A Book You Can Count On		$12	$18	$25	Lois Ehlert	NYT	HBJ
1991	Red Leaf, Yellow Leaf		$12	$18	$25	Lois Ehlert		HBJ
1992	Circus		$12	$18	$25	Lois Ehlert		HCollins
1992	Moon Rope		$12	$18	$25	Lois Ehlert		HBJ
1993	Nuts To You!		$12	$16	$20	Lois Ehlert		HBJ
1993	Words		$12	$16	$20	Bill Martin		LSimon
1994	Crocodile Smile		$12	$16	$20	Sarah Weeks		HCollins
1994	Mole's Hill		$12	$16	$20	Lois Ehlert		HBrace
1995	Chicka Chicka Sticka Sticka		$10	$16	$20	Bill Martin		LSimon
1995	Snowballs		$10	$16	$20	Lois Ehlert		HBrace
1996	A Pair Of Socks		$10	$16	$20	Stuart J. Murphy		HCollins
1996	Under My Nose		$10	$16	$20	Lois Ehlert		RCOwen
1997	Cuckoo		$10	$16	$20	Lois Ehlert		HBrace
1997	Hands		$10	$16	$20	Lois Ehlert		HBrace
1998	Angel Hide And Seek		$10	$14	$18	Ann W. Turner		HCollins
1998	Top Cat		$10	$14	$18	Lois Ehlert		HBrace
2000	Market Day		$8	$12	$16	Lois Ehlert		HBrace
2001	Waiting For Wings		$8	$12	$16	Lois Ehlert		Harcort
2002	In My World		$8	$10	$14	Lois Ehlert		Harcort
2004	Chicka Chicka 1, 2, 3		$8	$10	$14	Bill Martin		S&S
2004	Pie In The Sky		$8	$10	$14	Lois Ehlert		Harcort

Eichenberg   Fritz

Year	Title	VG-	VG	VG+	Fine	Author	Award	Pub
1937	Dick Whittington And His Cat	$70	$90	$120		Fritz Eichenberg		Holiday
1937	Uncle Remus	$50	$60	$80		Joel Chandler Harris		PPauper
1938	Sticks Across The Chimney	$50	$60	$80		Nora Burglon		Holiday
1939	Animals To Africa	$50	$60	$80		Rosalys Haskell Hall		Holiday
1939	Littling Of Gaywood	$50	$60	$80		Edna Henry Lee Turpin		Random

Eichenberg   Fritz

Year	Title	VG-	VG	VG+	Fine	Author	Award	Pub
1939	Merry Tales From Spain	$50	$60	$80		Antonio Robles		Winston
1939	Padre Porko	$50	$60	$80		Robert Davis		Holiday
1939	The Mystery Of Dog Flip	$50	$60	$80		Thérèse Lenôtre		FStokes
1940	Big Road Walker	$100	$120	$160		Eula Griffin Duncan		FStokes
1940	Gulliver's Travels	$50	$60	$80		Jonathan Swift		THP
1940	Rowena, The Skating Cow	$50	$60	$80		Stewart Schackne		Scribnr
1941	All On A Summer's Day	$50	$60	$80		Marjorie Fischer		Random
1941	Fathers & Sons	$50	$60	$80		Ivan Sergeevich Turgenev		THP
1941	The Story Of Peer Gynt	$50	$60	$80		E. V. Sandys		Crowell
1941	The Tree That Ran Away	$50	$60	$80		Henry Beston		Macmil
1943	Mischief In Fez	$50	$60	$80		Eleanor Hoffmann		Holiday
1944	No Room	$50	$60	$80		Rose Dobbs		CM
1944	Sancho & His Stubborn Mule	$50	$60	$80		Mark Keats		WRScott
1944	Tales Of Edgar Allan Poe	$50	$60	$80		Edgar Allan Poe		Random
1945	Black Beauty	$40	$60	$70		Anna Sewell		G&D
1946	Mistress Masham's Repose	$40	$60	$70		T. H. White		Putnam
1948	Felix Salten's Favorite Animal Stories	$40	$60	$70		Felix Salten		Messner
1949	The Wonderful House-Boat-Train	$40	$60	$70		Ruth Stiles Gannett		Random
1952	Ape In A Cape	$120	$160	$200		Fritz Eichenberg	CH	HBJ
1955	Dancing In The Moon	$35	$50	$60		Fritz Eichenberg		HBJ
1958	The Peaceable Kingdom	$35	$50	$60		Elizabeth Coatsworth		Pan
1973	The Two Magicians		$25	$35	$50	John Langstaff		Athenm
1983	Poor Troll		$16	$25	$30	Fritz Eichenberg (retold)		Stemmer
1995	The Jungle Book		$10	$16	$20	Rudyard Kipling		G&D

Eitzen   Allan

Year	Title	VG-	VG	VG+	Fine	Author	Award	Pub
2001	Corduroy Makes A Cake		$8	$10	$14	Alison Inches		Viking
2001	Corduroy's Hike		$8	$10	$14	Alison Inches		Viking
2002	Corduroy Writes A Letter		$8	$10	$14	Alison Inches		Viking
2002	Corduroy's Garden		$8	$10	$14	Alison Inches		Viking

Elling   Lars

Year	Title	VG-	VG	VG+	Fine	Author	Award	Pub
1993	Anna's Art Adventure		$12	$16	$20	Bjorn Sortland		CRB
1997	The Faithful Bull		$8	$12	$16	Ernest Hemingway		CRB
2000	The Story For The Search For The Story		$8	$10	$14	Bjorn Sortland		CRB
2001	The Dream Factory		$8	$10	$14	Bjorn Sortland		CRB

Elzbieta

Year	Title	VG-	VG	VG+	Fine	Author	Award	Pub
1972	Here And There		$25	$35	$50	Elzbieta		AU
1972	Summer Riddles		$18	$25	$35	Elzbieta		AU
1972	What Could Be Nicer?		$18	$25	$35	Elzbieta		AU
1974	Little Mops And The Butterfly		$16	$25	$30	Elzbieta		DoubleD
1974	Little Mops And The Moon		$16	$25	$30	Elzbieta		DoubleD
1974	Little Mops At The Seashore		$16	$25	$30	Elzbieta		DoubleD
1985	Dikou And The Snively Snoak		$12	$18	$25	Elzbieta		Barrn
1985	Dikou, The Little Troon Who-Walks-At-Night		$12	$18	$25	Elzbieta		Barrn
1988	Dikou And The Baby Star		$12	$16	$20	Elzbieta		Crowell
1988	Dikou And The Mysterious Moon Sheep		$12	$16	$20	Elzbieta		Crowell
1989	Brave Babette & Sly Tom		$12	$16	$20	Elzbieta		Dial
1994	Jon-Jon And Annette		$10	$14	$18	Elzbieta		Holt

Emberley   Ed

Year	Title	VG-	VG	VG+	Fine	Author	Award	Pub
1961	The Wing On A Flea	$70	$90	$120		Ed Emberley		LBrown
1962	The Big Dipper	$50	$60	$80		Franklyn M. Branley		Crowell
1962	The Parade Book	$50	$60	$80		Ed Emberley		LBrown
1962	The White House	$50	$60	$80		Mary Kay Phelan		HR&W
1963	American Inventions	$50	$60	$80		Leslie Waller		HR&W
1963	Birds Eat And Eat And Eat	$50	$60	$80		Roma Gans		Crowell
1963	Night's Nice	$50	$60	$80		Barbara Emberley		DoubleD
1963	The Story Of Paul Bunyan	$50	$60	$80		Barbara Emberley		P-Hall
1964	Cock A Doodle Doo	$50	$60	$80		Ed Emberley		LBrown

Emberley   Ed

Year	Title	VG-	VG	VG+	Fine	Author	Award	Pub
1964	Flash, Crash, Rumble, And Roll	$50	$60	$80		Franklyn M. Branley		Crowell
1965	A Rhinoceros? Preposterous!	$40	$60	$70		Letta Schatz		Steck-V
1965	Punch & Judy	$40	$60	$70		Ed Emberley		LBrown
1965	Yankee Doodle	$40	$60	$70		Ed Emberley (adapted)		P-Hall
1966	One Wide River To Cross	$90	$120	$160		Barbara Emberley	CH	P-Hall
1966	Rosebud	$40	$60	$70		Ed Emberley		LBrown
1966	The American West	$40	$60	$70		Leslie Waller		HR&W
1967	Drummer Hoff	$220	$300	$380		Barbara Emberley	CM	P-Hall
1967	Ladybug, Ladybug, Fly Away Home	$40	$50	$70		Judy Hawes		Crowell
1967	London Bridge Is Falling Down	$40	$50	$70		Ed Emberley		LBrown
1968	Green Says Go	$40	$50	$70		Ed Emberley		LBrown
1968	The Fifty-First Dragon	$40	$50	$70		Heywood Broun		P-Hall
1969	Clothing	$40	$50	$70		Leslie Waller		HR&W
1969	Simon's Song	$40	$50	$70		Barbara Emberley		P-Hall
1970	Drawing Book Of Animals		$30	$50	$60	Ed Emberley		LBrown
1972	Drawing Book: Make A World		$30	$50	$60	Ed Emberley		LBrown
1973	Suppose You Met A Witch		$30	$50	$60	Ian Serraillier		LBrown
1974	Klippity Klop		$30	$40	$60	Ed Emberley		LBrown
1975	Ed Emberley's Drawing Book Of Faces		$30	$40	$60	Ed Emberley		LBrown
1975	The Wizard Of Op		$30	$40	$60	Ed Emberley		LBrown
1976	Krispin's Fair		$30	$40	$60	John G. Keller		LBrown
1977	A Birthday Wish		$25	$40	$50	Ed Emberley		LBrown
1977	Ed Emberley's Great Thumbprint Drawing Book		$25	$40	$50	Ed Emberley		LBrown
1978	Ed Emberley's ABC		$25	$40	$50	Ed Emberley		LBrown
1979	Ed Emberley's Amazing Look-Through Book		$25	$40	$50	Ed Emberley		LBrown
1979	Ed Emberley's Big Green Drawing Book		$25	$40	$50	Ed Emberley		LBrown
1980	Ed Emberley's Big Orange Drawing Book		$25	$35	$50	Ed Emberley		LBrown
1980	Ed Emberley's Halloween Drawing Book		$25	$35	$50	Ed Emberley		LBrown
1981	Ed Emberley's Big Purple Drawing Book		$25	$35	$50	Ed Emberley		LBrown
1981	Ed Emberley's Crazy Mixed-Up Face Game		$25	$35	$50	Ed Emberley		LBrown
1982	6 Nature Adventures		$25	$35	$50	Ed Emberley		LBrown
1982	Straight Hair, Curly Hair		$25	$35	$50	Augusta R. Goldin		Crowell
1984	Ed Emberley's Picture Pie		$20	$30	$40	Ed Emberley		LBrown
1987	Animals		$20	$30	$40	Ed Emberley		LBrown
1987	Cars, Boats, And Planes		$20	$30	$40	Ed Emberley		LBrown
1987	Ed Emberley's Big Red Drawing Book		$20	$30	$40	Ed Emberley		LBrown
1987	Ed Emberley's Christmas Drawing Book		$20	$30	$40	Ed Emberley		LBrown
1987	Home		$20	$30	$40	Ed Emberley		LBrown
1987	Sounds		$20	$30	$40	Ed Emberley		LBrown
1990	Ed Emberley's Little Drawing Book Of Horses		$16	$25	$30	Ed Emberley		LBrown
1990	Ed Emberley's Little Drawing Book Of More Weirdos		$16	$25	$30	Ed Emberley		LBrown
1990	Ed Emberley's Little Drawing Book Of Trucks		$16	$25	$30	Ed Emberley		LBrown
1992	Ed Emberley's Thumbprint Drawing Box		$16	$25	$30	Ed Emberley		LBrown
1992	Go Away, Big Green Monster!		$16	$25	$30	Ed Emberley		LBrown
1993	Space City		$16	$25	$30	Franklyn M. Branley		Crowell
1996	Ed Emberley's Picture Pie 2		$12	$18	$25	Ed Emberley		LBrown
1997	Glad Monster, Sad Monster		$12	$18	$25	Anne Miranda		LBrown
1998	Three: An Emberley Family Scrapbook		$12	$16	$20	Ed, R., & M. Emberley		LBrown
2000	Ed Emberley's Fingerprint Drawing Book		$10	$14	$18	Ed Emberley		LBrown
2001	Ed Emberley's Drawing Book Of Weirdos		$10	$14	$18	Ed Emberley		LBrown
2001	The Wing On A Flea		$10	$14	$18	Ed Emberley		LBrown
2002	Ed Emberley's Drawing Book Of Trucks & Trains		$8	$12	$16	Ed Emberley		LBrown
2003	Thanks, Mom!		$8	$12	$16	Ed Emberley		LBrown

Engelbreit   Mary

Year	Title	VG-	VG	VG+	Fine	Author	Award	Pub
1985	Another Birthday		$30	$40	$60	Mary Engelbreit		AM
1992	For Mother O' Mine		$16	$25	$30	Mary Engelbreit		AM
1992	Life Is Just A Chair Of Bowlies		$16	$25	$30	Mary Engelbreit		AM
1992	Pals		$16	$25	$30	Mary Engelbreit		AM
1992	The Baby Book		$16	$25	$30	Mary Engelbreit		AM
1993	Believe		$16	$25	$30	Mary Engelbreit		AM
1993	Don't Waste The Miracle		$16	$25	$30	Mary Engelbreit		AM
1993	Have Your Cake And Eat It Too!		$16	$25	$30	Mary Engelbreit		AM
1993	Mother O' Mine		$16	$25	$30	Mary Engelbreit		AM
1993	Take Good Care		$16	$25	$30	Mary Engelbreit		AM

Engelbreit   Mary

Year	Title	VG-	VG	VG+	Fine	Author	Award	Pub
1993	The Snow Queen		$16	$25	$30	Hans Christian Andersen		Workman
1993	There Is No Friend Like A Sister		$16	$25	$30	Mary Engelbreit		AM
1994	Growing Up		$14	$20	$30	Mary Engelbreit		AM
1994	Over The River And Through The Woods		$14	$20	$30	Mary Engelbreit		AM
1994	'Tis The Season		$14	$20	$30	Mary Engelbreit		AM
1995	All You Need Is A Friend		$14	$20	$25	Mary Engelbreit		AM
1995	Everyone Needs Their Own Spot		$14	$20	$25	Mary Engelbreit		AM
1995	It Never Hurts To Ask		$14	$20	$25	Mary Engelbreit		AM
1996	Something Tells Me It's Your Birthday--		$12	$18	$25	Mary Engelbreit		AM
1997	My Symphony		$12	$18	$25	William Henry Channing		AM
1999	Words To Live By		$12	$16	$20	Mary Engelbreit		AM
2000	Mother O'mine		$10	$14	$18	Mary Engelbreit		AM
2000	Words For Mothers To Live By		$10	$14	$18	Mary Engelbreit		AM
2001	Tiny Teeny Halloweeny Treasury		$10	$14	$18	Patrick Regan		AM
2001	Words For Friends To Live By		$10	$14	$18	Mary Engelbreit		AM
2002	All Hail The Birthday Queen		$8	$12	$16	Patrick Regan		AM
2002	The Blessings Of Friendship		$8	$12	$16	Mary Engelbreit		AM
2002	The Night Before Christmas		$8	$12	$16	Clement C. Moore		HCollins
2002	Words For Teachers To Live By		$8	$12	$16	Mary Engelbreit		AM
2003	Queen Of Christmas		$8	$12	$16	Mary Engelbreit		HCollins
2004	Mary Engelbreit's Mother Goose		$8	$10	$14	Mary Engelbreit		HCollins
2004	Queen Of The Class		$8	$10	$14	Mary Engelbreit		HCollins

Erdoes   Richard

Year	Title	VG-	VG	VG+	Fine	Author	Award	Pub
1965	The Green Tree House	$30	$40	$50		Richard Erdoes		DoddM
1966	Come Over To My House	$200	$260	$320		Theo LeSieg (pseud/Seuss)		BB
1966	Memoirs Of A Certain Mouse	$25	$30	$40		Alexander King		McHill
1967	A Picture History Of Ancient Rome.	$25	$30	$40		Richard Erdoes		Macmil
1967	Peddlers And Vendors Around The World	$25	$30	$40		Richard Erdoes		McHill
1967	The Pueblo Indians	$25	$30	$40		Richard Erdoes		F&W
1968	What's Inside?	$20	$30	$35		Barbara Shook Hazen		Lion
1971	Musicians Around The World		$18	$25	$35	Richard Erdoes		McHill
1971	The Big Book Of Jokes		$18	$25	$35	Helen Hoke		FWatts
1971	The Tortured Americans		$18	$25	$35	Robert Burnette		P-Hall
1976	The Sound Of Flutes & Other Indian Legends		$16	$25	$30	John Fire		Pan
1978	Native Americans, Navajos		$14	$20	$30	Marvin L. Reiter		Sterl
1978	The Spotted Stones		$14	$20	$30	Silvio A. Bedini		Pan
1982	Native Americans, The Sioux		$14	$20	$25	Marvin L. Reiter		Sterl
1983	Native Americans, The Pueblos		$14	$20	$25	Marvin L. Reiter		Sterl
1984	Treasury Of Classic Unlaundered Limericks		$12	$18	$25	Richard Erdoes		Balsam
1991	Tales From The American Frontier		$10	$16	$20	Richard Erdoes		Pan
1998	Legends And Tales Of The American West		$8	$12	$16	Richard Erdoes		Pan
1999	Thunderwoman		$8	$12	$16	Nancy C. Wood		Dutton

Ets   Marie Hall

Year	Title	VG-	VG	VG+	Fine	Author	Award	Pub
1935	Mister Penny	$160	$200	$260		Marie Hall Ets		Viking
1939	The Story Of A Baby	$70	$90	$120		Marie Hall Ets		Viking
1944	In The Forest	$140	$180	$220		Marie Hall Ets	CH	Viking
1946	My Dog Rinty	$60	$80	$100		Ellen Tarry		Viking
1947	Oley, The Sea Monster	$60	$80	$100		Marie Hall Ets		Viking
1948	Little Old Automobile	$60	$80	$100		Marie Hall Ets		Viking
1951	Mr. T. W. Anthony Woo	$120	$160	$200		Marie Hall Ets	CH	Viking
1952	Beasts And Nonsense	$50	$70	$90		Marie Hall Ets		Viking
1953	Another Day	$50	$70	$90		Marie Hall Ets		Viking
1955	Play With Me	$100	$140	$180		Marie Hall Ets	CH	Viking
1956	Mister Penny's Race Horse	$100	$140	$180		Marie Hall Ets	CH	Viking
1958	Cow's Party	$50	$60	$80		Marie Hall Ets		Viking
1959	Nine Days To Christmas	$220	$300	$380		Aurora Labastida	CM	Viking
1961	Mister Penny's Circus	$50	$60	$80		Marie Hall Ets		Viking
1963	Gilberto And The Wind	$50	$60	$80		Marie Hall Ets		Viking
1964	Automobiles For Mice	$50	$60	$80		Marie Hall Ets		Viking
1965	Just Me	$90	$120	$160		Marie Hall Ets	CH	Viking
1967	Bad Boy, Good Boy	$40	$50	$70		Marie Hall Ets		Crowell
1968	Talking Without Words	$40	$50	$70		Marie Hall Ets		Viking

Ets — Marie Hall

Year	Title	VG-	VG	VG+	Fine	Author	Award	Pub
1972	Elephant In A Well		$18	$25	$35	Marie Hall Ets		Viking
1974	Jay Bird		$16	$25	$30	Marie Hall Ets		Viking

Eulalie — (Eulalie Banks)

Year	Title	VG-	VG	VG+	Fine	Author	Award	Pub
1913	Bobby In Bubbleland	$160	$220	$280		Eulalie (Eulalie Banks)		G&P
1922	Fairy Stories Children Love	$100	$120	$160		Watty Piper (pseud.)		P&Munk
1922	Treasure Box Of Children's Stories	$100	$120	$160		Eulalie (Eulalie Banks)		P&Munk
1924	Favorite Mother Goose Rhymes	$100	$120	$160		Watty Piper (pseud.)		P&Munk
1925	Cock, The Mouse And The Little Red Hen	$50	$60	$80		Watty Piper (pseud.)		P&Munk
1925	Little Black Sambo	$140	$200	$240		Helen Bannerman		P&Munk
1925	Nursery Tales Children Love	$100	$120	$160		Watty Piper (pseud.)		P&Munk
1925	Rooster, The Mouse, And The Little Red Hen	$100	$120	$160		Watty Piper (pseud.)		P&Munk
1925	The Gateway To Storyland	$100	$120	$160		Watty Piper (pseud.)		P&Munk
1927	The Gingerbread Boy	$100	$120	$160		Watty Piper (pseud.)		P&Munk
1927	The Little Red Hen And The Grain Of Wheat	$100	$120	$160		Watty Piper (pseud.)		P&Munk
1928	The Rooster, The Mouse And The Little Red Hen	$90	$120	$160		Watty Piper (pseud.)		P&Munk
1928	The Tale Of Peter Rabbit	$90	$120	$160		Beatrix Potter		P&Munk
1928	Three Little Pigs	$90	$120	$160		Watty Piper (pseud.)		P&Munk
1929	A Child's Garden Of Verses	$90	$120	$160		Robert Louis Stevenson		P&Munk
1929	Brimful Book	$200	$280	$340		Watty Piper (pseud.)		P&Munk
1929	Dawn & Other Verses	$90	$120	$160		Doris Caldwell		WHebb
1930	Pelle's New Suit	$70	$100	$120		Elsa Beskow		P&Munk
1931	Tick-Tock Tales	$70	$100	$120		Watty Piper (pseud.)		P&Munk
1932	Chicken Little	$70	$100	$120		Eulalie (Eulalie Banks)		P&Munk
1932	Child Of The Sea	$70	$100	$120		Elizabeth Syle Madison		William
1932	Fairy Tales Children Love	$70	$100	$120		Watty Piper (pseud.)		P&Munk
1932	Famous Fairy Tales	$70	$100	$120		Watty Piper (pseud.)		P&Munk
1932	Famous Rhymes, Mother Goose	$70	$100	$120		Watty Piper (pseud.)		P&Munk
1932	Funny Grunt And Frisky Frog	$70	$100	$120		Mary Lennox		Sutton
1932	Mother Goose Nursery Rhymes	$70	$100	$120		Eulalie (Eulalie Banks)		P&Munk
1932	My Story Book Library	$70	$100	$120		Eulalie (Eulalie Banks)		P&Munk
1932	The Enchanted Canyon Fairy Story	$70	$100	$120		Homer Mitten		Sutton
1933	Children Of Other Lands	$70	$100	$120		Watty Piper (pseud.)		P&Munk
1933	Little Readers Library	$70	$100	$120		Watty Piper (pseud.)		P&Munk
1934	Children's Heart Delight Stories	$70	$100	$120		Watty Piper (pseud.)		P&Munk
1934	Eight Fairy Tales	$70	$100	$120		Watty Piper (pseud.)		P&Munk
1934	Favorite Nursery Tales	$70	$100	$120		Watty Piper (pseud.)		P&Munk
1934	Folk Tales Children Love	$70	$100	$120		Watty Piper (pseud.)		P&Munk
1934	Jack And The Beanstalk	$70	$100	$120		Mother Goose		P&Munk
1934	Little Red Riding Hood	$70	$100	$120		Jacob & Wilhelm Grimm		P&Munk
1934	Peter Pan	$70	$100	$120		J. M. Barrie		P&Munk
1934	Puss In Boots	$70	$100	$120		Mother Goose		P&Munk
1934	The Three Bears	$70	$100	$120		Robert Southey		P&Munk
1934	Tom Thumb	$70	$100	$120		Mother Goose		P&Munk
1935	Animal Friends Story Book	$70	$100	$120		Watty Piper (pseud.)		P&Munk
1935	My Indian Library	$70	$100	$120		Watty Piper (pseud.)		P&Munk
1935	The Wishing Tree	$70	$100	$120		Mary Lennox		Faralar
1938	Baby's Very First Book	$70	$90	$120		Constance Wickham		Collins
1938	Lil' Hannibal	$70	$90	$120		Carolyn Sherwin Bailey		P&Munk
1939	And A Duck Waddles Too	$70	$90	$120		William Maurice Culp		HWagner
1939	Jeremiah, The Cat	$70	$90	$120		William Maurice Culp		HWagner
1941	My Picture Story Book	$70	$90	$120		Watty Piper (pseud.)		P&Munk
1946	The Bumper Book	$60	$80	$100		Watty Piper (pseud.)		P&Munk
1948	Pied Piper Of Hamelin	$60	$80	$100		Robert Browning		D&S
1979	The True Mother Goose		$14	$20	$30	Eulalie Eulalie (Banks)		GingH
1985	Favorite Nursery Stories & Poems		$12	$18	$25	Watty Piper (pseud.)		P&Munk

Evans — Katherine

Year	Title	VG-	VG	VG+	Fine	Author	Award	Pub
1944	Adventure For Beginners	$60	$80	$100		Margaret Friskey		W&F
1944	Chuggety-Chug	$60	$80	$100		Margaret Friskey		W&F
1945	Michael Angelo Mouse	$40	$60	$70		Katherine Evans		W&F
1945	The Ladybug Who Couldn't Fly Home	$40	$60	$70		Katherine Evans		W&F
1945	Who Lives At My House	$40	$60	$70		Margaret Friskey		W&F
1946	Chicken Little, Count-To-Ten	$40	$60	$70		Margaret Friskey		CP

Evans   Katherine

Year	Title	VG-	VG	VG+	Fine	Author	Award	Pub
1946	Johnny And The Monarch	$40	$60	$70		Margaret Friskey		CP
1947	Captain Joe	$40	$60	$70		Margaret Friskey		CP
1947	The Littlest Angel	$100	$140	$180		Charles Tazewell		CP
1947	Tommy Tittlemouse	$40	$60	$70		Katherine Evans		CP
1948	Flowers For Mother	$40	$60	$70		Katherine Evans		DMcKay
1949	Cloud Hoppers	$40	$60	$70		James Frederick Eckrich		CP
1951	Mother Goose	$40	$50	$70		Katherine Evans		CP
1953	Miss Frances' Ding Dong School Book	$40	$50	$70		Frances Horwich		RandMc
1953	The Four Riders	$40	$50	$70		Charlotte Krum		W&F
1953	The Littlest Stork	$50	$70	$90		Charles Tazewell		CP
1955	Easter Kitten	$35	$50	$60		Janet Konkle		CP
1955	Puppy's House	$35	$50	$60		Miriam Schlein		AWhit
1956	Little Bear Bumble	$35	$50	$60		Katherine Evans		Whitman
1956	The Little Tree	$35	$50	$60		Katherine Evans		Bruce
1957	I Want To Be A Bus Driver	$35	$50	$60		Carla Greene		CP
1957	Nemo Meets The Emperor	$35	$50	$60		Laura Bannon		AWhit
1957	Six Foolish Fishermen	$35	$50	$60		Benjamin Elkin		CP
1958	I Want To Be A Postman	$35	$50	$60		Carla Greene		CP
1958	The Big Jump & Other Stories	$100	$140	$180		Benjamin Elkin		BB
1958	The Little Old Lady	$35	$50	$60		Robbie Trent		Broad
1958	The Man, The Boy, And The Donkey	$35	$50	$60		Katherine Evans		AWhit
1959	The Maid And Her Pail Of Milk	$35	$50	$60		Katherine Evans		AWhit
1960	The Boy Who Cried Wolf	$35	$40	$60		Katherine Evans		AWhit
1961	A Camel In The Tent	$35	$40	$60		Katherine Evans		AWhit
1961	Raphael's Cat	$35	$40	$60		Katherine Evans		Bobbs
1962	A Bundle Of Sticks	$35	$40	$60		Katherine Evans		AWhit
1962	Lucky And The Giant	$35	$40	$60		Benjamin Elkin		CP
1963	The Mice That Ate Iron	$35	$40	$60		Katherine Evans		AWhit
1964	A Donkey For Abou	$35	$40	$60		Katherine Evans		AS
1964	One Good Deed Deserves Another	$35	$40	$60		Katherine Evans		AWhit

Falconer   Ian

Year	Title	VG-	VG	VG+	Fine	Author	Award	Pub
2000	Olivia		$40	$60	$90	Ian Falconer	CH	Athenm
2001	Olivia Saves The Circus		$12	$18	$25	Ian Falconer		Athenm
2002	Olivia Counts		$12	$16	$20	Ian Falconer		Athenm
2002	Olivia's Opposites		$12	$16	$20	Ian Falconer		Athenm
2003	Olivia And The Missing Toy		$10	$16	$20	Ian Falconer		Athenm
2005	Dream Big With Attitude		$8	$10	$14	Ian Falconer		AM

Fayman   Lynn (photos)

Year	Title	VG-	VG	VG+	Fine	Author	Award	Pub
1962	I Was Kissed By A Seal At The Zoo	$70	$90	$120		Helen Palmer		BB
1963	Do You Know What I'm Going To Do Next Saturday?	$50	$60	$80		Helen Palmer		BB
1964	Why I Built The Boogle House	$60	$80	$100		Helen Palmer		BB

Feelings   Tom

Year	Title	VG-	VG	VG+	Fine	Author	Award	Pub
1967	Bola And The Oba's Drummer	$40	$50	$70		Letta Schatz		McHill
1968	Song Of The Empty Bottles	$40	$50	$70		Osmond Molarsky		Walck
1968	The Congo, River Of Mystery	$40	$50	$70		Robin McKown		McHill
1968	The Tuesday Elephant	$40	$50	$70		Nancy Garfield		Crowell
1968	To Be A Slave	$60	$80	$100		Julius Lester	NH	Dial
1968	When The Stones Were Soft	$40	$50	$70		Eleanor B. Heady		F&W
1969	A Quiet Place	$40	$50	$70		Rose Blue		FWatts
1969	Black Folktales	$40	$50	$70		Julius Lester		FWBaron
1969	Panther's Moon	$40	$50	$70		Ruskin Bond		Random
1969	Tales Of Temba	$40	$50	$70		Kathleen Arnott		Walck
1970	Zamani Goes To Market		$30	$50	$60	Muriel L. Feelings		Seabury
1971	Moja Means One		$70	$100	$140	Muriel L. Feelings	CH	Dial
1974	Jambo Means Hello		$60	$90	$120	Muriel L. Feelings	CH	Dial
1978	Something On My Mind		$25	$40	$50	Nikki Grimes		Dial
1981	Black Child		$25	$35	$50	Joyce Carol Thomas		Zamani
1981	Daydreamers		$25	$35	$50	Eloise Greenfield		Dial
1987	Now Sheba Sings The Song		$20	$30	$40	Maya Angelou		Dutton

Feelings   Tom

Year	Title	VG-	VG	VG+	Fine	Author	Award	Pub
1993	Soul Looks Back In Wonder		$30	$40	$60	Maya Angelou	CSKM	Dial
1995	The Middle Passage		$14	$20	$25	Tom Feelings		Dial
2003	A Way To Move		$8	$12	$16	Dale Jacobs		Heine
2004	I Saw Your Face		$8	$10	$14	Kwame Senu Neville Dawes		Dial

Feiffer   Jules

Year	Title	VG-	VG	VG+	Fine	Author	Award	Pub
1961	The Phantom Tollbooth	$1,000	$1,400	$1,800		Norton Juster		E&C
1993	The Man In The Ceiling		$16	$25	$30	Jules Feiffer		HCollins
1997	Meanwhile...		$12	$18	$25	Jules Feiffer		diCapua
1998	I Lost My Bear		$12	$16	$20	Jules Feiffer		Morrow
1999	Bark, George		$12	$16	$20	Jules Feiffer		HCollins
2000	Some Things Are Scary		$10	$14	$18	Florence Parry Heide		Candle
2001	I'm Not Bobby!		$10	$14	$18	Jules Feiffer		diCapua
2002	By The Side Of The Road		$8	$12	$16	Jules Feiffer		diCapua
2002	The House Across The Street		$8	$12	$16	Jules Feiffer		diCapua
2004	The Daddy Mountain		$8	$10	$14	Jules Feiffer		diCapua

Fern   Eugene

Year	Title	VG-	VG	VG+	Fine	Author	Award	Pub
1960	Pepito's Story	$35	$40	$60		Eugene Fern		Ariel
1961	The Most Frightened Hero	$25	$30	$40		Eugene Fern		CM
1961	What's He Been Up To Now?	$25	$30	$40		Eugene Fern		Dial
1966	The King Who Was Too Busy	$25	$30	$40		Eugene Fern		Ariel
1967	Birthday Presents	$25	$30	$40		Eugene Fern		FSG
1968	Lorenzo And Angelina	$20	$30	$35		Eugene Fern		FSG

Ferris   Lynn Bywaters

Year	Title	VG-	VG	VG+	Fine	Author	Award	Pub
1987	Basil Of Bywater Hollow		$12	$16	$20	Jill Baker		Holt
1987	Goldilocks And The Three Bears		$14	$20	$30	Armand Eisen (adapted)		Ariel
1988	Little Red Riding Hood		$12	$16	$20	Armand Eisen (adapted)		Knopf
1991	A Classic Treasury Of Christmas		$10	$16	$20	Lynn Bywaters Ferris		Ideals
1991	The Night Before Christmas		$10	$16	$20	Clement C. Moore		AM
1992	Cinderella		$10	$16	$20	Samantha Easton (adapted)		AM
1992	Sleeping Beauty		$10	$16	$20	Samantha Easton (adapted)		AM

Fetz   Ingrid

Year	Title	VG-	VG	VG+	Fine	Author	Award	Pub
1964	The Tiny Little House	$35	$40	$60		Eleanor L. Clymer		Athenm
1965	Kate And The Wild Kittens	$25	$30	$40		Phyllis La Farge		Knopf
1965	Laughable Limericks	$25	$30	$40		Sara & John Brewton		Crowell
1965	The Adventure Of Walter	$25	$30	$40		Eleanor L. Clymer		Athenm
1965	What's Good For A Six-Year-Old?	$25	$30	$40		William Cole		HR&W
1966	Maurice's Room	$25	$30	$40		Paula Fox		Macmil
1966	The Valentine Box	$25	$30	$40		Maud Hart Lovelace		Crowell
1967	Tecwyn	$25	$30	$40		Mary Dawson		PMagP
1967	The Holy Terror	$25	$30	$40		François Mauriac		F&W
1968	Before You Were A Baby	$20	$30	$35		Paul & Kay S. Showers		Crowell
1968	Shoots Of Green	$20	$30	$35		Ella Bramblett		Crowell
1968	The Boy Who Lived In The Railroad Depot	$20	$30	$35		Dale Fife		CM
1969	The Bear Seeds	$20	$30	$35		James C. Asendorf		LBrown
1970	Me And Arch And The Pest		$18	$25	$35	John Durham		4Winds
1970	Where The Good Luck Was		$18	$25	$35	Osmond Molarsky		Walck
1971	The Spider, The Cave, And The Pottery Bowl		$18	$25	$35	Eleanor L. Clymer		Athenm
1972	A Monster Too Many		$18	$25	$35	Janet McNeill		LBrown
1973	Pure Magic		$16	$25	$30	Elizabeth Coatsworth		Macmil
1973	Santiago's Silver Mine		$16	$25	$30	Eleanor L. Clymer		Athenm
1976	I Loved Rose Ann		$16	$25	$30	Lee Bennett Hopkins		Knopf
1976	When Lucy Went Away		$16	$25	$30	George Maxim Ross		Dutton
1988	The Raft		$12	$16	$20	Bess C. Haskell		KRP

Field   Rachel

Year	Title	VG-	VG	VG+	Fine	Author	Award	Pub
1918	Rise Up, Jennie Smith	$160	$200	$260		Rachel Field		SFrench

Field   Rachel

Year	Title	VG-	VG	VG+	Fine	Author	Award	Pub
1924	Six Plays	$100	$120	$160		Rachel Field		Scribnr
1924	The Pointed People	$100	$120	$160		Rachel Field		YaleUP
1926	An Alphabet For Boys And Girls	$100	$120	$160		Rachel Field		DP
1926	Taxis And Toadstools	$100	$120	$160		Rachel Field		DP
1927	A Little Book Of Days	$100	$120	$160		Rachel Field		DP
1927	The Cross-Stitch Heart	$100	$120	$160		Rachel Field		Scribnr
1928	Come Christmas	$90	$120	$160		Eleanor Farjeon		FStokes
1928	Little Dog Toby	$90	$120	$160		Rachel Field		Macmil
1928	Polly Patchwork	$90	$120	$160		Rachel Field		DD
1929	Pocket-Handkerchief Park	$90	$120	$160		Rachel Field		DD
1930	Patchwork Plays	$90	$120	$160		Rachel Field		DD
1930	Points East, Narratives Of New England	$90	$120	$160		Rachel Field		B&W
1930	The Pointed People	$90	$120	$160		Rachel Field		Macmil
1931	The House That Grew Smaller	$90	$120	$160		Margery W. Bianco		Macmil
1931	The Yellow Shop	$90	$120	$160		Rachel Field		DD
1933	Just Across The Street	$80	$120	$140		Rachel Field		Macmil
1934	Susanna B. And William C.	$80	$120	$140		Rachel Field		Morrow
1936	Fear Is The Thorn	$80	$120	$140		Rachel Field		Macmil
1936	First Class Matter	$80	$120	$140		Rachel Field		SFrench
1940	All Through The Night	$70	$90	$120		Rachel Field		Macmil
1941	Christmas Time	$70	$90	$120		Rachel Field		Macmil
1946	Let's Go Home, Little Bear	$60	$80	$100		Rachel Field		Aldus
1957	Poems	$50	$70	$90		Rachel Field		Macmil

Fine   Howard

Year	Title	VG-	VG	VG+	Fine	Author	Award	Pub
1995	Piggie Pie		$14	$20	$25	Margie Palatini		Clarion
1997	The Upstairs Cat		$10	$16	$20	Karla Kuskin		Clarion
1998	Zak's Lunch		$10	$14	$18	Margie Palatini		Clarion
1998	Zoom Broom		$10	$14	$18	Margie Palatini		Hyper
1999	Ding Dong Ding Dong		$10	$14	$18	Margie Palatini		Hyper
2000	A Piggie Christmas		$8	$12	$16	Howard Fine		Hyper
2001	Piggie's 12 Days Of Christmas		$8	$12	$16	Howard Fine		Hyper
2001	Steamboat Annie & The Thousand-Pound Catfish		$8	$12	$16	Catherine Wright		Philo
2003	Broom Mates		$8	$10	$14	Margie Palatini		Hyper
2003	Dinosailors		$8	$10	$14	Deb Lund		Harcort
2003	Raccoon Tune		$8	$10	$14	Nancy Shaw		Holt
2003	Seven Scary Monsters		$8	$10	$14	Mary Beth Lundgren		Clarion

Firmin   Peter

Year	Title	VG-	VG	VG+	Fine	Author	Award	Pub
1967	Nogbad	$35	$40	$60		Oliver Postgate		Dwhite
1967	Noggin And The Moon Mouse	$25	$30	$40		Oliver Postgate		Dwhite
1967	Noggin And The Whale	$25	$30	$40		Oliver Postgate		Dwhite
1968	King Of The Nogs	$25	$30	$40		Oliver Postgate		Holiday
1968	The Ice Dragon	$25	$30	$40		Oliver Postgate		Holiday
1971	Basil Brush And A Dragon		$25	$35	$50	Peter Firmin		P-Hall
1976	Basil Brush At The Beach		$20	$30	$40	Peter Firmin		P-Hall
1976	Basil Brush Goes Boating		$20	$30	$40	Peter Firmin		P-Hall
1977	Basil Brush Builds A House		$20	$30	$40	Peter Firmin		P-Hall
1977	Basil Brush Goes Flying		$20	$30	$40	Peter Firmin		P-Hall
1978	Basil Brush Gets A Medal		$20	$30	$40	Peter Firmin		P-Hall
1979	Basil Brush Finds Treasure		$18	$25	$35	Peter Firmin		P-Hall
1979	Basil Brush In The Jungle		$18	$25	$35	Peter Firmin		P-Hall
1979	Stanley, The Tale Of The Lizard		$14	$20	$30	Peter Meteyard		Deutsch
1980	Basil Brush And The Windmills		$18	$25	$35	Peter Firmin		P-Hall
1980	Basil Brush On The Trail		$18	$25	$35	Peter Firmin		P-Hall
1980	The Last Of The Dragons		$14	$20	$25	Edith Nesbit		McHill
1982	Chicken Stew		$14	$20	$25	Peter Firmin		Pelham
1985	Pinny And The Bird		$12	$18	$25	Peter Firmin		Deutsch
1986	Pinny Finds A House		$12	$16	$20	Peter Firmin		VK
1986	Pinny In The Snow		$12	$16	$20	Peter Firmin		VK
1989	Boastful Mr. Bear		$12	$16	$20	Peter Firmin		DelaP
1989	Foolish Miss Crow		$12	$16	$20	Peter Firmin		DelaP
1989	Happy Miss Rat		$12	$16	$20	Peter Firmin		DelaP

Firth   Barbara

Year	Title	VG-	VG	VG+	Fine	Author	Award	Pub
1977	Exciting Things To Do With Nature Materials		$60	$80	$120	Judy Allen		Lippin
1982	The Spider		$30	$50	$60	Margaret Lane		Dial
1986	Quack! Said The Billy-Goat		$30	$40	$60	Charles Causley		H&Row
1988	Can't You Sleep Little Bear?		$80	$120	$160	Martin Waddell	GM	Walker
1989	The Park In The Dark		$25	$40	$50	Martin Waddell		LL&S
1990	The Grumpalump		$25	$35	$50	Sarah Hayes		Clarion
1990	We Love Them		$25	$35	$50	Martin Waddell		Lothrop
1992	Can't You Sleep, Little Bear?		$30	$40	$60	Martin Waddell	GM	Candle
1992	Sam Vole And His Brothers		$20	$30	$40	Martin Waddell		Candle
1993	Let's Go Home, Little Bear		$20	$30	$40	Martin Waddell		Candle
1994	Bears In The Forest		$20	$30	$40	Karen Wallace		Candle
1994	Wag, Wag, Wag		$20	$30	$40	Peter Hansard		Candle
1996	You And Me, Little Bear		$16	$25	$30	Martin Waddell		Candle
1998	At The Edge Of The Forest		$14	$20	$30	Jonathan London		Candle
1999	Good Job, Little Bear!		$14	$20	$25	Martin Waddell		Candle
2001	Tom Rabbit		$12	$16	$20	Martin Waddell		Candle
2003	Hi, Harry!		$10	$14	$18	Martin Waddell		Candle

Fisher   Leonard Everett

Year	Title	VG-	VG	VG+	Fine	Author	Award	Pub
1956	The First Book Of The American Revolution	$25	$35	$50		Richard Brandon Morris		FWatts
1957	Mike Fink, Snapping Turtle Of The O-Hi-O-O	$25	$35	$50		James Cloyd Bowman		LBrown
1957	The First Book Of American History	$25	$35	$50		Henry Steele Commager		FWatts
1958	Here Come The Clowns	$25	$35	$50		Celeste Edell		Putnam
1958	The First Book Of The Constitution	$25	$35	$50		Richard Brandon Morris		FWatts
1958	Whaling Boy	$25	$35	$50		Peter Freuchen		Putnam
1959	Paul Bunyan	$25	$35	$50		Maurice Dolbier		Random
1959	The First Book Of The Indian Wars	$25	$35	$50		Richard Brandon Morris		FWatts
1960	Indy And Mr. Lincoln	$25	$30	$40		Natalia Belting		HR&W
1960	The First Book Of Civil War Land Battles	$25	$30	$40		Trevor Nevitt Dupuy		FWatts
1960	The First Book Of The Declaration Of Independence	$25	$30	$40		Leonard Everett Fisher		FWatts
1960	The First Book Of The Man Without A Country	$25	$30	$40		Edward Everett Hale		FWatts
1960	The Golden Hind	$25	$30	$40		Edith Thacher Hurd		Crowell
1960	The Song Of Roland	$25	$30	$40		Eleanor Clark		Random
1960	Verity Mullens And The Indian	$25	$30	$40		Natalia Belting		HR&W
1961	Heroes And Heroines	$25	$30	$40		David Stone		FWatts
1961	Pumpers, Boilers, Hooks And Ladders	$25	$30	$40		Leonard Everett Fisher		Dial
1961	Pushers, Spads, Jennies And Jets	$25	$30	$40		Leonard Everett Fisher		Dial
1961	The First Book Of Civil War Naval Actions	$25	$30	$40		Trevor Nevitt Dupuy		FWatts
1961	The First Book Of The War Of 1812	$25	$30	$40		Richard Brandon Morris		FWatts
1962	A Head Full Of Hats	$25	$30	$40		Leonard Everett Fisher		Dial
1962	But Not Our Daddy	$25	$30	$40		Margery M. Fisher		Dial
1962	Sergeant O'keefe And His Mule	$25	$30	$40		Harold W. Felton		DoddM
1963	Getting To Know The U. S. A	$25	$30	$40		Charles Wright Ferguson		CM
1963	The First Book Edition Of Paul Revere's Ride	$25	$30	$40		Henry Wadsworth Longfellow		FWatts
1963	The First Book Edition Of The Gettysburg Address	$25	$30	$40		Abraham Lincoln		FWatts
1963	The Golden Frog	$25	$30	$40		Anico Surany		Putnam
1964	Alexander The Great	$25	$30	$40		Robert C. Suggs		Macmil
1964	Our Presidents	$25	$30	$40		Richard Willard Armour		Norton
1964	Ride The Cold Wind	$25	$30	$40		Anico Surany		Putnam
1964	The First Book Edition Of Casey At The Bat	$25	$30	$40		Ernest Lawrence Thayer		FWatts
1964	The Glassmakers	$25	$30	$40		Leonard Everett Fisher		FWatts
1964	The Golden Spur	$25	$30	$40		Eugenia Miller		HR&W
1964	The Silversmiths	$25	$30	$40		Leonard Everett Fisher		FWatts
1965	Let's Find Out About John Fitzgerald Kennedy	$25	$30	$40		Martha Shapp		FWatts
1965	The First Book Of The White House	$25	$30	$40		Lois Perry Jones		FWatts
1965	The Hatters	$25	$30	$40		Leonard Everett Fisher		FWatts
1965	The Papermakers	$25	$30	$40		Leonard Everett Fisher		FWatts
1965	The Printers	$25	$30	$40		Leonard Everett Fisher		FWatts
1965	The Wigmakers	$25	$30	$40		Leonard Everett Fisher		FWatts
1966	A Jungle Jumble	$25	$30	$40		Anico Surany		Putnam
1966	Kati And Kormos	$25	$30	$40		Anico Surany		Holiday
1966	Rip Van Winkle	$25	$30	$40		Washington Irving		FWatts
1966	The Cabinetmakers	$25	$30	$40		Leonard Everett Fisher		FWatts
1966	The Legend Of Sleepy Hollow	$25	$30	$40		Washington Irving		FWatts
1966	The Story Of Aida	$25	$30	$40		Florence Stevenson		Putnam

Fisher   Leonard Everett

Year	Title	VG-	VG	VG+	Fine	Author	Award	Pub
1966	The Tanners	$25	$30	$40		Leonard Everett Fisher		FWatts
1966	The Weavers	$25	$30	$40		Leonard Everett Fisher		FWatts
1967	Monsieur Jolicoeur's Umbrella	$25	$30	$40		Anico Surany		Putnam
1967	The Covered Bridge	$25	$30	$40		Anico Surany		Holiday
1967	The Great Stone Face	$25	$30	$40		Nathaniel Hawthorne		FWatts
1967	The Journey With Jonah	$25	$30	$40		Madeleine L'Engle		FSG
1967	The Schoolmasters	$25	$30	$40		Leonard Everett Fisher		FWatts
1967	The Shoemakers	$25	$30	$40		Leonard Everett Fisher		FWatts
1967	The Story Of Science In America	$25	$30	$40		L. Sprague De Camp		Scribnr
1968	Malachy's Gold	$20	$30	$35		Anico Surany		Holiday
1968	The Doctors	$20	$30	$35		Leonard Everett Fisher		FWatts
1968	The First Book Of The Founding Of The Republic	$20	$30	$35		Richard Brandon Morris		FWatts
1968	The Luck Of Roaring Camp	$20	$30	$35		Bret Harte		FWatts
1968	The Peddlers	$20	$30	$35		Leonard Everett Fisher		FWatts
1969	Lora, Lorita	$20	$30	$35		Anico Surany		Putnam
1969	The Limners	$20	$30	$35		Leonard Everett Fisher		FWatts
1969	The Potters	$20	$30	$35		Leonard Everett Fisher		FWatts
1970	American Popular Music: The Beginning Years		$18	$25	$35	Berenice Robinson Morris		FWatts
1970	Picture Book Of Revolutionary War Heroes		$18	$25	$35	Leonard Everett Fisher		StackP
1970	The Architects		$18	$25	$35	Leonard Everett Fisher		FWatts
1970	Two If By Sea		$18	$25	$35	Leonard Everett Fisher		Random
1971	The Land Beneath The Sea		$18	$25	$35	Julian May		Holiday
1971	The Shipbuilders		$18	$25	$35	Leonard Everett Fisher		FWatts
1972	The Death Of Evening Star		$18	$25	$35	Leonard Everett Fisher		DoubleD
1972	The Wicked City		$18	$25	$35	Isaac Bashevis Singer		FSG
1973	The Homemakers		$16	$25	$30	Leonard Everett Fisher		FWatts
1974	Journey Of The Gray Whales		$16	$25	$30	Gladys P. Conklin		Holiday
1974	Juan Diego And The Lady		$16	$25	$30	Jan Wahl		Putnam
1974	The Warlock Of Westfall		$16	$25	$30	Leonard Everett Fisher		DoubleD
1975	Sweeney's Ghost		$16	$25	$30	Leonard Everett Fisher		DoubleD
1976	The Blacksmiths		$16	$25	$30	Leonard Everett Fisher		FWatts
1978	Alphabet Art		$14	$20	$30	Leonard Everett Fisher		4Winds
1978	Noonan		$14	$20	$30	Leonard Everett Fisher		DoubleD
1979	The Factories		$14	$20	$30	Leonard Everett Fisher		Holiday
1979	The Railroads		$14	$20	$30	Leonard Everett Fisher		Holiday
1980	A Russian Farewell		$14	$20	$25	Leonard Everett Fisher		4Winds
1980	All Times, All Peoples		$14	$20	$25	Milton Meltzer		H&Row
1980	The Hospitals		$14	$20	$25	Leonard Everett Fisher		Holiday
1980	The Sports		$14	$20	$25	Leonard Everett Fisher		Holiday
1981	Storm At The Jetty		$14	$20	$25	Leonard Everett Fisher		Viking
1981	The Newspapers		$14	$20	$25	Leonard Everett Fisher		Holiday
1981	The Seven Days Of Creation		$14	$20	$25	Leonard Everett Fisher		Holiday
1982	A Circle Of Seasons		$14	$20	$25	Myra Cohn Livingston		Holiday
1982	Number Art		$14	$20	$25	Leonard Everett Fisher		4Winds
1982	The Unions		$14	$20	$25	Leonard Everett Fisher		Holiday
1983	Star Signs		$14	$20	$25	Leonard Everett Fisher		Holiday
1983	The Schools		$14	$20	$25	Leonard Everett Fisher		Holiday
1984	Boxes! Boxes!		$12	$18	$25	Leonard Everett Fisher		Viking
1984	Sky Songs		$12	$18	$25	Myra Cohn Livingston		Holiday
1984	The Olympians		$12	$18	$25	Leonard Everett Fisher		Holiday
1985	Celebrations		$12	$18	$25	Myra Cohn Livingston		Holiday
1985	Symbol Art		$12	$18	$25	Leonard Everett Fisher		4Winds
1985	The American Revolution		$12	$18	$25	Richard Brandon Morris		Lerner
1985	The Constitution		$12	$18	$25	Richard Brandon Morris		Lerner
1985	The Founding Of The Republic		$12	$18	$25	Richard Brandon Morris		Lerner
1985	The Indian Wars		$12	$18	$25	Richard Brandon Morris		Lerner
1985	The Statue Of Liberty		$12	$18	$25	Leonard Everett Fisher		Holiday
1985	The War Of 1812		$12	$18	$25	Richard Brandon Morris		Lerner
1986	Earth Songs		$12	$16	$20	Myra Cohn Livingston		Holiday
1986	Ellis Island		$12	$16	$20	Leonard Everett Fisher		Holiday
1986	Sea Songs		$12	$16	$20	Myra Cohn Livingston		Holiday
1986	The Great Wall Of China		$12	$16	$20	Leonard Everett Fisher		Macmil
1987	Look Around		$12	$16	$20	Leonard Everett Fisher		VK
1988	Monticello		$12	$16	$20	Leonard Everett Fisher		Holiday
1988	Pyramid Of The Sun		$12	$16	$20	Leonard Everett Fisher		Macmil
1988	Space Songs		$12	$16	$20	Myra Cohn Livingston		Holiday
1988	Theseus And The Minotaur		$12	$16	$20	Leonard Everett Fisher		Holiday

Fisher   Leonard Everett

Year	Title	VG-	VG	VG+	Fine	Author	Award	Pub
1989	The Wailing Wall		$12	$16	$20	Leonard Everett Fisher		Macmil
1989	The White House		$12	$16	$20	Leonard Everett Fisher		Holiday
1989	Up In The Air		$12	$16	$20	Myra Cohn Livingston		Holiday
1990	Jason And The Golden Fleece		$10	$16	$20	Leonard Everett Fisher		Holiday
1990	Prince Henry The Navigator		$10	$16	$20	Leonard Everett Fisher		Macmil
1990	The Oregon Trail		$10	$16	$20	Leonard Everett Fisher		Holiday
1991	Cyclops		$10	$16	$20	Leonard Everett Fisher		Holiday
1991	Sailboat Lost		$10	$16	$20	Leonard Everett Fisher		Macmil
1992	Galileo		$10	$16	$20	Leonard Everett Fisher		Macmil
1992	If You Ever Meet A Whale		$10	$16	$20	Myra Cohn Livingston		Holiday
1992	Little Frog's Song		$10	$16	$20	Alice Schertle		HCollins
1992	The Spotted Pony		$10	$16	$20	Eric Kimmel		Holiday
1993	David And Goliath		$10	$16	$20	Leonard Everett Fisher		Holiday
1993	Gutenberg		$10	$16	$20	Leonard Everett Fisher		Macmil
1993	Stars & Stripes		$10	$16	$20	Leonard Everett Fisher		Holiday
1994	Kinderdike		$10	$14	$18	Leonard Everett Fisher		Macmil
1994	Marie Curie		$10	$14	$18	Leonard Everett Fisher		Macmil
1994	The Three Princes		$10	$14	$18	Eric Kimmel		Holiday
1995	Gandhi		$10	$14	$18	Leonard Everett Fisher		Athenm
1995	Moses		$10	$14	$18	Leonard Everett Fisher		Holiday
1996	Festivals		$8	$12	$16	Myra Cohn Livingston		Holiday
1996	Niagara Falls		$8	$12	$16	Leonard Everett Fisher		Holiday
1996	William Tell		$8	$12	$16	Leonard Everett Fisher		FSG
1997	Anasazi		$8	$12	$16	Leonard Everett Fisher		Athenm
1997	The Gods And Goddesses Of Ancient Egypt		$8	$12	$16	Leonard Everett Fisher		Holiday
1997	The Jetty Chronicles		$8	$12	$16	Leonard Everett Fisher		MCaven
1999	Alexander Graham Bell		$8	$12	$16	Leonard Everett Fisher		Athenm
1999	Gods And Goddesses Of The Ancient Maya		$8	$12	$16	Leonard Everett Fisher		Holiday
2000	The Two Mountains		$8	$10	$14	Eric Kimmel		Holiday
2001	Gods And Goddesses Of The Ancient Norse		$8	$10	$14	Leonard Everett Fisher		Holiday
2001	Sky, Sea, The Jetty, And Me		$8	$10	$14	Leonard Everett Fisher		MCaven
2004	Don Quixote And The Windmills		$6	$10	$12	Eric Kimmel		FSG

Flack   Marjorie

Year	Title	VG-	VG	VG+	Fine	Author	Award	Pub
1928	Here, There And Everywhere	$140	$180	$240		Dorothy Keeley Aldis		Minton
1928	Taktuk, An Arctic Boy	$140	$180	$240		Helen Lomen		DD
1929	All Around The Town	$140	$180	$240		Marjorie Flack		DD
1929	Marionettes	$140	$180	$240		Edith Flack Ackley		Pullman
1930	Angus And The Ducks	$380	$500	$620		Marjorie Flack		DD
1931	Angus And The Cat	$320	$420	$520		Marjorie Flack		DD
1932	Angus Lost	$260	$360	$440		Marjorie Flack		DD
1932	Ask Mr Bear	$160	$220	$280		Marjorie Flack		Macmil
1933	Angus and Wag-Tail Bess	$220	$280	$360		Marjorie Flack		GardenC
1934	Humphrey	$160	$200	$260		Marjorie Flack		DD
1934	Scamper	$160	$200	$260		Anna Roosevelt		Macmil
1934	Scampers Christmas	$160	$200	$260		Anna Roosevelt Dall		Macmil
1934	Tim Tadpole And The Great Bullfrog	$160	$200	$260		Marjorie Flack		DD
1935	Christopher	$160	$200	$260		Marjorie Flack		Scribnr
1935	Topsy	$160	$200	$260		Marjorie Flack		DD
1936	What To Do About Molly	$160	$200	$260		Marjorie Flack		HM
1936	Willy Nilly	$160	$200	$260		Marjorie Flack		Macmil
1937	Lucky Little Lena	$160	$200	$260		Marjorie Flack		Macmil
1937	The Restless Robin	$160	$200	$260		Marjorie Flack		HM
1937	Walter, The Lazy Mouse	$160	$200	$260		Marjorie Flack		DD
1938	William And His Kitten	$160	$200	$260		Marjorie Flack		HM
1939	The Country Bunny And The Little Gold Shoes	$140	$200	$240		Du Bose Heyward		HM
1940	A Black Velvet Story	$70	$90	$120		Dee Smith		FStokes
1941	Adolphus	$70	$90	$120		Marjorie Flack		HM
1943	The New Pet	$70	$90	$120		Marjorie Flack		DoubleD
1952	All Together	$50	$70	$90		Dorothy Keeley Aldis		Putnam

Fleming   Denise

Year	Title	VG-	VG	VG+	Fine	Author	Award	Pub
1983	The Charmkins Discover Big World		$16	$25	$30	Edith Adams		Random
1983	The Charmkins Sniffy Adventure		$14	$20	$25	Denise Fleming		Random

Fleming   Denise

Year	Title	VG-	VG	VG+	Fine	Author	Award	Pub
1984	All Through The Town		$12	$18	$25	Alice Low		Random
1984	It Feels Like Christmas!		$12	$18	$25	Denise Fleming		Random
1984	The Care Bears Help Santa		$12	$18	$25	Peggy Kahn		Random
1985	Count In The Dark With Glo Worm		$12	$18	$25	Denise Fleming		Random
1985	This Little Pig Went To Market		$12	$18	$25	Denise Fleming		Random
1986	The Merry Christmas Book		$12	$16	$20	Denise Fleming		Random
1988	Creating Entrepreneurs		$12	$16	$20	Denise Fleming		AU
1988	D Is For Doll		$12	$16	$20	Linda Hayward		Random
1988	Tea Party Manners		$12	$16	$20	Linda Hayward		Random
1988	This Is The House		$12	$16	$20	Linda Hayward		Random
1989	Dollhouse Mouse		$12	$16	$20	Natalie Standiford		Random
1991	In The Tall, Tall Grass		$10	$16	$20	Denise Fleming		Holt
1992	Count!		$10	$16	$20	Denise Fleming		Holt
1992	Lunch		$10	$16	$20	Denise Fleming		Holt
1993	In The Small, Small Pond		$30	$40	$60	Denise Fleming	CH	Holt
1994	Barnyard Banter		$10	$14	$18	Denise Fleming		Holt
1996	Where Once There Was A Wood		$8	$12	$16	Denise Fleming		Holt
1997	Time To Sleep		$8	$12	$16	Denise Fleming		Holt
1998	Mama Cat Has Three Kittens		$8	$12	$16	Denise Fleming		Holt
2000	The Everything Book		$8	$10	$14	Denise Fleming		Holt
2001	Pumpkin Eye		$8	$10	$14	Denise Fleming		Holt
2002	Alphabet Under Construction		$8	$10	$14	Denise Fleming		Holt
2002	Maker Of Things		$8	$10	$14	Denise Fleming		RCOwen
2003	Buster		$8	$10	$14	Denise Fleming		Holt

Florczak   Robert

Year	Title	VG-	VG	VG+	Fine	Author	Award	Pub
1995	The Rainbow Bridge		$10	$16	$20	Audrey Wood		HBJ
1996	Rough Sketch Beginning		$8	$12	$16	James Berry		HBrace
1997	Birdsong		$8	$12	$16	Audrey Wood		HBrace
1999	The Persian Cinderella		$8	$12	$16	Shirley Climo		HCollins
2000	A Cowboy Christmas		$8	$10	$14	Audrey Wood		S&S
2000	The Magic Fish-Bone		$8	$10	$14	Charles Dickens		HBrace
2003	Yikes!		$8	$10	$14	Robert Florczak		BSP
2004	Horses Of Myth		$6	$10	$12	Gerald & Loretta Hausman		Dutton

Florian   Douglas

Year	Title	VG-	VG	VG+	Fine	Author	Award	Pub
1977	Tit For Tat		$25	$40	$50	Dorothy Van Woerkom		Green
1980	A Bird Can Fly		$18	$25	$35	Douglas Florian		Green
1980	The Night It Rained Pancakes		$18	$25	$35	Mirra Ginsburg		Green
1982	The City		$16	$25	$30	Douglas Florian		Crowell
1983	People Working		$16	$25	$30	Douglas Florian		Crowell
1984	Airplane Ride		$16	$25	$30	Douglas Florian		Crowell
1986	Discovering Butterflies		$14	$20	$30	Douglas Florian		Scribnr
1986	Discovering Frogs		$14	$20	$30	Douglas Florian		Scribnr
1986	Discovering Seashells		$14	$20	$30	Douglas Florian		Scribnr
1986	Discovering Trees		$14	$20	$30	Douglas Florian		Scribnr
1987	A Winter Day		$14	$20	$30	Douglas Florian		Green
1987	What Is A Cat?		$14	$20	$30	Bill Adler		Morrow
1988	A Summer Day		$14	$20	$30	Douglas Florian		Green
1989	A Year In The Country		$14	$20	$25	Douglas Florian		Green
1989	Nature Walk		$14	$20	$25	Douglas Florian		Green
1989	Turtle Day		$14	$20	$25	Douglas Florian		Crowell
1990	A Beach Day		$12	$18	$25	Douglas Florian		Green
1990	City Street		$12	$18	$25	Douglas Florian		Green
1991	A Carpenter		$12	$18	$25	Douglas Florian		Green
1991	A Potter		$12	$18	$25	Douglas Florian		Green
1991	Vegetable Garden		$12	$18	$25	Douglas Florian		HBJ
1992	A Chef		$12	$18	$25	Douglas Florian		Green
1992	At The Zoo		$12	$18	$25	Douglas Florian		Green
1993	A Painter		$12	$16	$20	Douglas Florian		Green
1993	A Rumbly Tumbly Glittery Gritty Place		$12	$16	$20	Mary Lyn Ray		HBJ
1993	Monster Motel		$12	$16	$20	Douglas Florian		HBJ
1994	A Fisher		$12	$16	$20	Douglas Florian		Green
1994	An Auto Mechanic		$12	$16	$20	Douglas Florian		Mulbery

Florian   Douglas

Year	Title	VG-	VG	VG+	Fine	Author	Award	Pub
1994	Beast Feast		$12	$16	$20	Douglas Florian		HBrace
1994	Bing Bang Boing		$12	$16	$20	Douglas Florian		HBrace
1995	Very Scary		$10	$16	$20	Tony Johnston		HBrace
1996	On The Wing		$10	$16	$20	Douglas Florian		HBrace
1997	In The Swim		$10	$16	$20	Douglas Florian		HBrace
1998	Insectlopedia		$10	$14	$18	Douglas Florian		HBrace
1999	Laugh-Eteria		$10	$14	$18	Douglas Florian		HBrace
1999	Winter Eyes		$10	$14	$18	Douglas Florian		Green
2000	A Pig Is Big		$8	$12	$16	Douglas Florian		Green
2000	Mammalabilia		$8	$12	$16	Douglas Florian		Harcort
2001	Lizards, Frogs, And Polliwogs		$8	$12	$16	Douglas Florian		Harcort
2002	Summersaults		$8	$10	$14	Douglas Florian		Green
2003	Autumnblings		$8	$10	$14	Douglas Florian		Green
2003	Bow Wow Meow Meow		$8	$10	$14	Douglas Florian		Harcort
2004	Omnibeasts		$8	$10	$14	Douglas Florian		Harcort

Ford   Lauren

Year	Title	VG-	VG	VG+	Fine	Author	Award	Pub
1934	The Lttle Book About God	$50	$70	$90		Lauren Ford		DD
1935	Imagina	$35	$50	$60		Julia Ellsworth Ford		Sutton
1937	Claude	$35	$50	$60		Geneviève Fauconnier		Macmil
1939	The Ageless Story	$140	$200	$240		Lauren Ford	CH	DoddM
1962	Our Lady's Book	$25	$30	$40		Lauren Ford		DoddM
1963	Lauren Ford's Christmas Book	$25	$30	$40		Lauren Ford		DoddM
1969	Joan Of Arc	$40	$50	$70		Winston Churchill		DoddM

Foreman   Michael

Year	Title	VG-	VG	VG+	Fine	Author	Award	Pub
1961	The General	$70	$90	$120		Janet Charters		Dutton
1966	Making Music	$40	$60	$70		Gwen Clemens		Longman
1967	Comic Alphabets	$40	$50	$70		Eric Partridge		Hobbs
1967	I'm For You, And You're For Me	$40	$50	$70		Mabel Watts		AS
1967	The Bad Food Guide	$40	$50	$70		Derek Cooper		R&KPaul
1967	The Perfect Present	$60	$80	$100		Michael Foreman		CM
1967	The Two Giants	$50	$60	$80		Michael Foreman		Pan
1968	Let's Fight, & Other Russian Fables	$40	$50	$70		Sergei Mikhalkov		Pan
1969	The Great Sleigh Robbery	$40	$50	$70		Michael Foreman		Pan
1970	Adam's Balm		$30	$50	$60	Bill Martin		Bowmar
1970	Horatio		$30	$50	$60	Michael Foreman		HHamil
1970	The Birthday Unicorn		$30	$50	$60	Janice Elliott		Goll
1970	The Travels Of Horatio		$30	$50	$60	Michael Foreman		Pan
1972	Moose		$30	$50	$60	Michael Foreman		Pan
1973	Alexander In The Land Of Mog		$30	$50	$60	Freire Wright		Brock
1973	Dinosaurs And All That Rubbish		$30	$50	$60	Michael Foreman		Crowell
1973	Mr. Noah And The Second Flood		$30	$50	$60	Sheila (Every) Burnford		Potter
1974	Rainbow Rider		$30	$40	$60	Jane Yolen		Crowell
1974	War And Peas		$30	$40	$60	Michael Foreman		Crowell
1975	Private Zoo		$30	$40	$60	Georgess McHargue		Viking
1975	Teeny-Tiny And The Witch-Woman		$30	$40	$60	Barbara K. Walker		Pan
1976	The Stone Book		$30	$40	$60	Alan Garner		Collins
1977	All The King's Horses		$25	$40	$50	Michael Foreman		BradP
1977	Borrowed Feathers		$25	$40	$50	Bryna Stevens		Random
1977	Granny Reardun		$25	$40	$50	Alan Garner		Collins
1977	Monkey And The Three Wizards		$25	$40	$50	Cheng'en Wu		BradP
1977	Tom Fobble's Day		$25	$40	$50	Alan Garner		Collins
1978	Hans Andersen, His Classic Fairy Tales		$25	$40	$50	Erik Haugaard (adapted)		DoubleD
1978	Panda's Puzzle, And His Voyage Of Discovery		$25	$40	$50	Michael Foreman		BradP
1978	Popular Folk Tales		$25	$40	$50	Jacob & Wilhelm Grimm		DoubleD
1978	Seven In One Blow		$25	$40	$50	Freire Wright		Random
1978	The Selfish Giant		$25	$40	$50	Oscar Wilde		Metheun
1979	Alan Garner's Fairy Tales Of Gold		$25	$40	$50	Alan Garner		Philo
1979	How To Catch A Ghost		$25	$40	$50	Michael Foreman		HR&W
1979	The Aimer Gate		$25	$40	$50	Alan Garner		Collins
1980	City Of Gold & Other Stories From Old Testament		$25	$35	$50	Peter Dickinson (retold)		Pan
1980	The Faithful Bull		$25	$35	$50	Ernest Hemingway		HHamil
1980	The Tiger Who Lost His Stripes		$25	$35	$50	Anthony Paul		HBJ

Foreman　　　　Michael

Year	Title	VG-	VG	VG+	Fine	Author	Award	Pub
1981	The Nightingale And The Rose		$25	$35	$50	Oscar Wilde		Oxford
1981	The Pig Plantagenet		$25	$35	$50	Allen Andrews		Viking
1981	Trick A Tracker		$25	$35	$50	Michael Foreman		Philo
1982	Fairy Tales		$25	$35	$50	Terry Jones		Schock
1982	Land Of Dreams		$25	$35	$50	Michael Foreman		HR&W
1982	Long Neck And Thunder Foot		$70	$100	$140	Helen Piers	GM	Kestrel
1982	Sleeping Beauty & Other Favourite Fairy Tales		$25	$35	$50	Angela Carter (adapted)		Goll
1983	A Christmas Carol: A Ghost Story Of Christmas		$25	$35	$50	Charles Dickens		Dial
1983	The Crab That Played With The Sea		$25	$35	$50	Rudyard Kipling		H&Row
1983	The Saga Of Erik The Viking		$25	$35	$50	Terry Jones		Schock
1984	A Cat And Mouse Love Story		$20	$30	$40	Nanette Newman		Heine
1984	Panda And The Bunnyips		$20	$30	$40	Michael Foreman		TNelson
1984	The Brontosaurus Birthday Cake		$20	$30	$40	Robert McCrum		S&S
1985	A Child's Garden Of Verses		$20	$30	$40	Robert Louis Stevenson		DelaP
1985	Cat And Canary		$20	$30	$40	Melissa Reilly		Dial
1985	Seasons Of Splendour		$20	$30	$40	Madhur Jaffrey		Athenm
1985	Shakespeare Stories		$20	$30	$40	Leon Garfield		Goll
1986	Early In The Morning		$20	$30	$40	Charles Causley		VK
1986	I'll Take You To Mrs. Cole!		$20	$30	$40	Nigel Gray		Bergh
1986	Nicobobinus		$20	$30	$40	Terry Jones		Bedrik
1986	Panda And The Bushfire		$20	$30	$40	Michael Foreman		P-Hall
1986	Tales For The Telling		$20	$30	$40	Edna O'Brien		Athenm
1987	Ben's Baby		$20	$30	$40	Michael Foreman		H&Row
1987	Daphne Du Maurier's Classics Of The Macabre		$20	$30	$40	Daphne Du Maurier		DoubleD
1987	Just So Stories		$20	$30	$40	Rudyard Kipling		VK
1988	Edmond Went Far Away		$18	$25	$35	Martin Bax		HBJ
1988	Fun		$18	$25	$35	Jan Mark		VK
1988	Peter Pan & Wendy		$18	$25	$35	J. M. Barrie		Crown
1988	The Angel And The Wild Animal		$18	$25	$35	Michael Foreman		Athenm
1988	Worms Wiggle		$18	$25	$35	David Pelham		S&S
1989	Land Of The Long White Cloud		$18	$25	$35	Kiri Te Kanawa		Arcad
1989	The Sand Horse		$18	$25	$35	Ann Turnbull		Athenm
1989	The Shining Princess		$18	$25	$35	Eric Quayle		Arcad
1989	War Boy		$50	$80	$100	Michael Foreman	GM	Arcad
1990	One World		$16	$25	$30	Michael Foreman		Arcad
1990	Panda And The Bunnyips		$16	$25	$30	Michael Foreman		Schock
1991	Busy! Busy! Busy!		$16	$25	$30	Jonathan Shipton		DelaP
1991	Michael Foreman's Mother Goose		$16	$25	$30	Iona Opie (adapted)		HBJ
1991	Michael Foreman's World Of Fairy Tales		$16	$25	$30	Michael Foreman		Arcad
1992	I'll Take You To Mrs Cole		$16	$25	$30	Nigel Gray		KaneM
1992	Jack's Fantastic Voyage		$16	$25	$30	Michael Foreman		HBJ
1992	Over In The Meadow		$16	$25	$30	Michael Foreman		S&S
1992	The Boy Who Sailed With Columbus		$16	$25	$30	Michael Foreman		Arcad
1993	Fantastic Stories		$16	$25	$30	Terry Jones		Viking
1993	Spider The Horrible Cat		$16	$25	$30	Nanette Newman		HBJ
1993	War Game		$16	$25	$30	Michael Foreman		Arcad
1994	A Fish Of The World		$14	$20	$30	Terry Jones		Bedrik
1994	Grandfather's Pencil & The Room Of Stories		$14	$20	$30	Michael Foreman		HBrace
1994	The Beast With A Thousand Teeth		$14	$20	$30	Terry Jones		Bedrik
1994	The Fly-By-Night		$14	$20	$30	Terry Jones		Bedrik
1994	The Long Weekend		$14	$20	$30	Troon Harrison		HBJ
1994	The Sea Tiger		$14	$20	$30	Terry Jones		Bedrik
1994	There's A Bear In The Bath!		$14	$20	$30	Nanette Newman		HBrace
1995	Arthur, High King Of Britain		$14	$20	$25	Michael Morpurgo		HBrace
1995	Dad! I Can't Sleep		$14	$20	$25	Michael Foreman		HBrace
1995	Shakespeare Stories II		$14	$20	$25	Leon Garfield		HM
1995	Surprise! Surprise!		$14	$20	$25	Michael Foreman		HBrace
1995	The Arabian Nights		$14	$20	$25	Brian Alderson		Morrow
1996	After The War Was Over		$12	$18	$25	Michael Foreman		Arcad
1996	Beyond The Rainbow Warrior		$12	$18	$25	Michael Foreman		Pavil
1996	Peter's Place		$12	$18	$25	Sally Grindley		HBrace
1996	Robin Of Sherwood		$12	$18	$25	Michael Morpurgo		HBrace
1996	Seal Surfer		$12	$18	$25	Michael Foreman		HBrace
1996	The Little Reindeer		$12	$18	$25	Michael Foreman		Dial
1997	Ben's Box		$12	$18	$25	Michael Foreman		Piggy
1997	Creation: Read-Aloud Stories From Many Lands		$12	$18	$25	Ann Pilling (retold)		Candle
1997	The Little Ships		$12	$18	$25	Louise Borden		McEld

Foreman   Michael

Year	Title	VG-	VG	VG+	Fine	Author	Award	Pub
1999	Joan Of Arc Of Domrémy		$12	$16	$20	Michael Morpurgo		HBrace
2001	Cat In The Manger		$10	$14	$18	Michael Foreman		Holt
2002	Michael Foreman's Playtime Rhymes		$8	$12	$16	Michael Foreman		Candle
2002	Saving Sinbad		$8	$12	$16	Michael Foreman		KaneM
2002	The Wind In The Willows		$8	$12	$16	Kenneth Grahame		Harcort
2003	A Trip To Dinosaur Time		$8	$12	$16	Michael Foreman		Candle
2003	Bobby, Charlton And The Mountain		$8	$12	$16	Sophie Smiley		AP
2003	Hello, World		$8	$12	$16	Michael Foreman		Candle
2003	Wonder Goal!		$8	$12	$16	Michael Foreman		FSG
2004	Sir Gawain And The Green Knight		$8	$10	$14	Michael Morpurgo		Candle

Frasconi   Antonio

Year	Title	VG-	VG	VG+	Fine	Author	Award	Pub
1954	12 Fables Of Aesop	$80	$100	$140		Aesop		MMA
1958	The House That Jack Built	$100	$140	$180		Antonio Frasconi	CH	HBrace
1960	A Whitman Portrait	$70	$90	$120		Walt Whitman		Spiral
1961	The Snow And The Sun	$50	$60	$80		Antonio Frasconi		HBrace
1964	See Again, Say Again	$50	$60	$80		Antonio Frasconi		HBrace
1965	Love Lyrics	$40	$60	$70		Louis Untermeyer		Odyssey
1965	The Cantilever Rainbow	$60	$80	$100		Ruth Krauss		Pan
1968	Kaleidoscope In Woodcuts	$40	$50	$70		Antonio Frasconi		HBrace
1969	Overhead The Sun	$40	$50	$70		Walt Whitman		FSG
1970	Elijah The Slave		$30	$50	$60	Isaac Bashevis Singer		FSG
1971	On The Slain Collegians		$30	$50	$60	Herman Melville		FSG
1972	Crickets And Frogs		$30	$50	$60	Gabriela Mistral		Athenm
1974	The Elephant And His Secret		$30	$40	$60	Doris Dana		Athenm
1975	One Little Room, An Everywhere		$30	$40	$60	Myra Cohn Livingston		Athenm
1978	How The Left-Behind Beasts Built Ararat		$25	$40	$50	Norma Farber		Walker
1979	Beginnings		$25	$40	$50	Penelope Farmer		Athenm
1981	Leaves Of Grass		$25	$35	$50	Walt Whitman		Frank
1981	The Little Blind Goat		$25	$35	$50	Jan Wahl		Stemmer
1983	The First Editor		$25	$35	$50	Theodore L. De Vinne		WTang
1983	Two Tales		$25	$35	$50	Mercè Rodoreda		ROzier
1983	Yentl The Yeshiva Boy		$25	$35	$50	Isaac Bashevis Singer		FSG
1984	Monkey Puzzle & Other Poems		$20	$30	$40	Myra Cohn Livingston		Athenm
1985	Sun At Midnight		$20	$30	$40	Merwin Muso Soseki		Nadja
1990	If The Owl Calls Again		$16	$25	$30	Myra Cohn Livingston		McEld
1992	At Christmastime		$16	$25	$30	Valerie Worth		HCollins
1993	Friendship		$16	$25	$30	Ralph Waldo Emerson		KellyW
1995	The Zoo At Night		$14	$20	$25	Martha Robinson		McEld

Frasier   Debra

Year	Title	VG-	VG	VG+	Fine	Author	Award	Pub
1991	On The Day You Were Born		$12	$18	$25	Debra Frasier		HBrace
1992	The Animal That Drank Up Sound		$10	$16	$20	William Stafford		HBJ
1994	We Got Here Together		$10	$14	$18	Kim R. Stafford		HBrace
1998	Out Of The Ocean		$8	$12	$16	Debra Frasier		Harcort
2000	Miss Alaineus		$8	$10	$14	Debra Frasier		HBrace
2002	In The Space Of The Sky		$8	$10	$14	Richard Lewis		Harcort
2004	The Incredible Water Show		$6	$10	$12	Debra Frasier		Harcort

Frazee   Marla

Year	Title	VG-	VG	VG+	Fine	Author	Award	Pub
1990	World Famous Muriel & The Magic Mystery		$12	$18	$25	Sue Alexander		Crowell
1995	That Kookoory!		$10	$14	$18	Margaret W. Froehlich		Bdeer
1997	The Seven Silly Eaters		$8	$12	$16	Mary Ann Hoberman		HBrace
1998	On The Morn Of Mayfest		$8	$12	$16	Erica Silverman		S&S
1999	Hush, Little Baby		$8	$12	$16	Marla Frazee		Bbear
2000	Harriet, You'll Drive Me Wild!		$8	$10	$14	Mem Fox		Harcort
2001	Everywhere Babies		$8	$10	$14	Susan Meyers		Harcort
2002	Mrs. Biddlebox		$8	$10	$14	Linda Smith		HCollins
2003	Roller Coaster		$8	$10	$14	Marla Frazee		Harcort
2004	New Baby Train		$6	$10	$12	Woody Guthrie		LBrown
2005	How Does Santa Know?		$6	$10	$12	Marla Frazee		Harcort

Freeman   Don

Year	Title	VG-	VG	VG+	Fine	Author	Award	Pub
1940	My Name Is Aram	$70	$90	$120		William Saroyan		HBrace
1945	It Shouldn't Happen--	$40	$60	$70		Don Freeman		HBrace
1945	The White Deer	$40	$60	$70		James Thurber		HBrace
1951	Chuggy And The Blue Caboose	$40	$50	$70		Lydia Freeman		Viking
1953	Pet Of The Met	$40	$50	$70		Lydia Freeman		Viking
1954	Beady Bear	$40	$50	$70		Don Freeman		Viking
1954	Hobo Hill	$40	$50	$70		Elizabeth Philbrook		Viking
1954	Mike's House	$40	$50	$70		Julia L. Sauer		Viking
1955	Mop Top	$35	$50	$60		Don Freeman		Viking
1955	The Circus In Peter's Closet	$35	$50	$60		Jane Randolph		Crowell
1956	Third Monkey	$35	$50	$60		Ann Nolan Clark		Viking
1957	Fly High, Fly Low	$100	$140	$180		Don Freeman	CH	Viking
1957	Ghost Town Treasure	$35	$50	$60		Clyde Robert Bulla		Crowell
1958	Hector Goes Fishing	$35	$50	$60		Priscilla C. Hallowell		Viking
1958	The Kid Sister	$35	$50	$60		Margaret Embry		Holiday
1959	Norman The Doorman	$35	$50	$60		Don Freeman		Viking
1962	Monkeys Are Funny That Way	$35	$40	$60		Dorothy Koch		Holiday
1963	Ski Pup	$35	$40	$60		Don Freeman		Viking
1964	Dandelion	$35	$40	$60		Don Freeman		Viking
1964	The Turtle And The Dove	$35	$40	$60		Don Freeman		Viking
1965	This For That	$30	$40	$50		Ann Nolan Clark		GGate
1966	A Rainbow Of My Own	$30	$40	$50		Don Freeman		Viking
1967	Best Friends	$30	$40	$50		Myra Berry Brown		GGate
1967	The Guard Mouse	$30	$40	$50		Don Freeman		Viking
1967	Voltaire's Micromegas	$30	$40	$50		Elizabeth Hall (adapted)		GGate
1968	Corduroy	$30	$40	$50		Don Freeman		Viking
1968	Seven In A Bed	$30	$40	$50		Ruth A. Sonneborn		Viking
1969	Best Of Luck	$25	$35	$50		Myra Berry Brown		GGate
1969	Joey's Cat	$25	$35	$50		Robert Burch		Viking
1969	Quiet! There's A Canary In The Library	$25	$35	$50		Don Freeman		GGate
1969	Tilly Witch	$25	$35	$50		Don Freeman		Viking
1970	Burnish Me Bright		$25	$35	$50	Julia Cunningham		Pan
1970	Hattie The Backstage Bat		$25	$35	$50	Don Freeman		Viking
1971	Edward And The Night Horses		$25	$35	$50	Jacklyn Meek Matthews		GGate
1972	Far In The Day		$25	$35	$50	Julia Cunningham		Pan
1972	Inspector Peckit		$25	$35	$50	Don Freeman		Viking
1972	The Wild Cats Of Rome		$25	$35	$50	Elizabeth K. Cooper		GGate
1973	Flash The Dash		$25	$35	$50	Don Freeman		CP
1974	The Paper Party		$20	$30	$40	Don Freeman		Viking
1974	The Seal And The Slick		$20	$30	$40	Don Freeman		Viking
1975	Will's Quill		$20	$30	$40	Don Freeman		Viking
1976	Bearymore		$20	$30	$40	Don Freeman		Viking
1976	The Chalk Box Story		$20	$30	$40	Don Freeman		Lippin
1976	The Christmas Strangers		$20	$30	$40	Marjorie Thayer		CP
1977	Monster Night At Grandma's House		$20	$30	$40	Richard Peck		Viking
1978	A Pocket For Corduroy		$20	$30	$40	Don Freeman		Viking
1978	Dinosaur, My Darling		$20	$30	$40	Edith Thacher Hurd		H&Row
1978	The April Foolers		$20	$30	$40	Marjorie Thayer		CP
1980	The Day Is Waiting		$18	$25	$35	Linda Z. Knab		Viking
2000	Gregory's Shadow		$8	$12	$16	Don Freeman		Viking
2001	Corduroy & Company		$8	$12	$16	Don Freeman		Viking
2004	Manuelo The Playing Mantis		$8	$10	$14	Don Freeman		Viking

French   Fiona

Year	Title	VG-	VG	VG+	Fine	Author	Award	Pub
1970	Jack Of Hearts		$30	$50	$60	Fiona French		HBrace
1972	The Blue Bird		$30	$50	$60	Fiona French		Walck
1973	King Tree		$30	$50	$60	Fiona French		Walck
1974	City Of Gold		$30	$40	$60	Fiona French		Walck
1975	Aio The Rainmaker		$30	$40	$60	Fiona French		Oxford
1976	Matteo		$30	$40	$60	Fiona French		Oxford
1978	Hunt The Thimble		$25	$40	$50	Fiona French		Oxford
1979	The Star Child		$25	$40	$50	Jennifer Westwood		4Winds
1984	Future Story		$20	$30	$40	Fiona French		Bedrik
1985	Going To Squintum's		$20	$30	$40	Jennifer Westwood		Dial
1986	Snow White In New York		$40	$60	$80	Fiona French	GM	Oxford

French   Fiona

Year	Title	VG-	VG	VG+	Fine	Author	Award	Pub
1989	Rise And Shine!		$18	$25	$35	Fiona French		LBrown
1991	Anancy And Mr. Dry-Bone		$16	$25	$30	Fiona French		LBrown
1992	King Of Another Country		$16	$25	$30	Fioni French		Scholas
1994	Little Inchkin		$14	$20	$30	Fiona French		Dial
1995	Pepi And The Secret Names		$14	$20	$25	Jill Paton Walsh		LL&S
1995	The Dragon Takes A Wife		$14	$20	$25	Walter Dean Myers		Scholas
1997	Lord Of The Animals		$12	$18	$25	Fiona French		Millbk
1999	The Glass Garden		$12	$16	$20	Joyce Dunbar		Lincoln
2001	Bethlehem		$10	$14	$18	Fiona French		HCollins
2002	Easter		$8	$12	$16	Fiona French		HCollins

Froud   Brian

Year	Title	VG-	VG	VG+	Fine	Author	Award	Pub
1972	A Midsummer Night's Dream		$70	$100	$140	Charles & Mary Lamb (adapted)		FWatts
1972	The Man Whose Mother Was A Pirate		$70	$100	$140	Margaret Mahy		Athenm
1975	Are All The Giants Dead?		$90	$120	$180	Mary Norton		HBJ
1975	Ultra-Violet Catastrophe!		$40	$60	$80	Margaret Mahy		PMagP
1977	The Land Of Froud		$60	$80	$120	David Larkin (edited)		Peacock
1978	Are All The Giants Dead?		$80	$120	$160	Mary Norton		HBJ
1978	Faeries		$50	$80	$100	David Larkin (edited)		Abrams
1979	Master Snickup's Cloak		$50	$80	$100	Alexander Theroux		PTiger
1982	The World Of The Dark Crystal		$160	$220	$300	J. J. Llewellyn		Knopf
1983	Goblins		$40	$60	$90	Brian Froud		Macmil
1986	The Goblins Of Labyrinth		$40	$60	$80	Terry Jones		Holt
1990	The Dreaming Place		$35	$50	$70	Charles De Lint		Athenm
1994	Lady Cottington's Pressed Fairy Book		$25	$40	$50	Terry Jones		AM
1994	The Wild Wood		$14	$20	$30	Charles De Lint		Bantam
1996	Strange Stains And Mysterious Smells		$12	$18	$25	Terry Jones		S&S
1996	The Goblin Companion		$12	$18	$25	Terry Jones		Turner
1997	Are All The Giants Dead?		$8	$12	$16	Mary Norton		Magic
1998	Good Faeries/Bad Faeries		$12	$16	$20	Terri Windling		S&S
2000	The Faeries' Oracle		$16	$25	$30	Jessica Macbeth		Fogel
2002	Lady Cottington's Pressed Fairy Album		$12	$18	$25	Brian Froud		Abrams
2003	The Runes Of Elfland		$12	$16	$20	Ari Berk		Abrams
2003	The World Of The Dark Crystal		$12	$16	$20	J. J. Llewellyn		Abrams
2004	Brian Fround's Goblins!		$10	$14	$18	Ari Berk		ST&C

Gackenbach   Dick

Year	Title	VG-	VG	VG+	Fine	Author	Award	Pub
1970	The First Book Of Music		$30	$50	$60	Gertrude Norman		FWatts
1974	Claude The Dog		$20	$30	$40	Dick Gackenbach		Seabury
1975	Do You Love Me?		$20	$30	$40	Dick Gackenbach		Seabury
1975	Is Milton Missing?		$20	$30	$40	Steven Kroll		Holiday
1976	Claude And Pepper		$20	$30	$40	Dick Gackenbach		Seabury
1976	Hattie Rabbit		$20	$30	$40	Dick Gackenbach		H&Row
1976	Hound And Bear The Long Night		$20	$30	$40	Dick Gackenbach		Clarion
1976	What's In A Map?		$20	$30	$40	Sally Cartwright		CM&G
1977	Harry And The Terrible Whatzit		$20	$30	$40	Dick Gackenbach		Seabury
1977	Hattie Be Quiet, Hattie Be Good		$20	$30	$40	Dick Gackenbach		H&Row
1977	Mother Rabbit's Son Tom		$20	$30	$40	Dick Gackenbach		H&Row
1977	The Leatherman		$20	$30	$40	Dick Gackenbach		Seabury
1977	What Is Papa Up To Now?		$20	$30	$40	Miriam Anne Bourne		CM&G
1978	Ida Fanfanny		$20	$30	$40	Dick Gackenbach		H&Row
1978	Pepper And All The Legs		$20	$30	$40	Dick Gackenbach		Seabury
1978	The Pig Who Saw Everything		$20	$30	$40	Dick Gackenbach		Seabury
1979	Crackle Gluck And The Sleeping Toad		$18	$25	$35	Dick Gackenbach		Seabury
1979	More From Hound And Bear		$18	$25	$35	Dick Gackenbach		HM
1979	Rat's Christmas Party		$18	$25	$35	Jim Murphy		P-Hall
1980	Amanda And The Giggling Ghost		$18	$25	$35	Steven Kroll		Holiday
1980	Hattie, Tom, And The Chicken Witch		$18	$25	$35	Dick Gackenbach		H&Row
1980	One, Two, Three-Ah-Choo!		$18	$25	$35	Marjorie N. Allen		CM&G
1981	A Bag Full Of Pups		$18	$25	$35	Dick Gackenbach		Clarion
1981	Friday The 13th		$18	$25	$35	Steven Kroll		Holiday
1981	Little Bug		$18	$25	$35	Dick Gackenbach		HM
1981	Mcgoogan Moves The Mighty Rock		$18	$25	$35	Dick Gackenbach		H&Row
1981	The Monster In The Third Dresser Drawer		$18	$25	$35	Janice Lee Smith		H&Row

Gackenbach   Dick

Year	Title	VG-	VG	VG+	Fine	Author	Award	Pub
1982	Adventures Of Albert, The Running Bear		$16	$25	$30	Barbara Isenberg		Clarion
1982	Annie And The Mud Monster		$16	$25	$30	Dick Gackenbach		LL&S
1982	Arabella And Mr. Crack		$16	$25	$30	Dick Gackenbach		Macmil
1983	Binky Gets A Car		$16	$25	$30	Dick Gackenbach		Clarion
1983	I Hate My Brother Harry		$16	$25	$30	Crescent Dragonwagon		H&Row
1983	Mr. Wink And His Shadow Ned		$16	$25	$30	Dick Gackenbach		H&Row
1983	The Princess And The Pea		$16	$25	$30	Hans Christian Andersen		Macmil
1984	King Wacky		$16	$25	$30	Dick Gackenbach		Crown
1984	Poppy, The Panda		$16	$25	$30	Dick Gackenbach		Clarion
1984	The Dog And The Deep Dark Woods		$16	$25	$30	Dick Gackenbach		H&Row
1984	The Kid Next Door & Other Headaches		$16	$25	$30	Janice Lee Smith		H&Row
1984	The Perfect Mouse		$16	$25	$30	Dick Gackenbach		Macmil
1984	What's Claude Doing?		$16	$25	$30	Dick Gackenbach		Clarion
1985	Mag The Magnificent		$16	$25	$30	Dick Gackenbach		Clarion
1986	Hurray For Hattie Rabbit		$14	$20	$30	Dick Gackenbach		H&Row
1986	My Dog And The Green Sock Mystery		$14	$20	$30	David A. Adler		Holiday
1986	Timid Timothy's Tongue Twisters		$14	$20	$30	Dick Gackenbach		Holiday
1987	Dog For A Day		$14	$20	$30	Dick Gackenbach		Clarion
1987	Jack And The Whoopee Wind		$14	$20	$30	Mary Calhoun		Morrow
1987	My Dog And The Birthday Mystery		$14	$20	$30	David A. Adler		Holiday
1988	Harvey, The Foolish Pig		$14	$20	$30	Dick Gackenbach (retold)		Clarion
1988	The Show-And-Tell War		$14	$20	$30	Janice Lee Smith		H&Row
1988	The Wonderful Hay Tumble		$14	$20	$30	Kathleen McKinley Harris		Morrow
1989	It's Not Easy Being George		$14	$20	$25	Janice Lee Smith		H&Row
1989	Supposes		$14	$20	$25	Dick Gackenbach		HBJ
1989	With Love From Gran		$14	$20	$25	Dick Gackenbach		Clarion
1990	Beauty, Brave And Beautiful		$12	$18	$25	Dick Gackenbach		Clarion
1990	The Turkeys' Side Of It		$12	$18	$25	Janice Lee Smith		H&Row
1991	Alice's Special Room		$12	$18	$25	Dick Gackenbach		Clarion
1991	There's A Ghost In The Coatroom		$12	$18	$25	Janice Lee Smith		HCollins
1992	Mighty Tree		$12	$18	$25	Dick Gackenbach		HBJ
1992	Nelson In Love		$12	$18	$25	Janice Lee Smith		HCollins
1992	Roll Over, Rosie		$12	$18	$25	Trinka Enell		Clarion
1993	Claude Has A Picnic		$12	$16	$20	Dick Gackenbach		Clarion
1993	Serious Science		$12	$16	$20	Janice Lee Smith		HCollins
1993	Tiny For A Day		$12	$16	$20	Dick Gackenbach		Clarion
1994	The Baby Blues		$12	$16	$20	Janice Lee Smith		HCollins
1994	When I Am Eight		$12	$16	$20	Joan Lowery Nixon		Dial
1994	Where Are Momma, Poppa, And Sister June?		$12	$16	$20	Dick Gackenbach		Clarion
1996	Barker's Crime		$10	$16	$20	Dick Gackenbach (retold)		HBrace

Gág   Flavia

Year	Title	VG-	VG	VG+	Fine	Author	Award	Pub
1936	Sing A Song Of Seasons	$70	$100	$120		Frances Carpenter		CM
1939	The Story Of Kattor	$50	$60	$80		Alam Olivia Schmidt Scott		CM
1941	The Lost Handkerchiefs	$50	$60	$80		Eva Knox Evans		Putnam
1945	Christmas House	$40	$60	$70		Thyra Turner		Scribnr
1946	The Wily Woodchucks	$40	$60	$70		Alam Olivia Schmidt Scott		CM
1952	Four Legs And A Tail	$40	$50	$70		Flavia Gág		Holt
1955	Fourth Floor Menagerie	$35	$50	$60		Flavia Gág		Holt
1957	Tweeter Of Prairie Dog Town	$35	$50	$60		Flavia Gág		Holt
1958	A Wish For Mimi	$35	$50	$60		Flavia Gág		Holt
1960	Chubby's First Year	$35	$40	$60		Flavia Gág		Holt
1964	The Melon Patch Mystery	$35	$40	$60		Flavia Gág		McKay
1969	The Florida Snow Party	$25	$35	$50		Flavia Gág		McKay

Gág   Wanda

Year	Title	VG-	VG	VG+	Fine	Author	Award	Pub
1928	Millions Of Cats	$2,400	$3,200	$4,000		Wanda Gág	NH	CM
1929	The Funny Thing	$560	$760	$940		Wanda Gág		CM
1931	Snippy And Snappy	$560	$740	$920		Wanda Gág		CM
1932	Wanda Gag's Story Book	$360	$480	$600		Wanda Gág		CM
1933	The ABC Bunny	$840	$1,200	$1,400		Wanda Gág	NH	CM
1935	Gone Is Gone	$340	$460	$580		Wanda Gág		CM
1936	Tales From Grimm	$340	$460	$580		Wanda Gág		CM
1938	Snow White And The Seven Dwarfs	$500	$680	$840		Wanda Gág		CM

Gág   Wanda

Year	Title	VG-	VG	VG+	Fine	Author	Award	Pub
1940	Growing Pains	$140	$200	$240		Wanda Gág		CM
1941	Nothing At All	$220	$300	$380		Wanda Gág	CH	CM
1943	Three Gay Tales From Grimm	$160	$220	$280		Wanda Gág		CM
1947	More Tales From Grimm	$160	$200	$260		Wanda Gág		CM

Gál   László

Year	Title	VG-	VG	VG+	Fine	Author	Award	Pub
1967	El Cid	$40	$50	$70		María Luisa Gefaell		Hamlyn
1967	Siegfried, The Mightly Warrior	$40	$50	$70		László Gál		McHill
1970	Cartier Discovers The St. Lawrence		$30	$50	$60	William Toye		Walck
1970	Raven, Creator Of The World		$30	$50	$60	Ronald Melzack		LBrown
1971	The Moon Painters		$30	$50	$60	Selve Maas		Viking
1977	My Name Is Not Odessa Yarker		$25	$40	$50	Marian Engel		KidsCan
1979	The Twelve Dancing Princesses		$25	$40	$50	Janet L.S. Lunn		Metheun
1984	Canadian Fairy Tales		$20	$30	$40	Eva Martin		D&M
1985	The Willow Maiden		$20	$30	$40	Meghan Collins		Dial
1986	Tales Of The Far North		$20	$30	$40	Eva Martin		Dial
1987	The Enchanted Tapestry		$20	$30	$40	Robert D. San Souci		Dial
1988	Iduna And The Magic Apples		$18	$25	$35	Marianna Mayer		Macmil
1990	Pome & Peel		$16	$25	$30	Amy Ehrlich		Dial
1990	The Spirit Of The Blue Light		$16	$25	$30	Marianna Mayer		Macmil
1991	Prince Ivan And The Firebird		$16	$25	$30	Laszlo Gal		M&S
1991	Sea Witches		$16	$25	$30	Joanne Robertson		Dial
1995	Merlin's Castle		$14	$20	$25	László Gál		Stodd
1996	Tiktala		$12	$18	$25	Margaret Shaw-MacKinnon		Holiday
1997	Dracula		$12	$18	$25	Tim Wynne-Jones (adapted)		KPorter
1997	The Parrot		$12	$18	$25	László Gál		Ground

Galdone   Paul

Year	Title	VG-	VG	VG+	Fine	Author	Award	Pub
1951	Miss Pickerell Goes To Mars	$50	$70	$90		Ellen MacGregor		Whittle
1951	Nine Lives	$50	$70	$90		Edward Fenton		Pan
1951	Of Mikes And Men	$30	$40	$50		Jane Woodfin		McHill
1951	Tallie	$30	$40	$50		Mildred Lawrence		HBrace
1951	The Kid Who Batted 1.000	$30	$40	$50		Bob Allison		DoubleD
1952	Monkey Shines	$30	$40	$50		Earl Schenck Miers		World
1952	Secret Of The Old Books	$30	$40	$50		Betty Baxter Anderson		TNelson
1952	Space Cat	$50	$70	$90		Ruthven Todd		Scribnr
1952	The Cub Scout Mystery	$30	$40	$50		Dorothy Sterling		DoubleD
1952	The Silver Purse	$30	$40	$50		Elisa Bialk		World
1952	Upside Down In The Magnolia Tree	$30	$40	$50		Mary Bancroft		LBrown
1953	Buckskin Scout	$30	$40	$50		Marion Renick		World
1953	Miss Pickerell And The Geiger Counter	$50	$70	$90		Ellen MacGregor		Whittle
1953	Miss Pickerell Goes Undersea	$50	$70	$90		Ellen MacGregor		Whittle
1953	Rocket Away!	$50	$70	$90		Frances Frost		Whittle
1953	Rocky's Road	$30	$40	$50		Jerrold Beim		HBrace
1953	Star Of Wonder	$50	$70	$90		Robert Reed Coles		McHill
1953	The Fishing Cat	$30	$40	$50		Grayce Silverton Myers		Abing
1953	The Heart For Baseball	$30	$40	$50		Marion Renick		Scribnr
1953	The Rosemont Riddle	$30	$40	$50		John & Maxine Drury		TNelson
1953	Touchdown Trouble	$30	$40	$50		Earl Schenck Miers		World
1953	Wilderness Journey	$30	$40	$50		William O. Steele		HBrace
1954	Hans Brinker	$30	$40	$50		Mary Mapes Dodge		GardenC
1954	How Do You Travel?	$30	$40	$50		Miriam Schlein		Abing
1954	Miss Pickerell Goes To The Arctic	$50	$70	$90		Ellen MacGregor		Whittle
1954	Skeleton Cave	$30	$40	$50		Cora Cheney		HR&W
1954	The Green Song	$30	$40	$50		Doris Troutman Plenn		DMcKay
1954	The Kid Who Beat The Dodgers	$30	$40	$50		Earl Schenck Miers		World
1954	Winter Danger	$30	$40	$50		William O. Steele		HBrace
1955	Island Secret	$25	$35	$50		Mildred Lawrence		HBrace
1955	Key Of Gold	$25	$35	$50		Cora Cheney		HR&W
1955	Mrs. Perrywinkle's Pets	$50	$70	$90		Catherine Woolley		Morrow
1955	Playing Possum	$25	$35	$50		Edward Eager		Putnam
1955	Space Cat Visits Venus	$25	$35	$50		Ruthven Todd		Scribnr
1955	The Battery For Madison High	$25	$35	$50		Albert Hirshberg		LBrown
1955	The Long Journey	$25	$35	$50		Florence S. Norman		Lippin

Galdone   Paul

Year	Title	VG-	VG	VG+	Fine	Author	Award	Pub
1955	Theodore Turtle	$50	$70	$90		Ellen MacGregor		Whittle
1955	Tomahawks And Trouble	$25	$35	$50		William O. Steele		HBrace
1956	Anatole	$160	$220	$280		Eve Titus	CH	Whittle
1956	Ball Of Fire	$25	$35	$50		Earl Schenck Miers		World
1956	Darcy's Harvest	$25	$35	$50		Evelyn Sibley Lampman		DoubleD
1956	Did You Feed My Cow?	$25	$35	$50		Margaret T. Burroughs		Crowell
1956	Down And Away Below	$25	$35	$50		Edwin E. Rols		Bobbs
1956	Sea Beach Adventure	$25	$35	$50		Gladys Relyea Saxon		HR&W
1956	The Lone Hunt	$25	$35	$50		William O. Steele		HBrace
1956	The Rocking Chair Buck	$25	$35	$50		Cora Cheney		HR&W
1956	The Sword In The Tree	$25	$35	$50		Clyde Robert Bulla		Crowell
1957	Anatole And The Cat	$140	$180	$240		Eve Titus	CH	Whittle
1957	Flaming Arrows	$25	$35	$50		William O. Steele		HBrace
1957	Making The Mississippi Shout	$25	$35	$50		Mary Calhoun		Morrow
1957	Mister Jim	$25	$35	$50		Rutherford Montgomery		World
1957	Mr. Pingle And Mr. Buttonhouse	$50	$70	$90		Ellen MacGregor		Whittle
1957	Night Cat	$25	$35	$50		Irma Simonton Black		Holiday
1957	Old Charlie	$25	$35	$50		Clyde Robert Bulla		Crowell
1957	Rusty Rings A Bell	$25	$35	$50		Franklyn M. Branley		Crowell
1957	Space Cat Meets Mars	$25	$35	$50		Ruthven Todd		Scribnr
1957	The Malibu Monster	$25	$35	$50		Jessica Ryan		Bobbs
1957	The Man In The Moon	$25	$35	$50		Margaret Otto		HR&W
1957	Where The Trail Divides	$25	$35	$50		Lorna Callahan		Whittle
1958	Bascombe, The Fastest Hound Alive	$50	$60	$80		Adam Smith		Morrow
1958	Basil Of Baker Street	$25	$35	$50		Eve Titus		Whittle
1958	Bayou Hunter	$25	$35	$50		Louise Reynes Jenkins		Bobbs
1958	My Dog And I	$50	$60	$80		Nancy Lord		Whittle
1958	One Little Drum	$25	$35	$50		Margaret Hodges		Follett
1958	Pancho	$25	$35	$50		Bruce Grant		World
1958	Space Cat And The Kittens	$25	$35	$50		Ruthven Todd		Scribnr
1958	The Perilous Road	$25	$35	$50		William O. Steele		HBrace
1958	The Tiptop Wish	$25	$35	$50		Ruth Hubbell Dudley		Crowell
1958	What Cabrillo Found	$25	$35	$50		Maud Hart Lovelace		Crowell
1959	At Jesus' House	$25	$35	$50		Carolyn M. Wolcott		Broad
1959	Grandfather And I	$25	$35	$50		Helen Elizabeth Buckley		LL&S
1959	Little Tuck	$25	$35	$50		Clara Baldwin		DoubleD
1959	That Big Broozer	$25	$35	$50		Benzell Graham		Morrow
1959	The Far Frontier	$25	$35	$50		William O. Steele		HBrace
1959	The Jamesville Jets	$25	$35	$50		C. Paul Jackson		Follett
1959	The Mysterious Schoolmaster	$25	$35	$50		Karin Anckarsvärd		HBrace
1959	The Tail Of The Terrible Tiger	$25	$35	$50		Marion Renick		Scribnr
1959	The Whales Go By	$100	$140	$180		Fred Phleger		BB
1959	Timmy And The Tin-Can Telephone	$25	$35	$50		Franklyn M. Branley		Crowell
1960	A Gaggle Of Geese	$25	$30	$40		Eve Merriam		Knopf
1960	Anatole And The Robot	$25	$30	$40		Eve Titus		Whittle
1960	Heroines Of The Early West	$25	$30	$40		Nancy Wilson Ross		Random
1960	Old Mother Hubbard And Her Dog	$25	$30	$40		Sarah Catherine Martin		Whittle
1960	Small Clown	$25	$30	$40		Nancy Faulkner		DoubleD
1960	The Different Dog	$25	$30	$40		Dale Everson		Morrow
1960	The Lemonade Trick	$25	$30	$40		Scott Corbett		LBrown
1961	Anatole Over Paris	$25	$30	$40		Eve Titus		Whittle
1961	Benjie Goes Into Business	$25	$30	$40		Patricia Miles Martin		Putnam
1961	Boy At Bat	$25	$30	$40		Marion Renick		Scribnr
1961	Drovers' Gold	$25	$30	$40		Julia Montgomery Street		DoddM
1961	Grandmother And I	$25	$30	$40		Helen Elizabeth Buckley		LL&S
1961	The Cowboy Surprise	$25	$30	$40		William Wise		Putnam
1961	The House That Jack Built	$25	$30	$40		Paul Galdone		Whittle
1961	The Mailbox Trick	$25	$30	$40		Scott Corbett		LBrown
1961	The Robber Ghost	$25	$30	$40		Karin Anckarsvärd		HBrace
1961	The Three Wishes	$25	$30	$40		Paul Galdone		Whittle
1961	The Wonderful Visit To Miss Liberty	$25	$30	$40		Elizabeth Starr Hill		HR&W
1962	Counting Carnival	$25	$30	$40		Feenie Ziner		CM
1962	How Many Teeth?	$25	$30	$40		Paul Showers		Crowell
1962	Jeff And Mr. James' Pond	$25	$30	$40		Esther MacBain Meeks		LL&S
1962	Look At Your Eyes	$25	$30	$40		Paul Showers		Crowell
1962	Madcap Mystery	$25	$30	$40		Karin Anckarsvärd		HBrace
1962	Sunnyvale Fair	$25	$30	$40		Alice E. Goudey		Scribnr

Galdone   Paul

Year	Title	VG-	VG	VG+	Fine	Author	Award	Pub
1962	The First Seven Days	$25	$30	$40		Paul Galdone (adapted)		Crowell
1962	The Hare And The Tortoise	$25	$30	$40		Aesop		Whittle
1962	The Two Old Bachelors	$25	$30	$40		Edward Lear		Whittle
1963	A Capital Ship	$25	$30	$40		Charles E. Carryl		Whittle
1963	Follow Your Nose	$25	$30	$40		Paul Showers		Crowell
1963	Miss Osborne-The-Mop	$25	$30	$40		Wilson Gage		World
1963	My Sister And I	$25	$30	$40		Helen Elizabeth Buckley		LL&S
1963	Soupbone	$25	$30	$40		Sidney Offit		StMart
1963	The Big Basketball Prize	$25	$30	$40		Marion Renick		Scribnr
1963	The Blind Men And The Elephant	$25	$30	$40		John Godfrey Saxe		Whittle
1963	The Disappearing Dog Trick	$25	$30	$40		Scott Corbett		LBrown
1964	Basil And The Lost Colony	$25	$30	$40		Eve Titus		Whittle
1964	Edie Changes Her Mind	$25	$30	$40		Johanna Johnston		Putnam
1964	Liselott And The Goloff	$25	$30	$40		Hans Peterson		CM
1964	Peek The Piper	$25	$30	$40		Vitalii Bianki		Black
1964	The Battle Of The Kegs	$25	$30	$40		Francis Hopkinson		Crowell
1964	The Limerick Trick	$25	$30	$40		Scott Corbett		LBrown
1964	The Year Santa Went Modern	$25	$30	$40		Richard Willard Armour		McHill
1964	Tom, Tom The Piper's Son	$25	$30	$40		Paul Galdone		Whittle
1965	Adventures Of Egbert The Easter Egg	$25	$30	$40		Richard Willard Armour		McHill
1965	Anatole And The Poodle	$25	$30	$40		Eve Titus		Whittle
1965	Brownie	$25	$30	$40		Hans Peterson		LL&S
1965	Shadrach, Meshach, And Abednego	$25	$30	$40		Paul Galdone (adapted)		Whittle
1965	The Baseball Trick	$25	$30	$40		Scott Corbett		LBrown
1965	The Little Boy And The Birthdays	$25	$30	$40		Helen Elizabeth Buckley		LL&S
1965	Who's In Charge Of Lincoln?	$25	$30	$40		Dale Fife		CM
1965	Your Skin And Mine	$25	$30	$40		Paul Showers		Crowell
1966	A Camel In The Sea	$25	$30	$40		Lee Garrett Goetz		McHill
1966	Anatole And The Piano	$25	$30	$40		Eve Titus		McHill
1966	Animals On The Ceiling	$25	$30	$40		Richard Willard Armour		McHill
1966	Koko And The Ghosts	$25	$30	$40		Ivan Kusan		HBrace
1966	That's Right, Edie	$25	$30	$40		Johanna Johnston		Putnam
1966	The Adventures Of Homer Fink	$25	$30	$40		Sidney Offit		StMart
1966	The Deacon's Masterpiece	$25	$30	$40		Oliver Wendell Holmes		WorldsW
1966	The History Of Simple Simon	$25	$30	$40		Paul Galdone		McHill
1966	Two Laughable Lyrics	$25	$30	$40		Edward Lear		Putnam
1967	A Dozen Dinosaurs	$25	$30	$40		Richard Willard Armour		McHill
1967	Elbert, The Mind Reader	$25	$30	$40		Barbara Rinkoff		LL&S
1967	High Sounds, Low Sounds	$25	$30	$40		Franklyn M. Branley		Crowell
1967	Little Tuppen	$25	$30	$40		Paul Galdone		Seabury
1967	Pandora's Box	$25	$30	$40		Nathaniel Hawthorne		McHill
1967	The Turnabout Trick	$25	$30	$40		Scott Corbett		LBrown
1967	Wallace, The Wandering Pig	$25	$30	$40		Judy Van der Veer		HBrace
1967	Whiskers, My Cat	$25	$30	$40		Letta Schatz		McHill
1967	Woody's Big Trouble	$25	$30	$40		Patricia Miles Martin		Putnam
1968	A Visit From St. Nicholas	$20	$30	$35		Clement C. Moore		McHill
1968	Budd's Noisy Wagon	$20	$30	$35		Richard Shaw		FWarne
1968	Henny Penny	$20	$30	$35		Paul Galdone		Seabury
1968	Odd Old Mammals	$20	$30	$35		Richard Willard Armour		McHill
1968	The Boy With A Billion Pets	$20	$30	$35		Peggy Mann		CM
1968	The Bremen Town Musicians	$20	$30	$35		Jacob & Wilhelm Grimm		McHill
1968	The Sunlit Sea	$20	$30	$35		Augusta R. Goldin		Crowell
1968	The Wise Fool	$20	$30	$35		Paul Galdone (adapted)		Random
1969	Anatole And The Thirty Thieves	$20	$30	$35		Eve Titus		McHill
1969	George Washington's Breakfast	$20	$30	$35		Jean Fritz		CM
1969	Oté	$20	$30	$35		Pura Belpré		Pan
1969	Sidney's Ghost	$20	$30	$35		Carol Iden		World
1969	The Hairy Horror Trick	$20	$30	$35		Scott Corbett		LBrown
1969	The Life Of Jack Sprat	$20	$30	$35		Paul Galdone		McHill
1969	To The Rescue	$20	$30	$35		Judy Van der Veer		HBrace
1970	All Sizes And Shapes Of Monkeys And Apes		$18	$25	$35	Richard Willard Armour		McHill
1970	Anatole And The Toyshop		$18	$25	$35	Eve Titus		McHill
1970	Androcles And The Lion		$18	$25	$35	Paul Galdone		McHill
1970	Little Tom Tucker		$18	$25	$35	Paul Galdone		McHill
1970	The Three Little Pigs		$18	$25	$35	Paul Galdone		Seabury
1970	Try It Again, Sam		$18	$25	$35	Judith Viorst		LL&S
1970	Two And Me Makes Three		$18	$25	$35	Roberta Greene		CM

Galdone   Paul

Year	Title	VG-	VG	VG+	Fine	Author	Award	Pub
1970	What's New, Lincoln?		$18	$25	$35	Dale Fife		CM
1971	Basil And The Pygmy Cats		$18	$25	$35	Eve Titus		McHill
1971	Dogs And Cats And Things Like That		$18	$25	$35	John Knoepfle		McHill
1971	The Hateful Plateful Trick		$18	$25	$35	Scott Corbett		LBrown
1971	The Town Mouse And The Country Mouse		$18	$25	$35	Paul Galdone		McHill
1971	What's The Prize, Lincoln?		$18	$25	$35	Dale Fife		CM&G
1971	Who's In Holes?		$18	$25	$35	Richard Willard Armour		McHill
1972	100 Hamburgers		$18	$25	$35	Mary Lynn Solot		LL&S
1972	Dance Of The Animals		$18	$25	$35	Pura Belpré		FWarne
1972	Improbable Adventures Marvelous O'hara Soapstone		$18	$25	$35	Zibby Oneal		Viking
1972	It Does Not Say Meow		$18	$25	$35	Beatrice S. De Regniers		Seabury
1972	The Moving Adventures Of Old Dame Trot		$18	$25	$35	Paul Galdone		McHill
1972	The Three Bears		$18	$25	$35	Paul Galdone (adapted)		Seabury
1972	Three Aesop Fox Fables		$18	$25	$35	Paul Galdone		WorldsW
1973	Adventures Of Old Dame Trot & Her Comical Cat		$16	$25	$30	Paul Galdone		McHill
1973	Anatole In Italy		$16	$25	$30	Eve Titus		McHill
1973	Clarence And The Burglar		$16	$25	$30	F. N. Monjo		CM&G
1973	Hereafterthis		$16	$25	$30	Joseph Jacobs		McHill
1973	The Cool Ride In The Sky		$16	$25	$30	Diane Wolkstein		Knopf
1973	The Home Run Trick		$16	$25	$30	Scott Corbett		LBrown
1973	The Little Red Hen		$16	$25	$30	Paul Galdone		Seabury
1973	The Three Billy Goats Gruff		$16	$25	$30	Peter Christen Asbjønsen		Seabury
1974	Jack-O'-Lantern		$16	$25	$30	Edna Barth		Seabury
1974	Little Red Riding Hood		$16	$25	$30	Paul Galdone		McHill
1974	Sea Full Of Whales		$16	$25	$30	Richard Willard Armour		McHill
1974	Speak Up, Edie!		$16	$25	$30	Johanna Johnston		Putnam
1974	The Frog Prince		$16	$25	$30	Paul Galdone (adapted)		McHill
1974	The History Of Mother Twaddle		$16	$25	$30	Paul Galdone		Seabury
1974	The Hockey Trick		$16	$25	$30	Scott Corbett		LBrown
1975	Because Of The Sand Witches There		$16	$25	$30	Mary Q. Steele		Green
1975	Gertrude, The Goose Who Forgot		$16	$25	$30	Joanna Galdone		FWatts
1975	The Lady Who Saw The Good Side Of Everything		$16	$25	$30	Pat Decker Tapio		Seabury
1975	The Queen Who Couldn't Bake Gingerbread		$16	$25	$30	Dorothy Van Woerkom		Knopf
1975	Who Goes There, Lincoln?		$16	$25	$30	Dale Fife		CM&G
1976	Basil In Mexico		$16	$25	$30	Eve Titus		McHill
1976	Puss In Boots		$16	$25	$30	Paul Galdone		Seabury
1976	The Black Mask Trick		$16	$25	$30	Scott Corbett		LBrown
1976	The Magic Porridge Pot		$16	$25	$30	Paul Galdone		Seabury
1976	The Table, The Donkey, And The Stick		$16	$25	$30	Paul Galdone		McHill
1977	A Strange Servant		$16	$25	$30	Paul Galdone		Knopf
1977	Clarence And The Cat		$16	$25	$30	Patricia Lauber		CM&G
1977	The Gorilla In The Hall		$16	$25	$30	Alice Schertle		LL&S
1977	The Hangman's Ghost Trick		$16	$25	$30	Scott Corbett		LBrown
1977	The Tailypo		$16	$25	$30	Joanna Galdone		Seabury
1977	Who'll Vote For Lincoln?		$16	$25	$30	Dale Fife		CM&G
1978	Amber Day		$14	$20	$30	Joanna Galdone		McHill
1978	Cinderella		$14	$20	$30	Paul Galdone (adapted)		McHill
1978	The Hungry Fox And The Foxy Duck		$14	$20	$30	Kathleen Leverich		PMagP
1978	The Princess And The Pea		$14	$20	$30	Hans Christian Andersen		Seabury
1978	Wriggles, The Little Wishing Pig		$14	$20	$30	Pauline Watson		Seabury
1979	Anatole And The Pied Piper		$14	$20	$30	Eve Titus		McHill
1979	Hans In Luck		$14	$20	$30	Paul Galdone		PMagP
1979	Strange Monsters Of The Sea		$14	$20	$30	Richard Willard Armour		McHill
1979	The Steadfast Tin Soldier		$14	$20	$30	Hans Christian Andersen		Clarion
1979	The Talking Turnip		$14	$20	$30	Anne K. Rose		PMagP
1979	Three Ducks Went Wandering		$14	$20	$30	Ron Roy		Seabury
1979	Zed And The Monsters		$14	$20	$30	Peggy Parish		DoubleD
1980	King Of The Cats		$14	$20	$25	Paul Galdone (adapted)		Clarion
1980	The Little Girl And The Big Bear		$14	$20	$25	Joanna Galdone		Clarion
1981	Insects All Around Us		$14	$20	$25	Richard Willard Armour		McHill
1981	The Amazing Pig		$14	$20	$25	Paul Galdone		Clarion
1981	The Three Sillies		$14	$20	$25	Paul Galdone (adapted)		Clarion
1982	Basil In The Wild West		$14	$20	$25	Eve Titus		McHill
1982	Hansel And Gretel		$14	$20	$25	Jacob & Wilhelm Grimm		McHill
1982	The Monster And The Tailor		$14	$20	$25	Paul Galdone		Clarion
1982	What's In Fox's Sack?		$14	$20	$25	Paul Galdone		Clarion
1983	Norma Lee I Don't Knock On Doors		$14	$20	$25	Charles Keller		P-Hall

Galdone   Paul

Year	Title	VG-	VG	VG+	Fine	Author	Award	Pub
1983	The Greedy Old Fat Man		$14	$20	$25	Paul Galdone		Clarion
1983	The Turtle And The Monkey		$14	$20	$25	Paul Galdone		Clarion
1984	The Elves And The Shoemaker		$12	$18	$25	Paul Galdone		Clarion
1984	The Teeny-Tiny Woman		$12	$18	$25	Paul Galdone		Clarion
1985	Cat Goes Fiddle-I-Fee		$12	$18	$25	Paul Galdone		Clarion
1985	Rumpelstiltskin		$12	$18	$25	Paul Galdone		Clarion
1986	Little Bo-Peep		$12	$16	$20	Paul Galdone		Clarion
1986	Over In The Meadow		$12	$16	$20	Paul Galdone		P-Hall
1986	Three Little Kittens		$12	$16	$20	Paul Galdone		Clarion
1987	The Complete Story Of The Three Blind Mice		$12	$16	$20	John W. Ivimey		Clarion
1987	The Owl And The Pussy-Cat		$12	$16	$20	Edward Lear		Clarion
2001	Nursery Classics		$8	$10	$14	Paul Galdone		Clarion

Gammell   Stephen

Year	Title	VG-	VG	VG+	Fine	Author	Award	Pub
1973	A Nutty Business		$60	$90	$120	Ida Chittum		Putnam
1974	Let Me Hear You Whisper		$40	$60	$80	Paul Zindel		H&Row
1974	The Glory Horse		$40	$60	$80	Ramona Maher		CM&G
1975	Nabby Adams' Diary		$30	$40	$60	Miriam Anne Bourne		CM&G
1975	Thunder At Gettysburg		$30	$40	$60	Patricia Lee Gauch		CM&G
1976	Ghosts		$30	$40	$60	Seymour Simon		Lippin
1976	Meet The Werewolf		$30	$40	$60	Georgess McHargue		Lippin
1976	The Kelpie's Pearls		$30	$40	$60	Mollie Hunter		H&Row
1977	A Furl Of Fairy Wind: Four Stories		$25	$40	$50	Mollie Hunter		H&Row
1977	Alice Yazzie's Year		$25	$40	$50	Ramona Maher		CM&G
1978	Day Of The Blizzard		$25	$40	$50	Marietta Moskin		CM&G
1978	The Ghost Of Tillie Jean Cassaway		$25	$40	$50	Ellen Harvey Showell		4Winds
1978	The Hawks Of Chelney		$25	$40	$50	Adrienne Jones		H&Row
1979	A Net To Catch The Wind		$25	$40	$50	Margaret Greaves		H&Row
1979	Leo Possessed		$25	$40	$50	Dilys Owen		HBJ
1979	Meet The Vampire		$25	$40	$50	Georgess McHargue		Lippin
1979	Stonewall		$25	$40	$50	Jean Fritz		Putnam
1979	Whitepaws: A Coyote-Dog		$25	$40	$50	Michael Fox		CM&G
1979	Yesterday's Island		$25	$40	$50	Eve Bunting		FWarne
1980	And Then The Mouse ...: Three Stories		$25	$35	$50	Malcolm Hall		4Winds
1980	Blackbird Singing		$25	$35	$50	Eve Bunting		Macmil
1980	Terrible Things		$25	$35	$50	Eve Bunting		H&Row
1980	The Real Tom Thumb		$25	$35	$50	Helen Reeder Cross		4Winds
1981	Demo And The Dolphin		$25	$35	$50	Nathaniel Benchley		H&Row
1981	Flash And The Swan		$25	$35	$50	Ann Brophy		FWarne
1981	Once Upon Macdonald's Farm		$25	$35	$50	Stephen Gammell		4Winds
1981	Scary Stories To Tell In The Dark		$25	$35	$50	Alvin Schwartz (retold)		Lippin
1981	Wake-Up, Bear--It's Christmas!		$25	$35	$50	Stephen Gammell		LL&S
1981	Where The Buffaloes Begin		$100	$160	$220	Olaf Baker	CH	FWarne
1982	The Best Way To Ripton		$25	$35	$50	Maggie S. Davis		Holiday
1982	The Story Of Mr. And Mrs. Vinegar		$25	$35	$50	Stephen Gammell		LL&S
1983	Git Along, Old Scudder		$25	$35	$50	Stephen Gammell		LL&S
1983	The Old Banjo		$25	$35	$50	Dennis Haseley		Macmil
1984	More Scary Stories To Tell In The Dark		$20	$30	$40	Alvin Schwartz (retold)		Lippin
1984	Thaddeus		$20	$30	$40	A. Herzig & J. Mali		LBrown
1984	Waiting To Waltz, A Childhood: Poems		$20	$30	$40	Cynthia Rylant		BradP
1985	Thanksgiving Poems		$20	$30	$40	Myra C. Livingston (selected)		Holiday
1985	The Relatives Came		$60	$90	$120	Cynthia Rylant	CH	BradP
1985	Who Kidnapped The Sheriff?		$20	$30	$40	Larry Callen		AMP
1986	A Regular Rolling Noah		$20	$30	$40	George Ella Lyon		BradP
1987	Old Henry		$20	$30	$40	Joan W. Blos		Morrow
1987	Song And Dance Man		$120	$180	$240	Karen Ackerman	CM	Knopf
1987	The Great Dimpole Oak		$20	$30	$40	Janet Taylor Lisle		Orchard
1988	Air Mail To The Moon		$18	$25	$35	Tom Birdseye		Holiday
1989	Dancing Teepees		$18	$25	$35	Virginia Sneve (selected)		Holiday
1989	Halloween Poems		$18	$25	$35	Myra C. Livingston (selected)		Holiday
1989	Will's Mammoth		$18	$25	$35	Rafe Martin		Putnam
1990	Come A Tide		$16	$25	$30	George Ella Lyon		Orchard
1990	Wing-A-Ding		$16	$25	$30	Lyn Littlefield Hoopes		Joy
1991	Old Black Fly		$16	$25	$30	Jim Aylesworth		Holt
1991	Scary Stories 3: More Tales To Chill Your Bones		$16	$25	$30	Alvin Schwartz (retold)		HCollins

Gammell   Stephen

Year	Title	VG-	VG	VG+	Fine	Author	Award	Pub
1991	The Wing Shop		$16	$25	$30	Elvira Woodruff		Holiday
1993	Monster Mama		$16	$25	$30	Liz Rosenberg		Philo
1997	Is That You, Winter?: A Story		$12	$18	$25	Stephen Gammell		Whistle
1998	I Did It Anyway		$12	$16	$20	Liz Rosenberg		HBrace
1999	The Art Contest		$12	$16	$20	Stephen Gammell		Whistle
2000	Once Upon Macdonald's Farm		$10	$14	$18	Stephen Gammell		S&S
2000	Twigboy		$10	$14	$18	Stephen Gammell		Whistle
2001	How About Going For A Ride		$10	$14	$18	Stephen Gammell		Whistle
2001	The Burger And The Hot Dog		$10	$14	$18	Jim Aylesworth		Athenm
2002	Humble Pie		$8	$12	$16	Jennifer Donnelly		Athenm
2003	Hey, Pancakes!		$8	$12	$16	Tamson Weston		Harcort

Gannett   Ruth

Year	Title	VG-	VG	VG+	Fine	Author	Award	Pub
1940	Paco Goes To The Fair	$70	$90	$120		Richard Gill		Holt
1942	Hi-Po The Hippo	$70	$90	$120		Dorothy Thomas		Random
1945	My Mother Is The Most Beautiful Woman In The World	$140	$180	$220		Becky Reyher	CH	Lothrop
1946	Miss Hickory	$300	$400	$500		Carolyn Sherwin Bailey	NM	Viking
1948	My Father's Dragon	$120	$160	$220		Ruth Stiles Gannett	NH	Random
1950	Elmer And The Dragon	$60	$80	$100		Ruth Stiles Gannett		Random
1951	The Dragons Of Blueland	$50	$70	$90		Ruth Stiles Gannett		Random
1961	Katie And The Sad Noise	$50	$60	$80		Ruth Stiles Gannett		Random
1966	The Home Place	$40	$60	$70		Dorothy Thomas		UNeb

Garland   Michael

Year	Title	VG-	VG	VG+	Fine	Author	Award	Pub
1995	Dinner At Magritte's		$10	$16	$20	Michael Garland		Dutton
1998	Angel Cat		$8	$12	$16	Michael Garland		Boyds
1999	An Elf For Christmas		$8	$12	$16	Michael Garland		Dutton
2001	Christmas Magic		$8	$10	$14	Michael Garland		Dutton
2002	The President And Mom's Apple Pie		$8	$10	$14	Michael Garland		Dutton
2004	Santa Kid		$6	$10	$12	James Patterson		LBrown

Gay   Romney

Year	Title	VG-	VG	VG+	Fine	Author	Award	Pub
1932	The Tale Of Corally Crothers	$50	$70	$90		Romney Gay		G&D
1934	Cinder	$40	$50	$70		Romney Gay		G&D
1935	The Funny Noise	$35	$50	$60		Romney Gay		G&D
1936	Mother Goose	$35	$50	$60		Romney Gay		G&D
1937	Toby And Sue	$35	$50	$60		Romney Gay		G&D
1938	Bonny's Wish	$35	$50	$60		Romney Gay		G&D
1939	Tommy Grows Wise	$35	$50	$60		Romney Gay		G&D
1940	Picture Book Of Poems	$35	$50	$60		Romney Gay		G&D
1941	Conny And Uncle Dick	$35	$40	$60		Romney Gay		G&D
1941	Five Little Playmates: A Book Of Finger-Play	$35	$40	$60		Romney Gay		G&D
1941	Let's Go Outdoors	$35	$40	$60		Romney Gay		G&D
1942	A Home For Sandy	$35	$40	$60		Romney Gay		Heath
1942	Book Of Nursery Tales	$35	$40	$60		Romney Gay		G&D
1943	Cinder's Secret	$35	$40	$60		Romney Gay		G&D
1943	Come Play With Corally Crothers	$35	$40	$60		Romney Gay		G&D
1944	A Joke On Cinder	$35	$40	$60		Romney Gay		G&D
1944	Corally Crothers' Birthday	$35	$40	$60		Romney Gay		G&D
1944	Hi-Ho For The Country	$35	$40	$60		Romney Gay		G&D
1946	The Romney Gay ABC	$35	$40	$60		Romney Gay		G&D
1948	The Tale Of Jeremy Gay	$35	$40	$60		Romney Gay		G&D

Gazsi   Edward S.

Year	Title	VG-	VG	VG+	Fine	Author	Award	Pub
1993	Kimbo's Marble		$10	$16	$20	Amy Herrick		HCollins
1994	The Seven Ravens		$10	$14	$18	Jacob & Wilhelm Grimm		HCollins
1996	Hans Christian Andersen's The Snow Queen		$8	$12	$16	Richard Kennedy (adapted)		LauraG
2000	Once Upon An Easter		$8	$10	$14	William Goetz		Horizon

Geisert   Arthur

Year	Title	VG-	VG	VG+	Fine	Author	Award	Pub
1980	Prisoners Of The Scrambling Dragon		$25	$35	$50	F. N. Monjo		HR&W
1984	Pa's Balloon & Other Pig Tales		$16	$25	$30	Arthur Geisert		HM
1986	Pigs From A To Z		$30	$40	$60	Arthur Geisert	NYT	HM
1988	The Ark		$14	$20	$30	Arthur Geisert		HM
1991	Aesop & Company		$12	$18	$25	Barbara Bader (prepared)		HM
1991	Oink		$12	$18	$25	Arthur Geisert		HM
1992	Pigs From 1 To 10		$12	$18	$25	Arthur Geisert		HM
1993	Oink Oink		$12	$16	$20	Arthur Geisert		HM
1994	After The Flood		$12	$16	$20	Arthur Geisert		HM
1995	Haystack		$10	$16	$20	Bonnie Geisert		HM
1996	Roman Numerals I To Mm		$10	$16	$20	Arthur Geisert		HM
1997	The Etcher's Studio		$10	$16	$20	Arthur Geisert		HM
1998	Prairie Town		$10	$14	$18	Bonnie Geisert		HM
1999	River Town		$10	$14	$18	Bonnie Geisert		HM
2000	Mountain Town		$8	$12	$16	Bonnie Geisert		HM
2001	Desert Town		$8	$12	$16	Bonnie Geisert		HM
2001	Nursery Crimes		$8	$12	$16	Arthur Geisert		HM
2002	Prairie Summer		$8	$10	$14	Bonnie Geisert		HM
2002	The Giant Ball Of String		$8	$10	$14	Arthur Geisert		HM
2003	Mystery		$8	$10	$14	Arthur Geisert		HM
2004	Pigaroons		$8	$10	$14	Arthur Geisert		HM

George   Lindsay Barrett

Year	Title	VG-	VG	VG+	Fine	Author	Award	Pub
1987	William And Boomer		$14	$20	$30	Lindsay Barrett George		Green
1988	Beaver At Long Pond		$12	$16	$20	William T. George		Green
1989	Box Turtle At Long Pond		$12	$16	$20	William T. George		Green
1991	Fishing At Long Pond		$10	$16	$20	William T. George		Green
1992	Christmas At Long Pond		$10	$16	$20	William T. George		Green
1995	In The Snow: Who's Been Here?		$10	$14	$18	Lindsay Barrett George		Green

Gergely   Tibor

Year	Title	VG-	VG	VG+	Fine	Author	Award	Pub
1938	The Very Stupid Folk	$70	$90	$120		Toivo David Rosvall		Dutton
1940	Tell Me A Story	$50	$60	$80		Dorothy Canfield Fisher		UnivPub
1940	The Talking Typewriter	$50	$60	$80		Margaret Pratt		LL&S
1940	Topsy Turvy Circus	$50	$60	$80		Georges Duplaix		H&B
1941	True Monkey Stories	$50	$60	$80		Frances Margaret Fox		LL&S
1942	Sweeny's Adventure	$50	$60	$80		Joseph Krumgold		Random
1942	The Merry Shipwreck	$50	$60	$80		Georges Duplaix		H&B
1943	A Day In The Jungle	$140	$180	$240		Janette Lowrey		Golden
1943	Bobo	$50	$60	$80		Margaret McConnell		LL&S
1943	Peewee The Mousedeer	$50	$60	$80		Hendrik De Leeuw		DMcKay
1943	The Red, White And Blue Auto	$50	$60	$80		Lucy Sprague Mitchell		WRScott
1943	Two Logs Crossing	$50	$60	$80		Walter Edmonds		DoddM
1944	Jenny	$50	$60	$80		Maurice Dolbier		Random
1944	Watch Me Said The Jeep	$50	$60	$80		Helen Josephine Ferris		GardenC
1946	Scuffy The Tugboat	$140	$180	$220		Gertrude Crampton		Golden
1946	The Taxi That Hurried	$140	$180	$220		Lucy Sprague Mitchell		Golden
1946	Tootle	$140	$180	$220		Gertrude Crampton		Golden
1946	When It Rained Cats And Dogs	$40	$60	$70		Nancy Byrd Turner		Lippin
1948	A Year In The City	$40	$60	$70		Lucy Sprague Mitchell		S&S
1948	Circus Time	$120	$160	$220		Marion Conger		Golden
1948	Five Little Firemen	$40	$60	$70		Margaret Wise Brown		S&S
1948	Little Pond In The Woods	$40	$60	$70		Muriel Ward		Golden
1948	The Golden Book Of Nursery Tales	$40	$60	$70		Jane Werner Watson		S&S
1949	Train Stories	$40	$60	$70		Robert Garfield		S&S
1950	A Day At The Zoo	$40	$50	$70		Marion Conger		S&S
1950	The Great Big Fire Engine Book	$40	$50	$70		Tibor Gergely		S&S
1950	The Happy Man And His Dump Truck	$40	$50	$70		Miryam Yardumian		S&S
1950	The Jolly Barnyard	$40	$50	$70		Annie North Bedford		S&S
1951	Christopher And The Columbus	$40	$50	$70		Kathryn Jackson		S&S
1952	Dog In The Sky	$40	$50	$70		Norman Lewis Corwin		S&S
1952	Seven Little Postmen	$40	$50	$70		Margaret Wise Brown		S&S
1953	The Little Red Caboose	$40	$50	$70		Marian Potter		S&S
1954	Daddies	$40	$50	$70		Janet Frank		S&S

Gergely   Tibor

Year	Title	VG-	VG	VG+	Fine	Author	Award	Pub
1954	Gergely's Golden Circus	$40	$50	$70		Peter Archer		S&S
1954	Wheel On The Chimney	$160	$220	$280		Margaret Wise Brown	CH	Lippin
1956	Animal Gym	$35	$50	$60		Beth Greiner Hoffman		S&S
1956	My Little Golden Book About The Sky	$35	$50	$60		Rose Wyler		S&S
1957	A Little Golden Book About The Seashore	$35	$50	$60		Kathleen N. Daly		S&S
1957	Golden Picture Book Of Questions And Answers	$35	$50	$60		Horace Elmo		S&S
1963	Nursery Tales	$35	$40	$60		Jane Werner Watson		Golden
1963	The Jungle Books	$35	$40	$60		Rudyard Kipling		Golden
1966	The Noah's Ark Book	$30	$40	$50		Tibor Gergely		Western
1968	The Happy Little Whale	$30	$40	$50		Kathleen Norris		Golden
1969	Golden Favorites	$25	$35	$50		Various Authors		Golden
1969	No Room For The Baker	$25	$35	$50		Käthe Recheis		4Winds
1969	The Golden Story Book Of River Bend	$25	$35	$50		Patricia M. Scarry		Golden
1972	Bedtime Stories		$25	$35	$50	Tibor Gergely		Golden
1973	Baby Wild Animals From A To Z		$25	$35	$50	Tibor Gergely		Golden
1974	The Me Book		$20	$30	$40	Jean Tymms		Golden
1987	Trains, Boats, And Trucks		$10	$14	$18	Tibor Gergely		Western
2001	Animal Orchestra		$6	$10	$12	Ilo Orleans		Golden
2001	The Fire Engine Book		$6	$10	$12	Tibor Gergely		Golden
2001	The Good Humor Man		$6	$10	$12	Kathleen N. Daly		Golden

Gerrard   Roy

Year	Title	VG-	VG	VG+	Fine	Author	Award	Pub
1983	Matilda Jane		$25	$35	$50	Jean Gerrard		FSG
1983	The Favershams		$30	$50	$60	Roy Gerrard	NYT	FSG
1984	Sir Cedric		$20	$30	$40	Roy Gerrard	NYT	FSG
1986	Sir Cedric Rides Again		$20	$30	$40	Roy Gerrard		FSG
1988	Sir Francis Drake		$18	$25	$35	Roy Gerrard	NYT	FSG
1989	Rosie And The Rustlers		$18	$25	$35	Roy Gerrard		FSG
1990	Mik's Mammoth		$16	$25	$30	Roy Gerrard		FSG
1991	A Pocket Full Of Posies		$16	$25	$30	Roy Gerrard		FSG
1992	Jocasta Carr, Movie Star		$16	$25	$30	Roy Gerrard		FSG
1994	Croco'nile		$14	$20	$30	Roy Gerrard		FSG
1996	Wagons West		$12	$18	$25	Roy Gerrard		FSG
1998	The Roman Twins		$12	$16	$20	Roy Gerrard		FSG

Gerstein   Mordicai

Year	Title	VG-	VG	VG+	Fine	Author	Award	Pub
1973	Something Queer Is Going On (A Mystery)		$30	$50	$60	Mordicai Gerstein		DelaP
1974	Nice Little Girls		$40	$60	$80	Mordicai Gerstein		DelaP
1975	Something Queer At The Ballpark, A Mystery		$30	$40	$60	Mordicai Gerstein		DelaP
1977	Something Queer At The Library: A Mystery		$25	$40	$50	Elizabeth Levy		DelaP
1979	Frankenstein Moved In On The Fourth Floor		$25	$40	$50	Elizabeth Levy		H&Row
1979	There Are Rocks In My Socks		$25	$40	$50	Patricia Thomas		LL&S
1980	Something Queer On Vacation: A Mystery		$25	$35	$50	Elizabeth Levy		DelaP
1982	Something Queer At The Haunted School		$25	$35	$50	Elizabeth Levy		DelaP
1982	Something Queer At The Lemonade Stand		$25	$35	$50	Elizabeth Levy		DelaP
1983	Arnold Of The Ducks		$30	$50	$60	Mordicai Gerstein		H&Row
1983	David's First Bicycle		$25	$35	$50	Rosalie Silver		Golden
1983	Dracula Is A Pain In The Neck		$25	$35	$50	Elizabeth Levy		H&Row
1983	Follow Me!		$25	$35	$50	Mordicai Gerstein		Morrow
1983	The Shadow Nose		$25	$35	$50	Elizabeth Levy		Morrow
1984	Prince Sparrow		$20	$30	$40	Mordicai Gerstein		4Winds
1984	Roll Over!		$20	$30	$40	Mordicai Gerstein		Crown
1984	The Room		$20	$30	$40	Mordicai Gerstein		H&Row
1985	William, Where Are You?		$20	$30	$40	Mordicai Gerstein		Crown
1986	Tales Of Pan		$20	$30	$40	Mordicai Gerstein		H&Row
1986	The Seal Mother		$20	$30	$40	Mordicai Gerstein		Dial
1987	Something Queer In Rock 'N' Roll		$20	$30	$40	Elizabeth Levy		DelaP
1987	The Mountains Of Tibet		$25	$40	$50	Mordicai Gerstein	NYT	H&Row
1989	Beauty And The Beast		$18	$25	$35	Mordicai Gerstein		Dutton
1989	The Sun's Day		$18	$25	$35	Mordicai Gerstein		H&Row
1990	Something Queer At The Birthday Party		$16	$25	$30	Elizabeth Levy		DelaP
1991	The Cataract Of Lodore		$16	$25	$30	Robert Southey		Dial
1991	The New Creatures		$16	$25	$30	Mordicai Gerstein		HCollins
1993	Something Queer In Outer Space		$16	$25	$30	Elizabeth Levy		Hyper

Gerstein   Mordicai

Year	Title	VG-	VG	VG+	Fine	Author	Award	Pub
1993	The Story Of May		$16	$25	$30	Mordicai Gerstein		HCollins
1994	Something Queer In The Cafeteria		$14	$20	$30	Elizabeth Levy		Hyper
1994	The Shadow Of A Flying Bird		$14	$20	$30	Mordicai Gerstein		Hyper
1995	Something Queer At The Scary Movie		$14	$20	$25	Elizabeth Levy		Hyper
1995	The Giant		$14	$20	$25	Mordicai Gerstein		Hyper
1996	Bedtime, Everybody!		$12	$18	$25	Mordicai Gerstein		Hyper
1996	Behind The Couch		$12	$18	$25	Mordicai Gerstein		Hyper
1997	Jonah And The Two Great Fish		$12	$18	$25	Mordicai Gerstein		S&S
1997	Something Queer In The Wild West		$12	$18	$25	Elizabeth Levy		Hyper
1998	Noah And The Great Flood		$12	$16	$20	Mordicai Gerstein		S&S
1998	Stop Those Pants!		$12	$16	$20	Mordicai Gerstein		HBrace
1998	The Wild Boy		$12	$16	$20	Mordicai Gerstein		FSG
1998	Victor		$12	$16	$20	Mordicai Gerstein		FSG
1999	The Absolutely Awful Alphabet		$12	$16	$20	Mordicai Gerstein		HBrace
2000	Albert And The Angels		$10	$14	$18	Leslie Norris		FSG
2000	Queen Esther The Morning Star		$10	$14	$18	Mordicai Gerstein		S&S
2000	The Jar Of Fools		$10	$14	$18	Eric Kimmel		Holiday
2001	Fox Eyes		$10	$14	$18	Mordicai Gerstein		Golden
2001	I Am Arachne		$10	$14	$18	Elizabeth Spires		FFoster
2002	What Charlie Heard		$8	$12	$16	Mordicai Gerstein		FSG
2003	Sparrow Jack		$8	$12	$16	Mordicai Gerstein		FFoster
2003	The Man Who Walked Between The Towers		$35	$50	$70	Mordicai Gerstein	CM	RoarB
2003	Three Samurai Cats		$8	$12	$16	Eric Kimmel		Holiday
2004	Sholom's Treasure		$8	$10	$14	Erica Silverman		FSG

Getz   Arthur

Year	Title	VG-	VG	VG+	Fine	Author	Award	Pub
1972	Hamilton Duck		$25	$35	$50	Arthur Getz		Golden
1973	Jennifer's Walk		$16	$25	$30	Anne Carriere		Golden
1974	Hamilton Duck's Springtime Story		$16	$25	$30	Arthur Getz		Golden
1979	Mr. Goat's Bad Good Idea		$14	$20	$30	Marileta Robinson		Crowell
1979	Tar Beach		$14	$20	$30	Arthur Getz		Dial
1980	Humphrey, The Dancing Pig		$14	$20	$25	Arthur Getz		Dial
1981	Gator And Mary's Traveling Band		$14	$20	$25	David Martin		Dial

Gibbons   Gail

Year	Title	VG-	VG	VG+	Fine	Author	Award	Pub
1979	The Missing Maple Syrup Sap Mystery		$18	$25	$35	Gail Gibbons		FWarne
1985	The Milk Makers		$16	$25	$30	Gail Gibbons		Macmil
1986	Up Goes The Skyscraper		$14	$20	$30	Gail Gibbons		4Winds

Gilchrist   Guy

Year	Title	VG-	VG	VG+	Fine	Author	Award	Pub
1984	Jim Henson's Muppet's Moving Right Along!		$16	$25	$30	Guy Gilchrist		S&S
1987	Little Wrinkle's Surprise		$12	$16	$20	Bobbi Katz		HHouse
1988	Bronty And The Birdosaur		$12	$16	$20	Guy Gilchrist		Warner
1988	Counting Tiny Dinos		$12	$16	$20	Guy Gilchrist		Warner
1988	Goodnight, Tiny Dinos		$12	$16	$20	Guy Gilchrist		Warner
1988	Steggie Makes A Friend		$12	$16	$20	Guy Gilchrist		Warner
1988	Thanks A Lot, Tricerator		$12	$16	$20	Guy Gilchrist		Warner
1988	Tiny Dinos ABC		$12	$16	$20	Guy Gilchrist		Warner
1988	Tiny Dinos Fun At The Beach		$12	$16	$20	Guy Gilchrist		Warner
1988	Tiny Dinos Playing Together		$12	$16	$20	Guy Gilchrist		Warner
1988	Tiny Dinos Silly Safari!		$12	$16	$20	Guy Gilchrist		Warner
1988	Tiny Dinos Sir Waldo's Island Adventure		$12	$16	$20	Corey Nash		Warner
1989	Night Lights & Pillow Fights		$12	$16	$20	Guy Gilchrist		Warner
1989	Strummer, The One-Of-A-Kind Duck		$12	$16	$20	Guy Gilchrist		Warner
1989	Too Many Bunnies!		$12	$16	$20	Guy Gilchrist		Warner
1990	Just Imagine		$10	$16	$20	Guy Gilchrist		Western
1995	Genetic Meltdown		$10	$14	$18	Cynthia Alvarez (adapted)		Random
1997	Night Lights & Pillow Fights Two		$8	$12	$16	Guy Gilchrist		Gil

Gillen   Denver

Year	Title	VG-	VG	VG+	Fine	Author	Award	Pub
1939	Rudolph The Red-Nosed Reindeer	$140	$200	$240		Robert May		MWard
1946	Rudolph The Red-Nosed Reindeer	$90	$120	$160		Robert May		MWard
1959	The First Transatlantic Cable	$25	$35	$50		Adele Gutman Nathan		Random
1970	Up From Slavery		$30	$50	$60	Booker T. Washington		LEC
1980	Rudolph The Red-Nosed Reindeer		$14	$20	$25	Robert May		Apple

Glanzman   Louis S.

Year	Title	VG-	VG	VG+	Fine	Author	Award	Pub
1950	Pippi Longstocking	$280	$360	$460		Astrid Lindgren		Viking
1957	Pippi Goes On Board	$200	$280	$340		Astrid Lindgren		Viking
1959	Ben Hur	$25	$35	$50		Felix Sutton (adapted)		G&D
1959	Pippi In The South Seas	$160	$220	$280		Astrid Lindgren		Viking
1964	The Chagres, Power Of The Panama Canal	$25	$30	$40		Jean Lee Latham		Garrard
1968	The Sword Of King Arthur	$20	$30	$35		Jay Williams (adapted)		Crowell
1968	Veronica Ganz	$20	$30	$35		Marilyn Sachs		DoubleD
1969	Peter And Veronica	$20	$30	$35		Marilyn Sachs		DoubleD
1970	It's America For Me		$18	$25	$35	Bill Martin		Bowmar
1970	Juan		$18	$25	$35	Mary Stolz		H&Row
1970	Man In Space To The Moon		$18	$25	$35	Franklyn M. Branley		Crowell
1970	Marv		$18	$25	$35	Marilyn Sachs		DoubleD
1970	Papeek		$18	$25	$35	Dirk Van Loon		Lippin
1971	My Brother, Angel		$18	$25	$35	Hilary Beckett		DoddM
1971	The Bears' House		$18	$25	$35	Marilyn Sachs		DoubleD
1972	The Mayo Brothers		$18	$25	$35	Jane Goodsell		Crowell
1973	The Truth About Mary Rose		$16	$25	$30	Marilyn Sachs		DoubleD
1974	Three Little Indians		$16	$25	$30	Gene S. Stuart		NGS
1994	Colonial Williamsburg ABC		$10	$14	$18	Amy Watson		Cwill
2001	The Dream Catchers		$8	$10	$14	Lisa Suhay		MarshM

Glass   Andrew

Year	Title	VG-	VG	VG+	Fine	Author	Award	Pub
1994	Soap! Soap! Don't Forget The Soap!		$12	$16	$20	Tom Birdseye		Holiday
1995	The Sweetwater Run		$10	$14	$18	Andrew Glass		Holiday
1996	Folks Call Me Appleseed John		$8	$12	$16	Andrew Glass		Holiday
1997	A Key To The Cupboard		$8	$12	$16	Susan Whitcher		FSG
1997	A Right Fine Life		$8	$12	$16	Andrew Glass		Holiday
1998	Easy Work!		$8	$12	$16	Eric Kimmel		Holiday

Glasser   Robin Preiss

Year	Title	VG-	VG	VG+	Fine	Author	Award	Pub
1995	Alexander, Who's Not Going To Move		$10	$16	$20	Judith Viorst		Athenm
1997	Absolutely Positively Alexander		$8	$12	$16	Judith Viorst		Athenm
1998	You Can't Take A Balloon Into The Met. Museum		$10	$14	$18	Jacqueline Preiss Weitzman		Dial
1999	Doctor Dolittle And His Animal Family		$8	$12	$16	N. H. Kleinbaum (adapted)		Bantam
1999	Doctor Dolittle And Tommy Stubbins		$8	$12	$16	N. H. Kleinbaum (adapted)		Bantam
1999	Doctor Dolittle Meets The Pushmi-Pullyu		$8	$12	$16	N. H. Kleinbaum (adapted)		Bantam
1999	Doctor Dolittle's Journey		$8	$12	$16	N. H. Kleinbaum (adapted)		Bantam
1999	You're Officially A Grown-Up		$8	$12	$16	Judith Viorst		S&S
2000	You Can't Take A Ballon Into The Nat'l Gallery		$8	$12	$16	Jacqueline Preiss Weitzman		Dial
2001	Super-Completely And Totally The Messiest		$8	$10	$14	Judith Viorst		Athenm
2002	America		$8	$10	$14	Lynne V. Cheney		S&S
2002	Taking Care Of Trouble		$8	$10	$14	Bonnie B. Graves		Dutton
2002	You Can't Take A Balloon Into The Museum Of Fine Arts		$8	$10	$14	Jacqueline Preiss Weitzman		Dial
2003	A Is For Abigail		$8	$10	$14	Lynne V. Cheney		S&S
2003	A Sock Is A Pocket For Your Toes		$8	$10	$14	Elizabeth Garton Scanlon		HCollins

Gliori   Debi

Year	Title	VG-	VG	VG+	Fine	Author	Award	Pub
1990	Dulcie Dando		$16	$25	$30	Sue Stops		Deutsch
1991	New Big Sister		$12	$18	$25	Debi Gliori		BradP
1992	My Little Brother		$12	$18	$25	Debi Gliori		Candle
1992	New Big House		$12	$18	$25	Debi Gliori		Candle
1993	Lizzie And Her Dolly		$12	$16	$20	David Martin		Candle
1993	Lizzie And Her Friend		$12	$16	$20	David Martin		Candle
1993	Lizzie And Her Kitty		$12	$16	$20	David Martin		Candle

Gliori   Debi

Year	Title	VG-	VG	VG+	Fine	Author	Award	Pub
1993	Lizzie And Her Puppy		$12	$16	$20	David Martin		Candle
1993	Oliver's Alphabets		$12	$16	$20	Lisa Bruce		BradP
1994	A Lion At Bedtime		$12	$16	$20	Debi Gliori		Barrn
1994	Mr. Bear Babysits		$12	$16	$20	Debi Gliori		Golden
1994	The Snowchild		$12	$16	$20	Debi Gliori		BradP
1994	When I'm Big		$12	$16	$20	Debi Gliori		Candle
1995	Little Bear And The Wish Fish		$10	$16	$20	Debi Gliori		Lincoln
1995	Mr. Bear's Picnic		$10	$16	$20	Debi Gliori		Golden
1995	Willie Bear And The Wish Fish		$10	$16	$20	Debi Gliori		Macmil
1996	Mr. Bear To The Rescue		$10	$16	$20	Debi Gliori		Orchard
1996	The Princess And The Pirate King		$10	$16	$20	Debi Gliori		Kfisher
1996	The Snow Lambs		$10	$16	$20	Debi Gliori		Scholas
1997	Poems Go Clang!: A Collection Of Noisy Verse		$10	$16	$20	Debi Gliori		Candle
1998	Tell Me Something Happy Before I Go To Sleep		$10	$14	$18	Joyce Dunbar		HBrace
1999	Mr. Bear's New Baby		$10	$14	$18	Debi Gliori		Orchard
1999	No Matter What		$10	$14	$18	Debi Gliori		HBrace
2000	Mr. Bear's Vacation		$8	$12	$16	Debi Gliori		Orchard
2000	Polar Bolero		$8	$12	$16	Debi Gliori		Harcort
2001	Flora's Blanket		$8	$12	$16	Debi Gliori		Orchard
2001	Pure Dead Magic		$40	$60	$80	Debi Gliori		Knopf
2001	Storm Maker's Tipi		$8	$12	$16	Paul Goble		Athenm
2001	Tell Me What It's Like To Be Big		$8	$12	$16	Joyce Dunbar		Harcort
2002	Bedtime Stories		$8	$10	$14	Debi Gliori		DK
2002	Penguin Post		$8	$10	$14	Debi Gliori		Harcort
2002	Pure Dead Wicked		$30	$40	$60	Debi Gliori		DoubleD
2003	Flora's Surprise		$8	$10	$14	Debi Gliori		Orchard
2003	Pure Dead Brilliant		$20	$30	$40	Debi Gliori		Knopf
2004	Always And Forever		$8	$10	$14	Alan Durant		Harcort
2005	Pure Deep Trouble		$10	$14	$18	Debi Gliori		Knopf

Goble   Paul

Year	Title	VG-	VG	VG+	Fine	Author	Award	Pub
1969	Red Hawk's Account Of Custer's Last Battle	$80	$120	$140		Paul And Dorothy Goble		Pan
1972	Brave Eagle's Account Of The Fetterman Fight		$30	$50	$60	Paul And Dorothy Goble		Pan
1973	Lone Bull's Horse Raid		$30	$50	$60	Paul And Dorothy Goble		BradP
1974	The Friendly Wolf		$30	$40	$60	Paul And Dorothy Goble		BradP
1976	The Sound Of Flutes & Other Indian Legends		$30	$40	$60	Richard Erdoes (adapted)		Pan
1978	The Gift Of The Sacred Dog		$25	$40	$50	Paul Goble		BradP
1978	The Girl Who Loved Wild Horses		$180	$260	$340	Paul Goble	CM	BradP
1983	Star Boy		$25	$35	$50	Paul Goble (retold)		BradP
1984	Buffalo Woman		$20	$30	$40	Paul Goble		BradP
1985	The Great Race Of The Birds And Animals		$20	$30	$40	Paul Goble		BradP
1987	Death Of The Iron Horse		$20	$30	$40	Paul Goble		BradP
1988	Her Seven Brothers		$18	$25	$35	Paul Goble		BradP
1988	Iktomi And The Boulder		$18	$25	$35	Paul Goble		Orchard
1989	Beyond The Ridge		$18	$25	$35	Paul Goble		BradP
1989	Iktomi And The Berries		$18	$25	$35	Paul Goble (retold)		Orchard
1990	Dream Wolf		$16	$25	$30	Paul Goble		BradP
1991	I Sing For The Animals		$16	$25	$30	Paul Goble		BradP
1991	Iktomi And The Buffalo Skull		$16	$25	$30	Paul Goble		Orchard
1992	Crow Chief: A Plains Indian Story		$16	$25	$30	Paul Goble		Orchard
1992	Love Flute: Story And Illustrations		$16	$25	$30	Paul Goble		BradP
1993	The Lost Children		$16	$25	$30	Paul Goble		BradP
1994	Adopted By The Eagles		$14	$20	$30	Paul Goble		BradP
1994	Hau Kola = Hello Friend		$14	$20	$30	Paul Goble		RCOwen
1994	Iktomi And The Buzzard		$14	$20	$30	Paul Goble		Orchard
1994	Iktomi And The Ducks		$14	$20	$30	Paul Goble (retold)		Orchard
1996	Remaking The Earth		$12	$18	$25	Paul Goble		Orchard
1998	Iktomi and the Coyote		$12	$16	$20	Paul Goble		Orchard
1998	The Legend Of The White Buffalo Woman		$12	$16	$20	Paul Goble		NGS
1999	Iktomi Loses His Eyes		$12	$16	$20	Paul Goble		Orchard
2001	Storm Maker's Tipi		$10	$14	$18	Paul Goble		Athenm
2003	Mystic Horse		$8	$12	$16	Paul Goble		HCollins
2004	Song of Creation		$8	$10	$14	Paul Goble		EerdB

Goffe   Toni

Year	Title	VG-	VG	VG+	Fine	Author	Award	Pub
1974	Ohia And The Animals		$30	$40	$60	Jennifer Vaughan		MacD
1979	A Book Of Sounds, A, B, C		$18	$25	$35	Anne Hughes		Rain
1979	A Book Of Sounds, Blends And Ends		$18	$25	$35	Anne Hughes		Rain
1979	A Book Of Sounds, Ee, Oo, Ai		$18	$25	$35	Anne Hughes		Rain
1979	A Book Of Sounds, Sl, Ch, Pr		$18	$25	$35	Anne Hughes		Rain
1987	A Fast Move		$14	$20	$30	Catherine Storr		SBurdet
1987	Building A House		$14	$20	$30	Catherine Storr		SBurdet
1987	Find The Specs		$14	$20	$30	Catherine Storr		SBurdet
1987	Grandpa's Birthday		$14	$20	$30	Catherine Storr		SBurdet
1988	Clap Your Hands: Finger Rhymes		$14	$20	$30	Sarah Hayes (selected)		LL&S
1988	My Little Box Of Prayers		$14	$20	$30	Felicity Henderson		LL&S
1988	Stamp Your Feet: Action Rhymes		$14	$20	$30	Sarah Hayes (selected)		LL&S
1989	I Wanted To Go To The Circus		$14	$20	$25	Constance Andrea Keremes		Herb
1989	In The Kingdom Of The Carpet Dragon		$14	$20	$25	Ralph Batten		Lion
1989	Mother Halverson's New Cat		$14	$20	$25	Jim Aylesworth		Athenm
1989	Sid Seal, Houseman		$14	$20	$25	Will Watkins		Orchard
1989	Stories For The Very Young		$14	$20	$25	Sally Grindley (selected)		Kfisher
1989	The Day Teddy Didn't Clean Up		$14	$20	$25	Ann Jungman		Barrn
1989	The Day Teddy Got Very Worried		$14	$20	$25	Ann Jungman		Barrn
1989	The Day Teddy Made New Friends		$14	$20	$25	Ann Jungman		Barrn
1989	The Day Teddy Wanted Grandpa To Notice Him		$14	$20	$25	Ann Jungman		Barrn
1989	The Little Red House		$14	$20	$25	Norma Jean Sawicki		LLee
1990	Joe Giant's Missing Boot		$12	$18	$25	Toni Goffe		LL&S
1990	Magnificent Max		$12	$18	$25	Terrance Dicks		Barrn
1990	Max And The Quiz Kids		$12	$18	$25	Terrance Dicks		Barrn
1990	Ms. Wiz Spells Trouble		$12	$18	$25	Terence Blacker		Barrn
1990	The Read-To-Me Treasury		$12	$18	$25	Sally Grindley (selected)		DoubleD
1990	You're Under Arrest, Ms. Wiz		$12	$18	$25	Terence Blacker		Barrn
1991	Bully For You		$12	$18	$25	Toni Goffe		ChildP
1991	Charm School		$12	$18	$25	Toni Goffe		ChildP
1991	My Little Box Of Bible Friends		$12	$18	$25	Felicity Henderson (retold)		Lion
1991	Rocks In My Pockets		$12	$18	$25	M. Harshman & B. Collins		Cobble
1991	War And Peace		$12	$18	$25	Toni Goffe		ChildP
1992	Just In Case You Ever Wonder		$12	$18	$25	Max Lucado		Word
1992	Max's Amazing Summer		$12	$18	$25	Terrance Dicks		Barrn
1992	No Smoking		$12	$18	$25	Toni Goffe		ChildP
1992	President Citizen		$12	$18	$25	Toni Goffe		ChildP
1992	The President		$12	$18	$25	Toni Goffe		ChildP
1992	The Prince Who Wrote A Letter		$12	$18	$25	Ann Love		ChildP
1992	Zoom On A Broom!: Six Fun-Filled Stories		$12	$18	$25	Judy Hindley		Kfisher
1993	Chief: Who Is In Charge?		$12	$16	$20	Toni Goffe		ChildP
1993	Jesus Is Risen!		$12	$16	$20	Lavonne Neff (retold)		Tynd
1993	Ma, You're Driving Me Crazy!		$12	$16	$20	Toni Goffe		ChildP
1993	Relax		$12	$16	$20	Catherine O'Neill		ChildP
1993	Stories Jesus Told		$12	$16	$20	Lavonne Neff (retold)		Tynd
1993	The Giant That Sneezed		$12	$16	$20	Norman Leach		ChildP
1993	The Legend Of Lightning Larry		$12	$16	$20	Aaron Shepard		Scribnr
1993	The Legend Of Slappy Hooper		$12	$16	$20	Aaron Shepard		Scribnr
1993	The Monster		$12	$16	$20	Toni Goffe		ChildP
1994	Fisherman Fred		$12	$16	$20	T.D. Triggs & M. Twinn		ChildP
1994	The Children Of The King		$12	$16	$20	Max Lucado		Crossw
1994	The Knight Who Was Afraid To Fight		$12	$16	$20	Barbara Shook Hazen		Dial
1995	Do Animals Take Baths?		$10	$16	$20	Neil Morriss		RDigest
1995	The Song Of The King		$10	$16	$20	Max Lucado		Crossw
1996	Around The World With Phineas Frog		$10	$16	$20	Paul S. Adshead		ChildP
1996	Beginning School		$10	$16	$20	Irene Small		Silver
1996	The Rhyme Bible		$10	$16	$20	L.J. Sattgast		G&H
1997	The Rhyme Bible Activity Book		$10	$16	$20	L.J. Sattgast		G&H
1997	The Rhyme Bible Prayer Book		$10	$16	$20	L.J. Sattgast		G&H
1998	Miss Fannie's Hat		$10	$14	$18	Jan Karon		Augsb
1998	The Rhyme Bible For Toddlers		$10	$14	$18	L.J. Sattgast		G&H
1999	Ice Cream At The Castle		$10	$14	$18	Ann Love		ChildP
1999	The Jesus Book		$10	$14	$18	LaVonne Neff		Loyola
1999	The Rhyme Bible Storybook For Toddlers		$10	$14	$18	L.J. Sattgast		G&H
2002	Rocks In My Pockets		$8	$10	$14	Marc Harshman		Quarr
2003	Bride Away		$8	$10	$14	Heather Gemmen		FKidz
2004	Look For Jesus		$8	$10	$14	Heather Gemmen		FKidz

Goffe   Toni

Year	Title	VG-	VG	VG+	Fine	Author	Award	Pub
2004	Neighbor		$8	$10	$14	Heather Gemmen		FKidz

Goffin   Josse

Year	Title	VG-	VG	VG+	Fine	Author	Award	Pub
1991	Oh!		$10	$16	$20	Josse Goffin		Abrams
1991	Silent Christmas		$12	$18	$25	Josse Goffin		Boyds
1992	Ah!		$10	$16	$20	Josse Goffin		Abrams
1992	Who Is The Boss?		$10	$16	$20	Josse Goffin		Clarion
1993	Yes		$10	$16	$20	Josse Goffin		LL&S
1994	The Christmas Story		$10	$14	$18	Josse Goffin		Ticnor
1997	The Amazing ABC Book		$8	$12	$16	Josse Goffin		Abrams

Goffstein   M. B.

Year	Title	VG-	VG	VG+	Fine	Author	Award	Pub
1966	Sleepy People	$40	$60	$70		M. B. Goffstein		FSG
1966	The Gats!	$30	$40	$50		M. B. Goffstein		Pan
1967	Brookie And Her Lamb	$30	$40	$50		M. B. Goffstein		FSG
1968	Across The Sea	$30	$40	$50		M. B. Goffstein		FSG
1969	Goldie, The Dollmaker	$25	$35	$50		M. B. Goffstein		FSG
1970	Two Piano Tuners		$25	$35	$50	M. B. Goffstein		FSG
1972	The Underside Of The Leaf		$25	$35	$50	M. B. Goffstein		FSG
1974	Me And My Captain		$20	$30	$40	M. B. Goffstein		FSG
1975	Daisy Summerfield's Style		$20	$30	$40	M. B. Goffstein		DelaP
1976	Fish For Supper		$70	$100	$140	M. B. Goffstein	CH	Dial
1976	My Crazy Sister		$20	$30	$40	M. B. Goffstein		Dial
1978	Family Scrapbook		$20	$30	$40	M. B. Goffstein		FSG
1978	My Noah's Ark		$20	$30	$40	M. B. Goffstein		H&Row
1979	Natural History		$18	$25	$35	M. B. Goffstein		FSG
1979	Neighbors		$18	$25	$35	M. B. Goffstein		H&Row
1979	The First Books		$18	$25	$35	M. B. Goffstein		Avon
1980	An Artist		$25	$35	$50	M. B. Goffstein	NYT	H&Row
1980	Laughing Latkes		$18	$25	$35	M. B. Goffstein		FSG
1981	Lives Of The Artists		$18	$25	$35	M. B. Goffstein		FSG
1984	A Writer		$16	$25	$30	M. B. Goffstein		H&Row
1985	An Artists Album		$16	$25	$30	M. B. Goffstein		H&Row
1985	My Editor		$16	$25	$30	M. B. Goffstein		FSG
1986	Our Snowman		$14	$20	$30	M. B. Goffstein		H&Row
1986	School Of Names		$14	$20	$30	M. B. Goffstein		H&Row
1986	Your Lone Journey		$14	$20	$30	Rosa Lee Watson		H&Row
1987	An Actor		$14	$20	$30	M. B. Goffstein		H&Row
1987	Artists' Helpers Enjoy The Evenings		$14	$20	$30	M. B. Goffstein		H&Row
1988	Our Prairie Home		$14	$20	$30	M. B. Goffstein		H&Row
1989	A House, A Home		$14	$20	$25	M. B. Goffstein		H&Row

Goodall   John S.

Year	Title	VG-	VG	VG+	Fine	Author	Award	Pub
1968	The Adventures Of Paddy Pork	$50	$60	$80		John S. Goodall		HBrace
1969	The Ballooning Adventures Of Paddy Pork	$40	$50	$70		John S. Goodall		HBrace
1971	Shrewbettina's Birthday		$25	$35	$50	John S. Goodall		HBJ
1972	Jacko		$25	$35	$50	John S. Goodall		HBJ
1972	Midnight Adventures Of Kelly, Dot, & Esmeralda		$25	$35	$50	John S. Goodall		Athenm
1973	Paddy's Evening Out		$25	$40	$50	John S. Goodall		Athenm
1975	Creepy Castle		$20	$30	$40	John S. Goodall		Athenm
1975	Naughty Nancy		$20	$30	$40	John S. Goodall		Athenm
1976	An Edwardian Summer		$20	$30	$40	John S. Goodall		Athenm
1976	Paddy Pork's Holiday		$20	$30	$40	John S. Goodall		Athenm
1977	The Surprise Picnic		$20	$30	$40	John S. Goodall		Athenm
1978	An Edwardian Christmas		$20	$30	$40	John S. Goodall		Athenm
1979	An Edwardian Holiday		$18	$25	$35	John S. Goodall		Athenm
1979	The Story Of An English Village		$18	$25	$35	John S. Goodall		Athenm
1980	Paddy's New Hat		$18	$25	$35	John S. Goodall		Athenm
1981	Before The War, 1908-1939		$18	$25	$35	John S. Goodall		Athenm
1981	Paddy Finds A Job		$18	$25	$35	John S. Goodall		Athenm
1981	Shrewbettina Goes To Work		$18	$25	$35	John S. Goodall		Athenm
1981	Victorians Abroad		$18	$25	$35	John S. Goodall		Athenm

Goodall   John S.

Year	Title	VG-	VG	VG+	Fine	Author	Award	Pub
1982	Edwardian Entertainments		$16	$25	$30	John S. Goodall		Athenm
1983	Above And Below Stairs		$16	$25	$30	John S. Goodall		McEld
1983	Lavinia's Cottage		$16	$25	$30	John S. Goodall		Athenm
1983	Paddy Pork--Odd Jobs		$16	$25	$30	John S. Goodall		Athenm
1984	Paddy Under Water		$16	$25	$30	John S. Goodall		Athenm
1985	Naughty Nancy Goes To School		$16	$25	$30	John S. Goodall		Athenm
1985	Paddy To The Rescue		$16	$25	$30	John S. Goodall		Athenm
1986	The Story Of A Castle		$14	$20	$30	John S. Goodall		McEld
1988	Little Red Riding Hood		$14	$20	$30	John S. Goodall		McEld
1989	The Story Of A Farm		$14	$20	$25	John S. Goodall		McEld
1990	Puss In Boots		$12	$18	$25	John S. Goodall		McEld
1990	The Story Of The Seashore		$12	$18	$25	John S. Goodall		McEld
1992	Great Days Of A Country House		$12	$18	$25	John S. Goodall		McEld

Goode   Diane

Year	Title	VG-	VG	VG+	Fine	Author	Award	Pub
1975	Little Pieces Of The West Wind		$30	$50	$60	Christian Garrison		BradP
1975	The Selchie's Seed		$30	$50	$60	Shulamith Oppenheim		BradP
1976	Flim And Flam & The Big Cheese		$30	$40	$60	Christian Garrison		BradP
1976	Tattercoats: An Old English Tale		$30	$40	$60	Flora Annie Steel		BradP
1978	Beauty And The Beast		$25	$40	$50	Madame de Beaumont		BradP
1978	The Dream Eater		$25	$40	$50	Christian Garrison		BradP
1981	The Good-Hearted Youngest Brother		$25	$35	$50	Emoke de Papp Severo		BradP
1982	The Unicorn And The Plow		$25	$35	$50	Louise Moeri		Dutton
1982	When I Was Young In The Mountains		$60	$80	$120	Cynthia Rylant	CH	Dutton
1983	Christmas Carols		$25	$35	$50	Diane Goode		Random
1983	Peter Pan		$25	$35	$50	J. M. Barrie		Random
1983	The Adventures Of Pinocchio		$25	$35	$50	Carlo Collodi		Random
1983	The Fir Tree		$25	$35	$50	Hans Christian Andersen		Random
1983	The Night Before Christmas		$25	$35	$50	Clement C. Moore		Random
1983	The Nutcracker: The Story Based On The Ballet		$25	$35	$50	Diane Goode		Random
1985	The Random House Book Of Fairy Tales		$20	$30	$40	Amy Ehrlich		Random
1985	Watch The Stars Come Out		$20	$30	$40	Riki Levinson		Dutton
1986	I Go With My Family To Grandma's		$20	$30	$40	Riki Levinson		Dutton
1986	The Story Of The Nutcracker Ballet		$20	$30	$40	Deborah Hautzig		Random
1987	Rumpty-Dudget's Tower		$20	$30	$40	Julian Hawthorne		Knopf
1988	Cinderella		$18	$25	$35	Charles Perrault		Knopf
1988	I Hear A Noise		$18	$25	$35	Diane Goode		Dutton
1989	Diane Goode Book Of American Folk Tales & Songs		$18	$25	$35	Ann Durell (selected)		Dutton
1990	Diane Goode's American Christmas		$16	$25	$30	Diane Goode		Dutton
1991	Ballet Shoes		$16	$25	$30	Noel Streatfeild		Random
1991	Where's Our Mama?		$16	$25	$30	Diane Goode		Dutton
1992	Diane Goode's Book Of Silly Stories & Songs		$16	$25	$30	Diane Goode		Dutton
1992	Diane Goode's Christmas Magic		$16	$25	$30	Diane Goode		Random
1993	The Little Book Of Cats		$16	$25	$30	Diane Goode		Dutton
1993	The Little Book Of Farm Friends		$16	$25	$30	Diane Goode		Dutton
1993	The Little Book Of Mice		$16	$25	$30	Diane Goode		Dutton
1993	The Little Book Of Pigs		$16	$25	$30	Diane Goode		Dutton
1994	Alice In Wonderland		$14	$20	$30	Lewis Carroll		Random
1994	Diane Goode's Book Of Scary Stories & Songs		$14	$20	$30	Diane Goode		Dutton
1995	The House Gobbaleen		$14	$20	$25	Lloyd Alexander		Dutton
1996	Mama's Perfect Present		$12	$18	$25	Diane Goode		Dutton
1997	Diane Goode's Book Of Giants & Little People		$12	$18	$25	Diane Goode		Dutton
1998	A Child's Garden Of Verses		$12	$16	$20	Robert Louis Stevenson		Morrow
1999	The Dinosaur's New Clothes		$12	$16	$20	Diane Goode		BSP
2000	Cinderella, the Dog and Her Little Glass Slipper		$10	$14	$18	Diane Goode		BSP
2001	Tiger Trouble		$10	$14	$18	Diane Goode		BSP
2002	Christmas in the Country		$8	$12	$16	Cynthia Rylant		BSP
2002	Monkey Mo Goes To Sea		$8	$12	$16	Diane Goode		BSP
2003	Thanksgiving is Here!		$8	$12	$16	Diane Goode		HCollins
2004	Christmas In The Barn		$8	$10	$14	Margaret Wise Brown		HCollins

Gorey   Edward

Year	Title	VG-	VG	VG+	Fine	Author	Award	Pub
1936	The Police Applicant	$220	$300	$380		Edward Gorey		LincP
1951	Case Record From A Sonnetorium	$160	$200	$260		Merrill Moore		Twayne

Gorey　　　　　Edward

Year	Title	VG-	VG	VG+	Fine	Author	Award	Pub
1953	The Unstrung Harp	$220	$280	$360		Edward Gorey		DS&P
1954	Merrill Moore And The American Sonnet	$140	$180	$240		Edward Gorey		Pagasus
1954	The Listing Attic	$140	$180	$240		Edward Gorey		DS&P
1957	The Doubtful Guest	$140	$180	$220		Edward Gorey		DoubleD
1958	In The Cage	$140	$180	$220		Henry James		DoubleD
1958	The Object-Lesson	$140	$180	$220		Edward Gorey		DoubleD
1959	The Haunted Looking Glass	$120	$160	$220		Edward Gorey		LGL
1960	The Bug Book (S/L)	$440	$580	$720		Edward Gorey		E&C
1960	The Fatal Lozenge	$100	$140	$180		Edward Gorey		Obolsky
1961	The Curious Sofa	$100	$120	$160		Edward Gorey		Obolsky
1961	The Hapless Child	$100	$120	$160		Edward Gorey		Obolsky
1961	The Man Who Sang The Sillies	$70	$90	$120		John Ciardi		Lippin
1962	The Beastly Baby	$480	$640	$800		Edward Gorey		Fantod
1962	The Willowdale Handcar	$100	$120	$160		Edward Gorey		Bobbs
1962	You Read To Me, I'll Read To You	$70	$90	$120		John Ciardi		Lippin
1963	Adders On The Heath	$70	$90	$120		Gladys Mitchell		London
1963	The Gashlycrumb Tinies	$100	$120	$160		Edward Gorey		S&S
1963	The Insect God	$100	$120	$160		Edward Gorey		S&S
1963	The West Wing	$100	$120	$160		Edward Gorey		S&S
1963	The Wuggly Ump	$100	$120	$160		Edward Gorey		Lippin
1964	The Nursery Frieze (S/L)	$560	$760	$940		Edward Gorey		Fantod
1965	Alvin Steadfast On Vernacular Island	$60	$80	$100		Frank Jacobs		Dial
1965	Monster Festival	$60	$80	$100		Eric Protter		Vnguard
1965	The Recently Deflowered Girl	$60	$80	$100		Hyacinthe Phypps		Chel
1965	The Remembered Visit	$90	$120	$160		Edward Gorey		S&S
1965	The Sinking Spell	$90	$120	$160		Edward Gorey		Obolsky
1966	Cultural Slag	$60	$80	$100		Felicia Lamport		HM
1966	The Gilded Bat	$90	$120	$160		Edward Gorey		S&S
1966	The Monster Den	$60	$80	$100		John Ciardi		Lippin
1967	Brer Rabbit And His Tricks	$60	$80	$100		Ennis Rees (adapted)		YScott
1967	The Christmas Bower	$60	$80	$100		Polly Redford		Dutton
1967	The Utter Zoo	$80	$120	$140		Edward Gorey		Mered
1968	Cobweb Castle	$80	$120	$140		Jan Wahl		HR&W
1968	More Of Brer Rabbit's Tricks	$60	$80	$100		Ennis Rees (adapted)		YScott
1968	The Jumblies	$80	$120	$140		Edward Lear		YScott
1968	The Other Statue	$80	$120	$140		Edward Gorey		S&S
1968	The Very Fine Clock	$60	$80	$100		Muriel Spark		Knopf
1969	Donald And The ..	$60	$80	$100		Peter F. Neumeyer		AW
1969	He Was There From The Day We Moved In	$60	$80	$100		Rhoda Levine		HQuist
1969	Merry, Rose, And Christmas-Tree June	$60	$80	$100		Doris Orgel		Knopf
1969	The Blue Aspic	$80	$120	$140		Edward Gorey		Mered
1969	The Dong With A Luminous Nose	$80	$120	$140		Edward Lear		YScott
1969	The Epiplectic Bicycle	$80	$120	$140		Edward Gorey		DoddM
1969	The Iron Tonic	$80	$120	$140		Edward Gorey		Harcort
1970	At The Top Of My Voice		$50	$70	$90	Felice Holman		Norton
1970	Penny Candy		$50	$70	$90	Edward Fenton		HR&W
1970	Someone Could Win A Polar Bear		$70	$100	$140	John Ciardi		Lippin
1970	Why We Have Day And Night		$50	$70	$90	Peter F. Neumeyer		YScott
1971	Fletcher And Zenobia Save The Circus		$70	$100	$140	Edward Gorey		DoddM
1971	Lions And Lobsters And Foxes And Frogs		$40	$60	$90	Ennis Rees		YScott
1971	Miss Clafooty And The Demon		$40	$60	$90	J. David Townsend		LL&S
1971	Sam And Emma		$40	$60	$90	Donald Nelsen		PMagP
1971	The Disrespectful Summons		$70	$100	$140	Edward Gorey		Fantod
1971	The Eleventh Episode		$70	$100	$140	Edward Gorey		Fantod
1971	The Shrinking Of Treehorn		$40	$60	$90	Florence Parry Heide	NYT	Holiday
1971	The Sopping Thursday		$70	$100	$140	Edward Gorey		Capra
1972	Amphigorey		$70	$100	$140	Edward Gorey		Putnam
1972	Freaky Friday		$80	$120	$160	Mary Rodgers		H&Row
1972	Leaves From A Mislaid Album		$70	$100	$140	Edward Gorey		Gotham
1972	Red Riding Hood		$40	$60	$90	Beatrice S. De Regniers		Athenm
1972	The Abandoned Sock		$70	$100	$140	Edward Gorey		Fantod
1972	The Awdrey-Gore Legacy		$70	$100	$140	Edward Gorey		DoddM
1973	Category		$60	$90	$120	Edward Gorey		Gotham
1973	The Black Doll		$60	$90	$120	Edward Gorey		Gotham
1973	The House With A Clock In Its Walls		$50	$80	$100	John Bellairs		Dial
1973	The Lost Lions		$60	$90	$120	Edward Gorey		Fantod
1974	Rumpelstiltskin		$40	$60	$80	Edith Tarcov		4Winds

Gorey   Edward

Year	Title	VG-	VG	VG+	Fine	Author	Award	Pub
1975	Amphigorey Too		$60	$80	$120	Edward Gorey		Putnam
1975	The Glorious Nosebleed		$60	$80	$120	Edward Gorey		DoddM
1976	The Broken Spoke		$60	$80	$120	Edward Gorey		DoddM
1977	The Loathsome Couple		$60	$80	$120	Edward Gorey		DoddM
1978	The Green Beads		$50	$80	$100	Edward Gorey		AP
1979	Dracula		$50	$80	$100	Edward Gorey		Scribnr
1979	Gorey Games		$50	$80	$100	Edward Gorey		Trouba
1979	Gorey Posters		$50	$80	$100	Edward Gorey		Abrams
1980	Dancing Cats & Neglected Murderesses (S/L)		$260	$380	$500	Edward Gorey		Workman
1981	Treehorn's Treasure		$35	$50	$70	Florence Parry Heide		Holiday
1982	Donald Has A Difficulty		$50	$70	$90	Edward Gorey		Capra
1982	Light Metres		$30	$50	$60	Felicia Lamport		Everest
1982	Old Possum's Book Of Practical Cats		$30	$50	$60	T. S. Eliot		HBJ
1982	The Dwindling Party		$50	$70	$90	Edward Gorey		Random
1982	The Water Flowers		$50	$70	$90	Edward Gorey		C&W
1983	Amphigorey Also		$40	$60	$90	Edward Gorey		C&W
1983	Gorey Stories		$30	$50	$60	David Aldrich		SFrench
1983	The Prune People (S/L)		$340	$500	$660	Edward Gorey		AP
1984	Edward Gorey's Haunted Looking Glass		$40	$60	$90	Edward Gorey		Avenel
1984	Treehorn's Wish		$30	$50	$60	Florence Parry Heide		Holiday
1985	The Eclectic Abecedarium		$40	$60	$80	Edward Gorey		Adama
1985	The Prune People II (S/L)		$240	$360	$480	Edward Gorey		AP
1986	The Eyes Of The Killer Robot		$30	$40	$60	John Bellairs		Dial
1986	The Improbable Landscape (S/L)		$220	$340	$440	Edward Gorey		AP
1989	Q.R.V. (S/L)		$200	$280	$380	Edward Gorey		Black
1990	The Fraught Settee (S/L)		$180	$280	$360	Edward Gorey		Fantod
1991	You Know Who		$25	$35	$50	John Ciardi		Wordsng
1992	The Betrayed Confidence		$30	$40	$60	Edward Gorey		Parnss
1992	The Mansion In The Mist		$20	$30	$40	John Bellairs		Dial
1993	The Ghost In The Mirror		$20	$30	$40	John Bellairs		Dial
1993	The Vengeance Of The Witch-Finder		$20	$30	$40	John Bellairs		Dial
1994	Figbash Acrobate		$25	$40	$50	Edward Gorey		Fantod
1995	The Unknown Vegetable		$25	$35	$50	Edward Gorey		Fantod
1997	The Deadly Blotter		$20	$30	$40	Edward Gorey		Fantod
1997	The Haunted Tea-Cosy		$20	$30	$40	Edward Gorey		HBrace
1999	The Headless Bust		$18	$25	$35	Edward Gorey		HBrace
2000	The Battles That Changed History		$12	$18	$25	Fletcher Pratt		Dover
2001	Ascending Peculiarity		$14	$20	$30	Edward Gorey		Harcort
2002	Cautionary Tales For Children		$10	$16	$20	Hilaire Belloc		Harcort
2003	Elephant House		$10	$14	$18	Kevin McDermott		Potter

Graham   Bob

Year	Title	VG-	VG	VG+	Fine	Author	Award	Pub
1981	A Boggle Of Bunyips		$25	$35	$50	Edna Wignell		H&S
1984	Jenny's Baby Brother		$16	$25	$30	Peter Smith		Viking
1984	Pete And Roland		$16	$25	$30	Bob Graham		Viking
1985	Bath Time For John		$16	$25	$30	Bob Graham		LBrown
1985	Libby, Oscar & Me		$16	$25	$30	Bob Graham		Bedrik
1985	Pearl's Place		$16	$25	$30	Bob Graham		Bedrik
1987	Crusher Is Coming!		$14	$20	$30	Bob Graham		VK
1987	The Adventures Of Charlotte And Henry		$14	$20	$30	Bob Graham		VK
1987	The Red Woollen Blanket		$14	$20	$30	Bob Graham		Walker
1987	The Wild		$14	$20	$30	Bob Graham		Bedrik
1988	Here Comes John		$14	$20	$30	Bob Graham		LBrown
1988	Here Comes Theo		$14	$20	$30	Bob Graham		LBrown
1988	Where Is Sarah?		$14	$20	$30	Bob Graham		LBrown
1989	Grandad's Magic		$14	$20	$25	Bob Graham		LBrown
1989	Has Anyone Here Seen William?		$14	$20	$25	Bob Graham		LBrown
1990	Greetings From Sandy Beach		$12	$18	$25	Bob Graham		Lothian
1992	Rose Meets Mr. Wintergarten		$12	$18	$25	Bob Graham		Candle
1993	Poems For The Very Young		$12	$16	$20	Michael Rosen		Kfisher
1996	Spirit Of Hope		$10	$16	$20	Bob Graham		Mondo
1996	This Is Our House		$10	$16	$20	Michael Rosen		Candle
1997	Queenie The Bantam		$10	$16	$20	Bob Graham		Walker
1997	Queenie, One Of The Family		$10	$16	$20	Bob Graham		Candle
1999	Benny		$10	$14	$18	Bob Graham		Candle

Graham   Bob

Year	Title	VG-	VG	VG+	Fine	Author	Award	Pub
1999	Buffy		$10	$14	$18	Bob Graham		Walker
2000	Max		$8	$12	$16	Bob Graham		Candle
2001	Let's Get A Pup! Said Kate		$8	$12	$16	Bob Graham		Candle
2002	Jethro Byrd		$25	$35	$50	Bob Graham	GM	Candle
2003	The Nine Lives Of Aristotle		$8	$10	$14	Dick King-Smith		Candle
2004	Tales From The Waterhole		$8	$10	$14	Bob Graham		Candle
2005	Oscar's Half Birthday		$6	$10	$12	Bob Graham		Candle

Graham   Margaret Bloy

Year	Title	VG-	VG	VG+	Fine	Author	Award	Pub
1950	Mr. Upstairs And Mr. Downstairs	$80	$120	$140		Charles Norman		H&B
1951	All Falling Down	$180	$240	$300		Gene Zion	CH	H&B
1951	The Crumb That Walked	$50	$70	$90		Charles Norman		H&B
1952	Hunch, Munch, And Crunch	$50	$70	$90		Charles Norman		H&B
1952	The Storm Book	$160	$200	$260		Charlotte Zolotow	CH	HCollins
1953	Big Mose	$50	$70	$90		Katherine Binney Shippen		H&B
1954	Hide And Seek Day	$50	$70	$90		Gene Zion		H&B
1954	To A Different Drum	$50	$70	$90		Charles Norman		H&B
1955	The Summer Snowman	$50	$70	$90		Gene Zion		H&B
1956	Harry, The Dirty Dog	$70	$100	$120		Gene Zion		H&B
1956	Really Spring	$50	$70	$90		Gene Zion		H&B
1957	Dear Garbage Man	$50	$70	$90		Gene Zion		H&B
1957	Jeffie's Party	$50	$70	$90		Gene Zion		H&B
1958	No Roses For Harry	$50	$60	$80		Gene Zion		H&B
1959	The Plant Sitter	$50	$60	$80		Gene Zion		H&B
1960	Harry And The Lady Next Door	$50	$60	$80		Gene Zion		H&B
1964	The Sugar Mouse Cake	$50	$60	$80		Gene Zion		Scribnr
1965	Harry By The Sea	$40	$60	$70		Gene Zion		H&Row
1967	Be Nice To Spiders	$60	$80	$100		Margaret Bloy Graham		H&Row
1970	The Green Hornet Lunchbox		$30	$50	$60	Shirley Gordon		HM
1970	The Meanest Squirrel I Ever Met		$30	$50	$60	Gene Zion		Scribnr
1971	Benjy And The Barking Bird		$40	$60	$90	Margaret Bloy Graham		H&Row
1973	Benjy's Dog House		$40	$60	$90	Margaret Bloy Graham		H&Row
1974	The Pack Rat's Day & Other Poems		$30	$40	$60	Jack Prelutsky		Macmil
1977	Benjy's Boat Trip		$40	$60	$80	Margaret Bloy Graham		H&Row
1987	What If?		$20	$30	$40	Else Holmelund Minarik		Green
1988	Benjy And His Friend Fifi		$18	$25	$35	Margaret Bloy Graham		H&Row
1989	It's Spring!		$18	$25	$35	Else Holmelund Minarik		Green

Gramatky   Hardie

Year	Title	VG-	VG	VG+	Fine	Author	Award	Pub
1939	Little Toot	$720	$960	$1,200		Hardie Gramatky		Putnam
1940	Hercules	$220	$280	$360		Hardie Gramatky		Putnam
1940	Skwee-Gee	$140	$200	$240		Darwin Le Ora Teilhet		DD
1941	Loopy	$140	$180	$240		Hardie Gramatky		Putnam
1948	Creeper's Jeep	$120	$160	$220		Hardie Gramatky		Putnam
1952	Sparky, The Story Of A Little Trolley Car	$120	$160	$200		Hardie Gramatky		Putnam
1957	Homer And The Circus Train	$100	$140	$180		Hardie Gramatky		Putnam
1961	Bolivar	$70	$90	$120		Hardie Gramatky		Putnam
1963	Nikos & The Sea God	$70	$90	$120		Hardie Gramatky		Putnam
1964	Little Toot On The Thames	$90	$120	$160		Hardie Gramatky		Putnam
1968	Little Toot On The Grand Canal	$80	$120	$140		Hardie Gramatky		Putnam
1970	Happy's Christmas		$50	$70	$90	Hardie Gramatky		Putnam
1973	Little Toot On The Mississippi		$60	$90	$120	Hardie Gramatky		Putnam
1975	Little Toot Through The Golden Gate		$60	$80	$120	Hardie Gramatky		Putnam
1989	Little Toot And The Loch Ness Monster		$35	$50	$70	Hardie Gramatky		Putnam

GrandPré   Mary

Year	Title	VG-	VG	VG+	Fine	Author	Award	Pub
1983	The Snow Storm		$30	$50	$60	Aleksandr Pushkin		Creat
1993	Chin Yu Min And The Ginger Cat		$16	$25	$30	Jennifer Armstrong		Crown
1994	The Vegetables Go To Bed		$14	$20	$30	Christopher King		Crown
1995	The Thread Of Life		$14	$20	$25	Domenico Vittorini		Crown
1997	Batwings And The Curtain Of Night		$12	$18	$25	Marguerite Davol		Orchard
1998	Harry Potter And The Sorcerer's Stone		$800	$1,200	$1,600	J.K. Rowling		Levine

GrandPré   Mary

Year	Title	VG-	VG	VG+	Fine	Author	Award	Pub
1998	Pockets		$12	$16	$20	Jennifer Armstrong		Crown
1999	Harry Potter And The Chamber Of Secrets		$140	$220	$300	J.K. Rowling		Levine
1999	Harry Potter And The Prisoner Of Azkaban		$60	$80	$120	J.K. Rowling		Levine
1999	The House Of Wisdom		$12	$16	$20	Judith/Florence Gilliland/Heide		DK
2000	Harry Potter And The Goblet Of Fire		$16	$25	$30	J.K. Rowling		Levine
2000	The Purple Snerd		$10	$14	$18	Rozanne Lanczak Williams		Harcort
2001	Aunt Claire's Yellow Beehive Hair		$10	$14	$18	Deborah Blumenthal		Dial
2002	The Sea Chest		$8	$12	$16	Toni Buzzeo		Dial
2003	Harry Potter And The Order Of The Phoenix		$12	$16	$20	J.K. Rowling		Levine
2003	Plum		$8	$12	$16	Tony Mitten		Levine
2004	Henry And Pawl		$8	$10	$14	Mary GrandPré		Dial
2005	Harry Potter And The Half-Blood Prince		$8	$10	$14	J.K. Rowling		Levine
2005	Sweep Dreams		$6	$10	$12	Nancy Willard		LBrown
2006	Henry And Pawl And The Round Yellow Ball		$6	$10	$12	Tom Casmer		Dial

Graves   Keith

Year	Title	VG-	VG	VG+	Fine	Author	Award	Pub
1984	Clovis Crawfish And Petit Papillon		$16	$25	$30	Mary Alice Fontenot		Pelican
1985	Clovis Crawfish And His Friends		$12	$18	$25	Mary Alice Fontenot		Pelican
1999	Frank Was A Monster Who Wanted To Dance		$8	$12	$16	Keith Graves		Chron
2000	Armadillo Tattletale		$8	$10	$14	Helen Ketteman		Scholas
2000	Pet Boy		$8	$10	$14	Keith Graves		Chron
2001	Uncle Blubbafink's Ridiculous Stories		$8	$10	$14	Keith Graves		Scholas
2001	Uncle Blubbafink's Seriously Ridiculous Stories		$8	$10	$14	Keith Graves		Scholas
2002	Loretta		$8	$10	$14	Keith Graves		Scholas
2003	Three Nasty Gnarlies		$8	$10	$14	Keith Graves		Scholas
2004	Moo Who?		$6	$10	$12	Margie Palatini		Tegen

Grebu   Devis

Year	Title	VG-	VG	VG+	Fine	Author	Award	Pub
1986	Joseph Who Loved The Sabbath		$14	$20	$30	Marilyn Hirsh		Viking
1987	The Book Of Miracles		$12	$16	$20	Lawrence Kushner		UAHC
1988	The King's Chessboard		$12	$16	$20	David Birch		Dial
1990	Follow That Fish		$10	$16	$20	Joanne Oppenheim		Bantam

Greenwald   Sheila

Year	Title	VG-	VG	VG+	Fine	Author	Award	Pub
1960	The Little Leftover Witch	$35	$40	$60		Florence Laughlin		Macmil
1961	The Man Who Never Snoozed	$25	$30	$40		Jean Lee Latham		Macmil
1962	A Metropolitan Love Story	$25	$30	$40		Sheila Greenwald		DoubleD
1965	Come A-Witching	$25	$30	$40		Grace Voris Curl		Bobbs
1965	Who'll Mind Henry?	$25	$30	$40		Anne Mallet		DoubleD
1966	The Seventh Cousin	$25	$30	$40		Florence Laughlin		Macmil
1966	The Snow Queen, & Other Tales	$25	$30	$40		Pat Shaw Iversen (adapted)		NAL
1967	The New Boy On The Sidewalk	$25	$30	$40		M. Jean Craig		Norton
1967	The Pretender Princess	$25	$30	$40		Mary Jane Roth		Morrow
1968	The Mystery Cup	$20	$30	$35		Jean Bothwell		Dial
1971	Willie Bryant And The Flying Otis		$18	$25	$35	Sheila Greenwald		G&D
1972	Mat Pit And The Tunnel Tenants		$18	$25	$35	Sheila Greenwald		Lippin
1972	Miss Amanda Snap		$18	$25	$35	Sheila Greenwald		Bobbs
1972	The Hot Day		$18	$25	$35	Sheila Greenwald		Bobbs
1974	The Secret Museum		$16	$25	$30	Sheila Greenwald		Lippin
1977	The Mariah Delany Lending Library Disaster		$16	$25	$30	Sheila Greenwald		HM
1977	The Secret In Miranda's Closet		$16	$25	$30	Sheila Greenwald		HM
1978	The Atrocious Two		$14	$20	$30	Sheila Greenwald		HM
1979	All The Way To Wits' End		$14	$20	$30	Sheila Greenwald		LBrown
1980	It All Began With Jane Eyre		$14	$20	$25	Sheila Greenwald		LBrown
1981	Give Us A Great Big Smile, Rosy Cole		$14	$20	$25	Sheila Greenwald		LBrown
1982	Blissful Joy And The Sats		$14	$20	$25	Sheila Greenwald		LBrown
1983	Will The Real Gertrude Hollings Please Stand Up?		$14	$20	$25	Sheila Greenwald		LBrown
1984	Valentine Rosy		$12	$18	$25	Sheila Greenwald		LBrown
1985	Rosy Cole's Great American Guilt Club		$12	$18	$25	Sheila Greenwald		Joy
1987	Alvin Webster's Surefire Plan For Success		$12	$16	$20	Sheila Greenwald		LBrown
1988	Write On, Rosy!		$12	$16	$20	Sheila Greenwald		Joy
1989	Rosy's Romance		$12	$16	$20	Sheila Greenwald		Joy

Greenwald   Sheila

Year	Title	VG-	VG	VG+	Fine	Author	Award	Pub
1990	Mariah Delany's Author-Of-The-Month Club		$10	$16	$20	Sheila Greenwald		Joy
1991	Here's Hermione		$10	$16	$20	Sheila Greenwald		Joy
1992	Rosy Cole Discovers America!		$10	$16	$20	Sheila Greenwald		Joy
1993	My Fabulous New Life		$10	$16	$20	Sheila Greenwald		Bdeer
1994	Rosy Cole		$10	$14	$18	Sheila Greenwald		LBrown
2000	Stucksville		$8	$10	$14	Sheila Greenwald		DK
2003	Rosy Cole's Worst Ever, Best Ever Tour Of NY City		$8	$10	$14	Sheila Greenwald		Kroupa

Gretz   Susanna

Year	Title	VG-	VG	VG+	Fine	Author	Award	Pub
1969	Teddy Bears 1 To 10	$25	$35	$50		Susanna Gretz		4Winds
1970	Teddy Bears Stay Indoors		$18	$25	$35	Susanna Gretz		4Winds
1973	Rilloby-Rill		$16	$25	$30	Henry John Newbolt		Ohara
1973	The Bears Who Went To The Seaside		$16	$25	$30	Susanna Gretz		Follett
1975	Teddybears ABC		$16	$25	$30	Susanna Gretz		Follett
1981	Teddy Bear's Moving Day		$14	$20	$25	Susanna Gretz		4Winds
1982	Teddy Bears Go Shopping		$14	$20	$25	Susanna Gretz		4Winds
1984	Teddy Bears Cure A Cold		$12	$18	$25	S. Getz & A. Sage		4Winds
1985	It's Your Turn, Roger!		$12	$18	$25	Susanna Gretz		Dial
1986	Hide-And-Seek		$12	$16	$20	Susanna Gretz		4Winds
1986	I'm Not Sleepy		$12	$16	$20	Susanna Gretz		4Winds
1986	Ready For Bed		$12	$16	$20	Susanna Gretz		4Winds
1986	Say It Again, Granny!		$12	$16	$20	John Agard		Bodley
1986	Too Dark!		$12	$16	$20	Susanna Gretz		4Winds
1987	Roger Takes Charge!		$12	$16	$20	Susanna Gretz		Dial
1987	Teddy Bears Stay Indoors		$12	$16	$20	S. Getz & A. Sage		4Winds
1987	Teddy Bears Take The Train		$12	$16	$20	S. Getz & A. Sage		4Winds
1988	Roger Loses His Marbles!		$12	$16	$20	Susanna Gretz		Dial
1989	Teddy Bears At The Seaside		$12	$16	$20	S. Getz & A. Sage		4Winds
1991	Duck Takes Off		$10	$16	$20	Susanna Gretz		4Winds
1991	Frog In The Middle		$10	$16	$20	Susanna Gretz		4Winds
1992	Frog, Duck, And Rabbit		$10	$16	$20	Susanna Gretz		4Winds
1992	Rabbit Rambles On		$10	$16	$20	Susanna Gretz		4Winds
1999	Rabbit Food		$8	$12	$16	Susanna Gretz		Candle

Grifalconi   Ann

Year	Title	VG-	VG	VG+	Fine	Author	Award	Pub
1963	Camping Through Europe By Car	$50	$60	$80		Ann Grifalconi		Crown
1965	City Rhythms	$40	$60	$70		Ann Grifalconi		Bobbs
1965	Voices In The Night	$30	$40	$50		Rhoda W/ Bacmeister		Bobbs
1966	American Steamboat Stories	$30	$40	$50		Edwin Palmer Hoyt		AS
1966	Peg-Leg Willy	$30	$40	$50		Margaret Embry		Holiday
1966	The Jazz Man	$30	$40	$50		Mary Hays Weik		Athenm
1967	A Special Bravery	$30	$40	$50		Johanna Johnston		DoddM
1967	Carlo's Cricket	$30	$40	$50		Barbara Reid		McHill
1967	Half-Breed	$30	$40	$50		Evelyn Sibley Lampman		DoubleD
1967	Pepito	$30	$40	$50		Nathan Zimelman		Reilly
1967	The Africans Knew	$30	$40	$50		Tillie S. Pine		McHill
1967	The Treasure Of Tolmec	$30	$40	$50		Louise A. Stinetorf		JohnDay
1968	America Forever New	$30	$40	$50		Sara Brewton		Crowell
1968	Antonio	$30	$40	$50		Bronson Potter		Athenm
1968	Shadows And Light	$30	$40	$50		Anton Chekhov		DoubleD
1968	The Ballad Of The Burglar Of Babylon	$30	$40	$50		Elizabeth Bishop		FSG
1968	The Incas Knew	$30	$40	$50		Tillie S. Pine		McHill
1968	The Midnight Fox	$30	$40	$50		Betsy Cromer Byars		Viking
1968	The Toy Trumpet: Story And Pictures	$40	$50	$70		Ann Grifalconi		Bobbs
1969	Don't You Turn Back	$25	$35	$50		Langston Hughes		Knopf
1969	The Boy Who Wouldn't Talk	$25	$35	$50		Lois Kalb Bouchard		DoubleD
1969	Venture For Freedom	$25	$35	$50		Ruby Zagoren		World
1970	Sunflowers For Tina		$25	$35	$50	Anne Norris Baldwin		4Winds
1970	This Street's For Me!		$25	$35	$50	Lee Bennett Hopkins		Crown
1971	David He No Fear		$25	$35	$50	Lorenz B. Graham		Crowell
1971	The Maya Knew		$25	$35	$50	Tillie S. Pine		McHill
1972	The Dragon Takes A Wife		$25	$35	$50	Walter Dean Myers		Bobbs
1972	The Night Of The Radishes		$25	$35	$50	Toby Talbot		Putnam
1973	A House On Liberty Street		$25	$35	$50	Mary Hays Weik		Athenm

Grifalconi   Ann

Year	Title	VG-	VG	VG+	Fine	Author	Award	Pub
1973	The Matter With Lucy		$25	$35	$50	Ann Grifalconi		Bobbs
1974	Everett Anderson's Year		$20	$30	$40	Lucille Clifton		HR&W
1974	The Day The Hurricane Happened		$20	$30	$40	John Lonzo Anderson		Scribnr
1975	Banji's Magic Wheel		$20	$30	$40	Letta Schatz		Follett
1975	The Secret Soldier		$20	$30	$40	Ann McGovern		4Winds
1976	Everett Anderson's Friend		$20	$30	$40	Lucille Clifton		HR&W
1977	Everett Anderson's 1 2 3		$20	$30	$40	Lucille Clifton		HR&W
1978	Everett Anderson's Nine Month Long		$20	$30	$40	Lucille Clifton		HR&W
1978	How Far, Felipe?		$20	$30	$40	Genevieve Gray		H&Row
1983	Everett Anderson's Goodbye		$16	$25	$30	Lucille Clifton		HR&W
1986	The Village Of Round And Square Houses		$40	$60	$80	Ann Grifalconi	CH	LBrown
1987	Darkness And The Butterfly		$14	$20	$30	Ann Grifalconi		LBrown
1990	Osa's Pride		$12	$18	$25	Ann Grifalconi		LBrown
1992	Who Painted The Porcupine Purple?		$12	$18	$25	Lael Littke		SBurdet
1993	Kinda Blue		$16	$25	$30	Ann Grifalconi		LBrown
1994	Jasmine's Parlour Day		$12	$16	$20	Lynn Joseph		LL&S
1994	The Bravest Flute		$14	$20	$30	Ann Grifalconi		LBrown
1995	Not Home		$14	$20	$25	Ann Grifalconi		LBrown
1995	The Lion's Whiskers		$10	$16	$20	Nancy Raines Day		Scholas
1996	Don't Leave An Elephant To Go And Chase A Bird		$10	$16	$20	James Berry		S&S
1997	Electric Yancy		$10	$16	$20	Ann Grifalconi		LL&S
1998	Tío Armando		$10	$14	$18	Florence Parry Heide		LL&S
1999	Tiny's Hat		$10	$14	$18	Ann Grifalconi		HCollins
2000	In The Rainfield		$8	$12	$16	Isaac Olaleye		BSP
2001	One Of The Problems Of Everett Anderson		$8	$12	$16	Lucille Clifton		Holt
2001	Patrol		$8	$12	$16	Walter Dean Myers		HCollins
2002	The Village That Vanished		$8	$10	$14	Ann Grifalconi		Dial

Grimly   Gris

Year	Title	VG-	VG	VG+	Fine	Author	Award	Pub
2001	Monster Museum		$12	$16	$20	Marilyn Singer		Hyper
2002	Pinocchio		$8	$12	$16	Carlo Collodi		Tor
2003	Gris Grimly's Wicked Nursery Rhymes		$8	$12	$16	Gris Grimly		BTB
2004	Boris And Bella		$8	$10	$14	Carolyn Crimi		Harcort
2004	Creature Carnival		$8	$10	$14	Marilyn Singer		Hyper
2004	Edgar Allan Poe's Tales Of Mystery		$8	$10	$14	Edgar Allan Poe		Athenm
2005	Grimericks		$6	$10	$12	Susan Pearson		MCaven

Gruelle   Johnny

Year	Title	VG-	VG	VG+	Fine	Author	Award	Pub
1914	Grimm's Fairy Stories	$300	$400	$500		Jacob & Wilhelm Grimm		C&L
1915	All About Little Red Riding Hood	$200	$260	$320		Jacob & Wilhelm Grimm		C&L
1916	All About Cinderella	$200	$260	$320		Charles Perrault		C&L
1916	All About Little Boy Blue	$200	$260	$320		Johnny Gruelle (adapted)		C&L
1916	All About Mother Goose	$200	$260	$320		Johnny Gruelle (adapted)		C&L
1916	Rhymes For Kindly Children	$200	$260	$320		Fairmont Snyder		Volland
1917	All About Hansel And Grethel	$200	$260	$320		Jacob & Wilhelm Grimm		C&L
1917	All About Little Black Sambo	$380	$500	$620		Helen Bannerman		C&L
1917	All About The Little Small Red Hen	$200	$260	$320		Johnny Gruelle (adapted)		C&L
1917	My Very Own Fairy Stories	$280	$380	$480		Johnny Gruelle		Volland
1918	Raggedy Ann Stories	$2,000	$2,800	$3,400		Johnny Gruelle		Volland
1918	Sunny Bunny	$440	$580	$720		Nina Wilcox Putnam		Volland
1919	Friendly Fairies	$420	$560	$700		Johnny Gruelle		Volland
1920	Raggedy Andy Stores	$960	$1,200	$1,600		Johnny Gruelle		Volland
1921	Eddie Elephant	$420	$560	$700		Johnny Gruelle		Volland
1921	Orphant Annie Story Book	$420	$560	$700		Johnny Gruelle		Bobbs
1922	The Magical Land Of Noom	$280	$360	$460		Johnny Gruelle		Volland
1922	The Man In The Moon Stories	$280	$360	$460		Josephine Lawrence		Volland
1924	Raggedy Ann & Andy And Camel With Wrinkled Knees	$400	$520	$660		Johnny Gruelle		Volland
1925	Raggedy Ann's Alphabet Book	$400	$520	$660		Johnny Gruelle		Volland
1926	Beloved Belindy	$260	$360	$440		Johnny Gruelle		Volland
1926	The Paper Dragon	$260	$360	$440		Johnny Gruelle		Volland
1927	Wooden Willie	$260	$340	$420		Johnny Gruelle		Volland
1928	Raggedy Ann's Magical Wishes	$380	$520	$640		Johnny Gruelle		Volland
1929	A Mother Goose Parade	$260	$340	$420		Justin C. Gruelle		Volland
1929	Marcella, A Raggedy Ann Story	$380	$500	$620		Johnny Gruelle		Volland

Gruelle Johnny

Year	Title	VG-	VG	VG+	Fine	Author	Award	Pub
1930	Raggedy Ann In The Deep, Deep Woods	$380	$500	$620		Johnny Gruelle		Volland
1930	Raggedy Ann In The Deep, Deep Woods	$40	$50	$70		Johnny Gruelle		Donohue
1931	Raggedy Ann In Cookie Land	$240	$320	$400		Johnny Gruelle		Volland
1935	Beloved Belindy	$35	$50	$60		Johnny Gruelle		Donohue
1937	Rhymes For Kindly Children	$160	$200	$260		Ethel Fairmont		Wis-P
1939	Raggedy Ann In The Magic Book	$70	$90	$120		Johnny Gruelle		Gruelle
1940	Raggedy Ann And The Golden Butterfly	$70	$90	$120		Johnny Gruelle		Gruelle
1940	Raggedy Ann Helps Grandpa Hoppergrass	$70	$90	$120		Johnny Gruelle		McLough
1943	Raggedy Ann And Betsy Bonnet String	$70	$90	$120		Johnny Gruelle		Gruelle
1946	Raggedy Ann In The Snow White Castle	$60	$80	$100		Johnny Gruelle		Gruelle
1947	Raggedy Ann Stories	$60	$80	$100		Johnny Gruelle		Gruelle

Gurney Eric

Year	Title	VG-	VG	VG+	Fine	Author	Award	Pub
1960	How To Live With A Neurotic Dog	$25	$30	$40		Stephen Baker		P-Hall
1962	How To Live With A Calculating Cat	$25	$30	$40		Eric Gurney		P-Hall
1963	Gilbert	$25	$30	$40		Eric Gurney		P-Hall
1964	And How Do We Feel This Morning?	$25	$30	$40		Corey Ford		P-Hall
1965	How To Live With A Pampered Pet	$25	$30	$40		Willian Nettleton		P-Hall
1965	The King, The Mice And The Cheese	$70	$90	$120		Nancy Gurney		BB
1966	Punctured Poems	$25	$30	$40		Richard Willard Armour		P-Hall
1967	The Digging-Est Dog	$60	$80	$100		Al Perkins		BB
1968	Gurney's Guide To Feathered Friends	$20	$30	$35		Nancy Gurney		Morrow
1969	Hand, Hand, Fingers, Thumb	$60	$80	$100		Al Perkins		BB
1969	Mind In A Maze	$20	$30	$35		Jessica Davidson		P-Hall
1970	Impossible Dogs And Troublesome Cats		$18	$25	$35	Nancy Gurney		AHP
1973	The Strange Dreams Of Rover Jones		$16	$25	$30	Richard Willard Armour		McHill
1974	Someone Is Eating The Sun		$16	$25	$30	Ruth A. Sonneborn		Random
1978	The Calculating Cat Returns		$14	$20	$30	Nancy Prevo		P-Hall
1981	Schnoodle And Sam		$14	$20	$25	Eric Gurney		P-Hall
1983	Gurney's Gallery Of Dogs & Doggie Dictionary		$14	$20	$25	Eric Gurney		Woodbrg
1983	How To Live With A Headstrong Horse		$14	$20	$25	Eric Gurney		P-Hall

Gurney James

Year	Title	VG-	VG	VG+	Fine	Author	Award	Pub
1993	Dinotopia		$30	$40	$60	James Gurney		Turner

Gurney John

Year	Title	VG-	VG	VG+	Fine	Author	Award	Pub
1985	The Temptation Of Wilfred Malachey		$16	$25	$30	William F. Buckley		Workman
1991	On Our Way To Market		$10	$16	$20	Dayle Ann Dodds		S&S
1993	The Jumbaroo		$10	$16	$20	Joy Cowley		Oxford
1993	The Search For Sidney's Smile		$10	$16	$20	Marc Kornblatt		S&S
1994	The Hog Call To End All!		$10	$14	$18	SuAnn Kiser		Orchard
1996	Christmas Magic		$8	$12	$16	Patricia Hermes		Scholas
1997	The Absent Author		$8	$12	$16	Ron Roy		Random
1997	The Bald Bandit		$8	$12	$16	Ron Roy		Random
1998	Phantoms Don't Drive Sports Cars		$8	$12	$16	D. Dadey & M. Jones		Scholas
1998	The Canary Caper		$8	$12	$16	Ron Roy		Random
1998	The Deadly Dungeon		$8	$12	$16	Ron Roy		Random
1998	The Empty Envelope		$8	$12	$16	Ron Roy		Random
1998	The Falcon's Feathers		$8	$12	$16	Ron Roy		Random
1999	Stubby And The Puppy Pack		$8	$12	$16	Nicki Wallace		Pocket
1999	The Haunted Hotel		$8	$12	$16	Ron Roy		Random
1999	The Invisible Island		$8	$12	$16	Ron Roy		Random
2000	The Jaguar's Jewel		$8	$10	$14	Ron Roy		Random
2000	The Kidnapped King		$8	$10	$14	Ron Roy		Random
2000	The Lucky Lottery		$8	$10	$14	Ron Roy		Random
2001	Bub Moose		$8	$10	$14	Carol & Bill Wallace		Pocket
2001	Chomps, Flea, And Gray Cat (That's Me!)		$8	$10	$14	Carol & Bill Wallace		Pocket
2001	The Missing Mummy		$8	$10	$14	Ron Roy		Random
2001	The Ninth Nugget		$8	$10	$14	Ron Roy		Random
2001	The Orange Outlaw		$8	$10	$14	Ron Roy		Random
2002	Because It's My Body!		$8	$10	$14	Joanne Sherman		SAFE
2002	Bub, Snow, And The Burly Bear Scare		$8	$10	$14	Carol & Bill Wallace		S&S

Gurney   John

Year	Title	VG-	VG	VG+	Fine	Author	Award	Pub
2002	Dinosaur Train		$8	$10	$14	John Steven Gurney		HCollins
2002	Stubby And The Puppy Pack To The Rescue		$8	$10	$14	Nicki & Bill Wallace		S&S
2002	The Panda Puzzle		$8	$10	$14	Ron Roy		Random
2002	The Quicksand Question		$8	$10	$14	Ron Roy		Random
2002	The Runaway Racehorse		$8	$10	$14	Ron Roy		Random
2003	The School Skeleton		$8	$10	$14	Ron Roy		Random
2003	The Talking T. Rex		$8	$10	$14	Ron Roy		Random
2004	On The Farm		$6	$10	$12	Kirsten Hall		CP
2004	The Unwilling Umpire		$6	$10	$12	Ron Roy		Random
2004	The Vampire's Vacation		$6	$10	$12	Ron Roy		Random
2004	The White Wolf		$6	$10	$12	Ron Roy		Random

Gwynne   Fred

Year	Title	VG-	VG	VG+	Fine	Author	Award	Pub
1960	What's Nude?	$35	$40	$60		Fred Gwynne		Obolsky
1962	The Battle Of The Frogs And The Mice	$70	$90	$120		George Martin		DoddM
1970	God's First World		$25	$35	$50	Fred Gwynne		H&Row
1970	The King Who Rained		$40	$60	$90	Fred Gwynne		Windmil
1971	Ick's ABC		$30	$50	$60	Fred Gwynne		Windmil
1971	The Story Of Ick		$30	$50	$60	Fred Gwynne		Windmil
1976	A Chocolate Moose For Dinner		$30	$40	$60	Fred Gwynne		Windmil
1980	The Sixteen Hand Horse		$25	$35	$50	Fred Gwynne		Windmil
1981	The King's Trousers		$25	$35	$50	Robert Kraus		Windmil
1988	A Little Pigeon Toad		$18	$25	$35	Fred Gwynne		S&S
1990	Pondlarker		$16	$25	$30	Fred Gwynne		S&S
1993	Easy To See Why		$16	$25	$30	Fred Gwynne		S&S

Haas   Irene

Year	Title	VG-	VG	VG+	Fine	Author	Award	Pub
1954	A Little House Of Your Own	$60	$80	$100		Beatrice S. De Regniers		HBrace
1954	The Mysterious Leaf	$60	$80	$100		Richard Banks		HBrace
1956	Was It A Good Trade?	$50	$70	$90		Beatrice S. De Regniers		HBrace
1958	Something Special	$50	$60	$80		Beatrice S. De Regniers		HBrace
1963	Tatsinda	$50	$60	$80		Elizabeth Enright		HBrace
1965	Zeee	$40	$60	$70		Elizabeth Enright		HBrace
1966	Emily's Vogage	$40	$60	$70		Emma Smith		HBrace
1974	Come Away		$30	$40	$60	Myra Cohn Livingston		Athenm
1975	The Maggie B		$30	$40	$60	Irene Haas		Athenm
1979	Carrie Hepple's Garden		$25	$40	$50	Ruth Craft		Athenm
1981	The Little Moon Theater		$25	$35	$50	Irene Haas		Athenm
1997	A Summertime Song		$12	$18	$25	Irene Haas		McEld

Hader   Berta & Elmer

Year	Title	VG-	VG	VG+	Fine	Author	Award	Pub
1927	Chicken Little and the Little Half Chick	$220	$280	$360		Berta & Elmer Hader		Macmil
1927	Hansel And Gretel	$220	$280	$360		Berta & Elmer Hader		Macmil
1927	Humpty Dumpty	$220	$280	$360		Berta & Elmer Hader		Macmil
1927	The Ugly Ducking	$220	$280	$360		Berta & Elmer Hader		Macmil
1928	The Little Red Hen	$140	$180	$240		Berta & Elmer Hader		Macmil
1928	The Old Woman The Crooked Sixpence	$140	$180	$240		Berta & Elmer Hader		Macmil
1928	The Picture Book Of Travel	$90	$120	$160		Berta & Elmer Hader		Macmil
1928	The Story Of The Three Bears	$140	$180	$240		Berta Hader (adapted)		Macmil
1928	The Wonderful Locomotive	$90	$120	$160		Cornelia Meigs		Macmil
1929	Two Funny Clowns	$140	$180	$240		Berta & Elmer Hader		CM
1929	What'll You Do When You Grow Up???	$90	$120	$160		Berta & Elmer Hader		Longman
1930	A Good Little Dog	$90	$120	$160		Anne Stoddard		Century
1930	Baby Bear	$90	$120	$160		Hamilton Williamson		DD
1930	Hader's Picture Book Of Mother Goose	$180	$240	$300		Berta & Elmer Hader		CM
1930	Lions And Tigers And Elephants Too	$140	$180	$220		Berta & Elmer Hader		Longman
1930	Sonny Elephant	$90	$120	$160		Hamilton Williamson		LBrown
1930	Under The Pig-Nut Tree	$140	$180	$220		Berta & Elmer Hader		Knopf
1931	A Monkey Tale	$100	$140	$180		Berta & Elmer Hader		DD
1931	Bingo Is My Name	$70	$100	$120		Anne Stoddard		Century
1931	Lion Cub	$70	$100	$120		Hamilton Williamson		DD
1931	The Farmer In The Dell	$100	$140	$180		Berta & Elmer Hader		Macmil

Hader   Berta & Elmer

Year	Title	VG-	VG	VG+	Fine	Author	Award	Pub
1931	Tooky	$100	$140	$180		Berta & Elmer Hader		Longman
1932	Hader's Picture Book Of The States	$100	$140	$180		Berta & Elmer Hader		H&B
1932	Here Bingo!	$70	$100	$120		Anne Stoddard		Century
1933	Chuck-A-Luck And His Reindeer	$100	$140	$180		Berta & Elmer Hader		HM
1933	Spunky:The Story Of A Shetland Pony	$100	$140	$180		Berta & Elmer Hader		Macmil
1933	Whiffy Mcmann	$100	$140	$180		Berta & Elmer Hader		Oxford
1934	Midget And Bridget	$100	$140	$180		Berta & Elmer Hader		Macmil
1935	Jamaica Johnny	$100	$140	$180		Berta & Elmer Hader		Macmil
1936	Billy Butter	$100	$140	$180		Berta & Elmer Hader		Macmil
1936	Green And Gold	$100	$140	$180		Berta & Elmer Hader		Macmil
1936	Stop, Look, Listen	$100	$140	$180		Berta & Elmer Hader		Longman
1937	Humpy, Son Of The Sands	$70	$90	$120		Hamilton Williamson		DD
1937	Marcos	$70	$90	$120		Melicent Humason Lee		AWhit
1937	The Farmer	$70	$90	$120		Henry Bolles Lent		Macmil
1937	Tommy Thatcher Goes To Sea	$100	$140	$180		Berta & Elmer Hader		Macmil
1938	Banana Tree House	$70	$90	$120		Phillis Garrard		CM
1938	Cricket	$100	$120	$160		Berta & Elmer Hader		Macmil
1939	Cock-A-Doodle Doo	$200	$280	$340		Berta & Elmer Hader	CH	Macmil
1939	Stripey	$70	$90	$120		Hamilton Williamson		DD
1940	The Cat And The Kitten	$100	$120	$160		Berta & Elmer Hader		Macmil
1941	Little Town	$100	$120	$160		Berta & Elmer Hader		Macmil
1942	Story Of Pancho & The Bull With The Crooked Tail	$90	$120	$160		Berta & Elmer Hader		Macmil
1943	The Mighty Hunter	$200	$280	$340		Berta & Elmer Hader	CH	Macmil
1943	Timothy Has Ideas	$70	$90	$120		Miriam Evangeline Mason		Macmil
1944	Hader's Picture Book Of Mother Goose	$60	$80	$100		Berta & Elmer Hader		CM
1944	The Little Stone House	$90	$120	$160		Berta & Elmer Hader		Macmil
1945	Rainbow's End	$90	$120	$160		Berta & Elmer Hader		Macmil
1946	The Skyrocket	$90	$120	$160		Berta & Elmer Hader		Macmil
1947	Big City	$80	$120	$140		Berta & Elmer Hader		Macmil
1947	Mr Peck's Pets	$60	$80	$100		Louise S. Bechtel		Macmil
1948	The Big Snow	$440	$580	$720		Berta & Elmer Hader	CM	Macmil
1949	Little Appaloosa	$80	$120	$140		Berta & Elmer Hader		Macmil
1950	Squirrely Of Willow Hill	$80	$120	$140		Berta & Elmer Hader		Macmil
1951	Lost In The Zoo	$70	$90	$120		Berta & Elmer Hader		Macmil
1952	Little White Foot	$60	$80	$100		Berta & Elmer Hader		Macmil
1953	The Friendly Phoebe	$60	$80	$100		Berta & Elmer Hader		Macmil
1954	Wish On The Moon	$60	$80	$100		Berta & Elmer Hader		Macmil
1955	Home On The Range	$60	$80	$100		Berta & Elmer Hader		Macmil
1956	The Runaways	$60	$80	$100		Berta & Elmer Hader		Macmil
1957	Ding, Dong, Bell	$60	$80	$100		Berta & Elmer Hader		Macmil
1958	Little Chip Of Willow Hill	$60	$80	$100		Berta & Elmer Hader		Macmil
1959	Reindeer Trail	$60	$80	$100		Berta & Elmer Hader		Macmil
1960	Mister Billy's Gun	$50	$70	$90		Berta & Elmer Hader		Macmil
1961	Quack Quack	$50	$70	$90		Berta & Elmer Hader		Macmil
1962	Little Antelope	$50	$70	$90		Berta & Elmer Hader		Macmil
1963	Snow In The City	$50	$70	$90		Berta & Elmer Hader		Macmil
1965	Two Is Company, Three's A Crowd	$50	$60	$80		Berta & Elmer Hader		Macmil
1993	The Ugly Duckling		$16	$25	$30	Hans Christian Andersen		G&D
1994	Chicken Little And Little Half Chick		$16	$25	$30	Berta Hader		Dover
1994	The Story Of Hansel And Gretel		$16	$25	$30	Berta Hader		Dover

Hafner   Marylin

Year	Title	VG-	VG	VG+	Fine	Author	Award	Pub
1949	Bonnie Bess	$60	$80	$100		Alvin R. Tresselt		LL&S
1965	Fun With ABC And 1-2-3	$30	$40	$50		Hal Dareff		PMagP
1967	The Story Of Zachary Zween	$30	$40	$50		Mabel Watts		PMagP
1968	Poetry Please	$30	$40	$50		Charlotte Reynolds		Singer
1972	Too Many Girls		$25	$35	$50	LouAnn Gaeddert		CM&G
1972	X Marks The Spot		$25	$35	$50	Eleanor Felder		CM&G
1973	Water Is Wet		$25	$35	$50	Sally Cartwright		CM&G
1974	Sunlight		$20	$30	$40	Sally Cartwright		CM&G
1975	Bright Lights To See By		$20	$30	$40	Miriam Anne Bourne		CM&G
1976	Something To Shout About		$20	$30	$40	Patricia Beatty		Morrow
1977	Cricket's Cookery		$20	$30	$40	Pauline Watson		Random
1977	It's Halloween		$20	$30	$40	Jack Prelutsky		Green
1977	P. T. Barnum		$20	$30	$40	Anne Edwards		Putnam

Hafner   Marylin

Year	Title	VG-	VG	VG+	Fine	Author	Award	Pub
1977	The Mango Tooth		$20	$30	$40	Charlotte Pomerantz		Green
1977	The Marble Cake Cat		$20	$30	$40	Marjorie & Carl Allen		CM&G
1978	Jenny And The Tennis Nut		$20	$30	$40	Janet Schulman		Green
1978	Mind Your Manners!		$20	$30	$40	Peggy Parish		Green
1978	Robbers, Bones, And Mean Dogs		$20	$30	$40	Barry & Velma Berkey		AW
1978	The Wobbly Tooth		$20	$30	$40	Nancy Evans Cooney		Putnam
1979	Camp Keewee's Secret Weapon		$18	$25	$35	Janet Schulman		Green
1979	I Wish Laura's Mommy Was My Mommy		$18	$25	$35	Barbara Power		Lippin
1979	Mrs. Gaddy And The Ghost		$18	$25	$35	Wilson Gage		Green
1979	The Candy Witch		$18	$25	$35	Steven Kroll		Holiday
1980	I Can--Can You?		$18	$25	$35	Peggy Parish		Green
1980	Little Devil Gets Sick		$18	$25	$35	Marjorie Weinman Sharmat		DoubleD
1980	M And M And The Haunted House Game		$18	$25	$35	Pat Ross		Pan
1980	Meet M And M		$18	$25	$35	Pat Ross		Pan
1980	Next Year I'll Be Special		$18	$25	$35	Patricia Reilly Giff		Dutton
1980	Rainy Rainy Saturday		$18	$25	$35	Jack Prelutsky		Green
1981	Big Sisters Are Bad Witches		$18	$25	$35	Morse Hamilton		Green
1981	Families		$18	$25	$35	Meredith Tax		LBrown
1981	It's Christmas		$18	$25	$35	Jack Prelutsky		Green
1981	M And M And The Big Bag		$18	$25	$35	Pat Ross		Pan
1981	Rollo And Juliet, Forever!		$18	$25	$35	Marjorie Weinman Sharmat		DoubleD
1982	Are You Pirates?		$16	$25	$30	Steven Kroll		Pan
1982	It's Thanksgiving		$16	$25	$30	Jack Prelutsky		Green
1982	Time's Up!		$16	$25	$30	Florence Parry Heide		Holiday
1983	Katharine's Doll		$16	$25	$30	Elizabeth Winthrop		Dutton
1983	M And M And The Bad News Babies		$16	$25	$30	Pat Ross		Pan
1983	That Dog!		$16	$25	$30	Nanette Newman		Crowell
1983	The Poison Ivy Case		$16	$25	$30	Joan M. Lexau		Dial
1984	The Crow And Mrs. Gaddy		$16	$25	$30	Wilson Gage		Green
1984	Time Flies!		$16	$25	$30	Florence Parry Heide		Holiday
1985	Germs Make Me Sick!		$16	$25	$30	Melvin Berger		Crowell
1985	Happy Mother's Day		$16	$25	$30	Steven Kroll		Holiday
1985	M & M And The Mummy Mess		$16	$25	$30	Pat Ross		VK
1985	M & M And The Santa Secrets		$16	$25	$30	Pat Ross		VK
1985	Mrs. Gaddy And The Fast-Growing Vine		$16	$25	$30	Wilson Gage		Green
1985	The Dog Food Caper		$16	$25	$30	Joan M. Lexau		Dial
1986	Best Friends, Hands Down		$14	$20	$30	Terry Wolfe Phelan		ShoeT
1986	My Brother, Will		$14	$20	$30	Joan Robins		Green
1986	The Laugh Book		$14	$20	$30	Joanna Cole		DoubleD
1986	The Purple Turkey & Other Thanksgiving Riddles		$14	$20	$30	David A. Adler		Holiday
1987	M & M And The Super Child Afternoon		$14	$20	$30	Pat Ross		VK
1988	Dinosaurs Are 568		$14	$20	$30	Jean Rogers		Green
1988	The Missing Tooth		$14	$20	$30	Joanna Cole		Random
1989	Bully Trouble		$14	$20	$25	Joanna Cole		Random
1989	Feeding Yourself		$14	$20	$25	Vicki Cobb		Lippin
1989	Getting Dressed		$14	$20	$25	Vicki Cobb		Lippin
1989	Keeping Clean		$14	$20	$25	Vicki Cobb		Lippin
1989	Sports Riddles		$14	$20	$25	Everett M. Hafner		VK
1989	Writing It Down		$14	$20	$25	Vicki Cobb		Lippin
1990	Hanukkah!		$12	$18	$25	Roni Schotter		Joy
1990	I'm Santa Claus And I'm Famous		$12	$18	$25	Marjorie Weinman Sharmat		Holiday
1990	Raymond's Best Summer		$12	$18	$25	Jean Rogers		Green
1991	Fathers, Mothers, Sisters, Brothers		$12	$18	$25	Mary Ann Hoberman		Joy
1991	M & M And The Halloween Monster		$12	$18	$25	Pat Ross		Viking
1991	Me Baby!		$12	$18	$25	Riki Levinson		Dutton
1991	My Stars, It's Mrs. Gaddy!		$12	$18	$25	Wilson Gage		Green
1992	Kevin And The School Nurse		$12	$18	$25	Martine Davison		Random
1992	Maggie And The Emergency Room		$12	$18	$25	Martine Davison		Random
1992	Red Day, Green Day		$12	$18	$25	Edith Kunhardt		Green
1993	An Egg And Seven Socks		$12	$16	$20	Judith Mathews		HCollins
1993	And Then What?		$12	$16	$20	Jake Wolf		Green
1993	Chatter-Box Jamie		$12	$16	$20	Nancy Evans Cooney		Putnam
1994	Don't Tease The Guppies		$12	$16	$20	Pat Lowery Collins		Putnam
1995	A Pocketful Of Laughs		$10	$16	$20	Joanna Cole		DoubleD
1995	Mommies Don't Get Sick		$10	$16	$20	Marylin Hafner		Candle
1995	Passover Magic		$10	$16	$20	Roni Schotter		LBrown
1996	Daddy, Could I Have An Elephant?		$10	$16	$20	Jake Wolf		Green

Hafner   Marylin

Year	Title	VG-	VG	VG+	Fine	Author	Award	Pub
1996	Lunch Bunnies		$10	$16	$20	Kathryn Lasky		LBrown
1997	A Year With Molly And Emmett		$10	$16	$20	Marylin Hafner		Candle
1997	Purim Play		$10	$16	$20	Roni Schotter		LBrown
1998	Show And Tell Bunnies		$10	$14	$18	Kathryn Lasky		Candle
2000	A Carnival Of Animals		$8	$12	$16	Sid Fleischman		Green
2000	Lucille's Snowsuit		$8	$12	$16	Kathryn Lasky		Crown
2000	Molly And Emmett's Camping Adventure		$8	$12	$16	Marylin Hafner		Cricket
2000	Molly And Emmett's Surprise Garden		$8	$12	$16	Marylin Hafner		Cricket
2000	Science Fair Bunnies		$8	$12	$16	Kathryn Lasky		Candle
2001	Starring Lucille		$8	$12	$16	Kathryn Lasky		Knopf
2002	Emmett's Dream		$8	$10	$14	Marylin Hafner		Cricket
2003	Lucille Camps In		$8	$10	$14	Kathryn Lasky		Knopf
2004	Pocket Poems		$8	$10	$14	Bobbi Katz		Dutton
2004	The Pepins And Their Problems		$8	$10	$14	Polly Horvath		FSG

Hague   Michael

Year	Title	VG-	VG	VG+	Fine	Author	Award	Pub
1978	The Cabbage Moth And The Shamrock		$40	$60	$80	Ethel Marbach		Stan&E
1979	A Necklace Of Fallen Stars		$25	$35	$50	Beth Hilgartner		LBrown
1979	Dream Weaver		$30	$45	$60	Jane Yolen		Collins
1980	A Mouse Called Junction		$18	$25	$35	Julia Cunningham		Pan
1980	Demetrius And The Golden Goblet		$18	$25	$35	Eve Bunting		HBJ
1980	East Of The Sun And West Of The Moon		$18	$25	$35	Kathleen & Michael Hague		HBJ
1980	Moments		$18	$25	$35	Lee Bennett Hopkins		HBJ
1980	The Wind In The Willows		$18	$25	$35	Kenneth Grahame		Ariel
1981	Hans Christian Andersen Fairy Tales		$18	$25	$35	Hans Christian Andersen		Holt
1981	The Man Who Kept House		$18	$25	$35	Kathleen & Michael Hague		HBJ
1981	The Night Before Christmas		$18	$25	$35	Clement C. Moore		HR&W
1981	The Pilgrim's Regress		$18	$25	$35	C.S. Lewis		EerdB
1982	The Dragon Kite		$16	$25	$30	Nancy Luenn		HBJ
1982	The Unicorn And The Lake		$16	$25	$30	Marianna Mayer		Dial
1982	The Wizard Of Oz		$16	$25	$30	L. Frank Baum		HR&W
1983	Beauty And The Beast		$16	$25	$30	Deborah Apy		HR&W
1983	The Lion, The Witch, And The Wardrobe		$16	$25	$30	C.S. Lewis		Macmil
1983	The Reluctant Dragon		$16	$25	$30	Kenneth Grahame		HR&W
1983	The Velveteen Rabbit		$16	$25	$30	Margery Williams		HR&W
1984	Alphabears: An ABC Book		$16	$25	$30	Kathleen Hague		HR&W
1984	Mother Goose		$16	$25	$30	Michael Hague		HR&W
1984	Rapunzel		$16	$25	$30	Jacob & Wilhelm Grimm		Creat
1984	The Frog Princess		$16	$25	$30	Elizabeth Isele		Crowell
1984	The Hobbit		$16	$25	$30	J. R. R. Tolkien		HM
1985	A Child's Book Of Prayers		$16	$25	$30	Michael Hague		HR&W
1985	Aesop's Fables		$16	$25	$30	Aesop		HR&W
1985	Alice's Adventures In Wonderland		$16	$25	$30	Lewis Carroll		HR&W
1985	The Legend Of The Veery Bird		$16	$25	$30	Kathleen Hague		HBJ
1986	Numbears		$14	$20	$30	Kathleen Hague		Holt
1986	Out Of The Nursery, Into The Night		$14	$20	$30	Kathleen Hague		Holt
1987	Peter Pan		$14	$20	$30	J. M. Barrie		Holt
1987	The Secret Garden		$14	$20	$30	Frances Hodgson Burnett		Holt
1988	The Land Of Nod		$14	$20	$30	Robert Louis Stevenson		Holt
1989	Bear Hugs		$14	$20	$25	Kathleen Hague		Holt
1989	Cinderella, & Other Tales From Perrault		$14	$20	$25	Charles Perrault		Holt
1989	Rootabaga Stories		$14	$20	$25	Carl Sandburg		HBJ
1989	The Fairies: A Poem		$14	$20	$25	William Allingham		Holt
1989	The Unicorn Alphabet		$14	$20	$25	Marianna Meyer		Dial
1990	Jingle Bells		$12	$18	$25	James Pierpont		Holt
1990	Old Mother West Wind		$12	$18	$25	Thornton W. Burgess		Holt
1990	The Lord Of The Rings		$12	$18	$25	J. R. R. Tolkien		Easton
1990	We Wish You A Merry Christmas		$12	$18	$25	Michael Hague		Holt
1991	Deck The Halls		$12	$18	$25	Michael Hague		Holt
1991	O Christmas Tree		$12	$18	$25	Michael Hague		Holt
1991	The Borrowers		$12	$18	$25	Mary Norton		HBJ
1992	South Pacific		$12	$18	$25	James Michener		HBJ
1992	The Teddy Bears Picnic		$12	$18	$25	Jimmy Kennedy		Holt
1992	Twinkle Twinkle Little Star		$12	$18	$25	Jane Taylor		Morrow
1993	Little Women Or Meg, Jo, Beth And Amy		$12	$16	$20	Louisa May Alcott		Holt

Hague   Michael

Year	Title	VG-	VG	VG+	Fine	Author	Award	Pub
1993	Teddy Bear, Teddy Bear		$12	$16	$20	Michael Hague		Morrow
1993	The Fairy Tales Of Oscar Wilde		$12	$16	$20	Oscar Wilde		Holt
1993	The Rainbow Fairy Book		$12	$16	$20	Andrew Lang (edited)		Morrow
1994	Sleep, Baby, Sleep		$12	$16	$20	Michael Hague (selected)		Morrow
1994	The Little Mermaid		$12	$16	$20	Hans Christian Andersen		Holt
1995	The Book Of Dragons		$10	$16	$20	Michael Hague (selected)		Morrow
1995	The Children's Book Of Virtues		$10	$16	$20	William J. Bennett		S&S
1995	The Owl And The Pussy-Cat		$10	$16	$20	Edward Lear		NSBooks
1996	Michael Hague's Family Christmas Treasury		$10	$16	$20	Michael Hague		Holt
1996	Michael Hague's Family Easter Treasury		$10	$16	$20	Michael Hague		Holt
1996	The Perfect Present		$10	$16	$20	Michael Hague		Morrow
1997	Calendarbears		$10	$16	$20	Kathleen Hague		Holt
1997	Little Treasury Of Christmas Carols		$10	$16	$20	Michael Hague		Garrard
1997	The 23rd Psalm		$10	$16	$20	Bible		Holt
1997	The Children's Book Of Heroes		$10	$16	$20	William J. Bennett		S&S
1997	The Story Of Doctor Dolittle		$10	$16	$20	Hugh Lofting		Morrow
1999	Michael Hague's World Of Unicorns		$10	$14	$18	Michael Hague		Holt
1999	Ten Little Bears		$10	$14	$18	Kathleen Hague		Morrow
2000	A Wind In The Willows Christmas		$8	$12	$16	Kenneth Grahame		SeaStar
2001	Book Of Pirates		$8	$12	$16	Michael Hague		HCollins
2001	Kate Culhane		$8	$12	$16	Michael Hague		SeaStar
2001	Teddy Bears' Mother Goose		$8	$12	$16	Michael Hague		Holt
2001	The Tale Of Peter Rabbit		$8	$12	$16	Beatrix Potter		SeaStar
2001	The Voyages Of Doctor Dolittle		$8	$12	$16	Hugh Lofting		HCollins
2002	Good Night, Fairies		$8	$10	$14	Kathleen Hague		SeaStar
2002	Michael Hague's Book Of Fairy Poetry		$8	$10	$14	Michael Hague (selected)		HCollins
2002	The Children's Book Of Home And Family		$8	$10	$14	William J. Bennett		DoubleD
2002	The Teddy Bears' Picnic		$8	$10	$14	Jimmy Kennedy		Holt
2003	Peter Pan		$8	$10	$14	J. M. Barrie		Holt
2003	The Life And Adventures Of Santa Claus		$8	$10	$14	L. Frank Baum		Holt
2003	The Nutcracker		$8	$10	$14	E. T. A. Hoffmann		SeaStar

Haley   Gail E.

Year	Title	VG-	VG	VG+	Fine	Author	Award	Pub
1962	My Kingdom For A Dragon	$70	$90	$120		Gail Haley		Crozet
1964	One, Two, Buckle My Shoe	$50	$60	$80		Gail Haley		DoubleD
1965	Koalas	$40	$60	$70		Bernice Kohn Hunt		P-Hall
1965	The Peek-A-Boo Book Of Puppies & Kittens	$40	$60	$70		Hannah Rush		TNelson
1966	Which Is Which?	$40	$60	$70		Solveig Paulson Russell		P-Hall
1970	A Story, A Story		$180	$260	$340	Gail Haley	CM	Athenm
1971	Altogether, One At A Time		$30	$50	$60	E L Konigsburg		Athenm
1971	Noah's Ark		$30	$50	$60	Gail Haley		Athenm
1973	Jack Jouett's Ride		$30	$50	$60	Gail Haley		Viking
1975	The Abominable Swamp Man		$30	$40	$60	Gail Haley		Viking
1976	The Post Office Cat		$60	$80	$120	Gail Haley	GM	Scribnr
1977	Go Away, Stay Away!		$25	$40	$50	Gail Haley		Scribnr
1978	Costumes For Plays And Playing		$25	$40	$50	Gail Haley		Metheun
1980	The Green Man		$25	$35	$50	Gail Haley		Scribnr
1984	Birdsong		$20	$30	$40	Gail Haley		Crown
1986	Jack And The Bean Tree		$20	$30	$40	Gail Haley		Crown
1988	Jack And The Fire Dragon		$18	$25	$35	Gail Haley		Crown
1990	Sea Tale		$16	$25	$30	Gail Haley		Dutton
1991	Puss In Boots		$16	$25	$30	Gail Haley		Dutton
1992	Mountain Jack Tales		$16	$25	$30	Gail Haley		Dutton
1993	Dream Peddler		$16	$25	$30	Gail Haley		Dutton
1994	Imagine That		$14	$20	$30	David M Considine		TIP
1996	Two Bad Boys		$12	$18	$25	Gail Haley		Dutton

Halperin   Wendy

Year	Title	VG-	VG	VG+	Fine	Author	Award	Pub
1991	The Lampfish Of Twill		$16	$25	$30	Janet Taylor Lisle		Orchard
1993	Hunting The White Cow		$12	$16	$20	Tres Seymour		Orchard
1995	Homeplace		$10	$16	$20	Anne Shelby Shelby		Orchard
1996	When Chickens Grow Teeth		$10	$16	$20	Wendy Halperin		Orchard
1997	A White Heron		$10	$16	$20	Sarah Orne Jewett		Candle
1998	A Little Shopping		$10	$14	$18	Cynthia Rylant		S&S

Halperin   Wendy

Year	Title	VG-	VG	VG+	Fine	Author	Award	Pub
1998	In Aunt Lucy's Kitchen		$10	$14	$18	Cynthia Rylant		S&S
1998	Once Upon A Company		$10	$14	$18	Wendy Halperin		Orchard
1998	Sophie And Rose		$10	$14	$18	Kathryn Lasky		Candle
1999	Full Belly Bowl		$10	$14	$18	Jim Aylesworth		Athenm
2000	Bonaparte		$8	$12	$16	Marsha Wilson Chall		DK
2001	Love Is...		$8	$12	$16	Wendy Halperin		S&S
2001	Summer Party		$8	$12	$16	Cynthia Rylant		S&S
2002	Let's Go Home		$8	$10	$14	Cynthia Rylant		S&S
2002	Wedding Flowers		$8	$10	$14	Cynthia Rylant		S&S
2003	The Secret Remedy Book		$8	$10	$14	Karin Cates		Orchard
2003	Turn! Turn! Turn!		$8	$10	$14	Pete Seeger		S&S
2004	The Visit		$8	$10	$14	Reeve Lindbergh		Dial

Handford   Martin

Year	Title	VG-	VG	VG+	Fine	Author	Award	Pub
1987	Where's Waldo?		$80	$120	$160	Martin Handford		LBrown
1987	Where's Wally?		$60	$80	$120	Martin Handford		Walker
1988	Find Waldo Now		$30	$50	$60	Martin Handford		LBrown
1988	Where's Wally Now?		$14	$20	$25	Martin Handford		Walker
1989	The Great Waldo Search		$14	$20	$25	Martin Handford		LBrown
1993	Where's Waldo?: In Hollywood		$12	$16	$20	Martin Handford		Candle
1997	Where's Waldo Now?		$10	$14	$18	Martin Handford		Candle
1997	Where's Waldo?: The Fantastic Journey		$10	$14	$18	Martin Handford		Candle
1997	Where's Waldo?: The Wonder Book		$10	$14	$18	Martin Handford		Candle

Handforth   Thomas

Year	Title	VG-	VG	VG+	Fine	Author	Award	Pub
1929	Toutou In Bondage	$160	$220	$280		Elizabeth Coatsworth		Macmil
1930	Tranquilina's Paradise	$70	$100	$120		Susan Smith		Minton
1938	Mei Li	$960	$1,200	$1,600		Thomas Handforth	CM	DD
1939	Faraway Meadow	$140	$200	$240		Thomas Handforth		DD
1944	The Dragon & The Eagle	$140	$180	$220		Delia Goetz		FPA

Harris   Jim

Year	Title	VG-	VG	VG+	Fine	Author	Award	Pub
1992	The Three Little Javelinas		$20	$30	$40	Susan Lowell		North
1993	A Tree In Sprocket's Pocket		$12	$16	$20	Paulette Nehemias		Concord
1993	Wiggler's Worms: Stories About God's Green Earth		$10	$16	$20	Paulette Nehemias		Concord
1994	Goose And The Mountain Lion		$14	$20	$30	Marian Harris		North
1994	The Tortoise And The Jackrabbit		$14	$20	$30	Susan Lowell		North
1995	Rapunzel		$10	$16	$20	Marian Harris		Accord
1995	The Legend Of The Whistle Pig Wrangler		$14	$20	$25	Kate Allen		Kumquat
1995	The Lizard Who Followed Me Home		$14	$20	$25	Kate Allen		Kumquat
1995	The Three Little Pigs		$10	$16	$20	Marian Harris		Accord
1996	All The Alternatives To Aging Are Bad		$10	$16	$20	R. Knight Steel (selected)		Cracom
1996	Ten Little Dinosaurs		$10	$16	$20	Pattie L. Schnetzler		Accord
1997	Jack And The Giant: A Story Full Of Beans		$10	$16	$20	Jim Harris		RMoon
1997	Mystery In Bugtown		$10	$16	$20	William Boniface		Accord
1998	Bible ABC		$10	$14	$18	Eric Metaxas		TNelson
1998	Slim And Miss Prim		$10	$14	$18	Robert Kinerk		RMoon
1998	The Treasure Hunter		$10	$14	$18	William Boniface		Accord
1998	Tuesday In Arizona		$10	$14	$18	Marian Harris		Pelican
1999	The Three Little Dinosaurs		$10	$14	$18	Jim Harris		Pelican
2001	Petite Rouge		$8	$12	$16	Mike Artell		Dial
2002	The Trouble With Cauliflower		$8	$10	$14	Jane Sutton		Dial
2003	Three Little Cajun Pigs		$8	$10	$14	Mike Artell		Dial

Hauman   George and Doris

Year	Title	VG-	VG	VG+	Fine	Author	Award	Pub
1934	Bread & Cheese	$70	$100	$120		George Hauman		Macmil
1935	I Know A Surprise	$50	$70	$90		Dorothy Walter Baruch		LL&S
1935	Three Circus Days	$50	$70	$90		Edna Henry Lee Turpin		Macmil
1936	Buttons	$50	$60	$80		George Hauman		Macmil
1937	The Air Pilot	$50	$60	$80		Henry Bolles Lent		Macmil
1937	The Storekeeper	$50	$60	$80		Henry Bolles Lent		Macmil

Hauman   George and Doris

Year	Title	VG-	VG	VG+	Fine	Author	Award	Pub
1938	Happy Harbor	$50	$60	$80		George Hauman		Macmil
1938	Stories That Never Grow Old	$50	$60	$80		Watty Piper (pseud.)		P&Munk
1939	Border Girl	$50	$60	$80		Genevieve May Fox		LBrown
1941	Tales From Storyland	$50	$60	$80		Watty Piper (pseud.)		P&Munk
1942	The Snow Queen	$50	$60	$80		Hans Christian Andersen		Macmil
1944	Decky's Secret	$50	$60	$80		Anne Stearns Molloy		HM
1944	Little Jonathan	$50	$60	$80		Miriam Evangeline Mason		Macmil
1945	Happy Jack	$40	$60	$70		Miriam Evangeline Mason		Macmil
1945	The Children's Christmas	$40	$60	$70		Wayne Norman		Boston
1946	Surprise For Timmy	$40	$60	$70		George Hauman		Macmil
1954	The Little Engine That Could	$80	$100	$140		Watty Piper (pseud.)		P&Munk

Hawkes   Kevin

Year	Title	VG-	VG	VG+	Fine	Author	Award	Pub
1991	Hey, Hay!: A Wagonful Of Funny Homonym Riddles		$16	$25	$30	Marvin Terbian		Clarion
1991	Lady Bugatti		$12	$18	$25	Joyce Maxner		LL&S
1991	Then The Troll Heard The Squeak		$12	$18	$25	Kevin Hawkes		LL&S
1992	His Royal Buckliness		$12	$18	$25	Kevin Hawkes		LL&S
1992	The Turnip		$12	$18	$25	Walter De La Mare		Godine
1993	By The Light Of The Halloween Moon		$12	$16	$20	Caroline Stutson		LL&S
1994	The Librarian Who Measured The Earth		$12	$16	$20	Kathryn Lasky		Joy
1994	The Nose		$12	$16	$20	Catherine Cowan (retold)		LL&S
1995	The Enormous Snore		$10	$16	$20	M. L. Miller		Putnam
1996	Dreamland		$10	$16	$20	Roni Schotter		Orchard
1996	My Little Sister Ate One Hare		$10	$16	$20	Bill Grossman		Crown
1996	Painting The Wind		$10	$16	$20	Michelle Dionetti		LBrown
1997	Boogie Bones		$10	$16	$20	Elizabeth Loredo		Putnam
1997	Marven Of The Great North Woods		$10	$16	$20	Kathryn Lasky		HBrace
1998	Imagine That!: Poems Of Never-Was		$10	$14	$18	Jack Perlutsky (selected)		Knopf
1998	My Friend The Piano		$10	$14	$18	Catherine Cowan		LL&S
1998	The Liars' Book		$10	$14	$18	Jane, Linda Yolen, Mannheim		BSP
1998	The Poombah Of Badoombah		$10	$14	$18	Dee Lillegard		Putnam
1999	And To Think That We Thought We'd Never Be Friends		$10	$14	$18	Mary Ann Hoberman		Crown
1999	Cow Pokes		$10	$14	$18	Caroline Stutson		LL&S
1999	Weslandia		$10	$14	$18	Paul Fleischman		Candle
2000	I Was A Rat!		$8	$12	$16	Philip Pullman		Knopf
2000	Island Of The Aunts		$8	$12	$16	Eva Ibbotson		Dutton
2000	Jason's Bears		$8	$12	$16	Marion Dane Bauer		Hyper
2000	Timothy Tunny Swallowed A Bunny		$8	$12	$16	Bill Grossman		LauraG
2001	A Christmas Treasury		$8	$12	$16	Kevin Hawkes		HCollins
2001	A Necklace Of Raindrops & Other Stories		$8	$12	$16	Joan Aiken		Knopf
2001	Dial-A-Ghost		$8	$12	$16	Eva Ibbotson		Dutton
2001	Handel		$8	$12	$16	M. T. Anderson		Candle
2001	Journey To The River Sea		$8	$12	$16	Eva Ibbotson		Dutton
2002	The Great Ghost Rescue		$8	$10	$14	Eva Ibbotson		Dutton
2003	Not Just A Witch		$8	$10	$14	Eva Ibbotson		Dutton
2003	The Man Who Made Time Travel		$8	$10	$14	Kathryn Lasky		Kroupa
2003	The Worry Week		$8	$10	$14	Anne Lindbergh		Godine
2004	Granite Baby		$8	$10	$14	Lynne Bertrand		FSG
2004	Me, All Alone, At The End Of The World		$8	$10	$14	M. T. Anderson		Candle
2004	My Little Sister Hugged An Ape		$8	$10	$14	Bill Grossman		Knopf
2004	Sidewalk Circus		$8	$10	$14	Paul Fleischman		Candle
2004	The Haunting Of Hiram		$8	$10	$14	Eva Ibbotson		Dutton
2004	The Star Of Kazan		$8	$10	$14	Eva Ibbotson		Dutton

Hawkins   Colin

Year	Title	VG-	VG	VG+	Fine	Author	Award	Pub
1982	The Social Climbing Cat		$16	$25	$30	Stewart Cowley		S&S
1983	Adding Animals		$14	$20	$25	Colin Hawkins		Putnam
1983	Boo! Who?		$25	$35	$50	Colin & Jacqui Hawkins		HR&W
1983	Pat The Cat		$25	$35	$50	Colin & Jacqui Hawkins		Putnam
1983	What Time Is It, Mr. Wolf?		$25	$35	$50	Colin & Jacqui Hawkins		Putnam
1984	Mig The Pig		$16	$25	$30	Colin & Jacqui Hawkins		Putnam
1984	Snap! Snap!		$16	$25	$30	Colin & Jacqui Hawkins		Putnam
1984	Take Away Monsters		$12	$18	$25	Colin Hawkins		Putnam
1985	Incy Wincy Spider		$16	$25	$30	Colin & Jacqui Hawkins		VK

Hawkins — Colin

Year	Title	VG-	VG	VG+	Fine	Author	Award	Pub
1985	Jen The Hen		$16	$25	$30	Colin & Jacqui Hawkins		Putnam
1985	My First Book		$16	$25	$30	Colin & Jacqui Hawkins		VK
1985	Old Mother Hubbard		$16	$25	$30	Colin & Jacqui Hawkins		Putnam
1985	Round The Garden		$16	$25	$30	Colin & Jacqui Hawkins		VK
1985	Spooks		$16	$25	$30	Colin & Jacqui Hawkins		SBurdet
1985	The Elephant		$16	$25	$30	Colin & Jacqui Hawkins		VK
1985	This Little Pig		$16	$25	$30	Colin & Jacqui Hawkins		VK
1985	Vampires		$16	$25	$30	Enid Von Bluoton		SBurdet
1985	Witches		$16	$25	$30	Colin & Jacqui Hawkins		SBurdet
1986	Dip, Dip, Dip		$12	$16	$20	Colin Hawkins		AMP
1986	Farmyard Sounds		$14	$20	$30	Colin & Jacqui Hawkins		Crown
1986	I'm Not Sleepy!		$14	$20	$30	Colin & Jacqui Hawkins		Crown
1986	Jungle Sounds		$14	$20	$30	Colin & Jacqui Hawkins		Crown
1986	Max And The Magic Word		$14	$20	$30	Colin & Jacqui Hawkins		VK
1986	One Finger, One Thumb		$14	$20	$30	Colin & Jacqui Hawkins		AMP
1986	Oops-A-Daisy		$14	$20	$30	Colin & Jacqui Hawkins		AMP
1986	See You Later		$12	$16	$20	Tony Bradman		Dial
1986	Tog The Dog		$14	$20	$30	Colin & Jacqui Hawkins		Piccad
1986	Where's Bear?		$14	$20	$30	Colin & Jacqui Hawkins		AMP
1986	Where's My Mommy?		$14	$20	$30	Colin & Jacqui Hawkins		Crown
1987	Busy ABC		$14	$20	$30	Colin & Jacqui Hawkins		VK
1987	Mr. Wolf's Birthday Surprise		$12	$16	$20	Colin Hawkins		Heine
1987	Terrible, Terrible Tiger		$14	$20	$30	Colin & Jacqui Hawkins		Walker
1987	The Wizard's Cat		$14	$20	$30	Colin & Jacqui Hawkins		Walker
1988	Here's A Happy Elephant		$14	$20	$30	Colin & Jacqui Hawkins		Walker
1988	Here's A Happy Pig		$14	$20	$30	Colin & Jacqui Hawkins		Walker
1988	How Many Are In This Old Car?		$14	$20	$30	Colin & Jacqui Hawkins		Putnam
1988	Zug The Bug		$14	$20	$30	Colin & Jacqui Hawkins		Putnam
1989	Crocodile Creek		$14	$20	$25	Colin & Jacqui Hawkins		DoubleD
1989	Noah Built An Ark One Day		$14	$20	$25	Colin & Jacqui Hawkins		Putnam
1990	The House That Jack Built		$12	$18	$25	Colin & Jacqui Hawkins		Putnam
1990	When I Was One		$12	$18	$25	Colin & Jacqui Hawkins		Viking
1991	Number Five		$12	$18	$25	Colin & Jacqui Hawkins		Bodley
1991	Number Four		$12	$18	$25	Colin & Jacqui Hawkins		Bodley
1991	Number One		$12	$18	$25	Colin & Jacqui Hawkins		Bodley
1991	Number Three		$12	$18	$25	Colin & Jacqui Hawkins		Bodley
1991	Number Two		$12	$18	$25	Colin & Jacqui Hawkins		Bodley
1992	Hey Diddle Diddle		$12	$18	$25	Colin & Jacqui Hawkins		Candle
1992	Humpty Dumpty		$12	$18	$25	Colin & Jacqui Hawkins		Candle
1993	Come For A Ride On The Ghost Train		$12	$16	$20	Colin & Jacqui Hawkins		Candle
1994	Pirate Ship		$10	$14	$18	Colin Hawkins		Cobble
1995	Pat The Cat And Friends		$10	$16	$20	Colin & Jacqui Hawkins		DK
1996	Here's A Happy Kitten		$10	$16	$20	Colin & Jacqui Hawkins		Candle
1996	Here's A Happy Puppy		$10	$16	$20	Colin & Jacqui Hawkins		Candle
1998	Whose House?		$10	$14	$18	Colin & Jacqui Hawkins		Barrn
2000	Number Eight		$8	$12	$16	Colin & Jacqui Hawkins		DK
2000	Number Nine		$8	$12	$16	Colin & Jacqui Hawkins		DK
2000	Number Seven		$8	$12	$16	Colin & Jacqui Hawkins		DK
2000	Number Six		$8	$12	$16	Colin & Jacqui Hawkins		DK
2000	Number Ten		$8	$12	$16	Colin & Jacqui Hawkins		DK
2001	Creepy Castle		$8	$12	$16	Colin & Jacqui Hawkins		Barrn
2001	One, Two, Guess Who?		$8	$12	$16	Colin & Jacqui Hawkins		Barrn
2004	Fairytale News		$8	$10	$14	Colin & Jacqui Hawkins		Candle

Hawkinson — John

Year	Title	VG-	VG	VG+	Fine	Author	Award	Pub
1967	Indian Two Feet And His Eagle Feather	$30	$40	$50		Margaret Friskey		CP
1971	Indian Two Feet And The Wolf Cubs		$25	$35	$50	Margaret Friskey		CP
1974	Indian Two Feet And The Grizzly Bear		$20	$30	$40	Margaret Friskey		CP
1977	Indian Two Feet And The ABC Moose Hunt		$20	$30	$40	Margaret Friskey		CP
1980	Indian Two Feet Rides Alone		$18	$25	$35	Margaret Friskey		CP

Hayes — Geoffrey

Year	Title	VG-	VG	VG+	Fine	Author	Award	Pub
1976	Bear By Himself		$30	$40	$60	Geoffrey Hayes		H&Row
1977	The Alligator And His Uncle Tooth		$25	$40	$50	Geoffrey Hayes		H&Row

Hayes   Geoffrey

Year	Title	VG-	VG	VG+	Fine	Author	Award	Pub
1977	When The Wind Blew		$25	$40	$50	Margaret Wise Brown	NYT	H&Row
1978	Muffie Mouse And The Busy Birthday		$20	$30	$40	Joan Lowery Nixon		Seabury
1978	Patrick Comes To Puttyville		$20	$30	$40	Geoffrey Hayes		H&Row
1980	The Secret Inside		$18	$25	$35	Geoffrey Hayes		H&Row
1982	Elroy And The Witch's Child		$16	$25	$30	Geoffrey Hayes		H&Row
1982	Moon Dragon		$16	$25	$30	Fran Manushkin		Macmil
1983	Hocus And Pocus At The Circus		$16	$25	$30	Fran Manushkin		H&Row
1984	Patrick And Ted		$16	$25	$30	Geoffrey Hayes		4Winds
1985	Christmas In Puttyville		$16	$25	$30	Geoffrey Hayes		Random
1985	Patrick Buys A Coat		$16	$25	$30	Geoffrey Hayes		Knopf
1985	Patrick Eats His Dinner		$16	$25	$30	Geoffrey Hayes		Knopf
1985	Patrick Goes To Bed		$16	$25	$30	Geoffrey Hayes		Knopf
1985	Patrick Takes A Bath		$16	$25	$30	Geoffrey Hayes		Knopf
1985	The Mystery Of The Pirate Ghost		$16	$25	$30	Geoffrey Hayes		Random
1986	The Lantern Keeper's Bedtime Book		$14	$20	$30	Geoffrey Hayes		Random
1987	Patrick And Ted At The Beach		$14	$20	$30	Geoffrey Hayes		Random
1988	Patrick And Ted Ride The Train		$14	$20	$30	Geoffrey Hayes		Random
1988	The Secret Of Foghorn Island		$14	$20	$30	Geoffrey Hayes		Random
1991	The Treasure Of The Lost Lagoon		$12	$18	$25	Geoffrey Hayes		Random
1994	The Curse Of The Cobweb Queen		$12	$16	$20	Geoffrey Hayes		Random
1995	The Night Of The Circus Monsters		$10	$16	$20	Geoffrey Hayes		Random
1996	Swamp Of The Hideous Zombies		$10	$16	$20	Geoffrey Hayes		Random
1997	House Of The Horrible Ghosts		$10	$16	$20	Geoffrey Hayes		Random
1999	Patrick's Christmas Tree		$10	$14	$18	Geoffrey Hayes		Random
2000	Thump And Plunk		$8	$12	$16	Janice May Udry		HCollins
2001	Brave Little Monster		$8	$12	$16	Ken Baker		HCollins
2001	Patrick And The Big Bully		$8	$12	$16	Geoffrey Hayes		Hyper
2002	Patrick At The Circus		$8	$10	$14	Geoffrey Hayes		Hyper
2003	A Night-Light For Bunny		$8	$10	$14	Geoffrey Hayes		HCollins
2003	Patrick Perks Up		$8	$10	$14	Geoffrey Hayes		Hyper

Haynes   Max

Year	Title	VG-	VG	VG+	Fine	Author	Award	Pub
1992	Sparky's Rainbow Repair		$12	$18	$25	Max Haynes		LL&S
1997	In The Driver's Seat		$8	$12	$16	Max Haynes		Bantam
1998	Bunny Isabel's Easter Egg Hunt		$8	$12	$16	Max Haynes		Dutton
1998	Trick Or Treat, Fraidy Cat		$8	$12	$16	Max Haynes		Dutton
1999	Love And Kisses, Kitty		$8	$12	$16	Max Haynes		Dutton
1999	Ticklemonster And Me		$8	$12	$16	Max Haynes		DoubleD
2000	Grandma's Gone To Live In The Stars		$8	$10	$14	Max Haynes		AWhit

Hays   Michael

Year	Title	VG-	VG	VG+	Fine	Author	Award	Pub
1986	Abiyoyo		$20	$30	$40	Pete Seeger		Macmil
1987	The Gold Cadillac		$14	$20	$30	Mildred D. Taylor		Dial
1988	My Father Doesn't Know About The Woods And Me		$14	$20	$30	Dennis Haseley		Athenm
1989	A Birthday For Blue		$14	$20	$25	Kerry Raines Lydon		AWhit
1990	The Tin Heart		$12	$18	$25	Karen Ackerman		Athenm
1991	Hello, Tree!		$12	$18	$25	Joanne Ryder		LodeS
1992	Jonathan And His Mommy		$12	$18	$25	Irene Smalls		LBrown
1992	Three Wishes		$12	$18	$25	Lucille Clifton		DoubleD
1993	Storm		$12	$16	$20	W. Nikola-Lisa		Athenm
1993	The Boy Who Loved Morning		$12	$16	$20	Shannon K. Jacobs		LBrown
1994	K Is For Kiss Good Night		$12	$16	$20	Jill Sardegna		DelaP
1995	Holding Onto Sunday		$10	$16	$20	Kathryn Osebold Galbraith		McEld
1995	The Hundredth Name		$10	$16	$20	Shulamith Oppenheim		Boyds
1996	Jackie Robinson		$10	$16	$20	Kenneth Rudeen		Harper
1996	Pedro And The Monkey		$10	$16	$20	Robert D. San Souci		Morrow
1997	Because You're Lucky		$10	$16	$20	Irene Smalls		LBrown
1997	The History Of Counting		$10	$16	$20	Denise Schmandt-Besserat		Morrow
1999	Kevin And His Dad		$10	$14	$18	Irene Smalls		LBrown
2001	Abiyoyo Returns		$8	$12	$16	Pete Seeger		S&S
2002	The Boy Who Was Generous With Salt		$8	$10	$14	Corinne Demas		MCaven

Hearn   Diane Dawson

Year	Title	VG-	VG	VG+	Fine	Author	Award	Pub
1975	See My Lovely Poison Ivy		$30	$40	$60	Hearn Lilian.		Athenm
1976	Nora Maeve And Sebi		$20	$30	$40	Andrew M Greeley		Paulist
1976	Spots Are Special!		$20	$30	$40	Kathryn Osebold Galbraith		Athenm
1977	The Wind Thief		$20	$30	$40	Judi Barrett		Athenm
1978	Larry		$20	$30	$40	Diane Dawson Hearn		NAVH
1978	Mother, Mother, I Want Another		$20	$30	$40	Maria Polushkin		Crown
1978	Ms. Glee Was Waiting		$20	$30	$40	Donna Hill		Athenm
1978	My Favorite Teeny Tiny Strawberry Animal Story Library		$20	$30	$40	Maria Polushkin		Straw
1979	Awful Evelina		$18	$25	$35	Susan Beth Pfeffer		AWhit
1979	I Am Not A Pest		$18	$25	$35	Marjorie Weinman Sharmat		Dutton
1979	Jenny, The Halloween Spy		$18	$25	$35	Lillie Patterson		Garrard
1979	Three Foolish Tales		$18	$25	$35	Ann Tompert		Crown
1979	Wish Upon A Birthday		$18	$25	$35	Norma Q. Hare		Garrard
1980	Gloria Chipmunk, Star!		$18	$25	$35	Joan Lowery Nixon		HM
1980	Mixed-Up Mother Goose		$18	$25	$35	Leonard Kessler		Garrard
1980	On The Way To The Movies		$18	$25	$35	Charlotte Herman		Dutton
1980	The Day I Was Born		$18	$25	$35	Marjorie Weinman Sharmat		Dutton
1981	The Blanket That Had To Go		$18	$25	$35	Nancy Evans Cooney		Putnam
1981	The Mouse Family's New Home		$18	$25	$35	Edith Kunhardt		Golden
1982	Roger On His Own		$16	$25	$30	Marcia Keyser		Crown
1983	Good Night, Aunt Lilly		$16	$25	$30	Margaret Madigan		Golden
1983	Monster Birthday Party		$16	$25	$30	Sally Freedman		Whitman
1983	The Christmas Tree Book		$16	$25	$30	Carol North		Golden
1984	Once Upon A Test		$16	$25	$30	Vivian Vande Velde		AWhit
1984	The Doozer Disaster		$16	$25	$30	Michaela Muntean		HR&W
1985	Bert And The Broken Teapot		$16	$25	$30	Tish Sommers		Western
1985	Fraggle Countdown		$16	$25	$30	Michaela Muntean		HR&W
1985	Gobo And The River		$16	$25	$30	Joseph Killorin Brennan		HR&W
1985	Happy Easter, Mother Duck		$16	$25	$30	Elizabeth Winthrop		Western
1986	Whinnie The Lovesick Dragon		$14	$20	$30	Mercer Mayer		Macmil
1987	Jim Henson Presents The Tale Of The Bunny Picnic		$14	$20	$30	Louise Gikow		Scholas
1990	My Brother The Star		$12	$18	$25	Alison Jackson		Dutton
1990	Princess Horrid		$12	$18	$25	Erik Haugaard		Macmil
1991	Crane's Rebound		$12	$18	$25	Alison Jackson		Dutton
1991	Dining With Prunella		$12	$18	$25	Teddy Slater		Silver
1991	Shopping With Samantha		$12	$18	$25	Teddy Slater		Silver
1992	Happy Birthday, Hector		$12	$18	$25	Laura Kingston		Golden
1993	Dad's Dinosaur Day		$12	$16	$20	Diane Dawson Hearn		Macmil
1994	Anna In The Garden		$12	$16	$20	Diane Dawson Hearn		SMoon
1994	Down Dairy Farm Road		$12	$16	$20	C. L. G. Martin		Macmil
1995	Bad Luck Boswell		$10	$16	$20	Diane Dawson Hearn		S&S
1997	The Little Pirate Ship		$10	$16	$20	Mallory Loehr		Random
1997	Turtle Dreams		$10	$16	$20	Marion Dane Bauer		Holiday
1998	Bear's Hiccups		$10	$14	$18	Marion Dane Bauer		Holiday
1998	Christmas In The Forest		$10	$14	$18	Marion Dane Bauer		Holiday
2001	Death Valley		$8	$12	$16	Nancy Smiler Levinson		Holiday
2002	Frog's Best Friend		$8	$10	$14	Marion Dane Bauer		Holiday
2002	North Pole, South Pole		$8	$10	$14	Nancy Smiler Levinson		Holiday

Hedderwick   Mairi

Year	Title	VG-	VG	VG+	Fine	Author	Award	Pub
1972	The Old Woman Who Lived In A Vinegar Bottle		$40	$60	$90	Rumer Godden		Viking
1975	Brave Janet Reachfar		$30	$40	$60	Jane Duncan		Seabury
1975	Herself And Janet Reachfar		$30	$40	$60	Jane Duncan		Macmil
1976	Janet Reachfar And The Kelpie		$30	$40	$60	Jane Duncan		Seabury
1978	Janet Reachfar And Chickabird		$25	$40	$50	Jane Duncan		Seabury
1986	Katie Morag And The Tiresome Ted		$20	$30	$40	Mairi Hedderwick		LBrown
1986	Katie Morag And The Two Grandmothers		$20	$30	$40	Mairi Hedderwick		LBrown
1987	Katie Morag And The Big Boy Cousins		$20	$30	$40	Mairi Hedderwick		LBrown
1987	Katie Morag Delivers The Mail		$20	$30	$40	Mairi Hedderwick		LBrown
1989	P.D. Peebles' Summer Or Winter Book		$18	$25	$35	Mairi Hedderwick		LBrown
1992	Venus Peter Saves The Whale		$16	$25	$30	Christopher Rush		Pelican
2001	Callum's Big Day		$10	$14	$18	Tom Pow		Inyx

Heine   Helme

Year	Title	VG-	VG	VG+	Fine	Author	Award	Pub
1979	The Pigs' Wedding		$25	$40	$50	Helme Heine		Athenm
1980	Merry-Go-Round		$18	$25	$35	Helme Heine		Barrn
1980	Mr. Miller, The Dog		$25	$35	$50	Helme Heine	NYT	Athenm
1982	Friends		$16	$25	$30	Helme Heine		Athenm
1982	King Bounce The 1st		$16	$25	$30	Helme Heine		Neuge
1983	Richard		$16	$25	$30	Helme Heine		Metheun
1983	The Most Wonderful Egg In The World		$16	$25	$30	Helme Heine		Athenm
1985	The Alarm Clock		$16	$25	$30	Helme Heine		Athenm
1985	The Pearl		$16	$25	$30	Helme Heine		Athenm
1985	The Racing Cart		$16	$25	$30	Helme Heine		Athenm
1985	The Visitor		$16	$25	$30	Helme Heine		Athenm
1986	One Day In Paradise		$14	$20	$30	Helme Heine		Athenm
1988	Seven Wild Pigs		$14	$20	$30	Helme Heine		McEld
1989	Prince Bear		$14	$20	$25	Helme Heine		McEld
1990	The Marvelous Journey Through The Night		$12	$18	$25	Helme Heine		FSG
1991	Mollywoop		$12	$18	$25	Helme Heine		FSG
1995	Friends Go Adventuring		$10	$16	$20	Helme Heine		McEld
1998	The Boxer And The Princess		$10	$14	$18	Helme Heine		McEld

Heller   Linda

Year	Title	VG-	VG	VG+	Fine	Author	Award	Pub
1979	Lily At The Table		$18	$25	$35	Linda Heller		Macmil
1980	Alexis And The Golden Ring		$14	$20	$25	Linda Heller		Macmil
1980	Horace Morris		$14	$20	$25	Linda Heller		Macmil
1981	A Picture Book Of Jewish Holidays		$14	$20	$25	David A. Adler		Holiday
1981	Trouble At Goodewoode Manor		$14	$20	$25	Linda Heller		Macmil
1982	A Picture Book Of Hanukkah		$14	$20	$25	David A. Adler		Holiday
1982	A Picture Book Of Passover		$14	$20	$25	David A. Adler		Holiday
1982	The Castle On Hester Street		$14	$20	$25	Linda Heller		JPS
1983	The Magic Stove		$14	$20	$25	Mirra Ginsburg		CM&G

Heller   Ruth

Year	Title	VG-	VG	VG+	Fine	Author	Award	Pub
1981	Chickens Aren't The Only Ones		$18	$25	$35	Ruth Heller		G&D
1982	Animals Born Alive And Well		$14	$20	$25	Ruth Heller		G&D
1983	Purim		$14	$20	$25	Miriam Schlein		Behman
1983	The Reason For A Flower		$14	$20	$25	Ruth Heller		G&D
1984	Plants That Never Ever Bloom		$12	$18	$25	Ruth Heller		G&D
1985	Ruth Heller's How To Hide A Butterfly		$12	$18	$25	Ruth Heller		G&D
1985	Ruth Heller's How To Hide A Polar Bear		$12	$18	$25	Ruth Heller		G&D
1985	Ruth Heller's How To Hide An Octopus		$12	$18	$25	Ruth Heller		G&D
1986	Ruth Heller's How To Hide A Crocodile		$12	$16	$20	Ruth Heller		G&D
1986	Ruth Heller's How To Hide A Gray Treefrog		$12	$16	$20	Ruth Heller		G&D
1986	Ruth Heller's How To Hide A Whip-Poor-Will		$12	$16	$20	Ruth Heller		G&D
1987	A Cache Of Jewels & Other Collective Nouns		$12	$16	$20	Ruth Heller		G&D
1988	King Of The Birds		$12	$16	$20	Shirley Climo		Crowell
1988	Kites Sail High		$12	$16	$20	Ruth Heller		G&D
1989	Many Luscious Lollipops		$12	$16	$20	Ruth Heller		G&D
1989	The Egyptian Cinderella		$12	$16	$20	Shirley Climo		Crowell
1990	Merry-Go-Round		$10	$16	$20	Ruth Heller		G&D
1991	Up, Up, And Away		$10	$16	$20	Ruth Heller		G&D
1993	The Korean Cinderella		$10	$16	$20	Shirley Climo		HCollins
1994	Blue Potatoes, Orange Tomatoes		$10	$14	$18	Rosalind Creasy		Sierra
1994	King Solomon And The Bee		$10	$14	$18	Dalia Hardof Renberg		HCollins
1995	Behind The Mask		$10	$14	$18	Ruth Heller		G&D
1995	Color, Color, Color, Color		$10	$14	$18	Ruth Heller		Putnam
1995	Ruth Heller's How To Hide A Meadow Frog		$10	$14	$18	Ruth Heller		G&D
1995	Ruth Heller's How To Hide A Parakeet		$10	$14	$18	Ruth Heller		G&D
1997	Mine, All Mine		$8	$12	$16	Ruth Heller		G&D
1998	Fantastic! Wow! And Unreal!		$8	$12	$16	Ruth Heller		G&D
2000	A Sea Within A Sea		$8	$10	$14	Ruth Heller		G&D
2000	Gálapagos Means "Tortoises"		$8	$10	$14	Ruth Heller		Sierra

Helquist — Brett

Year	Title	VG-	VG	VG+	Fine	Author	Award	Pub
1999	The Bad Beginning		$240	$340	$460	Lemony Snicket		HCollins
1999	The Reptile Room		$200	$280	$380	Lemony Snicket		HCollins
2000	The Austere Academy		$100	$160	$220	Lemony Snicket		HCollins
2000	The Miserable Mill		$120	$180	$240	Lemony Snicket		HCollins
2000	The Wide Window		$140	$220	$300	Lemony Snicket		Harper
2001	The Ersatz Elevator		$50	$80	$100	Lemony Snicket		HCollins
2001	The Hostile Hospital		$50	$80	$100	Lemony Snicket		HCollins
2001	The Revenge Of Randal Reese-Rat		$10	$14	$18	Tor Seidler		FSG
2001	The Vile Village		$50	$80	$100	Lemony Snicket		HCollins
2002	Howie Monroe And The Doghouse Of Doom		$8	$12	$16	James Howe		Athenm
2002	Invasion Of The Mind Swappers From Asteroid 6		$8	$12	$16	James Howe		Athenm
2002	Milly And The Macy's Parade		$8	$12	$16	Shana Corey		Scholas
2002	The Book Of Alfar		$8	$12	$16	Peter Hassinger		LauraG
2002	The Carnivorous Carnival		$25	$35	$50	Lemony Snicket		HCollins
2003	Amazing Odorous Adventures Of Stinky Dog		$8	$12	$16	James Howe		Athenm
2003	Bud Barkin, Private Eye		$8	$12	$16	James Howe		Athenm
2003	Chasing Vermeer		$35	$50	$70	Blue Balliett		Scholas
2003	Screaming Mummies Of The Pharaoh's Tomb II		$8	$12	$16	James Howe		Athenm
2003	The Slippery Slope		$18	$25	$35	Lemony Snicket		HCollins
2004	Roger, The Jolly Pirate		$8	$10	$14	Brett Helquist		HCollins

Henkes — Kevin

Year	Title	VG-	VG	VG+	Fine	Author	Award	Pub
1981	All Alone		$35	$50	$70	Kevin Henkes		Green
1982	Clean Enough		$25	$35	$50	Kevin Henkes		Green
1983	Margaret & Taylor		$25	$35	$50	Kevin Henkes		Green
1984	Return To Sender		$20	$30	$40	Kevin Henkes		Green
1985	Bailey Goes Camping		$20	$30	$40	Kevin Henkes		Green
1986	A Weekend With Wendell		$20	$30	$40	Kevin Henkes		Green
1986	Grandpa & Bo		$20	$30	$40	Kevin Henkes		Green
1987	Sheila Rae, The Brave		$20	$30	$40	Kevin Henkes		Green
1987	Two Under Par		$20	$30	$40	Kevin Henkes		Green
1988	Chester's Way		$18	$25	$35	Kevin Henkes		Green
1988	The Zebra Wall		$18	$25	$35	Kevin Henkes		Green
1989	Jessica		$18	$25	$35	Kevin Henkes		Green
1989	Shhhh		$18	$25	$35	Kevin Henkes		Green
1990	Julius, The Baby Of The World		$16	$25	$30	Kevin Henkes		Green
1991	Chrysanthemum		$16	$25	$30	Kevin Henkes		Green
1992	Words Of Stone		$16	$25	$30	Kevin Henkes		Green
1993	Owen		$40	$60	$80	Kevin Henkes	CH	Green
1995	Good-Bye, Curtis		$14	$20	$25	Marisabina Russo		Green
1995	Protecting Marie		$14	$20	$25	Kevin Henkes		Green
1996	Lilly's Purple Plastic Purse		$12	$18	$25	Kevin Henkes		Green
1997	Sun & Spoon		$12	$18	$25	Kevin Henkes		Green
1999	The Birthday Room		$12	$16	$20	Kevin Henkes		Green
2000	Wemberly Worried		$10	$14	$18	Kevin Henkes		Green
2001	Sheila Rae's Peppermint Stick		$10	$14	$18	Kevin Henkes		HFest
2002	Owen's Marshmallow Chick		$8	$12	$16	Kevin Henkes		HFest
2003	Julius's Candy Corn		$8	$12	$16	Kevin Henkes		HFest
2003	Olive's Ocean		$25	$35	$50	Kevin Henkes	NH	Green
2003	Owen's Marshmallow Chick Book & Finger Puppet		$8	$12	$16	Kevin Henkes		Green
2003	Sheila Rae's Peppermint Stick Book & Finger Puppet		$8	$12	$16	Kevin Henkes		Green
2003	Wemberly's Ice-Cream Star		$8	$12	$16	Kevin Henkes		HFest
2004	Kitten's First Full Moon		$25	$40	$50	Kevin Henkes	CM	Green
2004	Lilly's Chocolate Heart		$8	$10	$14	Kevin Henkes		Green

Henry — Marie H.

Year	Title	VG-	VG	VG+	Fine	Author	Award	Pub
1985	Bunnies All Day Long		$16	$25	$30	Amy Ehrlich		Dial
1985	Bunnies And Their Grandma		$16	$25	$30	Amy Ehrlich		Dial
1989	The Wedding Of Brown Bear & White Bear		$12	$16	$20	Martine Beck		LBrown
1991	The Rescue Of Brown Bear & White Bear		$10	$16	$20	Martine Beck		LBrown
1994	Christmas Is Coming		$10	$14	$18	Claire Masurel		Chron

Henstra Friso

Year	Title	VG-	VG	VG+	Fine	Author	Award	Pub
1969	School For Sillies	$40	$50	$70		Jay Williams		PMagP
1969	The Practical Princess	$25	$35	$50		Jay Williams		PMagP
1970	Stupid Marco		$25	$35	$50	Jay Williams		PMagP
1970	The Round Sultan And The Straight Answer		$25	$35	$50	Barbara K. Walker		PMagP
1971	The Silver Whistle		$25	$35	$50	Jay Williams		PMagP
1972	Seven At One Blow		$25	$35	$50	Jay Williams		PMagP
1972	The Youngest Captain		$25	$35	$50	Jay Williams		PMagP
1973	Petronella		$25	$35	$50	Jay Williams		PMagP
1974	Forgetful Fred		$20	$30	$40	Jay Williams		PMagP
1975	The Little Spotted Fish		$20	$30	$40	Jane Yolen		Seabury
1978	The Wicked Tricks Of Tyl Uilenspiegel		$20	$30	$40	Jay Williams		4Winds
1978	Wait And See		$20	$30	$40	Friso Henstra		AW
1979	Johnny Appleseed		$18	$25	$35	Herb Montgomery		WP
1979	Space Cats		$18	$25	$35	Steven Kroll		Holiday
1983	Mighty Mizzling Mouse		$16	$25	$30	Friso Henstra		Lippin
1983	The Terrible Tales Of Happy Days School		$16	$25	$30	Lois Duncan		LBrown
1984	Mighty Mizzling Mouse & The Red Cabbage House		$16	$25	$30	Friso Henstra		LBrown
1988	The Tsar & The Amazing Cow		$14	$20	$30	J. Patrick Lewis		Dial
1989	Pig And Bear		$14	$20	$25	Vít Horejs		4Winds
1989	The Tale Of Caliph Stork		$14	$20	$25	Lenny Hort (adapted)		Dial
1991	Pedro & The Padre		$12	$18	$25	Verna Aardema		Dial
1991	Why Not?		$12	$18	$25	Sylvia A. Hofsepian		4Winds
1992	Cynthia And The Runaway Gazebo		$12	$18	$25	Elsa Marston		Tambour
1992	The Future Of Yen-Tzu		$12	$18	$25	Winifred Morris		Athenm
1993	The Last Snow Of Winter		$12	$16	$20	Tony Johnston		Tambour
1993	The Mouse Who Owned The Sun		$12	$16	$20	Sally Derby		4Winds
1995	Sophie The Circus Princess		$10	$16	$20	Stig Claesson		GreenT

Henterly Jamichael

Year	Title	VG-	VG	VG+	Fine	Author	Award	Pub
1986	A Fairy Went A-Marketing		$20	$30	$40	Rose Fyleman		Dutton
1988	Good King Wenceslas		$14	$20	$30	J. M. Neale		Dutton
1988	Where The Wild Geese Go		$14	$20	$30	Meredith Ann Pierce		Dutton
1990	Buried Moon		$12	$18	$25	Margaret Hodges		LBrown
1991	Night Is Coming		$12	$18	$25	W. Nikola-Lisa		Dutton
1993	Young Guinevere		$12	$16	$20	Robert D. San Souci		DoubleD
1995	Heart Of A Tiger		$10	$16	$20	Marsha Diane Arnold		Dial
1996	Young Lancelot		$10	$16	$20	Robert D. San Souci		DoubleD
1997	Young Arthur		$10	$16	$20	Robert D. San Souci		DoubleD
2001	Good Night, Garden Gnome		$8	$12	$16	Jamichael Henterly		Dial

Henwood Simon

Year	Title	VG-	VG	VG+	Fine	Author	Award	Pub
1988	The King Who Sneezed		$14	$20	$30	Angela McAllister		Morrow
1989	The Clock Shop		$12	$16	$20	Simon Henwood		Aurum
1990	A Piece Of Luck		$10	$16	$20	Simon Henwood		FSG
1990	The Postman's Palace		$10	$16	$20	Adrian Henri		Athenm
1991	The Troubled Village		$10	$16	$20	Simon Henwood		FSG
1992	The Hidden Jungle		$10	$16	$20	Simon Henwood		FSG
1992	The View		$10	$16	$20	Harry Yoaker		Dial

Hepworth Catherine

Year	Title	VG-	VG	VG+	Fine	Author	Award	Pub
1991	While You Are Asleep		$12	$18	$25	Gwynne Isaacs		Walker
1992	Antics!		$10	$16	$20	Catherine Hepworth		Putnam
1994	Hattie Baked A Wedding Cake		$10	$14	$18	Toby Speed		Putnam
1998	Bug Off!		$8	$12	$16	Catherine Hepworth		Putnam

Herrera Velino

Year	Title	VG-	VG	VG+	Fine	Author	Award	Pub
1941	In My Mother's House	$140	$180	$240		Ann Nolan Clark	CH	Viking
1943	Young Hunters Of Picaris	$35	$40	$60		Ann Nolan Clark		Chil

Hewitt   Kathryn

Year	Title	VG-	VG	VG+	Fine	Author	Award	Pub
1984	Two By Two		$16	$25	$30	Kathryn Hewitt		HBJ
1985	The Worry Week		$12	$18	$25	Anne Lindbergh		HBJ
1986	The Three Sillies		$12	$16	$20	Kathryn Hewitt		HBJ
1987	King Midas And The Golden Touch		$12	$16	$20	Nathaniel Hawthorne		HBJ
1989	Animals From Mother Goose		$12	$16	$20	Lee Bennett Hopkins		HBJ
1989	People From Mother Goose		$12	$16	$20	Lee Bennett Hopkins		HBJ
1993	Lives Of The Musicians		$10	$16	$20	Kathleen Krull		HBJ
1994	Flower Garden		$10	$14	$18	Eve Bunting		HBJ
1994	Lives Of The Writers		$10	$14	$18	Kathleen Krull		HBrace
1995	Lives Of The Artists		$10	$14	$18	Kathleen Krull		HBrace
1996	Sunflower House		$8	$12	$16	Eve Bunting		HBrace
1997	Lives Of The Athletes		$8	$12	$16	Kathleen Krull		HBrace
1998	Lives Of The Presidents		$8	$12	$16	Kathleen Krull		HBrace
2000	Lives Of Extraordinary Women		$8	$10	$14	Kathleen Krull		Harcort
2001	Godiva		$8	$10	$14	Lynn Cullen		Golden

Heyer   Marilee

Year	Title	VG-	VG	VG+	Fine	Author	Award	Pub
1986	The Weaving Of A Dream		$30	$40	$60	Marilee Heyer		Viking
1988	The Forbidden Door		$18	$25	$35	Marilee Heyer		Viking
1993	Iron Hans		$16	$25	$30	Jacob & Wilhelm Grimm		Viking
1995	The Girl, The Fish & The Crown		$14	$20	$25	Marilee Heyer (adapted)		Viking
1999	We Goddesses		$12	$16	$20	Doris Orgel		DK

Hill   Eric

Year	Title	VG-	VG	VG+	Fine	Author	Award	Pub
1980	First Adventure Of The S.S. Happiness Crew		$25	$35	$50	June Dutton		DetProd
1980	Where's Spot?		$18	$25	$35	Eric Hill		Putnam
1981	Second Adventure Of The S.S. Happiness Crew		$18	$25	$35	June Dutton		DetProd
1981	Spot's First Walk		$18	$25	$35	Eric Hill		Putnam
1982	Puppy Love		$16	$25	$30	Eric Hill		Putnam
1982	Spot's Birthday Party		$16	$25	$30	Eric Hill		Putnam
1982	Third Adventure Of The S.S. Happiness Crew		$16	$25	$30	June Dutton		DetProd
1983	Fourth Adventure Of The S.S. Happiness Crew		$16	$25	$30	June Dutton		DetProd
1983	Spot's First Christmas		$16	$25	$30	Eric Hill		Putnam
1984	Baby Bear's Bedtime		$16	$25	$30	Eric Hill		Random
1984	Eric Hill's Crazy Mix Or Match		$16	$25	$30	Eric Hill		Random
1984	Good Morning, Baby Bear		$16	$25	$30	Eric Hill		Random
1984	Spot Goes To School		$16	$25	$30	Eric Hill		Putnam
1985	Spot At Play		$16	$25	$30	Eric Hill		Putnam
1985	Spot At The Fair		$16	$25	$30	Eric Hill		Putnam
1985	Spot Goes On Holiday		$16	$25	$30	Eric Hill		Heine
1985	Spot Goes To The Beach		$16	$25	$30	Eric Hill		Putnam
1985	Spot On The Farm		$16	$25	$30	Eric Hill		Putnam
1986	Spot Goes To The Circus		$14	$20	$30	Eric Hill		Putnam
1986	Spot Looks At Colors		$14	$20	$30	Eric Hill		Putnam
1986	Spot Looks At Shapes		$14	$20	$30	Eric Hill		Putnam
1986	Spot's First Words		$14	$20	$30	Eric Hill		Putnam
1987	Spot Goes To The Farm		$14	$20	$30	Eric Hill		Putnam
1987	Spot Visits The Hospital		$14	$20	$30	Eric Hill		Putnam
1987	Spot's First Picnic		$14	$20	$30	Eric Hill		Putnam
1988	Spot's Big Book Of Words		$14	$20	$30	Eric Hill		Putnam
1988	Spot's First Easter		$14	$20	$30	Eric Hill		Heine
1989	Spot Counts 1 To 10		$14	$20	$25	Eric Hill		Putnam
1989	Spot Looks At Opposites		$14	$20	$25	Eric Hill		Putnam
1989	Spot Looks At Weather		$14	$20	$25	Eric Hill		Putnam
1989	Spot's Baby Sister		$14	$20	$25	Eric Hill		Putnam
1990	Spot Sleeps Over		$12	$18	$25	Eric Hill		Putnam
1991	Spot At Home		$12	$18	$25	Eric Hill		Putnam
1991	Spot Goes To The Park		$12	$18	$25	Eric Hill		Putnam
1991	Spot In The Garden		$12	$18	$25	Eric Hill		Putnam
1991	Spot's Toy Box		$12	$18	$25	Eric Hill		Putnam
1992	Spot Goes To A Party		$12	$18	$25	Eric Hill		Putnam
1994	Spot Bakes A Cake		$12	$16	$20	Eric Hill		Putnam
1994	Spot's Big Book Of Colors, Shapes & Numbers		$12	$16	$20	Eric Hill		Putnam
1994	Spot's First 1, 2, 3 Frieze		$12	$16	$20	Eric Hill		FWarne

Hill   Eric

Year	Title	VG-	VG	VG+	Fine	Author	Award	Pub
1995	Spot's Magical Christmas		$10	$16	$20	Eric Hill		Putnam
1996	Spot And Friends Dress Up		$10	$16	$20	Eric Hill		Putnam
1996	Spot And Friends Play		$10	$16	$20	Eric Hill		Putnam
1996	Spot Visits His Grandparents		$10	$16	$20	Eric Hill		Putnam
1997	Spot's Favorite Baby Animals		$10	$16	$20	Eric Hill		Putnam
1997	Spot's Favorite Colors		$10	$16	$20	Eric Hill		Putnam
1997	Spot's Favorite Numbers		$10	$16	$20	Eric Hill		Putnam
1997	Spot's Favorite Words		$10	$16	$20	Eric Hill		Putnam
1998	Spot And His Grandparents Go To The Carnival		$10	$14	$18	Eric Hill		Putnam
1998	Spot Joins The Parade		$10	$14	$18	Eric Hill		Putnam
1998	Spot's Bedtime Storybook		$10	$14	$18	Eric Hill		Putnam
1998	Spot's Noisy Walk		$10	$14	$18	Eric Hill		PubIntl
1999	Bones Of Fire		$10	$14	$18	Eric Hill		Hill
1999	Good Night, Spot		$10	$14	$18	Eric Hill		Putnam
1999	Spot Can Count		$10	$14	$18	Eric Hill		Putnam
1999	Spot Helps Out		$10	$14	$18	Eric Hill		Putnam
2000	Spot Goes Splash! & Other Stories		$8	$12	$16	Eric Hill		G&D
2000	Spot's Windy Day & Other Stories		$8	$12	$16	Eric Hill		G&D
2002	Good Job, Spot		$8	$10	$14	Eric Hill		Weber
2002	Spot's Treasure Hunt		$8	$10	$14	Eric Hill		Putnam
2003	Spot's Halloween		$8	$10	$14	Eric Hill		Putnam
2003	Spot's Little Book Of Fun At Home		$8	$10	$14	Eric Hill		Putnam
2003	Spot's Little Book Of Fun At The Beach		$8	$10	$14	Eric Hill		Putnam
2003	Spot's Little Book Of Fun At The Farm		$8	$10	$14	Eric Hill		Putnam
2003	Spot's Little Book Of Fun In The Garden		$8	$10	$14	Eric Hill		Putnam
2003	Spot's Thanksgiving		$8	$10	$14	Eric Hill		Putnam
2004	Hello, Spot!		$8	$10	$14	Eric Hill		Putnam
2004	Spot's Christmas		$8	$10	$14	Eric Hill		Putnam
2004	Spot's Jigsaw Puzzle		$8	$10	$14	Eric Hill		Putnam
2004	Spot's Playtime Storybook		$8	$10	$14	Eric Hill		Putnam

Hillenbrand   Will

Year	Title	VG-	VG	VG+	Fine	Author	Award	Pub
1989	Awfully Short For The Fourth Grade		$18	$25	$35	Elvira Woodruff		Holiday
1991	Back In Action		$12	$18	$25	Elvira Woodruff		Holiday
1991	I'm The Best!		$12	$18	$25	Marjorie Weinman Sharmat		Holiday
1991	Traveling To Tondo		$12	$18	$25	Verna Aardema		Knopf
1992	Go Ask Giorgio!		$12	$18	$25	Patricia Wittman		Macmil
1992	Moon Was Tired Of Walking On Air		$12	$18	$25	Natalia Belting		HM
1992	The Magic Rocket		$12	$18	$25	Steven Kroll		Holiday
1993	Asher And The Capmakers		$12	$16	$20	Eric Kimmel		Holiday
1994	Cat, Mouse And Moon		$12	$16	$20	Roxanne Dyer Powell		HM
1994	The King Who Tried To Fry An Egg On His Head		$12	$16	$20	Mirra Ginsburg		Macmil
1995	The House That Drac Built		$10	$16	$20	Judy Sierra		HBrace
1995	The Treasure Chest		$10	$16	$20	Rosalind C. Wang		Holiday
1995	Wicked Jack		$10	$16	$20	Connie Nordhielm Wooldridge		Holiday
1996	Coyote And The Fire Stick		$10	$16	$20	Barbara Diamond Goldin		GB
1996	Sam Sunday & Mystery At The Ocean Beach Hotel		$10	$16	$20	Robyn Supraner		Viking
1996	The Tale Of Ali Baba And The Forty Thieves		$10	$16	$20	Eric Kimmel		Holiday
1997	Counting Crocodiles		$10	$16	$20	Judy Sierra		HBrace
1998	The Biggest, Best Snowman		$10	$14	$18	Margery Cuyler		Scholas
1998	The Golden Sandal		$10	$14	$18	Rebecca Hickox		Holiday
1998	The Many Troubles Of Andy Russell		$10	$14	$18	David A. Adler		HBrace
1999	Andy And Tamika		$10	$14	$18	David A. Adler		HBrace
1999	Down By The Station		$10	$14	$18	Will Hillenbrand		GB
1999	School Trouble For Andy Russell		$10	$14	$18	David A. Adler		HBrace
1999	The Last Snake In Ireland		$10	$14	$18	Sheila MacGill-Callahan		Holiday
2000	Kiss The Cow		$8	$12	$16	Phyllis Root		Candle
2000	Parachuting Hamsters And Andy Russell		$8	$12	$16	David A. Adler		Harcort
2001	Look Out, Jack! The Giant Is Back!		$8	$12	$16	Tom Birdseye		Holiday
2001	Preschool To The Rescue		$8	$12	$16	Judy Sierra		HBrace
2002	Fiddle-I-Fee		$8	$10	$14	Will Hillenbrand		GB
2002	'Twas The Fright Before Christmas		$8	$10	$14	Judy Sierra		HBrace
2003	Here We Go Round The Mulberry Bush		$8	$10	$14	Will Hillenbrand		Harcort
2004	Asleep In The Stable		$8	$10	$14	Will Hillenbrand		Holiday
2004	Down On The Farm		$8	$10	$14	Merrily Kutner		Holiday

Hillenbrand   Will

Year	Title	VG-	VG	VG+	Fine	Author	Award	Pub
2004	One, Two, Three O'leary		$8	$10	$14	Malachy Doyle		McEld
2004	Please Say Please!		$8	$10	$14	Margery Cuyler		Scholas

Himler   Ronald

Year	Title	VG-	VG	VG+	Fine	Author	Award	Pub
1972	Baby		$30	$50	$60	Fran Manushkin		H&Row
1972	Bunk Beds		$25	$35	$50	Elizabeth Winthrop		H&Row
1972	Exploring A Coral Reef		$25	$35	$50	Robert Forrest Burgess		Macmil
1972	Glad Day & Other Classical Poems For Children		$25	$35	$50	Ronald Himler		Putnam
1972	I Am Going Nowhere		$25	$35	$50	Millicent Brower		Putnam
1973	Indian Harvests		$25	$35	$50	William Carey Grimm		McHill
1973	Janey		$25	$35	$50	Charlotte Zolotow		H&Row
1973	Morris Brookside, A Dog		$25	$35	$50	Marjorie Weinman Sharmat		Holiday
1974	After The Goat Man		$20	$30	$40	Betsy Cromer Byars		Viking
1974	Bubblebath!		$20	$30	$40	Fran Manushkin		H&Row
1974	Hut School And The Wartime Home-Front Heroes		$20	$30	$40	Robert Burch		Viking
1974	Little Owl, Keeper Of The Trees		$20	$30	$40	Ann Himler		H&Row
1974	Morris Brookside Is Missing		$20	$30	$40	Marjorie Weinman Sharmat		Holiday
1975	Bruno		$20	$30	$40	Achim Bröger		Morrow
1975	Make A Circle, Keep Us In		$20	$30	$40	Arnold Adoff		DelaP
1975	Pea Patch Island		$20	$30	$40	Polly Curren		Golden
1976	The Blue Stone		$20	$30	$40	Richard Kennedy		Holiday
1976	The Girl On The Yellow Giraffe		$20	$30	$40	Ronald Himler		H&Row
1976	The House On Deer Track Trail		$20	$30	$40	Marty Kelly		McHill
1976	Wind Rose		$20	$30	$40	Crescent Dragonwagon		H&Row
1977	Daddy		$20	$30	$40	Jeannette Franklin Caines		H&Row
1977	Good Wife, Good Wife		$20	$30	$40	Louise McClenathan		McHill
1977	Harriet And The Runaway Book		$20	$30	$40	Johanna Johnston		H&Row
1977	Sadako And The Thousand Paper Cranes		$20	$30	$40	Eleanor Coerr		Putnam
1977	Tornado! Poems		$20	$30	$40	Arnold Adoff		DelaP
1978	Bus Ride		$20	$30	$40	Nancy Jewell		H&Row
1978	Conquista!		$20	$30	$40	Clyde Robert Bulla		Crowell
1978	Little Arliss		$20	$30	$40	Fred Gipson		H&Row
1978	Under The Early Morning Trees		$20	$30	$40	Arnold Adoff		Dutton
1979	Curly And The Wild Boar		$18	$25	$35	Fred Gipson		H&Row
1979	I Am The Running Girl		$18	$25	$35	Arnold Adoff		H&Row
1979	Inside My Feet		$18	$25	$35	Richard Kennedy		H&Row
1979	Trouble For Lucy		$18	$25	$35	Carla Stevens		HM
1979	Wake Up, Jeremiah		$18	$25	$35	Ronald Himler		H&Row
1980	The Bedtime Mother Goose		$18	$25	$35	Ronald Himler		Golden
1980	The Lion's Tail		$18	$25	$35	Douglas F. Davis		Athenm
1981	Allison's Grandfather		$18	$25	$35	Linda S Peavy		Scribnr
1981	The Upside-Down Cat		$18	$25	$35	Elizabeth Parsons		Athenm
1982	Jem's Island		$16	$25	$30	Kathryn Lasky		Scribnr
1982	Moon Song		$16	$25	$30	Byrd Baylor		Scribnr
1983	The Best Town In The World		$16	$25	$30	Byrd Baylor		Scribnr
1984	Kon-Tiki, A Ture Adventure Of Survival At Sea		$16	$25	$30	Thor Heyerdahl		Random
1985	Dakota Dugout		$16	$25	$30	Ann W. Turner		Macmil
1987	Edith Herself		$14	$20	$30	Ellen Howard		Athenm
1987	Eli's Ghost		$14	$20	$30	Betsy Gould Hearne		McEld
1987	Happy Birthday, Grample		$14	$20	$30	Susan Pearson		Dial
1987	Nettie's Trip South		$14	$20	$30	Ann W. Turner		Macmil
1988	The Bridge		$14	$20	$30	Emily Cheney Neville		H&Row
1988	The King Of Prussia & A Peanut Butter Sandwich		$14	$20	$30	Alice Mulcahey Fleming		Scribnr
1989	A World Of Cats		$14	$20	$25	Della Rowland		ContB
1989	Someday Rider		$14	$20	$25	Ann Herbert Scott		Clarion
1990	A Grass Green Gallop		$12	$18	$25	Patricia Hubbell		Athenm
1990	Animals Of The Night		$12	$18	$25	Merry Banks		Scribnr
1990	Dancing On The Table		$12	$18	$25	Liza Ketchum		Holiday
1990	George Washington And Presidents' Day		$12	$18	$25	Dorothy & Thomas Hoobler		Silver
1990	The Wall		$12	$18	$25	Eve Bunting		Clarion
1990	Winter Holding Spring		$12	$18	$25	Crescent Dragonwagon		Macmil
1991	Fly Away Home		$12	$18	$25	Eve Bunting		Clarion
1991	I'm Going To Pet A Worm Today		$12	$18	$25	Constance Levy		McEld
1991	Pearl Harbor Is Burning!		$12	$18	$25	Kathleen V. Kudlinski		Viking
1991	The Day It Rained Forever		$12	$18	$25	Virginia T. Gross		Viking

Himler   Ronald

Year	Title	VG-	VG	VG+	Fine	Author	Award	Pub
1992	Joey's Way		$12	$18	$25	Kate Aver		McEld
1992	Katie's Trunk		$12	$18	$25	Ann W. Turner		Macmil
1992	One Small Blue Bead		$12	$18	$25	Byrd Baylor		Scribnr
1992	The Lily Cupboard		$12	$18	$25	Shulamith Oppenheim		HCollins
1993	A Brand Is Forever		$12	$16	$20	Ann Herbert Scott		Clarion
1993	Earthquake!		$12	$16	$20	Kathleen V. Kudlinski		Viking
1993	Someday A Tree		$12	$16	$20	Eve Bunting		Clarion
1993	The Navajos		$12	$16	$20	Virginia Sneve		Holiday
1993	The Sioux		$12	$16	$20	Virginia Sneve		Holiday
1994	A Day's Work		$12	$16	$20	Eve Bunting		Clarion
1994	Lone Star		$12	$16	$20	Kathleen V. Kudlinski		Viking
1994	Squish!		$12	$16	$20	Nancy Luenn		Athenm
1994	The Nez Perce		$12	$16	$20	Virginia Sneve		Holiday
1994	The Seminoles		$12	$16	$20	Virginia Sneve		Holiday
1995	Bess's Log Cabin Quilt		$10	$16	$20	D. Anne Love		Holiday
1995	Dakota Spring		$10	$16	$20	D. Anne Love		Holiday
1995	Sand In My Shoes		$10	$16	$20	Wendy Kesselman		Hyper
1995	Sara's City		$10	$16	$20	Sue Alexander		Clarion
1995	The Hopis		$10	$16	$20	Virginia Sneve		Holiday
1995	The Iroquois		$10	$16	$20	Virginia Sneve		Holiday
1996	Desert Trip		$10	$16	$20	Barbara A Steiner		Sierra
1996	The Cherokees		$10	$16	$20	Virginia Sneve		Holiday
1996	The Cheyennes		$10	$16	$20	Virginia Sneve		Holiday
1996	The Log Cabin Quilt		$10	$16	$20	Ellen Howard		Holiday
1996	Train To Somewhere		$10	$16	$20	Eve Bunting		Clarion
1997	A Christmas Star		$10	$16	$20	Linda Oatman High		Holiday
1997	Hook Moon Night		$10	$16	$20	Faye Gibbons		Morrow
1997	The Apaches		$10	$16	$20	Virginia Sneve		Holiday
1998	The Roses In My Carpets		$10	$14	$18	Rukhsana Khan		Holiday
1999	Mark Twain And Huckleberry Finn		$10	$14	$18	Stewart Ross		Viking
1999	Redcoats And Petticoats		$10	$14	$18	Katherine Kirkpatrick		Holiday
1999	Rudi's Pond		$10	$14	$18	Eve Bunting		Clarion
1999	The Snoop		$10	$14	$18	Jane Resh Thomas		Clarion
1999	Why Not, Lafayette?		$10	$14	$18	Jean Fritz		Putnam
2000	The Log Cabin Christmas		$8	$12	$16	Ellen Howard		Holiday
2000	Voices Of The Alamo		$8	$12	$16	Sherry Garland		Scholas
2000	William Penn, Founder Of Pennsyslvania		$8	$12	$16	Steven Kroll		Holiday
2001	A Thanksgiving Turkey		$8	$12	$16	Julian Scheer		Holiday
2001	By The Light Of The Captured Moon		$8	$12	$16	Julian Scheer		Holiday
2001	The Caged Birds Of Phnom Penh		$8	$12	$16	Frederick Lipp		Holiday
2002	Baby, Come Out!		$8	$10	$14	Fran Manushkin		StarB
2002	Six Is So Much Less Than Seven		$8	$10	$14	Ronald Himler		StarB
2002	The Legend Of Blue Jacket		$8	$10	$14	Michael Spradlin		HCollins
2002	The Log Cabin Church		$8	$10	$14	Ellen Howard		Holiday
2002	The Story Of Levi's		$8	$10	$14	Michael Burgan		Scholas
2003	A Picture Book Of Lewis And Clark		$8	$10	$14	David A. Adler		Holiday
2003	I Wonder As I Wander		$8	$10	$14	Gwenyth Swain		EerdB
2003	The Blizzard		$8	$10	$14	Betty Ren Wright		Holiday
2004	Crooked Creek		$8	$10	$14	Laurie Lawlor		Holiday
2004	The Best Cat In The World		$8	$10	$14	Lesléa Newman		EerdB
2004	Wash Day		$8	$10	$14	Barbara Hancock Cole		StarB

Hirsh   Marilyn

Year	Title	VG-	VG	VG+	Fine	Author	Award	Pub
1969	The Runaway Hat	$35	$40	$60		Adelaide Holl		Singer
1969	The Tale Of Polly Polloo	$35	$40	$60		Beatrice Curtis Brown		Seabury
1969	Where Is Yonkela?	$70	$90	$120		Marilyn Hirsh		Crown
1970	Bravo, Burro!		$25	$35	$50	John Fante		HawB
1970	The Elephants And The Mice		$30	$50	$60	Marilyn Hirsh		World
1970	The Pink Suit		$30	$50	$60	Marilyn Hirsh		Crown
1971	Leela And The Watermelon		$25	$35	$50	Maya Narayan		Crown
1972	George And The Goblins		$30	$50	$60	Marilyn Hirsh		Crown
1972	How The World Got Its Color		$30	$50	$60	Marilyn Hirsh		Crown
1973	Ben Goes Into Business		$30	$50	$60	Marilyn Hirsh		Holiday
1973	Mushy Eggs		$25	$35	$50	Florence Adams		Putnam
1974	Could Anything Be Worse?		$30	$40	$60	Marilyn Hirsh		Holiday

Hirsh — Marilyn

Year	Title	VG-	VG	VG+	Fine	Author	Award	Pub
1974	The Polynesians Knew		$20	$30	$40	Tillie S. Pine		McHill
1975	The Pirate Hero Of New Orleans		$20	$30	$40	Carl Lamson Carmer		Harvey
1976	Captain Jiri And Rabbi Jacob		$30	$40	$60	Marilyn Hirsh		Holiday
1976	The House On The Roof		$20	$30	$40	David A. Adler		Bonim
1976	The Rabbi And The Twenty-Nine Witches		$30	$40	$60	Marilyn Hirsh		Holiday
1977	Hannibal And His 37 Elephants		$25	$40	$50	Marilyn Hirsh		Holiday
1977	The Hanukkah Story		$25	$40	$50	Marilyn Hirsh		Bonim
1978	Deborah The Dybbuk		$25	$40	$50	Marilyn Hirsh		Holiday
1978	Potato Pancakes All Around		$25	$40	$50	Marilyn Hirsh		Bonim
1979	One Little Goat		$25	$40	$50	Marilyn Hirsh (adapted)		Holiday
1979	The Secret Dinosaur		$25	$40	$50	Marilyn Hirsh		Holiday
1980	The Best Of K'Tonton		$18	$25	$35	Sadie Rose Weilerstein		JPS
1980	Wales' Tale		$18	$25	$35	Susan Saunders		Viking
1981	K'tonton In The Circus		$18	$25	$35	Sadie Rose Weilerstein		JPS
1981	The Tower Of Babel		$25	$35	$50	Marilyn Hirsh		Holiday
1984	Butchers And Bakers, Rabbis And Kings		$16	$25	$30	Jacqueline Dembar Greene		KarBen
1984	I Love Hanukkah		$20	$30	$40	Marilyn Hirsh		Holiday
1985	I Love Passover		$20	$30	$40	Marilyn Hirsh		Holiday
1997	Saying Goodbye To Grandpa		$10	$16	$20	Moshe HaLevi Spero		Potter

Hoban — Lillian

Year	Title	VG-	VG	VG+	Fine	Author	Award	Pub
1961	Herman The Loser	$100	$120	$160		Russell Hoban		H&B
1962	London Men And English Men	$70	$90	$120		Russell Hoban		Harper
1962	The Song In My Drum	$70	$90	$120		Russell Hoban		Harper
1963	Some Snow Said Hello	$70	$90	$120		Russell Hoban		H&Row
1964	A Baby Sister For Frances	$200	$280	$340		Russell Hoban		H&Row
1964	Bread And Jam For Frances	$120	$160	$220		Russell Hoban		H&Row
1964	Nothing To Do	$60	$80	$100		Russell Hoban		H&Row
1964	The Sorely Trying Day	$60	$80	$100		Russell Hoban		H&Row
1965	The Story Of Hester Mouse Who Became A Writer	$60	$80	$100		Russell Hoban		Norton
1965	Tom And The Two Handles	$60	$80	$100		Russell Hoban		H&Row
1965	When I Am Big	$40	$60	$70		Robert Paul Smith		H&Row
1966	A Gift-Bear For The King	$40	$60	$70		Carl Memling		Dutton
1966	Charlie The Tramp	$60	$80	$100		Russell Hoban		4Winds
1966	Goodnight	$60	$80	$100		Russell Hoban		Norton
1966	The Forest In The Wind	$40	$60	$70		Mitchell F Jayne		Bobbs
1966	The Little Brute Family	$60	$80	$100		Russell Hoban		Macmil
1966	When Jack & Daisy Tried To Fool The Tooth Fairies	$60	$80	$100		Russell Hoban		4Winds
1967	Save My Place	$60	$80	$100		Russell Hoban		Norton
1967	The Mouse And His Child	$60	$80	$100		Russell Hoban		H&Row
1967	Will I Have A Friend?	$60	$80	$100		Miriam Cohen		Macmil
1968	A Birthday For Frances	$80	$120	$140		Russell Hoban		H&Row
1968	The Pedaling Man	$60	$80	$100		Russell Hoban		Norton
1968	The Stone Doll Of Sister Brute	$60	$80	$100		Russell Hoban		Macmil
1969	A Wolf Of My Own	$40	$50	$70		Jan Wahl		Macmil
1969	Best Friends For Frances	$80	$120	$140		Russell Hoban		H&Row
1969	Harvey's Hideout	$60	$80	$100		Russell Hoban		PMagP
1969	In One Door And Out The Other	$40	$50	$70		Aileen Fisher		Crowell
1969	The Mole Family's Christmas	$60	$80	$100		Russell Hoban		PMagP
1969	Ugly Bird	$60	$80	$100		Russell Hoban		Macmil
1970	A Bargain For Frances		$50	$70	$90	Russell Hoban		H&Row
1971	Best Friends		$30	$50	$60	Miriam Cohen		Macmil
1971	Emmet Otter's Jug-Band Christmas		$40	$60	$90	Russell Hoban		PMagP
1971	Just Awful		$30	$50	$60	Alma Marshak Whitney		AW
1971	Rainy Day Together		$30	$50	$60	Ellen Parsons		H&Row
1971	The Easter Cat		$30	$50	$60	Meindert De Jong		Macmil
1972	Arthur's Christmas Cookies		$40	$60	$90	Lillian Hoban		H&Row
1972	Egg Thoughts & Other Frances Songs		$40	$60	$90	Russell Hoban		H&Row
1972	The New Teacher		$30	$50	$60	Miriam Cohen		Macmil
1973	Sophie And Gussie		$30	$50	$60	Marjorie Weinman Sharmat		Macmil
1973	The Sugar Snow Spring		$40	$60	$90	Lillian Hoban		H&Row
1974	Arthur's Honey Bear		$40	$60	$80	Lillian Hoban		H&Row
1974	Tough Jim		$30	$40	$60	Miriam Cohen		Macmil
1974	What's Good For A Three-Year-Old?		$30	$40	$60	William Cole		HR&W
1975	Strawberry Dress Escape		$30	$40	$60	Crescent Dragonwagon		Scribnr

Hoban   Lillian

Year	Title	VG-	VG	VG+	Fine	Author	Award	Pub
1976	Arthur's Pen Pal		$40	$60	$80	Lillian Hoban		H&Row
1976	Squirrel's Song		$30	$40	$60	Diane Wolkstein		Random
1976	The Big Hello		$30	$40	$60	Janet Schulman		Green
1976	The Trip, & Other Sophie And Gussie Stories		$30	$40	$60	Marjorie Weinman Sharmat		Macmil
1977	Here Come Raccoons!		$40	$60	$80	Lillian Hoban		HR&W
1977	I Don't Care		$25	$40	$50	Marjorie Weinman Sharmat		Macmil
1977	I Met A Traveller		$40	$60	$80	Lillian Hoban		H&Row
1977	Mr. Pig And Sonny Too		$40	$60	$80	Lillian Hoban		H&Row
1977	Nora And Mrs Mind-Your-Own-Business		$25	$40	$50	Johanna Hurwitz		Morrow
1977	Stick-In-The-Mud Turtle		$40	$60	$80	Lillian Hoban		Green
1977	When Will I Read?		$25	$40	$50	Miriam Cohen		Green
1978	Arthur's Prize Reader		$35	$50	$70	Lillian Hoban		H&Row
1978	Bee My Valentine!		$25	$40	$50	Miriam Cohen		Green
1978	No Nap For Me		$25	$40	$50	Theresa Zagone		Dutton
1978	Turtle Spring		$35	$50	$70	Lillian Hoban		Green
1979	Awful Thursday		$25	$40	$50	Ron Roy		Pan
1979	Lost In The Museum		$25	$40	$50	Miriam Cohen		Green
1979	Papa's Panda		$25	$40	$50	Nancy Willard		HBJ
1979	Say Hello, Vanessa		$25	$40	$50	Marjorie Weinman Sharmat		Holiday
1979	Seymour Therince		$25	$40	$50	Sue Alexander		Pan
1979	The Great Big Dummy		$25	$40	$50	Janet Schulman		Green
1979	The New Girl At School		$25	$40	$50	Judy Delton		Dutton
1979	Where Does The Teacher Live?		$25	$40	$50	aula Kurzband Feder		Dutton
1980	First Grade Takes A Test		$25	$35	$50	Miriam Cohen		Green
1980	Harry's Song		$35	$50	$70	Lillian Hoban		Green
1980	Mr. Pig And Family		$35	$50	$70	Lillian Hoban		H&Row
1980	No Good In Art		$25	$35	$50	Miriam Cohen		Green
1980	The Big Kite Contest		$25	$35	$50	Dorotha Ruthstrom		Pan
1981	Arthur's Funny Money		$35	$50	$70	Lillian Hoban		H&Row
1981	Jim Meets The Thing		$25	$35	$50	Miriam Cohen		Green
1981	No, No, Sammy Crow		$35	$50	$70	Lillian Hoban		Green
1981	The Balancing Girl		$25	$35	$50	Berniece Rabe		Dutton
1982	It's Really Christmas		$30	$50	$60	Lillian Hoban		Green
1982	Ready-Set-Robot!		$30	$50	$60	Lillian Hoban		H&Row
1982	So What?		$25	$35	$50	Miriam Cohen		Green
1983	I'm Telling You Now		$25	$35	$50	Judy Delton		Dutton
1983	Rip-Roaringrussell		$25	$35	$50	Johanna Hurwitz		Morrow
1983	See You Tomorrow, Charles		$25	$35	$50	Miriam Cohen		Green
1983	The Laziest Robot In Zone One		$30	$50	$60	Lillian Hoban		H&Row
1984	Arthur's Halloween Costume		$30	$50	$60	Lillian Hoban		H&Row
1984	Grandparents' Houses		$20	$30	$40	Corrine Streich		Green
1984	Jim's Dog Muffins		$20	$30	$40	Miriam Cohen		Green
1984	The Day The Teacher Went Bananas		$20	$30	$40	James Howe		Dutton
1984	The Story Of Bentley Beaver		$20	$30	$40	Marjorie Weinman Sharmat		H&Row
1985	Arthur's Loose Tooth		$30	$40	$60	Lillian Hoban		H&Row
1985	Attila The Angry		$20	$30	$40	Marjorie Weinman Sharmat		Holiday
1985	Liar, Liar, Pants On Fire!		$20	$30	$40	Miriam Cohen		Green
1985	Russell Rides Again		$20	$30	$40	Johanna Hurwitz		Morrow
1985	Starring First Grade		$20	$30	$40	Miriam Cohen		Green
1985	Tough Eddie		$20	$30	$40	Elizabeth Winthrop		Dutton
1986	The Case Of The Two Masked Robbers		$30	$40	$60	Lillian Hoban		H&Row
1987	Don't Eat Too Much Turkey!		$20	$30	$40	Miriam Cohen		Green
1987	My Dad The Magnificent		$20	$30	$40	Kristy Parker		Dutton
1987	Russell Sprouts		$20	$30	$40	Johanna Hurwitz		Morrow
1987	Silly Tilly And The Easter Bunny		$25	$40	$50	Lillian Hoban		H&Row
1988	Amy Loves The Sun		$18	$25	$35	Julia Hoban		H&Row
1988	Amy Loves The Wind		$18	$25	$35	Julia Hoban		H&Row
1988	It's George!		$18	$25	$35	Miriam Cohen		Green
1988	Tales Of Fuzzy Mouse		$18	$25	$35	Jan Wahl		Golden
1989	Amy Loves The Rain		$18	$25	$35	Julia Hoban		H&Row
1989	Amy Loves The Snow		$18	$25	$35	Julia Hoban		H&Row
1989	Arthur's Great Big Valentine		$25	$40	$50	Lillian Hoban		H&Row
1989	Caps, Hats, Socks, And Mittens		$18	$25	$35	Louise Borden		Scholas
1989	Quick Chick		$18	$25	$35	Julia Hoban		Dutton
1989	Russell And Elisa		$18	$25	$35	Johanna Hurwitz		Morrow
1989	See You In Second Grade!		$18	$25	$35	Miriam Cohen		Green
1990	Busybody Nora		$16	$25	$30	Johanna Hurwitz		Morrow

Hoban   Lillian

Year	Title	VG-	VG	VG+	Fine	Author	Award	Pub
1990	I'm Gonna Tell Mama I Want An Iguana		$16	$25	$30	Tony Johnston		Putnam
1990	Silly Tilly's Thanksgiving Dinner		$16	$25	$30	Lillian Hoban		H&Row
1990	Superduper Teddy		$16	$25	$30	Johanna Hurwitz		Morrow
1990	The Real-Skin Rubber Monster Mask		$16	$25	$30	Miriam Cohen		Green
1990	Waiting For Noah		$16	$25	$30	Shulamith Oppenheim		H&Row
1991	E Is For Elisa		$16	$25	$30	Johanna Hurwitz		Morrow
1991	Little Bear Sleeping		$16	$25	$30	Tony Johnston		Putnam
1991	New Neighbors For Nora		$16	$25	$30	Johanna Hurwitz		Morrow
1993	A Baby Sister For Frances		$12	$16	$20	Russell Hoban		HCollins
1993	Arthur's Camp-Out		$16	$25	$30	Lillian Hoban		HCollins
1993	Make Room For Elisa		$16	$25	$30	Johanna Hurwitz		Morrow
1993	The Big Seed		$16	$25	$30	Ellen Howard		S&S
1993	Will You Be My Valentine?		$16	$25	$30	Steven Kroll		Holiday
1994	A Plant Called Spot		$14	$20	$30	Nancy J Peteraf		DoubleD
1994	Like Me And You		$14	$20	$30	Raffi & Debi Pike		Crown
1995	Elisa In The Middle		$14	$20	$25	Johanna Hurwitz		Morrow
1995	I Never Did That Before		$14	$20	$25	Lilian Moore		Athenm
1995	Joe And Betsy The Dinosaur		$14	$20	$25	Lillian Hoban		HCollins
1996	Arthur's Back To School Day		$12	$18	$25	Lillian Hoban		HCollins
1997	Big Little Lion		$12	$18	$25	Lillian Hoban		HFest
1997	Big Little Otter		$12	$18	$25	Lillian Hoban		HFest
1997	Ever-Clever Elisa		$12	$18	$25	Johanna Hurwitz		Morrow
1998	Silly Tilly's Valentine		$12	$16	$20	Lillian Hoban		HCollins
1999	Arthur's Birthday Party		$12	$16	$20	Lillian Hoban		HCollins

Hobbie   Holly

Year	Title	VG-	VG	VG+	Fine	Author	Award	Pub
1976	The Night Before Christmas		$30	$40	$60	Clement C. Moore		P&Munk
1977	Holly Hobbie's Nursery Rhymes		$25	$40	$50	Holly Hobbie		Offen
1977	The Days Of Holly Hobbie		$25	$40	$50	Holly Hobbie		P&Munk
1978	Holly Hobbie's Special Days		$25	$40	$50	Holly Hobbie		Offen
1979	A Treasury Of Holly Hobbie		$25	$40	$50	Holly Hobbie		RandMc
1979	Holly Hobbie's Alphabet Book		$25	$40	$50	Holly Hobbie		WaterT
1979	Holly Hobbie's Cookbook		$25	$40	$50	Holly Hobbie		GingH
1979	Holly Hobbie's Time Book		$25	$40	$50	Holly Hobbie		WaterT
1980	Holly Hobbie's Christmas Book		$25	$35	$50	Holly Hobbie		Offen
1991	Bloodroot		$16	$25	$30	Holly Hobbie		Crown
1997	Toot & Puddle		$20	$30	$40	Holly Hobbie		LBrown
1998	Toot & Puddle A Present For Toot		$14	$20	$30	Holly Hobbie		LBrown
1999	Toot & Puddle You Are My Sunshine		$14	$20	$25	Holly Hobbie		LBrown
2000	Puddle's ABC		$12	$18	$25	Holly Hobbie		LBrown
2001	I'll Be Home For Christmas		$10	$14	$18	Holly Hobbie		LBrown
2001	Toot & Puddle Welcome To Woodcock Pocket		$10	$14	$18	Holly Hobbie		LBrown
2002	Toot & Puddle Top Of The World		$8	$12	$16	Holly Hobbie		LBrown
2003	Toot & Puddle Charming Opal		$8	$12	$16	Holly Hobbie		LBrown
2004	Toot & Puddle The New Friend		$8	$10	$14	Holly Hobbie		LBrown
2005	Toot & Puddle Wish You Were Here		$6	$10	$12	Holly Hobbie		LBrown

Hodges   C. Walter

Year	Title	VG-	VG	VG+	Fine	Author	Award	Pub
1935	Plays In Verse And Mime	$70	$100	$120		Rosalind Vallance		TNelson
1938	New Tales From Shakespeare	$50	$60	$80		George Bagshawe Harrison		TNelson
1939	Columbus Sails	$50	$60	$80		C. Walter Hodges		CM
1941	The Ship Aground	$50	$60	$80		C. Fox Smith		Oxford
1946	The Little White Horse	$40	$60	$70		Elizabeth Goudge		Gregg
1948	The Story Of The Treasure Seekers	$40	$60	$70		Edith Nesbit		CM
1949	Shakespeare And The Players	$40	$60	$70		C. Walter Hodges		CM
1952	Brother Dusty-Feet	$40	$50	$70		Rosemary Sutcliff		Oxford
1954	The Globe Restored	$40	$50	$70		C. Walter Hodges		CM
1955	Cold Hazard	$35	$50	$60		Richard Armstrong		HM
1957	The Three Musketeers	$35	$50	$60		Alexandre Dumas		World
1964	Shakespeare's Theatre	$60	$80	$100		C. Walter Hodges	GM	CM
1964	The Namesake	$35	$40	$60		C. Walter Hodges		CM
1965	Flight To Adventure	$30	$40	$50		Ian Serraillier		JCape
1965	Growing Up With The Norman Conquest	$30	$40	$50		Alfred Leo Duggan		Faber
1966	Hannibal And The Bears	$30	$40	$50		Margaret Joyce Baker		FSG

Hodges   C. Walter

Year	Title	VG-	VG	VG+	Fine	Author	Award	Pub
1966	Magna Carta	$30	$40	$50		C. Walter Hodges		CM
1966	The Norman Conquest	$30	$40	$50		C. Walter Hodges		CM
1967	Bows Against The Barons	$30	$40	$50		Geoffrey Trease		Mered
1967	Ransom For A Knight	$30	$40	$50		Barbara Leonie Picard		Walck
1967	The Marsh King	$30	$40	$50		C. Walter Hodges		CM
1968	The Spanish Armada	$30	$40	$50		C. Walter Hodges		CM
1970	Shakespeare & The Players		$25	$35	$50	C. Walter Hodges		CM
1970	The Overland Launch		$25	$35	$50	C. Walter Hodges		CM
1971	The Pied Piper Of Hamelin		$25	$35	$50	Robert Browning		CM&G
1971	The Rime Of The Ancient Mariner		$25	$35	$50	Samuel Taylor Coleridge		CM&G
1972	The English Civil War		$25	$35	$50	C. Walter Hodges		Oxford
1972	The Puritan Revolution		$25	$35	$50	C. Walter Hodges		CM&G
1973	Shakespeare's Second Globe		$25	$35	$50	C. Walter Hodges		Oxford
1974	Playhouse Tales		$20	$30	$40	C. Walter Hodges		CM&G
1974	The Sea Beggar's Son		$20	$30	$40	F. N. Monjo		CM&G
1978	Here Come The Clowns		$20	$30	$40	Lowell Swortzell		Viking
1978	Plain Lane Christmas		$20	$30	$40	C. Walter Hodges		CM&G
1980	Shakespeare's Theatre		$10	$14	$18	C. Walter Hodges	GM	CM&G
1980	The Battlement Garden		$18	$25	$35	C. Walter Hodges		HM
1986	The Boar's Head Playhouse		$14	$20	$30	Herbert Berry		Folger
1999	Enter The Whole Army		$10	$14	$18	C. Walter Hodges		CUP

Hoff   Syd

Year	Title	VG-	VG	VG+	Fine	Author	Award	Pub
1945	Mom, I'm Home!	$90	$120	$160		Syd Hoff		DD
1958	Danny And The Dinosaur	$160	$220	$280		Syd Hoff		H&B
1959	Julius	$120	$160	$200		Syd Hoff		H&B
1959	Sammy The Seal	$140	$200	$240		Syd Hoff		H&B
1960	Ogluk The Eskimo	$50	$70	$90		Syd Hoff		HR&W
1960	Oliver	$100	$140	$180		Syd Hoff		H&B
1960	Stanley	$100	$140	$180		Syd Hoff		H&B
1960	Where's Prancer	$100	$140	$180		Syd Hoff		H&B
1960	Who Will Be My Friends?	$100	$140	$180		Syd Hoff		H&B
1961	Albert The Albatross	$100	$120	$160		Syd Hoff		H&B
1961	Chester The Horse	$100	$120	$160		Syd Hoff		H&B
1961	Little Chief	$100	$120	$160		Syd Hoff		H&B
1963	Grizzwold	$50	$70	$90		Syd Hoff		H&Row
1964	Hello Muddah, Hello Faddah	$90	$120	$160		Allan Sherman		H&Row
1964	I Can't Dance	$90	$120	$160		Allan Sherman		H&Row
1966	Mrs. Switch	$50	$60	$80		Syd Hoff		Putnam
1966	The Homework Caper	$40	$60	$70		Joan Lexau		H&Row
1967	Irving And Me	$50	$60	$80		Syd Hoff		H&Row
1968	Slithers	$50	$60	$80		Syd Hoff		Putnam
1968	The Rooftop Mystery	$40	$50	$70		Joan Lexau		H&Row
1968	The Witch, Cat, And The Baseball Hat	$50	$60	$80		Syd Hoff		G&D
1968	Wanda's Wand	$50	$60	$80		Syd Hoff		Gibson
1969	Baseball Mouse	$50	$60	$80		Syd Hoff		Putnam
1969	Herschel The Hero	$50	$60	$80		Syd Hoff		Putnam
1969	Jeffrey At Camp	$50	$60	$80		Syd Hoff		Putnam
1969	Mahatma	$50	$60	$80		Syd Hoff		Putnam
1969	Roberto And The Bull	$50	$60	$80		Syd Hoff		McHill
1970	Horse In Harry's Room		$35	$50	$70	Syd Hoff		H&Row
1970	Litter Knight		$30	$50	$60	Syd Hoff		McHill
1970	Palace Bug		$30	$50	$60	Syd Hoff		Putnam
1970	Siegfried, Dog Of The Alps		$35	$50	$70	Syd Hoff		G&D
1970	The Horse In Harry's Room		$30	$50	$60	Syd Hoff		H&Row
1970	Wilfred The Lion		$30	$50	$60	Syd Hoff		Putnam
1971	Mule Who Struck It Rich		$30	$50	$60	Syd Hoff		LBrown
1971	Thunderhoff		$30	$50	$60	Syd Hoff		H&Row
1972	Ida, The Bareback Rider		$30	$50	$60	Syd Hoff		Putnam
1972	My Aunt Rosie		$30	$50	$60	Syd Hoff		H&Row
1972	Pedro And The Bananas		$30	$50	$60	Syd Hoff		Putnam
1973	Walk Past Ellen's House		$30	$50	$60	Syd Hoff		McHill
1974	Kip Van Winkle		$30	$40	$60	Syd Hoff		Putnam
1975	Barkley		$30	$40	$60	Syd Hoff		H&Row
1975	Katy's Kitty		$30	$40	$60	Syd Hoff		Windmil

Hoff   Syd

Year	Title	VG-	VG	VG+	Fine	Author	Award	Pub
1976	Little Leaguer		$30	$40	$60	Syd Hoff		Windmil
1977	Henrietta Lays Somes Eggs		$25	$40	$50	Syd Hoff		Garrard
1977	Walpole		$25	$40	$50	Syd Hoff		H&Row
1978	Boss Tweed And The Man Who Drew Him		$25	$40	$50	Syd Hoff		CM&G
1978	Henrietta, Circus Star		$25	$40	$50	Syd Hoff		Garrard
1978	Henrietta, The Early Bird		$25	$40	$50	Syd Hoff		Garrard
1979	Henrietta Goes To The Fair		$25	$40	$50	Syd Hoff		Garrard
1979	Santa's Moose		$25	$40	$50	Syd Hoff		H&Row
1979	Slugger Sal's Slump		$25	$40	$50	Syd Hoff		Windmil
1980	Henrietta's Halloween		$25	$35	$50	Syd Hoff		Garrard
1980	Merry Christmas, Henrietta!		$25	$35	$50	Syd Hoff		Garrard
1980	Scarface Al And His Uncle Sam		$25	$35	$50	Syd Hoff		CM&G
1981	Henrietta's Fourth Of July		$25	$35	$50	Syd Hoff		Garrard
1981	Soft Skull Sam		$25	$35	$50	Syd Hoff		HBJ
1982	The Man Who Loved Animals		$25	$35	$50	Syd Hoff		CM&G
1983	Happy Birthday, Henrietta!		$25	$35	$50	Syd Hoff		Garrard
1987	Barnie's Horse		$20	$30	$40	Syd Hoff		H&Row
1988	Mrs. Brice's Mice		$18	$25	$35	Syd Hoff		H&Row
1993	Bernard On His Own		$16	$25	$30	Syd Hoff		Clarion
1993	Captain Cat		$16	$25	$30	Syd Hoff		HCollins
1994	Duncan The Dancing Duck		$14	$20	$30	Syd Hoff		Clarion
1994	Lighthouse Children		$14	$20	$30	Syd Hoff		HCollins
1996	Danny And The Dinosaur Go To Camp		$12	$18	$25	Syd Hoff		HCollins
1997	Gentleman Jim And The Great John L		$12	$18	$25	Syd Hoff		CM&G

Hoffman   Rosekrans

Year	Title	VG-	VG	VG+	Fine	Author	Award	Pub
1973	Walter In Love		$30	$50	$60	Alicen White		LL&S
1974	Where Did That Naughty Little Hamster Go?		$20	$30	$40	Patty Wolcott		AW
1975	Anna Banana		$20	$30	$40	Rosekrans Hoffman		Knopf
1978	Alexandra The Rock Eater		$20	$30	$40	Dorothy Van Woerkom		Knopf
1978	An Egg Is To Sit On		$20	$30	$40	Christine Tanz		LL&S
1979	Go To Bed!: A Book Of Bedtime Poems		$18	$25	$35	L.B. Hopkins (selected)		Knopf
1979	My Mother Sends Her Wisdom		$18	$25	$35	Louise McClenathan		Morrow
1980	Come Home, Wilma		$18	$25	$35	Mitchell Sharmat		AWhit
1980	Elves, Fairies & Gnomes: Poems		$18	$25	$35	L.B. Hopkins (selected)		Knopf
1982	Sister Sweet Ella		$16	$25	$30	Rosekrans Hoffman		Morrow
1982	The Case Of The Missing Hat		$16	$25	$30	Gregory Williams		Muppet
1982	The Easter Pig		$16	$25	$30	Louise McClenathan		Morrow
1983	How Do You Make An Elephant Float?		$16	$25	$30	Lee Bennett Hopkins		AWhit
1983	The Truth About The Moon		$16	$25	$30	Clayton Bess		HM
1986	Creepy, Crawly Critter Riddles		$14	$20	$30	Joanne E. Bernstein		AWhit
1986	Three Sisters		$14	$20	$30	Audrey Wood		Dial
1988	The Horrible Holidays		$14	$20	$30	Audrey Wood		Dial
1989	Sue Patch And The Crazy Clocks		$14	$20	$25	Ann Tornbert		Dial
1990	Jet Black Pickup Truck		$12	$18	$25	Patricia Lakin		Orchard
1991	The Best Cat Suit Of All		$12	$18	$25	Sylvia Cassedy		Dial
1993	Where Do Little Girls Grow?		$12	$16	$20	Milly Jane Limmer		AWhit
1994	Jane Yolen's Old Macdonald Songbook		$12	$16	$20	Jane Yolen		Boyds
1996	Pignic		$10	$16	$20	Anne Miranda		Boyds

Hogrogian   Nonny

Year	Title	VG-	VG	VG+	Fine	Author	Award	Pub
1960	King Of The Kerry Fair	$70	$90	$120		Nicolete Meredith		Crowell
1961	Down Come The Leaves	$50	$60	$80		Henrietta Bancroft		Crowell
1963	Gaelic Ghosts	$50	$60	$80		Sorche Nic Leodhas		HR&W
1964	Poems of Stephen Crane	$50	$60	$80		Stephen Crane		Crowell
1965	Always Room For One More	$200	$280	$340		Sorche Nic Leodhas	CM	HR&W
1965	Arbor Day	$40	$60	$70		Aileen Fisher		Crowell
1965	Ghosts Go Haunting	$40	$60	$70		Sorche Nic Leodhas		HR&W
1965	Hand In Hand We'll Go	$40	$60	$70		Robert Burns		Crowell
1965	The Kitchen Knight	$40	$60	$70		Barbara Schiller (adapted)		HR&W
1966	A Tale Of Stolen Time	$40	$60	$70		Evgenii Shvarts		P-Hall
1966	The White Palace	$40	$60	$70		Mary Le Duc O'Neill		Crowell
1967	The Day Everybody Cried	$40	$50	$70		Beatrice S. De Regniers		Viking
1967	The Fearsome Inn	$80	$120	$140		Isaac Bashevis Singer	NH	Scribnr

Hogrogian   Nonny

Year	Title	VG-	VG	VG+	Fine	Author	Award	Pub
1967	The Renowned History Of Little Red Riding-Hood	$40	$50	$70		Nonny Hogrogian		Crowell
1968	Story Of Prince Ivan, The Firebird, & The Gray Wolf	$40	$50	$70		Thomas P Whitney		Scribnr
1968	The Thirteen Days Of Yule	$40	$50	$70		Nonny Hogrogian		Crowell
1968	The Three Sparrows	$40	$50	$70		Max Knight (translated)		Scribnr
1969	In School	$40	$50	$70		Esther Rudomin Hautzig		Macmil
1969	Sir Ribbeck Of Ribbeck Of Havelland	$40	$50	$70		Elizabeth Shub		Macmil
1969	The Time-Ago Tales Of Jahdu	$40	$50	$70		Virginia Hamilton		Macmil
1970	Deirdre		$30	$50	$60	James Stephens		Macmil
1970	Favorite Fairy Tales Told In Greece		$30	$50	$60	Virginia Haviland		LBrown
1970	Vasilisa The Beautiful		$30	$50	$60	Nonny Hogrogian		Macmil
1971	About Wise Men And Simpletons		$30	$50	$60	Jacob & Wilhelm Grimm		Macmil
1971	One Fine Day		$180	$260	$340	Nonny Hogrogian	CM	Macmil
1971	Paz		$30	$50	$60	Cheli Durán		Macmil
1971	Three Apples Fell From Heaven		$30	$50	$60	Virginia A. Tashjian		LBrown
1972	Billy Goat And His Well-Fed Friends		$30	$50	$60	Nonny Hogrogian		H&Row
1972	Looking Over Hills		$30	$50	$60	David Kherdian		Giligia
1972	One I Love, Two I Love		$30	$50	$60	Nonny Hogrogian		Dutton
1972	The Hermit And Harry And Me		$30	$50	$60	Nonny Hogrogian		LBrown
1973	Visions Of America		$30	$50	$60	David Kherdian		Macmil
1975	Handmade Secret Hiding Places		$30	$40	$60	Nonny Hogrogian		Over
1976	Poems Here And Now		$30	$40	$60	David Kherdian		Green
1976	The Contest		$70	$100	$140	Nonny Hogrogian	CH	Green
1977	Carrot Cake		$25	$40	$50	Nonny Hogrogian		Green
1977	Country Cat, City Cat		$25	$40	$50	David Kherdian		4Winds
1977	Housebuilding		$25	$40	$50	Les Walker		Over
1977	The Dog Writes On The Window With His Nose		$25	$40	$50	David Kherdian		4Winds
1978	I Am Eyes		$25	$40	$50	Leila Ward		Green
1979	The Pearl		$25	$40	$50	Nonny Hogrogian		2Rivers
1981	Cinderella		$25	$35	$50	Nonny Hogrogian		Green
1983	Right Now		$25	$35	$50	David Kherdian		Knopf
1983	The Devil With The Three Golden Hairs		$25	$35	$50	Nonny Hogrogian		Knopf
1984	Root River Run		$20	$30	$40	David Kherdian		CRB
1984	The Animal		$20	$30	$40	David Kherdian		Knopf
1985	The Glass Mountain		$20	$30	$40	Nonny Hogrogian		Knopf
1986	Noah's Ark		$20	$30	$40	Nonny Hogrogian		Knopf
1988	The Cat Who Loved To Sing		$18	$25	$35	Nonny Hogrogian		Knopf
1988	The Day Boy And The Night Girl		$18	$25	$35	George MacDonald		Knopf
1989	A Song For Uncle Harry		$18	$25	$35	David Kherdian		Philo
1990	The Cat's Midsummer Jamboree		$16	$25	$30	David Kherdian		Philo
1991	Candy Floss		$16	$25	$30	Rumer Godden		Philo
1991	The Great Fishing Contest		$16	$25	$30	David Kherdian		Philo
1992	Feathers And Tails		$16	$25	$30	David Kherdian		Philo
1993	Asking The River		$16	$25	$30	David Kherdian		Orchard
1993	By Myself		$16	$25	$30	David Kherdian		Holt
1993	Juna's Journey		$16	$25	$30	David Kherdian		Philo
1995	Lullaby For Emily		$14	$20	$25	David Kherdian		Holt
1995	The First Christmas		$14	$20	$25	David Kherdian (retold)		Green
1997	The Golden Bracelet		$12	$18	$25	David Kherdian		Holiday
2002	The Tiger Of Turkestan		$8	$12	$16	Nonny Hogrogian		Hampton

Holbrook   Ruth

Year	Title	VG-	VG	VG+	Fine	Author	Award	Pub
1937	Timothy Titus	$50	$60	$80		Blanche Elliott		DD
1938	Cap'n Benny's Birdhouses ...	$50	$60	$80		Ruth Holbrook		DD
1939	Camping Down At Highgate	$50	$60	$80		Hildreth Tyler Wristen		DD
1940	Katy's Quilt	$50	$60	$80		Ruth Holbrook		DD

Holder   Heidi

Year	Title	VG-	VG	VG+	Fine	Author	Award	Pub
1981	Aesop's Fables		$25	$35	$50	Heidi Holder		Viking
1982	The Mousewife		$25	$35	$50	Rumor Gooden		Viking
1987	Crows		$20	$30	$40	Heidi Holder		FSG
1992	Carmine The Crow		$16	$25	$30	Heidi Holder		FSG
2004	The Lord's Prayer		$8	$10	$14	Heidi Holder		Front

Holland   Marion

Year	Title	VG-	VG	VG+	Fine	Author	Award	Pub
1947	You Never Can Tell	$35	$40	$60		Elizabeth Hart Ritter		G&D
1952	Billy Had A System	$30	$40	$50		Marion Holland		Knopf
1955	Billy's Clubhouse	$25	$35	$50		Marion Holland		Knopf
1956	Everygirls Horse Stories	$25	$35	$50		Marion Holland		Lantern
1956	No Children, No Pets	$25	$35	$50		Marion Holland		Knopf
1957	A Tree For Teddy	$25	$35	$50		Marion Holland		Knopf
1958	A Big Ball Of String	$100	$140	$180		Marion Holland		BB
1959	Muggsy	$25	$35	$50		Marion Holland		Knopf
1959	No Room For A Dog.	$25	$35	$50		Marion Holland		Random
1959	The Secret Horse	$25	$35	$50		Marion Holland		LBrown
1963	Teddy's Camp Out	$25	$30	$40		Marion Holland		Knopf
1964	Casey Jones Rides Vanity	$25	$30	$40		Marion Holland		LBrown

Holling   Holling Clancy

Year	Title	VG-	VG	VG+	Fine	Author	Award	Pub
1926	Little Big-Bye-And-Bye	$140	$180	$240		Holling Clancy Holling		Volland
1928	Claws Of The Thunderbird	$90	$120	$160		Holling Clancy Holling		Volland
1928	Rocky Billy	$90	$120	$160		Holling Clancy Holling		Macmil
1929	Little Folks Of Other Lands	$90	$120	$160		Watty Piper (pseud.)		P&Munk
1930	The Blot	$70	$100	$120		Phyllis Crawford		JCape
1931	The Twins Who Flew Around The World	$70	$100	$120		Holling Clancy Holling		P&Munk
1935	The Book Of Indians	$100	$140	$180		Holling Clancy Holling		P&Munk
1936	The Book Of Cowboys	$100	$140	$180		Holling Clancy Holling		P&Munk
1939	Little Buffalo Boy	$70	$90	$120		Holling Clancy Holling		GardenC
1941	Paddle-To-The-Sea	$220	$280	$360		Holling Clancy Holling	CH	HM
1942	Tree In The Trail	$70	$90	$120		Holling Clancy Holling		HM
1948	Seabird	$160	$200	$260		Holling Clancy Holling	NH	HM
1951	Minn Of The Mississippi	$140	$180	$240		Holling Clancy Holling	NH	HM
1952	The Road In Storyland	$50	$70	$90		Watty Piper (pseud.)		P&Munk
1957	Pagoo	$50	$70	$90		Holling Clancy Holling		HM
1964	The Magic Story Tree	$50	$60	$80		Holling Clancy Holling		P&Munk

Holmes   Sally

Year	Title	VG-	VG	VG+	Fine	Author	Award	Pub
1987	The Life Of Our Lord		$14	$20	$30	Neil Philip (adapted)		SBurdet
1988	The Twig Thing		$12	$16	$20	Jan Mark		VK
1989	The Snow Queen		$12	$16	$20	Neil Philip (adapted)		LL&S
1993	Complete Fairy Tales Of Charles Perrault		$10	$16	$20	Charles Perrault		Clarion
1995	Sleeping Beauty		$10	$14	$18	Tim & Jenny Wood (adapted)		AM
1995	Swan Lake		$10	$14	$18	Tim & Jenny Wood (adapted)		AM
1995	The Nutcracker		$10	$14	$18	Tim & Jenny Wood (adapted)		AM

Horse   Harry

Year	Title	VG-	VG	VG+	Fine	Author	Award	Pub
1983	Magus, The Lollipop Man		$16	$25	$30	Michael Mullen		Wolf
1993	The Last Polar Bears		$10	$16	$20	Harry Horse		Viking
1995	Horror Stories		$10	$14	$18	Susan Price		Kfisher
1996	A Friend For Little Bear		$8	$12	$16	Harry Horse		Candle
2000	Abu Ali Counts His Donkeys		$8	$10	$14	Dorothy Van Woerkom		Candle
2002	Little Rabbit Lost		$8	$10	$14	Harry Horse		Peach
2004	Anything For You		$6	$10	$12	John Wallace		HCollins
2004	Little Rabbit Goes To School		$6	$10	$12	Harry Horse		Peach

Houston   James A.

Year	Title	VG-	VG	VG+	Fine	Author	Award	Pub
1965	Tikta Liktak, An Eskimo Legend	$30	$40	$50		James A. Houston		HBrace
1966	Eagle Mask	$25	$30	$40		James A. Houston		HBrace
1966	The Unicorn Was There	$25	$30	$40		Elizabeth Routh Pool		Barre
1967	The White Archer	$25	$30	$40		James A. Houston		HBrace
1968	Akavak	$30	$40	$50		James A. Houston		HBrace
1971	Wolf Run, A Caribou Eskimo Tale		$18	$25	$35	James A. Houston		HBJ
1972	Ghost Paddle		$18	$25	$35	James A. Houston		HBJ
1972	Songs Of The Dream People		$18	$25	$35	James A. Houston		Athenm
1973	Kiviok's Magic Journey		$16	$25	$30	James A. Houston		Athenm
1981	Long Claws		$14	$20	$25	James A. Houston		Athenm

Houston — James A.

Year	Title	VG-	VG	VG+	Fine	Author	Award	Pub
1983	First Came The Indians		$14	$20	$25	M. J. Wheeler		Athenm
1986	The Falcon Bow		$12	$16	$20	James A. Houston		McEld
1998	Fire Into Ice		$8	$12	$16	James A. Houston		Tundra

Howard — Arthur

Year	Title	VG-	VG	VG+	Fine	Author	Award	Pub
1994	Mr. Putter And Tabby Bake The Cake		$12	$16	$20	Cynthia Rylant		HBrace
1994	Mr. Putter And Tabby Pour The Tea		$12	$16	$20	Cynthia Rylant		HBrace
1994	Mr. Putter And Tabby Walk The Dog		$12	$16	$20	Cynthia Rylant		HBrace
1995	Gooseberry Park		$10	$14	$18	Cynthia Rylant		HBrace
1995	Mr. Putter And Tabby Pick The Pears		$10	$14	$18	Cynthia Rylant		HBrace
1996	When I Was Five		$8	$12	$16	Arthur Howard		HBrace
1997	Mr. Putter And Tabby Fly The Plane		$8	$12	$16	Cynthia Rylant		HBrace
1997	Mr. Putter And Tabby Row The Boat		$8	$12	$16	Cynthia Rylant		HBrace
1998	Mr. Putter & Tabby Take The Train		$8	$12	$16	Cynthia Rylant		HBrace
1998	Mr. Putter & Tabby Toot The Horn		$8	$12	$16	Cynthia Rylant		HBrace
1999	Cosmo Zooms		$8	$12	$16	Arthur Howard		HBrace
1999	The Battlefield Ghost		$8	$12	$16	Margery Cuyler		Scholas
2000	100th Day Worries		$8	$10	$14	Margery Cuyler		S&S
2000	Mr. Putter & Tabby Paint The Porch		$8	$10	$14	Cynthia Rylant		Harcort
2001	Hoodwinked		$8	$10	$14	Arthur Howard		Harcort
2001	Mr. Putter & Tabby Feed The Fish		$8	$10	$14	Cynthia Rylant		Harcort
2001	Stop Drop And Roll		$8	$10	$14	Margery Cuyler		S&S
2002	Bubba And Beau, Best Friends		$8	$10	$14	Kathi Appelt		Harcort
2002	Mr. Putter & Tabby Catch The Cold		$8	$10	$14	Cynthia Rylant		Harcort
2003	Bubba And Beau Go Night-Night		$8	$10	$14	Kathi Appelt		Harcort
2003	Mr. Putter & Tabby Stir The Soup		$8	$10	$14	Cynthia Rylant		Harcort
2003	Serious Trouble		$8	$10	$14	Arthur Howard		Harcort
2004	Bubba And Beau Meet The Relatives		$6	$10	$12	Kathi Appelt		Harcort
2004	Mr. Putter & Tabby Write The Book		$6	$10	$12	Cynthia Rylant		Harcort
2004	The SOS File		$6	$10	$12	Betsy Cromer Byars		Holt

Howard — Kim

Year	Title	VG-	VG	VG+	Fine	Author	Award	Pub
1970	I Wonder... About The Sea.		$18	$25	$35	Enid Field		ElkG
1991	The Lovables In The Kingdom Of Self-Esteem		$10	$16	$20	Diane Loomans		Kramer
1991	The Other Side Of The Wall		$10	$16	$20	Denis Woychuk		LL&S
1992	Mimi & Gustav In Pirates!		$10	$16	$20	Denis Woychuk		LL&S
1994	A Cloak For The Dreamer		$10	$14	$18	Aileen Friedman		Scholas
1994	In Wintertime		$10	$14	$18	Kim Howard		LL&S
1995	Favorite Fairy Tales Told In Russia		$10	$14	$18	Virginia Haviland		Beech
1997	The Chief's Blanket		$8	$12	$16	Michael Chanin		Starsed
1997	Where Does God Live?		$8	$12	$16	Holly Bea		Starsed
1997	Zorro And Quwi		$8	$12	$16	Rebecca Hickox		DoubleD
1998	Percy To The Rescue		$8	$12	$16	Steven J. Simmons		Charles
1999	Rosa's Parrot		$8	$12	$16	Jan Wahl		WCoyote
2000	Good Night, God		$8	$10	$14	Holly Bea		Starsed
2000	My Spiritual Alphabet Book		$8	$10	$14	Holly Bea		Kramer
2001	Bless Your Heart		$8	$10	$14	Holly Bea		Kramer
2003	Thank You, God		$8	$10	$14	Holly Bea		Starsed
2004	God Believes In You		$6	$10	$12	Holly Bea		Starsed

Huang — Benrei

Year	Title	VG-	VG	VG+	Fine	Author	Award	Pub
1989	Surprise!		$14	$20	$25	Mary Packard		Grolier
1989	The Kite		$14	$20	$25	Mary Packard		Grolier
1990	Boo! Guess Who?		$10	$16	$20	Benrei Huang		Random
1991	A Visit To China		$10	$16	$20	Mary Packard		Western
1991	A Visit To France		$10	$16	$20	Kirsten Hall		Western
1991	A Visit To Great Britain		$10	$16	$20	Mary Packard		Western
1991	A Visit To The Soviet Union		$10	$16	$20	Mary Packard		Western
1992	A Visit To Australia		$10	$16	$20	Mary Packard		Western
1992	A Visit To Mexico		$10	$16	$20	Mary Packard		Western
1992	Merry Christmas		$10	$16	$20	Benrei Huang		G&D
1992	Monster Party		$10	$16	$20	Benrei Huang		G&D

Huang Benrei

Year	Title	VG-	VG	VG+	Fine	Author	Award	Pub
1992	Santa's Workshop		$10	$16	$20	Benrei Huang		G&D
1992	Spooky Night		$10	$16	$20	Benrei Huang		G&D
1993	Let's Go Riding In Our Strollers		$10	$16	$20	Fran Manushkin		Hyper
1993	The Teeny Tiny Woman		$10	$16	$20	Benrei Huang		G&D
1994	Jonah And The Whale		$10	$14	$18	Mary Josephs		Random
1994	One Hundred Is A Family		$10	$14	$18	Pam Muñoz Ryan		Hyper
1994	What Can A Giant Do?		$10	$14	$18	Mary Louise Cuneo		HCollins
1995	A Visit To Kenya		$10	$14	$18	Mary Packard		Western
1995	A Visit To Russia And Ukraine		$10	$14	$18	Mary Packard		Western
1995	Jack And The Beanstalk		$10	$14	$18	Benrei Huang		G&D
1995	The Quiet Way Home		$10	$14	$18	Bonny Becker		Holt
1996	Young Clara Barton		$8	$12	$16	Susan Alcott		Troll
1997	Little Slam-Dunker		$8	$12	$16	Heather Feldman		Random
1997	Man On The Moon		$8	$12	$16	Anastasia Suen		Viking
1997	Mr. Pak Buys A Story		$8	$12	$16	Carol J. Farley		AWhit
1998	The Bedtime Rhyme		$8	$12	$16	Walter, Jr. Wangerin		Augsb
1998	The Imp That Ate My Homework		$8	$12	$16	Laurence Yep		HCollins
1999	Moon Sandwich Mom		$8	$12	$16	Jennifer Jacobson		AWhit
2000	Big Daddy, Frog Wrestler		$8	$10	$14	Maribeth Boelts		AWhit
2000	This Is The Earth That God Made		$8	$10	$14	Lynn Downey		Augsb
2001	A Cat In The Stable		$8	$10	$14	Troon Harrison		Augsb
2001	The Shy Scarecrow		$8	$10	$14	Mary Packard		Scholas
2002	Are You Sleeping?		$8	$10	$14	Debbie Trafton O'Neal		Augsb
2002	Hunting The Daddyosaurus		$8	$10	$14	Teresa Bateman		AWhit
2002	Rainbow Fish: Spike And The Substitute		$8	$10	$14	Leslie Goldman		HFest
2002	Rainbow Fish: The Dangerous Deep		$8	$10	$14	Leslie Goldman		HFest
2002	Twinkle, Twinkle, Little Star		$8	$10	$14	Jane Taylor		Augsb
2003	Sheep Don't Count Sheep		$8	$10	$14	Margaret Wise Brown		McEld

Hubbard Woodleigh

Year	Title	VG-	VG	VG+	Fine	Author	Award	Pub
1990	C Is For Curious		$12	$18	$25	Woodleigh Hubbard		Chron
1991	2 Is For Dancing		$10	$16	$20	Woodleigh Hubbard		Chron
1993	Hip Cat		$10	$16	$20	Jonathan London		Chron
1993	The Friendship Book		$10	$16	$20	Woodleigh Hubbard		Chron
1993	The Moles And The Mireuk		$10	$16	$20	Holly H. Kwon		HM
1994	Four Fur Feet		$10	$14	$18	Margaret Wise Brown		Hyper
1996	The Precious Gift		$8	$12	$16	Ellen Jackson		S&S
1996	Woodleigh Marx Hubbard's 12 Days Of Christmas		$8	$12	$16	Woodleigh Hubbard		Chron
1997	Imaginary Menagerie		$8	$12	$16	Layne Longfellow		Chron
1999	Once I Was...		$8	$12	$16	Nikia Leopold		Putnam
2000	All That You Are		$8	$10	$14	Woodleigh Hubbard		Putnam
2001	Park Beat		$8	$10	$14	Jonathan London		HCollins
2002	Whoa, Jealousy		$8	$10	$14	Woodleigh Hubbard		Putnam
2003	For The Love Of A Pug		$8	$10	$14	Woodleigh Hubbard		Putnam

Hughes Shirley

Year	Title	VG-	VG	VG+	Fine	Author	Award	Pub
1959	The Curious Adventures Of Tabby	$70	$100	$120		E. H. Lang		Barnes
1960	Lucy And Tom's Day	$50	$60	$80		Shirley Hughes		WRScott
1966	The Faber Book Of Nursery Stories	$40	$60	$70		Barbara Ireson		Faber
1966	The Smallest Doll	$40	$60	$70		Margaret Storey		Faber
1967	Porterhouse Major	$40	$50	$70		Margaret Joyce Baker		P-Hall
1968	A Crown For A Queen	$40	$50	$70		Ursula Moray Williams		Mered
1968	The New Tenants	$40	$50	$70		Margaret M. MacPherson		HBrace
1968	Voices In The Fog	$40	$50	$70		Elizabeth Cheatham Walton		AS
1969	Flutes And Cymbals	$40	$50	$70		Leonard Clark		Crowell
1969	Stories For Seven-Year-Olds	$40	$50	$70		Sara & Stephen Corrin		FWatts
1969	Stories For Six-Year-Olds	$40	$50	$70		Sara & Stephen Corrin		FWatts
1969	The Holiday Map	$40	$50	$70		Ann Thwaite		Follett
1969	The Toymaker's Daughter	$40	$50	$70		Ursula Moray Williams		Mered
1970	Moshie Cat		$30	$50	$60	Helen Griffiths		Holiday
1970	Satchkin Patchkin		$30	$50	$60	Helen Axford Morgan		MacSm
1970	The Ruth Ainsworth Book		$30	$50	$60	Ruth Ainsworth		FWatts
1970	The Wood Street Secret		$30	$50	$60	Mabel Esther Allan		AS
1971	Cinderella		$30	$50	$60	Charles Perrault		Walck

Hughes   Shirley

Year	Title	VG-	VG	VG+	Fine	Author	Award	Pub
1971	Stories For Eight-Year-Olds		$30	$50	$60	Sara & Stephen Corrin		Faber
1971	The Three Toymakers		$30	$50	$60	Ursula Moray Williams		TNelson
1972	Malkin's Mountain		$30	$50	$60	Ursula Moray Williams		TNelson
1972	Mary Kate		$30	$50	$60	Helen Axford Morgan		TNelson
1972	The Little Broomstick		$30	$50	$60	Mary Stewart		Morrow
1973	Sally's Secret		$30	$50	$60	Shirley Hughes		Bodley
1973	Stories For Five-Year-Olds		$30	$50	$60	Sara & Stephen Corrin		Faber
1973	The Family Tree		$30	$50	$60	Margaret Storey		TNelson
1974	The Thirteen Days Of Christmas		$30	$40	$60	Jenny Overton		TNelson
1977	A Throne For Sesame		$25	$40	$50	Helen Young		Deutsch
1977	Dogger		$60	$80	$120	Shirley Hughes	GM	Bodley
1977	George, The Babysitter		$25	$40	$50	Shirley Hughes		P-Hall
1977	Make Hay While The Sun Shines		$25	$40	$50	Alison M. Abel		Faber
1977	Tattercoats		$25	$40	$50	Winifred Finlay		Harvey
1978	David And Dog		$25	$40	$50	Shirley Hughes		P-Hall
1978	Haunted House		$25	$40	$50	Shirley Hughes		P-Hall
1978	More Stories For Seven-Year-Olds		$25	$40	$50	Sara & Stephen Corrin		Faber
1978	The Phantom Carousel		$25	$40	$50	Ruth Ainsworth		Follett
1978	The Snailman		$25	$40	$50	Brenda Sivers		LBrown
1978	Trouble With Dragons		$25	$40	$50	Oliver G. Selfridge		AW
1979	Hans Andersen's Fairy Tales		$25	$40	$50	E. Jean Roberton (adapted)		Schock
1979	Moving Molly		$25	$40	$50	Shirley Hughes		P-Hall
1979	Stories For Nine-Year-Olds		$25	$40	$50	Sara & Stephen Corrin		Faber
1979	Up And Up		$25	$40	$50	Shirley Hughes		P-Hall
1980	The Phantom Fisherboy		$25	$35	$50	Ruth Ainsworth		Deutsch
1981	My Naughty Little Sister And Bad Harry's Rabbit		$25	$35	$50	Dorothy Edwards		P-Hall
1982	A Cat's Tale		$25	$35	$50	Rikki Cate		HBJ
1982	Alfie Gets In First		$40	$60	$80	Shirley Hughes		LL&S
1982	Alfie's Feet		$35	$50	$70	Shirley Hughes		LL&S
1982	Charlie Moon And The Big Bonanza Bust-Up		$25	$35	$50	Shirley Hughes		Bodley
1983	Alfie Gives A Hand		$30	$40	$60	Shirley Hughes		LL&S
1984	An Evening At Alfie's		$20	$30	$40	Shirley Hughes		LL&S
1985	Bathwater's Hot		$20	$30	$40	Shirley Hughes		LL&S
1985	More Naughty Little Sister Stories		$20	$30	$40	Dorothy Edwards		Metheun
1985	My Naughty Little Sister		$20	$30	$40	Dorothy Edwards		Metheun
1985	Noisy		$20	$30	$40	Shirley Hughes		LL&S
1985	When We Went To The Park		$20	$30	$40	Shirley Hughes		LL&S
1986	All Shapes And Sizes		$20	$30	$40	Shirley Hughes		LL&S
1986	Chips And Jessie		$20	$30	$40	Shirley Hughes		LL&S
1986	Colors		$20	$30	$40	Shirley Hughes		LL&S
1986	Here Comes Charlie Moon		$20	$30	$40	Shirley Hughes		LL&S
1986	Lucy & Tom's A.B.C		$20	$30	$40	Shirley Hughes		VK
1986	Lucy & Tom's Christmas		$20	$30	$40	Shirley Hughes		VK
1986	Two Shoes, New Shoes		$20	$30	$40	Shirley Hughes		LL&S
1987	Another Helping Of Chips		$20	$30	$40	Shirley Hughes		LL&S
1987	Lucy & Tom's 1,2,3		$20	$30	$40	Shirley Hughes		VK
1988	Dogger		$18	$25	$35	Shirley Hughes		LL&S
1988	Out And About		$18	$25	$35	Shirley Hughes		LL&S
1989	Angle Mae		$18	$25	$35	Shirley Hughes		LL&S
1989	The Big Alfie And Annie Rose Storybook		$18	$25	$35	Shirley Hughes		LL&S
1989	The Secret Garden		$18	$25	$35	Frances Hodgson Burnett		VK
1990	My Naughty Little Sister's Friends		$16	$25	$30	Dorothy Edwards		Mammoth
1990	The Big Concrete Lorry		$16	$25	$30	Shirley Hughes		LL&S
1990	The Snow Lady		$16	$25	$30	Shirley Hughes		LL&S
1991	My Naughty Little Sister Storybook		$16	$25	$30	Dorothy Edwards		Clarion
1991	Wheels		$16	$25	$30	Shirley Hughes		Walker
1992	The Big Alfie Out Of Doors Storybook		$16	$25	$30	Shirley Hughes		LL&S
1992	The Girl With The Green Ear		$16	$25	$30	Margaret Mahy		Knopf
1993	Bouncing		$16	$25	$30	Shirley Hughes		Candle
1993	Giving		$16	$25	$30	Shirley Hughes		Candle
1993	Stories By Firelight		$16	$25	$30	Shirley Hughes		LL&S
1993	The Nursery Collection		$16	$25	$30	Shirley Hughes		LL&S
1994	Chatting		$14	$20	$30	Shirley Hughes		Candle
1994	Hiding		$14	$20	$30	Shirley Hughes		Candle
1994	The Railway Children		$14	$20	$30	Edith Nesbit		Holt
1995	Rhymes For Annie Rose		$14	$20	$25	Shirley Hughes		LL&S
1996	Enchantment In The Garden		$12	$18	$25	Shirley Hughes		LL&S

Hughes   Shirley

Year	Title	VG-	VG	VG+	Fine	Author	Award	Pub
1997	Alfie And The Birthday Surprise		$12	$18	$25	Shirley Hughes		LL&S
1997	All About Alfie		$12	$18	$25	Shirley Hughes		LL&S
1997	Being Together		$12	$18	$25	Shirley Hughes		Candle
1997	Playing		$12	$18	$25	Shirley Hughes		Candle
1997	Tales Of Trotter Street		$12	$18	$25	Shirley Hughes		Candle
1998	Alfie's ABC		$12	$16	$20	Shirley Hughes		LL&S
1999	Abel's Moon		$12	$16	$20	Shirley Hughes		DK
1999	Helping		$12	$16	$20	Shirley Hughes		Candle
1999	Keeping Busy		$12	$16	$20	Shirley Hughes		Candle
1999	Let's Join In		$12	$16	$20	Shirley Hughes		Candle
1999	The Lion And The Unicorn		$12	$16	$20	Shirley Hughes		DK
2000	Alfie's 1 2 3		$10	$14	$18	Shirley Hughes		LL&S
2003	Annie Rose Is My Little Sister		$8	$12	$16	Shirley Hughes		Candle
2004	Ella's Big Chance		$25	$40	$50	Shirley Hughes	GM	S&S
2004	Olly And Me		$8	$10	$14	Shirley Hughes		Candle

Hull   Richard

Year	Title	VG-	VG	VG+	Fine	Author	Award	Pub
1990	The Living World		$12	$18	$25	Steve Parker		Hend
1991	Jellyfish To Insects		$10	$16	$20	William Hemsley		GloucP
1992	The Cat & The Fiddle & More		$10	$16	$20	Jim Aylesworth		Athenm
1994	The Alphabet From Z To A		$10	$14	$18	Judith Viorst		Athenm
1995	Sad Underwear		$10	$14	$18	Judith Viorst		Athenm
1996	My Sister's Rusty Bike		$8	$12	$16	Jim Aylesworth		Athenm
1998	Laura Ingalls Wilder's Fairy Poems		$20	$30	$40	Laura Ingalls Wilder		Bantam

Hurd   Clement

Year	Title	VG-	VG	VG+	Fine	Author	Award	Pub
1938	Bumble Bugs And Elephants	$100	$120	$160		Margaret Wise Brown		WRScott
1939	Country	$70	$90	$120		Clement Hurd		WRScott
1939	The World Is Round	$180	$240	$300		Gertrude Stein		WRScott
1939	Town	$70	$90	$120		Clement Hurd		WRScott
1940	Engine, Engine, No 9	$70	$90	$120		Edith Thacher Hurd		LL&S
1940	The Race	$70	$90	$120		Clement Hurd		Random
1941	Seraphine Went Walking	$70	$90	$120		Jane Serrage		Dutton
1941	Sky High	$70	$90	$120		Edith Thacher Hurd		LL&S
1942	Speedy, The Hook & Ladder Truck	$90	$120	$160		Edith Thacher Hurd		LL&S
1942	The Runaway Bunny	$90	$120	$160		Margaret Wise Brown		H&B
1947	Benny The Bulldozer	$60	$80	$100		Edith Thacher Hurd		LL&S
1947	Goodnight Moon	$80	$120	$140		Margaret Wise Brown		H&B
1947	The Bad Little Duckhunter	$80	$120	$140		Margaret Wise Brown		WRScott
1948	Hello Peter	$60	$80	$100		Morrell Gipson		DoubleD
1948	Toughy And His Trailer Truck	$60	$80	$100		Edith Thacher Hurd		LL&S
1949	My World	$80	$120	$140		Margaret Wise Brown		H&B
1949	Willy's Farm	$60	$80	$100		Edith Thacher Hurd		LL&S
1950	Caboose	$80	$120	$140		Edith Thacher Hurd		LL&S
1950	The Peppermint Family	$60	$80	$100		Margaret Wise Brown		H&B
1951	Old Silversides	$50	$70	$90		Edith Thacher Hurd		LL&S
1952	St George's Day In Williamsburg	$50	$70	$90		Edith Thacher Hurd		Cwill
1952	The Lion On Scott Street	$50	$70	$90		Jane Siepmann		Walck
1953	Somebody's House	$50	$70	$90		Edith Thacher Hurd		LL&S
1954	Nino And His Fish	$50	$70	$90		Edith Thacher Hurd		LL&S
1954	The Devil's Tail	$50	$70	$90		Edith Thacher Hurd		DoubleD
1955	Mr Charlie's Chicken House	$50	$70	$90		Edith Thacher Hurd		Lippin
1955	The Cat From Telegraph Hill	$50	$70	$90		Edith Thacher Hurd		LL&S
1955	The Little Brass Band	$70	$100	$120		Margaret Wise Brown		H&B
1956	Mary's Scary House	$100	$140	$180		Edith Thacher Hurd		Sterl
1956	Mr Charlie's Gas Station	$50	$70	$90		Edith Thacher Hurd		Lippin
1956	Windy And The Willow Whistle	$50	$70	$90		Edith Thacher Hurd		Sterl
1957	Christmas At Rancho Los Alamitos	$50	$70	$90		Katharine Bixby Hotchkis		CHS
1957	Fox In A Box	$50	$70	$90		Edith Thacher Hurd		DoubleD
1957	Johnny Littlejohn	$50	$70	$90		Edith Thacher Hurd		LL&S
1957	Mr Charlie's Camping Trip	$50	$70	$90		Edith Thacher Hurd		Lippin
1958	Mr Charlie, The Fireman's Friend	$50	$60	$80		Edith Thacher Hurd		Lippin
1958	The Faraway Christmas	$50	$60	$80		Edith Thacher Hurd		LL&S
1959	Last One Home Is A Green Pig	$50	$60	$80		Edith Thacher Hurd		H&B

Hurd   Clement

Year	Title	VG-	VG	VG+	Fine	Author	Award	Pub
1959	Mr Charlie's Pet Shop	$50	$60	$80		Edith Thacher Hurd		Lippin
1960	Hurry Hurry	$50	$60	$80		Edith Thacher Hurd		H&B
1960	Mr Charlie's Farm	$50	$60	$80		Edith Thacher Hurd		Lippin
1960	The Diggers	$70	$90	$120		Margaret Wise Brown		H&B
1961	Stop, Stop	$50	$60	$80		Edith Thacher Hurd		H&B
1962	Christmas Eve	$50	$60	$80		Edith Thacher Hurd		Harper
1962	Come And Have Fun	$50	$60	$80		Edith Thacher Hurd		Harper
1962	No Funny Business	$50	$60	$80		Edith Thacher Hurd		Harper
1962	Wingfin And Topple	$50	$60	$80		Evans G Valens		World
1963	Follow Tomas	$50	$60	$80		Edith Thacher Hurd		Dial
1963	Wildfire	$50	$60	$80		Evans G Valens		World
1965	Johnny Lion's Book	$40	$60	$70		Edith Thacher Hurd		H&Row
1965	The Day The Sun Danced	$40	$60	$70		Edith Thacher Hurd		H&Row
1965	The So-So Cat	$40	$60	$70		Edith Thacher Hurd		H&Row
1965	Winter's Birds	$40	$60	$70		May Garelick		YScott
1966	What Whale? Where?	$40	$60	$70		Edith Thacher Hurd		H&Row
1967	Little Dog, Dreaming	$40	$50	$70		Edith Thacher Hurd		H&Row
1968	Monkey In The Jungle	$40	$50	$70		Edna Mitchell Preston		Viking
1968	Rain And The Valley	$40	$50	$70		Edith Thacher Hurd		CM
1968	Stop Stop	$40	$50	$70		Edith Thacher Hurd		H&Row
1968	The Blue Heron Tree	$40	$50	$70		Edith Thacher Hurd		Viking
1969	This Is The Forest	$40	$50	$70		Edith Thacher Hurd		CM
1970	Catfish		$30	$50	$60	Edith Thacher Hurd		Viking
1970	Johnny Lion's Bad Day		$30	$50	$60	Edith Thacher Hurd		H&Row
1971	The Mother Beaver		$30	$50	$60	Edith Thacher Hurd		LBrown
1971	Wilson's World		$30	$50	$60	Edith Thacher Hurd		H&Row
1972	Johnny Lion's Rubber Boots		$30	$50	$60	Edith Thacher Hurd		H&Row
1972	The Mother Deer		$30	$50	$60	Edith Thacher Hurd		LBrown
1972	The Runaway Bunny		$18	$25	$35	Margaret Wise Brown		HCollins
1973	The Mother Whale		$30	$50	$60	Edith Thacher Hurd		LBrown
1973	Wilkie's World		$30	$50	$60	Edith Thacher Hurd		Faber
1974	Catfish And The Kidnapped Cat		$30	$40	$60	Edith Thacher Hurd		H&Row
1974	The Mother Owl		$30	$40	$60	Edith Thacher Hurd		LBrown
1975	Nicholas		$30	$40	$60	Ginny Cowles		Seabury
1976	The Mother Kangaroo		$30	$40	$60	Edith Thacher Hurd		LBrown
1977	Look For A Bird		$25	$40	$50	Edith Thacher Hurd		H&Row
1978	The Mother Chimpanzee		$25	$40	$50	Edith Thacher Hurd		LBrown
1980	Under The Lemon Tree		$25	$35	$50	Edith Thacher Hurd		LBrown
1984	The Goodnight Moon Room		$20	$30	$40	Margaret Wise Brown		H&Row
1986	The World Is Not Flat		$20	$30	$40	Edith Thacher Hurd		Arion
1991	Goodnight Moon		$10	$16	$20	Margaret Wise Brown		HFest
2002	Goodnight Moon Touch And Feel		$8	$10	$14	Margaret Wise Brown		HFest

Hurd   Thacher

Year	Title	VG-	VG	VG+	Fine	Author	Award	Pub
1978	The Old Chair		$25	$40	$50	Thacher Hurd		Green
1978	The Quiet Evening		$20	$30	$40	Thacher Hurd		Green
1981	Axle The Freeway Cat		$18	$25	$35	Thacher Hurd		H&Row
1983	Mystery On The Docks		$16	$25	$30	Thacher Hurd		H&Row
1984	Mama Don't Allow		$16	$25	$30	Thacher Hurd		H&Row
1986	The Pea Patch Jig		$14	$20	$30	Thacher Hurd		Crown
1988	Mattie And The Chicken Thief		$14	$20	$30	Ida Luttrell		DoddM
1989	Blackberry Ramble		$14	$20	$25	Thacher Hurd		Crown
1989	Wheel Away!		$14	$20	$25	Dayle Ann Dodds		H&Row
1990	Little Mouse's Big Valentine		$12	$18	$25	Thacher Hurd		H&Row
1991	Dinosaur Chase		$12	$18	$25	Carolyn Otto		HCollins
1992	Little Mouse's Birthday Cake		$12	$18	$25	Thacher Hurd		HCollins
1992	Tomato Soup		$12	$18	$25	Thacher Hurd		Crown
1995	Fritzi Fox Flew In From Florida		$10	$16	$20	Leah Komaiko		HCollins
1996	Art Dog		$10	$16	$20	Thacher Hurd		HCollins
1998	Santa Mouse And The Ratdeer		$10	$14	$18	Thacher Hurd		HCollins
1998	Zoom City		$10	$14	$18	Thacher Hurd		HCollins
2001	Cat's Pajamas		$8	$12	$16	Thacher Hurd		HFest
2003	Moo Cow Kaboom!		$8	$10	$14	Thacher Hurd		HCollins

Hutchins — Laurence

Year	Title	VG-	VG	VG+	Fine	Author	Award	Pub
1975	The House That Sailed Away		$30	$40	$60	Pat Hutchins		Green
1977	Follow That Bus!		$20	$30	$40	Pat Hutchins		Green
1981	The Mona Lisa Mystery		$18	$25	$35	Pat Hutchins		Green
1983	The Curse Of The Egyptian Mummy		$16	$25	$30	Pat Hutchins		Green
1989	Rats!		$14	$20	$25	Pat Hutchins		Green

Hutchins — Pat

Year	Title	VG-	VG	VG+	Fine	Author	Award	Pub
1967	Rosie's Walk	$40	$50	$70		Pat Hutchins		Macmil
1968	Tom And Sam.	$30	$40	$50		Pat Hutchins		Macmil
1969	The Surprise Party.	$25	$35	$50		Pat Hutchins		Macmil
1970	Clocks And More Clocks.		$25	$35	$50	Pat Hutchins		Macmil
1971	Changes, Changes		$30	$50	$60	Pat Hutchins	NYT	Macmil
1971	Titch		$25	$35	$50	Pat Hutchins		Macmil
1972	Good Night, Owl!		$25	$35	$50	Pat Hutchins		Macmil
1974	The Silver Christmas Tree.		$20	$30	$40	Pat Hutchins		Macmil
1974	The Wind Blew.		$60	$90	$120	Pat Hutchins	GM	Macmil
1976	Don't Forget The Bacon!		$20	$30	$40	Pat Hutchins		Green
1978	Happy Birthday, Sam		$20	$30	$40	Pat Hutchins		Green
1978	The Best Train Set Ever		$20	$30	$40	Pat Hutchins		Green
1979	One-Eyed Jake		$18	$25	$35	Pat Hutchins		Green
1980	The Tale Of Thomas Mead		$18	$25	$35	Pat Hutchins		Green
1982	1 Hunter		$16	$25	$30	Pat Hutchins		Green
1983	King Henry's Palace		$16	$25	$30	Pat Hutchins		Green
1983	You'll Soon Grow Into Them, Titch		$16	$25	$30	Pat Hutchins		Green
1985	The Very Worst Monster		$16	$25	$30	Pat Hutchins		Green
1986	The Doorbell Rang		$14	$20	$30	Pat Hutchins		Green
1988	Where's The Baby?		$14	$20	$30	Pat Hutchins		Green
1989	Which Witch Is Which?		$14	$20	$25	Pat Hutchins		Green
1990	What Game Shall We Play?		$12	$18	$25	Pat Hutchins		Green
1991	Tidy Titch		$12	$18	$25	Pat Hutchins		Green
1992	Silly Billy!		$12	$18	$25	Pat Hutchins		Green
1993	My Best Friend		$12	$16	$20	Pat Hutchins		Green
1994	Little Pink Pig		$12	$16	$20	Pat Hutchins		Green
1994	Three-Star Billy		$12	$16	$20	Pat Hutchins		Green
1996	Titch And Daisy		$10	$16	$20	Pat Hutchins		Green
1997	Shrinking Mouse		$10	$16	$20	Pat Hutchins		Green
1998	It's My Birthday!		$10	$14	$18	Pat Hutchins		Green
2000	Ten Red Apples		$8	$12	$16	Pat Hutchins		Green
2002	We're Going On A Picnic!		$8	$10	$14	Pat Hutchins		Green
2003	There's Only One Of Me!		$8	$10	$14	Pat Hutchins		Green
2004	Don't Get Lost!		$8	$10	$14	Pat Hutchins		Green

Hutton — Warwick

Year	Title	VG-	VG	VG+	Fine	Author	Award	Pub
1977	Noah And The Great Flood		$20	$30	$40	Warwick Hutton		Athenm
1979	The Sleeping Beauty		$14	$20	$30	Warwick Hutton		Athenm
1981	The Nose Tree		$14	$20	$25	Warwick Hutton		Athenm
1983	Jonah And The Great Fish		$14	$20	$25	Warwick Hutton	NYT	Athenm
1983	The Silver Cow		$25	$35	$50	Susan Cooper		Athenm
1985	Beauty And The Beast		$12	$18	$25	Warwick Hutton		Athenm
1986	Moses In The Bulrushes		$12	$16	$20	Warwick Hutton		Athenm
1986	The Selkie Girl		$20	$30	$40	Susan Cooper		McEld
1987	Adam And Eve		$12	$16	$20	Warwick Hutton		McEld
1988	The Tinderbox		$12	$16	$20	Hans Christian Andersen		McEld
1989	Theseus And The Minotaur		$12	$16	$20	Warwick Hutton	NYT	McEld
1990	To Sleep		$10	$16	$20	James Sage		McEld
1991	Tam Lin		$12	$18	$25	Susan Cooper		McEld
1992	The Trojan Horse		$10	$16	$20	Warwick Hutton		McEld
1993	Perseus		$10	$16	$20	Warwick Hutton		McEld
1994	Persephone		$10	$14	$18	Warwick Hutton		McEld
1994	The Cricket Warrior		$10	$14	$18	Margaret Chang		McEld
1995	Odysseus And The Cyclops		$10	$14	$18	Warwick Hutton		McEld

Hyman   Trina Schart

Year	Title	VG-	VG	VG+	Fine	Author	Award	Pub
1964	Billy Celebrates	$60	$80	$100		Edna B. Trickey		UCP
1964	Curl Up Small	$60	$80	$100		Sandol Stoddard		HM
1966	Billy Finds Out	$40	$60	$70		Edna B. Trickey		UCP
1966	Favorite Fairy Tales Told In Czechoslovakia	$40	$60	$70		Virginia Haviland		LBrown
1966	Joy To The World	$30	$40	$50		Ruth Sawyer		LBrown
1967	Cinnamon Seed	$60	$80	$100		John Travers Moore		HM
1967	Moon Eyes	$30	$40	$50		Josephine Poole		LBrown
1967	Stuck With Luck	$40	$50	$70		Elizabeth Johnson		LBrown
1967	The Five Trials Of The Pansy Bed	$60	$80	$100		J. David Townsend		HM
1967	The Magic Maker	$30	$40	$50		Joyce Varney		Bobbs
1968	All In Free But Janey	$60	$80	$100		Elizabeth Johnson		LBrown
1968	Epaminondas	$80	$120	$140		Eve Merriam		Follett
1968	The Cabin On The Fjord	$30	$40	$50		Susan Meyers		DoubleD
1968	The Half-Time Gypsy	$30	$40	$50		Joyce Varney		Bobbs
1968	The Little Red Flower	$60	$80	$100		Paul Tripp		DoubleD
1969	A Walk Out Of The World	$25	$35	$50		Ruth Nichols		HBrace
1969	Benjamin The True	$40	$50	$70		Claudea Paley		LBrown
1969	Dragon Stew	$60	$80	$100		Tom McGowen		Follett
1969	How Six Found Christmas	$60	$80	$100		Trina S. Hyman		LBrown
1969	The Coming Of Pout	$25	$35	$50		Peter Hunter Blair		LBrown
1969	The Moon Singer	$60	$80	$100		Clyde Robert Bulla		Crowell
1970	Greta The Strong		$25	$35	$50	Donald J. Sobol		Follett
1970	Let's Steal The Moon		$25	$35	$50	Blanche Serwer-Bernstein		LBrown
1970	Sir Machinery		$200	$280	$380	Tom McGowen		Follett
1970	The Pumpkin Giant		$25	$35	$50	Ellin Greene		LL&S
1970	The Shy Little Girl		$30	$50	$60	Phyllis Krasilovsky		HM
1970	The Vi-Daylin Book Of Minnie The Mump		$30	$50	$60	Paul Tripp		Ross
1970	The Walking Stones		$25	$35	$50	Mollie Hunter		H&Row
1971	A Room Made Of Windows		$25	$35	$50	Eleanor Cameron		LBrown
1971	Break A Magic Circle		$30	$50	$60	Elizabeth Johnson		LBrown
1971	Princess Rosetta And The Popcorn Man		$40	$60	$90	Ellin Greene		LL&S
1971	Take It Or Leave It		$25	$35	$50	Osmond Molarsky		Walck
1971	The Bigger They Come		$40	$60	$90	Osmond Molarsky		Walck
1971	The Bread Book		$25	$35	$50	Carolyn Meyer		HBJ
1971	The Ghost Next Door		$25	$35	$50	Wylly Folk St. John		H&Row
1972	Boy In The Middle		$25	$35	$50	Gladys Baker Bond		Ginn
1972	How I Went Shopping And What I Got		$30	$50	$60	Eleanor L. Clymer		HR&W
1972	Listen, Children, Listen		$25	$35	$50	Myra Cohn Livingston		HBJ
1972	Magic Heart		$40	$60	$90	Jan Wahl		Seabury
1972	Sarah And Katie		$25	$35	$50	Dori White		H&Row
1972	The Bad Times Of Irma Baumlein		$25	$35	$50	Carol Ryrie Brink		Macmil
1972	The Marrow Of The World		$25	$35	$50	Ruth Nichols		Athenm
1972	The Popular Girls Club		$40	$60	$90	Phyllis Krasilovsky		S&S
1972	The Wanderers		$25	$35	$50	Elizabeth Coatsworth		4Winds
1972	Who Says So?		$25	$35	$50	Paula Hendrich		LL&S
1973	Caddie Woodlawn		$40	$60	$90	Carol Ryrie Brink	NM	Macmil
1973	Clever Cooks		$25	$35	$50	Ellin Greene		LL&S
1973	Figgie Hobbin		$30	$50	$60	Charles Causley		Walker
1973	Joanna Runs Away		$40	$60	$90	Phyllis La Farge		HR&W
1973	King Stork		$40	$60	$90	Howard Pyle		LBrown
1974	Greedy Mariani & Other Folktales Of The Antilles		$20	$30	$40	Dorothy Carter		Athenm
1974	Snow White		$30	$40	$60	Paul Heins		LBrown
1974	The Big Green Bean		$30	$40	$60	Marcia Wiesbauer		Ginn
1974	The Everything Book		$20	$30	$40	Eleanor Graham Vance		Golden
1974	Two Queens Of Heaven: Aphrodite, Demeter		$30	$40	$60	Doris Gates		Viking
1974	Why Don't You Get A Horse, Sam Adams?		$30	$40	$60	Jean Fritz		CM&G
1974	You've Come A Long Way, Sybil Macintosh		$20	$30	$40	Charlotte Herman		Ohara
1975	Among The Dolls		$30	$40	$60	William Sleator		Dutton
1975	Magic In The Mist		$20	$30	$40	Margaret Mary Kimmel		Athenm
1975	Star Mother's Youngest Child		$30	$40	$60	Louise Moeri		HM
1975	The Quitting Deal		$30	$40	$60	Tobi Tobias		Viking
1976	Will You Sign Here, John Hancock?		$30	$40	$60	Jean Fritz		CM&G
1976	Witch Poems		$30	$40	$60	Daisy Wallace (edited)		Holiday
1977	And A Sunflower Grew		$25	$40	$50	Aileen Fisher		Bowmar
1977	Jane, Wishing		$25	$40	$50	Tobi Tobias		Viking
1977	Meet Guguze		$25	$40	$50	Spiridon Vangeli		AW
1977	South Star		$25	$40	$50	Betsy Gould Hearne		Athenm

Hyman　　　　　　Trina Schart

Year	Title	VG-	VG	VG+	Fine	Author	Award	Pub
1977	The Sleeping Beauty		$60	$80	$120	Trina S. Hyman		LBrown
1978	On To Widecombe Fair		$25	$40	$50	Patricia Lee Gauch		Putnam
1979	Home		$18	$25	$35	Betsy Gould Hearne		Athenm
1979	How Does It Feel To Be Old?		$35	$50	$70	Norma Farber		Dutton
1979	The Mechanical Doll		$25	$40	$50	Pamela Stearns		HM
1979	Tight Times		$25	$40	$50	Barbara Shook Hazen		Viking
1980	A Little Alphabet		$25	$35	$50	Trina S. Hyman		LBrown
1980	Fairy Poems		$35	$50	$70	Daisy Wallace		Holiday
1980	Peter Pan		$18	$25	$35	J. M. Barrie		Scribnr
1981	The Man Who Loved Books		$25	$35	$50	Jean Fritz		Putnam
1981	The Night Journey		$18	$25	$35	Kathryn Lasky		FWarne
1982	Rapunzel		$25	$35	$50	Barbara Rogasky (adapted)		Holiday
1983	A Christmas Carol		$16	$25	$30	Charles Dickens		Holiday
1983	Big Sixteen		$25	$35	$50	Mary Calhoun		Morrow
1983	Little Red Riding Hood		$100	$140	$200	Trina S. Hyman (adapted)	CH	Holiday
1984	Christmas Poems		$20	$30	$40	Myra Cohn Livingston		Holiday
1984	Saint George And The Dragon		$160	$220	$300	Margaret Hodges (adapted)	CM	LBrown
1984	The Cat Walked Through The Casserole		$20	$30	$40	Pamela Espeland		CRB
1985	A Child's Christmas In Wales		$16	$25	$30	Dylan Thomas		Holiday
1985	A Hidden Magic		$16	$25	$30	Vivian Vande Velde		Crown
1985	The Castle In The Attic		$16	$25	$30	Elizabeth Winthrop		Holiday
1986	The Water Of Life		$20	$30	$40	Barbara Rogasky		Holiday
1987	Cat Poems		$20	$30	$40	Myra Cohn Livingston		Holiday
1988	A Connecticut Yankee In King Arthur's Court		$14	$20	$30	Mark Twain		BOW
1988	Canterbury Tales		$18	$25	$35	Barbara Cohen (adapted)		LL&S
1989	Hershel And The Hanukkah Goblins		$50	$80	$100	Eric Kimmel	CH	Holiday
1989	Swan Lake		$18	$25	$35	Margot Fonteyn (adapted)		HBJ
1990	The Kitchen Knight		$16	$25	$30	Margaret Hodges		Holiday
1992	Ghost Eye		$12	$18	$25	Marion Dane Bauer		Scholas
1992	The Fortune Tellers		$16	$25	$30	Lloyd Alexander		Dutton
1994	Iron John		$14	$20	$30	Eric Kimmel		Holiday
1994	Winter Poems		$14	$20	$30	Barbara Rogasky		Scholas
1995	The Adventures Of Hershel Of Ostropol		$14	$20	$25	Eric Kimmel		Holiday
1996	Comus		$10	$16	$20	Margaret Hodges (adapted)		Holiday
1996	Haunts: Five Hair-Raising Tales		$10	$16	$20	Angela Shelf Medearis		Holiday
1996	The Ballad Of Lucy Whipple		$10	$16	$20	Karen Cushman		Clarion
1996	The Golem: A Version		$10	$16	$20	Barbara Rogasky		Holiday
1997	Bearskin		$10	$16	$20	Howard Pyle		Morrow
1997	Serpent Slayer & Other Stories Of Strong Women		$10	$16	$20	Katrin Tchana		LBrown
1998	A Smile So Big		$10	$14	$18	Kathleen Abel		HBrace
1999	A Child's Calendar		$35	$50	$70	John Updike	CH	Holiday
2000	The Alphabet Game		$8	$12	$16	Trina S. Hyman		SeaStar
2000	The Serpent Slayer		$8	$12	$16	Katrin Tchana		LBrown
2001	Children Of The Dragon		$8	$12	$16	Sherry Garland		Harcort
2002	Little Women		$8	$10	$14	Louisa May Alcott		HCollins
2002	Sense Pass King		$8	$10	$14	Katrin Tchana		Holiday
2004	Merlin And The Making Of A King		$8	$10	$14	Margaret Hodges (adapted)		Holiday

Ichikawa　　　　　　Satomi

Year	Title	VG-	VG	VG+	Fine	Author	Award	Pub
1976	A Child's Book Of Seasons		$30	$40	$60	Satomi Ichikawa		PMagP
1977	Friends		$20	$30	$40	Satomi Ichikawa		PMagP
1977	From Morn To Midnight		$20	$30	$40	Elaine Moss		Crowell
1977	Suzanne And Nicholas At The Market		$20	$30	$40	Satomi Ichikawa		FWatts
1977	Suzanne And Nicholas In The Garden		$20	$30	$40	Satomi Ichikawa		FWatts
1978	Keep Running, Allen!		$20	$30	$40	Clyde Robert Bulla		Crowell
1979	Playtime		$18	$25	$35	Cynthia Mitchell		Collins
1979	Under The Cherry Tree		$18	$25	$35	Cynthia Mitchell		Collins
1980	Sun Through Small Leaves		$18	$25	$35	Satomi Ichikawa		Collins
1980	Suzette & Nicholas And The Sunijudi Circus		$18	$25	$35	Michèle Lochak		Philo
1981	Let's Play		$18	$25	$35	Satomi Ichikawa		Philo
1982	Suzette & Nicholas And The Seasons Clock		$16	$25	$30	Marie-France Mangin		Philo
1983	Merry Christmas		$16	$25	$30	Robina Beckles Willson		Philo
1983	The Wonderful Rainy Week		$16	$25	$30	Martine Jaureguiberry		Philo
1985	Here A Little Child I Stand		$16	$25	$30	Cynthia Mitchell (selected)		Philo
1986	Nora's Castle		$14	$20	$30	Satomi Ichikawa		Philo

Ichikawa   Satomi

Year	Title	VG-	VG	VG+	Fine	Author	Award	Pub
1986	Suzette And Nicholas In The Garden		$14	$20	$30	Satomi Ichikawa		StMart
1988	Happy Birthday!		$14	$20	$30	Elizabeth Laird		Philo
1988	Sophie And Simon		$14	$20	$30	Marie-France Mangin		Macmil
1989	Dance, Tany		$14	$20	$25	Patricia Lee Gauch		Philo
1989	Nora's Stars		$14	$20	$25	Satomi Ichikawa		Philo
1990	Rosy's Garden		$12	$18	$25	Elizabeth Laird		Philo
1991	Nora's Duck		$12	$18	$25	Satomi Ichikawa		Philo
1992	Brave, Tanya		$12	$18	$25	Patricia Lee Gauch		Philo
1993	Fickle Barbara		$12	$16	$20	Satomi Ichikawa		Philo
1993	Nora's Roses		$12	$16	$20	Satomi Ichikawa		Philo
1994	Nora's Surprise		$12	$16	$20	Satomi Ichikawa		Philo
1994	Tanya And Emily In A Dance For Two		$12	$16	$20	Patricia Lee Gauch		Philo
1995	Isabela's Ribbons		$10	$16	$20	Satomi Ichikawa		Philo
1996	Tanya Steps Out		$10	$16	$20	Patricia Lee Gauch		Philo
1997	Tanya And The Magic Wardrobe		$10	$16	$20	Patricia Lee Gauch		Philo
1999	Grandpa's Soup		$10	$14	$18	Eiko Kadono		EerdB
1999	Presenting Tanya, The Ugly Duckling		$10	$14	$18	Patricia Lee Gauch		Philo
2001	The First Bear In Africa!		$8	$12	$16	Satomi Ichikawa		Philo
2001	What The Little Fir Tree Wore To Christmas Party		$8	$12	$16	Satomi Ichikawa		Philo
2001	You Are My I Love You		$8	$12	$16	Maryann K. Cusimano		Philo
2002	Tanya And The Red Shoes		$8	$10	$14	Patricia Lee Gauch		Philo
2002	The Tanya Treasury		$8	$10	$14	Patricia Lee Gauch		Philo
2003	My Pig Amarillo		$8	$10	$14	Satomi Ichikawa		Philo
2004	La La Rose		$8	$10	$14	Satomi Ichikawa		Philo

Ingpen   Robert

Year	Title	VG-	VG	VG+	Fine	Author	Award	Pub
1974	Storm-Boy		$30	$40	$60	Colin Thiele		Rigby
1975	Robe: A Portrait Of The Past		$20	$30	$40	Robert Ingpen		Rigby
1976	The Runaway Punt		$20	$30	$40	Michael Page		Rigby
1978	Lincoln's Place		$20	$30	$40	Colin Thiele		Rigby
1978	Tasmania, Paradise And Beyond		$20	$30	$40	Nick Evers		Rigby
1979	Australian Gnomes		$18	$25	$35	Robert Ingpen		Rigby
1979	Marking Time: Australia's Abandoned Buildings		$18	$25	$35	Robert Ingpen		Rigby
1980	The Voyage Of The Poppykettle		$18	$25	$35	Robert Ingpen		Rigby
1982	Aussie Battlers		$16	$25	$30	Michael Page		Rigby
1983	Lifetimes: Beautiful Way To Explain Death To Children		$16	$25	$30	Bryan Mellonie		Bantam
1987	Encyclopedia Of Things That Never Were		$20	$30	$40	Michael Page		Viking
1987	The Idle Bear		$14	$20	$30	Robert Ingpen		Bedrik
1987	The Stolen White Elephant		$14	$20	$30	Mark Twain		PubIntl
1988	A Strange Expedition		$14	$20	$30	Mark Twain		PubIntl
1988	The Age Of Acorns		$14	$20	$30	Robert Ingpen		Bedrik
1988	The Great Bullocky Race		$14	$20	$30	Michael Page		DoddM
1988	Worldly Dogs		$14	$20	$30	Michael Page		Lothian
1990	Peace Begins With You		$12	$18	$25	Katherine Schles		LBrown
1990	The Encyclopedia Of Mysterious Places:		$12	$18	$25	Philip Wilkinson		Viking
1990	The Great Deeds Of Superheroes		$12	$18	$25	Maurice Saxby (retold)		Bedrik
1990	The Making Of Australians		$12	$18	$25	Michael Page		HM
1991	Encyclopedia Of Events That Changed The World		$12	$18	$25	Philip Wilkinson		Viking
1992	Treasure Island		$12	$18	$25	Robert Louis Stevenson		Viking
1993	Encyclopedia Of Ideas That Changed The World		$12	$16	$20	Philip Wilkinson		Viking
1994	Folk Tales & Fables Of Asia & Australia		$12	$16	$20	Barbara Hayes		Chel
1994	Folk Tales & Fables Of Europe		$12	$16	$20	Barbara Hayes		Chel
1994	Folk Tales & Fables Of The Americas & The Pacific		$12	$16	$20	Barbara Hayes		Chel
1994	Folk Tales & Fables Of The Middle East And Africa		$12	$16	$20	Barbara Hayes		Chel
1994	Generals Who Changed The World		$12	$16	$20	J. Dineen & P. Wilkinson		Chel
1994	People Who Changed The World		$12	$16	$20	J. Dineen & P. Wilkinson		Chel
1994	River Through The Ages		$12	$16	$20	Philip Steele		Troll
1994	Statesmen Who Changed The World		$12	$16	$20	J. Dineen & P. Wilkinson		Chel
1994	The Lands Of The Bible		$12	$16	$20	J. Dineen & P. Wilkinson		Chel
1994	The Magical East		$12	$16	$20	M. Pollard & P. Wilkinson		Chel
1994	The Master Builders		$12	$16	$20	M. Pollard & P. Wilkinson		Chel
1995	Art And Technology Through The Ages		$10	$16	$20	J. Dineen & P. Wilkinson		Chel
1995	The Early Inventions		$10	$16	$20	J. Dineen & P. Wilkinson		Chel
1995	The Industrial Revolution		$10	$16	$20	J. Dineen & P. Wilkinson		Chel
1995	Transportation		$10	$16	$20	J. Dineen & P. Wilkinson		Chel

288

Ingpen Robert

Year	Title	VG-	VG	VG+	Fine	Author	Award	Pub
1996	A Celebration Of Customs & Rituals Of The World		$10	$16	$20	Philip Wilkinson		FOF
1996	Ghouls And Monsters		$10	$16	$20	Molly Perham		Chel
1996	Gods And Goddesses		$10	$16	$20	Molly Perham		Chel
1996	Heroes And Heroines		$10	$16	$20	Molly Perham		Chel
1996	Magicians And Fairies		$10	$16	$20	Molly Perham		Chel
1998	Feasts And Festivals		$10	$14	$18	Jacqueline Dineen		Chel
1998	Hunting, Harvesting, And Home		$10	$14	$18	Jacqueline Dineen		Chel
1999	Living With The Gods		$10	$14	$18	Jacqueline Dineen		Chel
1999	Rites Of Passage		$10	$14	$18	Jacqueline Dineen		Chel
2000	Who Is The World For?		$8	$12	$16	Tom Pow		Candle
2001	Shakespeare		$8	$12	$16	Michael Rosen		Candle
2002	Chief Seattle		$8	$10	$14	Anna Carew-Miller		Mason
2002	Halloween Circus At The Graveyard Lawn		$8	$10	$14	Charise Neugebauer		NSBooks
2003	Halloween Circus		$8	$10	$14	Charise Neugebauer		NSBooks
2003	Marco Polo		$8	$10	$14	John Riddle		Mason
2003	Mother Theresa		$8	$10	$14	Anne Marie Sullivan		Mason
2003	Robert F. Scott		$8	$10	$14	John Riddle		Mason
2004	Peter Pan And Wendy		$8	$10	$14	J. M. Barrie		Orchard

Ingraham Erick

Year	Title	VG-	VG	VG+	Fine	Author	Award	Pub
1977	Harry And Shellburt		$20	$30	$40	Dorothy Van Woerkom		Macmil
1977	The Hidden World		$20	$30	$40	Laurence Pringle		Macmil
1979	Cross-Country Cat		$14	$20	$30	Mary Calhoun		Morrow
1980	Old Blue		$14	$20	$25	Sibyl Hancock		Putnam
1980	Wide-Angle Lens		$14	$20	$25	Phyllis R. Fenner		Morrow
1981	Hot-Air Henry		$14	$20	$25	Mary Calhoun		Morrow
1982	Porcupine Stew		$14	$20	$25	Beverly Major Schwartz		Morrow
1988	Little Daylight		$12	$16	$20	George MacDonald		Morrow
1991	High-Wire Henry		$10	$16	$20	Mary Calhoun		Morrow
1993	The Animals' Lullaby		$10	$16	$20	Tom Paxton		Morrow
1994	Henry The Sailor Cat		$10	$14	$18	Mary Calhoun		Morrow
1995	Night In The Barn		$10	$14	$18	Faye Gibbons		Morrow
1997	Flood!		$8	$12	$16	Mary Calhoun		Morrow
1998	Blue-Ribbon Henry		$8	$12	$16	Mary Calhoun		Morrow
2002	Henry The Christmas Cat		$8	$10	$14	Mary Calhoun		HCollins

Inkpen Mick

Year	Title	VG-	VG	VG+	Fine	Author	Award	Pub
1985	The Nativity Play		$20	$30	$40	Nick Butterworth		LBrown
1986	The House On The Rock		$14	$20	$30	Nick Butterworth		Mult
1986	The Lost Sheep		$14	$20	$30	Nick Butterworth		Mult
1986	The Precious Pearl		$14	$20	$30	Nick Butterworth		Mult
1986	The Two Sons		$14	$20	$30	Nick Butterworth		Mult
1987	Nice Or Nasty		$14	$20	$30	Nick Butterworth		LBrown
1987	One Bear At Bedtime		$20	$30	$40	Mick Inkpen		H&S
1988	If I Had A Pig		$18	$25	$35	Mick Inkpen		Macmil
1988	If I Had A Sheep		$18	$25	$35	Mick Inkpen		Macmil
1989	Just Like Jasper		$14	$20	$25	Nick Butterworth		LBrown
1990	The Blue Balloon		$12	$18	$25	Mick Inkpen		LBrown
1990	Threadbear		$12	$18	$25	Mick Inkpen		H&S
1992	Billy's Beetle		$12	$18	$25	Mick Inkpen		HBJ
1992	Kipper		$25	$35	$50	Mick Inkpen		LBrown
1992	Kipper's Toybox		$20	$30	$40	Mick Inkpen		HBJ
1993	Anything Cuddly Will Do!		$12	$16	$20	Mick Inkpen		Orchard
1993	Crocodile!		$12	$16	$20	Mick Inkpen		Orchard
1993	Jasper's Beanstalk		$12	$16	$20	Nick Butterworth		BradP
1993	Kipper's Birthday		$12	$16	$20	Mick Inkpen		HBJ
1993	Penguin Small		$12	$16	$20	Mick Inkpen		HBJ
1994	Kipper's Book Of Counting		$12	$16	$20	Mick Inkpen		H&S
1994	Lullabyhullaballoo!		$12	$16	$20	Mick Inkpen		AWG
1995	Kipper's Book Of Colors		$10	$16	$20	Mick Inkpen		HBrace
1995	Kipper's Book Of Numbers		$10	$16	$20	Mick Inkpen		HBrace
1995	Kipper's Book Of Opposites		$10	$16	$20	Mick Inkpen		HBrace
1995	Kipper's Book Of Weather		$10	$16	$20	Mick Inkpen		HBrace
1995	Where, Oh Where, Is Kipper's Bear?		$10	$16	$20	Mick Inkpen		RWagon

Inkpen   Mick

Year	Title	VG-	VG	VG+	Fine	Author	Award	Pub
1995	Wibbly Pig Can Dance!		$10	$16	$20	Mick Inkpen		Golden
1995	Wibbly Pig Can Make A Tent		$10	$16	$20	Mick Inkpen		Golden
1995	Wibbly Pig Is Upset		$10	$16	$20	Mick Inkpen		Golden
1995	Wibbly Pig Likes Bananas		$10	$16	$20	Mick Inkpen		Golden
1995	Wibbly Pig Makes Pictures		$10	$16	$20	Mick Inkpen		Golden
1995	Wibbly Pig Opens His Presents		$10	$16	$20	Mick Inkpen		Golden
1996	Kipper's Snowy Day		$10	$16	$20	Mick Inkpen		HBrace
1997	Everyone Hide From Wibbly Pig		$10	$16	$20	Mick Inkpen		Viking
1998	Arnold		$10	$14	$18	Mick Inkpen		HBrace
1998	Honk! / Mick Inkpen		$10	$14	$18	Mick Inkpen		HBrace
1998	Nothing		$10	$14	$18	Mick Inkpen		Orchard
1998	Sandcastle		$10	$14	$18	Mick Inkpen		HBrace
1998	Splosh! / Mick Inkpen		$10	$14	$18	Mick Inkpen		HBrace
1998	Wonderful Earth!		$10	$14	$18	Nick Butterworth		TNelson
1999	Butterfly		$10	$14	$18	Mick Inkpen		Harcort
1999	Hissss!		$10	$14	$18	Mick Inkpen		Harcort
1999	Kipper's Christmas Eve		$10	$14	$18	Mick Inkpen		H&S
1999	The Great Pet Sale		$10	$14	$18	Mick Inkpen		Orchard
2000	In Wibbly's Garden		$8	$12	$16	Mick Inkpen		Viking
2000	Kipper's A To Z		$8	$12	$16	Mick Inkpen		Harcort
2000	Meow!		$8	$12	$16	Mick Inkpen		HBrace
2000	Swing! / Mick Inkpen		$8	$12	$16	Mick Inkpen		HBrace
2000	Wibbly Pig Is Happy!		$8	$12	$16	Mick Inkpen		Viking
2001	Kipper And Roly		$8	$12	$16	Mick Inkpen		Harcort
2001	Kipper's Rainy Day		$8	$12	$16	Mick Inkpen		HBrace
2001	Kipper's Sunny Day		$8	$12	$16	Mick Inkpen		RWagon
2001	Picnic		$8	$12	$16	Mick Inkpen		Harcort
2001	Rocket		$8	$12	$16	Mick Inkpen		Harcort
2001	Skates		$8	$12	$16	Mick Inkpen		Harcort
2002	Kipper's Kite		$8	$10	$14	Mick Inkpen		Harcort
2002	Kipper's Monster		$8	$10	$14	Mick Inkpen		Harcort
2002	Kipper's Surprise		$8	$10	$14	Mick Inkpen		Harcort

Ipcar   Dahlov

Year	Title	VG-	VG	VG+	Fine	Author	Award	Pub
1945	The Little Fisherman	$90	$120	$160		Margaret Wise Brown		WRScott
1946	All Babies Have Mummies & Daddies Just Like You	$60	$80	$100		Evelyn Beyer		WRScott
1947	Animal Hide & Seek	$60	$80	$100		Dahlov Ipcar		WRScott
1948	Good Work!	$60	$80	$100		John G. McCullough		WRScott
1950	One Horse Farm	$60	$80	$100		Dahlov Ipcar		DoubleD
1955	World Full Of Horses	$50	$70	$90		Dahlov Ipcar		DoubleD
1958	Ten Big Farms	$50	$60	$80		Dahlov Ipcar		Knopf
1958	The Wonderful Egg	$50	$60	$80		Dahlov Ipcar		DoubleD
1959	Brown Cow Farm	$50	$60	$80		Dahlov Ipcar		DoubleD
1960	I Like Animals	$50	$60	$80		Dahlov Ipcar		Knopf
1961	Deep Sea Farm	$50	$60	$80		Dahlov Ipcar		Knopf
1961	Stripes And Spots	$50	$60	$80		Dahlov Ipcar		DoubleD
1962	Lobsterman	$50	$60	$80		Dahlov Ipcar		Knopf
1962	Wild And Tame Animals	$50	$60	$80		Dahlov Ipcar		DoubleD
1963	Black And White	$50	$60	$80		Dahlov Ipcar		Knopf
1964	I Love My Anteater With An A	$50	$60	$80		Dahlov Ipcar		Knopf
1965	Horses Of Long Ago	$40	$60	$70		Dahlov Ipcar		DoubleD
1965	The Calico Jungle	$40	$60	$70		Dahlov Ipcar		Knopf
1966	Bright Barnyard	$40	$60	$70		Dahlov Ipcar		Knopf
1967	The Song Of The Day Birds & The Night Birds	$40	$50	$70		Dahlov Ipcar		DoubleD
1967	Whisperings & Other Things	$40	$50	$70		Dahlov Ipcar		Knopf
1968	The Wild Whirlwind	$40	$50	$70		Dahlov Ipcar		Knopf
1969	The Cat At Night	$40	$50	$70		Dahlov Ipcar		DoubleD
1969	The Warlock Of Night	$40	$50	$70		Dahlov Ipcar		Viking
1970	The Marvelous Merry-Go-Round		$30	$50	$60	Dahlov Ipcar		DoubleD
1971	Sir Addlepate And The Unicorn		$30	$50	$60	Dahlov Ipcar		DoubleD
1971	The Cat Came Back		$30	$50	$60	Dahlov Ipcar		Knopf
1972	The Biggest Fish In The Sea		$30	$50	$60	Dahlov Ipcar		Viking
1973	A Flood Of Creatures		$30	$50	$60	Dahlov Ipcar		Holiday
1973	The Queen Of Spells		$30	$50	$60	Dahlov Ipcar		Viking
1974	The Land Of Flowers		$30	$40	$60	Dahlov Ipcar		Viking

Ipcar   Dahlov

Year	Title	VG-	VG	VG+	Fine	Author	Award	Pub
1975	Bug City		$30	$40	$60	Dahlov Ipcar		Holiday
1976	Hard Scrabble Harvest		$30	$40	$60	Dahlov Ipcar		DoubleD
1978	A Dark Horn Blowing		$25	$40	$50	Dahlov Ipcar		Viking
1981	Lost And Found		$25	$35	$50	Dahlov Ipcar		DoubleD
1986	My Wonderful Christmas Tree		$20	$30	$40	Dahlov Ipcar		Gannett
1990	The Nightmare And Her Foal		$16	$25	$30	Dahlov Ipcar		NCP

Isadora   Rachel

Year	Title	VG-	VG	VG+	Fine	Author	Award	Pub
1976	Max		$30	$40	$60	Rachel Isadora		Macmil
1977	The Potters' Kitchen		$20	$30	$40	Rachel Isadora		Green
1977	Willaby		$20	$30	$40	Rachel Isadora		Macmil
1978	Backstage		$20	$30	$40	Robert Maiorano		Green
1978	Francisco		$20	$30	$40	Robert Maiorano		Macmil
1979	Ben's Trumpet		$50	$80	$100	Rachel Isadora	CH	Green
1979	Seeing Is Believing		$20	$30	$40	Elizabeth Shub		Green
1980	A Little Interlude		$18	$25	$35	Robert Maiorano		CM&G
1980	My Ballet Class		$18	$25	$35	Rachel Isadora		Green
1980	No, Agatha!		$18	$25	$35	Rachel Isadora		Green
1981	Jesse & Abe		$18	$25	$35	Rachel Isadora		Green
1981	The Nutcracker		$18	$25	$35	Rachel Isadora (adapted)		Macmil
1982	The White Stallion		$18	$25	$35	Elizabeth Shub		Green
1983	City Seen From A To Z		$18	$25	$35	Rachel Isadora		Green
1984	Opening Night		$16	$25	$30	Rachel Isadora		Green
1985	I Hear		$16	$25	$30	Rachel Isadora		Green
1985	I See		$16	$25	$30	Rachel Isadora		Green
1985	I Touch		$16	$25	$30	Rachel Isadora		Green
1986	Cutlass In The Snow		$16	$25	$30	Elizabeth Shub		Green
1986	Flossie & The Fox		$16	$25	$30	Patricia McKissack		Dial
1987	The Little Match Girl		$16	$25	$30	Hans Christian Andersen		Putnam
1988	The Pirates Of Bedford Street		$14	$20	$30	Rachel Isadora		Green
1989	The Princess And The Frog		$14	$20	$30	Jacob & Wilhelm Grimm		Green
1990	Babies		$14	$20	$25	Rachel Isadora		Green
1990	Friends		$14	$20	$25	Rachel Isadora		Green
1991	At The Crossroads		$14	$20	$25	Rachel Isadora		Green
1991	Swan Lake		$14	$20	$25	Rachel Isadora (adapted)		Putnam
1992	Golden Bear		$12	$18	$25	Ruth Young		Viking
1992	Over The Green Hills		$12	$18	$25	Rachel Isadora		Green
1992	Prayers, Praises, And Thanksgivings		$12	$18	$25	Sandol Stoddard (compiled)		Dial
1993	Grandfather's Lovesong		$12	$18	$25	Reeve Lindbergh		Viking
1993	Lili At Ballet		$12	$18	$25	Rachel Isadora		Putnam
1994	Firebird		$12	$18	$25	Rachel Isadora (adapted)		Putnam
1995	Lili On Stage		$12	$16	$20	Rachel Isadora		Putnam
1996	The Steadfast Tin Soldier		$10	$16	$20	Rachel Isadora (adapted)		Putnam
1997	Lili Backstage		$10	$16	$20	Rachel Isadora		Putnam
1997	Young Mozart		$10	$16	$20	Rachel Isadora		Viking
1998	A South African Night		$10	$16	$20	Rachel Isadora		Green
1998	Caribbean Dream		$10	$16	$20	Rachel Isadora		Putnam
1998	Isadora Dances		$10	$16	$20	Rachel Isadora		Viking
1998	The Little Mermaid		$10	$16	$20	Hans Christian Andersen		Putnam
1999	ABC Pop!		$10	$14	$18	Rachel Isadora		Viking
1999	Sophie Skates		$10	$14	$18	Rachel Isadora		Putnam
2000	123 Pop!		$8	$12	$16	Rachel Isadora		Viking
2000	Listen To The City		$8	$12	$16	Rachel Isadora		Putnam
2001	Nick Plays Baseball		$8	$12	$16	Rachel Isadora		Putnam
2002	Bring On That Beat		$8	$12	$16	Rachel Isadora		Putnam
2002	Mr. Moon		$8	$12	$16	Rachel Isadora		Green
2002	Peekaboo Morning		$8	$12	$16	Rachel Isadora		Putnam
2003	In The Beginning		$8	$10	$14	Rachel Isadora		Putnam
2003	Not Just Tutus		$8	$10	$14	Rachel Isadora		Putnam
2003	On Your Toes		$8	$10	$14	Rachel Isadora		Green
2004	Saving Strawberry Farm		$8	$10	$14	Deborah Hopkinson		Green

Ivory   Lesley Anne

Year	Title	VG-	VG	VG+	Fine	Author	Award	Pub
1979	Selections From The Owl And The Pussycat		$18	$25	$35	Lesley Anne Ivory		Burke

Ivory   Lesley Anne

Year	Title	VG-	VG	VG+	Fine	Author	Award	Pub
1988	Cats Know Best		$12	$16	$20	Colin Eisler		Dial
1989	Glorious Cats		$12	$16	$20	Lesley Anne Ivory		Crown
1989	Meet My Cats		$12	$16	$20	Lesley Anne Ivory		Dial
1991	Cats In The Sun		$10	$16	$20	Lesley Anne Ivory		Dial
1993	The Birthday Cat		$10	$16	$20	Lesley Anne Ivory		Dial
1995	Cats And Carols		$10	$14	$18	Lesley Anne Ivory		LBrown
1998	Star Cats		$8	$12	$16	Lesley Anne Ivory		LBrown

Jackson   Shelley

Year	Title	VG-	VG	VG+	Fine	Author	Award	Pub
1993	Do You Know Me		$12	$16	$20	Nancy Farmer		Orchard
1994	Great Aunt Martha		$10	$14	$18	Rebecca C. Jones		Dutton
1997	Willy's Silly Grandma		$8	$12	$16	Cynthia C. DeFelice		Orchard
1998	The Old Woman And The Wave		$8	$12	$16	Shelley Jackson		DK
2000	Escape South		$8	$10	$14	Kim L. Siegelson		Golden
2000	Sophia, The Alchemist's Dog		$8	$10	$14	Shelley Jackson		DK

James   Robin

Year	Title	VG-	VG	VG+	Fine	Author	Award	Pub
1974	In Search of the Saveopotomas		$16	$25	$30	Stephen Cosgrove		Serend
1974	Serendipity		$16	$25	$30	Stephen Cosgrove		Serend
1974	The Dream Tree		$16	$25	$30	Stephen Cosgrove		Serend
1974	The Gnome from Nome		$16	$25	$30	Stephen Cosgrove		Serend
1974	The Muffin Muncher		$16	$25	$30	Stephen Cosgrove		Creat
1974	Wheedle on the Needle		$14	$20	$25	Stephen Cosgrove		Serend
1975	Creole		$12	$18	$25	Stephen Cosgrove		Serend
1975	Hucklebug		$12	$18	$25	Stephen Cosgrove		Serend
1975	Jake O'Shawnasey		$12	$18	$25	Stephen Cosgrove		Serend
1975	Morgan and me		$12	$18	$25	Stephen Cosgrove		Serend
1976	Flutterby		$12	$18	$25	Stephen Cosgrove		Creat
1977	Leo the Lop		$12	$18	$25	Stephen Cosgrove		Serend
1978	Catundra		$12	$18	$25	Stephen Cosgrove		Creat
1978	Kartusch		$12	$18	$25	Stephen Cosgrove		Creat
1978	Little Mouse on the Prairie		$12	$18	$25	Stephen Cosgrove		Creat
1979	Bangalee		$12	$18	$25	Stephen Cosgrove		Creat
1979	Cap'n Smudge		$12	$18	$25	Stephen Cosgrove		Creat
1983	Morgan and Yew		$10	$16	$20	Stephen Cosgrove		PriceSS
1984	Feather Fin		$10	$16	$20	Stephen Cosgrove		Rourke
1984	Gabby		$10	$16	$20	Stephen Cosgrove		Rourke
1984	Grampa-Lop		$10	$16	$20	Stephen Cosgrove		Rourke
1984	Ming Ling		$10	$16	$20	Stephen Cosgrove		Rourke
1984	Morgan mine		$10	$16	$20	Stephen Cosgrove		Rourke
1984	Morgan morning		$10	$16	$20	Stephen Cosgrove		Rourke
1984	Raz-Ma-Taz		$10	$16	$20	Stephen Cosgrove		Rourke
1984	Tee-Tee		$10	$16	$20	Stephen Cosgrove		Rourke
1984	Trapper		$10	$16	$20	Stephen Cosgrove		Rourke
1985	Crabby Gabby		$10	$16	$20	Stephen Cosgrove		Rourke
1985	Dragolin		$10	$16	$20	Stephen Cosgrove		Rourke
1985	Flutterby fly		$10	$16	$20	Stephen Cosgrove		Rourke
1985	Glitterby Baby		$10	$16	$20	Stephen Cosgrove		Rourke
1985	Jingle Bear		$10	$16	$20	Stephen Cosgrove		Rourke
1985	Kiyomi		$10	$16	$20	Stephen Cosgrove		Rourke
1985	Minikin		$10	$16	$20	Stephen Cosgrove		Rourke
1985	Squeakers		$10	$16	$20	Stephen Cosgrove		Rourke
1986	Buttermilk		$10	$16	$20	Stephen Cosgrove		Rourke
1986	Fanny		$10	$16	$20	Stephen Cosgrove		Rourke
1986	Mumkin		$10	$16	$20	Stephen Cosgrove		Rourke
1986	Pish-Posh		$10	$16	$20	Stephen Cosgrove		Rourke
1987	Buttermilk-Bear		$10	$16	$20	Stephen Cosgrove		Rourke
1987	Crickle-Crack		$10	$16	$20	Stephen Cosgrove		Rourke
1987	Memily		$10	$16	$20	Stephen Cosgrove		Rourke
1987	Misty Morgan		$10	$16	$20	Stephen Cosgrove		Rourke
1988	Persnickity		$10	$14	$18	Stephen Cosgrove		PriceSS
1988	Rhubarb		$10	$14	$18	Stephen Cosgrove		PriceSS
1988	Sassafras		$10	$14	$18	Stephen Cosgrove		PriceSS
1988	Sniffles		$10	$14	$18	Stephen Cosgrove		PriceSS

James   Robin

Year	Title	VG-	VG	VG+	Fine	Author	Award	Pub
1988	The Gigglesnitcher		$10	$14	$18	Stephen Cosgrove		PriceSS
1989	Andy McLark, the Aardvark		$10	$14	$18	Kitty Higgins		PriceSS
1989	Perry P. Plum, the Possum		$10	$14	$18	Kitty Higgins		PriceSS
1989	Polly Porter, the Platypus		$10	$14	$18	Kitty Higgins		PriceSS
1989	Poppyseed		$10	$14	$18	Stephen Cosgrove		PriceSS
1989	The Grumpling		$10	$14	$18	Stephen Cosgrove		PriceSS
1989	Tickle's Tale		$10	$14	$18	Stephen Cosgrove		PriceSS
1989	Tippy Potter, the Otter		$10	$14	$18	Kitty Higgins		PriceSS
1989	Zippity Zoom		$10	$14	$18	Stephen Cosgrove		PriceSS
1990	Frazzle		$10	$14	$18	Stephen Cosgrove		PriceSS
1990	Jalopy		$10	$14	$18	Stephen Cosgrove		PriceSS
1990	Lady Rose		$10	$14	$18	Stephen Cosgrove		PriceSS
1990	Squabbles		$10	$14	$18	Stephen Cosgrove		PriceSS
1991	A House Full of Cats		$10	$14	$18	Kitty Higgins		PriceSS
1993	Maynard's Mermaid		$8	$12	$16	Robin James		PriceSS
1994	Napoleon's Rainbow		$8	$12	$16	Robin James		PriceSS
1994	Sadie		$8	$12	$16	Robin James		PriceSS
1995	Maui-Maui		$8	$12	$16	Stephen Cosgrove		PriceSS
2001	Muffin Dragon		$8	$10	$14	Stephen Cosgrove		PriceSS
2003	Shimmeree		$6	$10	$12	Stephen Cosgrove		PriceSS
2003	Sooty Foot		$6	$10	$12	Stephen Cosgrove		PriceSS
2003	The Puddle Pine		$6	$10	$12	Stephen Cosgrove		PriceSS

James   Simon

Year	Title	VG-	VG	VG+	Fine	Author	Award	Pub
1991	Dear Mr. Blueberry		$10	$16	$20	Simon James		McEld
1991	My Friend Whale		$12	$18	$25	Simon James		Bantam
1991	Sally And The Limpet		$10	$16	$20	Simon James		McEld
1993	The Wild Woods		$10	$16	$20	Simon James		Candle
1997	Leon And Bob		$8	$12	$16	Simon James		Candle
2000	Days Like This		$8	$10	$14	Simon James		Candle
2002	Jake And His Cousin Sidney		$8	$10	$14	Simon James		Candle
2002	Jake And The Babysitter		$8	$10	$14	Simon James		Candle
2002	The Birdwatchers		$8	$10	$14	Simon James		Candle
2002	The Day Jake Vacuumed		$8	$10	$14	Simon James		Candle
2003	Little One Step		$8	$10	$14	Simon James		Candle
2004	Baby Brains		$6	$10	$12	Simon James		Candle

Jeffers   Susan

Year	Title	VG-	VG	VG+	Fine	Author	Award	Pub
1967	Everyhow Remarkable	$60	$80	$100		Victoria Lincoln		Crowell
1969	The Buried Moon	$40	$60	$70		Joseph Jacobs		BradP
1969	Why You Look Like You	$40	$60	$70		Rosemary Wells		YScott
1970	The Spirit Of Spring		$30	$40	$60	Penelope Proddow		BradP
1971	The Circus Detectives		$35	$50	$70	Harriette Abels		Ginn
1973	The First Of The Penguins		$25	$40	$50	Mary Q. Steele		Macmil
1973	Three Jovial Huntsmen		$120	$180	$240	Susan Jeffers	CH	BradP
1974	All The Pretty Horses		$30	$50	$60	Susan Jeffers		Macmil
1976	Wild Robin		$30	$40	$60	Susan Jeffers		Dutton
1978	Close Your Eyes		$30	$40	$60	Jean Marzollo		Dial
1978	Stopping By Woods On A Snowy Evening		$30	$40	$60	Robert Frost		Dutton
1979	If Wishes Were Horses & Other Rhymes		$30	$40	$60	Mother Goose		Dutton
1979	Thumbelina		$50	$80	$100	Hans Christian Andersen		Dial
1980	Hansel And Gretel		$35	$50	$70	Jacob & Wilhelm Grimm		Dial
1980	Little People's Book Of Baby Animals		$25	$40	$50	Susan Jeffers		Random
1981	Snow White And The Seven Dwarfs		$35	$50	$70	Freya Littledale		4Winds
1981	The Wild Swans		$35	$50	$70	Amy Ehrlich (retold)		Dial
1982	The Snow Queen		$30	$50	$60	Amy Ehrlich (retold)		Dial
1982	Wynken, Blynken, And Nod		$25	$35	$50	Eugene Field		Dutton
1983	Hiawatha		$30	$50	$60	Henry Wadsworth Longfellow		Dial
1984	Silent Night		$25	$35	$50	Joseph Mohr		Dutton
1985	Cinderella		$30	$40	$60	Amy Ehrlich (retold)		Dial
1986	Black Beauty		$20	$30	$40	Robin McKinley (adapted)		Random
1987	Feel The Fear And Do It Anyway		$20	$30	$40	Susan Jeffers		HBJ
1987	The Midnight Farm		$20	$30	$40	Reeve Lindbergh		Dial
1988	Forest Of Dreams		$20	$30	$40	Rosemary Wells		Dial

Jeffers   Susan

Year	Title	VG-	VG	VG+	Fine	Author	Award	Pub
1989	Baby Animals		$18	$25	$35	Margaret Wise Brown		Random
1989	Opening Our Hearts To Men		$18	$25	$35	Susan Jeffers		FC
1990	Benjamin's Barn		$18	$25	$35	Reeve Lindbergh		Dial
1991	Brother Eagle, Sister Sky		$18	$25	$35	Chief Seattle		Dial
1993	Waiting For The Evening Star		$14	$20	$25	Rosemary Wells		Dial
1995	Lassie Come-Home		$12	$18	$25	Rosemary Wells		Holt
1997	McDuff And The Baby		$14	$20	$25	Rosemary Wells		Hyper
1997	McDuff Comes Home		$14	$20	$25	Rosemary Wells		Hyper
1997	McDuff Moves In		$14	$20	$25	Rosemary Wells		Hyper
1997	McDuff Shows The Way		$14	$20	$25	Rosemary Wells		HFest
1998	McDuff's New Friend		$12	$18	$25	Rosemary Wells		Hyper
1999	Rachel Field's Hitty, Her First Hundred Years		$10	$16	$20	Rosemary Wells		S&S
2000	The McDuff Stories		$10	$14	$18	Rosemary Wells		Hyper
2001	Love Songs Of The Little Bear		$8	$12	$16	Margaret Wise Brown		Hyper
2001	McDuff Goes To School		$8	$12	$16	Rosemary Wells		Hyper
2002	If I Had A Pony		$8	$12	$16	Susan Jeffers		Hyper
2002	K Is For Kitten		$8	$12	$16	Nikia Leopold		Putnam
2002	McDuff Saves The Day		$8	$12	$16	Rosemary Wells		Hyper
2004	Blueberries For The Queen		$8	$10	$14	Katherine Paterson		HCollins
2004	McDuff Steps Out		$8	$10	$14	Rosemary Wells		Hyper

Jeram   Anita

Year	Title	VG-	VG	VG+	Fine	Author	Award	Pub
1991	Bill's Belly Button		$12	$18	$25	Anita Jeram		Walker
1991	It Was Jake!		$10	$16	$20	Anita Jeram		LBrown
1993	All Pigs Are Beautiful		$10	$16	$20	Dick King-Smith		Candle
1994	My Hen Is Dancing		$10	$14	$18	Karen Wallace		Candle
1994	The Most Obedient Dog In The World		$10	$14	$18	Anita Jeram		Candle
1995	Contrary Mary		$10	$14	$18	Anita Jeram		Candle
1995	Daisy Dare		$10	$14	$18	Anita Jeram		Candle
1995	Guess How Much I Love You		$35	$50	$70	Sam McBratney		Candle
1995	I Love Guinea Pigs		$10	$14	$18	Dick King-Smith		Candle
1996	Dick King-Smith's Animal Friends		$8	$12	$16	Dick King-Smith		Candle
1998	Birthday Happy, Contrary Mary		$8	$12	$16	Anita Jeram		Candle
1999	All Together Now		$8	$12	$16	Anita Jeram		Candle
1999	Bunny, My Honey		$8	$12	$16	Anita Jeram		Candle
2001	Kiss Good Night		$8	$10	$14	Amy Hest		Candle
2002	Don't You Feel Well, Sam?		$8	$10	$14	Amy Hest		Candle
2002	I Love My Little Storybook		$8	$10	$14	Anita Jeram		Candle
2003	Bunny Love		$8	$10	$14	Anita Jeram		Candle
2003	You Can Do It, Sam		$8	$10	$14	Amy Hest		Candle
2004	You're All My Favorites		$6	$10	$12	Sam McBratney		Candle

Jeschke   Susan

Year	Title	VG-	VG	VG+	Fine	Author	Award	Pub
1973	Wild Boy		$25	$35	$50	Joan Tate		H&Row
1974	Firerose		$16	$25	$30	Susan Jeschke		HR&W
1974	The Times They Used To Be		$16	$25	$30	Lucille Clifton		HR&W
1975	Sidney		$16	$25	$30	Susan Jeschke		HR&W
1975	The Devil Did It		$16	$25	$30	Susan Jeschke		HR&W
1976	Busybody Nora		$16	$25	$30	Johanna Hurwitz		Morrow
1976	Outrageous Kasimir		$16	$25	$30	Achim Bröger		Morrow
1976	Rima And Zeppo		$16	$25	$30	Susan Jeschke		Windmil
1976	Victoria's Adventure		$16	$25	$30	Susan Jeschke		HR&W
1977	Nora And Mrs. Mind-Your-Own-Business		$16	$25	$30	Johanna Hurwitz		Morrow
1978	A Mitzvah Is Something Special		$14	$20	$30	Phyllis Rose Eisenberg		H&Row
1978	Mia, Grandma And The Genie		$14	$20	$30	Susan Jeschke		HR&W
1979	Angela And Bear		$14	$20	$30	Susan Jeschke		HR&W
1979	New Neighbors For Nora		$14	$20	$30	Johanna Hurwitz		Morrow
1980	Perfect, The Pig		$14	$20	$25	Susan Jeschke		HR&W
1980	Superduper Teddy		$14	$20	$25	Johanna Hurwitz		Morrow
1980	Tamar And The Tiger		$14	$20	$25	Susan Jeschke		HR&W
1981	Saturday I Ran Away		$14	$20	$25	Susan Pearson		Lippin
1981	Sometimes It Happens		$14	$20	$25	Elinor Lander Horwitz		H&Row
1983	Bats Aren't Sweet		$14	$20	$25	Marilyn Jeffers Walton		Rain
1983	Possum Crest's Greatest Christmas Show		$14	$20	$25	Marilyn Jeffers Walton		Rain

Jeschke   Susan

Year	Title	VG-	VG	VG+	Fine	Author	Award	Pub
1983	Sparky's Valentine Victory		$14	$20	$25	Marilyn Jeffers Walton		Rain
1983	Tea And Whoppers		$14	$20	$25	Marilyn Jeffers Walton		Rain
1987	Lucky's Choice		$12	$16	$20	Susan Jeschke		Scholas
1990	Scary Night Visitors		$10	$16	$20	Irene & Paul Marcus		Magin
1992	Into The Great Forest		$10	$16	$20	Irene & Paul Marcus		Magin

Johnson   Crockett

Year	Title	VG-	VG	VG+	Fine	Author	Award	Pub
1943	Barnaby	$200	$280	$340		Crockett Johnson		Holt
1943	This Rich World	$140	$180	$240		Constance Jackson Foster		McBride
1944	Barnaby And Mr. O'malley	$140	$180	$220		Crockett Johnson		Holt
1945	The Carrot Seed	$300	$400	$500		Ruth Krauss		H&B
1950	Story Of Money	$120	$160	$200		Constance Jackson Foster		McBride
1952	Who's Upside Down!	$140	$180	$240		Crockett Johnson		WRScott
1954	How To Make An Earthquake	$160	$200	$260		Ruth Krauss		H&B
1954	Willie's Adventures	$260	$340	$420		Margaret Wise Brown		WRScott
1955	Harold And The Purple Crayon	$1,800	$2,400	$3,000		Crockett Johnson		H&B
1956	Barkis	$100	$140	$180		Crockett Johnson		S&S
1956	Mickey's Magnet	$100	$140	$180		Franklyn M. Branley		Crowell
1957	Harold's Trip To The Sky	$540	$720	$900		Crockett Johnson		H&B
1957	Terrible Terrifying Toby	$120	$160	$220		Crockett Johnson		H&B
1957	Time For Spring	$100	$140	$180		Crockett Johnson		H&B
1958	Merry Go Round	$100	$140	$180		Crockett Johnson		H&B
1958	The Blue Ribbon Puppies	$100	$140	$180		Crockett Johnson		H&B
1959	Ellen's Lion	$140	$200	$240		Crockett Johnson		H&B
1959	Frowning Prince	$100	$140	$180		Crockett Johnson		H&B
1959	Harold's Circus	$520	$680	$860		Crockett Johnson		H&B
1960	A Picture For Harold's Room	$500	$680	$840		Crockett Johnson		H&B
1963	The Lion's Own Story	$100	$120	$160		Crockett Johnson		H&Row
1964	We Wonder What Will Walter Be?	$90	$120	$160		Crockett Johnson		HR&W
1965	Gordy And The Pirate	$90	$120	$160		Crockett Johnson		Putnam
1967	The Happy Egg	$120	$160	$220		Ruth Krauss		Ohara

Johnson   David

Year	Title	VG-	VG	VG+	Fine	Author	Award	Pub
1997	The Beggar's Magic		$8	$12	$16	Margaret Chang		McEld
1997	The Bremen Town Musicians		$8	$12	$16	David Johnson		Rabbit
1998	Old Mother Hubbard		$8	$12	$16	David Johnson		McEld
2002	Abraham Lincoln		$8	$10	$14	Amy Cohn		Scholas

Johnson   Paul Brett

Year	Title	VG-	VG	VG+	Fine	Author	Award	Pub
1993	Saint Patrick And The Peddler		$12	$16	$20	Margaret Hodges		Orchard
1993	The Cow Who Wouldn't Come Down		$12	$16	$20	Paul Brett Johnson		Orchard
1994	Frank Fister's Hidden Talent		$10	$14	$18	Paul Brett Johnson		Orchard
1995	Insects Are My Life		$10	$14	$18	Megan McDonald		Orchard
1996	Lost		$8	$12	$16	Celeste Lewis		Orchard
1996	The Wild Ride Of Miss Impala George		$8	$12	$16	Eric Metaxas		Orchard
1997	Farmers' Market		$8	$12	$16	Paul Brett Johnson		Orchard
1997	Too Quiet For These Old Bones		$8	$12	$16	Tres Seymour		Orchard
1998	A Perfect Pork Stew		$8	$12	$16	Paul Brett Johnson		Orchard
1998	A Traveling Cat		$8	$12	$16	George Ella Lyon		Orchard
1998	An Appalachian Mother Goose		$8	$12	$16	James Still		UofK
1999	Bedbugs		$8	$12	$16	Megan McDonald		Orchard
1999	Old Dry Frye		$8	$12	$16	Paul Brett Johnson		Scholas
1999	The Pig Who Ran A Red Light		$8	$12	$16	Paul Brett Johnson		Orchard
2000	Bearhide And Crow		$8	$10	$14	Paul Brett Johnson		Holiday
2000	Mr. Persnickety And Cat Lady		$8	$10	$14	Paul Brett Johnson		Orchard
2001	Fearless Jack		$8	$10	$14	Paul Brett Johnson		McEld
2001	Reptiles Are My Life		$8	$10	$14	Megan McDonald		Orchard
2001	The Goose Who Went Off In A Huff		$8	$10	$14	Paul Brett Johnson		Orchard
2002	Jack Outwits The Giants		$8	$10	$14	Paul Brett Johnson		McEld
2003	The Best Kind Of Gift		$8	$10	$14	Kathi Appelt		HCollins
2004	Little Bunny Foo Foo		$6	$10	$12	Paul Brett Johnson		Scholas

Johnson — Stephen T.

Year	Title	VG-	VG	VG+	Fine	Author	Award	Pub
1992	The Nutcracker Ballet		$16	$25	$30	Melissa Hayden		AM
1992	The Samurai's Daughter		$12	$18	$25	Robert D. San Souci		Dial
1993	A Christmas Carol		$12	$16	$20	Donna Martin (adapted)		AM
1993	The Snow Wife		$12	$16	$20	Robert D. San Souci		Dial
1995	Alphabet City		$35	$50	$70	Stephen Johnson	CH	Viking
1995	The Tie Man's Miracle		$10	$16	$20	Steven Schnur		Morrow
1995	When Solomon Was King		$10	$16	$20	Sheila MacGill-Callahan		Dial
1996	The Girl Who Wanted A Song		$10	$16	$20	Steve Sanfield		HBrace
1997	Hoops		$10	$16	$20	Robert Burleigh		Whistle
1998	City By Numbers		$10	$14	$18	Stephen T. Johnson		Viking
1999	Love As Strong As Ginger		$10	$14	$18	Lenore Look		Athenm
2000	Goal		$8	$12	$16	Robert Burleigh		HBrace
2000	My Little Red Toolbox		$8	$12	$16	Stephen T. Johnson		HBrace
2000	On A Wintry Morning		$8	$12	$16	Dori Chaconas		Viking
2001	The Hurrying Child		$8	$12	$16	Jane Yolen		Whistle
2002	As The City Sleeps		$8	$10	$14	Stephen Johnson		Viking
2002	My Little Blue Robot		$8	$10	$14	Stephen T. Johnson		Whistle
2003	Tour America		$8	$10	$14	Diane Siebert		SeaStar

Johnson — Steve

Year	Title	VG-	VG	VG+	Fine	Author	Award	Pub
1989	No Star Nights		$14	$20	$25	Anna Egan Smucker		Knopf
1991	The Frog Prince Continued		$16	$25	$30	Jon Scieszka		Viking
2002	Robin's Room		$8	$10	$14	Margaret Wise Brown		Hyper

Jonas — Ann

Year	Title	VG-	VG	VG+	Fine	Author	Award	Pub
1982	When You Were A Baby		$16	$25	$30	Ann Jonas		Green
1984	Holes And Peeks		$12	$18	$25	Ann Jonas		Green
1985	The Trek		$12	$18	$25	Ann Jonas		Green
1990	Aardvarks, Disembark		$10	$16	$20	Ann Jonas		Green

Jones — Elizabeth Orton

Year	Title	VG-	VG	VG+	Fine	Author	Award	Pub
1937	David	$160	$200	$260		Elizabeth Orton Jones		Macmil
1937	Ragman Of Paris And His Ragamuffins	$160	$200	$260		Elizabeth Orton Jones		Oxford
1938	Brownies - Hush!	$100	$120	$160		Gladys L. Adshead		Oxford
1938	The Scarlet Oak	$100	$120	$160		Cornelia Meigs		Macmil
1939	Minnie The Mermaid	$100	$120	$160		Thomas Orton Jones		Oxford
1939	Told Under The Magic Umbrella	$100	$120	$160		Elizabeth Orton Jones		Macmil
1940	Maminka's Children	$100	$120	$160		Elizabeth Orton Jones		Macmil
1942	Twig	$140	$180	$240		Elizabeth Orton Jones		Macmil
1943	Small Rain	$160	$220	$280		Jessie Mae Orton Jones	CH	Viking
1943	The Peddler's Clock	$90	$120	$160		Mabel Leigh Hunt		G&D
1944	Prayer For A Child	$220	$280	$360		Rachel Field	CM	Macmil
1944	What Miranda Knew	$90	$120	$160		Gladys L. Adshead		Oxford
1945	A Prayer For Little Things	$90	$120	$160		Eleanor Farjean		HM
1945	Secrets	$90	$120	$160		Jessie Mae Orton Jones		Viking
1946	A Little Child	$90	$120	$160		Jessie Mae Orton Jones		Viking
1947	Big Susan	$120	$160	$220		Elizabeth Orton Jones		Macmil
1948	Little Red Riding Hood	$120	$160	$220		Elizabeth Orton Jones		Golden
1951	This Is The Way	$80	$100	$140		Jessie Mae Orton Jones		Viking
1952	Song Of The Sun	$80	$100	$140		Elizabeth Orton Jones		Macmil
1955	Deep River	$70	$100	$120		Howard Thurman		H&B
1955	How Far Is It To Bethlehem?	$70	$100	$120		Elizabeth Orton Jones		Horn
1955	Lullaby For Eggs	$70	$100	$120		Betty Bridgman		Macmil
1956	To Church We Go	$70	$100	$120		Robbie Trent		Follett

Jonke — Tim

Year	Title	VG-	VG	VG+	Fine	Author	Award	Pub
1989	The Tale Of Three Trees		$14	$20	$25	Angela Elwell Hunt		Lion
1994	Somewhere Angels		$10	$14	$18	Larry Libby		G&H
1995	Someone Awesome		$10	$14	$18	Larry Libby		G&H
1996	A Night The Stars Danced For Joy		$8	$12	$16	Bob Hartman		Lion
1998	God's Joyful Noise		$8	$12	$16	Nancy Sweetland		EerdB

Jonke   Tim

Year	Title	VG-	VG	VG+	Fine	Author	Award	Pub
1998	Little Rose Of Sharon		$8	$12	$16	Nan Gurley		Chariot
1999	The Easter Angels		$8	$12	$16	Bob Hartman		Lion
2001	I'll Love You Anyway & Always		$8	$10	$14	Bryan Chapell		Crossw

Joyce   William

Year	Title	VG-	VG	VG+	Fine	Author	Award	Pub
1983	My First Book Of Nursery Tales		$40	$60	$90	Marianna Mayer		Random
1984	Mother Goose		$30	$50	$60	Mother Goose		Random
1984	Waiting-For-Spring Stories		$20	$30	$40	Bethany Roberts		H&Row
1985	George Shrinks		$60	$90	$120	William Joyce		H&Row
1986	Shoes		$20	$30	$40	Elizabeth Winthrop		H&Row
1987	Humphrey's Bear		$20	$30	$40	Jan Wahl		Holt
1988	Dinosaur Bob		$50	$80	$100	William Joyce		H&Row
1989	Nicholas Crickett		$35	$50	$70	Joyce Maxner	NYT	H&Row
1990	A Day With Wilbur Robinson		$35	$50	$70	William Joyce		HCollins
1990	Some Of The Adventures Of Rhode Island Red		$16	$25	$30	Stephen Manes		Lippin
1992	Bentley And Egg		$20	$30	$40	William Joyce		HCollins
1993	Santa Calls		$20	$30	$40	William Joyce		LauraG
1996	The Leaf Men And The Brave Good Bugs		$16	$25	$30	William Joyce		LauraG
1997	Buddy		$16	$25	$30	William Joyce		HCollins
1998	Life With Bob		$12	$16	$20	William Joyce		LauraG
1999	Baseball Bob		$12	$16	$20	William Joyce		LauraG
1999	Rolie Polie Olie		$35	$50	$70	William Joyce		LauraG
2000	Be My Pal!		$10	$14	$18	William Joyce		MouseW
2000	Little Spot Of Color		$10	$14	$18	William Joyce		MouseW
2000	Snowie Rolie		$16	$25	$30	William Joyce		HCollins
2001	Sleepy Time Olie		$10	$14	$18	William Joyce		LauraG
2002	Big Time Olie		$8	$12	$16	William Joyce		LauraG
2004	True Story Of E. Astor Bunnyman & The Eggs Of Wonder		$6	$10	$12	William Joyce		LauraG

Karas   G. Brian

Year	Title	VG-	VG	VG+	Fine	Author	Award	Pub
1983	Shaggy Dog Riddles		$25	$35	$50	Lori Miescke		AWhit
1985	Arnold Plays Baseball		$16	$25	$30	Patricia Whitehead		Troll
1985	Here Comes Hungry Albert		$16	$25	$30	Patricia Whitehead		Troll
1985	Home For A Dinosaur		$16	$25	$30	Eileen Curran		Troll
1985	The Scoop On Ice Cream		$16	$25	$30	Vicki Cobb		LBrown
1986	Good Luck, Bad Luck		$14	$20	$30	Rita Schlachter		Troll
1986	Squeaky Shoes		$14	$20	$30	Morgan Matthews		Troll
1986	The Great Potato Book		$14	$20	$30	Meredith Sayles Hughes		Macmil
1987	I'm Telling!		$14	$20	$30	Eric H. Arnold		LBrown
1988	101 Questions And Answers About Pets & People		$14	$20	$30	Ann Squire		Macmil
1988	Here Comes Winter		$14	$20	$30	Janet Palazzo-Craig		Troll
1988	Playground Fun		$14	$20	$30	Sharon Gordon		Troll
1989	Madison Moves To The Country		$14	$20	$25	Melanie Martin		Troll
1989	Morris The Millionaire Mouse		$14	$20	$25	Melanie Martin		Troll
1989	Simple Science Says--Take One Mirror		$14	$20	$25	Melvin Berger		Scholas
1989	Who's There?		$14	$20	$25	Porter Gold		Rain
1990	Brenda's Private Swing		$12	$18	$25	G. Maccarone & B. Chardiet		Scholas
1990	Freddie The Frightened & Wondrous Ms. Wardrobe		$12	$18	$25	Pamela Shrapnel		Knopf
1990	If You're Not Here, Please Raise Your Hand		$12	$18	$25	Kalli Dakos		4Winds
1990	Merry Christmas, What's Your Name?		$12	$18	$25	G. Maccarone & B. Chardiet		Scholas
1990	The Best Teacher In The World		$12	$18	$25	G. Maccarone & B. Chardiet		Scholas
1990	Who Goes Out On Halloween?		$12	$18	$25	Sue Alexander		Bantam
1991	Martin And The Tooth Fairy		$12	$18	$25	G. Maccarone & B. Chardiet		Scholas
1991	The Forever Secret		$12	$18	$25	Neal Starkman		CHE
1991	The Holiday Handwriting School		$12	$18	$25	Robin Pulver		4Winds
1992	Eek! Stories To Make You Shriek		$12	$18	$25	Jane O'Connor		G&D
1992	Math Fun With A Pocket Calculator		$12	$18	$25	Rose Wyler		Messner
1992	Nobody's Mother Is In Second Grade		$12	$18	$25	Robin Pulver		Dial
1992	Pigeon, Pigeon		$12	$18	$25	Caron Lee Cohen		Dutton
1992	The Snowball War		$12	$18	$25	G. Maccarone & B. Chardiet		Scholas
1992	We Scream For Ice Cream		$12	$18	$25	G. Maccarone & B. Chardiet		Scholas
1992	Westward Ho Ho Ho!		$12	$18	$25	Victoria Hartman		Viking
1993	Dear Mr. President		$12	$16	$20	Stuart E. Hample		Workman
1993	Don't Read This Book Whatever You Do!		$12	$16	$20	Kalli Dakos		4Winds

Karas   G. Brian

Year	Title	VG-	VG	VG+	Fine	Author	Award	Pub
1993	Into This Night We Are Rising		$12	$16	$20	Jonathan London		Viking
1993	Odds 'N' Ends Alvy		$12	$16	$20	John Frank		4Winds
1994	Cinder-Elly		$12	$16	$20	Frances Minters		Viking
1994	I Know An Old Lady		$20	$30	$40	G. Brian Karas		Scholas
1994	Outdoor Science Adventures		$12	$16	$20	Melvin Berger		Scholas
1994	Three Little Bikers		$12	$16	$20	Tony Johnston		Knopf
1994	Truman's Aunt Farm		$12	$16	$20	Jama Kim Rattigan		HM
1994	We Dare You!		$12	$16	$20	Harriet Ziefert		S&S
1995	Like Butter On Pancakes		$10	$16	$20	Jonathan London		Viking
1995	Martin And The Teacher's Pets		$10	$16	$20	G. Maccarone & B. Chardiet		Scholas
1995	On The Trail With Miss Pace		$10	$16	$20	Sharon Phillips Denslow		S&S
1995	Scare The Moon		$10	$16	$20	Harriet Ziefert		Candle
1996	A Dog Named Sam		$10	$16	$20	Janice Boland		Dial
1996	Give Me Half!		$10	$16	$20	Stuart J. Murphy		HCollins
1996	Home On The Bayou		$16	$25	$30	G. Brian Karas		S&S
1996	Mr. Carey's Garden		$10	$16	$20	Jane Cutler		HM
1996	My Crayons Talk		$10	$16	$20	Patricia Hubbard		Holt
1996	No Way, Winky Blue!		$10	$16	$20	Pamela Jane		Mondo
1996	Saving Sweetness		$10	$16	$20	Diane Stanley		Putnam
1996	Sid And Sam		$10	$16	$20	Nola Buck		HCollins
1996	Sleepless Beauty		$10	$16	$20	Frances Minters		Viking
1996	The Nature Of The Beast		$10	$16	$20	Jan Carr		Tambour
1996	The Spider Who Created The World		$10	$16	$20	Amy MacDonald		Orchard
1997	Bootsie Barker Ballerina		$10	$16	$20	Barbara Bottner		HCollins
1997	Elevator Magic		$10	$16	$20	Stuart J. Murphy		HCollins
1997	Puddles		$10	$16	$20	Jonathan London		Viking
1998	Carlita Ropes The Twister		$10	$14	$18	Yanitzia Canetti		Steck-V
1998	Good Knight		$10	$14	$18	Linda R Rymill		Holt
1998	In The Hush Of The Evening		$10	$14	$18	Nancy Price Graff		HCollins
1998	It's A Deal, Dogboy		$10	$14	$18	Christine McDonnell		Viking
1998	The Windy Day		$14	$20	$30	G. Brian Karas		S&S
1998	Throw Your Tooth On The Roof		$10	$14	$18	Selby B Beeler		HM
1999	I Like Bugs		$14	$20	$25	Margaret Wise Brown		Golden
1999	Raising Sweetness		$10	$14	$18	Diane Stanley		Putnam
1999	The Bone Keeper		$10	$14	$18	Megan McDonald		DK
2000	Bebe's Bad Dream		$10	$14	$18	G. Brian Karas		Green
2000	Daniel's Mystery Egg		$8	$12	$16	Alma Flor Ada		Harcort
2000	Follow The Leader		$8	$12	$16	Erica Silverman		FSG
2000	Penelope Jane		$8	$12	$16	Rosanne Cash		Cotler
2000	The High Rise Private Eyes		$8	$12	$16	Cynthia Rylant		Green
2000	The Seals On The Bus		$8	$12	$16	Lenny Hort		Holt
2001	Car Wash		$8	$12	$16	Sandra & Susan Steen		Putnam
2001	Missing Mittens		$8	$12	$16	Stuart J. Murphy		HCollins
2001	The Class Artist		$8	$12	$16	G. Brian Karas		Green
2001	The High-Rise Private Eyes		$8	$12	$16	Cynthia Rylant		Green
2001	Toad Food & Measle Soup		$8	$12	$16	Christine McDonnell		Viking
2002	7 X 9 = Trouble!		$8	$10	$14	Claudia Mills		FSG
2002	Atlantic		$8	$10	$14	G. Brian Karas		Putnam
2002	Daniel's Pet		$8	$10	$14	Alma Flor Ada		Harcort
2002	Incredible Me!		$8	$10	$14	Kathi Appelt		HCollins
2002	Muncha! Muncha! Muncha!		$8	$10	$14	Candace Fleming		Athenm
2002	Princess Fishtail		$8	$10	$14	Frances Minters		Viking
2002	Skidamarink		$8	$10	$14	G. Brian Karas		HFest
2002	The Case Of The Puzzling Possum		$8	$10	$14	Cynthia Rylant		Harper
2003	Oh No, Gotta Go!		$8	$10	$14	Susan Middleton Elya		Putnam
2003	Put Your Eyes Up Here		$8	$10	$14	Kalli Dakos		S&S
2003	Ten Little Mummies		$8	$10	$14	Philip Yates		Viking
2003	That Crazy Barb'ra		$8	$10	$14	Milton Schafer		Dial
2003	The Case Of The Fidgety Fox		$8	$10	$14	Cynthia Rylant		Green
2004	Barfburger Baby, I Was Here First!		$8	$10	$14	Paula Danziger		Putnam
2004	Best Friends		$8	$10	$14	Anna Michaels		Harcort
2004	I Like Where I Am		$8	$10	$14	Jessica Harper		Putnam
2004	The Case Of The Baffled Bear		$8	$10	$14	Cynthia Rylant		Green

Kastner   Jill

Year	Title	VG-	VG	VG+	Fine	Author	Award	Pub
1989	Aurora Means Dawn		$14	$20	$25	Scott R. Sanders		BradP
1989	With A Name Like Lulu, Who Needs More Trouble?		$14	$20	$25	Tricia Springstubb		DelaP
1990	Lulu Vs. Love		$10	$16	$20	Tricia Springstubb		DelaP
1990	Night Owls		$10	$16	$20	Sharon Phillips Denslow		BradP
1990	Sarah's Surprise		$10	$16	$20	Sally H. Alexander		Macmil
1991	Mrs. Mcclosky's Monkeys		$10	$16	$20	Elvira Woodruff		Scholas
1992	I Want To Go Home		$10	$16	$20	Alice McLerran		Tambour
1992	You're My Nikki		$10	$16	$20	Phyllis Rose Eisenberg		Dial
1993	Naomi Knows It's Springtime		$10	$16	$20	Virginia L. Kroll		Boyds
1993	Snake Hunt		$10	$16	$20	Jill Kastner		4Winds
1993	Song For The Ancient Forest		$10	$16	$20	Nancy Luenn		Athenm
1994	Down At Angel's		$10	$14	$18	Sharon Chmielarz		Ticnor
1994	El Niño Pastor		$10	$14	$18	Kristine L. Franklin		Athenm
1994	The Shepherd Boy		$10	$14	$18	Kristine L. Franklin		Athenm
1995	The Stone Dancers		$10	$14	$18	Nora Martin		Athenm
1997	Barnyard Big Top		$8	$12	$16	Jill Kastner		S&S
1997	Beardream		$8	$12	$16	Will Hobbs		Athenm
1998	Howling Hill		$8	$12	$16	Will Hobbs		Morrow
1998	The Waterfall		$8	$12	$16	Jonathan London		Viking
1999	The Lizard Man Of Crabtree County		$8	$12	$16	Lucy A. Nolan		MCaven
2000	In November		$8	$10	$14	Cynthia Rylant		HBrace
2001	Princess Dinosaur		$8	$10	$14	Jill Kastner		Green
2001	White Water		$8	$10	$14	Jonathan London		Viking
2002	Merry Christmas, Princess Dinosaur!		$8	$10	$14	Jill Kastner		Green

Keats   Ezra Jack

Year	Title	VG-	VG	VG+	Fine	Author	Award	Pub
1954	Animal Stories	$50	$70	$90		Joel Chandler Harris		Junior
1954	Chester	$50	$70	$90		Eleanor L. Clymer		DoddM
1954	Jubilant For Sure	$120	$160	$200		Elizabeth H. Lansing		Crowell
1955	Mystery On The Isle Of Skye	$50	$70	$90		Phyllis A. Whitney		Westmin
1955	The Peterkin Papers	$50	$70	$90		Lucretia Hale		Junior
1955	Wonder Tales Of Dogs And Cats	$50	$70	$90		Frances Carpenter		DoubleD
1956	Sure Thing For Shep	$50	$70	$90		Elizabeth H. Lansing		Crowell
1956	Three Young Kings	$50	$70	$90		George S. Albee		FWatts
1957	Danny Dunn On A Desert Island	$50	$70	$90		J. Williams & R. Abrashkin		Whittle
1957	Little Hawk And The Free Horses	$50	$70	$90		Glenn Balch		Crowell
1957	Song Of The River	$50	$70	$90		Billy C. Clark		Crowell
1957	The Indians Knew	$50	$70	$90		Tillie S. Pine		Whittle
1957	The Pilgrims Knew	$50	$70	$90		T. Pine & J. Levine		Whittle
1957	Wee Joseph	$50	$70	$90		William Mac Kellar		McHill
1958	Danny Dunn And The Homework Machine	$50	$60	$80		J. Williams & R. Abrashkin		Whittle
1958	The Chinese Knew	$50	$60	$80		T. Pine & J. Levine		Whittle
1959	And Long Remember	$50	$60	$80		Dorothy Canfield Fisher		Whittle
1959	Danny Dunn And The Weather Machine	$50	$60	$80		J. Williams & R. Abrashkin		Whittle
1959	That First Easter	$50	$60	$80		Henry Denker		Crowell
1959	The Brave Riders	$50	$60	$80		Glenn Balch		Crowell
1960	My Dog Is Lost!	$50	$60	$80		Pat Cherr		Crowell
1960	Nihal	$50	$60	$80		Eleanor Albertson Murphey		Crowell
1960	The Peg-Legged Pirate Of Sulu	$50	$60	$80		Cora Cheney		Knopf
1960	The Tournament Of The Lions	$50	$60	$80		Jay Williams		Walck
1961	A Flood In Still River	$50	$60	$80		Bianca Bradbury		Dial
1961	In The Night	$50	$60	$80		Paul Showers		Crowell
1961	Three Children Of Chile	$50	$60	$80		Ella Huff Kepple		Friend
1962	The Eskimos Knew	$50	$60	$80		T. Pine & J. Levine		Whittle
1962	The Rice Bowl Pet	$50	$60	$80		Patricia Miles Martin		Crowell
1962	The Snowy Day	$220	$280	$360		Ezra Jack Keats	CM	Viking
1962	The Time Of The Wolves	$50	$60	$80		Verne T. Davis		Morrow
1962	What Good Is A Tail?	$50	$60	$80		Solveig Paulson Russell		Bobbs
1963	Farm Dog	$50	$60	$80		David Malcolmson		LBrown
1963	Jim Can Swim	$50	$60	$80		Helen Diehl Olds		Knopf
1963	Our Rice Village In Cambodia	$50	$60	$80		Ruth Tooze		Viking
1963	The Buffalo And The Bell	$50	$60	$80		Myra Scovel		Friend
1963	The Flying Cow	$50	$60	$80		Ruth Philpott Collins		Walck
1963	The Gobbler Called	$50	$60	$80		Verne T. Davis		Morrow
1963	Tía María's Garden	$50	$60	$80		Ann Nolan Clark		Viking

Keats   Ezra Jack

Year	Title	VG-	VG	VG+	Fine	Author	Award	Pub
1964	Speedy Digs Downside Up	$50	$60	$80		Maxine Kumin		Putnam
1964	The Egyptians Knew	$50	$60	$80		T. Pine & J. Levine		McHill
1964	Whistle For Willie	$90	$120	$160		Ezra Jack Keats		Viking
1964	Zoo, Where Are You?	$50	$60	$80		Ann McGovern		H&Row
1965	In A Spring Garden	$40	$60	$70		Richard Lewis		Dial
1965	John Henry	$90	$120	$160		Ezra Jack Keats		Pan
1965	The Naughty Boy	$40	$60	$70		John Keats		Viking
1966	Danny Dunn And The Anti-Gravity Paint	$40	$60	$70		J. Williams & R. Abrashkin		McHill
1966	God Is In The Mountain	$60	$80	$100		Ezra Jack Keats		HR&W
1966	How To Be A Nature Detective	$40	$60	$70		Millicent Selsam		H&Row
1966	Jennie's Hat	$90	$120	$160		Ezra Jack Keats		H&Row
1967	Peter's Chair	$60	$80	$100		Ezra Jack Keats		H&Row
1968	A Letter To Amy	$60	$80	$100		Ezra Jack Keats		H&Row
1968	In The Park	$40	$50	$70		Esther Rudomin Hautzig		Macmil
1968	The Little Drummer Boy	$40	$50	$70		Katherine Davis		Macmil
1969	Goggles!	$80	$120	$140		Ezra Jack Keats	CH	Macmil
1970	Hi, Cat!		$50	$70	$90	Ezra Jack Keats		Macmil
1971	Apt 3		$40	$60	$90	Ezra Jack Keats		Macmil
1971	Over In The Meadow		$40	$60	$90	Ezra Jack Keats		4Winds
1971	The King's Fountain		$30	$50	$60	Lloyd Alexander		Dutton
1971	Two Tickets To Freedom		$30	$50	$60	Florence B. Freedman		S&S
1972	Penny Tunes And Princesses		$30	$50	$60	Myron Levoy		H&Row
1972	Pet Show!		$35	$50	$70	Ezra Jack Keats		Macmil
1974	Dreams		$35	$50	$70	Ezra Jack Keats		Collier
1975	Louie		$30	$50	$60	Ezra Jack Keats		Green
1978	The Trip		$30	$50	$60	Ezra Jack Keats		Green
1979	Maggie And The Pirate		$30	$40	$60	Ezra Jack Keats		4Winds
1980	Louie's Search		$30	$40	$60	Ezra Jack Keats		4Winds
1981	Regards To The Man In The Moon		$25	$40	$50	Ezra Jack Keats		4Winds
1981	Skates!		$25	$40	$50	Ezra Jack Keats		4Winds
1982	Clementina's Cactus		$25	$40	$50	Ezra Jack Keats		Viking
1982	Kitten For A Day		$25	$40	$50	Ezra Jack Keats		4Winds

Keeping   Charles

Year	Title	VG-	VG	VG+	Fine	Author	Award	Pub
1959	The Silver Branch	$70	$100	$120		Rosemary Sutcliff		Walck
1962	Beowulf	$50	$60	$80		Rosemary Sutcliff		Dutton
1963	Grimbold's Other World	$50	$60	$80		Nicholas Stuart Gray		Mered
1964	The Treasure Of Siegfried	$50	$60	$80		E. M. Almedingen		Bodley
1965	Heroes And History	$40	$60	$70		Rosemary Sutcliff		Putnam
1965	The Life Of Our Lord	$40	$60	$70		Henri Daniel-Rops		HawB
1966	Celtic Folk And Fairy Tales	$40	$60	$70		Eric & Nancy Protter		DS&P
1966	King Horn	$40	$60	$70		Kevin Crossley-Holland		Dutton
1966	Molly O' The Moors	$60	$80	$100		Charles Keeping		World
1966	Shaun And The Cart-Horse	$60	$80	$100		Charles Keeping		FWatts
1967	Bent Is The Bow	$40	$50	$70		Geoffrey Trease		TNelson
1967	Charley, Charlotte, And The Golden Canary	$80	$120	$140		Charles Keeping	GM	FWatts
1967	Mainly In Moonlight	$40	$50	$70		Nicholas Stuart Gray		Mered
1967	Swords From The North	$40	$50	$70		Henry Treece		Pan
1967	The Red Towers Of Granada	$40	$50	$70		Geoffrey Trease		Vnguard
1967	With Books On Her Head	$40	$50	$70		Edna Walker Chandler		Mered
1968	Alfie And The Ferryboat	$60	$80	$100		Charles Keeping		Oxford
1968	Alfie Finds The Other Side Of The World	$60	$80	$100		Charles Keeping		FWatts
1968	Poko And The Golden Demon	$40	$50	$70		James Holding		AS
1968	The Dream Time	$40	$50	$70		Henry Treece		Mered
1969	Joseph's Yard	$60	$80	$100		Charles Keeping		FWatts
1969	Knights, Beasts, And Wonders	$40	$50	$70		Margaret J. Miller		Dwhite
1969	The Apple Stone	$40	$50	$70		Nicholas Stuart Gray		Mered
1969	The Christmas Story	$60	$80	$100		Charles Keeping		FWatts
1969	The Cold Flame	$40	$50	$70		James Reeves		Mered
1969	The Tale Of Ancient Israel	$40	$50	$70		Roger Lancelyn Green		DentD
1969	Tinker, Tailor	$40	$50	$70		K. Neil Slater		World
1970	Five Fables From France		$30	$50	$60	Lee Cooper		AS
1970	Over The Hills To Fabylon		$70	$100	$140	Nicholas Stuart Gray		HawB
1970	Through The Window		$50	$70	$90	Charles Keeping		FWatts
1971	The Poet's Tales		$30	$50	$60	William Cole		World

Keeping   Charles

Year	Title	VG-	VG	VG+	Fine	Author	Award	Pub
1971	The Valley Of The Frost Giants		$30	$50	$60	M. S. Craig		LL&S
1972	The Invaders		$30	$50	$60	Henry Treece		Crowell
1972	The Spider's Web		$40	$60	$90	Charles Keeping		Oxford
1972	The Twelve Labors Of Hercules		$30	$50	$60	Robert Newman		Crowell
1972	Wizards And Wampum		$30	$50	$60	Roger Squire		AS
1973	The Golden Shadow		$30	$50	$60	Leon Garfield		Pan
1973	Weland, Smith Of The Gods		$30	$50	$60	Ursula Synge		Phillip
1974	Monsters, Monsters, Monsters		$30	$40	$60	Helen Hoke		FWatts
1974	The Nanny Goat And The Fierce Dog		$40	$60	$80	Charles Keeping		Phillip
1975	About The Sleeping Beauty		$40	$60	$80	P.L. Travers		McHill
1975	Tower Blocks		$30	$40	$60	Marian Lines		FWatts
1976	Les Misérables		$30	$40	$60	Victor Hugo		Folio
1976	The Magic Horns		$30	$40	$60	Forbes Stuart		AW
1977	Haunts, Haunts, Haunts		$25	$40	$50	Helen Hoke		FWatts
1977	Spectres, Spooks And Suddery Shades		$25	$40	$50	Helen Hoke		FWatts
1977	Terry On The Fence		$25	$40	$50	Bernard Ashley		Phillip
1978	Miss Emily And The Bird Of Make-Believe		$35	$50	$70	Charles Keeping		Hutch
1980	Break In The Sun		$25	$35	$50	Bernard Ashley		Phillip
1980	Willie's Fire-Engine		$35	$50	$70	Charles Keeping		Oxford
1981	The Highwayman		$50	$70	$100	Alfred Noyes	GM	Oxford
1983	The Beginning Of The Armadilloes		$25	$35	$50	Rudyard Kipling		Bedrik
1986	Charles Keeping's Book Of Classic Ghost Stories		$30	$40	$60	Charles Keeping		Bedrik
1986	Two Tales		$20	$30	$40	Edgar Allan Poe		Chim
1987	Charles Keeping's Classic Tales Of The Macabre		$25	$40	$50	Charles Keeping		Bedrik
1987	Jack The Treacle Eater		$20	$30	$40	Charles Causley		Macmil
1987	The Tale Of Sir Gawain		$20	$30	$40	Neil Philip		Philo
1994	Warrior Scarlet		$14	$20	$30	Rosemary Sutcliff		FSG
1999	The Highwayman		$12	$16	$20	Alfred Noyes		Oxford

Kellogg   Steven

Year	Title	VG-	VG	VG+	Fine	Author	Award	Pub
1967	Gwot! Horribly Funny Hairticklers	$80	$120	$140		George Mendoza		H&Row
1969	Brave Johnny O'hare	$50	$70	$90		Eleanor B. Heady		PMagP
1969	Martha Matilda O'toole	$50	$70	$90		Jim Copp.		BradP
1969	The Rotten Book	$60	$80	$100		Steven Kellogg		H&Row
1970	Can't You Pretend?		$30	$50	$60	Miriam Young.		Putnam
1970	Granny And The Desperadoes		$50	$70	$90	Steven Kellogg		Macmil
1970	Matilda Who Told Lies And Was Burned To Death		$50	$70	$100	Steven Kellogg		Dial
1970	Mister Rogers' Songbook		$30	$50	$60	Fred Rogers		Random
1970	Mrs. Purdy's Children		$50	$70	$90	Steven Kellogg		Dial
1970	The Wicked Kings Of Bloon		$50	$70	$90	Steven Kellogg		P-Hall
1971	Can I Keep Him?		$40	$60	$90	Steven Kellogg		Dial
1971	Crabapple Night		$30	$50	$60	Jan Wahl		HR&W
1971	Here Comes Tagalong		$40	$60	$90	Steven Kellogg		PMagP
1971	The Mystery Beast Of Ostergeest		$40	$60	$90	Steven Kellogg		Dial
1972	The Castles Of The Two Brothers		$30	$50	$60	Aileen Friedman		HR&W
1972	The Orchard Cat		$40	$60	$90	Steven Kellogg		Dial
1972	The Very Peculiar Tunnel		$40	$60	$90	Steven Kellogg		Putnam
1972	Won't Somebody Play With Me?		$40	$60	$90	Steven Kellogg		Dial
1973	Abby		$40	$60	$90	Steven Kellogg		H&Row
1973	Come Here, Cat		$30	$50	$60	Joan L. Nodset		H&Row
1973	The Island Of The Skog		$40	$60	$90	Steven Kellogg		Dial
1973	You Ought To See Herbert's House		$40	$60	$90	Steven Kellogg		FWatts
1974	Kisses And Fishes		$30	$40	$60	Liesel Moak Skorpen		H&Row
1974	The Mystery Of The Missing Red Mitten		$40	$60	$80	Steven Kellogg		Dial
1974	There Was An Old Woman		$40	$60	$80	Steven Kellogg		PMagP
1975	How The Witch Got Alf		$30	$40	$60	Cora Annett		FWatts
1975	The Boy Who Was Followed Home		$30	$40	$60	Margaret Mahy		Dial
1975	The Great Christmas Kidnaping Caper		$30	$40	$60	Jean Van Leeuwen		Dial
1975	The Smartest Bear And His Brother Oliver		$30	$40	$60	Alice Bach		H&Row
1975	The Yak, The Python, The Frog		$40	$60	$80	Steven Kellogg		PMagP
1976	Awful Alexander		$30	$40	$60	Judith Choate		DoubleD
1976	Gustav The Gourmet Giant		$30	$40	$60	LouAnn Gaeddert		Dial
1976	Much Bigger Than Martin		$40	$60	$80	Steven Kellogg		Dial
1976	Steven Kellogg's Yankee Doodle		$30	$40	$60	Edward Bangs.		PMagP
1976	The Most Delicious Camping Trip Ever		$30	$40	$60	Alice Bach		H&Row

Kellogg   Steven

Year	Title	VG-	VG	VG+	Fine	Author	Award	Pub
1977	Barney Bipples Magic Dandelions		$25	$40	$50	Carol Chapman		Dutton
1977	Grouchy Uncle Otto		$25	$40	$50	Alice Bach		H&Row
1977	The Mysterious Tadpole		$40	$60	$80	Steven Kellogg		Dial
1978	Appelard And Liverwurst		$35	$50	$70	Mercer Mayer		4Winds
1978	Millicent The Magnificent		$25	$40	$50	Alice Bach		H&Row
1978	The Mystery Of The Magic Green Ball		$35	$50	$70	Steven Kellogg		Dial
1978	The Pickle Plan		$25	$40	$50	Marilyn Singer		Dutton
1979	Jill The Pill		$25	$40	$50	Julie Castiglia		Athenm
1979	Molly Moves Out		$25	$40	$50	Susan Pearson		Dial
1979	Once, Said Darlene		$25	$40	$50	William Sleator		Dutton
1979	Pinkerton, Behave!		$35	$50	$70	Steven Kellogg		Dial
1979	There's An Elephant In The Garage		$25	$40	$50	Douglas F. Davis		Dutton
1980	The Day Jimmy's Boa Ate The Wash		$25	$35	$50	Trinka Hakes Noble		Dial
1980	The Mystery Of The Flying Orange Pumpkin		$35	$50	$70	Steven Kellogg		Dial
1980	Uproar On Hollercat Hill		$25	$35	$50	Jean Marzollo		Dial
1981	A Rose For Pinkerton		$35	$50	$70	Steven Kellogg		Dial
1981	Leo, Zack, And Emmie		$25	$35	$50	Amy Ehrlich		Dial
1981	Liverwurst Is Missing		$35	$50	$70	Mercer Mayer		Morrow
1982	A Change Of Plans		$25	$35	$50	Alan Benjamin		4Winds
1982	Tallyho, Pinkerton!		$30	$50	$60	Steven Kellogg		Dial
1982	The Mystery Of The Stolen Blue Paint		$30	$50	$60	Steven Kellogg		Dial
1983	Ralph's Secret Weapon		$30	$50	$60	Steven Kellogg		Dial
1983	The Ten-Alarm Camp-Out		$25	$35	$50	Cathy Warren		LL&S
1984	A, My Name Is Alice		$20	$30	$40	Jane E. Bayer		Dial
1984	Jimmy's Boa Bounces Back		$20	$30	$40	Trinka Hakes Noble		Dial
1984	Paul Bunyan, A Tall Tale		$30	$50	$60	Steven Kellogg		Morrow
1985	Best Friends		$30	$40	$60	Steven Kellogg		Dial
1985	Chicken Little		$30	$40	$60	Steven Kellogg		Morrow
1985	How Much Is A Million?		$20	$30	$40	David Schwartz		LL&S
1985	Iva Dunnit And The Big Wind		$20	$30	$40	Carol Purdy		Dial
1986	Pecos Bill: A Tall Tale		$30	$40	$60	Steven Kellogg		Morrow
1987	Aster Aardvark's Alphabet Adventures		$25	$40	$50	Steven Kellogg		Morrow
1987	Leo, Zack, And Emmie Together Again		$20	$30	$40	Amy Ehrlich		Dial
1987	Prehistoric Pinkerton		$25	$40	$50	Steven Kellogg		Dial
1988	Barney Bipples Magic Dandelions		$18	$25	$35	Carol Chapman		Dutton
1988	Johnny Appleseed: A Tall Tale		$25	$40	$50	Steven Kellogg		Morrow
1989	If You Made A Million		$18	$25	$35	David Schwartz		LL&S
1989	Is Your Mama A Llama?		$18	$25	$35	Deborah Guarino		Scholas
1989	Jimmy's Boa And The Big Splash Birthday Bash		$18	$25	$35	Trinka Hakes Noble		Dial
1990	Englebert The Elephant		$16	$25	$30	Ton Paxton		Morrow
1990	The Day The Goose Got Loose		$16	$25	$30	Reeve Lindbergh		Dial
1991	Jack And The Beanstalk		$25	$35	$50	Steven Kellogg		Morrow
1992	Mike Fink: A Tall Tale		$20	$30	$40	Steven Kellogg		Morrow
1992	The Christmas Witch		$20	$30	$40	Steven Kellogg		Dial
1993	Parents In The Pigpen, Pigs In The Tub		$14	$20	$25	Amy Ehrlich		Dial
1993	The Wizard Next Door		$14	$20	$25	Peter Glassman		Morrow
1994	Adventures Of Huckleberry Finn		$12	$18	$25	Mark Twain		Morrow
1994	The Great Quillow		$12	$18	$25	James Thurber		HBJ
1994	The Rattlebang Picnic		$12	$18	$25	Margaret Mahy		Dial
1995	Sally Ann Thunder Ann Whirlwind Crockett		$16	$25	$30	Steven Kellogg		Morrow
1995	Snuffles And Snouts		$12	$16	$20	Laura Robb		Dial
1996	Frogs Jump A Counting Book		$12	$16	$20	Alan Brooks		Scholas
1996	I Was Born About 10,000 Years Ago		$14	$20	$30	Steven Kellogg		Morrow
1996	Library Lil		$12	$16	$20	Suzanne Williams		Dial
1997	The Three Little Pigs		$14	$20	$25	Steven Kellogg		Morrow
1998	A-Hunting We Will Go!		$12	$18	$25	Steven Kellogg		Morrow
1999	A Beasty Story		$10	$16	$20	Bill Martin Jr.		HBrace
1999	The Three Sillies		$12	$18	$25	Steven Kellogg		Candle
2000	Give The Dog A Bone		$10	$14	$18	Steven Kellogg		SeaStar
2000	The Baby Beebee Bird		$10	$14	$18	Diane Redfield Massie		HCollins
2000	The Missing Mitten		$10	$16	$20	Steven Kellogg		Dial
2001	A Penguin Pup For Pinkerton		$10	$16	$20	Steven Kellogg		Dial
2002	Big Bear Ball		$8	$12	$16	Joanne Ryder		HCollins
2002	Ready! Set! Measure		$8	$12	$16	David Schwartz		HCollins
2003	Clorinda		$8	$10	$14	Robert Kinerk		S&S
2003	Jimmy's Boa And The Bungee Jump Slam Dunk		$8	$10	$14	Trinka Hakes Noble		Dial
2004	Pinkerton & Friends		$8	$10	$14	Steven Kellogg		Dial

Kellogg Steven

Year	Title	VG-	VG	VG+	Fine	Author	Award	Pub
2004	Santa Claus Is Comin' To Town		$8	$10	$14	Steven Kellogg		HCollins
2004	Santa Claus Is Coming To Town		$8	$10	$14	Fred J. Coots		HCollins
2005	Clorinda The Fearless		$6	$10	$12	Robert Kinerk		S&S

Kelly Walt

Year	Title	VG-	VG	VG+	Fine	Author	Award	Pub
1952	The Glob	$120	$160	$200		Walt Kelly		Viking
1969	Can't	$80	$120	$140		Walt Kelly		Lance
1969	Walt Kelly's No	$80	$120	$140		Walt Kelly		Lance

Kennaway Adrienne

Year	Title	VG-	VG	VG+	Fine	Author	Award	Pub
1966	Jande's Ambition	$60	$80	$100		Asenath Odaga		EAPH
1967	Game Park Holiday	$40	$50	$70		William Lewis Radford		EAPH
1967	The Hare's Blanket	$40	$50	$70		Asenath Odaga		EAPH
1968	The Angry Flames	$40	$50	$70		Asenath Odaga		EAPH
1968	The Elephant's Heart	$40	$50	$70		William Lewis Radford		EAPH
1968	The Speck Of Gold	$40	$50	$70		Cynthia E. Hunter		EAPH
1968	The Tales Of Wamugumo	$40	$50	$70		Peter Kuguru		EAPH
1969	Captured By Raiders	$40	$50	$70		Benjamin S. Wegesa		EAPH
1969	Cock And Lion	$40	$50	$70		Kalondu Kyendo		EAPH
1969	The Girl Who Couldn't Keep A Secret	$40	$50	$70		Clare Omanga		EAPH
1971	Mother Of Twins		$30	$50	$60	Sala Nagenda		EAPH
1972	The Hippo Who Couldn't Stop Crying		$30	$50	$60	Susie Muthoni		EAPH
1974	Chameleon Who Couldn't Stop Changing His Mind		$30	$40	$60	Sally Nyokabi		TransAf
1976	How The Leopard Got His Claws		$30	$40	$60	Chinua Achebe		EAPH
1976	Island Of Yo		$30	$40	$60	Eutychus Ndirangu		EAPH
1984	Greedy Zebra		$40	$60	$90	Mwenye Hadithi		LBrown
1986	Hot Hippo		$20	$30	$40	Mwenye Hadithi		LBrown
1987	Crafty Chameleon		$60	$80	$120	Mwenye Hadithi	GM	LBrown
1987	Lend Me Your Wings		$20	$30	$40	John Agard		LBrown
1988	Tricky Tortoise		$18	$25	$35	Mwenye Hadithi		LBrown
1989	Awful Aardvark		$18	$25	$35	Mwalimu		LBrown
1990	Curious Clownfish		$16	$25	$30	Eric Maddern		LBrown
1990	Lazy Lion		$16	$25	$30	Mwenye Hadithi		LBrown
1991	Bushbaby		$16	$25	$30	Mwenye Hadithi		LBrown
1992	Little Elephant's Walk		$16	$25	$30	Mwenye Hadithi		HCollins
1993	Baby Baboon		$16	$25	$30	Mwenye Hadithi		H&S
1994	Hungry Hyena		$14	$20	$30	Mwenye Hadithi		H&S
1999	Arctic Song		$12	$16	$20	Miriam Moss		BWB
1999	Baby Rhino's Escape		$12	$16	$20	Adrienne Kennaway		StarB
2000	This Is The Tree		$10	$14	$18	Miriam Moss		KaneM

Kepes Juliet

Year	Title	VG-	VG	VG+	Fine	Author	Award	Pub
1952	Five Little Monkeys	$120	$160	$200		Juliet Kepes	CH	HM
1955	Beasts From A Brush	$50	$70	$90		Juliet Kepes		Pan
1960	Two Little Birds And Three	$50	$60	$80		Juliet Kepes		HM
1961	Frogs Merry	$50	$60	$80		Juliet Kepes		Pan
1964	Lady Bird, Quickly	$50	$60	$80		Juliet Kepes		LBrown
1965	Five Little Monkey Business	$40	$60	$70		Juliet Kepes		HM
1967	The Seed That Peacock Planted	$40	$50	$70		Juliet Kepes		LBrown
1968	Birds	$40	$50	$70		Juliet Kepes		Walker
1974	Run, Little Monkeys! Run, Run, Run!		$30	$40	$60	Juliet Kepes		Pan
1978	Cock-A-Doodle-Doo		$25	$40	$50	Juliet Kepes		Pan
1983	The Story Of A Bragging Duck		$25	$35	$50	Juliet Kepes		HM

Kessler Leonard

Year	Title	VG-	VG	VG+	Fine	Author	Award	Pub
1961	What Have I Got?	$50	$60	$80		Mike McClintock		H&B
1962	What Do They Do? Policemen And Firemen	$35	$40	$60		Carla Greene		Harper
1963	Doctors And Nurses: What Do They Do?	$35	$40	$60		Carla Greene		H&Row
1963	Soldiers And Sailors:What Do They Do?	$35	$40	$60		Carla Greene		H&Row
1964	Railroad Engineers And Airplane Pilots	$35	$40	$60		Carla Greene		H&Row
1965	Here Comes The Strikeout	$30	$40	$50		Leonard Kessler		H&Row

Kessler   Leonard

Year	Title	VG-	VG	VG+	Fine	Author	Award	Pub
1966	Kick, Pass, And Run	$30	$40	$50		Leonard Kessler		H&Row
1967	Animal Doctors	$30	$40	$50		Carla Greene		H&Row
1967	Truck Drivers	$30	$40	$50		Carla Greene		H&Row
1968	Binky Brothers, Detectives	$30	$40	$50		James Lawrence		H&Row
1969	Last One In Is A Rotten Egg	$25	$35	$50		Leonard Kessler		H&Row
1970	Binky Brothers And The Fearless Four		$25	$35	$50	James Lawrence		H&Row
1972	Cowboys: What Do They Do?		$25	$35	$50	Carla Greene		H&Row

Kincaid   Eric

Year	Title	VG-	VG	VG+	Fine	Author	Award	Pub
1977	Horse And Pony Care In Pictures		$40	$60	$80	Edward Holmes		Arco
1981	The Magic Of Rhymes		$25	$35	$50	Lucy Kincaid		Derry
1981	Time For A Rhyme		$25	$35	$50	Lucy Kincaid		Derry
1983	Chicken Licken		$25	$35	$50	Lucy Kincaid		Rourke
1983	Cinderella		$25	$35	$50	Lucy Kincaid		Rourke
1983	Foolish Jack		$25	$35	$50	Lucy Kincaid		Rourke
1983	Goldilocks And The Three Bears		$25	$35	$50	Lucy Kincaid (adapted)		Rourke
1983	Jack And The Beanstalk		$25	$35	$50	Lucy Kincaid		Rourke
1983	Little Red Hen		$25	$35	$50	Lucy Kincaid		Rourke
1983	Little Red Riding Hood		$25	$35	$50	Lucy Kincaid		Rourke
1983	Puss In Boots		$25	$35	$50	Lucy Kincaid		Rourke
1983	Rapunzel		$25	$35	$50	Lucy Kincaid		Rourke
1983	Rumpelstiltskin		$25	$35	$50	Lucy Kincaid		Rourke
1983	Sleeping Beauty		$25	$35	$50	Lucy Kincaid		Rourke
1983	Snow White And The Seven Dwarfs		$25	$35	$50	Lucy Kincaid		Rourke
1983	The Elves And The Shoemaker		$25	$35	$50	Lucy Kincaid		Rourke
1983	The Frog Prince		$25	$35	$50	Lucy Kincaid		Rourke
1983	The Gingerbread Man		$25	$35	$50	Lucy Kincaid		Rourke
1983	The Three Billygoats Gruff		$25	$35	$50	Lucy Kincaid		Rourke
1983	The Ugly Duckling		$25	$35	$50	Lucy Kincaid		Rourke
1983	Three Little Pigs		$25	$35	$50	Lucy Kincaid		Rourke
1989	Aesop's Fables		$18	$25	$35	Graeme Kent		Check
1995	Hideaway House		$14	$20	$25	Gill Davies		Brimax
1996	I Can't Sleep		$12	$18	$25	Gill Davies		Brimax

Kinstler   E. Raymond

Year	Title	VG-	VG	VG+	Fine	Author	Award	Pub
1959	Cowboy Andy	$100	$140	$180		Edna Walker Chandler		BB
1964	Fury	$25	$30	$40		Albert G. Miller		G&D

Kirk   Daniel

Year	Title	VG-	VG	VG+	Fine	Author	Award	Pub
1984	Dune		$16	$25	$30	Maida Silverman		G&D
1992	Skateboard Monsters		$10	$16	$20	Daniel Kirk		ChildU
1994	How The Wind Plays		$10	$14	$18	Michael Lipson		Hyper
1995	The Diggers		$10	$14	$18	Margaret Wise Brown		Hyper
1996	Lucky's Twenty-Four Hour Garage		$8	$12	$16	Daniel Kirk		Hyper
1997	Breakfast At The Liberty Diner		$8	$12	$16	Daniel Kirk		Hyper
1997	Trash Trucks!		$8	$12	$16	Daniel Kirk		Putnam
1998	Bigger		$8	$12	$16	Daniel Kirk		Putnam
1999	Chugga-Chugga Choo-Choo		$8	$12	$16	Kevin Lewis		Hyper
1999	Hush, Little Alien		$8	$12	$16	Daniel Kirk		Hyper
1999	Moondogs		$8	$12	$16	Daniel Kirk		Putnam
2000	Humpty Dumpty		$8	$10	$14	Daniel Kirk		Putnam
2000	The Snow Family		$8	$10	$14	Daniel Kirk		Hyper
2001	Bus Stop, Bus Go!		$8	$10	$14	Daniel Kirk		Putnam
2001	Go!		$8	$10	$14	Daniel Kirk		Hyper
2002	Hello, Hello!		$8	$10	$14	Miriam Schlein		S&S
2002	My Truck Is Stuck		$8	$10	$14	Kevin Lewis		Hyper
2003	Dogs Rule!		$8	$10	$14	Daniel Kirk		Hyper
2003	Jack And Jill		$8	$10	$14	Daniel Kirk		Putnam
2004	Lunchroom Lizard		$6	$10	$12	Daniel Kirk		Putnam
2004	Rex Tabby		$6	$10	$12	Daniel Kirk		Orchard

Kirk David

Year	Title	VG-	VG	VG+	Fine	Author	Award	Pub
1994	Miss Spider's Tea Party		$40	$60	$80	David Kirk		Scholas
1995	Miss Spider's Wedding		$25	$35	$50	David Kirk		Scholas
1997	Miss Spider's New Car		$16	$25	$30	David Kirk		Scholas
1998	Miss Spider's ABC		$12	$16	$20	David Kirk		Scholas
1998	Nova's Ark		$12	$16	$20	David Kirk		Scholas
2000	Little Miss Spider At Sunny Patch School		$10	$14	$18	David Kirk		Scholas
2001	Little Bird Biddle Bird		$10	$14	$18	David Kirk		Scholas
2001	Little Miss Spider: A Christmas Wish		$10	$14	$18	David Kirk		Scholas
2001	Little Pig Biddle Pig		$10	$14	$18	David Kirk		Scholas
2002	Little Bunny, Biddle Bunny		$8	$12	$16	David Kirk		Scholas
2002	Little Mouse, Biddle Mouse		$8	$12	$16	David Kirk		Scholas
2004	Miss Spider's Babies		$8	$10	$14	David Kirk		Scholas

Kitamura Satoshi

Year	Title	VG-	VG	VG+	Fine	Author	Award	Pub
1982	Angry Arthur		$40	$60	$80	Hiawyn Oram		HBJ
1983	Ned And The Joybaloo		$60	$80	$120	Hiawyn Oram		AP
1985	In The Attic		$25	$35	$50	Hiawyn Oram		HR&W
1985	What's Inside?: The Alphabet Book		$25	$35	$50	Satoshi Kitamura		FSG
1986	When Sheep Cannot Sleep		$25	$35	$50	Satoshi Kitamura		FSG
1987	Captain Toby		$25	$35	$50	Satoshi Kitamura		Dutton
1987	Lily Takes A Walk		$25	$35	$50	Satoshi Kitamura		Dutton
1987	My Friend Mr. Morris		$25	$35	$50	Pat Thomson		DelaP
1989	UFO Diary		$20	$30	$40	Satoshi Kitamura		FSG
1991	A Boy Wants A Dinosaur		$16	$25	$30	Hiawyn Oram		FSG
1992	From Acorn To Zoo		$16	$25	$30	Satoshi Kitamura		FSG
1996	Cat Is Sleepy		$12	$18	$25	Satoshi Kitamura		FSG
1996	Dog Is Thirsty		$12	$18	$25	Satoshi Kitamura		FSG
1996	Duck Is Dirty		$12	$18	$25	Satoshi Kitamura		FSG
1996	Fly With The Birds		$12	$18	$25	Richard Edwards		Orchard
1996	Sheep In Wolves' Clothing		$12	$18	$25	Satoshi Kitamura		FSG
1996	Squirrel Is Hungry		$12	$18	$25	Satoshi Kitamura		FSG
1997	Bath-Time Boots		$12	$18	$25	Satoshi Kitamura		FSG
1997	Goldfish Hide-And-Seek		$12	$18	$25	Satoshi Kitamura		FSG
1998	A Friend For Boots		$12	$16	$20	Satoshi Kitamura		FSG
2000	Me And My Cat?		$10	$14	$18	Satoshi Kitamura		FSG
2002	Comic Adventures Of Boots		$8	$12	$16	Satoshi Kitamura		FSG

Kitchen Bert

Year	Title	VG-	VG	VG+	Fine	Author	Award	Pub
1971	Dud & Pete: The Dagenham Dialogues		$30	$50	$60	D. Moore & P. Cook		Metheun
1973	Christopher Logue's True Stories From Private Eye		$25	$35	$50	Christopher Logue		Rush
1975	Cobbett's Country Book		$20	$30	$40	Richard Ingrams (edited)		Schock
1976	Stroke, Hole Or Match?		$20	$30	$40	Peter Dobereiner		Newton
1977	Abecedary: Verse		$20	$30	$40	Christopher Logue		JCape
1977	Talpa: The Story Of A Mole		$20	$30	$40	Kenneth Mellanby		Collins
1983	Feet & Other Stories		$16	$25	$30	Jan Mark		Penguin
1984	Animal Alphabet		$40	$60	$90	Bert Kitchen	NYT	Dial
1987	Animal Numbers		$25	$40	$50	Bert Kitchen		Dial
1989	Tenrec's Twigs		$14	$20	$25	Bert Kitchen		Philo
1990	Gorilla/Chinchilla		$12	$18	$25	Bert Kitchen		Dial
1990	The Deeper Meaning Of Liff		$12	$18	$25	L. Davis D. Adams		Harmony
1991	Pig In A Barrow		$12	$18	$25	Bert Kitchen		Dial
1992	Somewhere Today		$12	$18	$25	Bert Kitchen		Candle
1993	And So They Build		$12	$16	$20	Bert Kitchen		Walker
1994	When Hunger Calls		$12	$16	$20	Bert Kitchen		Candle
1998	Tom's Rabbit		$10	$14	$18	Meredith Hooper		NGS
1999	The Barn Owl		$10	$14	$18	Bert Kitchen		Kfisher
1999	The Other		$10	$14	$18	Bert Kitchen		Kfisher
2000	The Lion & The Mouse & Other Aesop's Fables		$8	$12	$16	Doris Orgel		DK
2003	The Bremen Town Musicians		$8	$10	$14	Doris Orgel		DK

Kleven Elisa

Year	Title	VG-	VG	VG+	Fine	Author	Award	Pub
1989	Ernst		$14	$20	$25	Elisa Kleven		Dutton

Kleven   Elisa

Year	Title	VG-	VG	VG+	Fine	Author	Award	Pub
1990	B Is For Bethlehem		$10	$16	$20	Isabel Wilner		Dutton
1991	Abuela		$10	$16	$20	Arthur Dorros		Dutton
1992	The Lion And The Little Red Bird		$10	$16	$20	Elisa Kleven		Dutton
1993	Snowsong Whistling		$10	$16	$20	Karen E. Lotz		Dutton
1993	The City By The Bay		$10	$16	$20	Tricia Brown		Chron
1994	The Paper Princess		$10	$14	$18	Elisa Kleven		Dutton
1995	Isla		$10	$14	$18	Arthur Dorros		Dutton
1996	Hooray! A Piñata!		$8	$12	$16	Elisa Kleven		Dutton
1996	The Magic Maguey		$8	$12	$16	Tony Johnston		HBrace
1997	The Puddle Pail		$8	$12	$16	Elisa Kleven		Dutton
1998	A Monster In The House		$8	$12	$16	Elisa Kleven		Dutton
1999	City Of Angels		$8	$12	$16	Julie Jaskol		Dutton
2000	Our Big Home		$8	$10	$14	Linda Glaser		Millbk
2001	Sun Bread		$8	$10	$14	Elisa Kleven		Dutton
2002	Fiestas		$8	$10	$14	José-Luis Orozco		Dutton
2002	The Dancing Deer And The Foolish Hunter		$8	$10	$14	Elisa Kleven		Dutton

Knight   Hilary

Year	Title	VG-	VG	VG+	Fine	Author	Award	Pub
1955	Eloise	$1,800	$2,400	$3,000		Kay Thompson		S&S
1957	Eloise In Paris	$200	$260	$320		Kay Thompson		S&S
1957	Hello, Mrs. Piggle-Wiggle	$120	$160	$220		Betty MacDonald.		Lippin
1957	Mrs. Piggle-Wiggle	$100	$140	$180		Betty MacDonald.		Lippin
1957	Mrs. Piggle-Wiggle's Magic	$100	$140	$180		Betty MacDonald.		Lippin
1957	Tiger's Chance	$100	$140	$180		Jan Henry		HBrace
1958	Roger	$100	$140	$180		Hilary Knight		Lippin
1958	The Wonderful World Of Aunt Tuddy	$100	$140	$180		Jeremy Gury		Random
1959	Eloise At Christmastime	$180	$240	$300		Kay Thompson		S&S
1959	Eloise In Moscow	$180	$240	$300		Kay Thompson		S&S
1960	Beginning With Mrs. McBee	$50	$60	$80		Cecil Maiden		Vnguard
1960	Tortoise And Turtle	$160	$200	$260		Evelyn Gendel		S&S
1962	Hilary Knight's Mother Goose	$70	$90	$120		Hilary Knight		Golden
1962	Speaking Of Mrs McCluskie	$50	$60	$80		Cecil Maiden		Vnguard
1963	Christmas Nutshell Library	$100	$120	$160		Hilary Knight		H&Row
1963	The Night Before Christmas	$70	$90	$120		Hilary Knight		H&Row
1963	The Tortoise The Turtle Abroad	$70	$90	$120		Evelyn Gendel		S&S
1964	Captain Boldheart/The Magic Fishbone	$50	$60	$80		Mary McCarthy		Macmil
1964	Where's Wallace?	$100	$140	$180		Hilary Knight		H&Row
1965	The Animal Garden: A Story	$40	$60	$70		Ogden Nash		MEvans
1965	When I Have A Little Girl	$40	$60	$70		Charlotte Zolotow		H&Row
1967	When I Have A Son	$40	$50	$70		Charlotte Zolotow		H&Row
1968	Sunday Morning	$40	$50	$70		Hilary Knight		H&Row
1969	A Child's Book Of Natural History	$40	$50	$70		Margaret Fishback		P&Munk
1969	Sylvia	$40	$50	$70		Hilary Knight		H&Row
1969	The Jeremy Mouse Book	$40	$50	$70		Patricia M. Scarry		AHP
1971	Angie		$30	$50	$60	Hilary Knight		H&Row
1971	Feldman Fieldmouse		$70	$100	$140	Hilary Knight		H&Row
1971	The Book Of Wishes And Wishmaking		$30	$50	$60	Hilary Knight		AHP
1974	Most-Of-The-Time Maxie		$30	$40	$60	Hilary Knight		Xerox
1975	I'm A Monkey		$30	$40	$60	Robert Kraus		Windmil
1975	Matt's Mitt		$30	$40	$60	Hilary Knight		DoubleD
1976	That Makes Me Mad!		$30	$40	$60	Steven Kroll		Pan
1976	The Golden Picture Dictionary		$30	$40	$60	L. Ogle & T. Thoburn		Golden
1977	Pettifur: A Story		$25	$40	$50	Jay Williams		4Winds
1977	The Good Mousekeeper		$25	$40	$50	Robert Kraus		Windmil
1978	The Circus Is Coming: A Picture Parade		$25	$40	$50	Hilary Knight		Golden
1980	Algonquin Cat		$35	$50	$70	Val Schaffner		DelaP
1980	Warren Weasel's Worse Than Measles		$25	$35	$50	Alice Bach		H&Row
1981	Hilary Knight's Cinderella		$25	$35	$50	Hilary Knight (adapted)		Random
1981	Hilary Knight's The Twelve Days Of Christmas		$25	$35	$50	Hilary Knight (adapted)		Macmil
1982	Never Take A Pig To Lunch		$25	$35	$50	Stephanie Calmenson (selected)		DoubleD
1983	Hilary Knight's The Owl And The Pussy-Cat		$25	$35	$50	Edward Lear		Macmil
1983	Screamy Mimi		$25	$35	$50	Robert Kraus		Windmil
1986	Sunday Morning: A Story		$20	$30	$40	Judith Viorst		Aladd
1986	Telephone Time		$20	$30	$40	Ellen Weiss		Random
1987	The Best Little Monkeys In The World		$20	$30	$40	Natalie Standiford		Random

Knight   Hilary

Year	Title	VG-	VG	VG+	Fine	Author	Award	Pub
1988	Side By Side: Poems To Read Together		$18	$25	$35	L.B. Hopkins (selected)		S&S
1989	The Golden Picture Dictionary		$18	$25	$35	L. Ogle & T. Thoburn		Western
1990	Beauty And The Beast		$16	$25	$30	Richard Howard		S&S
1991	Happy Birthday: Poems		$16	$25	$30	L.B. Hopkins (selected)		S&S
1991	Ten Tall Soldiers: A Story		$16	$25	$30	Nancy Robison		Holt
1994	The Mrs. Piggle-Wiggle Treasury		$14	$20	$30	Betty MacDonald		HCollins
2002	Eloise Takes A Bawth		$10	$16	$20	Kay Thompson		S&S
2004	A Firefly In A Fir Tree		$8	$10	$14	Kay Thompson		Tegen

Kraner   Florian

Year	Title	VG-	VG	VG+	Fine	Author	Award	Pub
1944	The Long-Ago Book	$35	$40	$60		George Arthur Hornby		Fischer
1945	The Bible Picture Book	$35	$40	$60		Florian Kraner (adapted)		GardenC
1945	Wonder Tales Of Giants And Dwarfs	$35	$40	$60		Janet Murtaugh		Random
1946	Come With Us To Story Book Land	$35	$40	$60		Various Authors		DomesD
1947	Famous Myths Of The Golden Age	$35	$40	$60		Beatrice Alexander		Random

Kraus   Robert

Year	Title	VG-	VG	VG+	Fine	Author	Award	Pub
1955	All The Mice Came	$50	$70	$90		Robert Kraus		H&B
1955	Junior	$35	$40	$60		Robert Kraus		Oxford
1957	Ladybug, Ladybug!	$35	$40	$60		Robert Kraus		H&B
1958	I, Mouse	$35	$40	$60		Robert Kraus		H&B
1959	Mouse At Sea	$35	$40	$60		Robert Kraus		H&B
1961	The Littlest Rabbit	$30	$40	$50		Robert Kraus		H&B
1962	The Trouble With Spider	$30	$40	$50		Robert Kraus		Harper
1964	Miranda's Beautiful Dream	$30	$40	$50		Robert Kraus		H&Row
1964	Penguin's Pal	$30	$40	$50		Robert Kraus		H&Row
1965	Amanda Remembers	$25	$35	$50		Robert Kraus		H&Row
1965	Juniper	$25	$35	$50		Robert Kraus		H&Row
1965	Springfellow's Parade	$25	$35	$50		Robert Kraus		H&Row
1965	The Bunny's Nutshell Library	$25	$35	$50		Robert Kraus		H&Row
1965	The First Robin	$25	$35	$50		Robert Kraus		H&Row
1965	The Silver Dandelion	$25	$35	$50		Robert Kraus		H&Row
1966	My Son The Mouse	$25	$35	$50		Robert Kraus		H&Row
1967	The Little Giant	$25	$35	$50		Robert Kraus		H&Row
1969	Hello, Hippopotamus	$25	$35	$50		Robert Kraus		Windmil
1969	Rumple Nose-Dimple And The 3 Horrible Snaps	$25	$35	$50		Mischa Richter		Windmil
1970	Daddy Long Ears		$20	$30	$40	Robert Kraus		Windmil
1970	How Spider Saved Christmas		$20	$30	$40	Robert Kraus		Windmil
1971	Lillian, Morgan And Teddy		$20	$30	$40	Edna Eicke		Windmil
1971	Ludwig: The Dog Who Snored Symphonies		$20	$30	$40	Robert Kraus		Windmil
1971	Pip Squeak, Mouse In Shining Armor		$20	$30	$40	Richard Oldden		Windmil
1971	Shaggy Fur Face		$20	$30	$40	Robert Kraus		Windmil
1971	The Tail Who Wagged The Dog		$20	$30	$40	Robert Kraus		Windmil
1973	Big Brother		$20	$30	$40	Robert Kraus		PMagP
1973	How Spider Saved Halloween		$20	$30	$40	Robert Kraus		PMagP
1973	Pip Squeaks Through		$20	$30	$40	Richard Oldden		Spring
1980	See The Moon		$16	$25	$30	Robert Kraus		Windmil
1981	How Spider Saved Turkey		$16	$25	$30	Robert Kraus		Windmil
1985	Bumpy The Car		$14	$20	$30	Robert Kraus		G&D
1985	Freddy, The Fire Engine		$14	$20	$30	Robert Kraus		G&D
1985	Tony The Tow Truck		$14	$20	$30	Robert Kraus		G&D
1986	Mrs. Elmo Of Elephant House		$14	$20	$30	Robert Kraus		DelaP
1987	Robert Kraus' A Sunny Day In Babytown		$14	$20	$25	Robert Kraus		LSimon
1987	Robert Kraus' Babytown Express		$14	$20	$25	Robert Kraus		LSimon
1987	Robert Kraus' Meet The Babies		$14	$20	$25	Robert Kraus		LSimon
1987	Robert Kraus' Welcome To Babytown		$14	$20	$25	Robert Kraus		LSimon
1987	The Hoodwinking Of Mrs. Elmo		$14	$20	$25	Robert Kraus		DelaP
1988	How Spider Saved Easter		$14	$20	$25	Robert Kraus		Scholas
1988	Noah Count Vampire Detective In Mummy Vanishes		$14	$20	$25	Robert Kraus		Warner
1988	Private Eyes Don't Blink		$14	$20	$25	Robert Kraus		Warner
1988	The Phantom Of Creepy Hollow		$14	$20	$25	Robert Kraus		Warner
1989	Buggy Bear Cleans Up		$14	$20	$25	Robert Kraus		Silver
1989	Daddy Long Ears' Christmas Surprise		$14	$20	$25	Robert Kraus		LSimon
1989	Ella The Bad Speller		$14	$20	$25	Robert Kraus		Silver

Kraus   Robert

Year	Title	VG-	VG	VG+	Fine	Author	Award	Pub
1989	Good Morning, Miss Gator		$14	$20	$25	Robert Kraus		Silver
1989	Here Comes Tardy Toad		$14	$20	$25	Robert Kraus		Silver
1989	Phil The Ventriloquist		$14	$20	$25	Robert Kraus		Green
1990	Daddy Long Ears' Halloween		$12	$18	$25	Robert Kraus		LSimon
1990	Klunky Monkey, New Kid In Class		$12	$18	$25	Robert Kraus		Silver
1990	Squirmy's Big Secret		$12	$18	$25	Robert Kraus		Silver
1990	The Boogie Woogie Bears Go Back To Nature		$12	$18	$25	Robert Kraus		Warner
1990	The Boogie Woogie Bears' Picnic		$12	$18	$25	Robert Kraus		Warner
1990	The Mixed-Up Mice Clean House		$12	$18	$25	Robert Kraus		Warner
1990	The Mixed-Up Mice In The Big Birthday Mix-Up		$12	$18	$25	Robert Kraus		Warner
1991	How Spider Saved Thanksgiving		$12	$18	$25	Robert Kraus		Scholas
1991	How Spider Saved The Flea Circus		$12	$18	$25	Robert Kraus		Scholas
1991	How Spider Stopped The Litterbugs		$12	$18	$25	Robert Kraus		Scholas
1992	Dr. Mouse, Bungle Jungle Doctor		$12	$16	$20	Robert Kraus		Western
1993	All My Chickens		$12	$16	$20	Robert Kraus		Western
1993	Dance, Spider, Dance!		$12	$16	$20	Robert Kraus		Western
1993	Jack O'Lantern's Scary Halloween		$12	$16	$20	Robert Kraus		Western
1993	The Adventures Of Wise Old Owl		$12	$16	$20	Robert Kraus		Troll
1993	Wise Old Owl's Canoe Trip Adventure		$12	$16	$20	Robert Kraus		Troll
1994	Fables Aesop Never Wrote		$12	$16	$20	Robert Kraus		Viking
1995	Strudwick		$10	$16	$20	Robert Kraus		Viking
1996	Near Myths		$10	$16	$20	Robert Kraus		Viking
1997	Little Beep		$10	$14	$18	Robert Kraus		LSimon
1997	Tiny Tow Truck		$10	$14	$18	Robert Kraus		LSimon

Krauss   Ruth

Year	Title	VG-	VG	VG+	Fine	Author	Award	Pub
1967	This Thumbprint	$60	$80	$100		Ruth Krauss		HCrest

Krupinski   Loretta

Year	Title	VG-	VG	VG+	Fine	Author	Award	Pub
1979	The Ghost At Penniman House		$25	$40	$50	Wilma Pitchford Hays		Xerox
1990	Lost In The Fog		$12	$16	$20	Irving Bacheller		LBrown
1991	Sailing To The Sea		$12	$16	$20	Mary-Claire Helldorfer		Viking
1991	The Old Ladies Who Liked Cats		$12	$16	$20	Carol Greene		HCollins
1992	Celia's Island Journal		$10	$16	$20	Celia Thaxter		LBrown
1992	How A Seed Grows		$10	$16	$20	Helene J. Jordan		HCollins
1992	Wonderful Worms		$10	$16	$20	Linda Glaser		Millbk
1993	Dear Rebecca, Winter Is Here		$10	$16	$20	Jean Craighead George		HCollins
1994	A New England Scrapbook		$10	$16	$20	Loretta Krupinski		HCollins
1994	The Runaway Christmas Toy		$10	$16	$20	Linda Hayward		Random
1994	Why Do Leaves Change Color?		$10	$16	$20	Betsy Maestro		HCollins
1995	Bluewater Journal: Voyage Of The Sea Tiger		$10	$14	$18	Loretta Krupinski		HCollins
1995	The Story Of Christmas		$10	$14	$18	Barbara Cooney		HCollins
1996	Heidi		$10	$14	$18	Johanna Spyri		HCollins
1996	The Irish Cinderlad		$10	$14	$18	Shirley Climo		HCollins
1996	The Velveteen Rabbit		$10	$14	$18	Margery Williams		Hyper
1997	Into The Woods: A Woodland Scrapbook		$10	$14	$18	Loretta Krupinski		HCollins
1997	The Quiet Morning		$10	$14	$18	Pamela Duncan Edwards		Hyper
1998	Best Friends		$8	$12	$16	Loretta Krupinski		Hyper
1998	Visit From St. Nicholas And Santa Mouse, Too!		$8	$12	$16	Clement C. Moore		Hyper
2001	Mouse Of My Heart		$8	$10	$14	Margaret Wise Brown		Hyper
2002	My World Of Color		$8	$10	$14	Margaret Wise Brown		Hyper

Kunhardt   Dorothy M.

Year	Title	VG-	VG	VG+	Fine	Author	Award	Pub
1933	Junket Is Nice	$160	$200	$260		Dorothy M. Kunhardt		HBrace
1934	Now Open The Box	$80	$120	$140		Dorothy M. Kunhardt		HBrace
1935	Brave Mr Buckingham	$80	$120	$140		Dorothy M. Kunhardt		HBrace
1936	Wise Old Aard-Vark	$80	$120	$140		Dorothy M. Kunhardt		Viking
1940	David's Birthday Party	$70	$90	$120		Dorothy M. Kunhardt		RandMc
1940	Pat The Bunny	$70	$90	$120		Dorothy M. Kunhardt		S&S
1947	Rennet Dessert Is Nice	$60	$80	$100		Dorothy M. Kunhardt		Forbes
1948	Little Peewee	$60	$80	$100		Dorothy M. Kunhardt		S&S
1962	Dr. Dick	$50	$60	$80		Dorothy M. Kunhardt		H&B

Kunhardt   Dorothy M.

Year	Title	VG-	VG	VG+	Fine	Author	Award	Pub
1965	Twenty Days	$40	$60	$70		Philip B. Kunhardt		H&Row

Kuskin   Karla

Year	Title	VG-	VG	VG+	Fine	Author	Award	Pub
1956	Roar And More	$35	$50	$60		Karla Kuskin		H&B
1957	James And The Rain	$30	$40	$50		Karla Kuskin		H&B
1958	In The Middle Of The Trees	$25	$35	$50		Karla Kuskin		H&B
1958	The Animals And The Ark	$25	$35	$50		Karla Kuskin		H&B
1959	Just Like Everyone Else	$25	$35	$50		Karla Kuskin		H&B
1959	Which Horse Is William?	$25	$35	$50		Karla Kuskin		H&B
1959	Xingu	$25	$35	$50		Violette Viertel		Macmil
1960	Square As A House	$25	$30	$40		Karla Kuskin		H&B
1961	The Bear Who Saw The Spring	$25	$30	$40		Karla Kuskin		H&B
1961	The Dog That Lost His Family	$25	$30	$40		Jean Lee Latham		Macmil
1962	Alexander Soames: His Poems	$25	$30	$40		Karla Kuskin		Harper
1962	All Sizes Of Noises	$25	$30	$40		Karla Kuskin		Harper
1963	ABCDEFGHIJKLMNOPQRSTUVWXYZ	$25	$30	$40		Karla Kuskin		H&Row
1964	Credos & Quips	$25	$30	$40		Virginia Cary Hudson		Macmil
1964	The Rose On My Cake	$25	$30	$40		Karla Kuskin		H&Row
1965	Sand And Snow	$25	$30	$40		Karla Kuskin		H&Row
1967	Look At Me	$25	$30	$40		Marguerita Rudolph		McHill
1967	The Walk The Mouse Girls Took	$25	$30	$40		Karla Kuskin		H&Row
1968	Watson, The Smartest Dog In The U.S.A.	$20	$30	$35		Karla Kuskin		H&Row
1969	In The Flaky Frosty Morning	$20	$30	$35		Karla Kuskin		H&Row
1970	Big Enough		$18	$25	$35	Sherry Kafka		Putnam
1970	What Shall We Do And Allee Galloo!		$18	$25	$35	Marie Winn		H&Row
1972	Any Me I Want To Be		$18	$25	$35	Karla Kuskin		H&Row
1973	What Did You Bring Me?		$16	$25	$30	Karla Kuskin		H&Row
1975	Near The Window Tree		$16	$25	$30	Karla Kuskin		H&Row
1976	A Boy Had A Mother Who Bought Him A Hat		$16	$25	$30	Karla Kuskin		HM
1979	Herbert Hated Being Small		$14	$20	$30	Karla Kuskin		HM
1980	Dogs & Dragons, Trees & Dreams		$14	$20	$25	Karla Kuskin		H&Row
1981	Night Again		$14	$20	$25	Karla Kuskin		LBrown
1985	Something Sleeping In The Hall		$12	$18	$25	Karla Kuskin		H&Row
1992	Soap Soup & Other Verses		$10	$16	$20	Karla Kuskin		HCollins
1994	City Dog		$10	$14	$18	Karla Kuskin		Clarion
1995	Thoughts, Pictures, And Words		$10	$14	$18	Nicholas Kuskin		RCOwen

Kyte   Dennis

Year	Title	VG-	VG	VG+	Fine	Author	Award	Pub
1983	The Last Elegant Bear		$16	$25	$30	Dennis Kyte		LSimon
1985	Puppy Gets Around		$12	$18	$25	Dennis Kyte		LSimon
1985	Puppy In The Garden		$12	$18	$25	Dennis Kyte		LSimon
1985	Puppy Plays A Song		$12	$18	$25	Dennis Kyte		LSimon
1985	Puppy Tidies-Up		$12	$18	$25	Dennis Kyte		LSimon
1985	To The Heart Of A Bear: The Last Elegant Bear		$12	$18	$25	Dennis Kyte		LSimon
1988	Mattie And Cataragus		$12	$16	$20	Dennis Kyte		DoubleD
1989	Zackary Raffles		$12	$16	$20	Dennis Kyte		DoubleD
1990	Merry Christmas, Bigelow Bear		$10	$16	$20	Dennis Kyte		DoubleD
1998	The Adventures Of Puppy		$8	$12	$16	Dennis Kyte		SmithM
1998	The Botanical Footwear		$8	$12	$16	Dennis Kyte		SmithM

LaMarche   Jim

Year	Title	VG-	VG	VG+	Fine	Author	Award	Pub
1978	My Daddy Don't Go To Work		$20	$30	$40	Madeena Spray Nolan		CRB
1979	Two Places To Sleep		$16	$25	$30	Joan Schuchman		CRB
1980	My Minnie Is A Jewel		$14	$20	$30	Tricia Springstubb		CRB
1981	A Matter Of Pride		$14	$20	$30	Emily Crofford		CRB
1991	Mandy		$12	$16	$20	Barbara D Booth		LL&S
1991	Night Parachuting		$12	$16	$20	Jim LaMarche		SpirSky
1992	The Rainbabies		$10	$16	$20	Laura Krauss Melmed		LL&S
1994	The Walloping Window-Blind		$10	$16	$20	Charles E. Carryl		LL&S
1995	The Carousel		$10	$14	$18	Liz Rosenberg		HBrace
1996	Grandmother's Pigeon		$10	$14	$18	Louise Erdrich		Hyper
1997	Little Oh		$10	$14	$18	Laura Krauss Melmed		LL&S

LaMarche   Jim

Year	Title	VG-	VG	VG+	Fine	Author	Award	Pub
2000	The Raft		$8	$10	$14	Jim LaMarche		HCollins
2001	Albert		$8	$10	$14	Donna Jo Napoli		HBrace
2002	A Story For Bear		$8	$10	$14	Dennis Haseley		Whistle
2002	Old Town In The Green Groves		$8	$10	$14	Cynthia Rylant		HCollins
2003	The Elves And The Shoemaker		$8	$10	$14	Susan Pearson		Chron

Lane   Daniel

Year	Title	VG-	VG	VG+	Fine	Author	Award	Pub
1991	Santa Cows		$12	$18	$25	Cooper Edens		GreenT
1994	Santa Cow Island		$10	$14	$18	Cooper Edens		GreenT
1994	Shawnee Bill's Enchanted Five-Ride Carousel		$10	$14	$18	Cooper Edens		GreenT
1995	Santa Cow Studios		$10	$14	$18	Cooper Edens		S&S

Lantz   Paul

Year	Title	VG-	VG	VG+	Fine	Author	Award	Pub
1940	Blue Willow	$50	$60	$80		Doris Gates		Viking
1941	The Matchlock Gun	$320	$440	$540		Walter Edmonds	NM	DoddM
1941	Young Shannon	$35	$40	$60		Grace Voris Curl		H&B
1942	Island Boy	$35	$40	$60		Betty Holdridge		Holiday
1942	Tom Whipple	$35	$40	$60		Walter Edmonds		DoddM
1943	Little Navajo Bluebird	$35	$40	$60		Ann Nolan Clark		Viking
1958	When The Cows Got Out	$25	$35	$50		Dorothy Koch		Holiday
1960	Three-Dollar Mule	$25	$30	$40		Clyde Robert Bulla		Crowell
1961	Patrick Visits The Library	$25	$30	$40		Maureen Daly		DoddM

Lathrop   Dorothy P.

Year	Title	VG-	VG	VG+	Fine	Author	Award	Pub
1919	The Three Mulla-Mulgars	$180	$240	$300		Walter De La Mare		Knopf
1920	A Little Boy Lost	$160	$200	$260		W. H. Hudson		Knopf
1921	Grim: The Story Of A Pike	$160	$200	$260		Sven Fleuron		Knopf
1922	Down-Adown-Derry	$160	$200	$260		Walter De La Mare		Const
1923	The Grateful Elephant	$140	$200	$240		Eugene W. Burlingame		YaleUP
1929	Hitty, Her First Hundred Years	$560	$760	$940		Rachel Field	NM	Macmil
1930	Stars To-Night	$100	$140	$180		Sara Teasdale		Macmil
1931	The Dutch Cheese	$100	$140	$180		Walter De La Mare		Knopf
1931	The Fairy Circus	$320	$420	$520		Dorothy P. Lathrop	NH	Macmil
1934	The Lost Merry-Go-Round	$160	$200	$260		Dorothy P. Lathrop		Macmil
1934	The Snail Who Ran	$160	$200	$260		Dorothy P. Lathrop		FStokes
1935	Who Goes There?	$160	$200	$260		Dorothy P. Lathrop		Macmil
1936	Bouncing Betsy	$160	$200	$260		Dorothy P. Lathrop		Macmil
1936	Fierce-Face	$120	$160	$220		Dhan Gopal Mukerji		Dutton
1937	Animals Of The Bible	$960	$1,200	$1,600		Helen Dean Fish	CM	FStokes
1938	Hide And Go Seek	$160	$200	$260		Dorothy P. Lathrop		Macmil
1939	The Happy Flute	$100	$120	$160		Sant Ram. Mandal		FStokes
1939	The Little Mermaid	$100	$120	$160		Hans Christian Andersen		Macmil
1940	Presents For Lupe	$140	$200	$240		Dorothy P. Lathrop		Macmil
1941	The Colt From Moon Mountain	$140	$180	$240		Dorothy P. Lathrop		Macmil
1942	Bells And Grass	$90	$120	$160		Walter De La Mare		Viking
1942	Mr. Bumps And His Monkey	$90	$120	$160		Walter De La Mare		Winston
1943	Puppies For Keeps	$90	$120	$160		Dorothy P. Lathrop		Macmil
1945	The Skittle-Skattle Monkey	$90	$120	$160		Dorothy P. Lathrop		Macmil
1947	An Angel In The Woods	$80	$120	$140		Dorothy P. Lathrop		Macmil
1951	Let Them Live	$80	$100	$140		Dorothy P. Lathrop		Macmil
1954	Puffy And The Seven Leaf Clover	$80	$100	$140		Dorothy P. Lathrop		Macmil
1955	The Littlest Mouse	$70	$100	$120		Dorothy P. Lathrop		Macmil
1960	Follow The Brook	$70	$90	$120		Dorothy P. Lathrop		Macmil
1962	The Dog In The Tapestry Garden	$70	$90	$120		Dorothy P. Lathrop		Macmil

Lawson   Robert

Year	Title	VG-	VG	VG+	Fine	Author	Award	Pub
1922	Wonderful Adventures Of Little Prince Toofat	$600	$800	$1,000		George R. Chester		McCann
1931	From The Horn Of The Moon	$160	$220	$280		Arthur Mason		DD
1936	Seven Beads Of Wampum	$100	$140	$180		Elizabeth Gale		Putnam
1936	The Story Of Ferdinand	$3,000	$4,000	$5,000		Munro Leaf		Viking
1937	Four & Twenty Blackbirds	$220	$300	$380		Helen Dean Fish	CH	FStokes

Lawson   Robert

Year	Title	VG-	VG	VG+	Fine	Author	Award	Pub
1937	The Prince And The Pauper	$160	$200	$260		Mark Twain		Winston
1937	The Story Of Jesus For Young People	$100	$140	$180		Walter Russell Bowie		Scribnr
1938	Mr Popper's Penguins	$240	$320	$400		Richard & Florence Atwater	NH	LBrown
1938	Walt Disney's Ferdinand The Bull	$70	$90	$120		Munro Leaf		Whitman
1938	Wee Gillis	$220	$280	$360		Munro Leaf	CH	Viking
1939	Ben And Me	$220	$280	$360		Robert Lawson		LBrown
1939	Pilgrim's Progress	$70	$90	$120		John Bunyan		FStokes
1940	Gaily We Parade	$100	$120	$160		John Brewton		Macmil
1940	Just For Fun	$140	$200	$240		Robert Lawson		RandMc
1940	They Were Strong And Good	$560	$740	$920		Robert Lawson	CM	Viking
1941	Aesop's Fable	$100	$120	$160		Munro Leaf		THP
1941	I Discover Columbus	$100	$120	$160		Robert Lawson		LBrown
1941	The Story Of Simpson And Sampson	$100	$120	$160		Munro Leaf		Viking
1942	Adam Of The Road	$240	$320	$400		Elizabeth Gray Vining	NM	Viking
1942	Poo-Poo And The Dragons	$460	$620	$780		C.S. Forester		LBrown
1942	Prince Prigio	$140	$180	$240		Andrew Lang		LBrown
1942	The Crock Of Gold	$90	$120	$160		James Stephens		LEC
1943	The Little Woman Wanted Noise	$90	$120	$160		Val Teal		RandMc
1943	Watchwords Of Liberty	$90	$120	$160		Robert Lawson		LBrown
1944	Country Colic	$90	$120	$160		Robert Lawson		LBrown
1944	Rabbit Hill	$220	$280	$360		Robert Lawson	NM	Viking
1945	Mr. Wilmer	$100	$120	$160		Robert Lawson		LBrown
1945	The Shoelace Robin	$90	$120	$160		William Hall		Crowell
1946	Greylock And The Robins	$90	$120	$160		Thomas P. Robinson		Viking
1947	At That Time	$80	$120	$140		Robert Lawson		Viking
1947	Mr Twigg's Mistake	$80	$120	$140		Robert Lawson		LBrown
1948	Robbut	$80	$120	$140		Robert Lawson		Viking
1949	Dick Whittington & His Cat	$80	$120	$140		Robert Lawson		LEC
1949	The Fabulous Flight	$80	$120	$140		Robert Lawson		LBrown
1950	Smeller Martin	$80	$120	$140		Robert Lawson		Viking
1951	McWhinney's Jaunt	$80	$100	$140		Robert Lawson		LBrown
1952	Edward, Hoppy, And Joe	$80	$100	$140		Robert Lawson		Knopf
1953	Mr. Revere And I	$80	$100	$140		Robert Lawson		LBrown
1956	Captain Kidd's Cat	$70	$100	$120		Robert Lawson		LBrown
1957	The Great Wheel	$160	$220	$280		Robert Lawson	NH	Viking
1969	Aesop's Fable	$40	$50	$70		Munro Leaf		THP

Le Cain   Errol

Year	Title	VG-	VG	VG+	Fine	Author	Award	Pub
1970	Collected Rhymes And Verses		$50	$70	$90	Errol Le Cain		Faber
1970	Sir Orfeo, A Legend From England		$30	$50	$60	Anthea Davies (adapted)		BradP
1971	The Child In The Bamboo Grove		$30	$50	$60	Rosemary Harris		Phillip
1972	Cinderella; Or, The Little Glass Slipper		$40	$60	$90	Errol Le Cain (adapted)		Faber
1972	The Beachcombers		$30	$50	$60	Errol Le Cain		Faber
1972	The Caine Mutiny		$30	$50	$60	Herman Wouk		FWatts
1973	The King's White Elephant		$30	$50	$60	Errol Le Cain		Faber
1973	The White Cat		$30	$50	$60	Errol Le Cain (adapted)		Faber
1974	King Orville And The Bullfrogs		$30	$40	$60	Errol Le Cain		LBrown
1974	The Lotus And The Grail		$30	$40	$60	Errol Le Cain		Faber
1974	Wigger		$30	$40	$60	Errol Le Cain		HBJ
1975	The Flying Ship		$30	$40	$60	Rosemary Harris		Faber
1975	The Green Glass Bottle		$30	$40	$60	Zena M. Carus		Black
1976	The Little Dog Of Fo		$30	$40	$60	Rosemary Harris		Faber
1976	The Rat, The Ox, And The Zodiac		$30	$40	$60	Dorothy Van Woerkom (adapted)		Crown
1977	Cupid And Psyche		$25	$40	$50	Walter Pater (adapted)		Faber
1977	The Sly Cormorant And The Fishes		$25	$40	$50	Brian Patten		Kestrel
1977	Thorn Rose		$25	$40	$50	Errol Le Cain (adapted)		BradP
1978	The Twelve Dancing Princesses		$25	$40	$50	Errol Le Cain (adapted)		Faber
1979	Beauty And The Beast		$25	$40	$50	Rosemary Harris (retold)		DoubleD
1979	The Snow Queen		$25	$40	$50	Naomi Lewis (adapted)		Viking
1980	Mrs. Fox's Wedding		$25	$35	$50	Sara & Stephen Corrin (retold)		DoubleD
1980	The Three Magic Gifts		$25	$35	$50	James Riordan		Oxford
1981	Aladdin And The Wonderful Lamp		$25	$35	$50	Andrew Lang (retold)		Viking
1983	Molly Whuppie		$25	$35	$50	Walter De La Ma (retold)		FSG
1984	Hiawatha's Childhood		$50	$80	$100	Henry Wadsworth Longfellow	GM	FSG
1987	Christmas Or, Santa's Last Ride:		$20	$30	$40	Leslie Bricusse		Faber

Le Cain   Errol

Year	Title	VG-	VG	VG+	Fine	Author	Award	Pub
1987	Growltiger's Last Stand		$20	$30	$40	T. S. Eliot		FSG
1987	The Christmas Stockings		$20	$30	$40	Mathew Price		Barrn
1987	The Enchanters Daughter		$20	$30	$40	Antonia Barber		JCape
1988	Alfi And The Dark		$18	$25	$35	Sally Miles		Chron
1989	The Pied Piper Of Hamelin		$18	$25	$35	Sara & Stephen Corrin (retold)		HBJ
1991	Have You Seen My Sister?		$16	$25	$30	Mathew Price		HBJ
1991	Mr. Mistoffele; With, Mungojerrie & Rumpelteazer		$16	$25	$30	T. S. Eliot		HBJ

Leaf   Munro

Year	Title	VG-	VG	VG+	Fine	Author	Award	Pub
1934	Grammar Can Be Fun	$180	$240	$300		Munro Leaf		FStokes
1934	Lo, The Poor Indian	$100	$140	$180		Munro Leaf		Seidel
1935	Robert Francis Weatherbee	$70	$100	$120		Munro Leaf		FStokes
1936	Manners Can Be Fun	$160	$200	$260		Munro Leaf		FStokes
1938	Safety Can Be Fun	$100	$140	$180		Munro Leaf		FStokes
1939	Fair Play.	$70	$90	$120		Munro Leaf		FStokes
1939	More Watchbirds	$120	$160	$220		Munro Leaf		FStokes
1939	The Watchbirds	$140	$200	$240		Munro Leaf		FStokes
1940	John Henry Davis	$70	$90	$120		Munro Leaf		FStokes
1941	Fly Away, Watchbird!	$70	$90	$120		Munro Leaf		FStokes
1942	A War-Time Handbook For Young Americans	$70	$90	$120		Munro Leaf		FStokes
1943	Health Can Be Fun	$90	$120	$160		Munro Leaf		FStokes
1944	3 And 30 Watchbirds	$100	$120	$160		Munro Leaf		Lippin
1944	Gordon The Goat	$60	$80	$100		Munro Leaf		Lippin
1945	Let's Do Better	$60	$80	$100		Munro Leaf		Lippin
1946	Flock Of Watchbirds	$80	$100	$140		Munro Leaf		Lippin
1946	How To Behave And Why	$60	$80	$100		Munro Leaf		Lippin
1948	Sam And The Superdroop	$60	$80	$100		Munro Leaf		Viking
1949	Arithmetic Can Be Fun	$60	$80	$100		Munro Leaf		Lippin
1950	History Can Be Fun	$60	$80	$100		Munro Leaf		Lippin
1951	Geography Can Be Fun	$50	$70	$90		Munro Leaf		Lippin
1953	Reading Can Be Fun	$50	$70	$90		Munro Leaf		Lippin
1955	Lucky You	$50	$70	$90		Munro Leaf		Lippin
1957	Three Promises To You	$50	$70	$90		Munro Leaf		Lippin
1958	Manners Can Be Fun	$50	$60	$80		Munro Leaf		Lippin
1958	Science Can Be Fun	$50	$60	$80		Munro Leaf		Lippin
1960	The Wishing Pool	$50	$60	$80		Munro Leaf		Lippin
1961	Safety Can Be Fun	$50	$60	$80		Munro Leaf		Lippin
1964	Being An American Can Be Fun	$50	$60	$80		Munro Leaf		Lippin
1967	Turnabout	$40	$50	$70		Munro Leaf		Lippin
1971	Who Cares? I Do		$30	$50	$60	Munro Leaf		Lippin
1976	Metric Can Be Fun!		$30	$40	$60	Munro Leaf		Lippin

Lee   Alan

Year	Title	VG-	VG	VG+	Fine	Author	Award	Pub
1976	The Golden Book Of The Mysterious		$40	$60	$80	Jane Werner Watson		Golden
1982	The Mabinogion		$25	$35	$50	Gwyn & Thomas Jones		Dragon
1986	The Mirrorstone		$20	$30	$40	Michael. Palin		Knopf
1987	The Moon's Revenge		$20	$30	$40	Joan Aiken		Knopf
1988	Merlin Dreams		$18	$25	$35	Peter Dickinson		DelaP
1991	The Lord Of The Rings		$120	$180	$240	J. R. R. Tolkien		HCollins
1993	Black Ships Before Troy		$40	$60	$80	Rosemary Sutcliff	GM	DelaP
1994	Tolkien's Ring		$14	$20	$30	David Day		HCollins
1996	The Wanderings Of Odysseus		$12	$18	$25	Rosemary Sutcliff		DelaP
1997	The Hobbit		$40	$60	$80	J. R. R. Tolkien		HM
2002	The Fellowship Of The Ring		$20	$30	$40	J. R. R. Tolkien		HM
2002	The Return Of The King		$20	$30	$40	J. R. R. Tolkien		HM
2002	The Two Towers		$20	$30	$40	J. R. R. Tolkien		HM

Lee   Jared D.

Year	Title	VG-	VG	VG+	Fine	Author	Award	Pub
1979	Upside Down Day		$16	$25	$30	Betty Wright		Whitman
1985	Cream Of Creature From The School Cafeteria		$12	$16	$20	Mike Thaler		Avon
1989	The Teacher From The Black Lagoon		$10	$16	$20	Mike Thaler		Scholas
1993	My Cat Is Going To The Dogs		$10	$14	$18	Mike Thaler		Troll

Lee — Jared D.

Year	Title	VG-	VG	VG+	Fine	Author	Award	Pub
1993	The Bully Brothers		$10	$14	$18	Mike Thaler		G&D
1993	The Bully Brothers Trick The Tooth Fairy		$10	$14	$18	Mike Thaler		G&D
1993	The Principal From The Black Lagoon		$10	$14	$18	Mike Thaler		Scholas
1994	Camp Rotten Time		$10	$14	$18	Mike Thaler		Troll
1994	Fang The Dentist		$10	$14	$18	Mike Thaler		Troll
1994	Miss Yonkers Goes Bonkers		$10	$14	$18	Mike Thaler		Avon
1994	The Gym Teacher From The Black Lagoon		$10	$14	$18	Mike Thaler		Scholas
1995	Bad Day At Monster Elementary		$8	$12	$16	Mike Thaler		Avon
1995	The Bully Brothers--Making The Grade		$8	$12	$16	Mike Thaler		Scholas
1995	The Schmo Must Go On		$8	$12	$16	Mike Thaler		Troll
1995	The School Nurse From The Black Lagoon		$8	$12	$16	Mike Thaler		Scholas
1997	Make Your Beds, Bananaheads		$8	$12	$16	Mike Thaler		Troll
1997	Schmoe White And The Seven Dorfs		$8	$12	$16	Mike Thaler		Scholas
1997	The Princess And The Pea-Ano		$8	$12	$16	Mike Thaler		Scholas
1998	The Cafeteria Lady From The Black Lagoon		$8	$12	$16	Mike Thaler		Scholas
1999	The School Bus Driver From The Black Lagoon		$8	$12	$16	Mike Thaler		Scholas
2000	The Music Teacher From The Black Lagoon		$8	$10	$14	Mike Thaler		Scholas
2001	The Custodian From The Black Lagoon		$8	$10	$14	Mike Thaler		Scholas
2003	The Talent Show From The Black Lagoon		$6	$10	$12	Mike Thaler		Scholas

Lehman — Barbara

Year	Title	VG-	VG	VG+	Fine	Author	Award	Pub
1991	Abracadabra To Zigzag		$12	$18	$25	Nancy Lecourt		LL&S
1992	Mattie		$10	$16	$20	Marsha Wilson Chall		LL&S
1993	Moonfall		$10	$16	$20	Susan Whitcher		FSG
1993	Timothy Twinge		$10	$16	$20	Florence Parry Heide		LL&S
1994	A Chartreuse Leotard In A Magenta Limousine		$10	$14	$18	Lynda Graham-Barber		Hyper
1995	Something For Everyone		$10	$14	$18	Susan Whitcher		FSG
1996	Say Boo!		$8	$12	$16	Lynda Graham-Barber		Candle
2003	Christmas Cookies!		$8	$10	$14	Susan Devins		Candle
2004	The Red Book	$18	$25	$35		Barbara Lehman	CH	HM

Lenski — Lois

Year	Title	VG-	VG	VG+	Fine	Author	Award	Pub
1924	The Peep-Show Man	$220	$280	$360		Padraic Colum		Macmil
1925	Chimney Corner Stories	$180	$240	$300		Veronica S. Hutchinson		Minton
1927	A Book Of Princess Stories	$160	$200	$260		K. Adams & F. Atchinson		DoddM
1927	A Merry-Go-Round Of Modern Tales	$160	$200	$260		Caroline Dwight Emerson		Dutton
1927	Fireside Stories	$160	$200	$260		Veronica S. Hutchinson		Minton
1927	Skipping Village	$220	$280	$360		Lois Lenski		FStokes
1928	A Book Of Enchantment	$160	$200	$260		K. Adams & F. Atchinson		DoddM
1928	A Little Girl Of Nineteen Hundred	$200	$280	$340		Lois Lenski		FStokes
1928	Candle-Light Stories	$160	$200	$260		Veronica S. Hutchinson		Minton
1928	Prudence & Peter Their Adventures With Pots & Pans	$160	$200	$260		E. Robins & O. Wilberforce		Morrow
1929	Chimney Corner Poems	$160	$200	$260		Veronica S. Hutchinson		Minton
1929	There Were Giants	$160	$200	$260		K. Adams & F. Atchinson		DoddM
1929	Two Brothers And Their Animal Friends .	$180	$240	$300		Lois Lenski		FStokes
1930	Fireside Poems	$100	$140	$180		Veronica S. Hutchinson		Minton
1930	Little Rag Doll	$100	$140	$180		Ethel Calvert Phillips		HM
1930	Mr. Nip And Mr. Tuck	$100	$140	$180		Caroline Dwight Emerson		Dutton
1930	Rustam, Lion Of Persia	$100	$140	$180		Alan Lake Chidsey		Minton
1930	Spinach Boy	$160	$220	$280		Lois Lenski		FStokes
1930	The Little Engine That Could	$560	$740	$920		Watty Piper (pseud.)		P&Munk
1930	The Twilight Of Magic	$200	$260	$320		Hugh Lofting		FStokes
1930	Two Brothers And Their Baby Sister	$160	$220	$280		Lois Lenski		FStokes
1931	Benny And His Penny	$160	$220	$280		Lois Lenski		Knopf
1931	Golden Tales Of New England	$100	$140	$180		May Lamberton Becker		DoddM
1931	Grandmother Tippytoe	$160	$220	$280		Lois Lenski		FStokes
1931	Odysseus, The Sage Of Greece	$100	$140	$180		Alan Lake Chidsey		Minton
1932	Arabella And Her Aunts	$160	$220	$280		Lois Lenski		FStokes
1932	Golden Tales Of The Prairie States	$100	$140	$180		May Lamberton Becker		DoddM
1932	The Little Family	$580	$780	$980		Lois Lenski		DD
1934	Gooseberry Garden	$160	$200	$260		Lois Lenski		H&B
1934	Surprise For Mother	$160	$200	$260		Lois Lenski		FStokes
1934	The Little Auto	$420	$560	$700		Lois Lenski		Oxford
1935	Golden Tales Of The Far West	$80	$120	$140		May Lamberton Becker		DoddM

Lenski Lois

Year	Title	VG-	VG	VG+	Fine	Author	Award	Pub
1935	Little Baby Ann	$160	$200	$260		Lois Lenski		Oxford
1936	Phoebe Fairchild	$220	$300	$380		Lois Lenski	NH	FStokes
1936	The Easter Rabbit's Parade	$160	$200	$260		Lois Lenski		Oxford
1937	A-Going To The Westward	$160	$200	$260		Lois Lenski		FStokes
1937	The Little Sailboat	$340	$440	$560		Lois Lenski		Oxford
1938	Bound Girl Of Cobble Hill	$160	$200	$260		Lois Lenski		FStokes
1938	Edgar: The 7:58	$100	$120	$160		Phil Stong		F&R
1938	Golden Tales Of Canada	$100	$120	$160		May Lamberton Becker		DoddM
1938	Once On Christmas	$160	$200	$260		Dorothy Thompson		Oxford
1938	The Little Airplane	$340	$440	$560		Lois Lenski		Oxford
1939	Golden Tales Of The Southwest	$100	$120	$160		May Lamberton Becker		DoddM
1939	Ocean-Born Mary	$140	$200	$240		Lois Lenski		FStokes
1939	Susie Mariar	$140	$200	$240		Lois Lenski		Oxford
1940	Betsy-Tacy	$140	$200	$240		Maud Hart Lovelace		Crowell
1940	Mother Makes Christmas	$120	$160	$200		Cornelia Meigs		G&D
1940	The Little Train	$320	$440	$540		Lois Lenski		Oxford
1940	The Pleasure Of Your Company	$100	$120	$160		Frances Lester Warner		HM
1941	A Name For Obed	$100	$120	$160		Ethel Calvert Phillips		HM
1941	Animals For Me	$140	$180	$240		Lois Lenski		Oxford
1941	Betsy-Tacy And Tib	$140	$180	$240		Maud Hart Lovelace		Crowell
1941	Indian Captive	$200	$260	$320		Lois Lenski	NH	FStokes
1941	Indigo Treasure	$100	$120	$160		Frances Rogers		FStokes
1942	A Letter To Popsey	$90	$120	$160		Mabel Guinnip La Rue		G&D
1942	Over The Big Hill	$90	$120	$160		Maud Hart Lovelace		Crowell
1942	The First Thanksgiving	$90	$120	$160		Lena Barksdale		Knopf
1942	The Little Farm	$200	$280	$340		Lois Lenski		Oxford
1943	Bayou Suzette	$140	$180	$240		Lois Lenski		FStokes
1943	Betsy And Tacy Go Downtown	$100	$140	$180		Maud Hart Lovelace		Crowell
1943	Davy's Day	$140	$180	$240		Lois Lenski		Oxford
1943	Five And Ten	$90	$120	$160		Roberta Whitehead		HM
1943	They Came From France	$90	$120	$160		Clara Ingram Judson		HM
1944	Let's Play House	$140	$180	$220		Lois Lenski		Oxford
1944	Puritan Adventure	$140	$180	$220		Lois Lenski		Lippin
1945	Spring Is Here	$140	$180	$220		Lois Lenski		Oxford
1945	Strawberry Girl	$720	$960	$1,200		Lois Lenski	NM	Lippin
1945	The Surprise Place	$70	$100	$120		Mary Graham Bonner		Knopf
1946	Blue Ridge Billy	$140	$180	$220		Lois Lenski		Lippin
1946	Pinocchio	$80	$100	$140		Allen Chaffee (adapted)		Random
1946	The Donkey Cart	$100	$140	$180		Clyde Robert Bulla		Crowell
1946	The Little Fire Engine	$140	$180	$220		Lois Lenski		Oxford
1947	Judy's Journey	$120	$160	$220		Lois Lenski		Lippin
1948	Boom Town Boy	$120	$160	$220		Lois Lenski		Lippin
1948	Mr. And Mrs. Noah	$120	$160	$220		Lois Lenski		Crowell
1948	Now It's Fall	$120	$160	$220		Lois Lenski		Walker
1949	Cotton In My Sack	$120	$160	$220		Lois Lenski		Lippin
1949	Cowboy Small	$200	$280	$340		Lois Lenski		Oxford
1950	I Like Winter	$120	$160	$200		Lois Lenski		Oxford
1950	Texas Tomboy	$120	$160	$200		Lois Lenski		Lippin
1951	Papa Small	$200	$260	$320		Lois Lenski		Oxford
1951	Prairie School	$120	$160	$200		Lois Lenski		Lippin
1952	Peanuts For Billy Ben	$100	$140	$180		Lois Lenski		Lippin
1952	We Are Thy Children	$80	$100	$140		Clyde Robert Bulla		Crowell
1952	We Live In The South	$100	$140	$180		Lois Lenski		Lippin
1953	Mama Hattie's Girl	$100	$120	$160		Lois Lenski		Lippin
1954	Corn Farm Boy	$80	$120	$140		Lois Lenski		Lippin
1954	Project Boy	$80	$120	$140		Lois Lenski		Lippin
1954	Songs Of Mr Small	$120	$160	$200		Clyde Robert Bulla		Oxford
1954	We Live In The City	$80	$120	$140		Lois Lenski		Lippin
1956	Big Little Davy	$80	$100	$140		Lois Lenski		Oxford
1958	Little Sioux Girl	$80	$100	$140		Lois Lenski		Lippin
1960	We Live In The Country	$70	$100	$120		Lois Lenski		Lippin
1962	Policeman Small	$140	$200	$240		Lois Lenski		Walck
1962	We Live In The Southwest	$70	$100	$120		Lois Lenski		Lippin
1965	We Live In The North	$70	$90	$120		Lois Lenski		Lippin
1966	High-Rise Secret	$70	$90	$120		Lois Lenski		Lippin
1966	More Mr. Small	$70	$90	$120		Lois Lenski		Walck
1967	Debbie And Her Grandma	$60	$80	$100		Lois Lenski		Walck

Lenski　　　　Lois

Year	Title	VG-	VG	VG+	Fine	Author	Award	Pub
1968	Deer Valley Girl	$60	$80	$100		Lois Lenski		Lippin
1968	Lois Lenski's Christmas Stories	$60	$80	$100		Lois Lenski		Lippin
1977	Lois Lenski's Big Book Of Mr. Small		$25	$40	$50	Lois Lenski		Walck
1985	Lois Lenski's Big Big Book Of Mr. Small		$20	$30	$40	Lois Lenski		Derry

Lent　　　　Blair

Year	Title	VG-	VG	VG+	Fine	Author	Award	Pub
1964	Pistachio	$60	$80	$100		Blair Lent		LBrown
1964	The Wave	$100	$140	$180		Margaret Hodges	CH	HM
1965	Oasis Of The Stars	$40	$60	$70		Olga Economakis		CM
1965	The Miracle Of The Talking Jungle	$40	$60	$70		Ruth Bartlett		VNost
1966	Baba Yaga	$40	$60	$70		Ernest Small		HM
1966	John Tabor's Ride	$40	$60	$70		Blair Lent		LBrown
1966	The Christmas Sky	$40	$60	$70		Franklyn M. Branley		Crowell
1967	From King Boggen's Hall To Nothing-At-All	$40	$50	$70		Blair Lent		LBrown
1968	The Little Match Girl	$40	$50	$70		Hans Christian Andersen		HM
1968	Tikki Tikki Tembo	$40	$50	$70		Arlene Mosel		HR&W
1968	Why The Sun And The Moon Live In The Sky	$100	$120	$160		Elphinstone Dayrell	CH	HM
1969	May Horses	$40	$50	$70		Jan Wahl		DelaP
1970	The Angry Moon		$80	$120	$160	William Sleator	CH	LBrown
1972	Blackbriar		$30	$50	$60	William Sleator		Dutton
1972	The Funny Little Woman		$220	$320	$420	Arlene Mosel	CM	Dutton
1973	Favorite Fairy Tales Told In India		$30	$50	$60	Virginia Haviland		LBrown
1977	The Telephone		$25	$40	$50	Kornei Chukovsky		DelaP
1979	I Stood Upon A Mountain		$25	$40	$50	Aileen Fisher		Crowell
1987	Bayberry Bluff		$20	$30	$40	Blair Lent		HM
1992	Molasses Flood		$16	$25	$30	Blair Lent		HM
1998	The Beastly Feast		$12	$16	$20	Bruce Goldstone		Holt
2000	Ruby And Fred		$10	$14	$18	Blair Lent		Holt

Lester　　　　Alison

Year	Title	VG-	VG	VG+	Fine	Author	Award	Pub
1982	Thing		$16	$25	$30	Robin Klein		Oxford
1984	Ratbags And Rascals		$12	$18	$25	Robin Klein		Dent
1986	Clive Eats Alligators		$12	$16	$20	Alison Lester		HM
1987	Summer		$12	$16	$20	June Factor		Viking
1988	Ruby		$12	$16	$20	Alison Lester		HM
1989	Rosie Sips Spiders		$12	$16	$20	Alison Lester		HM
1990	Imagine		$10	$16	$20	Alison Lester		HM
1991	Isabella's Bed		$10	$16	$20	Alison Lester		Oxford
1991	Tessa Snaps Snakes		$10	$16	$20	Alison Lester		HM
1991	The Journey Home		$10	$16	$20	Alison Lester		HM
1993	Yikes!		$10	$16	$20	Alison Lester		AU
1994	My Farm		$10	$14	$18	Alison Lester		HM
1996	When Frank Was Four		$8	$12	$16	Alison Lester		HM
1997	Alice And Aldo		$8	$12	$16	Alison Lester		HM
1999	Celeste Sails To Spain		$8	$12	$16	Alison Lester		HM
2000	Ernie Dances To The Didgeridoo		$8	$10	$14	Alison Lester		HM
2003	The Snow Pony		$8	$10	$14	Alison Lester		HM

Levin　　　　Ted

Year	Title	VG-	VG	VG+	Fine	Author	Award	Pub
1995	Creepy Crawly Creatures		$10	$14	$18	Warren Cutler		NGS
1995	Up River		$10	$14	$18	Frank Asch		S&S
1996	Sawgrass Poems		$8	$12	$16	Frank Asch		HBrace
1998	Cactus Poems		$8	$12	$16	Frank Asch		HBrace
1999	Song Of The North		$8	$12	$16	Frank Asch		HBrace

Lewin　　　　Betsy

Year	Title	VG-	VG	VG+	Fine	Author	Award	Pub
1980	Animal Snackers		$25	$35	$50	Betsy Lewin		DoddM
1981	Cat Count		$20	$30	$40	Betsy Lewin		DoddM
1982	Hip, Hippo, Hooray!		$20	$30	$40	Betsy Lewin		DoddM
1986	Furlie Cat		$14	$20	$30	Berniece Freschet		LL&S
1987	Penny		$14	$20	$30	Beatrice S. De Regniers		LL&S

Lewin   Betsy

Year	Title	VG-	VG	VG+	Fine	Author	Award	Pub
1988	Greens		$14	$20	$30	Arnold Adoff		LL&S
1988	Kitten In Trouble		$14	$20	$30	Maria Polushkin		BradP
1989	Here's That Kitten!		$14	$20	$25	Maria Polushkin		BradP
1989	Weird!		$14	$20	$25	Peter R. Limburg		BradP
1990	Araminta's Paint Box		$12	$18	$25	Karen Ackerman		Athenm
1990	What If The Shark Wears Tennis Shoes?		$12	$18	$25	Winifred Morris		Athenm
1991	Gobble		$12	$18	$25	Lynda Graham-Barber		BradP
1991	Mushy!		$12	$18	$25	Lynda Graham-Barber		BradP
1991	The Hummingbirds' Day		$12	$18	$25	Harry Allard		HM
1992	Doodle Dandy!		$12	$18	$25	Lynda Graham-Barber		BradP
1992	Eddie And The Fire Engine		$12	$18	$25	Carolyn Haywood		Beech
1992	Itchy, Itchy Chicken Pox		$12	$18	$25	Grace Maccarone		Scholas
1992	Jim Hedgehog And The Lonesome Tower		$12	$18	$25	Russell Hoban		Clarion
1992	Jim Hedgehog's Supernatural Christmas		$12	$18	$25	Russell Hoban		Clarion
1993	First Grade Ladybugs		$12	$16	$20	Joanne Ryder		Troll
1993	First Grade Valentines		$12	$16	$20	Joanne Ryder		Troll
1993	Fraidy Cats		$12	$16	$20	Stephen Krensky		Scholas
1993	Hello, First Grade		$12	$16	$20	Joanne Ryder		Troll
1993	Ho Ho Ho!		$12	$16	$20	Lynda Graham-Barber		BradP
1993	Mattie's Little Possum Pet		$12	$16	$20	Ida Luttrell		Athenm
1993	Somebody Catch My Homework		$12	$16	$20	David Lee Harrison		Boyds
1993	Yo, Hungry Wolf!		$12	$16	$20	David Vozar		DoubleD
1994	Detective Stars & Case Of The Super Soccer Team		$12	$16	$20	Caroline Anne Levine		Cobble
1994	First Grade Elves		$12	$16	$20	Joanne Ryder		Troll
1994	I'm George Washington, And You're Not!		$12	$16	$20	Steven Kroll		Hyper
1994	The Boy Who Counted Stars		$12	$16	$20	David Lee Harrison		Wordsng
1994	What's Black And White And Came To Visit		$12	$16	$20	Evan Levine		Orchard
1995	Booby Hatch		$10	$16	$20	Betsy Lewin		Clarion
1995	M.C. Turtle And The Hip Hop Hare		$10	$16	$20	David Vozar		DoubleD
1995	My Tooth Is About To Fall Out		$10	$16	$20	Grace Maccarone		Scholas
1995	The Classroom Pet		$10	$16	$20	Grace Maccarone		Scholas
1995	The Lunch Box Surprise		$10	$16	$20	Grace Maccarone		Scholas
1995	Walk A Green Path		$10	$16	$20	Betsy Lewin		LL&S
1996	A Thousand Cousins		$10	$16	$20	David Lee Harrison		Wordsng
1996	Chubbo's Pool		$10	$16	$20	Betsy Lewin		Clarion
1996	Recess Mess		$10	$16	$20	Grace Maccarone		Scholas
1996	Sharing Time Troubles		$10	$16	$20	Grace Maccarone		Cart
1996	The Gym Day Winner		$10	$16	$20	Grace Maccarone		Scholas
1997	Bug Boy		$10	$16	$20	Carol Sonenklar		Holt
1997	No Such Thing		$10	$16	$20	Jackie French Koller		Boyds
1997	What's The Matter, Habibi?		$10	$16	$20	Betsy Lewin		Clarion
1998	Bug Girl		$10	$14	$18	Carol Sonenklar		Holt
1998	I Have A Cold		$10	$14	$18	Grace Maccarone		Scholas
1998	Rapunzel, A Happenin' Rap		$10	$14	$18	David Vozar		DoubleD
1998	Snake Alley Band		$10	$14	$18	Elizabeth Nygaard		DoubleD
1998	Wiley Learns To Spell		$10	$14	$18	Betsy Lewin		Scholas
1999	Aunt Minnie Mcgranahan		$10	$14	$18	Mary Skillings Prigger		Clarion
1999	Gorilla Walk		$10	$14	$18	Ted Lewin		LL&S
1999	The Class Trip		$10	$14	$18	Grace Maccarone		Scholas
2000	Click, Clack, Moo		$30	$50	$60	Doreen Cronin	CH	S&S
2000	Elephant Quest		$8	$12	$16	Ted Lewin		HCollins
2000	Groundhog Day		$8	$12	$16	Betsy Lewin		Scholas
2000	Is It Far To Zanzibar?		$8	$12	$16	Nikki Grimes		LL&S
2000	Promises		$8	$12	$16	Elizabeth Winthrop		Clarion
2000	Purrfectly Purrfect		$8	$12	$16	Patricia Lauber		HCollins
2001	A Houseful Of Christmas		$8	$12	$16	Barbara M. Joosse		Holt
2001	Dumpy La Rue		$8	$12	$16	Elizabeth Winthrop		Holt
2001	First Grade Friends		$8	$12	$16	Grace Maccarone		Scholas
2002	A Hug Goes Around		$8	$10	$14	Laura Krauss Melmed		HCollins
2002	Aunt Minnie And The Twister		$8	$10	$14	Mary Skillings Prigger		Clarion
2002	Giggle, Giggle, Quack		$8	$10	$14	Doreen Cronin		S&S
2003	The Sleepover		$8	$10	$14	Grace Maccarone		Scholas
2003	Two Eggs, Please		$8	$10	$14	Sarah Weeks		Athenm
2004	Duck For President		$8	$10	$14	Doreen Cronin		S&S
2005	Cowgirl Kate And Cocoa		$6	$10	$12	Erica Silverman		Harcort
2005	Top To Bottom Down Under		$6	$10	$12	Ted Lewin		HCollins
2005	What Is It Like To Be A Cat?		$6	$10	$12	Karla Kuskin		Athenm

Lewin   Ted

Year	Title	VG-	VG	VG+	Fine	Author	Award	Pub
1968	A Blind Man Can!	$40	$50	$70		Jack McClellan		HM
1968	The Look-It-Up Book Of Presidents	$40	$50	$70		Wyatt Blassingame		Random
1969	Meet Robert E. Lee	$25	$35	$50		George Swift Trow		Random
1969	Up, Out, And Over!	$25	$35	$50		Jack McClellan		HM
1970	Jasper, The Drummin' Boy		$25	$35	$50	Margaret T. Burroughs		Follett
1971	A Surprise For Carlotta		$25	$35	$50	Nellie Burchardt		FWatts
1971	Mr. Big Britches		$25	$35	$50	Darrell A. Rolerson		DoddM
1971	Not Enough Indians		$25	$35	$50	Betty F. Horvath		FWatts
1971	Pioneers Of Ecology		$25	$35	$50	Donald W. Cox		Hamlyn
1971	The Visitor		$25	$35	$50	Gene Smith		Cowles
1972	A Month Of Sundays		$25	$35	$50	Rose Blue		FWatts
1972	Chicano, Amigo		$25	$35	$50	Maurine H. Gee		Morrow
1972	Getting It All Together		$25	$35	$50	Michael Capizzi		DelaP
1972	Grandma Didn't Wave Back		$25	$35	$50	Rose Blue		FWatts
1972	In Sheep's Clothing		$25	$35	$50	Darrell A. Rolerson		DoddM
1972	Nikki 108		$25	$35	$50	Rose Blue		FWatts
1972	Sugar Bee		$25	$35	$50	Rita Micklish		DelaP
1973	Lion On The Run		$25	$35	$50	Marian Rumsey		Morrow
1973	The Cheese Stands Alone		$25	$35	$50	Marjorie M. Prince		HM
1973	The Ghost Of Grannoch Moor		$25	$35	$50	William MacKellar		DoddM
1974	A Boy Called Plum		$20	$30	$40	Darrell A. Rolerson		DoddM
1974	Gabriel		$20	$30	$40	Jean Slaughter Doty		Macmil
1974	The Hayburners		$20	$30	$40	Gene Smith		DelaP
1975	Earthquake		$20	$30	$40	Matt Christopher		LBrown
1975	One Small Dog		$20	$30	$40	Shih-chin Tung		DoddM
1975	Rufus, Red Rufas		$20	$30	$40	Patricia Beatty		Morrow
1975	The Preacher's Kid		$20	$30	$40	Rose Blue		FWatts
1975	Up In Sister Bay		$20	$30	$40	Charles Ferry		HM
1975	Winter Pony		$20	$30	$40	Jean Slaughter Doty		Macmil
1976	Listen To The Crows		$20	$30	$40	Laurence Pringle		Crowell
1976	Puffin, Bird Of The Open Seas		$20	$30	$40	Lynne Martin		Morrow
1976	World Within A World--Everglades		$30	$40	$60	Ted Lewin		DoddM
1977	Bird Of Passage		$20	$30	$40	Mildred Teal		LBrown
1977	Carolina Hurricane		$20	$30	$40	Marian Rumsey		Morrow
1977	Ghostly Animals Of America		$20	$30	$40	Patricia Edwards Clyne		DoddM
1977	Patooie		$20	$30	$40	Robert Newton Peck		Knopf
1977	Straight On Till Morning		$20	$30	$40	Helen Hill		Crowell
1977	The Deserter		$20	$30	$40	Nigel Gray		H&Row
1977	The Shadow-Cage		$20	$30	$40	Philippa Pearce		Crowell
1978	Merlin & The Snake's Egg		$20	$30	$40	Leslie Norris		Viking
1978	Soup For President		$20	$30	$40	Robert Newton Peck		Knopf
1978	The Silent Bells		$20	$30	$40	William MacKellar		DoddM
1978	The Witch Of Glen Gowrie		$20	$30	$40	William MacKellar		DoddM
1978	World Within A World--Baja		$20	$30	$40	Ted Lewin		DoddM
1979	Barney And The Ufo		$18	$25	$35	Margaret Goff Clark		DoddM
1979	High Ridge Gobbler		$18	$25	$35	David Stemple		Collins
1979	Hub		$18	$25	$35	Robert Newton Peck		Knopf
1979	Strange And Supernatural Animals		$18	$25	$35	Patricia Edwards Clyne		DoddM
1980	Can I Get There By Candlelight?		$18	$25	$35	Jean Slaughter Doty		Macmil
1980	My Mother, The Witch		$18	$25	$35	Rose Blue		McHill
1980	World Within A World--Pribilofs		$18	$25	$35	Ted Lewin		DoddM
1981	Barney In Space		$18	$25	$35	Margaret Goff Clark		DoddM
1981	Bermuda Petrel		$18	$25	$35	Francine Jacobs		Morrow
1982	The Adventures Of Tom Sawyer		$16	$25	$30	Mark Twain		Wander
1983	Barney On Mars		$16	$25	$30	Margaret Goff Clark		DoddM
1983	The Horse In The Attic		$16	$25	$30	Eleanor L. Clymer		BradP
1983	The Willow Whistle		$16	$25	$30	Priscilla Homola		DoddM
1985	Babe Didrikson		$16	$25	$30	R. Rozanne Knudson		VK
1985	National Velvet		$16	$25	$30	Enid Bagnold		Morrow
1985	The Search For Grissi		$16	$25	$30	Mary Francis Shura		DoddM
1986	A Brown Bird Singing		$14	$20	$30	Frances Wosmek		LL&S
1986	A Dolphin Goes To School		$14	$20	$30	Elizabeth Simpson Smith		Morrow
1986	Mother Teresa, Sister To The Poor		$14	$20	$30	Patricia Reilly Giff		VK
1987	Margaret Mead		$14	$20	$30	Susan Saunders		VK
1987	The Serpent Never Sleeps		$14	$20	$30	Scott O'Dell		HM
1988	Faithful Elephants		$14	$20	$30	Yukio Tsuchiya		HM
1988	Rachel Carson		$14	$20	$30	Kathleen V. Kudlinski		VK

Lewin   Ted

Year	Title	VG-	VG	VG+	Fine	Author	Award	Pub
1989	Herds Of Thunder, Manes Of Gold		$14	$20	$25	Bruce Coville		DoubleD
1989	The Secret Of The Indian		$14	$20	$25	Lynne Reid Banks		DoubleD
1989	Young Nick And Jubilee		$14	$20	$25	Leon Garfield		DelaP
1990	Bird Watch		$12	$18	$25	Jane Yolen		Philo
1990	Island Of The Blue Dolphins		$12	$18	$25	Scott O'Dell		HM
1990	Judy Scuppernong		$12	$18	$25	Brenda Seabrooke		Cobble
1990	Shanghai Passage		$12	$18	$25	Greg Patent		Clarion
1990	The Day Of Ahmed's Secret		$12	$18	$25	Florence Parry Heide		LL&S
1990	Tiger Trek		$12	$18	$25	Ted Lewin		Macmil
1991	Brother Francis And The Friendly Beasts		$12	$18	$25	Margaret Hodges		Scribnr
1991	I Wonder If I'll See A Whale		$12	$18	$25	Frances Ward Weller		Philo
1991	The Potato Man		$12	$18	$25	Megan McDonald		Orchard
1992	Matthew Wheelock's Wall		$12	$18	$25	Frances Ward Weller		Macmil
1992	Matthew's Meadow		$12	$18	$25	Corinne Demas		HBJ
1992	Sami And The Time Of The Troubles		$12	$18	$25	Florence Parry Heide		Clarion
1992	The Great Pumpkin Switch		$12	$18	$25	Megan McDonald		Orchard
1992	When The Rivers Go Home		$12	$18	$25	Ted Lewin		Macmil
1993	Amazon Boy		$12	$16	$20	Ted Lewin		Macmil
1993	Cowboy Country		$12	$16	$20	Ann Herbert Scott		Clarion
1993	I Was A Teenage Professional Wrestler		$12	$16	$20	Ted Lewin		Orchard
1993	Peppe The Lamplighter		$30	$40	$60	Elisa Bartone	CH	LL&S
1994	Just In Time For Christmas		$12	$16	$20	Louise Borden		Scholas
1994	Sacred River		$12	$16	$20	Ted Lewin		Clarion
1994	The Always Prayer Shawl		$12	$16	$20	Sheldon Oberman		Boyds
1994	The Reindeer People		$12	$16	$20	Ted Lewin		Macmil
1995	Lost Moose		$10	$16	$20	Jan Slepian		Philo
1996	American Too		$10	$16	$20	Elisa Bartone		LL&S
1996	Market!		$10	$16	$20	Ted Lewin		LL&S
1996	Paperboy		$10	$16	$20	Mary Kay Kroeger		Clarion
1996	Sea Watch		$10	$16	$20	Jane Yolen		Philo
1997	Ali, Child Of The Desert		$10	$16	$20	Jonathan London		LL&S
1997	Fair!		$10	$16	$20	Ted Lewin		LL&S
1998	The Originals		$10	$14	$18	Jane Yolen		Philo
1998	The Storytellers		$10	$14	$18	Ted Lewin		LL&S
1999	A. Lincoln And Me		$10	$14	$18	Louise Borden		Scholas
1999	Barn Savers		$10	$14	$18	Linda Oatman High		Boyds
1999	How Whales Walked Into The Sea		$10	$14	$18	Faith McNulty		Scholas
1999	Nilo And The Tortoise		$10	$14	$18	Ted Lewin		Scholas
1999	Touch And Go		$10	$14	$18	Ted Lewin		LL&S
2000	The Disappearing Island		$8	$12	$16	Corinne Demas		S&S
2000	The Doorman		$8	$12	$16	Jacob & Wilhelm Grimm		Orchard
2001	Red Legs		$8	$12	$16	Ted Lewin		HCollins
2001	Winter Shoes For Shadow Horse		$8	$12	$16	Linda Oatman High		Boyds
2002	Big Jimmy's Kum Kau Chinese Take Out		$8	$10	$14	Ted Lewin		HCollins
2002	Sunsets Of The West		$8	$10	$14	Tony Johnston		Putnam
2003	Lost City		$8	$10	$14	Ted Lewin		Philo
2003	The Girl On The High-Diving Horse		$8	$10	$14	Linda Oatman High		Philo
2003	Tooth And Claw		$8	$10	$14	Ted Lewin		HCollins
2004	High As A Hawk		$8	$10	$14	T. A. Barron		Philo

Lewis   Earl B.

Year	Title	VG-	VG	VG+	Fine	Author	Award	Pub
1994	Fire On The Mountain		$12	$16	$20	Jane Kurtz		S&S
1995	Big Boy		$10	$14	$18	Tololwa Mollel		Clarion
1995	Down The Road		$10	$14	$18	Alice Schertle		Bdeer
1995	The New King		$10	$14	$18	Doreen Rappaport		Dial
1996	Magid Fasts For Ramadan		$8	$12	$16	Mary Matthews		Clarion
1996	The Magic Moonberry Jump Ropes		$8	$12	$16	Dakari Hru		Dial
1997	Creativity		$8	$12	$16	John Steptoe		Clarion
1997	I Love My Hair!		$8	$12	$16	Natasha Tarpley		LBrown
1997	Only A Pigeon		$8	$12	$16	Jane & Christopher Kurtz		S&S
1997	Staying Cool		$8	$12	$16	Nancy Antle		Dial
1998	The Bat Boy & His Violin		$8	$12	$16	Gavin Curtis		S&S
1998	The Jazz Of Our Street		$8	$12	$16	Fatima Shaik		Dial
1999	Little Cliff And The Porch People		$8	$12	$16	Clifton L. Taulbert		Dial
1999	My Rows And Piles Of Coins		$8	$12	$16	Tololwa Mollel		Clarion

Lewis — Earl B.

Year	Title	VG-	VG	VG+	Fine	Author	Award	Pub
1999	The Magic Tree		$8	$12	$16	T. Obinkaram Echewa		Morrow
1999	Virgie Goes To School With Us Boys		$8	$12	$16	Elizabeth F. Howard		S&S
2000	Dirt On Their Skirts		$8	$10	$14	Doreen Rappaport		Dial
2000	Faraway Home		$8	$10	$14	Jane Kurtz		Harcort
2000	The Times They Used To Be		$8	$10	$14	Lucille Clifton		DelaP
2001	Little Cliff's First Day Of School		$8	$10	$14	Clifton L. Taulbert		Dial
2001	The Other Side		$8	$10	$14	Jacqueline Woodson		Putnam
2002	Bippity Bop Barbershop		$8	$10	$14	Natasha Tarpley		LBrown
2002	Little Cliff And The Cold Place		$8	$10	$14	Clifton L. Taulbert		Dial
2002	Talkin' About Bessie		$8	$10	$14	Nikki Grimes		Orchard
2003	Joe-Joe's First Flight		$8	$10	$14	Natasha Tarpley		Knopf
2003	Sometimes My Mommy Gets Angry		$8	$10	$14	Bebe Moore Campbell		Putnam
2004	Circle Unbroken		$6	$10	$12	Margot Theis Raven		FSG
2004	Coming On Home Soon		$25	$40	$50	Jacqueline Woodson	CH	Putnam
2004	When You Were Born		$6	$10	$12	Dianna Hutts Aston		Candle

Lewis — Paul Owen

Year	Title	VG-	VG	VG+	Fine	Author	Award	Pub
1988	Davy's Dream		$18	$25	$35	Paul Owen Lewis		BW
1988	The Starlight Bride		$14	$20	$30	Paul Owen Lewis		BW
1989	You Are Cordially Invited To P. Bear's New Year's Party!		$14	$20	$30	Paul Owen Lewis		BW
1991	Ever Wondered?		$14	$20	$25	Paul Owen Lewis		BW
1993	Grasper		$12	$18	$25	Paul Owen Lewis		BW
1995	Storm Boy		$12	$16	$20	Paul Owen Lewis		BW
1997	Frog Girl		$10	$16	$20	Paul Owen Lewis		BW
2003	The Jupiter Stone		$8	$10	$14	Paul Owen Lewis		Tricyc

Lionni — Leo

Year	Title	VG-	VG	VG+	Fine	Author	Award	Pub
1959	Little Blue And Little Yellow	$200	$260	$320		Leo Lionni		Obolsky
1960	Inch By Inch	$220	$300	$380		Leo Lionni	CH	Obolsky
1961	On My Beach There Are Many Pebbles	$140	$180	$240		Leo Lionni		Obolsky
1963	Swimmy	$180	$240	$300		Leo Lionni	CH	Pan
1964	Tico And The Golden Wings	$90	$120	$160		Leo Lionni		Pan
1967	Frederick	$160	$200	$260		Leo Lionni	CH	Pan
1968	Alphabet Tree	$80	$120	$140		Leo Lionni		Pan
1968	Biggest House In The World	$80	$120	$140		Leo Lionni		Pan
1969	Alexander And The Wind-Up Mouse	$140	$180	$220		Leo Lionni	CH	Pan
1971	Theodore And The Talking Mushroom		$40	$60	$90	Leo Lionni		Pan
1973	Greentail Mouse		$40	$60	$90	Leo Lionni		Pan
1975	Color Of His Own		$40	$60	$80	Leo Lionni		Pan
1975	In The Rabbit Garden		$40	$60	$80	Leo Lionni		Pan
1975	Pezzettino		$40	$60	$80	Leo Lionni		Pan
1977	A Flea Story: I Want To Stay Here!		$30	$50	$60	Leo Lionni		Pan
1979	Geraldine, The Music Mouse		$30	$40	$60	Leo Lionni		Pan
1981	Mouse Days : A Book Of Seasons		$25	$40	$50	Hannah Solomon		Pan
1982	Let's Make Rabbits : A Fable		$25	$40	$50	Leo Lionni		Pan
1983	Cornelius : A Fable		$25	$40	$50	Leo Lionni		Pan
1983	Pictures To Talk About		$25	$40	$50	Leo Lionni		Pan
1985	Colors To Talk About		$25	$35	$50	Leo Lionni		Pan
1985	Frederick's Fables		$25	$35	$50	Leo Lionni		Pan
1985	Letters To Talk About		$25	$35	$50	Leo Lionni		Pan
1985	Numbers To Talk About		$25	$35	$50	Leo Lionni		Pan
1986	It's Mine!		$25	$35	$50	Leo Lionni		Knopf
1987	Nicholas Where Have You Been?		$20	$30	$40	Leo Lionni		Knopf
1988	Six Crows : A Fable		$20	$30	$40	Leo Lionni		Knopf
1991	Matthew's Dream		$18	$25	$35	Leo Lionni		Knopf
1992	Busy Year		$18	$25	$35	Leo Lionni		Knopf
1992	Let's Make Rabbits : A Fable		$12	$18	$25	Leo Lionni		Knopf
1992	Mr McMouse		$18	$25	$35	Leo Lionni		Knopf
1994	Extraordinary Egg		$16	$25	$30	Leo Lionni		Knopf
1994	Leo Lionni Favorites : Six Classic Stories		$16	$25	$30	Leo Lionni		Knopf

Lloyd   Megan

Year	Title	VG-	VG	VG+	Fine	Author	Award	Pub
1983	Chicken Tricks		$16	$25	$30	Megan Lloyd		H&Row
1984	Lonesome Lester		$12	$18	$25	Ida Luttrell		H&Row
1984	Surprises		$12	$18	$25	Lee Bennett Hopkins		H&Row
1985	All Those Mothers At The Manger		$12	$18	$25	Norma Farber		H&Row
1985	There Goes The Ghost		$12	$18	$25	Victoria Sherrow		H&Row
1986	Farmer Mack Measures His Pig		$12	$16	$20	Tony Johnston		H&Row
1986	Little Old Lady Who Was Not Afraid Of Anything		$12	$16	$20	Linda Williams		Crowell
1986	The Atlantic Free Balloon Race		$12	$16	$20	Thom Roberts		Avon
1987	More Surprises		$12	$16	$20	Lee Bennett Hopkins		H&Row
1990	How We Learned The Earth Is Round		$10	$16	$20	Patricia Lauber		Crowell
1990	That Sky, That Rain		$10	$16	$20	Carolyn Otto		Crowell
1991	Baba Yaga		$10	$16	$20	Eric Kimmel		Holiday
1991	Cactus Hotel		$10	$16	$20	Brenda Z. Guiberson		Holt
1991	Super Cluck		$10	$16	$20	Jane O'Connor		HCollins
1992	How You Talk		$10	$16	$20	Paul Showers		HCollins
1992	Look Out For Turtles!		$10	$16	$20	Melvin Berger		HCollins
1992	Spoonbill Swamp		$10	$16	$20	Brenda Z. Guiberson		Holt
1992	The Christmas Tree Ride		$10	$16	$20	Mary Neville		Holiday
1993	Lobster Boat		$10	$16	$20	Brenda Z. Guiberson		Holt
1993	The Gingerbread Doll		$10	$16	$20	Susan Tews		Clarion
1993	The Gingerbread Man		$10	$16	$20	Eric Kimmel		Holiday
1994	A Regular Flood Of Mishap		$10	$14	$18	Tom Birdseye		Holiday
1994	The Perfectly Orderly House		$10	$14	$18	Ellen Kindt McKenzie		Holt
1995	Dance With Me		$10	$14	$18	Barbara Juster Esbensen		HCollins
1995	Winter Wheat		$10	$14	$18	Brenda Z. Guiberson		Holt
1996	Falcons Nest On Skyscrapers		$8	$12	$16	Priscilla Belz Jenkins		HCollins
1996	Too Many Pumpkins		$8	$12	$16	Linda White		Holiday
1996	What Color Is Camouflage?		$8	$12	$16	Carolyn Otto		HCollins
1998	Chirping Crickets		$8	$12	$16	Melvin Berger		HCollins
1998	Pioneer Church		$8	$12	$16	Carolyn Otto		Holt
1998	Seven At One Blow		$8	$12	$16	Eric Kimmel		Holiday
2002	Horse In The Pigpen		$8	$10	$14	Linda Williams		HCollins
2003	Fancy That		$8	$10	$14	Esther Hershenhorn		Holiday
2003	Thanksgiving At The Tappletons'		$8	$10	$14	Eileen Spinelli		HCollins
2005	Earthquakes		$6	$10	$12	Franklyn M. Branley		HCollins

Lobel   Anita

Year	Title	VG-	VG	VG+	Fine	Author	Award	Pub
1965	Sven's Bridge	$90	$120	$160		Anita Lobel		H&Row
1966	Puppy Summer	$40	$60	$70		Meindert De Jong		H&Row
1966	The Troll Music	$50	$70	$90		Anita Lobel		H&Row
1967	Potatoes, Potatoes	$40	$50	$70		Anita Lobel		H&Row
1967	The Wishing Penny, & Other Stories	$35	$50	$60		Anita Lobel		PMagP
1968	Indian Summer	$35	$50	$60		F. N. Monjo		H&Row
1968	The Little Wooden Farmer	$35	$50	$60		Alice Dalgliesh		Macmil
1968	The Wisest Man In The World	$35	$50	$60		Benjamin Elkin		PMagP
1969	Someone Small	$35	$40	$60		Barbara Borack		H&Row
1970	The Seamstress Of Salzburg		$30	$40	$60	Anita Lobel		H&Row
1970	The Uproar		$30	$40	$60	Doris Orgel		McHill
1970	Three Rolls And One Doughnut		$30	$40	$60	Mirra Ginsburg		Dial
1970	Under A Mushroom		$30	$40	$60	Anita Lobel		H&Row
1971	How The Tsar Drinks Tea		$30	$40	$60	Benjamin Elkin		PMagP
1972	Little John		$25	$40	$50	Theodor Storm		FSG
1972	One For The Price Of Two		$25	$40	$50	Cynthia Jameson		PMagP
1972	Soldier, Soldier, Won't You Marry Me?		$25	$40	$50	John Langstaff		DoubleD
1973	A Birthday For The Princess		$25	$40	$50	Anita Lobel		H&Row
1973	Clever Kate		$25	$40	$50	Jacob & Wilhelm Grimm		Macmil
1975	King Rooster, Queen Hen		$25	$35	$50	Anita Lobel		Green
1976	Peter Penny's Dance		$25	$35	$50	Janet Quin-Harkin		Dial
1977	How The Rooster Saved The Day		$25	$35	$50	Arnold Lobel		Green
1978	The Pancake		$25	$35	$50	Anita Lobel		Green
1979	A Treeful Of Pigs		$25	$35	$50	Arnold Lobel		Green
1980	Fanny's Sister		$20	$30	$40	Penelope Lively		Dutton
1981	On Market Street		$80	$120	$160	Arnold Lobel	CH	Green
1982	Singing Bee!		$20	$30	$40	Jane Hart		LL&S
1983	The Straw Maid		$20	$30	$40	Anita Lobel		Green

Lobel   Anita

Year	Title	VG-	VG	VG+	Fine	Author	Award	Pub
1984	The Night Before Christmas		$18	$25	$35	Clement C. Moore		Knopf
1984	The Rose In My Garden		$18	$25	$35	Arnold Lobel		Green
1986	A New Coat For Anna		$18	$25	$35	Harriet Ziefert		Knopf
1986	Once, A Lullaby		$18	$25	$35	B. P. Nichol		Green
1988	Looking For Daniela		$16	$25	$30	Steven Kroll		Holiday
1989	Princess Furball		$16	$25	$30	Charlotte Huck		Green
1990	Alison's Zinnia		$16	$25	$30	Anita Lobel		Green
1991	The Dwarf Giant		$14	$20	$30	Anita Lobel		Holiday
1992	Pierrot's ABC Garden		$14	$20	$30	Anita Lobel		Golden
1992	This Quiet Lady		$14	$20	$30	Charlotte Zolotow		Green
1994	Away From Home		$14	$20	$25	Anita Lobel		Green
1995	Cat And The Cook & Other Fables Of Krylov		$12	$18	$25	Ethel Heins (retold)		Green
1995	Toads And Diamonds		$12	$18	$25	Charlotte Huck		Green
1997	Mangaboom		$12	$16	$20	Charlotte Pomerantz		Green
1998	My Day In The Garden		$10	$16	$20	Miela Ford		Green
1998	Not Everyday An Aurora Borealis For Your Birthday		$10	$16	$20	Carl Sandburg		Knopf
2000	One Lighthouse One Moon		$10	$14	$18	Anita Lobel		Green
2001	The Black Bull Of Norroway		$8	$12	$16	Charlotte Huck		Green
2001	The Stable Rat		$8	$12	$16	Julia Cunningham		Green
2003	All The World's A Stage		$8	$10	$14	Rebecca Platt Davidson		Green
2003	My Grandmother's Stories		$8	$10	$14	Adele Geras		Knopf

Lobel   Arnold

Year	Title	VG-	VG	VG+	Fine	Author	Award	Pub
1958	My Holiday Story Book	$100	$140	$180		Morris Epstain		Ktav
1959	The Complete Book Of Hanukkah	$70	$100	$120		Kinneret Chiel		FHP
1962	A Zoo For Mister Muster	$70	$90	$120		Arnold Lobel		Harper
1962	Let's Be Indians	$50	$60	$80		Peggy Parish		Harper
1962	Little Runner Of The Longhouse	$50	$60	$80		Betty Baker		Harper
1962	Terry And The Caterpillars	$50	$60	$80		Millicent Selsam		Harper
1963	A Holiday Of Mister Muster	$50	$70	$90		Arnold Lobel		H&Row
1963	Greg's Microscope	$50	$60	$80		Millicent Selsam		H&Row
1963	Prince Bertram The Bad	$50	$70	$90		Arnold Lobel		H&Row
1963	The Secret Three	$50	$60	$80		Mildred Myrick		H&Row
1964	Giant John	$50	$70	$90		Arnold Lobel		H&Row
1964	Lucille	$50	$70	$90		Arnold Lobel		H&Row
1964	Miss Suzy	$50	$60	$80		Miriam Young		PMagP
1964	Red Fox And His Canoe	$50	$60	$80		Nathaniel Benchley		H&Row
1965	Let's Get Turtles	$40	$60	$70		Millicent Selsam		H&Row
1965	Someday	$50	$60	$80		Charlotte Zolotow		H&Row
1965	The Bears Of The Air	$50	$60	$80		Arnold Lobel		H&Row
1966	Benny's Animals	$40	$60	$70		Millicent Selsam		H&Row
1966	Martha The Movie Mouse	$40	$60	$70		Arnold Lobel		HCrest
1966	Oscar Otter	$40	$60	$70		Nathaniel Benchley		H&Row
1966	The Witch On The Corner	$40	$60	$70		Felice Holman		Norton
1967	Let's Be Early Settlers With Daniel Boone	$40	$50	$70		Peggy Parish		H&Row
1967	The Star Thief	$40	$50	$70		Andrea Di Noto		Macmil
1967	The Strange Disappearance Of Arthur Cluck	$40	$50	$70		Nathaniel Benchley		H&Row
1968	Ants Are Fun	$40	$50	$70		Mildred Myrick		H&Row
1968	Comic Adventures Of Old Mother Hubbard & Her Dog	$40	$50	$70		Sarah Catherine Martin		BradP
1968	Four Little Children Who Went Around The World	$40	$50	$70		Edward Lear		Macmil
1968	The Great Blueness & Other Predicaments	$40	$50	$70		Arnold Lobel		H&Row
1969	I'll Fix Anthony	$40	$50	$70		Judith Viorst		H&Row
1969	Junk Day On Juniper Street	$40	$50	$70		Lilian Moore		PMagP
1969	Sam, The Minuteman	$40	$50	$70		Nathaniel Benchley		H&Row
1969	Small Pig	$40	$50	$70		Arnold Lobel		H&Row
1969	The Terrible Tiger	$40	$50	$70		Jack Prelutsky		Macmil
1970	Frog And Toad Are Friends		$90	$140	$180	Arnold Lobel	CH	H&Row
1970	The New Vestments		$30	$50	$60	Edward Lear		BradP
1970	Tot Botot And His Little Flute		$30	$50	$60	Laura Cathon		Macmil
1971	Hansel And Gretel		$30	$50	$60	Jacob & Wilhelm Grimm		DelaP
1971	Hildilid's Night		$70	$100	$140	Cheli Duran Ryan	CH	Macmil
1971	On The Day Peter Stuyvesant Sailed Into Town		$30	$50	$60	Arnold Lobel		H&Row
1971	The Ice-Cream Cone Coot		$30	$50	$60	Arnold Lobel		PMagP
1971	The Master Of Miracle		$30	$50	$60	Sulamith Ish-Kishor		H&Row
1972	Frog And Toad Together		$90	$120	$180	Arnold Lobel	NH	H&Row

Lobel   Arnold

Year	Title	VG-	VG	VG+	Fine	Author	Award	Pub
1972	Miss Suzy's Easter Surprise		$30	$50	$60	Miriam Young		PMagP
1972	Mouse Tales		$30	$50	$60	Arnold Lobel		H&Row
1972	Seahorse		$30	$50	$60	Robert A. Morris		H&Row
1973	Good Ethan		$30	$50	$60	Paula Fox		BradP
1973	The Clay Pot Boy		$30	$50	$60	Cynthia Jameson		CM&G
1974	Circus		$30	$40	$60	Jack Prelutsky		Macmil
1974	Dinosaur Time		$30	$40	$60	Peggy Parish		H&Row
1974	Miss Suzy's Birthday		$30	$40	$60	Miriam Young		PMagP
1974	The Man Who Took The Indoors Out		$30	$40	$60	Arnold Lobel		H&Row
1975	As I Was Crossing Boston Common		$30	$40	$60	Norma Farber		Dutton
1975	Owl At Home		$30	$40	$60	Arnold Lobel		H&Row
1976	As Right As Right Can Be		$30	$40	$60	Anne K. Rose		Dial
1976	Frog And Toad All Year		$30	$40	$60	Arnold Lobel		H&Row
1976	Nightmares: Poems To Trouble Your Sleep		$30	$40	$60	Jack Prelutsky		Green
1977	Merry Merry Fibruary		$25	$40	$50	Doris Orgel		PMagP
1977	Mouse Soup		$60	$80	$120	Arnold Lobel		H&Row
1978	Grasshopper On The Road		$25	$40	$50	Arnold Lobel		H&Row
1978	Gregory Griggs & Other Nursery Rhyme People		$25	$40	$50	Arnold Lobel (selected)		Green
1978	The Mean Old Mean Hyena		$25	$40	$50	Jack Prelutsky		Green
1979	Days With Frog And Toad		$25	$40	$50	Arnold Lobel		H&Row
1979	Tales Of Oliver Pig		$25	$40	$50	Jean Van Leeuwen		Dial
1980	Fables		$100	$160	$200	Arnold Lobel	CM	H&Row
1980	The Headless Horseman Rides Tonight		$25	$35	$50	Jack Prelutsky		Green
1980	The Tale Of Meshka The Kvetch		$25	$35	$50	Carol Chapman		Dutton
1981	More Tales Of Oliver Pig		$25	$35	$50	Jean Van Leeuwen		Dial
1981	Uncle Elephant		$25	$35	$50	Arnold Lobel		H&Row
1982	Ming Lo Moves The Mountain		$25	$35	$50	Arnold Lobel		Green
1983	The Book Of Pigericks: Pig Limericks		$25	$35	$50	Arnold Lobel		H&Row
1983	The Random House Book Of Poetry		$25	$35	$50	Jack Prelutsky		Random
1984	The Microscope		$20	$30	$40	Maxine Kumin		H&Row
1985	A Three Hat Day		$20	$30	$40	L.G. Bass		LauraG
1985	Whiskers & Rhymes		$20	$30	$40	Arnold Lobel		Green
1986	Bear All Year		$20	$30	$40	Harriet Ziefert		H&Row
1986	Bear Gets Dressed		$20	$30	$40	Harriet Ziefert		H&Row
1986	Bear Goes Shopping		$20	$30	$40	Harriet Ziefert		H&Row
1986	Bear's Busy Morning		$20	$30	$40	Harriet Ziefert		H&Row
1986	The Frog And Toad Pop-Up Book		$20	$30	$40	Arnold Lobel		H&Row
1986	The Just Right Mother Goose		$20	$30	$40	Arnold Lobel		Random
1986	The Random House Book Of Mother Goose		$20	$30	$40	Arnold Lobel		Random
1987	The Devil And Mother Crump		$20	$30	$40	Valerie Scho Carey		H&Row
1988	The Turnaround Wind		$18	$25	$35	Arnold Lobel		H&Row
1988	Tyrannosaurus Was A Beast: Dinosaur Poems		$18	$25	$35	Jack Prelutsky		Green
1997	The Arnold Lobel Book Of Mother Goose		$12	$18	$25	Arnold Lobel		Knopf
2004	Arnold Lobel's Mother Goose For Babies		$8	$10	$14	Arnold Lobel		Knopf

Locker   Thomas

Year	Title	VG-	VG	VG+	Fine	Author	Award	Pub
1984	Where The River Begins		$16	$25	$30	Thomas Locker	NYT	Dial
1985	The Mare On The Hill		$12	$18	$25	Thomas Locker		Dial
1986	Sailing With The Wind		$12	$16	$20	Thomas Locker		Dial
1987	The Boy Who Held Back The Sea		$12	$16	$20	Lenny Hort (adapted)		Dial
1987	The Ugly Duckling		$12	$16	$20	Marianna Mayer (adapted)		Macmil
1988	Family Farm		$12	$16	$20	Thomas Locker		Dial
1988	Washington Irving's Rip Van Winkle		$12	$16	$20	Washington Irving		Dial
1989	The Young Artist		$12	$16	$20	Thomas Locker		Dial
1990	Snow Toward Evening		$10	$16	$20	Josette Frank		Dial
1991	Catskill Eagle		$10	$16	$20	Herman Melville		Philo
1991	The Land Of Gray Wolf		$10	$16	$20	Thomas Locker		Dial
1992	Calico And Tin Horns		$10	$16	$20	Candace Christiansen		Dial
1992	Thirteen Moons On Turtle's Back		$10	$16	$20	Joseph Bruchac		Philo
1993	The First Thanksgiving		$10	$16	$20	Jean Craighead George		Philo
1993	The Ice Horse		$10	$16	$20	Candace Christiansen		Dial
1994	Anna And The Bagpiper		$10	$14	$18	Thomas Locker		Philo
1994	Miranda's Smile		$10	$14	$18	Thomas Locker		Dial
1995	Sky Tree		$10	$14	$18	Candace Christiansen		HCollins
1995	The Earth Under Sky Bear's Feet		$10	$14	$18	Joseph Bruchac		Philo

Locker   Thomas

Year	Title	VG-	VG	VG+	Fine	Author	Award	Pub
1995	To Climb A Waterfall		$10	$14	$18	Jean Craighead George		Philo
1996	Between Earth & Sky		$8	$12	$16	Joseph Bruchac		HBrace
1997	Water Dance		$8	$12	$16	Thomas Locker		HBrace
1998	Home		$8	$12	$16	Thomas Locker		HBrace
1999	Grandfather's Christmas Tree		$8	$12	$16	Keith Strand		Whistle
2000	Cloud Dance		$8	$10	$14	Thomas Locker		Whistle
2000	In Blue Mountains		$8	$10	$14	Thomas Locker		Pond
2001	Mountain Dance		$8	$10	$14	Thomas Locker		Whistle
2002	Walking With Henry		$8	$10	$14	Thomas Locker		Fulcrum
2003	John Muir, America's Naturalist		$8	$10	$14	Thomas Locker		Fulcrum
2004	Rachel Carson		$6	$10	$12	Joseph Bruchac		Fulcrum
2004	The Hudson		$6	$10	$12	Robert C. Baron		Fulcrum

Lonette   Reisie

Year	Title	VG-	VG	VG+	Fine	Author	Award	Pub
1957	Raphael, The Herald Angel	$35	$50	$60		David H. Appel		ChanIP
1959	Ludmila	$25	$35	$50		Paul Gallico		DoubleD
1959	The Blue Fairy Book	$25	$35	$50		Andrew Lang		LGL
1960	The Green Fairy Book	$25	$30	$40		Andrew Lang		LGL
1960	The Red Fairy Book	$25	$30	$40		Andrew Lang		LGL
1962	Traveling Shoes	$100	$120	$160		Noel Streatfeild		Random
1965	Jared's Gift	$25	$30	$40		Marguerite Vance		Dutton
1965	One Day Means A Lot	$25	$30	$40		Marisa		Bobbs
1965	Pigeon On My Head	$25	$30	$40		Vincent Nucera		Bobbs
1966	A Walk On An Iceberg	$25	$30	$40		Mary Chase		Norton
1967	Moving Away	$25	$30	$40		Alice R. Viklund		McHill
1970	The Haunted Birdhouse		$18	$25	$35	Flora Gill Jacobs		CM
1971	The Library		$18	$25	$35	Dorothy Clewes		CM
1973	The Tree House Mystery		$16	$25	$30	Carol Beach York		CM&G
1975	Rose Kennedy		$16	$25	$30	Ann Hawkes		Putnam
1977	The Sunday Whirligig		$16	$25	$30	Alberta Eiseman		Athenm

Long   Loren

Year	Title	VG-	VG	VG+	Fine	Author	Award	Pub
2000	My Dog, My Hero		$10	$14	$18	Betsy Cromer Byars		Holt
2002	The Wonders Of Donal O'Donnell		$8	$12	$16	Gary D. Schmidt		Holt
2003	I Dream Of Trains		$8	$12	$16	Angela Johnson		S&S
2003	My. Peabody's Apples		$8	$12	$16	Madonna		Calla
2003	The Day The Animals Came		$8	$12	$16	Frances Ward Weller		Philo
2004	When I Heard The Learn'd Astronomer		$8	$12	$16	Walt Whitman		S&S
2005	The Little Engine That Could		$8	$12	$16	Watty Piper (pseud.)		Philo

Long   Sylvia

Year	Title	VG-	VG	VG+	Fine	Author	Award	Pub
1983	The Western ABC		$16	$25	$30	Geoffrey O'Gara		Trote
1991	Ten Little Rabbits		$10	$16	$20	Virginia Grossman		Chron
1992	The Most Timid In The Land		$10	$16	$20	Oliver Herford		Chron
1993	Fire Race		$10	$16	$20	Jonathan London		Chron
1994	Alejandro's Gift		$10	$14	$18	Richard E. Albert		Chron
1994	Liplap's Wish		$10	$14	$18	Jonathan London		Chron
1995	Any Bear Can Wear Glasses		$10	$14	$18	Matthew & Thomas Long		Chron
1996	Hawk Hill		$8	$12	$16	Suzie Gilbert		Chron
1997	Hush Little Baby		$8	$12	$16	Sylvia Long		Chron
1999	Bugs For Lunch		$8	$12	$16	Margery Facklam		Charles
1999	Sylvia Long's Mother Goose		$8	$12	$16	Sylvia Long		Chron
2000	Deck The Hall		$8	$10	$14	Sylvia Long		Chron
2001	Sylvia Long's Mother Goose Nesting Blocks		$8	$10	$14	Sylvia Long		Chron
2001	Twinkle, Twinkle, Little Star		$8	$10	$14	Jane Taylor		Chron
2004	Snug As A Bug		$6	$10	$12	Michael Elsohn Ross		Chron

Longtemps   Kenneth

Year	Title	VG-	VG	VG+	Fine	Author	Award	Pub
1967	General Felice	$30	$40	$50		Dahlov Ipcar		McHill
1968	The Chalet At Saint-Marc	$20	$30	$35		Suzanne Butler		LBrown
1968	The Day It Snowed In Summer	$20	$30	$35		Florence Parry Heide		F&W

Longtemps   Kenneth

Year	Title	VG-	VG	VG+	Fine	Author	Award	Pub
1969	Our Tree	$20	$30	$35		Herbert H. Wong		AW
1969	The Secret People	$20	$30	$35		Madelaine Duke		DoubleD
1970	Danny Dougal, The Wanting Boy		$18	$25	$35	Barbara Shook Hazen		Lion
1970	Sound Of Sunshine, Sound Of Rain		$18	$25	$35	Florence Parry Heide		PMagP
1970	The Little One		$18	$25	$35	Florence Parry Heide		Lion
1973	Sometimes I Dance Mountains		$16	$25	$30	Byrd Baylor		Scribnr
1973	The Stairs That Kept Going Down		$16	$25	$30	Compton Mackenzie		DoubleD

Lopshire   Robert

Year	Title	VG-	VG	VG+	Fine	Author	Award	Pub
1959	Ann Can Fly	$100	$140	$180		Fred Phleger		BB
1960	Put Me In The Zoo	$200	$260	$320		Robert Lopshire		BB
1964	How To Make Flibbers	$90	$120	$160		Robert Lopshire		BB
1965	Big Max	$40	$60	$70		Kin Platt		H&Row
1968	I Am Better Than You!	$30	$40	$50		Robert Lopshire		H&Row
1969	It's Magic	$25	$35	$50		Robert Lopshire		Macmil
1969	The Pig War	$25	$35	$50		Betty Baker		H&Row
1972	Wish Again, Big Bear		$25	$35	$50	Richard J. Margolis		Macmil
1973	Little New Kangaroo		$25	$35	$50	Bernard Wiseman		Macmil
1975	Big Bear To The Rescue		$20	$30	$40	Richard J. Margolis		Green
1977	Big Max In The Mystery Of The Missing Moose		$20	$30	$40	Kin Platt		H&Row
1977	How To Make Snop Snappers		$20	$30	$40	Robert Lopshire		Green
1980	Biggest, Smallest, Fastest, Tallests Things		$18	$25	$35	Robert Lopshire		Crowell
1986	ABC Games		$14	$20	$30	Robert Lopshire		Crowell
1986	I Want To Be Somebody New!		$14	$20	$30	Robert Lopshire		BB
1993	Shut The Door!		$12	$16	$20	Robert Lopshire		Western
1996	New Tricks I Can Do!		$10	$16	$20	Robert Lopshire		BB

Lorenz   Lee

Year	Title	VG-	VG	VG+	Fine	Author	Award	Pub
1967	The Teddy Bear Habit	$25	$30	$40		James Lincoln Collier		Norton
1968	Here It Comes	$20	$30	$35		Lee Lorenz		Bobbs
1971	The Upside-Down King		$16	$25	$30	Richard J. Margolis		Windmil
1977	Now Look What You've Done!		$14	$20	$30	Lee Lorenz		Pan
1979	Sylvester Bear Overslept		$14	$20	$25	Jan Wahl		PMagP
1980	Scornful Simkin		$12	$18	$25	Geoffrey Chaucer		P-Hall
1981	Pinchpenny John		$12	$18	$25	Lee Lorenz		P-Hall
1981	Smokey The Shark		$12	$18	$25	Charles Keller		P-Hall
1981	The Feathered Ogre		$12	$18	$25	Lee Lorenz		P-Hall
1982	Big Gus And Little Gus		$12	$18	$25	Lee Lorenz		P-Hall
1983	Hugo And The Spacedog		$12	$18	$25	Lee Lorenz		P-Hall
1983	Remember The A La Mode		$12	$18	$25	Charles Keller		P-Hall
1985	A Weekend In The Country		$12	$16	$20	Lee Lorenz		P-Hall
1986	Waiter, There's A Fly In My Soup		$12	$16	$20	Charles Keller		P-Hall
1989	Driving Me Crazy		$10	$16	$20	Charles Keller		Pippin
1989	Mr. Munday And The Space Creatures		$10	$16	$20	Bonnie Pryor		S&S
1990	Dinah's Egg		$10	$14	$18	Lee Lorenz		S&S
1990	Seven Times Eight		$10	$14	$18	David Updike		Pippin
1997	Mad Amadeus Sued A Madam		$8	$12	$16	Allan Miller		Godine

Love   Judy

Year	Title	VG-	VG	VG+	Fine	Author	Award	Pub
1992	The Treasure Tree		$10	$16	$20	John Trent		Word
1993	There's A Duck In My Closet!		$10	$14	$18	John Trent		Word
1994	I'd Choose You!		$10	$14	$18	John Trent		Word
1996	Spider Sisters		$8	$12	$16	John Trent		Word
1998	Kirby Kelvin And The Not Laughing Lessons		$8	$12	$16	Ivon Cecil		WCoyote
1998	The Two Trails		$8	$12	$16	John Trent		TNelson
1999	The Black & White Rainbow		$8	$12	$16	John Trent		Water
2000	First Day Jitters		$8	$10	$14	Julie Danneberg		Charles
2002	Gobble, Quack, Moon		$8	$10	$14	Mathew Gollub		Tortuga
2002	The Witch Who Wanted To Be A Princess		$8	$10	$14	Lois G. Grambling		WCoyote
2003	First Year Letters		$6	$10	$12	Julie Danneberg		Charles

Low   Joseph

Year	Title	VG-	VG	VG+	Fine	Author	Award	Pub
1947	Rubáiyát	$35	$40	$60		Omar Khayyam		World
1953	Mother Goose	$50	$70	$90		Ruth Low (edited)		HBrace
1960	Heads	$50	$60	$80		Joseph Low		Eden
1960	How A Seed Grows	$25	$30	$40		Helene J. Jordan		Crowell
1960	Pulcinella; Or, Punch's Merry Pranks	$25	$30	$40		Laura Mincieli		Knopf
1962	Adam's Book Of Odd Creatures	$25	$30	$40		Joseph Low		Athenm
1963	Smiling Duke	$25	$30	$40		Joseph Low		HM
1964	Spider Silk	$25	$30	$40		Augusta R. Goldin		Crowell
1964	St. Nicholas And The Tub	$25	$30	$40		Brian Burland		Holiday
1966	Cat And The Mouse, & Other Spanish Tales	$25	$30	$40		Maria De La Iglesia		Pan
1966	How The Mouse Deer Became King	$25	$30	$40		Margueritte Bro		DoubleD
1967	Poems Of Robert Burns	$25	$30	$40		Lloyd Frankenberg		Crowell
1967	Shrimps	$25	$30	$40		Judy Hawes		Crowell
1967	Telephones	$25	$30	$40		Bernice Kohn		CM
1968	Friction	$20	$30	$35		Howard Liss		Crowell
1968	Hear Your Heart	$20	$30	$35		Paul Showers		Crowell
1968	Knight Of The Lion	$20	$30	$35		Constance B. Hieatt		Crowell
1968	Legend Of The Willow Plate	$20	$30	$35		Alvin R. Tresselt		PMagP
1968	Lost Zoo	$20	$30	$35		Countee Cullen		Follett
1969	Beastly Alphabet	$20	$30	$35		George Mendoza		G&D
1969	Flowers And Grasses And Weeds	$20	$30	$35		George Mendoza		F&W
1969	Greece	$20	$30	$35		Sophia Harvati Fenton		HR&W
1969	Poems From India	$20	$30	$35		Daisy Aldan		Crowell
1969	There Was A Wise Crow	$20	$30	$35		Joseph Low		Follett
1971	Speak Roughly To Your Little Boy		$18	$25	$35	Myra Cohn Livingston		HBJ
1972	White Sparrow		$18	$25	$35	Padraic Colum		McHill
1972	Your Bones Are Alive		$18	$25	$35	Sigmund Kalina		LL&S
1973	Land Of The Taffeta Dawn		$16	$25	$30	Natalia Belting		Dutton
1973	Paul Revere's Ride		$16	$25	$30	Henry Wadsworth Longfellow		Windmil
1973	Raucous Auk: A Menagerie Of Poems		$16	$25	$30	Mary Ann Hoberman		Viking
1974	Mouse And The Song		$16	$25	$30	Marilynne K. Roach		PMagP
1974	Snow Of Ohreeganu		$16	$25	$30	Russell E. Erickson		LL&S
1974	Trust Reba		$16	$25	$30	Joseph Low		McHill
1975	Boo To A Goose		$16	$25	$30	Joseph Low		Athenm
1975	Five Men Under One Umbrella		$16	$25	$30	Joseph Low		Macmil
1975	Roots Are Food Finders		$16	$25	$30	Franklyn M. Branley		Crowell
1976	Little Though I Be		$16	$25	$30	Joseph Low		McHill
1976	What If … ? : Fourteen Encounters		$16	$25	$30	Joseph Low		Athenm
1977	Christmas Grump		$16	$25	$30	Joseph Low		Athenm
1977	Mad Wet Hen & Other Riddles		$16	$25	$30	Joseph Low		Green
1977	Museum People		$16	$25	$30	Peggy Thomson		P-Hall
1978	Benny Rabbit And The Owl		$14	$20	$30	Joseph Low		Green
1978	Devil Himself		$14	$20	$30	Joseph Low		McHill
1978	Lollygag Of Limericks		$14	$20	$30	Myra Cohn Livingston		Athenm
1978	My Dog, Your Dog		$14	$20	$30	Joseph Low		Macmil
1980	Mice Twice		$50	$70	$100	Joseph Low	CH	McEld
1982	Alex And The Cat		$14	$20	$25	Helen Griffith		Green
1983	Beastly Riddles: Fishy, Flighty, And Buggy, Too		$14	$20	$25	Joseph Low		Macmil
1983	Don't Drag Your Feet		$14	$20	$25	Joseph Low		Athenm
1985	Learical Lexicon: From The Works Of Edward Lear		$12	$18	$25	Myra Cohn Livingston		Athenm

Lund   Jillian

Year	Title	VG-	VG	VG+	Fine	Author	Award	Pub
1993	Way Out West Lives A Coyote Named Frank		$16	$25	$30	Jillian Lund		Dutton
1997	Tortoise Brings The Mail		$10	$16	$20	Dee Lillegard		Dutton
1999	Two Cool Coyotes		$10	$14	$18	Jillian Lund		Dutton

Lynch   P.J.

Year	Title	VG-	VG	VG+	Fine	Author	Award	Pub
1986	A Bag Of Moonshine		$20	$30	$40	Alan Garner		DelaP
1988	The Raggy Taggy Toys		$18	$25	$35	Joyce Dunbar		Barrn
1989	Melisande		$18	$25	$35	Edith Nesbit		HBJ
1990	Fairy Tales Of Ireland		$16	$25	$30	W. B. Yeats		DelaP
1991	Stories		$16	$25	$30	Oscar Wilde		Macmil
1992	East O' The Sun And West O' The Moon		$16	$25	$30	George Webbe Dasent		Candle
1992	The Steadfast Tin Soldier		$16	$25	$30	Naomi Lewis (adapted)		HBJ

Lynch   P.J.

Year	Title	VG-	VG	VG+	Fine	Author	Award	Pub
1993	The Candlewick Book Of Fairy Tales		$16	$25	$30	Sarah Hayes		Candle
1994	Catkin		$14	$20	$30	Antonia Barber		Candle
1994	The Snow Queen		$14	$20	$30	Caroline Peachey 9adapted)		HBrace
1995	The Christmas Miracle Of Jonathan Toomey		$35	$50	$70	Susan Wojciechowski	GM	Candle
1997	The King Of Ireland's Son		$12	$18	$25	Brendan Behan		Orchard
1997	When Jessie Came Across The Sea		$30	$40	$60	Amy Hest	GM	Candle
1999	Grandad's Prayers Of The Earth		$12	$16	$20	Douglas Wood		Candle
2000	The Names Upon The Harp		$10	$14	$18	Marie Heaney		Levine
2001	Ignis		$10	$14	$18	Gina Wilson		Candle
2003	The Bee-Man Of Orn		$8	$12	$16	Frank R. Stockton		Candle

Macaulay   David

Year	Title	VG-	VG	VG+	Fine	Author	Award	Pub
1973	Cathedral: The Story Of Its Construction		$60	$90	$120	David Macaulay	CH	HM
1974	City: A Story Of Roman Planning And Construction		$30	$40	$60	David Macaulay		HM
1975	Pyramid		$30	$40	$60	David Macaulay		HM
1976	Underground		$30	$40	$60	David Macaulay		HM
1977	Castle		$40	$60	$80	David Macaulay	CH	HM
1978	Great Moments In Architecture		$25	$40	$50	David Macaulay		HM
1979	Motel Of The Mysteries		$25	$40	$50	David Macaulay		HM
1980	Unbuilding		$25	$35	$50	David Macaulay		HM
1982	Carpentry		$25	$35	$50	David Macaulay		Over
1982	Help! Let Me Out!		$25	$35	$50	David Lord Porter		HM
1983	Mill		$25	$35	$50	David Macaulay		HM
1984	The Amazing Brain		$18	$25	$35	R. Thompson & R. Ornstein		HM
1985	Baaa		$20	$30	$40	David Macaulay		HM
1987	Why The Chicken Crossed The Road		$20	$30	$40	David Macaulay		HM
1988	The Way Things Work		$16	$25	$30	David Macaulay		HM
1990	Black And White		$60	$80	$120	David Macaulay	CM	HM
1993	Ship		$14	$20	$25	David Macaulay		HM
1995	Shortcut		$12	$16	$20	David Macaulay		HM
1997	Rome Antics		$10	$16	$20	David Macaulay		HM
1998	The New Way Things Work		$10	$16	$20	David Macaulay		HM
1999	Pinball Science		$10	$16	$20	David Macaulay		Irwin
2002	Angelo		$8	$12	$16	David Macaulay		HM
2003	Mosque		$8	$10	$14	David Macaulay		HM

MacDonald   Suse

Year	Title	VG-	VG	VG+	Fine	Author	Award	Pub
1986	Alphabatics		$40	$60	$80	Suse MacDonald	CH	BradP
1988	Numblers		$12	$16	$20	Bill Oakes		Dial
1989	Puzzlers		$12	$16	$20	Bill Oakes		Dial
1990	Once Upon Another		$10	$16	$20	Bill Oakes		Dial
1991	Space Spinners		$10	$16	$20	Suse MacDonald		Dial
1993	Who Says A Dog Goes Bow-Wow?		$10	$16	$20	Hank De Zutter		DoubleD
1994	Sea Shapes		$10	$14	$18	Suse MacDonald		HBrace
1995	Nanta's Lion		$10	$14	$18	Suse MacDonald		Morrow
1997	Peck, Slither And Slide		$8	$12	$16	Suse MacDonald		HBrace
1999	Elephants On Board		$8	$12	$16	Suse MacDonald		HBrace
2000	I Love You : A Rebus Poem		$8	$10	$14	Jean Marzollo		Scholas
2000	Look Whooo's Counting		$8	$10	$14	Suse MacDonald		Scholas
2002	I See A Star		$8	$10	$14	Jean Marzollo		Scholas

MacKenzie   Garry

Year	Title	VG-	VG	VG+	Fine	Author	Award	Pub
1947	Freddie The Owl	$35	$40	$60		Guy. Andros		Oxford
1947	Town And Country Games	$35	$40	$60		Robert North		Crowell
1948	April Showers	$30	$40	$50		Elizabeth Foreman Lewis		Crowell
1948	Christmas Is Shaped Like Stars	$30	$40	$50		Frances Frost		Crowell
1948	Mr Flip Flop	$30	$40	$50		Helen Garrett		Viking
1948	The Wind And Peter	$30	$40	$50		Alvin R. Tresselt		Oxford
1949	Mother Goose	$30	$40	$50		Garry MacKenzie		Crowell
1950	The Taming Of Giants	$25	$35	$50		Joan Howard		Viking
1950	Uncle Sylvester	$25	$35	$50		Joan Howard		Oxford
1951	Quillenback For Fire Chief	$25	$35	$50		Joan Howard		Oxford

MacKenzie   Garry

Year	Title	VG-	VG	VG+	Fine	Author	Award	Pub
1953	Homer Sees The Queen	$25	$35	$50		Margaret Joyce Baker		Whittle
1953	The Heir To Christmas	$25	$35	$50		Joan Howard		Viking
1953	The Oldest Secret	$25	$35	$50		Joan Howard		Viking
1954	Two For A Walk	$25	$35	$50		Nathan Kravetz		Oxford
1955	Here Come The Deer!	$25	$30	$40		Alice E. Goudey		Scribnr
1955	Here Come The Elephants!	$25	$30	$40		Alice E. Goudey		Scribnr
1955	Miss Brimble's Happy Birthday	$25	$30	$40		Jane Quigg		Oxford
1956	Here Come The Lions!	$25	$30	$40		Alice E. Goudey		Scribnr
1956	Here Come The Whales!	$25	$30	$40		Alice E. Goudey		Scribnr
1956	Mining Round The World	$25	$30	$40		June M. Metcalfe		Oxford
1957	Here Come The Seals!	$25	$30	$40		Alice E. Goudey		Scribnr
1957	The Garden Under The Sea	$25	$30	$40		George Selden		Viking
1957	Up And Over The Hill	$25	$30	$40		Norma Simon		Lippin
1958	Here Come The Wild Dogs!	$25	$30	$40		Alice E. Goudey		Scribnr
1959	Here Come The Raccoons!	$25	$30	$40		Alice E. Goudey		Scribnr
1960	Here Come The Bees!	$25	$30	$40		Alice E. Goudey		Scribnr
1961	Here Come The Dolphins!	$25	$30	$40		Alice E. Goudey		Scribnr
1962	Flickertail	$25	$30	$40		Carolyn Sherwin Bailey		Walck
1962	Here Come The Squirrels!	$25	$30	$40		Alice E. Goudey		Scribnr
1965	Here Come The Cottontails!	$20	$25	$35		Alice E. Goudey		Scribnr
1965	Small Fry	$20	$25	$35		Eve Merriam		Knopf
1966	A Treasury Of Games	$20	$25	$35		Carl Withers		G&D

Maddison   Kevin

Year	Title	VG-	VG	VG+	Fine	Author	Award	Pub
1977	The Pobble Who Has No Toes		$16	$25	$30	Edward Lear		Viking
1980	The Courtship Of The Yonghy-Bonghy-Bo		$14	$20	$25	Edward Lear		Viking
1981	The Pelican Chorus & The Quangle Wangle's Hat		$14	$20	$25	Edward Lear		Viking

Maeno   Itoko

Year	Title	VG-	VG	VG+	Fine	Author	Award	Pub
1987	Minou		$12	$16	$20	Mindy Bingham		Advoc
1988	Kylie's Song		$10	$16	$20	Patty Sheehan		Advoc
1988	My Way Sally		$10	$16	$20	Mindy Bingham		Advoc
1988	Tonia The Tree		$10	$16	$20	Sandy Stryker		Advoc
1989	Berta Benz And The Motorwagen		$10	$16	$20	Mindy Bingham		Advoc
1990	Mother Nature Nursery Rhymes		$10	$14	$18	Sandy Stryker		Advoc
1990	Time For Horatio		$10	$14	$18	Penelope Colville Paine		Advoc
1992	Clarissa		$10	$14	$18	Carol Talley		MarshM
1992	Hana's Year		$10	$14	$18	Carol Talley		MarshM
1992	Papa Piccolo		$10	$14	$18	Carol Talley		MarshM
1993	Gumbo Goes Downtown		$10	$14	$18	Carol Talley		MarshM
1993	Kylie's Concert		$10	$14	$18	Patty Sheehan		MarshM
1993	Nature's Wonderful World In Rhyme		$10	$14	$18	William Sheehan		Advoc
1994	Pequeña The Burro		$10	$14	$18	Jami Parkison		MarshM
1994	Shadow And The Ready Time		$10	$14	$18	Patty Sheehan		Advoc
1994	Tessa On Her Own		$10	$14	$18	Alyssa Chase		MarshM
1995	Molly's Magic		$8	$12	$16	Penelope Colville Paine		MarshM
1996	Amazing Mallika		$8	$12	$16	Jami Parkison		MarshM
1997	Plato's Journey		$8	$12	$16	Linda Talley		MarshM
1999	Thank You, Meiling		$8	$12	$16	Linda Talley		MarshM
2001	Bastet		$8	$10	$14	Linda Talley		MarshM
2001	Toad In Town		$8	$10	$14	Linda Talley		MarshM

Maitland   Antony

Year	Title	VG-	VG	VG+	Fine	Author	Award	Pub
1961	Mrs. Cockle's Cat	$100	$120	$160		Philippa Pearce	GM	Lippin
1963	The Secret Of The Shed	$50	$60	$80		Antony Maitland		DS&P
1967	Ben Goes To The City	$30	$40	$50		Antony Maitland		DelaP
1967	Smith	$30	$40	$50		Leon Garfield		Pan
1968	More Tales Of Shellover	$30	$40	$50		Ruth Ainsworth		Roy
1968	The Quest	$30	$40	$50		Hanna Stephan		LBrown
1968	The Ten Tales Of Shellover	$30	$40	$50		Ruth Ainsworth		Roy
1968	To London! To London!	$30	$40	$50		Barbara Willard		LYoung
1969	Black Jack	$25	$35	$50		Leon Garfield		Pan

Maitland   Antony

Year	Title	VG-	VG	VG+	Fine	Author	Award	Pub
1969	Captain Sintar	$25	$35	$50		Richard Gavin Robinson		Dutton
1969	Mr. Corbett's Ghost & Other Stories	$25	$35	$50		Leon Garfield		LYoung
1969	The Drummer Boy	$25	$35	$50		Leon Garfield		Pan
1971	The Usurping Ghost		$25	$35	$50	Susan Dickinson		Dutton
1972	Child O'War		$25	$35	$50	Leon Garfield		HR&W
1972	The Ghost Downstairs		$25	$35	$50	Leon Garfield		Pan
1973	The Ghost Of Thomas Kempe		$25	$35	$50	Penelope Lively		Dutton
1974	The Phantom Cyclist		$20	$30	$40	Ruth Ainsworth		Folio
1976	Mirror, Mirror		$20	$30	$40	Leon Garfield		Heine
1977	The Wonder-Dog		$20	$30	$40	Richard Hughes		Green
1978	Green Fairy Book		$20	$30	$40	Andrew Lang		Kestrel
1978	The Bear Who Liked Hugging People		$20	$30	$40	Ruth Ainsworth		Russak
1979	Idle Jack		$18	$25	$35	Antony Maitland		FSG
1980	John Diamond		$18	$25	$35	Leon Garfield		Kestrel

Majewska   Maria

Year	Title	VG-	VG	VG+	Fine	Author	Award	Pub
1985	Oscar Mouse Finds A Home		$16	$25	$30	Moira Miller		Dial
1988	A Friend For Oscar Mouse		$12	$16	$20	Joe Majewski		Dial
1990	Ten Little Mice		$10	$16	$20	Joyce Dunbar		HBJ

Mallat   Kathy

Year	Title	VG-	VG	VG+	Fine	Author	Award	Pub
1997	The Picture That Mom Drew		$8	$12	$16	Kathy Mallat		Walker
1998	Seven Stars, More!		$8	$10	$14	Kathy Mallat		Walker
1999	Brave Bear		$8	$10	$14	Kathy Mallat		Walker
2001	Trouble On The Tracks		$8	$10	$14	Kathy Mallat		Walker
2002	Just Ducky		$6	$10	$12	Kathy Mallat		Walker
2003	Oh, Brother		$6	$10	$12	Kathy Mallat		Walker
2004	Mama Love		$6	$10	$12	Kathy Mallat		Walker

Malvern   Corinne

Year	Title	VG-	VG	VG+	Fine	Author	Award	Pub
1938	Land Of Surprise!	$100	$120	$160		Gladys Malvern		McLough
1939	Brownie	$70	$90	$120		Gladys Malvern		McLough
1940	The Story Book Of Brownie And Rusty	$70	$90	$120		Gladys Malvern		McLough
1942	Nursery Songs	$140	$180	$240		Leah Gale		Golden
1943	Mary Mapes Dodge Of St. Nicholas	$50	$60	$80		Alice B. Howard		Messner
1944	Nursery Rhymes And Songs	$60	$80	$100		Helen Dallam		Whitman
1945	Jonica's Island	$40	$60	$70		Gladys Malvern		Messner
1945	Tales About Timothy	$40	$60	$70		Gertrude Blumenthal		Whitman
1946	Christmas Carols	$140	$180	$220		Marjorie Elaine Wyckoff		Golden
1946	Counting Rhymes	$140	$180	$220		Corinne Malvern		Golden
1947	The Little Golden Book Of Poetry	$120	$160	$220		Corinne Malvern		Golden
1948	Up In The Attic	$40	$60	$70		Margaret Julia McElroy		Golden
1949	How Big?	$40	$60	$70		Corinne Malvern		Golden
1950	Doctor Dan	$180	$240	$300		Helen Gaspard		Golden
1950	Frosty The Snow Man	$40	$50	$70		Annie North Bedford		Golden
1950	Jerry At School	$40	$50	$70		Kathryn & Byron Jackson		Golden
1950	Storytime Tales	$40	$50	$70		Corinne Malvern		Golden
1950	Surprise For Sally	$40	$50	$70		Ethel Crowninshield		Golden
1950	Susie's New Stove	$40	$50	$70		Annie North Bedford		Golden
1950	When I Grow Up	$40	$50	$70		Katherine & Harry Mace		Golden
1953	Corinne Malvern's Mother Goose.	$40	$50	$70		Corinne Malvern		Golden

Manning   Jane

Year	Title	VG-	VG	VG+	Fine	Author	Award	Pub
1996	The Ghost Who Ate Chocolate		$8	$12	$16	Susan Saunders		HCollins
1996	The Haunted Skateboard		$8	$12	$16	Susan Saunders		Harper
1997	The Curse Of The Cat Mummy		$8	$10	$14	Susan Saunders		Harper
1997	The Ghost Of Spirit Lake		$8	$10	$14	Susan Saunders		Harper
1997	The Phantom Pen Pal		$8	$10	$14	Susan Saunders		HCollins
1997	The Revenge Of The Pirate Ghost		$8	$10	$14	Susan Saunders		HCollins
1997	This Little Piggy		$8	$10	$14	Jane Manning		HFest
1998	My First Songs		$8	$10	$14	Jane Manning		HFest

Manning   Jane

Year	Title	VG-	VG	VG+	Fine	Author	Award	Pub
1998	The Case Of The Eyeball Surprise		$8	$10	$14	Susan Saunders		Harper
1998	The Chilling Tale Of Crescent Pond		$8	$10	$14	Susan Saunders		HCollins
1998	The Creature Double Feature		$8	$10	$14	Susan Saunders		Harper
1998	The Creepy Camp-Out		$8	$10	$14	Susan Saunders		Harper
1999	Lost Little Angel		$8	$10	$14	M.M. Ragz		S&S
1999	The Witch Who Was Afraid Of Witches		$8	$10	$14	Alice Low		HCollins
2000	Cindy Ellen		$8	$10	$14	Susan Lowell		HCollins
2000	Drip, Drop		$8	$10	$14	Sarah Weeks		HCollins
2001	Cobweb Christmas		$8	$10	$14	Shirley Climo		HCollins
2001	My First Baby Games		$8	$10	$14	Jane Manning		HFest
2001	Who Stole The Cookies From The Cookie Jar?		$8	$10	$14	Jane Manning		HFest
2002	The Eensy Weensy Spider		$6	$10	$12	Jane Manning		HFest
2002	The Green Dog		$6	$10	$12	Melinda Luke		Kane
2003	A Pet For Me		$6	$10	$12	Lee Bennett Hopkins		HCollins
2003	There Was An Old Woman Who Lived In A Boot		$6	$10	$12	Linda Smith		HCollins
2004	Baa-Choo!		$6	$10	$12	Sarah Weeks		HCollins
2004	Beetle Mcgrady Eats Bugs!		$6	$10	$12	Megan McDonald		Green
2004	Fast 'N Snappy		$6	$10	$12	Pattie L. Schnetzler		CRB

Marcellino   Fred

Year	Title	VG-	VG	VG+	Fine	Author	Award	Pub
1979	When The Tree Sings		$35	$50	$70	Stratis Haviaras		S&S
1980	Ebb Of The River		$25	$35	$50	Richard C. Mears		Wyndham
1980	The Picnic & Other Inimitable Stories		$25	$35	$50	Gerald Durrel		S&S
1986	A Rat's Tale		$20	$30	$40	Tor Seidler		FSG
1990	Puss In Boots		$50	$70	$100	Malcolm Arthur (translated)	CH	FSG
1992	The Steadfast Tin Soldier		$16	$25	$30	Tor Seidler (retold)		HCollins
1993	The Wainscott Weasel		$16	$25	$30	Tor Seidler		HCollins
1995	The Pelican Chorus & Other Nonsense		$14	$20	$25	Edward Lear		HCollins
1998	Ouch!		$12	$16	$20	Natalie Babbitt		HCollins
1999	I, Crocodile		$12	$16	$20	Fred Marcellino		HCollins

Marciano   John Bemelmans

Year	Title	VG-	VG	VG+	Fine	Author	Award	Pub
2001	Madeline Says Merci		$8	$10	$14	John Bemelmans Marciano		Viking
2002	Delilah		$8	$10	$14	John Bemelmans Marciano		Viking
2003	Harold's Tale		$8	$10	$14	John Bemelmans Marciano		Viking

Mariana

Year	Title	VG-	VG	VG+	Fine	Author	Award	Pub
1945	The Journey Of Bangwell Putt	$90	$120	$160		Marian Curtis Foster		FAR
1949	Miss Flora McFlimsey's Christmas Eve	$120	$160	$220		Marian Curtis Foster		LL&S
1950	Miss Flora McFlimsey's Birthday	$100	$140	$180		Marian Curtis Foster		LL&S
1950	P'sich	$220	$300	$380		Marian Curtis Foster		FarG
1951	Miss Flora McFlimsey And The Baby New Year	$80	$120	$140		Marian Curtis Foster		LL&S
1951	Miss Flora McFlimsey's Easter Bonnet	$80	$120	$140		Marian Curtis Foster		LL&S
1953	Hotspur	$50	$70	$90		Marian Curtis Foster		LL&S
1954	Miss Flora McFlimsey And Little Laughing Water	$70	$100	$120		Marian Curtis Foster		LL&S
1957	Miss Flora McFlimsey And Little Red School House	$70	$90	$120		Marian Curtis Foster		LL&S
1962	Miss Flora McFlimsey's Valentine	$60	$80	$100		Marian Curtis Foster		LL&S
1969	Miss Flora McFlimsey's May Day	$50	$70	$90		Marian Curtis Foster		LL&S
1972	Miss Flora McFlimsey's Halloween		$40	$60	$80	Marian Curtis Foster		LL&S
1987	Miss Flora McFlimsey's Birthday		$10	$16	$20	Marian Curtis Foster		LL&S
1987	Miss Flora McFlimsey's Easter Bonnet		$10	$16	$20	Marian Curtis Foster		LL&S
1987	Miss Flora McFlimsey's Halloween		$10	$16	$20	Marian Curtis Foster		LL&S
1987	Miss Flora McFlimsey's May Day		$10	$16	$20	Marian Curtis Foster		LL&S
1987	Miss Flora McFlimsey's Valentine		$10	$16	$20	Marian Curtis Foster		LL&S
1988	Miss Flora McFlimsey And The Baby New Year		$10	$14	$18	Marian Curtis Foster		LL&S
1988	Miss Flora McFlimsey's Christmas Eve		$10	$14	$18	Marian Curtis Foster		LL&S

Marshall   James

Year	Title	VG-	VG	VG+	Fine	Author	Award	Pub
1971	Plink, Plink, Plink		$30	$50	$60	Byrd Baylor		HM
1972	George And Martha		$30	$50	$60	James Marshall		HM
1972	What's The Matter With Carruthers?		$30	$50	$60	James Marshall		HM

Marshall   James

Year	Title	VG-	VG	VG+	Fine	Author	Award	Pub
1972	Yummers!		$30	$50	$60	James Marshall		HM
1973	All The Way Home		$20	$30	$40	Lore Segal		FSG
1973	George And Martha Encore		$20	$30	$40	James Marshall		HM
1973	Miss Dog's Christmas Treat		$20	$30	$40	James Marshall		HM
1974	Dinosaur's Housewarming Party		$20	$30	$40	Norma Klein		Crown
1974	The Frog Prince		$20	$30	$40	Edith Tarcov		4Winds
1974	The Piggy In The Puddle		$20	$30	$40	Charlotte Pomerantz		Macmil
1974	The Stupids Step Out		$20	$30	$40	Harry Allard		HM
1974	Willis		$20	$30	$40	James Marshall		HM
1975	A Day With Whisker Wickles		$20	$30	$40	Cynthia Jameson		CM&G
1975	Dinner At Alberta's		$20	$30	$40	Russell Hoban		Crowell
1975	Four Little Troubles		$20	$30	$40	Laurette Murdock		HM
1975	Mary Alice, Operator Number 9		$20	$30	$40	Jeffrey Allen		LBrown
1975	The Guest		$20	$30	$40	James Marshall		HM
1975	The Tutti-Frutti Case		$20	$30	$40	Harry Allard		P-Hall
1976	Bonzini! The Tattooed Man		$18	$25	$35	Jeffrey Allen		LBrown
1976	George And Martha Rise And Shine		$18	$25	$35	James Marshall		HM
1976	Lazy Stories		$18	$25	$35	Diane Wolkstein		Seabury
1976	Speedboat		$18	$25	$35	James Marshall		HM
1977	A Summer In The South		$18	$25	$35	James Marshall		HM
1977	It's So Nice To Have A Wolf Around The House		$18	$25	$35	Harry Allard		DoubleD
1977	Miss Nelson Is Missing!		$18	$25	$35	Harry Allard		HM
1978	Carrot Nose		$18	$25	$35	Jan Wahl		FSG
1978	George And Martha, One Fine Day		$18	$25	$35	James Marshall		HM
1978	Macgooses' Grocery		$18	$25	$35	Frank Asch		Dial
1978	The Stupids Have A Ball		$18	$25	$35	Harry Allard		HM
1979	Bumps In The Night		$18	$25	$35	Harry Allard		DoubleD
1979	I Will Not Go To Market Today		$18	$25	$35	Harry Allard		Dial
1979	James Marshall's Mother Goose		$18	$25	$35	James Marshall		FSG
1979	Portly Mcswine		$18	$25	$35	James Marshall		HM
1980	George And Martha, Tons Of Fun		$16	$25	$30	James Marshall		HM
1980	How Beastly!		$16	$25	$30	Jane Yolen		Collins
1980	Space Case		$16	$25	$30	Edward Marshall		Dial
1980	Troll Country		$16	$25	$30	Edward Marshall		Dial
1981	Taking Care Of Carruthers		$16	$25	$30	James Marshall		HM
1981	The Exploding Frog & Other Fables From Aesop		$16	$25	$30	John B. McFarland		LBrown
1981	The Stupids Die		$16	$25	$30	Harry Allard		HM
1981	There's A Party At Mona's Tonight		$16	$25	$30	Harry Allard		DoubleD
1981	Three By The Sea		$16	$25	$30	Edward Marshall		Dial
1982	Fox And His Friends		$16	$25	$30	Edward Marshall		Dial
1982	Fox In Love		$16	$25	$30	Edward Marshall		Dial
1982	Miss Nelson Is Back		$16	$25	$30	Harry Allard		HM
1982	Roger's Umbrella		$16	$25	$30	Daniel Pinkwater		Dutton
1983	Fox At School		$16	$25	$30	Edward Marshall		Dial
1983	Fox On Wheels		$16	$25	$30	Edward Marshall		Dial
1983	Rapscallion Jones		$16	$25	$30	James Marshall		Viking
1984	Fox All Week		$16	$25	$30	Edward Marshall		Dial
1984	George And Martha Back In Town		$16	$25	$30	James Marshall		HM
1984	The Cut-Ups		$16	$25	$30	James Marshall		VK
1985	Four On The Shore		$14	$20	$30	Edward Marshall		Dial
1985	Miss Nelson Has A Field Day		$14	$20	$30	Harry Allard		HM
1985	Nosey Mrs. Rat		$14	$20	$30	Jeffrey Allen		VK
1985	The Night Before Christmas		$14	$20	$30	Clement C. Moore		Scholas
1986	Mary Alice Returns		$14	$20	$30	Jeffrey Allen		LBrown
1986	Merry Christmas, Space Case		$14	$20	$30	James Marshall		Dial
1986	Three Up A Tree		$14	$20	$30	James Marshall		Dial
1986	Wings		$14	$20	$30	James Marshall		VK
1986	Yummers Too		$14	$20	$30	James Marshall		HM
1987	Haunted House Jokes		$14	$20	$25	Louis Phillips		VK
1987	Red Riding Hood		$14	$20	$25	James Marshall		Dial
1987	The Cut-Ups Cut Loose		$14	$20	$25	James Marshall		VK
1988	Fox On The Job		$14	$20	$25	James Marshall		Dial
1988	George And Martha 'Round And 'Round		$14	$20	$25	James Marshall		HM
1988	Goldilocks And The Three Bears		$50	$80	$100	James Marshall	CH	Dial
1989	Cinderella		$14	$20	$25	Barbara Karlin		LBrown
1989	Hey, Diddle, Daddle		$14	$20	$25	James Marshall		Heath
1989	My Friends The Frogs		$14	$20	$25	James Marshall		Heath

Marshall   James

Year	Title	VG-	VG	VG+	Fine	Author	Award	Pub
1989	The Cut-Ups At Camp Custer		$14	$20	$25	James Marshall		VK
1989	The Three Little Pigs		$14	$20	$25	James Marshall		Dial
1990	Fox Be Nimble		$12	$18	$25	James Marshall		Dial
1990	Hansel And Gretel		$12	$18	$25	James Marshall		Dial
1990	The Cut-Ups Carry On		$12	$18	$25	James Marshall		Viking
1991	Old Mother Hubbard And Her Wonderful Dog		$12	$18	$25	Sarah Catherine Martin		FSG
1991	Rats On The Roof & Other Stories		$12	$18	$25	James Marshall		Dial
1991	The Adventures Of Isabel		$12	$18	$25	Ogden Nash		Joy
1992	Fox Outfoxed		$12	$16	$20	James Marshall		Dial
1992	The Cut-Ups Crack Up		$12	$16	$20	James Marshall		Viking
1993	Fox On Stage		$12	$16	$20	James Marshall		Dial
1993	Pocketful Of Nonsense		$12	$16	$20	James Marshall		AWG
1993	Rats On The Range & Other Stories		$12	$16	$20	James Marshall		Dial
1994	Hey Diddle Diddle		$12	$16	$20	James Marshall		FSG
1997	George And Martha		$10	$14	$18	James Marshall		HM
1998	The Owl And The Pussycat		$10	$14	$18	Edward Lear		HCollins
2000	Eugene		$8	$12	$16	James Marshall		HM
2000	Sing Out, Irene		$8	$12	$16	James Marshall		HM
2000	Snake		$8	$12	$16	James Marshall		HM
2001	James Marshall's Cinderella		$8	$12	$16	Barbara Karlin		Dial

Martin   Bernard

Year	Title	VG-	VG	VG+	Fine	Author	Award	Pub
1945	Little Squeegy Bug	$100	$120	$160		Bill Martin		TelWel
1946	Chicken Chuck	$80	$100	$140		Bill Martin		TelWel
1946	Rosy Nose	$80	$100	$140		Dorothy Tyler Reed		TelWel
1947	Smoky Poky	$70	$90	$120		Bill Martin		TelWel
1948	Bunny's Easter Gift	$70	$90	$120		Bill Martin		TelWel
1948	Hook And Ladder No. 3	$70	$90	$120		Bill Martin		TelWel
1948	Lightning A Cowboy's Colt	$70	$90	$120		Bill Martin		TelWel
1949	Christmas Puppy	$70	$90	$120		Bill Martin		TelWel
1949	Silver Stallion	$70	$90	$120		Bill Martin		TelWel
1950	Golden Arrow	$70	$90	$120		Bill Martin		TelWel
1950	Teach Me To Pray	$70	$90	$120		Bill Martin		TelWel
1950	Wild Horse Roundup	$70	$90	$120		Bill Martin		TelWel
1951	Five Little Rabbits	$50	$70	$90		Bill Martin		TelWel
1951	The Brave Little Indian	$50	$70	$90		Bill Martin		TelWel
1952	Palomino Pony	$50	$70	$90		Bill Martin		TelWel
1952	Thank You, God	$50	$70	$90		Bill Martin		TelWel
1953	The Green-Eyed Stallion	$50	$70	$90		Bill Martin		TelWel
1964	How Birds Keep Warm In Winter	$50	$60	$80		Bernard Martin		HR&W
1967	The Little Squeegy Bug	$40	$50	$70		Bill Martin		HR&W
1970	Once There Were Bluebirds		$30	$50	$60	Bill Martin		Bowmar
1970	Ten Little Squirrels		$30	$50	$60	Bill Martin		HR&W

Martin   Charles E.

Year	Title	VG-	VG	VG+	Fine	Author	Award	Pub
1969	The Big Orange Thing	$20	$30	$35		Jerry Juhl		BradP
1976	Hooper Humperdink ... ? Not Him!		$100	$160	$220	Theo LeSieg (pseud/Seuss)		BB
1978	Noah's Ark		$14	$20	$30	Lawrence T. Lorimer		Random
1981	The Story Of Jonah		$14	$20	$25	Juliana Bragg		Golden
1983	Dunkel Takes A Walk		$14	$20	$25	Charles E. Martin		Green
1984	Island Winter		$12	$18	$25	Charles E. Martin		Green
1984	Summer Business		$12	$18	$25	Charles E. Martin		Green
1985	Island Rescue		$12	$18	$25	Charles E. Martin		Green
1986	For Rent		$12	$16	$20	Charles E. Martin		Green
1987	Sam Saves The Day		$12	$16	$20	Charles E. Martin		Green

Masha   (Marie Simchow Stern)

Year	Title	VG-	VG	VG+	Fine	Author	Award	Pub
1940	The Good Shepherd	$100	$120	$160		Gunnar Gunnarsson		Bobbs
1941	A Child's Book Of Prayers	$70	$90	$120		Louise Raymond (selected)		Random
1941	Singing Words	$70	$90	$120		Alice G. Thorn		Scribnr
1942	A Child's Book Of Christmas Carols	$70	$90	$120		Inez Bertail (selected)		Random
1942	Tap-A-Tan!	$70	$90	$120		Janette Lowrey		S&S

Masha (Marie Simchow Stern)

Year	Title	VG-	VG	VG+	Fine	Author	Award	Pub
1942	Three Little Kittens	$70	$90	$120		Mary Reed		S&S
1943	A Child's Story Of The Nativity	$70	$90	$120		Louise Raymond		Random
1943	Nursery Tales	$70	$90	$120		Marie Stern		S&S
1944	A Child's Book Of Bible Stories	$60	$80	$100		Elsa Jane Werner		Random
1944	The Golden Almanac	$60	$80	$100		Dorothy Bennett		S&S
1945	A Child's Book Of Hymns	$60	$80	$100		Marjorie Wyckoff (arranged)		Random
1945	A Woods Story	$60	$80	$100		Elsa Ruth Nast		H&B
1945	The White Bunny And His Magic Nose	$60	$80	$100		Lily Duplaix		S&S
1946	A Farm Story	$60	$80	$100		Elsa Ruth Nast		H&B
1946	Bedtime Stories	$60	$80	$100		Eleanor Graham		Wonder

Matje Martin

Year	Title	VG-	VG	VG+	Fine	Author	Award	Pub
1998	The Ink Drinker		$8	$12	$16	Eric Sanvoisin		DelaP
1998	When It Starts To Snow		$8	$10	$14	Phillis Gershator		Holt
1999	A Straw For Two		$8	$10	$14	Eric Sanvoisin		DelaP
1999	Celeste		$8	$10	$14	Martin Matje		Athenm
1999	Harry And Lulu		$8	$10	$14	Arthur Yorinks		Hyper
1999	Wallace Hoskins, The Boy Who Grew Down		$8	$10	$14	Cynthia Zarin		DK
2000	Irene's Wish		$8	$10	$14	Jerdine Nolen		Whistle
2002	A Pig Named Perrier		$6	$10	$12	Elizabeth Spurr		Hyper
2002	Little Red Ink Drinker		$6	$10	$12	Eric Sanvoisin		DelaP
2002	Stuart's Cape		$6	$10	$12	Sara Pennypacker		Orchard
2002	The City Of Ink Drinkers		$6	$10	$12	Eric Sanvoisin		DelaP
2003	Stuart Goes To School		$6	$10	$12	Sara Pennypacker		Scholas

Mayer Mercer

Year	Title	VG-	VG	VG+	Fine	Author	Award	Pub
1967	A Boy, A Dog, And A Frog	$80	$120	$140		Mercer Mayer		Dial
1967	The Great Brain	$40	$50	$70		John Dennis Fitzgerald		Dial
1968	If I Had ..	$60	$80	$100		Mercer Mayer		Dial
1968	Outside My Window	$40	$50	$70		Liesel Moak Skorpen		H&Row
1968	Terrible Troll	$60	$80	$100		Mercer Mayer		Dial
1968	The Boy Who Made A Million	$40	$50	$70		Sidney Offit		StMart
1968	The Crack In The Wall	$40	$50	$70		George Mendoza		Dial
1968	The Gillygoofang	$40	$50	$70		George Mendoza		Dial
1968	There's A Nightmare In My Closet	$80	$120	$140		Mercer Mayer		Dial
1969	Boy, Was I Mad!	$40	$50	$70		Kathryn Hitte		PMagP
1969	Frog, Where Are You?	$60	$80	$100		Mercer Mayer		Dial
1969	Golden Butter	$40	$50	$70		Sheila LaFarge		Dial
1969	I Am A Hunter	$60	$80	$100		Mercer Mayer		Dial
1969	More Adventures Of The Great Brain	$40	$50	$70		John Dennis Fitzgerald		Dial
1970	A Special Trick		$50	$70	$90	Mercer Mayer		Dial
1970	Jack Tar		$30	$50	$60	Jean Russell Larson		MacSm
1970	Mine		$30	$50	$60	Marianna Mayer		S&S
1970	The Mousechildren And The Famous Collector		$30	$50	$60	Warren Fine		H&Row
1971	A Boy, A Dog, A Frog, And A Friend		$30	$50	$60	Marianna Mayer		Dial
1971	Let Me Fall Before I Fly		$30	$50	$60	Barbara Wersba		Athenm
1971	Margaret's Birthday		$30	$50	$60	Jan Wahl		4Winds
1971	Me And My Flying Machine		$30	$50	$60	Marianna Mayer		PMagP
1971	Me And My Little Brain		$30	$50	$60	John Dennis Fitzgerald		Dial
1971	The Bird Of Time		$30	$50	$60	Jane Yolen		Crowell
1971	The Queen Always Wanted To Dance		$40	$60	$90	Mercer Mayer		S&S
1972	A Silly Story		$40	$60	$90	Mercer Mayer		PMagP
1972	Good-Bye, Kitchen		$30	$50	$60	Mildred Kantrowitz		PMagP
1972	Grandmother Told Me		$30	$50	$60	Jan Wahl		LBrown
1972	Kim Ann And The Yellow Machine		$30	$50	$60	Candida Palmer		Ginn
1972	The Great Brain At The Academy		$30	$50	$60	John Dennis Fitzgerald		Dial
1973	Amanda Dreaming		$30	$50	$60	Barbara Wersba		Athenm
1973	Bubble Bubble		$40	$60	$90	Mercer Mayer		PMagP
1973	Frog On His Own		$40	$60	$90	Mercer Mayer		Dial
1973	Mrs. Beggs And The Wizard		$40	$60	$90	Mercer Mayer		PMagP
1973	The Great Brain Reforms		$30	$50	$60	John Dennis Fitzgerald		Dial
1973	What Do You Do With A Kangaroo?		$40	$60	$90	Mercer Mayer		4Winds
1973	While The Horses Galloped To London		$30	$50	$60	Mabel Watts		PMagP
1974	Frog Goes To Dinner		$40	$60	$80	Mercer Mayer		Dial

Mayer   Mercer

Year	Title	VG-	VG	VG+	Fine	Author	Award	Pub
1974	One Monster After Another		$140	$200	$280	Mercer Mayer		Golden
1974	The Return Of The Great Brain		$30	$40	$60	John Dennis Fitzgerald		Dial
1974	Two Moral Tales		$40	$60	$80	Mercer Mayer		4Winds
1974	Two More Moral Tales		$40	$60	$80	Mercer Mayer		4Winds
1974	Walk, Robot, Walk		$40	$60	$80	Mercer Mayer		Ginn
1974	You're The Scaredy-Cat		$40	$60	$80	Mercer Mayer		PMagP
1975	Just For You		$140	$200	$260	Mercer Mayer		Golden
1975	One Frog Too Many		$30	$40	$60	Marianna Mayer		Dial
1975	The Figure In The Shadows		$30	$40	$60	John Bellairs		Dial
1975	The Great Brain Does It Again		$30	$40	$60	John Dennis Fitzgerald		Dial
1975	The Great Cat Chase		$40	$60	$80	Mercer Mayer		4Winds
1976	Ah-Choo		$60	$80	$120	Mercer Mayer		Dial
1976	Everyone Knows What A Dragon Looks Like		$60	$80	$120	Jay Williams	NYT	4Winds
1976	Hiccup		$60	$80	$120	Mercer Mayer		Dial
1976	Liza Lou And The Yeller Belly Swamp		$60	$80	$120	Mercer Mayer		PMagP
1976	Professor Wormbog In Search For The Zipperump-A-Zoo		$60	$80	$120	Mercer Mayer		Golden
1977	A Poison Tree & Other Poems		$40	$60	$80	Mercer Mayer		Scribnr
1977	Just Me And My Dad		$80	$120	$160	Mercer Mayer		Golden
1977	Little Monster's Word Book		$80	$120	$160	Mercer Mayer		Golden
1977	Oops		$40	$60	$80	Mercer Mayer		Dial
1977	Professor Wormbog's Gloomy Kerploppus		$40	$60	$80	Mercer Mayer		Golden
1977	The Reward Worth Having		$25	$40	$50	Jay Williams		4Winds
1978	Beauty And The Beast		$25	$40	$50	Marianna Mayer		4Winds
1978	Little Monster At Home		$40	$60	$90	Mercer Mayer		Golden
1978	Little Monster At School		$40	$60	$90	Mercer Mayer		Golden
1978	Little Monster At Work		$40	$60	$90	Mercer Mayer		Golden
1978	Little Monster's Alphabet Book		$40	$60	$90	Mercer Mayer		Golden
1978	Little Monster's Bedtime Book		$40	$60	$90	Mercer Mayer		Golden
1978	Little Monster's Counting Book		$40	$60	$90	Mercer Mayer		Golden
1978	Little Monster's Neighborhood		$40	$60	$90	Mercer Mayer		Golden
1979	How The Trollusk Got His Hat		$35	$50	$70	Mercer Mayer		Golden
1979	Little Monster's Mother Goose		$40	$60	$80	Mercer Mayer		Golden
1980	East Of The Sun & West Of The Moon		$35	$50	$70	Mercer Mayer		4Winds
1980	Herbert The Timid Dragon		$35	$50	$70	Mercer Mayer		Golden
1980	Little Monster's Scratch And Sniff Mystery		$35	$50	$70	Mercer Mayer		Golden
1982	Favorite Tales From Grimm		$25	$35	$50	Jacob & Wilhelm Grimm		4Winds
1982	Merry Christmas Mom And Dad		$20	$30	$40	Mercer Mayer		Golden
1982	Play With Me		$20	$30	$40	Mercer Mayer		Golden
1983	All By Myself		$18	$25	$35	Mercer Mayer		Golden
1983	Bat Child's Haunted House		$18	$25	$35	Mercer Mayer		Random
1983	Gator Cleans House		$18	$25	$35	Mercer Mayer		Random
1983	I Was So Mad		$18	$25	$35	Mercer Mayer		Golden
1983	Just Grandma And Me		$18	$25	$35	Mercer Mayer		Golden
1983	Me Too!		$18	$25	$35	Mercer Mayer		Golden
1983	Sweetmeat's Birthday		$18	$25	$35	Mercer Mayer		Scholas
1983	The New Baby		$18	$25	$35	Mercer Mayer		Golden
1983	Too's Bracelet		$18	$25	$35	Mercer Mayer		Scholas
1983	When I Get Bigger		$18	$25	$35	Mercer Mayer		Golden
1984	The Sleeping Beauty		$18	$25	$35	Mercer Mayer		Macmil
1985	Just Grandpa And Me		$18	$25	$35	Mercer Mayer		Golden
1985	Just Me And My Puppy		$18	$25	$35	Mercer Mayer		Golden
1985	Tonk Gives A Magic Show		$18	$25	$35	Mercer Mayer		Tink
1985	Zoomer Builds A Racing Car		$14	$20	$30	Mercer Mayer		Tink
1986	A Christmas Carol: Being A Ghost Story Of Christmas		$14	$20	$30	Charles Dickens		Macmil
1986	Just Me And My Babysitter		$14	$20	$30	Mercer Mayer		Golden
1986	Just Me And My Little Sister		$14	$20	$30	Mercer Mayer		Golden
1987	Baby Sister Says No!		$14	$20	$30	Mercer Mayer		Golden
1987	Construction Critter		$14	$20	$30	Mercer Mayer		S&S
1987	Doctor Critter		$14	$20	$30	Mercer Mayer		S&S
1987	Just A Mess		$14	$20	$30	Mercer Mayer		Western
1987	Little Critter's Bedtime Storybook		$14	$20	$30	Mercer Mayer		Golden
1987	The Pied Piper Of Hamelin		$14	$20	$30	Mercer Mayer (adapted)		Macmil
1987	There's An Alligator Under My Bed		$14	$20	$30	Mercer Mayer		Dial
1988	Just My Friend And Me		$14	$20	$25	Mercer Mayer		Golden
1988	Little Critter's Little Sister's Birthday		$14	$20	$25	Mercer Mayer		Western
1988	Little Critter's Staying Overnight		$14	$20	$25	Mercer Mayer		Golden
1988	Little Critter's The Picnic		$14	$20	$25	Mercer Mayer		Golden

Mayer   Mercer

Year	Title	VG-	VG	VG+	Fine	Author	Award	Pub
1988	Little Critter's The Trip		$14	$20	$25	Mercer Mayer		Golden
1988	Little Critters These Are My Pets		$14	$20	$25	Mercer Mayer		Golden
1988	Little Critter's These Are My Pets		$14	$20	$25	Mercer Mayer		Golden
1988	Little Critters This Is My House		$14	$20	$25	Mercer Mayer		Golden
1988	Little Critter's This Is My House		$14	$20	$25	Mercer Mayer		Golden
1988	There's Something In My Attic		$14	$20	$25	Mercer Mayer		Dial
1989	Just A Daydream		$14	$20	$25	Mercer Mayer		Golden
1989	Just A Nap		$14	$20	$25	Mercer Mayer		Western
1989	Just Camping Out		$14	$20	$25	Mercer Mayer		Golden
1989	Just Shopping With Mom		$14	$20	$25	Mercer Mayer		Western
1989	Little Critter's Christmas Book		$14	$20	$25	Mercer Mayer		Golden
1989	Little Critter's The Fussy Princess		$14	$20	$25	Mercer Mayer		Golden
1989	Little Critter's This Is My Friend		$14	$20	$25	Mercer Mayer		Golden
1989	Mercer Mayer's Little Critter At Play		$14	$20	$25	Mercer Mayer		Golden
1989	Mercer Mayer's Little Critter's Day		$14	$20	$25	Mercer Mayer		Golden
1990	Just A Rainy Day		$12	$18	$25	Mercer Mayer		Western
1990	Just Going To The Dentist		$12	$18	$25	Mercer Mayer		Western
1990	Just Me And My Mom		$12	$18	$25	Mercer Mayer		Western
1990	Little Critter's This Is My School		$12	$18	$25	Mercer Mayer		Western
1990	Two-Minute Little Critter Stories		$12	$18	$25	Mercer Mayer		Western
1991	Just Me And My Little Brother		$12	$18	$25	Mercer Mayer		Western
1991	Little Critter At Scout Camp		$12	$18	$25	Mercer Mayer		Golden
1991	Little Critter's Hansel And Gretel		$12	$18	$25	Mercer Mayer		Random
1991	Little Critter's Jack And The Beanstalk		$12	$18	$25	Mercer Mayer		Dalton
1991	Little Critter's Little Red Riding Hood		$12	$18	$25	Mercer Mayer		Dalton
1991	Little Critter's Where Is My Frog?		$12	$18	$25	Mercer Mayer		Random
1991	Little Critter's Where's Kitty?		$12	$18	$25	Mercer Mayer		Random
1991	Mercer Mayer's A Monster Followed Me To School		$12	$18	$25	Mercer Mayer		Golden
1991	Mercer Mayer's Herbert The Timid Dragon		$12	$18	$25	Mercer Mayer		Western
1991	Thrills And Spills		$12	$18	$25	Mercer Mayer		Delmar
1991	When I Grow Up		$12	$18	$25	Mercer Mayer		Golden
1991	Where Is My Frog?		$12	$18	$25	Mercer Mayer		Dalton
1991	Where's Kitty?		$12	$18	$25	Mercer Mayer		Dalton
1991	Where's My Sneaker?		$12	$18	$25	Mercer Mayer		Dalton
1992	I Am Helping		$12	$18	$25	Mercer Mayer		Dalton
1992	I Am Hiding		$12	$18	$25	Mercer Mayer		Dalton
1992	I Am Playing		$12	$18	$25	Mercer Mayer		Dalton
1992	I Am Sharing		$12	$18	$25	Mercer Mayer		Dalton
1992	Just Me And My Cousin		$12	$18	$25	Gina Mayer		Golden
1992	Little Critter Colors		$12	$18	$25	Mercer Mayer		Dalton
1992	Little Critter Numbers		$12	$18	$25	Mercer Mayer		Random
1992	Little Critter Shapes		$12	$18	$25	Mercer Mayer		Dalton
1992	Little Critter's The Night Before Christmas		$12	$18	$25	Mercer Mayer (adapted)		GFrog
1992	Rosie's Mouse		$12	$18	$25	Gina Mayer		Western
1992	The New Potty		$12	$18	$25	Gina Mayer		Western
1992	This Is My Family		$12	$18	$25	Gina Mayer		Western
1992	What A Bad Dream		$12	$18	$25	Mercer Mayer		Golden
1993	A Very Special Critter		$12	$16	$20	Gina Mayer		Western
1993	Going To The Races		$12	$16	$20	Gina Mayer		Western
1993	It's Mine		$12	$16	$20	Gina Mayer		Western
1993	Just A Gum Wrapper		$12	$16	$20	Gina Mayer		Western
1993	Just A Thunderstorm		$12	$16	$20	Gina Mayer		Western
1993	Just Like Dad		$12	$16	$20	Gina Mayer		Western
1993	Just Me And My Bicycle		$12	$16	$20	Gina Mayer		Western
1993	Just Say Please		$12	$16	$20	Gina Mayer		Western
1993	Just Too Little		$12	$16	$20	Gina Mayer		Western
1993	Little Critter's Camp Out		$12	$16	$20	Mercer Mayer		Western
1993	Little Critter's Joke Book		$12	$16	$20	Mercer Mayer		Western
1993	Little Critter's Read-It-Yourself Storybook		$12	$16	$20	Mercer Mayer		Western
1993	Taking Care Of Mom		$12	$16	$20	Gina Mayer		Western
1993	That's Not Fair		$12	$16	$20	Gina Mayer		Western
1993	This Is My Body		$12	$16	$20	Gina Mayer		Western
1993	Trick Or Treat, Little Critter		$12	$16	$20	Gina Mayer		Western
1994	Just Lost!		$12	$16	$20	Gina Mayer		Western
1994	Just Me In The Tub		$12	$16	$20	Gina Mayer		Western
1994	Mercer Mayer's The Cat's Meow		$12	$16	$20	Mercer Mayer		Golden
1994	The Purple Kiss		$12	$16	$20	Erica Farber		Western

Mayer   Mercer

Year	Title	VG-	VG	VG+	Fine	Author	Award	Pub
1995	Golden Eagle		$10	$16	$20	Erica Farber		Western
1995	I Didn't Know That		$10	$16	$20	Gina Mayer		RDigest
1995	I Didn't Mean To		$10	$16	$20	Gina Mayer		RDigest
1995	I Said I Was Sorry		$10	$16	$20	Mercer Mayer		Golden
1995	I Was So Sick		$10	$16	$20	Gina Mayer		RDigest
1995	Jaguar Paw		$10	$16	$20	Erica Farber		Western
1995	Just A Bad Day		$10	$16	$20	Gina Mayer		RDigest
1995	Just A Little Different		$10	$16	$20	Gina Mayer		RDigest
1995	Just An Airplane		$10	$16	$20	Gina Mayer		RDigest
1995	Just Leave Me Alone		$10	$16	$20	Gina Mayer		RDigest
1995	Little Critter In Search Of The Beautiful Princess		$10	$16	$20	Mercer Mayer		Random
1995	Little Critter Jack And The Beanstalk		$10	$16	$20	Mercer Mayer		Random
1995	Little Critter Little Red Riding Hood		$10	$16	$20	Mercer Mayer		Random
1995	Little Critter's ABC		$10	$16	$20	Mercer Mayer		Dalton
1995	Little Critter's Night Before Christmas		$10	$16	$20	Mercer Mayer		Random
1995	My Big Sister		$10	$16	$20	Gina Mayer		Western
1995	The Alien		$10	$16	$20	Erica Farber		Western
1995	The Loose Tooth		$10	$16	$20	Gina Mayer		RDigest
1995	The Prince		$10	$16	$20	Erica Farber		Western
1995	The School Play		$10	$16	$20	Gina Mayer		RDigest
1995	The Swamp Thing		$10	$16	$20	Erica Farber		Western
1996	Bun Bun's Birthday		$10	$16	$20	Mercer Mayer		Random
1996	If You Dream A Dragon		$10	$16	$20	Erica Farber		Random
1996	I'm Sorry		$10	$16	$20	Gina Mayer		RDigest
1996	Little Sister's Bracelet		$10	$16	$20	Mercer Mayer		Random
1996	Mercer Mayer Look-Look Bindp-Up		$10	$16	$20	Mercer Mayer		Golden
1996	Old Howl Hall		$10	$16	$20	Mercer Mayer		Random
1996	The Goblin's Birthday Party		$10	$16	$20	Erica Farber		Random
1996	To Catch A Little Fishy		$10	$16	$20	Mercer Mayer		Random
1997	Midnight Snack		$10	$14	$18	Erica Farber		Random
1997	Night Of The Walking Dead		$10	$14	$18	Erica Farber		Random
1999	Just A Bully		$10	$14	$18	Gina Mayer		Golden
1999	Little Critter Sleeps Over		$10	$14	$18	Mercer Mayer		Golden
1999	Shibumi And The Kitemaker		$10	$14	$18	Mercer Mayer		MCaven
2000	Just A Toy		$8	$12	$16	Gina Mayer		Golden
2000	Little Critter's The Best Present		$8	$12	$16	Mercer Mayer		Golden
2000	The Rocking Horse Angel		$8	$12	$16	Mercer Mayer		MCaven
2001	A Yummy Lunch		$8	$12	$16	Mercer Mayer		McHill
2001	Our Friend Sam		$8	$12	$16	Mercer Mayer		McHill
2001	Surprise		$8	$12	$16	Mercer Mayer		McHill
2002	Camping Out		$8	$10	$14	Mercer Mayer		McHill
2002	Class Trip		$8	$10	$14	Mercer Mayer		McHill
2002	Field Day		$8	$10	$14	Mercer Mayer		McHill
2002	Grandma's Garden		$8	$10	$14	Mercer Mayer		McHill
2002	Helping Mom		$8	$10	$14	Mercer Mayer		McHill
2002	Just A Secret		$8	$10	$14	Gina Mayer		Golden
2002	Just Not Invited		$8	$10	$14	Gina Mayer		Golden
2002	My Trip To The Farm		$8	$10	$14	Mercer Mayer		McHill
2002	My Trip To The Zoo		$8	$10	$14	Mercer Mayer		McHill
2002	No One Can Play		$8	$10	$14	Mercer Mayer		McHill
2002	Our Park		$8	$10	$14	Mercer Mayer		McHill
2002	Play Ball		$8	$10	$14	Mercer Mayer		McHill
2002	Snow Day		$8	$10	$14	Mercer Mayer		McHill
2002	The Mixed-Up Morning		$8	$10	$14	Mercer Mayer		McHill
2003	A Day At Camp		$8	$10	$14	Mercer Mayer		McHill
2003	Beach Day		$8	$10	$14	Mercer Mayer		McHill
2003	Country Fair		$8	$10	$14	Mercer Mayer		McHill
2003	Goodnight, Little Critter		$8	$10	$14	Mercer Mayer		McHill
2003	Just Fishing With Grandma		$8	$10	$14	Gina Mayer		Golden
2003	New Kid In Town		$8	$10	$14	Mercer Mayer		McHill
2003	Our Tree House		$8	$10	$14	Mercer Mayer		McHill
2003	Purple Pickle Juice		$8	$10	$14	Erica Farber		Random
2003	Show And Tell		$8	$10	$14	Mercer Mayer		McHill
2003	The New Fire Truck		$8	$10	$14	Mercer Mayer		McHill
2003	The Wizard Comes To Town		$8	$10	$14	Mercer Mayer		GreenT
2003	Tiger's Birthday		$8	$10	$14	Mercer Mayer		McHill
2004	Bye-Bye, Mom And Dad		$8	$10	$14	Mercer Mayer		HFest

Mayer   Mercer

Year	Title	VG-	VG	VG+	Fine	Author	Award	Pub
2004	Christmas For Miss Kitty		$8	$10	$14	Mercer Mayer		McHill
2004	Happy Halloween, Little Critter!		$8	$10	$14	Mercer Mayer		HFest
2004	Harvest Time		$8	$10	$14	Mercer Mayer		McHill
2004	Just A Dump Truck		$8	$10	$14	Mercer Mayer		HFest
2004	Just A Science Project		$8	$10	$14	Mercer Mayer		HFest
2004	Just A Snowman		$8	$10	$14	Mercer Mayer		HFest
2004	Just A Tugboat		$8	$10	$14	Mercer Mayer		HFest
2004	Just Big Enough		$8	$10	$14	Mercer Mayer		HFest
2004	Little Critter's Picture Dictionary		$8	$10	$14	Mercer Mayer		McHill
2004	Merry Christmas, Little Critter!		$8	$10	$14	Mercer Mayer		HFest
2004	The Little Christmas Tree		$8	$10	$14	Mercer Mayer		McHill

McCaffery   Janet

Year	Title	VG-	VG	VG+	Fine	Author	Award	Pub
1964	The Witch Of Hissing Hill	$35	$40	$60		Mary Calhoun		Morrow
1965	The Incompetent Wizard	$20	$25	$30		Robert M. Oksner		Morrow
1967	The Runaway Brownie	$20	$25	$30		Mary Calhoun		Morrow
1967	The Thieving Dwarfs	$20	$25	$30		Mary Calhoun		Morrow
1968	The Goblin Under The Stairs	$20	$25	$30		Mary Calhoun		Morrow
1968	The Last Two Elves In Denmark	$20	$25	$30		Mary Calhoun		Morrow
1969	The Pixy And The Lazy Housewife	$20	$25	$30		Mary Calhoun		Morrow
1969	Traveling Ball Of String	$20	$25	$30		Mary Calhoun		Morrow
1970	I Wonder What's Under		$14	$20	$30	Doris Herold Lund		PMagP
1970	Mermaid Of Storms		$14	$20	$30	Mary Calhoun		Morrow
1970	The Swamp Witch		$25	$35	$50	Janet McCaffery		Morrow
1971	Daisy, Tell Me!		$14	$20	$30	Mary Calhoun		Morrow
1972	Cristóbal And The Witch		$14	$20	$30	Jan Wahl		Putnam
1972	Mrs. Dog's Own House		$14	$20	$30	Mary Calhoun		Morrow
1972	The Flower Mother		$14	$20	$30	Mary Calhoun		Morrow
1973	The Battle Of Reuben Robin & Kite Uncle John		$14	$20	$30	Mary Calhoun		Morrow
1974	Hey-How For Halloween!		$14	$20	$30	Lee Bennett Hopkins		HBJ
1974	Way Down Yonder On Troublesome Creek		$14	$20	$30	James Still		Putnam
1975	The Wolfpen Rusties		$14	$20	$25	James Still		Putnam
1976	Nailheads & Potato Eyes		$14	$20	$25	Cynthia Basil		Morrow
1977	Sporty Creek		$14	$20	$25	James Still		Putnam
1977	Waza Wins At Windy Gulch		$14	$20	$25	Eleanor Coerr		Putnam
1977	What Makes A Lemon Sour?		$14	$20	$25	Gail Kay Haines		Morrow
1979	Breakfast In The Afternoon		$12	$18	$25	Cynthia Basil		Morrow
1980	How Ships Play Cards		$12	$16	$20	Cynthia Basil		Morrow
1989	Rusties And Riddles & Gee-Haw Whimmy-Diddles		$10	$16	$20	James Still		UofK

McCarthy   Bobette

Year	Title	VG-	VG	VG+	Fine	Author	Award	Pub
1987	Buffalo Girls		$12	$16	$20	Bobette McCarthy		Crown
1992	Counting Sheep To Sleep		$10	$14	$18	Mary O'Brien		LBrown
1992	Ten Little Hippos		$10	$14	$18	Bobette McCarthy		BradP
1993	The Tantrum		$8	$12	$16	Kathryn Lasky		Macmil
1994	Dreaming		$8	$12	$16	Bobette McCarthy		Candle
1994	Happy Hiding Hippos		$8	$12	$16	Bobette McCarthy		BradP
1994	The Solo		$8	$12	$16	Kathryn Lasky		Macmil
1995	See You Later, Alligator		$8	$12	$16	Bobette McCarthy		Macmil

McCarty   Peter

Year	Title	VG-	VG	VG+	Fine	Author	Award	Pub
1996	Night Driving		$10	$16	$20	John Coy		Holt
1997	Life On Mars		$8	$12	$16	David Getz		Holt
1998	Frozen Girl		$8	$12	$16	David Getz		Holt
1998	Mary On Horseback		$8	$12	$16	Rosemary Wells		Dial
1999	Little Bunny On The Move		$8	$12	$16	Peter McCarty		Holt
2000	Baby Steps		$8	$10	$14	Peter McCarty		Holt
2000	Purple Death		$8	$10	$14	David Getz		Holt
2002	Brothers Below Zero		$8	$10	$14	Tor Seidler		LauraG
2002	Hondo & Fabian		$30	$50	$60	Peter McCarty	CH	Holt
2002	Terpin		$8	$10	$14	Tor Seidler		LauraG
2004	T Is For Terrible		$6	$10	$12	Peter McCarty		Holt

McClintock   Barbara

Year	Title	VG-	VG	VG+	Fine	Author	Award	Pub
1977	Potbellied Possums		$20	$30	$40	Elizabeth Winthrop		Holiday
1979	The Little Red Hen		$18	$25	$35	Barbara McClintock		Random
1984	Marooned In Fraggle Rock		$12	$18	$25	David Young		HR&W
1984	The Legend Of The Doozer Who Didn't		$12	$18	$25	Louise Gikow		HR&W
1984	What's A Fraggle?		$12	$18	$25	Louise Gikow		HR&W
1985	The Revolt Of The Teddy Bears: A May Gray Mystery		$12	$18	$25	James Duffy		Crown
1985	Waggleby Of Fraggle Rock		$12	$18	$25	Stephanie Calmenson		HR&W
1985	Why Wembley Fraggle Couldn't Sleep		$12	$18	$25	H.B. Gilmour		HR&W
1988	The Heartaches Of A French Cat		$12	$18	$25	Barbara McClintock		Godine
1989	The Christmas Gang: A May Gray Mystery		$12	$16	$20	James Duffy		Scribnr
1991	Animal Fables From Aesop		$12	$16	$20	Barbara McClintock (apapted)		Godine
1994	The Battle Of Luke And Longnose		$10	$16	$20	Barbara McClintock		HM
1996	The Fantastic Drawings Of Danielle		$10	$14	$18	Barbara McClintock		HM
1998	The Gingerbread Man		$8	$12	$16	Jim Aylesworth (retold)		Scholas
1998	When Mindy Saved Hanukkah		$8	$12	$16	Eric Kimmel		Scholas
1999	Aunt Pitty Patty's Piggy		$8	$12	$16	Jim Aylesworth		Scholas
1999	The Prog Frince		$8	$12	$16	C. Drew Lamm		Orchard
2000	A Little Princess		$8	$10	$14	Frances Hodgson Burnett		HCollins
2001	Molly And The Magic Wishbone		$8	$10	$14	Barbara McClintock		FSG
2001	The Tale Of Tricky Fox		$8	$10	$14	Jim Aylesworth		Scholas
2002	Dahlia		$8	$10	$14	Barbara McClintock		FSG
2003	A Child's Garden Of Verses		$8	$10	$14	Robert Louis Stevenson		HCollins
2003	Goldilocks And The Three Bears		$8	$10	$14	Jim Aylesworth (retold)		Scholas
2004	Adele And Simon		$6	$10	$12	Barbara McClintock		FSG

McCloskey   Robert

Year	Title	VG-	VG	VG+	Fine	Author	Award	Pub
1940	Lentil	$320	$440	$540		Robert McCloskey		Viking
1941	Make Way For Ducklings	$4,400	$6,000	$7,400		Robert McCloskey	CM	Viking
1942	The Man Who Lost His Head	$180	$240	$300		Claire Huchet Bishop		Viking
1942	Tree Toad	$180	$240	$300		Robert Hobert Davis		FStokes
1943	Homer Price	$380	$520	$640		Robert McCloskey		Viking
1948	Blueberries For Sal	$840	$1,200	$1,400		Robert McCloskey	CH	Viking
1951	Centerburg Tales	$160	$200	$260		Robert McCloskey		Viking
1952	One Morning In Maine	$340	$440	$560		Robert McCloskey	CH	Viking
1953	Journey Cake, Ho!	$720	$960	$1,200		Ruth Sawyer	CH	Viking
1957	Time Of Wonder	$540	$720	$900		Robert McCloskey	CM	Viking
1963	Burt Dow, Deep-Water Man	$100	$120	$160		Robert McCloskey		Viking
1963	Henry Reed's Journey	$100	$120	$160		Keith Robertson		Viking
1966	Henry Reed's Baby-Sitting Service	$90	$120	$160		Keith Robertson		Viking
1970	Henry Reed's Big Show		$70	$100	$140	Keith Robertson		Viking

McCue   Lisa

Year	Title	VG-	VG	VG+	Fine	Author	Award	Pub
1987	Bear Island		$12	$16	$20	Katherine Ross		Random
1992	Corduroy's Christmas		$10	$14	$18	B. G. Hennessy		Viking
1995	Corduroy's Halloween		$8	$12	$16	B. G. Hennessy		Viking
1997	Corduroy's Birthday		$8	$10	$14	B. G. Hennessy		Viking
1998	Corduroy's Easter		$8	$10	$14	B. G. Hennessy		Viking
2000	Bunny's Noisy Book		$8	$10	$14	Margaret Wise Brown		Hyper
2000	Corduroy At The Zoo		$8	$10	$14	B. G. Hennessy		Viking
2000	Corduroy's Christmas Surprise		$8	$10	$14	Don Freeman		G&D
2002	Rhymes And Riddles With Corduroy		$6	$10	$12	Don Freeman		G&D

McCully   Emily Arnold

Year	Title	VG-	VG	VG+	Fine	Author	Award	Pub
1962	Pennsylvania: Seed Of A Nation	$70	$90	$120		Paul A. Wallace		Harper
1967	Luigi Of The Streets	$40	$50	$70		Natalie Carlson		H&Row
1968	A Year To Grow	$30	$40	$50		Felice Holman		Norton
1968	Gooney	$30	$40	$50		Barbara Borack		H&Row
1968	Journey From Peppermint Street	$30	$40	$50		Meindert De Jong		H&Row
1968	That Mean Man	$30	$40	$50		Liesel Moak Skorpen		H&Row
1969	Here I Am	$30	$40	$50		Virginia Olsen Baron		Dutton
1969	Tales Of The Rue Broca	$30	$40	$50		Pierre Gripari		Bobbs
1969	The Fishermen	$30	$40	$50		Jan Wahl		Norton

McCully   Emily Arnold

Year	Title	VG-	VG	VG+	Fine	Author	Award	Pub
1969	The Mouse And The Elephant	$30	$40	$50		Barbara K. Walker		PMagP
1969	Twin Spell	$30	$40	$50		Janet L.S. Lunn		H&Row
1970	Friday Night Is Papa Night		$25	$35	$50	Ruth A. Sonneborn		Viking
1970	Gertrude's Pocket		$25	$35	$50	Miska Miles		LBrown
1970	Hobo Toad And The Motorcycle Gang		$25	$35	$50	Jane Yolen		World
1970	Maxie		$25	$35	$50	Mildred Kantrowitz		PMagP
1970	Slip! Slop! Gobble!		$25	$35	$50	Jeanne B. Hardendorff		Lippin
1970	Steffie And Me		$25	$35	$50	Phyllis Hoffman		H&Row
1971	Finders Keepers		$25	$35	$50	Alix Kates Shulman		BradP
1971	Finding Out With Your Senses		$25	$35	$50	Seymour Simon		McHill
1971	Go And Hush The Baby		$25	$35	$50	Betsy Cromer Byars		Viking
1971	Hurray For Captain Jane!		$25	$35	$50	Sam Reavin		PMagP
1971	Ma Nda La		$25	$35	$50	Arnold Adoff		H&Row
1971	Michael Is Brave		$25	$35	$50	Helen Elizabeth Buckley		LL&S
1972	Girls Can, Too!		$25	$35	$50	Lee Bennett Hopkins		FWatts
1972	Grandpa's Long Red Underwear		$25	$35	$50	Lynn Schoettle		LL&S
1972	Henry's Pennies		$25	$35	$50	Louise Greep McNamara		FWatts
1972	Jane's Blanket		$25	$35	$50	Arthur Miller		Viking
1972	The Boyhood Of Grace Jones		$25	$35	$50	Jane Langton		H&Row
1973	Black Is Brown Is Tan		$25	$35	$50	Arnold Adoff		H&Row
1973	How To Eat Fried Worms		$25	$35	$50	Thomas Rockwell		FWatts
1973	Isabelle The Itch		$25	$35	$50	Constance C. Greene		Viking
1973	That New Boy		$25	$35	$50	Mary H. Lystad		Crown
1973	When Violet Died		$25	$35	$50	Mildred Kantrowitz		PMagP
1974	I Want Mama		$25	$35	$50	Marjorie Weinman Sharmat		H&Row
1974	Jenny's Revenge		$25	$35	$50	Anne Norris Baldwin		4Winds
1974	Tree House Town		$25	$35	$50	Miska Miles		LBrown
1975	Amanda, The Panda, And The Redhead		$20	$30	$40	Susan Terris		DoubleD
1976	My Street's A Morning Cool Street		$20	$30	$40	Ianthe Thomas		H&Row
1976	The Bed Book		$50	$70	$100	Sylvia Plath		H&Row
1977	Martha's Mad Day		$20	$30	$40	Miranda Hapgood		Crown
1977	Professor Coconut And The Thief		$20	$30	$40	Rita Golden Gelman		HR&W
1977	That's Mine		$20	$30	$40	Elizabeth Winthrop		Holiday
1978	Edward Troy And The Witch Cat		$20	$30	$40	Sarah Sargent		Follett
1978	I And Sproggy		$20	$30	$40	Constance C. Greene		Viking
1978	No Help At All		$20	$30	$40	Betty Baker		Green
1978	Partners		$20	$30	$40	Betty Baker		Green
1978	The Highest Hit		$20	$30	$40	Nancy Willard		HBJ
1978	The Twenty-Elephant Restaurant		$20	$30	$40	Russell Hoban		Athenm
1978	What I Did Last Summer		$20	$30	$40	Glory St. John		Athenm
1978	Where Wild Willie		$20	$30	$40	Arnold Adoff		H&Row
1979	Last Look		$20	$30	$40	Clyde Robert Bulla		Crowell
1979	My Island Grandma		$20	$30	$40	Kathryn Lasky		FWarne
1979	Ookie-Spooky		$20	$30	$40	Mirra Ginsburg		Crown
1979	Whatever Happened To Beverly Bigler's Birthday?		$20	$30	$40	Barbara Williams		HBJ
1980	How I Found Myself At The Fair		$18	$25	$35	Pat Rhoads Mauser		Athenm
1980	How We Got Our First Cat		$18	$25	$35	Tobi Tobias		FWatts
1980	Oliver And Alison's Week		$18	$25	$35	Jane Breskin Zalben		FSG
1980	The Black Dog Who Went Into The Woods		$20	$30	$40	Edith Thacher Hurd		H&Row
1981	Joseph On The Subway Trains		$18	$25	$35	Kathleen Benson		AW
1981	Mail-Order Wings		$18	$25	$35	Beatrice Gormley		Dutton
1981	Pajama Walking		$18	$25	$35	Vicki Kimmel Artis		HM
1981	The April Fool		$18	$25	$35	Alice Schertle		LL&S
1981	The New Friend		$25	$35	$50	Charlotte Zolotow		Crowell
1981	The Seeing Summer		$18	$25	$35	Jeannette Eyerly		Lippin
1982	Fifth Grade Magic		$18	$25	$35	Beatrice Gormley		Dutton
1982	I Dance In My Red Pajamas		$18	$25	$35	Edith Thacher Hurd		H&Row
1982	Mitzi And The Terrible Tyrannosaurus Rex		$18	$25	$35	Barbara Williams		Dutton
1982	The Halloween Candy Mystery		$18	$25	$35	Marion M. Markham		HM
1983	Alice And The Boa Constrictor		$18	$25	$35	Laurie Adams		HM
1983	Best Friend Insurance		$18	$25	$35	Beatrice Gormley		Dutton
1983	Good Dog, Bad Dog		$18	$25	$35	Corinne Gerson		Athenm
1983	Mitzi's Honeymoon With Nana Potts		$18	$25	$35	Barbara Williams		Dutton
1983	The Playground		$30	$50	$60	Emily Arnold McCully		Golden
1984	For I Will Consider My Cat Jeoffry		$16	$25	$30	Christopher Smart		Athenm
1984	Mitzi And Frederick The Great		$16	$25	$30	Barbara Williams		Dutton
1984	Picnic		$20	$30	$40	Emily Arnold McCully		H&Row

McCully   Emily Arnold

Year	Title	VG-	VG	VG+	Fine	Author	Award	Pub
1984	The Christmas Present Mystery		$16	$25	$30	Marion M. Markham		HM
1984	The Thing In Kat's Attic		$16	$25	$30	Charlotte Graeber		Dutton
1985	First Snow		$20	$30	$40	Emily Arnold McCully		H&Row
1985	Fourth Of July		$16	$25	$30	Barbara M. Joosse		Knopf
1985	Mitzi And The Elephants		$16	$25	$30	Barbara Williams		Dutton
1985	The Explorer Of Barkham Street		$16	$25	$30	Mary Stolz		H&Row
1985	The Ghastly Glasses		$16	$25	$30	Beatrice Gormley		Dutton
1986	Lulu And The Witch Baby		$16	$25	$30	Jane O'Connor		H&Row
1986	Wheels		$16	$25	$30	Jane Resh Thomas		Clarion
1987	Jam Day		$16	$25	$30	Barbara M. Joosse		H&Row
1987	Lulu Goes To Witch School		$16	$25	$30	Jane O'Connor		H&Row
1987	Molly		$16	$25	$30	Ruth Radlauer		P-Hall
1987	Molly Goes Hiking		$16	$25	$30	Ruth Radlauer		P-Hall
1987	Richard And The Vratch		$16	$25	$30	Beatrice Gormley		Avon
1987	School		$20	$30	$40	Emily Arnold McCully		H&Row
1987	The Show Must Go On		$20	$30	$40	Emily Arnold McCully		Golden
1988	Breakfast By Molly		$14	$20	$30	Ruth Radlauer		S&S
1988	Molly At The Library		$14	$20	$30	Ruth Radlauer		S&S
1988	New Baby		$18	$25	$35	Emily Arnold McCully		H&Row
1988	The Baby Bubble Book		$14	$20	$30	Rhoda Josephs		G&D
1988	The Boston Coffee Party		$14	$20	$30	Doreen Rappaport		H&Row
1988	The Christmas Gift		$18	$25	$35	Emily Arnold McCully		H&Row
1988	The Grandma Mix-Up		$18	$25	$35	Emily Arnold McCully		H&Row
1988	You Lucky Duck!		$18	$25	$35	Emily Arnold McCully		Golden
1989	Dinah's Mad, Bad Wishes		$14	$20	$30	Barbara M. Joosse		H&Row
1989	It Always Happens To Leona		$14	$20	$30	Juanita Havill		Crown
1989	More Fifth Grade Magic		$14	$20	$30	Beatrice Gormley		Dutton
1989	Selene Goes Home		$14	$20	$30	Lucy Diggs		Athenm
1989	The Grandpa Days		$14	$20	$30	Joan W. Blos		S&S
1989	The Take-Along Dog		$14	$20	$30	Barbara Ann Porte		Green
1989	Zaza's Big Break		$18	$25	$35	Emily Arnold McCully		H&Row
1990	Grandmas At The Lake		$14	$20	$25	Emily Arnold McCully		H&Row
1990	Stepbrother Sabotage		$14	$20	$25	Sally Wittman		H&Row
1990	The Day Chubby Became Charles		$14	$20	$25	Achim Bröger		Lippin
1990	The Evil Spell		$14	$20	$25	Emily Arnold McCully		H&Row
1990	Wanted, UFO		$14	$20	$25	Beatrice Gormley		Dutton
1991	Leona And Ike		$14	$20	$25	Juanita Havill		Crown
1991	Meatball		$14	$20	$25	Phyllis Hoffman		HCollins
1991	Sky Guys To White Cat		$14	$20	$25	Beatrice Gormley		Dutton
1991	Speak Up, Blanche!		$14	$20	$25	Emily Arnold McCully		HCollins
1991	The Butterfly Birthday		$14	$20	$25	Ann Bixby Herold		Macmil
1992	Beavers Beware!		$12	$18	$25	Barbara Brenner		Bantam
1992	In My Tent		$12	$18	$25	Marilyn Singer		Macmil
1992	Meet The Lincoln Lions Band		$12	$18	$25	Patricia Reilly Giff		Dell
1992	Mirette On The High Wire		$70	$100	$140	Emily Arnold McCully	CM	Putnam
1992	Yankee Doodle Drumsticks		$12	$18	$25	Patricia Reilly Giff		Dell
1993	Amzat And His Brothers		$12	$18	$25	Paula Fox		Orchard
1993	Annie Flies The Birthday Bike		$12	$18	$25	Crescent Dragonwagon		Macmil
1993	Grandmas At Bat		$12	$18	$25	Emily Arnold McCully		HCollins
1993	If You Grew Up With George Washington		$12	$18	$25	Ruth Belov Gross		Scholas
1993	The Amazing Felix		$12	$18	$25	Emily Arnold McCully		Putnam
1993	The Great Shamrock Disaster		$12	$18	$25	Patricia Reilly Giff		Dell
1994	Crossing The New Bridge		$12	$18	$25	Emily Arnold McCully		Putnam
1994	My Real Family		$12	$18	$25	Emily Arnold McCully		HBJ
1994	Pizza Party		$12	$18	$25	Grace Maccarone		Cart
1995	Little Kit, Or, The Industrias Flea Circle Girl		$12	$16	$20	Emily Arnold McCully		Dial
1995	The Pirate Queen		$12	$16	$20	Emily Arnold McCully		Putnam
1996	Leo The Magnificat		$10	$16	$20	Ann M. Martin		Scholas
1996	Old Home Day		$10	$16	$20	Donald Hall		Bdeer
1996	The Ballot Box Battle		$10	$16	$20	Emily Arnold McCully		Knopf
1996	The Bobbin Girl		$10	$16	$20	Emily Arnold McCully		Dial
1997	Popcorn At The Palace		$10	$16	$20	Emily Arnold McCully		Bdeer
1997	Starring Mirette And Bellini		$10	$16	$20	Emily Arnold McCully		Putnam
1997	The Divide		$10	$16	$20	Michael Bedard		DoubleD
1998	An Outlaw Thanksgiving		$10	$16	$20	Emily Arnold McCully		Dial
1998	Beautiful Warrior		$10	$16	$20	Emily Arnold McCully		Levine
1999	Mouse Practice		$10	$14	$18	Emily Arnold McCully		Levine

McCully   Emily Arnold

Year	Title	VG-	VG	VG+	Fine	Author	Award	Pub
1999	Rabbit Pirates		$10	$14	$18	Judy Cox		Bdeer
2000	Hurry!		$8	$12	$16	Harry Hartwick (adapted)		HBrace
2000	Mirette & Bellini Cross Niagara Falls		$8	$12	$16	Emily Arnold McCully		Putnam
2000	Monk Camps Out		$8	$12	$16	Emily Arnold McCully		Levine
2000	Ten Go Tango		$8	$12	$16	Arthur Dorros		HCollins
2001	Four Hungry Kittens		$8	$12	$16	Emily Arnold McCully		Dial
2001	Grandmas Trick-Or-Treat		$8	$12	$16	Emily Arnold McCully		HCollins
2001	The Field Of The Dogs		$8	$12	$16	Katherine Paterson		HCollins
2001	The Orphan Singer		$8	$12	$16	Emily Arnold McCully		Levine
2002	Sing A Song Of Piglets		$8	$12	$16	Eve Bunting		Clarion
2002	The Battle For St. Michaels		$8	$12	$16	Emily Arnold McCully		HCollins
2003	Katie's Wish		$8	$10	$14	Barbara Shook Hazen		Dial
2003	The Secret Seder		$8	$10	$14	Doreen Rappaport		Hyper
2003	What Do Angels Wear?		$8	$10	$14	Eileen Spinelli		HCollins
2004	1, 2, I Love You		$8	$10	$14	Alice Schertle		Chron
2004	School		$8	$10	$14	Emily Arnold McCully		HCollins
2004	So Many Kinds Of Kisses		$8	$10	$14	Marilyn Singer		Athenm
2004	Squirrel And John Muir		$8	$10	$14	Emily Arnold McCully		FSG

McCurdy   Michael

Year	Title	VG-	VG	VG+	Fine	Author	Award	Pub
1973	Light Of Paradise		$25	$35	$50	William Ferguson		Penmaen
1973	Please Explain		$30	$50	$60	Isaac Asimov	NYT	HM
1974	Celebrations After The Death Of John Brennan		$16	$25	$30	X. J. Kennedy		Penmaen
1975	Founding Mothers		$16	$25	$30	Linda Grant De Pauw		HM
1975	Poems To Poets		$16	$25	$30	Richard Eberhart		Penmaen
1979	King Harald And The Icelanders		$14	$20	$30	Pardee Lowe		Penmaen
1981	Everything That Has Been Shall Be Again		$14	$20	$25	John Gilgun		Bieler
1984	The Very Best Christmas Tree		$12	$18	$25	B. A. King		Godine
1984	Two Prose Sketches		$12	$18	$25	Weldon Kees		Arali
1985	The Soul Of The Night		$12	$18	$25	Chet Raymo		P-Hall
1986	The Owl Scatterer		$20	$30	$40	Howard Norman		AMP
1986	The Winged Life		$12	$16	$20	Henry David Thoreau		Sierra
1987	The Christmas Junk Box		$12	$16	$20	B. A. King		Godine
1987	The Devils Who Learned To Be Good		$14	$20	$30	Michael McCurdy		Joy
1988	Hannah's Farm		$14	$20	$30	Michael McCurdy		Holiday
1989	An Old-Fashioned Thanksgiving		$12	$16	$20	Louisa May Alcott		Holiday
1989	How Glooskap Outwits The Ice Giants		$12	$16	$20	Howard Norman		LBrown
1991	American Tall Tales		$10	$16	$20	Mary Pope Osborne		Knopf
1992	The Beasts Of Bethlehem		$10	$16	$20	X. J. Kennedy		McEld
1992	The Old Man And The Fiddle		$12	$18	$25	Michael McCurdy		Putnam
1993	Giants In The Land		$10	$16	$20	Diana Karter Appelbaum		HM
1993	The Way West		$10	$16	$20	Lillian Schlissel		S&S
1994	Escape From Slavery		$10	$14	$18	Frederick Douglass		Knopf
1994	Lucy's Christmas		$10	$14	$18	Donald Hall		Bbear
1995	Lucy's Summer		$10	$14	$18	Donald Hall		HBrace
1995	Passover		$10	$14	$18	David Mamet		StMart
1995	The Gettysburg Address		$10	$14	$18	Abraham Lincoln		HM
1996	American Fairy Tales		$8	$12	$16	Neil Philip		Hyper
1996	The Seasons Sewn		$8	$12	$16	Ann Whitford Paul		Bdeer
1997	The Bone Man		$8	$12	$16	Laura Simms		Hyper
1997	Trapped By The Ice!		$8	$12	$16	Michael McCurdy		Walker
1998	Johnny Tremain		$8	$12	$16	Esther Forbes		HM
1998	The Sailor's Alphabet		$8	$12	$16	Michael McCurdy		HM
1999	Iron Horses		$8	$12	$16	Verla Kay		Putnam
1999	Tarzan		$8	$12	$16	Robert D. San Souci (adapted)		Hyper
1999	The Wonderful Wizard Of Oz		$8	$12	$16	L. Frank Baum		UKansas
2000	An Algonquian Year		$8	$10	$14	Michael McCurdy		HM
2000	Something Special		$8	$10	$14	Iris Murdoch		Norton
2000	Take Command, Captain Farragut!		$8	$10	$14	Peter & Connie Roop		Athenm
2002	The Signers		$8	$10	$14	Dennis B. Fradin		Walker
2003	The Train They Call The City Of New Orleans		$8	$10	$14	Steve Goodman		Putnam

McDermott   Dennis

Year	Title	VG-	VG	VG+	Fine	Author	Award	Pub
1991	Oom Razoom		$10	$16	$20	Diane Wolkstein		Morrow

McDermott   Dennis

Year	Title	VG-	VG	VG+	Fine	Author	Award	Pub
1992	The Listening Silence		$10	$14	$18	Phyllis Root		HCollins
1994	Gilly Martin The Fox		$8	$12	$16	Mollie Hunter		Hyper
1995	The Flying Ship		$8	$12	$16	Andrew Lang		Morrow
2000	The Golden Goose		$8	$10	$14	Dennis McDermott (adapted)		Morrow

McDermott   Gerald

Year	Title	VG-	VG	VG+	Fine	Author	Award	Pub
1972	Anansi The Spider		$140	$220	$280	Gerald McDermott	CH	HR&W
1973	The Magic Tree		$60	$90	$120	Gerald McDermott		HR&W
1974	Arrow To The Sun		$220	$320	$420	Gerald McDermott	CM	Viking
1975	The Stonecutter		$60	$80	$120	Gerald McDermott		Viking
1977	The Voyage Of Osiris		$40	$60	$80	Gerald McDermott		Windmil
1979	The Knight Of The Lion		$35	$50	$70	Gerald McDermott		4Winds
1980	Papagayo, The Mischief Maker		$25	$35	$50	Gerald McDermott		Windmil
1980	Sun Flight		$35	$50	$70	Gerald McDermott		4Winds
1981	The Adventures Of Pinocchio		$25	$35	$50	Marianna Mayer		4Winds
1984	Daughter Of Earth		$20	$30	$40	Gerald McDermott		DelaP
1985	Aladdin And The Enchanted Lamp		$20	$30	$40	Marianna Mayer		Macmil
1985	Alley Oop!		$20	$30	$40	Marianna Mayer		Macmil
1986	Daniel O'rourke		$20	$30	$40	Gerald McDermott		VK
1987	Brambleberrys Animal Book Of Big & Small Shapes		$20	$30	$40	Marianna Mayer		LongMed
1987	Brambleberrys Animal Family Learning Books Boxed		$20	$30	$40	Marianna Mayer		LongMed
1987	The Brambleberrys Animal Alphabet		$20	$30	$40	Marianna Mayer		StMart
1990	Tim O'Toole And The Wee Folk		$16	$25	$30	Gerald McDermott		Viking
1991	Marcel The Pastry Chef		$16	$25	$30	Marianna Mayer		Bantam
1991	The Brambleberrys Animal Book Of Colors		$16	$25	$30	Marianna Mayer		Bell
1991	The Brambleberrys Animal Book Of Counting		$16	$25	$30	Marianna Mayer		Bell
1992	Zomo The Rabbit		$16	$25	$30	Gerald McDermott		HBJ
1993	Raven		$16	$25	$30	Gerald McDermott		HBJ
1994	Coyote		$14	$20	$30	Gerald McDermott		HBrace
1994	Musicians Of The Sun		$14	$20	$30	Gerald McDermott		BSP
1998	The Light Of The World		$12	$16	$20	Gerald McDermott		S&S
1999	The Fox And The Stork		$12	$16	$20	Jean de La Fontaine		HBrace
2001	Jabutí The Tortoise		$10	$14	$18	Gerald McDermott		Harcort

McEwan   Chris

Year	Title	VG-	VG	VG+	Fine	Author	Award	Pub
1978	Fairground Games To Make And Play		$20	$30	$40	Neil & Ruth Thomson		Lippin
1989	The Little Penguin		$14	$20	$25	Chris McEwan		DoubleD
1990	Pinocchio		$10	$16	$20	Chris McEwan		DoubleD
1995	The 9 Tasks Of Mistry		$10	$14	$18	Chris McEwan		LBrown
2002	Word Bird Makes Words With Cat		$8	$10	$14	Jane Belk Moncure		CW
2002	Word Bird Makes Words With Dog		$8	$10	$14	Jane Belk Moncure		CW
2002	Word Bird Makes Words With Duck		$8	$10	$14	Jane Belk Moncure		CW
2002	Word Bird Makes Words With Hen		$8	$10	$14	Jane Belk Moncure		CW
2002	Word Bird Makes Words With Pig		$8	$10	$14	Jane Belk Moncure		CW
2002	Word Bird's Christmas Words		$8	$10	$14	Jane Belk Moncure		CW
2002	Word Bird's Easter Words		$8	$10	$14	Jane Belk Moncure		CW
2002	Word Bird's Fall Words		$8	$10	$14	Jane Belk Moncure		CW
2002	Word Bird's Halloween Words		$8	$10	$14	Jane Belk Moncure		CW
2002	Word Bird's Spring Words		$8	$10	$14	Jane Belk Moncure		CW
2002	Word Bird's Summer Words		$8	$10	$14	Jane Belk Moncure		CW
2002	Word Bird's Thanksgiving Words		$8	$10	$14	Jane Belk Moncure		CW
2002	Word Bird's Valentine's Day Words		$8	$10	$14	Jane Belk Moncure		CW
2002	Word Bird's Winter Words		$8	$10	$14	Jane Belk Moncure		CW
2003	Happy Birthday, Word Bird!		$8	$10	$14	Jane Belk Moncure		CW
2003	Hide-And-Seek Word Bird		$8	$10	$14	Jane Belk Moncure		CW
2003	No! No! Word Bird		$8	$10	$14	Jane Belk Moncure		CW
2003	Watch Out, Word Bird!		$8	$10	$14	Jane Belk Moncure		CW
2003	What Does Word Bird See?		$8	$10	$14	Jane Belk Moncure		CW
2003	Word Bird Asks: What? What? What?		$8	$10	$14	Jane Belk Moncure		CW
2003	Word Bird Builds A City		$8	$10	$14	Jane Belk Moncure		CW
2003	Word Bird's Circus Surprise		$8	$10	$14	Jane Belk Moncure		CW
2003	Word Bird's Dinosaur Days		$8	$10	$14	Jane Belk Moncure		CW
2003	Word Bird's Hats		$8	$10	$14	Jane Belk Moncure		CW
2003	Word Bird's Magic Wand		$8	$10	$14	Jane Belk Moncure		CW

McEwan   Chris

Year	Title	VG-	VG	VG+	Fine	Author	Award	Pub
2003	Word Bird's New Friend		$8	$10	$14	Jane Belk Moncure		CW
2003	Word Bird's Rainy-Day Dance		$8	$10	$14	Jane Belk Moncure		CW
2003	Word Bird's Shapes		$8	$10	$14	Jane Belk Moncure		CW

McKee   David

Year	Title	VG-	VG	VG+	Fine	Author	Award	Pub
1968	Elmer; The Story Of A Patchwork Elephant	$80	$120	$140		David McKee		McHill
1968	Mark And The Motorcycle	$30	$40	$50		David McKee		AS
1968	Mr. Benn: Red Knight	$30	$40	$50		David McKee		McHill
1968	The Pegasus Book Of Good English	$30	$40	$50		David McKee		Dobson
1970	123456789 Benn		$18	$25	$35	David McKee		McHill
1971	Mr. Drackle And His Dragons		$18	$25	$35	David McKee		FWatts
1972	Joseph, The Border Guard		$18	$25	$35	David McKee		PMagP
1972	Kids' London		$18	$25	$35	M. Perham E. Holt		AS
1973	The Man Who Was Going To Mind The House		$16	$25	$30	David McKee (retold)		AS
1974	Joachim The Dustman		$16	$25	$30	Kurt Baumann		ACB
1974	The Magician And The Sorcerer		$16	$25	$30	David McKee		PMagP
1975	The Day The Tide Went Out		$16	$25	$30	David McKee		AS
1976	The Magician And The Petnapping		$16	$25	$30	David McKee		HM
1977	A Book Of Elephants		$16	$25	$30	Katie Wales (compiled)		PMagP
1977	Two Admirals		$16	$25	$30	David McKee		HM
1978	The Parents' Day School Book		$14	$20	$30	Jonathan Croall		Pavil
1979	King Rollo And The Birthday		$14	$20	$30	David McKee		LBrown
1979	King Rollo And The Bread		$14	$20	$30	David McKee		LBrown
1979	King Rollo And The New Shoes		$14	$20	$30	David McKee		LBrown
1980	Not Now, Bernard		$14	$20	$25	David McKee		Metheun
1983	King Rollo's Playroom & Other Stories		$14	$20	$25	David McKee		AP
1984	I Hate My Teddy Bear		$12	$18	$25	David McKee		Clarion
1985	Paddington And The Knickerbocker Rainbow		$12	$18	$25	Michael Bond		Putnam
1985	Paddington At The Zoo		$12	$18	$25	Michael Bond		Putnam
1985	Paddington's Painting Exhibition		$12	$18	$25	Michael Bond		Collins
1985	The Hill And The Rock		$12	$18	$25	David McKee		Clarion
1986	Paddington At The Fair		$12	$16	$20	Michael Bond		Putnam
1986	Paddington At The Palace		$12	$16	$20	Michael Bond		Putnam
1986	Paddington Cleans Up		$12	$16	$20	Michael Bond		Putnam
1986	Paddington Minds The House		$12	$16	$20	Michael Bond		Collins
1986	Paddington's Art Exhibition		$12	$16	$20	Michael Bond		Putnam
1986	The Magician And The Balloon		$12	$16	$20	David McKee		Bedrik
1986	The Magician And The Dragon		$12	$16	$20	David McKee		Bedrik
1986	Two Monsters		$12	$16	$20	David McKee		BradP
1988	King Rollo And The Letter		$12	$16	$20	David McKee		AP
1989	Elmer		$12	$16	$20	David McKee		LL&S
1989	Snow Woman		$12	$16	$20	David McKee		LLee
1989	Who's A Clever Baby?		$12	$16	$20	David McKee		LLee
1990	Tusk Tusk		$10	$16	$20	David McKee		KaneM
1991	Elmer Again		$30	$50	$60	David McKee		LL&S
1991	The Sad Story Of Veronica Who Played The Violin		$10	$16	$20	David McKee		KaneM
1991	Zebra's Hiccups		$10	$16	$20	David McKee		AP
1993	Out Of The Blue: Poems About Color		$10	$16	$20	Hiawyn Oram		Hyper
1994	Elmer's Colors		$14	$20	$30	David McKee		LL&S
1994	Elmer's Day		$14	$20	$30	David McKee		LL&S
1994	Elmer's Friends		$14	$20	$30	David McKee		LL&S
1994	Elmer's Weather		$14	$20	$30	David McKee		LL&S
1994	The School Bus Comes At Eight O'clock		$10	$14	$18	David McKee		Hyper
1996	Elmer And Wilbur		$12	$18	$25	David McKee		LL&S
1997	Prince Peter And The Teddy Bear		$8	$12	$16	David McKee		FSG
1998	Elmer And The Wind		$12	$16	$20	David McKee		LL&S
1998	Elmer Takes Off		$12	$16	$20	David McKee		LL&S
1999	Elmer And The Lost Teddy		$12	$16	$20	David McKee		LL&S
2000	Elmer And The Kangaroo		$10	$14	$18	David McKee		HCollins

McKie   Roy

Year	Title	VG-	VG	VG+	Fine	Author	Award	Pub
1960	Bennett Cerf's Book Of Riddles	$100	$140	$180		Bennett Cerf		BB
1960	Melisande	$50	$60	$80		Margery Sharp		LBrown
1961	Bennett Cerf's More Riddles	$80	$120	$140		Bennett Cerf		BB

McKié   Roy

Year	Title	VG-	VG	VG+	Fine	Author	Award	Pub
1961	Ten Apples Up On Top!	$220	$280	$360		Theo LeSieg (pseud/Seuss)		BB
1962	Snow	$80	$120	$140		P. D. Eastman		BB
1963	Summer	$80	$100	$140		Alice Low		BB
1964	A Day Of Your Own	$90	$120	$160		Alice Low		BB
1964	Aesop Up-To-Date	$50	$60	$80		Robert Zimler		Potter
1964	Bennett Cerf's Book Of Animal Riddles	$70	$90	$120		Bennett Cerf		BB
1964	Night Before Christmas	$50	$60	$80		Clement Moore		Random
1968	Eye Book	$420	$560	$700		Theo LeSieg (pseud/Seuss)		BB
1969	My Book About Me	$120	$160	$200		Theo LeSieg (pseud/Seuss)		BB
1970	Nose Book		$70	$100	$140	Al Perkins		BB
1972	In A People House		$220	$320	$420	Theo LeSieg (pseud/Seuss)		BB
1973	The Many Mice Of Mr. Brice		$160	$240	$320	Theo LeSieg (pseud/Seuss)		BB
1975	Would You Rather Be A Bullfrog?		$160	$220	$300	Theo LeSieg (pseud/Seuss)		BB
1979	Hair Book		$50	$80	$100	Graham Tether		BB
1979	The Joke Book		$50	$80	$100	Roy McKié		BB
1981	Tooth Book		$100	$160	$220	Theo LeSieg (pseud/Seuss)		BB
1984	Noah's Ark		$40	$60	$90	Roy McKié		Random
1991	Nose, Toes, Antlers, Tail		$16	$25	$30	Michael Berenstain		Western
1992	Who Will Be My Pet?		$16	$25	$30	Stan Tusan		Western

McPhail   David

Year	Title	VG-	VG	VG+	Fine	Author	Award	Pub
1971	The Run, Jump, Bump Book		$40	$60	$90	Robert Brooks		LBrown
1972	Leave Herbert Alone		$30	$50	$60	Alma Marshak Whitney		AW
1972	The Bear's Toothache		$30	$50	$60	David McPhail		LBrown
1972	The Glerp		$40	$60	$90	David McPhail		Ginn
1973	Oh, No, Go (A Play)		$25	$40	$50	David McPhail		LBrown
1974	Sailing To Cythera, & Other Anatole Stories		$25	$35	$50	David McPhail		HBJ
1974	The Bear's Bicycle		$20	$30	$40	Emilie Warren McLeod		LBrown
1974	The Cereal Box		$25	$35	$50	David McPhail		LBrown
1975	One Winter Night In August		$20	$30	$40	X. J. Kennedy		Athenm
1976	Henry Bear's Park		$20	$30	$40	David McPhail		LBrown
1977	Strangers' Bread		$20	$30	$40	Nancy Willard		HBJ
1977	The Train		$25	$40	$50	David McPhail		LBrown
1978	A Big Fat Enormous Lie		$20	$30	$40	Marjorie Weinman Sharmat		Dutton
1978	Captain Toad And The Motorbike		$20	$30	$40	David McPhail		Athenm
1978	Mistletoe		$20	$30	$40	David McPhail		Dutton
1978	The Devil's Tail: Based On An Old French Legend		$20	$30	$40	Nanine Valen		Scribnr
1978	The Magical Drawings Of Moony B. Finch		$20	$30	$40	David McPhail		DoubleD
1979	Grandfather's Cake		$20	$30	$40	David McPhail		Scribnr
1979	I Want To Be Big		$20	$30	$40	Genie Iverson		Dutton
1979	Stanley, Henry Bear's Friend		$20	$30	$40	David McPhail		LBrown
1979	The Island Of The Grass King		$18	$25	$35	Nancy Willard		HBJ
1979	The Phantom Ice Cream Man		$18	$25	$35	X. J. Kennedy		Athenm
1979	Where Can An Elephant Hide?		$20	$30	$40	David McPhail		DoubleD
1980	Alligators Are Awful		$18	$25	$35	David McPhail		DoubleD
1980	Bumper Tubbs		$18	$25	$35	David McPhail		HM
1980	Pig Pig Grows Up		$18	$25	$35	David McPhail		Dutton
1980	Those Terrible Toy-Breakers		$18	$25	$35	David McPhail		PMagP
1981	A Wolf Story		$18	$25	$35	David McPhail		Scribnr
1982	Great Cat		$16	$25	$30	David McPhail		Dutton
1982	Pig Pig Rides		$16	$25	$30	David McPhail		Dutton
1982	Snow Lion		$16	$25	$30	David McPhail		PMagP
1982	That Grand Master Jumping Teacher		$16	$25	$30	David McPhail		FWarne
1982	Uncle Terrible: More Adventures Of Anatole		$16	$25	$30	Nancy Willard		HBJ
1983	Pig Pig Goes To Camp		$16	$25	$30	David McPhail		Dutton
1983	The Nightgown Of The Sullen Moon		$16	$25	$30	Nancy Willard		HBJ
1984	Andrew's Bath		$16	$25	$30	David McPhail		LBrown
1984	Fix-It		$16	$25	$30	David McPhail		Dutton
1984	Lorenzo		$16	$25	$30	David McPhail		DoubleD
1984	Sisters		$16	$25	$30	David McPhail		HBJ
1985	Emma's Pet		$16	$25	$30	David McPhail		Dutton
1985	Farm Morning		$16	$25	$30	David McPhail		HBJ
1985	The Dream Child		$16	$25	$30	David McPhail		Dutton
1986	Pig Pig And The Magic Photo Album		$14	$20	$30	David McPhail		Dutton
1987	Adam's Smile		$14	$20	$30	David McPhail		Dutton

McPhail   David

Year	Title	VG-	VG	VG+	Fine	Author	Award	Pub
1987	Emma's Vacation		$14	$20	$30	David McPhail		Dutton
1987	First Flight		$14	$20	$30	David McPhail		LBrown
1988	David Mcphail's Animals A To Z		$14	$20	$30	David McPhail		Scholas
1988	Moonhorse		$14	$20	$30	Mary Pope Osborne		Knopf
1989	Goldilocks And The Three Bears		$14	$20	$25	David McPhail (retold)		Heath
1989	The Tale Of Peter Rabbit		$14	$20	$25	Beatrix Potter		Scholas
1990	Ed And Me		$12	$18	$25	David McPhail		HBJ
1990	Lost		$12	$18	$25	David McPhail		LBrown
1990	Pig Pig Gets A Job		$12	$18	$25	David McPhail		Dutton
1990	The Mother Goose Songbook		$12	$18	$25	Tom Glazer		DoubleD
1990	The Party		$12	$18	$25	David McPhail		Joy
1991	Annie & Co.		$12	$18	$25	David McPhail		Holt
1991	The Ice Cream Store		$12	$18	$25	Dennis Lee		Scholas
1992	Farm Boy's Year		$12	$18	$25	David McPhail		Athenm
1992	Who Gets The Sun Out Of Bed?		$12	$18	$25	Nancy Carlstrom		LBrown
1993	Pigs Aplenty, Pigs Galore!		$12	$16	$20	David McPhail		Dutton
1993	The Return Of Moony B. Finch		$12	$16	$20	David McPhail		DoubleD
1994	Moony B. Finch, Fastest Draw In The West		$12	$16	$20	David McPhail		AWG
1994	Night Sounds, Morning Colors		$12	$18	$25	Rosemary Wells		Dial
1994	On A Starry Night		$12	$16	$20	Natalie Kinsey-Warnock		Orchard
1994	Ten Cats Have Hats: A Counting Book		$12	$16	$20	Jean Marzollo		Scholas
1995	Little Red Riding Hood		$10	$16	$20	David McPhail (retold)		Scholas
1995	Pigs Ahoy!		$10	$16	$20	David McPhail		Dutton
1995	The Glerp		$10	$16	$20	David McPhail		Silver
1995	The Three Little Pigs		$10	$16	$20	David McPhail (retold)		Scholas
1995	Yesterday I Lost A Sneaker		$10	$16	$20	David McPhail		SBurdet
1996	If You Were My Bunny		$10	$16	$20	Kate McMullan		Scholas
1996	In Flight With David Mcphail		$10	$16	$20	David McPhail		Heine
1996	The Day The Dog Said, "Cock-A-Doodle Doo!		$10	$16	$20	David McPhail		Scholas
1996	The Furry Bedtime Book: Lovey Bear's Story		$10	$16	$20	Margo Lundell		Scholas
1996	Those Can-Do Pigs		$10	$16	$20	David McPhail		Dutton
1997	Angel Pig And The Hidden Christmas		$10	$16	$20	Jan L. Waldron		Dutton
1997	The Great Race		$10	$16	$20	David McPhail		Scholas
1997	The Puddle		$10	$16	$20	David McPhail		FSG
1998	David Mcphail A Bug, A Bear, And A Boy		$10	$14	$18	David McPhail		Scholas
1998	John Pig's Halloween		$10	$14	$18	Jan L. Waldron		Dutton
1998	The Day The Sheep Showed Up		$10	$14	$18	David McPhail		Scholas
1998	Tinker And Tom And The Star Baby		$10	$14	$18	David McPhail		LBrown
1999	A Friend For Growl Bear		$10	$14	$18	Margot Austin		HCollins
1999	Tall In The Saddle		$10	$14	$18	Anne Carter		Orca
2000	A Girl, A Goat, And A Goose		$8	$12	$16	David McPhail		Scholas
2000	Bubblegum Delicious		$8	$12	$16	Dennis Lee		HCollins
2000	Drawing Lessons From A Bear		$8	$12	$16	David McPhail		LBrown
2000	Just Clowning Around		$8	$12	$16	Steven MacDonald		GLR
2000	Sail Away		$8	$12	$16	Florence McNeil		Orca
2001	Big Pig And Little Pig		$8	$12	$16	David McPhail		Harcort
2001	I Love You Because You're You		$8	$12	$16	Liza Baker		Scholas
2001	Little Horse		$8	$12	$16	Betsy Cromer Byars		Holt
2002	A Pot O' Gold		$8	$10	$14	Kathleen Krull		Hyper
2002	Edward In The Jungle		$8	$10	$14	David McPhail		LBrown
2002	Fix-It		$8	$10	$14	David McPhail		Dutton
2002	Jack And Rick		$8	$10	$14	David McPhail		Harcort
2002	Mud Is Cake		$8	$10	$14	Pam Muñoz Ryan		Hyper
2002	Piggy's Pancake Parlor		$8	$10	$14	David McPhail		Dutton
2002	The Teddy Bear		$8	$10	$14	David McPhail		Holt
2003	Big Brown Bear's Up And Down Day		$8	$10	$14	David McPhail		Harcort
2003	Emma's Pet		$8	$10	$14	David McPhail		Dutton
2003	Henry Bear's Christmas		$8	$10	$14	David McPhail		Athenm
2003	Thirsty Baby		$8	$10	$14	Catherine Ann Cullen		LBrown
2004	Little Horse On His Own		$8	$10	$14	Betsy Cromer Byars		Holt
2004	My Little Brother		$8	$10	$14	David McPhail		Harcort
2004	Rick Is Sick		$8	$10	$14	David McPhail		Harcort
2004	Wynken, Blynken, And Nod		$8	$10	$14	Eugene Field		Scholas
2005	A Place For Nicholas		$6	$10	$12	Lucy Floyd		Harcort

Meade   Holly

Year	Title	VG-	VG	VG+	Fine	Author	Award	Pub
1993	Rata-Pata-Scata-Fata		$18	$25	$35	Phillis Gershator		Joy
1994	Small Green Snake		$16	$25	$30	Libba Moore Gray		Orchard
1995	Sleep, Sleep, Sleep		$14	$20	$25	Nancy Van Laan		LBrown
1996	Hush!: A Thai Lullaby		$30	$50	$60	Minfong Ho	CH	Orchard
1996	Pie's In The Oven		$10	$16	$20	Betty G. Birney		HM
1997	Cocoa Ice		$10	$16	$20	Diana Karter Appelbaum		Orchard
1998	Boss Of The Plains		$10	$14	$18	Laurie M. Carlson		DK
1998	John Willy And Freddy Mcgee		$10	$14	$18	Holly Meade		MCaven
2000	Steamboat!		$8	$12	$16	Judith Heide Gilliland		DK
2000	When Papa Snores		$8	$12	$16	Melinda Long		S&S
2001	A Place To Sleep		$8	$12	$16	Holly Meade		MCaven
2001	The Rabbit's Bride		$8	$12	$16	Jacob & Wilhelm Grimm		MCaven
2002	Goose's Story		$8	$10	$14	Cari Best		Kroupa
2002	On Morning Wings		$8	$10	$14	Reeve Lindbergh		Candle
2002	Queenie Farmer Had Fifteen Daughters		$8	$10	$14	Ann-Jeanette Campbell		Whistle
2003	That's What Friends Are For		$8	$10	$14	Florence Parry Heide		Candle
2004	Blue Bowl Down		$8	$10	$14	C. M. Millen		Candle
2004	Peek!		$8	$10	$14	Minfong Ho		Candle

Meddaugh   Susan

Year	Title	VG-	VG	VG+	Fine	Author	Award	Pub
1977	Good Stones		$30	$50	$60	Anne Merrick Epstein		HM
1978	Too Short Fred		$35	$50	$70	Susan Meddaugh		HM
1980	Maude And Claude Go Abroad		$20	$30	$40	Susan Meddaugh		HM
1981	Beast		$18	$25	$35	Susan Meddaugh		HM
1982	My Friend Bear		$16	$25	$30	Carol-Lynn Rössel Waugh		LBrown
1982	Too Many Monsters		$16	$25	$30	Susan Meddaugh		HM
1983	Red Sun Girl		$16	$25	$30	Jean & Claudio Marzollo		Dial
1984	Blue Sun Ben		$16	$25	$30	Jean & Claudio Marzollo		Dial
1984	Ruthie's Rude Friends		$16	$25	$30	Jean & Claudio Marzollo		Dial
1985	Bimwili & The Zimwi		$16	$25	$30	Verna Aardema		Dial
1987	The Silver Bear		$14	$20	$30	Jean Marzollo		Dial
1988	The Way I Feel-- Sometimes		$14	$20	$30	Beatrice S. De Regniers		Clarion
1988	Two Ways To Count To Ten		$14	$20	$30	Ruby Dee		Holt
1989	No Nap		$14	$20	$25	Eve Bunting		Clarion
1989	The Hopeful Trout & Other Limericks		$14	$20	$25	John Ciardi		HM
1990	In The Haunted House		$12	$18	$25	Eve Bunting		Clarion
1990	Tree Of Birds		$12	$18	$25	Susan Meddaugh		HM
1991	The Witches' Supermarket		$12	$18	$25	Susan Meddaugh		HM
1992	Martha Speaks		$12	$18	$25	Susan Meddaugh		HM
1992	The Best Halloween Of All		$12	$18	$25	Susan Wojciechowski		Crown
1993	Amanda's Perfect Hair		$12	$16	$20	Linda Breiner Milstein		Tambour
1994	Martha Calling		$12	$16	$20	Susan Meddaugh		HM
1994	That Terrible Baby		$12	$16	$20	Jennifer Armstrong		Tambour
1995	Good Zap, Little Grog		$10	$16	$20	Sarah Wilson		Candle
1995	Hog-Eye		$10	$16	$20	Susan Meddaugh		HM
1996	Martha Blah Blah		$10	$16	$20	Susan Meddaugh		HM
1996	The Most Beautiful Kid In The World		$10	$16	$20	Jennifer A. Ericsson		Tambour
1997	Cinderella's Rat		$10	$16	$20	Susan Meddaugh		HM
1998	Five Little Piggies		$10	$14	$18	David Martin		Candle
1998	Martha Walks The Dog		$10	$14	$18	Susan Meddaugh		HM
1999	The Best Place		$10	$14	$18	Susan Meddaugh		HM
2000	Martha And Skits		$8	$12	$16	Susan Meddaugh		HM
2002	Lulu's Hat		$8	$10	$14	Susan Meddaugh		HM
2003	Harry On The Rocks		$8	$10	$14	Susan Meddaugh		HM
2004	Perfectly Martha		$8	$10	$14	Susan Meddaugh		HM

Mikolaycak   Charles

Year	Title	VG-	VG	VG+	Fine	Author	Award	Pub
1967	Great Wolf And The Good Woodsman	$60	$80	$100		Helen Hoover		PMagP
1968	Banner Over Me	$40	$50	$70		Margery Greenleaf		Follett
1968	Little Red Riding-Hood	$40	$50	$70		Jacob & Wilhelm Grimm		Gibson
1969	Mourka, The Mighty Cat	$40	$50	$70		Lee Wyndham		Random
1970	In The Morning Of Time		$25	$35	$50	Cynthia King		4Winds
1970	The Pretzel Hero; A Story Of Old Vienna		$25	$35	$50	Barbara Rinkoff		PMagP
1971	The Feral Child		$25	$35	$50	Eric Sundell		AS

Mikolaycak   Charles

Year	Title	VG-	VG	VG+	Fine	Author	Award	Pub
1972	How The Hare Told The Truth About His Horse		$25	$35	$50	Barbara K. Walker		PMagP
1972	The Gorgon's Head		$25	$35	$50	Margaret Hodges (retold)		LBrown
1973	The Feast Day		$25	$35	$50	Edwin Jr. Fadiman		LBrown
1974	Shipwreck		$20	$30	$40	Vera Cumberlege		Follett
1975	How Wilka Went To Sea		$20	$30	$40	Mirra Ginsburg (adapted)		Crown
1975	The Tall Man From Boston		$20	$30	$40	Marion L. Starkey		Crown
1976	A Fair Wind For Troy		$20	$30	$40	Doris Gates		Viking
1976	Little Red Riding-Hood		$20	$30	$40	Jacob & Wilhelm Grimm		Gibson
1976	Sister Of The Birds, & Other Gypsy Tales		$20	$30	$40	Jerzy Ficowski		Abing
1977	Captain Grey		$20	$30	$40	Avi		Pan
1978	The Binding Of Isaac		$20	$30	$40	Barbara Cohen		LL&S
1978	The Cobbler's Reward		$20	$30	$40	Barbara & Ewa Reid		Macmil
1978	Three Wanderers From Wapping		$20	$30	$40	Norma Farber		AW
1979	Journey To The Bright Kingdom		$18	$25	$35	Elizabeth Winthrop		Holiday
1979	The Surprising Things Maui Did		$18	$25	$35	Jay Williams		4Winds
1979	The Tale Of Tawny And Dingo		$18	$25	$35	William H. Armstrong		H&Row
1979	The Twelve Clever Brothers		$18	$25	$35	Mirra Ginsburg (adapted)		Lippin
1980	I Am Joseph		$18	$25	$35	Barbara Cohen		Lothrop
1980	Johnny's Egg		$18	$25	$35	Earlene Long		AW
1980	The Christmas Spider: A Puppet Play From Poland		$18	$25	$35	Loretta Holz		Philo
1980	The Nine Crying Dolls: A Story From Poland		$18	$25	$35	Anne Pellowski (retold)		Philo
1981	Perfect Crane		$18	$25	$35	Anne Laurin		H&Row
1981	Signs & Wonders: Tales From The Old Testament		$18	$25	$35	Bernard Evslin		4Winds
1982	Peter And The Wolf		$16	$25	$30	Sergei Prokofiev		Viking
1982	Tiger Watch		$16	$25	$30	Jan Wahl		HBJ
1983	A Child Is Born: The Christmas Story		$16	$25	$30	Elizabeth Winthrop (adapted)		Holiday
1983	The Highwayman		$16	$25	$30	Alfred Noyes		LL&S
1984	Babushka: An Old Russian Folktale		$40	$60	$90	Charles Mikolaycak (retold)	NYT	Holiday
1984	The Man Who Could Call Down Owls		$16	$25	$30	Eve Bunting		Macmil
1985	He Is Risen: The Easter Story		$16	$25	$30	Elizabeth Winthrop (adapted)		Holiday
1985	The Changing Maze		$16	$25	$30	Zilpha Keatley Snyder		Macmil
1986	Juma And The Magic Jinn		$14	$20	$30	Joy Anderson		Lothrop
1986	The Lullaby Songbook		$16	$25	$30	Jane Yolen		HBJ
1987	Exodus		$14	$20	$30	Miriam Chaikin (adapted)		Holiday
1988	A Gift From Saint Nicholas		$14	$20	$30	Carole Kismaric (adapted)		Holiday
1988	The Rumor Of Pavel And Paali		$14	$20	$30	Carole Kismaric (adapted)		H&Row
1988	Voyages: Poems		$14	$20	$30	Walt Whitman		HBJ
1990	Tam Lin: An Old Ballad		$14	$20	$30	Jane Yolen (adapted)		HBJ
1990	The Legend Of The Christmas Rose		$12	$18	$25	Ellin Greene (retold)		Holiday
1991	Bearhead: A Russian Folktale		$12	$18	$25	Eric Kimmel (adapted)		Holiday
1992	Orpheus		$12	$18	$25	Charles Mikolaycak (retold)		HBJ
1993	The Hero Of Bremen		$12	$16	$20	Margaret Hodges (retold)		Holiday

Miles   Elizabeth

Year	Title	VG-	VG	VG+	Fine	Author	Award	Pub
1985	Mokey's Birthday Present		$16	$25	$30	Ellen Weiss		HR&W
1988	The Night Before Christmas		$12	$16	$20	Clement C. Moore		Troll
1989	Dorothy Of Oz		$12	$16	$20	Roger S. Baum		BOW
1991	Goldilocks and the Three Bears		$10	$16	$20	Jennifer Greenway		AM
1992	Little Red Riding Hood		$10	$16	$20	Jennifer Greenway		AM
1996	Molly Limbo		$8	$12	$16	Margaret Hodges		Athenm
1997	Louie And Dan Are Friends		$8	$12	$16	Bonnie Pryor		Morrow
2001	Jennifer's Rabbit		$8	$10	$14	Tom Paxton		HCollins

Milhous   Katherine

Year	Title	VG-	VG	VG+	Fine	Author	Award	Pub
1938	Once On A Time	$90	$120	$160		Alice Dalgliesh		Scribnr
1939	Happily Ever After	$80	$100	$140		Alice Dalgliesh		Scribnr
1940	A Book For Jennifer	$70	$90	$120		Alice Dalgliesh		Scribnr
1940	Lovina, A Story Of The Pennsylvania Country	$80	$100	$140		Katherine Milhous		Scribnr
1941	Billy Buttons Butter'd Biscuit	$70	$90	$120		Mabel Leigh Hunt		FStokes
1941	Wings Around South America	$70	$90	$120		Alice Dalgliesh		Scribnr
1942	Herodia	$70	$90	$120		Katherine Milhous		Scribnr
1942	Peter Piper's Pickled Peppers	$70	$90	$120		Mabel Leigh Hunt		FStokes
1942	They Live In South America	$70	$90	$120		Alice Dalgliesh		Scribnr
1943	Corporal Keeperupper	$70	$90	$120		Katherine Milhous		Scribnr

Milhous   Katherine

Year	Title	VG-	VG	VG+	Fine	Author	Award	Pub
1943	The Little Angel	$70	$90	$120		Katherine Milhous		Scribnr
1944	The First Christmas Crib	$60	$80	$100		Katherine Milhous		Scribnr
1944	The Silver Pencil	$120	$160	$200		Alice Dalgliesh	NH	Scribnr
1945	Snow Over Bethlehem	$60	$80	$100		Katherine Milhous		Scribnr
1946	Along Janet's Road	$60	$80	$100		Alice Dalgliesh		Scribnr
1946	Old Abe, American Eagle	$60	$80	$100		Lorraine Sherwood		Scribnr
1946	The Brownies	$60	$80	$100		Juliana Horatia Ewing		Scribnr
1950	The Egg Tree	$320	$440	$540		Katherine Milhous	CM	Scribnr
1951	Patrick And The Golden Slippers	$50	$70	$90		Katherine Milhous		Scribnr
1954	Appolonia's Valentine	$50	$70	$90		Katherine Milhous		Scribnr
1955	With Bells On	$50	$70	$90		Katherine Milhous		Scribnr

Miller   Jane

Year	Title	VG-	VG	VG+	Fine	Author	Award	Pub
1941	A Dog Of His Own	$50	$60	$80		Laura Hobson		Viking
1943	Miss Lizzie	$35	$40	$60		Jane Miller		Viking
1946	Linda Just Right	$35	$40	$60		Jane Miller		Vnguard
1953	A Dance For Susie	$140	$180	$240		Lee Wyndham		DoddM
1953	Up And Down The Street	$30	$40	$50		Esther Watson Reno		Oxford
1954	Susie And The Dancing Cat	$120	$160	$200		Lee Wyndham		DoddM
1954	The Wet World	$30	$40	$50		Norma Simon		Lippin
1955	Susie And The Ballet Family	$100	$120	$160		Jane Hyndman		DoddM
1957	The Ill-Tempered Tiger	$25	$35	$50		Jane Miller		Lippin
1958	On Your Toes, Susie	$80	$100	$140		Lee Wyndham		DoddM
1959	A Part-Time Dog For Nick	$25	$35	$50		Carol Denison		DoddM
1960	Scrappy, The Pup	$25	$30	$40		John Ciardi		Lippin
1961	Flower Girl	$25	$30	$40		Myra Berry Brown		FWatts
1961	Mercy Percy	$25	$30	$40		Suzanne Gleaves		Lippin
1962	Henrietta And The Hat	$25	$30	$40		Mabel Watts		PMagP
1962	Nine Fine Gifts	$25	$30	$40		Mabel Watts		PMagP
1965	Dumb Stupid David	$25	$30	$40		Dorothy Keeley Aldis		Putnam
1968	Balloon	$20	$30	$35		Jane Carlisle		Follett

Miller   Mitchell

Year	Title	VG-	VG	VG+	Fine	Author	Award	Pub
1968	Martze	$40	$50	$70		Jack Sendak		FSG
1969	A Monkey's Uncle	$25	$35	$50		Doris Orgel (retold)		FSG
1969	How The Children Stopped The Wars	$25	$35	$50		Jan Wahl		FSG
1971	One Misty Moisty Morning		$25	$35	$50	Mother Goose		FSG
1971	The Magic Tears		$25	$35	$50	Jack Sendak		H&Row
1981	The Glass Slipper		$18	$25	$35	John Bierhorst		4Winds

Mills   Lauren

Year	Title	VG-	VG	VG+	Fine	Author	Award	Pub
1988	At The Back Of The North Wind		$14	$20	$30	George MacDonald		Godine
1989	Anne Of Green Gables		$14	$20	$25	L. M. Montgomery		Godine
1990	Elfabet		$16	$25	$30	Jane Yolen		LBrown
1991	The Rag Coat		$12	$18	$25	Lauren Mills		LBrown
1992	The Tsar's Promise		$12	$18	$25	Robert D. San Souci		Philo
1993	Tatterhood And The Hobgoblins		$12	$16	$20	Lauren Mills		LBrown
1995	Fairy Wings		$10	$16	$20	Lauren Mills		LBrown
1997	The Book Of Little Folk		$10	$16	$20	Lauren Mills		Dial
1999	The Goblin Baby		$10	$14	$18	Lauren Mills		Dial
2001	The Dog Prince		$8	$12	$16	Dennis Nolan		LBrown
2002	Fia & The Imp		$8	$10	$14	Dennis Nolan		LBrown
2002	The Tsar's Promise		$8	$10	$14	Robert D. San Souci		Philo
2003	Thumbelina		$8	$10	$14	Hans Christian Andersen		LBrown

Miyake   Yoshi

Year	Title	VG-	VG	VG+	Fine	Author	Award	Pub
1979	The Beaver		$12	$18	$25	Paula Hogan		Rain
1979	The Dandelion		$12	$18	$25	Paula Hogan		Rain
1979	The Salmon		$12	$18	$25	Paula Hogan		Rain
1980	Rudolph, The Red-Nosed Reindeer		$12	$16	$20	Eileen Daly (adapted)		Western
1980	Touching		$12	$16	$20	Richard L. Allington		Rain

Miyake   Yoshi

Year	Title	VG-	VG	VG+	Fine	Author	Award	Pub
1980	Writing		$12	$16	$20	Richard L. Allington		Rain
1981	Take A Walk, Johnny		$12	$16	$20	Margaret Hillert		Follett
1982	Earth Invaded		$16	$25	$30	Isaac Asimov		Rain
1982	The Boy And The Goats		$12	$16	$20	Margaret Hillert		Follett
1982	What Makes It Rain?		$12	$16	$20	Keith Brandt		Troll
1982	Wonders Of Rivers		$12	$16	$20	Rae Bains		Troll
1983	Time		$10	$16	$20	Richard L. Allington		Rain
1984	Paul Bunyan And Babe The Blue Ox		$10	$16	$20	Jan/Kathleen Gleiter/Thompson		Rain
1985	The Disappearing Man & Other Mysteries		$16	$25	$30	Isaac Asimov		Walker
1987	Annie Oakley		$10	$16	$20	Jan/Kathleen Gleiter/Thompson		Rain
1987	Sacagawea		$10	$16	$20	Jan/Kathleen Gleiter/Thompson		Rain
1988	John James Audubon		$10	$14	$18	Jan/Kathleen Gleiter/Thompson		Rain
1989	Diego Rivera		$10	$14	$18	Jan/Kathleen Gleiter/Thompson		Rain
1989	Gulliver's Travels		$10	$14	$18	Kathleen Thompson		Rain
1990	Caves		$10	$14	$18	Judith E. Greenberg		Rain
1990	Mozart, Young Music Genius		$10	$14	$18	Francene Sabin		Troll
1990	Plenty Coups		$10	$14	$18	Michael Doss		Rain
1990	Wonders Of Plants And Flowers		$10	$14	$18	Laura Damon		Troll
1991	Miloli's Orchids		$10	$14	$18	Alisandra Jezek		Rain
1992	Ahyoka And The Talking Leaves		$10	$14	$18	Peter Roop		LL&S
1992	All About Pets		$10	$14	$18	Kathleen Kain		World
1992	The Elves & The Shoemaker		$10	$14	$18	Seva Spanos (adapted)		World
1992	The Pegasus Club And Me		$10	$14	$18	Amanda Beck		RainSV
1992	Where Lies Butch Cassidy?		$10	$14	$18	Gail Stewart		CrestH
1992	Young Abigail Adams		$10	$14	$18	Francene Sabin		Troll
1993	Captain Cook		$8	$12	$16	Jon Noonan		CrestH
1993	Ferdinand Magellan		$8	$12	$16	Jon Noonan		CrestH
1993	Lewis And Clark		$8	$12	$16	Jon Noonan		CrestH
1993	Osceola		$8	$12	$16	Herman J. Viola		RainSV
1993	Rachel Carson		$8	$12	$16	Francene Sabin		Troll
1994	Obon		$8	$12	$16	Ruth Suyenaga		MCP
1994	Owl Eyes		$8	$12	$16	Frieda Gates		LL&S
1994	The Christmas Story		$8	$12	$16	Deborah Hautzig		Random
1995	Inspector Mcq Presents All About Pets		$8	$12	$16	Kathleen Kain		World
1995	Oni Wa Soto		$8	$12	$16	Cathy Spagnoli		Oxford
1996	The Blue-Eyed Goose		$8	$12	$16	Kristine L. Franklin		LL&S
1997	Selena Who Speaks In Silence		$8	$10	$14	Evangeline Nicholas		Oxford
1998	Moshi Moshi		$8	$10	$14	Jonathan London		Millbk
1998	The Little Drummer Boy		$8	$10	$14	Katherine Davis		Troll
1999	The Inclusive Classroom		$8	$10	$14	Sirinam S. Khalsa		GoodY

Modarressi   Mitra

Year	Title	VG-	VG	VG+	Fine	Author	Award	Pub
1993	Tumble Tower		$16	$25	$30	Anne Tyler		Orchard
1994	The Dream Pillow		$12	$16	$20	Mitra Modarressi		Orchard
1995	The Parent Thief		$10	$16	$20	Mitra Modarressi		Orchard
1996	The Beastly Visits		$10	$16	$20	Mitra Modarressi		Orchard
1998	Monster Stew		$10	$14	$18	Mitra Modarressi		DK
2000	Yard Sale		$8	$12	$16	Mitra Modarressi		DK
2005	Timothy Tugbottom Says No!		$6	$10	$12	Anne Tyler		Putnam

Montresor   Beni

Year	Title	VG-	VG	VG+	Fine	Author	Award	Pub
1961	Belling The Tiger	$70	$90	$120		Mary Stolz		H&B
1961	Mommies At Work	$70	$90	$120		Eve Merriam		Knopf
1961	On Christmas Eve	$70	$90	$120		Margaret Wise Brown		YScott
1961	The Great Rebellion	$70	$90	$120		Mary Stolz		H&B
1962	The Princesses	$50	$60	$80		Sally Patrick Johnson		Harper
1963	Siri The Conquistador	$50	$60	$80		Mary Stolz		H&Row
1963	Sounds Of A Summer Night	$50	$60	$80		May Garelick		YScott
1963	The Witches Of Venice	$50	$60	$80		Beni Montresor		Knopf
1964	May I Bring A Friend?	$200	$280	$340		Beatrice S. De Regniers	CM	Athenm
1964	The Last Savage	$50	$60	$80		Gian Carlo Menotti		NYGS
1965	Cinderella	$40	$60	$70		Gioacchino Rossini		Knopf
1966	The Magic Flute	$40	$60	$70		Stephen Spender		Putnam
1967	I Saw A Ship A-Sailing	$40	$50	$70		Beni Montresor		Knopf

Montresor Beni

Year	Title	VG-	VG	VG+	Fine	Author	Award	Pub
1968	Willy O'dwyer Jumped In The Fire	$40	$50	$70		Beatrice S. De Regniers		Athenm
1978	Bedtime!		$20	$30	$40	Beni Montresor		H&Row
1982	The Birthday Of The Infanta		$16	$25	$30	Oscar Wilde		Athenm
1985	The Nightingale		$16	$25	$30	Alan Benjamin (adapted)		Crown
2001	Hansel And Gretel		$8	$12	$16	Beni Montresor		Athenm

Moore Inga

Year	Title	VG-	VG	VG+	Fine	Author	Award	Pub
1976	Brella: The Story Of A Young Fruit Bat		$20	$30	$40	Josephine Croser Croser		TNelson
1980	Aktils Big Swim		$14	$20	$25	Inga Moore		Oxford
1980	Barnaby And The Horses		$14	$20	$25	Lydia Pender		Oxford
1981	Aktils Bicycle Ride		$14	$20	$25	Inga Moore		Oxford
1984	The Vegetable Thieves		$12	$18	$25	Inga Moore		Viking
1986	Read Me A Poem		$12	$16	$20	Caroline Royds (compiled)		Kfisher
1987	Away In A Manger		$12	$16	$20	Sarah Hayes		LSimon
1987	The Truffle Hunter		$12	$16	$20	Inga Moore		KaneM
1988	Fifty Red Night-Caps		$12	$16	$20	Inga Moore		Chron
1989	Prayers for Children		$12	$16	$20	Caroline Royds (compiled)		DoubleD
1989	The Sorcerer's Apprentice		$12	$16	$20	Inga Moore		Macmil
1990	Rose And The Nightingale		$10	$16	$20	Inga Moore		Knopf
1991	Little Dog Lost		$10	$16	$20	Inga Moore		Macmil
1991	Six-Dinner Sid		$10	$16	$20	Inga Moore		S&S
1992	Favorite Mowgli Stories From The Jungle Book		$10	$16	$20	Rudyard Kipling		S&S
1992	Oh, Little Jack		$10	$16	$20	Inga Moore		Candle
1993	The Little Book Of Prayers		$10	$16	$20	Caroline Walsh (selected)		Kfisher
1994	A Big Day For Little Jack		$10	$14	$18	Inga Moore		Candle
1994	Anne Of Green Gables		$10	$14	$18	L. M. Montgomery		Holt
1995	A Spider Bought A Bicycle		$10	$14	$18	Michael Rosen (adapted)		Kfisher
1996	The River Bank		$8	$12	$16	Kenneth Grahame		Candle
1997	The Canterville Ghost		$8	$12	$16	Oscar Wilde		Candle
1998	The Adventures of Mr. Toad		$8	$12	$16	Inga Moore		Candle
2001	The Book of Beasts		$8	$10	$14	Edith Nesbit		Candle
2003	The Wind in the Willows		$8	$10	$14	Inga Moore		Candle
2004	The Reluctant Dragon		$6	$10	$12	Kenneth Grahame		Candle

Mordvinoff Nicholas

Year	Title	VG-	VG	VG+	Fine	Author	Award	Pub
1940	Picture Story Life Of Christ	$70	$90	$120		William Lipkind		Warner
1950	Russet And The Two Reds	$140	$200	$240		William Lipkind	CH	HBrace
1951	Finders Keepers	$260	$360	$440		William Lipkind	CM	HBrace
1952	Boy With A Harpoon	$50	$70	$90		William Lipkind		HBrace
1952	Even Steven	$50	$70	$90		William Lipkind		HBrace
1953	Star Man's Son 2250 A.D.	$120	$160	$200		Andre Norton		HBrace
1953	The Christmas Bunny	$50	$70	$90		William Lipkind		HBrace
1954	Alphonse That Bearded One	$50	$70	$90		Natalie Carlson		HBrace
1954	Boy Of The Islands	$50	$70	$90		William Lipkind		HBrace
1954	Circus Ruckus	$50	$70	$90		William Lipkind		HBrace
1956	Perry The Imp	$50	$70	$90		William Lipkind		HBrace
1958	The Magic Feather Duster	$50	$60	$80		William Lipkind		HBrace
1960	The Little Tiny Rooster	$50	$60	$80		William Lipkind		HBrace
1961	Billy the Kid	$50	$60	$80		William Lipkind		HBJ
1964	The Boy And The Forest	$50	$60	$80		William Lipkind		HBrace

Morgan Mary

Year	Title	VG-	VG	VG+	Fine	Author	Award	Pub
1987	All Things Bright And Beautiful		$12	$16	$20	Cecil F. Alexander		P&Munk
1989	Let's Trade		$10	$14	$18	Harriet Ziefert		VK
1989	Singing Birds And Flashing Fireflies		$10	$14	$18	Dorothy Hinshaw Patent		FWatts
1989	The Pudgy Merry Christmas Book		$10	$14	$18	Mary Morgan-Vanroyen		G&D
1990	Jake Baked The Cake		$10	$14	$18	B. G. Hennessy		Viking
1990	The Guppies Of Hilly Dale House		$10	$14	$18	Anne Baird		S&S
1991	Animal Tracks And Traces		$10	$14	$18	Kathleen V. Kudlinski		FWatts
1991	Buba Leah And Her Paper Children		$10	$14	$18	Lillian Hammer Ross		JPS
1992	Guess Who I Love?		$10	$14	$18	Mary Morgan-Vanroyen		G&D
1992	Puddle Wonderful		$10	$14	$18	Bobbi Katz		Random

Morgan   Mary

Year	Title	VG-	VG	VG+	Fine	Author	Award	Pub
1992	What Can Baby Do?		$10	$14	$18	Lauren Ariev		Western
1992	Who Are Baby's Friends?		$10	$14	$18	Lauren Ariev		Golden
1993	Asleep In A Heap		$8	$12	$16	Elizabeth Winthrop		Holiday
1993	Baby's First Mother Goose		$8	$12	$16	Wendy Cheyette Lewison		Western
1993	Bloomers!		$8	$12	$16	Rhoda Blumberg		BradP
1993	Christmas Cookies		$8	$12	$16	Wendy Cheyette Lewison		G&D
1993	Happy Thanksgiving!		$8	$12	$16	Wendy Cheyette Lewison		G&D
1993	Hugs		$8	$12	$16	Alice McLerran		Scholas
1993	Kisses		$8	$12	$16	Alice McLerran		Scholas
1994	Benjamin's Bugs		$8	$12	$16	Mary Morgan-Vanroyen		BradP
1994	I'm The Boss!		$8	$12	$16	Elizabeth Winthrop		Holiday
1996	Daddies		$8	$12	$16	Dian Curtis Regan		Scholas
1996	Hannah And Jack		$8	$12	$16	Mary Nethery		Athenm
1996	I Wear My Tutu Everywhere!		$8	$12	$16	Wendy Cheyette Lewison		G&D
1996	Mommies		$8	$12	$16	Dian Curtis Regan		Scholas
1997	Night Ride		$8	$10	$14	Mary Morgan-Vanroyen		Athenm
1998	Little Miss Muffet		$8	$10	$14	Mary Morgan-Vanroyen		PubIntl
1998	Our Puppies Are Growing		$8	$10	$14	Carolyn Otto		HCollins
1998	Where Do Bears Sleep?		$8	$10	$14	Barbara Shook Hazen		HCollins
1999	Gentle Rosie		$8	$10	$14	Mary Morgan-Vanroyen		Hyper
1999	The Tiger Has A Toothache		$8	$10	$14	Patricia Lauber		NGS
1999	Wild Rosie		$8	$10	$14	Mary Morgan-Vanroyen		Hyper
2000	Curious Rosie		$8	$10	$14	Mary Morgan-Vanroyen		Hyper
2000	Patient Rosie		$8	$10	$14	Mary Morgan-Vanroyen		Hyper
2000	The Way To Wyatt's House		$8	$10	$14	Nancy Carlstrom		Walker
2002	What The Baby Hears		$6	$10	$12	Laura Godwin		Hyper
2002	Wild Women Of The Wild West		$6	$10	$12	Jonah Winter		Holiday
2003	My Good Night Book		$6	$10	$12	Mary Morgan		Dutton
2003	Sleep Tight, Little Mouse		$6	$10	$12	Mary Morgan-Vanroyen		Knopf

Morimoto   Junko

Year	Title	VG-	VG	VG+	Fine	Author	Award	Pub
1983	The White Crane		$16	$25	$30	Helen Smith		Collins
1986	Kojuro And The Bears		$14	$20	$30	Helen Smith		Collins
1986	The Inch Boy		$14	$20	$30	Junko Morimoto		VK
1986	The Mouse's Marriage		$14	$20	$30	Junko Morimoto		VK
1990	My Hiroshima		$35	$50	$70	Junko Morimoto		Viking
1992	A Piece Of Straw		$12	$18	$25	Junko Morimoto		Collins
1995	One Hand Clapping		$10	$16	$20	Rafe Martin		Reynal
1997	The Two Bullies		$10	$16	$20	Junko Morimoto		Crown

Morrissey   Dean

Year	Title	VG-	VG	VG+	Fine	Author	Award	Pub
1979	Jewels Of Gwahlur		$25	$40	$50	Robert Ervin Howard		DGrant
1987	The Speckled Band		$25	$40	$50	Arthur Conan Doyle		StMart
1994	Ship Of Dreams		$16	$25	$30	Dean Morrissey		Abrams
1997	The Great Kettles		$10	$16	$20	Dean Morrissey		Abrams
1998	The Song Of Celestine		$10	$16	$20	J. Redfield & D. Lillegard		LBrown
2000	The Christmas Ship		$10	$14	$18	Dean Morrissey		HCollins
2001	A Christmas Carol		$8	$12	$16	Stephen Krensky		HCollins
2001	The Moon Robber		$8	$12	$16	Stephen Krensky		HCollins
2002	The Winter King		$8	$12	$16	Stephen Krensky		HCollins
2003	Monsters On The Radio		$8	$10	$14	Dean Morrissey		HCollins
2003	The Monster Trap		$8	$10	$14	Stephen Krensky		HCollins

Moser   Barry

Year	Title	VG-	VG	VG+	Fine	Author	Award	Pub
1976	Director Of Alienation: A Poem		$30	$40	$60	Lawrence Ferlinghetti		Main
1976	Late, Passing Prairie Farm: A Poem		$30	$40	$60	William Stafford		Main
1976	Rhode Island: An Historical Guide		$30	$40	$60	Sheila Steinberg		RIB
1976	The Invasion Of Italy: A Poem		$30	$40	$60	Louis Simpson		Main
1976	The Siren & The Seashell		$30	$40	$60	Octavio Paz		UTexas
1977	Man In A Metal Cage: Thirty-Three Poems		$80	$120	$160	Arthur MacAlpine		Penny
1977	The Song Of Songs		$25	$40	$50	Marcia Falk (translated)		HBJ
1977	Thistles And Thorns		$25	$40	$50	Paul Smyth		Abatt

MOSER   BARRY

Year	Title	VG-	VG	VG+	Fine	Author	Award	Pub
1979	Flowering Plants Of Massachusetts		$60	$90	$120	Vernon Ahmadjian		UMass
1979	Moby Dick, Or, The Whale		$50	$80	$100	Herman Melville		Arion
1979	The Adventurous Gardener		$25	$40	$50	Nancy Wilkes Bubel		Godine
1980	John Brown's Body		$25	$35	$50	Stephen Vincent Benét		BOM
1981	The Aeneid Of Virgil: A Verse Translation		$25	$35	$50	Allen Mandelbaum		UCal
1982	Alice's Adventures In Wonderland		$25	$35	$50	Lewis Carroll		UCal
1983	The Hunting Of The Snark		$25	$35	$50	Lewis Carroll		UCal
1983	Through The Looking-Glass		$25	$35	$50	Lewis Carroll		UCal
1984	Fifty Years Of American Poetry		$20	$30	$40	Robert Penn Warren		Abrams
1984	Frankenstein, Or, The Modern Prometheus		$20	$30	$40	Mary Shelley		UCal
1984	Rip Van Winkle		$20	$30	$40	Washington Irving		Penny
1985	Above The Oxbow: Selected Writings		$20	$30	$40	Sylvia Plath		Cataw
1985	Adventures Of Huckleberry Finn		$20	$30	$40	Mark Twain		UCal
1985	Tap Dancing For The Relatives: Poems		$20	$30	$40	Richard Michelson		Florida
1986	Bhagavad-Gita: Krishna's Counsel In Time Of War		$20	$30	$40	Barbara Stoler Miller		ColP
1986	Henry Thoreau: A Life Of The Mind		$20	$30	$40	Robert Richardson		UCal
1986	Jump!: The Adventures Of Brer Rabbit		$20	$30	$40	Joel Chandler Harris		HBJ
1986	Master Richard's Bestiary Of Love And Response		$20	$30	$40	Jeanette Beer (translated)		UCal
1986	Rip Van Winkle And The Legend Of Sleepy Hollow		$20	$30	$40	Washington Irving		HBJ
1986	The Scarlet Letter: A Romance		$20	$30	$40	Nathaniel Hawthorne		HBJ
1986	The Wonderful Wizard Of Oz		$20	$30	$40	L. Frank Baum		UCal
1987	I Remember Grandpa		$20	$30	$40	Truman Capote		Peach
1987	The Red Badge Of Courage		$20	$30	$40	Stephen Crane		HBJ
1987	The Robber Bridegroom		$20	$30	$40	Eudora Welty		HBJ
1988	Around The World In Eighty Days		$18	$25	$35	Jules Verne		BOW
1988	Casey At The Bat		$18	$25	$35	Ernest Lawrence Thayer		Godine
1988	In The Beginning		$35	$50	$70	Virginia Hamilton	NH	HBJ
1989	A River Runs Through It		$50	$80	$100	Norman Maclean		UChic
1989	East Of The Sun & West Of The Moon		$18	$25	$35	Nancy Willard		HBJ
1989	Jump On Over!		$18	$25	$35	Joel Chandler Harris		HBJ
1989	Sook's Cookbook		$18	$25	$35	Marie Rudisill		LP
1989	The Adventures Of Tom Sawyer		$18	$25	$35	Mark Twain		BOW
1989	The Ballad Of Biddy Early		$18	$25	$35	Nancy Willard		Knopf
1990	Little Tricker The Squirrel Meets Big Double The Bear		$16	$25	$30	Ken Kesey		Viking
1990	Sky Dogs		$25	$35	$50	Jane Yolen		HBJ
1990	Strange Case Of Dr. Jekyll And Mr. Hyde		$16	$25	$30	Robert Louis Stevenson		UNeb
1990	The King		$16	$25	$30	Donald Barthelme		H&Row
1990	The Tinderbox		$16	$25	$30	Hans Christian Andersen		LBrown
1991	Alice's Adventures In Wonderland		$16	$25	$30	Lewis Carroll		HBJ
1991	And Still The Turtle Watched		$16	$25	$30	Sheila MacGill-Callahan		Dial
1991	Appalachia: The Voices Of Sleeping Birds		$16	$25	$30	Cynthia Rylant		HBJ
1991	Kashtanka		$16	$25	$30	Anton Chekhov		Putnam
1991	St. Jerome And The Lion		$16	$25	$30	Margaret Hodges (retold)		Orchard
1991	The All Jahdu Storybook		$16	$25	$30	Virginia Hamilton		HBJ
1991	The Ghost Horse Of The Mounties		$16	$25	$30	Sean O Huigin		Godine
1991	The Tales Of Edgar Allan Poe		$16	$25	$30	Edgar Allan Poe		BOW
1992	Beauty And The Beast		$16	$25	$30	Nancy Willard		HBJ
1992	Messiah: The Wordbook For The Oratorio		$16	$25	$30	George Frideric Handel		Perfman
1992	Noah's Cats And The Devil's Fire		$16	$25	$30	Arielle North Olson		Orchard
1992	Polly Vaughn: A Traditional British Ballad		$20	$30	$40	Barry Moser		LBrown
1992	Prayers From The Ark: Selected Poems		$16	$25	$30	C. Bernos de Gasztold		Viking
1992	The Adventures Of Sherlock Holmes		$16	$25	$30	Arthur Conan Doyle		Morrow
1992	The Magic Wood: A Poem		$16	$25	$30	Henry Treece		HCollins
1992	The People's Text: A Citizen Reads The Constitution		$16	$25	$30	E.L. Doctorow		Nouveau
1992	Through The Mickle Woods		$16	$25	$30	Valiska Gregory		LBrown
1993	Fly!: A Brief History Of Flight Illustrated		$20	$30	$40	Barry Moser		Perfman
1993	Grass Songs		$16	$25	$30	Ann W. Turner		HBJ
1993	The Dreamer		$16	$25	$30	Cynthia Rylant		BSP
1993	The Magic Hare		$16	$25	$30	Lynne Reid Banks		Morrow
1993	The Mushroom Man		$16	$25	$30	Ethel Pochocki		GreenT
1993	The Other Wise Man		$16	$25	$30	Ruth Wells (retold)		Picture
1994	A Game Of Catch		$14	$20	$30	Richard Wilbur		HBrace
1994	Ariadne, Awake!		$14	$20	$30	Doris Orgel		Viking
1994	Big Mistreatin' Bittersweet'n' Blues		$14	$20	$30	Anna Olswanger		Bantam
1994	Cloud Eyes		$14	$20	$30	Kathryn Lasky		HBrace
1994	I Am The Dog, I Am The Cat		$14	$20	$30	Donald Hall		Dial
1994	John Bunyan's Pilgrim's Progress		$14	$20	$30	Gary D. Schmidt		EerdB

Moser   Barry

Year	Title	VG-	VG	VG+	Fine	Author	Award	Pub
1994	My Dog Rosie		$14	$20	$30	Isabelle Harper		BSP
1994	The Call Of The Wild		$14	$20	$30	Jack London		Macmil
1994	The Farm Summer 1942		$14	$20	$30	Donald Hall		Dial
1994	Tucker Pfeffercorn		$20	$30	$40	Barry Moser		LBrown
1994	Turtle Island ABC		$14	$20	$30	Gerald Hausman		HCollins
1995	Bingleman's Midway		$14	$20	$25	Karen Ackerman		Boyds
1995	My Cats Nick And Nora		$14	$20	$25	Isabelle Harper		BSP
1995	Prayer For The Opening Of Little League Season		$14	$20	$25	Willie Morris		HBrace
1995	The Iron Woman		$14	$20	$25	Ted Hughes		Dial
1995	What You Know First		$14	$20	$25	Patricia MacLachlan		HCollins
1995	Whistling Dixie		$14	$20	$25	Marcia Vaughan		HCollins
1996	A Brilliant Streak: The Making Of Mark Twain		$12	$18	$25	Kathryn Lasky		HBrace
1996	Eagle Boy: A Traditional Navajo Legend		$12	$18	$25	Gerald Hausman		HCollins
1996	First Love: A Gothic Tale		$12	$18	$25	Joyce Carol Oates		Ecco
1996	Good and Perfect Gifts		$12	$18	$25	O. Henry		LBrown
1996	Just So Stories		$12	$18	$25	Rudyard Kipling		BOW
1996	Sixty Years Of American Poetry		$12	$18	$25	Robert Penn Warren		Abrams
1996	When Birds Could Talk & Bats Could Sing		$12	$18	$25	Virginia Hamilton		BSP
1996	When Willard Met Babe Ruth		$12	$18	$25	Donald Hall		Bdeer
1997	A Ring Of Tricksters		$12	$18	$25	Virginia Hamilton		BSP
1997	Dippers		$12	$18	$25	Barbara Nichol		Tundra
1997	On Call Back Mountain		$12	$18	$25	Eve Bunting		BSP
1997	The Trojan War & The Adventures Of Odysseus		$12	$18	$25	Padraic Colum		Morrow
1998	Telling Time With Big Mama Cat		$12	$16	$20	Dan Harper		HBrace
1998	The Bird House		$12	$16	$20	Cynthia Rylant		BSP
1998	Trail Of Tears		$12	$16	$20	Tony Johnston		BSP
1998	Witches And Witch Hunts		$12	$16	$20	Milton Meltzer		BSP
1999	Grandpa's Gamble		$12	$16	$20	Richard Michelson		MCaven
2001	One Small Garden		$10	$14	$18	Barbara Nichol		Tundra
2001	Sister Tricksters		$10	$14	$18	Robert D. San Souci		S&S
2001	Sit, Truman		$10	$14	$18	Dan Harper		Harcort
2001	The Three Little Pigs		$12	$16	$20	Barry Moser (adapted0		LBrown
2001	The Witch Of Blackbird Pond		$10	$14	$18	Elizabeth George Speare		HM
2001	Those Building Men		$10	$14	$18	Angela Johnson		BSP
2002	Earthquack		$8	$12	$16	Margie Palatini		S&S
2002	That Summer		$8	$12	$16	Tony Johnston		Harcort
2003	A Year With Emerson		$8	$12	$16	Ralph Waldo Emerson		Godine
2003	Is He Dead?		$8	$12	$16	Mark Twain		UCal
2003	Voices Of Ancient Egypt		$8	$12	$16	Kay Winters		NGS
2003	Winter		$8	$12	$16	Gary D. Schmidt		Skylite
2004	Hummingbird Nest		$8	$10	$14	Kristine O'Connell George		Harcort
2004	Tales From Shakespeare		$8	$10	$14	Tina Packer		Scholas
2004	The Three Silly Billies		$8	$10	$14	Margie Palatini		S&S
2004	Wee Winnie Witch's Skinny		$8	$10	$14	Virginia Hamilton		BSP

Most   Bernard

Year	Title	VG-	VG	VG+	Fine	Author	Award	Pub
1978	If The Dinosaurs Came Back		$25	$40	$50	Bernard Most		HBJ
1978	Whatever Happened To The Dinosaurs?		$25	$40	$50	Bernard Most		HBJ
1980	Boo!		$18	$25	$35	Bernard Most		P-Hall
1980	My Very Own Octopus		$18	$25	$35	Bernard Most		HBJ
1980	There's An Ant In Anthony		$18	$25	$35	Bernard Most		Morrow
1980	Turn Over		$18	$25	$35	Bernard Most		P-Hall
1981	There's An Ape Behind The Drape		$18	$25	$35	Bernard Most		Morrow
1987	Dinosaur Cousins?		$14	$20	$30	Bernard Most		HBJ
1989	The Littlest Dinosaurs		$14	$20	$25	Bernard Most		HBJ
1990	Four & Twenty Dinosaurs		$12	$18	$25	Bernard Most		H&Row
1990	The Cow That Went Oink		$12	$18	$25	Bernard Most		HBJ
1991	A Dinosaur Named After Me		$12	$18	$25	Bernard Most		HBJ
1991	Pets In Trumpets		$12	$18	$25	Bernard Most		HBJ
1992	Happy Holidaysaurus!		$12	$18	$25	Bernard Most		HBJ
1992	Zoodles		$12	$18	$25	Bernard Most		HBJ
1993	Can You Find It?		$12	$16	$20	Bernard Most		HBrace
1993	Where To Look For A Dinosaur		$12	$16	$20	Bernard Most		HBJ
1994	Hippopotamus Hunt		$12	$16	$20	Bernard Most		HBrace
1994	How Big Were The Dinosaurs		$12	$16	$20	Bernard Most		HBrace

Most — Bernard

Year	Title	VG-	VG	VG+	Fine	Author	Award	Pub
1995	Catbirds & Dogfish		$10	$16	$20	Bernard Most		HBrace
1995	Dinosaur Questions		$10	$16	$20	Bernard Most		HBrace
1996	Cock-A-Doodle-Moo!		$10	$16	$20	Bernard Most		HBrace
1997	Moo-Ha!		$10	$16	$20	Bernard Most		HBrace
1997	Oink-Ha!		$10	$16	$20	Bernard Most		HBrace
1998	A Pair Of Protoceratops		$10	$14	$18	Bernard Most		HBrace
1998	A Trio Of Triceratops		$10	$14	$18	Bernard Most		HBrace
1998	Peek-A-Moo!		$10	$14	$18	Bernard Most		HBrace
1998	Row, Row, Row Your Goat		$10	$14	$18	Bernard Most		HBrace
1999	Catch Me If You Can!		$10	$14	$18	Bernard Most		HBrace
1999	The Very Boastful Kangaroo		$10	$14	$18	Bernard Most		HBrace
1999	Z-Z-Zoink!		$10	$14	$18	Bernard Most		HBrace
2000	ABC T-Rex		$8	$12	$16	Bernard Most		HBrace

Mozley — Charles

Year	Title	VG-	VG	VG+	Fine	Author	Award	Pub
1959	Black Beauty	$25	$35	$50		Anna Sewell		FWatts
1960	The First Book Of Tales Of Ancient Araby	$25	$30	$40		Charles Mozley (adapted)		FWatts
1966	Children Of The Bible	$25	$30	$40		Norman J. Bull		World
1968	A Shropshire Lad	$20	$30	$35		A. E. Housman		FWatts
1968	King Arthur	$20	$30	$35		Andrew Lang		FWatts
1968	The Psalms	$20	$30	$35		Elvajean Hall		FWatts
1969	A Christmas Carol	$20	$30	$35		Charles Dickens		FWatts
1969	Sonnets	$20	$30	$35		William Shakespeare		FWatts
1969	The Procession	$20	$30	$35		Margaret Mahy		FWatts
1969	The Rime Of The Ancient Mariner	$20	$30	$35		Samuel Taylor Coleridge		FWatts
1970	Selected Poems Of John Keats		$18	$25	$35	John Keats		FWatts
1970	Selected Poems Of Robert Browning		$18	$25	$35	Robert Browning		FWatts
1970	The Little Witch		$18	$25	$35	Margaret Mahy		FWatts
1970	The Proverbs		$18	$25	$35	Elvajean Hall		FWatts
1971	The Red Badge Of Courage		$18	$25	$35	Stephen Crane		Dutton

Muller — Jorg

Year	Title	VG-	VG	VG+	Fine	Author	Award	Pub
1976	The Bear Who Wanted to Be a Bear		$60	$80	$120	Jorg Steiner		Athenm
1977	The Changing City		$25	$40	$50	Jorg Muller		McEld
1977	The Changing Countryside		$25	$40	$50	Jorg Muller		Athenm
1978	Rabbit Island		$25	$40	$50	Jorg Steiner		HBJ
1982	The Sea People		$30	$50	$60	Jorg Steiner		Schock
1986	Peter And The Wolf		$20	$30	$40	Sergei Prokofiev		Knopf

Muller — Robin

Year	Title	VG-	VG	VG+	Fine	Author	Award	Pub
1986	The Sorcerer's Apprentice		$12	$16	$20	Robin Muller		SBurdet
1990	The Magic Paintbrush		$10	$14	$18	Robin Muller		VK
1991	The Nightwood		$10	$14	$18	Robin Muller		DoubleD
1993	Mollie Whuppie And The Giant		$8	$12	$16	Robin Muller		Scholas
1994	Little Wonder		$8	$12	$16	Robin Muller		NWP
2001	Oscar Wilde's The Happy Prince		$8	$10	$14	Oscar Wilde		Stodd
2002	Badger's New House		$6	$10	$12	Robin Muller		Holt

Munsinger — Lynn

Year	Title	VG-	VG	VG+	Fine	Author	Award	Pub
1978	An Arkful Of Animals		$25	$40	$50	William Cole		HM
1978	The Rootomom Tree		$25	$40	$50	Meg. Elbow		HM
1979	Martin By Himself		$25	$40	$50	Gloria Skurzynski		HM
1979	The Lizard Hunt		$25	$40	$50	Nancy Robison		LL&S
1979	What Should A Hippo Wear?		$25	$40	$50	Jane Sutton		HM
1980	Boris And The Monsters		$25	$35	$50	Elaine Macmann Willoughby		HM
1980	Hugh Pine		$25	$35	$50	Janwillem Van de Wetering		HM
1981	A Very Mice Joke Book		$25	$35	$50	Karen Jo Gounaud		HM
1981	Bedtime Mouse		$25	$35	$50	Sandol Stoddard		HM
1982	A Pet For Duck And Bear		$25	$35	$50	Judy Delton		AWhit
1982	Don't Tell Me A Ghost Story		$25	$35	$50	Phyllis Rose Eisenberg		HBJ
1982	How The Alligator Missed Breakfast		$25	$35	$50	Galway Kinnell		HM

Munsinger   Lynn

Year	Title	VG-	VG	VG+	Fine	Author	Award	Pub
1982	Howliday Inn		$25	$35	$50	James Howe		Athenm
1983	Duck Goes Fishing		$25	$35	$50	Judy Delton		AWhit
1983	The Mean, Clean, Giant Canoe Machine		$25	$35	$50	Joseph Slate		Crowell
1983	The Wizard, The Fairy, And The Magic Chicken		$30	$50	$60	Helen Lester		HM
1984	Bear And Duck On The Run		$20	$30	$40	Judy Delton		AWhit
1984	Monkey In The Middle		$20	$30	$40	Eve Bunting		HBJ
1984	My Mother Never Listens To Me		$20	$30	$40	Marjorie Weinman Sharmat		AWhit
1984	Nothing Sticks Like A Shadow		$20	$30	$40	Ann Tompert		HM
1984	Silly School Riddles		$20	$30	$40	Caroline Anne Levine		AWhit
1984	This Little Pig Had A Riddle		$20	$30	$40	Richard Latta		AWhit
1985	A Playhouse For Monster		$20	$30	$40	Virginia Mueller		AWhit
1985	Bedtime For Bear: Story		$20	$30	$40	Sandol Stoddard		HM
1985	It Wasn't My Fault		$30	$40	$60	Helen Lester		HM
1985	Monster And The Baby		$20	$30	$40	Virginia Mueller		AWhit
1985	The Elephant In Duck's Garden		$20	$30	$40	Judy Delton		AWhit
1985	When Small Is Tall & Other Read-Together Tales		$20	$30	$40	Seymour Reit		Random
1986	A Halloween Mask For Monster		$20	$30	$40	Virginia Mueller		AWhit
1986	A Porcupine Named Fluffy		$30	$40	$60	Helen Lester		HM
1986	Hugh Pine And The Good Place		$20	$30	$40	Janwillem Van de Wetering		HM
1986	Monster Can't Sleep		$20	$30	$40	Virginia Mueller		AWhit
1986	My New Boy		$20	$30	$40	Joan Phillips		Random
1986	Rabbit Goes To Night School		$20	$30	$40	Judy Delton		AWhit
1986	Read-A-Rebus		$20	$30	$40	W.H. Hooks		Random
1987	Norma Jean, Jumping Bean		$20	$30	$40	Joanna Cole		Random
1987	Pookins Gets Her Way		$25	$40	$50	Helen Lester		HM
1987	Zoo Song		$20	$30	$40	Barbara Bottner		Scholas
1988	A Week Of Raccoons		$18	$25	$35	Gloria Whelan		Knopf
1988	Hello, House!		$18	$25	$35	Linda Hayward		Random
1988	Spiffen, A Tale Of A Tidy Pig		$18	$25	$35	Mary Ada Schwartz		AWhit
1988	Tacky The Penguin		$25	$40	$50	Helen Lester		HM
1988	Underwear!		$18	$25	$35	Mary Elise Monsell		AWhit
1989	Ho For A Hat!		$18	$25	$35	William Jay Smith		Joy
1989	One Hungry Monster		$18	$25	$35	Susan Heyboer O'Keefe		Joy
1990	Don't Call Me Names		$16	$25	$30	Joanna Cole		Random
1990	Hedgehog Bakes A Cake		$16	$25	$30	Maryann Macdonald		Bantam
1990	The Revenge Of The Magic Chicken		$25	$35	$50	Helen Lester		HM
1990	Tomorrow, Up And Away!		$16	$25	$30	Pat Lowery Collins		HM
1991	Monster Goes To School		$16	$25	$30	Virginia Mueller		AWhit
1991	Monster's Birthday Hiccups		$16	$25	$30	Virginia Mueller		AWhit
1991	Rabbit's Birthday Kite		$16	$25	$30	Maryann Macdonald		Bantam
1991	Rooter Remembers		$16	$25	$30	Joanne Oppenheim		Viking
1991	The Rainbow Ribbon		$16	$25	$30	W.H. Hooks & B.D. Boegehold		Viking
1992	A Zooful Of Animals		$16	$25	$30	William Cole		HM
1992	Group Soup		$16	$25	$30	Barbara Brenner		Viking
1992	Me First		$20	$30	$40	Helen Lester		HM
1992	Rough, Tough, Rowdy		$16	$25	$30	William H. Hooks		Viking
1993	Babysitting For Benjamin		$16	$25	$30	Valiska Gregory		LBrown
1993	Just A Little Bit		$16	$25	$30	Ann Tompert		HM
1993	Lin's Backpack		$20	$30	$40	Helen Lester		ScottF
1994	Three Cheers For Tacky		$20	$30	$40	Helen Lester		HM
1995	Listen, Buddy		$18	$25	$35	Helen Lester		HM
1995	The Gator Girls		$14	$20	$25	J. & S. Cole & Calmenson		Morrow
1995	The Tale Of Custard The Dragon		$14	$20	$25	Ogden Nash		LBrown
1995	The Three Blind Mice Mystery		$14	$20	$25	Stephen Krensky		Yearlng
1995	Turtle Time: A Bedtime Story		$14	$20	$25	Sandol Stoddard		HM
1996	Custard The Dragon And The Wicked Knight		$12	$18	$25	Ogden Nash		LBrown
1996	Princess Penelope's Parrot		$16	$25	$30	Helen Lester		HM
1997	Bugs!		$12	$18	$25	David Greenberg		LBrown
1997	Rockin' Reptiles		$12	$18	$25	S. Calmenson & J. Cole		Morrow
1997	Tacky In Trouble		$16	$25	$30	Helen Lester		HM
1997	The Teeny Tiny Ghost		$12	$18	$25	Kay Winters		HCollins
1997	Wanted--Best Friend		$12	$18	$25	A.M. Monson		Dial
1998	Get Well, Gators!		$12	$16	$20	S. Calmenson & J. Cole		Morrow
1998	Mothers/Fathers		$12	$16	$20	Laura Joffe Numeroff		S&S
1998	What Daddies Do Best/What Mommies Do Best		$12	$16	$20	Laura Joffe Numeroff		S&S
1999	Hooway For Wodney		$14	$20	$25	Helen Lester		HM
1999	One Monkey Too Many		$12	$16	$20	Jackie French Koller		HBrace

Munsinger   Lynn

Year	Title	VG-	VG	VG+	Fine	Author	Award	Pub
1999	Who's Haunting The Teeny Tiny Ghost?		$12	$16	$20	Kay Winters		HCollins
2001	A Stormy Ride On Noah's Ark		$10	$14	$18	Patricia Hooper		Putnam
2001	Score One For The Sloths		$12	$16	$20	Helen Lester		HM
2001	Skunks		$10	$14	$18	David Greenberg		LBrown
2002	Birthday Zoo		$8	$12	$16	Deborah Rose		AWhit
2002	God Bless America		$8	$12	$16	Irving Berlin		HCollins
2002	Hunter's Best Friend At School		$8	$12	$16	Laura Elliott		HCollins
2002	Tackylocks And The Three Bears		$10	$16	$20	Helen Lester		HM
2003	My New Boy		$8	$12	$16	Joan Phillips		Random
2003	Snakes!		$8	$12	$16	David Greenberg		LBrown
2003	Something Might Happen		$10	$14	$18	Helen Lester		HM
2003	What Sisters Do Best		$8	$12	$16	Laura Joffe Numeroff		S&S
2004	Beatrice Doesn't Want To		$8	$10	$14	Laura Joffe Numeroff		Candle
2004	Hurty Feelings		$8	$12	$16	Helen Lester		HM
2004	The Teeny Tiny Ghost And The Monster		$8	$10	$14	Kay Winters		HCollins
2005	Seven Spunky Monkeys		$6	$10	$12	Jackie French Koller		Harcort

Murphy   Jill

Year	Title	VG-	VG	VG+	Fine	Author	Award	Pub
1977	The Duke Who Had Too Many Giraffes		$20	$30	$40	Fiona Macdonald		A&B
1980	Peace At Last		$14	$20	$25	Jill Murphy		Dial
1982	A Bad Spell For The Worst Witch		$14	$20	$25	Jill Murphy		VK
1983	Whatever Next!		$14	$20	$25	Jill Murphy		Macmil
1984	What Next, Baby Bear!		$12	$18	$25	Jill Murphy		Dial
1986	Five Minutes' Peace		$12	$16	$20	Jill Murphy		Putnam
1987	All In One Piece		$12	$16	$20	Jill Murphy		Putnam
1988	The Worst Witch		$12	$16	$20	Jill Murphy		VK
1988	The Worst Witch Strikes Again		$12	$16	$20	Jill Murphy		VK
1988	Worlds Apart		$12	$16	$20	Jill Murphy		Putnam
1992	Jeffrey Strangeways		$10	$16	$20	Jill Murphy		Candle
1994	A Quiet Night In		$10	$14	$18	Jill Murphy		Candle
1995	The Last Noo-Noo		$10	$14	$18	Jill Murphy		Candle
1995	The Worst Witch At Sea		$10	$14	$18	Jill Murphy		Candle
1998	A Piece Of Cake		$8	$12	$16	Jill Murphy		Candle
2002	All For One		$8	$10	$14	Jill Murphy		Candle

Muth   Jon J.

Year	Title	VG-	VG	VG+	Fine	Author	Award	Pub
1999	Come On, Rain		$12	$16	$20	Karen Hesse		Scholas
1999	Putnam And Pennyroyal		$12	$16	$20	Patrick Jennings		Scholas
2000	Gershon's Monster		$10	$14	$18	Eric Kimmel		Scholas
2000	Why I Will Never Ever Have Time To Read This Book		$10	$14	$18	Remy Charlip		Tricyc
2002	Our Gracie Aunt		$8	$12	$16	Jacqquelin Woodson		Hyper
2002	The Three Questions		$8	$12	$16	Leo Tolstoy		Scholas
2003	Old Turtle And The Broken Truth		$8	$12	$16	Douglas Wood		Scholas
2003	Stone Soup		$8	$12	$16	Jon J. Muth (retold)		Scholas
2004	Mr. George Baker		$8	$10	$14	Amy Hest		Candle
2004	No Dogs Allowed!		$8	$10	$14	Sonia Manzano		Athenm
2005	Zen Shorts		$14	$20	$30	Jon Muth	CH	Scholas
2006	I Will Hold You 'Til You Sleep		$6	$10	$12	Linda Zuckerman		Levine

Myers   Christopher

Year	Title	VG-	VG	VG+	Fine	Author	Award	Pub
1995	Shadow Of The Red Moon		$14	$20	$25	Walter Dean Myers		Scholas
1997	Harlem		$25	$35	$50	Walter Dean Myers	CH	Scholas
1998	This I Know		$10	$14	$18	Arlene Harris Mitchell		Scholas
1999	Black Cat		$18	$25	$35	Christopher Myers	CSKH	Scholas
1999	Monster		$35	$50	$70	Walter Dean Myers	Printz	HCollins
2000	Wings		$8	$12	$16	Christopher Myers		Scholas
2001	Fly		$8	$12	$16	Christopher Myers		Hyper
2002	A Time To Love		$8	$10	$14	Walter Dean Myers		Scholas

Natchev   Alexi

Year	Title	VG-	VG	VG+	Fine	Author	Award	Pub
1992	Matreshka		$16	$25	$30	Becky Ayres		DoubleD

Natchev   Alexi

Year	Title	VG-	VG	VG+	Fine	Author	Award	Pub
1994	Nathaniel Willy		$10	$14	$18	Judith Mathews		BradP
1994	The Hobyahs		$10	$14	$18	Robert D. San Souci		DoubleD
1995	Forri The Baker		$10	$14	$18	Edward Myers		Dial
1995	Monster Mischief		$10	$14	$18	Pamela Jane		Macmil
1995	Tom, Babette & Simon		$10	$14	$18	Avi		Macmil
1995	Wet World		$10	$14	$18	Norma Simon		Candle
1996	A Wagonload Of Fish		$8	$12	$16	Judit Bodnar		LL&S
1997	Harmonica Night		$8	$12	$16	Mary-Claire Helldorfer		Athenm
1999	The Night Of The Goat Children		$8	$12	$16	J. Patrick Lewis		Dial
2000	Peter And The Blue Witch Baby		$8	$10	$14	Robert D. San Souci		DoubleD
2001	The Magic Apple		$8	$10	$14	Corinne Demas		Golden
2003	The Tale Of Urso Brunov		$8	$10	$14	Brian Jacques		Philo

Nelson   Kadir

Year	Title	VG-	VG	VG+	Fine	Author	Award	Pub
1999	Brothers Of The Knight		$14	$20	$25	Debbie Allen		Dial
2000	Big Jabe		$10	$14	$18	Jerdine Nolen		Lothrop
2000	Dancing In The Wings		$10	$14	$18	Debbie Allen		Dial
2000	Salt In His Shoes		$10	$14	$18	Deloris & Roslyn Jordan		S&S
2002	Please, Baby, Please		$8	$12	$16	Spike Lee		S&S
2002	Under The Christmas Tree		$8	$12	$16	Nikki Grimes		HCollins
2004	Ellington Was Not A Street		$10	$14	$18	Ntozake Shange	CSKM	S&S

Nelvana Studios

Year	Title	VG-	VG	VG+	Fine	Author	Award	Pub
2001	Billy		$8	$10	$14	William Joyce		Disney
2001	Olie		$8	$10	$14	William Joyce		Disney
2001	Spot		$8	$10	$14	William Joyce		Disney
2001	Zowie		$8	$10	$14	William Joyce		Disney
2002	Peekaboo, You!		$8	$10	$14	William Joyce		Disney
2002	Rocket Up, Rolie!		$8	$10	$14	William Joyce		Disney
2002	Rolie Polie Olie And Friends		$8	$10	$14	William Joyce		Disney
2002	Rolie Polie Shapes		$8	$10	$14	William Joyce		Disney

Ness   Evaline

Year	Title	VG-	VG	VG+	Fine	Author	Award	Pub
1954	The Story Of Ophelia	$140	$180	$220		Mary Le Duc Gibbons		DoubleD
1957	The Bridge	$90	$120	$160		Charlton Ogburn		HM
1960	Lonely Maria	$50	$60	$80		Elizabeth Coatsworth		Pan
1960	Ondine	$50	$60	$80		Maurice Machado Osborne		HM
1961	Listen-The Birds	$50	$60	$80		Mary Britton Miller		Pan
1962	Macaroon	$50	$60	$80		Julia Cunningham		Pan
1962	Where Did Josie Go?	$50	$60	$80		Helen Elizabeth Buckley		LL&S
1963	A Gift For Sula Sula	$70	$90	$120		Evaline Ness		Scribnr
1963	All In The Morning Early	$140	$200	$240		Leclaire Alger	CH	HR&W
1963	Funny Town	$50	$60	$80		Eve Merriam		Crowell
1963	Josefina February	$70	$90	$120		Evaline Ness		Scribnr
1963	Some Cheese For Charles	$50	$60	$80		Helen Elizabeth Buckley		LL&S
1963	The Princess And The Lion	$50	$60	$80		Elizabeth Coatsworth		Pan
1963	Thistle And Thyme	$50	$60	$80		Sorche Nic Leodhas		HR&W
1964	A Pocketful Of Cricket	$140	$180	$240		Rebecca Caudill	CH	HR&W
1964	Candle Tales	$50	$60	$80		Julia Cunningham		Pan
1964	Exactly Alike	$60	$80	$100		Evaline Ness		Scribnr
1964	Josie And The Snow	$50	$60	$80		Helen Elizabeth Buckley		LL&S
1964	Pavo And The Princess	$60	$80	$100		Evaline Ness		Scribnr
1965	A Double Discovery	$60	$80	$100		Evaline Ness		Scribnr
1965	Coll And His White Pig	$40	$60	$70		Lloyd Alexander		HR&W
1965	Favorite Fairy Tales Told In Italy	$40	$60	$70		Virginia Haviland		LBrown
1965	Tom Tit Tot	$140	$180	$220		Evaline Ness	CH	Scribnr
1966	Pierino And The Bell	$40	$60	$70		Sylvia Cassedy		DoubleD
1966	Sam, Bangs, And Moonshine	$300	$400	$500		Evaline Ness	CM	HR&W
1967	Josie's Buttercup	$40	$50	$70		Helen Elizabeth Buckley		LL&S
1967	Mr. Miacca	$60	$80	$100		Evaline Ness		HR&W
1967	The Truthful Harp	$40	$50	$70		Lloyd Alexander		HR&W
1968	Kellyburn Braes	$40	$50	$70		Sorche Nic Leodhas		HR&W

Ness   Evaline

Year	Title	VG-	VG	VG+	Fine	Author	Award	Pub
1969	A Scottish Songbook	$40	$50	$70		Leclaire Alger		HR&W
1969	Long, Broad & Quickeye	$60	$80	$100		Evaline Ness		Scribnr
1970	Some Of The Days Of Everett Anderson		$30	$50	$60	Lucille Clifton		HR&W
1970	The Girl And The Goatherd		$50	$70	$90	Evaline Ness		Dutton
1971	Do You Have The Time, Lydia?		$40	$60	$90	Evaline Ness		Dutton
1971	Everett Anderson's Christmas Coming		$30	$50	$60	Lucille Clifton		HR&W
1971	Joey And The Birthday Present		$30	$50	$60	Maxine Kumin		McHill
1972	Old Mother Hubbard And Her Dog		$30	$50	$60	Sarah Catherine Martin		HR&W
1973	Don't You Remember?		$30	$50	$60	Lucille Clifton		Dutton
1973	The Woman Of The Wood		$30	$50	$60	Algernon Black		HR&W
1974	The Steamroller		$30	$40	$60	Margaret Wise Brown		Walker
1974	Yeck Eck		$40	$60	$80	Evaline Ness		Dutton
1975	Amelia Mixed The Mustard & Other Poems		$40	$60	$80	Evaline Ness		Scribnr
1975	The Wizard's Tears		$30	$40	$60	Maxine Kumin		McHill
1976	The Lives Of My Cat Alfred		$30	$40	$60	Nathan Zimelman		Dutton
1976	The Warmint		$30	$40	$60	Walter De La Mare		Scribnr
1978	The Devil's Bridge		$25	$40	$50	Charles Scribners		Scribnr
1978	What Color Is Caesar?		$25	$40	$50	Maxine Kumin		McHill
1979	Marcella's Guardian Angel		$35	$50	$70	Evaline Ness		Holiday
1980	Fierce The Lion		$35	$50	$70	Evaline Ness		Holiday
1983	The Hand-Me-Down Doll		$25	$35	$50	Steven Kroll		Holiday

Newberry   Clare Turlay

Year	Title	VG-	VG	VG+	Fine	Author	Award	Pub
1931	Herbert The Lion	$380	$500	$620		Clare Turlay Newberry		B&W
1936	Mittens	$160	$200	$260		Clare Turlay Newberry		H&B
1937	Babette	$160	$200	$260		Clare Turlay Newberry		H&B
1938	Barkis	$220	$280	$360		Clare Turlay Newberry	CH	H&B
1939	Cousin Toby	$140	$200	$240		Clare Turlay Newberry		H&B
1939	Herbert The Lion	$100	$120	$160		Clare Turlay Newberry		H&B
1940	April's Kittens	$200	$260	$320		Clare Turlay Newberry	CH	H&B
1940	Drawing A Cat	$70	$90	$120		Clare Turlay Newberry		Studio
1941	Lambert's Bargain	$100	$120	$160		Clare Turlay Newberry		H&B
1942	Marshmallow	$200	$260	$320		Clare Turlay Newberry	CH	H&B
1943	Cats	$90	$120	$160		Clare Turlay Newberry		H&B
1944	Pandora	$90	$120	$160		Clare Turlay Newberry		H&B
1946	The Kittens' ABC	$90	$120	$160		Clare Turlay Newberry		H&B
1948	Smudge	$80	$120	$140		Clare Turlay Newberry		H&B
1950	T-Bone, The Baby-Sitter	$180	$240	$300		Clare Turlay Newberry	CH	H&B
1952	Percy, Polly, And Pete	$120	$160	$200		Clare Turlay Newberry		H&B
1953	Ice Cream For Two	$80	$100	$140		Clare Turlay Newberry		H&B
1956	Cats & Kittens	$70	$100	$120		Clare Turlay Newberry		H&B
1958	Widget	$70	$100	$120		Clare Turlay Newberry		H&B
1959	Drawing Cats	$70	$100	$120		Clare Turlay Newberry		Studio
1961	Frosty	$70	$90	$120		Clare Turlay Newberry		H&B

Ninon   (Ninon MacKnight)

Year	Title	VG-	VG	VG+	Fine	Author	Award	Pub
1938	Hickory Lane	$40	$60	$70		Jane Quigg		TNelson
1938	Little Kari	$40	$60	$70		Ingrid Treider		LL&S
1939	Here Is A Book	$40	$60	$70		Marshall McClintock		Vnguard
1939	Little Amish Schoolhouse	$40	$60	$70		Ella Marie Seyfert		Crowell
1939	Time for Bed	$35	$50	$60		Inez Bertail		DD
1940	Along The Erie Towpath	$35	$50	$60		Enid La Monte Meadowcroft		Crowell
1941	Parasols Is For Ladies	$35	$40	$60		Elizabeth Hart Ritter		Winston
1941	Sing For Your Supper	$100	$120	$160		Lenora Mattingly Weber		Crowell
1941	The House In The Mountains	$35	$40	$60		Averli Demuth		H&B
1945	Fish Hook Island Mystery	$35	$40	$60		Lavinia R. Davis		DD
1946	Snow White	$35	$40	$60		Jacob & Wilhelm Grimm		GardenC
1947	For A Child	$35	$40	$60		Wilma McFarland		Westmin
1948	Kit Koala	$35	$40	$60		Ninon MacKnight		Rinehrt
1949	Bush Holiday	$60	$80	$100		Stephen Fennimore		GardenC
1950	Mr. Apple's Family	$30	$40	$50		Jean McDevitt		DoubleD
1952	Captain Apple's Ghost	$30	$40	$50		Evelyn Lampman		DoubleD
1956	ABC Of Cars And Trucks	$25	$35	$50		Anne Alexander		DoubleD
1962	The Very Little Boy	$25	$30	$40		Phyllis Krasilovsky		DoubleD

Nobens — Cheryl Ann

Year	Title	VG-	VG	VG+	Fine	Author	Award	Pub
1979	The Happy Baker		$18	$25	$35	Cheryl Ann Nobens		CRB
1982	Stories From The Blue Road		$14	$20	$25	Emily Crofford		CRB
1983	April Fools' Day		$14	$20	$25	Emily Kelley		CRB
1987	Shy Charlene And Sharyl		$12	$16	$20	Cheryl Ann Nobens		LBrown
1990	Montgomery's Time Zone		$10	$16	$20	Cheryl Ann Nobens		CRB
1992	Fun With E/E		$10	$16	$20	Shelly Nielsen		Abdo
1992	Fun With U/U		$10	$16	$20	Shelly Nielsen		Abdo

Noble — Trinka Hakes

Year	Title	VG-	VG	VG+	Fine	Author	Award	Pub
1979	The King's Tea		$35	$50	$70	Trinka Hakes Noble		Dial
1979	The Witch Who Lost Her Shadow		$25	$40	$50	Mary Calhoun		H&Row
1980	Karin's Christmas Walk		$18	$25	$35	Susan Pearson		Dial
1981	Will You Take Me To Town On Strawberry Day?		$18	$25	$35	Marilyn Singer		H&Row
1983	Hansy's Mermaid		$25	$35	$50	Trinka Hakes Noble		Dial
1984	Apple Tree Christmas		$20	$30	$40	Trinka Hakes Noble		Dial

Nolan — Dennis

Year	Title	VG-	VG	VG+	Fine	Author	Award	Pub
1976	Big Pig		$20	$30	$40	Dennis Nolan		P-Hall
1976	Monster Bubbles		$20	$30	$40	Dennis Nolan		P-Hall
1977	Alphabrutes		$16	$25	$30	Dennis Nolan		P-Hall
1977	Wizard McBean And His Flying Machine		$16	$25	$30	Dennis Nolan		P-Hall
1979	Llama Beans		$16	$25	$30	Charles Keller		P-Hall
1979	Witch Bazooza		$16	$25	$30	Dennis Nolan		P-Hall
1981	The Joy Of Chickens		$14	$20	$30	Dennis Nolan		P-Hall
1987	The Castle Builder		$12	$18	$25	Dennis Nolan		Macmil
1988	Step Into The Night		$12	$18	$25	Joanne Ryder		4Winds
1988	The Legend Of The White Doe		$12	$18	$25	William H. Hooks		Macmil
1989	Dove Isabeau		$12	$18	$25	Jane Yolen		HBJ
1989	Mockingbird Morning		$12	$18	$25	Joanne Ryder		4Winds
1989	Wolf Child		$12	$18	$25	Dennis Nolan		Macmil
1990	Dinosaur Dream		$12	$16	$20	Dennis Nolan		Macmil
1990	Heather Hiding		$12	$16	$20	Nancy Carlstrom		Macmil
1990	Under Your Feet		$12	$16	$20	Joanne Ryder		4Winds
1991	No Nap For Benjamin Badger		$12	$16	$20	Nancy Carlstrom		Macmil
1991	Savina, The Gypsy Dancer		$12	$16	$20	Ann Tompert		Macmil
1991	Wings		$12	$16	$20	Jane Yolen		HBJ
1992	An Ellis Island Christmas		$10	$16	$20	Maxinne Rhea Leighton		Viking
1993	The Sword In The Stone		$10	$16	$20	T. H. White		Philo
1994	The Gentleman And The Kitchen Maid		$10	$16	$20	Diane Stanley		Dial
1996	A Midsummer Night's Dream		$10	$14	$18	Bruce Coville		Dial
1997	Androcles And The Lion		$10	$14	$18	Dennis Nolan		HBrace
1999	Red Flower Goes West		$8	$12	$16	Ann W. Turner		Hyper
1999	Romeo And Juliet		$8	$12	$16	Bruce Coville		Dial
2000	Sherwood		$8	$10	$14	Jane Yolen		Philo
2001	Shadow Of The Dinosaurs		$8	$10	$14	Dennis Nolan		S&S
2001	The Dog Prince		$8	$10	$14	Lauren Mills		LBrown
2002	Fia & The Imp		$8	$10	$14	Lauren Mills		LBrown
2004	St. Francis Of Assisi		$6	$10	$12	Robert Francis Kennedy		Hyper
2004	The Perfect Wizard		$6	$10	$12	Jane Yolen		Dutton

Novak — Matt

Year	Title	VG-	VG	VG+	Fine	Author	Award	Pub
1986	Rolling		$14	$20	$30	Matt Novak		BradP
1987	Claude And Sun		$12	$16	$20	Matt Novak		BradP
1990	Mr. Floop's Lunch		$10	$16	$20	Matt Novak		Orchard
1991	While The Shepherd Slept		$10	$16	$20	Matt Novak		Orchard
1991	Who Does This Job?		$10	$16	$20	Pat Upton		Bell
1992	Elmer Blunt's Open House		$10	$16	$20	Matt Novak		Orchard
1993	It's About Time: Poems		$10	$16	$20	L.B. Hopkins (selected)		S&S
1993	The Last Christmas Present		$10	$16	$20	Matt Novak		Orchard
1994	Mouse TV		$10	$14	$18	Matt Novak		Orchard
1995	Gertie And Gumbo		$10	$14	$18	Matt Novak		Orchard
1995	Ghost And Pete		$10	$14	$18	Dayle Ann Dodds		Random

Novak   Matt

Year	Title	VG-	VG	VG+	Fine	Author	Award	Pub
1996	Newt		$8	$12	$16	Matt Novak		HCollins
1997	Little Slugger		$8	$12	$16	Heather Lowenberg		Random
1997	Twelve Snails To One Lizard		$8	$12	$16	Susan Hightower		S&S
1998	The Pillow War		$8	$12	$16	Matt Novak		Orchard
1999	Jazzbo Goes To School		$8	$12	$16	Matt Novak		Hyper
1999	The Robobots		$8	$12	$16	Matt Novak		DK
2000	Jazzbo And Googy		$8	$10	$14	Matt Novak		Hyper
2000	Little Wolf, Big Wolf		$8	$10	$14	Matt Novak		HCollins
2001	No Zombies Allowed		$8	$10	$14	Matt Novak		Athenm
2001	On Halloween Street		$8	$10	$14	Matt Novak		LSimon
2004	Too Many Bunnies		$6	$10	$12	Matt Novak		RoarB

Oakley   Graham

Year	Title	VG-	VG	VG+	Fine	Author	Award	Pub
1963	The White Dragon	$70	$90	$120		Richard Garnett		Vnguard
1966	Jack Of Dover	$30	$40	$50		Richard Garnett		Vnguard
1968	The Three Feathers	$30	$40	$50		Mollie Clarke		Follett
1971	The Dragon Hoard		$30	$50	$60	Tanith Lee		FSG
1973	The Church Cat Abroad		$60	$90	$120	Graham Oakley		Macmil
1973	The Church Mouse		$70	$100	$140	Graham Oakley		Macmil
1974	The Church Mice And The Moon		$60	$90	$120	Graham Oakley		Athenm
1976	The Church Mice Spread Their Wings		$60	$80	$120	Graham Oakley		Athenm
1977	The Church Mice Adrift		$60	$80	$120	Graham Oakley		Athenm
1979	The Church Mice At Bay		$50	$80	$100	Graham Oakley		Athenm
1980	Graham Oakley's Magical Changes		$35	$50	$70	Graham Oakley		Athenm
1980	The Church Mice At Christmas		$50	$70	$100	Graham Oakley		Athenm
1982	Hetty And Harriet		$25	$35	$50	Graham Oakley		Athenm
1983	The Church Mice In Action		$40	$60	$90	Graham Oakley		Athenm
1986	Henry's Quest		$20	$30	$40	Graham Oakley		Athenm
1992	The Church Mice And The Ring		$20	$30	$40	Graham Oakley		Athenm
1994	The Foxbury Force		$14	$20	$30	Graham Oakley		Athenm

O'Brian   William

Year	Title	VG-	VG	VG+	Fine	Author	Award	Pub
1968	Ear Book	$120	$160	$220		Al Perkins		BB

Offen   Hilda

Year	Title	VG-	VG	VG+	Fine	Author	Award	Pub
1981	A Treasury Of Bedtime Stories		$18	$25	$35	Linda Yeatman (retold)		LSimon
1987	My Favorite Goodnight Stories		$12	$16	$20	Linda Yeatman (retold)		LSimon
1987	My Favorite Nursery Rhymes		$12	$16	$20	Linda Yeatman (retold)		LSimon
1991	Nice Work, Little Wolf!		$12	$18	$25	Hilda Offen		Dutton
1993	A Fox Got My Socks		$10	$16	$20	Hilda Offen		Dutton
1993	Elephant Pie		$10	$16	$20	Hilda Offen		Dutton
1994	As Quiet As A Mouse		$10	$14	$18	Hilda Offen		Dutton
1994	Beauty And The Beast & Other Stories		$10	$14	$18	Margaret Carter (retold)		Kfisher
1994	Cinderella & Other Stories		$10	$14	$18	Margaret Carter (retold)		Kfisher
1994	Goldilocks & Other Stories		$10	$14	$18	Margaret Carter (retold)		Kfisher
1994	Little Red Riding Hood & Other Stories		$10	$14	$18	Margaret Carter (retold)		Kfisher
1994	Sleeping Beauty & Other Stories		$10	$14	$18	Margaret Carter (retold)		Kfisher
1994	Snow White & Other Stories		$10	$14	$18	Margaret Carter (retold)		Kfisher
1994	The Sheep Made A Leap		$10	$14	$18	Hilda Offen		Dutton
1994	The Three Little Pigs & Other Stories		$10	$14	$18	Margaret Carter (retold)		Kfisher
1994	The Ugly Duckling & Other Stories		$10	$14	$18	Margaret Carter (retold)		Kfisher
1996	Good Girl, Gracie Growler!		$8	$12	$16	Hilda Offen		GarethS

Olds   Elizabeth

Year	Title	VG-	VG	VG+	Fine	Author	Award	Pub
1941	Another Tiny Tim	$70	$90	$120		Elizabeth Olds		Sutton
1945	The Big Fire	$40	$60	$70		Elizabeth Olds		HM
1948	Riding The Rails	$40	$60	$70		Elizabeth Olds		HM
1951	Feather Mountain	$120	$160	$200		Elizabeth Olds	CH	HM
1958	Deep Treasure	$35	$50	$60		Elizabeth Olds		HM
1962	Plop Plop Ploppie	$35	$40	$60		Elizabeth Olds		Scribnr
1963	Little Una	$35	$40	$60		Elizabeth Olds		Scribnr

O'Malley   Kevin

Year	Title	VG-	VG	VG+	Fine	Author	Award	Pub
1992	Froggy Went A-Courtin		$16	$25	$30	Kevin O'Malley		ST&C
1993	Bruno, You're Late For School		$12	$16	$20	Kevin O'Malley		ST&C
1993	Row, Row, Row Your Boat		$12	$16	$20	Joanne Oppenheim		Bantam
1993	The Box		$12	$16	$20	Kevin O'Malley		ST&C
1993	Who Killed Cock Robin?		$12	$16	$20	Kevin O'Malley		LL&S
1994	Cinder Edna		$12	$16	$20	Ellen Jackson		LL&S
1994	What's For Lunch?		$12	$16	$20	John Schindel		LL&S
1995	Miss Malarkey Doesn't Live In Room 10		$10	$16	$20	Judy Finchler		Walker
1995	Roller Coaster		$10	$16	$20	Kevin O'Malley		LL&S
1995	Run! Run!		$10	$16	$20	Joann Vandine		Mondo
1995	There Was A Crooked Man		$10	$16	$20	Kevin O'Malley		LSimon
1996	Big Squeak, Little Squeak		$10	$16	$20	Robert Kraus		Orchard
1996	Carl Caught A Flying Fish		$10	$16	$20	Kevin O'Malley		S&S
1996	Too Many Kangaroo Things To Do!		$10	$16	$20	Stuart J. Murphy		HCollins
1997	Chanukah In Chelm		$10	$16	$20	David A. Adler		LL&S
1997	Colliding With Chris		$10	$16	$20	Dan Harder		Hyper
1997	Rosie's Fiddle		$10	$16	$20	Phyllis Root		LL&S
1997	Velcome		$10	$16	$20	Kevin O'Malley		Walker
1998	The Planets In Our Solar System		$10	$14	$18	Franklyn M. Branley		HCollins
1999	Jump, Kangaroo, Jump		$10	$14	$18	Stuart J. Murphy		HCollins
1999	Leo Cockroach Toy Tester		$10	$14	$18	Kevin O'Malley		Walker
2000	Bud		$8	$12	$16	Kevin O'Malley		Walker
2000	Miss Malarkey Won't Be In Today		$8	$12	$16	Judy Finchler		Walker
2000	Testing Miss Malarkey		$8	$12	$16	Judy Finchler		Walker
2000	The Lucky Lizard		$8	$12	$16	Ellen A. Kelley		Dutton
2001	Big And Noisy Simon		$8	$12	$16	Joseph E. Wallace		Hyper
2001	Dinosaur Deals		$8	$12	$16	Stuart J. Murphy		HCollins
2001	Humpty Dumpty Egg-Splodes		$8	$12	$16	Kevin O'Malley		Walker
2002	Little Buggy		$8	$10	$14	Kevin O'Malley		Harcort
2002	Making Plum Jam		$8	$10	$14	John W. Stewig		Hyper
2002	Twelve Days		$8	$10	$14	Gordon Snell		HCollins
2002	You're A Good Sport, Miss Malarkey		$8	$10	$14	Judy Finchler		Walker
2003	Herbert Fieldmouse, Secret Agent		$8	$10	$14	Kevin O'Malley		Mondo
2003	Little Buggy Runs Away		$8	$10	$14	Kevin O'Malley		GB
2003	Mount Olympus Basketball		$8	$10	$14	Kevin O'Malley		Walker
2003	Straight To The Pole		$8	$10	$14	Kevin O'Malley		Walker
2004	Lucky Leaf		$8	$10	$14	Kevin O'Malley		Walker
2004	Miss Malarkey's Field Trip		$8	$10	$14	Judy Finchler		Walker

Ormerod   Jan

Year	Title	VG-	VG	VG+	Fine	Author	Award	Pub
1981	Hairs In The Palm of Your Hand		$25	$35	$50	Jan Mark		Kestrel
1981	Sunshine		$25	$35	$50	Jan Ormerod		LL&S
1982	Moonlight		$16	$25	$30	Jan Ormerod		LL&S
1983	Be Brave, Billy		$16	$25	$30	Jan Ormerod		Dent
1983	Lanky Longlegs		$16	$25	$30	Karin Lorentzen		Athenm
1983	Rhymes around the day		$16	$25	$30	Jan Ormerod		LL&S
1984	101 Things To Do With A Baby		$16	$25	$30	Jan Ormerod		LL&S
1985	Dad's Back		$16	$25	$30	Jan Ormerod		LL&S
1985	Messy Baby		$16	$25	$30	Jan Ormerod		LL&S
1985	Reading		$16	$25	$30	Jan Ormerod		LL&S
1985	Sleeping		$16	$25	$30	Jan Ormerod		LL&S
1986	Happy Christmas, Gemma		$14	$20	$30	Sarah Hayes		LL&S
1986	Just Like Me		$14	$20	$30	Jan Ormerod		LL&S
1986	Our Ollie		$14	$20	$30	Jan Ormerod		LL&S
1986	Silly Goose		$14	$20	$30	Jan Ormerod		LL&S
1986	The Story of Chicken Licken		$14	$20	$30	Jan Ormerod		LL&S
1986	Young Joe		$14	$20	$30	Jan Ormerod		LL&S
1987	Bend and Stretch		$14	$20	$30	Jan Ormerod		LL&S
1987	Making Friends		$14	$20	$30	Jan Ormerod		LL&S
1987	Mum's Home		$14	$20	$30	Jan Ormerod		Walker
1987	This Little Nose		$14	$20	$30	Jan Ormerod		LL&S
1988	Eat Up, Gemma		$14	$20	$30	Sarah Hayes		LL&S
1988	Peter Pan		$14	$20	$30	J. M. Barrie		VK
1989	Kitten Day		$14	$20	$25	Jan Ormerod		Walker
1989	The Saucepan Game		$14	$20	$25	Jan Ormerod		LL&S

Ormerod   Jan

Year	Title	VG-	VG	VG+	Fine	Author	Award	Pub
1991	One Ballerina Two		$12	$18	$25	Vivian French		Walker
1991	The Chewing-Gum Rescue		$12	$18	$25	Margaret Mahy		Over
1991	When We Went To The Zoo		$12	$18	$25	Jan Ormerod		LL&S
1992	Come Back, Kittens		$12	$18	$25	Jan Ormerod		LL&S
1992	Come Back, Puppies		$12	$18	$25	Jan Ormerod		LL&S
1992	Sunflakes		$12	$18	$25	Lilian Moore		Clarion
1992	The Magic Skateboard		$12	$18	$25	Enid Richemont		Candle
1993	Father Christmas and the Donkey		$12	$16	$20	Elizabeth Clark		Viking
1993	Joe Can Count		$12	$16	$20	Jan Ormerod		Mulbery
1993	Midnight Pillow Fight		$12	$16	$20	Jan Ormerod		Candle
1994	Grandfather and I		$12	$16	$20	Helen Elizabeth Buckley		LL&S
1994	Grandmother and I		$12	$16	$20	Helen Elizabeth Buckley		LL&S
1994	Jan Ormerod's To Baby With Love		$12	$16	$20	Jan Ormerod		LL&S
1995	Cloud Nine		$10	$16	$20	Norman Silver		Clarion
1996	Ms. MacDonald Has A Class		$10	$16	$20	Jan Ormerod		Clarion
1996	Sky Dancer		$10	$16	$20	Jack Bushnell		LL&S
1998	A Twist in the Tail		$10	$14	$18	Mary Hoffman		Holt
1998	Rock-A-Baby		$10	$14	$18	Jan Ormerod		Dutton
1998	The Water Babies		$10	$14	$18	Josephine Poole		Millbk
1998	Who's Whose?		$10	$14	$18	Jan Ormerod		LL&S
1999	Ben Goes Swimming		$10	$14	$18	Jan Ormerod		HCollins
1999	Emily Dances		$10	$14	$18	Jan Ormerod		Tupelo
1999	One, Two, Three, Jump!		$10	$14	$18	Penelope Lively		McEld
1999	Where Did Josie Go?		$10	$14	$18	Helen Elizabeth Buckley		LL&S
2001	Goodbye, Mousie		$8	$12	$16	Robie H. Harris		McEld
2001	Miss Mouse Takes Off		$8	$12	$16	Jan Ormerod		HCollins
2001	Miss Mouse's Day		$8	$12	$16	Jan Ormerod		HCollins
2001	Ten in a Bed		$8	$12	$16	Jan Ormerod		DK
2002	Hat Off, Baby!		$8	$10	$14	Jan Ormerod		Barrn
2003	I Am Not Going to School Today		$8	$10	$14	Robie H. Harris		McEld
2003	If You're Happy And You Know It!		$8	$10	$14	Jan Ormerod		StarB
2004	Emily and Albert		$8	$10	$14	Jan Ormerod		Chron

Owens   Gail

Year	Title	VG-	VG	VG+	Fine	Author	Award	Pub
1972	Sprout And The Dogsitter		$40	$60	$90	Jenifer Wayne		McHill
1974	Sprout And The Helicopter		$30	$40	$60	Jenifer Wayne		McHill
1974	Stranded		$20	$30	$40	Matt Christopher		LBrown
1974	The Winds Of Time		$20	$30	$40	Barbara Corcoran		Athenm
1975	A Bedtime Story		$30	$40	$60	Joan Goldman Levine		Dutton
1975	Romansgrove		$20	$30	$40	Mabel Esther Allan		Athenm
1975	The Santa Claus Mystery		$30	$40	$60	Joan Goldman Levine		Dutton
1975	Witch's Sister		$20	$30	$40	Phyllis Reynolds Naylor		Athenm
1976	Connie		$20	$30	$40	Anne Alexander		Athenm
1976	F*T*C Superstar		$20	$30	$40	Mary Anderson		Athenm
1976	I'll Tell On You		$30	$40	$60	Joan M. Lexau		Dutton
1976	Sprout		$30	$40	$60	Jenifer Wayne		McHill
1976	Sprout And The Magician		$30	$40	$60	Jenifer Wayne		McHill
1976	Sprout's Window Cleaner		$30	$40	$60	Jenifer Wayne		McHill
1976	The Eels' Strange Journey		$30	$40	$60	Judi Friedman		Crowell
1977	A Horse For X.Y.Z		$25	$40	$50	Louise Moeri		Dutton
1977	Julia And The Hand Of God		$20	$30	$40	Eleanor Cameron		Dutton
1977	Witch Water		$20	$30	$40	Phyllis Reynolds Naylor		Athenm
1978	Ella Of All Of A Kind Family		$20	$30	$40	Sydney Taylor		Dutton
1978	Hail, Hail, Camp Timberwood		$20	$30	$40	Ellen Conford		LBrown
1978	Jaky Or Dodo?		$25	$40	$50	Natalie Carlson		Scribnr
1978	Something About A Mermaid		$25	$40	$50	Carolyn Polese		Dutton
1978	Spider In The Sky		$25	$40	$50	Anne K. Rose (adapted)		H&Row
1978	The Witch Herself		$20	$30	$40	Phyllis Reynolds Naylor		Athenm
1978	Trees Are Forever		$25	$40	$50	Eleanor B. Heady		PMagP
1978	Unhurry Harry		$25	$40	$50	Eve Merriam		4Winds
1979	Fog In The Meadow		$25	$40	$50	Joanne Ryder		H&Row
1979	I Hate Red Rover		$25	$40	$50	Joan M. Lexau		Dutton
1979	Safe As The Grave		$25	$40	$50	Caroline B. Cooney		CM&G
1979	The Magic Grandfather		$18	$25	$35	Jay Williams		4Winds
1980	Danny Loves A Holiday		$25	$35	$50	Sydney Taylor		Dutton

Owens   Gail

Year	Title	VG-	VG	VG+	Fine	Author	Award	Pub
1980	Out In The Dark And Daylight		$18	$25	$35	Aileen Fisher		H&Row
1980	The Way To Windra		$18	$25	$35	Patricia Goehner Baehr		FWarne
1981	Angie's First Case		$18	$25	$35	Donald J. Sobol		4Winds
1981	Just Like Sisters		$18	$25	$35	LouAnn Gaeddert		Dutton
1981	The Cybil War		$18	$25	$35	Betsy Cromer Byars		Viking
1981	The Oldest Kid		$25	$35	$50	Elaine Knox-Wagner		AWhit
1981	The Paper Caper		$25	$35	$50	Caroline B. Cooney		CM&G
1982	A Bundle Of Sticks		$16	$25	$30	Pat Rhoads Mauser		Athenm
1982	Katy Did It		$16	$25	$30	Victoria Boutis		Green
1982	Mr. Adams's Mistake		$25	$35	$50	Peggy Parish		Macmil
1982	That Julia Redfern		$16	$25	$30	Eleanor Cameron		Dutton
1983	Hurricane		$25	$35	$50	Faith McNulty		H&Row
1984	Ash Brooks, Super Ranger		$16	$25	$30	Wanda VanHoy Smith		Scribnr
1984	Julia's Magic		$16	$25	$30	Eleanor Cameron		Dutton
1984	Making Room For Uncle Joe		$20	$30	$40	Ada Bassett Litchfield		AWhit
1984	Stall Buddies		$20	$30	$40	Penny Pollock		Putnam
1984	The Hot & Cold Summer		$16	$25	$30	Johanna Hurwitz		Morrow
1985	Benjy The Football Hero		$16	$25	$30	Jean Van Leeuwen		Dial
1985	Cassie Bowen Takes Witch Lessons		$16	$25	$30	Anna Grossnickle Hines		Dutton
1985	Ency. Brown - Case Of The Mysterious Handprints		$20	$30	$40	Donald J. Sobol		Morrow
1985	The Adventures Of Ali Baba Bernstein		$20	$30	$40	Johanna Hurwitz		Morrow
1986	Addie Across The Prairie		$14	$20	$30	Laurie Lawlor		AWhit
1986	Tac's Island		$20	$30	$40	Ruth Yaffe Radin		Macmil
1987	I Had A Friend Named Peter		$20	$30	$40	Janice Cohn		Morrow
1987	Tac's Turn		$20	$30	$40	Ruth Yaffe Radin		Macmil
1987	The Daring Rescue Of Marlon The Swimming Pig		$20	$30	$40	Susan Saunders		Random
1987	Vinegar Pancakes And Vanishing Cream		$14	$20	$30	Bonnie Pryor		Morrow
1988	Ency. Brown And The Case Of The Treasure Hunt		$18	$25	$35	Donald J. Sobol		Morrow
1989	Good-Bye, Sammy		$18	$25	$35	Liza Ketchum		Holiday
1989	Hurray For Ali Baba Bernstein		$14	$20	$25	Johanna Hurwitz		Morrow
1989	I'm The Big Sister Now		$18	$25	$35	Michelle Emmert		AWhit
1990	Amy, Ben, And Catalpa The Cat		$16	$25	$30	Alma S. Coon		Cwill
1990	Ency. Brown - Case Of The Disgusting Sneakers		$12	$18	$25	Donald J. Sobol		Morrow
1991	Annabelle's Un-Birthday		$12	$18	$25	Steven Kroll		Macmil
1991	Going Places		$16	$25	$30	Harriet Webster		Scribnr
1991	The Cat Next Door		$16	$25	$30	Betty Ren Wright		Holiday
1992	Great-Grandma Tells Of Threshing Day		$16	$25	$30	Verda Cross		Whitman
1993	Poison Ivy And Eyebrow Wigs		$12	$16	$20	Bonnie Pryor		Morrow
1993	The Up & Down Spring		$12	$16	$20	Johanna Hurwitz		Morrow
1994	Molly's Rosebush		$14	$20	$30	Janice Cohn		AWhit
1994	Why Did It Happen?		$14	$20	$30	Janice Cohn		Morrow
1995	Sad Days, Glad Days		$14	$20	$25	DeWitt Hamilton		AWhit
1996	The Down & Up Fall		$10	$16	$20	Johanna Hurwitz		Morrow

Oxenbury   Helen

Year	Title	VG-	VG	VG+	Fine	Author	Award	Pub
1968	Helen Oxenbury's Numbers Of Things	$60	$80	$100		Helen Oxenbury		DelaP
1968	The Great Big Enormous Turnip	$40	$50	$70		Alexei Tolstoy		FWatts
1969	Letters Of Thanks	$40	$50	$70		Manghanita Kempadoo		S&S
1969	The Dragon Of An Ordinary Family	$40	$50	$70		Margaret Mahy		FWatts
1970	The Hunting Of The Snark		$30	$50	$60	Lewis Carroll		FWatts
1970	The Quangle Wangle's Hat		$70	$100	$140	Helen Oxenbury	GM	FWatts
1971	Helen Oxenbury's ABC Of Things		$40	$60	$90	Helen Oxenbury		Heine
1971	Meal One		$30	$50	$60	Ivor Cutler		FWatts
1974	Cakes And Custard: Children's Rhymes		$30	$40	$60	Brian Alderson (selected)		Heine
1975	Balooky Klujypop		$30	$40	$60	Ivor Cutler		Heine
1976	Elephant Girl		$30	$40	$60	Ivor Cutler		Morrow
1976	The Animal House		$30	$40	$60	Ivor Cutler		Heine
1978	A Child's Book Of Manners		$25	$40	$50	Fay Maschler		JCape
1979	The Queen And Rosie Randall		$35	$50	$70	Helen Oxenbury		Morrow
1980	729 Curious Creatures		$35	$50	$70	Helen Oxenbury		H&Row
1980	729 Merry Mix-Ups		$35	$50	$70	Helen Oxenbury		H&Row
1980	729 Puzzle People		$35	$50	$70	Helen Oxenbury		H&Row
1981	Dressing		$25	$35	$50	Helen Oxenbury		Wander
1981	Family		$25	$35	$50	Helen Oxenbury		Wander
1981	Friends		$25	$35	$50	Helen Oxenbury		Wander

Oxenbury — Helen

Year	Title	VG-	VG	VG+	Fine	Author	Award	Pub
1981	Playing		$25	$35	$50	Helen Oxenbury		Wander
1981	Tiny Tim: Verses		$25	$35	$50	Jill Bennett (selected)		DelaP
1981	Working		$25	$35	$50	Helen Oxenbury		Wander
1982	Beach Day		$25	$35	$50	Helen Oxenbury		Dial
1982	Good Night, Good Morning		$25	$35	$50	Helen Oxenbury		Dial
1982	Mother's Helper		$25	$35	$50	Helen Oxenbury		Dial
1982	Shopping Trip		$25	$35	$50	Helen Oxenbury		Dial
1983	Eating Out		$25	$35	$50	Helen Oxenbury		Dutton
1983	First Day Of School		$25	$35	$50	Helen Oxenbury		Dial
1983	Playschool		$25	$35	$50	Helen Oxenbury		Walker
1983	The Birthday Party		$25	$35	$50	Helen Oxenbury		Dutton
1983	The Car Trip		$25	$35	$50	Helen Oxenbury		Dial
1983	The Checkup		$25	$35	$50	Helen Oxenbury		Dial
1983	The Dancing Class		$25	$35	$50	Helen Oxenbury		Dial
1983	The Drive		$25	$35	$50	Helen Oxenbury		Walker
1984	Grandma And Grandpa		$20	$30	$40	Helen Oxenbury		Dial
1984	Our Dog		$20	$30	$40	Helen Oxenbury		Dial
1984	The Important Visitor		$20	$30	$40	Helen Oxenbury		Dial
1985	I Hear		$20	$30	$40	Helen Oxenbury		Walker
1985	The Helen Oxenbury Nursery Story Book		$20	$30	$40	Helen Oxenbury		Knopf
1986	The Helen Oxenbury Nursery Rhyme Book		$20	$30	$40	Brian Alderson (selected)		Morrow
1988	Tom And Pippo In The Garden		$18	$25	$35	Helen Oxenbury		Aladd
1989	Pippo Gets Lost		$18	$25	$35	Helen Oxenbury		Aladd
1989	We're Going On A Bear Hunt		$18	$25	$35	Michael Rosen (adapted)		McEld
1991	Monkey See, Monkey Do		$16	$25	$30	Helen Oxenbury		Dial
1992	Farmer Duck		$16	$25	$30	Martin Waddell		Candle
1993	The Three Little Wolves And The Big Bad Pig		$16	$25	$30	Eugene Trivizas		McEld
1993	Tom And Pippo And The Bicycle		$16	$25	$30	Helen Oxenbury		Candle
1993	Tom And Pippo On The Beach		$16	$25	$30	Helen Oxenbury		Candle
1994	Favorite Nursery Stories		$14	$20	$30	Helen Oxenbury		Macmil
1994	First Nursery Stories		$14	$20	$30	Helen Oxenbury		Macmil
1994	It's My Birthday		$14	$20	$30	Helen Oxenbury		Candle
1994	So Much		$14	$20	$30	Trish Cooke		Candle
1995	I Can		$14	$20	$25	Helen Oxenbury		Candle
1995	I See		$14	$20	$25	Helen Oxenbury		Candle
1995	I Touch		$14	$20	$25	Helen Oxenbury		Candle
1995	Puzzle People		$14	$20	$25	Helen Oxenbury		Candle
1996	The Candlewick Book Of First Rhymes		$12	$18	$25	Helen Oxenbury		Candle
1998	Tom And Pippo Go For A Walk		$12	$16	$20	Helen Oxenbury		LSimon
1998	Tom And Pippo Read A Story		$12	$16	$20	Helen Oxenbury		LSimon
1998	Tom And Pippo's Day		$12	$16	$20	Helen Oxenbury		LSimon
1999	Alice's Adventures In Wonderland		$35	$50	$70	Lewis Carroll	GM	Candle
1999	Alice's Adventures In Wonderland (S/N)		$100	$160	$220	Lewis Carroll	GM	Candle
2000	Franny B. Kranny, There's A Bird In Your Hair!		$10	$14	$18	Harriet Lerner		HCollins
2000	The Growing Story		$10	$14	$18	Ruth Krauss		HCollins
2002	Big Momma Makes The World		$8	$12	$16	Phyllis Root		Candle

Paflin — Roberta

Year	Title	VG-	VG	VG+	Fine	Author	Award	Pub
1941	Little Dog That Would Not Wag His Tail	$50	$60	$80		Edna Groff Deihl		Gabriel
1942	This Little Piggy	$35	$40	$60		Phyllis Fraser		S&S
1945	Mother Goose Tells Time	$35	$40	$60		Alice Schneider		Cit
1945	Tales From Grimm	$35	$40	$60		Sarah Wright		Dutton
1946	Storyland	$35	$40	$60		Mary Patric (adapted)		PiedP
1946	Tales From Andersen	$35	$40	$60		Sarah Wright		Dutton

Palazzo — Tony

Year	Title	VG-	VG	VG+	Fine	Author	Award	Pub
1941	Forest Patrol	$50	$60	$80		Jim Kjelgaard		Holiday
1946	Timothy Turtle	$140	$180	$220		Al Graham	CH	RWelch
1947	The Mouse With The Small Guitar	$40	$60	$70		Al Graham		RWelch
1951	Federico The Flying Squirrel	$50	$70	$90		Tony Palazzo		Viking
1951	The Story Of Serapina	$40	$50	$70		Anne H. White		Viking
1952	Hubbub In The Hollow	$40	$50	$70		Irene Smith		Whittle
1953	An Otter's Story	$40	$50	$70		Emil E. Liers		Viking
1956	Nonsense Book	$35	$50	$60		Edward Lear		GardenC

Palazzo   Tony

Year	Title	VG-	VG	VG+	Fine	Author	Award	Pub
1956	The Chicken In The Tunnel	$35	$50	$60		Jane Thayer		Morrow
1957	The Giant Nursery Book	$35	$50	$60		Tony Palazzo		GardenC
1958	Animals 'Round The Mulberry Bush	$35	$50	$60		Tony Palazzo		GardenC
1958	Tales Of Don Quixote And His Friends	$35	$50	$60		M.I de Cervantes Saavedra		GardenC
1958	The Little Red Hen	$35	$50	$60		Tony Palazzo		GardenC
1959	Goldilocks And The Three Bears	$35	$50	$60		Tony Palazzo (adapted)		GardenC
1959	Simple Simon	$35	$50	$60		Tony Palazzo		GardenC
1959	The Giant Playtime Nursery Book	$35	$50	$60		Tony Palazzo		GardenC
1960	Animal Babies	$35	$40	$60		Tony Palazzo		GardenC
1960	The Mother Goose Nursery Almanac	$35	$40	$60		Tony Palazzo		GardenC
1961	Animal Folk Tales Of America	$35	$40	$60		Tony Palazzo		DoubleD
1961	Let's Go To The Circus	$35	$40	$60		Tony Palazzo		DoubleD
1961	The Story Of Peter And The Wolf	$35	$40	$60		Sergei Prokofiev		DoubleD
1961	The Three Little Pigs	$35	$40	$60		Tony Palazzo		DoubleD
1961	Three Little Kittens	$35	$40	$60		Tony Palazzo		DoubleD
1962	A Horse Alphabet	$35	$40	$60		Tony Palazzo		DS&P
1962	A Monkey Alphabet	$35	$40	$60		Tony Palazzo		DS&P
1962	Let's Go To The Jungle	$35	$40	$60		Tony Palazzo		DoubleD
1962	Songs For A Small Guitar	$35	$40	$60		Al Graham		DS&P
1962	The Four Musicians	$35	$40	$60		Jacob & Wilhelm Grimm		DoubleD
1962	The Story Of Snowman, The Cinderella Horse	$35	$40	$60		Tony Palazzo		DS&P
1963	Down With Dinosaurs!	$35	$40	$60		Al Graham		DS&P
1963	The Pied Piper	$35	$40	$60		Al Graham		DS&P
1964	A Bird Alphabet	$35	$40	$60		Tony Palazzo		DS&P
1964	Ramona Knew What She Wanted!	$35	$40	$60		Tony Palazzo		AS
1965	Hey, Horses	$30	$40	$50		Elizabeth M. Graves		Garrard
1965	The Lord Is My Shepherd	$30	$40	$50		Tony Palazzo		Walck
1966	A Time For All Things	$30	$40	$50		Tony Palazzo		Walck
1966	Charley The Horse	$30	$40	$50		Tony Palazzo		AS
1966	Thai, Kao, And Tone	$30	$40	$50		Tony Palazzo		AS
1967	The Animal Family Album	$30	$40	$50		Tony Palazzo		Lion
1968	A Passel Of 'Possums & Other Animal Families	$30	$40	$50		Robin Fox		Lion
1968	Wings Of The Morning	$30	$40	$50		Robin Palmer		Walck
1970	The Biggest And The Littlest Animals		$25	$35	$50	Tony Palazzo		Lion

Palladini   David

Year	Title	VG-	VG	VG+	Fine	Author	Award	Pub
1972	The Sword And The Grail		$30	$50	$60	Constance B. Hieatt (retold)		Crowell
1973	People Of The Ice Age		$25	$35	$50	Ruth Goode		Crowell
1974	The End Of The World		$20	$30	$40	Franklyn M. Branley		Crowell
1974	The Girl Who Cried Flowers		$30	$40	$60	Jane Yolen		Crowell
1976	The Moon Ribbon: & Other Tales		$30	$40	$60	Jane Yolen		Crowell
1977	The Hundredth Dove & Other Tales		$25	$40	$50	Jane Yolen		Crowell
1978	Fortunes & Misfortunes Of The Famous Moll Flanders		$20	$30	$40	Daniel Defoe		Frank
1980	Justine		$18	$25	$35	Lawrence Durrell		Frank
1980	Twenty-Six Starlings Will Fly Through Your Mind		$18	$25	$35	Barbara Wersba		H&Row
1981	If You Call My Name		$18	$25	$35	Crescent Dragonwagon		H&Row
1987	The Eyes Of The Dragon		$70	$100	$140	Stephen King		Viking
1988	Rosalie		$14	$20	$30	Arthur Yorinks		LBrown
1988	The Prince In The Golden Tower		$14	$20	$30	Florence Karpin		VK

Pallandt   Nicolas van

Year	Title	VG-	VG	VG+	Fine	Author	Award	Pub
1992	The Butterfly Night Of Old Brown Bear		$12	$18	$25	Nicolas van Pallandt		FSG
1994	Troll's Search For Summer		$12	$16	$20	Nicolas van Pallandt		FSG
1996	Eddie's Monster		$10	$16	$20	Michael Abrams		Abbe

Paraskevas   Michael

Year	Title	VG-	VG	VG+	Fine	Author	Award	Pub
1992	On The Edge Of The Sea		$16	$25	$30	Betty Paraskevas		Dial
1993	Junior Kroll		$12	$16	$20	Betty Paraskevas		HBJ
1993	Shamlanders		$12	$16	$20	Betty Paraskevas		HBrace
1993	The Strawberry Dog		$12	$16	$20	Betty Paraskevas		Dial
1994	A Very Kroll Christmas		$12	$16	$20	Betty Paraskevas		HBrace
1994	Junior Kroll And Company		$12	$16	$20	Betty Paraskevas		HBJ

Paraskevas   Michael

Year	Title	VG-	VG	VG+	Fine	Author	Award	Pub
1995	Gracie Graves And The Kids From Room 402		$10	$16	$20	Betty Paraskevas		HBrace
1995	Monster Beach		$10	$16	$20	Betty Paraskevas		HBrace
1996	Cecil Bunions And The Midnight Train		$10	$16	$20	Betty Paraskevas		HBrace
1996	The Ferocious Beast With The Polka-Dot Hide		$10	$16	$20	Betty Paraskevas		HBrace
1997	The Tangerine Bear		$10	$16	$20	Betty Paraskevas		HCollins
1999	Hoppy & Joe		$10	$14	$18	Betty Paraskevas		S&S
1999	Maggie And The Ferocious Beast		$10	$14	$18	Betty Paraskevas		S&S
1999	The Big Scare		$10	$14	$18	Betty Paraskevas		S&S
2000	Did You See That Eagle?		$8	$12	$16	Betty Paraskevas		S&S
2001	Marvin The Tap Dancing Horse		$8	$12	$16	Betty Paraskevas		S&S
2001	Nibbles O'Hare		$8	$12	$16	Betty Paraskevas		S&S

Parker   Nancy Winslow

Year	Title	VG-	VG	VG+	Fine	Author	Award	Pub
1974	Oh, A-Hunting We Will Go		$30	$40	$60	John Langstaff		McEld
1976	Mrs. Wilson Wanders Off		$30	$40	$60	Nancy Winslow Parker		DoddM
1977	Love From Uncle Clyde		$20	$30	$40	Nancy Winslow Parker		DoddM
1978	No Bath Tonight		$25	$40	$50	Jane Yolen		Crowell
1978	The Crocodile Under Louis Finneberg's Bed		$20	$30	$40	Nancy Winslow Parker		DoddM
1979	Ordeal of Bryon B. Blackbear		$18	$25	$35	Nancy Winslow Parker		DoddM
1980	Puddums		$18	$25	$35	Nancy Winslow Parker		Athenm
1980	Puffy Loves Company		$18	$25	$35	Nancy Winslow Parker		DoddM
1980	The Spotted Dog		$18	$25	$35	Nancy Winslow Parker		DoddM
1981	My Mom Travels A Lot		$25	$35	$50	Caroline Feller Bauer	NYT	FWarne
1981	The President's Car		$18	$25	$35	Nancy Winslow Parker		Crowell
1983	Love From Aunt Betty		$16	$25	$30	Nancy Winslow Parker		DoddM
1985	Paul Revere's Ride		$16	$25	$30	Henry Wadsworth Longfellow		Green
1987	Bugs		$14	$20	$30	Joan Richards Wright		Green
1988	Aren't You Coming Too?		$14	$20	$30	Eve Rice		HCollins
1989	Peter's Pockets		$14	$20	$25	Eve Rice		Green
1989	Willy Bear		$14	$20	$25	Mildred Kantrowitz		Macmil
1990	At Grammy's House		$12	$18	$25	Eve Rice		HCollins
1991	When the Rooster Crowed		$12	$18	$25	Patricia Lillie		Green
1992	Barbara Frietchie		$12	$18	$25	John Whittier		Green
1993	Sheridan's Ride		$12	$16	$20	Thomas Read		Green
1999	I'm Taking A Trip On My Train		$10	$14	$18	Shirley Neitzel		Green

Parker   Robert Andrew

Year	Title	VG-	VG	VG+	Fine	Author	Award	Pub
1969	Pop Corn & Ma Goodness	$80	$120	$140		Edna Mitchell Preston	CH	Viking
1971	King Fox, & Other Old Tales		$25	$35	$50	Freya Littledale		DoubleD
1971	The Trees Stand Shining		$30	$50	$60	Hettie Jones		Dial
1972	Liam's Catch		$25	$35	$50	Dorothy D. Parker		Viking
1972	Zeek Silver Moon		$25	$35	$50	Amy Ehrlich		Dial
1973	A Book Of Animal Poems		$25	$35	$50	William Cole		Viking
1973	The Mermaid And The Whale		$25	$35	$50	Georgess McHargue		HR&W
1974	The Green Isle		$20	$30	$40	Philip Burton		Dial
1975	Izzie		$20	$30	$40	Susan Pearson		Dial
1975	The Winter Wife		$20	$30	$40	Anne Eliot Crompton		LBrown
1975	When Light Turns Into Night		$20	$30	$40	Crescent Dragonwagon		H&Row
1977	Guess Who My Favorite Person Is		$20	$30	$40	Byrd Baylor		Scribnr
1977	Oliver Hyde's Dishcloth Concert		$20	$30	$40	Richard Kennedy		LBrown
1977	The Impossible Major Rogers		$20	$30	$40	Patricia Lee Gauch		Putnam
1978	Sweet Betsy From Pike		$20	$30	$40	Robert Andrew Parker		Viking
1983	Beautiful My Mane In The Wind		$16	$25	$30	Catherine Petroski		HM
1983	The Magic Wings		$16	$25	$30	Diane Wolkstein		Dutton
1985	A Winter Journey		$16	$25	$30	David Updike		P-Hall
1985	Brothers		$16	$25	$30	Florence B. Freedman		H&Row
1985	Father Time And The Day Boxes		$16	$25	$30	George Ella Lyon		BradP
1987	Gunga Din		$14	$20	$30	Rudyard Kipling		GB
1988	An Autumn Tale		$14	$20	$30	David Updike		Pippin
1989	A Spring Story		$14	$20	$25	David Updike		Pippin
1989	The Dancing Skeleton		$14	$20	$25	Cynthia C. DeFelice		Macmil
1990	Grandfather Tang's Story		$12	$18	$25	Ann Tompert		Crown
1990	Haunted Houses		$12	$18	$25	Lewann Sotnak		CrestH
1990	The Fox And The Kingfisher		$12	$18	$25	Judith Mellecker		Knopf

Parker　　Robert Andrew

Year	Title	VG-	VG	VG+	Fine	Author	Award	Pub
1991	Randolph's Dream		$12	$18	$25	Judith Mellecker		Knopf
1991	The Year Of No More Corn		$12	$18	$25	Helen Ketteman		Orchard
1993	A Great Miracle Happened There		$12	$16	$20	Karla Kuskin		Perlman
1993	The Magician's Visit		$12	$16	$20	Barbara Diamond Goldin		Viking
1993	The Sounds Of Summer		$12	$16	$20	David Updike		Pippin
1993	The Woman Who Fell From The Sky		$12	$16	$20	John Bierhorst		Morrow
1994	Aunt Skilly And The Stranger		$12	$16	$20	Kathleen Stevens		Ticnor
1994	Circus Of The Wolves		$12	$16	$20	Jack Bushnell		LL&S
1994	Full Worm Moon		$12	$16	$20	Margo Lemieux		Tambour
1994	The Great Shaking		$12	$16	$20	Jo Carson		Orchard
1998	The Hatmaker's Sign		$10	$14	$18	Candace Fleming		Orchard
2000	Cold Feet		$8	$12	$16	Cynthia C. DeFelice		DK
2000	The People With Five Fingers		$8	$12	$16	John Bierhorst		MCaven
2002	Action Jackson		$8	$10	$14	Jan Greenberg		RoarB
2003	Orville		$8	$10	$14	Haven Kimmel		Clarion

Parker-Rees　　Guy

Year	Title	VG-	VG	VG+	Fine	Author	Award	Pub
2000	Big Bad Bunny		$8	$12	$16	Alan Durant		Dutton
2001	Giraffes Can't Dance		$8	$10	$14	Giles Andreae		Orchard
2002	Down By The Cool Of The Pool		$8	$10	$14	Tony Mitton		Orchard
2002	Flying Friends		$8	$10	$14	Julia Jarman		Scholas
2003	Dinosaurumpus		$8	$10	$14	Tony Mitton		Orchard
2003	K Is For Kissing A Cool Kangaroo		$8	$10	$14	Giles Andreae		Orchard
2003	Quiet!		$8	$10	$14	Paul Bright		Orchard
2003	The Hippo-Not-Amus		$8	$10	$14	Tony & Jan Payne		Orchard
2004	Spooky Hour		$6	$10	$12	Tony Mitton		Orchard

Parnall　　Peter

Year	Title	VG-	VG	VG+	Fine	Author	Award	Pub
1967	A Dog's Book Of Bugs	$60	$80	$100		Elizabeth Griffen		Athenm
1967	Knee-Deep In Thunder	$60	$80	$100		Sheila Moon		Athenm
1967	The Psychology Of Birds	$60	$80	$100		Harold E. Burtt		Macmil
1968	Desert Solitaire	$340	$440	$560		Edward Abbey		McHill
1968	Kävik The Wolf Dog	$40	$50	$70		Walt Morey		Dutton
1968	Malachi Mudge	$40	$50	$70		Cecil Maiden		McHill
1968	The Moon Of The Wild Pigs	$40	$50	$70		Jean Craighead George		Crowell
1968	The Underground Hideaway	$40	$50	$70		Murray Goodwin		H&Row
1969	A Beastly Circus	$40	$50	$70		Peggy Parish		S&S
1969	Apricot ABC	$40	$50	$70		Miska Miles		LBrown
1969	The Gruesome Green Witch	$40	$50	$70		Patricia Coffin		Walker
1970	But Ostriches ..		$30	$50	$60	Aileen Fisher		Crowell
1970	Doctor Rabbit		$30	$50	$60	Jan Wahl		DelaP
1970	The Inspector		$30	$50	$60	George Mendoza		DoubleD
1971	Annie And The Old One		$30	$50	$60	Miska Miles	NH	LBrown
1971	Big Frog, Little Pond		$30	$50	$60	George Mendoza		McCall
1971	Moonfish And Owl Scratchings		$30	$50	$60	George Mendoza		G&D
1971	The Mountain		$35	$50	$70	Peter Parnall		DoubleD
1971	The Nightwatchers		$30	$50	$60	Angus Cameron		4Winds
1971	The Six Voyages Of Pleasant Fieldmouse		$30	$50	$60	Jan Wahl		DelaP
1971	When The Porcupine Moved In		$30	$50	$60	Cora Annett		FWatts
1972	Gifts Of An Eagle		$35	$50	$70	Peter Parnall		S&S
1972	The Fire Bringer		$30	$50	$60	Margaret Hodges		LBrown
1973	A Little Book Of Little Beasts		$30	$50	$60	Mary Ann Hoberman		S&S
1973	Emma's Search For Something		$30	$50	$60	Mary Anderson		Athenm
1973	Seven Houses		$30	$50	$60	Josephine W. Johnson		S&S
1973	The Great Fish		$35	$50	$70	Peter Parnall		DoubleD
1973	The Rabbit's World		$30	$50	$60	Miriam Schlein		4Winds
1973	Twist, Wiggle, And Squirm		$35	$50	$70	Laurence Pringle		Crowell
1974	Everybody Needs A Rock		$35	$50	$70	Byrd Baylor		Scribnr
1974	Tales Of Myrtle The Turtle		$30	$40	$60	Keith Robertson		Viking
1974	Year On Muskrat Marsh		$30	$40	$60	Berniece Freschet		Scribnr
1975	Alfalfa Hill		$30	$50	$60	Peter Parnall		DoubleD
1975	The Desert Is Theirs		$70	$100	$140	Byrd Baylor	CH	Scribnr
1975	The Peregrine Falcons		$30	$40	$60	Alice Schick		Dial
1975	The Pig With One Nostril		$30	$40	$60	Millard Lampell		DoubleD

Parnall   Peter

Year	Title	VG-	VG	VG+	Fine	Author	Award	Pub
1975	The Twilight Seas		$30	$40	$60	Sally Carrighar		W&T
1976	A Natural History Of Marine Mammals		$30	$40	$60	Victor B. Scheffer		Scribnr
1976	Hawk, I'm Your Brother		$70	$100	$140	Byrd Baylor	CH	Scribnr
1977	A Dog's Book Of Birds		$25	$40	$50	Peter Parnall		Scribnr
1978	Little Wild Chimpanzee		$25	$40	$50	Anna Michel		Pan
1978	The Other Way To Listen		$25	$40	$50	Byrd Baylor		Scribnr
1978	The Way To Start A Day		$60	$90	$120	Byrd Baylor	CH	Scribnr
1979	Little Wild Elephant		$25	$40	$50	Anna Michel		Pan
1979	The Spawning Run		$25	$40	$50	William Humphrey		DelaP
1979	Your Own Best Secret Place		$30	$40	$60	Byrd Baylor		Scribnr
1980	If You Are A Hunter Of Fossils		$30	$40	$60	Byrd Baylor		Scribnr
1980	Roadrunner		$25	$35	$50	Naomi Judd		Dutton
1981	Desert Voices		$25	$40	$50	Byrd Baylor		Scribnr
1984	The Daywatchers		$20	$30	$40	Peter Parnall		Macmil
1985	Between Cattails		$20	$30	$40	Terry Tempest Williams		Scribnr
1986	Cat Will Rhyme With Hat		$20	$30	$40	Jean Chapman (compiled)		Scribnr
1986	I'm In Charge Of Celebrations		$25	$35	$50	Byrd Baylor		Scribnr
1986	Winter Barn		$20	$30	$40	Peter Parnall		Macmil
1987	Apple Tree		$20	$30	$40	Peter Parnall		Macmil
1988	Feet!		$18	$25	$35	Peter Parnall		Macmil
1989	Cats From Away		$18	$25	$35	Peter Parnall		Macmil
1989	Quiet		$18	$25	$35	Peter Parnall		Morrow
1990	Woodpile		$16	$25	$30	Peter Parnall		Macmil
1991	Marsh Cat		$16	$25	$30	Peter Parnall		Macmil
1991	The Rock		$16	$25	$30	Peter Parnall		Macmil
1992	Become A Bird And Fly!		$16	$25	$30	Michael Elsohn Ross		Millbk
1992	Stuffer		$16	$25	$30	Peter Parnall		Macmil
1993	Spaces		$16	$25	$30	Peter Parnall		Millbk
1993	Water Pup		$16	$25	$30	Peter Parnall		Macmil
1994	The Table Where Rich People Sit		$14	$20	$30	Byrd Baylor		Scribnr

Patton   Lucia

Year	Title	VG-	VG	VG+	Fine	Author	Award	Pub
1937	Prayers For Little Children	$35	$50	$60		Mary Alice Jones		RandMc
1940	Seven Diving Ducks	$25	$35	$50		Margaret Friskey		DMcKay
1940	Surprise On Wheels	$25	$35	$50		Margaret Friskey		AWhit
1941	Grandfather Frog	$25	$35	$50		Margaret Friskey		DMcKay
1941	Wings Over The Woodshed	$25	$35	$50		Margaret Friskey		AWhit
1942	A Goat Afloat	$25	$35	$50		Margaret Friskey		AWhit
1942	Annie And The Wooden Skates	$25	$35	$50		Margaret Friskey		Oxford
1942	Three Smart Squirrels And Squee	$25	$35	$50		Margaret Friskey		DMcKay
1942	Today We Fly	$25	$35	$50		Margaret Friskey		AWhit
1943	Pepito At Capistrano	$25	$35	$50		Joan Costantino		Whitman
1943	Scuttlebutt Goes To War	$70	$90	$120		Margaret Friskey		W&F
1943	The House That Ran Away	$25	$35	$50		Margaret Friskey		AWhit
1944	Adventure For Beginners	$25	$35	$50		Margaret Friskey		W&F
1944	Corporal Crow	$25	$35	$50		Margaret Friskey		DMcKay
1944	Randy And The Crimson Rocket	$25	$35	$50		Margaret Friskey		AWhit
1944	Scuttlebutt And The Carrier Kitten	$50	$60	$80		Margaret Friskey		W&F
1944	Tad Lincoln And The Green Umbrella	$25	$35	$50		Margaret Friskey		Oxford
1946	Chipmunk Moves	$25	$35	$50		Margaret Friskey		DMcKay
1946	Johnny Cottontail	$25	$35	$50		Margaret Friskey		DMcKay
1946	The Little River Of Gold	$25	$35	$50		Lucia Patton		AWhit
1946	The Lost Little Boy	$25	$35	$50		Alma Kehoe Reck		AWhit
1948	The Little House On Stilts	$25	$35	$50		Lucia Patton		AWhit
1950	Little Echo In The Hills	$25	$30	$40		Lucia Patton		AWhit

Payne   C.F.

Year	Title	VG-	VG	VG+	Fine	Author	Award	Pub
1999	True Heart		$12	$16	$20	Marissa Moss		Whistle
2000	The Remarkable Farkle Mcbride		$10	$14	$18	John Lithgow		S&S
2002	Micawber		$8	$12	$16	John Lithgow		S&S
2002	Shoeless Joe & Black Betsy		$8	$10	$14	Phil Bildner		S&S
2004	Mighty Jackie		$6	$10	$12	Marissa Moss		S&S
2005	The Curse of the Bambino		$6	$10	$12	Dan Shaughnessy		S&S

Peat   Fern Bisel

Year	Title	VG-	VG	VG+	Fine	Author	Award	Pub
1928	Jiji Lou	$160	$220	$280		Lurline Bowles Mayol		SaalF
1929	A Christmas Carol	$160	$220	$280		Charles Dickens		SaalF
1929	A Wonder-Book For Boys And Girls	$160	$220	$280		Nathaniel Hawthorne		SaalF
1929	Mother Goose	$200	$260	$320		Frank Edwin Peat (adapted)		SaalF
1929	The Long Eared Bat	$160	$220	$280		Horace Thomas Barnaby		SaalF
1929	Tommy And Jane And The Birds	$120	$160	$200		Daisy Semple		SaalF
1930	Rag-Doll Jane	$70	$100	$120		Carolyn Treffinger		SaalF
1930	Tanglewood Tales	$100	$140	$180		Nathaniel Hawthorne		SaalF
1930	The Animal Caravan	$70	$100	$120		Frank R. Leet		SaalF
1930	The Sugar-Plum Tree	$100	$140	$180		Eugene Field		SaalF
1930	Wynken, Blynken, And Nod	$50	$70	$90		Eugene Field		SaalF
1931	Little Black Sambo	$160	$220	$280		Helen Bannerman		Harter
1931	Purr And Miew	$70	$100	$120		Frank R. Leet		SaalF
1931	The Bird Book	$70	$100	$120		Frank North Shankland		SaalF
1931	The Cock, The Mouse, And The Little Red Hen	$70	$100	$120		Margaret Smith-Masters		SaalF
1931	The Ugly Duckling	$70	$100	$120		Hans Christian Andersen		SaalF
1932	Cinderella	$70	$100	$120		Katharine Gibson		Harter
1932	Forest Friends	$70	$100	$120		Frank North Shankland		SaalF
1932	The Cock	$50	$70	$90		Margaret Smith-Masters		SaalF
1932	The Three Little Pigs	$50	$70	$90		Fern Bisel Peat		SaalF
1932	The Ugly Duckling	$50	$70	$90		Hans Christian Andersen		SaalF
1933	Mother Goose	$50	$70	$90		Fern Bisel Peat (adapted)		SaalF
1933	Round The Mulberry Bush	$50	$70	$90		Marion McNeil		SaalF
1934	Little Housekeepers	$50	$70	$90		Fern Bisel Peat		SaalF
1935	Rag-Doll Jane	$50	$70	$90		Carolyn Treffinger		SaalF
1937	Christmas Carols	$70	$90	$120		Frank Edwin Peat		SaalF
1939	Mother Goose	$50	$60	$80		Fern Bisel Peat (adapted)		SaalF
1939	When Toys Could Talk	$50	$60	$80		Jane Randall		SaalF
1940	A Child's Garden Of Verses	$70	$90	$120		Robert Louis Stevenson		SaalF
1940	Forest Friends	$50	$60	$80		Marceline Dauzet		SaalF
1940	Three Little Kittens	$35	$50	$60		Fern Bisel Peat		SaalF
1941	The Gingerbread Boy	$35	$40	$60		Fern Bisel Peat (adapted)		SaalF

Peck   Anne Merriman

Year	Title	VG-	VG	VG+	Fine	Author	Award	Pub
1929	A Vagabond's Provence	$70	$90	$120		Anne Merriman Peck		DoddM
1929	Storybook Europe	$50	$60	$80		Anne Merriman Peck		H&B
1931	Roundabout Europe	$50	$60	$80		Anne Merriman Peck		H&B
1931	Young Germany	$50	$60	$80		Anne Merriman Peck		McBride
1932	Wings Over Holland	$50	$60	$80		Enid Johnson		Macmil
1933	Roundabout America	$40	$60	$70		Enid Johnson		H&B
1934	Young Mexico	$40	$60	$70		Anne Merriman Peck		McBride
1935	Young Americans From Many Lands	$40	$60	$70		Enid Johnson		AWhit
1936	France, Crossroads Of Europe	$40	$60	$70		Edmond Albert Méras		H&B
1937	Spain In Europe And America	$40	$60	$70		Edmond Albert Méras		H&B
1938	René And Patou	$40	$60	$70		Merriman Peck		AWhit
1938	Runaway Balboa	$40	$60	$70		Enid Johnson		H&B
1939	Ho For Californy!	$40	$50	$70		Enid Johnson		H&B
1940	Belgium	$35	$50	$60		Anne Merriman Peck		H&B
1940	Roundabout South America	$35	$50	$60		Anne Merriman Peck		H&B
1941	The Pageant Of South American History	$35	$40	$60		Anne Merriman Peck		Longman
1942	Cinder Ike	$35	$40	$60		Hope Hockenberry Newell		TNelson
1942	Steppin And Family	$35	$40	$60		Hope Hockenberry Newell		Oxford
1943	Manoel And The Morning Star	$35	$40	$60		Anne Merriman Peck		H&B
1943	The Pageant Of Canadian History	$35	$40	$60		Anne Merriman Peck		Longman
1943	Young Canada	$35	$40	$60		Anne Merriman Peck		McBride
1947	Big Bright Land	$35	$40	$60		Enid Johnson		Messner
1947	The Little Old Woman Carries On	$35	$40	$60		Hope Hockenberry Newell		TNelson
1947	The Pageant Of Middle American History	$35	$40	$60		Anne Merriman Peck		Longman
1950	Southwest Roundup	$30	$40	$50		Anne Merriman Peck		DoddM
1952	Jo Ann Of The Border Country	$30	$40	$50		Anne Merriman Peck		DoddM
1962	The March Of Arizona History	$25	$30	$40		Anne Merriman Peck		Ariz
1963	Wings Of An Eagle	$25	$30	$40		Anne Merriman Peck		HawB
1973	The Little Old Woman Who Used Her Head		$16	$25	$30	Hope Hockenberry Newell		TNelson

Peet   Bill

Year	Title	VG-	VG	VG+	Fine	Author	Award	Pub
1950	Walt Disney's So Dear To My Heart	$60	$80	$100		Sterling North		S&S
1959	Hubert's Hair-Raising Adventure	$70	$100	$120		Bill Peet		HM
1961	Huge Harold	$50	$60	$80		Bill Peet		HM
1962	Smokey	$50	$60	$80		Bill Peet		HM
1963	The Pinkish, Purplish, Bluish Egg	$50	$60	$80		Bill Peet		HM
1964	Ella	$50	$60	$80		Bill Peet		HM
1964	Randy's Dandy Lions	$50	$60	$80		Bill Peet		HM
1965	Chester	$40	$60	$70		Bill Peet		HM
1965	Kermit The Hermit	$40	$60	$70		Bill Peet		HM
1966	Capyboppy	$40	$60	$70		Bill Peet		HM
1966	Farewell To Shady Glade	$40	$60	$70		Bill Peet		HM
1967	Buford, The Little Bighorn	$40	$50	$70		Bill Peet		HM
1967	Jennifer And Josephine	$40	$50	$70		Bill Peet		HM
1970	The Whingdingdilly		$30	$50	$60	Bill Peet		HM
1970	The Wump World		$30	$50	$60	Bill Peet		HM
1971	How Droofus The Dragon Lost His Head		$30	$50	$60	Bill Peet		HM
1972	Countdown To Christmas		$30	$50	$60	Bill Peet		GGate
1972	The Ant And The Elephant		$30	$50	$60	Bill Peet		HM
1975	Cyrus The Unsinkable Sea Serpent		$30	$40	$60	Bill Peet		HM
1975	The Gnats Of Knotty Pine		$30	$40	$60	Bill Peet		HM
1977	Big Bad Bruce		$25	$40	$50	Bill Peet		HM
1978	Eli		$25	$40	$50	Bill Peet		HM
1979	Cowardly Clyde		$25	$40	$50	Bill Peet		HM
1981	Encore For Eleanor		$25	$35	$50	Bill Peet		HM
1982	The Luckiest One Of All		$25	$35	$50	Bill Peet		HM
1983	No Such Things		$25	$35	$50	Bill Peet		HM
1984	Pamela Camel		$20	$30	$40	Bill Peet		HM
1985	The Kweeks Of Kookatumdee		$20	$30	$40	Bill Peet		HM
1986	Zella, Zack, And Zodiac		$20	$30	$40	Bill Peet		HM
1987	Jethro And Joel Were A Troll		$20	$30	$40	Bill Peet		HM
1989	Bill Peet: An Autobiography		$40	$60	$80	Bill Peet	CH	HM
1990	Cock-A-Doodle Dudley		$16	$25	$30	Bill Peet		HM

Pelletier   David

Year	Title	VG-	VG	VG+	Fine	Author	Award	Pub
1996	The Graphic Alphabet		$25	$40	$50	David Pelletier	CH	Orchard

Pels   Winslow

Year	Title	VG-	VG	VG+	Fine	Author	Award	Pub
1985	Spectacles		$20	$30	$40	Ann Beattie		Goblin
1985	The Magic Fish		$20	$30	$40	Freya Littledale		Scholas
1986	Stone Soup		$14	$20	$30	Ann McGovern		Scholas
1987	Beauty And The Beast		$14	$20	$30	Mary Pope Osborne		Scholas
1988	Hansel And Gretel		$14	$20	$30	Ruth Belov Gross		Scholas
1988	Miss Baba In The Caribbean Foul Ball Caper		$14	$20	$30	Richard Pels		ContB
1989	Miss Baba In The Doorknob Of Destiny		$14	$20	$25	Winslow Pels		ContB
1990	Noble-Hearted Kate		$12	$18	$25	Marianna Mayer		Bantam
1995	Camelot		$10	$16	$20	Jane Yolen		Philo
1995	Turandot		$10	$16	$20	Marianna Mayer		Morrow
1998	Iron John		$10	$14	$18	Marianna Mayer		Morrow
2002	Ali And The Magic Stew		$8	$10	$14	Shulamith Oppenheim		Boyds

Percy   Graham

Year	Title	VG-	VG	VG+	Fine	Author	Award	Pub
1978	The Picnic Book		$20	$30	$40	Carol Wright		HartD
1980	Sleeping Beauty		$14	$20	$25	Charles Perrault		Knopf
1984	The Woodland Gospels		$12	$18	$25	Jeremy Lloyd		Faber
1986	Captain Cat And The Carol Singers		$12	$16	$20	Jeremy Lloyd		Faber
1987	The Fantastic Flying Journey		$12	$16	$20	Gerald Durrell		S&S
1988	When Dad Cuts Down The Chestnut Tree		$12	$16	$20	Pam Ayres		Knopf
1988	When Dad Fills In The Garden Pond		$12	$16	$20	Pam Ayres		Knopf
1989	Sam Pig And The Cuckoo Clock		$12	$16	$20	Alison Uttley		Faber
1989	Sam Pig And The Scarecrow		$12	$16	$20	Alison Uttley		Faber
1989	Sam Pig At The Theatre		$12	$16	$20	Alison Uttley		Faber
1989	The Fantastic Dinosaur Adventure		$12	$16	$20	Gerald Durrell		S&S

Percy   Graham

Year	Title	VG-	VG	VG+	Fine	Author	Award	Pub
1991	A Cup Of Sunshine		$10	$16	$20	Jill Bennett		HBJ
1991	Max And The Very Rare Bird		$10	$16	$20	Graham Percy		CW
1991	Meg And Her Circus Tricks		$10	$16	$20	Graham Percy		CW
1991	Reynard, The Fox		$10	$16	$20	Selina Hastings (retold)		Tambour
1991	The Wind In The Willows		$10	$16	$20	Kenneth Grahame		NTrust
1992	36 Strange Little Animals Waiting To Eat		$10	$16	$20	Roz Denney		ST&C
1992	Elephants Never Forget		$10	$16	$20	Graham Percy		Chron
1992	The Cock, The Mouse, And The Little Red Hen		$10	$16	$20	Graham Percy		Candle
1993	The City Mouse And The Country Mouse		$10	$16	$20	Graham Percy		Holt
1994	Arthouse		$10	$14	$18	Graham Percy		Chron
1994	Max And The Orange Door		$10	$14	$18	Graham Percy		CW
1994	Meg And The Great Race		$10	$14	$18	Graham Percy		CW
1995	Lullabies: Poems And Rhymes To Dream On		$10	$14	$18	Graham Percy		RunP
1996	24 Strange Little Animals In A Haunted House		$8	$12	$16	Graham Percy		Chron
1996	Pigasus		$8	$12	$16	Pat Murphy		Dial
1999	Elympics		$8	$12	$16	X. J. Kennedy		Philo
1999	Row Your Boat		$8	$12	$16	Anthony Lishak		DK
2001	Albert's Raccoon		$8	$10	$14	Karen Wallace		Kfisher
2001	Mama Tiger, Baba Tiger		$8	$10	$14	Juli Mahr		DK
2002	Elefantina's Dream		$8	$10	$14	X. J. Kennedy		Philo

Petersham   Maud & Miska

Year	Title	VG-	VG	VG+	Fine	Author	Award	Pub
1922	Five Little Friends	$280	$360	$460		Sherred Willcox Adams		Macmil
1922	Rootabaga Stories	$600	$800	$1,000		Carl Sandburg		HBrace
1923	Rootabaga Pigeons	$340	$450	$560		Carl Sandburg		HBrace
1925	Little Ugly Face	$260	$360	$440		Florence C. Coolidge		Macmil
1929	Miki	$200	$280	$340		Maud & Miska Petersham		DD
1929	The Magic Doll Of Roumania	$200	$280	$340		Petersham Marie		FStokes
1930	The Ark Of Father Noah And Mother Noah	$200	$280	$340		Maud & Miska Petersham		DD
1931	The Christ Child	$200	$280	$340		Maud & Miska Petersham		DD
1932	Auntie And Celia Jane And Miki	$200	$260	$320		Maud & Miska Petersham		DD
1932	Heidi	$200	$260	$320		Johanna Spyri		GardenC
1932	Pinocchio	$200	$260	$320		Carlo Collodi		GardenC
1933	Get-A-Way And Háry János	$240	$320	$400		Maud & Miska Petersham		Viking
1933	The Story Book Of Clothes	$50	$60	$80		Maud & Miska Petersham		Winston
1933	The Story Book Of Food	$50	$60	$80		Maud & Miska Petersham		Winston
1933	The Story Book Of Houses	$50	$60	$80		Maud & Miska Petersham		Winston
1933	The Story Book Of Things We Use	$50	$60	$80		Maud & Miska Petersham		Winston
1933	The Story Book Of Transportation	$50	$60	$80		Maud & Miska Petersham		Winston
1934	Miki And Mary	$240	$320	$400		Maud & Miska Petersham		Viking
1935	The Story Book Of Aircraft	$40	$60	$70		Maud & Miska Petersham		Winston
1935	The Story Book Of Coal	$40	$60	$70		Maud & Miska Petersham		Winston
1935	The Story Book Of Earth's Treasures	$40	$60	$70		Maud & Miska Petersham		Winston
1935	The Story Book Of Gold	$40	$60	$70		Maud & Miska Petersham		Winston
1935	The Story Book Of Iron And Steel	$40	$60	$70		Maud & Miska Petersham		Winston
1935	The Story Book Of Oil	$40	$60	$70		Maud & Miska Petersham		Winston
1935	The Story Book Of Ships	$40	$60	$70		Maud & Miska Petersham		Winston
1935	The Story Book Of Trains	$40	$60	$70		Maud & Miska Petersham		NTrunst
1935	The Story Book Of Wheels, Ships, Trains, Aircraft	$50	$70	$90		Maud & Miska Petersham		Winston
1936	Rootabaga Stories	$100	$140	$180		Carl Sandburg		HBrace
1936	The Story Book Of Corn	$40	$60	$70		Maud & Miska Petersham		Winston
1936	The Story Book Of Foods From The Field	$40	$60	$70		Maud & Miska Petersham		Winston
1936	The Story Book Of Rice	$40	$60	$70		Maud & Miska Petersham		Winston
1936	The Story Book Of Sugar	$40	$60	$70		Maud & Miska Petersham		Winston
1936	The Story Book Of Wheat	$40	$60	$70		Maud & Miska Petersham		Winston
1938	David	$70	$90	$120		Maud & Miska Petersham		Winston
1938	Joseph And His Brothers	$70	$90	$120		Maud & Miska Petersham		Winston
1938	Moses	$70	$90	$120		Maud & Miska Petersham		Winston
1938	Ruth, From The Story Told In The Book Of Ruth	$70	$90	$120		Maud & Miska Petersham		Winston
1938	Stories From The Old Testament	$70	$90	$120		Maud & Miska Petersham		Winston
1938	The Four And Lena	$70	$90	$120		Marie Barringer		DD
1939	The Story Book Of Cotton	$40	$60	$70		Maud & Miska Petersham		Winston
1939	The Story Book Of Rayon	$40	$60	$70		Maud & Miska Petersham		Winston
1939	The Story Book Of Silk	$40	$60	$70		Maud & Miska Petersham		Winston
1939	The Story Book Of Things We Wear	$40	$60	$70		Maud & Miska Petersham		Winston

Petersham — Maud & Miska

Year	Title	VG-	VG	VG+	Fine	Author	Award	Pub
1939	The Story Book Of Wool	$40	$60	$70		Maud & Miska Petersham		Winston
1941	A Little Book Of Prayers	$70	$90	$120		Emilie L. D. Johnson		Viking
1941	An American ABC	$220	$280	$360		Maud & Miska Petersham	CH	Macmil
1941	Susannah, The Pioneer Cow	$70	$90	$120		Miriam Evangeline Mason		Macmil
1942	Jesus' Story	$70	$90	$120		Maud & Miska Petersham		Macmil
1945	The Rooster Crows	$440	$600	$740		Maud & Miska Petersham	CM	Macmil
1947	America's Stamps	$40	$60	$70		Maud & Miska Petersham		Macmil
1949	The Box With Red Wheels	$80	$120	$140		Maud & Miska Petersham		Macmil
1950	The Circus Baby	$80	$120	$140		Maud & Miska Petersham		Macmil
1951	A Bird In The Hand	$50	$70	$90		Benjamin Franklin		Macmil
1953	In Clean Hay	$80	$100	$140		Eric Kelly		Macmil
1953	Story Of The Presidents Of The U.S.A.	$50	$70	$90		Maud & Miska Petersham		Macmil
1954	Off To Bed	$80	$100	$140		Maud & Miska Petersham		Macmil
1955	The Boy Who Had No Heart	$70	$100	$120		Maud & Miska Petersham		Macmil
1956	The Silver Mace	$70	$100	$120		Maud & Miska Petersham		Macmil
1958	The Peppernuts	$50	$60	$80		Maud & Miska Petersham		Macmil
1962	The Shepherd Psalm	$50	$60	$80		Maud & Miska Petersham		Macmil

Pfister — Marcus

Year	Title	VG-	VG	VG+	Fine	Author	Award	Pub
1986	The Sleepy Owl		$30	$40	$60	Marcus Pfister		NSBooks
1986	Where Is My Friend?		$30	$40	$60	Marcus Pfister		NSBooks
1987	Camomile Heads For Home		$14	$20	$30	Hermann Moers		NSBooks
1987	Four Candles For Simon		$14	$20	$30	Gerda Marie Scheidl		NSBooks
1987	Penguin Pete		$40	$60	$80	Marcus Pfister		NSBooks
1988	Penguin Pete's New Friends		$30	$40	$60	Marcus Pfister		NSBooks
1988	Santa Claus And The Woodcutter		$14	$20	$30	Kathrin Siegenthaler		NSBooks
1989	Miriam's Gift		$14	$20	$25	Gerda Marie Scheidl		NSBooks
1989	Penguin Pete And Pat		$25	$35	$50	Marcus Pfister		NSBooks
1990	Shaggy		$12	$18	$25	Marcus Pfister		NSBooks
1990	Sun And Moon		$12	$18	$25	Marcus Pfister		NSBooks
1991	Hopper		$12	$18	$25	Marcus Pfister		NSBooks
1991	I See The Moon		$12	$18	$25	Marcus Pfister (selected)		NSBooks
1992	Hopper Hunts For Spring		$12	$18	$25	Marcus Pfister		NSBooks
1992	The Rainbow Fish		$40	$60	$90	Marcus Pfister		NSBooks
1993	Hopper's Easter Surprise		$12	$16	$20	Kathrin Siegenthaler		NSBooks
1993	Penguin Pete, Ahoy!		$16	$25	$30	Marcus Pfister		NSBooks
1993	The Christmas Star		$12	$16	$20	Marcus Pfister		NSBooks
1994	Chris & Croc		$12	$16	$20	Marcus Pfister		NSBooks
1994	Dazzle The Dinosaur		$12	$16	$20	Marcus Pfister		NSBooks
1994	Penguin Pete And Little Tim		$14	$20	$30	Marcus Pfister		NSBooks
1995	Hang On, Hopper!		$10	$16	$20	Marcus Pfister		NSBooks
1995	Rainbow Fish To The Rescue!		$14	$20	$25	Marcus Pfister		NSBooks
1996	Wake Up, Santa Claus!		$10	$16	$20	Marcus Pfister		NSBooks
1997	Hopper's Treetop Adventure		$10	$16	$20	Marcus Pfister		NSBooks
1997	Milo And The Magical Stones		$10	$16	$20	Marcus Pfister		NSBooks
1998	How Leo Learned To Be King		$10	$14	$18	Marcus Pfister		NSBooks
1998	Rainbow Fish And The Big Blue Whale		$12	$16	$20	Marcus Pfister		NSBooks
1999	Make A Wish, Honey Bear		$10	$14	$18	Marcus Pfister		NSBooks
2000	Milo And The Mysterious Island		$8	$12	$16	Marcus Pfister		NSBooks
2000	The Happy Hedgehog		$8	$12	$16	Marcus Pfister		NSBooks
2001	Rainbow Fish And The Sea Monsters' Cave		$8	$12	$16	Marcus Pfister		NSBooks
2002	Just The Way You Are		$8	$10	$14	Marcus Pfister		NSBooks
2002	Rainbow Fish 1, 2, 3		$8	$10	$14	Marcus Pfister		NSBooks
2002	Rainbow Fish A,B,C		$8	$10	$14	Marcus Pfister		NSBooks
2003	The Magic Book		$8	$10	$14	Marcus Pfister		NSBooks

Pham — LeUyen

Year	Title	VG-	VG	VG+	Fine	Author	Award	Pub
1997	Sugarcane House		$10	$16	$20	Adrienne Moore Bond		HBrace
1999	Can You Do This, Old Badger?		$8	$12	$16	Eve Bunting		Harcort
2001	Little Badger, Terror Of The Seven Seas		$8	$10	$14	Eve Bunting		Harcort
2001	Whose Shoes?		$8	$10	$14	Anna Grossnickle Hines		Harcort
2002	A Perfect Name		$8	$10	$14	Charlene Costanzo		Dial
2002	Little Badger's Just-About Birthday		$8	$10	$14	Eve Bunting		Harcort
2002	One Little Mouse		$8	$10	$14	Dori Chaconas		Viking

Pham   LeUyen

Year	Title	VG-	VG	VG+	Fine	Author	Award	Pub
2002	Which Hat Is That?		$8	$10	$14	Anna Grossnickle Hines		Harcort
2003	Before I Was Your Mother		$8	$10	$14	Kathryn Lasky		Harcort
2003	Piggies In A Polka		$8	$10	$14	Kathi Appelt		Harcort
2003	Sweet Briar Goes To School		$8	$10	$14	Karma Wilson		Dial
2004	Sing-Along Song		$6	$10	$12	JoAnn Early Macken		Viking
2004	Twenty-One Elephants		$6	$10	$12	Phil Bildner		S&S
2005	Sweet Briar Goes To Camp		$6	$10	$12	Karma Wilson		Dial
2006	Benny And Beautiful Baby Delilah		$6	$10	$12	Jean Van Leeuwen		Dial
2006	Once Around The Sun		$6	$10	$12	Bobbi Katz		Harcort

Pienkowski   Jan

Year	Title	VG-	VG	VG+	Fine	Author	Award	Pub
1967	Annie, Bridget, And Charlie	$60	$80	$100		Jan Pienkowski		Pan
1968	A Necklace Of Raindrops	$80	$120	$140		Joan Aiken		DoubleD
1970	The Golden Bird		$30	$50	$60	Edith Brill		FWatts
1971	The Kingdom Under The Sea		$70	$100	$140	Joan Aiken	GM	JCape
1973	Meg And Mog		$30	$50	$60	Helen Nicoll		Athenm
1973	Meg's Eggs		$30	$50	$60	Helen Nicoll		Athenm
1973	Sizes		$30	$50	$60	Jan Pienkowski		Messner
1975	Colors		$30	$40	$60	Jan Pienkowski		Harvey
1975	Meg's Castle		$30	$40	$60	Helen Nicoll		Heine
1975	Weather		$30	$40	$60	Jan Pienkowski		Messner
1977	Homes		$25	$40	$50	Jan Pienkowski		Messner
1977	Jack And The Beanstalk		$25	$40	$50	Joseph Jacobs		Crowell
1978	Ghosts And Bogles		$25	$40	$50	Dinah Starkey		GoodR
1978	Hansel And Gretel		$25	$40	$50	Jacob & Wilhelm Grimm		Crowell
1978	Puss-In-Boots		$25	$40	$50	Charles Perrault		Crowell
1978	Snow White		$25	$40	$50	Jacob & Wilhelm Grimm		Crowell
1978	Tale Of A One-Way Street		$25	$40	$50	Joan Aiken		JCape
1978	The Sleeping Beauty		$25	$40	$50	Jacob & Wilhelm Grimm		Crowell
1979	The Haunted House		$50	$80	$100	Jan Pienkowski	GM	Heine
1980	Time		$25	$35	$50	Jan Pienkowski		Messner
1981	Dinnertime		$25	$35	$50	Jan Pienkowski		Orchard
1982	Mog At The Zoo		$25	$35	$50	Helen Nicoll		Heine
1984	Christmas, The King James Version		$20	$30	$40	Jan Pienkowski		Knopf
1985	Farm		$20	$30	$40	Jan Pienkowski		Heine
1985	I'm Frog		$20	$30	$40	Jan Pienkowski		Walker
1985	I'm Mouse		$20	$30	$40	Jan Pienkowski		Walker
1985	I'm Panda		$20	$30	$40	Jan Pienkowski		Walker
1985	Zoo		$20	$30	$40	Jan Pienkowski		Heine
1987	Mog's Box		$20	$30	$40	Helen Nicoll		Heine
1987	Past Eight O'Clock		$20	$30	$40	Joan Aiken		VK
1987	Small Talk		$20	$30	$40	Jan Pienkowski		Orchard
1989	Easter		$18	$25	$35	Jan Pienkowski		Knopf
1989	Fancy That!		$18	$25	$35	Jan Pienkowski		Orchard
1989	Oh My, A Fly!		$18	$25	$35	Jan Pienkowski		PriceSS
1990	Pet Food		$16	$25	$30	Jan Pienkowski		DoubleD
1991	A Foot In The Grave		$16	$25	$30	Joan Aiken		Viking
1991	Pets		$16	$25	$30	Jan Pienkowski		Heine
1991	Phone Book		$16	$25	$30	Jan Pienkowski		PriceSS
1991	Wheels		$16	$25	$30	Jan Pienkowski		Heine
1993	Road Hog		$16	$25	$30	Jan Pienkowski		PriceSS
1994	1001 Words		$14	$20	$30	Jan Pienkowski		Heine
1994	Toilet Book		$14	$20	$30	Jan Pienkowski		PriceSS
1995	Animals, Friends, Fun, Play		$14	$20	$25	Jan Pienkowski		Heine
1997	Batto The Bat		$12	$18	$25	Jan Pienkowski		DK
1997	Big Machines		$12	$18	$25	Jan Pienkowski		Dutton
1997	Froggo The Frog		$12	$18	$25	Jan Pienkowski		DK
1997	Legs The Spider		$12	$18	$25	Jan Pienkowski		AM
1997	Octo The Octopus		$12	$18	$25	Jan Pienkowski		DK
1997	Splash The Frog		$12	$18	$25	Jan Pienkowski		AM
1997	Squeak The Bat		$12	$18	$25	Jan Pienkowski		AM
1997	Tickles The Octopus		$12	$18	$25	Jan Pienkowski		AM
1997	Trucks & Other Working Wheels		$12	$18	$25	Jan Pienkowski		Dutton
1998	1 2 3		$12	$16	$20	Jan Pienkowski		LSimon
1998	ABC		$12	$16	$20	Jan Pienkowski		LSimon

Pienkowski   Jan

Year	Title	VG-	VG	VG+	Fine	Author	Award	Pub
1998	Jungle		$12	$16	$20	Jan Pienkowski		Piggy
1998	Sea		$12	$16	$20	Jan Pienkowski		Piggy
1999	Good Night		$12	$16	$20	Jan Pienkowski		Candle
2000	Bel And Bub And The Baby Bird		$10	$14	$18	Jan Pienkowski		DK
2000	Bel And Bub And The Bad Snowball		$10	$14	$18	Jan Pienkowski		DK
2000	Bel And Bub And The Big Brown Box		$10	$14	$18	Jan Pienkowski		DK
2000	Bel And Bub And The Black Hole		$10	$14	$18	Jan Pienkowski		DK
2002	Pizza!		$8	$12	$16	Jan Pienkowski		Candle
2003	The Animals Went In Two By Two		$8	$12	$16	Jan Pienkowski		Candle
2004	The First Noel		$8	$10	$14	Jan Pienkowski		Candle

Pilkey   Dav

Year	Title	VG-	VG	VG+	Fine	Author	Award	Pub
1987	World War Won		$20	$30	$40	Dav Pilkey		Landmrk
1988	Don't Pop Your Cork On Mondays!		$14	$20	$30	Adolph Moser		Landmrk
1990	'Twas The Night Before Thanksgiving		$12	$18	$25	Dav Pilkey		Orchard
1991	A Friend For Dragon		$12	$18	$25	Dav Pilkey		Orchard
1991	Dragon Gets By		$16	$25	$30	Dav Pilkey		Orchard
1991	Dragon's Merry Christmas		$16	$25	$30	Dav Pilkey		Orchard
1992	Dragon's Fat Cat		$16	$25	$30	Dav Pilkey		Orchard
1992	When Cats Dream		$12	$18	$25	Dav Pilkey		Orchard
1993	Dogzilla		$12	$16	$20	Dav Pilkey		HBJ
1993	Dragon's Halloween		$16	$25	$30	Dav Pilkey		Orchard
1993	Julius		$12	$16	$20	Angela Johnson		Orchard
1993	Kat Kong		$12	$16	$20	Dav Pilkey		HBJ
1994	Dog Breath!		$12	$16	$20	Dav Pilkey		BSP
1994	The Dumb Bunnies		$14	$20	$30	Sue Denim		BSP
1995	The Dumb Bunnies' Easter		$14	$20	$25	Sue Denim		BSP
1995	The Hallo-Wiener		$10	$16	$20	Dav Pilkey		BSP
1995	The Moonglow Roll-O-Rama		$10	$16	$20	Dav Pilkey		Orchard
1996	God Bless The Gargoyles		$10	$16	$20	Dav Pilkey		HBrace
1996	Make Way For Dumb Bunnies		$12	$18	$25	Sue Denim		BSP
1996	The Paperboy		$30	$50	$60	Dav Pilkey	CH	Orchard
1997	Big Dog And Little Dog		$10	$16	$20	Dav Pilkey		HBrace
1997	Big Dog And Little Dog Getting In Trouble		$10	$16	$20	Dav Pilkey		HBrace
1997	Big Dog And Little Dog Going For A Walk		$10	$16	$20	Dav Pilkey		HBrace
1997	The Adventures Of Captain Underpants		$20	$30	$40	Dav Pilkey		BSP
1997	The Dumb Bunnies Go To The Zoo		$12	$18	$25	Sue Denim		BSP
1997	The Silly Gooses		$10	$16	$20	Dav Pilkey		BSP
1998	Big Dog And Little Dog Wearing Sweaters		$10	$14	$18	Dav Pilkey		HBrace
1998	The Silly Gooses Build A House		$10	$14	$18	Dav Pilkey		BSP
1998	'Twas The Night Before Christmas 2		$10	$14	$18	Dav Pilkey		BSP
1999	Big Dog And Little Dog Making A Mistake		$10	$14	$18	Dav Pilkey		HBrace
1999	Capt Underpants - Attach Of The Takling Toilets		$12	$16	$20	Dav Pilkey		BSP
1999	Capt Underpants - Invasion Of The Incredibly Naughty Cafeteria Ladies		$12	$16	$20	Dav Pilkey		BSP
2000	Capt Underpants - Perilous Plot Of Professor Poopypants		$10	$14	$18	Dav Pilkey		BSP
2000	Silly Stories To Tickle Your Funny Bone		$8	$12	$16	Dav Pilkey		SeaStar
2001	Capt Underpants - Wrath Of The Wicked Wedgie Woman		$10	$14	$18	Dav Pilkey		BSP
2002	The Adventures Of Super Diaper Baby		$8	$10	$14	Dav Pilkey		BSP
2003	Capt Underpants - Big, Bad Battle Of The Bionic Booger Boy		$8	$12	$16	Dav Pilkey		BSP

Pinkney   Brian

Year	Title	VG-	VG	VG+	Fine	Author	Award	Pub
1989	The Boy And The Ghost		$25	$40	$50	Robert D. San Souci		S&S
1990	The Ballad Of Belle Dorcas		$16	$25	$30	William H. Hooks		Knopf
1991	A Wave In Her Pocket		$16	$25	$30	Lynn Joseph		Clarion
1992	Drylongso		$16	$25	$30	Virginia Hamilton		Harcort
1992	Sukey And The Mermaid		$16	$25	$30	Robert D. San Souci		4Winds
1992	The Dark Thirty		$40	$60	$90	Patricia McKissack	NH	Knopf
1992	The Elephant's Wrestling Match		$16	$25	$30	Judy Sierra		LodeS
1993	Alvin Ailey		$16	$25	$30	Andrea D. Pinkney		Hyper
1993	Happy Birthday Martin Luther King		$16	$25	$30	Jean Marzollo		Scholas
1993	Seven Candles For Kwanzaa		$16	$25	$30	Andrea D. Pinkney		Dial
1994	Day Of Delight		$14	$20	$30	Maxine Schur		Dial
1994	Dear Benjamin Banneker		$14	$20	$30	Andrea D. Pinkney		Harcort
1994	Dream Keeper		$14	$20	$30	Langston Hughes		Knopf

Pinkney   Brian

Year	Title	VG-	VG	VG+	Fine	Author	Award	Pub
1995	Jojo's Flying Side Kick		$14	$20	$25	Brian Pinkney		S&S
1995	Max Found Two Sticks		$14	$20	$25	Brian Pinkney		S&S
1995	The Faithful Friend		$35	$50	$70	Robert D. San Souci	CH	S&S
1996	Bill Pickett, Rodeo-Ridin' Cowboy		$12	$18	$25	Andrea D. Pinkney		GB
1996	When I Left My Village		$12	$18	$25	Maxine Schur		Dial
1996	Wiley And The Hairy Man		$12	$18	$25	Judy Sierra		Penguin
1997	The Adventures Of Sparrowboy		$12	$18	$25	Brian Pinkney		S&S
1998	Cendrillion		$12	$16	$20	Daniel San Souci		S&S
1998	Duke Ellington		$25	$40	$50	Andrea D. Pinkney	CH/CSKM	Hyper
1999	In The Time Of The Drums		$12	$16	$20	Kim L. Siegelson		Hyper
2000	Cosmo And The Robot		$10	$14	$18	Brian Pinkney		Green
2001	In The Forest Of Your Remembrance		$10	$14	$18	Gloria Jean Pinkney		Penguin
2001	Mim's Christmas Jam		$10	$14	$18	Andrea D. Pinkney		Harcort
2002	Ella Fitzgerald		$8	$12	$16	Andrea D. Pinkney		Jump
2002	The Stone Lamp		$8	$12	$16	Karen Hesse		Hyper
2003	Jackie's Bat		$8	$12	$16	Marybeth Lorbiecki		S&S
2003	Thumbelina		$8	$12	$16	Hans Christian Andersen		Green
2004	Sleeping Cutie		$8	$10	$14	Andrea D. Pinkney		GB

Pinkney   Jerry

Year	Title	VG-	VG	VG+	Fine	Author	Award	Pub
1964	The Adventures Of Spider	$90	$120	$160		Joyce C. Arkhurst (retold)		LBrown
1966	The Traveling Frog	$60	$80	$100		V.M. Garshin		McHill
1967	Even Tiny Ants Must Sleep	$60	$80	$100		Harold J. Saleh.		McHill
1967	The Beautiful Blue Jay, & Other Tales Of India	$60	$80	$100		John W. Spellman (collected)		LBrown
1967	The Clock Museum	$60	$80	$100		Ken Sobol		McHill
1968	Kostas The Rooster	$60	$80	$100		Traudl		LL&S
1969	Babushka And The Pig	$60	$80	$100		Ann Trofimuk		HM
1969	Juano And The Wonderful Fresh Fish	$60	$80	$100		Thelma Shaw		AW
1969	The Porcupine And The Tiger	$60	$80	$100		Fern Powell		LL&S
1969	The Twin Witches Of Fingle Fu	$60	$80	$100		Irv Phillips		Singer
1970	Cora Annett's Homerhenry		$50	$70	$90	Cora Annett		AW
1971	The King's Ditch		$40	$60	$90	Francine Jacobs (adapted)		CM&G
1972	Femi And Old Grandaddie		$40	$60	$90	Adjai Robinson		CM&G
1973	JD		$40	$60	$90	Mari Evans		DoubleD
1973	Kasho And The Twin Flutes		$40	$60	$90	Adjai Robinson		CM&G
1974	The Great Minu		$40	$60	$80	Beth P. Wilson.		Follett
1975	Song Of The Trees		$40	$60	$80	Mildred D. Taylor		Dial
1976	Roll Of Thunder, Hear My Cry		$120	$180	$260	Mildred Taylor	NM	Dial
1976	Yagua Days		$40	$60	$80	Cruz Martel		Dial
1977	Gulliver's Travels		$40	$60	$80	Jonathan Swift		Frank
1977	Mary Mcleod Bethune		$40	$60	$80	Eloise Greenfield		Crowell
1977	Mildred Murphy, How Does Your Garden Grow?		$40	$60	$80	Phyllis Green		AW
1978	Ji-Nongo-Nongo Means Riddles		$35	$50	$70	Verna Aardema		4Winds
1979	Tales From Africa		$35	$50	$70	Lila Green (selected)		SBurdet
1979	Tonweya And The Eagles		$35	$50	$70	Rosebud Yellow Robe (retold)		Dial
1980	Count On Your Fingers African Style		$35	$50	$70	Claudia Zaslavsky		Crowell
1980	Jahdu		$35	$50	$70	Virginia Hamilton		Green
1981	Monster Myths Of Ancient Greece		$35	$50	$70	William Wise		Putnam
1983	Apples On A Stick: The Folklore Of Black Children		$30	$50	$60	Barbara Michels (selected)		CM
1985	The Patchwork Quilt		$40	$60	$80	Valerie Flournoy	CSKM	Dial
1986	Half A Moon And One Whole Star		$30	$40	$60	Crescent Dragonwagon		Macmil
1987	The Tales Of Uncle Remus		$25	$40	$50	Julius Lester		Dial
1987	Wild, Wild Sunflower Child Anna		$25	$40	$50	Nancy Carlstrom		Macmil
1988	Mirandy And Brother Wind		$50	$80	$100	Patricia McKissack	CH	Knopf
1988	More Tales Of Uncle Remus		$25	$40	$50	Julius Lester		Dial
1988	The Green Lion Of Zion Street		$25	$40	$50	Julia Fields		McEld
1989	Rabbit Makes A Monkey Of Lion: A Swahili Tale		$25	$40	$50	Verna Aardema (retold)		Dial
1989	The Talking Eggs		$50	$80	$100	Robert D. San Souci (adapted)	CH	Dial
1989	Turtle In July		$25	$40	$50	Marilyn Singer		Macmil
1990	Further Tales Of Uncle Remus		$25	$35	$50	Julius Lester		Dial
1990	Pretend You're A Cat		$35	$50	$70	Jean Marzollo	CSKM	Dial
1991	In For Winter, Out For Spring		$25	$35	$50	Arnold Adoff		HBJ
1991	The Man Who Kept His Heart In A Bucket		$25	$35	$50	Sonia Levitin		Dial
1991	Their Eyes Were Watching God		$25	$35	$50	Zora Neale Hurston		UIll
1992	Back Home		$20	$30	$40	Gloria Jean Pinkney		Dial

Pinkney   Jerry

Year	Title	VG-	VG	VG+	Fine	Author	Award	Pub
1992	David's Songs: His Psalms And Their Story		$20	$30	$40	Colin Eisler		Dial
1992	Drylongso		$20	$30	$40	Virginia Hamilton		HBJ
1993	A Starlit Somersault Downhill		$20	$30	$40	Nancy Willard		LBrown
1993	Home Place		$20	$30	$40	Crescent Dragonwagon		Aladd
1993	I Want To Be		$20	$30	$40	Thylias Moss		Dial
1993	New Shoes For Silvia		$20	$30	$40	Johanna Hurwitz		Morrow
1994	John Henry		$40	$60	$80	Julius Lester	CH	Dial
1994	The Last Tales Of Uncle Remus		$20	$30	$40	Julius Lester		Dial
1994	The Sunday Outing		$20	$30	$40	Gloria Jean Pinkney		Dial
1995	Tanya's Reunion		$18	$25	$35	Valerie Flournoy		Dial
1995	The Jungle Book		$18	$25	$35	Rudyard Kipling		Morrow
1996	Fever Dream		$16	$25	$30	Jane Yolen		HCollins
1996	Sam And The Tigers		$16	$25	$30	Julius Lester		Dial
1997	Rikki-Tikki-Tavi		$16	$25	$30	Rudyard Kipling		Morrow
1997	The Hired Hand: An African-American Folktale		$16	$25	$30	Robert D. San Souci (adapted)		Dial
1998	Black Cowboy, Wild Horses: A True Story		$14	$20	$30	Julius Lester		Dial
1998	Meeting Elijah: Eight Tales Of The Prophet		$14	$20	$30	Barbara Diamond Goldin		HBrace
1999	The Little Match Girl		$14	$20	$25	Hans Christian Andersen		Fogel
1999	The Ugly Duckling		$35	$50	$70	Hans Christian Andersen	CH	Morrow
2000	Aesop's Fables		$12	$18	$25	Jerry Pinkney		SeaStar
2000	Albidaro And The Mischievous Dream		$12	$18	$25	Julius Lester		Fogel
2001	Goin' Someplace Special		$12	$16	$20	Patricia McKissack		Athenm
2002	Noah's Ark		$25	$35	$50	Jerry Pinkney	CH	SeaStar
2002	The Nightingale		$10	$16	$20	Hans Christian Andersen		PFogel
2004	God Bless The Child		$8	$12	$16	Julius Lester		Dial
2004	The Old African		$8	$12	$16	Julius Lester		Dial

Pinkwater   Daniel

Year	Title	VG-	VG	VG+	Fine	Author	Award	Pub
1973	Wizard Crystal		$60	$90	$120	Daniel Pinkwater		DoddM
1977	The Blue Thing		$60	$80	$120	Daniel Pinkwater		P-Hall
1979	Alan Mendelsohn, The Boy From Mars		$50	$80	$100	Daniel Pinkwater		Dutton
1979	Pickle Creature		$50	$80	$100	Daniel Pinkwater		4Winds
1979	Yobgorgle: Mystery Monster		$50	$80	$100	Daniel Pinkwater		HM
1980	Java Jack		$20	$40	$60	Luqman Keele		Crowell
1980	The Magic Moscow		$20	$40	$60	Daniel Pinkwater		4Winds
1981	Attila The Pun: A Magic Moscow Story		$20	$40	$60	Daniel Pinkwater		4Winds
1981	The Worms Of Kukumlima		$20	$40	$60	Daniel Pinkwater		Dutton
1981	Tooth-Gnasher Superflash		$18	$25	$35	Daniel Pinkwater		4Winds
1982	Slaves Of Spiegel: A Magic Moscow Story		$16	$25	$30	Daniel Pinkwater		4Winds
1982	The Snarkout Boys & The Avocado Of Death		$35	$50	$70	Daniel Pinkwater		LL&S
1982	Young Adult Novel		$16	$25	$30	Daniel Pinkwater		Crowell
1983	I Was A Second Grade Werewolf		$16	$25	$30	Daniel Pinkwater		Dutton
1984	Bear's Picture		$16	$25	$30	Daniel Pinkwater		Dutton
1984	Devil In The Drain		$16	$25	$30	Daniel Pinkwater		Dutton
1984	Ducks!		$16	$25	$30	Daniel Pinkwater		LBrown
1984	The Snarkout Boys And The Baconburg Horror		$30	$40	$60	Daniel Pinkwater		LL&S
1986	The Frankenbagel Monster		$14	$20	$30	Daniel Pinkwater		Dutton
1986	The Moosepire		$14	$20	$30	Daniel Pinkwater		LBrown
1986	The Muffin Fiend		$14	$20	$30	Daniel Pinkwater		LL&S
1988	Aunt Lulu		$14	$20	$30	Daniel Pinkwater		Macmil
1989	Guys From Space		$14	$20	$25	Daniel Pinkwater		Macmil
1989	Uncle Melvin		$14	$20	$25	Daniel Pinkwater		Macmil
1990	Borgel		$12	$18	$25	Daniel Pinkwater		Macmil
1991	Chicago Days/Hoboken Nights		$12	$18	$25	Daniel Pinkwater		AW
1991	Doodle Flute		$12	$18	$25	Daniel Pinkwater		Macmil
1991	Wempires		$12	$18	$25	Daniel Pinkwater		Macmil
1992	The Phantom Of The Lunch Wagon		$12	$18	$25	Daniel Pinkwater		Macmil
1993	Author's Day		$12	$16	$20	Daniel Pinkwater		Macmil
1993	Spaceburger: A Kevin Spoon & Mason Mintz Story		$12	$16	$20	Daniel Pinkwater		Macmil
1994	Ned Feldman, Space Pirate		$12	$16	$20	Daniel Pinkwater		Macmil
1995	Mush, A Dog From Space		$10	$16	$20	Daniel Pinkwater		Athenm
1995	The Afterlife Diet		$10	$16	$20	Daniel Pinkwater		Random
1997	5 Novels		$10	$16	$20	Daniel Pinkwater		FSG

Pinkwater   Jill

Year	Title	VG-	VG	VG+	Fine	Author	Award	Pub
1996	Wallpaper From Space		$10	$16	$20	Daniel Pinkwater		Athenm
1997	Second Grade Ape		$8	$12	$16	Daniel Pinkwater		Scholas
1997	Young Larry		$8	$12	$16	Daniel Pinkwater		MCaven
1998	At The Hotel Larry		$8	$12	$16	Daniel Pinkwater		MCaven
1998	Big Bob And The Thanksgiving Potatoes		$8	$12	$16	Daniel Pinkwater		Scholas
1998	Bongo Larry		$8	$12	$16	Daniel Pinkwater		MCaven
1998	Rainy Morning		$8	$12	$16	Daniel Pinkwater		Athenm
1998	Wolf Christmas		$8	$12	$16	Daniel Pinkwater		MCaven
1999	Big Bob And The Halloween Potatoes		$8	$12	$16	Daniel Pinkwater		Scholas
1999	Big Bob And The Magic Valentine's Day Potato		$8	$12	$16	Daniel Pinkwater		Scholas
1999	Big Bob And The Winter Holiday Potato		$8	$12	$16	Daniel Pinkwater		Scholas
1999	Ice-Cream Larry		$8	$12	$16	Daniel Pinkwater		MCaven
2000	The Lunchroom Of Doom		$8	$10	$14	Daniel Pinkwater		Athenm
2000	The Magic Pretzel		$8	$10	$14	Daniel Pinkwater		Athenm
2001	Cone Kong		$8	$10	$14	Daniel Pinkwater		Scholas
2001	Irving And Muktuk		$8	$10	$14	Daniel Pinkwater		HM
2001	Uncle Boris In The Yukon		$8	$10	$14	Daniel Pinkwater		S&S
2001	Werewolf Club Meets Dorkula		$8	$10	$14	Daniel Pinkwater		Athenm
2001	Werewolf Club Meets The Hound Of The Basketballs		$8	$10	$14	Daniel Pinkwater		Athenm
2002	Meets Oliver Twit		$8	$10	$14	Daniel Pinkwater		Athenm
2002	Superpuppy		$8	$10	$14	Daniel Pinkwater		Clarion
2003	Bad Bears In The Big City		$8	$10	$14	Daniel Pinkwater		HM
2004	Looking For Bobowicz		$6	$10	$12	Daniel Pinkwater		HCollins

Pizer   Abigail

Year	Title	VG-	VG	VG+	Fine	Author	Award	Pub
1987	Harry's Night Out		$12	$16	$20	Abigail Pizer		Dial
1987	Nosey Gilbert		$10	$16	$20	Abigail Pizer		Dial
1989	Charlie The Puppy		$10	$14	$18	Abigail Pizer		CRB
1989	Hattie The Goat		$10	$14	$18	Abigail Pizer		CRB
1989	Penelope Pig		$10	$14	$18	Abigail Pizer		CRB
1989	Percy The Duck		$10	$14	$18	Abigail Pizer		CRB
1990	It's A Perfect Day		$10	$14	$18	Abigail Pizer		Lippin
1990	Loppylugs		$10	$14	$18	Abigail Pizer		Viking
1994	The Unicorn Of The West		$8	$12	$16	Alma Flor Ada		Athenm
1995	Tippu		$8	$12	$16	A. Pizer & D. Day		Barrn

Plume   Ilse

Year	Title	VG-	VG	VG+	Fine	Author	Award	Pub
1980	The Bremen Town Musicians		$50	$70	$100	Ilse Plume	CH	DoubleD
1981	The Story Of Befana		$14	$20	$25	Ilse Plume		Godine
1983	The Velveteen Rabbit		$14	$20	$25	Margery W. Bianco		Godine
1985	The Hedgehog Boy		$12	$18	$25	Jane Langton		H&Row
1986	Night Story		$12	$16	$20	Nancy Willard		HBJ
1988	Sleepy Book		$12	$16	$20	Charlotte Zolotow		H&Row
1990	The Twelve Days Of Christmas		$10	$16	$20	Ilse Plume		H&Row
1991	The Christmas Witch		$10	$16	$20	Ilse Plume		Hyper
1991	The Shoemaker And The Elves		$10	$16	$20	Ilse Plume		HBJ
1992	Salt		$10	$16	$20	Jane Langton		Hyper
1994	Lullaby And Goodnight		$10	$14	$18	Ilse Plume		HCollins
1994	The Queen's Necklace		$10	$14	$18	Jane Langton		Hyper

Pogány   Willy

Year	Title	VG-	VG	VG+	Fine	Author	Award	Pub
1912	A Treasury Of Verse For Little Children	$240	$320	$400		M. G Edgar		Crowell
1915	The Children In Japan	$220	$300	$380		Grace Bartruse		McBride
1917	Gulliver's Travels	$340	$460	$580		Jonathan Swift		Macmil
1917	Tales Of The Persian Genii	$220	$300	$380		Frances Jenkins Olcott		HM
1917	The Wishing-Ring Man	$220	$300	$380		Margaret Widdemer		Holt
1918	Adventures Of Odysseus And The Tale Of Troy	$220	$300	$380		Padraic Colum		Macmil
1920	The Children Of Odin	$180	$240	$300		Padraic Colum		Macmil
1921	Golden Fleece & Heroes Who Lived Before Achilles	$280	$360	$460		Padraic Colum	NH	Macmil
1926	Fairy Flowers	$160	$220	$280		Isidora Newman		Holt
1928	Tisza Tales	$160	$220	$280		Rosika Schwimmer		DD
1928	Willy Pogány's Mother Goose	$400	$520	$660		Willy Pogány		TNelson

Pogány   Willy

Year	Title	VG-	VG	VG+	Fine	Author	Award	Pub
1929	Alice's Adventures In Wonderland	$380	$520	$640		Lewis Carroll		Dutton
1930	Magyar Fairy Tales From Old Hungarian Legends	$180	$240	$300		Nándor Pogány		Dutton
1935	The Wimp And The Woodle	$160	$220	$280		Helen von Kolnitz Hyer		Sutton
1936	Coppa Hamba	$160	$200	$260		Blanche Ashley Ambrose		Sutton
1936	How Santa Found The Cobbler's Shop	$160	$200	$260		Margaretta Harmon		Sutton
1936	The Goose Girl Of Nürnberg	$160	$200	$260		Harriet Smith Hawley		Sutton
1938	The Golden Cockerel	$160	$200	$260		Elaine Cox Pogány (adapted)		TNelson
1940	Peterkin	$120	$160	$200		Elaine Pogány		DMcKay
1943	The Frenzied Prince	$120	$160	$200		Padraic Colum		DMcKay
1944	Running Away With Nebby	$120	$160	$200		Phillis Garrard		DMcKay

Polacco   Patricia

Year	Title	VG-	VG	VG+	Fine	Author	Award	Pub
1987	Meteor!		$20	$30	$40	Patricia Polacco		DoddM
1988	Boat Ride With Lillian Two Blossom		$18	$25	$35	Patricia Polacco		Philo
1988	Casey At The Bat		$16	$25	$30	Ernest Lawrence Thayer		Putnam
1988	Rechenka's Eggs		$16	$25	$30	Patricia Polacco		Philo
1988	The Keeping Quilt		$35	$50	$70	Patricia Polacco		S&S
1989	Uncle Vova's Tree		$16	$25	$30	Patricia Polacco		Philo
1990	Babushka's Doll		$16	$25	$30	Patricia Polacco		S&S
1990	Just Plain Fancy		$16	$25	$30	Patricia Polacco		Bantam
1990	Thunder Cake		$16	$25	$30	Patricia Polacco		Philo
1991	Appelemando's Dreams		$14	$20	$30	Patricia Polacco		Philo
1991	Some Birthday!		$14	$20	$30	Patricia Polacco		S&S
1992	Chicken Sunday		$14	$20	$30	Patricia Polacco		Philo
1992	Mrs. Katz And Tush		$14	$20	$30	Patricia Polacco		Bantam
1992	Picnic At Mudsock Meadow		$14	$20	$30	Patricia Polacco		Putnam
1993	Babushka Baba Yaga		$14	$20	$25	Patricia Polacco		Philo
1993	The Bee Tree		$14	$20	$25	Patricia Polacco		Philo
1994	My Rotten Redheaded Older Brother		$14	$20	$25	Patricia Polacco		S&S
1994	Pink And Say		$14	$20	$25	Patricia Polacco		Philo
1994	Tikvah Means Hope		$14	$20	$25	Patricia Polacco		DoubleD
1995	Babushka's Mother Goose		$12	$18	$25	Patricia Polacco		Philo
1995	My Ol' Man		$12	$18	$25	Patricia Polacco		Philo
1996	Aunt Chip And The Great Triple Creek Dam Affair		$12	$16	$20	Patricia Polacco		Philo
1996	I Can Hear The Sun: A Modern Myth		$12	$16	$20	Patricia Polacco		Philo
1996	The Trees Of The Dancing Goats		$12	$16	$20	Patricia Polacco		S&S
1997	In Enzo's Splendid Gardens		$12	$16	$20	Patricia Polacco		Philo
1997	Uncle Isaaco		$12	$16	$20	Patricia Polacco		Philo
1998	Thank You, Mr. Falker		$10	$16	$20	Patricia Polacco		Philo
1999	Luba And The Wren		$10	$16	$20	Patricia Polacco		Philo
1999	Welcome Comfort		$10	$16	$20	Patricia Polacco		Philo
2000	The Butterfly		$10	$14	$18	Patricia Polacco		Philo
2000	The Calhoun Club		$10	$14	$18	Patricia Polacco		Philo
2001	Betty Doll		$8	$12	$16	Patricia Polacco		Philo
2001	Mr. Lincoln's Way		$8	$12	$16	Patricia Polacco		Philo
2002	A Christmas Tapestry		$8	$12	$16	Patricia Polacco		Philo
2002	When Lightning Comes In A Jar		$8	$12	$16	Patricia Polacco		Philo
2003	G Is For Goat		$8	$10	$14	Patricia Polacco		Philo
2003	The Graves Family		$8	$10	$14	Patricia Polacco		Philo
2004	An Orange For Frankie		$8	$10	$14	Patricia Polacco		Philo
2004	John Philip Duck		$8	$10	$14	Patricia Polacco		Philo
2004	Oh! Look!		$8	$10	$14	Patricia Polacco		Philo

Politi   Leo

Year	Title	VG-	VG	VG+	Fine	Author	Award	Pub
1938	Little Pancho	$220	$280	$360		Leo Politi		Viking
1941	The Least One	$140	$180	$240		Ruth Sawyer		Viking
1944	Angelo	$90	$120	$160		Helen Garrett		Viking
1944	Stories From The Americas	$90	$120	$160		Frank Henius		Scribnr
1946	Pedro, The Angel Of Olvera Street	$200	$260	$320		Leo Politi	CH	Scribnr
1946	The Three Miracles	$90	$120	$160		Catherine Blanton		JohnDay
1947	El Coyote, The Rebel	$80	$120	$140		Luis Perez		Holt
1948	Juanita	$160	$200	$260		Leo Politi	CH	Scribnr
1949	At The Palace Gates	$80	$120	$140		Helen Rand Parish		Viking
1949	Song Of The Swallows	$280	$360	$460		Leo Politi	CM	Scribnr

Politi   Leo

Year	Title	VG-	VG	VG+	Fine	Author	Award	Pub
1950	A Boat For Peppe	$80	$120	$140		Leo Politi		Scribnr
1951	Little Leo	$80	$100	$140		Leo Politi		Scribnr
1953	The Mission Bell	$80	$100	$140		Leo Politi		Scribnr
1955	The Columbus Story	$70	$100	$120		Alice Dalgliesh		Scribnr
1957	The Butterflies Come	$70	$100	$120		Leo Politi		Scribnr
1959	Saint Francis And The Animals	$70	$100	$120		Leo Politi		Scribnr
1960	Moy Moy	$70	$90	$120		Leo Politi		Scribnr
1961	The Noble Doll	$70	$90	$120		Elizabeth Coatsworth		Viking
1962	All Things Bright And Beautiful	$70	$90	$120		Cecil F. Alexander		Scribnr
1963	Rosa	$70	$90	$120		Leo Politi		Scribnr
1964	Bunker Hill	$50	$60	$80		Leo Politi		Desert
1964	Lito And The Clown	$60	$80	$100		Leo Politi		Scribnr
1965	Piccolo's Prank	$60	$80	$100		Leo Politi		Scribnr
1966	Tales Of The Los Angeles Parks	$60	$80	$100		Leo Politi		Best
1969	Mieko	$60	$80	$100		Leo Politi		GGate
1971	Emmet		$40	$60	$90	Leo Politi		Scribnr
1973	The Nicest Gift		$40	$60	$90	Leo Politi		Scribnr
1976	Three Stalks Of Corn		$40	$60	$80	Leo Politi		Scribnr
1978	Mr Fong's Toy Shop		$35	$50	$70	Leo Politi		Scribnr
1983	Redlands Impressions		$30	$50	$60	Leo Politi		Moore
1986	Around The World, Around Our Town		$30	$40	$60	Dolores S. Liscia		FSPL
1992	Lorenzo, The Naughty Parrot		$20	$30	$40	Tony Johnston		HBJ

Popp   Wendy

Year	Title	VG-	VG	VG+	Fine	Author	Award	Pub
1994	Moving Days		$10	$14	$18	Marc Harshman		Cobble
1995	Princess Florecita And The Iron Shoes		$10	$14	$18	John W. Stewig		Knopf
1998	Sister Anne's Hands		$8	$12	$16	Marybeth Lorbiecki		Dial
2002	One Candle		$8	$10	$14	Eve Bunting		Cotler

Prange   Beckie

Year	Title	VG-	VG	VG+	Fine	Author	Award	Pub
2005	Song Of The Water Boatman		$14	$20	$30	John Steptoe	CH	HM

Priceman   Marjorie

Year	Title	VG-	VG	VG+	Fine	Author	Award	Pub
1989	Friend Or Frog		$18	$25	$35	Marjorie Priceman		HM
1990	A Mouse In My House		$12	$18	$25	Nancy Van Laan		Knopf
1990	Rachel Fister's Blister		$12	$18	$25	Amy MacDonald		HM
1991	For Laughing Out Loud		$12	$18	$25	Jack Prelutsky (selected)		Knopf
1993	A. Nonny Mouse Writes Again!		$12	$16	$20	Jack Prelutsky (selected)		Knopf
1993	The Tiny, Tiny Boy And The Big, Big Cow		$12	$16	$20	Nancy Van Laan		Knopf
1994	How To Make An Apple Pie And See The World		$12	$16	$20	Marjorie Priceman		Knopf
1995	For Laughing Out Louder		$10	$16	$20	Jack Prelutsky (selected)		Knopf
1995	How Emily Blair Got Her Fabulous Hair		$10	$16	$20	Susan Garrison Beroza		BWB
1995	Zin! Zin! Zin!: A Violin		$35	$50	$70	Lloyd Moss	CH	S&S
1996	Cousin Ruth's Tooth		$10	$16	$20	Amy MacDonald		HM
1996	What Zeesie Saw On Delancey Street		$10	$16	$20	Elsa Okon Rael		S&S
1997	One Of Each		$10	$16	$20	Mary Ann Hoberman		LBrown
1997	When Zaydeh Danced On Eldridge Street		$10	$16	$20	Elsa Okon Rael		S&S
1998	Dancin' In The Kitchen		$10	$14	$18	Wendy and Frank Gelsanliter and Christian		Putnam
2005	Hot Air		$14	$20	$30	Marjorie Priceman	CH	Athenm

Primavera   Elise

Year	Title	VG-	VG	VG+	Fine	Author	Award	Pub
1981	Always Abigail		$18	$25	$35	Joyce St. Peter		Lippin
1981	The Joker And The Swan		$18	$25	$35	Dorothy Crayder		H&Row
1981	The Mermaid's Cape		$18	$25	$35	Margaret K. Wetterer		Athenm
1981	The Snug Little House		$18	$25	$35	Eils Moorhouse Lewis		Athenm
1982	The Giant's Apprentice		$14	$20	$25	Margaret K. Wetterer		Athenm
1983	Basil & Maggie		$25	$35	$50	Elise Primavera		Lippin
1983	Santa And Alex		$60	$80	$120	Delia Ephron		LBrown
1983	Surprise In The Mountains		$14	$20	$25	Natalie Carlson		H&Row
1983	The Bollo Caper		$14	$20	$25	Art Buchwald		Putnam
1983	Uncle George Washington And Harriot's Guitar		$14	$20	$25	Miriam Anne Bourne		CM

Primavera — Elise

Year	Title	VG-	VG	VG+	Fine	Author	Award	Pub
1985	Grandma's House		$12	$18	$25	Elaine Moore		LL&S
1985	What's One More?		$12	$18	$25	Margaret Poynter		Athenm
1986	Make Way For Sam Houston		$20	$30	$40	Jean Fritz		Putnam
1987	Christina Katerina And The Time She Quit The Family		$12	$16	$20	Patricia Lee Gauch		Putnam
1987	Hobie Hanson, You're Weird		$12	$16	$20	Jamie Gilson		LL&S
1988	Double Dog Dare		$12	$16	$20	Jamie Gilson		LL&S
1988	Grandma's Promise		$12	$16	$20	Elaine Moore		LL&S
1989	Best Witches		$12	$16	$20	Jane Yolen		Putnam
1990	Christina Katerina And The Great Bear Train		$10	$16	$20	Patricia Lee Gauch		Putnam
1991	Ralph's Frozen Tale		$10	$16	$20	Elise Primavera		Putnam
1992	Moe The Dog In Tropical Paradise		$10	$16	$20	Diane Stanley		Putnam
1993	The Three Dots		$10	$16	$20	Elise Primavera		Putnam
1994	Plantpet		$10	$14	$18	Elise Primavera		Putnam
1995	Woe Is Moe		$10	$14	$18	Diane Stanley		Putnam
1996	Jack, Skinny Bones, And The Golden Pancakes		$8	$12	$16	Mary-Claire Helldorfer		Viking
1997	Moonlight Kite		$8	$12	$16	Helen Elizabeth Buckley		LL&S
1998	Raising Dragons		$8	$12	$16	Jerdine Nolen		Whistle
1999	Auntie Claus		$8	$12	$16	Elise Primavera		Whistle
2002	Auntie Claus And The Key To Christmas		$8	$10	$14	Elise Primavera		Whistle

Provensen — Alice & Martin

Year	Title	VG-	VG	VG+	Fine	Author	Award	Pub
1947	Fireside Book Of Folk Songs	$120	$160	$220		Margaret Bradford (edited)		S&S
1948	Mr. Noah And His Family	$80	$100	$140		Jane Werner Watson		Golden
1948	The Golden Mother Goose	$80	$100	$140		Jane Werner Watson		Golden
1949	Katie The Kitten	$60	$80	$100		Kathryn Jackson		Golden
1949	The Color Kittens	$90	$120	$160		Margaret Wise Brown		Golden
1949	The Fuzzy Duckling	$60	$80	$100		Jane Werner Watson		Golden
1950	Funny Bunny	$60	$80	$100		Rachel Learnard		Golden
1950	The Little Fat Policeman	$80	$120	$140		Margaret Wise Brown		Golden
1951	A Child's Garden Of Verses	$50	$70	$90		Robert Louis Stevenson		Golden
1952	The Animal Fair	$80	$100	$140		Alice Provensen	NYT	Golden
1959	The First Noel	$50	$60	$80		Alice Provensen		Golden
1962	Introduction To The Instruments Of The Orchestra	$35	$40	$60		Jane Bunche		Golden
1962	Ten Great Plays	$35	$40	$60		William Shakespeare		Golden
1963	Karen's Curiosity	$50	$60	$80		Alice Provensen		Golden
1963	Karen's Opposites	$50	$60	$80		Alice Provensen		Golden
1963	Legendary Animals	$50	$60	$80		Bryna & Louis Untermeyer		Golden
1964	The Charge Of The Light Brigade	$35	$40	$60		Alfred Tennyson		Golden
1965	Aesop's Fables	$40	$60	$70		Louis Untermeyer (adapted)		Golden
1967	What Is A Color?	$40	$50	$70		Alice Provensen		Golden
1968	Tales From The Ballet	$30	$40	$50		Louis Untermeyer		Golden
1970	The Golden Book Of Fun And Nonsense		$30	$50	$60	Louis Untermeyer		Golden
1970	Who's In The Egg		$30	$50	$60	Alice Provensen		Golden
1971	The Provensen Book Of Fairy Tales		$30	$50	$60	Alice Provensen (selected)		Random
1972	Play On Words		$25	$35	$50	Alice Provensen		Random
1973	My Little Hen		$30	$50	$60	Alice & Martin Provensen		Random
1973	Roses Are Red. Are Violets Blue?		$30	$50	$60	Alice Provensen		Random
1974	Our Animal Friends At Maple Hill Farm		$30	$40	$60	Alice Provensen		Random
1976	A Book Of Seasons		$30	$40	$60	Alice Provensen		Random
1976	The Mother Goose Book		$40	$60	$80	Alice Provensen	NYT	Random
1977	Old Mother Hubbard		$25	$40	$50	Sarah Catherine Martin		Random
1978	A Peaceable Kingdom: The Shaker Abecedarius		$35	$50	$70	Alice Provensen	NYT	Viking
1978	The Year At Maple Hill Farm		$25	$40	$50	Alice Provensen		Athenm
1980	A Horse And A Hound, A Goat And A Gander		$25	$35	$50	Alice Provensen		Athenm
1980	The Golden Serpent		$25	$35	$50	Walter Dean Myers		Viking
1981	A Visit To William Blake's Inn		$160	$240	$320	Nancy Willard	CH / NM	HBJ
1981	An Owl And Three Pussycats		$25	$35	$50	Alice Provensen		Athenm
1982	Birds, Beasts, And The Third Thing		$25	$35	$50	D. H. Lawrence		Viking
1983	The Glorious Flight		$120	$180	$240	Alice & Martin Provensen	CM	Viking
1984	Leonardo Da Vinci		$20	$30	$40	Alice Provensen		Viking
1984	Town & Country		$20	$30	$40	Alice Provensen		JCape
1987	Shaker Lane		$20	$30	$40	Alice & Martin Provensen		VK
1987	The Voyage Of The Ludgate Hill		$20	$30	$40	Nancy Willard		HBJ
1988	Old Mother Goose & Other Nursery Rhymes		$18	$25	$35	Alice Provensen		Golden
1990	The Buck Stops Here:The Presidents Of The U.S		$16	$25	$30	Alice Provensen		HCollins

Quackenbush   Robert M.

Year	Title	VG-	VG	VG+	Fine	Author	Award	Pub
1964	A Long, Long Time	$35	$40	$60		Inez Rice		LL&S
1965	The Selfish Giant	$25	$30	$40		Oscar Wilde		HR&W
1966	Rakoto And The Drongo Bird	$25	$30	$40		Robin McKown		LL&S
1967	A Sunday In Autumn	$25	$30	$40		Anthony Rowley		Singer
1967	Election Day	$25	$30	$40		Mary Kay Phelan		Crowell
1967	I Feel The Same Way	$25	$30	$40		Lilian Moore		Athenm
1967	If I Drove A Truck	$25	$30	$40		Miriam Young		LL&S
1967	The Diamond Necklace	$25	$30	$40		Guy de Maupassant		FWatts
1968	Billy And Milly	$20	$30	$35		Miriam Young		LL&S
1968	Billy Budd	$20	$30	$35		Herman Melville		FWatts
1968	Busy Winds	$20	$30	$35		Irma Simonton Black		Holiday
1968	Horatio	$20	$30	$35		Eleanor L. Clymer		Athenm
1968	The Open Boat	$20	$30	$35		Stephen Crane		FWatts
1969	Befana's Gift	$20	$30	$35		Natalie Carlson		H&Row
1969	Little Hans	$20	$30	$35		Oscar Wilde		Bobbs
1969	The Dirt Book	$20	$30	$35		Eva Knox Evans		LBrown
1969	When The Monkeys Wore Sombreros	$25	$35	$50		Mariana B. de Prieto		Harvey
1970	Beware The Polar Bear!		$18	$25	$35	Miriam Young		LL&S
1970	D Is For Rover		$18	$25	$35	Leonore Klein		Harvey
1970	If I Flew A Plane		$18	$25	$35	Miriam Young		LL&S
1970	The Baker And The Basilisk		$18	$25	$35	Georgess McHargue		Bobbs
1970	The Key To The Kitchen		$18	$25	$35	John Stewart		LL&S
1971	A Home For Hopper		$18	$25	$35	Rosemary Pendery		Morrow
1971	Blue River		$18	$25	$35	Julian May		Holiday
1971	If I Drove A Car		$18	$25	$35	Miriam Young		LL&S
1971	If I Sailed A Boat		$18	$25	$35	Miriam Young		LL&S
1971	Six Silver Spoons		$18	$25	$35	Janette Lowrey		H&Row
1971	The Bellfounder's Sons		$18	$25	$35	Lini R. Grol		Bobbs
1971	The Peasant's Pea Patch		$18	$25	$35	Guy Daniels		DelaP
1971	The Scribbler		$18	$25	$35	George Mendoza		HR&W
1972	Giraffes At Home		$18	$25	$35	Ann Cooke		Crowell
1972	If I Drove A Train		$18	$25	$35	Miriam Young		LL&S
1972	Old Macdonald Had A Farm		$18	$25	$35	Robert M. Quackenbush		Lippin
1973	A Gift For Lonny		$16	$25	$30	Eve Bunting		Ginn
1973	Go Tell Aunt Rhody		$16	$25	$30	Robert M. Quackenbush		Lippin
1973	If I Drove A Bus		$16	$25	$30	Miriam Young		LL&S
1973	If I Drove A Tractor		$16	$25	$30	Miriam Young		LL&S
1973	If I Rode A Horse		$16	$25	$30	Miriam Young		LL&S
1973	Pronghorn On The Powder River		$16	$25	$30	Berniece Freschet		Crowell
1973	Seal Harbor		$16	$25	$30	John Frederick Waters		FWarne
1973	She'll Be Comin' 'Round The Mountain		$16	$25	$30	Robert M. Quackenbush		Lippin
1973	The Wizard Islands		$16	$25	$30	Jane Yolen		Crowell
1974	Clementine		$16	$25	$30	Robert M. Quackenbush		Lippin
1974	If I Rode A Dinosaur		$16	$25	$30	Miriam Young		LL&S
1974	If I Rode An Elephant		$16	$25	$30	Miriam Young		LL&S
1974	Leave Horatio Alone		$16	$25	$30	Eleanor L. Clymer		Athenm
1974	There'll Be A Hot Time In The Old Town Tonight		$16	$25	$30	Robert M. Quackenbush		Lippin
1975	Animal Cracks		$16	$25	$30	Robert M. Quackenbush		LL&S
1975	Engine Number Seven		$16	$25	$30	Eleanor L. Clymer		HR&W
1975	Skip To My Lou		$16	$25	$30	Robert M. Quackenbush		Lippin
1975	The Man On The Flying Trapeze		$16	$25	$30	Robert M. Quackenbush		Lippin
1975	Too Many Lollipops		$16	$25	$30	Robert M. Quackenbush		PMagP
1976	Detective Mole		$16	$25	$30	Robert M. Quackenbush		LL&S
1976	Horatio's Birthday		$16	$25	$30	Eleanor L. Clymer		Athenm
1976	Pete Pack Rat		$16	$25	$30	Robert M. Quackenbush		LL&S
1976	Pop! Goes The Weasel And Yankee Doodle		$16	$25	$30	Robert M. Quackenbush		Lippin
1976	Take Me Out To The Airfield!		$16	$25	$30	Robert M. Quackenbush		PMagP
1977	Detective Mole And The Secret Clues		$16	$25	$30	Robert M. Quackenbush		LL&S
1977	Sheriff Sally Gopher And The Haunted Dance Hall		$16	$25	$30	Robert M. Quackenbush		LL&S
1977	The House On Stink Alley		$16	$25	$30	F. N. Monjo		HR&W
1978	Along Came The Model T!		$14	$20	$30	Robert M. Quackenbush		PMagP
1978	Calling Doctor Quack		$14	$20	$30	Robert M. Quackenbush		LL&S
1978	Detective Mole And The Tip-Top Mystery		$14	$20	$30	Robert M. Quackenbush		LL&S
1978	Horatio Goes To The Country		$14	$20	$30	Eleanor Lowenton		Athenm
1978	Mr. Snow Bunting's Secret		$14	$20	$30	Robert M. Quackenbush		LL&S
1978	Pete Pack Rat And The Gila Monster Gang		$14	$20	$30	Robert M. Quackenbush		LL&S
1978	The Boy Who Dreamed Of Rockets		$14	$20	$30	Robert M. Quackenbush		PMagP

Quackenbush   Robert M.

Year	Title	VG-	VG	VG+	Fine	Author	Award	Pub
1978	The Most Welcome Visitor		$14	$20	$30	Robert M. Quackenbush		Windmil
1979	Detective Mole And The Seashore Mystery		$14	$20	$30	Robert M. Quackenbush		LL&S
1979	Moose's Store		$14	$20	$30	Robert M. Quackenbush		LL&S
1979	Who Threw That Pie?		$14	$20	$30	Robert M. Quackenbush		AWhit
1980	Detective Mole And The Circus Mystery		$14	$20	$25	Robert M. Quackenbush		LL&S
1980	Henry's Awful Mistake		$14	$20	$25	Robert M. Quackenbush		PMagP
1980	Horatio Solves A Mystery		$14	$20	$25	Eleanor L. Clymer		Athenm
1980	Movie Monsters And Their Masters		$14	$20	$25	Robert M. Quackenbush		AWhit
1980	Oh, What An Awful Mess!		$14	$20	$25	Robert M. Quackenbush		P-Hall
1980	Piet Potter Returns		$14	$20	$25	Robert M. Quackenbush		McHill
1980	Piet Potter's First Case		$14	$20	$25	Robert M. Quackenbush		McHill
1980	The Black Pearl And The Ghost		$14	$20	$25	Walter Dean Myers		Viking
1981	Ahoy! Ahoy! Are You There?		$14	$20	$25	Robert M. Quackenbush		P-Hall
1981	City Trucks		$14	$20	$25	Robert M. Quackenbush		AWhit
1981	Detective Mole And The Halloween Mystery		$14	$20	$25	Robert M. Quackenbush		LL&S
1981	Express Train To Trouble		$14	$20	$25	Robert M. Quackenbush		P-Hall
1981	Henry's Important Date		$14	$20	$25	Robert M. Quackenbush		PMagP
1981	No Mouse For Me!		$14	$20	$25	Robert M. Quackenbush		FWatts
1981	Pete Pack Rat's Christmas Eve Surprise		$14	$20	$25	Robert M. Quackenbush		LL&S
1981	Piet Potter Strikes Again		$14	$20	$25	Robert M. Quackenbush		McHill
1981	Piet Potter To The Rescue		$14	$20	$25	Robert M. Quackenbush		McHill
1981	The Boy Who Waited For Santa Claus		$14	$20	$25	Robert M. Quackenbush		FWatts
1981	What Has Wild Tom Done Now?		$14	$20	$25	Robert M. Quackenbush		P-Hall
1982	Cable Car To Catastrophe		$14	$20	$25	Robert M. Quackenbush		P-Hall
1982	Dig To Disaster		$14	$20	$25	Robert M. Quackenbush		P-Hall
1982	First Grade Jitters		$14	$20	$25	Robert M. Quackenbush		Lippin
1982	Henry Goes West		$14	$20	$25	Robert M. Quackenbush		PMagP
1982	Here A Plant, There A Plant, Everywhere A Plant!		$14	$20	$25	Robert M. Quackenbush		P-Hall
1982	Piet Potter On The Run		$14	$20	$25	Robert M. Quackenbush		McHill
1982	Piet Potter's Hot Clue		$14	$20	$25	Robert M. Quackenbush		McHill
1982	Sheriff Sally Gopher And The Thanksgiving Caper		$14	$20	$25	Robert M. Quackenbush		LL&S
1982	Watt Got You Started, Mr. Fulton?		$14	$20	$25	Robert M. Quackenbush		P-Hall
1983	Gondola To Danger		$14	$20	$25	Robert M. Quackenbush		P-Hall
1983	I Don't Want To Go, I Don't Know How To Act		$14	$20	$25	Robert M. Quackenbush		Lippin
1983	Quick, Annie, Give Me A Catchey Line!		$14	$20	$25	Robert M. Quackenbush		P-Hall
1983	Stairway To Doom		$14	$20	$25	Robert M. Quackenbush		P-Hall
1983	The Beagle And Mr. Flycatcher		$14	$20	$25	Robert M. Quackenbush		P-Hall
1984	Don't You Dare Shoot That Bear!		$12	$18	$25	Robert M. Quackenbush		P-Hall
1984	Funny Bunnies		$12	$18	$25	Robert M. Quackenbush		Clarion
1984	Investigator Ketchem's Crime Book		$12	$18	$25	Robert M. Quackenbush		Avon
1984	Mark Twain? What Kind Of Name Is That?		$12	$18	$25	Robert M. Quackenbush		P-Hall
1984	Rickshaw To Horror		$12	$18	$25	Robert M. Quackenbush		P-Hall
1984	Taxi To Intrigue		$12	$18	$25	Robert M. Quackenbush		P-Hall
1985	Bicycle To Treachery		$12	$18	$25	Robert M. Quackenbush		P-Hall
1985	Detective Mole And The Haunted Castle Mystery		$12	$18	$25	Robert M. Quackenbush		LL&S
1985	Once Upon A Time!		$12	$18	$25	Robert M. Quackenbush		P-Hall
1985	Stage Door To Terror		$12	$18	$25	Robert M. Quackenbush		P-Hall
1985	Who Said There's No Man On The Moon?		$12	$18	$25	Robert M. Quackenbush		P-Hall
1986	Chuck Lends A Paw		$12	$16	$20	Robert M. Quackenbush		Clarion
1986	Old Silver Leg Takes Over!		$12	$16	$20	Robert M. Quackenbush		P-Hall
1986	Sherlock Chick's First Case		$12	$16	$20	Robert M. Quackenbush		PMagP
1986	Surfboard To Peril		$12	$16	$20	Robert M. Quackenbush		P-Hall
1986	Texas Trail To Calamity		$12	$16	$20	Robert M. Quackenbush		P-Hall
1986	Who Let Muddy Boots Into The White House?		$12	$16	$20	Robert M. Quackenbush		P-Hall
1987	Dogsled To Dread		$12	$16	$20	Robert M. Quackenbush		S&S
1987	Quit Pulling My Leg!		$12	$16	$20	Robert M. Quackenbush		P-Hall
1987	Sherlock Chick And The Peekaboo Mystery		$12	$16	$20	Robert M. Quackenbush		PMagP
1987	Too Many Ducklings		$12	$16	$20	Robert M. Quackenbush		Golden
1988	It's Raining Cats And Dogs		$12	$16	$20	Charles Keller		Pippin
1988	Mouse Feathers		$12	$16	$20	Robert M. Quackenbush		Clarion
1988	Who's That Girl With The Gun?		$12	$16	$20	Robert M. Quackenbush		P-Hall
1989	Danger In Tibet		$12	$16	$20	Robert M. Quackenbush		Pippin
1989	Funny Bunnies On The Run		$12	$16	$20	Robert M. Quackenbush		Clarion
1989	I Did It With My Hatchet		$12	$16	$20	Robert M. Quackenbush		Pippin
1989	Pass The Quill, I'll Write A Draft		$12	$16	$20	Robert M. Quackenbush		Pippin
1989	Sherlock Chick And The Giant Egg Mystery		$12	$16	$20	Robert M. Quackenbush		PMagP
1990	Clear The Cow Pasture, I'm Coming In For A Landing!		$10	$16	$20	Robert M. Quackenbush		S&S

Quackenbush   Robert M.

Year	Title	VG-	VG	VG+	Fine	Author	Award	Pub
1990	Lost In The Amazon		$10	$16	$20	Robert M. Quackenbush		Pippin
1990	Sherlock Chick & The Case Of The Night Noises		$10	$16	$20	Robert M. Quackenbush		PMagP
1992	Henry's World Tour		$10	$16	$20	Robert M. Quackenbush		DoubleD
1992	Stop The Presses, Nellie's Got A Scoop!		$10	$16	$20	Robert M. Quackenbush		S&S
1993	Henry Babysits		$10	$16	$20	Robert M. Quackenbush		PMagP
1993	The Whole World In Your Hands		$10	$16	$20	Melvin & Gilda Berger		Ideals
1993	Where Did Your Family Come From?		$10	$16	$20	Melvin & Gilda Berger		Ideals
1994	Arthur Ashe And His Match With History		$10	$14	$18	Robert M. Quackenbush		S&S
1994	The Spinner's Daughter		$10	$14	$18	Amy Littlesugar		Pippin
1995	Abigail's Drum		$10	$14	$18	John A. Minahan		Pippin
1995	Clara Barton And Her Victory Over Fear		$10	$14	$18	Robert M. Quackenbush		S&S
1997	Batbaby		$8	$12	$16	Robert M. Quackenbush		Random
1998	Daughter Of Liberty		$8	$12	$16	Robert M. Quackenbush		Hyper
2001	Batbaby Finds A Home		$8	$10	$14	Robert M. Quackenbush		Random

Rand   Ted

Year	Title	VG-	VG	VG+	Fine	Author	Award	Pub
1970	America, I Know You		$25	$35	$50	Bill Martin		Martin
1979	The Phantom Athlete		$14	$20	$30	Ted Rand		HR&W
1985	The Ghost-Eye Tree		$12	$18	$25	B. Martin & J. Archambault		HR&W
1986	Barn Dance!		$12	$16	$20	B. Martin & J. Archambault		HR&W
1986	White Dynamite & Curly Kidd		$12	$16	$20	B. Martin & J. Archambault		HR&W
1987	Here Are My Hands		$12	$16	$20	B. Martin & J. Archambault		Holt
1987	Knots On A Counting Rope		$12	$16	$20	B. Martin & J. Archambault		Holt
1988	Once When I Was Scared		$12	$16	$20	Helena Clare Pittman		Dutton
1988	The Hornbeam Tree & Other Poems		$12	$16	$20	Charles Norman		Holt
1988	The Sun, The Wind, And The Rain		$12	$16	$20	Lisa Westberg Peters		Holt
1988	Up And Down On The Merry-Go-Round		$12	$16	$20	B. Martin & J. Archambault		Holt
1989	A Little Excitement		$12	$16	$20	Marc Harshman		Cobble
1989	Salt Hands		$12	$16	$20	Jane Chelsea Aragon		Dutton
1989	Salty Dog		$12	$16	$20	Gloria Rand		Holt
1989	The Jumblies		$25	$40	$50	Edward Lear		Putnam
1990	Christmas Trees		$10	$16	$20	Robert Frost		Holt
1990	My Shadow		$10	$16	$20	Robert Louis Stevenson		Putnam
1990	Paul Revere's Ride		$10	$16	$20	Henry Wadsworth Longfellow		Dutton
1990	Salty Sails North		$10	$16	$20	Gloria Rand		Holt
1990	The Wild Horses Of Sweetbriar		$25	$35	$50	Natalie Kinsey-Warnock		Cobble
1991	Country Crossing		$10	$16	$20	Jim Aylesworth		Athenm
1991	Night Tree		$10	$16	$20	Eve Bunting		HBJ
1991	Salty Takes Off		$10	$16	$20	Gloria Rand		Holt
1991	Water's Way		$10	$16	$20	Lisa Westberg Peters		Arcad
1992	Grandma According To Me		$40	$60	$90	Karen Magnuson Beil		DoubleD
1992	My Buddy		$10	$16	$20	Audrey Osofsky		Holt
1992	Prince William		$10	$16	$20	Gloria Rand		Holt
1992	The Walloping Window-Blind		$10	$16	$20	Charles E. Carryl		Arcad
1993	Arithmetic		$10	$16	$20	Carl Sandburg		HBJ
1993	Can I Be Good?		$10	$16	$20	Livingston Taylor		HBJ
1993	The Bear That Heard Crying		$10	$16	$20	Natalie Kinsey-Warnock		Cobble
1993	The Owl Who Became The Moon		$10	$16	$20	Jonathan London		Dutton
1994	A Snake In The House		$10	$14	$18	Faith McNulty		Scholas
1994	Backyard Rescue		$10	$14	$18	Hope Ryden		Tambour
1994	Don't Forget		$10	$14	$18	Patricia Lakin		Tambour
1994	Heidi		$10	$14	$18	Johanna Spyri		Holt
1994	The Cabin Key		$10	$14	$18	Gloria Rand		HBrace
1994	The Wizard's Promise		$10	$14	$18	Suzanna Marshak		S&S
1994	Whiffle Squeek		$10	$14	$18	Caron Lee Cohen		Penguin
1995	In The Palace Of The Ocean King		$10	$14	$18	Marilyn Singer		Athenm
1995	The Night Before Christmas		$10	$14	$18	Clement C. Moore		NSBooks
1995	The Tree That Would Not Die		$10	$14	$18	Ellen Levine		Scholas
1996	Aloha, Salty!		$8	$12	$16	Gloria Rand		Holt
1996	Keepers		$8	$12	$16	Alice Schertle		LL&S
1996	Mountain Wedding		$8	$12	$16	Faye Gibbons		Morrow
1996	Secret Place		$8	$12	$16	Eve Bunting		Clarion
1996	The Football That Won--		$8	$12	$16	Michael R. Sampson		Holt
1996	Willie Takes A Hike		$8	$12	$16	Gloria Rand		HBrace
1997	Baby In A Basket		$8	$12	$16	Gloria Rand		Cobble

Rand   Ted

Year	Title	VG-	VG	VG+	Fine	Author	Award	Pub
1997	Mailing May		$8	$12	$16	Michael O. Tunnell		Green
1997	Storm On The Desert		$8	$12	$16	Carolyn Lesser		HBrace
1998	A Home For Spooky		$8	$12	$16	Gloria Rand		Holt
1998	Jezebel's Spooky Spot		$8	$12	$16	Alice Ross		Dutton
1998	My Father's Boat		$8	$12	$16	Sherry Garland		Scholas
1998	The Hullabaloo ABC		$8	$12	$16	Beverly Cleary		Morrow
1999	Fighting For The Forest		$8	$12	$16	Gloria Rand		Holt
1999	Mama And Me And The Model-T		$8	$12	$16	Faye Gibbons		Morrow
2000	It's About Dogs		$8	$10	$14	Tony Johnston		Harcort
2000	Let's Play Rough		$8	$10	$14	Lynne Jonell		Putnam
2000	The Memory String		$8	$10	$14	Eve Bunting		Clarion
2000	With A Dog Like That, A Kid Like Me		$8	$10	$14	Michael Rosen		Dial
2001	Nutik & Amaroq Play Ball		$8	$10	$14	Jean Craighead George		HCollins
2001	Nutik, The Wolf Pup		$8	$10	$14	Jean Craighead George		HCollins
2001	Sailing Home		$8	$10	$14	Gloria Rand		NSBooks
2002	Country Kid, City Kid		$8	$10	$14	Julie Cummins		Holt
2002	Goodnight, Hattie, My Dearie, My Dove		$8	$10	$14	Alice Schertle		HCollins
2002	Once Upon A Farm		$8	$10	$14	Marie Bradby		Orchard
2003	Anna The Bookbinder		$8	$10	$14	Andrea Cheng		Walker
2003	Homespun Sarah		$8	$10	$14	Verla Kay		Putnam
2003	Ice Palace		$8	$10	$14	Deborah Blumenthal		Clarion
2004	Faraway Grandpa		$6	$10	$12	Roberta Karim		Holt
2004	If Not For The Cat		$6	$10	$12	Jack Prelutsky		Green
2004	Mary Was A Little Lamb		$6	$10	$12	Gloria Rand		Holt
2004	My Mountain Song		$6	$10	$12	Shutta Crum		Clarion

Raschka   Christopher

Year	Title	VG-	VG	VG+	Fine	Author	Award	Pub
1990	The Saga Of Shakespeare Pintlewood		$25	$35	$50	James H. Lehman		Bro
1991	Benjamin Brody's Backyard Bag		$16	$25	$30	Phyllis Wezeman		Breth
1991	The Owl And The Tuba		$16	$25	$30	James H. Lehman		Bro
1992	Charlie Parker Played Be Bop		$16	$25	$30	Christopher Raschka		Orchard
1993	Yo! Yes?		$40	$60	$80	Christopher Raschka	CH	Orchard
1994	Elizabeth Imagined An Iceberg		$14	$20	$30	Christopher Raschka		Orchard
1995	Can't Sleep		$14	$20	$25	Christopher Raschka		Orchard
1996	The Blushful Hippopotamus		$12	$18	$25	Christopher Raschka		Orchard
1996	The Genie In The Jar		$12	$18	$25	Nikki Giovanni		Holt
1997	Mysterious Thelonious		$12	$18	$25	Christopher Raschka		Orchard
1998	Arlene Sardine		$12	$16	$20	Christopher Raschka		Orchard
1998	Simple Gifts		$12	$16	$20	Christopher Raschka		Holt
1999	Another Important Book		$12	$16	$20	Margaret Wise Brown		HCollins
1999	Happy To Be Nappy		$12	$16	$20	Bell Hooks		Hyper
1999	Like Likes Like		$12	$16	$20	Christopher Raschka		DK
2000	Doggy Dog		$10	$14	$18	Christopher Raschka		Hyper
2000	Fishing In The Air		$10	$14	$18	Sharon Creech		Cotler
2000	Goosey Goose		$10	$14	$18	Christopher Raschka		Hyper
2000	Lamby Lamb		$10	$14	$18	Christopher Raschka		Hyper
2000	Moosey Moose		$10	$14	$18	Christopher Raschka		Hyper
2000	Movin'		$10	$14	$18	Dave Johnson		Orchard
2000	Ring! Yo?		$10	$14	$18	Christopher Raschka		DK
2000	Sluggy Slug		$10	$14	$18	Christopher Raschka		Hyper
2000	Snaily Snail		$10	$14	$18	Christopher Raschka		Hyper
2000	The Four Corners Of The Sky		$10	$14	$18	Steven J. Zeitlin		Holt
2000	Whaley Whale		$10	$14	$18	Christopher Raschka		Hyper
2000	Wormy Worm		$10	$14	$18	Christopher Raschka		Hyper
2001	A Poke In The I		$10	$14	$18	Paul B. Janeczko		Candle
2001	Little Tree		$10	$14	$18	E. E. Cummings		Hyper
2001	Table Manners		$10	$14	$18	Vladimir Radunsky		Candle
2001	Waffle		$10	$14	$18	Christopher Raschka		Athenm
2002	Be Boy Buzz		$8	$12	$16	Bell Hooks		Hyper
2002	I Pledge Allegiance		$8	$12	$16	Francis Bellamy		Candle
2002	John Coltrane's Giant Steps		$8	$12	$16	John Coltrane		Athenm
2003	Talk To Me About The Alphabet		$8	$12	$16	Christopher Raschka		Holt
2004	A Child's Christmas In Wales		$8	$10	$14	Dylan Thomas		Candle
2005	The Hello, Goodbye Window		$25	$40	$50	Norton Juster	CM	diCapua

Raskin   Ellen

Year	Title	VG-	VG	VG+	Fine	Author	Award	Pub
1966	Nothing Ever Happens On My Block	$40	$60	$70		Ellen Raskin		Athenm
1966	Songs Of Innocence	$40	$60	$70		William Blake		DoubleD
1967	Probability: The Science Of Chance	$30	$40	$50		Arthur G. Razzell		DoubleD
1967	Silly Songs And Sad	$30	$40	$50		Ellen Raskin		Crowell
1967	This Is 4	$30	$40	$50		Arthur G. Razzell		DoubleD
1968	A Paper Zoo	$30	$40	$50		Renée Karol Weiss		Macmil
1968	Books	$30	$40	$50		Susan Bartlett		HR&W
1968	Inatuk's Friend	$30	$40	$50		Suzanne Stark Morrow		LBrown
1968	Lady Ellen Grae	$30	$40	$50		Vera & Bill Cleaver		Lippin
1968	Spectacles	$40	$50	$70		Ellen Raskin	NYT	Athenm
1968	Symmetry	$30	$40	$50		Arthur G. Razzell		DoubleD
1969	A Question Of Accuracy	$25	$35	$50		Arthur G. Razzell		DoubleD
1969	And It Rained	$25	$35	$50		Ellen Raskin		Athenm
1969	Circles And Curves	$25	$35	$50		Arthur G. Razzell		DoubleD
1969	Come Along!	$25	$35	$50		Rebecca Caudill		HR&W
1969	Ghost In A Four-Room Apartment	$25	$35	$50		Ellen Raskin		Athenm
1969	Shrieks At Midnight	$25	$35	$50		Sara & John Brewton		Crowell
1969	Three And The Shape Of Three	$25	$35	$50		Arthur G. Razzell		DoubleD
1970	A & The		$25	$35	$50	Ellen Raskin		Athenm
1970	Goblin Market		$25	$35	$50	Christina Georgina Rossetti		Dutton
1971	Mysterious Disappearance Of Leon (I Mean Noel)		$25	$35	$50	Ellen Raskin		Dutton
1971	The World's Greatest Freak Show		$25	$35	$50	Ellen Raskin		Athenm
1972	Franklin Stein		$25	$35	$50	Ellen Raskin		Athenm
1973	Moe Q. Mcglutch		$25	$35	$50	Ellen Raskin		PMagP
1973	Who, Said Sue, Said Whoo!		$25	$35	$50	Ellen Raskin		Athenm
1974	Figgs & Phantoms		$40	$60	$80	Ellen Raskin	NH	Dutton
1974	Moose, Goose, And Little Nobody		$30	$40	$60	Ellen Raskin		PMagP
1975	The Tattooed Potato & Other Clues		$20	$30	$40	Ellen Raskin		Dutton
1976	Twenty-Two, Twenty-Three		$30	$40	$60	Ellen Raskin		Athenm
1978	The Westing Game		$120	$180	$240	Ellen Raskin	NM	Dutton

Rathmann   Peggy

Year	Title	VG-	VG	VG+	Fine	Author	Award	Pub
1991	Ruby The Copycat		$12	$18	$25	Peggy Rathmann		Scholas
1992	Bootsie Barker Bites		$12	$18	$25	Barbara Bottner		Putnam
1994	Good Night, Gorilla		$12	$16	$20	Peggy Rathmann		Putnam
1995	Officer Buckle And Gloria		$60	$80	$120	Peggy Rathmann	CM	Putnam
1998	10 Minutes Till Bedtime		$10	$14	$18	Peggy Rathmann		Putnam
2003	The Day The Babies Crawled Away		$8	$10	$14	Peggy Rathmann		Putnam
2004	Buenas Noches, Gorilla		$8	$10	$14	Peggy Rathmann		Putnam

Ratz de Tagyos   Paul

Year	Title	VG-	VG	VG+	Fine	Author	Award	Pub
1992	A Coney Tale		$12	$18	$25	Paul Ratz de Tagyos		Clarion
1994	Showdown At Lonesome Pellet		$12	$16	$20	Paul Ratz de Tagyos		Clarion
2004	Rooster Can't Cock-A-Doodle-Doo		$8	$10	$14	Karen Rostoker-Gruber		Dial

Rayevsky   Robert

Year	Title	VG-	VG	VG+	Fine	Author	Award	Pub
1985	Hitchety Hatchety, Up I Go!		$16	$25	$30	Patricia Brennan		Macmil
1986	Mister Cat-And-A-Half		$12	$16	$20	Richard Pevear (retold)		Macmil
1987	Our King Has Horns!		$12	$16	$20	Richard Pevear (retold)		Macmil
1987	The Riddle		$12	$16	$20	Adele Vernon		DoddM
1988	Aesop's Fables		$12	$16	$20	Tom Paxton (retold)		Morrow
1988	The Dragon Nanny		$12	$16	$20	C. L. G. Martin		Macmil
1990	Belling The Cat & Other Aesop's Fables		$10	$16	$20	Tom Paxton (retold)		Morrow
1990	The Talking Tree: An Old Italian Tale		$10	$16	$20	Inna Rayevsky (retold)		Putnam
1990	The Tzar's Bird		$10	$16	$20	Ann Tompert		Macmil
1991	Androcles And The Lion, & Other Aesop's Fables		$10	$16	$20	Tom Paxton (retold)		Morrow
1991	The Golden Heart Of Winter		$10	$16	$20	Marilyn Singer		Morrow
1993	Angels, Angels All Around: Bible Stories Retold		$10	$16	$20	Bob Hartman		Lion
1993	Birds Of A Feather & Other Aesop's Fables		$10	$16	$20	Tom Paxton (retold)		Morrow
1993	Three Sacks Of Truth		$10	$16	$20	Eric Kimmel (adapted)		Holiday
1994	A Word To The Wise: & Other Proverbs		$10	$14	$18	Johanna Hurwitz		Morrow
1994	Bernal & Florinda: A Spanish Tale		$10	$14	$18	Eric Kimmel		Holiday

Rayevsky   Robert

Year	Title	VG-	VG	VG+	Fine	Author	Award	Pub
1996	The Sleepy Men		$8	$12	$16	Margaret Wise Brown		Hyper
1997	Squash It!: A True And Ridiculous Tale		$8	$12	$16	Eric Kimmel (adapted)		Holiday
1999	Joan Of Arc		$8	$12	$16	Margaret Hodges		Holiday
2001	Under New York		$8	$10	$14	Linda Oatman High		Holiday
2002	Two Fools And A Horse		$8	$10	$14	Sally Derby		Holiday
2003	The Eyes Of The Unicorn		$8	$10	$14	Teresa Bateman		MCaven

Rayner   Mary

Year	Title	VG-	VG	VG+	Fine	Author	Award	Pub
1976	Mr. And Mrs. Pig's Evening Out		$20	$30	$40	Mary Rayner		Athenm
1976	The Witchfinder		$20	$30	$40	Mary Rayner		Morrow
1978	Cass The Brave		$14	$20	$30	Griselda Gifford		Goll
1978	Garth Pig And The Ice Cream Lady		$14	$20	$30	Mary Rayner		Athenm
1980	Daggie Dogfoot		$50	$70	$100	Dick King-Smith		Goll
1980	The Rain Cloud		$14	$20	$25	Mary Rayner		Macmil
1981	Mrs. Pig's Bulk Buy		$14	$20	$25	Mary Rayner		Athenm
1982	Pigs Might Fly		$25	$35	$50	Dick King-Smith		Viking
1983	The Dead Letter Box		$14	$20	$25	Jan Mark		HHamil
1984	Lost And Found		$12	$18	$25	Jill Paton Walsh		Deutsch
1984	Magnus Powermouse		$40	$60	$90	Dick King-Smith		H&Row
1984	The Sheep-Pig		$60	$90	$120	Dick King-Smith		Goll
1985	Babe		$60	$90	$120	Dick King-Smith		Crown
1986	Crocodarling		$12	$16	$20	Mary Rayner		BradP
1987	Mrs. Pig Gets Cross & Other Stories		$12	$16	$20	Mary Rayner		Dutton
1987	Thank You For The Tadpole		$12	$16	$20	Pat Thomson		DelaP
1989	Marathon And Steve		$12	$16	$20	Mary Rayner		Dutton
1989	Oh, Paul!		$12	$16	$20	Mary Rayner		Barrn
1993	Garth Pig Steals The Show		$10	$16	$20	Mary Rayner		Dutton
1994	One By One		$10	$14	$18	Mary Rayner		Dutton
1994	Ten Pink Piglets		$10	$14	$18	Mary Rayner		Dutton
2002	Hobart		$8	$10	$14	Anita Briggs		S&S

Reed   Philip

Year	Title	VG-	VG	VG+	Fine	Author	Award	Pub
1958	Many Moons	$50	$60	$80		James Thurber		Roe
1962	The 7 Voyages Of Sindbad The Sailor	$50	$60	$80		Philip Reed		Athenm
1963	Mother Goose And Nursery Rhymes	$70	$90	$120		Philip Reed (adapted)	CH	Athenm
1966	A Christmas Carol In Prose	$40	$60	$70		Charles Dickens		Athenm

Rey   H.A.

Year	Title	VG-	VG	VG+	Fine	Author	Award	Pub
1941	Curious George	$2,200	$3,000	$3,800		H.A. Rey		HM
1942	Anybody At Home?	$200	$280	$340		H.A. Rey		HM
1942	Cecily G. And The 9 Monkeys	$720	$960	$1,200		H.A. Rey		HM
1942	Don't Frighten The Lion!	$200	$280	$340		Margaret Wise Brown		H&B
1942	Elizabite	$200	$280	$340		H.A. Rey		H&B
1942	Tit For Tat	$200	$280	$340		H.A. Rey		H&B
1943	Tommy Helps, Too	$200	$280	$340		H.A. Rey		HM
1943	Where's My Baby?	$200	$280	$340		H.A. Rey		HM
1944	Egbert And His Marvelous Adventures	$140	$180	$220		Paul Thomas Gilbert		H&B
1944	Katy No-Pocket	$140	$180	$220		Emmy Payne		HM
1944	Pretzel	$140	$180	$220		Margret Rey		H&B
1944	The Park Book	$140	$180	$220		Charlotte Zolotow		H&B
1945	Look For The Letters	$140	$180	$220		H.A. Rey		H&B
1945	Spotty	$140	$180	$220		Margret Rey		H&B
1946	Pretzel And The Puppies	$140	$180	$220		Margret Rey		H&B
1947	Curious George Takes A Job	$1,400	$2,000	$2,400		H.A. Rey		HM
1948	Billy's Picture	$120	$160	$220		H.A. & Margret Rey		H&B
1952	Curious George Rides A Bike	$580	$780	$980		H.A. Rey		HM
1952	The Stars, A New Way Too See Them	$120	$160	$200		H.A. Rey		HM
1954	Find The Constellations	$120	$160	$200		H.A. Rey		HM
1957	Curious George Gets A Medal	$540	$720	$900		H.A. Rey		HM
1958	Curious George Flies A Kite	$520	$700	$880		Margret Rey		HM
1962	The Stars, A New Way Too See Them	$100	$120	$160		H.A. Rey		HM
1963	Curious George Learns The Alphabet	$320	$420	$520		H.A. Rey		HM

Rey   H.A.

Year	Title	VG-	VG	VG+	Fine	Author	Award	Pub
1966	The Stars, A New Way To See The Stars	$40	$60	$70		H.A. Rey		Hamlyn
1967	Zozo Goes to the Hospital	$40	$50	$70		H.A. & Margret Rey		C&Weed
1973	The Daynight Lamp		$30	$50	$60	Christian Morgenstern		HM

Rice   James

Year	Title	VG-	VG	VG+	Fine	Author	Award	Pub
1973	Cajun Night Before Christmas		$40	$60	$90	James Rice		Pelican
1974	Gaston The Green-Nosed Alligator		$16	$25	$30	James Rice		Pelican
1974	The Little Colonel		$16	$25	$30	James Rice		Pelican
1975	Cajun Columbus		$16	$25	$30	James Rice		Pelican
1975	Lyn And The Fuzzy		$16	$25	$30	James Rice		Pelican
1976	Cajun Alphabet		$16	$25	$30	James Rice		Pelican
1977	Prairie Christmas		$16	$25	$30	James Rice		Pelican
1978	Gaston Goes To Mardi Gras		$14	$20	$30	James Rice		Pelican
1978	Gaston Goes To Texas		$14	$20	$30	James Rice		Pelican
1978	Gaston Lays An Offshore Pipeline		$14	$20	$30	James Rice		Pelican
1983	Hillbilly Night Before Christmas		$14	$20	$25	James Rice		Pelican
1985	Gaston Goes To Nashville		$12	$18	$25	James Rice		Pelican
1986	Prairie Night Before Christmas		$12	$16	$20	James Rice		Pelican
1986	Texas Night Before Christmas		$12	$16	$20	James Rice		Pelican

Riddell   Chris

Year	Title	VG-	VG	VG+	Fine	Author	Award	Pub
1986	Ben And The Bear		$30	$40	$60	Chris Riddell		H&Row
1986	Ffangs The Vampire Bat And The Kiss Of Truth		$30	$40	$60	Ted Hughes		Faber
1986	Gruesome Giants		$30	$40	$60	Sarah Hayes (retold)		Derry
1986	Mr. Underbed		$30	$40	$60	Chris Riddell		Holt
1987	Bird's New Shoes		$20	$30	$40	Chris Riddell		Holt
1987	The Magician's Cat		$20	$30	$40	Jeff Williams		Faber
1988	The Trouble With Elephants		$18	$25	$35	Chris Riddell		Lippin
1989	Dracula's Daughter		$18	$25	$35	Mary Hoffman		Barrn
1989	Ellis And The Hummick		$18	$25	$35	Andrew Gibson		Faber
1989	The Dream Boat Brontosaurus		$18	$25	$35	Robert McCrum		Metheun
1990	The Abradizil		$16	$25	$30	Andrew Gibson		Faber
1990	The Bear Dance		$16	$25	$30	Chris Riddell		S&S
1990	The Wish Factory		$16	$25	$30	Chris Riddell		Ideals
1991	Jemima, Grandma, And The Great Lost Zone		$16	$25	$30	Andrew Gibson		Faber
1991	Out For The Count		$16	$25	$30	Kate Cave		Barrn
1996	Buddhism For Sheep		$12	$18	$25	Louise Howard		StMart
1997	Kasper In The Glitter		$12	$18	$25	Philip Ridley		Dutton
1997	The Swan's Stories		$12	$18	$25	Hans Christian Andersen		Candle
1997	Until I Met Dudley/How Everyday Things Really Work		$12	$18	$25	Roger McGough		Walker
1998	Beyond The Deepwoods		$500	$760	$1,000	Paul Stewart		DoubleD
1998	Something Else		$12	$16	$20	Kathryn Cave		Mondo
1999	A Little Bit Of Winter		$25	$35	$50	Paul Stewart		HCollins
1999	Buddhism For Bears		$12	$16	$20	Claire Nielson		StMart
1999	Castle Diary		$12	$16	$20	Richard Platt		Candle
1999	Stormchaser		$380	$580	$760	Paul Stewart		DoubleD
1999	The Birthday Presents		$12	$16	$20	Paul Stewart		AP
2000	Midnight Over Sanctaphrax		$260	$380	$500	Paul Stewart		DoubleD
2001	Pirate Diary		$35	$50	$70	Richard Platt	GM	Candle
2001	Platypus		$10	$14	$18	Chris Riddell		Harcort
2001	Rabbit's Wish		$25	$40	$50	Paul Stewart		HCollins
2001	The Curse Of The Gloamglozer		$100	$160	$220	Paul Stewart		DoubleD
2001	The Tao For Babies		$10	$14	$18	Claire Nielson		SaalF
2002	Platypus And The Lucky Day		$8	$12	$16	Chris Riddell		Harcort
2003	Platypus And The Birthday Party		$8	$12	$16	Chris Riddell		Harcort
2004	Beyond The Deepwoods		$30	$40	$60	Paul Stewart		DFick
2004	Fergus Crane		$25	$35	$50	Paul Stewart		DoubleD
2004	Free Lance And The Lake Of Skulls		$35	$50	$70	Paul Stewart		S&S
2004	Gulliver's Travels		$8	$10	$14	Martin Jenkins		Candle
2004	Midnight Over Sanctaphrax		$16	$25	$30	Paul Stewart		DFick
2004	Stormchaser		$16	$25	$30	Paul Stewart		DFick
2004	The Curse Of The Gloamglozer		$16	$25	$30	Paul Stewart		DFick
2005	Dragon's Hoard		$6	$10	$12	Paul Stewart		Athenm
2005	Joust Of Honor		$6	$10	$12	Paul Stewart		Athenm

Riddell   Chris

Year	Title	VG-	VG	VG+	Fine	Author	Award	Pub
2005	The Last Of The Sky Pirates		$6	$10	$12	Paul Stewart		DFick
2005	Vox		$6	$10	$12	Paul Stewart		DFick
2006	Corby Flood		$6	$10	$12	Paul Stewart		DFick
2006	Fergus Crane		$6	$10	$12	Paul Stewart		DFick
2006	Freeglader		$6	$10	$12	Paul Stewart		DFick

Riddle   Tohby

Year	Title	VG-	VG	VG+	Fine	Author	Award	Pub
1989	Careful With That Ball, Eugene!		$12	$16	$20	Tohby Riddle		PB
1994	A Most Unusual Dog		$10	$14	$18	Tohby Riddle		GSteve
1999	The Great Escape From City Zoo		$8	$12	$16	Tohby Riddle		FSG
2001	The Singing Hat		$8	$10	$14	Tohby Riddle		FSG

Ringgold   Faith

Year	Title	VG-	VG	VG+	Fine	Author	Award	Pub
1991	Tar Beach		$30	$50	$60	Faith Ringgold	CH	Crown
1992	Aunt Harriet's Underground Railroad		$16	$25	$30	Faith Ringgold		Crown
1993	Dinner At Aunt Connie's House		$10	$16	$20	Faith Ringgold		Hyper
1995	My Dream Of Martin Luther King		$10	$14	$18	Faith Ringgold		Crown
1996	Bonjour, Lonnie		$8	$12	$16	Faith Ringgold		Hyper
1999	Cassie's Colorful Day		$8	$12	$16	Faith Ringgold		Crown
1999	Counting To Tar Beach		$8	$12	$16	Faith Ringgold		Crown
1999	If A Bus Could Talk		$8	$12	$16	Faith Ringgold		S&S
1999	The Invisible Princess		$8	$12	$16	Faith Ringgold		Crown
2002	Cassie's Word Quilt		$8	$10	$14	Faith Ringgold		Knopf

Rockwell   Anne F.

Year	Title	VG-	VG	VG+	Fine	Author	Award	Pub
1964	Paul & Arthur Search For The Egg	$50	$60	$80		Anne F. Rockwell		DoubleD
1966	Gypsy Girl's Best Shoes	$35	$50	$60		Anne F. Rockwell		PMagP
1966	Sally's Caterpillar	$35	$50	$60		Anne F. Rockwell		PMagP
1967	Eric And The Little Canal Boat	$30	$40	$50		Lillian Bason		PMagP
1967	Filippo's Dome	$30	$40	$50		Anne F. Rockwell		Athenm
1967	The Minstrel And The Mountain	$30	$40	$50		Jane Yolen		World
1967	The Three Visitors	$30	$40	$50		Marjorie Hopkins		PMagP
1968	Glass, Stones And Crown	$30	$40	$50		Anne F. Rockwell		Macmil
1968	The Glass Valentine	$30	$40	$50		Marjorie Hopkins		PMagP
1968	The Good Llama	$30	$40	$50		Anne F. Rockwell		World
1968	The Stolen Necklace	$30	$40	$50		Anne F. Rockwell		World
1969	Temple On A Hill	$30	$40	$50		Anne F. Rockwell		Athenm
1969	The Wonderful Eggs Of Furicchia	$30	$40	$50		Anne F. Rockwell		World
1970	Legends Of The Saints		$25	$35	$50	Ann (Lane) Petry		Crowell
1970	Mexicali Soup		$25	$35	$50	Kathryn Hitte		PMagP
1970	Munachar & Manachar		$25	$35	$50	Joseph Jacobs		Crowell
1970	Olly's Polliwogs		$25	$35	$50	Anne F. Rockwell		DoubleD
1970	What Happens To A Hamburger		$25	$35	$50	Paul Showers		Crowell
1970	When The Drum Sang		$25	$35	$50	Anne F. Rockwell		PMagP
1971	Molly's Woodland Garden		$25	$35	$50	Anne F. Rockwell		DoubleD
1971	Paintbrush & Peacepipe		$25	$35	$50	Anne F. Rockwell		Athenm
1971	The Monkey's Whiskers		$25	$35	$50	Anne F. Rockwell		PMagP
1971	The Toolbox		$25	$35	$50	Anne F. Rockwell		Macmil
1971	Tuhurahura And The Whale		$25	$35	$50	Anne F. Rockwell		PMagP
1971	What Bobolino Knew		$25	$35	$50	Anne F. Rockwell		McCall
1972	A Gift For Tolum		$25	$35	$50	Marjorie Hopkins		PMagP
1972	Machines		$25	$35	$50	Anne F. Rockwell		Macmil
1972	Master Of All Masters		$25	$35	$50	Joseph Jacobs		G&D
1972	Paul & Arthur And The Little Explorer		$25	$35	$50	Anne F. Rockwell		PMagP
1972	The Dancing Stars		$25	$35	$50	Anne F. Rockwell		Crowell
1972	Thruway		$25	$35	$50	Anne F. Rockwell		Macmil
1972	Toad		$25	$35	$50	Anne F. Rockwell		DoubleD
1973	Games (And How To Play Them)		$25	$35	$50	Anne F. Rockwell		Crowell
1973	Head To Toe		$25	$35	$50	Anne F. Rockwell		DoubleD
1973	The Awful Mess		$25	$35	$50	Anne F. Rockwell		PMagP
1973	The Boy Who Drew Sheep		$25	$35	$50	Anne F. Rockwell		Athenm
1973	The Wolf Who Had A Wonderful Dream		$25	$35	$50	Anne F. Rockwell		Crowell

Rockwell   Anne F.

Year	Title	VG-	VG	VG+	Fine	Author	Award	Pub
1974	Befana		$25	$35	$50	Anne F. Rockwell		Athenm
1974	Gift For A Gift		$25	$35	$50	Anne F. Rockwell		PMagP
1974	The Gollywhopper Egg		$25	$35	$50	Anne F. Rockwell		Macmil
1974	The Story Snail		$25	$35	$50	Anne F. Rockwell		Macmil
1975	Big Boss		$20	$30	$40	Anne F. Rockwell		Macmil
1975	Cunningham's Rooster		$20	$30	$40	Barbara Brenner		PMagP
1975	The Three Bears & 15 Other Stories		$20	$30	$40	Anne F. Rockwell		Crowell
1976	No More Work		$20	$30	$40	Anne F. Rockwell		Green
1976	Poor Goose		$20	$30	$40	Anne F. Rockwell		Crowell
1977	A Bear, A Bobcat, And Three Ghosts		$20	$30	$40	Anne F. Rockwell		Macmil
1977	Albert B. Cub & Zebra		$20	$30	$40	Anne F. Rockwell		Crowell
1977	I Like The Library		$20	$30	$40	Anne F. Rockwell		Dutton
1977	Never Hit A Porcupine		$20	$30	$40	Barbara Williams		Dutton
1978	Buster And The Bogeyman		$20	$30	$40	Anne F. Rockwell		4Winds
1978	Gogo's Car Breaks Down		$20	$30	$40	Anne F. Rockwell		DoubleD
1978	Gogo's Pay Day		$20	$30	$40	Anne F. Rockwell		DoubleD
1978	Timothy Todd's Good Things Are Gone		$20	$30	$40	Anne F. Rockwell		Macmil
1978	Willy Runs Away		$20	$30	$40	Anne F. Rockwell		Dutton
1979	Bing Bong Bang And Fiddle Dee Dee		$20	$30	$40	Gerda Mantinband		DoubleD
1979	Blackout		$20	$30	$40	Anne F. Rockwell		Macmil
1979	The Bump In The Night		$20	$30	$40	Anne F. Rockwell		Green
1979	The Girl With A Donkey Tail		$20	$30	$40	Anne F. Rockwell		Dutton
1979	The Old Woman And Her Pig & 10 Other Stories		$20	$30	$40	Anne F. Rockwell		Crowell
1979	The Supermarket		$20	$30	$40	Anne F. Rockwell		Macmil
1980	Gray Goose And Gander		$18	$25	$35	Anne F. Rockwell		Crowell
1980	Henry The Cat And The Big Sneeze		$18	$25	$35	Anne F. Rockwell		Green
1980	Honk Honk!		$18	$25	$35	Anne F. Rockwell		Dutton
1980	Out To Sea		$18	$25	$35	Anne F. Rockwell		Macmil
1980	The Stubborn Old Woman		$18	$25	$35	Clyde Robert Bulla		Crowell
1980	Walking Shoes		$18	$25	$35	Anne F. Rockwell		DoubleD
1981	Happy Birthday To Me		$18	$25	$35	Anne F. Rockwell		Macmil
1981	I Play In My Room		$18	$25	$35	Anne F. Rockwell		Macmil
1981	My Barber		$18	$25	$35	Anne F. Rockwell		Macmil
1981	The Turtle And The Two Ducks		$18	$25	$35	Patricia Plante		Crowell
1981	Thump, Thump, Thump		$18	$25	$35	Anne F. Rockwell		Dutton
1981	When We Grow Up		$18	$25	$35	Anne F. Rockwell		Dutton
1982	Big Bad Goat		$18	$25	$35	Anne F. Rockwell		Dutton
1982	Boats		$18	$25	$35	Anne F. Rockwell		Dutton
1982	Can I Help?		$18	$25	$35	Anne F. Rockwell		Macmil
1982	How My Garden Grew		$18	$25	$35	Anne F. Rockwell		Macmil
1982	I Love My Pets		$18	$25	$35	Anne F. Rockwell		Macmil
1982	Sick In Bed		$18	$25	$35	Anne F. Rockwell		Macmil
1982	The Emperor's New Clothes		$18	$25	$35	Hans Christian Andersen		Crowell
1983	The Mother Goose Cookie-Candy Book		$18	$25	$35	Anne F. Rockwell		Random
1983	The Night We Slept Outside		$18	$25	$35	Anne F. Rockwell		Macmil
1983	Toot! Toot!		$18	$25	$35	Steven Kroll		Holiday
1984	Cars		$16	$25	$30	Anne F. Rockwell		Dutton
1984	My Back Yard		$16	$25	$30	Anne F. Rockwell		Macmil
1984	Nice And Clean		$16	$25	$30	Anne F. Rockwell		Macmil
1984	Trucks		$16	$25	$30	Anne F. Rockwell		Dutton
1984	When I Go Visiting		$16	$25	$30	Anne F. Rockwell		Macmil
1985	First Comes Spring		$16	$25	$30	Anne F. Rockwell		Crowell
1985	In Our House		$16	$25	$30	Anne F. Rockwell		Crowell
1985	My Baby-Sitter		$16	$25	$30	Anne F. Rockwell		Macmil
1985	Planes		$16	$25	$30	Anne F. Rockwell		Dutton
1985	The Emergency Room		$16	$25	$30	Anne F. Rockwell		Macmil
1986	At Night		$16	$25	$30	Anne F. Rockwell		Crowell
1986	At The Playground		$16	$25	$30	Anne F. Rockwell		Crowell
1986	Big Wheels		$16	$25	$30	Anne F. Rockwell		Dutton
1986	Fire Engines		$16	$25	$30	Anne F. Rockwell		Dutton
1986	In The Morning		$16	$25	$30	Anne F. Rockwell		Crowell
1986	In The Rain		$16	$25	$30	Anne F. Rockwell		Crowell
1986	Things That Go		$16	$25	$30	Anne F. Rockwell		Dutton
1987	At The Beach		$16	$25	$30	Anne F. Rockwell		Macmil
1987	Bear Child's Book Of Hours		$16	$25	$30	Anne F. Rockwell		Crowell
1987	Bikes		$16	$25	$30	Anne F. Rockwell		Dutton
1987	Come To Town		$16	$25	$30	Anne F. Rockwell		Crowell

Rockwell Anne F.

Year	Title	VG-	VG	VG+	Fine	Author	Award	Pub
1987	The First Snowfall		$16	$25	$30	Anne F. Rockwell		Macmil
1988	Handy Hank Will Fix It		$14	$20	$30	Anne F. Rockwell		Holt
1988	Hugo At The Window		$14	$20	$30	Anne F. Rockwell		Macmil
1988	Puss In Boots & Other Stories		$14	$20	$30	Anne F. Rockwell		Macmil
1988	Things To Play With		$14	$20	$30	Anne F. Rockwell		Dutton
1988	Trains		$14	$20	$30	Anne F. Rockwell		Dutton
1989	Bear Child's Book Of Special Days		$14	$20	$30	Anne F. Rockwell		Dutton
1989	On Our Vacation		$14	$20	$30	Anne F. Rockwell		Dutton
1989	Willy Can Count		$14	$20	$30	Anne F. Rockwell		Arcad
1990	Hugo At The Park		$14	$20	$25	Anne F. Rockwell		Macmil
1990	When Hugo Went To School		$14	$20	$25	Anne F. Rockwell		Macmil
1991	Root-A-Toot-Toot		$14	$20	$25	Anne F. Rockwell		Macmil
1992	What We Like		$12	$18	$25	Anne F. Rockwell		Macmil
1993	Mr. Panda's Painting		$12	$18	$25	Anne F. Rockwell		Macmil
1994	Space Vehicles		$12	$18	$25	David Brion		Dutton
1994	The Robber Baby		$12	$18	$25	Anne F. Rockwell		Green
1994	The Way To Captain Yankee's		$12	$18	$25	Anne F. Rockwell		Macmil
1995	No! No! No!		$12	$16	$20	Anne F. Rockwell		Macmil
1995	The Acorn Tree & Other Folktales		$12	$16	$20	Anne F. Rockwell		Green
1996	The One-Eyed Giant		$10	$16	$20	Anne F. Rockwell		Green
1997	Romulus And Remus		$10	$16	$20	Anne F. Rockwell		S&S
1998	Our Earth		$10	$16	$20	Anne F. Rockwell		Whistle
1999	Bumblebee, Bumblebee, Do You Know Me?		$10	$14	$18	Anne F. Rockwell		HCollins
1999	Long Ago Yesterday		$10	$14	$18	Anne F. Rockwell		Green
1999	Our Stars		$10	$14	$18	Anne F. Rockwell		Whistle
2000	The Boy Who Wouldn't Obey		$8	$12	$16	Anne F. Rockwell		Green
2001	Welcome To Kindergarten		$8	$12	$16	Anne F. Rockwell		Walker
2003	At The Firehouse		$8	$10	$14	Anne F. Rockwell		HCollins
2003	Seba The Scribe		$8	$10	$14	Anne F. Rockwell		HCollins

Rockwell Lizzy

Year	Title	VG-	VG	VG+	Fine	Author	Award	Pub
1989	Apples And Pumpkins		$12	$16	$20	Anne F. Rockwell		Macmil
1992	Our Yard Is Full Of Birds		$10	$14	$18	Anne F. Rockwell		Macmil
1993	Pots And Pans		$8	$12	$16	Anne F. Rockwell		Macmil
1994	Ducklings And Pollywogs		$8	$12	$16	Anne F. Rockwell		Macmil
1997	Halloween Day		$8	$10	$14	Anne F. Rockwell		HCollins
1997	Show & Tell Day		$8	$10	$14	Anne F. Rockwell		HCollins
1999	Thanksgiving Day		$8	$10	$14	Anne F. Rockwell		HCollins
2000	Career Day		$8	$10	$14	Anne F. Rockwell		HCollins
2000	What Good Are Alligators?		$8	$10	$14	Anne F. Rockwell		HCollins
2001	Valentine's Day		$8	$10	$14	Anne F. Rockwell		HCollins
2002	100 School Days		$6	$10	$12	Anne F. Rockwell		HCollins
2004	Mother's Day		$6	$10	$12	Anne F. Rockwell		HCollins

Rogers Gregory

Year	Title	VG-	VG	VG+	Fine	Author	Award	Pub
1992	Lucy's Bay		$10	$16	$20	Gary Crew		JamRoll
1992	Space Travelers		$10	$16	$20	Margaret Wild		Scholas
1994	Great-Grandpa		$10	$14	$18	Susan McQuade		SRA
1994	Way Home		$25	$40	$50	Elizabeth Hathorn	GM	Random
1996	Running Away From Home		$8	$12	$16	Nigel Gray		Crown
1996	Tracks		$8	$12	$16	Gary Crew		GarethS

Rohmann Eric

Year	Title	VG-	VG	VG+	Fine	Author	Award	Pub
1994	Time Flies		$40	$60	$80	Eric Rohmann	CH	Crown
1995	King Crow		$25	$35	$50	Jennifer Armstrong		Crown
1996	Golden Compass		$100	$140	$200	Philip Pullman		Knopf
1997	The Cinder-Eyed Cat		$20	$30	$40	Eric Rohmann		Crown
1997	The Prairie Train		$8	$12	$16	Antoine O. Flatharta		Crown
1998	Subtle Knife		$60	$80	$120	Philip Pullman		Knopf
2000	Amber Spyglass		$20	$30	$40	Philip Pullman		Knopf
2002	My Friend Rabbit		$40	$60	$90	Eric Rohmann	CM	RoarB
2003	Pumpkinhead		$8	$10	$14	Eric Rohmann		Knopf

Rojankovsky   Feodor

Year	Title	VG-	VG	VG+	Fine	Author	Award	Pub
1931	Daniel Boone	$200	$280	$340		Esther Holden Averill		Domino
1933	Powder	$200	$260	$320		Esther Holden Averill		SmithH
1935	Wild Animals And Their Little Ones	$120	$160	$220		Rose Celli		AWG
1936	Plouf	$120	$160	$220		Lily Duplaix (translated)		H&B
1936	Pompom, The Little Red Squirrel	$120	$160	$220		Lily Duplaix (translated)		H&B
1937	Bruin	$80	$120	$140		Lily Duplaix (translated)		H&B
1937	Fluff, The Little Wild Rabbit	$80	$120	$140		Lily Duplaix (translated)		H&B
1937	Scuff, The Seal	$80	$120	$140		Lily Duplaix (translated)		H&B
1937	The Children's Year	$80	$120	$140		Margaret Wise Brown		H&B
1937	The Voyages Of Jacques Cartier	$180	$240	$300		Esther Holden Averill		Domino
1938	Spiky, the Hedgehog	$80	$100	$140		Lily Duplaix (translated)		H&B
1938	Tales Of Poindi	$80	$100	$140		Jean Mariotti		Domino
1940	The Kingfisher	$70	$90	$120		Lily Duplaix (translated)		H&B
1940	The Old Man Is Always Right	$70	$90	$120		Hans Christian Andersen		H&B
1941	The Adventures Of Dudley And Gilderoy	$70	$90	$120		Marion Benedict Cothren		Dutton
1942	Cuckoo	$70	$90	$120		Lily Duplaix (translated)		H&B
1942	How The Camel Got His Hump	$50	$70	$90		Rudyard Kipling		GardenC
1942	How The Leopard Got His Spots	$50	$70	$90		Rudyard Kipling		GardenC
1942	How The Rhinoceras Got His Skin	$50	$70	$90		Rudyard Kipling		GardenC
1942	The Elephant's Child	$50	$70	$90		Rudyard Kipling		GardenC
1942	The Tall Book Of Mother Goose	$140	$180	$240		Feodor Rojankovsky		H&B
1943	The Golden Book Of Birds	$140	$180	$240		Hazel Lockwood		Golden
1944	Animal Stories	$60	$80	$100		Georges Duplaix		S&S
1944	The Tall Book Of Nursery Tales	$140	$180	$220		Feodor Rojankovsky		H&B
1945	Daniel Boone	$60	$80	$100		Esther Holden Averill		H&B
1945	Pictures From Mother Goose	$60	$80	$100		Feodor Rojankovsky		S&S
1945	The Ugly Duckling	$60	$80	$100		Hans Christian Andersen		G&D
1947	Cortez The Conqueror	$60	$80	$100		Covelle Newcomb		Random
1947	The Cat That Walked By Himself	$60	$80	$100		Rudyard Kipling		GardenC
1947	The Golden Bible	$60	$80	$100		Jane Werner Watson		Golden
1948	A Name For Kitty	$60	$80	$100		Phyllis McGinley		Golden
1948	Big Farmer Big	$60	$80	$100		Kathryn & Byron Jackson		Golden
1948	The Three Bears	$60	$80	$100		Feodor Rojankovsky (adapted)		Golden
1949	Favorite Fairy Tales	$60	$80	$100		Feodor Rojankovsky		Golden
1949	Gaston And Joséphine	$60	$80	$100		Georges Duplaix		Golden
1949	Our Puppy	$60	$80	$100		Elsa Ruth Nast		Golden
1950	The Great Big Animal Book	$60	$80	$100		Feodor Rojankovsky		Golden
1951	The Great Big Wild Animal Book	$50	$70	$90		Feodor Rojankovsky		Golden
1953	All Alone	$50	$70	$90		Claire Huchet Bishop		Viking
1955	Frog Went A-Courtin	$480	$640	$800		John Langstaff	CM	HBrace
1955	The True Story Of Smokey The Bear	$50	$70	$90		Jane Werner Watson		S&S
1957	Over In The Meadow	$70	$100	$120		John Langstaff		HBrace
1958	The Cabin Faced West	$50	$60	$80		Jean Fritz		CM
1960	Animal Dictionary	$50	$60	$80		Jane Werner Watson		Golden
1960	Robinson Crusoe	$50	$60	$80		Daniel Defoe		Golden
1960	Wild Animals	$50	$60	$80		Feodor Rojankovsky		Golden
1961	10 Little Animals	$50	$60	$80		Carl Memling		Golden
1961	The Whirly Bird	$50	$60	$80		Feodor Rojankovsky		Knopf
1962	Animals In The Zoo	$50	$60	$80		Feodor Rojankovsky		Knopf
1963	Cricket In A Thicket	$50	$60	$80		Aileen Fisher		Scribnr
1966	Christmas Bear	$40	$60	$70		Marie Colmont		Golden
1967	Animals On The Farm	$40	$50	$70		Feodor Rojankovsky		Knopf
1968	A Crowd Of Cows	$40	$50	$70		John Graham		HBrace
1969	The Falcon Under The Hat	$40	$50	$70		Guy Daniels		F&W
1969	To Make A Duck Happy	$40	$50	$70		Carol E. Lester		H&Row
1971	Rojankovsky's ABC		$30	$50	$60	Feodor Rojankovsky		Golden
1972	Over In The Meadow		$30	$50	$60	John Langstaff		HBJ
1972	Rojankovsky's Wonderful Picture Book		$30	$50	$60	Feodor Rojankovsky		Golden
1973	A Year In The Forest		$30	$50	$60	Bill Hall		McHill
1973	Kathryn And Byron Jackson's The Big Elephant		$30	$50	$60	Kathryn & Byron Jackson		Golden

Root   Barry

Year	Title	VG-	VG	VG+	Fine	Author	Award	Pub
1989	The Araboolies Of Liberty Street		$18	$25	$35	Sam Swope		Potter
1991	The Saint And The Circus		$10	$16	$20	Roberto Piumini		Tambour
1992	Pumpkins		$10	$16	$20	Mary Lyn Ray		HBJ

Root   Barry

Year	Title	VG-	VG	VG+	Fine	Author	Award	Pub
1992	The Christmas Box		$10	$16	$20	JoAnne Wetzel		Knopf
1992	The Singing Fir Tree		$10	$16	$20	Marti Stone		Putnam
1993	Chinook!		$10	$16	$20	Michael O. Tunnell		Tambour
1993	Old Devil Wind		$10	$16	$20	Bill Martin		HBJ
1994	Alvah And Arvilla		$10	$14	$18	Mary Lyn Ray		HBrace
1994	April, Bubbles, Chocolate		$10	$14	$18	Lee Bennett Hopkins		S&S
1994	Those Bottles!		$10	$14	$18	M. L. Miller		Putnam
1995	Someplace Else		$10	$14	$18	Carol Saul		S&S
1995	Two Cool Cows		$10	$14	$18	Toby Speed		Putnam
1995	Wan Hu Is In The Stars		$10	$14	$18	Jennifer Armstrong		Tambour
1996	Fishing Sunday		$8	$12	$16	Tony Johnston		Tambour
1996	Grandpa Takes Me To The Moon		$8	$12	$16	Timothy R. Gaffney		Tambour
1997	Whoosh! Went The Wish		$8	$12	$16	Toby Speed		Putnam
1998	Nobody's Dog		$8	$12	$16	Charlotte Graeber		Hyper
1998	The Giant Carrot		$8	$12	$16	Jan Peck		Dial
1999	Cowboy Dreams		$8	$12	$16	Kathi Appelt		HCollins
2000	Brave Potatoes		$8	$10	$14	Toby Speed		Putnam
2000	Messenger, Messenger		$8	$10	$14	Robert Burleigh		Athenm
2000	Saturday Night Jamboree		$8	$10	$14	Lee Wardlaw		Dial
2001	Backyard Bedtime		$8	$10	$14	Susan Hill		HFest
2002	Central Park Serenade		$8	$10	$14	Laura Godwin		Cotler
2002	Gumbrella		$8	$10	$14	Barry Root		Putnam
2003	The Cat Who Liked Potato Soup		$8	$10	$14	Terry Farish		Candle
2004	By My Brother's Side		$6	$10	$12	Robert Burleigh		S&S
2004	Giant Steps		$6	$10	$12	Elizabeth Loredo		Putnam

Root   Kimberly Bulcken

Year	Title	VG-	VG	VG+	Fine	Author	Award	Pub
1988	A Bed For The Wind		$12	$16	$20	Roger B. Goodman		S&S
1989	Granny, Will Your Dog Bite		$10	$14	$18	Gerald Milnes		Knopf
1989	Windows Of Gold & Other Golden Tales		$10	$14	$18	Selma G. Lanes (adapted)		S&S
1990	In A Messy, Messy Room		$10	$14	$18	Judith Gorog		Philo
1990	The Kids' Book Of Chess		$10	$14	$18	Harvey Kidder		Workman
1992	Boots And His Brothers		$12	$18	$25	Eric Kimmel		Holiday
1992	Hugh Can Do		$10	$14	$18	Jennifer Armstrong		Crown
1993	Beggars, Beasts & Easter Fire		$8	$12	$16	Carol Greene		Lion
1993	Papa's Bedtime Story		$8	$12	$16	Mary Lee Donovan		Knopf
1993	The Palace Of Stars		$8	$12	$16	Patricia Lakin		Tambour
1994	Billy Beg And His Bull: An Irish Tale		$8	$12	$16	Ellin Greene (retold)		Holiday
1994	If I'd Known Then What I Know Now		$8	$12	$16	Reeve Lindbergh		Viking
1995	Gulliver In Lilliput		$8	$12	$16	Margaret Hodges (retold)		Holiday
1995	The Toll-Bridge Troll		$8	$12	$16	Patricia Rae Wolff		Bdeer
1995	When The Whippoorwill Calls		$8	$12	$16	Candice Ransom		Tambour
1996	In A Creepy, Creepy Place		$8	$12	$16	Judith Gorog		HCollins
1996	The Year Of The Ranch		$8	$12	$16	Alice Mclerran		Viking
1997	Birdie's Lighthouse		$8	$10	$14	Deborah Hopkinson		Athenm
1997	Junk Pile!		$8	$10	$14	Lady Borton		Philo
1997	The True Tale Of Johnny Appleseed		$8	$10	$14	Margaret Hodges		Holiday
1998	Bronco Busters		$8	$10	$14	Alison Herzig		Putnam
1999	Granny, Will Your Dog Bite		$8	$10	$14	Gerald Milnes		AH
1999	The Peddler's Gift		$8	$10	$14	Maxine Schur		Dial
1999	Understood Betsy		$8	$10	$14	Dorothy Canfield Fisher		Holt
2000	Don't Forget Winona		$8	$10	$14	Jeanne Whitehouse Peterson		Cotler
2001	The Storytelling Princess		$8	$10	$14	Rafe Martin		Putnam
2001	The Wee Christmas Cabin		$8	$10	$14	Margaret Hodges		Holiday
2003	In The Piney Woods		$6	$10	$12	Roni Schotter		Kroupa
2003	The Doll With The Yellow Star		$6	$10	$12	Yona Zeldis McDonough		Holt

Rose   Carl

Year	Title	VG-	VG	VG+	Fine	Author	Award	Pub
1945	Stork Bites Man	$35	$40	$60		Louis Pollock		World
1946	One Dozen Roses	$35	$40	$60		Carl Rose		Random
1950	A New Leash On Life	$30	$40	$50		Richard Grossman		Random
1950	Great American Sports Humor	$30	$40	$50		Mac Davis		BRB
1950	Shake Well Before Using	$30	$40	$50		Bennett Cerf		GardenC
1959	Bennett Cerf's Book Of Laughs	$100	$140	$180		Bennett Cerf		BB

Rose   Carl

Year	Title	VG-	VG	VG+	Fine	Author	Award	Pub
1963	The Crazy Zoo That Dudley Drew	$25	$30	$40		Carl Rose		LBrown
1965	The Verse By The Side Of The Road	$25	$30	$40		Frank Rowsome		Greene
1968	The Wonderful Babies Of 1809 & Other Years	$20	$30	$35		Maxine Kumin		Putnam

Rose   Gerald

Year	Title	VG-	VG	VG+	Fine	Author	Award	Pub
1958	How Saint Francis Tamed The Wolves	$35	$50	$60		Elizabeth Rose		HBrace
1960	Old Winkle And The Seagulls	$100	$140	$180		Elizabeth Rose	GM	Barnes
1960	Wuffles Goes To Town	$35	$40	$60		Elizabeth Rose		Barnes
1964	Good King Wenceslas	$35	$40	$60		Elizabeth Rose		Faber
1964	Nessie The Mannerless Monster	$90	$120	$160		Ted Hughes		Faber
1964	Pete And The Mouse	$35	$40	$60		Irmengarde Eberle		AS
1964	St. George And The Fiery Dragon	$35	$40	$60		Elizabeth Rose		Norton
1965	The Gingerbread Man	$30	$40	$50		Barbara Ireson		Norton
1966	Baron Brandy's Boots	$30	$40	$50		Peter Hughes		AS
1966	The Giant Who Drank From His Shoe	$30	$40	$50		Léonce Bourliaguet		AS
1966	The Magic Suit	$30	$40	$50		Hans Christian Andersen		Faber
1966	Tim's Giant Marrow	$30	$40	$50		Elizabeth Rose		Bedrik
1968	A Sword To Slice Through Mountains	$30	$40	$50		Léonce Bourliaguet		AS
1968	Jabberwocky	$30	$40	$50		Lewis Carroll		Faber
1968	Mark And His Pictures	$30	$40	$50		Carol Odell		Walker
1968	The Sorcerer's Apprentice	$30	$40	$50		Elizabeth Rose		Walker
1969	Alexander's Flycycle	$25	$35	$50		Elizabeth Rose		Walker
1969	The Dong With A Luminous Nose	$25	$35	$50		Edward Lear		Faber
1969	The Walrus And The Carpenter	$25	$35	$50		Lewis Carroll		Dutton
1972	A Time To Laugh		$25	$35	$50	Sara & Stephen Corrin		Faber
1973	Ironhead		$25	$35	$50	Gerald Rose		Faber
1973	The Bird Who Saved The Jungle		$25	$35	$50	Jeremy Kingston		Faber
1973	The Bold Bad Bus		$25	$35	$50	Wilma Horsbrugh		BBC
1974	Wolf! Wolf!		$20	$30	$40	Elizabeth Rose		Faber
1977	Ahhh! Said Stork		$20	$30	$40	Gerald Rose		Faber
1978	Watch Out!		$20	$30	$40	Gerald Rose		Kestrel
1979	The Tiger Skin Rug		$18	$25	$35	Gerald Rose		P-Hall
1980	PB Takes A Holiday		$18	$25	$35	Gerald Rose		Bodley
1980	Rabbit Pie		$18	$25	$35	Gerald Rose		Faber
1989	Laugh Out Loud		$14	$20	$25	Sara & Stephen Corrin		Faber
1989	Trouble In The Ark		$14	$20	$25	Gerald Rose		MHouse
2001	Out There		$8	$12	$16	Gerald Rose		Rut
2002	Horrible Hair		$8	$10	$14	Gerald Rose		Barrn
2003	Mars And Beyond		$8	$10	$14	Gerald Rose		Rut

Ross   Tony

Year	Title	VG-	VG	VG+	Fine	Author	Award	Pub
1977	Hugo And The Man Who Stole Colors		$30	$50	$60	Tony Ross		Follett
1978	Little Red Riding Hood		$20	$30	$40	Tony Ross		AP
1978	The Pied Piper Of Hamelin		$25	$40	$50	Tony Ross		LL&S
1978	The Second Did I Ever Tell You ...? Book		$25	$40	$50	Iris Grender		Hutch
1980	Hugo And The Ministry Of Holidays		$18	$25	$35	Tony Ross		AP
1980	Jack And The Beanstalk		$18	$25	$35	Tony Ross		DelaP
1980	The Charge Of The Mouse Brigade		$18	$25	$35	Bernard Stone		Pan
1980	The Greedy Little Cobbler		$18	$25	$35	Tony Ross		Barrn
1981	Hare And Badger Go To Town		$18	$25	$35	Naomi Lewis		AP
1981	Invasion Of The Brain Sharpeners		$18	$25	$35	Philip Curtis		Knopf
1981	Mr. Browser And The Comet Crisis		$18	$25	$35	Philip Curtis		AP
1981	Puss In Boots		$18	$25	$35	Tony Ross		DelaP
1981	The Tale Of Admiral Mouse		$18	$25	$35	Bernard Stone		HR&W
1982	Hugo And Oddsock		$18	$25	$35	Tony Ross		RRourke
1982	Hugo And The Bureau Of Holidays		$18	$25	$35	Tony Ross		RRourke
1982	Naughty Nicky		$18	$25	$35	Tony Ross		HR&W
1982	The True Story Of Mother Goose And Her Son Jack		$18	$25	$35	Tony Ross		RRourke
1983	Invasion Of The Comet People		$18	$25	$35	Philip Curtis		Knopf
1983	Jack The Giantkiller		$18	$25	$35	Tony Ross		AP
1983	The Enchanted Pig		$18	$25	$35	Tony Ross		Bedrik
1983	The Three Pigs		$18	$25	$35	Tony Ross		Pan
1984	I'm Coming To Get You		$16	$25	$30	Tony Ross		Dial
1984	Marmalade Jim And The Fox		$16	$25	$30	Alan Sillitoe		Reynal

Ross   Tony

Year	Title	VG-	VG	VG+	Fine	Author	Award	Pub
1984	Towser And Sadie's Birthday		$16	$25	$30	Tony Ross		Pan
1984	Towser And The Terrible Thing		$16	$25	$30	Tony Ross		Pan
1984	Towser And The Water Rats		$16	$25	$30	Tony Ross		Pan
1985	Limericks		$16	$25	$30	Michael Palin		Hutch
1985	The Boy Who Cried Wolf		$16	$25	$30	Tony Ross		Dial
1985	Towser And The Funny Face		$16	$25	$30	Tony Ross		AP
1985	Towser And The Haunted House		$16	$25	$30	Tony Ross		AP
1985	Towser And The Magic Apple		$16	$25	$30	Tony Ross		AP
1986	Foxy Fables		$16	$25	$30	Tony Ross (adapted)		Dial
1986	I Want My Potty		$16	$25	$30	Tony Ross		KaneM
1986	Jenna And The Troublemaker		$16	$25	$30	Hiawyn Oram		Holt
1986	Lazy Jack		$16	$25	$30	Tony Ross		Dial
1986	The Treasure Sock		$16	$25	$30	Pat Thomson		Goll
1987	Meanwhile Back At The Ranch		$16	$25	$30	Trinka Hakes Noble		Dial
1987	Stone Soup		$16	$25	$30	Tony Ross		Dial
1988	Anyone Seen Harry Lately?		$14	$20	$30	Hiawyn Oram		AP
1988	Oscar Got The Blame		$14	$20	$30	Tony Ross		Dial
1988	Super Dooper Jezebel		$14	$20	$30	Tony Ross		FSG
1988	The Clever Potato		$14	$20	$30	Vernon Scannell		Hutch
1989	Earthlets, As Explained By Professor Xargle		$14	$20	$30	Jeanne Willis		Dutton
1989	Hansel And Gretel		$14	$20	$30	Tony Ross		AP
1989	I Want A Cat		$14	$20	$30	Tony Ross		FSG
1989	The Knight Who Was Afraid Of The Dark		$14	$20	$30	Barbara Shook Hazen		Dial
1990	Earth Hounds As Explained By Professor Xargle		$14	$20	$25	Jeanne Willis		Dutton
1990	Happy Blanket		$14	$20	$25	Tony Ross		FSG
1990	Love Shouts And Whispers		$14	$20	$25	Vernon Scannell		Hutch
1990	Mrs. Goat And Her Seven Little Kids		$14	$20	$25	Tony Ross		Athenm
1990	The Treasure Of Cozy Cove		$14	$20	$25	Tony Ross		FSG
1990	Well I Never!		$14	$20	$25	Heather Eyles		Over
1991	A Fairy Tale		$14	$20	$25	Tony Ross		LBrown
1991	Don't Do That!		$14	$20	$25	Tony Ross		Crown
1991	Earth Tigerlets As Explained By Professor Xargle		$14	$20	$25	Jeanne Willis		Dutton
1991	Michael		$14	$20	$25	Tony Bradman		Macmil
1991	Rhinestone Rhino & Other Poems		$14	$20	$25	Adrian Henri		Mammoth
1991	Travelling Light		$14	$20	$25	Vernon Scannell		Bodley
1992	Earth Mobiles As Explained By Professor Xargle		$12	$18	$25	Jeanne Willis		Dutton
1992	Goldilocks And The Three Bears		$12	$18	$25	Tony Ross		Over
1992	Reckless Ruby		$12	$18	$25	Hiawyn Oram		Crown
1993	Dr Xargle's Book Of Earth Relations		$12	$18	$25	Jeanne Willis		AP
1993	Earth Weather As Explained By Professor Xargle		$12	$18	$25	Jeanne Willis		Dutton
1993	I Want To Be		$12	$18	$25	Tony Ross		KaneM
1993	Landscapes		$12	$18	$25	Claude Delafosse		Scholas
1993	Paintings		$12	$18	$25	Claude Delafosse		Scholas
1993	Portraits		$12	$18	$25	Claude Delafosse		Scholas
1993	Through The Looking-Glass		$16	$25	$30	Lewis Carroll		Athenm
1994	Alice's Adventures In Wonderland		$14	$20	$30	Lewis Carroll		Athenm
1994	Amber Brown Is Not A Crayon		$12	$18	$25	Paula Danziger		Putnam
1994	Pets		$12	$18	$25	Tony Ross		HBrace
1994	Relativity, As Explained By Professor Xargle		$12	$18	$25	Jeanne Willis		Dutton
1994	The Second Princess		$12	$18	$25	Hiawyn Oram		AWG
1994	Weather		$12	$18	$25	Tony Ross		HBrace
1995	Animals		$12	$16	$20	Claude Delafosse		Scholas
1995	Bedtime		$12	$16	$20	Tony Ross		HBrace
1995	Shapes		$12	$16	$20	Tony Ross		RWagon
1995	You Can't Eat Your Chicken Pox, Amber Brown		$12	$16	$20	Paula Danziger		Putnam
1996	Amber Brown Wants Extra Credit		$10	$16	$20	Paula Danziger		Putnam
1996	Forever Amber Brown		$10	$16	$20	Paula Danziger		Putnam
1996	Horrid Henry And The Secret Club		$10	$16	$20	Francesca Simon		Dolphin
1996	Horrid Henry And The Tooth Fairy		$10	$16	$20	Francesca Simon		Orion
1996	I Want My Dinner		$10	$16	$20	Tony Ross		HBrace
1996	It Came Through The Wall		$10	$16	$20	Tim Healey		Mondo
1996	Seeing Red		$10	$16	$20	Sarah Garland		KaneM
1996	The Pet Person		$10	$16	$20	Jeanne Willis		Dial
1997	Amber Brown Sees Red		$10	$16	$20	Paula Danziger		Putnam
1997	Dad		$10	$16	$20	Michael Rosen		Sund
1997	Dad's Fig Bar		$10	$16	$20	Michael Rosen		Sund
1997	Harry The Poisonous Centipede		$10	$16	$20	Lynne Reid Banks		Morrow

Ross   Tony

Year	Title	VG-	VG	VG+	Fine	Author	Award	Pub
1997	Lisa's Letter		$10	$16	$20	Michael Rosen		Sund
1997	Norma's Notebook		$10	$16	$20	Michael Rosen		Sund
1998	Amber Brown Is Feeling Blue		$10	$16	$20	Paula Danziger		Putnam
1998	Why?		$10	$16	$20	Lindsay Camp		Putnam
1999	Horrid Henry		$10	$14	$18	Francesca Simon		Hyper
1999	I, Amber Brown		$10	$14	$18	Paula Danziger		Putnam
1999	Little Wolf's Book Of Badness		$10	$14	$18	Ian Whybrow		CRB
1999	The Kingfisher Treasury Of Pirate Stories		$10	$14	$18	Tony Bradman		Kfisher
2000	Horrid Henry Strikes It Rich		$8	$12	$16	Francesca Simon		Hyper
2000	Horrid Henry's Head Lice		$8	$12	$16	Francesca Simon		Hyper
2000	Horrid Henry's Nits		$8	$12	$16	Francesca Simon		Dolphin
2000	Little Wolf's Diary Of Daring Deeds		$8	$12	$16	Ian Whybrow		CRB
2000	Little Wolf's Haunted Hall For Small Horrors		$8	$12	$16	Ian Whybrow		CRB
2000	Susan Laughs		$8	$12	$16	Jeanne Willis		Holt
2000	The Boy Who Lost His Belly Button		$8	$12	$16	Jeanne Willis		DK
2000	Wash Your Hands!		$8	$12	$16	Tony Ross		KaneM
2000	What Did I Look Like When I Was A Baby?		$8	$12	$16	Jeanne Willis		Putnam
2001	Harry The Poisonous Centipede's Big Adventure		$8	$12	$16	Lynne Reid Banks		HCollins
2001	I Want To Be A Cowgirl		$8	$12	$16	Jeanne Willis		Holt
2001	It's Justin Time, Amber Brown		$8	$12	$16	Paula Danziger		Putnam
2001	Little Wolf		$8	$12	$16	Ian Whybrow		CRB
2001	The Cats Of Cuckoo Square		$8	$12	$16	Adèle Geras		DelaP
2001	The Picture Of Dorian Gray		$8	$12	$16	Oscar Wilde		Viking
2001	What A Trip, Amber Brown		$8	$12	$16	Paula Danziger		Putnam
2002	Dear Little Wolf		$8	$12	$16	Ian Whybrow		1stAve
2002	Don't Let Go!		$8	$12	$16	Jeanne Willis		AP
2002	Get Ready For Second Grade, Amber Brown		$8	$12	$16	Paula Danziger		Putnam
2002	It's A Fair Day, Amber Brown		$8	$12	$16	Paula Danziger		Putnam
2002	Little Wolf's Handy Book Of Poems		$8	$12	$16	Ian Whybrow		1stAve
2002	Young Robin's Hood		$8	$12	$16	Ian Whybrow		Mondo
2003	Amber Brown Is Green With Envy		$8	$10	$14	Paula Danziger		Putnam
2003	Centipede's 100 Shoes		$8	$10	$14	Tony Ross		Holt
2003	Little Wolf, Pack Leader		$8	$10	$14	Ian Whybrow		CRB
2004	I Don't Want To Go To Bed		$8	$10	$14	Tony Ross		KaneM
2004	I Hate School		$8	$10	$14	Jeanne Willis		Athenm
2004	I Want My Pacifier		$8	$10	$14	Tony Ross		KaneM
2004	Little Wolf, Terror Of The Shivery Sea		$8	$10	$14	Ian Whybrow		CRB
2004	Second Grade Rules, Amber Brown		$8	$10	$14	Paula Danziger		Putnam
2005	Orange You Glad It's Halloween, Amber Brown!		$6	$10	$12	Paula Danziger		Putnam

Roth   Roger

Year	Title	VG-	VG	VG+	Fine	Author	Award	Pub
1992	The Giraffe That Walked To Paris		$40	$60	$90	Nancy Milton		Crown
1993	The Invisible Dog		$10	$16	$20	Dick King-Smith		Crown
1993	The Sign Painter's Dream		$10	$16	$20	Roger Roth		Crown
1994	The Cat Hall Of Fame		$10	$14	$18	Terri Epstein		Oxford
1995	Harriet's Hare		$10	$14	$18	Dick King-Smith		Crown
1996	Alison's Wings		$8	$12	$16	Marion Dane Bauer		Hyper
1997	Billy The Ghost And Me		$8	$12	$16	Gery Greer		HCollins
1998	Fishing For Methuselah		$8	$12	$16	Roger Roth		HCollins
1998	Mr. Ape		$8	$12	$16	Dick King-Smith		Crown
1999	The Mary Celeste		$8	$12	$16	Jane Yolen		S&S
1999	The Merman		$8	$12	$16	Dick King-Smith		Crown
2001	The Wolf Girls		$8	$10	$14	Jane Yolen		S&S
2003	Roanoke		$8	$10	$14	Jane Yolen		S&S
2004	Stink Soup		$6	$10	$12	Jill Esbaum		FSG

Rounds   Glen

Year	Title	VG-	VG	VG+	Fine	Author	Award	Pub
1936	Ol' Paul, The Mightly Logger	$60	$80	$100		Glen Rounds		Holiday
1937	Lumbercamp	$60	$80	$100		Glen Rounds		Holiday
1938	Pay Dirt	$40	$60	$70		Glen Rounds		Holiday
1941	The Blind Colt	$35	$40	$60		Glen Rounds		Holiday
1944	Tall Tale America	$35	$40	$60		Walter Blair		CM
1944	Whitey Looks For A Job	$35	$40	$60		Glen Rounds		G&D
1946	Tatoosh	$35	$40	$60		Martha Hardy		Macmil

Rounds   Glen

Year	Title	VG-	VG	VG+	Fine	Author	Award	Pub
1946	Whitey And Jinglebob	$35	$40	$60		Glen Rounds		G&D
1951	Hunted Horses	$30	$40	$50		Glen Rounds		Holiday
1951	We Always Lie To Strangers	$30	$40	$50		Vance Randolph		CoIP
1952	Buffalo Harvest	$30	$40	$50		Glen Rounds		Holiday
1952	Who Blowed Up The Church House?	$30	$40	$50		Vance Randolph		CoIP
1953	Lone Muskrat	$30	$40	$50		Glen Rounds		Holiday
1954	Haunt Fox	$30	$40	$50		Jim Kjelgaard		Holiday
1954	Whitey Takes A Trip	$30	$40	$50		Glen Rounds		Holiday
1956	Firefly	$25	$35	$50		Paul McCutcheon Sears		Holiday
1957	The Talking Turtle	$25	$35	$50		Vance Randolph		CoIP
1958	Sticks In The Knapsack	$25	$35	$50		Vance Randolph		CoIP
1958	Wildlife At Your Doorstep	$25	$35	$50		Glen Rounds		P-Hall
1960	Whitey's First Roundup	$25	$30	$40		Glen Rounds		Holiday
1961	A Wild Goose Tale	$25	$30	$40		Wilson Gage		World
1961	Wild Orphan	$25	$30	$40		Glen Rounds		Holiday
1962	Dan And The Miranda	$25	$30	$40		Wilson Gage		World
1962	Whitey And The Colt-Killer	$25	$30	$40		Glen Rounds		Holiday
1963	Whitey's New Saddle	$25	$30	$40		Glen Rounds		Holiday
1964	Big Blue Island	$25	$30	$40		Mary Q. Steele		World
1964	Rain In The Woods & Other Small Matters	$25	$30	$40		Glen Rounds		World
1965	Trail Drive	$25	$30	$40		Andy Adams		Holiday
1966	Billy Boy	$25	$30	$40		Richard Chase		GGate
1966	Mountain Men	$25	$30	$40		George Ruxton		Holiday
1966	The Crocodile's Mouth	$25	$30	$40		Adrien Stoutenburg		Viking
1966	The Snake Tree	$25	$30	$40		Glen Rounds		World
1967	How The People Sang The Mountains Up	$25	$30	$40		Maria Leach		Viking
1967	The Boll Weevil	$25	$30	$40		Glen Rounds		GGate
1967	The Treeless Plains	$25	$30	$40		Glen Rounds		Holiday
1968	American Tall-Tale Animals	$20	$30	$35		Adrien Stoutenburg		Viking
1968	Lucky Ladybugs	$20	$30	$35		Gladys P. Conklin		Holiday
1968	The Prairie Schooners	$20	$30	$35		Glen Rounds		Holiday
1969	Contrary Jenkins	$20	$30	$35		Rebecca Caudill		HR&W
1969	Folklore Of The Great West	$20	$30	$35		John Greenway		AmWest
1969	Stolen Pony	$20	$30	$35		Glen Rounds		Holiday
1969	Wild Horses Of The Red Desert	$20	$30	$35		Glen Rounds		Holiday
1970	Ballads Of The Great West		$18	$25	$35	Austin E. Fife		AmWest
1970	Go Find Hanka!		$18	$25	$35	Alexander L. Crosby		GGate
1970	Mike's Toads		$18	$25	$35	Wilson Gage		World
1970	The Strawberry Roan		$18	$25	$35	Glen Rounds		GGate
1971	Farmer Hoo And The Baboons		$18	$25	$35	Ida Chittum		DelaP
1971	Once We Had A Horse		$18	$25	$35	Glen Rounds		Holiday
1972	A Twister Of Twists		$18	$25	$35	Alvin Schwartz		Lippin
1972	Tarantula, The Giant Spider		$18	$25	$35	Gladys P. Conklin		Holiday
1972	The Cowboy Trade		$18	$25	$35	Glen Rounds		Holiday
1973	I'm Going On A Bear Hunt		$16	$25	$30	Sandra Stroner Sivulich		Dutton
1973	Sweet Betsy From Pike		$16	$25	$30	Glen Rounds		CP
1973	Tomfoolery: Trickery And Foolery With Words		$16	$25	$30	Alvin Schwartz		Lippin
1973	Witcracks: Jokes & Jests From American Folklore		$16	$25	$30	Alvin Schwartz		Lippin
1974	Cross Your Fingers, Spit In Your Hat		$16	$25	$30	Alvin Schwartz		Lippin
1975	Jennie Jenkins		$16	$25	$30	Mark Taylor		LBrown
1975	Lizard Lying In The Sun		$16	$25	$30	Berniece Freschet		Scribnr
1975	Three Fools And A Horse		$16	$25	$30	Betty Baker		Macmil
1975	Whoppers		$16	$25	$30	Alvin Schwartz		Lippin
1976	Kickle Snifters & Other Fearsome Critters		$16	$25	$30	Alvin Schwartz		Lippin
1976	Mr. Yowder And The Lion Roar Capsules		$16	$25	$30	Glen Rounds		Holiday
1976	Squash Pie		$16	$25	$30	Wilson Gage		Green
1976	The Beaver, How He Works		$16	$25	$30	Glen Rounds		Holiday
1976	Toby, Granny, And George		$16	$25	$30	Robbie Branscum		DoubleD
1977	Down In The Boondocks		$16	$25	$30	Wilson Gage		Green
1977	Elephant & Friends		$16	$25	$30	Berniece Freschet		Scribnr
1977	Little Black Bear Goes For A Walk		$16	$25	$30	Berniece Freschet		Scribnr
1977	Mr. Yowder And The Steamboat		$16	$25	$30	Glen Rounds		Holiday
1977	The Happy Dromedary		$16	$25	$30	Berniece Freschet		Scribnr
1977	The Saving Of P.S.		$16	$25	$30	Robbie Branscum		DoubleD
1978	Halfway Up The Mountain		$14	$20	$30	Theo E. Gilchrist		Lippin
1978	Mr. Yowder And The Giant Bull Snake		$14	$20	$30	Glen Rounds		Holiday
1978	Praying Mantis, The Garden Dinosaur		$14	$20	$30	Gladys P. Conklin		Holiday

Rounds   Glen

Year	Title	VG-	VG	VG+	Fine	Author	Award	Pub
1979	The Lucky Man		$14	$20	$30	Mary Blount Christian		Macmil
1980	Blind Outlaw		$14	$20	$25	Glen Rounds		Holiday
1980	Hush Up!		$14	$20	$25	Jim Aylesworth		HR&W
1980	Mr. Yowder		$14	$20	$25	Glen Rounds		Holiday
1980	The Amazing Voyage Of The New Orleans		$14	$20	$25	Judith St. George		Putnam
1981	Mr. Yowder And The Train Robbers		$14	$20	$25	Glen Rounds		Holiday
1981	Uncle Lemon's Spring		$14	$20	$25	Jane Yolen		Dutton
1983	Mr. Yowder And The Windwagon		$14	$20	$25	Glen Rounds		Holiday
1983	Wild Appaloosa		$14	$20	$25	Glen Rounds		Holiday
1984	The Morning The Sun Refused To Rise		$12	$18	$25	Glen Rounds		Holiday
1984	You All Spoken Here		$12	$18	$25	Roy Wilder		Viking
1985	Shenandoah Noah		$12	$18	$25	Jim Aylesworth		HR&W
1985	Washday On Noah's Ark		$12	$18	$25	Glen Rounds		Holiday
1987	The Old Woman And The Willy Nilly Man		$12	$16	$20	Jill Wright		Putnam
1988	Wild Pill Hickok & Other Old West Riddles		$12	$16	$20	David A. Adler		Holiday
1989	Charlie Drives The Stage		$12	$16	$20	Eric Kimmel		Holiday
1989	Old Macdonald Had A Farm		$12	$16	$20	Glen Rounds		Holiday
1990	Four Dollars And Fifty Cents		$10	$16	$20	Eric Kimmel		Holiday
1990	I Know An Old Lady Who Swallowed A Fly		$10	$16	$20	Glen Rounds		Holiday
1990	The Old Woman And The Jar Of Uums		$10	$16	$20	Jill Wright		Putnam
1991	Cowboys		$10	$16	$20	Glen Rounds		Holiday
1992	Three Little Pigs And The Big Bad Wolf		$10	$16	$20	Glen Rounds		Holiday
1993	The Three Billy Goats Gruff		$10	$16	$20	Glen Rounds		Holiday
1995	Sod Houses On The Great Plains		$10	$14	$18	Glen Rounds		Holiday

Rowand   Phyllis

Year	Title	VG-	VG	VG+	Fine	Author	Award	Pub
1947	The Growing Story	$35	$40	$60		Ruth Krauss		H&B
1948	Bears	$35	$40	$60		Ruth Krauss		H&B

Rubel   Nicole

Year	Title	VG-	VG	VG+	Fine	Author	Award	Pub
1976	Rotten Ralph		$20	$30	$40	Jack Gantos		HM
1976	Sleepy Ronald		$20	$30	$40	Jack Gantos		HM
1977	Fair-Weather Friends		$16	$25	$30	Jack Gantos		HM
1978	Aunt Bernice		$14	$20	$30	Jack Gantos		HM
1978	Worse Than Rotten, Ralph		$14	$20	$30	Jack Gantos		HM
1979	Greedy Greeny		$14	$20	$30	Jack Gantos		DoubleD
1979	The Perfect Pal		$14	$20	$30	Jack Gantos		HM
1980	Swampy Alligator		$14	$20	$25	Jack Gantos		Windmil
1980	The Werewolf Family		$14	$20	$25	Jack Gantos		HM
1980	Willy's Raiders		$14	$20	$25	Jack Gantos		PMagP
1982	Sam And Violet's Birthday Book		$14	$20	$25	Nicole Rubel		Avon
1982	Woof, Woof!		$14	$20	$25	Steven Kroll		Dial
1983	Bruno Brontosaurus		$14	$20	$25	Nicole Rubel		Avon
1983	Me And My Kitty		$14	$20	$25	Nicole Rubel		Macmil
1984	Alligator's Garden		$12	$18	$25	Michaela Muntean		Dial
1984	Little Lamb Bakes A Cake		$12	$18	$25	Michaela Muntean		Dial
1984	Monkey's Marching Band		$12	$18	$25	Michaela Muntean		Dial
1984	Rotten Ralph's Rotten Christmas		$12	$18	$25	Jack Gantos		HM
1984	The House That Bear Built		$12	$18	$25	Michaela Muntean		Dial
1985	Pirate Jupiter And The Moondogs		$12	$18	$25	Nicole Rubel		Dial
1985	Sam And Violet's Bedtime Mystery		$12	$18	$25	Nicole Rubel		Avon
1985	Sam And Violet's Get Well Book		$12	$18	$25	Nicole Rubel		Avon
1986	Rotten Ralph's Trick Or Treat!		$12	$16	$20	Jack Gantos		HM
1986	This Is Weird		$12	$16	$20	Patty Wolcott		Scholas
1986	Uncle Henry & Aunt Henrietta's Honeymoon		$12	$16	$20	Nicole Rubel		Dial
1988	And Now, You're Getting Married		$12	$16	$20	Nicole Rubel		StMart
1988	It Came From The Swamp		$12	$16	$20	Nicole Rubel		Dial
1989	Goldie		$12	$16	$20	Nicole Rubel		H&Row
1989	Grizzly Riddles		$12	$16	$20	K. Hall & L. Eisenberg		Dial
1989	Rotten Ralph's Show And Tell		$12	$16	$20	Jack Gantos		HM
1990	Happy Birthday Rotten Ralph		$10	$16	$20	Jack Gantos		HM
1991	Goldie's Nap		$10	$16	$20	Nicole Rubel		HCollins
1992	The Ghost Family Meets Its Match		$10	$16	$20	Nicole Rubel		Dial
1993	Batty Riddles		$10	$16	$20	K. Hall & L. Eisenberg		Dial

Rubel Nicole

Year	Title	VG-	VG	VG+	Fine	Author	Award	Pub
1993	Conga Crocodile		$10	$16	$20	Nicole Rubel		HM
1994	Not So Rotten Ralph		$10	$14	$18	Jack Gantos		HM
1995	Cyrano The Bear		$10	$14	$18	Nicole Rubel		Dial
1997	Bunny Riddles		$8	$12	$16	K. Hall & L. Eisenberg		Dial
1997	Mummy Riddles		$8	$12	$16	K. Hall & L. Eisenberg		Dial
1997	No School For Penelope Pig		$8	$12	$16	Nicole Rubel		Troll
1997	Rotten Ralph's Rotten Romance		$8	$12	$16	Jack Gantos		HM
1998	Back To School For Rotten Ralph		$8	$12	$16	Jack Gantos		HCollins
1998	Rotten Ralph's Halloween Howl		$8	$12	$16	Jack Gantos		HFest
1998	The Christmas Spirit Strikes Rotten Ralph		$8	$12	$16	Jack Gantos		HFest
1999	Rotten Ralph's Thanksgiving Wish		$8	$12	$16	Jack Gantos		HFest
1999	Wedding Bells For Rotten Ralph		$8	$12	$16	Jack Gantos		HCollins
2000	The One And Only Me		$8	$10	$14	Marilyn Singer		HFest
2001	A Cowboy Named Ernestine		$8	$10	$14	Nicole Rubel		Dial
2001	Rotten Ralph Helps Out		$8	$10	$14	Jack Gantos		FSG
2002	Dino Riddles		$8	$10	$14	K. Hall & L. Eisenberg		Dial
2002	No More Vegetables!		$8	$10	$14	Nicole Rubel		FSG
2002	Practice Makes Perfect For Rotten Ralph		$8	$10	$14	Jack Gantos		FSG
2003	Grody's Not So Golden Rules		$8	$10	$14	Nicole Rubel		Harcort
2004	Rotten Ralph Feels Rotten		$6	$10	$12	Jack Gantos		FSG

Sabuda Robert

Year	Title	VG-	VG	VG+	Fine	Author	Award	Pub
1988	The Fiddler's Son		$18	$25	$35	Eugene Bradley Coco		GreenT
1988	The Wishing Well		$18	$25	$35	Eugene Bradley Coco		GreenT
1990	Walden		$12	$18	$25	Steve Lowe		Philo
1991	Earth Verses And Water Rhymes		$12	$18	$25	J. Patrick Lewis		Athenm
1991	I Hear America Singing		$12	$18	$25	Walt Whitman		Philo
1992	Saint Valentine		$12	$18	$25	Robert Sabuda		Athenm
1992	The Log Of Christopher Columbus		$12	$18	$25	Steve Lowe		Philo
1993	The Ibis And The Egret		$12	$16	$20	Roy Owen		Philo
1994	A Tree Place & Other Poems		$25	$40	$50	Constance Levy		McEld
1994	Creepy Crawly Halloween Fright		$100	$150	$200	Thomas Beach		Troll
1994	The Christmas Alphabet		$100	$150	$200	Robert Sabuda		Orchard
1994	The Knight's Castle		$25	$40	$50	Robert Sabuda		Golden
1994	The Mummy's Tomb		$25	$40	$50	Robert Sabuda		Golden
1994	Tutankhamen's Gift		$25	$40	$50	Robert Sabuda		Athenm
1995	A Kwanzaa Celebration		$50	$75	$100	Nancy Williams		LSimon
1995	Arthur And The Sword		$25	$35	$50	Thomas Malory		Athenm
1995	Help the Animals of North America		$40	$60	$80	Robert Sabuda		JMorris
1997	Cookie Count		$30	$45	$60	Robert Sabuda		LSimon
1997	The Paper Dragon		$20	$30	$40	Marguerite W. Davol		Athenm
1998	ABC Disney		$25	$35	$50	Robert Sabuda		Disney
1999	The Blizzard's Robe		$18	$25	$35	Robert Sabuda		Athenm
1999	The Movable Mother Goose		$25	$35	$50	Robert Sabuda		LSimon
2000	Wonderful Wizard Of Oz		$25	$35	$50	L. Frank Baum		LSimon
2001	Beetles		$14	$20	$30	Robert Sabuda		Hyper
2001	Butterflies		$14	$20	$30	Robert Sabuda		Hyper
2002	America the Beautiful		$20	$30	$40	Clement Moore		LSimon
2002	The Adventures Of Providence Traveler		$12	$18	$25	Robert Sabuda		Athenm
2002	The Night Before Christmas		$25	$35	$50	Clement C. Moore		S&S
2002	Uh-Oh, Leonardo!		$8	$12	$16	Robert Sabuda		Athenm
2003	Alice In Wonderland		$20	$30	$40	Lewis Carroll		S&S

San Souci Daniel

Year	Title	VG-	VG	VG+	Fine	Author	Award	Pub
1978	The Legend Of Scarface		$20	$30	$40	Robert D. San Souci		DoubleD
1981	Song Of Sedna		$14	$20	$25	Robert D. San Souci		DoubleD
1982	The Brave Little Tailor		$14	$20	$25	Jacob & Wilhelm Grimm		DoubleD
1983	Ceremony--In The Circle Of Life		$14	$20	$25	White Deer Of Autumn		Rain
1983	Hidden Places		$14	$20	$25	Phyllis Root		Rain
1983	Star Riders Of Ren		$14	$20	$25	Calvin Miller		H&Row
1984	Rip Van Winkle		$12	$18	$25	Morrel Gipson		DoubleD
1984	War Of The Moonrhymes		$12	$18	$25	Calvin Miller		H&Row
1985	Potter, Come Fly To The First Of The Earth		$12	$18	$25	Walter, Jr. Wangerin		Chariot
1985	The Bedtime Book		$12	$18	$25	Daniel San Souci (adapted)		Messner

San Souci   Daniel

Year	Title	VG-	VG	VG+	Fine	Author	Award	Pub
1986	The Legend Of Sleepy Hollow		$12	$16	$20	Robert D. San Souci		DoubleD
1986	The Little Mermaid		$12	$16	$20	Hans Christian Andersen		Scholas
1986	The Mother Goose Book		$12	$16	$20	Daniel San Souci (adapted)		LSimon
1987	A Season Of Joy		$12	$16	$20	Diane Arico (edited)		DoubleD
1987	The Ugly Duckling		$12	$16	$20	Hans Christian Andersen		Scholas
1988	Robert D. San Souci's The Six Swans		$12	$16	$20	Robert D. San Souci		S&S
1988	Vassilisa The Wise		$12	$16	$20	Josepha Sherman		HBJ
1989	Easter Treasures		$12	$16	$20	Diane Arico (edited)		DoubleD
1991	The Christmas Ark		$10	$16	$20	Robert D. San Souci		DoubleD
1992	Feathertop		$10	$16	$20	Robert D. San Souci		DoubleD
1992	The Golden Deer		$10	$16	$20	Margaret Hodges		Scribnr
1993	A Possible Tree		$10	$16	$20	Josephine H. Aldridge		Macmil
1993	Country Road		$10	$16	$20	Daniel San Souci		DoubleD
1994	Muir Of The Mountains		$10	$14	$18	William O. Douglas		Sierra
1994	Potter		$10	$14	$18	Walter, Jr. Wangerin		Augsb
1994	Sootface: An Ojibwa Cinderella Story		$10	$14	$18	Robert D. San Souci		DelaP
1995	The Gifts Of Wali Dad		$10	$14	$18	Aaron Shepard		Athenm
1996	Jigsaw Jackson		$8	$12	$16	David Birchman		LL&S
1996	Red Wolf Country		$8	$12	$16	Jonathan London		Dutton
1996	Waterman's Child		$8	$12	$16	Barbara Mitchell		LL&S
1997	Two Bear Cubs		$8	$12	$16	Robert D. San Souci		Yose
1998	Ice Bear And Little Fox		$8	$12	$16	Robert D. San Souci		Dutton
1998	Island Magic		$8	$12	$16	Martha Bennett Stiles		Athenm
1999	Cowpokes		$8	$12	$16	Caroline Stutson		Lothrop
1999	In The Moonlight Mist		$8	$12	$16	Eujin Kim Neilan		Boyds
2000	Montezuma And The Fall Of The Aztecs		$8	$10	$14	Eric Kimmel		Holiday
2000	Mustang Canyon		$8	$10	$14	Jonathan London		Dutton
2002	Frightful's Daughter		$8	$10	$14	Jean Craighead George		Dutton
2002	The Adventure Of Capitol Kitty		$8	$10	$14	Sharon Davis		Scholas
2002	The Rabbit And The Dragon King		$8	$10	$14	Daniel San Souci		Boyds
2003	The Flying Canoe		$8	$10	$14	Eric Kimmel		Holiday
2004	The Dangerous Snake And Reptile Club		$6	$10	$12	Daniel San Souci		Tricyc

Sanderson   Ruth

Year	Title	VG-	VG	VG+	Fine	Author	Award	Pub
1975	Grandma's Beach Surprise		$20	$30	$40	Ilka Katherine List		Putnam
1976	Buck, Wild		$16	$25	$30	Glenn Balch		Crowell
1976	First Serve		$16	$25	$30	Mary Towne		Athenm
1976	The Little Engine That Could		$16	$25	$30	Watty Piper (pseud.)		P&Munk
1976	The Season Of Silence		$16	$25	$30	Mary Francis Shura		Athenm
1977	A Child's Garden Of Verses		$16	$25	$30	Robert Louis Stevenson		P&Munk
1977	Don't Hurt Laurie!		$16	$25	$30	Willo Davis Roberts		Athenm
1977	Jimmy Carter		$16	$25	$30	Charles E. Mercer		Putnam
1977	The Beast Of Lor		$16	$25	$30	Clyde Robert Bulla		Crowell
1977	The Great Rat Island Adventure		$16	$25	$30	Charlene Joy Talbot		Athenm
1977	Walt Disney		$16	$25	$30	Greta Walker		Putnam
1978	On The Track Of The Mystery Animal		$14	$20	$30	Miriam Schlein		4Winds
1978	The Hideaway Summer		$14	$20	$30	Beverly Hollett Renner		H&Row
1978	The Mystery Of Pony Hollow		$14	$20	$30	Lynn Hall		Garrard
1979	Into The Dream		$14	$20	$30	William Sleator		Dutton
1979	Samantha On Stage		$14	$20	$30	Susan Clement Farrar		Dial
1979	The Poetry Of Horses		$14	$20	$30	William Cole		Scribnr
1979	The Sara Summer		$14	$20	$30	Mary Downing Hahn		Clarion
1979	The Triple Hoax		$14	$20	$30	Carolyn Keene		Wander
1979	We Remember Philip		$14	$20	$30	Norma Simon		AWhit
1980	Five Nests		$14	$20	$25	Caroline Arnold		Dutton
1980	Secret In The Pirate's Cave		$14	$20	$25	Laura Lee Hope		Wander
1980	The Flying Saucer Mystery		$14	$20	$25	Carolyn Keene		Wander
1980	The Mystery Of The Missing Pony		$14	$20	$25	Margaret Chittenden		Garrard
1980	The Secret In The Old Lace		$14	$20	$25	Carolyn Keene		Wander
1981	A Different Kind Of Gold		$14	$20	$25	Cecily Stern		H&Row
1981	Good Dog Poems		$14	$20	$25	William Cole		Scribnr
1981	One Of Us		$14	$20	$25	Nikki Amdur		Dial
1981	The Dune Buggy Mystery		$14	$20	$25	Laura Lee Hope		Wander
1981	The Greek Symbol Mystery		$14	$20	$25	Carolyn Keene		Wander
1981	The Missing Pony Mystery		$14	$20	$25	Laura Lee Hope		Wander

Sanderson   Ruth

Year	Title	VG-	VG	VG+	Fine	Author	Award	Pub
1981	The Mysterious Moortown Bridge		$14	$20	$25	Lynn Hall		Follett
1981	The Mystery Of The Caramel Cat		$14	$20	$25	Lynn Hall		Garrard
1981	The Rose Parade Mystery		$14	$20	$25	Laura Lee Hope		Wander
1982	The Animal, The Vegetable, And John D. Jones		$14	$20	$25	Betsy Cromer Byars		DelaP
1982	The Owl And The Pussycat		$14	$20	$25	Edward Lear		Golden
1982	When You Were A Baby		$14	$20	$25	Linda Hayward		Golden
1983	Caught In The Turtle		$14	$20	$25	Judith Gorog		Philo
1983	One Of The Family		$14	$20	$25	Peggy Archer		Golden
1983	Poochie And The Four Seasons Fair		$14	$20	$25	Joan Webb		Western
1983	The Store-Bought Doll		$14	$20	$25	Lois Meyer		Golden
1984	Heidi		$12	$18	$25	Johanna Spyri		Ariel
1985	Five Little Bunnies		$12	$18	$25	Linda Hayward		Western
1986	The Sleeping Beauty		$12	$16	$20	Jane Yolen		Ariel
1987	The Happy Times Storybook		$12	$16	$20	Phyllis Krasilovsky		Golden
1988	The Secret Garden		$12	$16	$20	Frances Hodgson Burnett		Knopf
1989	Puppies And Kittens		$12	$16	$20	Fran Manushkin		Golden
1990	The Twelve Dancing Princesses		$10	$16	$20	Ruth Sanderson		LBrown
1991	The Enchanted Wood		$10	$16	$20	Ruth Sanderson		LBrown
1992	Beauty And The Beast		$10	$16	$20	Samantha Easton		AM
1993	The Nativity		$10	$16	$20	Ruth Sanderson		LBrown
1994	The Night Before Christmas		$10	$14	$18	Clement C. Moore		Turner
1994	The Story Of The First Christmas		$10	$14	$18	Ruth Sanderson		Turner
1994	William Shakespeare's The Tempest		$10	$14	$18	Bruce Coville		DelaP
1995	Papa Gatto		$10	$14	$18	Ruth Sanderson		LBrown
1996	A Treasury Of Princesses		$8	$12	$16	Shirley Climo		HCollins
1997	Rose Red & Snow White		$8	$12	$16	Jacob & Wilhelm Grimm		LBrown
1998	Tapestries		$8	$12	$16	Ruth Sanderson		LBrown
1999	The Crystal Mountain		$8	$12	$16	Ruth Sanderson		LBrown
2000	Where Have The Unicorns Gone?		$8	$10	$14	Jane Yolen		S&S
2001	Golden Mare, The Firebird, And The Magic Ring		$8	$10	$14	Ruth Sanderson		LBrown
2002	Cinderella		$8	$10	$14	Charles Perrault		LBrown
2003	Mother Goose		$8	$10	$14	Ruth Sanderson		LBrown
2003	Saints		$8	$10	$14	Ruth Sanderson		EerdB
2004	The Snow Princess		$6	$10	$12	Ruth Sanderson		LBrown

Sandford   John

Year	Title	VG-	VG	VG+	Fine	Author	Award	Pub
1986	The Biggest Little House In The Forest		$12	$16	$20	Djemma Bider		Caed
1988	The Rinkey-Dink Cafe		$12	$16	$20	Maggie S. Davis		S&S
1991	Siegfried		$10	$16	$20	Diane Stanley		Bantam
1998	Tale Of A Tail		$8	$12	$16	Judit Bodnar		Lothrop

Sandlin   Joan

Year	Title	VG-	VG	VG+	Fine	Author	Award	Pub
1971	Hill Of Fire		$18	$25	$35	Tom Lewis		H&Row
1972	Small Wolf		$18	$25	$35	Nathaniel Benchley		H&Row
1974	Woodchuck		$16	$25	$30	Faith McNulty		H&Row

Santore   Charles

Year	Title	VG-	VG	VG+	Fine	Author	Award	Pub
1986	The Complete Tales Of Peter Rabbit		$20	$30	$40	Beatrix Potter		Courage
1988	Aesop's Fables		$16	$25	$30	Aesop		JellyB
1991	Tales Of Peter Rabbit		$14	$20	$25	Beatrix Potter		RunP
1991	The Wizard Of Oz		$14	$20	$25	L. Frank Baum		JellyB
1993	The Little Mermaid: The Original Story		$12	$18	$25	Hans Christian Andersen		JellyB
1996	Snow White		$10	$16	$20	Jacob & Wilhelm Grimm		Park
1997	William The Curious: Knight Of The Water Lilies		$10	$16	$20	Charles Santore		Random
1998	The Fox And The Rooster		$10	$16	$20	Charles Santore		Random
2000	A Stowaway On Noah's Ark		$8	$12	$16	Charles Santore		Random
2003	Paul Revere's Ride		$8	$10	$14	Henry Wadsworth Longfellow		HCollins
2004	The Camel's Lament		$8	$10	$14	Charles E. Carryl		Random

Santoro   Christopher

Year	Title	VG-	VG	VG+	Fine	Author	Award	Pub
1979	Animals Build Amazing Homes		$25	$40	$50	Hedda Nussbaum		Random

Santoro   Christopher

Year	Title	VG-	VG	VG+	Fine	Author	Award	Pub
1979	The Book Of Shapes		$25	$40	$50	Christopher Santoro		GingH
1980	The Incredible Dinosaurs		$18	$25	$35	Rita Golden Gelman		Random
1981	The Dinosaurs		$18	$25	$35	Mary Packard		Messner
1982	A Garden For Miss Mouse		$18	$25	$35	Michaela Muntean		PMagP
1982	Here Comes Santa Claus		$18	$25	$35	M. Hover		Golden
1982	Panda Bear's Secret		$18	$25	$35	Michaela Muntean		Golden
1984	Prehistoric Mammals		$16	$25	$30	Susanne Santoro Miller		S&S
1985	Pterosaurs, The Flying Reptiles		$16	$25	$30	Helen Roney Sattler		LL&S
1986	The Three Little Pigs & Other Nursery Tales		$16	$25	$30	Christopher Santoro (selected)		Western
1987	Lion's Mixed-Up Friends		$16	$25	$30	Lucille Hammond		Western
1987	Little Goat's Big Brother		$16	$25	$30	Marcia Leonard		Bantam
1987	Rudolph The Red-Nosed Reindeer		$16	$25	$30	Robert May		Random
1987	Sharks		$16	$25	$30	Gilda Berger		DoubleD
1987	Snakes & Other Reptiles		$16	$25	$30	Mary Elting		S&S
1987	The Little Rabbit Who Wanted Red Wings		$16	$25	$30	Carolyn Sherwin Bailey		P&Munk
1988	Busy Bunnies		$14	$20	$30	Alan Benjamin		S&S
1988	Ducky's Easter Surprise		$14	$20	$30	Alan Benjamin		S&S
1988	Hominids: A Look Back At Our Ancestors		$14	$20	$30	Helen Roney Sattler		LL&S
1988	The Big Golden Book Of Dinosaurs		$14	$20	$30	Mary Elting		Western
1989	Christmas Wishes		$14	$20	$30	Alan Benjamin		LSimon
1989	Favorite Mother Goose And Animal Tales		$14	$20	$30	Ann Schweninger		Western
1989	Giraffes, The Sentinels Of The Savannas		$14	$20	$30	Helen Roney Sattler		LL&S
1989	Little Treasury Of Dinosaurs		$14	$20	$30	Isaac Asimov		Chatham
1989	The Complete Frog		$14	$20	$30	Elizabeth A. Lacey		LL&S
1989	Those Mysterious Dinosaurs		$14	$20	$30	Gina Ingoglia		Golden
1989	Two-Minute Christmas Stories		$14	$20	$30	Kathryn Jackson		Golden
1990	Charlie The Caterpillar		$18	$25	$35	Dom DeLuise		S&S
1990	Flying Dinosaurs		$14	$20	$25	Steven Lindblom		Western
1990	Make Way For Trucks: Big Machines On Wheels		$14	$20	$25	Gail Herman		Random
1990	The Velveteen Rabbit		$14	$20	$25	Margery Williams		Western
1991	Quilted Elephant And The Green Velvet Dragon		$14	$20	$25	Alice Low		S&S
1992	Goldilocks		$16	$25	$30	Dom DeLuise		S&S
1992	The Cat That Climbed The Christmas Tree		$12	$18	$25	Susanne Santoro Whayne		Western
1992	The Glow-In-The-Dark Book Of Animal Skeletons		$12	$18	$25	Regina Kahney		Random
1993	Halloween Riddles		$12	$18	$25	Alan Benjamin		S&S
1993	Lift A Rock: A Chunky Flap Book		$12	$18	$25	Christopher Santoro		Random
1993	Open The Barn Door		$12	$18	$25	Christopher Santoro		Random
1993	Open The Hood		$12	$18	$25	Christopher Santoro		Random
1994	Peter Cottontail		$12	$18	$25	Amanda Stephens		Scholas
1995	Who's In My Christmas Tree?		$12	$16	$20	Christopher Santoro		Random
1995	Who's In My Gingerbread House?		$12	$16	$20	Christopher Santoro		Random
1996	I Can Read About Dinosaurs		$10	$16	$20	John Howard		Troll
1996	King Bob's New Clothes		$12	$18	$25	Dom DeLuise		S&S
1997	Bears Are Curious		$10	$16	$20	Joyce Milton		Random
1997	Dom Deluise's Hansel & Gretel		$12	$18	$25	Dom DeLuise		S&S
1997	Hansel And Gretel		$12	$18	$25	Dom DeLuise		S&S
1998	The Nightingale		$12	$16	$20	Dom DeLuise		S&S
2000	A Pie Went By		$8	$12	$16	Carolyn Dunn		HCollins
2001	Jumbo		$8	$12	$16	Bonnie Worth		Random
2001	Penguins		$8	$12	$16	Joy Bean		Random
2002	Bug Dance		$8	$12	$16	Stuart J. Murphy		HCollins
2002	Grandpappy Snippy Snappies		$8	$12	$16	Lynn Plourde		HCollins
2003	The Night The Martians Landed		$8	$10	$14	Kathleen Krull		HCollins
2004	Apples, Apples		$8	$10	$14	Kathleen Weidner Zoehfeld		HFest
2004	Pumpkin Time		$8	$10	$14	Kathleen Weidner Zoehfeld		HFest

Sargent   Robert E.

Year	Title	VG-	VG	VG+	Fine	Author	Award	Pub
1966	A Trick On A Lion	$30	$40	$50		Robert E. Sargent		McHill
1966	The Alligator's Problem	$30	$40	$50		Robert E. Sargent		Scribnr
1966	The Restless Rabbit	$30	$40	$50		Robert E. Sargent		McHill
1967	A Bug of Some Importance	$25	$30	$40		Robert E. Sargent		Scribnr
1967	The Small Seabird	$25	$30	$40		Robert E. Sargent		Scribnr
1968	Everything Is Difficult At First	$20	$30	$35		Robert E. Sargent		Scribnr
1968	Peter And The Wolf	$20	$30	$35		Sergei Prokofiev		Lance
1968	Six Magical Folk Tales	$20	$30	$35		Robert E. Sargent		Lance

Sargent   Robert E.

Year	Title	VG-	VG	VG+	Fine	Author	Award	Pub
1968	Ten Fairy Tales	$20	$30	$35		Robert E. Sargent		S&S
1968	The Adventurous Moth	$20	$30	$35		Robert E. Sargent		S&S
1968	The Lost Continent Of Atlantis	$20	$30	$35		James Wyckoff		Putnam
1969	Dogs Are Friends To Owls, And Cats Aren't	$20	$30	$35		Robert E. Sargent		Lance
1969	The Hungry Elephant	$20	$30	$35		Robert E. Sargent		Lance
1969	The Princess' Party	$20	$30	$35		Robert E. Sargent		Putnam
1969	What Is Beautiful?	$20	$30	$35		Robert E. Sargent		Lance

Sauber   Robert

Year	Title	VG-	VG	VG+	Fine	Author	Award	Pub
1990	The Golden Swan		$12	$18	$25	Marianna Mayer		Bantam
1991	All Is Well		$10	$16	$20	Frank E. Peretti		Word
1993	Gray Fox		$10	$16	$20	Jonathan London		Viking
1994	I-Know-Not-What, I-Know-Not-Where		$10	$14	$18	Eric Kimmel		Holiday
1994	The First Thanksgiving		$10	$14	$18	Robert Sauber		Western
1994	The Goose Girl		$10	$14	$18	Eric Kimmel (adapted)		Holiday
1994	The Storm		$10	$14	$18	Anne F. Rockwell		Hyper
1994	The Swan Maiden		$10	$14	$18	Ellin Greene		Holiday
1996	The Gift Of The Magi		$8	$12	$16	Penelope J. Stokes (adapted)		Victor
1996	The Story Of The Tooth Fairy		$8	$12	$16	Tom Paxton		Morrow
1997	Florence Robinson		$8	$12	$16	Dorothy & Thomas Hoobler		SBurdet
1997	Louis Braille		$8	$12	$16	Dennis B. Fradin		Silver
1997	Sirko And The Wolf		$8	$12	$16	Eric Kimmel		Holiday
2001	The Secret Garden		$8	$10	$14	Jane Parker Resnick (adapted)		Courage
2003	The Moon In My Room		$8	$10	$14	Ila Wallen		Random
2003	The Not Me Monster		$8	$10	$14	Ila Wallen		Random
2004	A Team Of One		$6	$10	$12	Ila Wallen		Random

Say   Allen

Year	Title	VG-	VG	VG+	Fine	Author	Award	Pub
1968	A Canticle To The Waterbirds	$80	$120	$140		William Everson		Equix
1972	Dr. Smith's Safari		$30	$50	$60	Allen Say		H&Row
1974	Once Under The Cherry Blossom Tree		$30	$40	$60	Allen Say		H&Row
1976	Morning Glories		$30	$40	$60	Shiga Naoya		Graham
1976	The Feast Of Lanterns		$30	$40	$60	Allen Say		H&Row
1978	Magic And The Night River		$25	$40	$50	Eve Bunting		H&Row
1979	The Ink-Keeper's Apprentice		$25	$40	$50	Allen Say		H&Row
1980	The Lucky Yak		$25	$35	$50	Annetta Lawson		Parnss
1981	The Secret Cross Of Lorraine		$25	$35	$50	Thea Brow		Parnss
1982	The Bicycle Man		$25	$35	$50	Allen Say		Parnss
1984	How My Parents Learned To Eat		$20	$30	$40	Ina R. Friedman		HM
1988	A River Dream		$18	$25	$35	Allen Say		HM
1988	The Boy Of The Three-Year Nap		$50	$80	$100	Dianne Snyder Snyder	CH	HM
1989	The Lost Lake		$18	$25	$35	Allen Say		HM
1990	El Chino		$16	$25	$30	Allen Say		HM
1991	Tree Of Cranes		$16	$25	$30	Allen Say		HM
1993	Grandfather's Journey		$70	$100	$140	Allen Say	CM	HM
1995	Stranger In The Mirror		$14	$20	$25	Allen Say		HM
1996	Emma's Rug		$12	$18	$25	Allen Say		HM
1997	Allison		$12	$18	$25	Allen Say		HM
1997	Under The Cherry Blossom Tree		$12	$18	$25	Allen Say		HM
1999	Tea With Milk		$12	$16	$20	Allen Say		HM
2000	The Sign Painter		$10	$14	$18	Allen Say		HM
2002	Home Of The Brave		$8	$12	$16	Allen Say		HM
2004	Music For Alice		$8	$10	$14	Allen Say		HM

Scarry   Richard

Year	Title	VG-	VG	VG+	Fine	Author	Award	Pub
1949	Christopher Bunny	$70	$90	$120		Jane Werner Watson		Golden
1949	Mouse's House	$80	$120	$140		Kathryn & Byron Jackson		Golden
1949	My Little Golden Dictionary	$60	$80	$100		Mary Maud Reed		Golden
1949	Two Little Miners	$120	$160	$220		Margaret Wise Brown		Golden
1950	Brave Cowboy Bill	$70	$90	$120		Kathryn & Byron Jackson		Golden
1950	Little Benny Wanted A Pony	$70	$90	$120		Oliver O'Connor Barret		Golden
1950	The Animals' Merry Christmas	$70	$90	$120		Kathryn Jackson		Golden

Scarry   Richard

Year	Title	VG-	VG	VG+	Fine	Author	Award	Pub
1951	Albert's Zoo	$50	$70	$90		Jane Werner		Golden
1951	The Great Big Car And Truck Book	$80	$100	$140		Richard Scarry		Golden
1952	The New Golden Almanac	$50	$70	$90		Kathryn Jackson		Golden
1953	Rabbit And His Friends	$60	$80	$100		Richard Scarry		Golden
1953	The Animals Of Farmer Jones	$50	$70	$90		Leah Gale		Golden
1953	Three Billy Goats Gruff	$50	$70	$90		Peter Christen Asbjønsen		Golden
1954	Little Indian	$80	$100	$140		Margaret Wise Brown		Golden
1954	Pierre Bear	$50	$70	$90		Patricia M. Scarry		S&S
1955	Naughty Bunny	$60	$80	$100		Richard Scarry		Golden
1955	Smokey the Bear	$50	$70	$90		Jane Werner		S&S
1955	The Golden Bedtime Book	$50	$70	$90		Kathryn Jackson		Golden
1958	Cowboys And Indians	$50	$60	$80		Willis Lindquist		Golden
1958	Rudolph, The Red-Nosed Reindeer	$50	$60	$80		Robert May		Golden
1959	A Little Golden Book About Colors	$50	$60	$80		Kathleen N. Daly		Golden
1959	The Chipmunk's Merry Christmas	$60	$80	$100		Richard Scarry		Golden
1960	Just For Fun	$50	$60	$80		Patricia M. Scarry		Golden
1960	Tinker And Tanker	$50	$70	$90		Richard Scarry		GardenC
1961	Tinker And Tanker And The Pirates	$80	$120	$140		Richard Scarry		DoubleD
1961	Tinker And Tanker And Their Space Ship	$80	$120	$140		Richard Scarry		DoubleD
1961	Tinker And Tanker Out West	$80	$120	$140		Richard Scarry		DoubleD
1962	A Nonsense Alphabet	$50	$60	$80		Edward Lear		DoubleD
1962	My Golden Book Of Manners	$50	$60	$80		Peggy Parish		Golden
1962	Tommy Visits The Doctor	$50	$60	$80		Jean Hortense Seligmann		Golden
1963	Chipmunk's ABC	$50	$60	$80		Richard Scarry		Golden
1963	I Am A Bunny	$50	$60	$80		Ole Risom		Golden
1963	The Rooster Struts	$50	$60	$80		Richard Scarry		Golden
1963	Tinker and Tanker in Africa	$70	$100	$120		Richard Scarry		DoubleD
1963	Tinker And Tanker Knights of the Round Table	$70	$100	$120		Richard Scarry		DoubleD
1964	Animal Mother Goose	$50	$60	$80		Richard Scarry		Golden
1964	Fables	$50	$60	$80		Jean de La Fontaine		DoubleD
1964	Is This the House of Mistress Mouse?	$90	$120	$160		Richard Scarry		Golden
1964	My Nursery Tale Book	$50	$60	$80		Richard Scarry		Golden
1965	Busy, Busy World	$140	$180	$220		Richard Scarry		Golden
1965	The Bunny Book	$40	$60	$70		Richard Scarry		Golden
1966	Storybook Dictionary	$40	$60	$70		Laura Norton (adapted)		Golden
1967	Boats	$40	$50	$70		Richard Scarry		Golden
1967	Cars	$40	$50	$70		Richard Scarry		Golden
1967	Egg in the Hole Book	$40	$50	$70		Richard Scarry		Western
1967	Planes	$40	$50	$70		Richard Scarry		Golden
1967	Trains	$40	$50	$70		Richard Scarry		Golden
1968	Smokey The Bear	$40	$50	$70		Jane Werner Watson		Golden
1968	What Do People Do All Day?	$40	$50	$70		Richard Scarry		Random
1969	Richard Scarry's Great Big Schoolhouse	$40	$50	$70		Richard Scarry		Random
1969	The Great Pie Robbery	$40	$50	$70		Richard Scarry		Random
1969	The Supermarket Mystery	$40	$50	$70		Richard Scarry		Random
1971	More Adventures Of Tinker And Tanker		$30	$50	$60	Richard Scarry		DoubleD
1971	Richard Scarry's Great Big Air Book		$30	$50	$60	Richard Scarry		Random
1972	Nicky Goes To The Doctor		$30	$50	$60	Richard Scarry		Golden
1972	Richard Scarry's Hop Aboard! Here We Go!		$30	$50	$60	Richard Scarry		Golden
1973	Richard Scarry's Silly Stories		$30	$50	$60	Richard Scarry		Golden
1976	All Year Long		$30	$40	$60	Richard Scarry		Golden
1976	Early Words		$30	$40	$60	Richard Scarry		Random
1976	In My Town		$30	$40	$60	Richard Scarry		Golden
1976	Learn To Count		$30	$40	$60	Richard Scarry		Golden
1976	Richard Scarry's About Animals		$30	$40	$60	Richard Scarry		Golden
1976	Richard Scarry's All Day Long		$30	$40	$60	Richard Scarry		Golden
1976	Richard Scarry's At Work		$30	$40	$60	Richard Scarry		Golden
1976	Richard Scarry's Busiest People Ever		$30	$40	$60	Richard Scarry		Random
1976	Richard Scarry's Favorite Mother Goose Rhymes		$30	$40	$60	Richard Scarry		Golden
1976	Richard Scarry's My House		$30	$40	$60	Richard Scarry		Golden
1976	Richard Scarry's On The Farm		$30	$40	$60	Richard Scarry		Golden
1976	Richard Scarry's On Vacation		$30	$40	$60	Richard Scarry		Golden
1976	Short And Tall		$30	$40	$60	Richard Scarry		Golden
1984	Pig Will and Pig Won't		$20	$30	$40	Richard Scarry		Random
1984	The Best Mistake Ever!		$20	$30	$40	Richard Scarry		Random
1987	Lowly Learns His ABC's		$20	$30	$40	Richard Scarry		Random
1987	Lowly Learns to Count		$20	$30	$40	Richard Scarry		Random

Scarry   Richard

Year	Title	VG-	VG	VG+	Fine	Author	Award	Pub
1987	Richard Scarry's Things To Love		$20	$30	$40	Richard Scarry		Golden
1988	Richard Scarry's Frances Fix-It		$14	$20	$25	Richard Scarry		Golden
1989	Richard Scarry's Best House Ever		$14	$20	$25	Kathryn & Byron Jackson		Golden
1991	Richard Scarry's Best Busy Year Ever		$12	$18	$25	Richard Scarry		Golden
1992	Huckle Cat's Busiest Day Ever		$12	$18	$25	Richard Scarry		Random
1992	Richard Scarry's Bananas Gorilla		$12	$18	$25	Richard Scarry		Golden
1992	Richard Scarry's Word Book		$12	$18	$25	Richard Scarry		Golden
1995	Richard Scarry's Best Story Book Ever		$10	$16	$20	Richard Scarry		Golden
1995	Richard Scarry's Happy Birthday, Hilda		$10	$16	$20	Richard Scarry		Golden
1995	Richard Scarry's Pig Will And Pig Won't		$10	$16	$20	Richard Scarry		Random
1995	The Adventures Of Lowly Worm		$10	$16	$20	Richard Scarry		Random
1997	Best Balloon Ride Ever!		$10	$14	$18	Richard Scarry		Golden
1997	Best Little Word Book Ever!		$10	$14	$18	Richard Scarry		Golden
1997	Busiest Fire Fighters Ever!		$10	$14	$18	Richard Scarry		Golden
1997	Cucumber To The Rescue!		$10	$14	$18	Richard Scarry		LSimon
1997	Mr. Frumble's Coffee Shop Disaster		$10	$14	$18	Richard Scarry		Golden
1997	Richard Scarry's Mr. Frumble's Bedtime Stories		$10	$14	$18	Richard Scarry		LSimon
1997	Sneef Saves The Day!		$10	$14	$18	Richard Scarry		LSimon
1998	Cars And Trucks And Things That Go!		$10	$14	$18	Richard Scarry		Golden
1998	Christmas Mice		$10	$14	$18	Naomi Kleinberg		Golden
1998	Good Night, Little Bear		$10	$14	$18	Richard Scarry		Golden
1998	Naughty Bunny		$10	$14	$18	Richard Scarry		Golden
1998	Polite Elephant		$10	$14	$18	Naomi Kleinberg		Golden
1998	Richard Scarry's A Story A Day		$10	$14	$18	Kathryn Jackson		Golden
1998	Richard Scarry's Best Mother Goose Ever		$10	$14	$18	Richard Scarry		Golden
1998	Richard Scarry's Best Word Book Ever		$10	$14	$18	Richard Scarry		Golden
1998	Richard Scarry's Biggest And Best Ever		$10	$14	$18	Margery Cuyler		Golden
1998	Richard Scarry's Mother Goose Rhymes		$10	$14	$18	Laura Norton (adapted)		Golden
1998	The Worst Helper Ever		$10	$14	$18	Richard Scarry		Golden
1999	Richard Scarry's Color Book		$10	$14	$18	Richard Scarry		Random
1999	The Early Bird		$10	$14	$18	Richard Scarry		Random
2000	Mr. Paint Pig's ABC's		$8	$12	$16	Richard Scarry		Random
2000	The Night Before The Night Before Christmas		$8	$12	$16	Richard Scarry		Random
2001	Is This The House Of Mistress Mouse?		$8	$12	$16	Richard Scarry		Golden
2002	Richard Scarry's Best Friend Ever		$8	$10	$14	Richard Scarry		Golden
2002	Richard Scarry's Frances Fix-It		$8	$10	$14	Richard Scarry		Golden
2002	Richard Scarry's What Will I Wear?		$8	$10	$14	Richard Scarry		Random
2002	Sergeant Murphy's Traffic Book		$8	$10	$14	Richard Scarry		Random
2003	Richard Scarry's A Day At The Fire Station		$8	$10	$14	Richard Scarry		Random
2003	Richard Scarry's Favorite Storybook Ever		$8	$10	$14	Richard Scarry		Golden
2003	Richard Scarry's Watch Your Step, Mr. Rabbit!		$8	$10	$14	Richard Scarry		Random
2004	A Day At The Police Station		$8	$10	$14	Richard Scarry		Golden
2004	Richard Scarry's Best Rainy Day Book Ever		$8	$10	$14	Richard Scarry		Random
2004	The Rooster Struts		$8	$10	$14	Richard Scarry		Random

Schindler   S. D.

Year	Title	VG-	VG	VG+	Fine	Author	Award	Pub
1981	Fair's Fair		$25	$35	$50	Leon Garfield		DoubleD
1982	Fish Fry		$16	$25	$30	Susan Saunders		Viking
1982	The First Tulips in Holland		$25	$35	$50	Phyllis Krasilovsky		DoubleD
1985	Every Living Thing		$16	$25	$30	Cynthia Rylant		BradP
1988	Catwings		$18	$25	$35	Ursula K. Le Guin		Orchard
1989	Catwing Returns		$16	$25	$30	Ursula K. Le Guin		Orchard
1989	Three Little Pigs and the Fox		$25	$40	$50	William Hooks		Macmil
1990	Is This A House For Hermit Crab?		$12	$18	$25	Megan McDonald		Orchard
1991	Not the Piano, Mrs. Medley!		$12	$18	$25	Evan Levine		Orchard
1992	Whoo-Oo Is It?		$12	$18	$25	Megan McDonald		Orchard
1993	Odds on Oliver		$12	$16	$20	Constance Greene		Viking
1993	The Great White Owl of Sissinghurst		$12	$16	$20	Dawn Simmons		McEld
1993	The Stinky Book		$12	$16	$20	Noah Lukas		Random
1994	Charlie Malarkey and the Singing Mouse		$12	$16	$20	William Kennedy		Viking
1994	Don't Fidget a Feather		$12	$16	$20	Erica Silverman		Macmil
1994	Great Aunt Ida and Her Great Dane		$12	$16	$20	Leah Komaiko		DoubleD
1994	I Love My Buzzard		$12	$16	$20	Tres Seymour		Orchard
1995	Full Moon Birthday		$10	$16	$20	Jeff Sheppard		S&S
1995	If You Should Hear A Honey Guide		$10	$16	$20	April Sayre		HM

Schindler   S. D.

Year	Title	VG-	VG	VG+	Fine	Author	Award	Pub
1995	The Smash-Up Crash-Up Derby		$14	$20	$25	Tres Seymour		Orchard
1996	Madame Lagrande And Her [...] Uproarious Pompadour		$10	$16	$20	Candace Fleming		Knopf
1996	The Ghost of Nicholas Greebe		$10	$16	$20	Tony Johnston		Dial
1997	A Tree Is Growing		$10	$16	$20	Arthur Dorros		Scholas
1997	Whatever Happened to Humpty Dumpty		$10	$16	$20	David Greenberg		LBrown
1997	Whuppity Stoorie		$10	$16	$20	Carolyn White		Putnam
1998	Clever Crow		$10	$14	$18	Cynthia De Felice		Athenm
1998	How Santa Got His Job		$10	$14	$18	Stephen Krensky		S&S
1999	Are We There Yet, Daddy?		$10	$14	$18	Virginia Walters		Penguin
1999	Gold Fever		$10	$14	$18	Kay Verla		Putnam
2000	Hog Music		$8	$12	$16	Mary-Claire Helldorfer		Penguin
2000	Sam's Wild West Christmas		$8	$12	$16	Nancy Antle		Penguin
2001	Cackle Cook's Monster Stew		$8	$12	$16	Patricia Rae Wolff		Golden
2001	Johnny Appleseed		$8	$12	$16	Vincent Benet		Scholas
2002	Don't Know Much About Pilgrims		$8	$10	$14	Kenneth Davis		HCollins
2002	Skeleton Hiccups		$8	$10	$14	Margery Cuyler		McEld
2003	The Runaway Pumpkin		$8	$10	$14	Kevin Lewis		Scholas
2003	Three Pebbles and a Song		$8	$10	$14	Eileen Spinelli		Penguin

Schoenherr   John

Year	Title	VG-	VG	VG+	Fine	Author	Award	Pub
1963	Rascal	$50	$70	$90		Sterling North		Dutton
1963	Storm Boy	$50	$60	$80		Colin Thiele		H&Row
1964	A Bat Is Born	$40	$50	$70		Randall Jarrell		DoubleD
1965	Gentle Ben	$35	$40	$60		Walt Morey		Dutton
1965	Mississippi Possum	$30	$40	$50		Miska Miles		LBrown
1965	The Golden Eagle	$30	$40	$50		Robert William Murphy		Dutton
1966	Fox And The Fire	$30	$40	$50		Miska Miles		LBrown
1966	Kangaroo Red	$30	$40	$50		Berniece Freschet		Scribnr
1966	The Phantom Setter	$30	$40	$50		Robert William Murphy		Dutton
1967	A Zebra Came To Drink	$30	$40	$50		Arthur Catherall		Dutton
1967	Rabbit Garden	$30	$40	$50		Miska Miles		LBrown
1967	The Dangerous Year	$30	$40	$50		Era Zistel		Random
1967	The Fox And The Hound	$30	$40	$50		Daniel Pratt Mannix		Dutton
1968	The Barn	$30	$40	$50		John Schoenherr		LBrown
1968	The Big Island	$30	$40	$50		Julian May		Follett
1968	The Moon Of The Chickarees	$40	$50	$70		Jean Craighead George		Crowell
1969	Nobody's Cat	$25	$35	$50		Miska Miles		LBrown
1969	The Wolfling	$25	$35	$50		Sterling North		Dutton
1970	Eddie's Bear		$25	$35	$50	Miska Miles		LBrown
1970	Hoagie's Rifle-Gun		$25	$35	$50	Miska Miles		LBrown
1971	Incident At Hawk's Hill		$25	$35	$50	Allan W. Eckert		LBrown
1971	The Jezebel Wolf		$25	$35	$50	F. N. Monjo		S&S
1972	Julie Of The Wolves		$120	$180	$240	Jean Craighead George	NM	H&Row
1972	Wharf Rat		$25	$35	$50	Miska Miles		LBrown
1973	Somebody's Dog		$25	$35	$50	Miska Miles		LBrown
1973	The Travels Of Atunga		$25	$35	$50	Theodore Clymer		LBrown
1974	Otter In The Cove		$20	$30	$40	Miska Miles		LBrown
1974	Susy's Scoundrel		$20	$30	$40	Harold Keith		Crowell
1975	Black Lightning		$20	$30	$40	John A. Giegling		CM&G
1975	River Song		$20	$30	$40	Alison Morgan		H&Row
1976	Simon Underground		$20	$30	$40	Joanne Ryder		H&Row
1976	Wapootin		$20	$30	$40	Jane & Paul Annixter		CM&G
1977	Kilroy And The Gull		$20	$30	$40	Nathaniel Benchley		H&Row
1978	Beaver Moon		$20	$30	$40	Miska Miles		LBrown
1978	The Wounded Wolf		$20	$30	$40	Jean Craighead George		H&Row
1987	Owl Moon		$160	$220	$300	Jane Yolen	CM	Philo
1991	Bear		$12	$18	$25	John Schoenherr		Philo
1991	Wild Voices		$12	$18	$25	Drew Nelson		Philo
1995	Rebel		$10	$16	$20	John Schoenherr		Philo
1997	Pigs In The Mud In The Middle Of The Rud		$10	$16	$20	Lynn Plourde		BSP

Schreiber   Georges

Year	Title	VG-	VG	VG+	Fine	Author	Award	Pub
1934	His First Million Women	$60	$80	$100		George Weston		F&R
1935	Marty Comes To Town	$60	$80	$100		Ethel Calvert Phillips		HM

Schreiber   Georges

Year	Title	VG-	VG	VG+	Fine	Author	Award	Pub
1947	Bambino The Clown	$120	$160	$220		Georges Schreiber	CH	Viking
1947	Pancakes-Paris	$80	$120	$140		Claire Huchet Bishop	NH	Viking
1951	The Light At Tern Rock	$40	$50	$70		Julia L. Sauer		Viking
1954	Professor Bull's Umbrella	$40	$50	$70		William Lipkind		Viking
1956	Ride On The Wind	$35	$50	$60		Alice Dalgliesh		Scribnr
1959	Bambino Goes Home	$35	$50	$60		Georges Schreiber		Viking
1960	William Tell	$35	$40	$60		Katharine Scherman		Random

Schucker   James

Year	Title	VG-	VG	VG+	Fine	Author	Award	Pub
1961	Little Black, A Pony	$70	$90	$120		Robert Farley		BB
1963	Little Black Goes To The Circus	$70	$90	$120		Walter Farley		BB

Schwartz   Amy

Year	Title	VG-	VG	VG+	Fine	Author	Award	Pub
1982	Bea And Mr. Jones		$14	$20	$25	Amy Schwartz		BradP
1983	Begin at the Beginning		$12	$16	$20	Amy Schwartz		H&Row
1984	Her Majesty, Aunt Essie		$12	$16	$20	Amy Schwartz		BradP
1984	Jane Martin, Dog Detective		$12	$18	$25	Eve Bunting		HBJ
1984	The Crack-Of-Dawn Walkers		$12	$16	$20	Amy Hest		Macmil
1985	The Witch Who Lives Down The Hall		$10	$16	$20	Donna Guthrie		HBJ
1986	The Purple Coat		$10	$16	$20	Amy Hest		4Winds
1987	Maggie Doesn't Want To Move		$10	$16	$20	Elizabeth Lee O'Donnell		4Winds
1987	Oma and Bobo		$10	$16	$20	Amy Schwartz		BradP
1988	Because of Lozo Brown		$10	$16	$20	Larry King		VK
1989	How I Captured a Dinosaur		$12	$16	$20	Henry Schwartz		Orchard
1989	The Lady Who Put Salt in Her Coffee		$10	$16	$20	Lucretia Hale		HBJ
1990	Blow Me A Kiss, Miss Lilly		$10	$14	$18	Nancy Carlstrom		H&Row
1990	Fancy Aunt Jess		$10	$14	$18	Amy Hest		Morrow
1990	Mother Goose's Little Misfortunes		$10	$14	$18	Leonard Marcus		BradP
1991	Camper Of The Week		$10	$14	$18	Amy Schwartz		Orchard
1992	Albert Goes Hollywood		$10	$14	$18	Amy Schwartz		Orchard
1994	A Teeny Tiny Baby		$8	$12	$16	Amy Schwartz		Orchard
1999	How To Catch An Elephant		$8	$10	$14	Amy Schwartz		DK
2003	What James Likes Best		$6	$10	$12	Amy Schwartz		Arcad

Schweninger   Ann

Year	Title	VG-	VG	VG+	Fine	Author	Award	Pub
1976	The Hunt For Rabbit's Galosh		$20	$30	$40	Kay Chorao		DoubleD
1979	A Dance For Three		$18	$25	$35	Ann Schweninger		Dial
1979	The Man In The Moon As He Sails The Sky		$14	$20	$30	Ann Schweninger (compiled)		DoddM
1980	Amy Goes Fishing		$12	$16	$20	Jean Marzollo		Dial
1981	On My Way To Grandpa's		$12	$16	$20	Ann Schweninger		Dial
1981	Thump And Plunk		$12	$16	$20	Janice May Udry		H&Row
1982	Amanda Pig And Her Big Brother Oliver		$12	$16	$20	Jean Van Leeuwen		Dial
1982	Animal Poems		$12	$16	$20	Dewitt Conyers (selected)		Golden
1982	Bedtime Story		$12	$16	$20	Jim Erskine		Crown
1982	Morning, Rabbit, Morning		$12	$16	$20	Mary Caldwell		H&Row
1983	ABC Cat		$10	$16	$20	Nancy Jewell		H&Row
1983	Ribtickle Town		$10	$16	$20	Alan Benjamin		4Winds
1983	Silent Night		$10	$16	$20	Reverend Joseph Mohr		Golden
1983	Tales Of Amanda Pig		$10	$16	$20	Jean Van Leeuwen		Dial
1983	The Musicians Of Bremen		$10	$16	$20	Ben Cruise (retold)		Golden
1984	Christmas Secrets		$10	$16	$20	Ann Schweninger		VK
1984	Halloween Surprises		$10	$16	$20	Ann Schweninger		VK
1985	Henrietta And The Hat		$10	$16	$20	Mabel Watts		Golden
1985	More Tales Of Amanda Pig		$10	$16	$20	Jean Van Leeuwen		Dial
1985	Peter's Welcome		$10	$16	$20	Maida Silverman		Golden
1986	Birthday Wishes		$10	$16	$20	Ann Schweninger		VK
1986	Godfather Cat And Mousie		$10	$16	$20	Doris Orgel (retold)		Macmil
1986	Mother Goose & Other Nursery Rhymes		$10	$16	$20	Clara A. Nestor (edited)		Golden
1987	My Christmas Tree & Other Poems Of The Season		$10	$16	$20	Ann Schweninger (compiled)		Golden
1987	Off To School!		$10	$16	$20	Ann Schweninger		VK
1987	Oliver, Amanda, And Grandmother Pig		$10	$16	$20	Jean Van Leeuwen		Dial
1987	The Mother Goose Word Book		$10	$16	$20	Melanie Donovan (selected)		Golden

Schweninger   Ann

Year	Title	VG-	VG	VG+	Fine	Author	Award	Pub
1988	The Read-Aloud Treasury		$10	$14	$18	S. Calmenson & J. Cole		DoubleD
1988	The Runaway Christmas Toy		$10	$14	$18	Linda Hayward		Random
1988	Two-Minute Fairy Tales		$10	$14	$18	Mary Packard (adapted)		Golden
1988	Valentine Friends		$10	$14	$18	Ann Schweninger		VK
1989	Alphabet School		$10	$14	$18	Linda Hayward		Random
1989	Oliver And Amanda's Christmas		$10	$14	$18	Jean Van Leeuwen		Dial
1989	The Teddy Bear Book		$10	$14	$18	Jean Marzollo		Dial
1990	Oliver Pig At School		$10	$14	$18	Jean Van Leeuwen		Dial
1990	Wintertime		$10	$14	$18	Ann Schweninger		Viking
1991	Amanda Pig On Her Own		$10	$14	$18	Jean Van Leeuwen		Dial
1991	Autumn Days		$10	$14	$18	Ann Schweninger		Viking
1992	Mary Had A Little Lamb		$10	$14	$18	Ann Schweninger		Western
1992	Oliver And Amanda's Halloween		$10	$14	$18	Jean Van Leeuwen		Dial
1992	Summertime		$10	$14	$18	Ann Schweninger		Viking
1992	The Tale Of Peter Rabbit		$10	$14	$18	Beatrix Potter		Western
1993	Springtime		$8	$12	$16	Ann Schweninger		Viking
1994	The Make-Something Club		$8	$12	$16	Frances Zweifel		Viking
1995	Oliver & Amanda And The Big Snow		$8	$12	$16	Jean Van Leeuwen		Dial
1996	The Littlest Duckling		$8	$12	$16	Frances Zweifel		Viking
1997	Amanda Pig, School Girl		$8	$10	$14	Jean Van Leeuwen		Dial
1997	The Make-Something Club Is Back!		$8	$10	$14	Frances Zweifel		Viking
1998	Amanda Pig And Her Best Friend Lollipop		$8	$10	$14	Jean Van Leeuwen		Dial
2000	Oliver And Albert, Friends Forever		$8	$10	$14	Jean Van Leeuwen		PFogel
2001	We're Going On A Ghost Hunt		$8	$10	$14	Marcia Vaughan		Whistle
2003	Amanda Pig And The Awful, Scary Monster		$6	$10	$12	Jean Van Leeuwen		PFogel
2003	Oliver The Mighty Pig		$6	$10	$12	Jean Van Leeuwen		PFogel

Scott   Janet Laura

Year	Title	VG-	VG	VG+	Fine	Author	Award	Pub
1917	Happy All Day Through	$400	$520	$660		John Gabbert Bowman		Volland
1918	Wild Flower Children	$320	$440	$540		Elizabeth Gordon		Volland
1921	Betty, Bobby and Bubbles	$260	$360	$440		Edith Mitchell		Volland
1922	The Princess Of Cozytown	$260	$360	$440		Ruth Plumly Thompson		Volland
1923	The Ladder Of Rickety Rungs	$260	$360	$440		T.C. O'Donnell		Volland
1926	Pudding Lane People	$120	$160	$200		Sarah Addington		LBrown
1927	Mrs. Cucumber Green	$100	$140	$180		Mary Graham Bonner		MB
1927	Shoes And Ships And Sealing-Wax	$100	$140	$180		Ethel Clere Chamberlin		SaalF
1935	Fifty Songs For Boys And Girls.	$80	$120	$140		Mary Nancy Graham		Whitman
1935	Sugar And Spice	$80	$120	$140		Rose Fyleman		Whitman
1935	The Turned-Into's	$80	$120	$140		Elizabeth Gordon		Wis-P
1938	A Story Teller's Holiday	$80	$100	$140		Mary Graham Bonner		McLough
1938	I Never Knew That Before	$80	$100	$140		Eric J. Bender		SaalF
1939	On Christmas Day In The Morning	$80	$100	$140		Edith Lowe		Whitman
1939	One Happy Day	$80	$100	$140		Marceline Dauzet		SaalF
1939	'Round The World We Sail	$80	$100	$140		Janet Laura Scott		SaalF

Scruton   Clive

Year	Title	VG-	VG	VG+	Fine	Author	Award	Pub
1980	Flat Cat		$12	$16	$20	Russell Hoban		Philo
1984	Jack And Nelly		$10	$14	$18	David Lloyd		Walker
1985	Bubble And Squeak		$10	$14	$18	Clive Scruton		Random
1985	Circus Cow		$10	$14	$18	Clive Scruton		Random
1985	Pig In The Air		$10	$14	$18	Clive Scruton		Random
1985	Scaredy Cat		$10	$14	$18	Clive Scruton		Random
1987	Cat And Dog		$10	$14	$18	David Lloyd		LL&S
1987	Four Black Puppies		$10	$14	$18	Sally Grindley		LL&S
1989	Mary's Pets		$8	$12	$16	Clive Scruton		LL&S
1991	The Secrets Of Santa		$8	$12	$16	Anne Civardi		S&S
1992	It's A Go-To-The-Park Day		$8	$12	$16	Vivian French		S&S
1998	A Goodnight Kind Of Feeling		$8	$10	$14	Tony Bradman		Holiday
1999	I Love You!		$8	$10	$14	Clive Scruton		PubIntl
1999	Where Are Mary's Pets?		$8	$10	$14	Clive Scruton		Candle
2000	Mrs. Hippo's Pizza Parlour		$6	$10	$12	Vivian French		Kfisher
2000	Teddy Bear, Piglet, Kitten & Me		$6	$10	$12	Catherine Maccabe		Augsb
2002	Crazy Christmas Chaos		$6	$10	$12	Quinlan B. Lee		HFest
2002	Silly Sweetheart Celebrations		$6	$10	$12	Quinlan B. Lee		HFest

Scruton   Clive

Year	Title	VG-	VG	VG+	Fine	Author	Award	Pub
2002	The Kingfisher Treasury Of Dinosaur Stories		$6	$10	$12	Jeremy Strong		Kfisher
2002	Tricky Turkey Tongue Twisters		$6	$10	$12	Quinlan B. Lee		HFest
2003	Super School Side-Splitters		$6	$10	$12	Quinlan B. Lee		HFest

Searle   Ronald

Year	Title	VG-	VG	VG+	Fine	Author	Award	Pub
1950	The Female Approach	$80	$120	$140		Ronald Searle		MacD
1952	The Terror Of St. Trinian's	$50	$70	$90		D.B. Wyndham Lewis		Parrish
1953	Souls In Torment	$80	$100	$140		Ronald Searle		Perpet
1954	Down With Skool!	$50	$70	$90		Geoffrey Willans		Vnguard
1954	How To Be Topp	$50	$70	$90		Geoffrey Willans		Vnguard
1955	The Rake's Progress	$70	$100	$120		Ronald Searle		Perpet
1956	Merry England	$70	$100	$120		Ronald Searle		Perpet
1956	Molesworth's Guide To The Atommic Age	$50	$70	$90		Geoffrey Willans		Vnguard
1956	The Investigator	$50	$70	$90		Reuben Ship		S&J
1956	Whizz For Atomms	$50	$70	$90		Geoffrey Willans		Pavil
1958	The Dog's Ear Book	$50	$60	$80		Geoffrey Willans		Crowell
1959	Molesworth Back In The Jug Agane	$50	$60	$80		Geoffrey Willans		Vnguard
1959	The St. Trinian's Story	$50	$60	$80		Kaye Webb		Perpet
1961	The Penguin Ronald Searle	$70	$90	$120		Ronald Searle		Penguin
1961	Which Way Did He Go?	$70	$90	$120		Ronald Searle		World
1962	Oliver Twist	$50	$60	$80		Charles Dickens		Norton
1964	From Frozen North To Filthy Lucre	$50	$60	$80		Jane Clapperton		Viking
1965	Those Magnificent Men In Their Flying Machines	$40	$60	$70		William Richardson		Dobson
1967	Searle's Cats	$60	$80	$100		Ronald Searle		Dobson
1968	The Square Egg	$60	$80	$100		Ronald Searle		W&N
1969	Hello - Where Did All The People Go?	$60	$80	$100		Ronald Searle		W&N
1969	The Adventures Of Baron Munchausen	$60	$80	$100		Ronald Searle		Pan
1969	Tiens!	$60	$80	$100		Ronald Searle		Pavil
1971	The Addict		$40	$60	$90	Ronald Searle		Greene
1975	Dick Deadeye		$30	$40	$60	W.S. Gilbert		HBJ
1975	More Cats		$40	$60	$80	Ronald Searle		Dobson
1977	Searle's Zoodiac		$40	$60	$80	Ronald Searle		Dobson
1977	Zoodiac		$40	$60	$80	Ronald Searle		Pan
1980	The King Of Beasts & Other Creatures		$35	$50	$70	Ronald Searle		Lane
1982	Ronald Searle's Big Fat Cat Book		$30	$50	$60	Ronald Searle		LBrown
1986	To The Kwai And Back		$30	$40	$60	Ronald Searle		AMP
1993	The Curse Of St. Trinian's		$20	$30	$40	Ronald Searle		Pavil
1994	The Tales Of Grandpa Cat		$14	$20	$30	Lee Warklaw		Dial
1995	The Hatless Man		$14	$20	$25	Sarah Kortum		Viking

Seiden   Art

Year	Title	VG-	VG	VG+	Fine	Author	Award	Pub
1950	The Little Engine That Laughed	$40	$50	$70		Alf Evers		G&D
1950	The Noisy Clock Shop	$40	$50	$70		Jean Horton Berg		Wonder
1950	Three Mice And A Cat	$40	$50	$70		Jean Horton Berg		Wonder
1953	Howdy Doody in Funland	$30	$40	$50		Edward Kean		S&S
1953	My ABC Book	$30	$40	$50		Art Seiden		Wonder
1953	The Big Treasure Book of Wheels	$30	$40	$50		Felix Sutton		G&D
1955	Snow White And The Seven Dwarfs	$25	$35	$50		Art Seiden		Treasur
1965	The Peek-A-Boo Book Of Animals	$25	$30	$40		Hannah Rush		TNelson
1965	The Picture Story And Biography Of Red Cloud	$25	$30	$40		Shannon Garst		Follett
1965	This Is A Newspaper	$25	$30	$40		Lawrence H. Feigenbaum		Follett
1965	Uncle Wiggily Stories	$25	$30	$40		Howard Roger Garis		G&D
1966	Animal Babies	$25	$30	$40		Joan Potter Elwart		Whitman
1967	A White Sweater Must Be White	$25	$30	$40		Solveig Paulson Russell		G&D
1969	The Big And Little Book Of ABC's	$20	$30	$35		Ann McFerran		Gibson
1970	Whatever Happened To Yes?		$18	$25	$35	Phyllis W. Goldman		Walker
1981	1 Nose, 10 Toes		$14	$20	$25	Janet Cnenery		G&D
1981	Fishing Basics		$14	$20	$25	John Randolph		P-Hall
1982	Bicycling Basics		$14	$20	$25	Tim & Glenda Wilhelm		P-Hall
1982	Little Bunny Learns Colors		$14	$20	$25	Art Seiden		Random
1982	Michael Shows Off Baltimore		$14	$20	$25	Art Seiden		Outdoor
1982	Sailing Basics		$14	$20	$25	Lorna Slocombe		P-Hall
1983	Tippet Shows Off Washington		$14	$20	$25	Patricia W. Romero		Outdoor
1983	Trucks		$14	$20	$25	Art Seiden		P&Munk

Seiden   Art

Year	Title	VG-	VG	VG+	Fine	Author	Award	Pub
1984	Electronics Basics		$12	$18	$25	Carl Laron		P-Hall
1985	Boating Basics		$12	$18	$25	Henry F. Halsted		P-Hall
1985	Easy-To-Make Water Toys That Really Work		$12	$18	$25	Mary & Dewey Blocksma		P-Hall
1985	Laser Basics		$12	$18	$25	Lawrence Stevens		P-Hall
1986	Diving Basics		$12	$16	$20	Bob Goldberg		P-Hall
1986	Space-Crafting		$12	$16	$20	Mary & Dewey Blocksma		P-Hall
1992	How On Earth Do We Recycle Glass?		$10	$16	$20	Joanna Randolph Rott		Millbk
1992	How On Earth Do We Recycle Metal?		$10	$16	$20	Rudy Kouhoupt		Millbk
1992	How On Earth Do We Recycle Paper?		$10	$16	$20	Helen Jill Fletcher		Millbk
1993	Soccer		$10	$16	$20	Barry Wilner		RainSV
1994	Baseball		$10	$14	$18	Mark Alan Teirstein		RainSV
1994	Basketball		$10	$14	$18	Tom Withers		RainSV
1994	Football		$10	$14	$18	Dave Raffo		RainSV
1994	Hockey		$10	$14	$18	Lisa Harris		RainSV
1994	Track And Field		$10	$14	$18	Bert Rosenthal		RainSV
1996	Bicycling		$8	$12	$16	John Francis		RainSV
1996	Jewish Heroes & Heroines Of America		$8	$12	$16	Seymour Brody		Life
1996	Karate And Judo		$8	$12	$16	Thomas J. Nardi		RainSV
1996	Swimming		$8	$12	$16	Barry Wilner		RainSV
1999	The Train To Timbuctoo		$8	$12	$16	Margaret Wise Brown		Golden

Selznick   Brian

Year	Title	VG-	VG	VG+	Fine	Author	Award	Pub
1991	The Houdini Box		$16	$25	$30	Brian Selznick		Knopf
1994	Doll Face Has A Party!		$12	$16	$20	Pam Conrad		HCollins
1995	Our House: The Stories Of Levittown		$10	$16	$20	Pam Conrad		Scholas
1995	The Robot King		$10	$16	$20	Brian Selznick		LauraG
1996	Frindle		$10	$16	$20	Andrew Clements		S&S
1997	The Boy Who Longed For A Lift		$10	$16	$20	Norma Farber		LauraG
1998	Riding Freedom		$10	$14	$18	Pam Muñoz Ryan		Scholas
1999	Amelia And Eleanor		$10	$14	$18	Pam Muñoz Ryan		Scholas
2000	Barnyard Prayers		$8	$12	$16	Laura Godwin		Hyper
2000	The Boy Of A Thousand Faces		$8	$12	$16	Brian Selznick		HCollins
2000	The Doll People		$10	$14	$18	A. Martin & L. Godwin		Hyper
2001	The Dinosaurs Of Waterhouse Hawkins		$25	$35	$50	Brian Selznick	CH	Scholas
2001	The School Story		$8	$12	$16	Andrew Clements		S&S
2002	When Marian Sang		$8	$10	$14	Pam Muñoz Ryan		Scholas
2002	Wingwalker		$8	$10	$14	Rosemary Wells		Hyper
2003	The Dulcimer Boy		$8	$10	$14	Tor Seidler		LauraG
2003	The Meanest Doll In The World		$8	$10	$14	A. Martin & L. Godwin		Hyper
2004	Walt		$8	$10	$14	Barbara Kerley		Scholas

Sendak   Maurice

Year	Title	VG-	VG	VG+	Fine	Author	Award	Pub
1951	Good Shabbos, Everybody!	$520	$680	$860		Robert Garvey		USC
1952	A Hole Is To Dig	$340	$440	$560		Ruth Krauss	NYT	H&B
1952	Maggie Rose, Her Birthday Christmas	$220	$280	$360		Ruth Sawyer		H&B
1953	A Very Special House	$720	$960	$1,200		Ruth Krauss	CH	H&B
1953	Hurry Home, Candy	$320	$440	$540		Meindert De Jong	NH	H&B
1953	Shadrach	$220	$280	$360		Meindert De Jong	NH	H&B
1953	The Giant Story	$160	$220	$280		Beatrice S. De Regniers		H&B
1954	I'll Be You And You Be Me	$220	$280	$360		Ruth Krauss		H&B
1954	Magic Pictures	$320	$440	$540		Marcel Ayme		H&B
1954	Mrs. Piggle-Wiggle's Farm	$320	$440	$540		Betty Bard MacDonald		Lippin
1954	The Wheel On The School	$480	$640	$800		Meindert De Jong	NM	H&B
1955	Charlotte and the White Horse	$320	$420	$520		Ruth Krauss		H&B
1955	Singing Family Of The Cumberlands	$140	$180	$240		Jean Ritchie		Oxford
1955	The Little Cow And The Turtle	$200	$280	$340		Meindert De Jong		H&B
1955	What Can You Do With A Shoe?	$200	$280	$340		Beatrice S. De Regniers		H&B
1956	Happy Rain	$240	$320	$400		Jack Sendak		H&B
1956	I Want To Paint My Bathroom Blue	$200	$280	$340		Ruth Krauss		H&B
1956	Kenny's Window	$380	$500	$620		Maurice Sendak		H&B
1956	The House Of Sixty Fathers	$320	$420	$520		Meindert De Jong	NH	H&B
1957	Little Bear	$360	$480	$600		Else Holmelund Minarik		H&B
1957	Very Far Away	$240	$320	$400		Maurice Sendak		H&B
1957	You Can't Get There From Here	$240	$320	$400		Maurice Sendak		LBrown

Sendak   Maurice

Year	Title	VG-	VG	VG+	Fine	Author	Award	Pub
1958	Along Came A Dog	$240	$320	$400		Meindert De Jong	NH	H&B
1958	No Fighting, No Biting!	$160	$220	$280		Else Holmelund Minarik		H&B
1958	Somebody's Else's Nut Tree	$160	$220	$280		Ruth Krauss		H&B
1958	What Do You Do, Dear?	$240	$320	$400		Sesyle Joslin	CH	YScott
1959	Father Bear Comes Home	$220	$300	$380		Else Holmelund Minarik		H&B
1959	Seven Tales By H.C. Anderson	$160	$200	$260		Eva Le Gallienne		HCollins
1959	The Moon Jumpers	$220	$300	$380		Janice May Udry	CH	H&B
1960	Dwarf Long-Nose	$160	$200	$260		Wilhelm Hauff		Random
1960	Little Bear's Friend	$160	$200	$260		Else Holmelund Minarik		H&B
1960	Open House for Butterflies	$160	$200	$260		Ruth Krauss		H&B
1960	The Sign On Rosie's Door	$160	$200	$260		Maurice Sendak		H&B
1961	Little Bear's Visit	$160	$200	$260		Else Holmelund Minarik	CH	H&B
1961	What Do You Do, Dear	$160	$200	$260		Sesyle Joslin		YScott
1962	Mr. Rabbit And The Lovely Present	$140	$200	$240		Charlotte Zolotow	CH	Harper
1962	Nutshell Library	$320	$440	$540		Maurice Sendak		Harper
1962	The Big Green Book	$140	$200	$240		Robert Graves		Macmil
1962	The Singing Hill	$140	$200	$240		Meindert De Jong		Harper
1963	How Little Lori Visited Times Square	$140	$200	$240		Amos Vogel		H&Row
1963	Sarah's Room	$140	$200	$240		Maurice Sendak		H&Row
1963	She Loves Me...She Loves Me Not...	$140	$200	$240		Robert Keeshan		H&Row
1963	The Griffin And The Minor Canon	$140	$200	$240		Frank R. Stockton		HR&W
1963	Where The Wild Things Are	$6,200	$8,200	$10,200		Maurice Sendak	CM	H&Row
1964	Little Stories	$200	$280	$340		Gladys Baker Bond		B'nai
1964	Pleasant Fieldmouse	$140	$180	$240		Jan Wahl		H&Row
1964	The Bat-Poet	$90	$120	$160		Randall Jarrell		Macmil
1964	The Bee-Man Of Orn	$140	$180	$240		Frank R. Stockton		HR&W
1965	Hector Protector	$140	$180	$220		Maurice Sendak		H&Row
1965	Lullabies And Night Songs	$140	$180	$220		William Engvick		H&Row
1965	The Animal Family	$200	$280	$340		Randall Jarrell	NH	Pan
1966	Zlateh The Goat & Other Stories	$140	$180	$220		Isaac Bashevis Singer		H&Row
1967	Higglety Pigglety Pop!	$120	$160	$220		Maurice Sendak		H&Row
1967	Poems From William Blake's Songs Of Innocence	$120	$160	$220		William Blake		Bodley
1967	The Golden Key	$120	$160	$220		George MacDonald		FSG
1968	A Kiss For Little Bear	$200	$260	$320		Else Holmelund Minarik		H&Row
1969	The Light Princess	$120	$160	$200		George MacDonald		FSG
1970	In The Night Kitchen		$160	$220	$300	Maurice Sendak	CH	H&Row
1973	King Grisly-Beard		$70	$100	$140	Jacob & Wilhelm Grimm	NYT	FSG
1973	The Juniper Tree, & Other Tales From Grimm		$70	$100	$140	Lore Segal (selected)		FSG
1975	Maurice Sendak's Really Rosie		$50	$70	$90	Carole King		H&Row
1975	Seven Little Monsters		$70	$100	$140	Maurice Sendak		H&Row
1976	Fly By Night		$50	$80	$100	Randall Jarrell		FSG
1976	Some Swell Pup		$35	$50	$70	Mathew Margolis		FSG
1981	Outside Over There		$40	$60	$90	Maurice Sendak	CH	H&Row
1984	Nutcracker		$40	$60	$80	E. T. A. Hoffmann		Crown
1984	The Love For Three Oranges		$30	$40	$60	Frank Corsaro		FSG
1985	In Grandpa's House		$25	$40	$50	Philip Sendak		H&Row
1985	The Cunning Little Vixen		$25	$40	$50	Rudolf Tesnohlídek		FSG
1988	Dear Mili		$25	$35	$50	Ralph Manheim (translated)		FSG
1988	Tail Feathers From Mother Goose		$25	$35	$50	Jacob & Wilhelm Grimm		FSG
1989	Where The Wild Things Are		$25	$35	$50	Maurice Sendak	CM	HCollins
1992	I Saw Esau		$20	$30	$40	Iona & Peter Opie		Candle
1993	We Are All In The Dumps With Jack And Guy		$18	$25	$35	Maurice Sendak		HCollins
1994	The Wonderful Farm		$18	$25	$35	Marcel Aymé		HCollins
1995	Pierre		$16	$25	$30	Herman Melville		HCollins
1995	The Miami Giant		$16	$25	$30	Arthur Yorinks		HCollins
1996	Frank & Joey Go To Work		$16	$25	$30	Arthur Yorinks		HFest
1998	Penthesilea		$14	$20	$30	Heinrich von Kleist		diCapua
1999	Swine Lake		$14	$20	$25	James Marshall		HCollins
2002	Little Bear's Egg		$10	$16	$20	Else Holmelund Minarik		HFest
2003	Brundibar		$10	$14	$18	Tony Kushner		Hyper

Seredy   Kate

Year	Title	VG-	VG	VG+	Fine	Author	Award	Pub
1932	From Hunters To Herdsmen	$100	$140	$180		Elizabeth Forbes O'Hara		Macmil
1932	Taming The Wild Grasses	$100	$140	$180		Elizabeth Forbes O'Hara		Macmil
1934	The Broken Song	$70	$100	$120		Sonia M. Daugherty		TNelson

Seredy   Kate

Year	Title	VG-	VG	VG+	Fine	Author	Award	Pub
1934	The Prince Commands	$70	$100	$120		Andre Norton		DApple
1935	Caddie Woodlawn	$600	$800	$1,000		Carol Ryrie Brink	NM	Macmil
1935	The Good Master	$160	$200	$260		Kate Seredy	NH	Viking
1935	The Selfish Giant & Other Stories	$70	$100	$120		Wilhelmina Harper		DMcKay
1936	Hoot-Owl	$70	$100	$120		Mabel Guinnip La Rue		Macmil
1936	Listening	$70	$100	$120		Kate Seredy		Viking
1936	Mademoiselle Misfortune	$70	$100	$120		Carol Ryrie Brink		Macmil
1936	The Gunniwolf & Other Merry Tales	$70	$100	$120		Wilhelmina Harper		DMcKay
1937	Bible Children	$70	$90	$120		Blanche Jennings Thompson		DoddM
1937	Smiling Hill Farm	$70	$90	$120		Miriam Evangeline Mason		Ginn
1937	The White Stag	$340	$440	$560		Kate Seredy	NM	Viking
1939	The Singing Tree	$140	$200	$240		Kate Seredy	NH	Viking
1939	Who Is Johnny?	$70	$90	$120		Leopold Gedö		Viking
1940	Michel's Island	$70	$90	$120		Mabel Leigh Hunt		FStokes
1941	A Tree For Peter	$70	$90	$120		Kate Seredy		Viking
1943	The Open Gate	$70	$90	$120		Kate Seredy		Viking
1944	The Christmas Anna Angel	$180	$240	$300		Ruth Sawyer	CH	Viking
1946	A Candle Burns For France	$60	$80	$100		Blanche Jennings Thompson		Bruce
1946	The Wonderful Year	$60	$80	$100		Helen Simmons Adams		Messner
1947	Adopted Jane	$60	$80	$100		Helen Fern Daringer		HBrace
1948	Mary Montgomery	$60	$80	$100		Helen Fern Daringer		HBrace
1948	The Chestry Oak	$60	$80	$100		Kate Seredy		Viking
1949	A House For Ten	$60	$80	$100		Miriam Evangeline Mason		Ginn
1949	Pilgrim Kate	$60	$80	$100		Helen Fern Daringer		HBrace
1951	Gypsy	$50	$70	$90		Kate Seredy		Viking
1951	Little Vic	$50	$70	$90		Doris Gates		Viking
1953	Finnegan II, His Nine Lives	$50	$70	$90		Carolyn Sherwin Bailey		Viking
1961	A Brand-New Uncle	$50	$60	$80		Kate Seredy		Viking
1962	Lazy Tinka	$50	$60	$80		Kate Seredy		Viking

Seuss, Dr.   [Theodor Seuss Geisel]

Year	Title	VG-	VG	VG+	Fine	Author	Award	Pub
1937	And To Think That I Saw It On Mulberry Street	$5,000	$6,800	$8,400		Theodor Geisel		Vnguard
1938	The 500 Hats Of Bartholomew Cubbins	$3,800	$5,000	$6,200		Theodor Geisel		Vnguard
1939	The King's Stilts	$3,200	$4,200	$5,200		Theodor Geisel		Random
1939	The Seven Lady Godivas	$320	$440	$540		Theodor Geisel		Random
1940	Horton Hatches The Egg	$4,400	$6,000	$7,400		Theodor Geisel		Random
1947	McElligot's Pool	$1,800	$2,400	$3,000		Theodor Geisel	CH	Random
1948	Thidwick: The Big-Hearted Moose	$1,800	$2,400	$3,000		Theodor Geisel		Random
1949	Bartholomew And The Oobleck	$1,400	$1,800	$2,200		Theodor Geisel	CH	Random
1950	If I Ran The Zoo	$960	$1,200	$1,600		Theodor Geisel	CH	Random
1953	Scrambled Eggs Super	$960	$1,200	$1,600		Theodor Geisel		Random
1954	Horton Hears A Who	$1,200	$1,600	$2,000		Theodor Geisel		Random
1955	On Beyond Zebra	$840	$1,200	$1,400		Theodor Geisel		Random
1956	If I Ran The Circus	$840	$1,200	$1,400		Theodor Geisel		Random
1957	How The Grinch Stole Christmas	$1,200	$1,600	$2,000		Theodor Geisel		Random
1957	The Cat In The Hat	$2,400	$3,200	$4,000		Theodor Geisel		BB
1958	Cat In The Hat Comes Back	$180	$240	$300		Theodor Geisel		BB
1958	Yertle The Turtle & Other Stories	$140	$180	$220		Theodor Geisel		Random
1959	Happy Birthday To You	$160	$200	$260		Theodor Geisel		Random
1960	Green Eggs And Ham	$2,800	$3,800	$4,800		Theodor Geisel		BB
1960	One Fish, Two Fish, Red Fish, Blue Fish	$380	$520	$640		Theodor Geisel		BB
1961	The Sneetches & Other Stories	$160	$200	$260		Theodor Geisel		Random
1962	Dr. Seuss's Sleep Book	$120	$160	$200		Theodor Geisel		Random
1963	Dr. Seuss's ABC	$320	$420	$520		Theodor Geisel		BB
1963	Hop On Pop	$320	$420	$520		Theodor Geisel		BB
1964	The Cat In The Hat Dictionary	$70	$100	$120		P. D. Eastman		BB
1965	Fox In Socks	$160	$200	$260		Theodor Geisel		BB
1965	I Had Trouble In Getting To Solla Sollew	$160	$200	$260		Theodor Geisel		Random
1967	The Cat In The Hat Song Book	$70	$90	$120		Theodor Geisel		Random
1968	Foot Book	$960	$1,200	$1,600		Theodor Geisel		BB
1969	I Can Lick 30 Tigers Today! & Other Stories	$140	$200	$240		Theodor Geisel		Random
1969	My Book About Me	$70	$90	$120		Roy McKié		BB
1970	I Can Draw It Myself		$60	$80	$120	Theodor Geisel		Random
1970	Mr. Brown Can Moo! Can You?		$120	$180	$240	Theodor Geisel		BB
1971	The Lorax		$80	$120	$160	Theodor Geisel		Random

Seuss, Dr.   [Theodor Seuss Geisel]

Year	Title	VG-	VG	VG+	Fine	Author	Award	Pub
1972	Marvin K. Mooney Will You Please Go Now!		$80	$120	$160	Theodor Geisel		Random
1973	Did I Ever Tell You How Lucky You Are?		$70	$100	$140	Theodor Geisel		Random
1973	The Shape Of Me & Other Stuff		$100	$160	$220	Theodor Geisel		BB
1974	Dr. Seuss Storytime		$90	$140	$180	Theodor Geisel		Random
1974	There's A Wocket In My Pocket!		$70	$100	$140	Theodor Geisel		BB
1975	Oh, The Thinks You Can Think!		$70	$100	$140	Theodor Geisel		BB
1976	The Cat's Quizzer		$70	$100	$140	Theodor Geisel		BB
1978	I Can Read With My Eyes Shut!		$90	$140	$180	Theodor Geisel		Random
1979	Oh Say Can You Say?		$60	$90	$120	Theodor Geisel		BB
1982	Hunches And Bunches		$60	$80	$120	Theodor Geisel		Random
1984	The Butter Battle Book		$40	$60	$80	Theodor Geisel		Random
1986	You're Only Old Once		$30	$40	$60	Theodor Geisel		Random
1987	The Seven Lady Godivas		$25	$40	$50	Theodor Geisel		Random
1987	The Tough Coughs As He Ploughs The Dough		$25	$40	$50	Theodor Geisel		Morrow
1990	Oh, The Places You'll Go!		$25	$35	$50	Theodor Geisel		Random
1991	Six By Seuss		$10	$16	$20	Theodor Geisel		Random
1994	Daisy-Head Mayzie		$10	$16	$20	Theodor Geisel		Random
1996	A Hatful Of Seuss: Five Favorite Dr. Seuss Stories		$10	$14	$18	Theodor Geisel		Random
1996	My Many Colored Days		$10	$14	$18	Steve Johnson		Knopf

Sewall   Marcia

Year	Title	VG-	VG	VG+	Fine	Author	Award	Pub
1972	Master Of All Masters		$25	$35	$50	Marcia Sewall		LBrown
1974	The Parrot And The Thief		$16	$25	$30	Richard Kennedy		LBrown
1975	The Squire's Bride; A Norwegian Folk Tale		$16	$25	$30	Peter Christen Asbjønsen		Athenm
1976	Come Again In The Spring		$16	$25	$30	Richard Kennedy		H&Row
1976	Coo-My-Dove, My Dear		$16	$25	$30	Joseph Jacobs		Athenm
1976	The Porcelain Man		$16	$25	$30	Richard Kennedy		LBrown
1977	The Wee, Wee Mannie And The Big, Big Coo		$16	$25	$30	Marcia Sewall		LBrown
1978	Little Things		$14	$20	$30	Anne Laurin		Athenm
1978	The Ballad Of Penelope Lou ... And Me		$14	$20	$30	Drew Stevenson		CrossP
1978	The Lifting Stone		$14	$20	$30	Anne Eliot Crompton		Holiday
1978	The Nutcrackers And The Sugar-Tongs		$14	$20	$30	Edward Lear		LBrown
1978	The Rise And Fall Of Ben Gizzard		$14	$20	$30	Richard Kennedy		LBrown
1979	The Birthday Tree		$14	$20	$30	Paul Fleischman		H&Row
1979	The Leprechaun's Story		$14	$20	$30	Richard Kennedy		Dutton
1979	The Little Wee Tyke: An English Folk Tale		$14	$20	$30	Marcia Sewall (adapted)		Athenm
1979	The Man Who Tried To Save Time		$14	$20	$30	Phyllis Krasilovsky		DoubleD
1980	Crazy In Love		$14	$20	$25	Richard Kennedy		Dutton
1980	Stone Fox		$14	$20	$25	John Reynolds Gardiner		Crowell
1981	Song Of The Horse		$14	$20	$25	Richard Kennedy		Dutton
1981	The Marzipan Moon		$14	$20	$25	Nancy Willard		HBJ
1981	The Story Of Old Mrs. Brubeck		$14	$20	$25	Lore Segal		Pan
1982	Poor Boy, Rich Boy		$14	$20	$25	Clyde Robert Bulla		H&Row
1982	The Cobbler's Song: A Fable		$14	$20	$25	Marcia Sewall (adapted)		Dutton
1983	Finzel The Farsighted		$14	$20	$25	Paul Fleischman		Dutton
1983	Thistle		$14	$20	$25	Walter, Jr. Wangerin		H&Row
1983	When I Was Little		$14	$20	$25	Lyn Littlefield Hoopes		Dutton
1985	Ridin' That Strawberry Roan		$12	$18	$25	Marcia Sewall		VK
1986	The Pilgrims Of Plimoth		$12	$16	$20	Marcia Sewall		Athenm
1986	The World Turned Upside Down		$12	$16	$20	Marcia Sewall (adapted)		AMP
1987	Richard Kennedy: Collected Stories		$12	$16	$20	Richard Kennedy		H&Row
1988	Animal Song		$12	$16	$20	Marcia Sewall (adapted)		Joy
1988	Saying Goodbye To Grandma		$12	$16	$20	Jane Resh Thomas		Clarion
1989	Captain Snap And The Children Of Vinegar Lane		$12	$16	$20	Roni Schotter		Orchard
1990	John And The Fiddler		$10	$16	$20	Patricia Foley		H&Row
1990	People Of The Breaking Day		$10	$16	$20	Marcia Sewall		Athenm
1991	Daisy's Taxi		$10	$16	$20	Ruth Young		Orchard
1992	Nobody's Cat		$10	$16	$20	Barbara M. Joosse		HCollins
1992	The Golden Locket		$10	$16	$20	Carol Greene		HBJ
1994	Sable		$10	$14	$18	Karen Hesse		Holt
1995	The Morning Chair		$10	$14	$18	Barbara M. Joosse		Clarion
1995	Thunder From The Clear Sky		$10	$14	$18	Marcia Sewall		Athenm
1996	Daddy Doesn't Have To Be A Giant Anymore		$8	$12	$16	Jane Resh Thomas		Clarion
1996	Rosa And Her Singing Grandfather		$8	$12	$16	Leon Rosselson		Philo
1997	Madaket Millie		$8	$12	$16	Frances Ward Weller		Philo

Sewall   Marcia

Year	Title	VG-	VG	VG+	Fine	Author	Award	Pub
1999	Nickommoh!		$8	$12	$16	Jackie French Koller		Athenm
1999	The Green Mist		$8	$12	$16	Marcia Sewall (adapted)		HM

Sewell   Helen

Year	Title	VG-	VG	VG+	Fine	Author	Award	Pub
1929	Mr. Hermit Crab	$200	$280	$340		Mimpsy Rhys		Macmil
1930	A B C For Everyday	$200	$280	$340		Helen Sewell		Macmil
1931	A Head For Happy	$200	$280	$340		Helen Sewell		Macmil
1932	Little House In The Big Woods	$2,200	$3,000	$3,800		Laura Ingalls Wilder		H&B
1932	The Dream Keeper & Other Poems	$90	$120	$160		Langston Hughes		Knopf
1932	Words To The Wise	$140	$180	$220		Helen Sewell		DoddM
1933	Blue Barns	$120	$160	$220		Helen Sewell		Macmil
1933	Farmer Boy	$960	$1,200	$1,600		Laura Ingalls Wilder		H&B
1934	Bluebonnets For Lucinda	$80	$120	$140		Frances Clarke Sayers		Viking
1934	Cinderella	$120	$160	$220		Helen Sewell		Macmil
1935	A Round Of Carols	$80	$120	$140		Thomas Tertius Noble		Oxford
1935	Little House On The Prairie	$1,800	$2,400	$3,000		Laura Ingalls Wilder		H&B
1935	Peter And Gretchen Of Old Nuremberg	$80	$120	$140		Viola May Jones		AWhit
1936	Ming And Mehitable	$120	$160	$220		Helen Sewell		Macmil
1936	Peggy And The Pony	$120	$160	$220		Helen Sewell		Oxford
1936	Ten Saints	$80	$120	$140		Eleanor Farjeon		Walck
1937	Baby Island	$80	$120	$140		Carol Ryrie Brink		Macmil
1937	On The Banks Of Plum Creek	$840	$1,200	$1,400		Laura Ingalls Wilder		H&B
1937	The Magic Hill	$180	$240	$300		A. A. Milne		G&D
1937	The Princess And The Apple Tree	$180	$240	$300		A. A. Milne		G&D
1938	Jane Eyre	$80	$100	$140		Charlotte Brontë		Oxford
1939	By The Shores Of Silver Lake	$720	$960	$1,200		Laura Ingalls Wilder		H&B
1939	Five Bushel Farm	$80	$100	$140		Elizabeth Coatsworth		Macmil
1940	Jimmy And Jemima	$100	$120	$160		Helen Sewell		Macmil
1940	The Fair American	$70	$90	$120		Elizabeth Coatsworth		Macmil
1940	The Long Winter	$720	$960	$1,200		Laura Ingalls Wilder	NH	H&B
1941	Little Town On The Prairie	$720	$960	$1,200		Laura Ingalls Wilder	NH	H&B
1941	Peggy And The Pup	$100	$120	$160		Helen Sewell		Oxford
1941	Tag-Along Tooloo	$70	$90	$120		Frances Clarke Sayers		Viking
1942	A Book Of Myths	$70	$90	$120		Thomas Bulfinch		Macmil
1942	The Blue-Eyed Lady	$70	$90	$120		Ferenc Molnár		Viking
1942	The White Horse	$70	$90	$120		Elizabeth Coatsworth		Macmil
1943	Birthdays For Robin	$90	$120	$160		Helen Sewell		Macmil
1943	These Happy Golden Years	$440	$580	$720		Laura Ingalls Wilder		H&B
1944	A Bee In Her Bonnet	$60	$80	$100		Eva M. Kristoffersen		Crowell
1944	Belinda The Mouse	$90	$120	$160		Helen Sewell		Oxford
1944	Boat Children Of Canton	$60	$80	$100		Marion Boss Ward		DMcKay
1944	Christmas Magic	$60	$80	$100		James S. Tippett		G&D
1944	The Big Green Umbrella	$60	$80	$100		Elizabeth Coatsworth		G&D
1946	Once There Was A Little Boy	$60	$80	$100		Dorothy M. Kunhardt		Viking
1946	The Brave Bantam	$60	$80	$100		Louise S. Bechtel		Macmil
1946	The Wonderful Day	$60	$80	$100		Elizabeth Coatsworth		Macmil
1947	Three Tall Tales	$60	$80	$100		Elena Eleska		Macmil
1951	Azor And The Blue-Eyed Cow	$50	$70	$90		Maude Crowley		Gregg
1952	Mrs. McThing	$50	$70	$90		Mary Chase		Oxford
1952	The Bears On Hemlock Mountain	$120	$160	$200		Alice Dalgliesh	NH	Scribnr
1954	The Thanksgiving Story	$140	$180	$220		Alice Dalgliesh	CH	Athenm

Shachat   Andrew

Year	Title	VG-	VG	VG+	Fine	Author	Award	Pub
1986	You Can't Catch Me		$14	$20	$30	Joanne Oppenheim		HM
1992	The Simple People		$10	$16	$20	Tedd Arnold		Dial
1993	Stop That Pickle!		$10	$16	$20	Peter Armour		HM

Shannon   David

Year	Title	VG-	VG	VG+	Fine	Author	Award	Pub
1989	All The Troubles Of The World		$25	$40	$50	Isaac Asimov		Creat
1989	Franchise		$25	$40	$50	Isaac Asimov		Creat
1989	How Many Spots Does A Leopard Have?		$18	$25	$35	Julius Lester		Scholas
1989	Robbie		$25	$40	$50	Isaac Asimov		Creat

Shannon David

Year	Title	VG-	VG	VG+	Fine	Author	Award	Pub
1989	Sally		$25	$40	$50	Isaac Asimov		Creat
1990	The Man Who Walked Like A Bear		$16	$25	$30	Stuart Kaminsky		Scribnr
1992	Encounter		$20	$30	$40	Jane Yolen		HBJ
1992	The Rough-Face Girl		$16	$25	$30	Rafe Martin		Putnam
1993	The Boy Who Lived With The Seals		$16	$25	$30	Rafe Martin		Putnam
1994	Gawain And The Green Knight		$14	$20	$30	Mark Shannon		Putnam
1994	How Georgie Radbourn Saved Baseball		$20	$30	$40	David Shannon		BSP
1995	The Amazing Christmas Extravaganza		$18	$25	$35	David Shannon		BSP
1995	The Ballad Of The Pirate Queens		$18	$25	$35	Jane Yolen		HBrace
1996	Sacred Places		$16	$25	$30	Jane Yolen		HBrace
1996	The Bunyans		$12	$18	$25	Audrey Wood		BSP
1997	Nicholas Pipe		$12	$18	$25	Robert D. San Souci		Dial
1998	A Bad Case Of Stripes		$12	$16	$20	David Shannon		BSP
1998	No, David!		$40	$60	$80	David Shannon	CH	BSP
1999	David Goes To School		$25	$35	$50	David Shannon		BSP
1999	The Acrobat And The Angel		$12	$16	$20	Mark Shannon		Putnam
2000	The Rain Came Down		$10	$14	$18	David Shannon		BSP
2001	The Shark God		$10	$14	$18	Rafe Martin		Levine
2002	David Gets In Trouble		$12	$18	$25	David Shannon		BSP
2002	Duck On A Bike		$8	$12	$16	David Shannon		BSP
2003	How I Became A Pirate		$8	$12	$16	Melinda Long		Harcort
2004	Alice The Fairy		$8	$10	$14	David Shannon		BSP

Shecter Ben

Year	Title	VG-	VG	VG+	Fine	Author	Award	Pub
1963	Emily, Girl Witch of New York	$35	$40	$60		Ben Shecter		Dial
1964	Jonathan And The Bank Robbers	$25	$30	$40		Ben Shecter		Dial
1966	Emilio's Summer Day	$25	$30	$40		Miriam Anne Bourne		H&Row
1966	If It Weren't For You	$25	$30	$40		Charlotte Zolotow		H&Row
1966	Partouche Plants A Seed	$25	$30	$40		Ben Shecter		H&Row
1966	The Mummy Market	$25	$30	$40		Nancy Burns Brelis		H&Row
1967	Conrad's Castle	$25	$30	$40		Ben Shecter		H&Row
1967	Every Day A Dragon	$25	$30	$40		Joan M. Lexau		H&Row
1967	Grandpa	$25	$30	$40		Barbara Borack		H&Row
1967	The Toad Hunt	$25	$30	$40		Janet Chenery		H&Row
1968	A Ghost Named Fred	$20	$30	$35		Nathaniel Benchley		H&Row
1968	John Patrick's Amazing Morning	$20	$30	$35		Mary Church		DoubleD
1968	My Friend John	$20	$30	$35		Charlotte Zolotow		H&Row
1969	Clean As A Whistle	$20	$30	$35		Aileen Fisher		Crowell
1969	Inspector Rose	$20	$30	$35		Ben Shecter		H&Row
1969	The Hating Book	$20	$30	$35		Charlotte Zolotow		H&Row
1970	If I Had A Ship		$18	$25	$35	Ben Shecter		DoubleD
1971	A Father Like That		$18	$25	$35	Charlotte Zolotow		H&Row
1971	Getting Something On Maggie Marmelstein		$18	$25	$35	Marjorie Weinman Sharmat		H&Row
1971	Someplace Else		$18	$25	$35	Ben Shecter		H&Row
1971	The Magic Convention		$18	$25	$35	Sandra Hochman		DoubleD
1972	Across The Meadow		$18	$25	$35	Ben Shecter		DoubleD
1972	Game For Demons		$18	$25	$35	Ben Shecter		H&Row
1972	More Potatoes!		$18	$25	$35	Millicent Selsam		H&Row
1972	What Will You Do Today, Little Russell?		$18	$25	$35	Robert Wahl		Putnam
1973	Stone House Stories		$16	$25	$30	Ben Shecter		H&Row
1973	The Toughest And Meanest Kid On The Block		$16	$25	$30	Ben Shecter		Putnam
1974	The Escape Of The Giant Hogstalk		$16	$25	$30	Felice Holman		Scribnr
1974	The Summer Night		$16	$25	$30	Charlotte Zolotow		H&Row
1974	The Whistling Whirligig		$16	$25	$30	Ben Shecter		H&Row
1975	Cheer Up, Pig!		$16	$25	$30	Nancy Jewell		H&Row
1975	Maggie Marmelstein For President		$16	$25	$30	Marjorie Weinman Sharmat		H&Row
1975	Molly Patch And Her Animal Friends		$16	$25	$30	Ben Shecter		H&Row
1976	Mooch The Messy		$16	$25	$30	Marjorie Weinman Sharmat		H&Row
1976	The Difference Of Ari Stein		$16	$25	$30	Charlotte Herman		H&Row
1976	The Stocking Child		$16	$25	$30	Ben Shecter		H&Row
1977	A Summer Secret		$16	$25	$30	Ben Shecter		H&Row
1977	Hester The Jester		$16	$25	$30	Ben Shecter		H&Row
1977	The Hiding Game		$16	$25	$30	Ben Shecter		PMagP
1977	Will It Be Okay?		$16	$25	$30	Crescent Dragonwagon		H&Row
1978	Merrily Comes Our Harvest In		$14	$20	$30	Lee Bennett Hopkins		HBJ

Shecter   Ben

Year	Title	VG-	VG	VG+	Fine	Author	Award	Pub
1978	Mooch The Messy Meets Prudence The Neat		$14	$20	$30	Marjorie Weinman Sharmat		CM&G
1979	Dudley Pippin's Summer		$14	$20	$30	Philip Ressner		H&Row
1979	The River Witches		$14	$20	$30	Ben Shecter		H&Row
1979	The Trolls Of Twelfth Street		$14	$20	$30	Marjorie Weinman Sharmat		CM&G
1980	The Discontented Mother		$14	$20	$25	Ben Shecter		HBJ
1981	Sparrow Song		$14	$20	$25	Ben Shecter		H&Row
1982	Mysteriously Yours, Maggie Marmelstein		$14	$20	$25	Marjorie Weinman Sharmat		H&Row
1989	Grandma Remembers		$12	$16	$20	Ben Shecter		H&Row
1991	The Big Stew		$10	$16	$20	Ben Shecter		HCollins
1993	When Will The Snow Trees Grow?		$10	$16	$20	Ben Shecter		HCollins
1996	Great-Uncle Alfred Forgets		$8	$12	$16	Ben Shecter		HCollins

Shed   Greg

Year	Title	VG-	VG	VG+	Fine	Author	Award	Pub
1994	Casey Over There		$10	$14	$18	Staton Rabin		HBJ
1995	Dandelions		$8	$12	$16	Eve Bunting		HBrace
1995	Moontellers: Myths Of The Moon		$8	$12	$16	Lynn Moroney		North
1996	I Remember Papa		$8	$12	$16	Helen Ketteman		Dial
1996	The Language Of Doves		$8	$12	$16	Rosemary Wells		Dial
1996	The Rose Horse		$8	$12	$16	Deborah Rose		HBrace
1997	A Net Of Stars		$8	$10	$14	Jennifer Jacobson		Dial
1997	The Milkman's Boy		$8	$10	$14	Donald Hall		Walker
1998	The Turning Of The Year		$8	$10	$14	Bill Martin Jr.		HBrace
1999	Butterfly House		$8	$10	$14	Eve Bunting		Scholas
2000	Harvest Home		$8	$10	$14	Jane Yolen		HBrace
2000	Squanto's Journey		$8	$10	$14	Joseph Bruchac		Whistle
2001	I Loved You Before You Were Born		$8	$10	$14	Anne Bowen		HCollins
2002	White Christmas		$6	$10	$12	Irving Berlin		HCollins
2004	Root Beer And Banana		$6	$10	$12	Sarah Sullivan		Candle

Shimin   Symeon

Year	Title	VG-	VG	VG+	Fine	Author	Award	Pub
1950	How Big Is Big?	$30	$40	$50		Herman & Nina Schneider		WRScott
1954	Elephant Herd	$30	$40	$50		Miriam Schlein		WRScott
1955	Young Kangaroo	$100	$140	$180		Margaret Wise Brown		WRScott
1959	Onion John	$25	$35	$50		Joseph Krumgold		Crowell
1965	One Small Blue Bead	$25	$30	$40		Byrd Baylor		Macmil
1965	Passover	$25	$30	$40		Norma Simon		Crowell
1965	The Turtle Net	$25	$30	$40		Shirley M. Gudmundson		GBraz
1966	All Except Sammy	$25	$30	$40		Gladys Y. Cretan		LBrown
1966	The Hurricane	$25	$30	$40		Shirley M. Gudmundson		GBraz
1967	A Kite Over Tenth Avenue	$25	$30	$40		Joan M. Lexau		DoubleD
1967	All Kinds Of Babies	$25	$30	$40		Millicent Selsam		4Winds
1967	David Was Mad	$25	$30	$40		Bill Martin		HR&W
1967	Good Morning, Good Night	$25	$30	$40		Betty Comden		HR&W
1967	Poems Of Earth And Space	$25	$30	$40		Claudia Louise Lewis		Dutton
1967	Sam	$25	$30	$40		Ann Herbert Scott		McHill
1967	Zeely	$25	$30	$40		Virginia Hamilton		Macmil
1968	Lighthouse Island	$30	$40	$50		Elizabeth Coatsworth		Norton
1968	The House In The Tree	$20	$30	$35		Molly Cone		Crowell
1968	The Man Who Talked To A Tree	$20	$30	$35		Byrd Baylor		Dutton
1969	A Star In The Sea	$20	$30	$35		Alvin Silverstein		FWarne
1969	Before The Indians	$20	$30	$35		Julian May		Holiday
1969	Dance In The Desert	$40	$50	$70		Madeleine L'Engle		FSG
1969	Santiago	$20	$30	$35		Pura Belpré		FWarne
1969	Sing, Little Mouse	$20	$30	$35		Aileen Fisher		Crowell
1970	All About Story Book		$18	$25	$35	Watty Piper (pseud.)		P&Munk
1970	Animals Near And Far		$18	$25	$35	Helen Hoover		PMagP
1970	I Am Freedom's Child		$18	$25	$35	Bill Martin		Bowmar
1970	Joseph And Koza		$50	$70	$90	Isaac Bashevis Singer		FSG
1970	The Wonderful Story Of How You Were Born		$18	$25	$35	Sidonie M. Gruenberg		DoubleD
1971	The Best New Thing		$25	$35	$50	Isaac Asimov		World
1971	The Pair Of Shoes		$18	$25	$35	Aline Glasgow		Dial
1971	Why People Are Different Colors		$18	$25	$35	Julian May		Holiday
1972	A Day In The Life Of A Baby Gibbon		$18	$25	$35	Helen Kay		AS
1972	Coyote Cry		$18	$25	$35	Byrd Baylor		LL&S

414

Shimin   Symeon

Year	Title	VG-	VG	VG+	Fine	Author	Award	Pub
1972	Grandpa And Me		$18	$25	$35	Patricia Lee Gauch		CM&G
1972	Marian Anderson		$18	$25	$35	Tobi Tobias		Crowell
1972	My Castle		$18	$25	$35	Florence Parry Heide		McHill
1973	Gorilla Gorilla		$16	$25	$30	Carol Fenner		Random
1973	The Knee-Baby		$16	$25	$30	Mary Jarrell		FSG
1973	The Paint-Box Sea		$16	$25	$30	Doris Herold Lund		McHill
1974	Send Wendell		$16	$25	$30	Genevieve Gray		McHill
1976	A Special Birthday		$16	$25	$30	Symeon Shimin		McHill
1976	I Wish There Were Two Of Me		$16	$25	$30	Symeon Shimin		FWarne
1977	Now That Spring Is Here		$16	$25	$30	Aileen Fisher		Bowmar
1977	The Wentletrap Trap		$16	$25	$30	Jean Craighead George		Dutton
1978	Petey		$14	$20	$30	Tobi Tobias		Putnam
1981	More Night		$14	$20	$25	Muriel Rukeyser		H&Row

Shinn   Everett

Year	Title	VG-	VG	VG+	Fine	Author	Award	Pub
1938	A Christmas Carol In Prose	$80	$100	$140		Charles Dickens		Winston
1939	Rip Van Winkle	$120	$160	$200		Washington Irving		GardenC
1939	The Life Of Our Lord	$60	$80	$100		Charles Dickens		GardenC
1940	Jerry At The Academy	$50	$60	$80		Elmer Ellsworth Ferris		DD
1940	The Happy Prince	$70	$90	$120		Oscar Wilde		Winston
1940	The Man Without A Country	$70	$90	$120		Edward Everett Hale		Random
1941	Christmas In Dickens	$70	$90	$120		Charles Dickens		GardenC
1941	The Mystery Of Edwin Drood	$70	$90	$120		Charles Dickens		THP
1941	The United States Army	$50	$60	$80		Earl C. Ewert		LBrown
1942	Frédéric Chopin	$70	$90	$120		André Maurois		H&B
1942	The Night Before Christmas	$90	$120	$160		Clement C. Moore		Winston
1943	Poems Of Childhood	$50	$60	$80		James Whitcomb Riley		G&D
1943	The Christ Story	$50	$60	$80		Everett Shinn		Winston
1946	The Sermon On The Mount	$40	$60	$70		Everett Shinn		Winston

Shortall   Leonard

Year	Title	VG-	VG	VG+	Fine	Author	Award	Pub
1947	Andy And The School Bus	$40	$60	$70		Jerrold Beim		Morrow
1950	Country Train	$30	$40	$50		Jerrold Beim		Morrow
1958	4-H Filly	$100	$140	$180		Patsey Gray		CM
1958	Country Mailman	$25	$35	$50		Jerrold Beim		Morrow
1959	Adventure At Black Rock Cave	$25	$35	$50		Patricia Lauber		Random
1960	Champ, Gallant Collie	$25	$30	$40		Patricia Lauber		Random
1960	Country Snowplow	$25	$30	$40		Leonard Shortall		Morrow
1960	The King's Wish & Other Stories	$70	$90	$120		Benjamin Elkin		BB
1961	John And His Thumbs	$25	$30	$40		Leonard Shortall		Morrow
1962	Sam's First Fish	$25	$30	$40		Leonard Shortall		Morrow
1963	Davey's First Boat	$25	$30	$40		Leonard Shortall		Morrow
1963	Mishmash And The Substitute Teacher	$25	$30	$40		Molly Cone		HM
1964	Danny On The Lookout	$25	$30	$40		Leonard Shortall		Morrow
1964	New Year's Day	$25	$30	$40		Lynn Groh		Garrard
1965	ABC Of Buses	$25	$30	$40		Dorothy E. Shuttlesworth		DoubleD
1965	Ben On The Ski Trail	$25	$30	$40		Leonard Shortall		Morrow
1965	Piper	$25	$30	$40		Osmond Molarsky		NYGS
1965	The Hat Book	$25	$30	$40		Leonard Shortall		Golden
1966	Encyclopedia Brown Finds The Clues	$90	$120	$160		Donald J. Sobol		TNelson
1966	One Day Everything Went Wrong	$25	$30	$40		Elizabeth Vreeken		Follett
1966	Steve's First Pony Ride	$25	$30	$40		Leonard Shortall		Morrow
1967	Encyclopedia Brown Gets His Man	$60	$80	$100		Donald J. Sobol		TNelson
1967	Eric In Alaska	$40	$50	$70		Leonard Shortall		Morrow
1967	I Know A Teacher	$25	$30	$40		Naomi Buchheimer		Putnam
1968	Andy, The Dog Walker	$20	$30	$35		Leonard Shortall		Morrow
1968	Encyclopedia Brown Solves Them All	$50	$60	$80		Donald J. Sobol		TNelson
1968	Mishmash And Uncle Looey	$20	$30	$35		Molly Cone		HM
1969	Encyclopedia Brown Keeps The Peace	$50	$60	$80		Donald J. Sobol		TNelson
1969	Harry's Homemade Robot	$20	$30	$35		Barbara Rinkoff		Crown
1969	Peter In Grand Central Station	$20	$30	$35		Leonard Shortall		Morrow
1970	Animals Grow		$18	$25	$35	Patricia A. Anthony		Putnam
1970	Encyclopedia Brown Saves The Day		$35	$50	$70	Donald J. Sobol		TNelson
1970	Jerry The Newsboy		$18	$25	$35	Leonard Shortall		Morrow

Shortall   Leonard

Year	Title	VG-	VG	VG+	Fine	Author	Award	Pub
1971	Encyclopedia Brown Tracks Them Down		$35	$50	$70	Donald J. Sobol		TNelson
1971	Plants Grow		$18	$25	$35	Thomas E. Tinsley		Putnam
1971	The Case Of The Stolen Code Book		$18	$25	$35	Barbara Rinkoff		Crown
1971	Tod On The Tugboat		$18	$25	$35	Leonard Shortall		Morrow
1972	Encyclopedia Brown Shows The Way		$35	$50	$70	Donald J. Sobol		TNelson
1972	Georgina And The Dragon		$18	$25	$35	Lee Kingman		HM
1972	Tony's First Dive		$18	$25	$35	Leonard Shortall		Morrow
1973	A Building On Your Street		$16	$25	$30	Seymour Simon		Holiday
1973	Encyclopedia Brown Takes The Case		$35	$50	$70	Donald J. Sobol		TNelson
1973	Just-In-Time Joey		$16	$25	$30	Leonard Shortall		Morrow
1973	Louder And Louder		$16	$25	$30	Thomas & Gretchen Perera		FWatts
1974	Animal Manners		$16	$25	$30	Barbara Shook Hazen		Golden
1974	Encyclopedia Brown Lends A Hand		$35	$50	$70	Donald J. Sobol		TNelson
1975	Ency. Brown And The Case Of The Dead Eagles		$30	$50	$60	Donald J. Sobol		TNelson
1975	One Way		$16	$25	$30	Leonard Shortall		P-Hall
1975	The Winnemah Spirit		$16	$25	$30	Carolyn Lane		HM
1976	Animal Crackers		$16	$25	$30	Wanda Cheyne		RandMc
1976	Bear Hunt		$16	$25	$30	Margaret Siewert		P-Hall
1976	Going My Way		$16	$25	$30	Stan Applebaum		HBJ
1977	Little Toad To The Rescue		$16	$25	$30	Leonard Shortall		Golden
1978	The Magic Pizza		$14	$20	$30	Beverly Major Schwartz		P-Hall
1979	Driving Your Bike Safely		$14	$20	$30	Corinne J. Naden		Messner
1979	Freaky Francie		$14	$20	$30	Sibyl Hancock		P-Hall
1979	I Can Bake Bread		$14	$20	$30	David Magill		DandP
1979	I Can Bake Cookies		$14	$20	$30	Judith Wolman		Random
1980	Here Comes A Train!		$14	$20	$25	Leonard Shortall		Golden
1980	Jake Mcgee And His Feet		$14	$20	$25	Mary Waldorf		HM
1982	Annie And The Kidnappers		$14	$20	$25	Amy Ehrlich		Random
1982	Annie Finds A Home		$14	$20	$25	Amy Ehrlich		Random
1982	Annie Joins The Circus		$14	$20	$25	James Howe		Random
1982	Mishmash And The Big Fat Problem		$14	$20	$25	Molly Cone		HM
1984	Old Macdonald Had A Farm		$12	$18	$25	Leonard Shortall		Random

Shulevitz   Uri

Year	Title	VG-	VG	VG+	Fine	Author	Award	Pub
1963	The Moon In My Room	$100	$120	$160		Uri Shulevitz		H&Row
1964	A Rose, A Bridge, And A Wild Black Horse	$60	$80	$100		Charlotte Zolotow		H&Row
1965	The Second Witch	$50	$60	$80		Uri Shulevitz		H&Row
1965	Who Knows Ten?	$40	$60	$70		Molly Cone		UAH
1966	The Carpet Of Solomon	$50	$60	$80		Uri Shulevitz		Pan
1966	The Twelve Dancing Princesses	$40	$60	$70		Elizabeth Shub (translated)		Scribnr
1967	One Monday Morning	$50	$60	$80		Uri Shulevitz		Scribnr
1967	Runaway Jonah, & Other Tales	$50	$60	$80		Uri Shulevitz		Macmil
1967	The Silkspinners	$50	$60	$80		Uri Shulevitz		Scribnr
1968	My Kind Of Verse	$40	$50	$70		Uri Shulevitz		Macmil
1968	The Fool Of The World And The Flying Ship	$200	$260	$320		Arthur Ransome (retold)	CM	FSG
1968	The Treasure Of The Turkish Pasha	$40	$50	$70		Uri Shulevitz		Scribnr
1969	Rain Rain Rivers	$40	$50	$70		Uri Shulevitz		FSG
1970	The Wonderful Kite		$30	$50	$60	Jan Wahl		DelaP
1971	Oh What A Noise!		$30	$50	$60	Uri Shulevitz		Macmil
1972	Soldier And Tsar In The Forest		$30	$50	$60	Uri Shulevitz		FSG
1973	The Fools Of Chelm And Their History		$30	$50	$60	Uri Shulevitz		FSG
1973	The Magician		$30	$50	$60	I.L. Peretz		Macmil
1974	Dawn		$30	$40	$60	Uri Shulevitz		FSG
1976	The Touchstone: A Fable		$30	$40	$60	Robert Louis Stevenson		Green
1978	Hanukah Money		$25	$40	$50	Sholem Aleichem		Green
1978	The Treasure		$50	$80	$100	Uri Shulevitz	CH	FSG
1979	The Lost Kingdom Of Karnica		$25	$40	$50	Richard Kennedy		Sierra
1982	The Golem		$50	$70	$90	Isaac Bashevis Singer		FSG
1986	Strange And Exciting Adventures Of Jeremiah Hush		$20	$30	$40	Uri Shulevitz		FSG
1988	Lilith's Cave: Jewish Tales Of The Supernatural		$18	$25	$35	Howard Schwartz		H&Row
1990	Toddlecreek Post Office		$16	$25	$30	Uri Shulevitz		FSG
1991	The Diamond Tree		$16	$25	$30	B. Rush H. Schwartz		HCollins
1993	The Secret Room		$16	$25	$30	Uri Shulevitz		FSG
1995	The Golden Goose		$14	$20	$25	Jacob & Wilhelm Grimm		FSG
1997	Hosni The Dreamer: An Arabian Tale		$12	$18	$25	Ehud Ben-Ezer		FSG

Shulevitz   Uri

Year	Title	VG-	VG	VG+	Fine	Author	Award	Pub
1998	Snow		$25	$40	$50	Uri Shulevitz	CH	FSG
2000	What Is A Wise Bird Doing In A Silly Tale Like This?		$10	$14	$18	Uri Shulevitz		FSG
2001	Daughters of Fire		$10	$14	$18	Uri Shulevitz		Whistle

Sidjakov   Nicolas

Year	Title	VG-	VG	VG+	Fine	Author	Award	Pub
1957	The Friendly Beasts	$50	$70	$90		Laura Baker		Parnss
1960	Baboushka And The Three Kings	$160	$200	$260		Ruth Robbins	CM	Parnss
1962	The Emperor And The Drummer Boy	$70	$90	$120		Ruth Robbins	NYT	Parnss
1965	Harlequin And Mother Goose	$40	$60	$70		Ruth Robbins		Parnss
1969	A Lodestone And A Toad Stone	$40	$50	$70		Irene Elmer		Knopf
1969	Staffan	$40	$50	$70		Nicholas Sidjakov		Parnss

Siebel   Fritz

Year	Title	VG-	VG	VG+	Fine	Author	Award	Pub
1958	A Fly Went By	$160	$200	$260		Mike McClintock		BB
1959	Stop That Ball!	$100	$140	$180		Mike McClintock		BB
1960	Cat And Dog	$70	$90	$120		Fritz Siebel		H&B
1960	David And The Giant	$70	$90	$120		Mike McClintock		H&B
1961	Tell Me Some More	$50	$60	$80		Crosby Bonsall		H&B
1963	Amelia Bedelia	$100	$120	$160		Peggy Parish		H&Row
1963	Who Took The Farmer's Hat?	$50	$60	$80		Joan L. Nodset		H&Row
1964	Terrible Thomas	$50	$60	$80		Helene Hanff		H&Row
1964	Thank You, Amelia Bedelia	$60	$80	$100		Peggy Parish		H&Row
1966	Amelia Bedelia And The Surprise Shower	$50	$70	$90		Peggy Parish		H&Row
1968	A House So Big	$40	$50	$70		Joan M. Lexau		H&Row

Silverstein   Shel

Year	Title	VG-	VG	VG+	Fine	Author	Award	Pub
1955	Take Ten, A Collection of Cartoons	$180	$240	$300		Shel Silverstein		Kyoya
1961	Uncle Shelby's ABZ Book	$220	$280	$360		Shel Silverstein		S&S
1963	Uncle Shelby's Story Of Lafcadio	$160	$200	$260		Shel Silverstein		H&Row
1964	The Giving Tree	$460	$620	$780		Shel Silverstein		H&Row
1964	Uncle Shelby's A Giraffe And A Half	$100	$140	$180		Shel Silverstein		H&Row
1964	Uncle Shelby's Zoo: Don't Bump The Glump!	$100	$140	$180		Shel Silverstein		S&S
1964	Who Wants A Cheap Rhinoceros?	$100	$140	$180		Shel Silverstein		Macmil
1974	Where The Sidewalk Ends		$50	$70	$100	Shel Silverstein		H&Row
1976	The Missing Piece		$50	$70	$90	Shel Silverstein		H&Row
1981	A Light In The Attic		$30	$50	$60	Shel Silverstein		H&Row
1981	The Missing Piece Meets The Big O		$30	$50	$60	Shel Silverstein		H&Row
1996	Falling Up		$8	$12	$16	Shel Silverstein		HCollins
1999	The Giving Tree		$8	$10	$14	Shel Silverstein		HCollins

Simont   Marc

Year	Title	VG-	VG	VG+	Fine	Author	Award	Pub
1939	Castle In The Silver Wood	$140	$200	$240		Ruth Bryan Owen		DoddM
1939	Pirate Of Chatham Square	$140	$200	$240		Emma Gelders Sterne		DoddM
1941	Isabella, Queen of Spain	$70	$90	$120		Mildred Criss		DoddM
1942	Welcome	$70	$90	$120		Babette Deutsch		H&B
1943	Pocohontas	$70	$90	$120		Mildred Criss		DoddM
1946	Billy and the Unhappy Bull	$60	$80	$100		Meindert DeJong		H&Row
1946	Music For Your Child	$60	$80	$100		William Krevit		DoddM
1947	Flying Ebony	$60	$80	$100		Iris Vinton		DoddM
1947	The First Story	$60	$80	$100		Margaret Wise Brown		H&B
1948	Red Fairy Book	$60	$80	$100		Andrew Lang		Longman
1948	The First Christmas	$60	$80	$100		Robbie Trent		H&B
1949	The Big World And The Little House	$60	$80	$100		Ruth Krauss		Schuman
1949	The Happy Day	$120	$160	$220		Ruth Krauss	CH	H&B
1950	Good Luck Duck	$60	$80	$100		Meindert De Jong		H&B
1950	The 13 Clocks	$120	$160	$200		James Thurber		S&S
1950	The Backward Day	$60	$80	$100		Ruth Krauss		H&B
1951	Polly's Oats	$50	$70	$90		Marc Simont		H&B
1952	Christmas Eve	$50	$70	$90		Alistair Cooke		Knopf
1952	How To Get To First Base	$50	$70	$90		Marc Simont		Schuman
1952	Jareb	$50	$70	$90		Mariam Powell		Crowell

Simont   Marc

Year	Title	VG-	VG	VG+	Fine	Author	Award	Pub
1952	The Lovely Summer	$50	$70	$90		Marc Simont		H&B
1952	Timmy And The Tiger	$50	$70	$90		Marjorie Paradis		H&B
1953	Deer Mountain Hideway	$50	$70	$90		Elizabeth H. Lansing		Crowell
1954	Fishhead	$50	$70	$90		Jean Fritz		CM
1954	Mimi	$50	$70	$90		Marc Simont		H&B
1954	View Of Sports	$50	$70	$90		Red Smith		Knopf
1955	Now I Know	$50	$70	$90		Julius Schwartz		Whittle
1955	The Plumber Out Of The Sea	$50	$70	$90		Marc Simont		H&B
1955	The Trail-Driving Rooster	$50	$70	$90		Fred Gipson		H&B
1957	A Tree Is Nice	$240	$320	$400		Janice May Udry	CM	H&B
1957	Goose That Almost Got Cooked	$50	$70	$90		Marc Simont		Scholas
1957	The Seal That Couldn't Swim	$50	$70	$90		Alexis Ladas		LBrown
1957	The Wonderful O	$50	$70	$90		James Thurber		S&S
1959	The Contest At Paca	$50	$60	$80		Marc Simont		H&B
1962	A Good Man And His Good Wife	$50	$60	$80		Ruth Krauss		Harper
1965	Afternoon In Spain	$40	$60	$70		Marc Simont		Morrow
1965	How Come Elephants?	$40	$60	$70		Marc Simont		H&Row
1967	Every Time I Climb A Tree	$40	$50	$70		David McCord		LBrown
1969	Glenda	$40	$50	$70		Janice May Udry		H&Row
1969	Wolfie	$40	$50	$70		Janet Chenery		H&Row
1971	The Lieutenant Colonel And The Gypsy		$30	$50	$60	Federico Garcia Lorca		DoubleD
1972	A Child's Eye View Of The World		$30	$50	$60	Marc Simont		DelaP
1972	Nate The Great		$30	$50	$60	Marjorie Weinman Sharmat		CM&G
1974	Nate The Great Goes Undercover		$30	$40	$60	Marjorie Weinman Sharmat		CM&G
1975	Nate The Great And The Lost List		$30	$40	$60	Marjorie Weinman Sharmat		CM&G
1975	Robert Louis Stevenson, Teller Of Tales		$30	$40	$60	Eulalie Osgood Grover		Gale
1975	The Contests At Cowlick		$30	$40	$60	Richard Kennedy		LBrown
1975	The Star In The Pail		$30	$40	$60	David McCord		LBrown
1976	The Beetle Bush		$30	$40	$60	Beverly Keller		CM&G
1977	Nate The Great And The Phony Clue		$25	$40	$50	Marjorie Weinman Sharmat		CM&G
1978	A Space Story		$25	$40	$50	Karla Kuskin		H&Row
1978	Danger In Dinosaur Valley		$25	$40	$50	Joan Lowery Nixon		Putnam
1978	Mouse And Tim		$25	$40	$50	Faith McNulty		H&Row
1978	Nate The Great And The Sticky Case		$25	$40	$50	Marjorie Weinman Sharmat		CM&G
1979	How To Dig A Hole To The Other Side Of The World		$25	$40	$50	Faith McNulty		H&Row
1979	Reddy Rattler And Easy Eagle		$25	$40	$50	Mitchell Sharmat		DoubleD
1980	If You Listen		$25	$35	$50	Charlotte Zolotow		H&Row
1980	Speak Up		$25	$35	$50	David McCord		LBrown
1980	Ten Copycats In A Boat		$25	$35	$50	Alvin Schwartz		H&Row
1980	The Elephant Who Couldn't Forget		$25	$35	$50	Faith McNulty		H&Row
1981	Chasing After Annie		$25	$35	$50	Marjorie Weinman Sharmat		H&Row
1981	Nate The Great And The Missing Key		$25	$35	$50	Marjorie Weinman Sharmat		CM&G
1981	No More Monsters For Me!		$25	$35	$50	Peggy Parish		H&Row
1982	Nate The Great And The Snowy Trail		$25	$35	$50	Marjorie Weinman Sharmat		CM&G
1982	The Philharmonic Gets Dressed		$30	$50	$60	Karla Kuskin	NYT	H&Row
1983	My Uncle Nikos		$25	$35	$50	Julie Delton		Crowell
1983	The Knight Of The Golden Plain		$25	$35	$50	Mollie Hunter		H&Row
1984	Bruno The Pretzel Man		$20	$30	$40	Edward E Davis		H&Row
1984	In The Year Of The Boar And Jackie Robinson		$20	$30	$40	Bette Lord		H&Row
1984	Martin's Hats		$20	$30	$40	Joan W. Blos		Morrow
1984	Top Secret		$20	$30	$40	John Reynolds Gardiner		LBrown
1985	Nate The Great And The Fishy Prize		$20	$30	$40	Marjorie Weinman Sharmat		CM&G
1985	The Three-Day Enchantment		$20	$30	$40	Mollie Hunter		H&Row
1985	Volcanoes		$20	$30	$40	Franklyn M. Branley		Crowell
1986	Journey Into A Black Hole		$20	$30	$40	Franklyn M. Branley		Crowell
1986	Nate The Great Stalks Stupidweed		$20	$30	$40	Marjorie Weinman Sharmat		CM
1986	The Dallas Titans Get Ready For Bed		$20	$30	$40	Karla Kuskin		H&Row
1987	Nate The Great And The Boring Beach Bag		$20	$30	$40	Marjorie Weinman Sharmat		CM&G
1988	Glaciers		$18	$25	$35	Wendell V Tangborn		H&Row
1989	Nate The Great And The Halloween Hunt		$18	$25	$35	Marjorie Weinman Sharmat		CM&G
1989	Nate The Great Goes Down In The Dumps		$18	$25	$35	Marjorie Weinman Sharmat		CM&G
1989	The Quiet Mother And The Noisy Little Boy		$18	$25	$35	Charlotte Zolotow		H&Row
1989	What Happened To The Dinosaurs?		$18	$25	$35	Franklyn M. Branley		Crowell
1990	Many Moons		$16	$25	$30	James Thurber		HBJ
1990	Nate The Great And The Musical Note		$16	$25	$30	Marjorie Weinman Sharmat		CM
1992	Nate The Great And The Stolen Base		$16	$25	$30	Marjorie Weinman Sharmat		CM
1992	The Lovely Summer		$16	$25	$30	Marc Simont		Bantam

Simont   Marc

Year	Title	VG-	VG	VG+	Fine	Author	Award	Pub
1993	Nate The Great And The Pillowcase		$16	$25	$30	Marjorie Weinman Sharmat		DelaP
1994	Nate The Great And The Mushy Valentine		$14	$20	$30	Marjorie Weinman Sharmat		DelaP
1995	Nate The Great And The Tardy Tortoise		$14	$20	$25	Marjorie Weinman Sharmat		DelaP
1995	Playing Right Field		$14	$20	$25	Willy Welch		Scholas
1996	My Brother, Ant		$12	$18	$25	Betsy Cromer Byars		Viking
1996	Nate The Great And The Crunchy Christmas		$12	$18	$25	Marjorie Weinman Sharmat		DelaP
1997	Ant Plays Bear		$12	$18	$25	Betsy Cromer Byars		Viking
1997	Nate The Great Saves The King Of Sweden		$12	$18	$25	Marjorie Weinman Sharmat		DelaP
1997	Richie And The Fritzes		$12	$18	$25	Marjorie Weinman Sharmat		HCollins
1997	The Goose That Almost Got Cooked		$12	$18	$25	Marc Simont		Scholas
1998	Nate The Great And Me		$12	$16	$20	Marjorie Weinman Sharmat		DelaP
1999	Nate The Great And The Monster Mess		$12	$16	$20	Marjorie Weinman Sharmat		CM
1999	Nate The Great Goes Down The Dumps		$12	$16	$20	Marjorie Weinman Sharmat		CM
2000	Nate The Great, San Francisco Detective		$10	$14	$18	Marjorie Weinman Sharmat		DelaP
2000	The Stray Dog		$20	$30	$40	Reiko Sassa	CH	HCollins

Sis   Peter

Year	Title	VG-	VG	VG+	Fine	Author	Award	Pub
1984	Bean Boy		$20	$30	$40	George Shannon		Green
1985	Stories To Solve: Folktales From Around The World		$16	$25	$30	George Shannon		Green
1986	Higgledy Piggledy		$14	$20	$30	Myra Cohn Livingston		Macmil
1986	Oaf		$14	$20	$30	Julia Cunningham		Knopf
1986	The Whipping Boy		$100	$160	$200	Sid Fleischman	NM	Green
1986	Three Yellow Dogs		$14	$20	$30	Caron Lee Cohen		Green
1987	After Good-Night		$14	$20	$30	Monica Mayper		H&Row
1987	City Night		$14	$20	$30	Eve Rice		Green
1987	Jed And The Space Bandits		$14	$20	$30	Jean & Claudio Marzollo		Dial
1987	Rainbow Rhino		$14	$20	$30	Peter Sis		Knopf
1987	The Scarebird		$14	$20	$30	Sid Fleishman		Green
1988	Alphabet Soup		$14	$20	$30	Kate Banks		Knopf
1988	Waving: A Counting Book		$14	$20	$30	Peter Sis		Green
1989	Going Up!: A Color Counting Book		$14	$20	$25	Peter Sis		Green
1989	Halloween: Stories And Poems		$14	$20	$25	Caroline Bauer (edited)		Lippin
1989	The Ghost In The Noonday Sun		$14	$20	$25	Sid Fleischman		Green
1990	Beach Ball		$12	$18	$25	Peter Sis		Green
1990	More Stories To Solve		$12	$18	$25	George Shannon		Green
1990	The Algonquin Literary Quiz Book		$12	$18	$25	Louis Rubin (compiled)		Algon
1990	The Midnight Horse		$12	$18	$25	Sid Fleischman		Green
1991	Follow The Dream/Story Of Christopher Columbus		$12	$18	$25	Peter Sis		Knopf
1992	An Ocean World		$12	$18	$25	Peter Sis		Green
1993	A Small Tall Tale From The Far Far North		$12	$16	$20	Peter Sis		Knopf
1993	Komodo		$12	$16	$20	Peter Sis		Green
1993	The Dragons Are Singing Tonight		$12	$16	$20	Jack Prelutsky		Green
1994	Still More Stories To Solve		$12	$16	$20	George Shannon		Green
1994	The Three Golden Keys		$12	$16	$20	Peter Sis		DoubleD
1995	Rumpelstiltskin		$10	$16	$20	Christopher Noel		Rabbit
1995	The 13th Floor: A Ghost Story		$10	$16	$20	Sid Fleischman		Green
1996	Monday's Troll		$10	$16	$20	Jack Prelutsky		Green
1996	Starry Messenger: Galileo Galilei		$30	$50	$60	Peter Sis	CH	FSG
1997	Fire Truck		$10	$16	$20	Peter Sis		Green
1997	Sleep Safe, Little Whale		$10	$16	$20	Miriam Schlein		Green
1998	Tibet Through The Red Box		$25	$40	$50	Peter Sis	CH	FSG
2000	Madlenka		$8	$12	$16	Peter Sis		FSG
2001	Ballerina		$8	$12	$16	Peter Sis		Green
2001	The Little Wing Giver		$8	$12	$16	Jacques Taravant		Holt
2002	Madlenka's Dog		$8	$10	$14	Peter Sis		FSG
2002	Scranimals		$8	$10	$14	Jack Prelutsky		Green
2003	Animal Sense		$8	$10	$14	Diane Ackerman		Knopf
2003	The Tree Of Life		$8	$10	$14	Peter Sis		FSG
2003	The Wicked, Wicked Ladies In The Haunted House		$8	$10	$14	Mary Chase		Knopf
2004	A Collection Of Rudyard Kipling's Just So Stories		$8	$10	$14	Rudyard Kipling		Candle
2004	Train Of States		$8	$10	$14	Peter Sis		Green

Slobodkin   Louis

Year	Title	VG-	VG	VG+	Fine	Author	Award	Pub
1941	The Moffats	$160	$220	$280		Eleanor Estes		HBrace

Slobodkin   Louis

Year	Title	VG-	VG	VG+	Fine	Author	Award	Pub
1942	The Middle Moffat	$220	$300	$380		Eleanor Estes	NH	HBrace
1943	Many Moons	$460	$620	$780		James Thurber	CM	HBrace
1943	Peter The Great	$70	$90	$120		Nina Brown Baker		Vnguard
1943	Rufus M.	$140	$180	$240		Eleanor Estes	NH	HBJ
1943	The Sun And The Wind And Mr Todd	$140	$180	$240		Eleanor Estes		HBrace
1944	Magic Michael	$140	$180	$220		Louis Slobodkin		Macmil
1944	The Friendly Animals	$140	$180	$220		Louis Slobodkin		Vnguard
1944	The Hundred Dresses	$140	$180	$220		Eleanor Estes	NH	HBrace
1944	Young Man Of The House	$35	$40	$60		Mabel Leigh Hunt		Lippin
1945	Clear The Track For Michael's Magic Train	$90	$120	$160		Louis Slobodkin		Macmil
1945	Fo'castle Waltz	$60	$80	$100		Louis Slobodkin		Vnguard
1945	Lenin	$40	$60	$70		Nina Brown Baker		Vnguard
1945	Russia & America	$60	$80	$100		Delia Goetz		FPA
1946	Robin Hood	$60	$80	$100		J Walker McSpadden		World
1946	The Adventures Of Arab	$60	$80	$100		Louis Slobodkin		Macmil
1946	The Adventures Of Tom Sawyer	$40	$60	$70		Mark Twain		World
1947	The Seaweed Hat	$60	$80	$100		Louis Slobodkin		Macmil
1948	Hustle And Bustle	$60	$80	$100		Louis Slobodkin		Macmil
1948	Jonathan And The Rainbow	$60	$80	$100		Jacob Blanck		HM
1949	Bixxy And The Secret Message	$60	$80	$100		Louis Slobodkin		Macmil
1950	Mr Mushroom	$60	$80	$100		Louis Slobodkin		Macmil
1950	The King And The Noble Blacksmith	$40	$50	$70		Jacob Blanck		HM
1951	Dinny And Danny	$50	$70	$90		Louis Slobodkin		Macmil
1951	Gertie the Horse Who Thought	$120	$160	$200		Margarite Glendinning		Whittle
1951	Ginger Pye	$260	$360	$440		Eleanor Estes	NM	HBrace
1951	Our Friendly Friends	$50	$70	$90		Louis Slobodkin		Vnguard
1951	Red Head	$120	$160	$200		Edward Eager		HM
1951	The Saucepan Journey	$40	$50	$70		Edith Unnerstad		Macmil
1952	The Space Ship Under The Apple Tree	$120	$160	$200		Louis Slobodkin		Macmil
1953	Circus, April 1st	$50	$70	$90		Louis Slobodkin		Macmil
1953	The Magic Fishbone	$40	$50	$70		Charles Dickens		Vnguard
1954	Mr Petersand's Cats	$50	$70	$90		Louis Slobodkin		Macmil
1954	The Horse With The High-Heeled Shoes	$50	$70	$90		Louis Slobodkin		Vnguard
1955	Millions And Millions And Millions!	$50	$70	$90		Louis Slobodkin		Vnguard
1955	Pysen	$35	$50	$60		Edith Unnerstad		Macmil
1955	The Amiable Giant	$50	$70	$90		Louis Slobodkin		Macmil
1956	One Is Good, But Two Are Better	$50	$70	$90		Louis Slobodkin		Vnguard
1956	The Little Mermaid Who Could Not Sing	$70	$100	$120		Louis Slobodkin		Macmil
1957	Melvin The Moose Child	$50	$70	$90		Louis Slobodkin		Macmil
1957	Thank You--You're Welcome	$50	$70	$90		Louis Slobodkin		Vnguard
1957	The Warmhearted Polar Bear	$35	$50	$60		Robert Murphy		LBrown
1958	The First Book Of Drawing	$50	$60	$80		Louis Slobodkin		FWatts
1958	The Space Ship Returns To The Apple Tree	$70	$100	$120		Louis Slobodkin		Macmil
1958	The Wide-Awake Owl	$50	$60	$80		Louis Slobodkin		Macmil
1958	Too Many Mittens	$50	$60	$80		Florence Slobodkin		Vnguard
1959	Excuse Me! Certainly!	$50	$60	$80		Louis Slobodkin		Vnguard
1959	Martin's Dinosaur	$50	$60	$80		Reda Davis		Crowell
1959	Trick Or Treat	$50	$60	$80		Louis Slobodkin		Macmil
1960	Gogo, the French Seagull	$35	$40	$60		Louis Slobodkin		Macmil
1960	Nomi And The Lovely Animals	$35	$40	$60		Louis Slobodkin		Vnguard
1960	The Cowboy Twins	$35	$40	$60		Florence & Louis Slobodkin		Vnguard
1960	Up High And Down Low	$35	$40	$60		Louis Slobodkin		Macmil
1961	A Good Place To Hide	$35	$40	$60		Louis Slobodkin		Macmil
1961	Mr. Spindles and the Spiders	$35	$40	$60		Andrew Packard		Macmil
1961	Picco, The Sad Italian Pony	$35	$40	$60		Louis Slobodkin		Vnguard
1962	The Late Cuckoo	$35	$40	$60		Louis Slobodkin		Vnguard
1962	The Three-Seated Space Ship	$70	$90	$120		Louis Slobodkin		Macmil
1963	Luigi And The Long-Nosed Soldier	$35	$40	$60		Louis Slobodkin		Macmil
1963	Moon Blossom And The Golden Penny	$35	$40	$60		Louis Slobodkin		Vnguard
1964	Mr Papadilly And Willy	$35	$40	$60		Florence Slobodkin		Vnguard
1964	The Polka-Dot Goat	$35	$40	$60		Louis Slobodkin		Macmil
1965	Colette And The Princess	$30	$40	$50		Louis Slobodkin		Dutton
1965	Yasu And The Strangers	$30	$40	$50		Louis Slobodkin		Macmil
1966	Read About The Policeman	$30	$40	$50		Louis Slobodkin		FWatts
1966	Read About The Postman	$30	$40	$50		Louis Slobodkin		FWatts
1967	Read About The Busman	$30	$40	$50		Louis Slobodkin		FWatts
1967	Read About The Fireman	$30	$40	$50		Louis Slobodkin		FWatts

Slobodkin   Louis

Year	Title	VG-	VG	VG+	Fine	Author	Award	Pub
1968	Round Trip Space Ship	$60	$80	$100		Louis Slobodkin		Macmil
1970	Sarah Somebody		$25	$35	$50	Florence Slobodkin		Vnguard
1972	The Space Ship In The Park		$25	$35	$50	Louis Slobodkin		Macmil
1972	Wilbur The Warrior		$25	$35	$50	Louis Slobodkin		Vnguard

Slobodkina   Esphyr

Year	Title	VG-	VG	VG+	Fine	Author	Award	Pub
1938	The Little Fireman	$180	$240	$300		Margaret Wise Brown		WRScott
1940	Caps For Sale	$100	$120	$160		Esphyr Slobodkina		WRScott
1948	The Little Cowboy	$200	$260	$320		Margaret Wise Brown		WRScott
1948	The Little Farmer	$200	$260	$320		Margaret Wise Brown		WRScott
1952	The Little Fireman	$80	$100	$140		Margaret Wise Brown		WRScott
1953	Sleepy ABC	$180	$240	$300		Margaret Wise Brown		Lothrop
1955	The Wonderful Feast	$70	$100	$120		Esphyr Slobodkina		LL&S
1956	Little Dog Lost, Little Dog Found	$50	$70	$90		Esphyr Slobodkina		AS
1956	The Clock	$50	$70	$90		Esphyr Slobodkina		AS
1958	Behind The Dark Window Shade	$50	$60	$80		Esphyr Slobodkina		LL&S
1958	The Little Dinghy	$50	$60	$80		Esphyr Slobodkina		AS
1959	Billie	$50	$60	$80		Esphyr Slobodkina		LL&S
1959	Pinky And The Petunias	$50	$60	$80		Esphyr Slobodkina		AS
1960	Moving Day For The Middlemans	$50	$60	$80		Esphyr Slobodkina		AS
1961	Jack And Jim	$50	$60	$80		Esphyr Slobodkina		AS
1961	The Long Island Ducklings	$50	$60	$80		Esphyr Slobodkina		Lantern
1967	Pezzo The Peddler And The Circus Elephant	$40	$50	$70		Esphyr Slobodkina		AS
1969	The Flame, The Breeze, And The Shadow	$40	$50	$70		Esphyr Slobodkina		RandMc
1970	Pezzo The Peddler And The Thirteen Silly Thieves		$30	$50	$60	Esphyr Slobodkina		AS
1980	Billy, The Condominium Cat		$25	$35	$50	Esphyr Slobodkina		AW
1987	Spots, Alias Prince		$20	$30	$40	Esphyr Slobodkina		ESlob
1987	Whole World Over, Magic Glass, And Yesterdays		$20	$30	$40	Esphyr Slobodkina		ESlob
1994	Sleepy ABC		$10	$14	$18	Margaret Wise Brown		HCollins
2002	Circus Caps For Sale		$8	$10	$14	Esphyr Slobodkina		HCollins

Small   David

Year	Title	VG-	VG	VG+	Fine	Author	Award	Pub
1982	Eulalie And The Hopping Head		$30	$50	$60	David Small		Macmil
1983	Gulliver's Travels		$25	$35	$50	Jonathan Swift		Morrow
1983	Mean Chickens And Wild Cucumbers		$25	$35	$50	Nathan Zimelman		Macmil
1984	Anna And The Seven Swans		$20	$30	$40	Maida Silverman		Morrow
1984	The Dragon Who Lived Downstairs		$30	$50	$60	Burr Tillstrom		Morrow
1985	Imogene's Antlers		$20	$30	$40	David Small		Crown
1985	The Christmas Box		$20	$30	$40	Eve Merriam		Morrow
1987	Paper John		$20	$30	$40	David Small		FSG
1987	The River In Winter		$20	$30	$40	David Small		Norton
1988	Company's Coming		$18	$25	$35	Arthur Yorinks		Crown
1988	The King Has Horse's Ears		$18	$25	$35	Peggy Thomson		S&S
1989	American Politics: How It Really Works		$18	$25	$35	Milton Meltzer		Morrow
1990	Box And Cox		$16	$25	$30	Grace Chetwin		BradP
1991	The Money Tree		$16	$25	$30	Sarah Stewart		FSG
1992	Fighting Words		$16	$25	$30	Eve Merriam		Morrow
1992	Ruby Mae Has Something To Say		$16	$25	$30	David Small		Crown
1993	Petey's Bedtime Story		$16	$25	$30	Beverly Cleary		Morrow
1994	George Washington's Cows		$14	$20	$30	David Small		FSG
1995	Hoover's Bride		$14	$20	$25	David Small		Crown
1995	The Library		$14	$20	$25	Sarah Stewart		FSG
1996	Fenwick's Suit		$12	$18	$25	David Small		FSG
1997	Talk Of Fame		$12	$18	$25	Jeffrey Zaslow (compiled)		Cader
1997	The Gardener		$30	$40	$60	Sarah Stewart	CH	FSG
1998	As Silly As Knees, As Busy As Bees		$12	$16	$20	Norton Juster		Beech
1998	The Christmas Crocodile		$12	$16	$20	Bonny Becker		S&S
1999	The Huckabuck Family		$12	$16	$20	Carl Sandburg		FSG
2000	Imogene's Antlers		$10	$14	$18	David Small		Crown
2000	So You Want To Be President?		$40	$60	$90	Judith St. George	CM	Philo
2001	Company's Going		$10	$14	$18	Arthur Yorinks		Hyper
2001	The Journey		$10	$14	$18	Sarah Stewart		FSG
2001	The Mouse And His Child		$10	$14	$18	Russell Hoban		Levine
2002	So You Want To Be An Inventor		$8	$12	$16	Judith St. George		Philo

Small   David

Year	Title	VG-	VG	VG+	Fine	Author	Award	Pub
2003	The Essential Worldwide Monster Guide		$8	$12	$16	Linda Ashman		S&S
2004	The Friend		$8	$10	$14	Sarah Stewart		FSG

Smath   Jerry

Year	Title	VG-	VG	VG+	Fine	Author	Award	Pub
1991	Seven Little Hippos		$10	$14	$18	Mike Thaler		S&S
1993	A Hat So Simple		$8	$12	$16	Jerry Smath		BWB
1994	Country Mouse and the City Mouse		$8	$12	$16	Maxine Fisher		Random
1994	Never Mail An Elephant		$8	$12	$16	Mike Thaler		Troll
1994	Uses For Mooses & Other Popular Pets		$8	$12	$16	Mike Thaler		Troll
1996	Never Give A Fish An Umbrella		$8	$10	$14	Mike Thaler		WStop
2000	The Animal's Christmas Carol		$6	$10	$12	Charles Dickens		Troll

Smith   Barry

Year	Title	VG-	VG	VG+	Fine	Author	Award	Pub
1989	Cumberland Road		$10	$14	$18	Barry Smith		HM
1989	Tom And Annie Go Shopping		$8	$12	$16	Barry Smith		HM
1990	Minnie And Ginger		$8	$12	$16	Barry Smith		Potter
1999	Grandma Rabbitty's Visit		$8	$10	$14	Barry Smith		DK
2003	Stuffed Animals		$6	$10	$12	Barry Smith		Iceni

Smith   Lane

Year	Title	VG-	VG	VG+	Fine	Author	Award	Pub
1987	Halloween A B C		$14	$20	$30	Eve Merriam		Macmil
1988	Flying Jake		$12	$16	$20	Lane Smith		Macmil
1989	The True Story Of The 3 Little Pigs		$12	$16	$20	Jon Scieszka		VK
1991	Glasses: Who Needs 'Em?		$10	$16	$20	Lane Smith		Viking
1991	Knights Of The Kitchen Table		$10	$16	$20	Jon Scieszka		Viking
1991	The Big Pets		$10	$16	$20	Lane Smith		Viking
1991	The Not-So-Jolly-Roger		$10	$16	$20	Jon Scieszka		Viking
1992	The Good, The Bad, And The Goofy		$10	$16	$20	Jon Scieszka		Viking
1992	The Stinky Cheese Man & Other Fairly Stupid Tales		$30	$40	$60	Jon Scieszka	CH	Viking
1993	The Happy Hocky Family!		$10	$16	$20	Lane Smith		Viking
1993	Your Mother Was A Neanderthal		$10	$16	$20	Jon Scieszka		Viking
1995	2095		$10	$14	$18	Jon Scieszka		Viking
1995	Math Curse		$10	$14	$18	Jon Scieszka		Viking
1996	James And The Giant Peach		$8	$12	$16	Karey Kirkpatrick		Disney
1996	Tut, Tut		$8	$12	$16	Jon Scieszka		Viking
1998	Hooray For Diffendoofer Day!		$8	$12	$16	Theodor Geisel		Knopf
1998	Squids Will Be Squids		$8	$12	$16	Jon Scieszka		Viking
1998	Summer Reading Is Killing Me!		$8	$12	$16	Jon Scieszka		Viking
1999	It's All Greek To Me		$8	$12	$16	Jon Scieszka		Viking
2000	The Very Persistent Gappers Of Frip		$8	$10	$14	George Saunders		Viking
2001	Baloney, Henry P.		$8	$10	$14	Jon Scieszka		Viking
2002	Pinocchio		$8	$10	$14	Lane Smith		Viking
2002	Spooky A B C		$8	$10	$14	Eve Merriam		S&S
2003	The Happy Hocky Family Moves To The Country!		$8	$10	$14	Lane Smith		Viking
2004	Science Verse		$6	$10	$12	Jon Scieszka		Viking

Sneed   Brad

Year	Title	VG-	VG	VG+	Fine	Author	Award	Pub
1991	An Occurrence At Owl Creek Bridge		$12	$18	$25	Ambrose Bierce		Potter
1991	Grandpa's Song		$12	$18	$25	Tony Johnston		Dial
1992	Lucky Russell		$12	$18	$25	Brad Sneed		Putnam
1993	The Legend Of The Cranberry		$10	$16	$20	Ellin Greene		S&S
1993	Turkey In The Straw		$10	$16	$20	Barbara Shook Hazen		Dial
1994	When The Fly Flew In		$10	$14	$18	Lisa Westberg Peters		Dial
1995	I Heard Said The Bird		$10	$14	$18	Polly Berrien Berends		Dial
1996	Higgins Bend Song And Dance		$8	$12	$16	Jacqueline Martin		HM
1996	The Unbeatable Bread		$8	$12	$16	Lyn Littlefield Hoopes		Dial
1997	Smoky Mountain Rose: An Appalachian Cinderella		$8	$12	$16	Alan Schroeder		Dial
1998	The Pumpkin Runner		$8	$12	$16	Marsha Diane Arnold		Dial
1998	The Strange And Wonderful Tale Of Robert Mcdoodle		$8	$12	$16	Steven Bauer		S&S
1998	Watch Out For Bears!		$8	$12	$16	Ferida Wolff		Random
2000	The Bravest Of Us All		$8	$10	$14	Marsha Diane Arnold		Dial

Sneed — Brad

Year	Title	VG-	VG	VG+	Fine	Author	Award	Pub
2001	Sorry		$8	$10	$14	Jean Van Leeuwen		Fogel
2002	Picture A Letter		$8	$10	$14	Brad Sneed		PFogel
2002	When Wishes Were Horses		$8	$10	$14	Sharon Hart Addy		HM
2003	Aesop's Tales		$8	$10	$14	Brad Sneed (retold)		Dial
2004	Thumbelina		$6	$10	$12	Brad Sneed (retold)		Dial

Snow — Alan

Year	Title	VG-	VG	VG+	Fine	Author	Award	Pub
1989	Animals, Birds, Bees, And Flowers		$12	$16	$20	Alan Snow		Derry
1989	Colors, Shapes, Words, And Numbers		$12	$16	$20	Alan Snow		Derry
1989	Machines, Cars, Boats, And Airplanes		$12	$16	$20	Alan Snow		Derry
1989	Vacations, Parties, People, And Places		$12	$16	$20	Alan Snow		Derry
1990	How To Deal With Babies		$10	$16	$20	Richard Powell		WaterM
1990	How To Deal With Parents		$10	$16	$20	Richard Powell		WaterM
1991	How To Deal With Friends		$10	$16	$20	Richard Powell		WaterM
1991	How To Deal With Monsters		$10	$16	$20	Richard Powell		WaterM
1991	The Monster Book Of ABC Sounds		$10	$16	$20	Alan Snow		Dial
1992	My First Dictionary		$10	$16	$20	Alan Snow		Troll
1992	My First Encyclopedia		$10	$16	$20	Alan Snow		Troll
1992	Reader's Digest Children's Book Of Poetry		$10	$16	$20	Beverly Mathias		RDigest
1993	Don't Climb Out Of The Window Tonight		$10	$16	$20	Richard McGilvray		Dial
1993	How Dogs Really Work!		$10	$16	$20	Alan Snow		LBrown
1993	Stories From Hans Christian Andersen		$10	$16	$20	Andrew Matthews (adapted)		Orchard
1996	The Dog Who Wanted To Be A Tiger		$8	$12	$16	Carmen Tafolla		CelebP
1996	The Truth About Cats		$8	$12	$16	Alan Snow		LBrown
2003	Here's What You Do When You Can't Find Your Shoe		$8	$10	$14	Andrea Perry		Athenm
2004	How Santa Really Works		$6	$10	$12	Alan Snow		Athenm

Snyder — Jerome

Year	Title	VG-	VG	VG+	Fine	Author	Award	Pub
1966	Umbrellas, Hats And Wheels	$25	$30	$40		Ann Rand		HBrace
1966	Why The Sun Was Late	$25	$30	$40		Benjamin Elkin		PMagP
1967	Jerome	$25	$30	$40		Philip Ressner		PMagP
1968	The Oak That Would Not Pay	$20	$30	$35		Maria De La Iglesia		Pan
1970	Santa Makes A Change		$18	$25	$35	Sol Chaneles		PMagP
1973	Martha Ann And The Mother Store		$16	$25	$30	Nathaniel Charnley		HBJ

Spier — Peter

Year	Title	VG-	VG	VG+	Fine	Author	Award	Pub
1953	Cocoa	$80	$100	$140		Margaret Otto		Holt
1957	Favorite Christmas Carols	$50	$70	$90		Margaret Bradford (edited)		S&S
1958	Hans Brinker	$50	$60	$80		Mary Mapes Dodge		Scribnr
1958	Hector the Stowaway Dog	$50	$60	$80		Kenneth Dodson		LBrown
1960	100 More Story Poems	$50	$60	$80		Elinor Milnor Parker		Crowell
1961	The Fox Went Out On A Chilly Night	$160	$200	$260		Peter Spier	CH	DoubleD
1965	Elizabethan England	$40	$60	$70		Anthony West		Odyssey
1967	Here And There	$40	$50	$70		Elinor Milnor Parker		Crowell
1967	London Bridge Is Falling Down!	$60	$80	$100		Peter Spier		DoubleD
1967	To Market! To Market!	$40	$50	$70		Peter Spier		DoubleD
1968	Hurrah, We're Outward Bound!	$40	$50	$70		Peter Spier		DoubleD
1969	And So My Garden Grows	$40	$50	$70		Peter Spier		DoubleD
1969	Frederica, Colonial Fort And Town	$40	$50	$70		Trevor R. Reese		FFA
1969	Of Dikes And Windmills	$40	$50	$70		Peter Spier		DoubleD
1970	The Erie Canal		$30	$50	$60	Thomas S. Allen		DoubleD
1971	Gobble, Growl, Grunt		$30	$50	$60	Peter Spier		DoubleD
1972	Crash! Bang! Boom!		$30	$50	$60	Peter Spier		DoubleD
1972	Fast-Slow, High-Low		$30	$50	$60	Peter Spier		DoubleD
1973	The Star-Spangled Banner		$30	$50	$60	Francis Scott Key		DoubleD
1975	Tin Lizzie		$30	$40	$60	Peter Spier		DoubleD
1977	Noah's Ark		$180	$280	$360	Peter Spier	CM	DoubleD
1978	Bored--Nothing To Do!		$25	$40	$50	Peter Spier		DoubleD
1978	Oh, Were They Ever Happy!		$25	$40	$50	Peter Spier		DoubleD
1979	The Legend Of New Amsterdam		$25	$40	$50	Peter Spier		DoubleD
1980	People		$25	$35	$50	Peter Spier		DoubleD
1981	Bill's Service Station		$25	$35	$50	Peter Spier		DoubleD

Spier   Peter

Year	Title	VG-	VG	VG+	Fine	Author	Award	Pub
1981	Fire House, Hook & Ladder Company		$25	$35	$50	Peter Spier		DoubleD
1981	Food Market		$25	$35	$50	Peter Spier		DoubleD
1981	My School		$25	$35	$50	Peter Spier		DoubleD
1981	The Pet Store		$25	$35	$50	Peter Spier		DoubleD
1981	The Toy Shop		$25	$35	$50	Peter Spier		DoubleD
1982	Peter Spier's Rain		$25	$35	$50	Peter Spier		DoubleD
1983	Peter Spier's Christmas!		$25	$35	$50	Peter Spier		DoubleD
1984	Peter Spier's Little Cats		$20	$30	$40	Peter Spier		DoubleD
1984	Peter Spier's Little Dogs		$20	$30	$40	Peter Spier		DoubleD
1984	Peter Spier's Little Ducks		$20	$30	$40	Peter Spier		DoubleD
1984	Peter Spier's Little Rabbits		$20	$30	$40	Peter Spier		DoubleD
1985	The Book Of Jonah		$20	$30	$40	Peter Spier		DoubleD
1986	Dreams		$20	$30	$40	Peter Spier		DoubleD
1987	We The People		$20	$30	$40	Peter Spier		DoubleD
1988	Big Trucks, Little Trucks		$18	$25	$35	Peter Spier		Random
1988	Fast Cars, Slow Cars		$18	$25	$35	Peter Spier		Random
1988	Here Come The Fire Trucks		$18	$25	$35	Peter Spier		Random
1988	Last Hurdle		$18	$25	$35	F. K. Brown		Linnet
1988	The Little Riders		$18	$25	$35	Margaretha Shemin		Putnam
1988	Trucks That Dig And Dump		$18	$25	$35	Peter Spier		Random
1992	Peter Spier's Circus!		$16	$25	$30	Peter Spier		DoubleD
1993	Father, May I Come?		$16	$25	$30	Peter Spier		DoubleD

Spirin   Gennady

Year	Title	VG-	VG	VG+	Fine	Author	Award	Pub
1985	Once There Was A Tree		$20	$30	$40	Natalia Romanova		Dial
1987	The Enchanter's Spell: Five Famous Tales		$14	$20	$30	Various Authors		Dial
1988	Mysterious Tale Of Gentle Jack And Lord Bumblebee		$14	$20	$30	George Sand		Dial
1989	The Tale Of The Unicorn		$14	$20	$25	Otfried Preussler		Dial
1990	Sorotchintzy Fair		$12	$18	$25	Nikolai Gogol		Godine
1990	The Fool And The Fish		$12	$18	$25	Alexander Afanasyev		Dial
1990	The White Cat: An Old French Fairy Tale		$12	$18	$25	Robert D. San Souci		Orchard
1991	Rumpelstiltskin		$12	$18	$25	Jacob & Wilhelm Grimm		Dial
1992	Boots & The Glass Mountain		$12	$18	$25	Claire Martin		Dial
1992	Snow White And Rose Red		$12	$18	$25	Jacob & Wilhelm Grimm		Philo
1993	Gulliver's Adventures In Lilliput		$12	$16	$20	Jonathan Swift		Philo
1993	The Children Of Lir		$12	$16	$20	Sheila MacGill-Callahan		Dial
1993	The Nose		$12	$16	$20	Nikolai Gogol		Godine
1994	The Frog Princess		$12	$16	$20	J. Patrick Lewis		Dial
1995	Kashtanka		$18	$25	$35	Anton Chekhov	NYT	HBrace
1996	The Nutcracker		$10	$16	$20	E. T. A. Hoffmann		ST&C
1996	The Tale Of Tsar Saltan		$10	$16	$20	Alexander Pushkin		Dial
1996	The Tempest		$10	$16	$20	Ann K. Beneduce (retold)		Philo
1997	The Sea King's Daughter		$10	$16	$20	Aaron Shepard (retold)		Athenm
1998	The Christmas Story		$10	$14	$18	King James Bible		Holt
1998	The Crane Wife		$10	$14	$18	Odds Bodkin (retold)		HBrace
1999	Jack And The Beanstalk		$10	$14	$18	Ann K. Beneduce (retold)		Philo
1999	The Easter Story		$10	$14	$18	Gennady Spirin		Holt
2000	Joy To The World		$8	$12	$16	Ann K. Beneduce (retold)		Athenm
2000	Philipok		$8	$12	$16	Ann K. Beneduce (retold)		Philo
2001	Little Mermaids And Ugly Ducklings		$8	$12	$16	Hans Christian Andersen		Chron
2002	The Tale Of The Firebird		$8	$10	$14	Gennady Spirin		Philo
2003	Simeon's Gift		$8	$10	$14	Julie Edwards		HCollins
2004	Moses		$8	$10	$14	Ann Keay Beneduce		Orchard
2004	The Story Of Noah And The Ark		$8	$10	$14	Gennady Spirin (adapted)		Holt
2004	Yakov And The Seven Thieves		$8	$10	$14	Gennady Madonna		Calla

Spohn   Kate

Year	Title	VG-	VG	VG+	Fine	Author	Award	Pub
1989	Clementine's Winter Wardrobe		$12	$16	$20	Kate Spohn		Orchard
1990	Ruth's Bake Shop		$10	$16	$20	Kate Spohn		Orchard
1991	Introducing Fanny		$12	$18	$25	Kate Spohn		Orchard
1992	Hide And Seek In The Yellow House		$10	$14	$18	Agatha Rose		Viking
1993	Christmas At Anna's		$10	$14	$18	Kate Spohn		Viking
1993	Fanny & Margarita		$10	$16	$20	Kate Spohn		Viking
1994	Broken Umbrellas		$8	$12	$16	Kate Spohn		Viking

Spohn   Kate

Year	Title	VG-	VG	VG+	Fine	Author	Award	Pub
1994	River		$8	$12	$16	Bill Staines		Viking
1995	Night Goes By		$8	$12	$16	Kate Spohn		Macmil
1996	Dog And Cat Shake A Leg		$8	$12	$16	Kate Spohn		Viking
1997	Dog And Cat Make A Splash		$8	$12	$16	Kate Spohn		Viking
1998	Chick's Daddy		$8	$10	$14	Kate Spohn		Random
1998	Kitten's Nap		$8	$10	$14	Kate Spohn		Random
1998	Piglet's Bath		$8	$10	$14	Kate Spohn		Random
1998	Puppy's Games		$8	$10	$14	Kate Spohn		Random
1998	The Mermaid's Lullaby		$8	$10	$14	Kate Spohn		Random
1999	Turtle And Snake At Work		$8	$10	$14	Kate Spohn		Viking
2000	Turtle And Snake And The Christmas Tree		$8	$10	$14	Kate Spohn		Viking
2000	Turtle And Snake Go Camping		$8	$10	$14	Kate Spohn		Viking
2001	Snow Play		$8	$10	$14	Kate Spohn		Scholas
2002	The Wet Dry Book		$6	$10	$12	Kate Spohn		Random
2002	Turtle And Snake Fix It		$6	$10	$12	Kate Spohn		Viking
2002	Turtle And Snake's Spooky Halloween		$6	$10	$12	Kate Spohn		Viking
2003	Turtle And Snake's Day At The Beach		$6	$10	$12	Kate Spohn		Viking
2003	Turtle And Snake's Valentine's Day		$6	$10	$12	Kate Spohn		Viking
2004	By Word Of Mouse		$6	$10	$12	Kate Spohn		Bloom
2004	Critter Love		$6	$10	$12	Kate Spohn		HFest

Spowart   Robin

Year	Title	VG-	VG	VG+	Fine	Author	Award	Pub
1987	A Rose, A Bridge, And A Wild Black Horse		$12	$16	$20	Charlotte Zolotow		H&Row
1987	The Three Bears		$10	$16	$20	Robin Spowart (adapted)		Knopf
1988	Vegetable Soup		$10	$14	$18	Jeanne Modesitt		Macmil
1989	Latkes And Applesauce		$10	$14	$18	Fran Manushkin		Scholas
1989	The Night Call		$10	$14	$18	Jeanne Modesitt		VK
1989	The Star Grazers		$10	$14	$18	Christine Barker Widman		H&Row
1989	To Rabbittown		$10	$14	$18	April Halprin Wayland		Scholas
1992	Sometimes I Feel Like A Mouse		$10	$14	$18	Jeanne Modesitt		Scholas
1993	Mama, If You Had A Wish		$8	$12	$16	Jeanne Modesitt		GreenT
1994	Lunch With Milly		$8	$12	$16	Jeanne Modesitt		BWB
1996	The Night The Moon Blew Kisses		$8	$12	$16	Lynn Manuel		HM
1998	Inside, Outside Christmas		$8	$10	$14	Robin Spowart		Holiday
1999	It's Hanukkah!		$8	$10	$14	Jeanne Modesitt		Holiday
1999	Little Bunny's Easter Surprise		$8	$10	$14	Jeanne Modesitt		S&S
2001	Love Me, Love You		$8	$10	$14	Susan Heyboer O'Keefe		Boyds
2001	Ten Little Bunnies		$8	$10	$14	Robin Spowart		Scholas
2003	Little Bunny's Christmas Tree		$6	$10	$12	Jeanne Modesitt		S&S
2004	Mouse's Halloween Party		$6	$10	$12	Jeanne Modesitt		Boyds

Spurll   Barbara

Year	Title	VG-	VG	VG+	Fine	Author	Award	Pub
1991	Rhinos For Lunch And Elephants For Supper!		$10	$14	$18	Tololwa Mollel		Clarion
1994	The Flying Tortoise		$8	$12	$16	Tololwa Mollel		Clarion
1999	Emma And The Coyote		$8	$10	$14	Margriet Ruurs		Stodd
2001	Emma's Cold Day		$8	$10	$14	Margriet Ruurs		Stodd
2001	Mooki, The Berry Bandit		$8	$10	$14	Kari Smalley Gibson		Zkidz

Stanley   Diane

Year	Title	VG-	VG	VG+	Fine	Author	Award	Pub
1979	Fiddle-I-Fee: A Traditional American Chant		$25	$40	$50	Diane Stanley		LBrown
1979	Half-A-Ball-Of-Kenki: An Ashanti Tale Retold		$18	$25	$35	Verna Aardema		FWarne
1979	Little Mouse Nibbling		$18	$25	$35	Tony Johnston		Putnam
1981	Onions, Onions		$14	$20	$25	Toni Hormann		Crowell
1981	Petrosinella, A Neapolitan Rapunzel		$14	$20	$25	John Edward Taylor (adapted)		FWarne
1981	Sleeping Ugly		$18	$25	$35	Jane Yolen		CM&G
1981	The Man Whose Name Was Not Thomas		$14	$20	$25	M. Jean Craig		DoubleD
1982	Beach Party		$14	$20	$25	Joanne Ryder		FWarne
1982	Robin Of Bray		$14	$20	$25	Jean & Claudio Marzollo		Dial
1983	Little Orphant Annie		$14	$20	$25	James Whitcomb Riley		Putnam
1983	The Conversation Club		$16	$25	$30	Diane Stanley		Macmil
1983	The Month-Brothers		$14	$20	$25	Samuel Marshak (retold)		Morrow
1984	All Wet! All Wet!		$12	$18	$25	James Skofield		H&Row

Stanley   Diane

Year	Title	VG-	VG	VG+	Fine	Author	Award	Pub
1985	A Country Tale		$16	$25	$30	Diane Stanley		Macmil
1985	Birdsong Lullaby: Story And Pictures		$16	$25	$30	Diane Stanley		Morrow
1986	Peter The Great		$14	$20	$30	Diane Stanley		4Winds
1987	Captain Whiz-Bang		$14	$20	$30	Diane Stanley		Morrow
1988	Shaka: King Of The Zulus		$12	$16	$20	Peter Vennema	NYT	Morrow
1990	Fortune		$12	$18	$25	Diane Stanley		Morrow
1990	Good Queen Bess: The Story Of Elizabeth I		$10	$16	$20	Peter Vennema		4Winds
1991	The Last Princess: The Story Of Princess Kaiulani		$10	$16	$20	Fay Stanley		4Winds
1992	Bard Of Avon: The Story Of William Shakespeare		$10	$16	$20	Peter Vennema		Morrow
1993	Charles Dickens/Man Who Had Great Expectations		$10	$16	$20	Peter Vennema		Morrow
1994	Cleopatra		$10	$14	$18	Peter Vennema		Morrow
1995	The True Adventure Of Daniel Hall		$10	$14	$18	Diane Stanley		Dial
1996	Elena		$8	$12	$16	Diane Stanley		Hyper
1996	Leonardo Da Vinci		$8	$12	$16	Diane Stanley		Morrow
1997	Rumpelstiltskin's Daughter		$8	$12	$16	Diane Stanley		Morrow
1998	Joan Of Arc		$8	$12	$16	Diane Stanley		Morrow
1999	A Time Apart		$8	$12	$16	Diane Stanley		Morrow
1999	Peter The Great		$8	$12	$16	Diane Stanley		Morrow
2000	Michaelangelo		$8	$10	$14	Diane Stanley		HCollins
2001	Good Queen Bess		$8	$10	$14	Peter Vennema		HCollins
2001	The Last Princess		$8	$10	$14	Fay Stanley		HCollins
2001	The Mysterious Matter Of I.M. Fine		$8	$10	$14	Diane Stanley		HCollins
2002	Saladin		$8	$10	$14	Diane Stanley		HCollins
2003	Goldie And The Three Bears		$8	$10	$14	Diane Stanley		HCollins
2004	The Giant And The Beanstalk		$6	$10	$12	Diane Stanley		HCollins

Steadman   Ralph

Year	Title	VG-	VG	VG+	Fine	Author	Award	Pub
1965	The Big Squirrel And The Little Rhinoceros	$90	$120	$160		Mischa Damjan		Norton
1966	Where Love Lies Deepest	$40	$60	$70		Daisy Ashford		HartD
1967	Lewis Carroll's Alice In Wonderland	$200	$260	$320		Lewis Carroll		Dobson
1968	The Little Prince And The Tiger Cat	$80	$120	$140		Mischa Damjan		McHill
1969	The Little Red Computer	$120	$160	$200		Ralph Steadman		McHill
1970	Fly Away Peter		$50	$70	$90	Frank Dickens		Scroll
1970	Jelly Book		$100	$160	$200	Ralph Steadman		Scroll
1970	The False Flamingoes		$50	$70	$90	Mischa Damjan		Scroll
1972	Lewis Carroll's Through The Looking Glass		$100	$160	$200	Lewis Carroll		M&K
1973	Lewis Carroll's Alice In Wonderland		$90	$120	$180	Lewis Carroll		Potter
1973	Lewis Carroll's Through The Looking Glass		$70	$100	$140	Lewis Carroll		Cpot
1974	America		$140	$200	$280	Ralph Steadman		Str8A
1974	The Bridge		$40	$60	$80	Ralph Steadman		Collins
1975	The Hunting Of The Snark		$90	$120	$180	Lewis Carroll		Dempsey
1981	Inspector Mouse		$25	$35	$50	Bernard Stone		HR&W
1982	Emergency Mouse		$25	$35	$50	Bernard Stone		RRourke
1983	I, Leonardo		$40	$60	$90	Ralph Steadman		JCape
1983	Two Donkeys And A Bridge		$25	$35	$50	Ralph Steadman		AP
1984	Quasimodo Mouse		$20	$30	$40	Bernard Stone		AP
1986	That's My Dad		$20	$30	$40	Ralph Steadman		AP
1989	No Room To Swing A Cat		$18	$25	$35	Ralph Steadman		AP
2000	Little.Com		$10	$14	$18	Ralph Steadman		AP
2003	Alice In Wonderland		$8	$12	$16	Lewis Carroll		Firefly

Steig   William

Year	Title	VG-	VG	VG+	Fine	Author	Award	Pub
1950	Giggle Box	$60	$80	$100		William Steig		Knopf
1968	C D B!	$120	$160	$220		William Steig		S&S
1968	Roland, The Minstrel Pig	$40	$50	$70		William Steig		H&Row
1969	Sylvester And The Magic Pebble	$280	$360	$460		William Steig	CM	Windmil
1969	The Bad Island	$120	$160	$200		William Steig		Windmil
1970	An Eye For Elephants		$30	$50	$60	William Steig		Windmil
1970	The Bad Speller		$30	$50	$60	William Steig		Windmil
1971	Amos & Boris		$70	$100	$140	William Steig	NYT	FSG
1971	Listen, Little Man!		$30	$50	$60	Ralph Manheim (translated)		Octagon
1972	Dominic		$30	$50	$60	William Steig		FSG
1973	The Real Thief		$30	$50	$60	William Steig		FSG
1974	Farmer Palmer's Wagon Ride		$30	$40	$60	William Steig		FSG

Steig   William

Year	Title	VG-	VG	VG+	Fine	Author	Award	Pub
1976	Abel's Island		$60	$80	$120	William Steig	NH	FSG
1976	The Amazing Bone		$90	$120	$180	William Steig	CH	FSG
1978	Caleb And Kate		$25	$40	$50	William Steig		FSG
1978	Tiffky Doofky		$25	$40	$50	William Steig		FSG
1979	Drawings		$25	$40	$50	William Steig		FSG
1980	Gorky Rises		$35	$50	$70	William Steig	NYT	FSG
1982	Doctor DeSoto		$50	$70	$90	William Steig	NH	FSG
1983	How To Become Extinct		$25	$35	$50	Will Cuppy		UChic
1984	C D C?		$20	$30	$40	William Steig		FSG
1984	Rotten Island		$20	$30	$40	William Steig		Godine
1984	Ruminations		$20	$30	$40	William Steig		FSG
1984	The Decline And Fall Of Practically Everybody		$20	$30	$40	Will Cuppy		Godine
1984	Yellow And Pink		$20	$30	$40	William Steig		FSG
1985	Solomon: The Rusty Nail		$20	$30	$40	William Steig		FSG
1986	Brave Irene		$30	$40	$60	William Steig	NYT	FSG
1987	Mr. Blandings Builds His Dream House		$20	$30	$40	Eric Hodgins		ACP
1987	The Zabajaba Jungle		$20	$30	$40	William Steig		FSG
1988	Consider The Lemming		$18	$25	$35	Jeanne Steig		FSG
1988	Spinky Sulks		$18	$25	$35	William Steig		FSG
1990	Our Miserable Life		$16	$25	$30	William Steig		Noonday
1990	Shrek!		$80	$120	$160	William Steig		FSG
1990	The Old Testament Made Easy		$16	$25	$30	Jeanne Steig		FSG
1992	Alpha Beta Chowder		$16	$25	$30	Jeanne Steig		HCollins
1992	Doctor De Soto Goes To Africa		$16	$25	$30	William Steig		HCollins
1994	Collected Drawings		$14	$20	$30	William Steig		Moyer
1994	Zeke Pippen		$14	$20	$30	William Steig		HCollins
1995	Grown-Ups Get To Do All The Driving		$14	$20	$25	William Steig		HCollins
1996	The Toy Brother		$12	$18	$25	William Steig		HCollins
1998	A Handful Of Beans		$12	$16	$20	Jeanne Steig		HCollins
1998	Pete's A Pizza		$12	$16	$20	William Steig		HCollins
1999	Arthur Yorinks's The Flying Latke		$12	$16	$20	Arthur Yorinks		S&S
2001	A Gift From Zeus		$10	$14	$18	Jeanne Steig		Cotler
2003	When Everybody Wore A Hat		$12	$16	$20	William Steig	NYT	HCollins

Steiner   Jorg

Year	Title	VG-	VG	VG+	Fine	Author	Award	Pub
1977	The Bear Who Wanted To Be A Bear		$20	$30	$40	Jorg Steiner		Athenm
1978	Rabbit Island		$14	$20	$30	Jorg Steiner		HBJ
1982	The Sea People		$14	$20	$25	Jorg Muller		Schock
1990	The Animals Rebellion		$10	$16	$20	Jorg Muller		Atom

Steptoe   John

Year	Title	VG-	VG	VG+	Fine	Author	Award	Pub
1969	Stevie	$60	$80	$100		John Steptoe		H&Row
1970	Uptown		$25	$35	$50	John Steptoe		H&Row
1971	Train Ride		$40	$60	$90	John Steptoe		H&Row
1972	Birthday		$25	$35	$50	John Steptoe		HR&W
1973	All Us Come Cross The Water		$25	$35	$50	Lucille Clifton		HR&W
1974	My Special Best Words		$20	$30	$40	John Steptoe		Viking
1974	She Come Bringing Me That Little Baby Girl		$20	$30	$40	Eloise Greenfield		Lippin
1976	Marcia		$20	$30	$40	John Steptoe		Viking
1980	Daddy Is A Monster ... Sometimes		$18	$25	$35	John Steptoe		Lippin
1981	Mother Crocodile		$18	$25	$35	Birago Diop		DelaP
1981	Outside Inside Poems		$18	$25	$35	Arnold Adoff		LL&S
1982	All The Colors Of The Race: Poems		$16	$25	$30	Arnold Adolf		LL&S
1983	Jeffrey Bear Cleans Up His Act		$16	$25	$30	John Steptoe		LL&S
1984	The Story Of A Jumping Mouse		$40	$60	$90	John Steptoe	CH	LL&S
1987	Mufaro's Beautiful Daughters: An African Tale		$60	$80	$120	John Steptoe	CH	LL&S
1987	The Little Tree Growin' In The Shade		$14	$20	$30	Camille Yarbrough		Putnam
1988	Baby Says		$14	$20	$30	John Steptoe		LL&S
1997	Creativity		$10	$16	$20	John Steptoe		Clarion

Stevens   Janet

Year	Title	VG-	VG	VG+	Fine	Author	Award	Pub
1978	Callooh! Callay!: Holiday Poems For Young Readers		$35	$50	$70	Myra C. Livingston (selected)		Athenm

Stevens   Janet

Year	Title	VG-	VG	VG+	Fine	Author	Award	Pub
1981	Animal Fair		$35	$50	$70	Janet Stevens		Holiday
1981	Lucretia The Unbearable		$25	$35	$50	Marjorie Weinman Sharmat		Holiday
1981	Twitchell The Wishful		$25	$35	$50	Marjorie Weinman Sharmat		Holiday
1982	Not Like That, Armadillo		$25	$35	$50	Ida Luttrell		HBJ
1982	The Big Bunny And The Easter Eggs		$25	$35	$50	Steven Kroll		Holiday
1982	The Princess And The Pea		$25	$35	$50	Hans Christian Andersen		Holiday
1983	The Owl And The Pussycat		$25	$35	$50	Edward Lear		Holiday
1984	Sasha The Silly		$20	$30	$40	Marjorie Weinman Sharmat		Holiday
1984	The Tortoise And The Hare: An Aesop Fable		$25	$35	$50	Janet Stevens (retold)		Holiday
1984	Trout The Magnificent		$20	$30	$40	Sheila Turnage		HBJ
1985	The Cabbages Are Chasing The Rabbits		$20	$30	$40	Arnold Adoff		HBJ
1985	The Emperor's New Clothes		$20	$30	$40	Hans Christian Andersen		Holiday
1985	The House That Jack Built		$25	$35	$50	Janet Stevens		Holiday
1985	The Weighty Word Book		$20	$30	$40	Burger & Guralnick Levitt		BG
1986	Goldilocks And The Three Bears		$25	$35	$50	Janet Stevens (retold)		Holiday
1986	Little David's Adventure		$20	$30	$40	Squire D. Rushnell		Word
1986	The Big Bunny And The Magic Show		$20	$30	$40	Steven Kroll		Holiday
1987	The Three Billy Goats Gruff		$20	$30	$40	Janet Stevens (retold)		HBJ
1987	The Town Mouse And The Country Mouse		$20	$30	$40	Janet Stevens (retold)		Holiday
1988	Anansi And The Moss-Covered Rock		$18	$25	$35	Eric Kimmel		Holiday
1988	It's Perfectly True		$18	$25	$35	Hans Christian Andersen		Holiday
1988	The Quangle Wangle's Hat		$18	$25	$35	Edward Lear		HBJ
1989	Androcles And The Lion		$20	$30	$40	Janet Stevens (retold)		Holiday
1989	I'm In The Zoo, Too!		$18	$25	$35	Brent Ashabranner		Dutton
1990	How The Manx Cat Lost Its Tail		$16	$25	$30	Janet Stevens		HBJ
1990	Nanny Goat And The Seven Little Kids		$16	$25	$30	Jacob & Wilhelm Grimm		Holiday
1990	Wally, The Worry-Warthog		$16	$25	$30	Barbara Shook Hazen		Clarion
1991	The Dog Who Had Kittens		$16	$25	$30	Polly M. Robertus		Holiday
1992	Anansi Goes Fishing		$16	$25	$30	Eric Kimmel		Holiday
1992	The Bremen Town Musicians		$16	$25	$30	Jacob & Wilhelm Grimm		Holiday
1993	Buddy Bear And The Bad Guys		$16	$25	$30	Margery Cuyler		Clarion
1993	Coyote Steals The Blanket: An Ute Tale		$16	$25	$30	Janet Stevens (retold)		Holiday
1994	Anansi And The Talking Melon		$14	$20	$30	Eric Kimmel		Holiday
1995	From Pictures To Words/Book About Making A Book		$14	$20	$25	Janet Stevens		Holiday
1995	The Gates Of The Wind		$14	$20	$25	Kathryn Lasky		Harcort
1995	Tops & Bottoms		$35	$50	$70	Janet Stevens	CH	HBrace
1996	Old Bag Of Bones: A Coyote Tale		$12	$18	$25	Janet Stevens		Holiday
1997	To Market, To Market		$12	$18	$25	Anne Miranda		HBrace
2001	Anansi And The Magic Stick		$10	$14	$18	Eric Kimmel		Holiday
2001	And The Dish Ran Away With The Spoon		$10	$14	$18	Susan S. Crummel		Harcort
2002	Epossumondas		$8	$12	$16	Colleen Salley		Harcort
2003	Jackalope		$8	$12	$16	Janet Stevens		Harcort
2004	Plaidypus Lost		$8	$10	$14	Susan S. Crummel		Holiday
2004	Why Epossumondas Has No Hair On His Tail		$8	$10	$14	Colleen Salley		Harcort

Stevenson   Harvey

Year	Title	VG-	VG	VG+	Fine	Author	Award	Pub
1990	Anna's Rain		$10	$14	$18	Fred Burstein		Orchard
1990	Gone Fishing		$10	$16	$20	Steven Kroll		Crown
1990	Good Books, Good Times!		$10	$14	$18	Lee Bennett Hopkins		H&Row
1991	As The Crow Flies		$10	$14	$18	Gail Hartman		BradP
1991	Violet's Finest Hour		$10	$14	$18	Alice Duggan		LL&S
1992	Elmer And The Chickens Vs. The Big League		$10	$14	$18	Brian McConnachie		Crown
1992	New Feet For Old		$10	$14	$18	Barrett Waller		4Winds
1993	Weekend Girl		$8	$12	$16	Amy Hest		Morrow
1994	Day Lights, Night Lights		$8	$12	$16	Cecile Schoberle		S&S
1994	Grandpa's House		$8	$12	$16	Harvey Stevenson		Hyper
1994	Little Rabbit Goes To Sleep		$8	$12	$16	Tony Johnston		HCollins
1994	Morning Sounds, Evening Sounds		$8	$12	$16	Cecile Schoberle		S&S
1994	The Bear Who Came To Stay		$8	$12	$16	Allen Woodman		BradP
1995	The Tangerine Tree		$8	$12	$16	Regina Hanson		Clarion
1996	The Chocolate Covered Cookie Tantrum		$8	$12	$16	Deborah Blumenthal		Clarion
1997	Big Scary Wolf		$8	$10	$14	Harvey Stevenson		Clarion
1997	Little Coyote Runs Away		$8	$10	$14	Craig Strete		Putnam
1998	Bye, Mis' Lela		$8	$10	$14	Dorothy Carter		FSG
1998	Sam The Zamboni Man		$8	$10	$14	James Stevenson		Green

Stevenson   Harvey

Year	Title	VG-	VG	VG+	Fine	Author	Award	Pub
1999	Wilhe'mina Miles After The Stork Night		$8	$10	$14	Dorothy Carter		FSG
2000	Grandpa Never Lies		$8	$10	$14	Ralph J. Fletcher		Clarion
2001	The Ticky-Tacky Doll		$8	$10	$14	Cynthia Rylant		HBrace
2002	Shadows		$6	$10	$12	April Pulley Sayre		Holt

Stevenson   James

Year	Title	VG-	VG	VG+	Fine	Author	Award	Pub
1962	Do Yourself A Favor, Kid	$50	$60	$80		James Stevenson		Macmil
1963	Sorry, Lady, This Beach Is Private	$40	$50	$70		James Stevenson		Macmil
1968	If I Owned A Candy Factory	$30	$40	$50		James Stevenson		LBrown
1969	Tony And The Toll Collector	$30	$40	$50		Eric Stevenson		LBrown
1969	Walker, The Witch, And The Striped Flying Saucer	$30	$40	$50		James Stevenson		LBrown
1971	Something Marvelous Is About To Happen		$25	$35	$50	James Stevenson		H&Row
1972	Alec's Sand Castle		$25	$35	$50	Lavinia Russ		H&Row
1972	The Bear Who Had No Place To Go		$25	$35	$50	James Stevenson		H&Row
1972	Tony's Hard Work Day		$25	$35	$50	Alan Arkin		H&Row
1973	Here Comes Herb's Hurricane!		$25	$35	$50	James Stevenson		H&Row
1975	Good Old James		$20	$30	$40	John Donovan		H&Row
1976	Cool Jack And The Beanstalk		$20	$30	$40	James Stevenson		Penguin
1976	Could Be Worse!		$20	$30	$40	James Stevenson		FSG
1977	Jack The Bum And The Halloween Handout		$20	$30	$40	Janet Schulman		Green
1977	Jack The Bum And The Haunted House		$20	$30	$40	Janet Schulman		Green
1977	Wilfred The Rat		$20	$30	$40	James Stevenson		Green
1978	Help! Yelled Maxwell		$20	$30	$40	Edwina Stevenson		Green
1978	Jack The Bum And The UFO		$20	$30	$40	Janet Schulman		Green
1978	Let's Boogie!		$20	$30	$40	James Stevenson		DoddM
1978	The Sea View Hotel		$25	$40	$50	James Stevenson		Green
1978	The Worst Person In The World		$20	$30	$40	James Stevenson		Green
1978	Winston, Newton, Elton, And Ed		$20	$30	$40	James Stevenson		Green
1979	Fast Friends		$18	$25	$35	James Stevenson		Green
1979	Monty		$18	$25	$35	James Stevenson		Green
1980	Clams Can't Sing		$18	$25	$35	James Stevenson		Green
1980	Howard		$18	$25	$35	James Stevenson		Green
1980	Say It!		$18	$25	$35	Charlotte Zolotow		Green
1980	That Terrible Halloween Night		$18	$25	$35	James Stevenson		Green
1981	The Night After Christmas		$18	$25	$35	James Stevenson		Green
1981	The Wish Card Ran Out!		$18	$25	$35	James Stevenson		Green
1982	Oliver, Clarence And Violet		$16	$25	$30	James Stevenson		Green
1982	The Baby Uggs Are Hatching		$16	$25	$30	Jack Prelutsky		Green
1982	We Can't Sleep		$16	$25	$30	James Stevenson		Green
1983	Barbara's Birthday		$16	$25	$30	James Stevenson		Green
1983	Cully Cully And The Bear		$16	$25	$30	Wilson Gage		Green
1983	Grandpa's Great City Tour		$16	$25	$30	James Stevenson		Green
1983	How Do You Get A Horse Out Of The Bathtub?		$16	$25	$30	Louis Phillips		Viking
1983	The Great Big Especially Beautiful Easter Egg		$16	$25	$30	James Stevenson		Green
1983	What's Under My Bed?		$16	$25	$30	James Stevenson		Green
1984	I Know A Lady		$16	$25	$30	Charlotte Zolotow		Green
1984	The New Kid On The Block		$16	$25	$30	Jack Prelutsky		Green
1984	Worse Than Willy!		$16	$25	$30	James Stevenson		Green
1984	Yuck!		$16	$25	$30	James Stevenson		Green
1985	263 Brain Busters		$16	$25	$30	Louis Phillips		VK
1985	Are We Almost There?		$16	$25	$30	James Stevenson		Green
1985	Emma		$16	$25	$30	James Stevenson		Green
1985	Otto Is Different		$16	$25	$30	Franz Brandenberg		Green
1985	That Dreadful Day		$16	$25	$30	James Stevenson		Green
1986	Fried Feathers For Thanksgiving		$14	$20	$30	James Stevenson		Green
1986	Georgia Music		$14	$20	$30	Helen Griffith		Green
1986	No Friends		$14	$20	$30	James Stevenson		Green
1986	There's Nothing To Do!		$14	$20	$30	James Stevenson		Green
1986	When I Was Nine		$14	$20	$30	James Stevenson		Green
1987	Grandaddy's Place		$14	$20	$30	Helen Griffith		Green
1987	Happy Valentine's Day, Emma!		$14	$20	$30	James Stevenson		Green
1987	Henry And Mudge		$14	$20	$30	Cynthia Rylant		BradP
1987	Higher On The Door		$14	$20	$30	James Stevenson		Green
1987	I Am Not Going To Get Up Today!		$80	$120	$160	Theodore Giesel		BB
1987	No Need For Monty		$14	$20	$30	James Stevenson		Green

Stevenson   James

Year	Title	VG-	VG	VG+	Fine	Author	Award	Pub
1987	Will You Please Feed Our Cat?		$14	$20	$30	James Stevenson		Green
1988	How Do You Lift A Walrus With One Hand?		$14	$20	$30	Louis Phillips		VK
1988	The Supreme Souvenir Factory		$14	$20	$30	James Stevenson		Green
1988	The Worst Person In The World At Crab Beach		$14	$20	$30	James Stevenson		Green
1988	We Hate Rain!		$14	$20	$30	James Stevenson		Green
1989	Grandpa's Too-Good Garden		$14	$20	$25	James Stevenson		Green
1989	Oh No, It's Waylon's Birthday!		$14	$20	$25	James Stevenson		Green
1989	Percy And The Five Houses		$14	$20	$25	Else Holmelund Minarik		Green
1989	Un-Happy New Year, Emma!		$14	$20	$25	James Stevenson		Green
1990	Emma At The Beach		$12	$18	$25	James Stevenson		Green
1990	July		$12	$18	$25	James Stevenson		Green
1990	National Worm Day		$12	$18	$25	James Stevenson		Green
1990	Quick! Turn The Page!		$12	$18	$25	James Stevenson		Green
1990	Something Big Has Been Here		$12	$18	$25	Jack Prelutsky		Green
1990	The Stowaway		$12	$18	$25	James Stevenson		Green
1990	Which One Is Whitney?		$12	$18	$25	James Stevenson		Green
1991	Brrr!		$12	$18	$25	James Stevenson		Green
1991	Explorer		$12	$18	$25	Rupert Matthews		Knopf
1991	That's Exactly The Way It Wasn't		$12	$18	$25	James Stevenson		Green
1991	The Worst Person's Christmas		$12	$18	$25	James Stevenson		Green
1992	Don't You Know There's A War On?		$12	$18	$25	James Stevenson		Green
1992	Loop The Loop		$12	$18	$25	Barbara Dugan		Green
1992	Rolling Rose		$12	$18	$25	James Stevenson		Green
1993	Grandaddy And Janetta		$12	$16	$20	Helen Griffith		Green
1993	The Flying Acorns		$12	$16	$20	James Stevenson		Green
1993	The Night After Christmas		$12	$16	$20	James Stevenson		Mulbery
1993	The Pattaconk Brook		$12	$16	$20	James Stevenson		Green
1994	Fun, No Fun		$12	$16	$20	James Stevenson		Green
1994	The Mud Flat Olympics		$12	$16	$20	James Stevenson		Green
1994	Worse Than The Worst		$12	$16	$20	James Stevenson		Green
1995	A Village Full Of Valentines		$10	$16	$20	James Stevenson		Green
1995	All Aboard!		$10	$16	$20	James Stevenson		Green
1995	Grandaddy's Stars		$10	$16	$20	Helen Griffith		Green
1995	I Had A Lot Of Wishes		$10	$16	$20	James Stevenson		Green
1995	Mrs. Donald's Dog Bun & His Home Away From Home		$10	$16	$20	William Maxwell		Knopf
1995	Sweet Corn		$10	$16	$20	James Stevenson		Green
1995	The Bones In The Cliff		$10	$16	$20	James Stevenson		Green
1995	The Royal Nap		$10	$16	$20	Charles C. Black		Viking
1995	The Worst Goes South		$10	$16	$20	James Stevenson		Green
1996	A Pizza The Size Of The Sun		$10	$16	$20	Jack Prelutsky		Green
1996	I Meant To Tell You		$10	$16	$20	James Stevenson		Green
1996	The Oldest Elf		$10	$16	$20	James Stevenson		Green
1996	Yard Sale		$10	$16	$20	James Stevenson		Green
1997	Happily Ever After		$10	$16	$20	Anna Quindlen		Viking
1997	Heat Wave At Mud Flat		$10	$16	$20	James Stevenson		Green
1997	Hooper Humperdink--? Not Him!		$10	$16	$20	James Stevenson		BB
1997	The Mud Flat Mystery		$10	$16	$20	James Stevenson		Green
1997	The Unprotected Witness		$10	$16	$20	James Stevenson		Green
1998	Mud Flat April Fool		$10	$14	$18	James Stevenson		Green
1998	Popcorn		$10	$14	$18	James Stevenson		Green
1999	Candy Corn		$10	$14	$18	James Stevenson		Green
1999	Don't Make Me Laugh		$10	$14	$18	James Stevenson		FSG
1999	Mud Flat Spring		$10	$14	$18	James Stevenson		Green
2000	Christmas At Mud Flat		$8	$12	$16	James Stevenson		Green
2000	Cornflakes		$8	$12	$16	James Stevenson		Green
2000	It's Raining Pigs & Noodles		$8	$12	$16	Jack Prelutsky		Green
2000	The Most Amazing Dinosaur		$8	$12	$16	James Stevenson		Green
2001	Grandaddy And Janetta Together		$8	$12	$16	Helen Griffith		Green
2001	Just Around The Corner		$8	$12	$16	James Stevenson		Green
2001	Rocks In His Head		$8	$12	$16	Carol Otis Hurst		Green
2002	Corn-Fed		$8	$10	$14	James Stevenson		Green
2002	The Castaway		$8	$10	$14	James Stevenson		Green
2003	Corn Chowder		$8	$10	$14	James Stevenson		Green
2003	Runaway Horse!		$8	$10	$14	James Stevenson		Green
2004	Flying Feet At Mud Flat		$8	$10	$14	James Stevenson		Green
2004	No Laughing, No Smiling, No Giggling		$8	$10	$14	James Stevenson		FSG

Stobbs   William

Year	Title	VG-	VG	VG+	Fine	Author	Award	Pub
1951	Jack And The Beanstalk	$50	$70	$90		Walter De La Mare		Hulton
1957	De Soto, Finder Of The Mississippi	$35	$50	$60		Ronald Syme		Morrow
1961	Kashtanka And A Bundle Of Ballads	$50	$60	$80		Anton Chekhov	GM	Walck
1963	Francisco Pizarro	$35	$40	$60		Ronald Syme		Morrow
1963	Rex And Mistigri	$35	$40	$60		René Guillot		Bodley
1965	Sir Henry Morgan	$30	$40	$50		Ronald Syme		Morrow
1965	The Story Of The Three Bears	$30	$40	$50		William Stobbs (adapted)		Whittle
1965	The Story Of The Three Little Pigs	$30	$40	$50		William Stobbs (adapted)		Whittle
1966	Round The World Fairy Tales	$30	$40	$50		Amabel Williams-Ellis		FWarne
1966	The Canal Trip	$30	$40	$50		Joan E. Cass		AS
1967	The Golden Goose	$30	$40	$50		William Stobbs		McHill
1967	The Three Brothers	$30	$40	$50		Mollie Clarke		Follett
1968	Captain John Paul Jones	$30	$40	$50		Ronald Syme		Morrow
1968	Greyling	$30	$40	$50		Jane Yolen		World
1968	The Three Billy Goats Gruff	$30	$40	$50		Peter Christen Asbjønsen		McHill
1969	A Frog He Would A-Wooing Go	$25	$35	$50		Joan Cass		AS
1969	Amerigo Vespucci	$25	$35	$50		Ronald Syme		Morrow
1969	The Cats Go To Market	$25	$35	$50		Joan E. Cass		AS
1970	Henny-Penny		$25	$35	$50	William Stobbs		Follett
1970	The Magpie's Nest		$25	$35	$50	Joseph Jacobs		Follett
1970	Vancouver		$25	$35	$50	Ronald Syme		Morrow
1971	Bye, Baby Bunting		$25	$35	$50	Elizabeth Poston		Bodley
1971	Girls And Boys Come Out To Play		$25	$35	$50	Elizabeth Poston		Bodley
1971	I Had A Little Nut Tree		$25	$35	$50	Elizabeth Poston		Bodley
1971	Rumpelstiltskin		$25	$35	$50	Jacob & Wilhelm Grimm		Walck
1971	The Cats' Adventure With Car Thieves		$25	$35	$50	Joan E. Cass		AS
1971	The Crock Of Gold		$25	$35	$50	Joseph Jacobs		Follett
1971	Where Are You Going To, My Pretty Maid?		$25	$35	$50	Elizabeth Poston		Bodley
1972	Achilles		$25	$35	$50	Compton Mackenzie		Aldus
1972	Guleesh		$25	$35	$50	Joseph Jacobs		Follett
1972	Jason		$25	$35	$50	Compton Mackenzie		Aldus
1972	John Cabot And His Son Sebastian		$25	$35	$50	Ronald Syme		Morrow
1972	The Little Red Riding Hood		$25	$35	$50	Charles Perrault		Walck
1972	Theseus		$25	$35	$50	Compton Mackenzie		Aldus
1973	Johnny-Cake		$25	$35	$50	Joseph Jacobs		Viking
1973	Verrazano		$25	$35	$50	Ronald Syme		Morrow
1974	A Is An Apple Pie		$20	$30	$40	William Stobbs		Bodley
1974	Marquette And Joliet		$20	$30	$40	Ronald Syme		Morrow
1975	Puss In Boots		$20	$30	$40	Charles Perrault		McHill
1975	The Derby Ram		$20	$30	$40	William Stobbs		Bodley
1977	A Gaping Wide-Mouthed Waddling Frog		$20	$30	$40	William Stobbs		Pelham
1977	Old Mother Goose And The Golden Egg		$20	$30	$40	William Stobbs		Bodley
1978	Mr. Gosling And The Runaway Chair		$20	$30	$40	John A. Cunliffe		Deutsch
1978	The Hare And The Frogs		$20	$30	$40	Aesop		Bodley
1979	Mr Gosling And The Great Art Robbery		$18	$25	$35	John A. Cunliffe		Deutsch
1981	Animal Pictures		$18	$25	$35	William Stobbs		Bodley
1981	Rainbow Warrior's Bride		$18	$25	$35	Marcus Crouch		Pelham
1981	This Little Piggy		$18	$25	$35	William Stobbs		Bodley
1983	The Cat That Walked By Himself		$16	$25	$30	Rudyard Kipling		Bedrik
1983	The House That Jack Built		$16	$25	$30	William Stobbs		Oxford
1984	Gregory's Dog		$16	$25	$30	William Stobbs		Oxford
1984	Gregory's Garden		$16	$25	$30	William Stobbs		Oxford
1984	One, Two, Buckle My Shoe		$16	$25	$30	William Stobbs		Bodley

Stock   Catherine

Year	Title	VG-	VG	VG+	Fine	Author	Award	Pub
1979	Shortchanged By History		$25	$40	$50	Vernon Pizer		Putnam
1980	All-By-Herself		$20	$30	$40	Betty Baker		Green
1980	The Princess And The Pumpkin		$20	$30	$40	Maggie Duff		Macmil
1982	A Royal Gift		$16	$25	$30	Marietta Moskin		CM&G
1982	Isabella Mine		$16	$25	$30	Helen Reeder Cross		LL&S
1983	Posy		$16	$25	$30	Charlotte Pomerantz		Green
1984	Emma's Dragon Hunt		$30	$50	$60	Catherine Stock		LL&S
1984	Sampson, The Christmas Cat		$30	$50	$60	Catherine Stock		Putnam
1985	Bella Arabella		$16	$25	$30	Liza Fosburgh		4Winds
1985	Owl At Night		$16	$25	$30	Ann Whitford Paul		Putnam

Stock   Catherine

Year	Title	VG-	VG	VG+	Fine	Author	Award	Pub
1985	Sophie's Bucket		$20	$30	$40	Catherine Stock		LL&S
1986	Justin And The Best Biscuits In The World		$14	$20	$30	Mildred Pitts Walter		LL&S
1986	Street Talk		$14	$20	$30	Ann W. Turner		HM
1986	That New Pet!		$14	$20	$30	Alane Ferguson		LL&S
1986	Timothy Tall Feather		$14	$20	$30	Charlotte Pomerantz		Green
1987	Midnight Snowman		$14	$20	$30	Caroline Feller Bauer		Athenm
1987	Trot, Trot, To Boston		$14	$20	$30	Carol F. Ra		LL&S
1988	A Tiger Called Thomas		$14	$20	$30	Charlotte Zolotow		LL&S
1988	Alexander's Midnight Snack		$18	$25	$35	Catherine Stock		Clarion
1988	Better With Two		$14	$20	$30	Barbara M. Joosse		H&Row
1988	Sea Swan		$14	$20	$30	Kathryn Lasky		Macmil
1988	Something Is Going To Happen		$14	$20	$30	Charlotte Zolotow		H&Row
1988	Sophie's Knapsack		$14	$20	$30	Catherine Stock		LL&S
1989	Mr. Meredith And The Truly Remarkable Stone		$14	$20	$25	Grace Chetwin		BradP
1989	The Copycat		$14	$20	$25	Kathleen & Donald Hersom		Athenm
1990	Armien's Fishing Trip		$12	$18	$25	Catherine Stock		Morrow
1990	Christmas Time		$12	$18	$25	Catherine Stock		BradP
1990	Galimoto		$12	$18	$25	Karen Lynn Williams		LL&S
1990	Halloween Monster		$12	$18	$25	Catherine Stock		BradP
1990	Thanksgiving Treat		$12	$18	$25	Catherine Stock		BradP
1991	Birthday Present		$12	$18	$25	Catherine Stock		BradP
1991	Easter Surprise		$12	$18	$25	Catherine Stock		BradP
1991	Eddie's Friend Boodles		$12	$18	$25	Carolyn Haywood		Morrow
1991	Mara In The Morning		$12	$18	$25	C. B. Christiansen		Athenm
1991	Oh, Emma		$12	$18	$25	Barbara Baker		Dutton
1991	Secret Valentine		$12	$18	$25	Catherine Stock		BradP
1991	When The Woods Hum		$12	$18	$25	Joanne Ryder		Morrow
1992	An Island Christmas		$12	$18	$25	Lynn Joseph		Clarion
1992	Taking Turns		$12	$18	$25	Bernice Wolman		Athenm
1993	Snowed In		$12	$16	$20	Barbara Lucas		BradP
1993	The Evening King		$12	$16	$20	David LaRochelle		Athenm
1993	The Willow Umbrella		$12	$16	$20	Christine Barker Widman		Macmil
1993	Where Are You Going Manyoni?		$12	$16	$20	Catherine Stock		Morrow
1994	By The Dawn's Early Light		$12	$16	$20	Karen Ackerman		Athenm
1994	Tap-Tap		$12	$16	$20	Karen Lynn Williams		Clarion
1995	A Very Important Day		$10	$16	$20	Maggie Rugg Herold		Morrow
1995	Mama Moon		$10	$16	$20	Jeannine Ouellette-Howitz		Orchard
1995	Too Far Away To Touch		$10	$16	$20	Lesléa Newman		Clarion
1996	Nellie Bly's Monkey		$10	$16	$20	Joan W. Blos		Morrow
1996	Today Is The Day		$10	$16	$20	Nancy Riecken		HM
1997	Gus And Grandpa		$10	$16	$20	Claudia Mills		FSG
1997	Gus And Grandpa And The Christmas Cookies		$10	$16	$20	Claudia Mills		FSG
1997	Kele's Secret		$10	$16	$20	Tololwa Mollel		LodeS
1998	Gus And Grandpa At The Hospital		$10	$14	$18	Claudia Mills		FSG
1998	Gus And Grandpa Ride The Train		$10	$14	$18	Claudia Mills		FSG
1998	Painted Dreams		$10	$14	$18	Karen Lynn Williams		LL&S
1998	The Sanyasin's First Day		$10	$14	$18	Ned Shank		MCaven
1999	An Island Summer		$10	$14	$18	Catherine Stock		LL&S
1999	Gus And Grandpa And The Two-Wheeled Bike		$10	$14	$18	Claudia Mills		FSG
1999	Miss Viola And Uncle Ed Lee		$10	$14	$18	Alice Faye Duncan		Athenm
2000	Doll Baby		$8	$12	$16	Eve Bunting		Clarion
2000	Gus And Grandpa And Show-And-Tell		$8	$12	$16	Claudia Mills		FSG
2001	Gugu's House		$8	$12	$16	Catherine Stock		Clarion
2001	Gus And Grandpa At Basketball		$8	$12	$16	Claudia Mills		FSG
2002	Gus And Grandpa And The Halloween Costume		$8	$10	$14	Claudia Mills		FSG
2002	Is This A Sack Of Potatoes?		$8	$10	$14	Crescent Dragonwagon		MCaven
2003	A Spree In Paree		$8	$10	$14	Catherine Stock		Holiday
2003	Gus And Grandpa Go Fishing		$8	$10	$14	Claudia Mills		FSG
2004	Gus And Grandpa And The Piano Lesson		$8	$10	$14	Claudia Mills		FSG
2004	Kaddish For Grandpa In Jesus' Name, Amen		$8	$10	$14	James Howe		Athenm
2005	The Bora-Bora Dress		$6	$10	$12	Carole Lexa Schaefer		Candle

Stone   Helen

Year	Title	VG-	VG	VG+	Fine	Author	Award	Pub
1944	Horse Who Lived Upstairs	$60	$80	$100		Phyllis McGinley		Lippin
1945	Exciting Adventures Of Waldo	$60	$80	$100		Earl Burton		McHill

Stone Helen

Year	Title	VG-	VG	VG+	Fine	Author	Award	Pub
1945	The Plain Princess	$60	$80	$100		Phyllis McGinley		Lippin
1947	Taffy And Joe	$60	$80	$100		Earl Burton		Whittle
1948	All Around The Town	$180	$240	$300		Phyllis McGinley	CH	Lippin
1949	A Pussycat's Christmas	$120	$160	$220		Margaret Wise Brown		Crowell
1950	The Most Wonderful Doll In The World	$160	$220	$280		Phyllis McGinley	CH	Lippin
1951	The Bundle Book	$80	$100	$140		Ruth Krauss		H&B
1951	The Horse Who Had His Picture In The Paper	$50	$70	$90		Phyllis McGinley		Lippin
1951	Violets Are Blue	$50	$70	$90		Mary Kennedy		LL&S
1952	Little Ballet Dancer	$50	$70	$90		Monica Stirling		LL&S
1953	Little Witch	$50	$70	$90		Anna Elizabeth Bennett		Lippin
1954	The Twirly Skirt	$50	$70	$90		Martha Goldberg		Holiday
1956	A Tree For Me	$50	$70	$90		Norma Simon		Lippin
1956	Little Flower Girl	$50	$70	$90		Elizabeth Tate		LL&S
1956	Sally Saucer	$50	$70	$90		Edna S. Weiss		HM
1957	Tell Me Mr. Owl	$50	$70	$90		Doris Foster		LL&S
1959	Let It Rain	$50	$60	$80		Dorothy Koch		Holiday
1959	Lucy Mclockett	$50	$60	$80		Phyllis McGinley		Lippin
1963	Snow Is Falling	$50	$60	$80		Franklyn M. Branley		Crowell
1964	Watch Honeybees With Me	$50	$60	$80		Judy Hawes		Crowell

Summers Leo

Year	Title	VG-	VG	VG+	Fine	Author	Award	Pub
1965	The Horse That Swam Away	$30	$40	$50		Walter Farley		Random
1967	Kinji Goes Fishing	$25	$30	$40		Harriet Johnson		Singer
1967	Missy And The Mountain Lion	$25	$30	$40		Iris Vinton		Singer
1967	The Space Hut	$25	$30	$40		Ester Wier		StackP
1968	Off To The Races	$60	$80	$100		Fred Phleger		BB
1979	Seven True Horse Stories		$14	$20	$30	Margaret Davidson		Hastings

Sweat Lynn

Year	Title	VG-	VG	VG+	Fine	Author	Award	Pub
1966	Cluck, The Captain's Chicken	$40	$60	$70		Lynn Sweat		Macmil
1976	Good Work, Amelia Bedelia		$20	$30	$40	Peggy Parish		Green
1977	Teach Us, Amelia Bedelia		$20	$30	$40	Peggy Parish		Green
1979	Amelia Bedelia Helps Out		$18	$25	$35	Peggy Parish		Green
1981	Amelia Bedelia And The Baby		$18	$25	$35	Peggy Parish		Green
1985	Amelia Bedelia Goes Camping		$16	$25	$30	Peggy Parish		Green
1986	Merry Christmas, Amelia Bedelia		$14	$20	$30	Peggy Parish		Green
1990	One Good Horse		$12	$18	$25	Ann Herbert Scott		Green
1995	Good Driving, Amelia Bedelia		$10	$16	$20	Herman Parish		Green
1997	Bravo, Amelia Bedelia!		$10	$16	$20	Herman Parish		Green
1999	Amelia Bedelia 4 Mayor!		$10	$14	$18	Herman Parish		Green
2002	Calling Doctor Amelia Bedelia		$8	$10	$14	Herman Parish		Green
2003	Amelia Bedelia And The Christmas List		$8	$10	$14	Herman Parish		HFest
2003	Amelia Bedelia, Bookworm		$8	$10	$14	Herman Parish		Green
2004	Amelia Bedelia Goes Back To School		$8	$10	$14	Herman Parish		HFest
2004	Be My Valentine, Amelia Bedelia		$8	$10	$14	Herman Parish		HFest
2004	Happy Haunting, Amelia Bedelia		$8	$10	$14	Herman Parish		Green

Szekeres Cyndy

Year	Title	VG-	VG	VG+	Fine	Author	Award	Pub
1961	New Shoes	$50	$60	$80		Sam Vaughan		DoubleD
1961	When Homer Honked	$100	$120	$160		Jean Lee Latham		Macmil
1963	Walter, The Lazy Mouse	$50	$60	$80		Marjorie Flack		DoubleD
1965	The Girl Who Was A Cowboy	$40	$60	$70		Phyllis Krasilovsky		DoubleD
1966	Humpty Dumpty's Storybook	$60	$80	$100		Cyndy Szekeres		PMagP
1967	Michael, The Upstairs Dog	$40	$50	$70		Edward Ormondroyd		Dial
1968	Macaroni	$40	$50	$70		Kathleen Lombardo		Random
1968	Small Clown And Tiger	$40	$50	$70		Nancy Faulkner		DoubleD
1969	Brian's Secret Errand	$40	$50	$70		Joy Lonergan		DoubleD
1969	Jumper Goes To School	$40	$50	$70		Peggy Parish		S&S
1969	Moon Mouse	$40	$50	$70		Adelaide Holl		Random
1969	The Fattest Bear In The First Grade	$40	$50	$70		Barbara Rinkoff		Random
1970	Little Richard		$70	$100	$140	Patricia M. Scarry		AHP
1971	Little Richard And Prickles		$40	$60	$90	Patricia M. Scarry		AHP

Szekeres   Cyndy

Year	Title	VG-	VG	VG+	Fine	Author	Award	Pub
1971	No! No!		$30	$50	$60	Lois Myller		S&S
1971	Waggy And His Friends		$30	$50	$60	Patricia M. Scarry		AHP
1971	What Can You Do Without A Place To Play?		$30	$50	$60	Kathryn Hitte		PMagP
1972	Good Night, Orange Monster		$30	$50	$60	Betty Jean Lifton		Athenm
1972	James The Jaguar		$30	$50	$60	Mary H. Lystad		Putnam
1973	Bedtime For Bears		$30	$50	$60	Adelaide Holl		Garrard
1973	Four-Ring Three		$30	$50	$60	Miriam Anne Bourne		CM&G
1973	Halloween Parade		$30	$50	$60	Mary H. Lystad		Putnam
1973	More About Waggy		$30	$50	$60	Patricia M. Scarry		McHill
1973	Pippa Mouse		$30	$50	$60	Betty V, Boegehold		Knopf
1974	Goodbye, Hello		$30	$40	$60	Robert Welber		Pan
1974	Little Bat's Secret		$30	$40	$60	Kathy Darling		Garrard
1974	Maybe, A Mole		$30	$40	$60	Julia Cunningham		Pan
1975	Gus And Buster Work Things Out		$30	$40	$60	Andrew Bronin		CM&G
1975	Here's Pippa Again!		$30	$40	$60	Betty V, Boegehold		Knopf
1975	The Clumpets Go Sailing		$30	$40	$60	Jan Wahl		PMagP
1975	The Muffletump Storybook		$30	$40	$60	Jan Wahl		Follett
1975	The Muffletumps' Christmas Party		$30	$40	$60	Jan Wahl		Follett
1976	Edgemont		$30	$40	$60	Marjorie Weinman Sharmat		CM&G
1976	Great-Grandmother Cat Tales		$30	$40	$60	Jan Wahl		Pan
1977	Doctor Rabbit's Foundling		$25	$40	$50	Jan Wahl		Pan
1977	Five Little Foxes And The Snow		$25	$40	$50	Tony Johnston		Putnam
1977	Long Ago		$40	$60	$80	Cyndy Szekeres		McHill
1977	Night Noises & Other Mole And Troll Stories		$25	$40	$50	Tony Johnston		Putnam
1977	The Muffletumps' Halloween Scare		$25	$40	$50	Jan Wahl		Follett
1978	Brimhall Comes To Stay		$25	$40	$50	Judy Delton		LL&S
1978	Little Chick's Story		$25	$40	$50	Mary DeBall Kwitz		H&Row
1978	Small Bear Builds A Playhouse		$25	$40	$50	Adelaide Holl		Garrard
1978	Who Will Believe Tim Kitten?		$25	$40	$50	Jan Wahl		Pan
1979	Argentaybee And The Boonie		$25	$40	$50	Catherine Hiller		CM&G
1979	Doctor Rabbit's Lost Scout		$25	$40	$50	Jan Wahl		Pan
1979	Happy Birthday, Mole And Troll		$25	$40	$50	Tony Johnston		Putnam
1979	Pippa Pops Out!		$25	$40	$50	Betty V, Boegehold		Knopf
1979	The 329th Friend		$25	$40	$50	Marjorie Weinman Sharmat		4Winds
1980	Hurray For Pippa!		$25	$35	$50	Betty V, Boegehold		Knopf
1980	Ladybug And Dog And The Night Walk		$25	$35	$50	Polly Berrien Berends		Random
1980	Patsy Scarry's Big Bedtime Storybook		$25	$35	$50	Patricia M. Scarry		Random
1981	A Child's First Book Of Poems		$35	$50	$70	Cyndy Szekeres		Golden
1982	Honey Rabbit		$25	$35	$50	Margo Hopkins		Golden
1982	Pepper's Good & Bad Day		$25	$35	$50	Marci McGill		Golden
1982	Six Little Possums, A Birthday ABC		$25	$35	$50	Marci McGill		Golden
1982	The Night Before Christmas		$25	$35	$50	Clement C. Moore		Golden
1982	The Six Little Possums And The Babysitter		$25	$35	$50	Marci McGill		Golden
1982	The Six Little Possums At Home		$25	$35	$50	Marci McGill		Golden
1983	A Child's First Book Of Nursery Tales		$25	$35	$50	Selma G. Lanes (adapted)		Golden
1983	Cyndy Szekeres' A B C		$25	$35	$50	Cyndy Szekeres		Golden
1984	Baby Bear's Surprise		$20	$30	$40	Cyndy Szekeres		Golden
1984	Cyndy Szekeres' Counting Book 1 To 10		$20	$30	$40	Cyndy Szekeres		Western
1984	Puppy Too Small		$20	$30	$40	Cyndy Szekeres		Golden
1984	Scaredy Cat		$20	$30	$40	Cyndy Szekeres		Golden
1984	Thumpity Thump Gets Dressed		$20	$30	$40	Cyndy Szekeres		Western
1985	Good Night, Sammy		$20	$30	$40	Cyndy Szekeres		Golden
1985	Hide-And-Seek Duck		$20	$30	$40	Cyndy Szekeres		Golden
1985	Nothing-To-Do Puppy		$20	$30	$40	Cyndy Szekeres		Golden
1985	Suppertime For Frieda Fuzzypaws		$20	$30	$40	Cyndy Szekeres		Golden
1986	Little Bear Counts His Favorite Things		$20	$30	$40	Cyndy Szekeres		Golden
1986	Melanie Mouse's Moving Day		$20	$30	$40	Cyndy Szekeres		Golden
1986	Puppy Lost		$20	$30	$40	Cyndy Szekeres		Golden
1986	Sammy's Special Day		$20	$30	$40	Cyndy Szekeres		Golden
1987	Cyndy Szekeres' Book Of Nursery Tales		$20	$30	$40	Selma G. Lanes		Golden
1987	Cyndy Szekeres' Book Of Poems		$20	$30	$40	Cyndy Szekeres		Golden
1987	Cyndy Szekeres' Mother Goose Rhymes		$20	$30	$40	Cyndy Szekeres		Golden
1988	Cyndy Szekeres' Book Of Fairy Tales		$18	$25	$35	Cyndy Szekeres		Western
1988	Cyndy Szekeres' Good Night, Sweet Mouse		$18	$25	$35	Cyndy Szekeres		Golden
1989	A Busy Day		$18	$25	$35	Cyndy Szekeres		Western
1989	A Fine Mouse Band		$18	$25	$35	Cyndy Szekeres		Western
1989	Cyndy Szekeres' Favorite Two-Minute Stories		$18	$25	$35	Cyndy Szekeres		Western

Szekeres   Cyndy

Year	Title	VG-	VG	VG+	Fine	Author	Award	Pub
1989	Here's Pippa		$18	$25	$35	Betty V, Boegehold		Knopf
1989	Moving Day		$18	$25	$35	Cyndy Szekeres		Western
1990	A Mouse Mess		$16	$25	$30	Cyndy Szekeres		Western
1990	Cyndy Szekeres' Nice Animals		$16	$25	$30	Cyndy Szekeres		Western
1990	Things Bunny Sees		$16	$25	$30	Cyndy Szekeres		Golden
1990	What Bunny Loves		$16	$25	$30	Cyndy Szekeres		Golden
1991	Favorite Fairy Tales		$16	$25	$30	Selma G. Lanes		Western
1991	Ladybug, Ladybug, Where Are You?		$16	$25	$30	Cyndy Szekeres		Western
1991	Little Puppy Learns To Share		$16	$25	$30	Cyndy Szekeres		Western
1992	Cyndy Szekeres' Colors		$16	$25	$30	Cyndy Szekeres		Golden
1992	Favorite Mother Goose Rhymes		$16	$25	$30	Cyndy Szekeres		Golden
1992	Fluffy Duckling		$16	$25	$30	Cyndy Szekeres		Western
1992	Teeny Mouse Counts Herself		$16	$25	$30	Cyndy Szekeres		Western
1992	The Whispering Rabbit		$20	$30	$40	Margaret Wise Brown		Western
1993	I Am A Kitten		$16	$25	$30	Ole Risom		Golden
1993	Kisses		$16	$25	$30	Cyndy Szekeres		Western
1993	Little Puppy Cleans His Room		$16	$25	$30	Cyndy Szekeres		Western
1993	The Tale Of Peter Rabbit		$16	$25	$30	Beatrix Potter		Golden
1994	Baby Animals		$14	$20	$30	Cyndy Szekeres		Western
1994	I Am A Puppy		$14	$20	$30	Ole Risom		Western
1995	Christmas Mouse		$14	$20	$25	Cyndy Szekeres		Golden
1996	Giggles		$12	$18	$25	Cyndy Szekeres		Western
1997	I Love My Busy Book		$12	$18	$25	Cyndy Szekeres		Scholas
1997	The Mouse That Jack Built		$12	$18	$25	Cyndy Szekeres		Scholas
1997	Yes, Virginia, There Is A Santa Claus		$12	$18	$25	Francis P. Church		Scholas
1998	A Very Merry Mouse Country Christmas		$12	$16	$20	Cyndy Szekeres		Scholas
1998	I Can Count 100 Bunnies		$12	$16	$20	Cyndy Szekeres		Scholas
1998	Kisses		$12	$16	$20	Cyndy Szekeres		Golden
1998	The Deep Blue Sky Twinkles With Stars		$12	$16	$20	Cyndy Szekeres		Scholas
1999	A Small Child's Book Of Cozy Poems		$12	$16	$20	Cyndy Szekeres		Scholas
1999	A Small Child's Book Of Prayers		$12	$16	$20	Cyndy Szekeres		Scholas
2000	Learn To Count		$10	$14	$18	Cyndy Szekeres		Scholas
2000	Toby Counts His Marbles		$10	$14	$18	Cyndy Szekeres		LSimon
2000	Toby's Alphabet Walk		$10	$14	$18	Cyndy Szekeres		LSimon
2000	Toby's Flying Lesson		$10	$14	$18	Cyndy Szekeres		LSimon
2000	Toby's Holiday Hugs And Kisses		$10	$14	$18	Cyndy Szekeres		LSimon
2000	Toby's New Brother		$10	$14	$18	Cyndy Szekeres		LSimon
2000	Toby's Rainbow Clothes		$10	$14	$18	Cyndy Szekeres		LSimon
2000	Wilbur Bunny's Funny Friends A To Z		$10	$14	$18	Cyndy Szekeres		Scholas
2001	Do You Love Me?		$10	$14	$18	Cyndy Szekeres		LSimon
2001	Santa Toby's Busy Christmas		$10	$14	$18	Cyndy Szekeres		LSimon
2001	Toby's Good Night		$10	$14	$18	Cyndy Szekeres		LSimon
2001	Toby's Please And Thank You		$10	$14	$18	Cyndy Szekeres		LSimon

Taback   Simms

Year	Title	VG-	VG	VG+	Fine	Author	Award	Pub
1964	Jabberwocky	$50	$60	$80		Lewis Carroll		HQuist
1965	Please Share That Peanut!	$40	$60	$70		Sesyle Joslin		HBrace
1967	Too Much Noise	$40	$50	$70		Ann McGovern		HM
1970	There's Motion Everywhere		$30	$50	$60	John Travers Moore		HM
1976	Euphonia And The Flood		$30	$40	$60	Mary Calhoun		PMagP
1977	Laughing Together : Giggles And Grins		$25	$40	$50	Barbara K. Walker		4Winds
1983	Fishy Riddles		$25	$35	$50	Katy Hall		Dial
1984	Where Is My Dinner?		$20	$30	$40	Harriet Ziefert		G&D
1984	Where Is My Friend?		$20	$30	$40	Harriet Ziefert		G&D
1984	Where Is My House?		$20	$30	$40	Harriet Ziefert		G&D
1985	On Our Way To The Barn		$20	$30	$40	Harriet Ziefert		H&Row
1985	On Our Way To The Forest		$20	$30	$40	Harriet Ziefert		H&Row
1985	On Our Way To The Water		$20	$30	$40	Harriet Ziefert		H&Row
1985	On Our Way To The Zoo		$20	$30	$40	Harriet Ziefert		H&Row
1986	Buggy Riddles		$20	$30	$40	Katy Hall		Dial
1987	Jason's Bus Ride		$20	$30	$40	Harriet Ziefert		VK
1990	Noisy Barn!		$16	$25	$30	Harriet Ziefert		H&Row
1990	Snakey Riddles		$16	$25	$30	Katy Hall		Dial
1990	Zoo Parade!		$16	$25	$30	Harriet Ziefert		H&Row
1992	Spacey Riddles		$16	$25	$30	Katy Hall		Dial

Taback   Simms

Year	Title	VG-	VG	VG+	Fine	Author	Award	Pub
1994	Road Builders		$14	$20	$30	B. G. Hennessy		Viking
1994	Where Is My Baby?		$14	$20	$30	Harriet Ziefert		HFest
1995	Sam's Wild West Show		$14	$20	$25	Nancy Antle		Dial
1996	Two Little Witches		$12	$18	$25	Harriet Ziefert		Candle
1996	Who Said Moo?		$12	$18	$25	Harriet Ziefert		HFest
1997	There Was An Old Lady Who Swallowed A Fly		$30	$40	$60	Simms Taback	CH	Viking
1998	When I First Came To This Land		$12	$16	$20	Harriet Ziefert		Putnam
1999	Joseph Had A Little Overcoat		$40	$60	$80	Simms Taback	CM	Viking
2002	This Is The House That Jack Built		$8	$12	$16	Simms Taback		Putnam

Tafuri   Nancy

Year	Title	VG-	VG	VG+	Fine	Author	Award	Pub
1978	My Hands Can		$20	$30	$40	Jean Holzenthaler		Dutton
1981	The Piney Woods Peddler		$14	$20	$25	George Shannon		Green
1982	Across The Stream		$14	$20	$25	Mirra Ginsburg		Green
1982	If I Had A Paka: Poems In Eleven Languages		$14	$20	$25	Charlotte Pomerantz		Green
1982	The Song		$14	$20	$25	Charlotte Zolotow		Green
1983	All Year Long		$14	$20	$25	Nancy Tafuri		Green
1983	Early Morning In The Barn		$14	$20	$25	Nancy Tafuri		Green
1984	All Asleep		$12	$18	$25	Charlotte Pomerantz		Green
1984	Coconut		$12	$18	$25	Crescent Dragonwagon		H&Row
1984	Have You Seen My Duckling?		$40	$60	$90	Nancy Tafuri	CH	Green
1985	Nata		$12	$18	$25	Helen Griffith		Green
1985	Rabbit's Morning		$12	$18	$25	Nancy Tafuri		Green
1986	Who's Counting?		$12	$16	$20	Nancy Tafuri		Green
1987	Do Not Disturb		$12	$16	$20	Nancy Tafuri		Green
1987	Four Brave Sailors		$12	$16	$20	Helen Griffith		Green
1987	In A Red House		$12	$16	$20	Nancy Tafuri		Green
1987	My Friends		$12	$16	$20	Nancy Tafuri		Green
1987	Where We Sleep		$12	$16	$20	Mirra Ginsburg		Green
1988	Junglewalk		$12	$16	$20	Nancy Tafuri		Green
1988	One Wet Jacket		$12	$16	$20	Nancy Tafuri		Green
1988	Spots, Feathers, And Curly Tails		$12	$16	$20	Nancy Tafuri		Green
1988	Two New Sneakers		$12	$16	$20	Nancy Tafuri		Green
1989	Flap Your Wings And Try		$12	$16	$20	Charlotte Pomerantz		Green
1989	The Ball Bounced		$12	$16	$20	Nancy Tafuri		Green
1990	Follow Me!		$10	$16	$20	Nancy Tafuri		Green
1992	Asleep, Asleep		$10	$16	$20	Mirra Ginsburg		Green
1993	Everything Has A Place		$10	$16	$20	Patricia Lillie		Green
1994	This Is The Farmer		$10	$14	$18	Nancy Tafuri		Green
1995	The Barn Party		$10	$14	$18	Nancy Tafuri		Green
1995	The Biggest Boy		$10	$14	$18	Kevin Henkes		Green
1996	The Brass Ring		$8	$12	$16	Nancy Tafuri		Green
1997	What The Sun Sees, What The Moon Sees		$8	$12	$16	Nancy Tafuri		Green
1998	Counting To Christmas		$8	$12	$16	Nancy Tafuri		Scholas
1998	I Love You, Little One		$8	$12	$16	Nancy Tafuri		Scholas
1999	Snowy Flowy Blowy		$8	$12	$16	Gregory Gander		Scholas
2000	Will You Be My Friend?		$8	$10	$14	Nancy Tafuri		Scholas
2001	Silly Little Goose!		$8	$10	$14	Nancy Tafuri		Scholas
2001	Where Did Bunny Go?		$8	$10	$14	Nancy Tafuri		Scholas
2002	Mama's Little Bears		$8	$10	$14	Nancy Tafuri		Scholas
2002	The Donkey's Christmas Song		$8	$10	$14	Nancy Tafuri		Scholas
2003	You Are Special, Little One		$8	$10	$14	Nancy Tafuri		Scholas

Talbott   Hudson

Year	Title	VG-	VG	VG+	Fine	Author	Award	Pub
1987	We're Back!		$14	$20	$30	Hudson Talbott		Crown
1988	Into The Woods		$50	$80	$100	Stephen Sondheim		Crown
1989	Going Hollywood		$12	$16	$20	Hudson Talbott		Crown
1991	The Lady At Liberty		$10	$16	$20	Hudson Talbott		Avon
1991	The Sword In The Stone		$10	$16	$20	Hudson Talbott		Morrow
1992	Your Pet Dinosaur		$10	$16	$20	Hudson Talbott		Morrow
1993	The Wildest Show On Earth		$10	$16	$20	Francine Hughes		G&D
1995	King Arthur And The Round Table		$10	$14	$18	Hudson Talbott		Morrow
1996	Amazon Diary		$8	$12	$16	Hudson Talbott		Putnam
1996	Excalibur		$8	$12	$16	Hudson Talbott		Morrow

Talbott   Hudson

Year	Title	VG-	VG	VG+	Fine	Author	Award	Pub
1999	Lancelot		$8	$12	$16	Hudson Talbott		Morrow
1999	O'Sullivan Stew		$8	$12	$16	Hudson Talbott		Putnam
2000	Forging Freedom		$8	$10	$14	Hudson Talbott		Putnam
2001	Leonardo's Horse		$8	$10	$14	Jean Fritz		Putnam
2003	Safari Journal		$8	$10	$14	Hudson Talbott		Harcort
2004	The Lost Colony Of Roanoke		$6	$10	$12	Jean Fritz		Putnam

Tavares   Matt

Year	Title	VG-	VG	VG+	Fine	Author	Award	Pub
2000	Zachary's Ball		$8	$12	$16	Matt Tavares		Candle
2002	Twas The Night Before Christmas		$8	$10	$14	Clement C. Moore		Candle
2004	Oliver's Game		$6	$10	$12	Matt Tavares		Candle
2005	Mudball		$6	$10	$12	Matt Tavares		Candle

Taylor   E.J.

Year	Title	VG-	VG	VG+	Fine	Author	Award	Pub
1984	Goose Eggs		$12	$18	$25	E.J. Taylor		Knopf
1984	Ivy Cottage		$12	$18	$25	E.J. Taylor		Knopf
1985	Rag Doll Press		$12	$18	$25	E.J. Taylor		Candle
1985	The Thorn Witch		$12	$18	$25	E.J. Taylor		Knopf

Teague   Mark

Year	Title	VG-	VG	VG+	Fine	Author	Award	Pub
1989	The Trouble With The Johnsons		$25	$40	$50	Mark Teague		Scholas
1990	Moog-Moog, Space Barber		$16	$25	$30	Mark Teague		Scholas
1991	Frog Medicine		$12	$18	$25	Mark Teague		Scholas
1992	The Field Beyond The Outfield		$12	$18	$25	Mark Teague		Scholas
1993	No Moon, No Milk!		$12	$16	$20	Chris Babcock		Crown
1994	Pigsty		$12	$16	$20	Mark Teague		Scholas
1994	Three Terrible Trins		$12	$16	$20	Dick King-Smith		Crown
1995	How I Spent My Summer Vacation		$10	$16	$20	Mark Teague		Crown
1995	The Iguana Brothers, A Perfect Day		$10	$16	$20	Tony Johnston		BSP
1996	Mr. Potter's Pet		$10	$16	$20	Dick King-Smith		Hyper
1996	The Flying Dragon Room		$10	$16	$20	Audrey Wood		BSP
1996	The Secret Shortcut		$10	$16	$20	Mark Teague		Scholas
1997	Baby Tamer		$10	$16	$20	Mark Teague		Scholas
1997	Poppleton		$18	$25	$35	Cynthia Rylant		BSP
1997	Poppleton And Friends: Book Two		$15	$20	$30	Cynthia Rylant		BSP
1998	Lost And Found		$10	$14	$18	Mark Teague		Scholas
1998	Poppleton Everyday		$10	$15	$20	Cynthia Rylant		BSP
1998	Poppleton Forever		$10	$15	$20	Cynthia Rylant		BSP
1998	Sweet Dream Pie		$10	$14	$18	Audrey Wood		BSP
1999	One Halloween Night		$10	$14	$18	Mark Teague		Scholas
1999	Poppleton In Fall		$10	$14	$18	Cynthia Rylant		BSP
2000	How Do Dinosaurs Say Good Night?		$15	$22	$30	Jane Yolen		BSP
2000	Poppleton Has Fun		$9	$14	$18	Cynthia Rylant		BSP
2001	First Graders From Mars		$8	$12	$16	Shana Corey		Scholas
2001	Poppleton In Winter		$8	$12	$16	Cynthia Rylant		BSP
2001	The Great Gracie Chase		$8	$12	$16	Cynthia Rylant		BSP
2002	Dear Mrs. Larue		$8	$10	$14	Mark Teague		Scholas
2003	How Do Dinosaurs Get Well Soon?		$8	$12	$16	Jane Yolen		BSP
2004	Detective Larue		$8	$10	$14	Mark Teague		Scholas
2004	How Do Dinosaurs Clean Their Rooms?		$8	$12	$16	Jane Yolen		BSP
2004	How Do Dinosaurs Count To Ten?		$8	$12	$16	Jane Yolen		BSP

Tejima

Year	Title	VG-	VG	VG+	Fine	Author	Award	Pub
1986	The Bear's Autumn		$20	$30	$40	Keizaburo Tejima		GreenT
1987	Fox's Dream		$20	$30	$40	Keizaburo Tejima	NYT	Philo
1987	Owl Lake		$14	$20	$30	Keizaburo Tejima		Philo
1988	Swan Sky		$18	$25	$35	Keizaburo Tejima	NYT	Philo
1989	Woodpecker Forest		$14	$20	$25	Keizaburo Tejima		Philo
1990	Ho-Limlim		$12	$18	$25	Keizaburo Tejima		Philo

Tenggren   Gustaf

Year	Title	VG-	VG	VG+	Fine	Author	Award	Pub
1923	A Wonder-Book And Tanglewood Tales	$140	$200	$240		Nathaniel Hawthorne		HM
1923	D'Aulnoy's Fairy Tales	$220	$280	$360		Marie-Catherine Aulnoy		DMcKay
1924	The Good Dog Book	$220	$280	$360		Gustaf Tenggren		HM
1924	The Red Fairy Book	$140	$200	$240		Andrew Lang		DMcKay
1925	A Dog Of Flanders	$100	$120	$160		Tenggren Ouida		Macmil
1926	Juan And Juanita	$100	$120	$160		Frances C. Baylor		HM
1927	Small Fry And The Winged Horse	$100	$120	$160		Ruth Campbell		Volland
1931	Pirate's Loot	$90	$120	$160		Carolyn Rodgers		Sears
1932	How They Carried The Goods	$90	$120	$160		Charles Geoffrey Muller		Sears
1932	Ring Of The Nibelung	$90	$120	$160		Gertrude Henderson		Knopf
1932	Sven The Wise	$90	$120	$160		Alicia O'Reardon Overbeck		H&B
1933	Seldom And The Golden Cheese	$80	$120	$140		Joseph Schrank		DoddM
1935	Anderson's Fairy Tales	$120	$160	$220		Hans Christian Andersen		AC
1940	Mother Goose	$140	$200	$240		Gustaf Tenggren		LBrown
1941	Favorite Hymns	$70	$90	$120		Inez Bertail		GardenC
1942	Bedtime Stories	$160	$220	$280		Gustaf Tenggren		Golden
1942	The Poky Little Puppy	$220	$300	$380		Janette Lowrey		Golden
1942	The Tenggren Tell-It-Again Book	$90	$120	$160		Katharine Gibson		LBrown
1943	Sing For Christmas	$90	$120	$160		Opal Wheeler		Dutton
1943	Stories From The Great Metropolitan Operas	$90	$120	$160		Helen Dike		Random
1943	The Lively Little Rabbit	$140	$180	$240		Georges Duplaix		Golden
1943	The Story Of England	$70	$90	$120		Beatrice Curtis Brown		Random
1944	Sing For America	$90	$120	$160		Opal Wheeler		Dutton
1944	Tenggren's Story Book	$140	$180	$220		Gustaf Tenggren		Golden
1944	The Little Match Girl	$90	$120	$160		Hans Christian Andersen		G&D
1946	Farm Stories	$140	$180	$220		Kathryn & Byron Jackson		Golden
1946	The Shy Little Kitten	$140	$180	$220		Cathleen Schurr		Golden
1947	The Big Brown Bear	$60	$80	$100		Georges Duplaix		Golden
1947	The Saggy Baggy Elephant	$60	$80	$100		Kathryn & Byron Jackson		Golden
1948	Little Black Sambo	$200	$260	$320		Helen Bannerman		Golden
1948	Tenggren's Cowboys And Indians	$80	$120	$140		Kathryn & Byron Jackson		Golden
1950	Pirates, Ships And Sailors	$80	$120	$140		Kathryn & Byron Jackson		Golden
1950	The Little Trapper	$80	$120	$140		Kathryn & Byron Jackson		Golden
1951	The Night Before Christmas	$50	$70	$90		Clement C. Moore		Golden
1952	Tawny Scrawny Lion	$50	$70	$90		Kathryn Jackson		Golden
1953	Tenggren's Jack And The Beanstalk	$50	$70	$90		Gustaf Tenggren		Golden
1953	Topsy Turvy Circus	$50	$70	$90		Georges Duplaix		Golden
1955	Snow White And Rose Red	$50	$70	$90		Gustaf Tenggren		Golden
1955	Tenggren's The Giant With Three Golden Hairs	$50	$70	$90		Jacob & Wilhelm Grimm		Golden

Thaler   Mike

Year	Title	VG-	VG	VG+	Fine	Author	Award	Pub
1961	Magic Boy	$50	$60	$80		Mike Thaler		H&B
1962	The Clown's Smile	$35	$40	$60		Mike Thaler		Harper
1963	Penny Pencil	$35	$40	$60		Mike Thaler		H&Row
1963	The King's Flower	$35	$40	$60		Mike Thaler		Orion
1964	Moonboy	$35	$40	$60		Mike Thaler		H&Row
1976	Knock Knocks, The Most Ever		$20	$30	$40	William Cole		FWatts
1976	Soup With Quackers		$20	$30	$40	Mike Thaler		FWatts
1977	Knock Knocks You've Never Heard Before		$20	$30	$40	William Cole		FWatts
1977	Never Tickle A Turtle		$20	$30	$40	Mike Thaler		FWatts
1978	Give Up?		$20	$30	$40	William Cole		FWatts
1978	Madge's Magic Show		$20	$30	$40	Mike Thaler		H&Row
1978	The Chocolate Marshmelephant Sundae		$20	$30	$40	Mike Thaler		FWatts
1978	The Yellow Brick Toad		$20	$30	$40	Mike Thaler		DoubleD
1987	Mr. Bananahead At Home		$14	$20	$30	Mike Thaler		Scholas

Tharlet   Eve

Year	Title	VG-	VG	VG+	Fine	Author	Award	Pub
1982	The Grasshopper And The Ants		$25	$35	$50	Eve Tharlet		SBurdet
1983	The Golden Goose		$16	$25	$30	Paula Franklin		SBurdet
1985	Dizzy From Fools		$16	$25	$30	M. L. Miller		Picture
1987	The Princess And The Pea		$14	$20	$30	Hans Christian Andersen		Picture
1988	The Wishing Table		$14	$20	$30	Jacob & Wilhelm Grimm		Picture
1989	Little Pig, Big Trouble		$14	$20	$25	Eve Tharlet		Picture
1989	The Brave Little Tailor		$14	$20	$25	Jacob & Wilhelm Grimm		Picture

Tharlet   Eve

Year	Title	VG-	VG	VG+	Fine	Author	Award	Pub
1990	Christmas Won't Wait		$12	$18	$25	Eve Tharlet		Picture
1991	Simon And The Holy Night		$12	$18	$25	Andrew Clements		Picture
1992	Jack In Luck		$12	$18	$25	Jacob & Wilhelm Grimm		Picture
1994	I Wish I Were-- A Baby		$12	$16	$20	Eve Tharlet		NSBooks
1994	I Wish I Were-- A Bird		$12	$16	$20	Eve Tharlet		NSBooks
1994	I Wish I Were-- A Lion		$12	$16	$20	Eve Tharlet		NSBooks
1994	I Wish I Were-- A Mouse		$12	$16	$20	Eve Tharlet		NSBooks
1996	What Have You Done, Davy?		$10	$16	$20	Brigitte Weninger		NSBooks
1996	Where Have You Gone, Davy?		$10	$16	$20	Brigitte Weninger		NSBooks
1997	Will You Mind The Baby, Davy?		$10	$16	$20	Brigitte Weninger		NSBooks
1998	Hans Im Glück		$10	$14	$18	Jacob & Wilhelm Grimm		Neuge
1998	Merry Christmas, Davy!		$10	$14	$18	Brigitte Weninger		NSBooks
1998	What's The Matter, Davy?		$10	$14	$18	Brigitte Weninger		NSBooks
1999	Why Are You Fighting, Davy?		$10	$14	$18	Brigitte Weninger		NSBooks
2000	Happy Birthday, Davy		$8	$12	$16	Brigitte Weninger		NSBooks
2000	How Will We Get To The Beach?		$8	$12	$16	Brigitte Luciani		NSBooks
2000	The Emperor's New Clothes		$8	$12	$16	Hans Christian Andersen		NSBooks
2001	Happy Easter, Davy!		$8	$12	$16	Brigitte Weninger		NSBooks
2001	Hugs And Kisses		$8	$12	$16	Christophe Loupy		NSBooks
2002	Davy, Help! It's A Ghost!		$8	$10	$14	Brigitte Weninger		NSBooks
2003	A Baby For Davy		$8	$10	$14	Brigitte Weninger		NSBooks
2003	Davy's Christmas Gift		$8	$10	$14	Brigitte Weninger		NSBooks
2003	Don't Fight, Davy		$8	$10	$14	Brigitte Weninger		NSBooks
2003	Don't Worry, Wags		$8	$10	$14	Christophe Loupy		NSBooks
2003	No Hugs For Davy		$8	$10	$14	Brigitte Weninger		NSBooks
2004	Davy In The Middle		$8	$10	$14	Brigitte Weninger		NSBooks

Thompson   Colin

Year	Title	VG-	VG	VG+	Fine	Author	Award	Pub
1992	The Paper Bag Prince		$30	$40	$60	Colin Thompson		Knopf
1993	Looking For Atlantis		$16	$25	$30	Colin Thompson		MacRae
1993	Pictures Of Home		$16	$25	$30	Colin Thompson		GreenT
1994	Ruby		$14	$20	$30	Colin Thompson		Knopf
1995	How To Live Forever		$14	$20	$25	Colin Thompson		Knopf
1996	The Tower To The Sun		$12	$18	$25	Colin Thompson		Knopf
1998	The Paradise Garden		$12	$16	$20	Colin Thompson		Knopf
1999	The Last Alchemist		$12	$16	$20	Colin Thompson		Knopf
1999	The Staircase Cat		$12	$16	$20	Colin Thompson		Hodder

Titherington   Jeanne

Year	Title	VG-	VG	VG+	Fine	Author	Award	Pub
1981	The Chronicles Of Pantouflia		$18	$25	$35	Andrew Lang		Godine
1982	A Taste For Quiet & Other Disquieting Tales		$14	$20	$25	Judith Gorog		Philo
1982	The Story-Teller		$14	$20	$25	Saki		Godine
1984	It's Snowing! It's Snowing!		$12	$18	$25	Jack Prelutsky		Green
1985	Big World, Small World		$16	$25	$30	Jeanne Titherington		Green
1986	Pumpkin, Pumpkin		$12	$16	$20	Jeanne Titherington		Green
1987	A Place For Ben		$12	$16	$20	Jeanne Titherington		Green
1988	Where Are You Going, Emma?		$12	$16	$20	Jeanne Titherington		Green
1989	A Child's Prayer		$12	$16	$20	Jeanne Titherington		Green
1992	Baby's Boat		$10	$16	$20	Jeanne Titherington		Green
1995	Sophy And Auntie Pearl		$10	$14	$18	Jeanne Titherington		Green
2001	Bonkers Fellini		$8	$10	$14	Jeanne Titherington		Green

Tobey   B.

Year	Title	VG-	VG	VG+	Fine	Author	Award	Pub
1965	I Wish That I Had Duck Feet	$300	$400	$500		Theo LeSieg (pseud/Seuss)		BB
1966	Don And Donna Go To Bat	$90	$120	$160		Al Perkins		BB
1968	Chitty Chitty Bang Bang	$80	$120	$140		Al Perkins (adapted)		BB

Tomes   Margot

Year	Title	VG-	VG	VG+	Fine	Author	Award	Pub
1965	In The Woods, In The Meadow, In The Sky	$40	$60	$70		Aileen Fisher		Scribnr
1967	Marzipan Day On Bridget Lane	$30	$40	$50		Sylvia Cassedy		DoubleD
1968	For Pepita, An Orange Tree	$30	$40	$50		Claire Oleson		DoubleD

Tomes   Margot

Year	Title	VG-	VG	VG+	Fine	Author	Award	Pub
1968	Joe And The Talking Christmas Tree	$30	$40	$50		Dale Fife		CM
1968	Size, Distance, Weight	$30	$40	$50		Solveig Paulson Russell		Walck
1969	I Saw Three Ships	$25	$35	$50		Elizabeth Goudge		CM
1970	A Secret House		$25	$35	$50	Patricia Lee Gauch		CM
1970	One, Two, Three, And Many		$25	$35	$50	Solveig Paulson Russell		Walck
1971	Plenty For Three		$25	$35	$50	Liesel Moak Skorpen		CM&G
1972	Aaron And The Green Mountain Boys		$25	$35	$50	Patricia Lee Gauch		CM&G
1972	The Secret Of The Sachem's Tree		$25	$35	$50	F. N. Monjo		CM&G
1973	And Then What Happened, Paul Revere!		$25	$35	$50	Jean Fritz		CM&G
1973	Lysbet And The Fire Kittens		$25	$35	$50	Marietta Moskin		CM&G
1974	Everything Under A Mushroom		$20	$30	$40	Ruth Krauss		4Winds
1974	King George's Head Was Made Of Lead		$20	$30	$40	F. N. Monjo		CM&G
1974	This Time, Tempe Wick?		$20	$30	$40	Patricia Lee Gauch		CM&G
1975	Becky And The Bear		$20	$30	$40	Dorothy Van Woerkom		Putnam
1975	Where Was Patrick Henry On The 29th Of May?		$20	$30	$40	Jean Fritz		CM&G
1976	By George, Bloomers!		$20	$30	$40	Judith St. George		CM&G
1976	Little Sister And The Month Brothers		$20	$30	$40	Beatrice S. De Regniers		Seabury
1976	What's The Big Idea, Ben Franklin?		$20	$30	$40	Jean Fritz		CM&G
1977	Jack And The Wonder Beans		$20	$30	$40	James Still		Putnam
1977	Phoebe And The General		$20	$30	$40	Judith Berry Griffin		CM&G
1977	Prize Performance		$20	$30	$40	Aileen Fisher		Bowmar
1977	Those Foolish Molboes		$20	$30	$40	Lillian Bason		CM&G
1978	A Curiosity For The Curious		$20	$30	$40	Helen Reeder Cross		CM&G
1978	Giant Poems		$20	$30	$40	Daisy Wallace		Holiday
1978	Jorinda And Joringel		$25	$40	$50	Wanda Gág		CM&G
1978	The Halloween Pumpkin Smasher		$20	$30	$40	Judith St. George		Putnam
1979	Everyone Is Good For Something		$18	$25	$35	Beatrice S. De Regniers		HM
1979	The Sorcerer's Apprentice		$25	$40	$50	Wanda Gág		CM&G
1979	The Teeny, Tiny Witches		$18	$25	$35	Jan Wahl		Putnam
1979	Turtle And Snail		$18	$25	$35	Zibby Oneal		Lippin
1980	Clever Gretchen & Other Forgotten Folktales		$18	$25	$35	Alison Lurie		Crowell
1980	Garlanda		$18	$25	$35	Penny Pollock		Putnam
1980	Ty's One-Man Band		$18	$25	$35	Mildred Pitts Walter		4Winds
1980	Where Do You Think You're Going, Chris Columbus?		$18	$25	$35	Jean Fritz		Putnam
1981	Sara Crewe		$18	$25	$35	Frances Hodgson Burnett		Putnam
1981	The Mysterious Girl In The Garden		$18	$25	$35	Judith St. George		Putnam
1982	Anna, Grandpa, And The Big Storm		$16	$25	$30	Carla Stevens		Clarion
1982	Chimney Sweeps		$16	$25	$30	James Giblin		Crowell
1982	Pot Full Of Luck		$16	$25	$30	Anne K. Rose		LL&S
1982	Wanda Gág's The Six Swans		$16	$25	$30	Wanda Gág		CM&G
1983	Cecelia And The Blue Mountain Boy		$16	$25	$30	Ellen Harvey Showell		LL&S
1984	A Song I Sang To You		$16	$25	$30	Myra Cohn Livingston		HBJ
1984	If There Were Dreams To Sell		$16	$25	$30	Barbara Lalicki		LL&S
1984	The Witch's Hat		$16	$25	$30	Tony Johnston		Putnam
1985	The Earth Gnome		$16	$25	$30	Wanda Gág		CM
1986	Snowy Day		$14	$20	$30	Caroline Feller Bauer		Lippin
1986	The Little Jewel Box		$14	$20	$30	Marianna Mayer		Dial
1987	Everything Glistens And Everything Sings		$14	$20	$30	Charlotte Zolotow		HBJ
1987	New Year's Poems		$14	$20	$30	Myra Cohn Livingston		Holiday
1987	The Shadowmaker		$14	$20	$30	Ron Hansen		H&Row
1988	A Norse Lullaby		$14	$20	$30	M. L. Van Vorst		LL&S
1988	The Fisherman And His Wife		$14	$20	$30	John W. Stewig		Holiday
1989	Birthday Poems		$14	$20	$25	Myra Cohn Livingston		Holiday
1989	Tattercoats		$14	$20	$25	Joseph Jacobs		Putnam
1990	The Soup Bone		$12	$18	$25	Tony Johnston		HBJ
1991	Stone Soup		$12	$18	$25	John W. Stewig		Holiday
1991	Witch Hazel		$12	$18	$25	Alice Schertle		HCollins
1994	If There Were Dreams To Sell		$12	$16	$20	Barbara Lalicki		4Winds

Torrey   Marjorie

Year	Title	VG-	VG	VG+	Fine	Author	Award	Pub
1938	Sarah's Idea	$70	$90	$120		Doris Gates		Viking
1943	Sensible Kate	$50	$60	$80		Doris Gates		Viking
1944	Far From Marlborough Street	$50	$60	$80		Elizabeth Philbrook		Viking
1944	Penny	$60	$80	$100		Marjorie Torrey		Howell
1944	Trouble For Jerry	$60	$80	$100		Doris Gates		Viking

Torrey   Marjorie

Year	Title	VG-	VG	VG+	Fine	Author	Award	Pub
1945	Artie And The Princess	$60	$80	$100		Marjorie Torrey		Howell
1945	Sing Mother Goose	$140	$180	$220		Opal Wheeler	CH	Dutton
1946	Sing In Praise	$140	$180	$220		Opal Wheeler	CH	Dutton
1947	Three Little Chipmunks	$60	$80	$100		Marjorie Torrey		G&D
1949	Merriweathers	$60	$80	$100		Marjorie Torrey		Viking
1952	Saturday Night Is My Delight	$50	$70	$90		Marjorie Torrey		Putnam
1955	Alice In Wonderland	$50	$70	$90		Lewis Carroll		Random
1955	Fairing Weather	$35	$50	$60		Elspeth Bragdon		Viking
1957	Peter Pan	$35	$50	$60		Frank Josette (edited)		Random

Trientja   (Engelbrecht Trientja)

Year	Title	VG-	VG	VG+	Fine	Author	Award	Pub
1947	Bad Mousie	$35	$40	$60		Martha Dudley		CP
1947	Farmer Collins	$35	$40	$60		Julilly House Kohler		CP
1947	Martin And Abraham Lincoln	$35	$40	$60		Catherine C. Coblentz		CP

Tripp   Wallace

Year	Title	VG-	VG	VG+	Fine	Author	Award	Pub
1967	Read Me Another Fairy Tale	$60	$80	$100		Andrew Lang		G&D
1967	Saint George	$60	$80	$100		Katherine Miller		HM
1968	Rabbits Rafferty	$40	$50	$70		Gerald Dumas		HM
1968	Sam Bottleby	$40	$50	$70		Ruth Christoffer Carlsen		HM
1968	The Tale Of A Pig	$60	$80	$100		Wallace Tripp		McHill
1969	Mrs. Fox	$40	$50	$70		John Erwin		S&S
1969	The Holiday Rat	$40	$50	$70		Felice Holman		Norton
1970	Jennifer's Rabbit		$50	$70	$90	Tom Paxton		Putnam
1970	Little Dog Lost		$30	$50	$60	René Guillot		LL&S
1970	No Flying In The House		$30	$50	$60	Betty Brock		H&Row
1970	Pirates In Panama		$30	$50	$60	F. N. Monjo		S&S
1970	Stubborn Bear		$30	$50	$60	Robert Sidney Bigelow		LBrown
1970	The Baseball Bargain		$30	$50	$60	Scott Corbett		LBrown
1971	Candle-Lighting Time In Bodidalee		$30	$50	$60	Julian Bagley		AHP
1971	Come Back, Amelia Bedelia		$40	$60	$90	Peggy Parish		H&Row
1971	Puppy Lost In Lapland		$30	$50	$60	Arthur Catherall		FWatts
1971	Stand Back, Said The Elephant		$40	$60	$90	Patricia Thomas		LL&S
1971	The Heart Of The Wood		$30	$50	$60	Victor Sharoff		CM&G
1971	The Magic Egg		$40	$60	$90	Marguerita Rudolph		LBrown
1971	Tigers In The Woods		$30	$50	$60	Miriam Anne Bourne		CM&G
1972	Catofy The Clever		$30	$50	$60	Cynthia Jameson		CM&G
1972	Old Arthur		$50	$80	$100	Liesel Moak Skorpen		H&Row
1972	Play Ball, Amelia Bedelia		$30	$50	$60	Peggy Parish		H&Row
1972	The Adventures Of Mole & Troll		$30	$50	$60	Tony Johnston		Putnam
1972	The Voices Of Greenwillow Pond		$30	$50	$60	Carolyn Lane		HM
1973	A Big Ugly Man Came Up And Tied His Horse To Me		$60	$90	$120	Wallace Tripp		LBrown
1973	Headlines		$30	$50	$60	Malcolm Hall		CM&G
1974	Mole And Troll Trim The Tree		$30	$40	$60	Tony Johnston		Putnam
1974	Pleasant Fieldmouse's Halloween Party		$30	$40	$60	Jan Wahl		Putnam
1975	My Uncle Podger		$30	$40	$60	Jerome K. Jerome		LBrown
1975	Three Friends		$30	$40	$60	Robert. Fremlin		LBrown
1976	Granfa' Grig Had A Pig		$60	$80	$120	Wallace Tripp		LBrown
1976	Sir Toby Jingle's Beastly Journey		$30	$40	$60	Wallace Tripp		CM&G
1978	Casey At The Bat		$25	$40	$50	Ernest Lawrence Thayer		CM&G
1981	Wallace Tripp's Wurst Seller		$25	$35	$50	Wallace Tripp		Sparhk
1982	The Bad Child's Book Of Beasts		$25	$35	$50	Hilaire Belloc		Sparhk
1985	Marguerite, Go Wash Your Feek		$20	$30	$40	William Tripp		HM
1999	Rose's Are Red, Violet's Are Blue		$12	$16	$20	Wallace Tripp		LBrown

Tryon   Leslie

Year	Title	VG-	VG	VG+	Fine	Author	Award	Pub
1985	Daniel Boone		$20	$30	$40	Jan Gleiter		Rain
1991	Albert's Alphabet		$12	$18	$25	Leslie Tryon		Athenm
1992	Albert's Play		$12	$18	$25	Leslie Tryon		Athenm
1992	Toohy And Wood		$12	$18	$25	Mary Elise Monsell		Athenm
1993	Albert's Field Trip		$12	$16	$20	Leslie Tryon		Athenm
1993	One Gaping Wide-Mouthed Hopping Frog		$12	$16	$20	Leslie Tryon		Athenm

Tryon   Leslie

Year	Title	VG-	VG	VG+	Fine	Author	Award	Pub
1994	Albert's Thanksgiving		$12	$16	$20	Leslie Tryon		Athenm
1994	Dear Peter Rabbit		$12	$16	$20	Alma Flor Ada		Athenm
1996	Albert's Ballgame		$10	$16	$20	Leslie Tryon		Athenm
1997	Albert's Christmas		$10	$16	$20	Leslie Tryon		Athenm
1998	Albert's Halloween		$10	$14	$18	Leslie Tryon		Athenm
1998	Yours Truly, Goldilocks		$10	$14	$18	Alma Flor Ada		Athenm
1999	Albert's Birthday		$10	$14	$18	Leslie Tryon		Athenm
2000	Patsy Says		$8	$12	$16	Leslie Tryon		Athenm
2001	With Love, Little Red Hen		$8	$12	$16	Alma Flor Ada		Athenm
2004	Pigs Can Fly!		$8	$10	$14	Deborah Chocolate		Cricket

Tudor   Tasha

Year	Title	VG-	VG	VG+	Fine	Author	Award	Pub
1938	Pumpkin Moonshine	$2,000	$2,800	$3,400		Tasha Tudor		Oxford
1939	Alexander The Gander	$960	$1,200	$1,600		Tasha Tudor		Oxford
1940	The County Fair	$480	$640	$800		Tasha Tudor		Oxford
1940	Thistly B	$480	$640	$800		Tasha Tudor		Oxford
1941	A Tale For Easter	$480	$640	$800		Tasha Tudor		Walck
1941	Snow Before Christmas	$480	$640	$800		Tasha Tudor		Oxford
1942	Dorcas Porkus	$460	$620	$780		Tasha Tudor		Oxford
1943	The White Goose	$320	$420	$520		Tasha Tudor		Oxford
1944	Mother Goose	$460	$600	$760		Tasha Tudor	CH	Oxford
1945	Fairy Tales From Hans Christian Andersen	$300	$400	$500		Hans Christian Andersen		Oxford
1946	Linsey Woolsey	$300	$400	$500		Tasha Tudor		Oxford
1947	A Child's Garden Of Verses	$280	$380	$480		Robert Louis Stevenson		Oxford
1948	Jackanapes	$200	$260	$320		Juliana Horatia Ewing		Oxford
1950	The Dolls' Christmas	$280	$360	$460		Tasha Tudor		Oxford
1951	Amanda And The Bear	$260	$360	$440		Tasha Tudor		Oxford
1952	First Prayers	$180	$240	$300		Tasha Tudor		Oxford
1953	Edgar Allan Crow	$400	$520	$660		Tasha Tudor		Oxford
1954	A Is For Annabelle	$160	$220	$280		Tasha Tudor		Walck
1955	First Graces	$100	$140	$180		Tasha Tudor		Oxford
1955	Pekin White	$380	$500	$620		T.L. McCready		FSG
1956	1 Is One	$240	$320	$400		Tasha Tudor	CH	Oxford
1957	Around The Year	$160	$220	$280		Tasha Tudor		Oxford
1958	And It Was So	$160	$200	$260		Tasha Tudor		Westmin
1958	Increase Rabbit	$520	$700	$880		T.L. McCready		Ariel
1959	First Graces	$100	$140	$180		Tasha Tudor		Walck
1960	Becky's Birthday	$220	$300	$380		Tasha Tudor		Viking
1961	Becky's Christmas	$160	$200	$260		Tasha Tudor		Viking
1961	Book Of Fairy Tales	$100	$120	$160		Tasha Tudor		P&Munk
1962	The Dolls' House	$100	$120	$160		Rumer Godden		Viking
1962	The Secret Garden	$100	$120	$160		Frances Hodgson Burnett		Lippin
1964	Wings From The Wind	$90	$120	$160		Tasha Tudor		Lippin
1965	Favorite Stories	$90	$120	$160		Tasha Tudor		Lippin
1965	The Twenty-Third Psalm	$90	$120	$160		Bible		Onge
1966	First Delights	$90	$120	$160		Tasha Tudor		P&Munk
1966	Take Joy!	$90	$120	$160		Tasha Tudor		World
1966	The Wind In The Willows	$90	$120	$160		Kenneth Grahame		World
1967	First Poems Of Childhood	$80	$120	$140		Tasha Tudor		P&Munk
1967	More Prayers	$80	$120	$140		Tasha Tudor		Walck
1967	The Real Diary Of A Real Boy	$80	$120	$140		Henry A. Shute		RRSmith
1968	Brite And Fair	$80	$120	$140		Henry A. Shute		Noone
1969	Little Women	$80	$120	$140		Louisa May Alcott		World
1971	Corgiville Fair		$70	$100	$140	Tasha Tudor		Crowell
1975	The Night Before Christmas		$60	$80	$120	Clement C. Moore		RandMc
1976	The Christmas Cat		$60	$80	$120	Efner Tudor Holmes		Crowell
1977	A Time To Keep		$60	$80	$120	Tasha Tudor		RandMc
1977	Amy's Goose		$60	$80	$120	Efner Tudor Holmes		Crowell
1977	Tasha Tudor's Bedtime Book		$60	$80	$120	Tasha Tudor		P&Munk
1977	Tasha Tudor's Sampler		$60	$80	$120	Tasha Tudor		McKay
1978	Carrie's Gift		$80	$120	$160	Efner Tudor Holmes		Collins
1978	Tasha Tudor's Five Senses		$50	$80	$100	Tasha Tudor		P&Munk
1979	A Book Of Christmas		$50	$80	$100	Tasha Tudor		Collins
1979	The Springs Of Joy		$50	$80	$100	Tasha Tudor		RandMc
1980	The Lord Is My Shepherd		$50	$70	$100	Bible		Philo

Tudor   Tasha

Year	Title	VG-	VG	VG+	Fine	Author	Award	Pub
1981	Rosemary For Remembrance		$50	$70	$100	Tasha Tudor		Philo
1983	A Basket Of Herbs		$40	$60	$90	Mary Mason Campbell		Greene
1984	All For Love		$40	$60	$90	Tasha Tudor		Philo
1985	A Little Princess		$40	$60	$80	Frances Hodgson Burnett		HFest
1987	Give Us This Day		$40	$60	$80	Bible		Philo
1988	Tasha Tudor's Fairy Tales		$35	$50	$70	Tasha Tudor		P&Munk
1989	A Brighter Garden		$35	$50	$70	Emily Dickinson		Philo
1992	The Real Pretend		$30	$40	$60	Joan Donaldson		Check
1997	The Great Corgiville Kidnapping		$20	$30	$40	Tasha Tudor		LBrown
2001	A Is For Annabelle		$14	$20	$30	Tasha Tudor		S&S
2003	Corgiville Christmas		$12	$16	$20	Tasha Tudor		Front

Turkle   Brinton

Year	Title	VG-	VG	VG+	Fine	Author	Award	Pub
1958	Ten Pairs Of Shoes	$50	$60	$80		Mae Hurley Ashworth		Friend
1958	The Aunt-Sitter	$35	$50	$60		Quail Hawkins		Holiday
1958	You Say You Saw A Camel?	$35	$50	$60		Elizabeth Coatsworth		Row&P
1960	Danny Dunn On The Ocean Floor	$50	$60	$80		Jay Williams		Whittle
1964	If You Lived In Colonial Times	$35	$40	$60		Ann McGovern		4Winds
1964	Indian Children Of America	$35	$40	$60		Margaret C. Farquhar		HR&W
1965	How Joe The Bear And Sam The Mouse Got Together	$60	$80	$100		Beatrice S. De Regniers		PMagP
1965	Obadiah The Bold	$40	$60	$70		Brinton Turkle		Viking
1965	Peter's Tent	$30	$40	$50		Norah Smaridge		Viking
1965	The Story Of Ben Franklin	$30	$40	$50		Eve Merriam		4Winds
1966	A Special Birthday Party For Someone Very Special	$30	$40	$50		Tamara Kitt		Norton
1966	Belinda And Me	$30	$40	$50		Bettye Hill Braucher		Viking
1966	High-Noon Rocket	$30	$40	$50		Charles Paul May		Holiday
1966	The Mystery Of The Red Tide	$30	$40	$50		Frank Bonham		Dutton
1967	Nicolau's Prize	$30	$40	$50		Mary Jane Foltz		McHill
1967	Sam And The Impossible Thing	$30	$40	$50		Tamara Kitt		Norton
1967	The Lollipop Party	$30	$40	$50		Ruth A. Sonneborn		Viking
1967	The Magic Of Millicent Musgrave	$30	$40	$50		Brinton Turkle		Viking
1967	The Troublesome Tuba	$30	$40	$50		Barbara Rinkoff		LL&S
1968	That's What Friends Are For	$30	$40	$50		Florence Parry Heide		4Winds
1968	The Fiddler Of High Lonesome	$40	$50	$70		Brinton Turkle		Viking
1969	Granny And The Indians	$25	$35	$50		Peggy Parish		Macmil
1969	Jake	$25	$35	$50		Tamara Kitt		AS
1969	The Sky Dog	$40	$50	$70		Brinton Turkle		Viking
1969	Thy Friend, Obediah	$80	$120	$140		Brinton Turkle	CH	Viking
1970	Anna And The Baby Buzzard		$25	$35	$50	Helga Sandburg		Dutton
1970	Catch A Little Fox		$25	$35	$50	Beatrice S. De Regniers		Seabury
1970	Mooncoin Castle		$30	$50	$60	Brinton Turkle		Viking
1970	Yvette		$25	$35	$50	Leon Harris		McHill
1971	C Is For Circus		$25	$35	$50	Bernice Chardiet		Walker
1972	The Adventures Of Obadiah		$30	$50	$60	Brinton Turkle		Viking
1972	The Ballad Of William Sycamore		$25	$35	$50	Stephen Vincent Benét		LBrown
1972	Who Likes It Hot?		$25	$35	$50	May Garelick		4Winds
1973	It's Only Arnold		$30	$50	$60	Brinton Turkle		Viking
1973	Poor Richard In France		$25	$35	$50	F. N. Monjo		HR&W
1973	The Boy Who Didn't Believe In Spring		$25	$35	$50	Lucille Clifton		Dutton
1974	Over The River And Through The Wood		$20	$30	$40	Lydia Maria Child		CM&G
1975	The Elves And The Shoemaker		$20	$30	$40	Freya Littledale		4Winds
1976	Deep In The Forest		$30	$40	$60	Brinton Turkle		Dutton
1976	Island Time		$20	$30	$40	Bette Lamont		Lippin
1978	Rachel And Obadiah		$20	$30	$40	Brinton Turkle		Dutton
1981	Do Not Open		$18	$25	$35	Brinton Turkle		Dutton

Turska   Krystyna

Year	Title	VG-	VG	VG+	Fine	Author	Award	Pub
1967	A Cavalcade Of Witches	$40	$50	$70		Jacynth Hope-Simpson		Walck
1968	William Mayne's Book Of Heroes	$30	$40	$50		William Mayne		Dutton
1969	A Cavalcade Of Goblins	$25	$35	$50		Alan Garner		Walck
1969	The Trojan Horse	$25	$35	$50		James Reeves		FWatts
1970	A Cavalcade Of Dragons		$25	$35	$50	Roger Lancelyn Green		Walck
1970	Pegasus		$25	$35	$50	Krystyna Turska		FWatts
1971	Authors' Choice		$25	$35	$50	Gillian Avery		Crowell

Turska   Krystyna

Year	Title	VG-	VG	VG+	Fine	Author	Award	Pub
1972	A Cavalcade Of Sea Legends		$25	$35	$50	Michael Brown		Walck
1972	Tamara And The Sea Witch		$25	$35	$50	Krystyna Turska		PMagP
1972	The Woodcutter's Duck		$40	$60	$90	Krystyna Turska	GM	Macmil
1974	Authors' Choice 2		$20	$30	$40	Joan Aiken		Crowell
1974	Ellen And The Queen		$20	$30	$40	Gillian Avery		TNelson
1974	Happy Families		$20	$30	$40	Barbara Willard		Macmil
1975	Marra's World		$20	$30	$40	Elizabeth Coatsworth		Green
1975	The Magician Of Cracow		$20	$30	$40	Krystyna Turska		Green
1976	Russian Tales		$20	$30	$40	James Riordan		Kestrel
1976	Tales From Central Russia		$20	$30	$40	James Riordan		Kestrel
1978	Great Grandmother Goose		$20	$30	$40	Helen Cooper		Green
1978	The King Of The Golden River		$20	$30	$40	John Ruskin		Green
1978	The Last King Of Cornwall		$20	$30	$40	Charles Causley		H&S
1981	The Mouse And The Egg		$18	$25	$35	William Mayne		Green
1981	The Palace Of The Moon		$18	$25	$35	Ruzena Wood		Deutsch
1985	Coppelia		$16	$25	$30	Linda M. Jennings		SBurdet
1986	Crispin And The Dancing Piglet		$14	$20	$30	Linda M. Jennings		SBurdet

Ungerer   Tomi

Year	Title	VG-	VG	VG+	Fine	Author	Award	Pub
1957	The Mellops Go Diving For Treasure	$100	$140	$180		Tomi Ungerer		H&B
1957	The Mellops Go Flying	$100	$140	$180		Tomi Ungerer		H&B
1958	Crictor	$100	$140	$180		Tomi Ungerer		H&B
1958	The Mellops Strike Oil	$100	$140	$180		Tomi Ungerer		H&B
1959	Adelaide	$70	$100	$120		Tomi Ungerer		H&B
1959	Seeds And More Seeds	$160	$200	$260		Millicent Selsam		H&B
1960	Christmas Eve At The Mellops'	$70	$90	$120		Tomi Ungerer		H&B
1960	Emile	$70	$90	$120		Tomi Ungerer		H&B
1961	Rufus	$70	$90	$120		Tomi Ungerer		H&B
1962	Snail, Where Are You?	$70	$90	$120		Tomi Ungerer		Harper
1962	The Three Robbers	$70	$90	$120		Tomi Ungerer		Athenm
1963	A Book Of Various Owls	$50	$60	$80		John Hollander		Norton
1963	A Cat-Hater's Handbook	$50	$60	$80		William Cole		Dial
1963	Frances Face-Maker	$50	$60	$80		William Cole		World
1963	The Mellops' Go Spelunking	$70	$90	$120		Tomi Ungerer		H&Row
1964	Beastly Boys And Ghastly Girls	$140	$180	$240		William Cole		Philo
1964	Flat Stanley	$90	$120	$160		Jeff Brown		H&Row
1964	One, Two, Where's My Shoe?	$60	$80	$100		Tomi Ungerer		H&Row
1964	The Clambake Mutiny	$50	$60	$80		Jerome Beatty		YScott
1966	Mr. Tall And Mr. Small	$40	$60	$70		Barbara Brenner		YScott
1966	Oh, What Nonsense!	$40	$60	$70		William Cole		Viking
1966	Orlando, The Brave Vulture	$60	$80	$100		Tomi Ungerer		H&Row
1966	Warwick's 3 Bottles	$40	$60	$70		André Hodeir		Grove
1967	A Case Of The Giggles	$40	$50	$70		William Cole		World
1967	Lear's Nonsense Verses	$40	$50	$70		Edward Lear		G&D
1967	Moon Man	$60	$80	$100		Tomi Ungerer		H&Row
1967	The Donkey Ride	$40	$50	$70		Jean B. Showalter		DoubleD
1967	What's Good For A Four-Year-Old?	$40	$50	$70		William Cole		HR&W
1967	Zeralda's Ogre	$60	$80	$100		Tomi Ungerer		H&Row
1968	Ask Me A Question	$60	$80	$100		Tomi Ungerer		H&Row
1968	Cleopatra Goes Sledding	$40	$50	$70		André Hodeir		Grove
1969	Limerick Giggles, Joke Giggles	$40	$50	$70		William Cole		Bodley
1969	The Sorcerer's Apprentice	$40	$50	$70		Barbara Shook Hazen		Lance
1970	Oh, How Silly!		$30	$50	$60	William Cole		Viking
1970	That Pest Jonathan		$30	$50	$60	William Cole		H&Row
1970	The Book Of Giggles		$30	$50	$60	William Cole		World
1970	The Hat		$30	$50	$60	Tomi Ungerer		PMagP
1970	Zeraldas Riese		$50	$70	$90	Tomi Ungerer		DV
1971	I Am Papa Snap/These Are My Favorite No Such Stories		$30	$50	$60	Tomi Ungerer		H&Row
1971	The Beast Of Monsieur Racine		$30	$50	$60	Tomi Ungerer		FSG
1972	Oh, That's Ridiculous!		$30	$50	$60	William Cole		Viking
1974	A Storybook From Tomi Ungerer		$30	$40	$60	Tomi Ungerer		FWatts
1974	Allumette		$30	$40	$60	Tomi Ungerer		PMagP
1978	The Great Song Book		$25	$40	$50	Timothy John		DoubleD
1981	Cat-Hater's Handbook		$25	$35	$50	William Cole		Avenel
1991	No Kiss For Mother		$16	$25	$30	Tomi Ungerer		H&Row

Ungerer   Tomi

Year	Title	VG-	VG	VG+	Fine	Author	Award	Pub
1994	Marianne Moore		$14	$20	$30	Dave Page		Creat
1998	Flix		$12	$16	$20	Tomi Ungerer		Rinehrt
1998	Tortoni Tremelo The Cursed Musician		$12	$16	$20	Tomi Ungerer		Rinehrt
1999	Otto		$12	$16	$20	Tomi Ungerer		Rinehrt

Vagin   Vladimir

Year	Title	VG-	VG	VG+	Fine	Author	Award	Pub
1989	Here Comes The Cat!		$12	$16	$20	Frank Asch		Scholas
1992	Dear Brother		$10	$16	$20	Frank Asch		Scholas
1992	King's Equal		$10	$16	$20	Katherine Paterson		HCollins
1993	The Flower Faerie		$10	$16	$20	Frank Asch		Scholas
1994	Insects From Outer Space		$10	$14	$18	Frank Asch		Scholas
1999	The Twelve Days Of Christmas		$8	$12	$16			HCollins

Van Allsburg   Chris

Year	Title	VG-	VG	VG+	Fine	Author	Award	Pub
1979	The Garden Of Abdul Gasazi		$480	$700	$940	Chris Van Allsburg	CH	HM
1981	Jumanji		$500	$760	$1,000	Chris Van Allsburg	CM	HM
1982	Ben's Dream		$100	$160	$200	Chris Van Allsburg		HM
1983	The Wreck Of The Zephyr		$100	$140	$200	Chris Van Allsburg		HM
1984	The Mysteries Of Harris Burdick		$90	$140	$180	Chris Van Allsburg	NYT	HM
1985	Polar Express		$700	$1,000	$1,400	Chris Van Allsburg	CM	HM
1986	The Stranger		$50	$70	$90	Chris Van Allsburg		HM
1987	The Z Was Zapped		$40	$60	$90	Chris Van Allsburg		HM
1988	Two Bad Ants		$40	$60	$90	Chris Van Allsburg		HM
1989	Swan Lake		$30	$40	$60	Mark Helprin		HM
1990	Just A Dream		$25	$40	$50	Chris Van Allsburg		HM
1991	The Wretched Stone		$25	$40	$50	Chris Van Allsburg		HM
1992	The Widows Broom		$25	$35	$50	Chris Van Allsburg		HM
1993	The Sweetest Fig		$25	$35	$50	Chris Van Allsburg		HM
1995	Bad Day At Riverbend		$20	$30	$40	Chris Van Allsburg		HM
1996	A City In Winter		$18	$25	$35	Mark Helprin		Viking
1997	The Veil Of Snows		$18	$25	$35	Mark Helprin		Viking
2002	Zathura		$15	$22	$30	Chris Van Allsburg		HM

Van Nutt   Robert

Year	Title	VG-	VG	VG+	Fine	Author	Award	Pub
1986	The Ugly Duckling		$12	$16	$20	Hans Christian Andersen	NYT	Knopf
1988	The Emperor And The Nightingale		$10	$14	$18	Joel Tuber (adapted)		Rabbit
1989	The Legend Of Sleepy Hollow		$10	$14	$18	Robert Van Nutt (adapted)		Rabbit
1991	The Emperor's New Clothes		$10	$14	$18	Eric Metaxas (adapted)		Rabbit
1992	The Savior Is Born		$10	$14	$18	Brian Gleeson		Rabbit
1994	The Junior Thunder Lord		$8	$12	$16	Laurence Yep		BWB
1995	The Gift Of A Traveler		$8	$12	$16	Wendy Matthews		BWB
1996	The Firebird		$8	$12	$16	Brad Kessler		Rabbit
1997	Charlotte Brontë And Jane Eyre		$8	$10	$14	Stewart Ross		Viking
1998	A Cobtown Christmas		$8	$10	$14	Julia Van Nutt		DoubleD
1999	Pumpkins From The Sky?		$8	$10	$14	Julia Van Nutt		DoubleD
1999	The Mystery Of Mineral Gorge		$8	$10	$14	Julia Van Nutt		DoubleD
2000	Pignapped!		$8	$10	$14	Julia Van Nutt		DoubleD
2000	The Monster In The Shadows		$8	$10	$14	Julia Van Nutt		DoubleD
2001	Skyrockets And Snickerdoodles		$8	$10	$14	Julia Van Nutt		DoubleD
2002	Camp Fortunate		$6	$10	$12	Ann Gold		Macmil

Varley   Susan

Year	Title	VG-	VG	VG+	Fine	Author	Award	Pub
1984	Badger's Parting Gifts		$12	$18	$25	Susan Varley		LL&S
1986	The Fox And The Cat		$10	$16	$20	Kevin Crossley-Holland		LL&S
1987	The Long Blue Blazor		$10	$16	$20	Jeanne Willis		Dutton
1987	The Monster Bed		$10	$16	$20	Jeanne Willis		LL&S
1988	The Long Blue Blazer		$10	$14	$18	Jeanne Willis		Dutton
1989	Jack And The Monster		$10	$14	$18	Richard Graham		HM
1990	After Dark		$10	$14	$18	Louis Baum		Over
1991	Lollopy		$10	$14	$18	Joyce Dunbar		Macmil
1995	Badger's Bring Something Party		$8	$12	$16	Hiawyn Oram		LL&S

Varley   Susan

Year	Title	VG-	VG	VG+	Fine	Author	Award	Pub
1995	The Monster Storm		$8	$12	$16	Jeanne Willis		LL&S
1997	Mole's Moon		$8	$10	$14	Hiawyn Oram		AP
1997	Why Is The Sky Blue?		$8	$10	$14	Sally Grindley		S&S
1998	Badger's Bad Mood		$8	$10	$14	Hiawyn Oram		Levine
1999	Princess Chamomile Gets Her Way		$8	$10	$14	Hiawyn Oram		Dutton
2000	Princess Chamomile's Garden		$8	$10	$14	Hiawyn Oram		Dutton
2002	The Boy Who Thought He Was A Teddy Bear		$6	$10	$12	Jeanne Willis		Peach

Ventura   Piero

Year	Title	VG-	VG	VG+	Fine	Author	Award	Pub
1973	Vanuk Vanuk		$16	$25	$30	Guido Sperandio		DoubleD
1975	Piero Ventura's Book Of Cities		$12	$18	$25	Piero Ventura		Random
1975	Ten Brothers With Camels		$12	$18	$25	Gladys Y. Cretan		Golden
1976	The Magic Well		$12	$18	$25	Piero Ventura		Random
1977	The Painter's Trick		$12	$18	$25	Marisa Ventura		Random
1978	Christopher Columbus		$12	$18	$25	Gian Paolo Ceserani		Random
1982	Man And The Horse		$12	$16	$20	Piero Ventura		Putnam
1982	Marco Polo		$12	$16	$20	Gian Paolo Ceserani		Putnam
1983	Grand Constructions		$10	$16	$20	Gian Paolo Ceserani		Putnam
1985	In Search Of Ancient Crete		$10	$16	$20	Gian Paolo Ceserani		SBurdet
1985	In Search Of Troy		$10	$16	$20	Gian Paolo Ceserani		SBurdet
1985	In Search Of Tutankhamun		$10	$16	$20	Gian Paolo Ceserani		SBurdet
1986	Journey To Egypt		$10	$16	$20	Joan Knight		VK
1987	There Once Was A Time		$10	$16	$20	Piero Ventura		Putnam
1988	Michelangelo's World		$10	$14	$18	Piero Ventura		Putnam
1988	Venice, The Birth Of A City		$10	$14	$18	Sergio Bettini		Putnam
1989	Great Composers		$10	$14	$18	Piero Ventura		Putnam
1992	1492		$10	$14	$18	Piero Ventura		Putnam
1993	Clothing		$8	$12	$16	Piero Ventura		HM
1993	Houses		$8	$12	$16	Piero Ventura		HM
1994	Food		$8	$12	$16	Piero Ventura		HM

Vestal   H. B. (Herman)

Year	Title	VG-	VG	VG+	Fine	Author	Award	Pub
1957	Favorite Just So Stories	$25	$35	$50		Rudyard Kipling		G&D
1961	Look Out For Pirates	$70	$90	$120		Iris Vinton		BB
1965	The Pirate Book	$25	$30	$40		Margaret Davidson		BB
1968	The Story Of California	$20	$30	$35		Edith Gilbert Stull		G&D
1968	Vikings Of The West	$20	$30	$35		Ruth Robins Holland		G&D
1969	Continents And Islands	$20	$30	$35		Leslie Waller		G&D
1969	The German Immigrants In America	$20	$30	$35		Ruth Robins Holland		G&D
1969	The Oriental Immigrants In America	$20	$30	$35		Ruth Robins Holland		G&D
1970	Brogeen And The Bronze Lizard		$18	$25	$35	Patricia Lynch		Macmil
1971	The Curtain Rises, The Story Of Ossie Davis		$18	$25	$35	Lewis Funke		G&D
1972	The Almost All-White Rabbity Cat		$18	$25	$35	Meindert De Jong		Macmil
1973	Fish Heads And Fire Ants		$16	$25	$30	George S. Cook		YScott

Vivas   Julie

Year	Title	VG-	VG	VG+	Fine	Author	Award	Pub
1983	Possum Magic		$16	$25	$30	Mem Fox		HBJ
1985	Wilfrid Gordon Mcdonald Partridge		$12	$18	$25	Mem Fox		KaneM
1987	Stories From Our House		$12	$16	$20	Richard Tulloch		CUP
1988	The Nativity		$18	$25	$35	Julie Vivas		HBJ
1989	Stories From Our Street		$12	$16	$20	Richard Tulloch		CUP
1989	The Tram To Bondi Beach		$12	$16	$20	Elizabeth Hathorn		KaneM
1990	I Went Walking		$10	$16	$20	Sue Williams		HBJ
1990	The Very Best Of Friends		$10	$16	$20	Margaret Wild		HBJ
1991	Let The Celebrations Begin!		$10	$16	$20	Margaret Wild		Orchard
1991	Nurse Lugton's Curtain		$10	$16	$20	Virginia Woolf		HBJ
1994	Our Granny		$10	$14	$18	Margaret Wild		Ticnor
1996	Let's Eat!		$8	$12	$16	Ana Zamorano		Omnibus
1998	Let's Go Visiting		$8	$12	$16	Sue Williams		HBrace
1999	Hello Baby		$8	$12	$16	Jenni Overend		ABC
2000	Welcome With Love		$8	$10	$14	Jenni Overend		KaneM
2002	Sleepy Pendoodle		$8	$10	$14	Malachy Doyle		Candle

Vivas   Julie

Year	Title	VG-	VG	VG+	Fine	Author	Award	Pub
2004	Cuddle Time		$6	$10	$12	Libby Gleeson		Candle

Voce   Louise

Year	Title	VG-	VG	VG+	Fine	Author	Award	Pub
1986	My First Book Of Animals		$12	$16	$20	Louise Voce		P&Munk
1988	Hello, Goodbye		$10	$14	$18	David Lloyd		LL&S
1992	My First Book		$10	$14	$18	Louise Voce		Candle
1994	Over In The Meadow		$8	$12	$16	Louise Voce		Candle
1995	Hello, Good-Bye		$8	$12	$16	David Lloyd		Candle
1996	What Newt Could Do For Turtle		$8	$12	$16	Jonathan London		Candle
2002	Snarlyhissopus		$6	$10	$12	Alan MacDonald		Tiger
2004	The Quangle Wangle's Hat		$6	$10	$12	Edward Lear		Candle

Vroman   Tom

Year	Title	VG-	VG	VG+	Fine	Author	Award	Pub
1962	An Elephant Is Not A Cat	$25	$30	$40		A. Tresselt & W. Wheaton		PMagP
1962	Jonathan And The Dragon	$20	$25	$35		Irwin Shapiro		Golden
1963	A Very, Very Special Day	$20	$25	$35		Frances DeArmand		PMagP
1964	A Maker Of Boxes	$20	$25	$35		H. R. Wright		HoltR
1964	Alexander	$20	$25	$35		Harold Littledale		PMagP
1965	Sandusky Sam	$18	$25	$30		Carmen Gould		HoltR

Waber   Bernard

Year	Title	VG-	VG	VG+	Fine	Author	Award	Pub
1961	Lorenzo	$70	$90	$120		Bernard Waber		HM
1962	The House On East 88th Street	$50	$60	$80		Bernard Waber		HM
1963	How To Go About Laying An Egg	$50	$60	$80		Bernard Waber		HM
1963	Rich Cat, Poor Cat	$50	$60	$80		Bernard Waber		HM
1964	Just Like Abraham Lincoln	$60	$80	$100		Bernard Waber		HM
1965	Lyle, Lyle, Crocodile	$140	$200	$240		Bernard Waber		HM
1966	Lyle And The Birthday Party	$120	$160	$200		Bernard Waber		HM
1966	You Look Ridiculous	$40	$60	$70		Bernard Waber		HM
1967	An Anteater Named Arthur	$40	$50	$70		Bernard Waber		HM
1967	Cheese	$40	$50	$70		Bernard Waber		HM
1968	A Rose For Mr. Bloom	$40	$50	$70		Bernard Waber		HM
1969	Lovable Lyle	$80	$120	$140		Bernard Waber		HM
1970	A Firefly Named Torchy		$30	$50	$60	Bernard Waber		HM
1972	Ira Sleeps Over		$30	$50	$60	Bernard Waber		HM
1974	Lyle Finds His Mother		$40	$60	$80	Bernard Waber		HM
1975	I Was All Thumbs		$30	$40	$60	Bernard Waber		HM
1976	But Names Will Never Hurt Me		$30	$40	$60	Bernard Waber		HM
1977	Goodbye, Funny Dumpy-Lumpy		$25	$40	$50	Bernard Waber		HM
1977	Mice On My Mind		$25	$40	$50	Bernard Waber		HM
1978	The Snake: A Very Long Story		$25	$40	$50	Bernard Waber		HM
1980	Dear Hildegarde		$25	$35	$50	Bernard Waber		HM
1980	You're A Little Kid With A Big Heart		$25	$35	$50	Bernard Waber		HM
1982	Bernard		$25	$35	$50	Bernard Waber		HM
1987	Funny, Funny Lyle		$25	$40	$50	Bernard Waber		HM
1988	Ira Says Goodbye		$18	$25	$35	Bernard Waber		HM
1994	Lyle At The Office		$20	$30	$40	Bernard Waber		HM
1995	Do You See A Mouse?		$14	$20	$25	Bernard Waber		HM
1995	Gina		$14	$20	$25	Bernard Waber		HM
1996	A Lion Named Shirley Williamson		$12	$18	$25	Bernard Waber		HM
1997	Bearsie Bear And The Surprise Sleepover Party		$12	$18	$25	Bernard Waber		HM
1998	Lyle At Christmas		$14	$20	$30	Bernard Waber		HM
2000	The Mouse That Snored		$10	$14	$18	Bernard Waber		HM
2001	Fast Food! Gulp! Gulp!		$10	$14	$18	Bernard Waber		HM
2002	Courage		$8	$12	$16	Bernard Waber		HM
2003	Evie And Marie		$8	$12	$16	Bernard Waber		HM

Waldman   Neil

Year	Title	VG-	VG	VG+	Fine	Author	Award	Pub
1974	Osceola's Head		$16	$25	$30	Walter L. Harter		P-Hall
1979	Pitcher In Left Field		$12	$18	$25	Jeri Waldman		P-Hall
1983	The Moving Coffins		$10	$16	$20	David C. Knight		P-Hall

Waldman   Neil

Year	Title	VG-	VG	VG+	Fine	Author	Award	Pub
1984	Best True Ghost Stories Of The 20th Century		$10	$16	$20	David C. Knight		P-Hall
1984	The Runt		$10	$16	$20	Patricia Tracy Lowe		Caed
1984	Toba		$10	$16	$20	Michael Mark		BradP
1985	Tales Of Terror		$10	$16	$20	Edgar Allan Poe		P-Hall
1986	The Headless Ghost		$10	$16	$20	William E. Warren		P-Hall
1987	The Screaming Skull		$10	$16	$20	William E. Warren		P-Hall
1988	Bring Back The Deer		$10	$14	$18	Jeffrey Prusski		HBJ
1990	A Horse Called Starfire		$10	$14	$18	Betty V, Boegehold		Bantam
1990	Nessa's Fish		$10	$14	$18	Nancy Luenn		Athenm
1990	The Highwayman		$10	$14	$18	Alfred Noyes		HBJ
1991	The Gold Coin		$10	$14	$18	Alma Flor Ada		Athenm
1991	The Sea Lion		$10	$14	$18	Ken Kesey		Viking
1992	Mother Earth		$10	$14	$18	Nancy Luenn		Athenm
1993	America The Beautiful		$8	$12	$16	Katharine Lee Bates		Athenm
1993	Light		$8	$12	$16	Sarah Waldman		HBJ
1993	The Tyger		$8	$12	$16	William Blake		HBrace
1994	Nessa's Story		$8	$12	$16	Nancy Luenn		Athenm
1994	The Passover Journey		$8	$12	$16	Barbara Diamond Goldin		Viking
1995	Bayou Lullaby		$8	$12	$16	Kathi Appelt		Morrow
1995	The Golden City		$8	$12	$16	Neil Waldman		Athenm
1996	And The Earth Trembled		$8	$12	$16	Shulamith Oppenheim		HBrace
1996	Next Year In Jerusalem		$8	$12	$16	Howard Schwartz		Viking
1996	Quetzal		$8	$12	$16	Dorothy Hinshaw Patent		Morrow
1997	By The Hanukkah Light		$8	$10	$14	Sheldon Oberman		Boyds
1997	The Never-Ending Greenness		$8	$10	$14	Neil Waldman		Morrow
1997	The Two Brothers		$8	$10	$14	Neil Waldman		Athenm
1998	Masada		$8	$10	$14	Neil Waldman		Morrow
1999	The Family Haggadah		$8	$10	$14	Ellen Schecter		Viking
1999	The Starry Night		$8	$10	$14	Neil Waldman		Boyds
2000	The Wisdom Bird		$8	$10	$14	Sheldon Oberman		Boyds
2001	They Came From The Bronx		$8	$10	$14	Neil Waldman		Boyds
2001	Wounded Knee		$8	$10	$14	Neil Waldman		Athenm
2002	The Promised Land		$6	$10	$12	Neil Waldman		Boyds
2003	Dream Makers		$6	$10	$12	Neil Waldman		Boyds
2003	The Snowflake		$6	$10	$12	Neil Waldman		Millbk
2004	Subway		$6	$10	$12	Larry Dane Brimner		Boyds

Wallner   John

Year	Title	VG-	VG	VG+	Fine	Author	Award	Pub
1975	Ethan's Favorite Teacher		$20	$30	$40	Hila Colman		Crown
1975	Follow Me Cried Bee		$20	$30	$40	Jan Wahl		Crown
1976	Little Fox Goes To The End Of The World		$16	$25	$30	Ann Tompert		Crown
1976	Lizzie Lies A Lot		$16	$25	$30	Elizabeth Levy		DelaP
1977	A January Fog Will Freeze A Hog		$16	$25	$30	Hubert Davis (compiled)		Crown
1977	Little Otter Remembers, & Other Stories		$16	$25	$30	Ann Tompert		Crown
1977	The Sick Story		$16	$25	$30	Linda Hirsch		Hastings
1977	Top Of The World		$16	$25	$30	John Rowe Townsend		Lippin
1978	Harvey, The Beer Can King		$14	$20	$30	Jamie Gilson		LL&S
1978	Much Ado About Aldo		$14	$20	$30	Johanna Hurwitz		Morrow
1978	Pepe's Private Christmas		$14	$20	$30	Dorothy Corey		PMagP
1978	The Night Stella Hid The Stars		$14	$20	$30	Gail Radley		Crown
1979	Aldo Applesauce		$14	$20	$30	Johanna Hurwitz		Morrow
1979	Charlotte & Charles		$14	$20	$30	Ann Tompert		Crown
1980	A Perfect Nose For Ralph		$14	$20	$25	Jane Breskin Zalben		Philo
1980	Gloomy Louie		$14	$20	$25	Phyllis Green		AWhit
1980	Good Night To Annie		$14	$20	$25	Eve Merriam		4Winds
1980	Sara And The Pinch		$14	$20	$25	Carla Stevens		HM
1981	Aldo Ice Cream		$14	$20	$25	Johanna Hurwitz		Morrow
1981	Grandpa Gus's Birthday Cake		$14	$20	$25	Jan Wahl		P-Hall
1981	Winter		$14	$20	$25	Richard L. Allington		Rain
1982	Case Of The Missing Dinosaur		$14	$20	$25	Keith Brandt		Troll
1982	Grandma's Secret Letter		$14	$20	$25	Maggie S. Davis		Holiday
1982	One Tough Turkey: A Thanksgiving Story		$14	$20	$25	Steven Kroll		Holiday
1982	The Macmillan Picture Wordbook		$14	$20	$25	Kathleen Daly		Macmil
1982	The Pipkins Go Camping		$14	$20	$25	Jan Wahl		P-Hall
1982	You're Going Out There A Kid, But You're Coming Back A Star		$14	$20	$25	Linda Hirsch		Hastings

Wallner   John

Year	Title	VG-	VG	VG+	Fine	Author	Award	Pub
1983	Frizzy The Fearful		$14	$20	$25	Marjorie Weinman Sharmat		Holiday
1983	More Room For The Pipkins		$14	$20	$25	Jan Wahl		P-Hall
1983	When The Dark Comes Dancing		$14	$20	$25	Nancy Larrick (compiled)		Philo
1984	Rumpelstiltskin		$12	$18	$25	Jacob & Wilhelm Grimm		P-Hall
1984	Snow White And Rose Red		$12	$18	$25	Jacob & Wilhelm Grimm		P-Hall
1985	Easter Poems		$12	$18	$25	Myra C. Livingston (selected)		Holiday
1985	Hansel And Gretel		$12	$18	$25	Jacob & Wilhelm Grimm		P-Hall
1985	Hello, My Name Is Scrambled Eggs		$12	$18	$25	Jamie Gilson		LL&S
1985	Milton, The Monster You Can Count On:		$12	$18	$25	John Wallner		PriceSS
1985	Mrs. Claus's Crazy Christmas		$12	$18	$25	Steven Kroll		Holiday
1986	Hooray For Mother's Day!		$12	$16	$20	Marjorie Weinman Sharmat		Holiday
1986	Ring Of Earth: A Child's Book Of Seasons		$12	$16	$20	Jane Yolen		HBJ
1987	City Mouse-Country Mouse And 2 More Mouse Tales		$12	$16	$20	Aesop		Scholas
1987	Remember Betsy Floss		$12	$16	$20	David A. Adler		Holiday
1988	My Favorite Time Of Year		$12	$16	$20	Susan Pearson		H&Row
1988	The Boy Who Ate The Moon		$12	$16	$20	Christopher King		Philo
1989	A Teacher On Roller Skates		$12	$16	$20	David A. Adler		Holiday
1989	Birthday In A Bathtub		$12	$16	$20	Marcia Leonard		Silver
1989	Hailstones And Halibut Bones		$12	$16	$20	Mary O'Neill		DoubleD
1989	Swimming In The Sand		$12	$16	$20	Marcia Leonard		Silver
1989	Tickle-Toe Rhymes		$12	$16	$20	Joan Knight		Orchard
1990	Good King Wenceslas		$10	$16	$20	John Wallner (adapted)		Philo
1990	That's What I Thought		$10	$16	$20	Alice Schertle		H&Row
1991	Balderdash The Brilliant		$10	$16	$20	Muff Singer		Time
1991	The Bed Who Ran Away From Home		$10	$16	$20	Dan Greenburg		HCollins
1992	Animal Mixups		$10	$16	$20	Millicent Selsam		Macmil
1992	Henry And The Haunted House		$10	$16	$20	Teddy Slater		Silver
1992	Min-Yo And The Moon Dragon		$10	$16	$20	Elizabeth Hillman		HBJ
1992	To The Zoo: Animal Poems		$10	$16	$20	L.B. Hopkins (selected)		LBrown
1992	Violet And The Pirates		$10	$16	$20	Marcia Leonard		Silver
1993	Things That Go Zoom		$10	$16	$20	Jim Dessing (designed)		PriceSS
1993	Where's That Pig?		$10	$16	$20	Lisa Rojany-Buccieri		PriceSS
1994	A Picture Book Of Robert E. Lee		$8	$12	$16	David A. Adler		Holiday
1995	A Picture Book Of Patrick Henry		$8	$12	$16	David A. Adler		Holiday
1995	A Picture Book Of Paul Revere		$8	$12	$16	David A. Adler		Holiday
1996	A Picture Book Of Davy Crockett		$8	$12	$16	David A. Adler		Holiday
1996	A Picture Book Of Thomas Alva Edison		$8	$12	$16	David A. Adler		Holiday
1997	A Picture Book Of Louis Braille		$8	$10	$14	David A. Adler		Holiday
2001	President George Washington		$8	$10	$14	David A. Adler		Holiday
2003	Helen Keller		$8	$10	$14	David A. Adler		Holiday

Walsh   Ellen Stoll

Year	Title	VG-	VG	VG+	Fine	Author	Award	Pub
1979	Brunus And The New Bear		$18	$25	$35	Ellen Stoll Walsh		HBJ
1981	Theodore All Grown Up		$14	$20	$25	Ellen Stoll Walsh		HBJ
1989	Mouse Paint		$18	$25	$35	Ellen Stoll Walsh		HBJ
1991	Mouse Count		$16	$25	$30	Ellen Stoll Walsh		HBJ
1992	You Silly Goose		$10	$16	$20	Ellen Stoll Walsh		HBJ
1993	Hop Jump		$10	$16	$20	Ellen Stoll Walsh		HBJ
1994	Pip's Magic		$10	$14	$18	Ellen Stoll Walsh		HBJ
1996	Samantha		$8	$12	$16	Ellen Stoll Walsh		HBrace
1997	Jack's Tale		$8	$12	$16	Ellen Stoll Walsh		HBrace
1998	For Pete's Sake		$8	$12	$16	Ellen Stoll Walsh		HBJ
2000	Mouse Magic		$8	$10	$14	Ellen Stoll Walsh		HBJ
2001	Dot & Jabber / Great Acorn Mystery		$8	$10	$14	Ellen Stoll Walsh		Harcort
2002	Dot & Jabber / Mystery Of The Missing Stream		$8	$10	$14	Ellen Stoll Walsh		Harcort
2003	Dot & Jabber / Big Bug Mystery		$8	$10	$14	Ellen Stoll Walsh		Harcort

Ward   Lynd

Year	Title	VG-	VG	VG+	Fine	Author	Award	Pub
1928	The Begging Deer	$160	$220	$280		Dorothy Rowe		Macmil
1929	God's Man	$160	$220	$280		Lynd Ward		World
1929	Little Blacknose	$100	$140	$180		Hildegarde Hoyt Swift		HBrace
1929	Prince Bantam	$100	$140	$180		May Yonge McNeer		Macmil
1929	Traveling Shops	$100	$140	$180		Dorothy Rowe		Macmil
1930	Hot Countries	$90	$120	$160		Alec Waugh		F&R

Ward   Lynd

Year	Title	VG-	VG	VG+	Fine	Author	Award	Pub
1930	Jockeys, Crooks And Kings	$90	$120	$160		Winfield Scott O'Connor		JCape
1930	Midsummernight	$90	$120	$160		Carl Wilhelmson		F&R
1930	Sir Bob	$90	$120	$160		Salvador de Madariaga		HBrace
1930	Spice And The Devil's Cave	$90	$120	$160		Agnes Danforth Hewes		Knopf
1930	Stop Tim!	$200	$280	$340		May Yonge McNeer		F&R
1930	The Cat Who Went To Heaven	$460	$620	$780		Elizabeth Coatsworth	NM	Macmil
1930	The Children Of The New Forest	$90	$120	$160		Frederick Marryat		Macmil
1930	Waif Maid	$90	$120	$160		May Yonge McNeer		Macmil
1930	Wonder Flights Of Long Ago	$90	$120	$160		Mary Elizabeth Barry		DApple
1931	Ching-Li and the Dragons	$200	$280	$340		Alice Howard		Macmil
1931	Most Women	$90	$120	$160		Alec Waugh		F&R
1932	A Christmas Poem	$90	$120	$160		Thomas Mann		Equix
1932	Wild Pilgrimage	$200	$260	$320		Lynd Ward		SmithH
1933	Southern Mail	$80	$120	$140		Antoine de Saint-Exupéry		SmithH
1933	The Flutter Of An Eyelid	$80	$120	$140		Myron Brinig		F&R
1933	The White Sparrow	$120	$160	$220		Padraic Colum		Macmil
1934	Man With Four Lives	$80	$120	$140		William Joyce Cowen		F&R
1934	The Cadaver Of Gideon Wyck	$80	$120	$140		Alexander Kinnan Laing		F&R
1935	One Of Us	$120	$160	$220		Granville Hicks		Equix
1935	Topgallant	$80	$120	$140		Marjorie Medary		SmithH
1936	The Motives Of Nicholas Holtz	$80	$120	$140		Thomas Painter		F&R
1937	A Book Of Hours	$80	$120	$140		Donald Culross Peattie		Putnam
1937	Bright Island	$80	$120	$140		Mabel Louise Robinson		Random
1937	The Haunted Omnibus	$80	$120	$140		Alexander Laing		F&R
1938	Birds Against Men	$80	$100	$140		Louis Joseph Halle		Viking
1938	House By The Sea	$80	$100	$140		Hildegarde Hoyt Swift		HBrace
1938	The Porpoise Of Pirate Bay	$80	$100	$140		F. Martin Howard		Random
1939	Great Ghost Stories Of The World	$80	$100	$140		Alexander Kinnan Laing		GardenC
1939	Runner Of The Mountain Tops	$80	$100	$140		Mabel Louise Robinson		Random
1940	The Last Hunt	$50	$60	$80		Maurice Genevoix		Random
1941	Pirate Waters	$50	$60	$80		Edwin Legrand Sabin		Lippin
1942	The Little Red Lighthouse And The Great Gray Bridge	$140	$180	$240		Hildegarde Hoyt Swift		HBrace
1942	The Sangamon	$35	$40	$60		Edgar Lee Masters		F&R
1943	Johnny Tremain	$320	$420	$520		Esther Forbes	NM	HM
1943	Journey Into America	$50	$60	$80		Donald Culross Peattie		HM
1944	The Gold Rush	$90	$120	$160		May Yonge McNeer		G&D
1945	Atoms And You .	$60	$80	$100		Tom O'Connor		Pamp
1945	Brave Companions	$40	$60	$70		Ruth Adams Knight		DD
1945	Reunion In Poland	$40	$60	$70		Jean Karsavina		IP
1946	America's Paul Revere	$60	$80	$100		Esther Forbes		HM
1946	The Life & Surprising Adventures Of Robinson Crusoe	$40	$60	$70		Daniel Defoe		G&D
1947	Many Mansions	$40	$60	$70		Jessie Mae Orton Jones		Viking
1947	North Star Shining	$60	$80	$100		Hildegarde Hoyt Swift		Morrow
1947	The Golden Flash	$40	$60	$70		May Yonge McNeer		Viking
1948	Kidnapped	$40	$60	$70		Robert Louis Stevenson		G&D
1948	The Palomino Boy	$40	$60	$70		D. L Emblen		Viking
1949	America's Ethan Allen	$120	$160	$220		Stewart Hall Holbrook	CH	HM
1949	The Swiss Family Robinson	$40	$60	$70		Johann David Wyss		G&D
1950	The California Gold Rush	$40	$50	$70		May Yonge McNeer		Random
1951	America's Robert E. Lee	$40	$50	$70		Henry Steele Commager		HM
1951	John Wesley	$50	$70	$90		May Yonge McNeer		Abing
1951	Strong Wings	$40	$50	$70		Mabel Louise Robinson		Random
1952	The Biggest Bear	$600	$800	$1,000		Hildegarde Hoyt Swift	CM	HM
1952	The Black Sombrero	$40	$50	$70		Nanda Ward		Ariel
1952	The Conquest Of The North And South Poles	$40	$50	$70		Russell Owen		Random
1952	The Golden Trail	$40	$50	$70		Margery Evernden		Random
1952	The Story Of Ulysses S. Grant	$40	$50	$70		Jeannette Covert Nolan		G&D
1952	Up A Crooked River	$40	$50	$70		May Yonge McNeer		Viking
1953	Martin Luther	$50	$70	$90		May Yonge McNeer		Abing
1953	The Arabian Nights	$40	$50	$70		Padraic Colum		Macmil
1954	Little Baptiste	$40	$50	$70		May Yonge McNeer		HM
1954	The Horn That Stopped The Band	$40	$50	$70		Arthur Hudson Parsons		FWatts
1954	The Sign Of The Seven Seas	$40	$50	$70		Carley Dawson		HM
1954	War Chief Of The Seminoles	$40	$50	$70		May Yonge McNeer		Random
1955	Dragon Run	$35	$50	$60		Carley Dawson		HM
1955	Explorers' Digest	$35	$50	$60		Leonard Clark		HM
1955	Santiago	$35	$50	$60		Ann Nolan Clark		Viking

Ward · Lynd

Year	Title	VG-	VG	VG+	Fine	Author	Award	Pub
1955	Story And Verse	$35	$50	$60		Miriam Blanton Huber		Macmil
1956	The High Flying Hat	$35	$50	$60		Nanda Ward		Ariel
1957	America's Abraham Lincoln	$35	$50	$60		May Yonge McNeer		HM
1957	Armed With Courage	$35	$50	$60		May Yonge McNeer		Abing
1958	The Canadian Story	$35	$50	$60		May Yonge McNeer		Ariel
1960	Brady	$35	$40	$60		Jean Fritz		CM
1960	Gaudenzia, Pride Of The Palio	$35	$40	$60		Marguerite Henry		RandMc
1960	My Friend Mac	$50	$60	$80		May Yonge McNeer		HM
1960	The Alaska Gold Rush	$35	$40	$60		May Yonge McNeer		Random
1960	The Wildest Horse Race In The World	$35	$40	$60		Marguerite Henry		RandMc
1962	America's Mark Twain	$35	$40	$60		May Yonge McNeer		HM
1962	From The Eagle's Wing	$35	$40	$60		Hildegarde Hoyt Swift		Morrow
1962	Hi Tom	$50	$60	$80		Nanda Ward		Hastings
1963	The American Indian Story	$50	$60	$80		May Yonge McNeer		Ariel
1964	Give Me Freedom	$35	$40	$60		May Yonge McNeer		Abing
1965	A Peculiar Magic	$30	$40	$50		Annabel Johnson		HM
1965	Nic Of The Woods	$40	$60	$70		Lynd Ward		HM
1966	Dream Of The Blue Heron	$30	$40	$50		Victor Barnouw		DelaP
1967	Early Thunder	$30	$40	$50		Jean Fritz		CM
1967	The Wolf Of Lambs Lane	$40	$50	$70		May Yonge McNeer		HM
1968	The Secret Journey Of The Silver Reindeer	$40	$50	$70		Lee Kingman		DoubleD
1970	Treasure Island		$25	$35	$50	Robert Louis Stevenson		AEP
1971	Stories From The Bible		$30	$50	$60	Alvin R. Tresselt		CM&G
1971	Stranger In The Pines		$25	$35	$50	May Yonge McNeer		HM
1972	The Treasure Of Topo-El-Bampo		$30	$50	$60	Scott O'Dell		HM
1973	The Silver Pony		$60	$90	$120	Lynn Ward		HM
1973	The Story Of George Washington		$30	$50	$60	May Yonge McNeer		Abing
1976	Bloomsday For Maggie		$20	$30	$40	May Yonge McNeer		HM

Warhola · James

Year	Title	VG-	VG	VG+	Fine	Author	Award	Pub
1987	The Pumpkinville Mystery		$20	$30	$40	Bruce B. Cole		P-Hall
1989	Jack And The Beanstalk		$14	$20	$25	Susan Pearson (retold)		S&S
1990	Well, I Never!		$12	$18	$25	Susan Pearson		S&S
1991	The Tinderbox		$12	$18	$25	Peggy Thomson (retold)		S&S
1992	Aunt Hilarity's Bustle		$12	$18	$25	Helen Ketteman		S&S
1992	The Brave Little Tailor		$12	$18	$25	Peggy Thomson (retold)		S&S
1993	Hurricane City		$12	$16	$20	Sarah Weeks		HCollins
1993	The Surrey With The Fringe On Top		$12	$16	$20	R. Rodgers & O. Hammerstein		S&S
1994	My Favorite Things		$12	$16	$20	R. Rodgers & O. Hammerstein		S&S
1994	The Mystery Of The Several Sevens		$12	$16	$20	Bill Brittain		HCollins
1994	The Wizards And The Monster		$12	$16	$20	Bill Brittain		HCollins
1995	The Christmas Blizzard		$10	$16	$20	Helen Ketteman		Scholas
1997	Bubba The Cowboy Prince: A Fractured Texas Tale		$10	$16	$20	Helen Ketteman		Scholas
1998	Bigfoot Cinderrrrella		$10	$14	$18	Tony Johnston		Putnam
1999	If You Hopped Like A Frog		$10	$14	$18	David Schwartz		Scholas
2001	The Bear Came Over To My House		$8	$12	$16	Rick Walton		Putnam
2003	Uncle Andy's		$8	$10	$14	James Warhola		Putnam
2004	Eddie		$8	$10	$14	Ed Koch		Putnam

Warnes · Tim

Year	Title	VG-	VG	VG+	Fine	Author	Award	Pub
1995	Tom's Tail		$10	$16	$20	Linda M. Jennings		LBrown
1996	I Don't Want To Go To Bed!		$8	$12	$16	Julie Sykes		LTiger
1996	Shhh!		$8	$12	$16	Julie Sykes		LTiger
1996	Who Likes Wofie?		$8	$12	$16	Ragnhild Scamell		LBrown
1997	Davy's Scary Journey		$8	$12	$16	Christine Leeson		LTiger
1997	I Don't Want To Take A Bath!		$8	$12	$16	Julie Sykes		LTiger
1998	Counting Leopard's Spots & Other Animal Stories		$8	$12	$16	Hiawyn Oram		LTiger
1998	Hurry, Santa!		$8	$12	$16	Julie Sykes		LTiger
1998	It Could Have Been Worse		$8	$12	$16	A. H. Benjamin		LTiger
1998	Little Bunny Bobkin		$8	$12	$16	James Riordan		LTiger
1998	Not-So-Grizzly Bear Stories		$8	$12	$16	Hiawyn Oram		LTiger
1998	We Love Preschool		$8	$12	$16	Tim Warnes		Millbk
1999	Little Tiger's Big Surprise		$8	$12	$16	Julie Sykes		LTiger
2000	Have You Got My Purr?		$8	$10	$14	Judy West		Dutton

Warnes   Tim

Year	Title	VG-	VG	VG+	Fine	Author	Award	Pub
2001	Can't You Sleep, Dotty?		$8	$10	$14	Tim Warnes		Tiger
2001	That's Not Fair, Hare!		$8	$10	$14	Julie Sykes		Barrn
2001	Wait For Me, Little Tiger!		$8	$10	$14	Julie Sykes		Tiger
2001	Who's That?		$8	$10	$14	Isobel Gamble		Barrn
2002	Careful, Santa!		$8	$10	$14	Julie Sykes		Tiger
2002	Scaredy Mouse		$8	$10	$14	Alan MacDonald		Tiger
2003	Happy Birthday, Dotty!		$8	$10	$14	Tim Warnes		Tiger
2004	Don't Be So Nosy, Posy!		$6	$10	$12	Nicola Grant		Tiger

Watson   Aldren

Year	Title	VG-	VG	VG+	Fine	Author	Award	Pub
1941	Aesop's Fables	$50	$60	$80		Aesop		PPauper
1942	Christmas In The Woods	$35	$40	$60		Frances Frost		H&B
1942	The Wonder Cat	$35	$40	$60		Dahris Martin		Crowell
1944	The 154 Sonnets Of William Shakespeare	$35	$40	$60		William Shakespeare		Crowell
1946	Miss Pennyfeather And The Pooka	$35	$40	$60		Eileen O'Faoláin		Random
1947	Gulliver's Travels	$35	$40	$60		Jonathan Swift		G&D
1950	John Henry And His Hammer	$30	$40	$50		Harold W. Felton		Knopf
1951	Chanticleer Of Wilderness Road	$30	$40	$50		Meridel Le Sueur		Knopf
1954	Whose Birthday Is It?	$30	$40	$50		Nancy Dingman Watson		Knopf
1956	What Does A Begin With?	$25	$35	$50		Nancy Dingman Watson		Knopf
1957	Annie's Spending Spree	$25	$35	$50		Nancy Dingman Watson		Viking
1958	John Greenleaf Whittier: Fighting Quaker	$25	$35	$50		Ruth Langland Holberg		Crowell
1960	The Clean Brook	$25	$30	$40		Margaret F. Bartlett		Crowell
1961	Where The Brook Begins	$25	$30	$40		Margaret F. Bartlett		Crowell
1962	My Garden Grows	$25	$30	$40		Aldren Auld Watson		Viking
1963	The River, A Story In Pictures	$25	$30	$40		Aldren Auld Watson		HR&W
1964	Sugar On Snow	$25	$30	$40		Nancy Dingman Watson		Viking
1965	Catch A Fish	$25	$30	$40		Marie Puccinelli		Bobbs
1965	Katie's Chickens	$25	$30	$40		Nancy Dingman Watson		Knopf
1965	The Snow Book	$25	$30	$40		Eva Knox Evans		LBrown
1966	Very First Words For Writing And Spelling	$25	$30	$40		Aldren Auld Watson		HR&W
1968	Just Right	$20	$30	$35		Lilian Moore		PMagP
1968	The Village Blacksmith	$20	$30	$35		Aldren Auld Watson		Crowell
1969	Carol To A Child	$20	$30	$35		Nancy Dingman Watson		World
1969	Our Terrariums	$20	$30	$35		Herbert H. Wong		AW
1970	A Maple Tree Begins		$18	$25	$35	Aldren Auld Watson		Viking
1970	New Under The Stars		$18	$25	$35	Nancy Dingman Watson		LBrown
1970	Tatty Mae & Catty Mae		$18	$25	$35	Bill Martin		HR&W
1971	Tommy's Mommy's Fish		$18	$25	$35	Nancy Dingman Watson		Viking
1974	Where Everyday Things Come From		$16	$25	$30	Aldren Auld Watson		P&Munk
1976	Uncle Wiggily's Happy Days		$16	$25	$30	Howard Roger Garis		P&Munk
1977	Uncle Wiggily And The Runaway Cheese		$16	$25	$30	Howard Roger Garis		P&Munk
1977	Uncle Wiggily And The Sugar Cookie		$16	$25	$30	Howard Roger Garis		P&Munk

Watson   Richard Jesse

Year	Title	VG-	VG	VG+	Fine	Author	Award	Pub
1986	Bronwen, The Traw And The Shape Shifter		$20	$30	$40	James Dickey		HBJ
1989	Tom Thumb		$14	$20	$25	Richard J. Watson (adapted)		HBJ
1990	High Rise Glorious Skittle Skat Roarious Sky Pie Angel Food Cake		$12	$18	$25	Nancy Willard		HBJ
1990	The Dream Stair		$12	$18	$25	Betsy James		H&Row
1994	One Wintry Night		$12	$16	$20	Ruth Bell Graham		Baker
2001	The Waterfall's Gift		$8	$12	$16	Joanne Ryder		Sierra
2002	The Legend Of Saint Christopher		$8	$10	$14	Margaret Hodges (adapted)		EerdB
2005	The Magic Rabbit		$6	$10	$12	Richard Jesse Watson		BSP

Watson   Wendy

Year	Title	VG-	VG	VG+	Fine	Author	Award	Pub
1967	Daughter Of Liberty	$40	$50	$70		Edna Boutwell		World
1967	Love Is A Laugh	$40	$50	$70		Margaret Greenman (edited)		PPauper
1967	Rosabel's Secret	$40	$50	$70		Alice E. Christgau		YScott
1967	The Country Mouse And The Town Mouse	$40	$50	$70		Wendy Watson		Stine
1967	The Cruise Of The Aardvark	$40	$50	$70		Wendy Watson		MEvans
1967	The Strawman Who Smiled By Mistake	$40	$50	$70		Wendy Watson		DoubleD
1968	Uncle Fonzo's Ford	$30	$40	$50		Wendy Watson		LBrown

Watson   Wendy

Year	Title	VG-	VG	VG+	Fine	Author	Award	Pub
1968	When Noodlehead Went To The Fair	$30	$40	$50		Wendy Watson		PMagP
1969	God Bless Us, Every One	$25	$35	$50		Louise Bachelder (edited)		PPauper
1969	The Hedgehog And The Hare	$25	$35	$50		Wendy Watson (adapted)		World
1970	Happy Thoughts		$25	$35	$50	Wendy Watson		PPauper
1970	How Dear To My Heart Are The Scenes Of My Childhood		$25	$35	$50	Wendy Watson		PPauper
1970	Lizzie, The Lost Toys Witch		$25	$35	$50	Wendy Watson		MacSm
1970	Magic In The Alley		$25	$35	$50	Wendy Watson		Athenm
1971	Father Fox's Pennyrhymes		$25	$35	$50	Clyde Watson		Crowell
1972	America! America! From Sea To Shining Sea!		$25	$35	$50	Wendy Watson		PPauper
1972	Open The Door And See All The People		$25	$35	$50	Wendy Watson		Crowell
1972	Tom Fox And The Apple Pie		$25	$35	$50	Wendy Watson		Crowell
1973	Upside Down And Inside Out		$25	$35	$50	Wendy Watson		FWatts
1974	Sleep Is For Everyone		$20	$30	$40	Wendy Watson		Crowell
1974	The Birthday Goat		$20	$30	$40	Wendy Watson		Crowell
1975	Quips & Quirks		$20	$30	$40	Clyde Watson		Crowell
1976	Hickory Stick Rag		$20	$30	$40	Clyde Watson		Crowell
1976	Lollipop		$20	$30	$40	Wendy Watson		Crowell
1976	Muncus Agruncus, A Bad Little Mouse		$20	$30	$40	Nancy Dingman Watson		Golden
1978	Catch Me & Kiss Me & Say It Again		$20	$30	$40	Clyde Watson		Collins
1978	Has Winter Come?		$20	$30	$40	Wendy Watson		Collins
1978	Moving		$20	$30	$40	Wendy Watson		Crowell
1979	Jenny's Cat		$18	$25	$35	Miska Miles		Dutton
1980	Button Eye's Orange		$18	$25	$35	Jan Wahl		FWarne
1980	How Brown Mouse Kept Christmas		$18	$25	$35	Clyde Watson		FSG
1981	Jamie's Story		$18	$25	$35	Wendy Watson		Philo
1981	Stairstep Farm: Anna Rose's Story		$18	$25	$35	Anne Pellowski		Philo
1981	Willow Wind Farm: Betsy's Story		$18	$25	$35	Anne Pellowski		Philo
1982	Applebet: An ABC		$16	$25	$30	Clyde Watson		FSG
1982	Biggest, Meanest, Ugliest Dog In Whole Wide World		$16	$25	$30	Rebecca C. Jones		Macmil
1982	First Farm In The Valley: Anna's Story		$16	$25	$30	Anne Pellowski		Philo
1982	Winding Valley Farm: Annie's Story		$16	$25	$30	Anne Pellowski		Philo
1983	Betsy's Up-And-Down Year		$16	$25	$30	Anne Pellowski		Philo
1983	The Bunnies' Christmas Eve		$16	$25	$30	Wendy Watson		Philo
1984	Belinda's Hurricane		$16	$25	$30	Elizabeth Winthrop		Dutton
1984	I Love My Baby Sister (Most Of The Time)		$16	$25	$30	Elaine Edelman		LL&S
1985	Little Brown Bear		$16	$25	$30	Wendy Watson		Golden
1987	Doctor Coyote: A Native American Aesop's Fables		$14	$20	$30	John Bierhorst (retold)		Macmil
1988	Angry		$14	$20	$30	Marcia Leonard		Bantam
1988	Happy		$14	$20	$30	Marcia Leonard		Bantam
1988	Scared		$14	$20	$30	Marcia Leonard		Bantam
1988	Silly		$14	$20	$30	Marcia Leonard		Bantam
1988	Tales For A Winter's Eve		$14	$20	$30	Wendy Watson		FSG
1989	A,B,C,D, Tummy, Toes, Hands, Knees		$14	$20	$25	B. G. Hennessy		VK
1989	Valentine Foxes		$14	$20	$25	Clyde Watson		Orchard
1989	Wendy Watson's Mother Goose		$14	$20	$25	Wendy Watson		LL&S
1990	The Night Before Christmas		$12	$18	$25	Clement C. Moore		Clarion
1990	Wendy Watson's Frog Went A-Courting		$12	$18	$25	Wendy Watson		LL&S
1991	A Valentine For You		$12	$18	$25	Wendy Watson		Clarion
1991	Thanksgiving At Our House		$12	$18	$25	Wendy Watson		Clarion
1992	Boo! It's Halloween		$12	$18	$25	Wendy Watson		Clarion
1992	Hurray For The Fourth Of July		$12	$18	$25	Wendy Watson		Clarion
1993	Happy Easter Day!		$12	$16	$20	Wendy Watson		Clarion
1994	Fox Went Out On A Chilly Night		$12	$16	$20	Wendy Watson		LL&S
1998	Love's A Sweet		$10	$14	$18	Clyde Watson		Viking
2000	Is My Friend At Home?		$8	$12	$16	John Bierhorst		FSG
2002	Holly's Christmas Eve		$8	$10	$14	Wendy Watson		HCollins
2002	Rabbit Moon		$8	$10	$14	Patricia Hubbell		MCaven
2003	Father Fox's Christmas Rhymes		$8	$10	$14	Clyde Watson		FSG
2004	The Cats In Krasinski Square		$8	$10	$14	Karen Hesse		Scholas

Weihs   Erika

Year	Title	VG-	VG	VG+	Fine	Author	Award	Pub
1944	Hello, I'm Adeline	$50	$60	$80		Frida Sarsen-Bucky		Anim
1944	Mother Goose	$50	$60	$80		Erika Weihs (adapted)		Whitman
1944	The Proud Little Kitten	$50	$60	$80		Muriel Lasky		Unicorn
1945	Hansel And Gretel	$35	$40	$60		Jacob & Wilhelm Grimm		S&S

Weihs   Erika

Year	Title	VG-	VG	VG+	Fine	Author	Award	Pub
1946	Heidi	$35	$40	$60		Johanna Spyri		Random
1946	Pandora	$35	$40	$60		Mary Patric		PiedP
1954	The Cello In The Belly Of The Plane	$30	$40	$50		Joseph Schrank		FWatts
1956	How The Rhinoceros Got His Skin	$25	$35	$50		Rudyard Kipling		RandMc
1956	Jeremy And The Torah	$25	$35	$50		Libby M Klaperman		Behman
1957	Terry's Ferry	$25	$35	$50		Marion Belden Cook		Dutton
1965	Alphabet Zoo.	$25	$30	$40		Jane K. Lansing		Hart
1965	The Roly-Poly Policeman	$25	$30	$40		Caroline Horowitz		Hart
1968	Indian Tales	$20	$30	$35		Te Ata		Singer
1976	Count The Cats		$16	$25	$30	Erika Weihs		DoubleD
1983	Rosh Hashanah And Yom Kippur		$14	$20	$25	Miriam Schlein		Behman
1983	Shavuot		$14	$20	$25	Miriam Schlein		Behman
1991	Cakes And Miracles		$10	$16	$20	Barbara Diamond Goldin		Viking
1991	Days Of Awe		$10	$16	$20	Eric Kimmel		Viking
1992	How A Shirt Grew In The Field		$10	$16	$20	Marguerita Rudolph		Clarion
1993	Two Very Little Sisters		$10	$16	$20	Carol Carrick		Clarion

Weil   Lisl

Year	Title	VG-	VG	VG+	Fine	Author	Award	Pub
1956	Pudding's Wonderful Bone	$50	$70	$90		Lisl Weil		Crowell
1961	Mimi	$35	$40	$60		Lisl Weil		HM
1961	Miss Polly's Animal School	$35	$40	$60		Lisl Weil		Wonder
1961	What Will I Wear?	$35	$40	$60		Lisl Weil		Knopf
1963	Sheep Ahoy	$25	$30	$40		Lisl Weil		HM
1967	Melissa's Friend Fabrizzio	$25	$30	$40		Lisl Weil		Macmil
1967	Shivers and the Case of the Secret Hamburgers	$25	$30	$40		Lisl Weil		HM
1967	The Fantastic Toy Shop	$25	$30	$40		Lisl Weil		AS
1970	Doctor George Owl		$18	$25	$35	Lisl Weil		HM
1970	The Hopping Knapsack		$18	$25	$35	Lisl Weil		Macmil
1971	A Visit With Rosalind		$18	$25	$35	Lisl Weil		Macmil
1971	The Wiggler		$18	$25	$35	Lisl Weil		HM
1971	What Is A Pet		$18	$25	$35	Lee Parr McGrath		Macmil
1972	What Makes Me Feel This Way?		$18	$25	$35	Eda Le Shan		Macmil
1973	Fat Ernest		$16	$25	$30	Lisl Weil		PMagP
1973	Master Of All Masters		$16	$25	$30	Lisl Weil		Scholas
1974	Mindy		$16	$25	$30	Lisl Weil		Macmil
1974	Ralphi Rhino		$16	$25	$30	Lisl Weil		Walker
1974	Your First Pet And How To Take Care Of It		$16	$25	$30	Lisl Weil		Macmil
1975	Deadline For McGurk		$16	$25	$30	E. W. Hildick		Macmil
1975	The Bed Just So		$16	$25	$30	Jeanne B. Hardendorff (retold)		4Winds
1975	The Candy Egg Bunny		$16	$25	$30	Lisl Weil		Holiday
1975	The Case Of The Condemned Cat		$16	$25	$30	E. W. Hildick		Macmil
1976	Chicken		$16	$25	$30	Lisl Weil		FWarne
1976	If Eggs Had Legs: Nonsense And Some Sense		$16	$25	$30	Lisl Weil		DoubleD
1976	The Case Of The Nervous Newsboy		$16	$25	$30	E. W. Hildick		Macmil
1976	The Lancelot Closes At Five		$16	$25	$30	Marjorie Weinman Sharmat		Macmil
1976	The Very First Story Ever Told		$16	$25	$30	Lisl Weil		Athenm
1977	Donkey Head		$16	$25	$30	Lisl Weil		Athenm
1977	Gertie & Gus		$16	$25	$30	Lisl Weil		PMagP
1977	The Case Of The Invisible Dog		$16	$25	$30	E. W. Hildick		Macmil
1977	The Great Rabbit Rip-Off		$16	$25	$30	E. W. Hildick		Macmil
1978	Gillie And The Flattering Fox		$14	$20	$30	Lisl Weil (adapted)		Athenm
1978	The Case Of The Secret Scribbler		$14	$20	$30	E. W. Hildick		Macmil
1979	The Case Of The Phantom Frog		$14	$20	$30	E. W. Hildick		Macmil
1980	Esther		$14	$20	$25	Lisl Weil		Athenm
1980	Owl & Other Scrambles		$14	$20	$25	Emilie McLeod (edited)		Dutton
1980	Step On It, Andrew		$14	$20	$25	Barbara Shook Hazen		Athenm
1980	The Case Of The Snowbound Spy		$14	$20	$25	E. W. Hildick		Macmil
1980	The Case Of The Treetop Treasure		$14	$20	$25	E. W. Hildick		Macmil
1981	Mother Goose Picture Riddles		$14	$20	$25	Lisl Weil (adapted)		Holiday
1981	The Case Of The Bashful Bank Robber		$14	$20	$25	E. W. Hildick		Macmil
1981	The Case Of The Four Flying Fingers		$14	$20	$25	E. W. Hildick		Macmil
1981	The Riddle Monster		$14	$20	$25	Lisl Weil		Clarion
1981	The Story Of The Wise Men And The Child		$14	$20	$25	Lisl Weil		Athenm
1982	Mcgurk Gets Good And Mad		$14	$20	$25	E. W. Hildick		Macmil
1982	The Case Of The Felon's Fiddle		$14	$20	$25	E. W. Hildick		Macmil

Weil   Lisl

Year	Title	VG-	VG	VG+	Fine	Author	Award	Pub
1982	The Foolish King		$14	$20	$25	Lisl Weil		Macmil
1982	When Animals Had Fire		$14	$20	$25	Lisl Weil		Athenm
1983	I, Christopher Columbus		$14	$20	$25	Lisl Weil		Athenm
1983	Our World To You With Love		$14	$20	$25	Lisl Weil		Athenm
1983	The Case Of The Slingshot Sniper		$14	$20	$25	E. W. Hildick		Macmil
1984	To Sail A Ship Of Treasures		$12	$18	$25	Lisl Weil		Athenm
1985	Of Witches And Monsters And Wondrous Creatures		$12	$18	$25	Lisl Weil		Athenm
1985	The Houses We Build		$12	$18	$25	Lisl Weil		Athenm
1986	Pandora's Box		$12	$16	$20	Lisl Weil (adapted)		Athenm
1987	Santa Claus Around The World		$12	$16	$20	Lisl Weil		Holiday
1987	What People Wore, From Cavemen To Astronauts		$12	$16	$20	Lisl Weil		Athenm
1988	Let's Go To The Circus		$12	$16	$20	Lisl Weil		Holiday
1989	Let's Go To The Museum		$12	$16	$20	Lisl Weil		Holiday
1989	The Magic Of Music		$12	$16	$20	Lisl Weil		Holiday
1990	Let's Go To The Library		$10	$16	$20	Lisl Weil		Holiday
1991	Wolferl: The First Six Years In The Life Of Mozart		$10	$16	$20	Lisl Weil		Holiday

Weisgard   Leonard

Year	Title	VG-	VG	VG+	Fine	Author	Award	Pub
1937	Suki, The Siamese Pussy	$180	$240	$300		Leonard Weisgard		TNelson
1938	Cinderella	$180	$240	$300		Leonard Weisgard		GardenC
1939	Noisy Book	$180	$240	$300		Margaret Wise Brown		WRScott
1939	The Pup Called Cinderella	$80	$100	$140		Esther Watson Reno		Bobbs
1940	Country Noisy Book	$140	$200	$240		Margaret Wise Brown		WRScott
1940	Little Joe	$100	$120	$160		Dorothy Clark		LL&S
1940	Punch & Judy	$140	$200	$240		Margaret Wise Brown		WRScott
1940	Under the Greenwood Tree	$140	$200	$240		Margaret Wise Brown		H&B
1941	Grab Bag	$50	$60	$80		Lavinia R. Davis		DD
1941	Pedro Of Santa Fe	$70	$90	$120		Frances Cavanah		DMcKay
1941	The Poodle And The Sheep	$70	$90	$120		Margaret Wise Brown		Dutton
1941	The Seashore Noisy Book	$70	$90	$120		Margaret Wise Brown		WRScott
1942	Americans Every One	$50	$60	$80		Lavinia R. Davis		DD
1942	Indoor Noisy Book	$70	$90	$120		Margaret Wise Brown		WRScott
1942	Night And Day	$70	$90	$120		Margaret Wise Brown		H&B
1942	Picture Book Of Musical Instruments	$50	$60	$80		Marion Lacey		LL&S
1942	The Water-Carrier's Secrets	$50	$60	$80		Maria Cristina Chambers		Oxford
1943	Big Dog, Little Dog	$70	$90	$120		Margaret Wise Brown		DD
1943	Little Chicken	$70	$90	$120		Margaret Wise Brown		H&B
1943	The Noisy Bird Book	$70	$90	$120		Margaret Wise Brown		WRScott
1944	Bucky Bear	$60	$80	$100		Elaine Wayne		LL&S
1944	Let's Play	$60	$80	$100		Leonard Weisgard		Schill
1944	Red Light, Green Light	$60	$80	$100		Margaret Wise Brown		DD
1944	Timid Timothy	$60	$80	$100		Gweneira Maureen Williams		WRScott
1944	Whose Little Bird Am I?	$60	$80	$100		Leonard Weisgard		Crowell
1945	Little Lost Lamb	$140	$180	$220		Golden MacDonald	CH	DD
1945	Would You Like To Be A Monkey?	$60	$80	$100		Leonard Weisgard		Crowell
1946	City Country ABC	$60	$80	$100		Morrell Gipson		GardenC
1946	Heidi	$40	$60	$70		Johanna Spyri		World
1946	Mrs Mallard's Ducklings	$60	$80	$100		Clelia C. Delafield		LL&S
1946	Rain Drop Splash	$140	$180	$220		Alvin R. Tresselt	CH	LL&S
1946	Round The Afternoon	$60	$80	$100		Charlotte E. Jackson		DoddM
1946	The Little Island	$300	$400	$500		Golden MacDonald	CM	DoubleD
1947	Down Huckleberry Hill	$60	$80	$100		Leonard Weisgard		Scribnr
1947	The Golden Egg Book	$60	$80	$100		Margaret Wise Brown		S&S
1948	Pelican Here, Pelican There	$60	$80	$100		Leonard Weisgard		Scribnr
1949	Alice's Adventures In Wonderland	$60	$80	$100		Charles L. Dodgson		H&B
1949	The Important Book	$80	$120	$140		Margaret Wise Brown		H&B
1949	The Night Before Christmas	$60	$80	$100		Clement C. Moore		G&D
1950	The Funny Bunny Factory	$40	$50	$70		Adam Green		G&D
1950	The Little Lost Squirrel	$40	$50	$70		Alvin R. Tresselt		G&D
1950	The Quiet Noisy Book	$120	$160	$200		Margaret Wise Brown		H&B
1950	Who Dreams Of Cheese?	$60	$80	$100		Leonard Weisgard		Scribnr
1951	Pantaloon	$40	$50	$70		Kathryn Jackson		S&S
1951	Pussy Willow	$50	$70	$90		Margaret Wise Brown		Golden
1951	The Family Mother Goose	$50	$70	$90		Leonard Weisgard		H&B
1951	The Summer Noisy Book	$50	$70	$90		Margaret Wise Brown		H&B

Weisgard   Leonard

Year	Title	VG-	VG	VG+	Fine	Author	Award	Pub
1952	The Clean Pig	$50	$70	$90		Leonard Weisgard		Scribnr
1952	The Noon Balloon	$50	$70	$90		Margaret Wise Brown		H&B
1953	A Book About God	$40	$50	$70		Florence Mary Fitch		Lothrop
1953	Let's Play Train	$50	$70	$90		Leonard Weisgard		Treasur
1953	Little Frightened Tiger	$50	$70	$90		Margaret Wise Brown		DoubleD
1953	My First Picture Book	$50	$70	$90		Leonard Weisgard		G&D
1953	Silly Willy Nilly	$50	$70	$90		Leonard Weisgard		Scribnr
1954	Gulliver's Travels	$40	$50	$70		Jonathan Swift		Junior
1954	Just Like Me	$50	$70	$90		Leonard Weisgard		Treasur
1954	The Courage Of Sarah Noble	$120	$160	$200		Alice Dalgliesh	NH	Scribnr
1955	Peter Rabbit	$35	$50	$60		Beatrix Potter		G&D
1955	Tales From Shakespeare	$35	$50	$60		Charles & Mary Lamb (adapted)		Junior
1955	The Big Book Of Train Stories	$50	$70	$90		Leonard Weisgard		G&D
1955	The Child Jesus	$35	$50	$60		Florence Mary Fitch		LL&S
1955	The Secret River	$35	$50	$60		Marjorie Kinnan Rawlings		Scribnr
1956	Mr. Peaceable Paints	$50	$70	$90		Leonard Weisgard		Scribnr
1956	Something For Now, Something For Later	$35	$50	$60		Miriam Schlein		H&B
1956	The Most Beautiful Tree In The World	$50	$70	$90		Leonard Weisgard		Wonder
1956	The Story Of Valentine	$35	$50	$60		Wilma Pitchford Hays		CM
1956	Treasures To See	$50	$70	$90		Leonard Weisgard		HBrace
1957	The Rabbit Story	$35	$50	$60		Alvin R. Tresselt		LL&S
1957	Who Ever Heard Of Kangaroo Eggs?	$35	$50	$60		Sam Vaughan		DoubleD
1958	The First People In The World	$35	$50	$60		Gerald Ames		H&B
1959	Adam And The Golden Cock	$35	$50	$60		Alice Dalgliesh		Scribnr
1959	Nibble Nibble	$50	$60	$80		Margaret Wise Brown		WRScott
1959	The Valentine Cat	$35	$50	$60		Clyde Robert Bulla		Crowell
1960	Who Is At The Door?	$35	$40	$60		Isabel & Frederick Eberstadt		LBrown
1961	Hailstones And Halibut Bones	$35	$40	$60		Mary Le Duc O'Neill		DoubleD
1961	Half-As-Big and the Tiger	$35	$40	$60		Bernice Frankel		FWatts
1961	See Along The Shore	$35	$40	$60		Millicent Selsam		H&B
1961	The Raccoon and Mrs. McGinnis	$35	$40	$60		Patricia Miles Martin		Putnam
1962	Good Hunting Little Indian	$35	$40	$60		Peggy Parish		YScott
1962	Like Nothing At All	$35	$40	$60		Aileen Fisher		Crowell
1962	Penguin's Way	$35	$40	$60		Johanna Johnston		DoubleD
1962	The Mouse And The Lion	$35	$40	$60		Eve Titus		PMagP
1962	Watch That Watch	$35	$40	$60		Hila Colman		Morrow
1962	When A Boy Wakes Up In The Morning	$35	$40	$60		Faith McNulty		Knopf
1963	Baby Elephant Goes to China	$35	$40	$60		Sesyle Joslin		HBrace
1963	The Athenians In The Classical Period	$50	$60	$80		Leonard Weisgard		CM
1963	The Golden Bunny	$35	$40	$60		Margaret Wise Brown		Golden
1963	When A Boy Goes To Bed At Night	$35	$40	$60		Faith McNulty		Knopf
1965	Favorite Poems Old And New	$30	$40	$50		Helen Josephine Ferris		Compton
1965	The Boat That Mooed	$30	$40	$50		Christopher Fry		Macmil
1965	Whale's Way	$30	$40	$50		Johanna Johnston		DoubleD
1966	Hawaiian Myths Of Earth, Sea, And Sky	$30	$40	$50		Vivian Laubach Thompson		Holiday
1966	The First Farmers In The New Stone Age	$40	$60	$70		Leonard Weisgard		CM
1966	White Bird	$30	$40	$50		Clyde Robert Bulla		Crowell
1967	A Wreath Of Christmas Legends	$30	$40	$50		Phyllis McGinley		Macmil
1967	Cynthia And The Unicorn	$30	$40	$50		Jean Todd Freeman		Norton
1967	The Plymouth Thanksgiving	$40	$50	$70		Leonard Weisgard		DoubleD
1968	Midnight Alarm	$30	$40	$50		Mary Kay Phelan		Crowell
1968	On The Sand Dune	$30	$40	$50		Doris Orgel		H&Row
1968	Salt Boy	$30	$40	$50		Mary Perrine		HM
1968	Su An	$30	$40	$50		Doris Johnson		Follett
1968	The Beginnings Of Cities	$40	$50	$70		Leonard Weisgard		CM
1969	Growing Time	$25	$35	$50		Sandol Stoddard		HM
1969	Journey To Jericho	$25	$35	$50		Scott O'Dell		HM
1969	Look At The Moon	$25	$35	$50		May Garelick		YScott
1969	Shepherdess Of France	$25	$35	$50		Judith Masefield		CM
1969	What Makes A Bird A Bird?	$25	$35	$50		May Garelick		Follett
1970	Nannabah's Friend		$25	$35	$50	Mary Perrine		HM
1970	Tom Sawyer		$25	$35	$50	Mark Twain		AEP
1971	And It Came To Pass		$25	$35	$50	Jean Slaughter Doty		Macmil
1971	Doctor Proctor And Mrs Merriwether		$25	$35	$50	Irma Black		AWhit
1971	The Magic Ringlet		$25	$35	$50	Konstantin Paustovsky		YScott
1971	Wake Up And Good Night		$25	$35	$50	Charlotte Zolotow		H&Row
1972	Try And Catch Me		$25	$35	$50	Nancy Jewell		H&Row

Weisgard   Leonard

Year	Title	VG-	VG	VG+	Fine	Author	Award	Pub
1973	Calf, Goodnight		$25	$35	$50	Nancy Jewell		H&Row
1973	Try On A Shoe		$25	$35	$50	Jane Belk Moncure		CW
1974	How The Rhinoceros Got His Skin		$20	$30	$40	Rudyard Kipling		Walker
1988	The Golden Christmas Tree		$12	$16	$20	Jan Wahl		Western
1989	The Golden Birthday Book		$12	$16	$20	Margaret Wise Brown		Western
1992	Red Light, Green Light		$10	$16	$20	Margaret Wise Brown		Scholas
1993	The Noisy Book		$10	$16	$20	Margaret Wise Brown		HCollins
1993	The Quiet Noisy Book		$10	$16	$20	Margaret Wise Brown		HCollins
1994	The Country Noisy Book		$10	$14	$18	Margaret Wise Brown		HCollins

Wells   Rosemary

Year	Title	VG-	VG	VG+	Fine	Author	Award	Pub
1968	A Song To Sing, O!	$60	$80	$100		A. Sullivan W.S. Gilbert		Macmil
1969	Hungry Fred	$40	$50	$70		Paula Fox		BradP
1969	John And The Rarey	$60	$80	$100		Rosemary Wells		F&W
1969	Michael And The Mitten Test	$60	$80	$100		Rosemary Wells		BradP
1969	The Shooting Of Dan Mcgrew	$40	$50	$70		Robert W, Service		YScott
1970	Martha's Birthday		$50	$70	$90	Rosemary Wells		BradP
1970	Marvin's Manhole		$30	$50	$60	Winifred Rosen		Dial
1970	Miranda's Pilgrims		$30	$50	$60	Rosemary Wells		BradP
1970	The Cat That Walked By Himself		$30	$50	$60	Rudyard Kipling		HawB
1970	The First Child		$50	$70	$90	Rosemary Wells		HawB
1971	A Hot Thirsty Day		$25	$35	$50	Marjorie Weinman Sharmat		Macmil
1971	Impossible, Possum		$25	$35	$50	Ellen Conford		LBrown
1972	The Fog Comes On Little Pig Feet		$40	$60	$90	Rosemary Wells		Dial
1972	Two Sisters And Some Hornets		$25	$35	$50	Beryl W. Epstein		Holiday
1972	Unfortunately Harriet		$40	$60	$90	Rosemary Wells		Dial
1973	Benjamin & Tulip		$40	$60	$90	Rosemary Wells		Dial
1973	Noisy Nora		$40	$60	$90	Rosemary Wells		Dial
1974	None Of The Above		$40	$60	$80	Rosemary Wells		Dial
1974	With A Deep Sea Smile		$20	$30	$40	Virginia A. Tashjian		LBrown
1975	Abdul		$30	$40	$60	Rosemary Wells		Dial
1975	Morris's Disappearing Bag		$30	$40	$60	Rosemary Wells		Dial
1977	Don't Spill It Again, James		$25	$40	$50	Rosemary Wells		Dial
1977	Tell Me A Trudy		$20	$30	$40	Lore Segal		FSG
1978	Stanley & Rhoda		$25	$40	$50	Rosemary Wells		Dial
1979	Max's First Word		$25	$40	$50	Rosemary Wells		Dial
1979	Max's New Suit		$25	$40	$50	Rosemary Wells		Dial
1979	Max's Ride		$25	$40	$50	Rosemary Wells		Dial
1979	Max's Toys		$25	$40	$50	Rosemary Wells		Dial
1980	When No One Was Looking		$18	$25	$35	Rosemary Wells		Dial
1981	Good Night, Fred		$18	$25	$35	Rosemary Wells		Dial
1981	Timothy Goes To School		$18	$25	$35	Rosemary Wells		Dial
1982	A Lion For Lewis		$16	$25	$30	Rosemary Wells		Dial
1983	Peabody		$16	$25	$30	Rosemary Wells		Dial
1984	The Man In The Woods		$16	$25	$30	Rosemary Wells		Dial
1985	Hazel's Amazing Mother		$16	$25	$30	Rosemary Wells		Dial
1985	Max's Bath		$16	$25	$30	Rosemary Wells		Dial
1985	Max's Bedtime		$16	$25	$30	Rosemary Wells		Dial
1985	Max's Birthday		$16	$25	$30	Rosemary Wells		Dial
1985	Max's Breakfast		$16	$25	$30	Rosemary Wells		Dial
1986	Max's Christmas		$14	$20	$30	Rosemary Wells		Dial
1987	Through The Hidden Door		$14	$20	$30	Rosemary Wells		Dial
1988	Shy Charles		$14	$20	$30	Rosemary Wells		Dial
1989	Max's Chocolate Chicken		$14	$20	$25	Rosemary Wells		Dial
1990	The Little Lame Prince		$12	$18	$25	Dinah M. M. Craik		Dial
1991	Fritz And The Mess Fairy		$12	$18	$25	Rosemary Wells		Dial
1991	Max's Dragon Shirt		$12	$18	$25	Rosemary Wells		Dial
1992	First Tomato		$12	$18	$25	Rosemary Wells		Dial
1992	Moss Pillows		$12	$18	$25	Rosemary Wells		Dial
1992	The Island Light		$12	$18	$25	Rosemary Wells		Dial
1993	Max And Ruby's First Greek Myth		$12	$16	$20	Rosemary Wells		Dial
1995	Edward In Deep Water		$10	$16	$20	Rosemary Wells		Dial
1995	Edward Unready For School		$10	$16	$20	Rosemary Wells		Dial
1995	Edward's Overwhelming Overnight		$10	$16	$20	Rosemary Wells		Dial
1995	Max And Ruby's Midas		$10	$16	$20	Rosemary Wells		Dial

Wells   Rosemary

Year	Title	VG-	VG	VG+	Fine	Author	Award	Pub
1996	My Very First Mother Goose		$10	$16	$20	Iona Opie (adapted)		Candle
1996	The Christmas Mystery		$40	$60	$80	Jostein Gaarder		FSG
1997	Bunny Cakes		$10	$16	$20	Rosemary Wells		Dial
1997	Bunny Money		$10	$16	$20	Rosemary Wells		HCollins
1998	Old MacDonald		$10	$14	$18	Rosemary Wells		Scholas
1998	Read To Your Bunny		$10	$14	$18	Rosemary Wells		Scholas
1998	The Bear Went Over The Mountain		$10	$14	$18	Rosemary Wells		Scholas
1998	The Itsy-Bitsy Spider		$10	$14	$18	Rosemary Wells		Scholas
1998	Yoko		$10	$14	$18	Rosemary Wells		Hyper
1999	Bingo		$10	$14	$18	Rosemary Wells		Scholas
1999	Here Comes Mother Goose		$10	$14	$18	Iona Opie (adapted)		Candle
2000	Emily's First 100 Days Of School		$8	$12	$16	Rosemary Wells		Hyper
2000	Goodnight Max		$8	$12	$16	Rosemary Wells		Viking
2000	Max Cleans Up		$8	$12	$16	Rosemary Wells		Viking
2000	Timothy's Lost And Found Day		$8	$12	$16	Rosemary Wells		Viking
2001	Benjamin's Treasure		$8	$12	$16	Garth Williams		HCollins
2001	Bunny Party		$8	$12	$16	Rosemary Wells		Viking
2001	Felix Feels Better		$8	$12	$16	Rosemary Wells		Candle
2001	Max In The Tub		$8	$12	$16	Rosemary Wells		G&D
2001	The Halloween Parade		$8	$12	$16	Rosemary Wells		Hyper
2001	Timothy's Class Trip		$8	$12	$16	Rosemary Wells		Viking
2001	Yoko's Paper Cranes		$8	$12	$16	Rosemary Wells		Hyper
2002	Getting To Know You!		$8	$10	$14	Rodgers & Hammerstein		HCollins
2002	Max And Ruby's Busy Week		$8	$10	$14	Rosemary Wells		G&D
2002	Play With Max And Ruby		$8	$10	$14	Rosemary Wells		G&D
2002	Ruby's Beauty Shop		$8	$10	$14	Rosemary Wells		Viking
2003	Emily's World Of Wonders		$8	$10	$14	Rosemary Wells		Hyper
2003	Felix And The Worrier		$8	$10	$14	Rosemary Wells		Candle
2003	Max And Ruby Play School		$8	$10	$14	Rosemary Wells		G&D
2003	Max's Christmas Stocking		$8	$10	$14	Rosemary Wells		Viking
2003	Only You		$8	$10	$14	Rosemary Wells		Viking
2004	Bunny Mail		$8	$10	$14	Rosemary Wells		Viking
2004	I Love You! A Bushel & A Peck		$8	$10	$14	Frank Loesser		HCollins

Wende   Philip

Year	Title	VG-	VG	VG+	Fine	Author	Award	Pub
1967	Hector, The Boy Who Loves Fleas	$30	$40	$50		Philip Wende		Singer
1967	Travels Of Doctor Dolittle	$60	$80	$100		Al Perkins (adapted)		BB
1968	Doctor Dolittle And The Pirates	$60	$80	$100		Al Perkins (adapted)		BB
1968	The Incredible Thrilling Adventures Of The Rock	$20	$30	$35		Michael O'Donoghue		Random
1969	Gaston's Ghastly Green Thumb	$20	$30	$35		Robert Littell		Cowles
1969	Hector Has A Flea Circus	$20	$30	$35		Philip Wende		Singer
1969	Left And Right With Lion And Ryan.	$20	$30	$35		Robert Littell		Cowles
1970	Animal Kingdom Dictionary		$18	$25	$35	S. Alan Cohen		Random
1970	Bird Boy		$18	$25	$35	Philip Wende		Cowles
1970	Let's Pretend Dictionary		$18	$25	$35	S. Alan Cohen		Random
1970	Playmates Dictionary		$18	$25	$35	S. Alan Cohen		Random
1970	Tell Me Why Dictionary		$18	$25	$35	S. Alan Cohen		Random
1970	Up And Away Dictionary		$18	$25	$35	S. Alan Cohen		Random
1971	The Hunter, The Tick, And The Gumberoo		$18	$25	$35	George Mendoza		Cowles
1972	Why Can't I Be William?		$18	$25	$35	Ellen Conford		LBrown

Wensell   Ulises

Year	Title	VG-	VG	VG+	Fine	Author	Award	Pub
1978	Come To Our House		$20	$30	$40	Charlotte Herman		RandMc
1979	Annie, The Invisible Girl		$14	$20	$30	José Luis García Sánchez		Metheun
1979	The Boy With Two Eyes		$14	$20	$30	José Luis García Sánchez		Metheun
1983	Little Lost Dog		$14	$20	$25	Howard Goldsmith		Santill
1983	Stormy Day Together		$14	$20	$25	Howard Goldsmith		Santill
1983	The Contest		$14	$20	$25	Howard Goldsmith		Santill
1983	The Greedy Monster		$14	$20	$25	Paloma Martínez		SBurdet
1983	Treasure Hunt		$14	$20	$25	Howard Goldsmith		Santill
1983	Welcome, Makoto!		$14	$20	$25	Howard Goldsmith		Santill
1986	A Walk In The Rain		$12	$16	$20	Ursel Scheffler		Putnam
1986	Ben Finds A Friend		$12	$16	$20	Anne-Marie Chapouton		Putnam
1987	I Wish I Were		$12	$16	$20	Geneviève Laurencin		Putnam

Wensell   Ulises

Year	Title	VG-	VG	VG+	Fine	Author	Award	Pub
1987	When The Lights Went Out		$12	$16	$20	Cris Baisch		Putnam
1988	Paul And Sebastian		$12	$16	$20	René Escudié		Kane
1994	They Followed A Bright Star		$10	$14	$18	Joan Alavedra		Putnam
1998	What Is God Like?		$8	$12	$16	Marie-Agnès Gaudrat		Litur
1998	Who Has Time For Little Bear?		$8	$12	$16	Ursel Scheffler		DoubleD
1999	Taking Care Of Sister Bear		$8	$12	$16	Ursel Scheffler		DoubleD

Werber   Adele

Year	Title	VG-	VG	VG+	Fine	Author	Award	Pub
1946	The Contented Little Pussy Cat	$40	$60	$70		Frances Ruth Keller		P&Munk
1947	Animal Babies	$35	$40	$60		Kathryn Jackson		S&S
1957	The Curious Little Owl	$25	$35	$50		Frances Ruth Keller		P&Munk
1958	Animal Alphabet A to Z	$25	$35	$50		Barbara Hazen		S&S
1963	Grimm's Fairy Tales	$25	$30	$40		Brothers Grimm		G&D

Werth   Kurt

Year	Title	VG-	VG	VG+	Fine	Author	Award	Pub
1946	Boniface The Bunny	$40	$60	$70		Muriel Laskey		PiedP
1946	Cyril The Squirrel	$40	$60	$70		Muriel Laskey		PiedP
1947	Hercules, The Gentle Giant	$35	$40	$60		Nina Schneider		Roy
1954	Little Teddy and the Big Sea	$30	$40	$50		Elizabeth Tate		LL&S
1955	Beech Tree	$100	$140	$180		Pearl S. Buck		JohnDay
1957	The Year Without A Santa Claus	$25	$35	$50		Phyllis McGinley		Lippin
1958	Seven for St. Nicholas	$25	$35	$50		Rosalyn Hall		Lippin
1959	Rainbow On The Rhine	$25	$35	$50		Helen Hilles		Lippin
1961	Tony's Birds	$25	$30	$40		Millicent Selsam		H&B
1964	Hear Ye Of Boston	$25	$30	$40		Polly Curren		LL&S
1965	Mr. Picklepaw's Popcorn	$25	$30	$40		Ruth Adams		LL&S
1965	The Valiant Tailor	$25	$30	$40		Kurt Werth		Viking
1966	Isabelle And The Library Cat	$25	$30	$40		Lillian Bason		LL&S
1966	Mcbroom Tells The Truth	$25	$30	$40		Sid Fleischman		Norton
1966	The Elf Who Didn't Believe In Himself	$25	$30	$40		Geraldine Ross		Steck-V
1967	Faraway Farm	$25	$30	$40		Maxine Kumin		Norton
1967	Mcbroom And The Big Wind	$25	$30	$40		Sid Fleischman		Norton
1967	The Cobbler's Dilemma	$25	$30	$40		Kurt Werth		McHill
1967	The Monkey, The Lion, And The Snake	$25	$30	$40		Kurt Werth		Viking
1968	Hear Ye Of Philadelphia	$20	$30	$35		Polly Curren		LL&S
1968	King Thrushbeard	$20	$30	$35		Kurt Werth		Viking
1968	Miranda's Dragon	$20	$30	$35		Rosalys Haskell Hall		McHill
1968	That Lincoln Boy	$20	$30	$35		Earl Schenck Miers		World
1969	Mcbroom's Ear	$20	$30	$35		Sid Fleischman		Norton
1969	One Dark Night	$20	$30	$35		Edna Mitchell Preston		Viking
1969	The Bright And Shining Breadboard	$20	$30	$35		Rosalys Haskell Hall		LL&S
1970	Lazy Jack		$18	$25	$35	Kurt Werth		Viking
1970	Mr. Picklepaw's Puppy		$18	$25	$35	Ruth & Guy Adams		LL&S
1970	Samuel Clemens		$18	$25	$35	Charles M. Daugherty		Crowell
1970	Who Are You Today?		$18	$25	$35	Richard Shaw		FWarne
1971	How A Piglet Crashed The Christmas Party		$18	$25	$35	Boris Vladimirovich Zakhoder		LL&S
1972	McBroom's Zoo		$18	$25	$35	Sid Fleischman		G&D
1973	Molly And The Giant		$16	$25	$30	Mabel Watts		PMagP
1974	Dick Whittington And His Cat		$16	$25	$30	Eva Moore		Seabury
1974	The Three Beggar Kings		$16	$25	$30	Rosalys Haskell Hall		Random

Wheeler   Cindy

Year	Title	VG-	VG	VG+	Fine	Author	Award	Pub
1980	A Good Day, A Good Night		$14	$20	$25	Cindy Wheeler		Lippin
1981	One Step, Two...		$14	$20	$25	Charlotte Zolotow		LL&S
1982	Marmalade's Snowy Day		$50	$70	$90	Cindy Wheeler		Knopf
1982	Marmalade's Yellow Leaf		$50	$70	$90	Cindy Wheeler		Knopf
1982	The Scaredy Cats And The Haunted House		$14	$20	$25	Cindy Wheeler		Random
1983	Dad Told Me Not To		$14	$20	$25	Susan Talanda		Rain
1983	Marmalade's Nap		$25	$35	$50	Cindy Wheeler		Knopf
1983	Marmalade's Picnic		$25	$35	$50	Cindy Wheeler		Knopf
1983	Someone Just Like Me		$14	$20	$25	Carol A. Marron		Rain
1984	Marmalade's Christmas Present		$20	$30	$40	Cindy Wheeler		Knopf

Wheeler   Cindy

Year	Title	VG-	VG	VG+	Fine	Author	Award	Pub
1985	Rose		$12	$18	$25	Cindy Wheeler		Knopf
1986	That Olive!		$12	$16	$20	Alice Schertle		LL&S
1988	Sally Wants To Help		$12	$16	$20	Cindy Wheeler		Random
1994	Bookstore Cat		$10	$14	$18	Cindy Wheeler		Random
1995	Simple Signs		$10	$14	$18	Cindy Wheeler		Viking
1996	The Emperor's Birthday Suit		$8	$12	$16	R.W. Alley (adapted)		Random
1998	Early Easter Morning		$8	$12	$16	Jane E. Gerver		LSimon
1998	More Simple Signs		$8	$12	$16	Cindy Wheeler		Viking
1998	What's In Your Basket?		$8	$12	$16	Jane E. Gerver		LSimon

Wheeler   Jody

Year	Title	VG-	VG	VG+	Fine	Author	Award	Pub
1993	The Tea Party Book		$12	$16	$20	Lucille Penner		Random
1997	The Teddy Bear Book		$8	$12	$16	Lucille Penner		Random
2001	Mama, Don't Go!		$8	$10	$14	Rosemary Wells		Hyper
2001	The School Play		$8	$10	$14	Rosemary Wells		Hyper
2002	Bubble-Gum Radar		$8	$10	$14	Rosemary Wells		Hyper
2002	Make New Friends		$8	$10	$14	Rosemary Wells		Viking
2002	Practice Makes Perfect		$8	$10	$14	Rosemary Wells		Hyper
2002	Read Me A Story		$8	$10	$14	Rosemary Wells		Hyper
2002	The Germ Busters		$8	$10	$14	Rosemary Wells		Hyper
2002	Timothy's Tales From Hilltop School		$8	$10	$14	Rosemary Wells		Viking
2003	When I Grow Up		$8	$10	$14	Rosemary Wells		Hyper

Whitman   Franklin

Year	Title	VG-	VG	VG+	Fine	Author	Award	Pub
1947	The Small One	$35	$40	$60		Charles Tazewell		WP

Wiberg   Harald

Year	Title	VG-	VG	VG+	Fine	Author	Award	Pub
1962	Christmas In The Stable	$40	$50	$70		Astrid Lindgren		CM&G
1965	The Tomten And The Fox	$30	$40	$50		Astrid Lindgren		CM&G
1968	Christmas At The Tomten's Farm	$30	$40	$50		Harald Wiberg		CM&G
1969	Dogs Of The World	$25	$35	$50		Ivan Swedrup		Arco
1969	Tomten	$25	$35	$50		Viktor Rydberg		Raben
1970	When Peter Was Lost In The Forest		$25	$35	$50	Hans Peterson		CM&G
1975	The Big Snowstorm		$20	$30	$40	Hans Peterson		CM&G
1981	The Christmas Tomten		$18	$25	$35	Viktor Rydberg		CM&G

Wickstrom   Sylvie

Year	Title	VG-	VG	VG+	Fine	Author	Award	Pub
1988	Wheels On The Bus		$14	$20	$30	Raffi		Crown
1989	Five Silly Fishermen		$12	$16	$20	Roberta Edwards		Random
1989	Mothers Can't Get Sick		$14	$20	$25	Sylvie Wickstrom		Crown
1989	The Christmas Coat		$12	$16	$20	Clyde Robert Bulla		Knopf
1990	The Squeaky Door		$10	$16	$20	Laura Simms		Crown
1990	Turkey On The Loose		$12	$18	$25	Sylvie Wickstrom		Dial
1990	Yours Till Niagara Falls		$10	$16	$20	Lillian Morrison		Crowell
1991	Armadillo		$10	$16	$20	Mary Elise Monsell		Athenm
1992	This Old House		$10	$16	$20	Karen Ackerman		Athenm
1994	Dog Days For Dudley		$10	$14	$18	Barbara A. Moe		BradP
1995	Hey! I'm Reading!		$10	$14	$18	Betty Miles		Knopf
1995	The Baby		$10	$14	$18	Amy Goldman Koss		OCP
1996	Walter The Warlock		$8	$12	$16	Deborah Hautzig		Random
1998	Little Witch Goes To School		$8	$12	$16	Deborah Hautzig		Random
1998	Silly Sadie, Silly Samuel		$8	$12	$16	Ann Whitford Paul		S&S
1999	Room For Ripley		$8	$12	$16	Stuart J. Murphy		HCollins
2000	Little Witch's Bad Dream		$8	$10	$14	Deborah Hautzig		Random
2002	Little Witch Goes To Camp		$8	$10	$14	Deborah Hautzig		Random
2002	Little Witch Takes Charge!		$8	$10	$14	Deborah Hautzig		Random
2002	Silly Sara		$8	$10	$14	Anna Jane Hays		Random
2003	Little Witch Learns To Read		$8	$10	$14	Deborah Hautzig		Random
2004	I Love You, Mister Bear		$6	$10	$12	Sylvie Wickstrom		HCollins
2004	Loose Tooth		$6	$10	$12	Lola M. Schaefer		HCollins

Wiese   Kurt

Year	Title	VG-	VG	VG+	Fine	Author	Award	Pub
1928	Bambi	$260	$340	$420		Felix Salten		S&S
1928	Don, The Story Of A Lion Dog	$260	$340	$420		Zane Grey		H&B
1928	Panther Magic	$160	$220	$280		Olaf Baker		DoddM
1928	The Three Little Kittens	$260	$340	$420		Kurt Wiese		Macmil
1929	A Book Of Mysteries	$70	$100	$120		Augusta Huiell Seaman		DD
1929	Karoo, The Kangaroo	$160	$220	$280		Kurt Wiese		CM
1929	Poodle-Oodle Of Doodle Farm	$100	$140	$180		Lawton Mackall		FStokes
1929	The Chinese Ink Stick	$70	$100	$120		Kurt Wiese		DD
1929	The Cradle Of The Deep	$70	$100	$120		Joan Lowell		S&S
1929	The Deliverymen	$100	$140	$180		Charlotte Kuh		Macmil
1929	The Engineer	$100	$140	$180		Charlotte Kuh		Macmil
1929	The Fireman	$100	$140	$180		Charlotte Kuh		Macmil
1929	The Motorman	$100	$140	$180		Charlotte Kuh		Macmil
1929	Wind On The Prairie	$70	$100	$120		Lenora Mattingly Weber		LBrown
1930	14th Street	$60	$80	$100		Percy Shostac		S&S
1930	Liang & Lo	$140	$180	$220		Kurt Wiese		DD
1930	Little Tooktoo	$140	$180	$220		Marie Ahnighito Peary		Morrow
1930	More To And Again	$460	$620	$780		Walter R. Brooks		Knopf
1930	The Adventures Of Mario	$60	$80	$100		Waldemar Bonsels		Boni
1930	The Gypsy Bridle	$90	$120	$160		Lenora Mattingly Weber		LBrown
1930	The Hound Of Florence	$60	$80	$100		Felix Salten		S&S
1930	The Life Story Of A Little Monkey	$60	$80	$100		Ferdynand Ossendowski		Dutton
1930	Wallie, The Walrus	$140	$180	$220		Kurt Wiese		CM
1931	Ella the Elephant	$140	$180	$220		Kurt Wiese		CM
1931	Joe Buys Nails	$140	$180	$220		Kurt Wiese		DD
1931	Muskox, Little Tooktoo's Friend	$90	$120	$160		Marie Peary		Morrow
1931	North America	$60	$80	$100		Lucy Sprague Mitchell		Macmil
1931	The White Leopard	$60	$80	$100		Inglis Fletcher		Bobbs
1932	Freddy The Detective	$460	$600	$760		Walter R. Brooks		Knopf
1932	The Jungle Book	$60	$80	$100		Rudyard Kipling		DD
1932	The Parrot Dealer	$60	$80	$100		Kurt Wiese		CM
1932	Wagtail	$60	$80	$100		Alice Crew Gall		Oxford
1932	Young Fu Of The Upper Yangtze	$460	$600	$760		Elizabeth Foreman Lewis	NM	HR&W
1933	The Story About Ping	$440	$600	$740		Marjorie Flack		Viking
1933	The Story of Little Black Sambo	$200	$260	$320		Helen Bannerman		GardenC
1934	Farm Boy	$80	$120	$140		Phil Stong		DD
1934	Ho-Ming	$60	$80	$100		Elizabeth Foreman Lewis		Winston
1934	Me An' Pete	$80	$120	$140		Wendell McKown		DD
1934	Odie Seeks A Friend	$80	$120	$140		Julius King		CM
1934	O-Go The Beaver	$60	$80	$100		Raymond Ransome Kelly		AWhit
1934	Our Planet The Earth Then And Now	$80	$120	$140		Lillian Rifkin		LL&S
1935	Camel Bells	$80	$120	$140		Anna Ratzesberger		AWhit
1935	Honk, The Moose	$280	$380	$480		Phil Stong	NH	DoddM
1935	Little Ones	$80	$120	$140		Dorothy M. Kunhardt		Viking
1935	The Blue Mittens	$60	$80	$100		Mary Katharine Reely		G&D
1935	Yen-Foh, A Chinese Boy	$80	$120	$140		Ethel J. Eldridge		AWhit
1936	All The Mowgli Stories	$60	$80	$100		Rudyard Kipling		DD
1936	Buddy The Bear	$120	$160	$220		Kurt Wiese		CM
1936	Gay Pippo	$80	$120	$140		Eleanor Fairchild Pease		AWhit
1936	Ling	$80	$120	$140		Ethel J. Eldridge		AWhit
1936	No-Sitch: The Hound	$80	$120	$140		Phil Stong		DoddM
1936	The Story Of Freginald	$440	$580	$720		Walter R. Brooks		Knopf
1937	Cheeky	$80	$120	$140		Josephine Sanger Lau		AWhit
1937	China Quest	$60	$80	$100		Elizabeth Foreman Lewis		Winston
1937	Each In His Way	$60	$80	$100		Alice Crew Gall		Oxford
1937	High Water	$80	$120	$140		Phil Stong		DoddM
1937	Jasmine	$60	$80	$100		Anna Ratzesberger		AWhit
1937	Ki-Ki	$80	$120	$140		Edith Janice Crane		AWhit
1937	Kurt Wiese's Picture Book Of Animals	$80	$120	$140		Kurt Wiese		CM
1937	Silver Chief To The Rescue	$60	$80	$100		John S O'Brien		Winston
1937	The Clockwork Twin	$340	$440	$560		Walter R. Brooks		Knopf
1938	Alice-Albert Elephant	$60	$80	$100		Marjorie Hayes		LBrown
1938	Carnival Time At Ströbeck	$80	$100	$140		May V Harris		AWhit
1938	Donkey Beads	$80	$100	$140		Anna Ratzesberger		AWhit
1938	Hamlet	$80	$100	$140		Irma Simonton Black		Holiday
1938	Jasper, The Gypsy Dog	$80	$100	$140		Mable Chesley Kahmann		Messner
1938	The Five Chinese Brothers	$80	$100	$140		Claire Huchet Bishop		CM

Wiese   Kurt

Year	Title	VG-	VG	VG+	Fine	Author	Award	Pub
1938	The Hidden Valley	$60	$80	$100		Laura Benét		DoddM
1938	The Streamlined Pig	$120	$160	$200		Margaret Wise Brown		H&B
1938	Yinka-Tu The Yak	$80	$100	$140		Alice Lide		Viking
1938	Young Settler	$80	$100	$140		Phil Stong		DoddM
1939	Amandus	$80	$100	$140		Elsie Glenn		MacSm
1939	Blackfellow Bundi	$80	$100	$140		Leila Gott Harris		AWhit
1939	Cats For The Tooseys	$80	$100	$140		Mabel Guinnip La Rue		TNelson
1939	Cowhand Goes To Town	$60	$80	$100		Phil Stong		DoddM
1939	Crunch	$80	$100	$140		Elizabeth Anne Bond		DoddM
1939	Dirk's Dog, Bello	$60	$80	$100		Meindert De Jong		H&B
1939	Hidden Valley	$60	$80	$100		Laura Benét		Harrap
1939	Horses And Americans	$60	$80	$100		Phil Stong		FStokes
1939	Joan And The Three Deer	$60	$80	$100		Marjorie Medary		Random
1939	Kip	$80	$100	$140		Irma Simonton Black		Holiday
1939	Saranga	$60	$80	$100		Attilio Gatti		Scribnr
1939	Silk And Satin Lane	$60	$80	$100		Esther Wood Brady		Longman
1939	The Penguin Twins	$60	$80	$100		Jane Tompkins McConnell		FStokes
1939	The Trail Of The Buffalo	$60	$80	$100		Rutherford Montgomery		HM
1939	Three Sisters	$60	$80	$100		Cornelia Spencer		JohnDay
1939	Wiggins For President	$320	$440	$540		Walter R. Brooks		Knopf
1940	Dogs	$50	$60	$80		Albert Payson Terhune		SaalF
1940	Freddy's Cousin Weedly	$260	$340	$420		Walter R. Brooks		Knopf
1940	Greased Lightning	$70	$90	$120		Sterling North		Winston
1940	On Safari	$50	$60	$80		Theodore J. Waldeck		Viking
1940	Pecos Bill And Lightning	$70	$90	$120		Leigh Peck		HM
1940	The King And The Princess	$70	$90	$120		Jack O'Brien		G&D
1940	The Rabbits' Revenge	$70	$90	$120		Kurt Wiese		CM
1940	Tito, The Pig Of Guatemala	$70	$90	$120		Charlotte E. Jackson		DoddM
1940	With Love And Irony	$50	$60	$80		Yutang Lin		JohnDay
1941	Alaska In Story And Pictures	$50	$60	$80		Marguerite Henry		AWhit
1941	Argentina In Story And Pictures	$50	$60	$80		Marguerite Henry		AWhit
1941	Bells Of The Harbor	$50	$60	$80		Meindert De Jong		H&B
1941	Brazil In Story And Pictures	$50	$60	$80		Marguerite Henry		AWhit
1941	Canada In Story And Pictures	$50	$60	$80		Marguerite Henry		AWhit
1941	Captain Kidd's Cow	$50	$60	$80		Phil Stong		DoddM
1941	Chile In Story And Pictures	$50	$60	$80		Marguerite Henry		AWhit
1941	Freddy And The Ignormus	$260	$340	$420		Walter R. Brooks		Knopf
1941	Mexico In Story And Pictures	$50	$60	$80		Marguerite Mexico		AWhit
1941	Muffy	$70	$90	$120		Laura Zenobia Le Fevre		AWhit
1941	Panama In Story And Pictures	$50	$60	$80		Marguerite Henry		AWhit
1941	Tapiola's Brave Regiment	$50	$60	$80		Robert Nathan		Knopf
1941	The Ferryman	$70	$90	$120		Claire Huchet Bishop		CM
1941	The White Panther	$50	$60	$80		Theodore J. Waldeck		Viking
1941	West Indies In Story And Pictures	$50	$60	$80		Marguerite Henry		AWhit
1941	Whampoa	$50	$60	$80		Hawthorne Daniel		Crowell
1942	Angleworms On Toast	$50	$60	$80		MacKinlay Kantor		CM
1942	Bolivia In Story And Pictures	$50	$60	$80		Bernadine Bailey		AWhit
1942	Corn-Belt Billy	$70	$90	$120		Mabel Leigh Hunt		G&D
1942	Ecuador In Story And Pictures	$50	$60	$80		Bernadine Bailey		AWhit
1942	Favorite Stories Old And New	$50	$60	$80		Sidonie M. Gruenberg		DD
1942	Freddy And The Perilous Adventure	$240	$320	$400		Walter R. Brooks		Knopf
1942	Greenland In Story And Pictures	$50	$60	$80		Bernadine Bailey		AWhit
1942	Guatemala In Story And Pictures	$50	$60	$80		Bernadine Bailey		AWhit
1942	Honduras In Story And Pictures	$50	$60	$80		Bernadine Bailey		AWhit
1942	Iceland In Story And Pictures	$50	$60	$80		Bernadine Bailey		AWhit
1942	Jamba The Elephant	$50	$60	$80		Theodore J. Waldeck		Viking
1942	Juneau, The Sleigh Dog	$50	$60	$80		West Lathrop		Random
1942	Lions On The Hunt	$50	$60	$80		Theodore J. Waldeck		Viking
1942	Little Boy Lost In Brazil	$70	$90	$120		Kurt Wiese		DoddM
1942	Nibs	$70	$90	$120		Don Lang		G&D
1942	Paddy's Christmas	$70	$90	$120		Helen Albee Monsell		Knopf
1942	Peru In Story And Pictures	$50	$60	$80		Bernadine Bailey		AWhit
1942	Spike Of Swift River	$50	$60	$80		Jack O'Brien		Winston
1942	Tents In The Wilderness	$50	$60	$80		Julius Lips		FStokes
1942	The Raccoon Twins	$50	$60	$80		Jane Tompkins McConnell		FStokes
1942	Way Down Cellar	$50	$60	$80		Phil Stong		DoddM
1942	When The Typhoon Blows	$50	$60	$80		Elizabeth Foreman Lewis		Winston

Wiese   Kurt

Year	Title	VG-	VG	VG+	Fine	Author	Award	Pub
1942	White Stars Of Freedom	$50	$60	$80		Mirim Isasi		AWhit
1943	A Puppy For Keeps	$70	$90	$120		Quail Hawkins		Holiday
1943	A Very Special Pet	$70	$90	$120		Lavinia R. Davis		G&D
1943	Adventure In Black And White	$50	$60	$80		Attilio Gatti		Scribnr
1943	Costa Rica In Story And Pictures	$50	$60	$80		Lois Donaldson		AWhit
1943	El Salvador In Story And Pictures	$50	$60	$80		Lois Donaldson		AWhit
1943	Freddy And The Bean Home News	$240	$320	$400		Walter R. Brooks		Knopf
1943	Igor's Summer	$70	$90	$120		Lorraine Beim		RWR
1943	Made In China	$50	$60	$80		Cornelia Spencer		Knopf
1943	Midnight And Jeremiah	$70	$90	$120		Sterling North		Winston
1943	Missouri Canary	$70	$90	$120		Phil Stong		DoddM
1943	Mr Red Squirrel	$70	$90	$120		Thomas P. Robinson		Viking
1943	Nicaragua In Story And Pictures	$50	$60	$80		Lois Donaldson		AWhit
1943	Oswald's Pet Dragon	$70	$90	$120		Carl Glick		CM
1943	Roger And The Fishes	$70	$90	$120		Charlotte E. Jackson		DoddM
1943	Sly Mongoose	$50	$60	$80		Katherine G. Pollock		Scribnr
1943	The Return Of Silver Chief	$70	$90	$120		Jack O'Brien		Winston
1943	Tramp, The Sheep Dog	$70	$90	$120		Don Lang		G&D
1943	Uruguay In Story And Pictures	$50	$60	$80		Lois Donaldson		AWhit
1944	Central American Roundabout	$50	$60	$80		Agnes Rothery		DoddM
1944	Colombia In Story And Pictures	$50	$60	$80		Lois Donaldson		AWhit
1944	Freddy And Mr. Camphor	$240	$320	$400		Walter R. Brooks		Knopf
1944	Guiana In Story And Pictures	$50	$60	$80		Lois Donaldson		AWhit
1944	Newfoundland In Story And Pictures	$50	$60	$80		Lois Donaldson		AWhit
1944	Paraguay In Story And Pictures	$50	$60	$80		Lois Donaldson		AWhit
1944	The Adventures Of Monkey	$50	$60	$80		Cheng'en Wu		JohnDay
1945	Censored, the Goat	$60	$80	$100		Phil Stong		DoddM
1945	Freddy And The Popinjay	$220	$300	$380		Walter R. Brooks		Knopf
1945	Hello, Alaska	$40	$60	$70		Sarah Litchfield		AWhit
1945	Mpengo Of The Congo	$40	$60	$70		Grace W McGavran		Friend
1945	The Eskimo Hunter	$40	$60	$70		Florence Hayes		Random
1945	The Wizard And His Magic Powder	$40	$60	$70		Alfred Stuart Campbell		Knopf
1945	You Can Write Chinese	$140	$180	$220		Kurt Wiese	CH	Viking
1946	Australia In Story And Pictures	$40	$60	$70		Marguerite Henry		AWhit
1946	Bermuda In Story And Pictures	$40	$60	$70		Marguerite Henry		AWhit
1946	British Honduras In Story And Pictures	$40	$60	$70		Marguerite Henry		AWhit
1946	Dominican Republic In Story And Pictures	$40	$60	$70		Marguerite Henry		AWhit
1946	Freddy The Pied Piper	$220	$300	$380		Walter R. Brooks		Knopf
1946	Hawaii In Story An Pictures	$40	$60	$70		Marguerite Henry		AWhit
1946	Jungle Journey	$40	$60	$70		Jo Besse McElveen Waldeck		Viking
1946	Mr 2 Of Everything	$60	$80	$100		M S Klutch		CM
1946	New Zealand In Story And Pictures	$40	$60	$70		Marguerite Henry		AWhit
1946	The Bahamas In Story And Pictures	$40	$60	$70		Marguerite Henry		AWhit
1946	The Four Friends	$60	$80	$100		Eleanor Hoffmann		Macmil
1946	The Home-Builders	$40	$60	$70		Warren H Miller		Winston
1946	The Picture Story Of China	$40	$60	$70		Emily Hahn		ReyHitc
1946	This Is The Moon	$40	$60	$70		Marion Benedict Cothren		CM
1946	Twenty Thousand Leagues Under The Sea	$40	$60	$70		Jules Verne		World
1946	Virgin Islands In Story And Pictures	$40	$60	$70		Marguerite Henry		AWhit
1946	Wild West Bill Rides Home	$60	$80	$100		Muriek Millen		AWhit
1947	Abraham, The Itinerant Mouse	$60	$80	$100		Donald Hutter		DoddM
1947	Dumblebum	$60	$80	$100		Elsie Glenn		MacSm
1947	Freddy The Magician	$220	$300	$380		Walter R. Brooks		Knopf
1947	Li Lun, Lad Of Courage	$40	$60	$70		Carolyn Treffinger		Abing
1947	Positive Pete	$60	$80	$100		Phil Stong		DoddM
1948	Daughter Of The Mountains	$40	$60	$70		Louise Rankin		Viking
1948	Fish In The Air	$60	$80	$100		Kurt Wiese		Viking
1948	Freddy And The Politician	$220	$300	$380		Walter R. Brooks		Knopf
1948	Freddy Goes Camping	$220	$300	$380		Walter R. Brooks		Knopf
1948	Freddy The Politician	$220	$300	$380		Walter R. Brooks		Knopf
1948	Rosie, The Rhino	$60	$80	$100		Marion Conger		Abing
1948	What Every Young Rabbit Should Know	$60	$80	$100		Carol Denison		DoddM
1949	Freddy Goes To Florida	$220	$280	$360		Walter R. Brooks		Knopf
1949	Freddy Plays Football	$220	$280	$360		Walter R. Brooks		Knopf
1949	Laughing Matter	$40	$60	$70		Helen R. Smith		Scribnr
1949	Little Circus Dog	$60	$80	$100		Jene Barr		AWhit
1949	Little Prairie Dog	$60	$80	$100		Jene Barr		AWhit

Wiese   Kurt

Year	Title	VG-	VG	VG+	Fine	Author	Award	Pub
1949	Mrs. Piggle-Wiggle's Magic	$120	$160	$220		Betty MacDonald		Lippin
1949	Picture Book Of California	$40	$60	$70		Bernadine Bailey		AWhit
1949	Picture Book Of Florida	$40	$60	$70		Bernadine Bailey		AWhit
1949	Picture Book Of Illinois	$40	$60	$70		Bernadine Bailey		AWhit
1949	Picture Book Of Massachusetts	$40	$60	$70		Bernadine Bailey		AWhit
1950	Freddy The Cowboy	$220	$280	$360		Walter R. Brooks		Knopf
1950	Picture Book Of Colorado	$40	$50	$70		Bernadine Bailey		AWhit
1950	Picture Book Of Indiana	$40	$50	$70		Bernadine Bailey		AWhit
1950	Picture Book Of Michigan	$40	$50	$70		Bernadine Bailey		AWhit
1950	Picture Book Of New York	$40	$50	$70		Bernadine Bailey		AWhit
1950	Picture Book Of North Carolina	$40	$50	$70		Bernadine Bailey		AWhit
1950	Picture Book Of Ohio	$40	$50	$70		Bernadine Bailey		AWhit
1950	Picture Book Of Pennsylvania	$40	$50	$70		Bernadine Bailey		AWhit
1950	Picture Book Of Texas	$40	$50	$70		Bernadine Bailey		AWhit
1950	Quest In The Desert	$40	$50	$70		Roy Chapman Andrews		Viking
1950	The Fables Of Aesop	$40	$50	$70		Joseph Jacobs		Macmil
1950	The Walking Hat	$60	$80	$100		William Hall		Knopf
1951	Freddy Goes To The North Pole	$220	$280	$360		Walter R. Brooks		Knopf
1951	Freddy Rides Again	$220	$280	$360		Walter R. Brooks		Knopf
1951	Picture Book Of Missouri	$40	$50	$70		Bernadine Bailey		AWhit
1951	Picture Book Of Virginia	$40	$50	$70		Bernadine Bailey		AWhit
1952	Children Of The Blizzard	$40	$50	$70		Heluiz Chandler Washburne		JohnDay
1952	Freddy The Pilot	$200	$280	$340		Walter R. Brooks		Knopf
1952	Happy Easter	$50	$70	$90		Kurt Wiese		Viking
1952	Picture Book Of Iowa	$40	$50	$70		Bernadine Bailey		AWhit
1952	Picture Book Of Oklahoma	$40	$50	$70		Bernadine Bailey		AWhit
1952	Picture Book Of Tennessee	$40	$50	$70		Bernadine Bailey		AWhit
1953	Freddy And The Space Ship	$200	$280	$340		Walter R. Brooks		Knopf
1953	Picture Book Of Alabama	$40	$50	$70		Bernadine Bailey		AWhit
1953	Picture Book Of Georgia	$40	$50	$70		Bernadine Bailey		AWhit
1953	Picture Book Of Minnesota	$40	$50	$70		Bernadine Bailey		AWhit
1953	The Collected Poems Of Freddy The Pig	$200	$280	$340		Walter R. Brooks		Knopf
1953	The Dog, The Fox, And The Fleas	$50	$70	$90		Kurt Wiese		DMcKay
1954	Freddy And The Men From Mars	$200	$280	$340		Walter R. Brooks		Knopf
1954	Picture Book Of Louisiana	$40	$50	$70		Bernadine Bailey		AWhit
1954	Picture Book Of Oregon	$40	$50	$70		Bernadine Bailey		AWhit
1955	Freddy And The Baseball Team From Mars	$200	$260	$320		Walter R. Brooks		Knopf
1955	Lions In The Barn	$50	$70	$90		Virginia Frances Voight		Holiday
1955	Picture Book Of Connecticut	$35	$50	$60		Bernadine Bailey		AWhit
1955	Picture Book Of Kentucky	$35	$50	$60		Bernadine Bailey		AWhit
1955	Picture Book Of Maryland	$35	$50	$60		Bernadine Bailey		AWhit
1956	Early Old Testament Stories	$35	$50	$60		Ethel Smither		Abing
1956	First To Be Called Christmas	$35	$50	$60		Ethel Smither		Abing
1956	Freddy And Simon The Dictator	$200	$260	$320		Walter R. Brooks		Knopf
1956	Later Old Testament Stories	$35	$50	$60		Ethel Smither		Abing
1956	Stories Of Jesus	$35	$50	$60		Ethel Smither		Abing
1956	The Cunning Turtle	$50	$70	$90		Kurt Wiese		Viking
1957	Freddy And The Flying Saucer Plans	$200	$260	$320		Walter R. Brooks		Knopf
1957	Picture Book Of Arizona	$35	$50	$60		Bernadine Bailey		AWhit
1957	Picture Book Of Arkansas	$35	$50	$60		Bernadine Bailey		AWhit
1957	Picture Book Of Maine	$35	$50	$60		Bernadine Bailey		AWhit
1957	Picture Book Of Utah	$35	$50	$60		Bernadine Bailey		AWhit
1958	Chipmunk Terrace	$50	$60	$80		John Oldrin		Viking
1958	Freddy And The Dragon	$180	$240	$300		Walter R. Brooks		Knopf
1958	Great Gravity the Cat	$50	$60	$80		Johanna Johnston		Knopf
1959	Picture Book Of Alaska	$35	$50	$60		Bernadine Bailey		AWhit
1959	Pika And The Roses	$50	$60	$80		Elizabeth Coatsworth		Pan
1959	The Groundhog And His Shadow	$50	$60	$80		Kurt Wiese		Viking
1960	Picture Book Of New Mexico	$35	$40	$60		Bernadine Bailey		AWhit
1960	What? Another Cat!	$50	$60	$80		John Beecroft		DoddM
1962	Picture Book Of Washington	$35	$40	$60		Bernadine Bailey		AWhit
1963	Rabbit Bros Circus	$50	$60	$80		Kurt Wiese		Viking
1963	The Yangtze: China's River Highway	$35	$40	$60		Cornelia Spencer		Garrard
1964	Picture Book Of Hawaii	$35	$40	$60		Bernadine Bailey		AWhit
1964	The Thames, London's River	$35	$40	$60		Noel Streatfeild		Garrard
1964	Twenty-Two Bears	$50	$60	$80		Claire Huchet Bishop		Viking
1965	Picture Book Of Nevada	$30	$40	$50		Bernadine Bailey		AWhit

464

Wiese   Kurt

Year	Title	VG-	VG	VG+	Fine	Author	Award	Pub
1965	Picture Book Of New Hampshire	$30	$40	$50		Bernadine Bailey		AWhit
1965	Picture Book Of New Jersey	$30	$40	$50		Bernadine Bailey		AWhit
1965	The Thief In The Attic	$40	$60	$70		Kurt Wiese		Viking
1966	Picture Book Of Delaware	$30	$40	$50		Bernadine Bailey		AWhit
1966	Picture Book Of Mississippi	$30	$40	$50		Bernadine Bailey		AWhit
1966	Picture Book Of North Dakota	$30	$40	$50		Bernadine Bailey		AWhit
1966	Picture Book Of Rhode Island	$30	$40	$50		Bernadine Bailey		AWhit
1966	Picture Book Of South Carolina	$30	$40	$50		Bernadine Bailey		AWhit
1966	Picture Book Of South Dakota	$30	$40	$50		Bernadine Bailey		AWhit
1966	Picture Book Of Wyoming	$30	$40	$50		Bernadine Bailey		AWhit
1967	Picture Book Of Idaho	$30	$40	$50		Bernadine Bailey		AWhit
1971	The Truffle Pig		$30	$50	$60	Claire Huchet Bishop		CM

Wiesner   David

Year	Title	VG-	VG	VG+	Fine	Author	Award	Pub
1980	Honest Andrew		$50	$70	$100	Gloria Skurzynski		HBJ
1980	Man From The Sky		$50	$70	$100	Avi		Knopf
1981	The Boy Who Spoke Chimp		$35	$50	$70	Jane Yolen		Knopf
1981	The One Bad Thing About Birthdays		$25	$35	$50	David R. Collins		HBJ
1981	The Ugly Princess		$25	$35	$50	Nancy Luenn		LBrown
1982	Neptune Rising: Songs And Tales Of The Undersea Folk		$30	$50	$60	Jane Yolen		Philo
1982	Owly		$25	$35	$50	Mike Thaler		H&Row
1983	Miranty And The Alchemist		$25	$35	$50	Vera Chapmen		Avon
1984	The Dark Green Tunnel		$20	$30	$40	Allan W. Eckert		LBrown
1985	E.T., The Storybook Of The Green Planet		$20	$30	$40	William Kotzwinkle		Putnam
1985	The Wand: The Return To Mesmeria		$20	$30	$40	Allan W. Eckert		LBrown
1986	Kite Flier		$20	$30	$40	Dennis Haseley		4Winds
1987	The Loathsome Dragon		$25	$40	$50	Kim Kahng (retold)		Putnam
1988	Firebrat		$18	$25	$35	Nancy Willard		Knopf
1988	Free Fall		$40	$60	$90	David Wiesner	CH	LL&S
1989	The Rainbow People		$18	$25	$35	Laurence Yep		H&Row
1989	The Sorcerer's Apprentice		$18	$25	$35	Marianna Mayer		Bantam
1990	Hurricane		$16	$25	$30	David Wiesner		Clarion
1991	Tongues Of Jade		$16	$25	$30	Laurence Yep		HCollins
1991	Tuesday		$100	$140	$200	David Wiesner	CM	Clarion
1992	June 29,1999		$16	$25	$30	David Wiesner		Clarion
1994	Night Of The Gargoyles		$14	$20	$30	Eve Bunting		Clarion
1996	Moo!		$12	$18	$25	David Wiesner		Clarion
1997	Looking For Merlyn		$12	$18	$25	Dilys Evans		Scholas
1999	Sector 7		$35	$50	$70	David Wiesner	CH	Clarion
2001	The Three Pigs		$35	$50	$70	David Wiesner	CM	Clarion
2005	The Loathsome Dragon		$6	$10	$12	Kim Kahng (retold)		Clarion

Wijngaard   Juan

Year	Title	VG-	VG	VG+	Fine	Author	Award	Pub
1981	Sir Gawain And The Green Knight		$25	$35	$50	Selina Hastings		LL&S
1982	Janni's Stork		$16	$25	$30	Rosemary Harris		Bedrik
1983	Jelly Belly		$16	$25	$30	Dennis Lee		Bedrik
1985	Sir Gawain And The Loathly Lady		$30	$40	$60	Selina Hastings (retold)	GM	LL&S
1987	Tiger's Railway		$20	$30	$40	William Mayne		Walker
1988	The Faber Book Of Favourite Fairy Tales		$14	$20	$30	Sara & Stephen Corrin (edited)		Faber
1989	Hanukkah: The Festival Of Lights		$14	$20	$25	Jenny Koralek		Walker
1989	The Nativity		$14	$20	$25	Juan Wijngaard		LL&S
1990	Bear		$12	$18	$25	Juan Wijngaard		Crown
1990	Cat		$12	$18	$25	Juan Wijngaard		Crown
1990	Dog		$12	$18	$25	Juan Wijngaard		Crown
1990	Duck		$12	$18	$25	Juan Wijngaard		Crown
1992	Going To Sleep On The Farm		$12	$18	$25	Wendy Cheyette Lewison		Dial
1993	Emma Bean		$12	$16	$20	Jean Van Leeuwen		Dial
1994	Thunderstorm!		$12	$16	$20	Nathaniel Tripp		Dial
1995	Buzz Buzz		$10	$16	$20	Juan Wijngaard		MacD
1995	Buzz! Buzz!		$10	$16	$20	Steve Augarde		LodeS
1996	A Piece Of Home		$10	$16	$20	Sonia Levitin		Dial
1996	Esther's Story		$10	$16	$20	Diane Wolkstein		Morrow
1998	Tales Of Wonder And Magic		$10	$14	$18	Berlie Doherty (selected)		Candle
1999	The Midas Touch		$10	$14	$18	Jan Mark		Candle

Wijngaard   Juan

Year	Title	VG-	VG	VG+	Fine	Author	Award	Pub
2000	The King Of The Golden River		$8	$12	$16	John Ruskin		Candle

Wildsmith   Brian

Year	Title	VG-	VG	VG+	Fine	Author	Award	Pub
1963	ABC	$70	$90	$120		Brian Wildsmith	GM	FWatts
1963	Oxford Book Of Poetry For Children	$50	$60	$80		Edward Blishen		FWatts
1963	The Lion And The Rat	$50	$60	$80		Jean de La Fontaine		FWatts
1964	Brian Wildsmith's Mother Goose	$60	$80	$100		Brian Wildsmith		FWatts
1964	The North Wind And The Sun	$50	$60	$80		Jean de La Fontaine		FWatts
1965	Brian Wildsmith's 1, 2, 3's	$60	$80	$100		Brian Wildsmith		FWatts
1965	Havelok The Dane	$40	$60	$70		Kevin Crossley-Holland		Dutton
1965	The Rich Man And The Shoe-Maker	$40	$60	$70		Jean de La Fontaine		FWatts
1966	A Child's Garden Of Verses	$40	$60	$70		Robert Louis Stevenson		FWatts
1967	Birds	$40	$50	$70		Brian Wildsmith		Oxford
1967	Brian Wildsmith's Birds	$60	$80	$100		Brian Wildsmith		FWatts
1967	The Hare And The Tortoise	$40	$50	$70		Jean de La Fontaine		FWatts
1967	Wild Animals	$40	$50	$70		Brian Wildsmith		FWatts
1968	Fishes	$40	$50	$70		Brian Wildsmith		FWatts
1969	Brian Wildsmith's Illustrated Bible Stories	$40	$50	$70		Philip Turner		FWatts
1969	The Miller, The Boy, And The Donkey	$40	$50	$70		Jean de La Fontaine		FWatts
1970	Brian Wildsmith's Circus		$30	$50	$60	Brian Wildsmith		FWatts
1971	Puzzles		$30	$50	$60	Brian Wildsmith		FWatts
1972	The Little Wood Duck		$30	$50	$60	Brian Wildsmith		Oxford
1972	The Owl And The Woodpecker		$30	$50	$60	Brian Wildsmith		FWatts
1972	The Twelve Days Of Christmas		$30	$50	$60	Brian Wildsmith		FWatts
1974	The Lazy Bear		$30	$40	$60	Brian Wildsmith		FWatts
1975	Python's Party		$30	$40	$60	Brian Wildsmith		FWatts
1975	Squirrels		$30	$40	$60	Brian Wildsmith		FWatts
1976	Maurice Maeterlinck's Blue Bird		$30	$40	$60	Maurice Maeterlinck		FWatts
1977	The True Cross		$25	$40	$50	Brian Wildsmith		Oxford
1978	What The Moon Saw		$25	$40	$50	Brian Wildsmith		Oxford
1979	Hunter And His Dog		$25	$40	$50	Brian Wildsmith		Oxford
1980	Animal Games		$25	$35	$50	Brian Wildsmith		Oxford
1980	Animal Homes		$25	$35	$50	Brian Wildsmith		Oxford
1980	Animal Shapes		$25	$35	$50	Brian Wildsmith		Oxford
1980	Animal Tricks		$25	$35	$50	Brian Wildsmith		Oxford
1980	Professor Noah's Spaceship		$25	$35	$50	Brian Wildsmith		Oxford
1980	Seasons		$25	$35	$50	Brian Wildsmith		Oxford
1981	Bear's Adventure		$25	$35	$50	Brian Wildsmith		Pan
1982	Pelican		$25	$35	$50	Brian Wildsmith		Pan
1984	Daisy		$20	$30	$40	Brian Wildsmith		Pan
1985	Brian Wildsmith's Book Of Bedtime Stories		$20	$30	$40	Brian Wildsmith		Pan
1985	Give A Dog A Bone		$20	$30	$40	Brian Wildsmith		Pan
1986	Goat's Trail		$20	$30	$40	Brian Wildsmith		Knopf
1988	Carousel		$18	$25	$35	Brian Wildsmith		Knopf
1989	A Christmas Story		$18	$25	$35	Brian Wildsmith		Knopf
1990	The Snow Country Prince		$16	$25	$30	G. McCaughrean (adapted)		Knopf
1992	Over The Deep Blue Sea		$16	$25	$30	G. McCaughrean (adapted)		Knopf
1992	The Cherry Tree		$16	$25	$30	G. McCaughrean (adapted)		Knopf
1992	The Princess And The Moon		$16	$25	$30	G. McCaughrean (adapted)		Knopf
1993	Look Closer		$16	$25	$30	Brian & Rebecca Wildsmith		GB
1993	Wake Up, Wake Up!		$16	$25	$30	Brian & Rebecca Wildsmith		HBJ
1993	What Did I Find?		$16	$25	$30	Brian & Rebecca Wildsmith		HBJ
1993	Whose Hat Was That?		$16	$25	$30	Brian & Rebecca Wildsmith		HBJ
1994	Brian Wildsmith's Noah's Ark		$14	$20	$30	Brian Wildsmith		Harper
1994	Jack And The Meanstalk		$14	$20	$30	Brian & Rebecca Wildsmith		Knopf
1994	The Easter Story		$14	$20	$30	Brian Wildsmith		Knopf
1995	The Creation		$14	$20	$25	Brian Wildsmith		Oxford
1996	Brian Wildsmith's Animals To Count		$12	$18	$25	Brian Wildsmith		StarB
1996	Brian Wildsmith's Opposites		$12	$18	$25	Brian Wildsmith		StarB
1996	Brian Wildsmith's Puzzles		$12	$18	$25	Brian Wildsmith		Millbk
1996	Katie And The Dream-Eater		$12	$18	$25	Miya Hisako Takamado		Oxford
1996	Saint Francis		$12	$18	$25	Brian Wildsmith		EerdB
1996	The Circus		$12	$18	$25	Brian Wildsmith		Millbk
1997	All Fall Down		$12	$18	$25	Brian Wildsmith		Oxford
1997	Brian Wildsmith's Amazing World Of Words		$12	$18	$25	Brian Wildsmith		Millbk

Wildsmith   Brian

Year	Title	VG-	VG	VG+	Fine	Author	Award	Pub
1997	If I Were You		$12	$18	$25	Brian Wildsmith		Oxford
1997	Joseph		$12	$18	$25	Brian Wildsmith		EerdB
1997	My Dream		$12	$18	$25	Brian Wildsmith		Oxford
1997	The Apple Bird		$12	$18	$25	Brian Wildsmith		Oxford
1997	The Trunk		$12	$18	$25	Brian Wildsmith		Oxford
1997	Toot, Toot		$12	$18	$25	Brian Wildsmith		Oxford
1997	What A Tale		$12	$18	$25	Brian Wildsmith		Oxford
1998	Exodus		$12	$16	$20	Brian Wildsmith		EerdB
2000	Jesus		$10	$14	$18	Brian Wildsmith		EerdB
2001	Brian Wildsmith's Animal Colors		$10	$14	$18	Brian Wildsmith		StarB
2001	Brian Wildsmith's Farm Animals		$10	$14	$18	Brian Wildsmith		StarB
2002	Brian Wildsmith's Zoo Animals		$8	$12	$16	Brian Wildsmith		StarB
2002	Mary		$8	$12	$16	Brian Wildsmith		EerdB

Willems   Mo

Year	Title	VG-	VG	VG+	Fine	Author	Award	Pub
2003	Don't Let The Pigeon Drive The Bus		$30	$40	$60	Mo Willems	CH	Hyper
2003	Time To Peel		$8	$12	$16	Mo Willems		Hyper
2004	Pigeon Finds A Hot Dog!		$8	$10	$14	Mo Willems		Hyper
2004	The Knuffle Bunny		$18	$25	$35	Mo Willems	CH	Hyper
2005	Leonardo the Terrible Monster		$6	$10	$12	Mo Wiillems		Hyper

Williams   Garth

Year	Title	VG-	VG	VG+	Fine	Author	Award	Pub
1945	Stuart Little	$300	$400	$500		E. B. White		H&B
1945	The Door Opens	$60	$80	$100		Garth Williams		DoubleD
1946	In Our Town	$160	$200	$260		Damon Runyon	CH	CAP
1946	Little Fur Family	$200	$260	$320		Margaret Wise Brown		H&B
1946	The Chicken Book	$90	$120	$160		Garth Williams		Howell
1948	Robin Hood	$60	$80	$100		Henry Gilbert		Lippin
1948	The Golden Sleepy Book	$80	$120	$140		Margaret Wise Brown		S&S
1948	Wait Till The Moon Is Full	$80	$120	$140		Margaret Wise Brown		H&B
1951	Fox Eyes	$80	$100	$140		Margaret Wise Brown		Pan
1951	Golden Books Treasury Of Elves & Fairies	$120	$160	$200		Jane Werner Watson		S&S
1951	The Adventures Of Benjamin Pink	$50	$70	$90		Garth Williams		H&B
1952	Baby Animals	$50	$70	$90		Garth Williams		S&S
1952	Charlotte's Web	$580	$780	$980		E. B. White	NH	H&B
1953	Baby Farm Animals	$40	$50	$70		Garth Williams		S&S
1953	Baby's First Book	$40	$50	$70		Garth Williams		S&S
1953	By The Shores Of Silver Lake	$100	$120	$160		Laura Ingalls Wilder		H&B
1953	Farmer Boy	$100	$120	$160		Laura Ingalls Wilder		H&B
1953	Little House In The Big Woods	$100	$120	$160		Laura Ingalls Wilder		H&B
1953	Little House On The Prairie	$100	$120	$160		Laura Ingalls Wilder		H&B
1953	Little Town On The Prairie	$100	$120	$160		Laura Ingalls Wilder		H&B
1953	My Bedtime Book	$50	$70	$90		Garth Williams		Golden
1953	On The Banks Of Plum Creek	$100	$120	$160		Laura Ingalls Wilder		H&B
1953	The Long Winter	$100	$120	$160		Laura Ingalls Wilder		H&B
1953	These Happy Golden Years	$100	$120	$160		Laura Ingalls Wilder		H&B
1954	The Golden Animal A. B. C	$40	$50	$70		Garth Williams		S&S
1955	The Golden Name Day	$35	$50	$60		Jennie D. Lindquist		H&B
1956	Three Little Animals	$70	$100	$120		Margaret Wise Brown		H&B
1957	Over And Over	$50	$70	$90		Charlotte Zolotow		HCollins
1957	The Happy Orpheline	$35	$50	$60		Natalie Carlson		H&B
1958	Do You Know What I'll Do?	$50	$60	$80		Charlotte Zolotow		H&B
1958	The Family Under The Bridge	$35	$50	$60		Natalie Carlson		H&B
1958	The Rabbits' Wedding	$50	$60	$80		Garth Williams		H&B
1958	Three Bedtime Stories:	$50	$60	$80		Garth Williams		S&S
1959	A Brother For The Orphelines	$35	$50	$60		Natalie Carlson		H&B
1959	Baby's First Book	$50	$60	$80		Garth Williams		Golden
1959	Emmett's Pig	$35	$50	$60		Mary Stolz		H&B
1959	The Rescuers	$100	$140	$180		Margery Sharp		LBrown
1960	Bedtime For Frances	$100	$140	$180		Russell Hoban		H&B
1960	The Cricket In Times Square	$160	$200	$260		George Selden	NH	Ariel
1963	Amigo	$50	$60	$80		Byrd Baylor		Macmil
1963	The Sky Was Blue	$50	$60	$80		Charlotte Zolotow		H&Row
1963	The Turret	$35	$40	$60		Margery Sharp		LBrown

Williams — Garth

Year	Title	VG-	VG	VG+	Fine	Author	Award	Pub
1964	Bread-And-Butter Indian	$35	$40	$60		Polly Anne Graff		HR&W
1964	The Gingerbread Rabbit	$35	$40	$60		Randall Jarrell		Macmil
1966	Miss Bianca In The Salt Mines	$30	$40	$50		Margery Sharp		LBrown
1966	The Golden Name Day	$30	$40	$50		Jennie D. Lindquist		H&Row
1968	Push Kitty	$40	$50	$70		Jan Wahl		H&Row
1969	Tucker's Countryside	$25	$35	$50		George Selden		FSG
1970	Bread-And-Butter Journey		$25	$35	$50	Polly Anne Graff		HR&W
1971	The First Four Years		$25	$35	$50	Laura Ingalls Wilder		H&Row
1971	The Golden Sleepy Book		$18	$25	$35	Garth Williams		Golden
1974	Harry Cat's Pet Puppy		$20	$30	$40	George Selden		FSG
1977	Fox Eyes		$16	$25	$30	Margaret Wise Brown		Pan
1981	Chester Cricket's Pigeon Ride		$18	$25	$35	George Selden		FSG
1983	Chester Cricket's New Home		$16	$25	$30	George Selden		FSG
1986	Harry Kitten And Tucker Mouse		$14	$20	$30	George Selden		FSG
1986	Ride A Purple Pelican		$14	$20	$30	Jack Prelutsky		Green
1987	Over And Over		$12	$16	$20	Charlotte Zolotow		HCollins
1987	The Old Meadow		$14	$20	$30	George Selden		FSG
1990	Beneath A Blue Umbrella		$12	$18	$25	Jack Prelutsky		Green
1991	King Emmett The Second		$12	$18	$25	Mary Stolz		Green
1992	J.B.'S Harmonica		$12	$18	$25	John Sebastian		HBJ
1992	The Sailor Dog		$12	$18	$25	Margaret Wise Brown		Western
1993	The Kitten Who Thought He Was A Mouse		$12	$16	$20	Miriam Norton		AWG
1994	A Little House Christmas		$12	$16	$20	Laura Ingalls Wilder		HCollins
1994	Home For A Bunny		$12	$16	$20	Margaret Wise Brown		Golden
1994	The Annotated Charlotte's Web		$12	$16	$20	E. B. White		HCollins
1996	The Gingerbread Rabbit		$8	$12	$16	Randall Jarrell		HCollins
1997	Little House Sisters		$10	$16	$20	Laura Ingalls Wilder		HCollins

Williams — Kit

Year	Title	VG-	VG	VG+	Fine	Author	Award	Pub
1983	Masquerade		$25	$35	$50	Kit Williams		Workman
1984	[The Bee On The Comb]		$20	$30	$40	Kit Williams		Knopf

Williams — Vera B.

Year	Title	VG-	VG	VG+	Fine	Author	Award	Pub
1975	Hooray For Me!		$30	$40	$60	Remy Charlip		PMagP
1978	It's A Gingerbread House: Bake It, Build It, Eat It!		$20	$30	$40	Vera B. Williams		Green
1978	Our Class Presents Ostrich Feathers		$20	$30	$40	Barbara Brenner		PMagP
1980	The Great Watermelon Birthday		$18	$25	$35	Vera B. Williams		Green
1981	Three Days On A River In A Red Canoe		$18	$25	$35	Vera B. Williams		Green
1982	A Chair For My Mother		$50	$70	$90	Vera B. Williams	CH	Green
1983	Something Special For Me		$16	$25	$30	Vera B. Williams		Green
1984	Music, Music For Everyone		$16	$25	$30	Vera B. Williams		Green
1986	Cherries And Cherry Pits		$14	$20	$30	Vera B. Williams		Green
1990	More More More Said The Baby: 3 Love Stories		$35	$50	$70	Vera B. Williams	CH	Green
1993	Scooter		$12	$16	$20	Vera B. Williams		Green
1997	Lucky Song		$10	$16	$20	Vera B. Williams		Green
2001	Amber Was Brave, Essie Was Smart		$8	$12	$16	Vera B. Williams		Green

Wilson — April

Year	Title	VG-	VG	VG+	Fine	Author	Award	Pub
1990	Look!		$16	$25	$30	A. J. Wood		Dial
1993	Look Again!		$16	$25	$30	A. J. Wood		Dial
1999	April Wilson's Magpie Magic		$12	$16	$20	April Wilson		Dial

Wilson — Rowland

Year	Title	VG-	VG	VG+	Fine	Author	Award	Pub
1971	Tubby and the Lantern		$40	$60	$90	Al Perkins		BB
1972	Tubby And The Poo-Bah		$40	$60	$90	Al Perkins		BB

Winborn — Marsha

Year	Title	VG-	VG	VG+	Fine	Author	Award	Pub
1981	I Have A Friend		$18	$25	$35	Michaela Muntean		Western
1981	Let's Pretend		$18	$25	$35	Rose Greydanus		Troll
1982	Mystery Of The Lost Ring (With Two Hearts)		$14	$20	$25	Robyn Supraner		Troll

468

Winborn Marsha

Year	Title	VG-	VG	VG+	Fine	Author	Award	Pub
1984	Come! Sit! Stay!		$12	$18	$25	Joan M. Lexau		FWatts
1984	Sir William And The Pumpkin Monster		$12	$18	$25	Margery Cuyler		HR&W
1985	Big Bird Brings Spring To Sesame Street		$12	$18	$25	Lauren Collier Swindler		Western
1985	Little Red Riding Hood		$12	$18	$25	Rebecca Heller		Golden
1985	My Dog And The Knock Knock Mystery		$12	$18	$25	David A. Adler		Holiday
1986	Freckles & Willie		$12	$16	$20	Margery Cuyler		HR&W
1986	Inside Sesame Street		$12	$16	$20	Marsha Winborn		Western
1987	Fat Santa		$12	$16	$20	Margery Cuyler		Holt
1988	Digby And Kate		$12	$16	$20	Barbara Baker		Dutton
1989	Digby And Kate Again		$12	$16	$20	Barbara Baker		Dutton
1990	I Like It When--		$10	$16	$20	Benjamin Auster		Rain
1991	One Hundred Monkeys		$10	$16	$20	Daniel S. Cutler		S&S
1995	All About Electricity		$10	$14	$18	Melvin Berger		Scholas
1995	The Pirates Of Snake Island		$10	$14	$18	Andreas Lord		Random
1996	Grandma's Cat		$8	$12	$16	Helen Ketteman		HM
1998	Digby And Kate And The Beautiful Day		$8	$12	$16	Barbara Baker		Dutton
1999	A Valentine For Norman Noggs		$8	$12	$16	Valiska Gregory		HCollins
2000	Pepper's Journal		$8	$10	$14	Stuart J. Murphy		HCollins
2001	Probably Pistachio		$8	$10	$14	Stuart J. Murphy		HCollins
2002	Bigger, Better, Best!		$8	$10	$14	Stuart J. Murphy		HCollins
2002	Egg-Napped!		$8	$10	$14	Marisa Montes		HCollins
2003	America's Promise		$8	$10	$14	Alma Powell		HCollins
2003	May Belle And The Ogre		$8	$10	$14	Bethany Roberts		Dutton
2004	Digby And Kate 1, 2, 3		$6	$10	$12	Barbara Baker		Dutton

Winship Florence Sarah

Year	Title	VG-	VG	VG+	Fine	Author	Award	Pub
1944	Woofus The Woolly Dog	$50	$60	$80		Jane Curry		Whitman
1947	Miss Sniff, The Fuzzy Cat	$40	$60	$70		Nan Gilbert		Whitman
1947	Sir Gruff The Woolly Dog	$40	$60	$70		Nan Gilbert		Whitman
1947	The Three Fuzzy Bears	$40	$60	$70		Nan Gilbert		Whitman

Wiseman Bernard

Year	Title	VG-	VG	VG+	Fine	Author	Award	Pub
1959	Morris The Moose	$50	$60	$80		Bernard Wiseman		H&B
1960	Morris Is A Cowboy, A Policeman, & A Baby Sitter	$35	$40	$60		Bernard Wiseman		H&B
1961	The Log And Admiral Frog	$35	$40	$60		Bernard Wiseman		H&B
1970	Morris Goes To School		$25	$35	$50	Bernard Wiseman		H&Row
1971	Detective Dog		$25	$35	$50	Bernard Wiseman		P&Munk
1971	Hats And Coats, Cows And Goats		$25	$35	$50	Bernard Wiseman		P&Munk
1971	The Nutty Nature Book		$25	$35	$50	Bernard Wiseman		P&Munk
1971	The Silly Science Book		$25	$35	$50	Bernard Wiseman		P&Munk
1974	Morris And Boris, Three Stories		$20	$30	$40	Bernard Wiseman		DoddM
1975	Halloween With Morris And Boris		$20	$30	$40	Bernard Wiseman		DoddM
1976	Billy Learns Karate		$20	$30	$40	Bernard Wiseman		HR&W
1977	Iglook's Seal		$20	$30	$40	Bernard Wiseman		DoddM
1978	Bobby And Boo, The Little Spaceman		$20	$30	$40	Bernard Wiseman		HR&W
1978	Morris Has A Cold		$20	$30	$40	Bernard Wiseman		DoddM
1979	Morris Tells Boris Mother Moose Stories & Rhymes		$18	$25	$35	Bernard Wiseman		DoddM
1979	My Googoo		$18	$25	$35	Bernard Wiseman		HR&W
1979	Quick Quackers		$18	$25	$35	Bernard Wiseman		Garrard
1979	The Lucky Runner		$18	$25	$35	Bernard Wiseman		Garrard
1980	Hooray For Patsy's Oink!		$18	$25	$35	Bernard Wiseman		Garrard
1980	Oscar Is A Mama!		$18	$25	$35	Bernard Wiseman		Garrard
1980	Penny's Poodle Puppy, Pickle		$18	$25	$35	Bernard Wiseman		Garrard
1980	Tails Are Not For Painting		$18	$25	$35	Bernard Wiseman		Garrard
1981	The Very Bumpy Bus Ride		$18	$25	$35	Michaela Muntean		PMagP
1982	Don't Make Fun!		$16	$25	$30	Bernard Wiseman		HM
1983	Christmas With Morris And Boris		$16	$25	$30	Bernard Wiseman		LBrown
1983	George's Store		$16	$25	$30	Frank Asch		PMagP
1983	Morris Has A Birthday Party!		$16	$25	$30	Bernard Wiseman		LBrown
1984	Cats! Cats! Cats!		$16	$25	$30	Bernard Wiseman		PMagP
1984	Doctor Duck And Nurse Swan		$16	$25	$30	Bernard Wiseman		Dutton
1987	Barber Bear		$14	$20	$30	Bernard Wiseman		LBrown
1987	Dolly Dodo		$14	$20	$30	Bernard Wiseman		Scholas
1987	Handy Hound		$14	$20	$30	Bernard Wiseman		LBrown

Wiseman   Bernard

Year	Title	VG-	VG	VG+	Fine	Author	Award	Pub
1988	Morris And Boris At The Circus		$14	$20	$30	Bernard Wiseman		H&Row

Wisniewski   David

Year	Title	VG-	VG	VG+	Fine	Author	Award	Pub
1989	The Warrior And The Wise Man		$25	$40	$50	David Wisniewski		LL&S
1990	Elfwyn's Saga		$16	$25	$30	David Wisniewski		LL&S
1991	Rain Player		$16	$25	$30	David Wisniewski		Clarion
1992	Sundiata: Lion King Of Mali		$16	$25	$30	David Wisniewski		Clarion
1994	The Wave Of The Sea-Wolf		$14	$20	$30	David Wisniewski		Clarion
1997	Ducky		$12	$18	$25	Eve Bunting		Clarion
1997	Golem		$40	$60	$80	David Wisniewski	CM	Clarion
1998	Kid's Guide To The Secret Knowledge Of Grown-Ups		$12	$16	$20	David Wisniewski		LL&S
1999	Tough Cookie		$12	$16	$20	David Wisniewski		Lothrop
1999	Workshop		$12	$16	$20	Andrew Clements		Clarion
2000	I'll Play With You		$10	$14	$18	Mary McKenna Siddals		HCollins
2001	Master Man		$10	$14	$18	David Wisniewski		HCollins
2001	The Second File		$10	$14	$18	David Wisniewski		HCollins
2002	Halloweenies		$8	$12	$16	David Wisniewski		HCollins
2002	Sumo Mouse		$8	$12	$16	David Wisniewski		HCollins

Wolff   Ashley

Year	Title	VG-	VG	VG+	Fine	Author	Award	Pub
1984	A Year Of Birds		$30	$50	$60	Ashley Wolff		DoddM
1985	Only The Cat Saw		$20	$30	$40	Ashley Wolff		DoddM
1985	The Bells Of London		$20	$30	$40	Ashley Wolff		DoddM
1986	A Year Of Beasts		$20	$30	$40	Ashley Wolff		Dutton
1988	Block City		$14	$20	$30	Robert Louis Stevenson		Dutton
1988	Who Is Coming To Our House?		$14	$20	$30	Joseph Slate		Putnam
1990	Baby Beluga		$12	$18	$25	Raffi		Crown
1990	Come With Me		$12	$18	$25	Ashley Wolff		Dutton
1991	A Garden Alphabet		$12	$18	$25	Isabel Wilner		Dutton
1991	I Love My Daddy Because--		$12	$18	$25	Laurel Porter-Gaylord		Dutton
1991	I Love My Mommy Because--		$12	$18	$25	Laurel Porter-Gaylord		Dutton
1993	Stella & Roy		$16	$25	$30	Ashley Wolff		Dutton
1993	The Gingerbread Man		$12	$16	$20	Jane Melick		Heath
1994	Goody O'Grumpity		$12	$16	$20	Carol Ryrie Brink		NSBooks
1995	How Chipmunk Got Tiny Feet		$10	$16	$20	Gerald Hausman		HCollins
1995	Little Donkey Close Your Eyes		$10	$16	$20	Margaret Wise Brown		HCollins
1996	Miss Bindergarten Gets Ready For Kindergarten		$10	$16	$20	Joseph Slate		Dutton
1997	A String Of Beads		$10	$16	$20	Margarette S. Reid		Dutton
1997	Home Sweet Home		$10	$16	$20	Jean Marzollo		HCollins
1998	Doctor Bird		$10	$14	$18	Gerald Hausman		Philo
1998	Miss Bindergarten Celebrates The 100th Day Of Kindergarten		$10	$14	$18	Joseph Slate		Dutton
1999	Some Things Go Together		$12	$16	$20	Charlotte Zolotow		HFest
1999	Splish Splash		$10	$14	$18	Sarah Weeks		HCollins
1999	Stella & Roy Go Camping		$12	$16	$20	Ashley Wolff		Dutton
2000	Each Living Thing		$8	$12	$16	Joanne Ryder		Harcort
2000	Miss Bindergarten Stays Home From Kindergarten		$8	$12	$16	Joseph Slate		Dutton
2000	Who Took The Cookies From The Cookie Jar?		$8	$12	$16	Bonnie Lass		LBrown
2001	Miss Bindergarten Takes A Field Trip With Kindergarten		$8	$12	$16	Joseph Slate		Dutton
2002	Miss Bindergarten Plans A Circus With Kindergarten		$8	$10	$14	Joseph Slate		Dutton
2002	My Somebody Special		$8	$10	$14	Sarah Weeks		Harcort
2002	Old Macdonald Had A Woodshop		$8	$10	$14	Lisa Shulman		Putnam
2003	The Baby Chicks Are Singing / Los Pollitos Dicen		$8	$10	$14	Ashley Wolff		LBrown
2003	The Colors		$8	$10	$14	Ashley Wolff		LBrown
2004	Me Baby, You Baby		$8	$10	$14	Ashley Wolff		Dutton
2004	She'll Be Comin' 'Round The Mountain		$8	$10	$14	Philemon Sturges		LBrown

Wolpin   Harriet

Year	Title	VG-	VG	VG+	Fine	Author	Award	Pub
1946	Hansel And Gretel	$35	$40	$60		Jacob & Wilhelm Grimm		Maxton
1946	Jack And The Beanstalk	$35	$40	$60		Harriet Wolpin (adapted)		Maxton
1946	King Thrushbeard	$35	$40	$60		Jacob & Wilhelm Grimm		Maxton
1946	Snow-White And Rose-Red	$35	$40	$60		Jacob & Wilhelm Grimm		Maxton
1946	The Princess And The Pea	$35	$40	$60		Hans Christian Andersen		Maxton

Wolpin — Harriet

Year	Title	VG-	VG	VG+	Fine	Author	Award	Pub
1946	The Shoes That Danced	$35	$40	$60		Jacob & Wilhelm Grimm		Maxton
1946	The Steadfast Tin Soldier	$35	$40	$60		Harriet Wolpin (adapted)		Maxton
1947	Cinderella	$35	$40	$60		Jacob & Wilhelm Grimm		Maxton
1948	The Emperor's New Clothes	$35	$40	$60		Hans Christian Andersen		Maxton

Wood — Audrey

Year	Title	VG-	VG	VG+	Fine	Author	Award	Pub
1980	Orlando's Little-While Friends		$25	$35	$50	Audrey Wood		ChildP
1982	The Princess And The Dragon		$16	$25	$30	Audrey Wood		ChildP
1983	Tugford Wanted To Be Bad		$16	$25	$30	Audrey Wood		HBJ
1987	Detective Valentine		$14	$20	$30	Audrey Wood		H&Row
1989	Little Penguin's Tale		$14	$20	$25	Audrey Wood		HBJ
1989	Presto Change-O		$14	$20	$25	Audrey Wood		ChildP
1989	Scaredy Cats		$14	$20	$25	Audrey Wood		ChildP
1990	Little Mouse, Red Ripe Strawberry, & Big Hungry Bear		$12	$18	$25	Don Wood		ChildP
1990	Oh My Baby Bear!		$12	$18	$25	Audrey Wood		HBJ
1990	Twenty-Four Robbers		$12	$18	$25	Audrey Wood		ChildP
1990	Weird Parents		$12	$18	$25	Audrey Wood		Dial
1991	Piggies		$12	$18	$25	Don Wood		HBJ
1992	Balloonia		$12	$18	$25	Audrey Wood		ChildP
1992	Silly Sally		$12	$18	$25	Audrey Wood		HBJ
1992	Tooth Fairy		$12	$18	$25	Audrey Wood		ChildP
1993	Rude Giants		$12	$16	$20	Audrey Wood		HBJ
1996	The Red Racer		$10	$16	$20	Audrey Wood		S&S
2001	A Book For Honey Bear		$8	$12	$16	Audrey Wood		LSimon
2003	Piggy Pie Po		$8	$10	$14	Audrey Wood		Harcort

Wood — Bruce

Year	Title	VG-	VG	VG+	Fine	Author	Award	Pub
1998	The Christmas Adventures Of Space Elf Sam		$12	$16	$20	Audrey Wood		BSP
2001	Alphabet Adventure		$8	$12	$16	Audrey Wood		BSP
2003	Alphabet Mystery		$8	$10	$14	Audrey Wood		BSP
2004	Ten Little Fish		$8	$10	$14	Audrey Wood		BSP

Wood — Don

Year	Title	VG-	VG	VG+	Fine	Author	Award	Pub
1980	Moonflute		$25	$35	$50	Audrey Wood		GreenT
1983	The Napping House		$25	$35	$50	Don & Audrey Wood	NYT	HBJ
1985	King Bidgood's In The Bathtub		$40	$60	$80	Don & Audrey Wood	CH	HBJ
1987	Heckedy Peg		$14	$20	$30	Don & Audrey Wood		HBJ
1988	Elbert's Bad Word		$14	$20	$30	Don & Audrey Wood		HBJ
1990	Quick As A Cricket		$12	$18	$25	Audrey Wood		ChildP
1990	The Little Mouse, The Red Ripe Strawberry, And The Big Hungry Bear		$12	$18	$25	Don & Audrey Wood		ChildP
1991	Piggies		$12	$18	$25	Don & Audrey Wood		HBJ
1993	Don Juan		$12	$16	$20	Nigel Wood (edited)		OUP
1994	The Napping House Wakes Up		$12	$16	$20	Audrey Wood		HBrace
1994	The Tickleoctopus		$12	$16	$20	Audrey Wood		HBrace
1996	Bright And Early Thursday Evening: A Tangled Tale		$10	$16	$20	Audrey Wood		HBrace
2000	Jubal's Wish		$8	$12	$16	Audrey Wood		BSP
2002	Merry Christmas, Big Hungry Bear		$8	$10	$14	Don Wood		BSP

Woodward — Hildegard

Year	Title	VG-	VG	VG+	Fine	Author	Award	Pub
1935	Everyday Children	$70	$100	$120		Hildegard Woodward		Oxford
1940	Yammy Buys A Bicycle	$50	$60	$80		Bernice Morgan Bryant		AWhit
1941	Time Was	$50	$60	$80		Hildegard Woodward		Scribnr
1942	Jared's Blessing	$50	$60	$80		Hildegard Woodward		Scribnr
1947	Roger And The Fox	$120	$160	$220		Lavinia R. Davis	CH	DoubleD
1949	The Wild Birthday Cake	$120	$160	$220		Lavinia R. Davis	CH	DoubleD
1950	Christmas	$40	$50	$70		Alice Dalgliesh		Scribnr
1953	Danny's Luck	$40	$50	$70		Lavinia R. Davis		DoubleD
1959	The Wonderful Story Of How You Were Born	$35	$50	$60		Sidonie M. Gruenberg		GardenC
1961	The House On Grandfather's Hill	$35	$40	$60		Hildegard Woodward		Scribnr

Wormell   Christopher

Year	Title	VG-	VG	VG+	Fine	Author	Award	Pub
1990	An Alphabet Of Animals		$12	$18	$25	Christopher Wormell		Dial
1992	Mowgli's Brothers		$10	$16	$20	Rudyard Kipling		Creat
1993	A Number Of Animals		$10	$16	$20	Kate Green		Creat
1996	What I Eat		$8	$12	$16	Christopher Wormell		Dial
1996	Where I Live		$8	$12	$16	Christopher Wormell		Dial
2000	Blue Rabbit And Friends		$8	$10	$14	Christopher Wormell		PFogel
2000	The Animal Train		$8	$10	$14	Christopher Wormell		JCape
2001	Blue Rabbit And The Runaway Wheel		$8	$10	$14	Christopher Wormell		PFogel
2001	Puff-Puff, Chugga-Chugga		$8	$10	$14	Christopher Wormell		McEld
2002	The New Alphabet Of Animals		$8	$10	$14	Christopher Wormell		RunP
2003	Swan Songs		$8	$10	$14	J. Patrick Lewis		Creat
2004	Teeth, Tails, And Tentacles		$6	$10	$12	Christopher Wormell		RunP
2004	The Big Ugly Monster And The Little Stone Rabbit		$6	$10	$12	Christopher Wormell		Knopf

Wright   Jane Chambless

Year	Title	VG-	VG	VG+	Fine	Author	Award	Pub
1980	You're Dumber In The Summer		$14	$20	$25	Jim Aylward		HR&W
1981	The Bookseller's Advice		$12	$16	$20	Sue Breitner		Viking
1984	The Soap Bandit		$10	$16	$20	Dennis Haseley		FWarne
1985	Superted And The Birthday Search		$10	$16	$20	Mike Young		Random
1986	Beauty And The Beast & Other Tales Of Enchantment		$10	$16	$20	Jane Chambless Wright		Golden
1986	Old Friends, New Friends		$10	$16	$20	Joanne Ryder		Golden
1987	The Real Mother Goose Clock Book		$10	$16	$20	Jane Chambless Wright		Check
1987	The Three Little Kittens		$10	$16	$20	Jane Chambless Wright		Western
1988	Uncle Wiggily To The Rescue		$10	$14	$18	Howard Roger Garis		P&Munk
1989	Tucker And The Bear		$10	$14	$18	Jane Chambless Wright		S&S
1990	The Three Little Pigs		$10	$14	$18	Margaret Driscoll Timmons		SBurdet
1996	The Sun Is Up		$8	$12	$16	William Jay Smith		Wordsng
2000	Kidding Around		$8	$10	$14	Claire Janosik Griffin		Denison

Yaccarino   Dan

Year	Title	VG-	VG	VG+	Fine	Author	Award	Pub
1993	Big Brother Mike		$16	$25	$30	Dan Yaccarino		Hyper
1994	The Sawfin Stickleback		$12	$16	$20	Catherine Friend		Hyper
1995	Bam, Bam, Bam		$10	$16	$20	Eve Merriam		Holt
1996	Carnival		$10	$16	$20	Mary-Claire Helldorfer		Viking
1996	If I Had A Robot		$10	$16	$20	Dan Yaccarino		Viking
1996	One Hole In The Road		$10	$16	$20	W. Nikola-Lisa		Holt
1997	An Octopus Followed Me Home		$10	$16	$20	Dan Yaccarino		Viking
1997	Good Night, Mr. Night		$10	$16	$20	Dan Yaccarino		HBrace
1997	Zoom! Zoom! Zoom! I'm Off To The Moon!		$10	$16	$20	Dan Yaccarino		Scholas
1998	Circle Dogs		$10	$14	$18	Kevin Henkes		Green
1998	Five Little Pumpkins		$10	$14	$18	Dan Yaccarino		HFest
1998	Little White Dog		$10	$14	$18	Laura Godwin		Hyper
1998	Move It!		$10	$14	$18	Ann Keech		RunP
1999	Bugs		$10	$14	$18	Dan Yaccarino		RunP
1999	Trashy Town		$10	$14	$18	Andrea Griffing Zimmerman		HCollins
2000	Away We Go!		$8	$12	$16	Rebecca Kai Dotlich		HFest
2000	Come With Me		$8	$12	$16	Naomi Shihab Nye		Green
2000	Deep In The Jungle		$8	$12	$16	Dan Yaccarino		Athenm
2000	First Day On A Strange New Planet		$8	$12	$16	Dan Yaccarino		Hyper
2000	Surviving Brick Johnson		$8	$12	$16	Laurie Myers		Clarion
2001	Baby Face		$8	$12	$16	Abigail Tabby		HFest
2001	I Love Going Through This Book		$8	$12	$16	Robert Burleigh		Cotler
2001	New Pet		$8	$12	$16	Dan Yaccarino		Hyper
2001	Oswald		$8	$12	$16	Dan Yaccarino		Athenm
2001	So Big!		$8	$12	$16	Dan Yaccarino		HFest
2001	Unlovable		$8	$12	$16	Dan Yaccarino		Holt
2002	Halloween Countdown		$8	$10	$14	Jack Prelutsky		HFest
2002	I Met A Bear		$8	$10	$14	Dan Yaccarino		HFest
2002	The Good Little Bad Little Pig		$8	$10	$14	Margaret Wise Brown		Hyper
2003	Dan Yaccarino's Mother Goose		$8	$10	$14	Dan Yaccarino		Golden
2003	Where The Four Winds Blow		$8	$10	$14	Dan Yaccarino		Cotler
2004	Bittle		$8	$10	$14	Patricia MacLachlan		Cotler
2004	Sammy Keyes And The Psycho Kitty Queen		$8	$10	$14	Wendelin Van Draanen		Knopf

Yashima   Taro

Year	Title	VG-	VG	VG+	Fine	Author	Award	Pub
1953	The Village Tree	$180	$240	$300		Taro Yashima		Viking
1954	Plenty To Watch	$120	$160	$200		Mitsu Yashima		Viking
1955	Crow Boy	$160	$220	$280		Taro Yashima	CH	Viking
1958	Umbrella	$160	$200	$260		Taro Yashima	CH	Viking
1960	The Golden Footprints	$70	$90	$120		Hatoju Muku		World
1961	Momo's Kitten	$70	$90	$120		Mitsu Yashima		Viking
1961	The Sugar Pear Tree	$70	$90	$120		Clyde Robert Bulla		Crowell
1962	Youngest One	$70	$90	$120		Taro Yashima		Viking
1967	Seashore Story	$120	$160	$220		Taro Yashima	CH	Viking
1971	The Fisherman And The Goblet		$40	$60	$90	Mark Taylor		GGate

Yeakey   Carol

Year	Title	VG-	VG	VG+	Fine	Author	Award	Pub
1945	The City Dog And The Country Cat	$35	$40	$60		George Arthur Hornby		DomesD
1946	Michael Finnegan	$35	$40	$60		Irene Little		G&D
1946	The Ugly Ducking	$35	$40	$60		Mary Patric (adapted)		PiedP

Yoshi

Year	Title	VG-	VG	VG+	Fine	Author	Award	Pub
1988	Big Al		$18	$25	$35	Andrew Elborn		Picture
1989	Magical Hands		$14	$20	$25	Marjorie Barker		Picture
1991	1,2,3		$12	$18	$25	Yoshi		Picture
1992	A To Zen		$12	$18	$25	Ruth Wells		Picture
1995	Skeleton Woman		$10	$16	$20	Alberto Villoldo		S&S
1996	The Farmer And The Poor God		$10	$16	$20	Ruth Wells		S&S
1996	The First Story Ever Told		$10	$16	$20	Erik Jendresen		S&S
2002	Big Al And Shrimpy		$8	$10	$14	Andrew Clements		S&S

Young   Ed

Year	Title	VG-	VG	VG+	Fine	Author	Award	Pub
1966	The Yellow Boat	$60	$80	$100		Margaret Hillert		Follett
1966	Turkey Girl: A Zuni Cinderella Story	$40	$60	$70		Penny Pollock		LBrown
1967	The Emperor And The Kite	$80	$120	$140		Jane Yolen	CH	World
1968	Chinese Mother Goose Rhymes	$40	$50	$70		Robert Wyndham		World
1969	The Golden Swans	$40	$50	$70		Kermit Krueger		World
1969	The Tiniest Sound	$40	$50	$70		Melvin Evans		DoubleD
1970	The Bird From The Sea		$30	$50	$60	Renée Karol Weiss		Crowell
1970	The Seventh Mandarin		$50	$70	$90	Jane Yolen		Seabury
1972	8,000 Stones, A Chinese Folktale		$30	$50	$60	Diane Wolkstein		DoubleD
1972	The Girl Who Loved The Wind		$40	$60	$90	Jane Yolen		Crowell
1973	Young Fu Of The Upper Yangtze		$30	$50	$60	Elizabeth Foreman Lewis		HR&W
1977	Cricket Boy: A Chinese Tale		$25	$40	$50	Feenie Ziner (retold)		DoubleD
1977	The Red Lion		$25	$40	$50	Diane Wolkstein		Crowell
1978	Tales From The Arabian Nights		$25	$40	$50	N. J. Dawood		DoubleD
1978	The Rooster's Horns		$25	$40	$50	Hilary Beckett		Collins
1978	The Terrible Nung Gwama		$25	$40	$50	Leslie Bonnet		Collins
1979	The Lion And The Mouse		$35	$50	$70	Ed Young		DoubleD
1979	White Wave: A Chinese Tale		$25	$40	$50	Diane Wolkstein (retold)		Crowell
1980	High On A Hill		$35	$50	$70	Ed Young		Collins
1981	Bo Rabbit Smart For True: Folktales From The Gullah		$25	$35	$50	Priscella Jaquith (retold)		Philo
1982	Yeh-Shen		$30	$50	$60	Ai-Ling Louie		Philo
1983	Bicycle Rider		$25	$35	$50	Mary Scioscia		H&Row
1983	The Double Life Of Pocahontas		$25	$35	$50	Jean Fritz		Putnam
1983	Up A Tree		$30	$50	$60	Ed Young	NYT	H&Row
1984	The Other Bone		$20	$30	$40	Ed Young		H&Row
1985	Foolish Rabbit's Big Mistake		$20	$30	$40	Rafe Martin		Putnam
1985	Moon Tiger		$20	$30	$40	Phyllis Root		HR&W
1987	Eyes Of The Dragon		$20	$30	$40	Margaret Leaf		LL&S
1987	I Wish I Were A Butterfly		$20	$30	$40	James Howe		HBJ
1987	Whale Song		$20	$30	$40	Tony Johnston		Putnam
1987	Who-Paddled-Backward-With-Trout		$20	$30	$40	Howard Norman		Joy
1988	Birches		$18	$25	$35	Robert Frost		Holt
1988	Cats Are Cats: Poems		$18	$25	$35	Nancy Larrick (compiled)		Philo
1988	China's Long March		$18	$25	$35	Jean Fritz		Putnam
1988	In The Night, Still Dark		$18	$25	$35	Richard Lewis		Athenm

Young   Ed

Year	Title	VG-	VG	VG+	Fine	Author	Award	Pub
1989	High In The Mountains		$18	$25	$35	Ruth Yaffe Radin		Macmil
1989	Lon Po Po		$90	$120	$180	Ed Young	CM	Philo
1989	Oscar Wilde's The Happy Prince		$18	$25	$35	Oscar Wilde		S&S
1989	The Voice Of The Great Bell		$18	$25	$35	Margaret Hodges		LBrown
1990	Mice Are Nice		$16	$25	$30	Nancy Larrick		Philo
1991	All Of You Was Singing		$16	$25	$30	Richard Lewis		Athenm
1991	Goodbye, Geese		$16	$25	$30	Nancy Carlstrom		Philo
1992	Dreamcatcher		$16	$25	$30	Audrey Osofsky		Orchard
1992	Seven Blind Mice		$60	$90	$120	Ed Young	CH	Philo
1992	The First Song Ever Sung		$16	$25	$30	Laura Krauss Melmed		LL&S
1992	The Rime Of The Ancient Mariner		$16	$25	$30	Samuel Taylor Coleridge		Athenm
1992	What Comes In Spring?		$16	$25	$30	Barbara Savadge Horton		Knopf
1992	While I Sleep		$16	$25	$30	Mary Calhoun		Morrow
1993	Moon Mother		$16	$25	$30	Ed Young		HCollins
1993	Red Thread		$16	$25	$30	Ed Young		Philo
1993	Sadako		$16	$25	$30	Eleanor Coerr		Putnam
1994	Bitter Bananas		$14	$20	$30	Isaac Olaleye		Boyds
1994	Iblis		$14	$20	$30	Shulamith Oppenheim		HBJ
1994	Little Plum		$14	$20	$30	Ed Young		Philo
1995	Cat And Rat		$14	$20	$25	Ed Young		Holt
1995	Donkey Trouble		$14	$20	$25	Ed Young		Athenm
1995	Night Visitors		$14	$20	$25	Ed Young		Philo
1995	The Turkey Girl		$14	$20	$25	Penny Pollock		LBrown
1996	October Smiled Back		$12	$18	$25	Lisa Westberg Peters		Holt
1996	Pinocchio		$12	$18	$25	Carlo Collodi		Philo
1997	Genesis		$12	$18	$25	Ed Young		LauraG
1997	Mouse Match		$12	$18	$25	Ed Young		Whistle
1998	The Lost Horse		$12	$16	$20	Ed Young		Whistle
2000	A Pup Just For Me		$10	$14	$18	Dorothea Seeber		Philo
2000	Desert Song		$10	$14	$18	Tony Johnston		Sierra
2000	The Hunter		$10	$14	$18	Mary Casanova		Athenm
2000	White Fang		$10	$14	$18	Jack London		Athenm
2001	Monkey King		$10	$14	$18	Ed Young		HCollins
2002	What About Me?		$8	$12	$16	Ed Young		Philo
2004	I, Doko		$8	$10	$14	Ed Young		Philo
2004	Tai Chi Morning		$8	$10	$14	Nikki Grimes		Cricket
2004	The Sons Of The Dragon King		$8	$10	$14	Ed Young		Athenm

Zelinsky   Paul O.

Year	Title	VG-	VG	VG+	Fine	Author	Award	Pub
1978	Emily Upham's Revenge		$25	$40	$50	Avi		Pan
1979	How I Hunted The Little Fellows		$50	$80	$100	Boris Zhitkov		DoddM
1980	The History Of Helpless Harry		$25	$35	$50	Avi		Pan
1981	The Maid And The Mouse		$35	$50	$70	Paul O. Zelinsky (adapted)		DoddM
1981	Three Romances: Love Stories From Camelot Retold		$25	$35	$50	Winifred Rosen		Knopf
1981	What Amanda Saw		$35	$50	$70	Naomi Lazard		Green
1982	Ralph S. Mouse		$25	$35	$50	Beverly Cleary		Morrow
1982	The Song In The Walnut Grove		$25	$35	$50	David Kherdian		Knopf
1982	The Sun's Asleep Behind The Hill		$30	$50	$60	Mirra Ginsburg		Green
1983	Dear Mr. Henshaw		$100	$140	$200	Beverly Cleary	NM	Morrow
1983	Zoo Doings: Animal Poems		$25	$35	$50	Jack Prelutsky		Green
1984	Hansel And Gretel		$60	$90	$120	Rika Lesser	CH	DoddM
1984	The Lion And The Stoat		$30	$50	$60	Paul O. Zelinsky		Green
1985	The Story Of Mrs. Lovewright And Purrless Her Cat		$20	$30	$40	Lore Segal	NYT	Knopf
1986	Rumpelstiltskin		$60	$80	$120	Jacob & Wilhelm Grimm	CH	Dutton
1988	The Random House Book Of Humor		$18	$25	$35	Pamela Pollack (selected)		Random
1989	The Maid And The Mouse And The Odd-Shaped House		$18	$25	$35	Paul O. Zelinsky		Dutton
1990	The Wheels On The Bus		$16	$25	$30	Paul O. Zelinsky		Dutton
1991	Strider		$16	$25	$30	Beverly Cleary		Morrow
1992	The Enchanted Castle		$16	$25	$30	Edith Nesbit		BOW
1993	More Rootabagas		$16	$25	$30	Carl Sandburg		Knopf
1994	Swamp Angel		$40	$60	$80	Anne Isaacs	CH	Dutton
1995	The History Of Helpless Harry		$14	$20	$25	Avi		Beech
1997	Rapunzel		$50	$70	$100	Paul O. Zelinsky (adapted)	CM	Dutton
1999	Five Children And It		$12	$16	$20	Edith Nesbit		HCollins

Zelinsky   Paul O.

Year	Title	VG-	VG	VG+	Fine	Author	Award	Pub
2000	The Sun's Asleep Behind The Hill		$10	$14	$18	Mirra Ginsburg		Walker
2001	Awful Ogre's Awful Day		$10	$14	$18	Jack Prelutsky		Green
2002	Knick-Knack Paddywhack		$8	$12	$16	Paul O. Zelinsky (adapted)		Dutton
2003	Doodler Doodling		$8	$12	$16	Rita Golden Gelman		Green

Zemach   Margot

Year	Title	VG-	VG	VG+	Fine	Author	Award	Pub
1963	The Three Sillies	$100	$120	$160		Margot Zemach		HR&W
1964	The Last Dragon	$60	$80	$100		Fleming Lee Blitch		Lippin
1965	Salt	$40	$60	$70		Harve Zemach		Follett
1965	The Little Tiny Woman	$60	$80	$100		Margot Zemach		Bobbs
1965	The Tricks Of Master Dabble	$40	$60	$70		Harve Zemach		HR&W
1966	Mommy, Buy Me A China Doll	$40	$60	$70		Harve Zemach		Follett
1966	The Fisherman And His Wife	$40	$60	$70		Jacob & Wilhelm Grimm		Norton
1966	The King Of The Hermits	$40	$60	$70		Jack Sendak		FSG
1967	Mazel And Shlimazel	$40	$50	$70		Isaac Bashevis Singer		FSG
1967	Too Much Nose	$40	$50	$70		Harve Zemach		HR&W
1968	When Shlemiel Went To Warsaw & Other Stories	$80	$120	$140		Isaac Bashevis Singer	NH	FSG
1969	The Judge, An Untrue Tale	$80	$120	$140		Harve Zemach	CH	FSG
1970	Awake And Dreaming		$30	$50	$60	Harve Zemach		FSG
1971	A Penny A Look		$30	$50	$60	Harve Zemach		FSG
1971	Alone In The Wild Forest		$30	$50	$60	Isaac Bashevis Singer		FSG
1971	Favorite Fairy Tales Told In Denmark		$30	$50	$60	Virginia Haviland		LBrown
1972	Simon Boom Gives A Wedding		$30	$50	$60	Yuri Suhl		4Winds
1973	Duffy And The Devil		$160	$240	$320	Harve Zemach	CM	FSG
1973	The Foundling, & Other Tales Of Prydain		$30	$50	$60	Lloyd Alexander		HR&W
1975	The Princess And Froggie		$30	$40	$60	Harve Zemach		FSG
1976	Hush, Little Baby		$30	$40	$60	Margot Zemach		Dutton
1976	It Could Always Be Worse		$60	$80	$120	Margot Zemach	CH	FSG
1976	Naftali The Storyteller And His Horse, Sus		$30	$40	$60	Isaac Bashevis Singer		FSG
1977	To Hilda For Helping		$25	$40	$50	Margot Zemach		FSG
1982	Come On, Patsy		$25	$35	$50	Zilpha Keatley Snyder		Athenm
1982	Jake And Honeybunch Go To Heaven		$25	$35	$50	Margot Zemach		FSG
1982	Molly, Mccollough, & Tom The Rogue		$25	$35	$50	Kathleen Stevens		Crowell
1982	The Cat's Elbow & Other Secret Languages		$25	$35	$50	Alvin Schwartz		FSG
1983	The Little Red Hen		$25	$35	$50	Margot Zemach		FSG
1985	The Sign In Mendel's Window		$20	$30	$40	Mildred Phillips		Macmil
1986	The Three Wishes		$20	$30	$40	Margot Zemach		FSG
1987	The Two Foolish Cats		$20	$30	$40	Yoshiko Uchida		McEld
1988	The Chinese Mirror		$18	$25	$35	Mirra Ginsburg		HBJ
1988	The Enchanted Umbrella		$18	$25	$35	Odette Meyers		HBJ
1988	The Three Little Pigs		$18	$25	$35	Margot Zemach		FSG
1989	All God's Critters Got A Place In The Choir		$18	$25	$35	Bill Staines		Dutton
1994	Shrewd Todie And Lyzer The Miser		$14	$20	$30	Isaac Bashevis Singer		BF
1995	Mother Goose Picture Book		$14	$20	$25	Margot Zemach		HCollins
2001	Some From The Moon, Some From The Sun		$10	$14	$18	Margot Zemach		FSG

Zimmer   Dirk

Year	Title	VG-	VG	VG+	Fine	Author	Award	Pub
1978	Felix In The Attic		$20	$30	$40	Larry Bograd		Harvey
1980	Egon		$14	$20	$25	Larry Bograd		Macmil
1981	Mean Jake And The Devils		$14	$20	$25	William H. Hooks		Dial
1982	The Star Rocker		$14	$20	$25	Joseph Slate		H&Row
1982	The Trick-Or-Treat Trap		$14	$20	$25	Dirk Zimmer		H&Row
1983	Bony-Legs		$14	$20	$25	Joanna Cole		4Winds
1983	Esteban And The Ghost		$14	$20	$25	Sibyl Hancock (adapted)		Dial
1983	The Sky Is Full Of Song		$14	$20	$25	L.B. Hopkins (selected)		H&Row
1984	In A Dark, Dark Room		$12	$18	$25	Alvin Schwartz (retold)		H&Row
1985	Buster Loves Buttons!		$12	$18	$25	Fran Manushkin		H&Row
1985	Someone Saw A Spider		$12	$18	$25	Shirley Climo		Crowell
1986	Perrywinkle And The Book Of Magic Spells		$12	$16	$20	Ross Martin Madsen		Dial
1986	Poor Gertie		$12	$16	$20	Larry Bograd		DelaP
1987	The Curse Of The Squirrel		$12	$16	$20	Laurence Yep		Random
1987	The Naked Bear: Folktales Of The Iroquois		$12	$16	$20	John Bierhorst (edited)		Morrow
1988	The Iron Giant		$35	$50	$70	Ted Hughes		H&Row
1988	Windy Day: Stories And Poems		$12	$16	$20	Caroline Bauer (edited)		Lippin
1989	John Tabor's Ride		$12	$16	$20	Edward C. Day		Knopf

Zimmer   Dirk

Year	Title	VG-	VG	VG+	Fine	Author	Award	Pub
1989	Ma And Pa Dracula		$12	$16	$20	Ann M. Martin		Holiday
1989	Weird Wolf		$12	$16	$20	Margery Cuyler		Holt
1990	The Adventures Of Ratman		$10	$16	$20	M. Friedman E. Weiss		Random
1991	Goody Sherman's Pig		$10	$16	$20	Mary Blount Christian		Macmil
1991	The Cow Is Mooing Anyhow		$10	$16	$20	L.G. Bass		LauraG
1992	The Moonbow Of Mr. B. Bones		$10	$16	$20	J. Patrick Lewis		Knopf
1992	The One That Got Away		$10	$16	$20	Percival Everett		Clarion
1993	Tsugele's Broom		$10	$16	$20	Valerie Scho Carey		HCollins
1994	Seven Spiders Spinning		$10	$14	$18	Gregory Maguire		Clarion
1994	The Curse Of The Calico Cat		$10	$14	$18	M. Friedman E. Weiss		Random
1995	Some Fine Grampa!		$10	$14	$18	Alan Arkin		HCollins
1996	One Eye, Two Eyes, Three Eyes: A Hutzul Tale		$8	$12	$16	Eric Kimmel (adapted)		Holiday
1996	The Great Turtle Drive		$8	$12	$16	Steve Stanfield		Knopf
1997	Perrywinkle's Magic Match		$8	$12	$16	Ross Martin Madsen		Dial
1998	King Of Magic, Man Of Glass		$8	$12	$16	Judith Kinter (retold)		Clarion
2003	Curse In Reverse		$8	$10	$14	Tom Coppinger		Athenm

Zwerger   Lisbeth

Year	Title	VG-	VG	VG+	Fine	Author	Award	Pub
1979	Hansel And Gretel		$35	$50	$70	Jacob & Wilhelm Grimm		Morrow
1980	Thumbelina		$25	$35	$50	Hans Christian Andersen		Morrow
1981	The Seven Ravens		$25	$35	$50	Jacob & Wilhelm Grimm		Morrow
1982	The Gift Of The Magi		$25	$35	$50	O. Henry		Picture
1982	The Swineherd		$25	$35	$50	Hans Christian Andersen		Morrow
1983	Little Red Cap		$25	$35	$50	Jacob & Wilhelm Grimm	NYT	Picture
1983	The Nutcracker And The Mouse-King		$25	$35	$50	E. T. A. Hoffmann		Picture
1984	The Nightingale		$20	$30	$40	Hans Christian Andersen		Picture
1984	The Selfish Giant		$20	$30	$40	Oscar Wilde		Picture
1984	The Strange Child		$20	$30	$40	E. T. A. Hoffmann		Picture
1985	The Deliverers Of Their Country		$20	$30	$40	Edith Nesbit		Picture
1985	The Legend Of Rosepetal		$20	$30	$40	Clemens Brentano		Picture
1986	The Canterville Ghost		$20	$30	$40	Oscar Wilde		Picture
1987	The Nutcracker		$20	$30	$40	E. T. A. Hoffmann		Picture
1988	A Christmas Carol		$18	$25	$35	Charles Dickens		Picture
1989	Aesop's Fables		$18	$25	$35	Lisbeth Zwerger (adapted)		S&S
1990	The Merry Pranks Of Till Eulenspiegel		$16	$25	$30	Anthea Bell		Picture
1991	Hans Christian Andersen Fairy Tales		$16	$25	$30	Hans Christian Andersen		Picture
1994	Dwarf Nose		$14	$20	$30	Wilhelm Hauff		NSBooks
1995	Little Hobbin		$14	$20	$25	Theodor Storm		NSBooks
1995	Lullabies, Lyrics And Gallows Songs		$14	$20	$25	Christian Morgenstern		NSBooks
1996	The Wizard Of Oz		$12	$18	$25	L. Frank Baum		NSBooks
1997	Noah's Ark		$12	$18	$25	Heinz Janisch		NSBooks
1999	Alice In Wonderland		$12	$16	$20	Lewis Carroll		NSBooks
2001	How The Camel Got His Bump		$10	$14	$18	Rudyard Kipling		NSBooks
2002	Stories From The Bible		$8	$12	$16	Lisbeth Zwerger (adapted)		NSBooks
2002	Swan Lake		$8	$12	$16	Lisbeth Zwerger (adapted)		NSBooks

ABBR	PUBLISHER
10Speed	Ten Speed Press
1stAve	First Avenue Editions
2Rivers	Two Rivers Press
4Seas	Four Seas Company
4Winds	Four Winds Press
A&B	Allison and Busby
Abatt	Abattoir Editions
Abbe	Abbeville Kids
ABC	ABC Books
Abdo	Abdo
Abing	Abingdon
Abrams	Harry N. Abrams
AC	Appleton-Century
ACB	A & C Black
ACC	Antique Collectors' Club
Accord	Accord
ACP	Academy Chicago Publishers
Adama	Adama Books
Adelphi	Adelphi Press
Advoc	Advocacy Press
AEP	American Education Publications
AG	American Girl
AH	August House Littlefolk
AHP	American Heritage Press
AIG	American Institute of Graphic Arts
Aladd	Aladdin Books
Aldus	Aldus Books
Algon	Algonquin Books
AM	Andrews McMeel
AMP	Altantic Monthly Press
AmWest	American West
Anim	Animated Book Co.
Annik	Annick Press
AP	Albondocani Press
AP	Anderson Press
Apple	Applewood Books
Arali	Aralia Press
Arcad	Arcade
Arco	Arco Pub. Co.
Ariel	Ariel Books
Arion	Arion Press
Ariz	Arizona Silhouettes
Arrow	Arrow Editions
AS	Abelard-Schuman
Ashlar	Ashlar Press
Athenm	Atheneum
Atom	Atomium
AU	Allen & Unwin
Augsb	Augsburg Books
Aurum	Aurum Books
Avenel	Avenel
Avon	Avon Books
AW	Addison-Wesley
AWG	Artists & Writers Guild
AWhit	Albert Whitman
B&W	Brewer & Warren
Baker	Baker Books
Ball	Ballantine Books
Balsam	Balsam Press
Bantam	Bantam Books
Barnes	A. S. Barnes
Barre	Barre Publishers
Barrn	Barron's
BB	Beginner Books
BBC	BBC Books
Bbear	Brownbear Press
Bdeer	Browndeer Press
Beacon	Beacon Press
Bedford	Thirty Bedford Square
Bedrik	Bedrick
Beech	Beech Tree Books
Behman	Behrman House

ABBR	PUBLISHER
Bell	Bell Books
Bellwd	Bellwood Press
Bergh	Bergh Pub.
Best	Best-West Publications
Bethny	Bethany Backyard
BF	Barefoot Books
BG	Bookmakers Guild
Bieler	Bieler Press
BIP	Black Ice Publishers
Black	Blackie
BLB	Blue Lantern Books
Bloom	Bloomsbury
B'nai	Anti-Defamation League of B'nai B'rith
Bobbs	Bobbs-Merrill
Bodley	Bodley Head
BOM	Book-of-the-Month Club
Boni	A & C Boni
Bonim	Bonim Books
Boston	Boston Music Co
BOW	Books of Wonder
Bowmar	Bowmar
Boyds	Boyds Mills Press
BradP	Bradbury Press
BRB	Blue Ribbon Books
Breth	Brethren Press
Brimax	Brimax
Bro	Brotherstone
Broad	Broadman Press
Brock	Brockhampton Press
Bruce	Bruce Publishing
BSP	Blue Sky Press
BTB	Baby Tattoo Books
Budget	Budget Books
Burke	Burke
BW	Beyond Words
BWB	BridgeWater Books
C&L	Cupples & Leon
C&W	Congdon & Weed
C&Weed	Chatto & Windus
Cader	Cader Books
Caed	Caedmon
Calico	Calico Book
Calla	Callaway Editions
Candle	Candlewick Press
CAP	Creative Age Press
Capra	Capra Press
Cart	Cartwheel Books
Carts	Celestial Arts
Cassel	Cassell
Cataw	Catawba Press
CBeach	Cooper Beach Books
CBS	CBS Books
Ccane	CandyCane Press
CCC	Caregivers' Comfort Creations
CelebP	Celebration Press
Century	The Century Company
CH	Caroline House
ChanlP	Channel Press
ChapP	Chapters Pub.
Chariot	Chariot Books
Charles	Charlesbridge
Chatham	Chatham River Press
CHE	Comprehensive Health Education Foundation
Check	Checkerboard Press
Chel	Chelsea House
Chil	Chilocco
ChildP	Child's Play
ChildU	Children's Universe
Chim	Chimaera Press
Chosen	Chosen Books
Chron	Chronicle Books
CHS	California Historical Society

ABBR	PUBLISHER
Cit	Citadel Press
Clarion	Clarion Books
CM	Coward, McCann
CM&G	Coward, McCann & Geoghegan
Cobble	Cobblehill Books
Collier	Collier Books
Collins	Collins
ColP	Columbia University Press
Compton	F.E. Compton
Concord	Concordia
Const	Constable
ContB	Contemporary Books
ContC	Container Corp.
Cotler	Joanna Cotler Books
Country	Countryman Press
Courage	Courage Books
Coward	Coward
Cowles	Cowles Book
Coyote	Coyote Love Press
CP	Childrens Press
Cpot	Clarkson Potter
Cracom	Beverly Cracom
CRB	Carolrhoda Books
Creat	Creative
CrestH	Crestwood House
Cricket	Cricket Books
Crit	Criterion Books
Croc	Crocodile Books
CrossP	Crossing Press
CrossR	Crossroads Books
Crossw	Crossway Books
Crowell	Crowell
Crown	Crown Publishers
Crozet	Crozet Print Shop
CUP	Cambridge University Press
CW	Child's World
Cwill	Colonial Williamsburg
D&M	Douglas & McIntyre
D&S	Dean & Sons
Dalton	B. Dalton
DandP	Dandelion Press
DApple	D. Appleton
DaughT	Daughters Pub.
DD	Doubleday, Doran
Debrett	Debrett's Peerage
DelaP	Delacorte Press
Dell	Dell
Delmar	Delmar Publishers
Dempsey	Michael Dempsey
Denison	TS Denison
Dent	J.M. Dent
DentD	Dent Dutton
Derry	Derrydale Books
Desert	Desert-Southwest
DetProd	Determined Productions
Deutsch	Andre Deutsch
DFick	David Fickling
DGrant	Donald M. Grant
Dial	Dial Books
diCapua	Michael di Capua Books
Dillon	Dillon Press
Disney	Disney Press
DK	Dorling Kindersley
DMcKay	David McKay
Dobson	Dobson
DoddM	Dodd, Mead
Dolphin	Dolphin
DomesD	Domesday Press
Domino	Domino Press
Donohue	M.A. Donohue
DoubleD	Doubleday
Dover	Dover Publications
DP	Doubleday, Page
Dragon	Dragon's

ABBR	PUBLISHER
Drexel	Drexel Press
DS&P	Duell, Sloan & Pearce
Dutton	Dutton
DV	Diogenes-Verlag
Dwhite	D. White
E&C	Epstein & Carroll
E&S	Eyre & Spottiswoode
EAPH	East African Pub. House
Easton	Easton Press
EB	Encyclopaedia Britannica Press
Ecco	Ecco Press
Eden	Eden Hill Press
EEC	Early Education Co.
EerdB	Eerdmans Books
ElkG	Elk Grove Press
EMC	EMC Pub.
EMHale	E.M. Hale
Equix	Equinox
ESlob	E. Slobodkina
Everest	Everest House
F&R	Farrar & Rinehart
F&W	Funk & Wagnalls
Faber	Faber
Fairfax	Fairfax Publishers
Fantod	Fantod Press
FAR	F.A.R. Gallery
Faralar	Faralar Press
FarG	Far Gallery
FC	Fawcett Columbine
FCC	First Choice Chapter Book
FFA	Fort Frederica Association
FFoster	Frances Foster Books
FHP	Friendly House Publishers
Firefly	Firefly Books
Firfield	Firfield Pamphlet Press
Fischer	L. B. Fischer
FKidz	Faith Kidz
FLinc	Frances Lincoln
Florida	Florida Press
Fly	Fly By Night Press
FOF	Facts On File
Fogel	Fogelman
Folger	Folger Shakespeare Library
Folio	Folio Press
Follett	Follett Publishing
Forbes	Forbes Lithograph
FPA	Foreign Policy Association
Frank	Franklin Library
Friend	Friendship Press
Front	Front Street
FSG	Farrar Straus Giroux
FSPL	Friends of the San Pedro Library
FStokes	Frederick Stokes
Fulcrum	Fulcrum Pub.
FWarne	Frederick Warne
FWatts	Franklin Watts
FWBaron	R. W. Baron
G&D	Grosset & Dunlap
G&H	Gold'n Honey Books
G&P	Gale and Poulden
Gabriel	S. Gabriel Sons
GAC	Graphic Arts Center
Gale	Gale Research Co.
Gallery	Gallery Press
Gannett	Gannett Books
GardenC	Garden City
GarethS	Gareth Stevens
Garrard	Garrard
GB	Gulliver Books
GBles	G. Bles
GBraz	G. Braziller
Gem	Gemstone Books
GFrog	Green Frog Publishers
GGate	Golden Gate Junior Books

ABBR	PUBLISHER
Gibson	C. R. Gibson
Gil	Gilchrist Publishing
Giligia	Giligia Press
GingH	Gingerbread House
Ginn	Ginn
GloucP	Gloucester Press
GLR	Green Light Readers
Goblin	Goblin Tales
Godine	David R. Godine
Golden	Golden Press
Goll	Gollancz
GoodB	Good Book
GoodR	Good Reading
GoodY	Good Year Books
Gotham	Gotham Book Mart
GP	Grossman Publishers
Graham	Graham Makintosh
Green	Greenwillow Books
Greene	S. Greene Press
GreenT	Green Tiger Press
Gregg	Gregg Press
Grolier	Grolier
Ground	Groundwood Books
Grove	Grove Press
Gruelle	Johnny Gruelle Co.
GSteve	G. Stevens
H&B	Harper & Brothers
H&R	Human & Rousseau
H&Row	Harper & Row
H&S	Hodder & Stoughton
Hamlyn	Hamlyn
Hampton	Hampton Roads
Hand	Handprint Books
Harcort	Harcourt
Harmony	Harmony Books
Harper	Harper
Harrap	George G. Harrap
Harrisn	Harrison Company
Hart	Hart Pub. Co.
HartD	Hart-Davis
Harter	Harter Publishing
Harvey	Harvey House
Hasbro	Hasbro Bradley
Hastings	Hastings House
HawB	Hawthorn Books
HBJ	Harcourt Brace Jovanovich
HBrace	Harcourt Brace
HCollins	HarperCollins
HCrest	HarperCrest
HeartS	HeartSpring Media
Heath	D.C. Heath
Heine	Heinemann
Hend	Henderson Pub.
Herb	Harbinger Pub.
HFest	HarperFestival
HHamil	H. Hamilton
HHouse	Happy House
Hill	Hill Publishing
HM	Houghton Mifflin
Hobbs	Hobbs, Dorman
Hodder	Hodder Headline
Holiday	Holiday House
Holt	Henry Holt
HoltR	Holt, Rinehart
Horizon	Horizon Books
Horn	Horn Book
Howard	Howard Publishing
Howell	Howell, Soskin
HQuist	Harlin Quist
HR&W	Holt, Rinehart & Winston
HShaw	Harold Shaw
Hulton	Hulton Press
Hutch	Hutchinson
HWagner	Harr Wagner

ABBR	PUBLISHER
Hyper	Hyperion
Iceni	Iceni Books
Ideals	Ideals Children's Books
Illum	Illumination Arts
Inyx	Inyx
IP	International Publishers
Irwin	Irwin Pub.
JamRoll	Jam Roll Press
JCape	Jonathan Cape
JellyB	JellyBean Press
JMDent	J. M. Dent
JMorris	Joshua Morris
JohnDay	John Day Co.
Joy	Joy Street Books
JPS	Jewish Publication Society
Jump	Jump at the Sun
Junior	Junior Deluxe Editions
JuniorL	Junior Literary
K&W	Kaye & Ward
Kane	Kane Press
KaneM	Kane/Miller Book Publishers
KarBen	Kar-Ben Copies
Kayak	Kayak Books
KellyW	Kelly-Winterton Press
Kestrel	Kestrel Books
Kfisher	Kingfisher Books
Kids	Kids Matter
KidsCan	Kids Can Press
Knopf	Knopf
KPorter	Key Porter Kids
Kramer	H.J. Kramer
Kroupa	Melanie Kroupa Books
KRP	Kennebec River Press
Ktav	Ktav Pub. House
Kumquat	Kumquat Press
Kwela	Kwela Books
Kyoya	Kyoya
L&B	Lockwood & Brainard
LadyB	Ladybird Books
Lance	Lancelot Press
Landmrk	Landmark Editions
Lane	A. Lane
LangArt	Laing Art Gallery
Lantern	Lantern Press
LauraG	Laura Geringer
LBrown	Little, Brown
LEC	Limited Editions Club
LeeLow	Lee & Low Books
Lerner	Lerner Publications
Levine	Arthur A. Levine
LGL	Looking Glass Library
Life	Lifetime Books
Lincoln	F. Lincoln
LincP	Lincoln Printing
Linnet	Linnet Books
Lion	Lion Press
Lippin	J. B. Lippincott
Litur	Liturgical Press
LL&S	Lothrop, Lee & Shepard
LLee	Lothrop Lee
LodeS	Lodestar Books
London	London House
Longman	Longmans, Green
LongMed	Longmeadow Press
Lothian	Lothian
Lothrop	Lothrop
Lowell	Lowell House
Loyola	Loyola Press
LP	Longstreet Press
LSimon	Little Simon
LTiger	Little Tiger Press
LUP	Lion and Unicorn Press
Lutten	Lutterworth
LYoung	Longmans, Young Books

478

Abbr	Publisher
M&K	MacGibbon & Kee
M&S	McClelland & Stewart
MacD	Macdonald
Macmil	Macmillan
MacRae	Julia MacRae Books
MacSm	Macrae Smith
Magic	Magic Carpet Books
Magin	Magination Press
Main	Main Street
Mammoth	Mammoth
Marchb	Marchbanks Press
Marlowe	Marlowe & Co.
MarshM	MarshMedia
Martin	Bill Martin Corp
Mason	Mason Crest
Maxton	Maxton Publishers
MB	Milton Bradley
MBrown	Marc Brown Studios
MCaven	Marshall Cavendish
McBride	McBride
McCall	McCall
McCann	McCann
McEld	Margaret K. McElderry
McHill	McGraw-Hill
McKay	McKay
McLough	McLoughlin Bros.
MCP	Modern Curriculum Press
Mered	Meredith Press
Messner	Julian Messner
Methuen	Methuen
MEvans	M. Evans
MHouse	Morehouse
Milk	Milk And Cookies Press
Millbk	Millbrook Press
Millik	Milliken
Minton	Minton, Balch
MJoseph	M. Joseph
MLF	MJF Books
MMA	Museum of Modern Art
Moffat	Moffat, Yark and Co
Mondo	Mondo
Moore	Moore Historical Foundation
Morrow	Morrow
MountP	Mountain Press
MouseW	MouseWorks
Moyer	Moyer Bell
Mulbery	Mulberry Books
Muller	F. Muller
Mult	Multnomah Press
Muppet	Muppet Press
MWard	Montgomery Ward
Nadja	Nadja Publishing
NAL	New American Library
NAVH	Nat'l Asso. for Visually Handicapped
NCP	North Country Press
NEP	New England Press
Neuge	Neugebauer
Newton	Newton, Abbot
NGS	National Geographic Society
Night	Night Sky Books
Noonday	Noonday Press
Noone	Noone House
North	Northland
Norton	Norton
Nouveau	Nouveau Press
NSBooks	North-South Books
NTrust	National Trust
NWP	North Winds Press
NYGS	New York Graphic Society
Obolsky	Obolensky
OCP	Open Court Pub.
Octagon	Octagon Books
Odyssey	Odyssey Press
Offen	Ottenheimer Publishers
Ohara	J. P. O'Hara
Omnibus	Omnibus
Onge	A.J. St. Onge
Orca	Orca Book Publishers
Orchard	Orchard Books
Orion	Orion Press
OUP	Open University Press
Outdoor	Outdoor Books
Over	Overlook Press
Oxford	Oxford University Press
P&C	Pellegrini & Cudahy
P&Munk	Platt & Munk
Pagasus	Pegasus Press
Pamp	Pamphlet Press
Pan	Pantheon Books
Park	Park Lane Press
Parker	Parker Bros
Parnss	Parnassus Press
Parrish	M. Parrish
Paulist	Paulist Press
Pavil	Pavilion
PB	Pan Books
PDavies	Peter Davies
Peach	Peachtree
Peacock	Peacock Press
Pelham	Pelham Books
Pelican	Pelican
Penguin	Penguin Books
Penmaen	Penmaen Press
Penny	Pennyroyal
Perfman	Perlman Books
Perlman	Willa Perlman Books
Perpet	Perpetua Books
PFogel	Phyllis Fogelman
P-Hall	Prentice-Hall
Phillip	S. G. Phillips
Philo	Philomel Books
Piccad	Piccadilly Press
Picture	Picture Book Studio
PiedP	Pied Piper Books
Piggy	Piggy Toes Press
Pippin	Pippin Press
Pleasnt	Pleasant Company
PMagP	Parents Magazine Press
Pocket	Pocket Books
Pond	Bell Pond Books
Potter	Potter
PPauper	Peter Pauper Press
PriceSS	Price Stern Sloan
PTiger	Paper Tiger
PublIntl	Publications International
Pullman	Pullman Couch
Putnam	Putnam
Quarr	Quarrier Press
R&KPaul	Routledge & K. Paul
Rabbit	Rabbit Ears Books
Raben	Rabén & Sjögren
Rain	Raintree
Rainbow	Rainbow Press
RainSV	Raintree Steck-Vaughn
RandMc	Rand McNally
Random	Random House
RBLuce	R. B. Luce
RCOwen	Richard C. Owen
RDigest	Reader's Digest
Redpth	Redpath Press
Reilly	Reilly & Lee
ReyHitc	Reynal & Hitchcock
Reynal	Reynal
RIB	Rhode Island Bicentennial Foundation
Rigby	Rigby
Rinehrt	Rinehart
RMoon	Rising Moon
RoarB	Roaring Brook Press
Roe	A. M. & R. W. Roe
Ross	Ross Laboratories
Rourke	Rourke
Row&P	Row, Peterson & Co.
Roy	Roy Publishers
ROzier	Red Ozier
RRourke	R. Rourke
RRSmith	R. R. Smith
RunP	Running Press
Rush	A. P. Rushton
Russak	C. Russak
Rut	Rutledge Books
RWagon	Red Wagon Books
RWelch	Robert Welch
RWR	Russian War Relief
S&J	Sidgwick and Jackson
S&S	Simon & Schuster
SaalF	Saalfield
SAB	Scientific American Books
Sadler	Sadler & Brown
SAFE	S.A.F.E. for Children Pub.
Santill	Santillana Publishers
SBurdet	Silver Burdett
Schill	Schilling Co.
Schock	Schocken Books
Scholas	Scholastic
Schuman	H. Schuman
ScottF	Scott Foresman
Scribnr	Scribners
Scroll	Scroll Press
Seabury	Seabury Press
Sears	Sears Publishing
SeaStar	SeaStar Books
Seidel	Seidel & Stokes
Serend	Serendipity Press
SFrench	S. French
Sheed	Sheed and Ward
Sheer	Sheer Bliss Communications
ShoeT	Shoe Tree Press
Sierra	Sierra Club Books
Silver	Silver Press
Singer	L. W. Singer
Skylite	SkyLight Paths Pub.
Sloane	Sloane
SmithH	H. Smith and R. Haas
SmithM	Smithmark
SMoon	Silver Moon Press
Songo	Songololo Books
Sparhk	Sparhawk Books
Sparrow	Sparrow Press
Spiral	Spiral Press
SpirSky	Spiral Sky Music
Spring	Springfellow Books
SRA	SRA School Group
ST&C	Stewart, Tabori & Chang
StackP	Stackpole Books
Stan&E	Star and Elephant Books
StandP	Standard Pub.
StarB	Star Bright Books
Starsed	Starseed Press
Steck-V	Steck-Vaughn
Stemmer	Stemmer House
Sten	Stenhouse Publishers
Sterl	Sterling
Stine	Stinehour Press
StMart	St. Martin's Press
Stodd	Stoddart
Stoll&E	Stoll & Edwards
Str8A	Straight Arrow
Straw	One Strawberry
Studio	The Studio
Sund	Sundance Pub.

Abbr	Publisher
Sutton	Suttonhouse
Tambour	Tambourine Books
Tegen	Katherine Tegen Books
TelWel	Tell-Well Press
Templar	Templar Pub.
Thames	Thameside Press
THP	The Heritage Press
Ticnor	Ticknor & Fields
Tiger	Tiger Tales
Time	Time-Life
Tink	Tink Tonk
TIP	Teacher Ideas Press
TNelson	Thomas Nelson
Tor	Tor
Tortuga	Tortuga Press
Town	Town Book Press
TransAf	Transafrica Publishers
Treasur	Treasure Books
Tricyc	Tricycle Press
Troll	Troll Associates
Trote	Trotevale
Trouba	Troubador Press
Tundra	Tundra Books
Tupelo	Tupelo Books
Turner	Turner Publications
Twayne	Twayne Publishers
Tynd	Tyndale House
UAH	Union of American Hebrew
UAHC	UAHC Press
UCal	University of California Press
UChic	University of Chicago Press
UCP	United Church Press
UHaw	Univ. Of Hawaii Press
UIll	University of Illinois Press
UKansas	University Press of Kansas
UMass	University of Massachusetts Press
UNeb	University of Nebraska Press
Unicorn	Unicorn
UnivPub	University Publishing
UofK	Univ. Press of Kentucky
USC	United Synagogue Commission
UTexas	University of Texas Press
VFC	Vermont Folklife Center
Victor	Victor Books
Viking	Viking
Vista	Vista Books
VK	Viking Kestrel
Vnguard	Vanguard Press
VNost	Van Nostrand
Volland	P.F. Volland
W&F	Wilcox & Follett
W&H	Wolgemuth & Hyatt
W&N	Weidenfeld & Nicolson
W&T	Weybright and Talley
Walck	Henry Z. Walck
Walker	Walker
Wander	Wanderer Books
Warner	Warner Books
Watcorn	Whatcom County Opportunity Council
Water	Waterbrook Press
WaterM	Watermill Press
WaterT	Watertower Books
WCoyote	Whispering Coyote
Weather	J. Weatherhill
Weber	Louis Weber
Western	Western Publishing
Westmin	Westminster Press
WGuptil	Watson-Guptill
WHBooks	WH Books
WHebb	Wallace Hebberd
WHHC	Woods Hole Historical Collection
Whistle	Silver Whistle

Abbr	Publisher
Whitman	Whitman
Whittle	Whittlesey House
WienAm	Wien American
William	Williams Printing Co
Windmil	Windmill Books
Winslow	Winslow House
Winston	John C. Winston
Wis-P	Wise-Parslow
WNorton	W. W. Norton
Wolf	Wolfhound Press
Wonder	Wonder books
Woodbrg	Woodbridge Press
Word	Word Pub.
Wordsng	Wordsong
Workman	Workman Publishing
World	World Publishing
WorldsW	World's Work
WP	Winston Press
WRichie	Ward Richie Press
WRScott	W. R. Scott
WStop	WhistleStop
WTang	W. Targ
Wyndham	Wyndham Books
Xerox	Xerox
YaleUP	Yale University Press
Yearlng	Yearling
Yose	Yosemite/Limited
YScott	Young Scott Books
Zamani	Zamani Productions
Ziff-D	Ziff-Davis
Zkidz	Zonderkidz
Zonder	Zondervan